STREET & SMITH'S GUIDE TO BASEBALL 1994

STREET & SMITH'S GUIDE TO BASEBALL 1994

by the editors of
Street & Smith's

Consulting Editor: Reuben Lattimore

BALLANTINE BOOKS • NEW YORK

 Published in the United States of America by Ballantine Books, a division of Random House, Inc., New York, and simultaneously in Canada by Random House of Canada Limited, Toronto.

Library of Congress Catalog Card Number: 93–90710

ISBN 0–345–38617–5

Manufactured in the United States of America

First Edition: March 1994

10 9 8 7 6 5 4 3 2 1

TABLE OF CONTENTS

Statistics, Facts and Other Information

ACKNOWLEDGEMENTS

Putting together a guide this thorough is quite an undertaking, and we'd like to thank the following people for all of their help.

First and foremost, we could never have completed this book without the generous assistance and cooperation of the Directors of Public Relations and Media Relations for all 28 major league teams, and their staffs, who answered our many requests quickly and helpfully.

We'd also like to thank everyone at Creative Graphics who worked so hard to help us bring this project to completion in time for the season.

Finally, many thanks to our editor Jeff Doctoroff, who helped conceive and execute every stage of this book, and to all of the others at Ballantine Books, especially Caron Harris, George Davidson, Nora Reichard, Joe McKeown, and Myles McDonnell.

Editor's Note

Players are classified by their primary position in '93 and ranked, in descending order, in various categories relative to other players at that position with at least 150 at bats, or 50 innings pitched. A number one ranking in home runs or wins indicates that a player had more home runs or wins than any other player in the major leagues at that position who had at least 150 at bats, or 50 inning pitched. Pitcher rankings for hits, runs, home runs allowed, walks and strikeouts are based on the rate per inning pitched, not the season total. For instance, although Randy Johnson led the majors with 308 total strikeouts over 255.1 innings, among eligible pitchers, his strikeouts per inning pitched rate of 1.207 ranked third, behind Toronto's Duane Ward (97 strikeouts in 71 innings, for a rate of 1.362 strikeouts per inning pitched) and Montreal's John Wetteland (113 strikeouts in 85 innings, for a rate of 1.328 strikeouts per inning pitched). So Randy Johnson's rank in strikeouts is third, not first.

Player projections are based upon a computerized analysis that takes into consideration whether 1993 was a player's best year. If 1993 was a player's best year, one set of assumptions is applied that assumes the player will continue to improve in various categories at the rate he has improved over his career. For instance, if Bill Smith went from 10 home runs in his first year to 20 home runs in his third year, and hasn't peaked, his rate of improvement is deemed to be 50% annual —and we'll project that he'll hit 30 home runs in 1994. If a player's best career year was a year other than 1993, the player's 1994 performance is estimated from a computer-generated performance curve that uses 1993 as the starting point to estimate future performance. The curve is generated by assuming that players steadily improve, and then, after they peak, steadily decline. Since the performance curve is solely based on the player's career stats, it is unique to that player.

The longer a player has been in the league, the more reliable the estimate should be. So estimated performance for Rickey Henderson, with 15 years in baseball, should be more reliable than that of Pat Listach, with just two years in baseball. This method should prove more accurate than three-year averages in estimating performance, because our method takes into account whether a player is improving, and will outperform his three year average (or declining, and will underperform his three year average). Remember, the analysis is mechanical—you may be convinced that Jeff Juden will pitch 20 games for the Phillies in 1994, but all the computer knows is that he's only made it into six games over two years (and with a 5.87 career ERA, it's easy to see why!) and makes its forecast accordingly. Forecasts are not furnished for players with just one year in baseball.

Due to a tight schedule, we've probably missed some late free agent signings, trades, and other developments. Still, this guide should give you a comprehensive overview of the 1994 season from spring training to the World Series.

NATIONAL LEAGUE

1993 Recap

NL East

Philadelphia went from worst to first in '93. Aided by a full season from spark plug Lenny Dykstra, the Phillies took over first place for good on April 11. They got off to a 57-32 start, then held off a late season charge by Montreal.

14.5 games back on August 20, the Expos went 21–3 to close to within four games of the Phillies on September 17. But Moises Alou's broken leg on September 16 doomed Montreal's chances.

St. Louis opened the season chasing Philadelphia, and was in second place into late August. But the Cardinals slipped from three games out on July 18 to eleven games out August 25, and finished the season 28–31.

Chicago's 84–78 campaign, good for fourth in the NL East, was only their seventh winning record in 25 years of division play. After their title hopes ended, Chicago finished strong, going 20–10 in September and October. But that finish didn't placate GM Larry Himes, who was convinced that the Cubs had the talent to contend. He fired manager Jim Lefebvre and hired former Milwaukee skipper Tom Trebelhorn.

Defending division champ Pittsburgh, one out away from the World Series in '92, reeled to a fifth-place finish in '93. Andy Van Slyke's injury problems deprived the Pirates of their best player for half the season. 42–46 at the All-Star break, Pittsburgh finished 33–41.

The Marlins marked their inaugural season by finishing ahead of the Mets in the NL East. Bryan Harvey was a pleasant surprise, saving 45 games. Florida peaked in June when they won eight of nine to reach 30–31 and place fourth in the division. But the Marlins slumped in the second half as their weak offense took its toll; they were 9–22 in September and October.

What a woeful season for the Mets! Manager Jeff Torborg was fired after a 13–25 start, but the Mets weren't any better under Dallas Green. And the on-field woes were matched by off-field travails, with Vince Coleman's firecracker injuring a child in Los Angeles, and two locker-room incidents involving Bret Saberhagen. GM Al Harazin left in June, and Joe McIlvaine returned from San Diego as the new GM.

NL West

Despite the best rotation in baseball, Atlanta lacked a power hitting first baseman and the Braves found themselves 9.5 games out on July 18. Then Atlanta acquired Fred McGriff and began a phenomenal run. McGriff homered in his first game as a Brave, and Atlanta started a 49–17 stretch to take the division by one game over a Giants team that won 103 games.

Rookie Manager Dusty Baker got San Francisco off to a fast start, with a 59–30 record at the All-Star break and the division title seemingly wrapped up. But the Giants lost ten games in the standings to charging Atlanta between July 22 and September 10—despite a 24–19 mark over that span. San Francisco was just one game back going into the season-ending series with Los Angeles, but the Giants lost their last game to the Dodgers, while Atlanta clinched the division with a 5–3 win over Colorado.

Houston, stuck in a division with two teams that won over 100 games, got disappointing seasons from free agent pitchers Doug Drabek and Greg Swindell. They were in first place as late as May 10, but fell steadily behind the Giants from that point on. By August 6, they were 18.5 games out.

Los Angeles won 18 more games in '93 than in '92 to finish at 81–81. Mike Piazza emerged as a star, winning Rookie of the Year honors. But Darryl Strawberry was hurt most of the year, and disappointing Eric Davis was traded to Detroit in August.

Cincinnati started off slowly, with a 20–24 record, so GM Jim Bowden replaced popular rookie manager Tony Perez with former Met manager Dave Johnson. The Reds closed 1993 by going 14–34 over their last 48 games, prompting an off-season housecleaning in Cincinnati.

Colorado set a record for wins by a National League expansion team. They started slow, going 15–36 in April and May. But manager Don Baylor kept the team playing hard, and Colorado responded with the third best record in the NL after August 7, 31–21.

San Diego trimmed its payroll, and the results showed up in the standings. After pledging to preserve the team's core, the Padres sent Darrin Jackson away before the season started, and traded Fred McGriff to Atlanta, Gary Sheffield to Florida, and Greg Harris to Colorado. Ticket holders revolted, going to court to win refunds on tickets already purchased, and San Diego ended up with the second-worst record in the major leagues.

NATIONAL LEAGUE PROJECTIONS

NL EAST	NL CENTRAL	NL WEST
1. Philadelphia	1. Houston	1. San Francisco
2. Atlanta	2. St. Louis	2. Los Angeles
3. Montreal	3. Chicago	3. Colorado
4. New York	4. Pittsburgh	4. San Diego
5. Florida	5. Cincinnati	

Playoffs: San Francisco over Atlanta, Philadelphia over Houston
Pennant Winner: San Francisco
World Series Winner: San Francisco over Chicago

The divisions might be different in the realigned National League, but the good teams stay the same. In the East, Atlanta and Philadelphia will battle for first, with Montreal close behind. Ex-Astro Doug Jones probably isn't the answer to their bullpen woes, but the Phils still should have the inside track to the top of the NL East. With a full-season of Fred McGriff added to a line-up that includes Ron Gant and Dave Justice, the Braves could pull out the race. The Expos will miss Delino DeShields and Dennis Martinez, but they have a strong young team and only finished three out in 1993. For Florida and the Mets, 1994 will be hard. They should battle to stay out of the cellar. Florida might come out on top, unless they trade closer Bryan Harvey.

Houston GM Bob Watson must be one of the happiest men in baseball. His Astros, also-rans behind the Braves and Giants in 1993, have landed in a division with no 90-game winners. Even without 18–4 Mark Portugal, the Astros should pull out a tight race in the NL Central on the strength of their starting rotation and young sluggers like Jeff Bagwell and Craig Biggio. The Cubs should also contend, but they lack the depth to take the division, and the Cardinals don't have the pitching to last all season. Pittsburgh and Cincinnati are trying to rebuild in small markets, and are in for long seasons. The Reds will particularly miss departed free agent Chris Sabo.

The Giants can't be sad to see the Braves go — San Francisco won 103 games in 1993, and didn't make the playoffs. Now, with free agent signee Mark Portugal, the Giants should dominate the NL West. None of the other teams in the division pose much of a threat. Manager Don Baylor's Rockies closed the season strong, and if additions Ellis Burks and Howard Johnson have big years, they might take second in a weak division. The Dodgers' rotation is getting old, and Tommy Lasorda's team might slip back below .500, unless they get unexpected help. The Padres are headed in the wrong direction. They might be the worst team in the league in 1994.

NATIONAL LEAGUE EAST—1993

TEAM	W	L	PCT	GB	HOME	ROAD	EAST	WEST	LHP	RHP	X-INN
PHILADELPHIA	97	65	.599	—	52–29	45–36	47–31	50–34	36–19	61–46	11–7
MONTREAL	94	68	.580	3.0	55–26	39–42	46–32	48–36	29–21	65–47	9–8
ST. LOUIS	87	75	.537	10.0	49–32	38–43	42–36	45–39	25–18	62–57	9–6
CHICAGO	84	78	.519	13.0	43–38	41–40	39–39	45–39	17–26	67–52	6–6
PITTSBURGH	75	87	.463	22.0	40–41	35–46	39–39	36–48	20–28	55–59	10–8
FLORIDA	64	98	.395	33.0	35–46	29–52	30–48	34–50	21–23	43–75	4–7
NEW YORK	59	103	.364	38.0	28–53	31–50	30–48	29–55	11–33	48–70	8–7

NATIONAL LEAGUE WEST—1993

TEAM	W	L	PCT	GB	HOME	ROAD	EAST	WEST	LHP	RHP	X-INN
ATLANTA	104	58	.642	—	51–30	53–28	49–35	55–23	29–15	75–43	7–6
SAN FRANCISCO	103	59	.636	1.0	50–31	53–28	50–34	53–25	32–21	71–38	8–5
HOUSTON	85	77	.525	19.0	44–37	41–40	51–33	34–44	28–28	57–49	4–8
LOS ANGELES	81	81	.500	23.0	41–40	40–41	42–42	39–39	21–22	60–59	10–12
CINCINNATI	73	89	.451	31.0	41–40	32–49	39–45	34–44	17–23	56–66	6–8
COLORADO	67	95	.414	37.0	39–42	28–53	36–48	31–47	13–20	54–75	8–4
SAN DIEGO	61	101	.377	43.0	34–47	27–54	34–50	27–51	23–27	38–74	5–13

NATIONAL LEAGUE CLUB BATTING—1993

	AB	R	H	2B	3B	HR	RBI	BB	SO	SB	BAT	SLG	OBA
SF	5557	808	1534	269	33	168	759	516	930	120	.276	.427	.340
PHI	5685	877	1555	297	51	156	811	665	1049	91	.274	.426	.351
COL	5517	758	1507	278	59	142	704	388	944	146	.273	.422	.323
STL	5551	758	1508	262	34	118	724	588	882	153	.272	.395	.341
CHC	5627	738	1521	259	32	161	706	446	923	100	.270	.414	.325
PIT	5549	707	1482	267	50	110	664	536	972	92	.267	.393	.335
HOU	5464	716	1459	288	37	138	656	497	911	103	.267	.409	.330
CIN	5517	722	1457	261	28	137	669	485	1025	142	.264	.396	.324
ATL	5515	767	1444	239	29	169	712	560	946	125	.262	.408	.331
LA	5588	675	1458	234	28	130	639	492	937	126	.261	.383	.321
MTL	5493	732	1410	270	36	122	682	542	860	228	.257	.386	.326
SD	5503	679	1386	239	28	153	633	443	1046	92	.252	.389	.312
NYM	5448	672	1350	228	37	158	632	448	879	79	.248	.390	.305
FLA	5475	581	1356	197	31	94	542	498	1054	117	.248	.346	.314

NATIONAL LEAGUE CLUB PITCHING—1993

	W	L	ERA	CG	SHO	SV	IP	H	R	ER	HR	BB	SO
ATL	104	58	3.14	18	16	46	1455.0	1297	559	507	101	480	1036
HOU	85	77	3.49	18	14	42	1441.1	1363	630	559	117	476	1056
LA	81	81	3.50	17	9	36	1472.2	1406	662	573	103	567	1043
MTL	94	68	3.55	8	7	61	1456.2	1369	682	574	119	521	934
SF	103	59	3.61	4	9	50	1456.2	1385	636	585	168	442	982
PHI	97	65	3.95	24	11	46	1472.2	1419	740	647	129	573	1117
NYM	59	103	4.05	16	8	22	1438.0	1483	744	647	139	434	867
STL	87	75	4.09	5	7	54	1453.0	1553	744	660	152	383	775
FLA	64	98	4.13	4	5	48	1440.1	1437	724	661	135	598	945
CHC	84	78	4.18	8	5	56	1449.2	1514	739	673	153	470	905
SD	61	101	4.23	8	6	32	1437.2	1470	772	675	148	558	957
CIN	73	89	4.51	11	8	37	1434.0	1510	785	718	158	508	996
PIT	75	87	4.77	12	5	34	1445.2	1557	806	766	153	485	832
COL	67	95	5.41	9	0	35	1431.1	1664	967	860	181	609	913

Atlanta

BRAVES

1994 Scouting Report

Hitting: (1993/.262 BA, ninth in NL; 169 HR, first in NL)

Atlanta has the most daunting lineup in the NL, with Jeff Blauser (.305 BA, 15 HR, 73 RBI), Ron Gant (.274, 36, 117), Dave Justice (.270, 40, 120), Terry Pendleton (.272, 17, 84), and Fred McGriff (.291, 37, 101). And except for Terry Pendleton, this corps is still in its prime.

The starters are looking over their shoulders, though, because there's young talent in the farm system looking to take their jobs. Javier Lopez hit .375 in eight games after his call-up from AAA Richmond and will start at catcher in '94, replacing Greg Olson. But Atlanta also has to make room for Chipper Jones, Ryan Klesko, and Tony Tarasco.

Pitching: (1993/3.14 ERA, first in NL)

Baseball's best starting rotation, starting with Greg Maddux, the NL Cy Young winner two years running. Although they started slow—as the Braves always seem to—the rotation of Maddux, Tom Glavine, John Smoltz, and Steve Avery was a combined 75–33. The Braves will go with Kent Mercker as the fifth starter in '94.

The team's major weakness is in the bullpen. The Braves still haven't come up with an overpowering closer. Mike Stanton (27 saves) had a 4.67 ERA in '93, and Greg McMichael (2.06 ERA, 19 saves) filled the closer's role by season's end. Middle relief features Steve Bedrosian in a set-up role.

Defense: (1993/.983 pct., third in NL)

Jeff Blauser is a reliable glove at shortstop, and Mark Lemke is outstanding at second base. Fred McGriff is a good fielding first baseman.

1994 Prospects:

The Braves simply have too much talent not to be a threat in the new NL East. They're not perfect—they did lose the pennant to the Phillies—but they won more games than anybody else in baseball, and the core of that team is returning in '94. Atlanta needs to look beyond the regular season to the playoffs and World Series, where a first-rate closer will be critical to erasing the frustration of the past three seasons.

Team Directory

Owner: R.E. "Ted" Turner
Chairman: Bill Bartholomay
President: Stan Kasten
Gen. Mgr.: John Schuerholz
Dir. of Public Relations: Jim Schultz
Traveling Secretary: Bill Acree

Minor League Affiliates:

Level	Team/League	1993 Record
AAA	Richmond – International	80–62
AA	Greenville – Southern	75–67
A	Durham – Carolina	69–69
A	Macon – South Atlantic	74–67
Rookie	Danville – Appalachian	38–30
	Idaho Falls – Pioneer	36–40
	West Palm Beach Braves – Gulf Coast	32–26

1993 Review

	Home		Away			Home		Away			Home		Away	
vs NL East	W	L	W	L	vs NL Cent.	W	L	W	L	vs NL West	W	L	W	L
Florida	3	3	4	2	Chicago	3	3	4	2	Colorado	6	0	7	0
Montreal	3	3	4	2	Cincinnati	6	1	4	2	Los Angeles	5	2	3	3
New York	4	2	5	1	Houston	3	3	5	2	San Diego	5	2	4	2
Philadelphia	3	3	3	3	Pittsburgh	3	3	4	2	S. Francisco	3	3	4	3
					St. Louis	4	2	2	4					
Total	13	11	16	8		19	12	19	12		19	7	18	8

1993 finish: 104–58 (51–30 home, 53–28 away), first in NL West, Lost NLCS 2–4 to Philadelphia

1994 Schedule

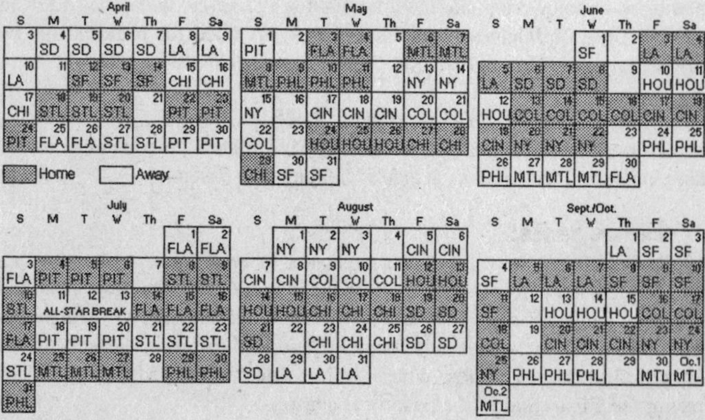

April

S	M	T	W	Th	F	Sa
3	4 SD	5 SD	6 SD	7 SD	8 LA	9 LA
10 LA	11	12 SF	13 SF	14 SF	15 CHI	16 CHI
17 CHI	18 STL	19 STL	20 STL	21	22 PIT	23 PIT
24 PIT	25 FLA	26 FLA	27 STL	28 STL	29 PIT	30 PIT

Home Away

May

S	M	T	W	Th	F	Sa
1 PIT	2	3 FLA	4 FLA	5	6 MTL	7 MTL
8 MTL	9 PHL	10 PHL	11 PHL	12	13 NY	14 NY
15 NY	16	17 CIN	18 CIN	19 CIN	20 COL	21 COL
22 COL	23	24 HOU	25 HOU	26 HOU	27 CHI	28 CHI
29 CHI	30 SF	31 SF				

June

S	M	T	W	Th	F	Sa
			1 SF	2	3 LA	4 LA
5 LA	6 SD	7 SD	8 SD	9	10 HOU	11 HOU
12 HOU	13 COL	14 COL	15 COL	16 COL	17 CIN	18 CIN
19 CIN	20 NY	21 NY	22 NY	23	24 PHL	25 PHL
26 PHL	27 MTL	28 MTL	29 MTL	30 FLA		

July

S	M	T	W	Th	F	Sa
					1 FLA	2 FLA
3 FLA	4 PIT	5 PIT	6 PIT	7	8 STL	9 STL
10 STL	11 ALL-STAR BREAK	12	13	14 FLA	15 FLA	16 FLA
17 FLA	18 PIT	19 PIT	20 PIT	21 STL	22 STL	23 STL
24 STL	25 MTL	26 MTL	27 MTL	28	29 PHL	30 PHL
31 PHL						

August

S	M	T	W	Th	F	Sa
	1 NY	2 NY	3 NY	4	5 CIN	6 CIN
7 CIN	8 CIN	9 COL	10 COL	11 COL	12 HOU	13 HOU
14 HOU	15 HOU	16 CHI	17 CHI	18 CHI	19 SD	20 SD
21 SD	22	23 CHI	24 CHI	25 CHI	26 SD	27 SD
28 SD	29 LA	30 LA	31 LA			

Sept./Oct.

S	M	T	W	Th	F	Sa
				1 LA	2 SF	3 SF
4 SF	5 LA	6 LA	7 LA	8 SF	9 SF	10 SF
11 SF	12	13 HOU	14 HOU	15 HOU	16 COL	17 COL
18 COL	19	20 CIN	21 CIN	22 CIN	23 NY	24 NY
25 NY	26 PHL	27 PHL	28 PHL	29	30 MTL	Oc.1 MTL
Oc.2 MTL						

ATLANTA BRAVES 1994 ROSTER

Manager: Bobby Cox (6)
Coaches: Jim Beauchamp, dugout (37); Pat Corrales, 1B (39); Clarence Jones, hitting (28); Leo Mazzone, pitching (54); Jimy Williams, 3B (22); Ned Yost, bullpen (42)

No.	PITCHERS	B	T	HT	WT	DOB	BIRTHPLACE	RESIDENCE
33	Avery, Steve	L	L	6–4	190	4–14–70	Trenton,MI	Taylor, MI
57	Bark, Brian	L	L	5–9	160	8–26–68	Baltimore, MD	Randallstown, MD
36	Bedrosian, Steve	R	R	6–3	205	12–6–57	Methuen, MA	Duluth, GA
	Birkbeck, Mike	R	R	6–2	188	3–10–61	Orrville, OH	Orrville, OH
51	Borbon, Pedro	L	L	6–1	205	11–15–67	Mao, DR	Texas City, TX
47	Glavine, Tom	L	L	6–1	190	3–25–66	Concord, MA	Alpharetta, GA
	Hill, Milt	R	R	6–0	180	8–22–65	Atlanta, GA	Dawsonville, GA
	Koller, Jerry	R	R	6–3	190	6–30–72	Beech Grove, IN	Martinsville, IN
31	Maddux, Greg	R	R	6–0	175	4–14–66	San Angelo, TX	Las Vegas, NV
38	McMichael, Greg	R	R	6–3	215	12–1–66	Knoxville, TN	Knoxville, TN
50	Mercker, Kent	L	L	6–2	195	2–1–68	Dublin, OH	Dublin, OH
63	Murray, Matt	L	R	6–6	200	9–26–70	Boston, MA	Swampscott, MA
59	Potts, Michael	L	L	5–9	170	9–5–70	Langdale, AL	Lithonia, GA
29	Smoltz, John	R	R	6–3	185	5–15–67	Warren, MI	Alpharetta, GA
30	Stanton, Mike	L	L	5–10	190	6–2–67	Houston, TX	Houston, TX
43	Wohlers, Mark	R	R	6–4	207	1–23–70	Holyoke, MA	Holyoke, MA
No.	**CATCHERS**	**B**	**T**	**HT**	**WT**	**DOB**	**BIRTHPLACE**	**RESIDENCE**
	Ayrault, Joe	R	R	6–3	190	10–8–71	Rochester, MI	Sarasota, FL
11	Berryhill, Damon	S	R	6–0	205	12–3–63	South Laguna, CA	Laguna Niguel, CA
61	Houston, Tyler	L	R	6–2	210	1–17–71	Las Vegas, NV	Las Vegas, NV
8	Lopez, Javier	R	R	6–3	185	11–5–70	Ponce, PR	Ponce, PR
22	O'Brien, Charlie	R	R	6–2	205	5–1–61	Tulsa, OK	Tulsa, OK
No.	**INFIELDERS**	**B**	**T**	**HT**	**WT**	**DOB**	**BIRTHPLACE**	**RESIDENCE**
2	Belliard, Rafael	R	R	5–6	160	10–24–61	Pueblo Nuevo Mao, DR	Boca Raton, FL
4	Blauser, Jeff	R	R	6–0	170	11–8–65	Los Gatos, CA	Alpharetta, GA
15	Carabello, Ramon	S	R	5–7	150	5–23–69	Rio San Juan, DR	Santo Domingo, DR
16	Jones, Chipper	S	R	6–3	185	4–24–72	DeLand, FL	Pierson, FL
18	Klesko, Ryan	L	L	6–3	220	6–12–71	Westminster, CA	Westminster, CA
20	Lemke, Mark	S	R	5–9	167	8–13–65	Utica, NY	Whitesboro, NY
27	McGriff, Fred	L	L	6–3	215	10–31–63	Tampa, FL	Tampa, FL
45	Oliva, Jose	R	R	6–1	150	3–3–71	S.P. de Macoris, DR	S.P de Macoris, DR
32	Pecota, Bill	R	R	6–2	195	2–16–60	Redwood City, CA	Overland Park, KS
9	Pendleton, Terry	S	R	5–9	195	7–16–60	Los Angeles, CA	Duluth, GA
No.	**OUTFIELDERS**	**B**	**T**	**HT**	**WT**	**DOB**	**BIRTHPLACE**	**RESIDENCE**
	Brown, Jarvis	R	R	5–7	177	3–26–67	Waukegan, IL	Waukegan, IL
	Gallagher, Dave	R	R	6–0	185	9–20–60	Trenton, NJ	Trenton, NJ
5	Gant, Ron	R	R	6–0	172	3–2–65	Victoria, TX	Smyrna, GA
66	Hughes, Troy	R	R	6–4	195	1–3–71	Mt. Vernon, IL	Mt. Vernon, IL
23	Justice, David	L	L	6–3	200	4–14–66	Cincinnati, OH	Atlanta, GA
	Kelly, Mike	R	R	6–4	195	6–2–70	Los Angeles, CA	Los Alamitos, CA
24	Sanders, Deion	L	L	6–1	195	8–9–67	Ft. Meyers, FL	Alpharetta, GA
26	Tarasco, Tony	L	R	6–1	205	12–9–70	New York, NY	Santa Monica, CA

Atlanta–Fulton County (52,709, grass)
Tickets: 404–522–7630
Ticket prices:
- $20 (dugout)
- $18 (club level)
- $15 (field level)
- $12 (lower pavilion)
- $10 (upper level)
- $5 (upper pavilion)

Field Dimensions (from home plate)
- To left field at foul line, 330 feet
- To center field, 402 feet
- To right field at foul line, 330 feet
- (OF wall is 10 feet high)

Jeff Blauser No. 4/SS

Full name: Jeffrey Michael Blauser
Bats: R **Throws:** R **HT:** 6–0 **WT:** 170
Born: 11–8–65, Los Gatos, CA
High school: Placer (Sacramento, CA)
College: Sacramento City (CA)
Blauser became the first Brave SS since Alvin Dark in 1948 to hit over .300. His 110 runs was fifth best in the NL.

	TEAM	LG	POS	G	AB	R	H	2B	3B	HR	RBI	BB	SO	SB	E	BA	SLG	SALARY
1987	ATL	NL	SS	51	165	11	40	6	3	2	15	18	34	7	9	.242	.352	N/A
1988	ATL	NL	2B-SS	18	67	7	16	3	1	2	7	2	11	0	4	.239	.403	N/A
1989	ATL	NL	3B-2B	142	456	63	123	24	2	12	46	38	101	5	21	.270	.410	N/A
1990	ATL	NL	SS	115	386	46	104	24	3	8	39	35	70	3	16	.269	.409	N/A
1991	ATL	NL	SS-2B	129	352	49	91	14	3	11	54	54	59	5	17	.259	.409	280,000
1992	ATL	NL	SS-2B	123	343	61	90	19	3	14	46	46	82	5	14	.262	.458	925,000
1993	ATL	NL	SS	161	597	110	182	29	2	15	73	85	109	16	19	.305	.436	2,000,000
7	YR	TOTALS		739	2366	347	646	119	17	64	280	278	466	41	100	.273	.419	
1993	RANK	MLB	SS	2	4	1	2	6	21	3	3	1	3	5	8	5	6	7
1994	PROJECTIONS			162	605	114	185	29	0	14	74	86	109	15	18	.306	.423	

Ron Gant No. 5/OF

Full name: Ronald Edwin Gant
Bats: R **Throws:** R **HT:** 6–0 **WT:** 172
Born: 3–2–65, Victoria, TX
High school: Victoria (TX)
Gant has been offered in proposed trades for a closer. He reached career highs for HR (36) and RBI (117) in '93. 18 of his 36 home runs gave Atlanta the lead or the win.

	TEAM	LG	POS	G	AB	R	H	2B	3B	HR	RBI	BB	SO	SB	E	BA	SLG	SALARY
1987	ATL	NL	2B	21	83	9	22	4	0	2	9	1	11	4	3	.265	.386	N/A
1988	ATL	NL	2B-3B	146	563	85	146	28	8	19	60	46	118	19	31	.259	.439	N/A
1989	ATL	NL	3B-OF	75	260	26	46	8	3	9	25	20	63	9	17	.177	.335	N/A
1990	ATL	NL	OF	152	575	107	174	34	3	32	84	50	86	33	8	.303	.539	N/A
1991	ATL	NL	OF	154	561	101	141	35	3	32	105	71	104	34	6	.251	.496	1,195,000
1992	ATL	NL	OF	153	544	74	141	22	6	17	80	45	101	32	4	.259	.415	2,650,000
1993	ATL	NL	OF	157	606	113	166	27	4	36	117	67	117	26	11	.274	.510	3,700,000
7	YR	TOTALS		858	3192	515	836	158	27	147	480	300	600	157	80	.262	.466	
1993	RANK	MLB	OF	8	7	6	17	28	32	6	6	19	13	23	6	61	14	14
1994	PROJECTIONS			152	576	99	151	30	5	29	94	61	113	26	16	.262	.483	

David Justice No. 23/OF

Full name: David Christopher Justice
Bats: L **Throws:** L **HT:** 6–3 **WT:** 200
Born: 4–14–66, Cincinnati, OH
High school: Covington Latin (KY)
College: Thomas Moore (KY)

This former NL rookie of the year really came into his own last year. '93's 120 RBI was the most by a Brave since Dale Murphy in 1983.

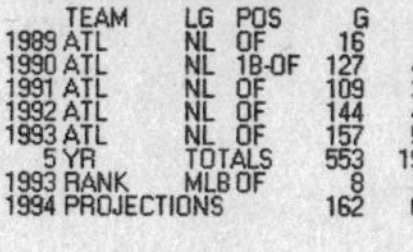
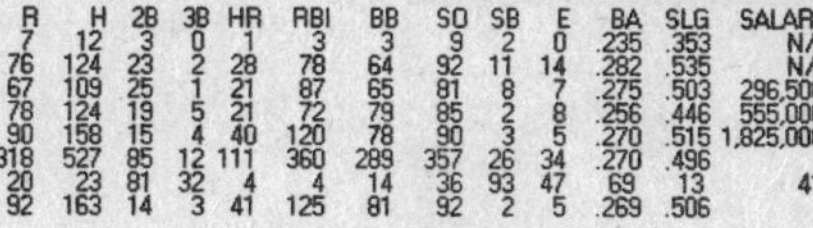

	TEAM	LG	POS	G	AB	R	H	2B	3B	HR	RBI	BB	SO	SB	E	BA	SLG	SALARY
1989	ATL	NL	OF	16	51	7	12	3	0	1	3	3	9	2	0	.235	.353	N/A
1990	ATL	NL	1B-OF	127	439	76	124	23	2	28	78	64	92	11	14	.282	.535	N/A
1991	ATL	NL	OF	109	396	67	109	25	1	21	87	65	81	8	7	.275	.503	296,500
1992	ATL	NL	OF	144	484	78	124	19	5	21	72	79	85	2	8	.256	.446	555,000
1993	ATL	NL	OF	157	585	90	158	15	4	40	120	78	90	3	5	.270	.515	1,825,000
5	YR	TOTALS		553	1955	318	527	85	12	111	360	289	357	26	34	.270	.496	
1993	RANK	MLB	OF	8	13	20	23	81	32	4	4	14	36	93	47	69	13	41
1994	PROJECTIONS			162	605	92	163	14	3	41	125	81	92	2	5	.269	.506	

Mark Lemke No. 20/2B

Full name: Mark Allen Lemke
Bats: S **Throws:** R **HT:** 5–9 **WT:** 167
Born: 8–13–65, Utica, NY
High school: Notre Dame (Utica, NY)

'93 was his first full season as the Braves' starting second baseman. Lemke hit .303 on artificial turf, and slugged .482 against left–handed pitching.

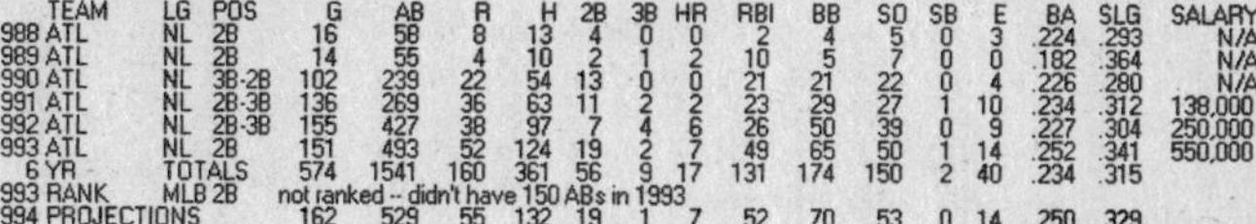

	TEAM	LG	POS	G	AB	R	H	2B	3B	HR	RBI	BB	SO	SB	E	BA	SLG	SALARY
1988	ATL	NL	2B	16	58	8	13	4	0	0	2	4	5	0	3	.224	.293	N/A
1989	ATL	NL	2B	14	55	4	10	2	1	2	10	5	7	0	0	.182	.364	N/A
1990	ATL	NL	3B-2B	102	239	22	54	13	0	0	21	21	22	0	4	.226	.280	N/A
1991	ATL	NL	2B-3B	136	269	36	63	11	2	2	23	29	27	1	10	.234	.312	138,000
1992	ATL	NL	2B-3B	155	427	38	97	7	4	6	26	50	39	0	9	.227	.304	250,000
1993	ATL	NL	2B	151	493	52	124	19	2	7	49	65	50	1	14	.252	.341	550,000
6	YR	TOTALS		574	1541	160	361	56	9	17	131	174	150	2	40	.234	.315	
1993	RANK	MLB	2B	not ranked -- didn't have 150 ABs in 1993														
1994	PROJECTIONS			162	529	55	132	19	1	7	52	70	53	0	14	.250	.329	

Javier Lopez — No. 8/C

Full name: Javier Torres Lopez
Bats: R **Throws:** R **HT:** 6–3 **WT:** 185
Born: 11–5–70, Ponce, PR
High school: Academia Cristo Rey (Ponce, PR)
In 100 games at AAA Richmond, Lopez hit .305, with 17 HR and 74 RBI. He hit .375 in eight games after his call-up from the minors, including a double, triple, and home run.

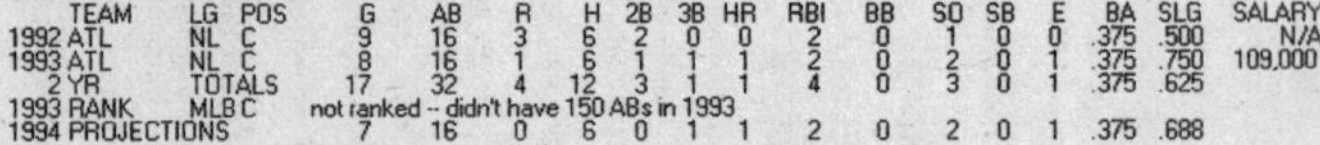

	TEAM	LG	POS	G	AB	R	H	2B	3B	HR	RBI	BB	SO	SB	E	BA	SLG	SALARY
1992	ATL	NL	C	9	16	3	6	2	0	0	2	0	1	0	0	.375	.500	N/A
1993	ATL	NL	C	8	16	1	6	1	1	1	2	0	2	0	1	.375	.750	109,000
2	YR	TOTALS		17	32	4	12	3	1	1	4	0	3	0	1	.375	.625	
1993	RANK	MLB	C	not ranked -- didn't have 150 ABs in 1993														
1994	PROJECTIONS			7	16	0	6	0	1	1	2	0	2	0	1	.375	.688	

Fred McGriff — No. 27/1B

Full name: Frederick Stanley McGriff
Bats: L **Throws:** L **HT:** 6–3 **WT:** 215
Born: 10–31–63, Tampa, FL
High school: Jefferson (Tampa, FL)
McGriff's .310 BA, 19 HR, and 55 RBI propelled the Braves to a 51–17 record after he arrived July 20. He's hit 30 HR for six straight years, only the twelfth major leaguer to do so.

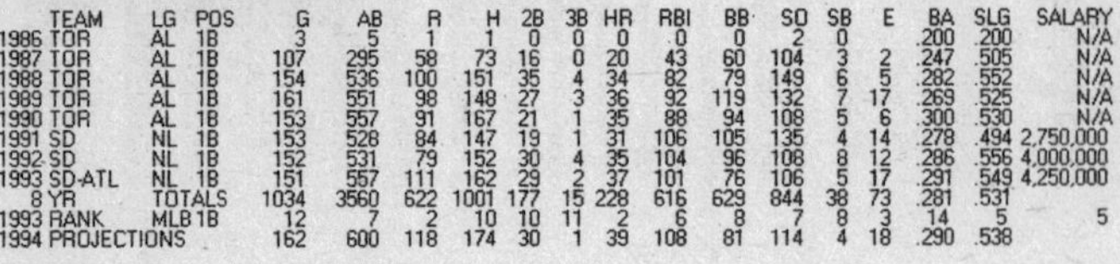

	TEAM	LG	POS	G	AB	R	H	2B	3B	HR	RBI	BB	SO	SB	E	BA	SLG	SALARY
1986	TOR	AL	1B	3	5	1	1	0	0	0	0	0	2	0		.200	.200	N/A
1987	TOR	AL	1B	107	295	58	73	16	0	20	43	60	104	3	2	.247	.505	N/A
1988	TOR	AL	1B	154	536	100	151	35	4	34	82	79	149	6	5	.282	.552	N/A
1989	TOR	AL	1B	161	551	98	148	27	3	36	92	119	132	7	17	.269	.525	N/A
1990	TOR	AL	1B	153	557	91	167	21	1	35	88	94	108	5	6	.300	.530	N/A
1991	SD	NL	1B	153	528	84	147	19	1	31	106	105	135	4	14	.278	.494	2,750,000
1992	SD	NL	1B	152	531	79	152	30	4	35	104	96	108	8	12	.286	.556	4,000,000
1993	SD-ATL	NL	1B	151	557	111	162	29	2	37	101	76	106	5	17	.291	.549	4,250,000
8	YR	TOTALS		1034	3560	622	1001	177	15	228	616	629	844	38	73	.281	.531	
1993	RANK	MLB	1B	12	7	2	10	10	11	2	6	8	7	8	3	14	5	5
1994	PROJECTIONS			162	600	118	174	30	1	39	108	81	114	4	18	.290	.538	

Terry Pendleton No. 9/3B

Full name: Terry Lee Pendleton
Bats: S **Throws:** R **HT:** 5–9 **WT:** 195
Born: 7–16–60, Los Angeles, CA
High school: Channel Island (CA)
College: Oxnard JC and Fresno State (CA)

Pendleton's .272 BA was due to a .148 BA through May 4; from then on, he hit .299. He hit just 8 HR in his first 125 games.

	TEAM	LG	POS	G	AB	R	H	2B	3B	HR	RBI	BB	SO	SB	E	BA	SLG	SALARY
1984	STL	NL	3B	67	262	37	85	16	3	1	33	16	32	20	13	.324	.420	N/A
1985	STL	NL	3B	149	559	56	134	16	3	5	69	37	75	17	18	.240	.306	N/A
1986	STL	NL	3B-OF	159	578	56	138	26	5	1	59	34	59	24	20	.239	.306	N/A
1987	STL	NL	3B	159	583	82	167	29	4	12	96	70	74	19	26	.286	.412	N/A
1988	STL	NL	3B	110	391	44	99	20	2	6	53	21	51	3	12	.253	.361	N/A
1989	STL	NL	3B	162	613	83	162	28	5	13	74	44	81	9	15	.264	.390	N/A
1990	STL	NL	3B	121	447	46	103	20	2	6	58	30	58	7	19	.230	.324	N/A
1991	ATL	NL	3B	153	586	94	187	34	8	22	86	43	70	10	24	.319	.517	1,750,000
1992	ATL	NL	3B	160	640	98	199	39	1	21	105	37	67	5	19	.311	.473	3,000,000
1993	ATL	NL	3B	161	633	81	172	33	1	17	84	36	97	5	19	.272	.408	2,250,000
10	YR	TOTALS		1401	5292	677	1446	261	34	104	717	368	664	119	185	.273	.394	
1993	RANK	MLB	3B	1	1	10	3	5	21	8	8	19	6	15	9	19	17	8
1994	PROJECTIONS			160	609	82	167	30	3	14	84	50	84	11	20	.274	.402	

Deion Sanders No. 24/OF

Full name: Deion Luwynn Sanders
Bats: L **Throws:** L **HT:** 6–1 **WT:** 195
Born:8–9–67, Ft. Meyers, FL
High school: North Ft. Meyers (FL)
College: Florida State

The poor man's Bo Jackson, Deion Sanders will be the Braves' starting center fielder in '94, with the departure of Otis Nixon.

	TEAM	LG	POS	G	AB	R	H	2B	3B	HR	RBI	BB	SO	SB	E	BA	SLG	SALARY
1989	NY	AL	OF	14	47	7	11	2	0	2	7	3	8	1	1	.234	.404	N/A
1990	NY	AL	OF	57	133	24	21	2	2	3	9	13	27	8	2	.158	.271	N/A
1991	ATL	NL	OF	54	110	16	21	1	2	4	13	12	23	11	3	.191	.345	N/A
1992	ATL	NL	OF	97	303	54	92	6	14	8	28	18	52	26	3	.304	.495	600,000
1993	ATL	NL	OF	95	272	42	75	18	6	6	28	16	42	19	2	.276	.452	1,416,666
5	YR	TOTALS		317	865	143	220	29	24	23	85	62	152	65	11	.254	.423	
1993	RANK	MLB	OF	98	94	87	88	61	13	87	98	117	97	34	97	56	44	51
1994	PROJECTIONS			68	171	27	39	7	3	4	16	13	30	12	2	.228	.380	

Steve Avery No. 33/P

Full name: Steven Thomas Avery
Bats: L **Throws:** L **HT:** 6–4 **WT:** 190
Born: 4–14–70, Trenton,MI
High school: John F. Kennedy (Taylor, MI)

Avery's 18 wins tied his '91 career high. Overall, the Braves were 28–7 when he started. Named to the All-Star team in '93, Avery led the NL in picking off runners with 15.

TM	LG	POS	W	L	ERA	G	GS	CG	SH	SV	IP	H	R	ER	HR	BB	SO	SALARY
1990 ATL	NL	P	3	11	5.64	21	20	1	1	0	99.0	121	79	62	7	45	75	N/A
1991 ATL	NL	P	18	8	3.38	35	35	3	1	0	210.1	189	89	79	21	65	137	110,000
1992 ATL	NL	P	11	11	3.20	35	35	2	2	0	233.2	216	95	83	14	71	129	355,000
1993 ATL	NL	P	18	6	2.94	35	35	3	1	0	223.1	216	81	73	14	43	125	560,000
4 YR	TOTALS		50	36	3.49	126	125	9	5	0	766.1	742	344	297	56	224	466	
1993 RANK	MLB Ps		8		39	134	6	37	23	102	24	113	31		52	15	200	127
1994 PROJECTIONS			13	8	3.61	30	30	2	1	0	177	175	83	71	14	51	112	

Tom Glavine No. 47/P

Full name: Thomas Michael Glavine
Bats: L **Throws:** L **HT:** 6–1 **WT:** 190
Born: 3–25–66, Concord, MA
High school: Billerica (MA)

Glavine tied for the league lead in wins with 22, and his 3.20 ERA placed eighth in the NL.

TM	LG	POS	W	L	ERA	G	GS	CG	SH	SV	IP	H	R	ER	HR	BB	SO	SALARY
1987 ATL	NL	P	2	4	5.54	9	9	0	0	0	50.1	55	34	31	5	33	20	N/A
1988 ATL	NL	P	7	17	4.56	34	34	1	0	0	195.1	201	111	99	12	63	84	N/A
1989 ATL	NL	P	14	8	3.68	29	29	6	4	0	186.0	172	88	76	20	40	90	N/A
1990 ATL	NL	P	10	12	4.28	33	33	1	0	0	214.1	232	111	102	18	78	129	N/A
1991 ATL	NL	P	20	11	2.55	34	34	9	1	0	246.2	201	83	70	17	69	192	722,000
1992 ATL	NL	P	20	8	2.76	33	33	7	5	0	225.0	197	81	69	6	70	129	2,925,000
1993 ATL	NL	P	22	6	3.20	36	36	4	2	0	239.1	236	91	85	16	90	120	4,850,000
7 YR	TOTALS		95	66	3.53	208	208	28	12	0	1357.0	1294	599	532	94	443	764	
1993 RANK	MLB Ps		1		61	124	1	25	8	102	11	124	42		58	160	237	7
1994 PROJECTIONS			17	8	3.38	34	34	4	2	0	226	221	94	85	13	79	126	

Greg Maddux No. 31/P

Full name: Gregory Alan Maddux
Bats: R **Throws:** R **HT:** 6–0 **WT:** 175
Born: 4–14–66, San Angelo, TX
High school: Valley (Las Vegas, NV)

Maddux' two straight Cy Young awards is a feat not seen in the NL since Sandy Koufax. (Roger Clemens did it in the AL in 1986–87.) Maddux led the NL in innings pitched.

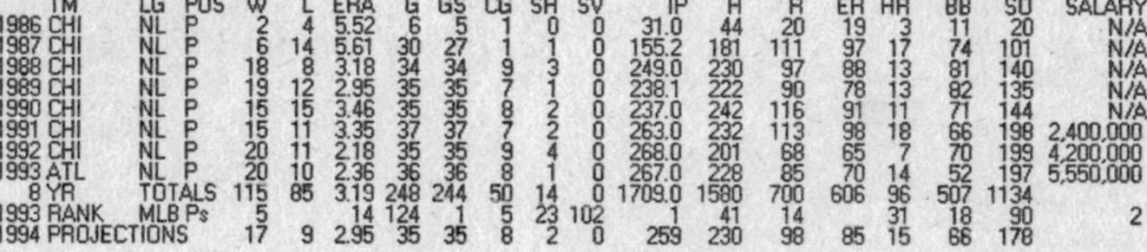

	TM	LG	POS	W	L	ERA	G	GS	CG	SH	SV	IP	H	R	ER	HR	BB	SO	SALARY
1986	CHI	NL	P	2	4	5.52	6	5	1	0	0	31.0	44	20	19	3	11	20	N/A
1987	CHI	NL	P	6	14	5.61	30	27	1	1	0	155.2	181	111	97	17	74	101	N/A
1988	CHI	NL	P	18	8	3.18	34	34	9	3	0	249.0	230	97	88	13	81	140	N/A
1989	CHI	NL	P	19	12	2.95	35	35	7	1	0	238.1	222	90	78	13	82	135	N/A
1990	CHI	NL	P	15	15	3.46	35	35	8	2	0	237.0	242	116	91	11	71	144	N/A
1991	CHI	NL	P	15	11	3.35	37	37	7	2	0	263.0	232	113	98	18	66	198	2,400,000
1992	CHI	NL	P	20	11	2.18	35	35	9	4	0	268.0	201	68	65	7	70	199	4,200,000
1993	ATL	NL	P	20	10	2.36	36	36	8	1	0	267.0	228	85	70	14	52	197	5,550,000
8	YR	TOTALS		115	85	3.19	248	244	50	14	0	1709.0	1580	700	606	96	507	1134	
1993	RANK	MLB Ps		5		14	124	1	5	23	102	1	41	14		31	18	90	2
1994	PROJECTIONS			17	9	2.95	35	35	8	2	0	259	230	98	85	15	66	178	

John Smoltz No. 29/P

Full name: John Andrew Smoltz
Bats: R **Throws:** R **HT:** 6–3 **WT:** 185
Born: 5–15–67, Warren, MI
High school: Waverly (Lansing, MI)

Smoltz' 208 strikeouts was second in the NL. He's already second on Atlanta's all-time strikeout list with 946 in six seasons (Phil Niekro leads with 2,855).

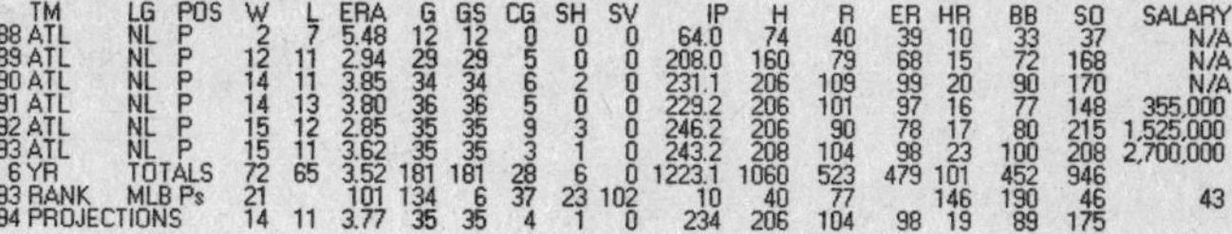

	TM	LG	POS	W	L	ERA	G	GS	CG	SH	SV	IP	H	R	ER	HR	BB	SO	SALARY
1988	ATL	NL	P	2	7	5.48	12	12	0	0	0	64.0	74	40	39	10	33	37	N/A
1989	ATL	NL	P	12	11	2.94	29	29	5	0	0	208.0	160	79	68	15	72	168	N/A
1990	ATL	NL	P	14	11	3.85	34	34	6	2	0	231.1	206	109	99	20	90	170	N/A
1991	ATL	NL	P	14	13	3.80	36	36	5	0	0	229.2	206	101	97	16	77	148	355,000
1992	ATL	NL	P	15	12	2.85	35	35	9	3	0	246.2	206	90	78	17	80	215	1,525,000
1993	ATL	NL	P	15	11	3.62	35	35	3	1	0	243.2	208	104	98	23	100	208	2,700,000
6	YR	TOTALS		72	65	3.52	181	181	28	6	0	1223.1	1060	523	479	101	452	946	
1993	RANK	MLB Ps		21		101	134	6	37	23	102	10	40	77		146	190	46	43
1994	PROJECTIONS			14	11	3.77	35	35	4	1	0	234	206	104	98	19	89	175	

Greg McMichael No. 38/P

Full name: Gregory Winston McMichael
Bats: R **Throws:** R **HT:** 6–3 **WT:** 215
Born: 12–1–66, Knoxville, TN
High school: Webb (TN)
College: Tennessee

McMichael converted his first 15 save opportunities. His 19 saves were the most by a rookie since Todd Worrell's 36 in '86.

TM	LG	POS	W	L	ERA	G	GS	CG	SH	SV	IP	H	R	ER	HR	BB	SO	SALARY
1993 ATL	NL	P	2	3	2.06	74	0	0	0	19	91.2	68	22	21	3	29	89	109,000
1 YR	TOTAL		2	3	2.06	74	0	0	0	19	91.2	68	22	21	3	29	89	
1993 RANK	MLB Ps		246		3	5	202	125	69	19	161	13	4		8	91	20	236

Bobby Cox No. 6/Mgr.

Full name: Robert Joe Cox
Bats: R **Throws:** R **HT:** 6–0 **WT:** 185
Born: 5–21–41, Tulsa, OK
High school: Selma (CA)
College: Reedley JC (CA)

Under Cox, Atlanta has won more games than anyone else in baseball over the past 3 years. He was NL manager of the year with the Braves in 1991.

				REG. SEASON				PLAYOFF			CHAMP. SERIES			WORLD SERIES		
	YEAR	TEAM	LG	W	L	PCT	POS	W	L	PCT	W	L	PCT	W	L	PCT
	1978	ATL	NL	69	93	.426	6			---			---			---
	1979	ATL	NL	66	94	.413	6			---			---			---
	1980	ATL	NL	81	80	.503	4			---			---			---
1ST HALF	1981	ATL	NL	25	29	.463	4			---			---			---
2ND HALF	1981	ATL	NL	25	27	.481	5			---			---			---
	1982	TOR	AL	78	84	.481	6			---			---			---
	1983	TOR	AL	89	73	.549	4			---			---			---
	1984	TOR	AL	89	73	.549	2			---			---			---
	1985	TOR	AL	99	62	.615	1			---	3	4	.429			---
	1990	ATL	NL	40	57	.412	6			---			---			---
	1991	ATL	NL	94	68	.580	1			---	4	3	.571	3	4	.429
	1992	ATL	NL	98	64	.605	1			---	4	3	.571	2	4	.333
	1993	ATL	NL	104	58	.642	1			---	2	4	.333			---
	12	YR TOTALS		957	862	.526		0	0	---	13	14	.481	5	8	.385

Steve Bedrosian No. 36/P

Full name: Stephen Wayne Bedrosian
Bats: R **Throws:** R **HT:** 6–3 **WT:** 205
Born:12–6–57, Methuen, MA
High school: Methuen (MA)
College: N. Essex CC (MA) and New Haven (CT)
Bedrosian had a 1.63 ERA in '93, his career best.

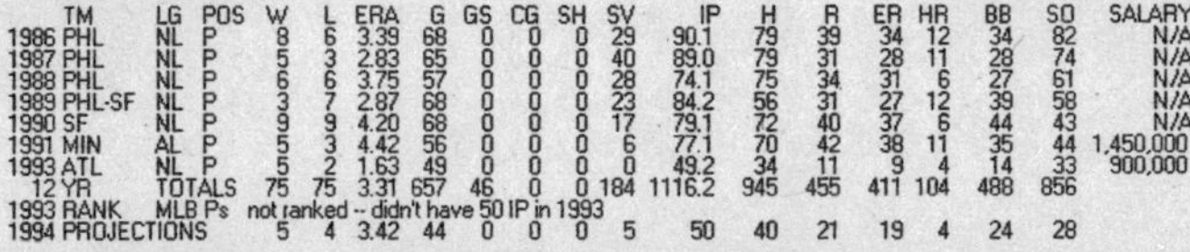

TM	LG	POS	W	L	ERA	G	GS	CG	SH	SV	IP	H	R	ER	HR	BB	SO	SALARY
1986 PHL	NL	P	8	6	3.39	68	0	0	0	29	90.1	79	39	34	12	34	82	N/A
1987 PHL	NL	P	5	3	2.83	65	0	0	0	40	89.0	79	31	28	11	28	74	N/A
1988 PHL	NL	P	6	6	3.75	57	0	0	0	28	74.1	75	34	31	6	27	61	N/A
1989 PHL-SF	NL	P	3	7	2.87	68	0	0	0	23	84.2	56	31	27	12	39	58	N/A
1990 SF	NL	P	9	9	4.20	68	0	0	0	17	79.1	72	40	37	6	44	43	N/A
1991 MIN	AL	P	5	3	4.42	56	0	0	0	6	77.1	70	42	38	11	35	44	1,450,000
1993 ATL	NL	P	5	2	1.63	49	0	0	0	0	49.2	34	11	9	4	14	33	900,000
12 YR	TOTALS		75	75	3.31	657	46	0	0	184	1116.2	945	455	411	104	488	856	
1993 RANK	MLB Ps		not ranked -- didn't have 50 IP in 1993															
1994 PROJECTIONS			5	4	3.42	44	0	0	0	5	50	40	21	19	4	24	28	

Rafael Belliard No. 2/2B

Full name: Rafael Leonidas Belliard
Bats: R **Throws:** R **HT:** 5–6 **WT:** 160
Born:10–24–61, Pueblo Nuevo Mao, DR
Belliard only started 16 games all season, but appeared in 61 games as a defensive replacement. He committed just one error in 153 chances.

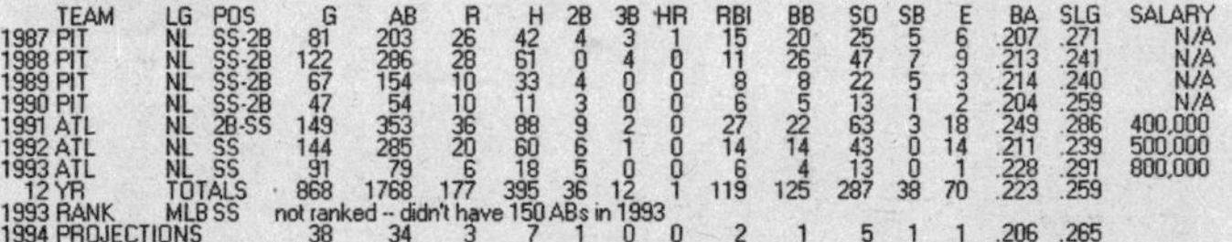

TEAM	LG	POS	G	AB	R	H	2B	3B	HR	RBI	BB	SO	SB	E	BA	SLG	SALARY
1987 PIT	NL	SS-2B	81	203	26	42	4	3	1	15	20	25	5	6	.207	.271	N/A
1988 PIT	NL	SS-2B	122	286	28	61	0	4	0	11	26	47	7	9	.213	.241	N/A
1989 PIT	NL	SS-2B	67	154	10	33	4	0	0	8	8	22	5	3	.214	.240	N/A
1990 PIT	NL	SS-2B	47	54	10	11	3	0	0	6	5	13	1	2	.204	.259	N/A
1991 ATL	NL	2B-SS	149	353	36	88	9	2	0	27	22	63	3	18	.249	.286	400,000
1992 ATL	NL	SS	144	285	20	60	6	1	0	14	14	43	0	14	.211	.239	500,000
1993 ATL	NL	SS	91	79	6	18	5	0	0	6	4	13	0	1	.228	.291	800,000
12 YR	TOTALS		868	1768	177	395	36	12	1	119	125	287	38	70	.223	.259	
1993 RANK	MLB SS		not ranked -- didn't have 150 ABs in 1993														
1994 PROJECTIONS			38	34	3	7	1	0	0	2	1	5	1	1	.206	.265	

Damon Berryhill No. 11/C

Full name: Damon Scott Berryhill
Bats: S **Throws:** R **HT:** 6–0 **WT:** 205
Born:12–3–63, South Laguna, CA
High school: Laguna Beach (CA)
College: Orange Coast (CA)
Split time with Greg Olson at catcher in '93.

TEAM	LG	POS	G	AB	R	H	2B	3B	HR	RBI	BB	SO	SB	E	BA	SLG	SALARY
1987 CHI	NL	C	12	28	2	5	1	0	0	1	3	5	0	4	.179	.214	N/A
1988 CHI	NL	C	95	309	19	80	19	1	7	38	17	56	1	9	.259	.395	N/A
1989 CHI	NL	C	91	334	37	86	13	0	5	41	16	54	1	4	.257	.341	N/A
1990 CHI	NL	C	17	53	6	10	4	0	1	9	5	14	0	2	.189	.321	N/A
1991 ATL	NL	C	63	160	13	30	7	0	5	14	11	42	1	8	.188	.325	N/A
1992 ATL	NL	C	101	307	21	70	16	1	10	43	17	67	0	1	.228	.384	325,000
1993 ATL	NL	C	115	335	24	82	18	2	8	43	21	64	0	6	.245	.382	1,000,000
7 YR	TOTALS		494	1526	122	363	78	4	36	189	90	302	3	34	.238	.365	
1993 RANK	MLB C		20	20	29	22	16	6	22	19	26	15	35	15	29	23	15
1994 PROJECTIONS			129	378	27	93	20	2	9	49	23	72	0	6	.246	.381	

Jarvis Brown — OF

Full name: Jarvis Ardel Brown
Bats: R **Throws:** R **HT:** 5–7 **WT:** 177
Born: 3–26–67, Waukegan, IL
High school: St. Joseph (Kenosha, WI)
College: Triton (IL)
Brown hit .308 with 22 SB for AAA Las Vegas.

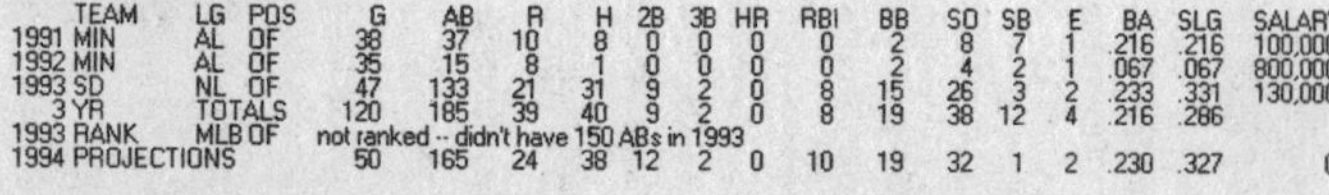

	TEAM	LG	POS	G	AB	R	H	2B	3B	HR	RBI	BB	SO	SB	E	BA	SLG	SALARY
1991	MIN	AL	OF	38	37	10	8	0	0	0	0	2	8	7	1	.216	.216	100,000
1992	MIN	AL	OF	35	15	8	1	0	0	0	0	2	4	2	1	.067	.067	800,000
1993	SD	NL	OF	47	133	21	31	9	2	0	8	15	26	3	2	.233	.331	130,000
3	YR	TOTALS		120	185	39	40	9	2	0	8	19	38	12	4	.216	.286	
1993	RANK	MLB	OF	not ranked -- didn't have 150 ABs in 1993														
1994	PROJECTIONS			50	165	24	38	12	2	0	10	19	32	1	2	.230	.327	0

Dave Gallagher — OF

Full name: Dave Gallagher
Bats: R **Throws:** R **HT:** 6–0 **WT:** 185
Born: 9–20–60, Trenton, NJ
High school: Steinert (Trenton, NJ)
College: Mercer County CC (NJ)
Obtained from the Mets for pitcher Pete Smith.

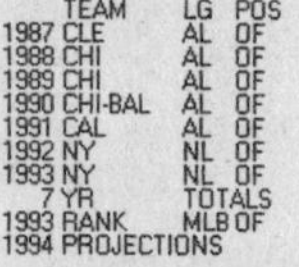

	TEAM	LG	POS	G	AB	R	H	2B	3B	HR	RBI	BB	SO	SB	E	BA	SLG	SALARY
1987	CLE	AL	OF	15	36	2	4	1	1	0	1	2	5	2	1	.111	.194	N/A
1988	CHI	AL	OF	101	347	59	105	15	3	5	31	29	40	5	0	.303	.406	N/A
1989	CHI	AL	OF	161	601	74	160	22	2	1	46	46	79	5	3	.266	.314	N/A
1990	CHI-BAL	AL	OF	68	126	12	32	4	1	0	7	7	12	1	2	.254	.302	N/A
1991	CAL	AL	OF	90	270	32	79	17	0	1	30	24	43	2	0	.293	.367	357,500
1992	NY	NL	OF	98	175	20	42	11	1	1	21	19	16	4	2	.240	.331	628,750
1993	NY	NL	OF	99	201	34	55	12	2	6	28	20	18	1	0	.274	.443	500,000
7	YR	TOTALS		632	1756	233	477	82	10	14	164	147	213	20	8	.272	.354	
1993	RANK	MLB	OF	93	119	95	111	96	76	87	98	104	134	116	131	62	55	81
1994	PROJECTIONS			88	167	22	43	9	1	2	18	15	15	2	1	.257	.365	

Chipper Jones — No. 16/SS

Full name: Larry Wayne Jones
Bats: S **Throws:** R **HT:** 6–3 **WT:** 185
Born: 4–24–72, DeLand, FL
High school: The Bolles (Jacksonville, FL)
Jones hit .325 with 13 HR and 89 RBI at AAA Richmond, and .667 in eight games with Atlanta.

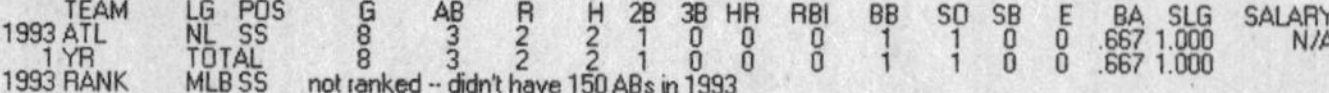

	TEAM	LG	POS	G	AB	R	H	2B	3B	HR	RBI	BB	SO	SB	E	BA	SLG	SALARY
1993	ATL	NL	SS	8	3	2	2	1	0	0	0	1	1	0	0	.667	1.000	N/A
1	YR	TOTAL		8	3	2	2	1	0	0	0	1	1	0	0	.667	1.000	
1993	RANK	MLB	SS	not ranked -- didn't have 150 ABs in 1993														

Ryan Klesko No. 18/1B–OF

Full name: Ryan Anthony Klesko
Bats: L **Throws:** L **HT:** 6–3 **WT:** 220
Born: 6–12–71, Westminster, CA
High school: Westminster (CA)
Klesko hit .274 with 22 HR and 74 RBI in 98 games at AAA Richmond.

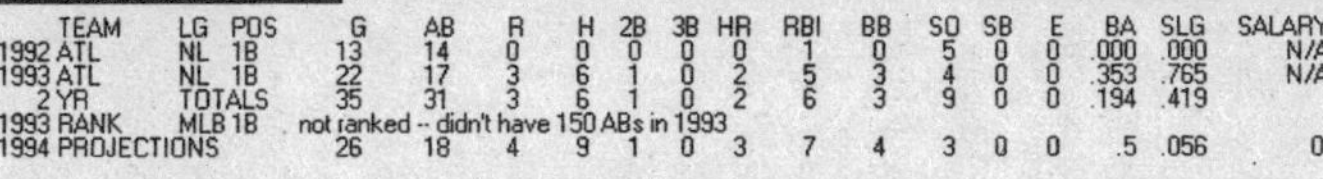

TEAM	LG	POS	G	AB	R	H	2B	3B	HR	RBI	BB	SO	SB	E	BA	SLG	SALARY
1992 ATL	NL	1B	13	14	0	0	0	0	0	1	0	5	0	0	.000	.000	N/A
1993 ATL	NL	1B	22	17	3	6	1	0	2	5	3	4	0	0	.353	.765	N/A
2 YR	TOTALS		35	31	3	6	1	0	2	6	3	9	0	0	.194	.419	
1993 RANK	MLB 1B		not ranked -- didn't have 150 ABs in 1993														
1994 PROJECTIONS			26	18	4	9	1	0	3	7	4	3	0	0	.5	.056	0

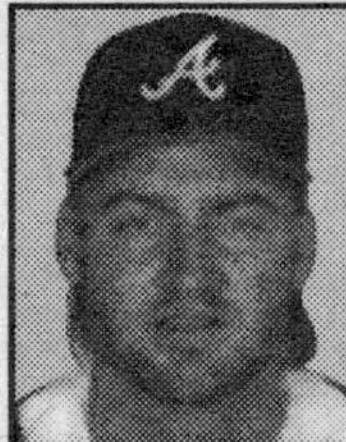

Kent Mercker No. 50/P

Full name: Kent Franklin Mercker
Bats: L **Throws:** L **HT:** 6–2 **WT:** 195
Born: 2–1–68, Dublin, OH
High school: Dublin (OH)
Mercker could become the fifth starter with Pete Smith's trade to New York.

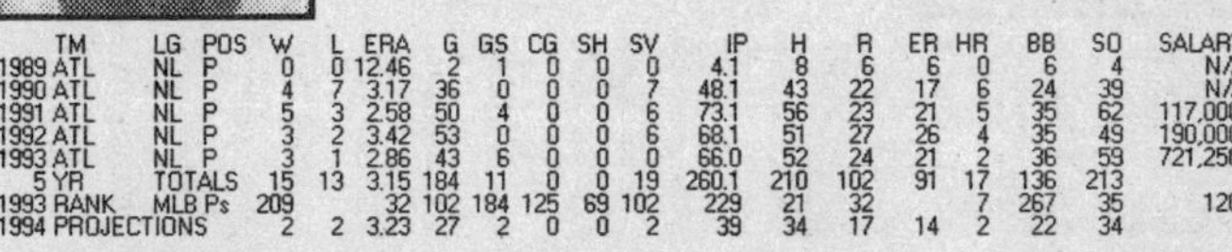

TM	LG	POS	W	L	ERA	G	GS	CG	SH	SV	IP	H	R	ER	HR	BB	SO	SALARY
1989 ATL	NL	P	0	0	12.46	2	1	0	0	0	4.1	8	6	6	0	6	4	N/A
1990 ATL	NL	P	4	7	3.17	36	0	0	0	7	48.1	43	22	17	6	24	39	N/A
1991 ATL	NL	P	5	3	2.58	50	4	0	0	6	73.1	56	23	21	5	35	62	117,000
1992 ATL	NL	P	3	2	3.42	53	0	0	0	6	68.1	51	27	26	4	35	49	190,000
1993 ATL	NL	P	3	1	2.86	43	6	0	0	0	66.0	52	24	21	2	36	59	721,250
5 YR	TOTALS		15	13	3.15	184	11	0	0	19	260.1	210	102	91	17	136	213	
1993 RANK	MLB Ps		209		32	102	184	125	69	102	229	21	32		7	267	35	120
1994 PROJECTIONS			2	2	3.23	27	2	0	0	2	39	34	17	14	2	22	34	

Charlie O'Brien No. 22/C

Full name: Charles Hugh O'Brien
Bats: R **Throws:** R **HT:** 6–2 **WT:** 205
Born: 5–1–61, Tulsa, OK
High school: Bishop Kelley (Tulsa, OK)
College: McLennan CC (TX) and Wichita State
This ex-Met will back up Javier Lopez in '94.

TEAM	LG	POS	G	AB	R	H	2B	3B	HR	RBI	BB	SO	SB	E	BA	SLG	SALARY
1985 OAK	AL	C	16	11	3	3	1	0	0	1	3	3	0	1	.273	.364	N/A
1987 MIL	AL	C	10	35	2	7	3	1	0	0	4	4	0	0	.200	.343	N/A
1988 MIL	AL	C	40	118	12	26	6	0	2	9	5	16	0	2	.220	.322	N/A
1989 MIL	AL	C	62	188	22	44	10	0	6	35	21	11	0	5	.234	.383	N/A
1990 MIL	AL	C	46	145	11	27	7	2	0	11	11	26	0	2	.186	.262	N/A
1990 NY	NL	C	28	68	6	11	3	0	0	9	10	8	0	3	.162	.206	N/A
1991 NY	NL	C	69	168	16	31	6	0	2	14	17	25	0	4	.185	.256	300,000
1992 NY	NL	C	68	156	15	33	12	0	2	13	16	18	0	7	.212	.327	370,000
1993 NY	NL	C	67	188	15	48	11	0	4	23	14	14	1	5	.255	.378	500,000
8 YR	TOTALS		406	1077	102	230	59	3	16	115	101	125	1	29	.214	.318	
1993 RANK	MLB C		38	36	39	36	27	25	30	35	35	41	21	23	22	26	22

Bill Pecota — No. 32/3B

Full name: William Joseph Pecota
Bats: R **Throws:** R **HT:** 6–2 **WT:** 195
Born: 2–16–60, Redwood City, CA
High school: Peterson (Sunnyvale, CA)
College: De Anza (CA)
This utility player didn't commit an error all season.

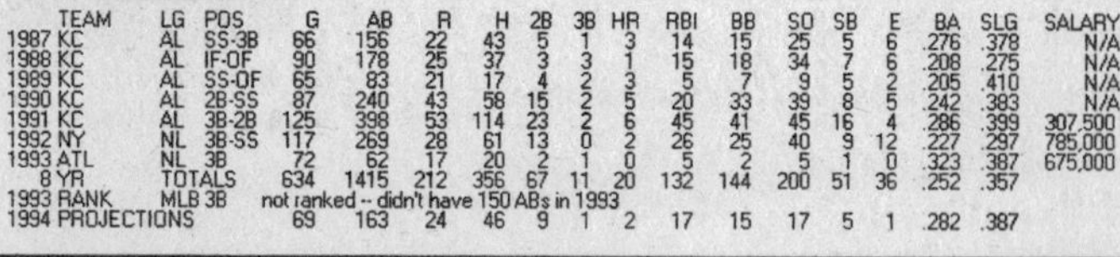

	TEAM	LG	POS	G	AB	R	H	2B	3B	HR	RBI	BB	SO	SB	E	BA	SLG	SALARY
1987	KC	AL	SS-3B	66	156	22	43	5	1	3	14	15	25	5	6	.276	.378	N/A
1988	KC	AL	IF-OF	90	178	25	37	3	3	1	15	18	34	7	6	.208	.275	N/A
1989	KC	AL	SS-OF	65	83	21	17	4	2	3	5	7	9	5	2	.205	.410	N/A
1990	KC	AL	2B-SS	87	240	43	58	15	2	5	20	33	39	8	5	.242	.383	N/A
1991	KC	AL	3B-2B	125	398	53	114	23	2	6	45	41	45	16	4	.286	.399	307,500
1992	NY	NL	3B-SS	117	269	28	61	13	0	2	26	25	40	9	12	.227	.297	785,000
1993	ATL	NL	3B	72	62	17	20	2	1	0	5	2	5	1	0	.323	.387	675,000
8	YR	TOTALS		634	1415	212	356	67	11	20	132	144	200	51	36	.252	.357	
1993	RANK	MLB 3B		not ranked -- didn't have 150 ABs in 1993														
1994	PROJECTIONS			69	163	24	46	9	1	2	17	15	17	5	1	.282	.387	

Mike Stanton — No. 30/P

Full name: William Michael Stanton
Bats: L **Throws:** L **HT:** 5–10 **WT:** 190
Born: 6–2–67, Houston, TX
High school: Midland (TX)
College: Alvin Community (TX)
Stanton converted 27 of 33 save opportunities.

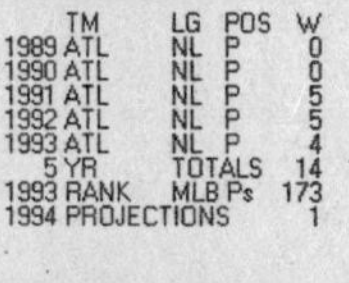

	TM	LG	POS	W	L	ERA	G	GS	CG	SH	SV	IP	H	R	ER	HR	BB	SO	SALARY
1989	ATL	NL	P	0	1	1.50	20	0	0	0	7	24.0	17	4	4	0	8	27	N/A
1990	ATL	NL	P	0	3	18.00	7	0	0	0	2	7.0	16	16	14	1	4	7	N/A
1991	ATL	NL	P	5	5	2.88	74	0	0	0	7	78.0	62	27	25	6	21	54	120,000
1992	ATL	NL	P	5	4	4.10	65	0	0	0	8	63.2	59	32	29	6	20	44	265,000
1993	ATL	NL	P	4	6	4.67	63	0	0	0	27	52.0	51	35	27	4	29	43	850,000
5	YR	TOTALS		14	19	3.97	229	0	0	0	51	224.2	205	114	99	17	82	175	
1993	RANK	MLB Ps		173		207	38	202	125	69	13	284	119	264		90	270	54	110
1994	PROJECTIONS			1	3	5.00	30	0	0	0	12	27	28	18	15	1	13	25	

Mark Wohlers — No. 43/P

Full name: Mark Edward Wohlers
Bats: R **Throws:** R **HT:** 6–4 **WT:** 207
Born:1–23–70, Holyoke, MA
High school: Holyoke (MA)
Wohlers has allowed just 3 HR in 95 major league games. Six wins in '93 was a career high.

	TM	LG	POS	W	L	ERA	G	GS	CG	SH	SV	IP	H	R	ER	HR	BB	SO	SALARY
1991	ATL	NL	P	3	1	3.20	17	0	0	0	2	19.2	17	7	7	1	13	13	100,000
1992	ATL	NL	P	1	2	2.55	32	0	0	0	4	35.1	28	11	10	0	14	17	114,000
1993	ATL	NL	P	6	2	4.50	46	0	0	0	0	48.0	37	25	24	2	22	45	140,000
3	YR	TOTALS		10	5	3.58	95	0	0	0	6	103.0	82	43	41	3	49	75	
1993	RANK	MLB Ps		not ranked -- didn't have 50 IP in 1993															
1994	PROJECTIONS			7	2	4.58	55	0	0	0	0	57	43	31	29	2	25	55	

Chicago
CUBS

1994 Scouting Report

Hitting: (1993/.270 BA, fifth in NL; 161 HR, third in NL)

Power is supplied by Sammy Sosa (33 HR, 93 RBI) and Rick Wilkins (.303 BA, 30 HR, 73 RBI). Mark Grace hit .325 with 14 HR and 98 HR. The Cubs lost Shawon Dunston for almost all of '93 with a herniated disk in his lower back. Rey Sanchez emerged as a capable replacement, hitting .282.

The Cubs lack team speed. They only stole 100 bases in '93, tenth in the NL, and they led the league in grounding into double plays. Chicago could use a true leadoff hitter who can get on and threaten to steal bases.

Pitching: (1993/4.18 ERA, tenth in NL)

No true ace, but the rotation features quality pitchers in Jose Guzman (12–10, 4.34 ERA) and Mike Harkey (10–10). Jose Bautista, a '93 non-roster invitee who was one of the last players to make the team, went 10–3 with a 2.82 ERA—despite not making his first start until June 16. The Cubs fortified the staff by trading for Willie Banks from Minnesota.

Randy Myers is a strong closer (53 saves, 3.11 ERA), but middle relief is a problem.

Defense: (1993/.982 pct., fourth in NL)

Cub OF defense needs improvement. Steve Buechele led NL third basemen with a .975 fielding percentage. Mark Grace is a good fielding first baseman, and catcher Rick Wilkins posted a .996 fielding percentage.

1994 Prospects:

GM Larry Himes is on the spot after dismissing Jim Lefebvre, who was popular with senior team officials, in favor of Tom Trebelhorn. But the Cubs aren't as talented as Himes believes they are. They have a solid nucleus, but their talent level drops significantly after the likes of Wilkins, Grace, and Sosa. Their pitching doesn't compare to division rivals Houston or St. Louis. And their offense isn't overwhelming—especially for a team that plays 81 games in the friendly confines of Wrigley Field. The Cubs don't figure to make the playoffs, let alone win the NL Central.

Team Directory

Chairman: Stanton R. Cook
General Mgr.: Larry Himes
Director of P.R.: Sharon Pannozzo
VP, Baseball Adm.: Ned Coletti
Asst. GM: Syd Thrift
Traveling Secretary: Jim Banks

Minor League Affiliates:

Level	Team/League	1993 Record
AAA	Iowa – American Association	85–59
AA	Orlando – Southern	71–70
A	Daytona/Florida State	57–76
	Peoria – Midwest	59–79
	Geneva – New York/Penn.*	43–34
Rookie	Huntington – Appalachian	33–35

*New York-Penn League franchise moving from Geneva, New York, to Williamsport, Pennsylvania for 1994.

1993 Review

	Home W	Home L	Away W	Away L		Home W	Home L	Away W	Away L		Home W	Home L	Away W	Away L
vs NL East	W	L	W	L	vs NL Cent.	W	L	W	L	vs NL West	W	L	W	L
Atlanta	2	4	3	3	Cincinnati	3	3	4	2	Colorado	5	1	3	3
Florida	4	2	2	5	Houston	2	4	2	4	Los Angeles	4	2	3	3
Montreal	3	3	2	5	Pittsburgh	3	4	2	4	San Diego	3	3	5	1
New York	4	3	4	2	St. Louis	4	3	4	2	S. Francisco	3	3	3	3
Philadelphia	3	3	4	3										
Total	16	15	15	18		12	14	12	12		15	9	14	10

1993 finish: 84–78 (43–38 home, 41–40 away), fourth in NL East, 13 games behind

1994 Schedule

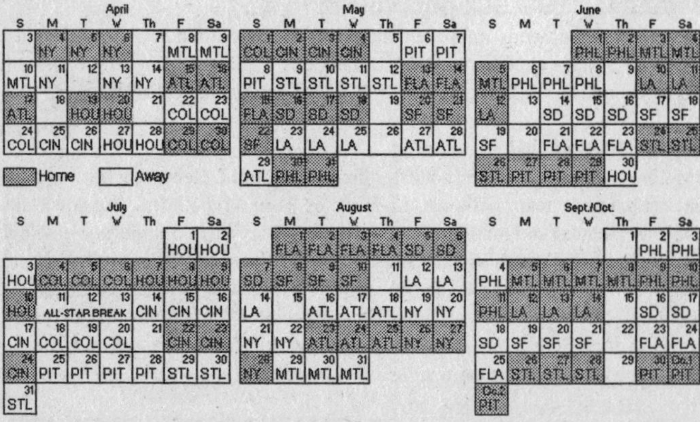

CHICAGO CUBS 1994 ROSTER

Manager: Tom Trebelhorn (41)
Coaches: Chuck Cottier (15); Moe Drabowsky; Marv Foley; Jose Martinez (3); Tony Muser (40); Billy Williams (26)

No.	PITCHERS	B	T	HT	WT	DOB	BIRTHPLACE	RESIDENCE
	Banks, Willie	R	R	6–1	203	2–27–69	Jersey City, NJ	Jersey City, NJ
38	Bautista, Jose	R	R	6–2	205	7–26–64	Bani, DR	Cooper City, FL
47	Boskie, Shawn	R	R	6–3	200	3–28–67	Hawthorne, NV	Scottsdale, AZ
52	Bullinger, Jim	R	R	6–2	185	8–21–65	New Orleans, LA	Metairie, LA
49	Castillo, Frank	R	R	6–1	190	4–1–69	El Paso, TX	El Paso, TX
33	Dickson, Lance	R	L	6–1	190	10–19–69	Fullerton, CA	San Diego, CA
29	Guzman, Jose	R	R	6–3	195	4–9–63	Santa Isabel, PR	Chicago, IL
22	Harkey, Mike	R	R	6–5	235	10–25–66	San Diego, CA	Chino Hills, CA
37	Hibbard, Greg	L	L	6–0	190	9–13–64	New Orleans, LA	Memphis, TN
48	Hollins, Jessie	R	R	6–3	235	1–27–70	Conroe, TX	Apple Springs, TX
	Ilsley, Blaise	L	L	6–1	195	4–9–64	Alpena, MI	Alpena, MI
26	Luebbers, Larry	R	R	6–6	190	10–11–69	Cincinnati, OH	
36	Morgan, Mike	R	R	6–2	220	10–8–59	Tulare, CA	Las Vegas, NV
28	Myers, Randy	L	L	6–1	230	9–19–62	Vancouver, WA	Vancouver, WA
32	Plesac, Dan	L	L	6–5	215	2–4–62	Gary, IN	St. Charles, IL
30	Scanlan, Bob	R	R	6–8	215	8–9–66	Los Angeles, CA	Beverly Hills, CA
48	Trachael, Steve	R	R	6–4	205	10–31–70	Oxnard, CA	Yorba Linda, CA
13	Wendell, Turk	S	R	6–2	190	5–19–67	Pittsfield, MA	Dalton, MA
No.	**CATCHERS**	**B**	**T**	**HT**	**WT**	**DOB**	**BIRTHPLACE**	**RESIDENCE**
2	Wilkins, Rick	L	R	6–2	210	6–4–67	Jacksonville, FL	Jacksonville, FL
No.	**INFIELDERS**	**B**	**T**	**HT**	**WT**	**DOB**	**BIRTHPLACE**	**RESIDENCE**
24	Buechele, Steve	R	R	6–2	200	9–26–61	Lancaster, CA	Arlington, TX
12	Dunston, Shawon	R	R	6–1	180	3–21–63	Brooklyn, NY	Fremont, CA
	Franco, Matt	L	R	6–2	200	8–19–69	Santa Monica, CA	Thousand Oaks, CA
17	Grace, Mark	L	L	6–2	190	6–28–64	Winston–Salem, NC	Chicago, IL
	Hernandez, Jose	R	R	6–1	180	7–14–69	Vega Alta, PR	Vega Alta, PR
11	Sanchez, Rey	R	R	5–9	170	10–5–67	Rio Piedras, PR	Port Charlotte, FL
23	Sandberg, Ryne	R	R	6–2	190	9–18–59	Spokane, WA	Phoenix, AZ
1	Shields, Tommy	R	R	6–0	185	8–14–64	Fairfax, VA	Evanston, IL
16	Vizcaino, Jose	S	R	6–1	180	3–26–68	San Cristobal, DR	El Cajon, CA
No.	**OUTFIELDERS**	**B**	**T**	**HT**	**WT**	**DOB**	**BIRTHPLACE**	**RESIDENCE**
	Glanville, Doug							
34	Hill, Glenallen	R	R	6–2	220	3–22–65	Santa Cruz, CA	Boca Raton, FL
27	May, Derrick	L	R	6–4	225	7–14–68	Rochester, NY	Newark, DE
25	Rhodes, Karl	L	L	6–0	195	8–21–68	Cincinnati, OH	Cincinnati, OH
19	Roberson, Kevin	S	R	6–4	210	1–29–68	Decatur, IL	Scottsdale, AZ
18	Smith, Dwight	L	R	5–11	190	11–8–63	Tallahassee, FL	Fairburn, GA
21	Sosa, Sammy	R	R	6–0	185	11–12–68	S.P. de Macoris, DR	S.P. de Macoris, DR
	Timmons, Ozzie							
6	Wilson, Willie	S	R	6–2	200	7–9–55	Montgomery, AL	Leawood, KS
39	Zambrano, Eddie	R	R	6–3	200	2–1–66	Maricaibo, VZ	Zulia, VZ

Wrigley Field (38,710, grass)
Tickets: 312–404–2827
Ticket prices:
- $19 (field box)
- $15 (terrace box)
- $15 (upper deck box)
- $12 (terrace reserved)
- $9 (adult upper deck reserved)
- $6 (under 14 upper deck reserved)
- $10 (bleachers)

Field Dimensions (from home plate)
- To left field at foul line, 355 feet
- To center field, 400 feet
- To right field at foul line, 353 feet
- (OF wall is 15' in LF and RF, 11.5' in CF)

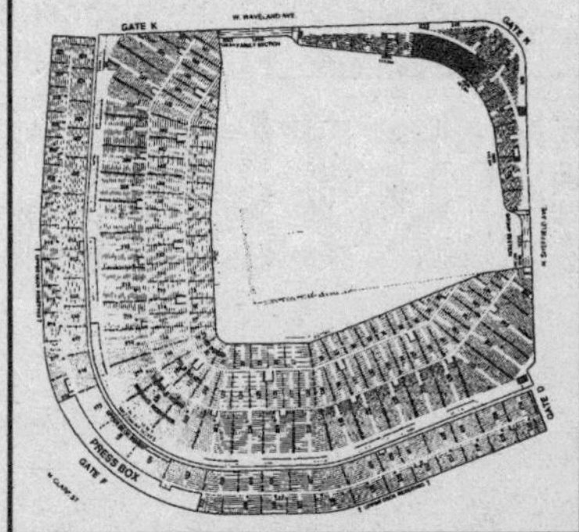

Steve Buechele No. 24/3B

Full name: Steven Bernard Buechele
Bats: R **Throws:** R **HT:** 6–2 **WT:** 200
Born: 9–26–61, Lancaster, CA
High school: Servite (Anaheim, CA)
College: Stanford

Buechele's .272 BA was a career high. He also had a career high 27 doubles, and hit safely in 13 straight games, his career best.

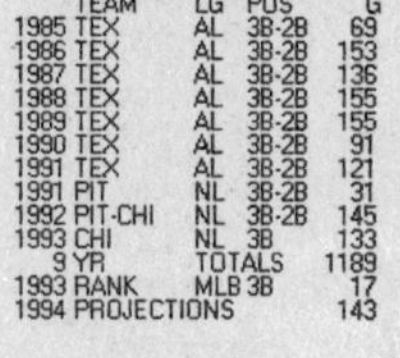
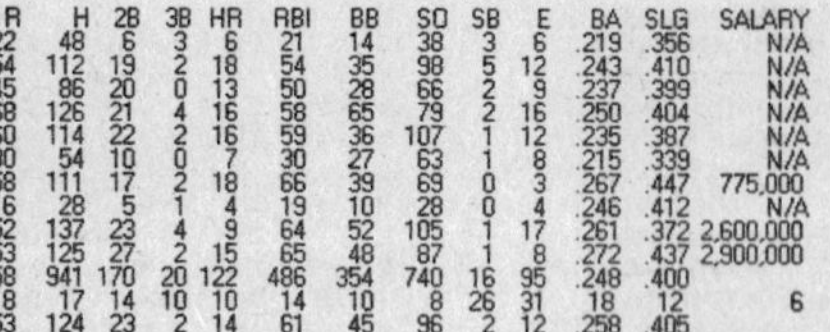

TEAM	LG	POS	G	AB	R	H	2B	3B	HR	RBI	BB	SO	SB	E	BA	SLG	SALARY
1985 TEX	AL	3B-2B	69	219	22	48	6	3	6	21	14	38	3	6	.219	.356	N/A
1986 TEX	AL	3B-2B	153	461	54	112	19	2	18	54	35	98	5	12	.243	.410	N/A
1987 TEX	AL	3B-2B	136	363	45	86	20	0	13	50	28	66	2	9	.237	.399	N/A
1988 TEX	AL	3B-2B	155	503	68	126	21	4	16	58	65	79	2	16	.250	.404	N/A
1989 TEX	AL	3B-2B	155	486	60	114	22	2	16	59	36	107	1	12	.235	.387	N/A
1990 TEX	AL	3B-2B	91	251	30	54	10	0	7	30	27	63	1	8	.215	.339	N/A
1991 TEX	AL	3B-2B	121	416	58	111	17	2	18	66	39	69	0	3	.267	.447	775,000
1991 PIT	NL	3B-2B	31	114	16	28	5	1	4	19	10	28	0	4	.246	.412	N/A
1992 PIT-CHI	NL	3B-2B	145	524	52	137	23	4	9	64	52	105	1	17	.261	.372	2,600,000
1993 CHI	NL	3B	133	460	53	125	27	2	15	65	48	87	1	8	.272	.437	2,900,000
9 YR	TOTALS		1189	3797	458	941	170	20	122	486	354	740	16	95	.248	.400	
1993 RANK	MLB	3B	17	18	18	17	14	10	10	14	10	8	26	31	18	12	6
1994 PROJECTIONS			143	481	53	124	23	2	14	61	45	96	2	12	.258	.405	

Mark Grace No. 17/1B

Full name: Mark Eugene Grace
Bats: L **Throws:** L **HT:** 6–2 **WT:** 190
Born: 6–28–64, Winston–Salem, NC
High school: Tustin (CA)
College: Saddleback (CA) and San Diego St.

Grace's .325 BA placed fifth in the NL. It was the highest average by a Cub since Bill Madlock hit .339 in 1976.

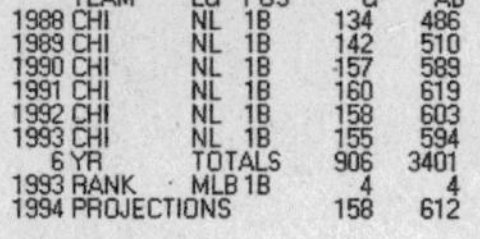

TEAM	LG	POS	G	AB	R	H	2B	3B	HR	RBI	BB	SO	SB	E	BA	SLG	SALARY
1988 CHI	NL	1B	134	486	65	144	23	4	7	57	60	43	3	17	.296	.403	N/A
1989 CHI	NL	1B	142	510	74	160	28	3	13	79	80	42	14	6	.314	.457	N/A
1990 CHI	NL	1B	157	589	72	182	32	1	9	82	59	54	15	12	.309	.413	N/A
1991 CHI	NL	1B	160	619	87	169	28	5	8	58	70	53	3	8	.273	.373	1,200,000
1992 CHI	NL	1B	158	603	72	185	37	5	9	79	72	36	6	4	.307	.430	2,262,500
1993 CHI	NL	1B	155	594	86	193	39	4	14	98	71	32	8	5	.325	.475	3,100,000
6 YR	TOTALS		906	3401	456	1033	187	22	60	453	412	260	49	52	.304	.425	
1993 RANK	MLB	1B	4	4	7	2	3	2	22	9	10	36	5	21	4	12	9
1994 PROJECTIONS			158	612	89	201	41	4	15	104	72	30	8	3	.328	.482	

Derrick May — No. 27/OF

Full name: Derrick Brant May
Bats: L **Throws:** R **HT:** 6–4 **WT:** 225
Born: 7–14–68, Rochester, NY
High school: Newark (NJ)

May hit .328 with runners in scoring position and .467, with 3 HR and 9 RBI, against Philadelphia. But he only hit .102 against the expansion Florida Marlins.

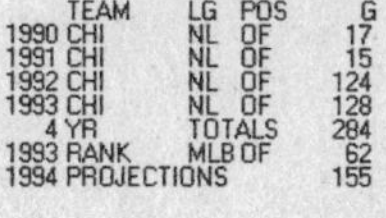
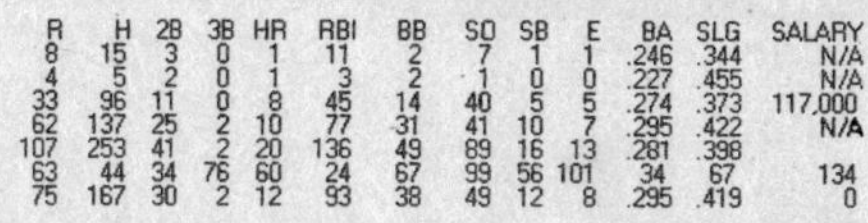

	TEAM	LG	POS	G	AB	R	H	2B	3B	HR	RBI	BB	SO	SB	E	BA	SLG	SALARY
1990	CHI	NL	OF	17	61	8	15	3	0	1	11	2	7	1	1	.246	.344	N/A
1991	CHI	NL	OF	15	22	4	5	2	0	1	3	2	1	0	0	.227	.455	N/A
1992	CHI	NL	OF	124	351	33	96	11	0	8	45	14	40	5	5	.274	.373	117,000
1993	CHI	NL	OF	128	465	62	137	25	2	10	77	31	41	10	7	.295	.422	N/A
4	YR	TOTALS		284	899	107	253	41	2	20	136	49	89	16	13	.281	.398	
1993	RANK	MLB	OF	62	56	63	44	34	76	60	24	67	99	56	101	34	67	134
1994	PROJECTIONS			155	566	75	167	30	2	12	93	38	49	12	8	.295	.419	0

Rey Sanchez — No. 11/SS

Full name: Rey Francisco Sanchez
Bats: R **Throws:** R **HT:** 5–9 **WT:** 170
Born: 10–5–67, Rio Piedras, PR
High school: Live Oak (Morgan Hill, CA)

Sanchez hit .481 (13 for 27) with two men out and runners in scoring position. He hit .324 during the first half of the '93 season, just .216 during the second half.

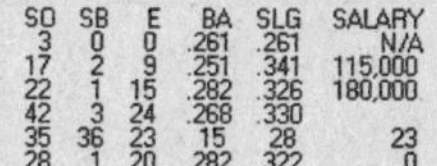

	TEAM	LG	POS	G	AB	R	H	2B	3B	HR	RBI	BB	SO	SB	E	BA	SLG	SALARY
1991	CHI	NL	SS-2B	13	23	1	6	0	0	0	2	4	3	0	0	.261	.261	N/A
1992	CHI	NL	SS-2B	74	255	24	64	14	3	1	19	10	17	2	9	.251	.341	115,000
1993	CHI	NL	SS	105	344	35	97	11	2	0	28	15	22	1	15	.282	.326	180,000
3	YR	TOTALS		192	622	60	167	25	5	1	49	29	42	3	24	.268	.330	
1993	RANK	MLB	SS	27	28	30	25	30	21	38	29	31	35	36	23	15	28	23
1994	PROJECTIONS			135	451	46	127	14	2	0	36	18	28	1	20	.282	.322	0

Ryne Sandberg No. 23/2B

Full name: Ryne Dee Sandberg
Bats: R **Throws:** R **HT:** 6–2 **WT:** 190
Born: 9–18–59, Spokane, WA
High school: North Central (Spokane, WA)
Sandberg's .309 BA was his best mark since 1984. He also recorded his career 2,000th hit in a year where recurring injuries held him to a career low 117 games.

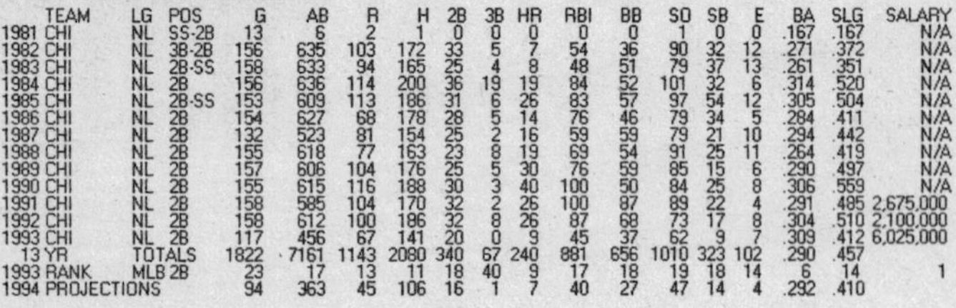

TEAM	LG	POS	G	AB	R	H	2B	3B	HR	RBI	BB	SO	SB	E	BA	SLG	SALARY
1981 CHI	NL	SS-2B	13	6	2	1	0	0	0	0	0	1	0	0	.167	.167	N/A
1982 CHI	NL	3B-2B	156	635	103	172	33	5	7	54	36	90	32	12	.271	.372	N/A
1983 CHI	NL	2B-SS	158	633	94	165	25	4	8	48	51	79	37	13	.261	.351	N/A
1984 CHI	NL	2B	156	636	114	200	36	19	19	84	52	101	32	6	.314	.520	N/A
1985 CHI	NL	2B-SS	153	609	113	186	31	6	26	83	57	97	54	12	.305	.504	N/A
1986 CHI	NL	2B	154	627	68	178	28	5	14	76	46	79	34	5	.284	.411	N/A
1987 CHI	NL	2B	132	523	81	154	25	2	16	59	59	79	21	10	.294	.442	N/A
1988 CHI	NL	2B	155	618	77	163	23	8	19	69	54	91	25	11	.264	.419	N/A
1989 CHI	NL	2B	157	606	104	176	25	5	30	76	59	85	15	6	.290	.497	N/A
1990 CHI	NL	2B	155	615	116	188	30	3	40	100	50	84	25	8	.306	.559	N/A
1991 CHI	NL	2B	158	585	104	170	32	2	26	100	87	89	22	4	.291	.485	2,675,000
1992 CHI	NL	2B	158	612	100	186	32	8	26	87	68	73	17	8	.304	.510	2,100,000
1993 CHI	NL	2B	117	456	67	141	20	0	9	45	37	62	9	7	.309	.412	6,025,000
13 YR	TOTALS		1822	7161	1143	2080	340	67	240	881	656	1010	323	102	.290	.457	
1993 RANK	MLB	2B	23	17	13	11	18	40	9	17	18	19	18	14	6	14	1
1994 PROJECTIONS			94	363	45	106	16	1	7	40	27	47	14	4	.292	.410	

Dwight Smith No. 18/OF

Full name: John Dwight Smith
Bats: L **Throws:** R **HT:** 5–11 **WT:** 190
Born: 11–8–63, Tallahassee, FL
High school: Wade Hampton (Varnville, SC)
College: Spartanburg Methodist (SC)
Dwight Smith holds the Cubs record for career pinch hits with 50. His 11 home runs in 1993 were a career high.

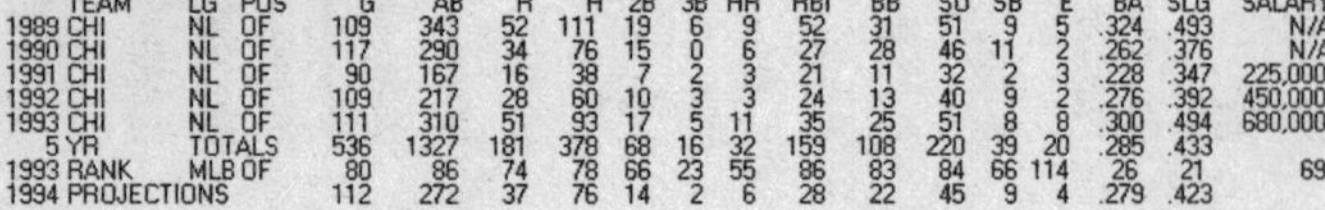

TEAM	LG	POS	G	AB	R	H	2B	3B	HR	RBI	BB	SO	SB	E	BA	SLG	SALARY
1989 CHI	NL	OF	109	343	52	111	19	6	9	52	31	51	9	5	.324	.493	N/A
1990 CHI	NL	OF	117	290	34	76	15	0	6	27	28	46	11	2	.262	.376	N/A
1991 CHI	NL	OF	90	167	16	38	7	2	3	21	11	32	2	3	.228	.347	225,000
1992 CHI	NL	OF	109	217	28	60	10	3	3	24	13	40	9	2	.276	.392	450,000
1993 CHI	NL	OF	111	310	51	93	17	5	11	35	25	51	8	8	.300	.494	680,000
5 YR	TOTALS		536	1327	181	378	68	16	32	159	108	220	39	20	.285	.433	
1993 RANK	MLB	OF	80	86	74	78	66	23	55	86	83	84	66	114	26	21	69
1994 PROJECTIONS			112	272	37	76	14	2	6	28	22	45	9	4	.279	.423	

Sammy Sosa No. 21/OF

Full name: Samuel Sosa
Bats: R **Throws:** R **HT:** 6–0 **WT:** 185
Born: 11–12–68, S.P. de Macoris, DR

Sosa became the first Cub ever to have 30 HR and 30 steals in the same season. 23 of his homers were hit off right-handed pitching. Sosa also had 17 outfield assists, the second-highest total in the NL.

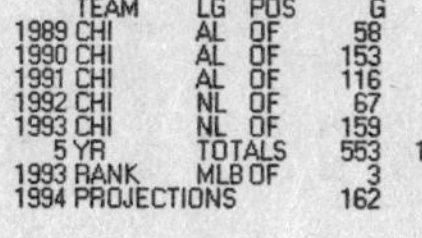
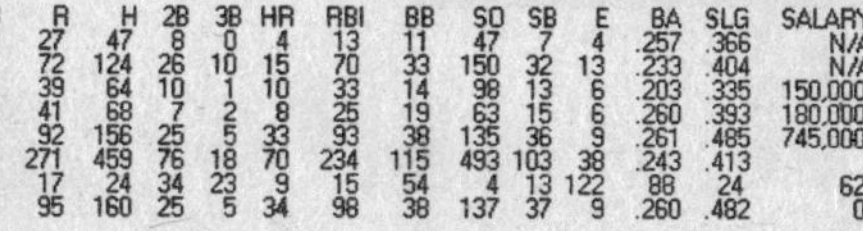

	TEAM	LG	POS	G	AB	R	H	2B	3B	HR	RBI	BB	SO	SB	E	BA	SLG	SALARY
1989	CHI	AL	OF	58	183	27	47	8	0	4	13	11	47	7	4	.257	.366	N/A
1990	CHI	AL	OF	153	532	72	124	26	10	15	70	33	150	32	13	.233	.404	N/A
1991	CHI	AL	OF	116	316	39	64	10	1	10	33	14	98	13	6	.203	.335	150,000
1992	CHI	NL	OF	67	262	41	68	7	2	8	25	19	63	15	6	.260	.393	180,000
1993	CHI	NL	OF	159	598	92	156	25	5	33	93	38	135	36	9	.261	.485	745,000
5	YR	TOTALS		553	1891	271	459	76	18	70	234	115	493	103	38	.243	.413	
1993	RANK	MLB	OF	3	9	17	24	34	23	9	15	54	4	13	122	88	24	62
1994	PROJECTIONS			162	616	95	160	25	5	34	98	38	137	37	9	.260	.482	0

Rick Wilkins No. 2/C

Full name: Richard David Wilkins
Bats: L **Throws:** R **HT:** 6–2 **WT:** 210
Born: 6–4–67, Jacksonville, FL
High school: Bolles (Jacksonville, FL)
College: Florida CC (Jacksonville, FL)

Wilkins was the first Cub catcher to hit 30 HR since Gabby Hartnett hit 37 in 1930. Wilkins hit .356 with 20 HR away from Wrigley Field.

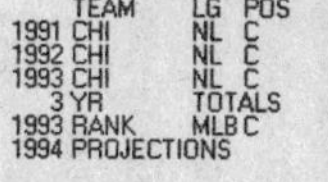
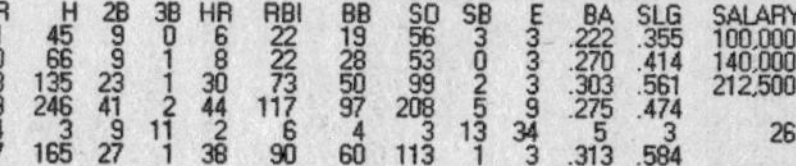

	TEAM	LG	POS	G	AB	R	H	2B	3B	HR	RBI	BB	SO	SB	E	BA	SLG	SALARY
1991	CHI	NL	C	86	203	21	45	9	0	6	22	19	56	3	3	.222	.355	100,000
1992	CHI	NL	C	83	244	20	66	9	1	8	22	28	53	0	3	.270	.414	140,000
1993	CHI	NL	C	136	446	78	135	23	1	30	73	50	99	2	3	.303	.561	212,500
3	YR	TOTALS		305	893	119	246	41	2	44	117	97	208	5	9	.275	.474	
1993	RANK	MLB	C	8	8	4	3	9	11	2	6	4	3	13	34	5	3	26
1994	PROJECTIONS			152	527	97	165	27	1	38	90	60	113	1	3	.313	.584	

Willie Banks — P

Full name: Willie Anthony Banks
Bats: R **Throws:** R **HT:** 6–1 **WT:** 203
Born: 2–27–69, Jersey City, NJ
High school: St. Anthony's (Jersey City, NJ)

1993 was the first full major league season for this young prospect. Drafted third in the June, 1987 free agent draft, Banks is the highest draft choice ever from New Jersey.

	TM	LG	POS	W	L	ERA	G	GS	CG	SH	SV	IP	H	R	ER	HR	BB	SO	SALARY
1991	MIN	AL	P	1	1	5.71	5	3	0	0	0	17.1	21	15	11	1	12	16	N/A
1992	MIN	AL	P	4	4	5.70	16	12	0	0	0	71.0	80	46	45	6	37	37	N/A
1993	MIN	AL	P	11	12	4.04	31	30	0	0	0	171.1	186	91	77	17	78	138	126,000
3	YR	TOTALS		16	17	4.61	52	45	0	0	0	259.2	287	152	133	24	127	191	
1993	RANK	MLB Ps		59		141	194	58	125	69	102	74	201	175		156	231	59	211
1994	PROJECTIONS			12	13	4.01	36	36	0	0	0	204	222	107	91	20	92	164	

Jose Guzman — No. 29/P

Full name: Jose Alberto (Mirabal) Guzman
Bats: R **Throws:** R **HT:** 6–3 **WT:** 195
Born: 4–9–63, Santa Isabel, PR

Guzman led the Cubs with 163 strikeouts. He struck out twelve against Montreal August 17, but developed tendinitis in his right shoulder September 7 and was out for thc season.

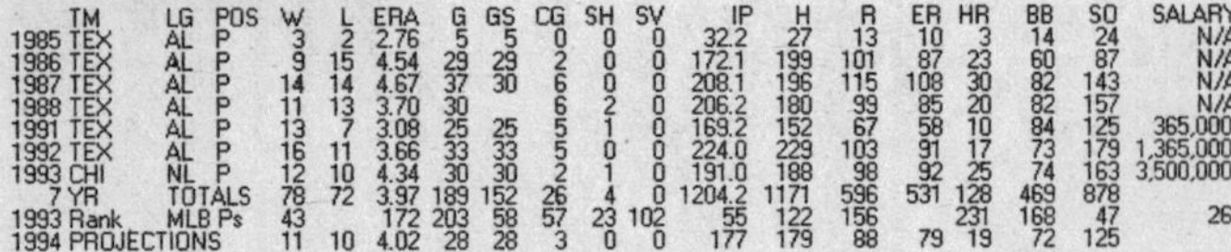

	TM	LG	POS	W	L	ERA	G	GS	CG	SH	SV	IP	H	R	ER	HR	BB	SO	SALARY
1985	TEX	AL	P	3	2	2.76	5	5	0	0	0	32.2	27	13	10	3	14	24	N/A
1986	TEX	AL	P	9	15	4.54	29	29	2	0	0	172.1	199	101	87	23	60	87	N/A
1987	TEX	AL	P	14	14	4.67	37	30	6	0	0	208.1	196	115	108	30	82	143	N/A
1988	TEX	AL	P	11	13	3.70	30		6	2	0	206.2	180	99	85	20	82	157	N/A
1991	TEX	AL	P	13	7	3.08	25	25	5	1	0	169.2	152	67	58	10	84	125	365,000
1992	TEX	AL	P	16	11	3.66	33	33	5	0	0	224.0	229	103	91	17	73	179	1,365,000
1993	CHI	NL	P	12	10	4.34	30	30	2	1	0	191.0	188	98	92	25	74	163	3,500,000
7	YR	TOTALS		78	72	3.97	189	152	26	4	0	1204.2	1171	596	531	128	469	878	
1993	Rank	MLB Ps		43		172	203	58	57	23	102	55	122	156		231	168	47	26
1994	PROJECTIONS			11	10	4.02	28	28	3	0	0	177	179	88	79	19	72	125	

Greg Hibbard No. 37/P

Full name: James Gregory Hibbard
Bats: L **Throws:** L **HT:** 6–0 **WT:** 190
Born: 9–13–64, New Orleans, LA
High school: Harrison Central (Gulfport, MS)
College: Miss. Gulf Coast JC and Alabama

Hibbard's 15 wins were the most by a Cubs left-hander since Ken Holtzman won 17 in 1970. He won his last five decisions.

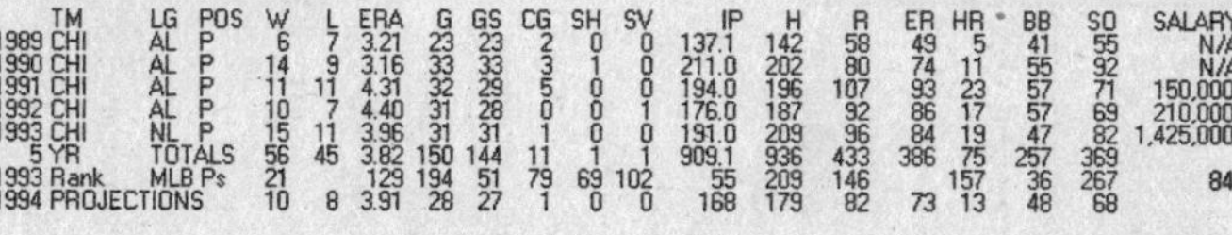

	TM	LG	POS	W	L	ERA	G	GS	CG	SH	SV	IP	H	R	ER	HR	BB	SO	SALARY
1989	CHI	AL	P	6	7	3.21	23	23	2	0	0	137.1	142	58	49	5	41	55	N/A
1990	CHI	AL	P	14	9	3.16	33	33	3	1	0	211.0	202	80	74	11	55	92	N/A
1991	CHI	AL	P	11	11	4.31	32	29	5	0	0	194.0	196	107	93	23	57	71	150,000
1992	CHI	AL	P	10	7	4.40	31	28	0	0	1	176.0	187	92	86	17	57	69	210,000
1993	CHI	NL	P	15	11	3.96	31	31	1	0	0	191.0	209	96	84	19	47	82	1,425,000
5	YR	TOTALS		56	45	3.82	150	144	11	1	1	909.1	936	433	386	75	257	369	
1993	Rank	MLB Ps		21		129	194	51	79	69	102	55	209	146		157	36	267	84
1994	PROJECTIONS			10	8	3.91	28	27	1	0	0	168	179	82	73	13	48	68	

Mike Morgan No. 36/P

Full name: Michael Thomas Morgan
Bats: R **Throws:** R **HT:** 6–2 **WT:** 220
Born: 10–8–59, Tulare, CA
High school: Valley (Las Vegas, NV)

Morgan led the staff in innings pitched with 207.2. But he started the season 1–4, and was 3–6 in his last 15 starts with six no-decisions.

	TM	LG	POS	W	L	ERA	G	GS	CG	SH	SV	IP	H	R	ER	HR	BB	SO	SALARY
1978	OAK	AL	P	0	3	7.30	3	3	1	0	0	12.1	19	12	10	1	8	0	N/A
1979	OAK	AL	P	2	10	6.63	13	13	2	0	0	77.1	102	67	57	7	50	17	N/A
1982	NY	AL	P	7	11	4.37	30	23	2	0	0	150.1	167	77	73	15	67	71	N/A
1983	TOR	AL	P	0	3	5.16	16	4	0	0	0	45.1	48	26	26	6	21	22	N/A
1985	SEA	AL	P	1	1	12.00	2	2	0	0	0	6.0	11	8	8	2	5	2	N/A
1986	SEA	AL	P	11	17	4.53	37	33	9	1	1	216.1	243	122	109	24	86	116	N/A
1987	SEA	AL	P	12	17	4.65	34	31	8	2	0	207.0	245	117	107	25	53	85	N/A
1988	BAL	AL	P	1	6	5.43	22		2	0	1	71.1	70	45	43	6	23	29	N/A
1989	LA	NL	P	8	11	2.53	40	19	0	0	0	152.2	130	51	43	6	33	72	N/A
1990	LA	NL	P	11	15	3.75	33	33	6	4	0	211.0	216	100	88	19	60	106	N/A
1991	LA	NL	P	14	10	2.78	34	33	5	1	1	236.1	197	85	73	12	61	140	650,000
1992	CHI	NL	P	16	8	2.55	34	34	6	1	0	240.0	203	80	68	14	79	123	2,875,000
1993	CHI	NL	P	10	15	4.03	32	32	1	1	0	207.2	206	100	93	15	74	111	3,375,000
12	YR	TOTALS		93	127	3.92	330	260	42	10	3	1833.2	1857	890	798	152	620	894	
1993	Rank	MLB Ps		75		139	175	39	79	23	102	46	129	121		72	140	214	31
1994	PROJECTIONS			11	16	4.41	34	32	6	1	0	210	231	113	103	21	71	104	

Randy Myers No. 28/P

Full name: Randall Kirk Myers
Bats: L **Throws:** L **HT:** 6–1 **WT:** 230
Born: 9–19–62, Vancouver, WA
High school: Evergreen (Vancouver, WA)
College: Clark CC (WA)

Myers won the Rolaids Relief Man Award. His 53 saves was an NL record and the second highest total in major league history.

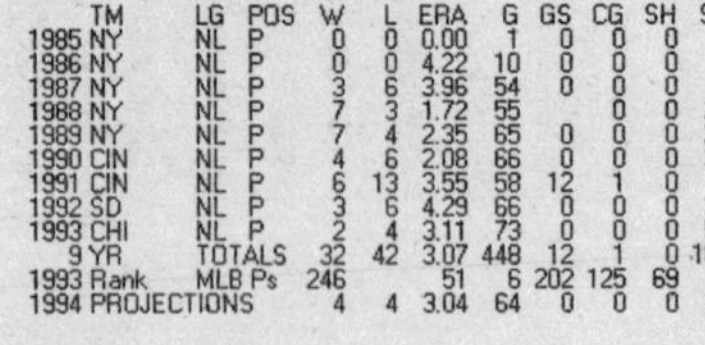
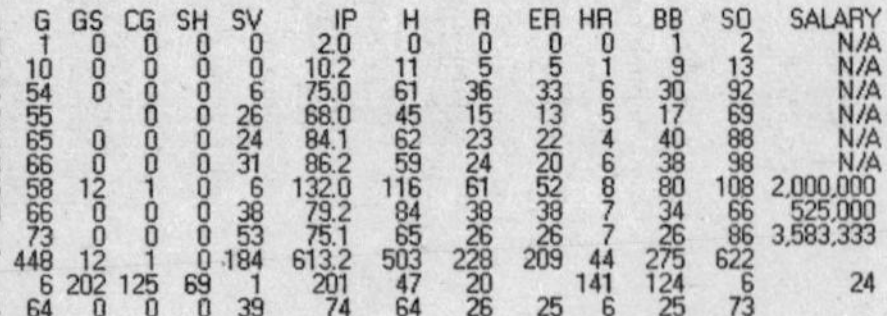

	TM	LG	POS	W	L	ERA	G	GS	CG	SH	SV	IP	H	R	ER	HR	BB	SO	SALARY
1985	NY	NL	P	0	0	0.00	1	0	0	0	0	2.0	0	0	0	0	1	2	N/A
1986	NY	NL	P	0	0	4.22	10	0	0	0	0	10.2	11	5	5	1	9	13	N/A
1987	NY	NL	P	3	6	3.96	54	0	0	0	6	75.0	61	36	33	6	30	92	N/A
1988	NY	NL	P	7	3	1.72	55		0	0	26	68.0	45	15	13	5	17	69	N/A
1989	NY	NL	P	7	4	2.35	65	0	0	0	24	84.1	62	23	22	4	40	88	N/A
1990	CIN	NL	P	4	6	2.08	66	0	0	0	31	86.2	59	24	20	6	38	98	N/A
1991	CIN	NL	P	6	13	3.55	58	12	1	0	6	132.0	116	61	52	8	80	108	2,000,000
1992	SD	NL	P	3	6	4.29	66	0	0	0	38	79.2	84	38	38	7	34	66	525,000
1993	CHI	NL	P	2	4	3.11	73	0	0	0	53	75.1	65	26	26	7	26	86	3,583,333
9	YR	TOTALS		32	42	3.07	448	12	1	0	184	613.2	503	228	209	44	275	622	
1993	Rank	MLB Ps		246		51	6	202	125	69	1	201	47	20		141	124	6	24
1994	PROJECTIONS			4	4	3.04	64	0	0	0	39	74	64	26	25	6	25	73	

Tom Trebelhorn No. 41/Mgr.

Full name: Thomas Lynn Trebelhorn
Bats: R **Throws:** R **HT:** 5–11 **WT:** 180
Born: 1-27-48, Portland, OR
College: Portland State (OR)

Trebelhorn was promoted from bench coach when the Cubs didn't renew Jim Lefebvre's contract. He won more games than any other manager in Milwaukee Brewer history.

			REG. SEASON				PLAYOFF			CHAMP. SERIES			WORLD SERIES		
YEAR	TEAM	LG	W	L	PCT	POS	W	L	PCT	W	L	PCT	W	L	PCT
1986	MIL	AL	6	3	.667	6			---			---			---
1987	MIL	AL	91	71	.562	3			---			---			---
1988	MIL	AL	87	75	.537	3			---			---			---
1989	MIL	AL	81	81	.500	4			---			---			---
1990	MIL	AL	74	88	.457	6			---			---			---
1991	MIL	AL	83	79	.512	4			---			---			---
6	YR TOTALS		422	397	.515		0	0	---	0	0	---	0	0	---

Jose Bautista No. 38/P

Full name: Jose Joaquin Bautista
Bats: R **Throws:** R **HT:** 6–2 **WT:** 205
Born: 7–26–64, Bani, DR
High school: Bani School (Bani, DR)
Bautista won eight of his last nine decisions. He was 6–1 with a 2.22 ERA out of the bullpen.

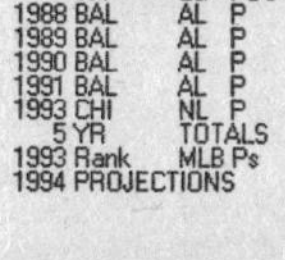

	TM	LG	POS	W	L	ERA	G	GS	CG	SH	SV	IP	H	R	ER	HR	BB	SO	SALARY
1988	BAL	AL	P	6	15	4.30	33	25	3	0	0	171.2	171	86	82	21	45	76	N/A
1989	BAL	AL	P	3	4	5.31	15	10	0	0	0	78.0	84	46	46	17	15	30	N/A
1990	BAL	AL	P	1	0	4.05	22	0	0	0	0	26.2	28	15	12	4	7	15	N/A
1991	BAL	AL	P	0	1	16.88	5	0	0	0	0	5.1	13	10	10	1	5	3	N/A
1993	CHI	NL	P	10	3	2.82	58	7	1	0	2	111.2	105	38	35	11	27	63	165,000
5	YR	TOTALS		20	23	4.23	133	42	4	0	2	393.1	401	195	185	54	99	187	
1993	Rank	MLB Ps		75		28	50	177	79	69	55	128	91	19		155	32	197	189
1994	PROJECTIONS			4	2	3.93	31	5	0	0	0	71	72	33	31	10	16	36	

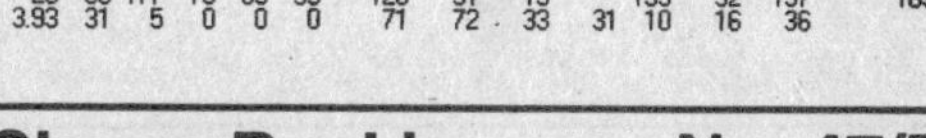

Shawn Boskie No. 47/P

Full name: Shawn Kealoha Boskie
Bats: R **Throws:** R **HT:** 6–3 **WT:** 200
Born: 3–28–67, Hawthorne, NV
High school: Reno (NV)
College: Modesto JC
Boskie was 4–2 as a reliever, 1–1 as a starter.

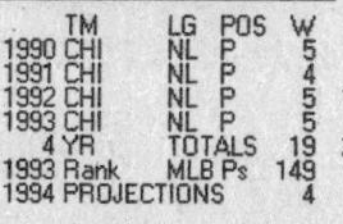

	TM	LG	POS	W	L	ERA	G	GS	CG	SH	SV	IP	H	R	ER	HR	BB	SO	SALARY
1990	CHI	NL	P	5	6	3.69	15	15	1	0	0	97.2	99	42	40	8	31	49	N/A
1991	CHI	NL	P	4	9	5.23	28	20	0	0	0	129.0	150	78	75	14	52	62	130,000
1992	CHI	NL	P	5	11	5.01	23	18	0	0	0	91.2	96	55	51	14	36	39	185,000
1993	CHI	NL	P	5	3	3.43	39	2	0	0	0	65.2	63	30	25	7	21	39	210,000
4	YR	TOTALS		19	29	4.48	105	55	1	0	0	384.0	408	205	191	43	140	189	
1993	Rank	MLB Ps		149		82	118	197	125	69	102	230	104	97		180	95	167	170
1994	PROJECTIONS			4	6	4.27	27	12	0	0	0	97	104	50	46	9	34	50	

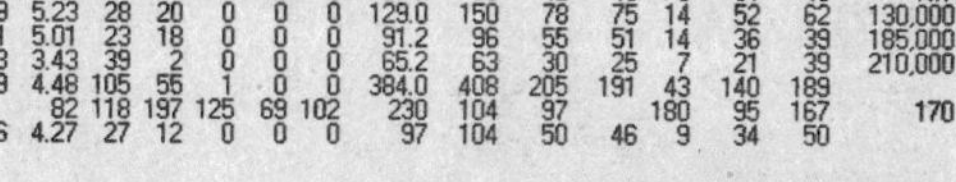

Frank Castillo No. 49/P

Full name: Frank Anthony Castillo
Bats: R **Throws:** R **HT:** 6–1 **WT:** 190
Born: 4–1–69, El Paso, TX
High school: Eastwood (El Paso, TX)
Castillo failed to win a game after July 30. He had a 4.84 ERA as a starter.

	TM	LG	POS	W	L	ERA	G	GS	CG	SH	SV	IP	H	R	ER	HR	BB	SO	SALARY
1991	CHI	NL	P	6	7	4.35	18	18	4	0	0	111.2	107	56	54	5	33	73	100,000
1992	CHI	NL	P	10	11	3.46	33	33	0	0	0	205.1	179	91	79	19	63	135	150,000
1993	CHI	NL	P	5	8	4.84	29	25	2	0	0	141.1	162	83	76	20	39	84	250,000
3	YR	TOTALS		21	26	4.10	80	76	6	0	0	458.1	448	230	209	44	135	292	
1993	Rank	MLB Ps		149		217	213	91	57	69	102	104	244	215		253	55	166	159
1994	PROJECTIONS			7	8	4.09	26	25	2	0	0	152	149	76	69	14	45	97	

Shawon Dunston — No. 12/SS

Full name: Shawon Donnell Dunston
Bats: R **Throws:** R **HT:** 6–1 **WT:** 180
Born: 3–21–63, Brooklyn, NY
High school: Thomas Jefferson (Brooklyn, NY)
Dunston was the starting shortstop before he was sidelined for the season with a herniated disk.

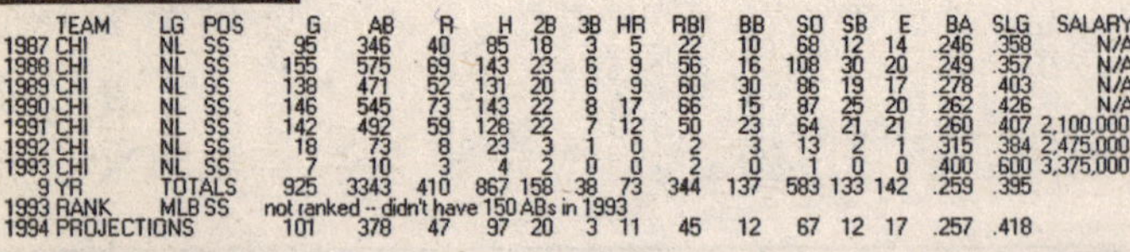

	TEAM	LG	POS	G	AB	R	H	2B	3B	HR	RBI	BB	SO	SB	E	BA	SLG	SALARY
1987	CHI	NL	SS	95	346	40	85	18	3	5	22	10	68	12	14	.246	.358	N/A
1988	CHI	NL	SS	155	575	69	143	23	6	9	56	16	108	30	20	.249	.357	N/A
1989	CHI	NL	SS	138	471	52	131	20	6	9	60	30	86	19	17	.278	.403	N/A
1990	CHI	NL	SS	146	545	73	143	22	8	17	66	15	87	25	20	.262	.426	N/A
1991	CHI	NL	SS	142	492	59	128	22	7	12	50	23	64	21	21	.260	.407	2,100,000
1992	CHI	NL	SS	18	73	8	23	3	1	0	2	3	13	2	1	.315	.384	2,475,000
1993	CHI	NL	SS	7	10	3	4	2	0	0	2	0	1	0	0	.400	.600	3,375,000
9	YR	TOTALS		925	3343	410	867	158	38	73	344	137	583	133	142	.259	.395	
1993	RANK	MLB	SS	not ranked -- didn't have 150 ABs in 1993														
1994	PROJECTIONS			101	378	47	97	20	3	11	45	12	67	12	17	.257	.418	

Mike Harkey — No. 22/P

Full name: Michael Anthony Harkey
Bats: R **Throws:** R **HT:** 6–5 **WT:** 235
Born: 10–25–66, San Diego, CA
High school: Ganesha (Pomona, CA)
College: Cal State–Fullerton
Harkey was 4–1 vs. Florida and Colorado.

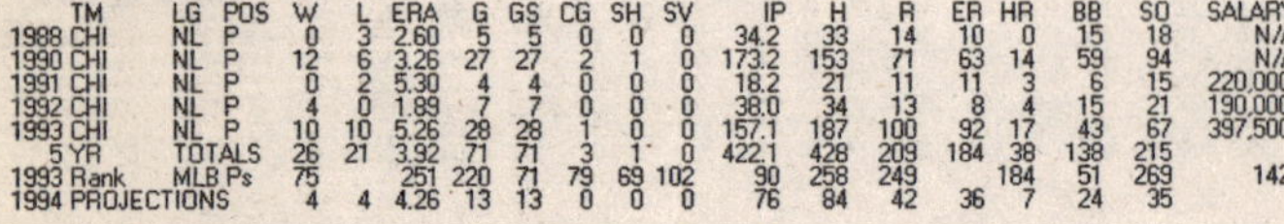

	TM	LG	POS	W	L	ERA	G	GS	CG	SH	SV	IP	H	R	ER	HR	BB	SO	SALARY
1988	CHI	NL	P	0	3	2.60	5	5	0	0	0	34.2	33	14	10	0	15	18	N/A
1990	CHI	NL	P	12	6	3.26	27	27	2	1	0	173.2	153	71	63	14	59	94	N/A
1991	CHI	NL	P	0	2	5.30	4	4	0	0	0	18.2	21	11	11	3	6	15	220,000
1992	CHI	NL	P	4	0	1.89	7	7	0	0	0	38.0	34	13	8	4	15	21	190,000
1993	CHI	NL	P	10	10	5.26	28	28	1	0	0	157.1	187	100	92	17	43	67	397,500
5	YR	TOTALS		26	21	3.92	71	71	3	1	0	422.1	428	209	184	38	138	215	
1993	Rank	MLB	Ps	75		251	220	71	79	69	102	90	258	249		184	51	269	142
1994	PROJECTIONS			4	4	4.26	13	13	0	0	0	76	84	42	36	7	24	35	

Glenallen Hill — No. 34/OF

Full name: Glenallen Hill
Bats: R **Throws:** R **HT:** 6–2 **WT:** 220
Born: 3–22–65, Santa Cruz, CA
High school: Santa Cruz (CA)
Hill had a .387 on-base average in 31 games for Chicago. He also hit two pinch-hit home runs.

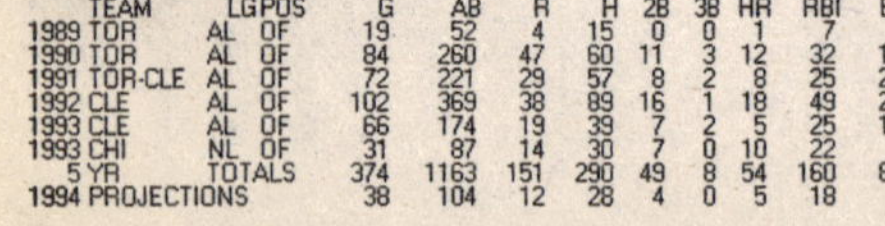
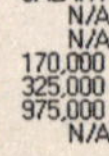

	TEAM	LG	POS	G	AB	R	H	2B	3B	HR	RBI	BB	SO	SB	E	BA	SLG	SALARY
1989	TOR	AL	OF	19	52	4	15	0	0	1	7	3	12	2	1	.288	.346	N/A
1990	TOR	AL	OF	84	260	47	60	11	3	12	32	18	62	8	2	.231	.435	N/A
1991	TOR-CLE	AL	OF	72	221	29	57	8	2	8	25	23	54	6	3	.258	.421	170,000
1992	CLE	AL	OF	102	369	38	89	16	1	18	49	20	73	9	6	.241	.436	325,000
1993	CLE	AL	OF	66	174	19	39	7	2	5	25	11	50	7	4	.224	.374	975,000
1993	CHI	NL	OF	31	87	14	30	7	0	10	22	6	21	1	2	.345	.770	N/A
5	YR	TOTALS		374	1163	151	290	49	8	54	160	81	272	33	18	0.249	0.445	
1994	PROJECTIONS			38	104	12	28	4	0	5	18	6	27	3	2	.269	.481	

Larry Luebbers No. 26/P

Full name: Larry Christopher Luebbers
Bats: R **Throws:** R **HT:** 6–6 **WT:** 190
Born: 10–11–69, Cincinnati, OH
High school: St. Henry (Erlanger, KY)
College: Kentucky
Allowed 3 or less earned runs in 10 of 14 starts.

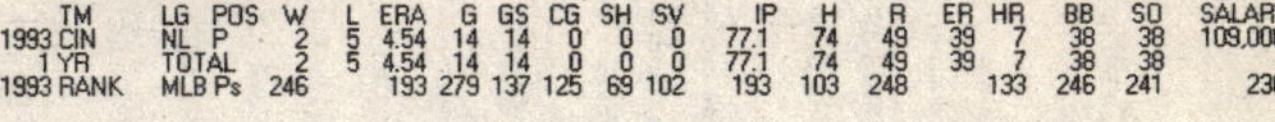

TM	LG	POS	W	L	ERA	G	GS	CG	SH	SV	IP	H	R	ER	HR	BB	SO	SALARY
1993 CIN	NL	P	2	5	4.54	14	14	0	0	0	77.1	74	49	39	7	38	38	109,000
1 YR	TOTAL		2	5	4.54	14	14	0	0	0	77.1	74	49	39	7	38	38	
1993 RANK	MLB	Ps	246		193	279	137	125	69	102	193	103	248		133	246	241	236

Dan Plesac No. 32/P

Full name: Daniel Thomas Plesac
Bats: L **Throws:** L **HT:** 6–5 **WT:** 215
Born: 2–4–62, Gary, IN
High school: Crown Point (IN)
College: North Carolina State
Plesac has 133 AL saves, but none with the Cubs.

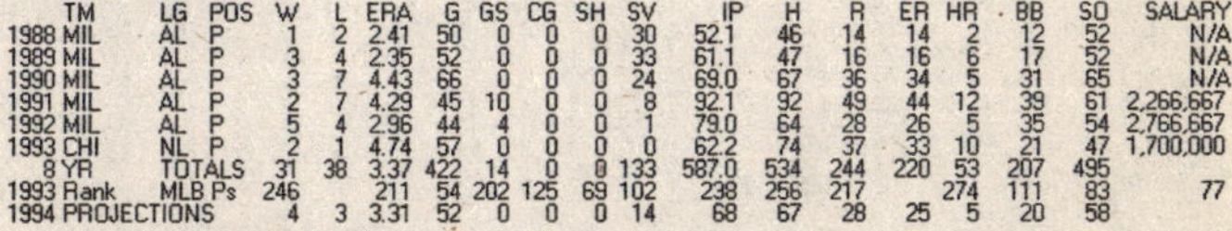

TM	LG	POS	W	L	ERA	G	GS	CG	SH	SV	IP	H	R	ER	HR	BB	SO	SALARY
1988 MIL	AL	P	1	2	2.41	50	0	0	0	30	52.1	46	14	14	2	12	52	N/A
1989 MIL	AL	P	3	4	2.35	52	0	0	0	33	61.1	47	16	16	6	17	52	N/A
1990 MIL	AL	P	3	7	4.43	66	0	0	0	24	69.0	67	36	34	5	31	65	N/A
1991 MIL	AL	P	2	7	4.29	45	10	0	0	8	92.1	92	49	44	12	39	61	2,266,667
1992 MIL	AL	P	5	4	2.96	44	4	0	0	1	79.0	64	28	26	5	35	54	2,766,667
1993 CHI	NL	P	2	1	4.74	57	0	0	0	0	62.2	74	37	33	10	21	47	1,700,000
8 YR	TOTALS		31	38	3.37	422	14	0	0	133	587.0	534	244	220	53	207	495	
1993 Rank	MLB	Ps	246		211	54	202	125	69	102	238	256	217		274	111	83	77
1994 PROJECTIONS			4	3	3.31	52	0	0	0	14	68	67	28	25	5	20	58	

Kevin Roberson No. 19/OF

Full name: Kevin Lynn Roberson
Bats: S **Throws:** R **HT:** 6–4 **WT:** 210
Born: 1–29–68, Decatur, IL
High school: Eisenhower (Decatur, IL)
College: Parkland Junior (Champaign, IL)
Roberson hit .304 with 16 HR and 50 RBI at Iowa.

TEAM	LG	POS	G	AB	R	H	2B	3B	HR	RBI	BB	SO	SB	E	BA	SLG	SALARY
1993 CHI	NL	OF	62	180	23	34	4	1	9	27	12	48	0	3	.189	.372	109,000
1 YR	TOTAL		62	180	23	34	4	1	9	27	12	48	0	3	.189	.372	
1993 RANK	MLB	OF	134	124	124	135	136	97	64	102	123	90	127	42	136	101	124

Bob Scanlan — No. 30/P

Full name: Robert Guy Scanlan Jr.
Bats: R **Throws:** R **HT:** 6–8 **WT:** 215
Born: 8–9–66, Los Angeles, CA
High school: Harvard (North Hollywood, CA)
Scanlan's ERA was 5.23 in the second half. In one stretch of 7.1 innings, he allowed 12 earned runs.

TM	LG	POS	W	L	ERA	G	GS	CG	SH	SV	IP	H	R	ER	HR	BB	SO	SALARY
1991 CHI	NL	P	7	8	3.89	40	13	0	0	1	111.0	114	60	48	5	40	44	100,000
1992 CHI	NL	P	3	6	2.89	69	0	0	0	14	87.1	76	32	28	4	30	42	150,000
1993 CHI	NL	P	4	5	4.54	70	0	0	0	0	75.1	79	41	38	6	28	44	245,000
3 YR	TOTALS		14	19	3.75	179	13	0	0	15	273.2	269	133	114	15	98	130	
1993 Rank	MLB Ps		173		194	14	202	125	69	102	201	178	185		107	157	176	162
1994 PROJECTIONS			4	6	3.76	59	4	0	0	5	91	89	44	38	5	32	43	

Jose Vizcaino — No. 16/SS

Full name: Jose Luis Vizcaino
Bats: S **Throws:** R **HT:** 6–1 **WT:** 180
Born: 3–26–68, San Cristobal, DR
High school: Americo Tolentino (DR)
Vizcaino became the second Cub middle infielder since 1979 to play 120 games and hit over .280.

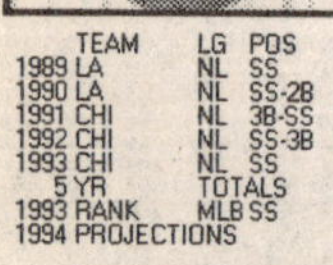

TEAM	LG	POS	G	AB	R	H	2B	3B	HR	RBI	BB	SO	SB	E	BA	SLG	SALARY
1989 LA	NL	SS	7	10	2	2	0	0	0	0	0	1	0	2	.200	.200	N/A
1990 LA	NL	SS-2B	37	51	3	14	1	1	0	2	4	8	1	2	.275	.333	N/A
1991 CHI	NL	3B-SS	93	145	7	38	5	0	0	10	5	18	2	7	.262	.297	114,000
1992 CHI	NL	SS-3B	86	285	25	64	10	4	1	17	14	35	3	9	.225	.298	177,000
1993 CHI	NL	SS	151	551	74	158	19	4	4	54	46	71	12	17	.287	.358	235,000
5 YR	TOTALS		374	1042	111	276	35	9	5	83	69	133	18	37	.265	.330	
1993 RANK	MLB	SS	11	7	9	6	20	10	17	13	16	13	8	28	10	21	21
1994 PROJECTIONS			162	596	79	171	19	3	3	57	49	76	12	18	.287	.344	0

Willie Wilson — No. 6/OF

Full name: Willie James Wilson
Bats: S **Throws:** R **HT:** 6–2 **WT:** 200
Born: 7–9–55, Montgomery, AL
High school: Summit (NJ)
His 145 career triples are the highest among active players. He hit .435 in his last 17 games.

TEAM	LG	POS	G	AB	R	H	2B	3B	HR	RBI	BB	SO	SB	E	BA	SLG	SALARY
1987 KC	AL		146	610	97	170	18	15	4	30	32	88	59	1	.279	.377	N/A
1988 KC	AL		147	591	81	155	17	11	1	37	22	106	35	4	.262	.333	N/A
1989 KC	AL		112	383	58	97	17	7	3	43	27	78	24	6	.253	.358	N/A
1990 KC	AL	OF	115	307	49	89	13	3	2	42	30	57	24	0	.290	.371	N/A
1991 OAK	AL		113	294	38	70	14	4	0	28	18	43	20	3	.238	.313	1,000,000
1992 OAK	AL		132	396	38	107	15	5	0	37	35	65	28	7	.270	.333	1,000,000
1993 CHI	NL	OF	105	221	29	57	11	3	1	11	11	40	7	1	.258	.348	700,000
18 YR	TOTALS		2137	7710	1165	2202	281	145	41	585	424	1138	667	65	.286	.376	
1993 RANK	MLB	OF	87	115	108	109	101	54	122	137	126	101	71	8	91	114	66
1994 PROJECTIONS			81	151	27	37	7	1	0	9	9	27	19	2	.245	.318	

Cincinnati *REDS*

1994 Scouting Report

Hitting: (1993/.264 BA, eighth in NL; 137 HR, ninth in NL)

Cincinnati has a solid offense—when healthy. Unfortunately, injuries devastated the Reds in '93. The Reds' main lineup of Hal Morris, Bip Roberts, Barry Larkin, Chris Sabo, Kevin Mitchell, Roberto Kelly, Reggie Sanders, and Joe Oliver played together only four times in '93. Kelly missed the second half of the season after putting up All-Star numbers (.319, 9 HR, 35 RBI, 21 steals) in the first half. Barry Larkin had thumb problems throughout the entire season and went on the DL for good in mid-August. Kevin Mitchell only played in 93 games. Hal Morris missed the first two months due to a separated shoulder.

The Reds are trying to scale down their payroll, and have rid themselves of veterans Chris Sabo and Bip Roberts. They signed as free agents infielders Lenny Harris, Kurt Stillwell, and Casey Candaele.

Pitching: (1993/4.51, twelfth in NL)

Jose Rijo is the staff ace. In '93, Rijo was 14–9, with a 2.48 ERA and 227 strikeouts. But John Smiley and Tom Browning were disappointments. Smiley's 3–9, 5.62 ERA season ended in July with bone spurs in his elbow. And Browning was 7–7 with a 4.74 ERA in an injury-shortened '93.

Rob Dibble led the team with 19 saves, but his ERA ballooned to 6.48, and many observers thought Dibble had lost his fastball. Scott Service appeared in 29 games with a 4.30 ERA.

Defense: (1993/.980 pct., fifth in NL)

Larkin's return will bolster the infield, but losing Sabo and Roberts will hurt.

1994 Prospects:

Reds have a solid talent core, starting with Barry Larkin, Hal Morris, John Smiley, and Tom Browning. But they're not as talented, or as deep, as the best teams in the NL. Fortunately for the Reds, the best teams in the NL don't play in the NL Central. Cincinnati could finish anywhere between first and fourth.

Team Directory

President & CEO: Marge Schott
General Mgr.: Jim Bowden
Director of Scouting: Julian Mock
Director of Player Dev.: Sheldon Bender
Director of P.R.: Jon Braude
Traveling Secretary: Joel Pieper

Minor League Affiliates:

Level	Team/League	1993 Record
AAA	Indianapolis – American Association	66–77
AA	Chattanooga – Southern	70–69
A	Winston-Salem – Carolina	72–68
	Charleston, W.Va. – South Atlantic	76–64
Rookie	Billings – Pioneer	49–26
	Princeton – Appalachian	26–42

1993 Review

	Home		Away			Home		Away			Home		Away	
vs NL East	W	L	W	L	vs NL Cent.	W	L	W	L	vs NL West	W	L	W	L
Atlanta	2	4	1	6	Chicago	2	4	3	3	Colorado	7	0	2	4
Florida	4	2	3	3	Houston	3	3	3	4	Los Angeles	3	4	2	4
Montreal	2	4	2	4	Pittsburgh	5	1	3	3	San Diego	5	2	4	2
New York	2	4	4	2	St. Louis	3	3	2	4	S. Francisco	1	5	1	6
Philadelphia	2	4	2	4										
Total	12	18	12	19		13	11	11	14		16	11	9	16

1993 finish: 73-89 (41-40 home, 32-49 away), fifth in NL West, 31 games behind

1994 Schedule

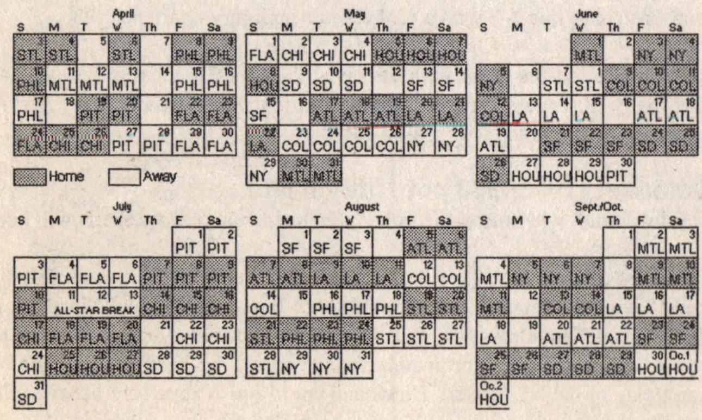

CINCINNATI REDS 1994 ROSTER

MANAGER: Dave Johnson (15)
COACHES: Don Gullett (35), Ray Knight (25) Bob Boone, bench; Mel Stottlemyre, pitching; Grant Jackson, bullpen; Joel Youngblood, 1B

No.	PITCHERS	B	T	HT	WT	DOB	BIRTHPLACE	RESIDENCE
32	Browning, Tom	L	L	6–1	195	4–28–60	Casper, WY	Edgewood, KY
61	Bushing, Chris	R	R	6–0	190	11–4–67	Rockville Center, NY	Danbury, CT
	Carrasco, Hector	R	R	6–2	175	10–22–69	S.P. de Macoris, DR	S.P. de Macoris, DR
	Courtright, John	L	L	6–2	185	5–30–70	Marion, OH	Columbus, OH
49	Dibble, Rob	L	R	6–4	230	1–24–64	Bridgeport, CT	Cincinnati, OH
64	Ferry, Mike	R	R	6–3	185	7–26–69	Appleton, WI	Auburn, AL
54	Foster, Steve	R	R	6–0	180	8–16–66	Dallas, TX	Richwood, KY
39	Hanson, Erik	R	R	6–6	215	5–18–65	Kinnelon, NJ	Kirkland, WA
36	Holman, Brian	R	R	6–4	190	1–25–65	Denver, CO	Bothell, WA
	Jarvis, Kevin	L	R	6–2	200	8–1–69	Lexington, KY	Lexington, KY
	McElroy, Chuck	L	L	6–0	195	10–1–67	Port Arthur, TX	Friendswood, TX
	Patterson, Ken	L	L	6–4	210	7–8–64	Costa Mesa, CA	Costa Mesa, CA
55	Powell, Ross	L	L	6–0	180	1–24–68	Grand Rapids, MI	Antioch, TN
40	Pugh, Tim	R	R	6–6	225	1–26–67	Lake Tahoe, CA	Bartlesville, OK
27	Rijo, Jose	R	R	6–2	210	5–13–65	San Cristobal, DR	Santo Domingo, DR
44	Roper, John	R	R	6–0	175	11–21–71	Southern Pines, NC	Raeford, NC
47	Ruffin, Johnny	R	R	6–3	175	7–29–71	Butler, AL	Butler, AL
34	Service, Scott	R	R	6–6	235	2–26–67	Cincinnati, OH	Cincinnati, OH
57	Smiley, John	L	L	6–4	200	3–17–65	Phoenixville, PA	Warrendale, PA
48	Spradlin, Jerry	S	R	6–7	220	6–14–67	Fullerton, CA	Anaheim, CA
53	Wickander, Kevin	L	L	6–3	200	1–4–65	Fort Dodge, IA	Glendale, AZ
No.	**CATCHERS**	**B**	**T**	**HT**	**WT**	**DOB**	**BIRTHPLACE**	**RESIDENCE**
33	Dorsett, Brian	R	R	6–4	220	4–9–61	Terre Haute, IN	Terre Haute, IN
	Lake, Steve	R	R	6–1	195	3–14–57	Inglewood, CA	Inglewood, CA
9	Oliver, Joe	R	R	6–3	210	7–24–65	Memphis, TN	Orlando, FL
No.	**INFIELDERS**	**B**	**T**	**HT**	**WT**	**DOB**	**BIRTHPLACE**	**RESIDENCE**
29	Boone, Bret	R	R	5–10	180	4–6–69	El Cajon, CA	Villa Park, CA
20	Branson, Jeff	L	R	6–0	180	1–26–67	Waynesboro, MS	Silas, AL
	Candaele, Casey	S	R	5–9	165	1–12–61	Lompoc, CA	
18	Costo, Tim	R	R	6–5	230	2–16–69	Melrose Park, IL	Glen Ellyn, IL
	Dismuke, Jamie	L	R	6–1	210	10–17–69	Syracuse, NY	Syracuse, NY
12	Greene, Willie	L	R	5–11	180	9–23–71	Milledgeville, GA	Haddock, GA
29	Harris, Lenny	L	R	5–10	220	10–28–64	Miami, FL	Miami, FL
	Koelling, Brian	R	R	6–1	185	6–11–69	Cincinnati, OH	Cleves, OH
11	Larkin, Barry	R	R	6–0	190	4–28–64	Cincinnati, OH	Cincinnati, OH
23	Morris, Hal	L	L	6–4	215	4–9–65	Fort Rucker, AL	Union, KY
	Stillwell, Kurt	R	R	5–11	185	6–4–65	Glendale, CA	Glendale,CA
No.	**OUTFIELDERS**	**B**	**T**	**HT**	**WT**	**DOB**	**BIRTHPLACE**	**RESIDENCE**
4	Brumfield, Jacob	R	R	6–0	180	5–27–65	Bogalusa, LA	Atlanta, GA
	Gibralter, Steve	R	R	6–0	185	10–9–72	Dallas, TX	Duncanville, TX
50	Gordon, Keith	R	R	6–1	200	1–22–69	Bethesda, MD	Olney, MD
22	Howard, Thomas	B	R	6–2	205	12–11–64	Middletown, OH	Elk Grove, CA
30	Kelly, Roberto	R	R	6–2	190	10–1–64	Panama City, PN	Panama City, PN
7	Mitchell, Kevin	R	R	5–11	210	1–13–62	San Diego, CA	Chula Vista, CA
16	Sanders, Reggie	R	R	6–1	180	12–1–67	Florence, SC	Cincinnati, OH

Riverfront Stadium (52,952, artificial)
Tickets: 513-421-7337
Ticket prices:
- $11.50 (blue level box seats)
- $10.00 (green level box seats)
- $10.00 (yellow level box seats)
- $9.00 (red level box seats)
- $8.00 (green level reserved seats)
- $6.50 (red level reserved seats)
- $3.50 ("top six" reserved seats)

Field Dimensions (from home plate)
- To left field at foul line, 330 feet
- To center field, 404 feet
- To right field at foul line, 330 feet

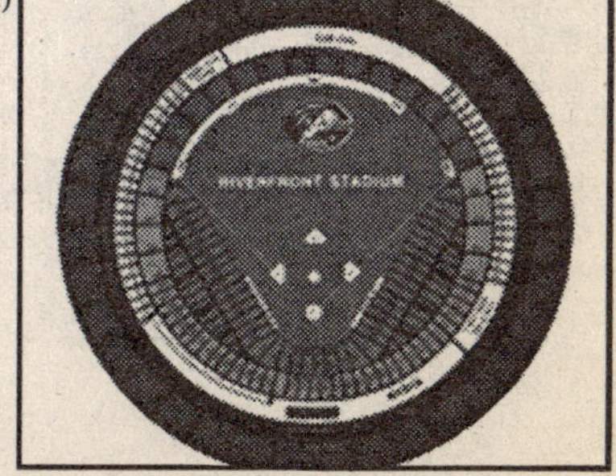

Bret Boone No. 29/2B

Full name: Bret Robert Boone
Bats: R **Throws:** R **HT:** 5–10 **WT:** 180
Born: 4–6–69, El Cajon, CA
High school: El Dorado (Yorba Linda, CA)
College: USC

Boone started 57 of Seattle's last 58 games. His 12 HR set a club record for HRs by a second baseman.

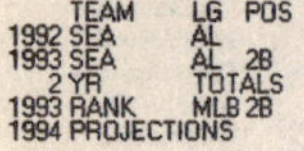
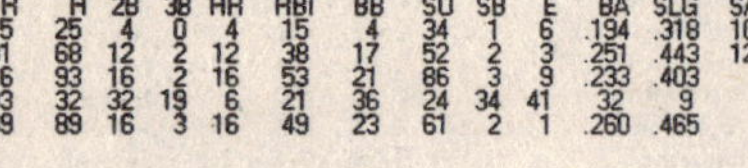

	TEAM	LG	POS	G	AB	R	H	2B	3B	HR	RBI	BB	SO	SB	E	BA	SLG	SALARY
1992	SEA	AL		33	129	15	25	4	0	4	15	4	34	1	6	.194	.318	109,000
1993	SEA	AL	2B	76	271	31	68	12	2	12	38	17	52	2	3	.251	.443	120,000
2	YR	TOTALS		109	400	46	93	16	2	16	53	21	86	3	9	.233	.403	
1993	RANK	MLB	2B	40	31	33	32	32	19	6	21	36	24	34	41	32	9	34
1994	PROJECTIONS			97	342	39	89	16	3	16	49	23	61	2	1	.260	.465	0

Casey Candaele 2B-SS

Full name: Casey Todd Candaele
Bats: S **Throws:** R **HT:** 5–9 **WT:** 165
Born: 1–12–61, Lompoc, CA
High school: Lompoc (CA)
College: Arizona

Free agent signee Candaele had just 7 RBI in 75 games for Houston in 1993.

	TEAM	LG	POS	G	AB	R	H	2B	3B	HR	RBI	BB	SO	SB	E	BA	SLG	SALARY
1986	MTL	NL	2B-3B	30	104	9	24	4	1	0	6	5	15	3	2	.231	.288	N/A
1987	MTL	NL	2B-OF	138	449	62	122	23	4	1	23	38	28	5	8	.272	.347	N/A
1988	MTL-HOU	NL	2B-OF	57	147	11	25	8	1	0	5	11	17	1	2	.170	.238	N/A
1990	HOU	NL	OF-2B	130	262	30	75	8	6	3	22	31	42	7	3	.286	.397	N/A
1991	HOU	NL	2B-OF	151	461	44	121	20	7	4	50	40	49	9	10	.262	.362	350,000
1992	HOU	NL	SS-3B	135	320	19	68	12	1	1	18	24	36	7	11	.213	.266	905,000
1993	HOU	NL	2B	75	121	18	29	8	0	1	7	10	14	2	3	.240	.331	775,000
7	YR	TOTALS		716	1864	193	464	83	20	10	131	159	201	34	39	.249	.331	
1993	RANK	MLB	2B	not ranked -- didn't have 150 ABs in 1993														
1994	PROJECTIONS			54	124	12	26	6	0	0	6	8	15	2	2	.210	.282	

Roberto Kelly No. 30/OF

Full name: Roberto Conrado Kelly
Bats: R **Throws:** R **HT:** 6–2 **WT:** 190
Born: 10–1–64, Panama City, Pan.
High school: Jose Delores Moscote (Panama City, PN)

Kelly had an All-Star first half of 1993 (.319 BA, 21 SB, 102 H), but missed the rest of the year due to a shoulder injury.

	TEAM	LG	POS	G	AB	R	H	2B	3B	HR	RBI	BB	SO	SB	E	BA	SLG	SALARY
1987	NY	AL	OF	23	52	12	14	3	0	1	7	5	15	9	2	.269	.385	N/A
1988	NY	AL	OF	38	77	9	19	4	1	1	7	3	15	5	1	.247	.364	N/A
1989	NY	AL	OF	137	441	65	133	18	3	9	48	41	89	35	6	.302	.417	N/A
1990	NY	AL	OF	162	641	85	183	32	4	15	61	33	148	42	5	.285	.418	N/A
1991	NY	AL	OF	126	486	68	130	22	2	20	69	45	77	32	4	.267	.444	900,000
1992	NY	AL	OF	152	580	81	158	31	2	10	66	41	96	28	7	.272	.384	2,150,000
1993	CIN	NL	OF	78	320	44	102	17	3	9	35	17	43	21	1	.319	.475	3,133,333
7	YR	TOTALS		716	2597	364	739	127	15	65	293	185	483	172	26	.285	.42	
1993	RANK	MLB	OF	118	84	81	72	66	54	64	86	113	96	29	8	7	34	21
1994	PROJECTIONS			46	149	21	45	8	1	3	16	8	24	11	1	.302	.443	

Barry Larkin No. 11/SS

Full name: Barry Louis Larkin
Bats: R **Throws:** R **HT:** 6–0 **WT:** 190
Born: 4–28–64, Cincinnati, OH
High school: Moeller (Cincinnati, OH)
College: Michigan

Larkin played only 100 games due to injury. He batted .321 with runners in scoring position, and struck out only 33 times in 384 AB.

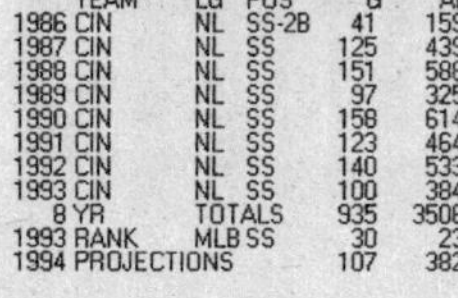

	TEAM	LG	POS	G	AB	R	H	2B	3B	HR	RBI	BB	SO	SB	E	BA	SLG	SALARY
1986	CIN	NL	SS-2B	41	159	27	45	4	3	3	19	9	21	8	4	.283	.403	N/A
1987	CIN	NL	SS	125	439	64	107	16	2	12	43	36	52	21	19	.244	.371	N/A
1988	CIN	NL	SS	151	588	91	174	32	5	12	56	41	24	40	29	.296	.429	N/A
1989	CIN	NL	SS	97	325	47	111	14	4	4	36	20	23	10	10	.342	.446	N/A
1990	CIN	NL	SS	158	614	85	185	25	6	7	67	49	49	30	17	.301	.396	N/A
1991	CIN	NL	SS	123	464	88	140	27	4	20	69	55	64	24	15	.302	.506	2,100,000
1992	CIN	NL	SS	140	533	76	162	32	6	12	78	63	58	15	11	.304	.454	4,300,000
1993	CIN	NL	SS	100	384	57	121	20	3	8	51	51	33	14	16	.315	.445	5,750,000
8	YR	TOTALS		935	3506	535	1045	170	33	78	419	324	324	162	121	.298	.432	
1993	RANK	MLB	SS	30	23	16	19	16	12	12	15	9	29	7	13	3	4	1
1994	PROJECTIONS			107	382	56	113	16	3	8	43	35	36	15	15	.296	.416	

Kevin Mitchell No. 7/OF

Full name: Kevin Darrell Mitchell
Bats: R **Throws:** R **HT:** 5–11 **WT:** 210
Born: 1–13–62, San Diego, CA
High school: Clairmont (San Diego, CA)

Mitchell is still trying to overcome injuries and find his power stroke; his 64 RBI was his lowest total since 1986. His .341 BA was his career-best by a wide margin.

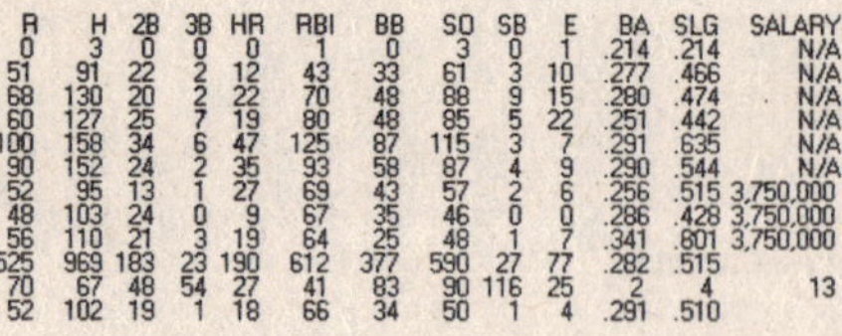

	TEAM	LG	POS	G	AB	R	H	2B	3B	HR	RBI	BB	SO	SB	E	BA	SLG	SALARY
1984	NY	NL	3B	7	14	0	3	0	0	0	1	0	3	0	1	.214	.214	N/A
1986	NY	NL	OF-SS	108	328	51	91	22	2	12	43	33	61	3	10	.277	.466	N/A
1987	SD/SF	NL	3B-OF	131	464	68	130	20	2	22	70	48	88	9	15	.280	.474	N/A
1988	SF	NL	3B-OF	148	505	60	127	25	7	19	80	48	85	5	22	.251	.442	N/A
1989	SF	NL	OF-3B	154	543	100	158	34	6	47	125	87	115	3	7	.291	.635	N/A
1990	SF	NL	OF	140	524	90	152	24	2	35	93	58	87	4	9	.290	.544	N/A
1991	SF	NL	OF-1B	113	371	52	95	13	1	27	69	43	57	2	6	.256	.515	3,750,000
1992	SEA	AL	OF	99	360	48	103	24	0	9	67	35	46	0	0	.286	.428	3,750,000
1993	CIN	NL	OF	93	323	56	110	21	3	19	64	25	48	1	7	.341	.801	3,750,000
9	YR	TOTALS		993	3432	525	969	183	23	190	612	377	590	27	77	.282	.515	
1993	RANK	MLB	OF	100	82	70	67	48	54	27	41	83	90	116	25	2	4	13
1994	PROJECTIONS			101	351	52	102	19	1	18	66	34	50	1	4	.291	.510	

Hal Morris No. 23/1B

Full name: William Harold Morris III
Bats: L **Throws:** L **HT:** 6–4 **WT:** 215
Born: 4–9–65, Fort Rucker, AL
High school: Munster (IN)
College: Michigan

Morris recovered from a shoulder injury and batted .335 after the All-Star break, but 95 of his 120 hits were singles.

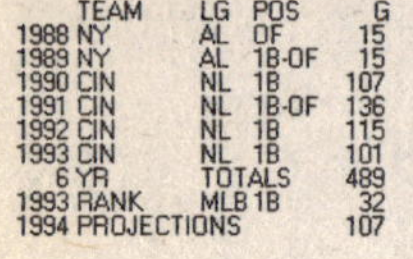

	TEAM	LG	POS	G	AB	R	H	2B	3B	HR	RBI	BB	SO	SB	E	BA	SLG	SALARY
1988	NY	AL	OF	15	20	1	2	0	0	0	0	0	9	0	0	.100	.100	N/A
1989	NY	AL	1B-OF	15	18	2	5	0	0	0	4	1	4	0	0	.278	.278	N/A
1990	CIN	NL	1B	107	309	50	105	22	3	7	36	21	32	9	4	.340	.498	N/A
1991	CIN	NL	1B-OF	136	478	72	152	33	1	14	59	46	61	10	9	.318	.479	180,000
1992	CIN	NL	1B	115	395	41	107	21	3	6	53	45	53	6	1	.271	.385	430,000
1993	CIN	NL	1B	101	379	48	120	18	0	7	49	34	51	2	5	.317	.420	1,275,000
6	YR	TOTALS		489	1599	214	491	94	7	34	201	147	210	27	19	.307	.438	
1993	RANK	MLB	1B	32	28	26	23	26	30	30	28	28	29	20	21	7	26	16
1994	PROJECTIONS			107	361	46	110	20	2	6	46	33	45	5	3	.305	.429	

Joe Oliver No. 9/C

Full name: Joseph Melton Oliver
Bats: R **Throws:** R **HT:** 6–3 **WT:** 210
Born: 7–24–65, Memphis, TN
High school: Orlando Boone (FL)
Oliver's career-high 75 RBI were third-best on the team, and he hit .291 against left-handers. He threw out only 43 of 143 (30%) base stealers.

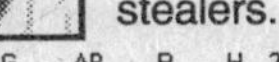

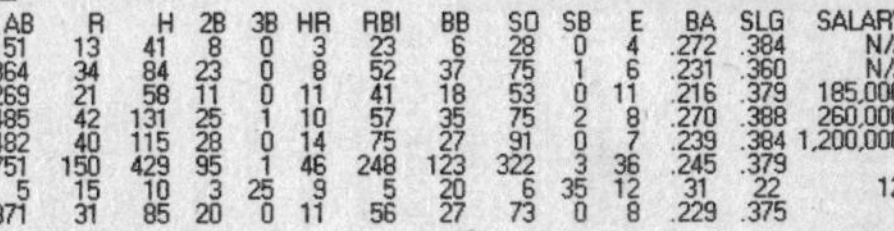

TEAM	LG	POS	G	AB	R	H	2B	3B	HR	RBI	BB	SO	SB	E	BA	SLG	SALARY
1989 CIN	NL	C	49	151	13	41	8	0	3	23	6	28	0	4	.272	.384	N/A
1990 CIN	NL	C	121	364	34	84	23	0	8	52	37	75	1	6	.231	.360	N/A
1991 CIN	NL	C	94	269	21	58	11	0	11	41	18	53	0	11	.216	.379	185,000
1992 CIN	NL	C-1B	143	485	42	131	25	1	10	57	35	75	2	8	.270	.388	260,000
1993 CIN	NL	C	139	482	40	115	28	0	14	75	27	91	0	7	.239	.384	1,200,000
5 YR	TOTALS		546	1751	150	429	95	1	46	248	123	322	3	36	.245	.379	
1993 RANK	MLB	C	4	5	15	10	3	25	9	5	20	6	35	12	31	22	12
1994 PROJECTIONS			118	371	31	85	20	0	11	56	27	73	0	8	.229	.375	

Reggie Sanders No. 16/OF

Full name: Reginald Laverne Sanders
Bats: R **Throws:** R **HT:** 6–1 **WT:** 180
Born: 12–1–67, Florence, SC
High school: Wilson (Florence, SC)
College: Spartanburg Methodist (SC)
An emerging star, Sanders established career-highs in HR (20), RBI (83), and SB (27). 14 of his 20 HRs were off of righties.

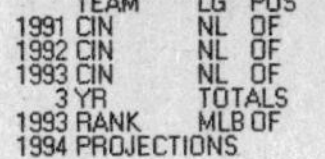

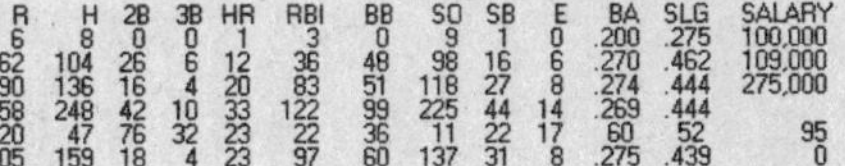

TEAM	LG	POS	G	AB	R	H	2B	3B	HR	RBI	BB	SO	SB	E	BA	SLG	SALARY
1991 CIN	NL	OF	9	40	6	8	0	0	1	3	0	9	1	0	.200	.275	100,000
1992 CIN	NL	OF	116	385	62	104	26	6	12	36	48	98	16	6	.270	.462	109,000
1993 CIN	NL	OF	138	496	90	136	16	4	20	83	51	118	27	8	.274	.444	275,000
3 YR	TOTALS		263	921	158	248	42	10	33	122	99	225	44	14	.269	.444	
1993 RANK	MLB	OF	45	45	20	47	76	32	23	22	36	11	22	17	60	52	95
1994 PROJECTIONS			162	579	105	159	18	4	23	97	60	137	31	8	.275	.439	0

Tom Browning No. 32/P

Full name: Thomas Leo Browning
Bats: L **Throws:** L **HT:** 6–1 **WT:** 195
Born: 4–28–60, Casper, WY
High school: Franklin Acad. (Malone, NY)
College: LeMoyne (NY) and Tenn. Wesleyan

A fractured finger ended Browning's season in August. He walked only 20 batters in 114.1 IP and had a 4–2 record at home.

	TM	LG	POS	W	L	ERA	G	GS	CG	SH	SV	IP	H	R	ER	HR	BB	SO	SALARY
1984	CIN	NL	P	1	0	1.54	3	3	0	0	0	23.1	27	4	4	0	5	14	N/A
1985	CIN	NL	P	20	9	3.55	38	38	6	4	0	261.1	242	111	103	29	73	155	N/A
1986	CIN	NL	P	14	13	3.81	39	39	4	2	0	243.1	225	123	103	26	70	147	N/A
1987	CIN	NL	P	10	13	5.02	32	31	2	0	0	183.0	201	107	102	27	61	117	N/A
1988	CIN	NL	P	18	5	3.41	36	36	5	2	0	250.2	205	98	95	36	64	124	N/A
1989	CIN	NL	P	15	12	3.39	37	37	9	2	0	249.2	241	109	94	31	64	118	N/A
1990	CIN	NL	P	15	9	3.80	35	35	2	1	0	227.2	235	98	96	24	52	99	N/A
1991	CIN	NL	P	14	14	4.18	36	36	1	0	0	230.1	241	124	107	32	56	115	2,650,000
1992	CIN	NL	P	6	5	5.07	16	16	0	0	0	87.0	108	49	49	6	28	33	3,250,000
1993	CIN	NL	P	7	7	4.74	21	20	0	0	0	114.0	159	61	60	15	20	53	2,250,000
10	YR	TOTALS		120	87	3.91	293	291	29	11	0	1870.1	1884	884	813	226	493	975	
1993	Rank	MLB	Ps	108		210	250	105	125	69	102	124	288	180		234	9	253	60
1994	PROJECTIONS			4	4	4.50	13	13	0	0	0	74	98	38	37	7	17	33	

Tim Pugh No. 40/P

Full name: Timothy Dean Pugh
Bats: R **Throws:** R **HT:** 6–6 **WT:** 225
Born: 1–26–67, Lake Tahoe, CA
High school: Bartlesville (OK)
College: Oklahoma State

Pugh's 15 losses were the most on the Reds staff; his 10 wins ranked second. He came within two outs of a no-hitter vs. San Diego.

	TM	LG	POS	W	L	ERA	G	GS	CG	SH	SV	IP	H	R	ER	HR	BB	SO	SALARY
1992	CIN	NL	P	4	2	2.58	7	7	0	0	0	45.1	47	15	13	2	13	18	N/A
1993	CIN	NL	P	10	15	5.26	31	27	3	1	0	164.1	200	102	96	19	59	94	115,000
2	YR	TOTALS		14	17	4.68	38	34	3	1	0	209.2	247	117	109	21	72	112	
1993	RANK	MLB	Ps	75		250	194	81	37	23	102	82	267	239		196	143	184	222
1994	PROJECTIONS			12	20	5.54	41	36	3	0	0	216	268	141	133	26	79	128	

Jose Rijo No. 27/P

Full name: Jose Antonio (Abreu) Rijo
Bats: R **Throws:** R **HT:** 6–2 **WT:** 210
Born: 5–13–65, San Cristobal, DR
High school: Santo Domingo, DR

Rijo's 237 strikeouts led the NL, while his 2.48 ERA ranked second. Healthy for the entire season for the first time in 6 years, he was 8–4 after the All-Star break.

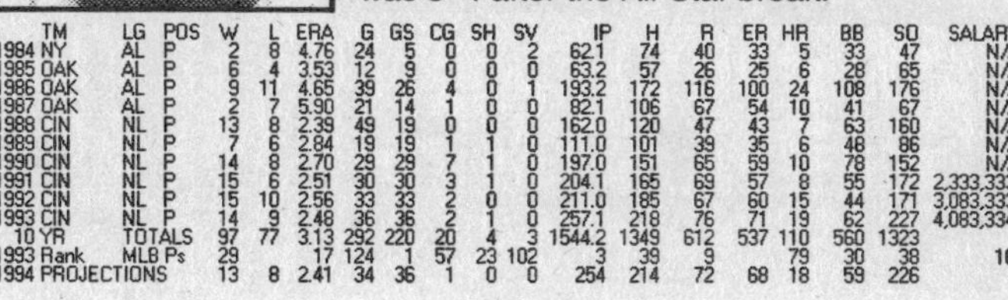

	TM	LG	POS	W	L	ERA	G	GS	CG	SH	SV	IP	H	R	ER	HR	BB	SO	SALARY
1984	NY	AL	P	2	8	4.76	24	5	0	0	2	62.1	74	40	33	5	33	47	N/A
1985	OAK	AL	P	6	4	3.53	12	9	0	0	0	63.2	57	26	25	6	28	65	N/A
1986	OAK	AL	P	9	11	4.65	39	26	4	0	1	193.2	172	116	100	24	108	176	N/A
1987	OAK	AL	P	2	7	5.90	21	14	1	0	0	82.1	106	67	54	10	41	67	N/A
1988	CIN	NL	P	13	8	2.39	49	19	0	0	0	162.0	120	47	43	7	63	160	N/A
1989	CIN	NL	P	7	6	2.84	19	19	1	1	0	111.0	101	39	35	6	48	86	N/A
1990	CIN	NL	P	14	8	2.70	29	29	7	1	0	197.0	151	65	59	10	78	152	N/A
1991	CIN	NL	P	15	6	2.51	30	30	3	1	0	204.1	165	69	57	8	55	172	2,333,333
1992	CIN	NL	P	15	10	2.56	33	33	2	0	0	211.0	185	67	60	15	44	171	3,083,333
1993	CIN	NL	P	14	9	2.48	36	36	2	1	0	257.1	218	76	71	19	62	227	4,083,334
10	YR	TOTALS		97	77	3.13	292	220	20	4	3	1544.2	1349	612	537	110	560	1323	
1993	Rank	MLB Ps		29		17	124	1	57	23	102	3	39	9		79	30	38	16
1994	PROJECTIONS			13	8	2.41	34	36	1	0	0	254	214	72	68	18	59	226	

John Smiley No. 57/P

Full name: John Patrick Smiley
Bats: L **Throws:** L **HT:** 6–4 **WT:** 200
Born: 3–17–65, Phoenixville, PA
High school: Perkiomen Valley (PA)

Smiley's first season with the Reds ended early due to shoulder surgery. He started very slowly (0-5, 7.08 ERA), but Cincinnati scored only 16 runs in his 9 losses.

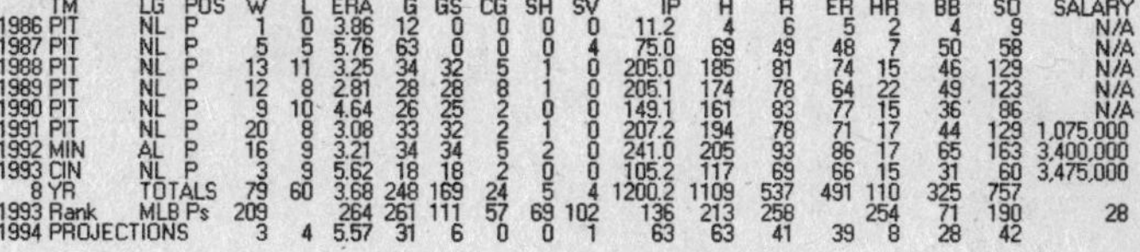

	TM	LG	POS	W	L	ERA	G	GS	CG	SH	SV	IP	H	R	ER	HR	BB	SO	SALARY
1986	PIT	NL	P	1	0	3.86	12	0	0	0	0	11.2	4	6	5	2	4	9	N/A
1987	PIT	NL	P	5	5	5.76	63	0	0	0	4	75.0	69	49	48	7	50	58	N/A
1988	PIT	NL	P	13	11	3.25	34	32	5	1	0	205.0	185	81	74	15	46	129	N/A
1989	PIT	NL	P	12	8	2.81	28	28	8	1	0	205.1	174	78	64	22	49	123	N/A
1990	PIT	NL	P	9	10	4.64	26	25	2	0	0	149.1	161	83	77	15	36	86	N/A
1991	PIT	NL	P	20	8	3.08	33	32	2	1	0	207.2	194	78	71	17	44	129	1,075,000
1992	MIN	AL	P	16	9	3.21	34	34	5	2	0	241.0	205	93	86	17	65	163	3,400,000
1993	CIN	NL	P	3	9	5.62	18	18	2	0	0	105.2	117	69	66	15	31	60	3,475,000
8	YR	TOTALS		79	60	3.68	248	169	24	5	4	1200.2	1109	537	491	110	325	757	
1993	Rank	MLB Ps		209		264	261	111	57	69	102	136	213	258		254	71	190	28
1994	PROJECTIONS			3	4	5.57	31	6	0	0	1	63	63	41	39	8	28	42	

Rob Dibble No. 49/P

Full name: Robert Keith Dibble
Bats: L **Throws:** R **HT:** 6–4 **WT:** 230
Born: 1–24–64, Bridgeport, CT
High school: Southington (CT)
College: Florida Southern (Lakeland, FL)

Through the end of July, Dibble was 1–0 with a 2.30 ERA and 15 saves in 19 chances before slumping badly.

	TM	LG	POS	W	L	ERA	G	GS	CG	SH	SV	IP	H	R	ER	HR	BB	SO	SALARY
1988	CIN	NL	P	1	1	1.82	37	0	0	0	0	59.1	43	12	12	2	21	59	N/A
1989	CIN	NL	P	10	5	2.09	74	0	0	0	2	99.0	62	23	23	4	39	141	N/A
1990	CIN	NL	P	8	3	1.74	68	0	0	0	11	98.0	62	22	19	3	34	136	N/A
1991	CIN	NL	P	3	5	3.17	67	0	0	0	31	82.1	67	32	29	5	25	124	475,000
1992	CIN	NL	P	3	5	3.07	63	0	0	0	25	70.1	48	26	24	3	31	110	1,400,000
1993	CIN	NL	P	1	4	6.48	45	0	0	0	19	41.2	34	33	30	8	42	49	2,500,000
6	YR	TOTALS		26	23	2.74	354	0	0	0	88	450.2	316	148	137	25	192	619	
1993	Rank	MLB Ps		not ranked -- didn't have 50 IP in 1993															
1994	PROJECTIONS			6	4	2.73	62	0	0	0	10	79	52	26	24	5	38	108	

Dave Johnson No. 15/Mgr.

Full name: David Allen Johnson
Bats: R **Throws:** R **HT:** 6–1 **WT:** 170
Born: 1–30–43, Orlando, FL

Johnson took over for Tony Perez, who was dismissed after only 44 games. Cincinnati was 20–24 (.455) pre-Johnson, 53–65 (.449) after Johnson was hired.

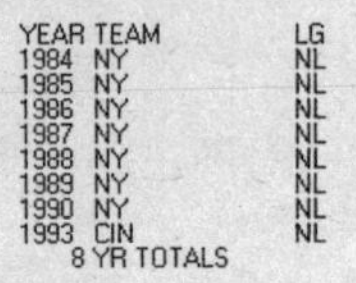

			REG. SEASON				PLAYOFF			CHAMP. SERIES			WORLD SERIES		
YEAR	TEAM	LG	W	L	PCT	POS	W	L	PCT	W	L	PCT	W	L	PCT
1984	NY	NL	90	72	.556	2			---			---			---
1985	NY	NL	98	64	.605	2			---			---			---
1986	NY	NL	108	54	.667	1			---	4	2	.667	4	3	.571
1987	NY	NL	92	70	.568	2			---			---			---
1988	NY	NL	100	60	.625	1			---	3	4	.429			---
1989	NY	NL	87	75	.537	2			---			---			---
1990	NY	NL	20	22	.476	4			---			---			---
1993	CIN	NL	53	65	.449	5			---			---			---
8 YR TOTALS			648	482	.573		0	0	---	7	6	.538	4	3	.571

Jeff Branson No. 20/SS

Full name: Jeffrey Glenn Branson
Bats: L **Throws:** R **HT:** 6–0 **WT:** 180
Born: 1–26–67, Waynesboro, MS
High school: Southern Choctaw (Silas, AL)
College: Livingston (AL)
Branson hit .353 as a pinch-hitter.

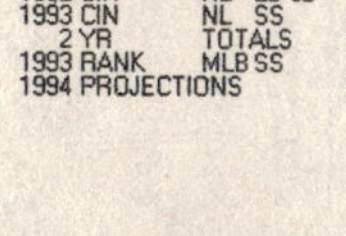

	TEAM	LG	POS	G	AB	R	H	2B	3B	HR	RBI	BB	SO	SB	E	BA	SLG	SALARY
1992	CIN	NL	2B-3B	72	115	12	34	7	1	0	15	5	16	0	7	.296	.374	109,000
1993	CIN	NL	SS	125	381	40	92	15	1	3	22	19	73	4	11	.241	.310	157,500
2	YR	TOTALS		197	496	52	126	22	2	3	37	24	89	4	18	.254	.325	
1993	RANK	MLB	SS	22	25	28	26	23	29	20	34	29	11	25	12	35	34	28
1994	PROJECTIONS			151	514	54	121	19	1	4	25	26	101	6	13	.235	.300	0

Jacob Brumfield No. 4/OF

Full name: Jacob Donnell Brumfield
Bats: R **Throws:** R **HT:** 6–0 **WT:** 180
Born: 5–27–65, Bogalusa, LA
High school: Hammond (LA)
Utilityman Brumfield saw action at 4 positions in 1994, and batted a solid .309 on the road.

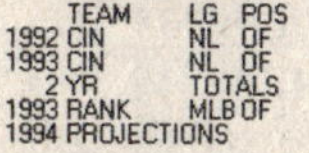

	TEAM	LG	POS	G	AB	R	H	2B	3B	HR	RBI	BB	SO	SB	E	BA	SLG	SALARY
1992	CIN	NL	OF	24	30	6	4	0	0	0	2	2	4	6	0	.133	.133	N/A
1993	CIN	NL	OF	103	272	40	73	17	3	6	23	21	47	20	7	.268	.419	117,500
2	YR	TOTALS		127	302	46	77	17	3	6	25	23	51	26	7	.255	.391	
1993	RANK	MLB	OF	89	94	90	92	66	54	87	117	99	93	32	101	74	68	123
1994	PROJECTIONS			142	393	57	107	25	4	9	33	30	68	27	10	.272	.425	0

Erik Hanson No. 39/P

Full name: Erik Brian Hanson
Bats: R **Throws:** R **HT:** 6–6 **WT:** 215
Born: 5–18–65, Kinnelon, NJ
High school: Peddie School (Highstown, NJ)
College: Wake Forest
Hanson tied for sixth in the AL in complete games.

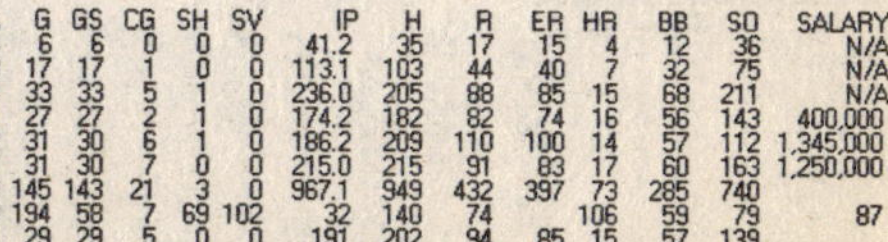

	TM	LG	POS	W	L	ERA	G	GS	CG	SH	SV	IP	H	R	ER	HR	BB	SO	SALARY
1988	SEA	AL	P	2	3	3.24	6	6	0	0	0	41.2	35	17	15	4	12	36	N/A
1989	SEA	AL	P	9	5	3.18	17	17	1	0	0	113.1	103	44	40	7	32	75	N/A
1990	SEA	AL	P	18	9	3.24	33	33	5	1	0	236.0	205	88	85	15	68	211	N/A
1991	SEA	AL	P	8	8	3.81	27	27	2	1	0	174.2	182	82	74	16	56	143	400,000
1992	SEA	AL	P	8	17	4.82	31	30	6	1	0	186.2	209	110	100	14	57	112	1,345,000
1993	SEA	AL	P	11	12	3.47	31	30	7	0	0	215.0	215	91	83	17	60	163	1,250,000
6	YR	TOTALS		56	54	3.69	145	143	21	3	0	967.1	949	432	397	73	285	740	
1993	Rank	MLB	Ps	59		88	194	58	7	69	102	32	140	74		106	59	79	87
1994	PROJECTIONS			9	12	4.01	29	29	5	0	0	191	202	94	85	15	57	139	

Lenny Harris — No. 29/IF

Full name: Leonard Anthony Harris
Bats: L **Throws:** R **HT:** 5–10 **WT:** 220
Born: 10–28–64, Miami, FL
High school: Jackson (Miami, FL)
Harris started only 26 games for the Dodgers in 1993. He batted .387 as a pinch-hitter.

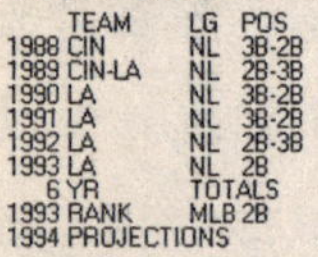
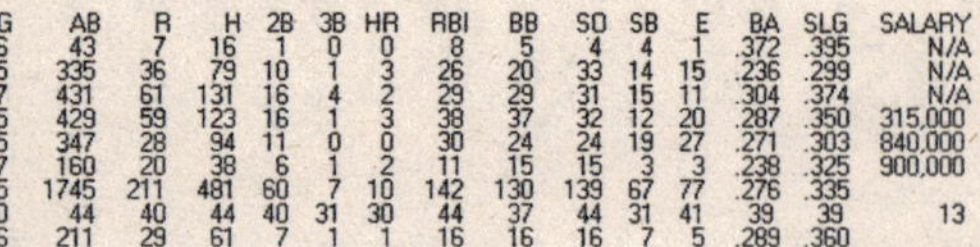

	TEAM	LG	POS	G	AB	R	H	2B	3B	HR	RBI	BB	SO	SB	E	BA	SLG	SALARY
1988	CIN	NL	3B-2B	16	43	7	16	1	0	0	8	5	4	4	1	.372	.395	N/A
1989	CIN-LA	NL	2B-3B	115	335	36	79	10	1	3	26	20	33	14	15	.236	.299	N/A
1990	LA	NL	3B-2B	137	431	61	131	16	4	2	29	29	31	15	11	.304	.374	N/A
1991	LA	NL	3B-2B	145	429	59	123	16	1	3	38	37	32	12	20	.287	.350	315,000
1992	LA	NL	2B-3B	135	347	28	94	11	0	0	30	24	24	19	27	.271	.303	840,000
1993	LA	NL	2B	107	160	20	38	6	1	2	11	15	15	3	3	.238	.325	900,000
6	YR	TOTALS		655	1745	211	481	60	7	10	142	130	139	67	77	.276	.335	
1993	RANK	MLB	2B	30	44	40	44	40	31	30	44	37	44	31	41	39	39	13
1994	PROJECTIONS			86	211	29	61	7	1	1	16	16	16	7	5	.289	.360	

Thomas Howard — No. 22/OF

Full name: Thomas Howard
Bats: B **Throws:** R **HT:** 6–2 **WT:** 205
Born: 12-11-64, Middletown, OH
High school: Valley View (Germantown, OH)
College: Ball State (IN)
Howard batted .313 left-handed and .138 right-handed.

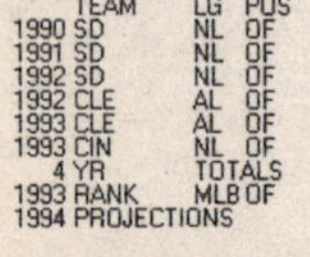
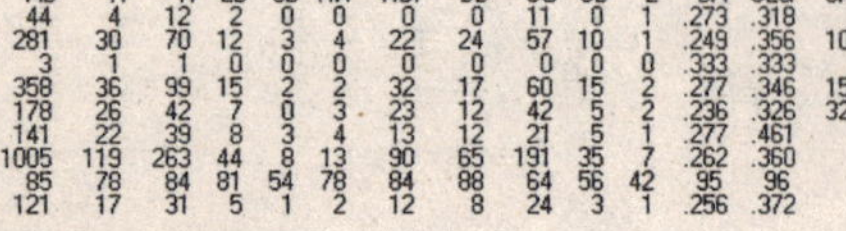

	TEAM	LG	POS	G	AB	R	H	2B	3B	HR	RBI	BB	SO	SB	E	BA	SLG	SALARY
1990	SD	NL	OF	20	44	4	12	2	0	0	0	0	11	0	1	.273	.318	N/A
1991	SD	NL	OF	106	281	30	70	12	3	4	22	24	57	10	1	.249	.356	105,000
1992	SD	NL	OF	5	3	1	1	0	0	0	0	0	0	0	0	.333	.333	N/A
1992	CLE	AL	OF	117	358	36	99	15	2	2	32	17	60	15	2	.277	.346	158,000
1993	CLE	AL	OF	74	178	26	42	7	0	3	23	12	42	5	2	.236	.326	325,000
1993	CIN	NL	OF	38	141	22	39	8	3	4	13	12	21	5	1	.277	.461	N/A
4	YR	TOTALS		360	1005	119	263	44	8	13	90	65	191	35	7	.262	.360	
1993	RANK	MLB	OF	78	85	78	84	81	54	78	84	88	64	56	42	95	96	
1994	PROJECTIONS			44	121	17	31	5	1	2	12	8	24	3	1	.256	.372	

Steve Lake — C

Full name: Steven Michael Lake
Bats: R **Throws:** R **HT:** 6–1 **WT:** 195
Born: 3–14–57, Inglewood, CA
High school: Lennox (CA)
Lake batted a weak .225, but 11 of his 27 hits were for extra bases.

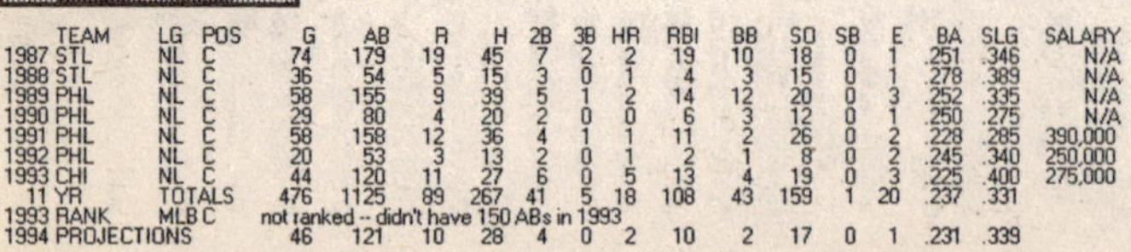

	TEAM	LG	POS	G	AB	R	H	2B	3B	HR	RBI	BB	SO	SB	E	BA	SLG	SALARY
1987	STL	NL	C	74	179	19	45	7	2	2	19	10	18	0	1	.251	.346	N/A
1988	STL	NL	C	36	54	5	15	3	0	1	4	3	15	0	1	.278	.389	N/A
1989	PHL	NL	C	58	155	9	39	5	1	2	14	12	20	0	3	.252	.335	N/A
1990	PHL	NL	C	29	80	4	20	2	0	0	6	3	12	0	1	.250	.275	N/A
1991	PHL	NL	C	58	158	12	36	4	1	1	11	2	26	0	2	.228	.285	390,000
1992	PHL	NL	C	20	53	3	13	2	0	1	2	1	8	0	2	.245	.340	250,000
1993	CHI	NL	C	44	120	11	27	6	0	5	13	4	19	0	3	.225	.400	275,000
11	YR	TOTALS		476	1125	89	267	41	5	18	108	43	159	1	20	.237	.331	
1993	RANK	MLB	C	not ranked -- didn't have 150 ABs in 1993														
1994	PROJECTIONS			46	121	10	28	4	0	2	10	2	17	0	1	.231	.339	

Chuck McElroy — No. 35/P

Full name: Charles Dwayne McElroy
Bats: L **Throws:** L **HT:** 6–0 **WT:** 195
Born: 10–1–67, Port Arthur, TX
High school: Lincoln (Port Arthur, TX)
McElroy didn't allow a homer in 22 second-half appearances.

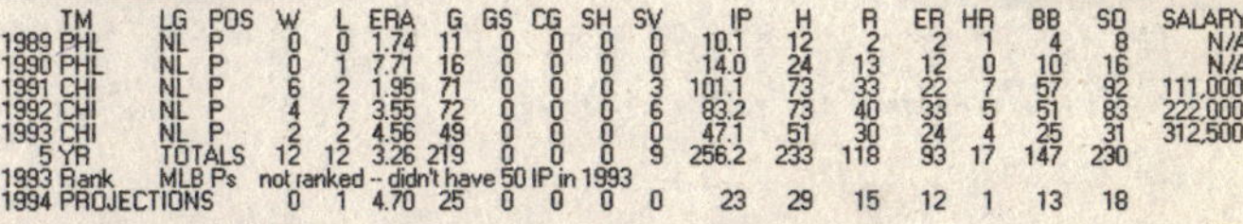

TM	LG	POS	W	L	ERA	G	GS	CG	SH	SV	IP	H	R	ER	HR	BB	SO	SALARY
1989 PHL	NL	P	0	0	1.74	11	0	0	0	0	10.1	12	2	2	1	4	8	N/A
1990 PHL	NL	P	0	1	7.71	16	0	0	0	0	14.0	24	13	12	0	10	16	N/A
1991 CHI	NL	P	6	2	1.95	71	0	0	0	3	101.1	73	33	22	7	57	92	111,000
1992 CHI	NL	P	4	7	3.55	72	0	0	0	6	83.2	73	40	33	5	51	83	222,000
1993 CHI	NL	P	2	2	4.56	49	0	0	0	0	47.1	51	30	24	4	25	31	312,500
5 YR	TOTALS		12	12	3.26	219	0	0	0	9	256.2	233	118	93	17	147	230	
1993 Rank	MLB Ps		not ranked -- didn't have 50 IP in 1993															
1994 PROJECTIONS			0	1	4.70	25	0	0	0	0	23	29	15	12	1	13	18	

Ken Patterson — P

Full name: Kenneth Brian Patterson
Bats: L **Throws:** L **HT:** 6–4 **WT:** 230
Born: 7–8–64, Costa Meas, CA
High school: McGregor (TX)
College: McLennan CC (TX) and Baylor
Patterson was in 46 games, his best since '89.

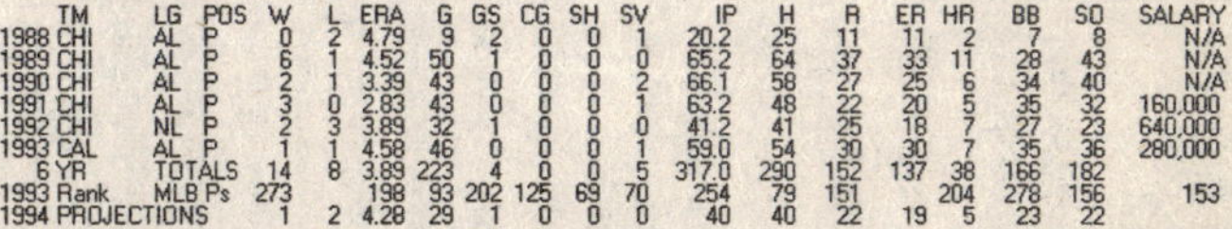

TM	LG	POS	W	L	ERA	G	GS	CG	SH	SV	IP	H	R	ER	HR	BB	SO	SALARY
1988 CHI	AL	P	0	2	4.79	9	2	0	0	1	20.2	25	11	11	2	7	8	N/A
1989 CHI	AL	P	6	1	4.52	50	1	0	0	0	65.2	64	37	33	11	28	43	N/A
1990 CHI	AL	P	2	1	3.39	43	0	0	0	2	66.1	58	27	25	6	34	40	N/A
1991 CHI	AL	P	3	0	2.83	43	0	0	0	1	63.2	48	22	20	5	35	32	160,000
1992 CHI	NL	P	2	3	3.89	32	1	0	0	0	41.2	41	25	18	7	27	23	640,000
1993 CAL	AL	P	1	1	4.58	46	0	0	0	1	59.0	54	30	30	7	35	36	280,000
6 YR	TOTALS		14	8	3.89	223	4	0	0	5	317.0	290	152	137	38	166	182	
1993 Rank	MLB Ps		273		198	93	202	125	69	70	254	79	151		204	278	156	153
1994 PROJECTIONS			1	2	4.28	29	1	0	0	0	40	40	22	19	5	23	22	

John Roper — No. 44/P

Full name: John Christopher Roper
Bats: R **Throws:** R **HT:** 6–0 **WT:** 175
Born: 11–21–71, Southern Pines, NC
High school: Raeford, NC
Roper allowed 92 hits and 36 walks in only 80 IP.

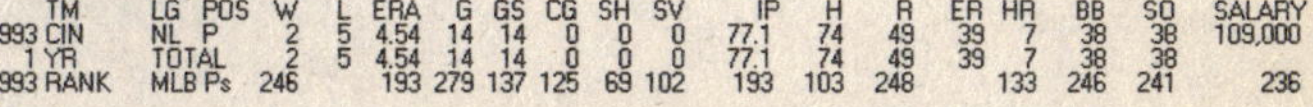

TM	LG	POS	W	L	ERA	G	GS	CG	SH	SV	IP	H	R	ER	HR	BB	SO	SALARY
1993 CIN	NL	P	2	5	4.54	14	14	0	0	0	77.1	74	49	39	7	38	38	109,000
1 YR	TOTAL		2	5	4.54	14	14	0	0	0	77.1	74	49	39	7	38	38	
1993 RANK	MLB Ps		246		193	279	137	125	69	102	193	103	248		133	246	241	236

Jerry Spradlin — No. 48/P

Full name: Jerry Carl Spradlin
Bats: S **Throws:** R **HT:** 6–7 **WT:** 220
Born: 6–14–67, Fullerton, CA
High school: Katella (Anaheim, CA)
College: Cal–Fullerton
Spradlin posted a 1.26 ERA in his last 11 games.

TM	LG	POS	W	L	ERA	G	GS	CG	SH	SV	IP	H	R	ER	HR	BB	SO	SALARY
1993 CIN	NL	P	2	1	3.49	37	0	0	0	2	49.0	44	20	19	4	9	24	109,000
1 YR	TOTAL		2	1	3.49	37	0	0	0	2	49.0	44	20	19	4	9	24	
1993 RANK	MLB Ps	not ranked -- didn't have 50 IP in 1993																

Kurt Stillwell — 2B

Full name: Kurt Andrew Stillwell
Bats: B **Throws:** R **HT:** 5–11 **WT:** 185
Born: 6–4–65, Glendale, CA
High school: Thousand Oaks (CA)
Stillwell was signed as a free agent. He broke into the majors with Cincinnati in 1986.

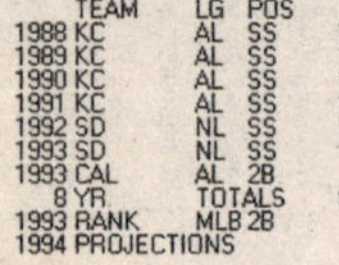
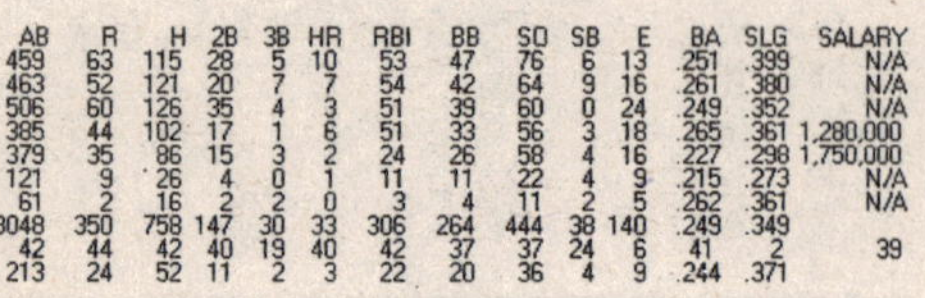

TEAM	LG	POS	G	AB	R	H	2B	3B	HR	RBI	BB	SO	SB	E	BA	SLG	SALARY
1988 KC	AL	SS	128	459	63	115	28	5	10	53	47	76	6	13	.251	.399	N/A
1989 KC	AL	SS	130	463	52	121	20	7	7	54	42	64	9	16	.261	.380	N/A
1990 KC	AL	SS	144	506	60	126	35	4	3	51	39	60	0	24	.249	.352	N/A
1991 KC	AL	SS	122	385	44	102	17	1	6	51	33	56	3	18	.265	.361	1,280,000
1992 SD	NL	SS	114	379	35	86	15	3	2	24	26	58	4	16	.227	.298	1,750,000
1993 SD	NL	SS	57	121	9	26	4	0	1	11	11	22	4	9	.215	.273	N/A
1993 CAL	AL	2B	22	61	2	16	2	2	0	3	4	11	2	5	.262	.361	N/A
8 YR	TOTALS		952	3048	350	758	147	30	33	306	264	444	38	140	.249	.349	
1993 RANK	MLB	2B	39	42	44	42	40	19	40	42	37	37	24	6	41	2	39
1994 PROJECTIONS			69	213	24	52	11	2	3	22	20	36	4	9	.244	.371	

Colorado
ROCKIES

1994 Scouting Report

Hitting: (1993/.273 BA, third in NL; 142 HR, seventh in NL)

The Rockies are an exciting, aggressive team, combining both power (fourth in runs scored) and speed (third in stolen bases). Andres Galarraga led the NL in hitting with a .370 average, and also had 22 HR and 98 RBI. Other offensive stars include Charlie Hayes (.305, 25 HR, 98 RBI), Dante Bichette (.310, 21 HR, 89 RBI), Jerald Clark (.292), Eric Young (.269, 42 SB), and Alex Cole (.256, 30 SB). Free agent signees Howard Johnson and Ellis Burks (as well as the returning Galarraga) should have big years playing 81 games at Mile High Stadium.

Pitching: (1993/5.41 ERA, fourteenth in NL)

Colorado was plagued with weak starting pitching. Armando Reynoso was the Rockies' best starter, going 12–11 with a 4.00 ERA, four complete games, and 117 strikeouts. The other starters in '93 were Kent Bottenfield (5–10, 5.07 ERA) and Willie Blair (6–10, 4.75 ERA). Colorado acquired Greg Harris from the Padres, but he was a disappointment, going just 1–8 with a 6.50 ERA for the Rockies. Colorado hopes prospects John Burke and Mark Thompson will soon bolster the starting rotation.

Colorado's starting woes obscured a pretty effective bullpen. Darren Holmes had a strong '93 performance as the Rockies' closer; he was 25 for 29 in save opportunities. Bruce Ruffin (6–5, 3.87 ERA, 59 appearances) held down the setup role.

Defense: (1993/.973 pct., fourteenth in NL)

Some of Colorado's defensive problems were caused by Mile High Stadium's infield, considered the worst in the major leagues.

1994 Prospects:

Mile High Stadium may be the most hitter-friendly stadium in the major leagues. It's certainly responsible for some of the Rockies' offensive prowess—they hit .306 in Colorado, just .240 on the road. And the Rockies' staff ERA was 5.82 at home, 4.97 on the road. The Rockies will score their share of runs, and win their share of games at home. But until their young pitchers develop, they won't advance much in the standings.

Team Directory

Chairman: Jerry D. McMorris	Executive VP: John McHale, Jr.
General Mgr.: Bob Gebhard	Director of Player Dev.: Dick Balderson
Dir. of Media Relations: Mike Swanson	Traveling Secretary: Peter Durso

Minor League Affiliates:

Level	Team/League	1993 Record
AAA	Colorado Springs – Pacific Coast	66–75
AA	none	
A	Central Valley– California	61–75
	Bend – Northwest	35–41
Rookie	Mesa – Arizona	21–32

Added the Asheville Tourists–South Atlantic League (A) as an affiliate through 1996.

1993 Review

	Home W	Home L	Away W	Away L
vs NL East				
Atlanta	0	7	0	6
Florida	4	2	3	3
Montreal	2	4	1	5
New York	4	2	2	4
Philadelphia	1	5	2	4
Total	11	20	8	22

	Home W	Home L	Away W	Away L
vs NL Cent.				
Chicago	3	3	1	5
Cincinnati	4	2	0	7
Houston	7	0	4	2
Pittsburgh	4	2	4	2
St. Louis	2	4	3	3
Total	20	11	12	19

	Home W	Home L	Away W	Away L
vs NL West				
Los Angeles	3	3	4	3
San Diego	4	2	2	5
S. Francisco	1	6	2	4
Total	8	11	8	12

1993 finish: 67–95 (39–42 home, 28–53 away), sixth in NL West, 37 games behind

1994 Schedule

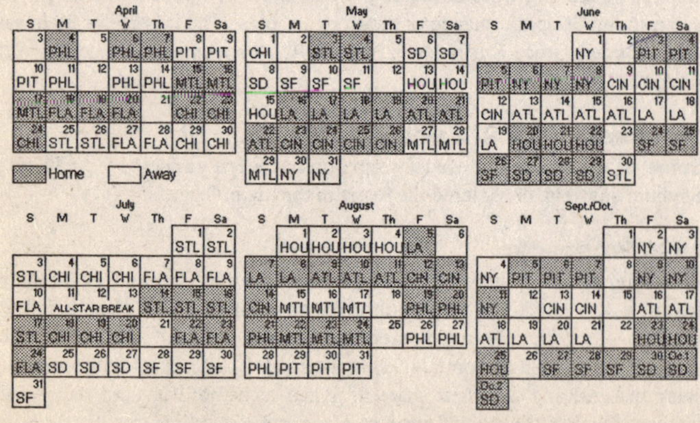

April

S	M	T	W	Th	F	Sa
3	4 PHL	5	6 PHL	7 PHL	8 PIT	9 PIT
10 PIT	11 PHL	12	13 PHL	14 PHL	15 MTL	16 MTL
17 MTL	18 FLA	19 FLA	20 FLA	21	22 CHI	23 CHI
24 CHI	25 STL	26 STL	27 FLA	28 FLA	29 CHI	30 CHI

Home Away

May

S	M	T	W	Th	F	Sa
1 CHI	2	3 STL	4 STL	5	6 SD	7 SD
8 SD	9 SF	10 SF	11 SF	12	13 HOU	14 HOU
15 HOU	16 LA	17 LA	18 LA	19 LA	20 ATL	21 ATL
22 ATL	23 CIN	24 CIN	25 CIN	26 CIN	27 MTL	28 MTL
29 MTL	30 NY	31 NY				

June

S	M	T	W	Th	F	Sa
			1 NY	2	3 PIT	4 PIT
5 PIT	6 NY	7 NY	8 NY	9 CIN	10 CIN	11 CIN
12 CIN	13 ATL	14 ATL	15 ATL	16 ATL	17 LA	18 LA
19 LA	20 HOU	21 HOU	22 HOU	23	24 SF	25 SF
26 SF	27 SD	28 SD	29 SD	30 STL		

July

S	M	T	W	Th	F	Sa
					1 STL	2 STL
3 STL	4 CHI	5 CHI	6 CHI	7 FLA	8 FLA	9 FLA
10 FLA	11 ALL-STAR BREAK	12	13	14 STL	15 STL	16 STL
17 STL	18 CHI	19 CHI	20 CHI	21	22 FLA	23 FLA
24 FLA	25 SD	26 SD	27 SD	28 SF	29 SF	30 SF
31 SF						

August

S	M	T	W	Th	F	Sa
	1 HOU	2 HOU	3 HOU	4 HOU	5 LA	6
7 LA	8 LA	9 ATL	10 ATL	11 ATL	12 CIN	13 CIN
14 CIN	15 MTL	16 MTL	17 MTL	18	19 PHL	20 PHL
21 PHL	22 MTL	23 MTL	24 MTL	25	26 PHL	27 PHL
28 PHL	29 PIT	30 PIT	31 PIT			

Sept./Oct.

S	M	T	W	Th	F	Sa
				1	2 NY	3 NY
4 NY	5 PIT	6 PIT	7 PIT	8	9 NY	10 NY
11 NY	12	13 CIN	14 CIN	15	16 ATL	17 ATL
18 ATL	19 LA	20 LA	21 LA	22	23 HOU	24 HOU
25 HOU	26	27 SF	28 SF	29 SF	30 SD	Oct.1 SD
Oct.2 SD						

COLORADO ROCKIES 1994 ROSTER

MANAGER: Don Baylor (25)

COACHES: Larry Bearnarth (36), Dwight Evans, Gene Glynn, Ron Hassey (29), Bill Plummer (41), Don Zimmer (23)

No.	PITCHERS	B	T	HT	WT	DOB	BIRTHPLACE	RESIDENCE
19	Blair, Willie	R	R	6–1	185	12–18–65	Paintsville, KY	Lexington, KY
46	Bottenfield, Kent	S	R	6–3	225	11–14–68	Portland, OR	W. Palm Beach, FL
49	Fredrickson, Scott	R	R	6–3	215	8–19–67	Manchester, NH	San Antonio, TX
44	Freeman, Marvin	R	R	6–7	222	4–10–63	Chicago, IL	Chicago, IL
27	Harris, Greg	R	R	6–2	195	12–1–63	Greensboro, NC	Cary, NC
48	Hawblitzel, Ryan	R	R	6–2	170	4–30–71	W. Palm Beach, FL	Lake Worth, FL
40	Holmes, Darren	R	R	6–0	199	4–25–66	Asheville, NC	Fletcher, NC
45	Leskanic, Curt	R	R	6–0	180	4–2–68	Homestead, PA	Pineville, LA
54	Moore, Marcus	S	R	6–5	195	11–2–70	Oakland, CA	Oakland, CA
43	Munoz, Mike	L	L	6–2	200	7–12–65	Baldwin Park, CA	South Lake, TX
17	Nied, David	R	R	6–2	185	12–22–68	Dallas, TX	Denver, CO
28	Painter, Lance	L	L	6–1	195	7–21–67	Bedford, England	Lakewood, CO
39	Reed, Steve	R	R	6–2	202	3–1–66	Los Angeles, CA	Arvada, CO
42	Reynoso, Armando	R	R	6–0	186	5–1–66	San Luis Potosi, MX	Jalisco, MX
18	Ruffin, Bruce	S	L	6–2	209	10–4–63	Lubbock, TX	Austin, TX
34	Sanford, Mo	R	R	6–6	225	12–24–66	Americus, GA	Starkville, MS
52	Shepherd, Keith	R	R	6–2	197	1–21–68	Wabash, IN	Wabash, IN
53	Wayne, Gary	L	L	6–3	193	11–30–62	Newton, MA	Lakewood, CO
No.	**CATCHERS**	**B**	**T**	**HT**	**WT**	**DOB**	**BIRTHPLACE**	**RESIDENCE**
7	Girardi, Joe	R	R	5–11	195	10–14–64	Peoria, IL	Lake Forest, IL
33	Owens, Jayhawk	R	R	6–1	200	2–10–69	Cincinnati, OH	Sardinia, OH
16	Shaeffer, Danny	R	R	6–0	190	8–21–61	Jacksonville, FL	Mt. Airy, NC
22	Wedge, Eric	R	R	6–3	215	1–27–68	Fort Wayne, IN	Fort Wayne, IN
No.	**INFIELDERS**	**B**	**T**	**HT**	**WT**	**DOB**	**BIRTHPLACE**	**RESIDENCE**
12	Benavides, Freddie	R	R	6–2	185	4–7–66	Laredo, TX	Laredo, TX
15	Castellano, Pedro	R	R	6–1	175	3–11–70	Lara, VZ	Lara, VZ
9	Castilla, Vinny	R	R	6–1	175	7–4–67	Oaxaca, MX	Oaxaca, MX
37	Gainer, Jay	L	L	6–0	190	10–8–66	Panama City, FL	Ellensburg, WA
14	Galarraga, Andres	R	R	6–3	235	6–18–61	Caracas, VZ	Caracas, VZ
13	Hayes, Charlie	R	R	6–0	207	5–29–65	Hattiesburg, MS	Hattiesburg, MS
4	Liriano, Nelson	S	R	5–10	165	6–3–64	Santo Domingo, DR	Puerto Plata, DR
8	Mejia, Roberto	R	R	5–11	160	4–14–72	Hato Mayor, DR	Hato Mayor, DR
	Tatum, Jim	R	R	6–2	200	10–9–67	San Diego, CA	Lakeside, CA
No.	**OUTFIELDERS**	**B**	**T**	**HT**	**WT**	**DOB**	**BIRTHPLACE**	**RESIDENCE**
10	Bichette, Dante	R	R	6–3	225	11–18–63	W. Palm Beach, FL	Palm Beach Gdns., FL
26	Burks, Ellis	R	R	6–2	205	9–11–64	Vicksburg, MS	Fort Worth, TX
24	Clark, Jerald	R	R	6–4	205	8–10–63	Crockett, TX	San Diego, CA
20	Johnson, Howard	S	R	5–10	195	11–29–60	Clearwater, FL	Poway, CA
33	Jones, Chris	R	R	6–2	205	12–16–65	Utica, NY	Cedar Rapids, IA
	Sherman, Darrell	L	L	5–9	160	12–4–67	Los Angeles, CA	Lynwood, CA
21	Young, Eric	R	R	5–9	180	11–26–66	Jacksonville, FL	New Brunswick, NJ

Mile High Stadium (76,037, grass)

Tickets: 303–292–0200

Ticket prices:

$16 (VIP field box — first eight rows)

$14 (infield plaza box)

$12 (VIP, OF plaza box, and IF mezz. box)

$10 (OF plaza box, OF mezz. and IF terr.)

$8 (outfield terr. and infield view)

$5 (OF view and reserved pavilion)

$4 (reserved general admission)

$1 (rockpile res.— day of game only)

Field Dimensions (from home plate)

To left field at foul line, 335 feet

To center field, 423 feet

To right field at foul line, 370 feet

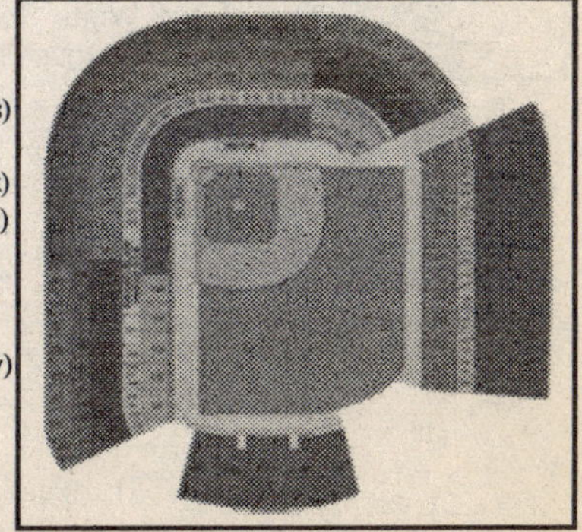

Dante Bichette No. 10/OF

Full name: Alphonse Dante Bichette
Bats: R **Throws:** R **HT:** 6–3 **WT:** 225
Born: 11–18–63, W. Palm Beach, FL
High school: Jupiter (FL)
College: Palm Beach Junior (FL)

Bichette had 41 doubles, third-best in the NL. He had 47 multi-hit games, and his 14 outfield assists tied for third in the league.

	TEAM	LG	POS	G	AB	R	H	2B	3B	HR	RBI	BB	SO	SB	E	BA	SLG	SALARY
1988	CAL	AL	OF	21	46	1	12	2	0	0	8	0	7	0	1	.261	.304	N/A
1989	CAL	AL	OF	48	138	13	29	7	0	3	15	6	24	3	1	.210	.326	N/A
1990	CAL	AL	OF	109	349	40	89	15	1	15	53	16	79	5	7	.255	.433	120,000
1991	MIL	AL	OF	134	445	53	106	18	3	15	59	22	107	14	7	.238	.393	185,000
1992	MIL	AL	OF-3B	112	387	37	111	27	2	5	41	16	74	18	2	.287	.406	230,000
1993	COL	NL	OF	141	538	93	167	43	5	21	89	28	99	14	9	.310	.526	735,000
6	YR	TOTALS		565	1903	237	514	112	11	59	265	88	390	54	27	.270	.434	
1993	RANK	MLB	OF	38	32	14	16	2	23	19	16	71	23	48	122	15	10	63
1994	PROJECTIONS			161	620	108	192	49	5	24	102	32	114	16	10	.310	.521	

Ellis Burks No. 26/OF

Full name: Ellis Rena Burks
Bats: R **Throws:** R **HT:** 6–2 **WT:** 205
Born: 9–11–64, Vicksburg, MS
High school: Everman (TX)

In 1993, Burks bounced back from two off-years, batting .275 with 17 HR and 74 RBI for the White Sox. He did not hit a home run after August 31.

	TEAM	LG	POS	G	AB	R	H	2B	3B	HR	RBI	BB	SO	SB	E	BA	SLG	SALARY
1987	BOS	AL	OF	133	558	94	152	30	2	20	59	41	98	27	4	.272	.441	N/A
1988	BOS	AL	OF	144	540	93	159	37	5	18	92	62	89	25	9	.294	.481	N/A
1989	BOS	AL	OF	97	399	73	121	19	6	12	61	36	52	21	6	.303	.471	N/A
1990	BOS	AL	OF	152	588	89	174	33	8	21	89	48	82	9	2	.296	.486	600,000
1991	BOS	AL	OF	130	474	56	119	33	3	14	56	39	81	6	2	.251	.422	1,825,000
1992	BOS	AL	OF	66	235	35	60	8	3	8	30	25	48	5	2	.255	.417	2,300,000
1993	CHI	AL	OF	146	499	75	137	24	4	17	74	60	97	6	6	.275	.441	2,050,000
7	YR	TOTALS		868	3293	515	922	184	31	110	461	311	547	99	31	.280	.455	
1993	RANK	MLB	OF	27	42	36	44	38	32	32	27	25	27	73	92	58	56	38
1994	PROJECTIONS			124	457	68	125	25	4	14	63	45	76	11	4	.274	.442	

Vinny Castilla No. 9/SS

Full name: Vinicio Soria Castilla
Bats: R **Throws:** R **HT:** 6–1 **WT:** 175
Born: 7–4–67, Oaxaca, MX
High school: Carlos Gracida (Oaxaca, MX)
College: Benito Suarez (MX)

Castilla's 7 triples tied for eighth in the NL. He batted an impressive .305 at home, just .206 on the road.

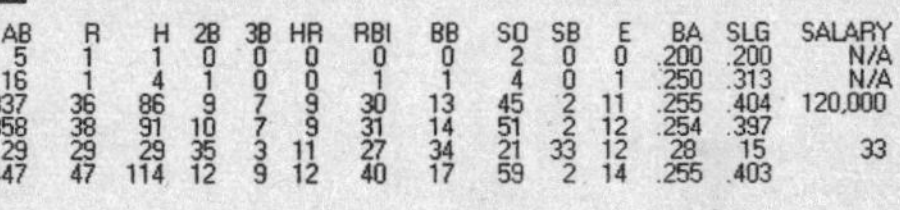

	TEAM	LG	POS	G	AB	R	H	2B	3B	HR	RBI	BB	SO	SB	E	BA	SLG	SALARY
1991	ATL	NL	SS	12	5	1	1	0	0	0	0	0	2	0	0	.200	.200	N/A
1992	ATL	NL	SS-3B	9	16	1	4	1	0	0	1	1	4	0	1	.250	.313	N/A
1993	COL	NL	SS	105	337	36	86	9	7	9	30	13	45	2	11	.255	.404	120,000
3	YR	TOTALS		126	358	38	91	10	7	9	31	14	51	2	12	.254	.397	
1993	RANK	MLB	SS	27	29	29	29	35	3	11	27	34	21	33	12	28	15	33
1994	PROJECTIONS			136	447	47	114	12	9	12	40	17	59	2	14	.255	.403	

Andres Galarraga No. 14/1B

Full name: Andres Jose Galarraga
Bats: R **Throws:** R **HT:** 6–3 **WT:** 240
Born: 6–18–61, Caracas, VZ
High school: Enrique Felmi (Caracas, VZ)

NL batting champ Galarraga recorded a career-best .370 BA. He also led the league in multi-hit games with 56.

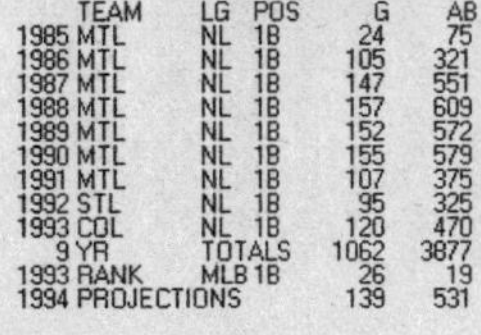

	TEAM	LG	POS	G	AB	R	H	2B	3B	HR	RBI	BB	SO	SB	E	BA	SLG	SALARY
1985	MTL	NL	1B	24	75	9	14	1	0	2	4	3	18	1	1	.187	.280	N/A
1986	MTL	NL	1B	105	321	39	87	13	0	10	42	30	79	6	4	.271	.405	N/A
1987	MTL	NL	1B	147	551	72	168	40	3	13	90	41	127	7	10	.305	.459	N/A
1988	MTL	NL	1B	157	609	99	184	42	8	29	92	39	153	13	15	.302	.540	N/A
1989	MTL	NL	1B	152	572	76	147	30	1	23	85	48	158	12	11	.257	.434	N/A
1990	MTL	NL	1B	155	579	65	148	29	0	20	87	40	169	10	10	.256	.409	N/A
1991	MTL	NL	1B	107	375	34	82	13	2	9	33	23	86	5	9	.219	.336	2,366,667
1992	STL	NL	1B	95	325	38	79	14	2	10	39	11	69	5	8	.243	.391	2,366,667
1993	COL	NL	1B	120	470	71	174	35	4	22	98	24	73	2	11	.370	.602	850,000
9	YR	TOTALS		1062	3877	503	1083	217	20	138	570	259	932	61	79	.279	.452	
1993	RANK	MLB	1B	26	19	19	5	7	2	11	9	36	15	20	9	1	2	19
1994	PROJECTIONS			139	531	73	163	35	2	19	91	37	119	7	10	.307	.492	

Joe Girardi — No. 7/C

Full name: Joseph Elliott Girardi
Bats: R **Throws:** R **HT:** 5–11 **WT:** 195
Born: 10–14–64, Peoria, IL
High school: Spalding Institute (Peoria, IL)
College: Northwestern (Evanston, IL)

Girardi hit .317 over the last two months of 1993. He led the Rockies in sacrifice bunts with 12.

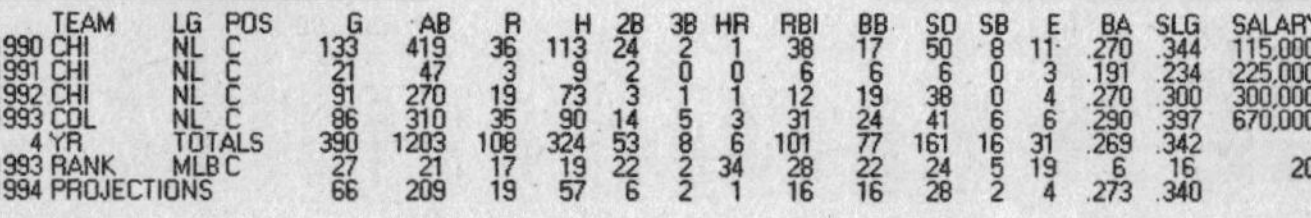

	TEAM	LG	POS	G	AB	R	H	2B	3B	HR	RBI	BB	SO	SB	E	BA	SLG	SALARY
1990	CHI	NL	C	133	419	36	113	24	2	1	38	17	50	8	11	.270	.344	115,000
1991	CHI	NL	C	21	47	3	9	2	0	0	6	6	6	0	3	.191	.234	225,000
1992	CHI	NL	C	91	270	19	73	3	1	1	12	19	38	0	4	.270	.300	300,000
1993	COL	NL	C	86	310	35	90	14	5	3	31	24	41	6	6	.290	.397	670,000
4	YR	TOTALS		390	1203	108	324	53	8	6	101	77	161	16	31	.269	.342	
1993	RANK	MLB	C	27	21	17	19	22	2	34	28	22	24	5	19	6	16	20
1994	PROJECTIONS			66	209	19	57	6	2	1	16	16	28	2	4	.273	.340	

Charlie Hayes — No. 13/3B

Full name: Charles Dewayne Hayes
Bats: R **Throws:** R **HT:** 6–0 **WT:** 207
Born: 5–29–65, Hattiesburg, MS
High school: Forest Co. Agr. (Brooklyn, MS)

Hayes totalled career bests in BA (.305), doubles (45), HR (25), and RBI (98). He hit .462 with the bases loaded and .313 with runners in scoring position.

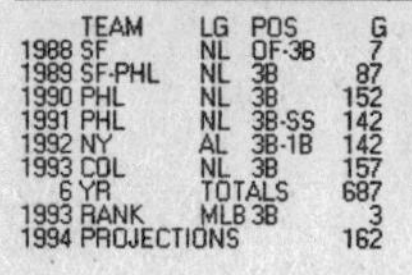

	TEAM	LG	POS	G	AB	R	H	2B	3B	HR	RBI	BB	SO	SB	E	BA	SLG	SALARY
1988	SF	NL	OF-3B	7	11	0	1	0	0	0	0	0	3	0	0	.091	.091	N/A
1989	SF-PHL	NL	3B	87	304	26	78	15	1	8	43	11	50	3	22	.257	.391	N/A
1990	PHL	NL	3B	152	561	56	145	20	0	10	57	28	91	4	20	.258	.348	150,000
1991	PHL	NL	3B-SS	142	460	34	106	23	1	12	53	16	75	3	15	.230	.363	280,000
1992	NY	AL	3B-1B	142	509	52	131	19	2	18	66	28	100	3	13	.257	.409	280,000
1993	COL	NL	3B	157	573	89	175	45	2	25	98	43	82	11	20	.305	.522	1,325,000
6	YR	TOTALS		687	2418	257	636	122	6	73	317	126	401	24	90	.263	.409	
1993	RANK	MLB	3B	3	4	3	2	1	10	3	3	15	11	5	34	1	2	12
1994	PROJECTIONS			162	592	91	181	46	1	25	101	44	84	10	20	.306	.514	

Howard Johnson No. 20/OF

Full name: Howard Michael Johnson
Bats: S **Throws:** R **HT:** 5–10 **WT:** 195
Born: 11–29–60, Clearwater, FL
High school: Clearwater (FL)
College: St. Petersburg Junior (FL)
Ex-Met Johnson played in a career-low 72 games for New York in 1993. He batted just .067 in Colorado's Mile High Stadium.

TEAM	LG	POS	G	AB	R	H	2B	3B	HR	RBI	BB	SO	SB	E	BA	SLG	SALARY
1982 DET	AL	3B-OF	54	155	23	49	5	0	4	14	16	30	7	7	.316	.426	N/A
1983 DET	AL	3B	27	66	11	14	0	0	3	5	7	10	0	7	.212	.348	N/A
1984 DET	AL	3B-SS	116	355	43	88	14	1	12	50	40	67	10	14	.248	.394	N/A
1985 NY	NL	3B-SS	126	389	38	94	18	4	11	46	34	78	6	18	.242	.393	N/A
1986 NY	NL	3B-SS	88	220	30	54	14	0	10	39	31	64	8	20	.245	.445	N/A
1987 NY	NL	3B-SS	157	554	93	147	22	1	36	99	83	113	32	26	.265	.504	N/A
1988 NY	NL	3B-SS	148	495	85	114	21	1	24	68	86	104	23	18	.230	.422	N/A
1989 NY	NL	3B-SS	153	571	104	164	41	3	36	101	77	126	41	24	.287	.559	N/A
1990 NY	NL	3B-SS	154	590	89	144	37	3	23	90	69	100	34	28	.244	.434	1,666,666
1991 NY	NL	3B-OF	156	564	108	146	34	4	38	117	78	120	30	31	.259	.535	2,216,667
1992 NY	NL	OF	100	350	48	78	19	0	7	43	55	79	22	4	.223	.337	2,266,667
1993 NY	NL	3B	72	235	32	56	8	2	7	26	43	43	6	11	.238	.379	2,100,000
12 YR	TOTALS		1351	4544	704	1148	233	19	211	698	619	934	219	208	.253	.452	
1993 RANK	MLB	3B	35	33	29	32	36	10	24	34	15	30	10	17	35	30	10
1994 PROJECTIONS			51	152	22	39	4	0	4	15	22	27	4	8	.257	.388	

Eric Young No. 21/OF

Full name: Eric Young
Bats: R **Throws:** R **HT:** 5–9 **WT:** 180
Born: 11–26–66, Jacksonville, FL
High school: New Brunswick (NJ)
College: Rutgers (New Brunswick, NJ)
Young was the sixth toughest batter to strike-out in the NL (1 K–13.8 AB) and hit safely in 18 of his last 20 games.

TEAM	LG	POS	G	AB	R	H	2B	3B	HR	RBI	BB	SO	SB	E	BA	SLG	SALARY
1992 LA	NL	2B	49	132	9	34	1	0	1	11	8	9	6	9	.258	.288	109,000
1993 COL	NL	OF	144	490	82	132	16	8	3	42	63	41	42	18	.269	.353	120,000
2 YR	TOTALS		193	622	91	166	17	8	4	53	71	50	48	27	.267	.339	
1993 RANK	MLB	OF	31	46	27	51	76	6	108	75	22	99	9	1	70	110	121
1994 PROJECTIONS			162	567	100	153	19	10	3	48	76	48	50	18	.270	.354	

Willie Blair No. 19/P

Full name: William Allen Blair
Bats: R **Throws:** R **HT:** 6–1 **WT:** 185
Born: 12–18–65, Paintsville, KY
High school: Johnson Central (KY)
College: Morehead State (KY)

Blair was 4–10 as a starter, but the Rockies scored just 14 runs in his 10 losses. He had an impressive 2 K–1 BB.

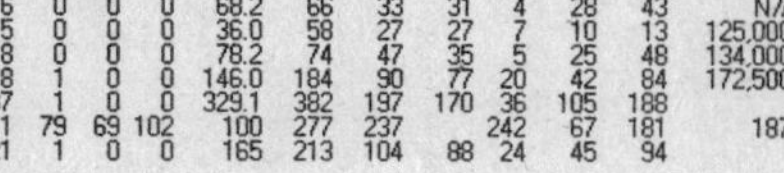

	TM	LG	POS	W	L	ERA	G	GS	CG	SH	SV	IP	H	R	ER	HR	BB	SO	SALARY
1990	TOR	AL	P	3	5	4.06	27	6	0	0	0	68.2	66	33	31	4	28	43	N/A
1991	CLE	AL	P	2	3	6.75	11	5	0	0	0	36.0	58	27	27	7	10	13	125,000
1992	HOU	NL	P	5	7	4.00	29	8	0	0	0	78.2	74	47	35	5	25	48	134,000
1993	COL	NL	P	6	10	4.75	46	18	1	0	0	146.0	184	90	77	20	42	84	172,500
4	YR	TOTALS		16	25	4.65	113	37	1	0	0	329.1	382	197	170	36	105	188	
1993	Rank	MLB Ps		128		212	93	111	79	69	102	100	277	237		242	67	181	187
1994	PROJECTIONS			6	11	4.80	50	21	1	0	0	165	213	104	88	24	45	94	

Kent Bottenfield No. 46/P

Full name: Kent Dennis Bottenfield
Bats: S **Throws:** R **HT:** 6–3 **WT:** 225
Born: 11–14–68, Portland, OR
High school: James Madison (Portland, OR)

In Bottenfield's 14 Colorado starts, opposing batters hit .301. He had more walks (82) than strikeouts (77).

	TM	LG	POS	W	L	ERA	G	GS	CG	SH	SV	IP	H	R	ER	HR	BB	SO	SALARY
1992	MTL	NL	P	1	2	2.23	10	4	0	0	1	32.1	26	9	8	1	11	14	N/A
1993	COL	NL	P	5	10	5.07	37	25	1	0	0	159.2	179	102	90	24	71	63	113,500
2	YR	TOTALS		6	12	4.59	47	29	1	0	1	192.0	205	111	98	25	82	77	
1993	Rank	MLB Ps		149		240	123	91	79	69	102	88	225	252		266	221	277	229
1994	PROJECTIONS			7	14	5.31	50	35	1	0	0	222	255	148	131	35	101	87	

Greg W. Harris No. 27/P

Full name: Gregory Wade Harris
Bats: R **Throws:** R **HT:** 6–2 **WT:** 195
Born: 12–1–63, Greensboro, NC
High school: J. Matthews (Siler City, NC)
College: Elon (NC)

Harris was touched for a NL-high 33 HR in 1993. He pitched into the seventh inning in 12 straight starts for the Padres.

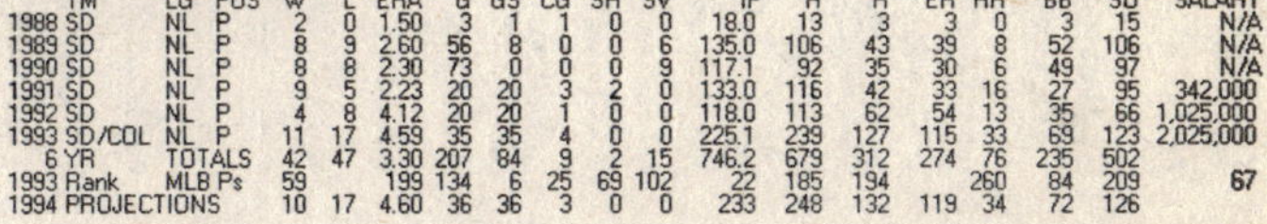

	TM	LG	POS	W	L	ERA	G	GS	CG	SH	SV	IP	H	R	ER	HR	BB	SO	SALARY
1988	SD	NL	P	2	0	1.50	3	1	1	0	0	18.0	13	3	3	0	3	15	N/A
1989	SD	NL	P	8	9	2.60	56	8	0	0	6	135.0	106	43	39	8	52	106	N/A
1990	SD	NL	P	8	8	2.30	73	0	0	0	9	117.1	92	35	30	6	49	97	N/A
1991	SD	NL	P	9	5	2.23	20	20	3	2	0	133.0	116	42	33	16	27	95	342,000
1992	SD	NL	P	4	8	4.12	20	20	1	0	0	118.0	113	62	54	13	35	66	1,025,000
1993	SD/COL	NL	P	11	17	4.59	35	35	4	0	0	225.1	239	127	115	33	69	123	2,025,000
6	YR	TOTALS		42	47	3.30	207	84	9	2	15	746.2	679	312	274	76	235	502	
1993	Rank	MLB	Ps	59		199	134	6	25	69	102	22	185	194		260	84	209	67
1994	PROJECTIONS			10	17	4.60	36	36	3	0	0	233	248	132	119	34	72	126	

Armando Reynoso No. 42/P

Full name: Martia Armando Gutierrez Reynoso
Bats: R **Throws:** R **HT:** 6–0 **WT:** 186
Born: 5–1–66, Sam Luis Potosi, MX
High school: Mita del Estado (Jalisco, MX)

Reynoso led the Rockies staff with 8 pickoffs. Of his 12 wins, 11 followed a Rockies loss.

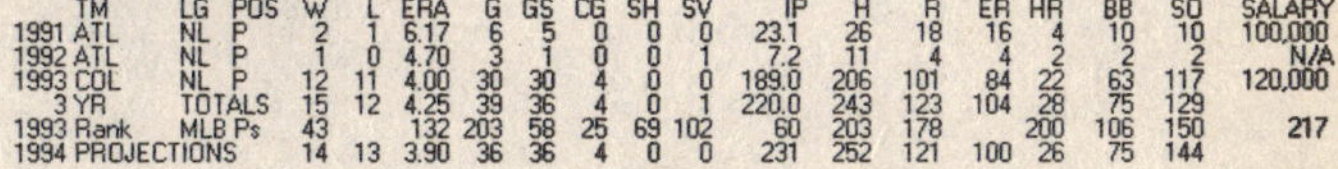

	TM	LG	POS	W	L	ERA	G	GS	CG	SH	SV	IP	H	R	ER	HR	BB	SO	SALARY
1991	ATL	NL	P	2	1	6.17	6	5	0	0	0	23.1	26	18	16	4	10	10	100,000
1992	ATL	NL	P	1	0	4.70	3	1	0	0	1	7.2	11	4	4	2	2	2	N/A
1993	COL	NL	P	12	11	4.00	30	30	4	0	0	189.0	206	101	84	22	63	117	120,000
3	YR	TOTALS		15	12	4.25	39	36	4	0	1	220.0	243	123	104	28	75	129	
1993	Rank	MLB	Ps	43		132	203	58	25	69	102	60	203	178		200	106	150	217
1994	PROJECTIONS			14	13	3.90	36	36	4	0	0	231	252	121	100	26	75	144	

Darren Holmes — No. 40/P

Full name: Darren Lee Holmes
Bats: R **Throws:** R **HT:** 6–0 **WT:** 199
Born: 4–25–66, Asheville, NC
High school: T.C. Roberson (Asheville, NC)
Holmes tied for ninth in the league with 25 saves. He posted a 17.19 ERA in his first 9 games, then had a 2.43 ERA over his final 52 appearances.

	TM	LG	POS	W	L	ERA	G	GS	CG	SH	SV	IP	H	R	ER	HR	BB	SO	SALARY
1990	LA	NL	P	0	1	5.19	14	0	0	0	0	17.1	15	10	10	1	11	19	N/A
1991	MIL	AL	P	1	4	4.72	40	0	0	0	3	76.1	90	43	40	6	27	59	102,500
1992	MIL	AL	P	4	4	2.55	41	0	0	0	6	42.1	35	12	12	1	11	31	130,000
1993	COL	NL	P	3	3	4.05	62	0	0	0	25	66.2	56	31	30	6	20	60	235,000
4	YR	TOTALS		8	12	4.09	157	0	0	0	34	202.2	196	96	92	14	69	169	
1993	Rank	MLB Ps		209		142	42	202	125	69	15	227	37	102		132	79	32	164
1994	PROJECTIONS			3	3	4.04	74	0	0	0	31	78	66	36	35	7	22	70	

Don Baylor — No. 25/Mgr.

Full name: Donald Edward Baylor
Bats: R **Throws:** R **HT:** 6–1 **WT:** 220
Born: 6–28–49, Austin, TX
High school: Stephen F. Austin (Austin, TX)
College: Miami–Dade JC (FL) and Blinn JC (TX)
Baylor was passed over for the Brewers' job in '92, but his expansion Rockies won just two fewer games than the '93 Brewers.

			REG. SEASON				PLAYOFF			CHAMP. SERIES			WORLD SERIES		
YEAR	TEAM	LG	W	L	PCT	POS	W	L	PCT	W	L	PCT	W	L	PCT
1993	COL	NL	67	95	.414	6			---			---			---
1	YR TOTAL		67	95	.414		0	0	---	0	0	---	0	0	---

Freddie Benavides No. 12/IF

Full name: Alfredo Benavides III
Bats: R **Throws:** R **HT:** 6–2 **WT:** 185
Born: 4–7–66, Laredo, TX
High school: Nixon (Laredo, TX)
College: Texas Christian
Benavides batted .387 at home.

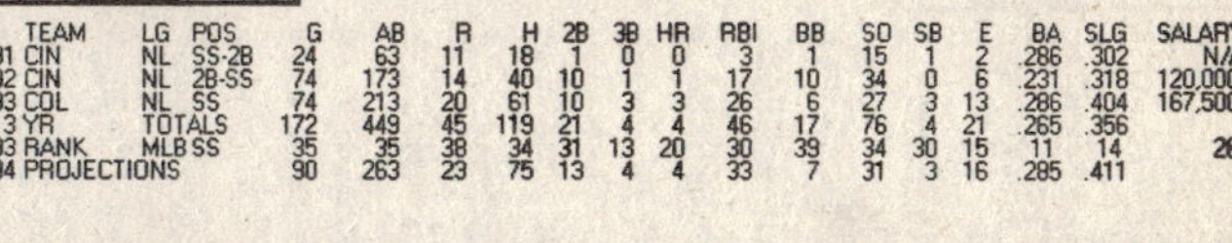

TEAM	LG	POS	G	AB	R	H	2B	3B	HR	RBI	BB	SO	SB	E	BA	SLG	SALARY
1991 CIN	NL	SS-2B	24	63	11	18	1	0	0	3	1	15	1	2	.286	.302	N/A
1992 CIN	NL	2B-SS	74	173	14	40	10	1	1	17	10	34	0	6	.231	.318	120,000
1993 COL	NL	SS	74	213	20	61	10	3	3	26	6	27	3	13	.286	.404	167,500
3 YR	TOTALS		172	449	45	119	21	4	4	46	17	76	4	21	.265	.356	
1993 RANK	MLB	SS	35	35	38	34	31	13	20	30	39	34	30	15	11	14	26
1994 PROJECTIONS			90	263	23	75	13	4	4	33	7	31	3	16	.285	.411	

Marvin Freeman No. 44/P

Full name: Marvin Freeman
Bats: R **Throws:** R **HT:** 6–7 **WT:** 222
Born: 4–10–63, Chicago, IL
High school: Chicago Vocational (IL)
College: Jackson State (MS)
Freeman had a 6.08 ERA in 21 games for Atlanta.

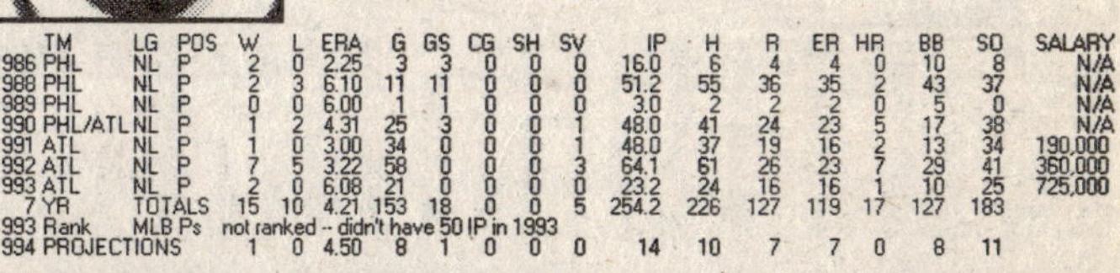

TM	LG	POS	W	L	ERA	G	GS	CG	SH	SV	IP	H	R	ER	HR	BB	SO	SALARY
1986 PHL	NL	P	2	0	2.25	3	3	0	0	0	16.0	6	4	4	0	10	8	N/A
1988 PHL	NL	P	2	3	6.10	11	11	0	0	0	51.2	55	36	35	2	43	37	N/A
1989 PHL	NL	P	0	0	6.00	1	1	0	0	0	3.0	2	2	2	0	5	0	N/A
1990 PHL/ATL	NL	P	1	2	4.31	25	3	0	0	1	48.0	41	24	23	5	17	38	N/A
1991 ATL	NL	P	1	0	3.00	34	0	0	0	1	48.0	37	19	16	2	13	34	190,000
1992 ATL	NL	P	7	5	3.22	58	0	0	0	3	64.1	61	26	23	7	29	41	360,000
1993 ATL	NL	P	2	0	6.08	21	0	0	0	0	23.2	24	16	16	1	10	25	725,000
7 YR	TOTALS		15	10	4.21	153	18	0	0	5	254.2	226	127	119	17	127	183	
1993 Rank	MLB	Ps	not ranked -- didn't have 50 IP in 1993															
1994 PROJECTIONS			1	0	4.50	8	1	0	0	0	14	10	7	7	0	8	11	

Chris Jones No. 33/OF

Full name: Christopher Carlos Jones
Bats: R **Throws:** R **HT:** 6–2 **WT:** 205
Born: 12–16–65, Utica, NY
High school: Liverpool (NY)
Jones struck out 48 times in only 209 AB for the Rockies. He batted .299 against righthanders.

TEAM	LG	POS	G	AB	R	H	2B	3B	HR	RBI	BB	SO	SB	E	BA	SLG	SALARY
1991 CIN	NL	OF	52	89	14	26	1	2	2	6	2	31	2	0	.292	.416	100,000
1992 HOU	NL	OF	54	63	7	12	2	1	1	4	7	21	3	2	.190	.302	N/A
1993 COL	NL	OF	86	209	29	57	11	4	6	31	10	48	9	2	.273	.450	140,000
3 YR	TOTALS		192	361	50	95	14	7	9	41	19	100	14	4	.263	.416	
1993 RANK	MLB	OF	108	118	108	109	101	32	87	94	130	90	60	26	64	45	113
1994 PROJECTIONS			97	249	34	67	14	4	7	39	12	53	11	2	.269	.442	

Jerald Clark No. 24/OF–1B

Full name: Jerald Clark
Bats: R **Throws:** R **HT:** 6–4 **WT:** 205
Born: 8–10–63, Crockett, TX
High school: Crockett (TX)
College: Lamar (Beaumont (TX)
After August 1, Clark hit .303 with 7 HR.

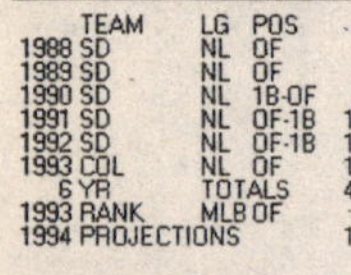

	TEAM	LG	POS	G	AB	R	H	2B	3B	HR	RBI	BB	SO	SB	E	BA	SLG	SALARY
1988	SD	NL	OF	6	15	0	3	1	0	0	3	0	4	0	0	.200	.267	N/A
1989	SD	NL	OF	17	41	5	8	2	0	1	7	3	9	0	1	.195	.317	N/A
1990	SD	NL	1B-OF	53	101	12	27	4	1	5	11	5	24	0	1	.267	.475	109,500
1991	SD	NL	OF-1B	118	369	26	84	16	0	10	47	31	90	2	2	.228	.352	127,500
1992	SD	NL	OF-1B	146	496	45	120	22	6	12	58	22	97	3	3	.242	.383	200,000
1993	COL	NL	OF	140	478	65	135	26	6	13	67	20	60	9	12	.282	.444	700,000
6	YR	TOTALS		480	1500	153	377	71	13	41	193	81	284	14	19	.251	.398	
1993	RANK	MLB	OF	41	53	59	48	31	13	42	36	104	68	60	133	49	53	66
1994	PROJECTIONS			162	555	75	157	30	7	15	77	23	69	10	14	.283	.443	

Nelson Liriano No. 4/IF

Full name: Nelson Arturo Liriano
Bats: S **Throws:** R **HT:** 5–10 **WT:** 165
Born: 6–3–64, Santo Domingo, DR
High school: Jose Debeaw (Puerto Plata, DR)
After recovering from a broken foot, Liriano had a 20-game hitting streak at AAA Colorado Springs.

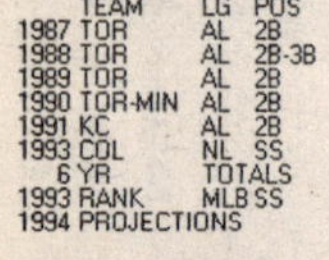

	TEAM	LG	POS	G	AB	R	H	2B	3B	HR	RBI	BB	SO	SB	E	BA	SLG	SALARY
1987	TOR	AL	2B	37	158	29	38	6	2	2	10	16	22	13	1	.241	.342	N/A
1988	TOR	AL	2B-3B	99	276	36	73	6	2	3	23	11	40	12	12	.264	.333	N/A
1989	TOR	AL	2B	132	418	51	110	26	3	5	53	43	51	16	12	.263	.376	N/A
1990	TOR-MIN	AL	2B	103	355	46	83	12	9	1	28	38	44	8	11	.234	.327	255,000
1991	KC	AL	2B	10	22	5	9	0	0	0	1	0	2	0	0	.409	.409	N/A
1993	COL	NL	SS	48	151	28	46	6	3	2	15	18	22	6	6	.305	.424	N/A
6	YR	TOTALS		429	1380	195	359	56	19	13	130	126	181	55	42	.260	.357	
1993	RANK	MLB	SS	38	38	33	37	37	12	25	36	29	34	19	36	6	7	36
1994	PROJECTIONS			31	110	20	31	4	1	1	8	11	15	6	2	.282	.382	

Roberto Mejia No. 8/IF

Full name: Roberto Antonio Mejia
Bats: R **Throws:** R **HT:** 5–11 **WT:** 160
Born: 4–14–72, Hato Mayor, DR
High school: Adventista (DR)
Eight of his first 11 major league hits went for extra bases (4 doubles, 3 triples, and a home run).

	TEAM	LG	POS	G	AB	R	H	2B	3B	HR	RBI	BB	SO	SB	E	BA	SLG	SALARY
1993	COL	NL	2B	65	229	31	53	14	5	5	20	13	63	4	12	.231	.402	109,000
1	YR	TOTAL		65	229	31	53	14	5	5	20	13	63	4	12	.231	.402	
1993	RANK	MLB	2B	44	37	33	38	28	7	17	38	40	17	29	14	40	17	39

Mike Munoz — No. 43/P

Full name: Michael Anthony Munoz
Bats: L **Throws:** L **HT:** 6–2 **WT:** 200
Born: 7–12–65, Baldwin Park, CA
College: Cal Poly Pomona
At AAA Colorado Springs, Munoz had a 1.67 ERA.

	TM	LG	POS	W	L	ERA	G	GS	CG	SH	SV	IP	H	R	ER	HR	BB	SO	SALARY
1989	LA	NL	P	0	0	16.88	3	0	0	0	0	2.2	5	5	5	1	2	3	N/A
1990	LA	NL	P	0	1	3.18	8	0	0	0	0	5.2	6	2	2	0	3	2	N/A
1991	DET	AL	P	0	0	9.64	6	0	0	0	0	9.1	14	10	10	0	5	3	N/A
1992	DET	AL	P	1	2	3.00	65	0	0	0	2	48.0	44	16	16	3	25	23	115,000
1993	DET	AL	P	0	1	6.00	8	0	0	0	0	3.0	4	2	2	1	6	1	180,000
1993	COL	NL	P	2	1	4.50	21	0	0	0	0	18.0	21	12	9	1	9	16	N/A
5	YR	TOTALS		3	5	4.57	111	0	0	0	2	86.2	94	47	44	6	50	48	
1993	Rank	MLB Ps		not ranked -- didn't have 50 IP in 1993															
1994	PROJECTIONS			0	0	6.30	11	0	0	0	0	10	13	8	7	0	6	6	

David Nied — No. 17/P

Full name: David Glen Nied
Bats: R **Throws:** R **HT:** 6–2 **WT:** 185
Born: 12–22–68, Dallas, TX
High school: Duncanville (TX)
The first pick in the expansion draft, Nied struggled as opponents hit him at a .296 clip.

	TM	LG	POS	W	L	ERA	G	GS	CG	SH	SV	IP	H	R	ER	HR	BB	SO	SALARY
1992	ATL	NL	P	3	0	1.17	6	2	0	0	0	23.0	10	3	3	0	5	19	N/A
1993	COL	NL	P	5	9	5.17	16	16	1	0	0	87.0	99	53	50	8	42	46	150,000
2	YR	TOTALS		8	9	4.34	22	18	1	0	0	110.0	109	56	53	8	47	65	
1993	Rank	MLB Ps		149		244	272	123	79	69	102	169	239	229		139	240	222	195
1994	PROJECTIONS			6	13	5.52	21	23	1	0	0	119	143	78	73	12	60	59	

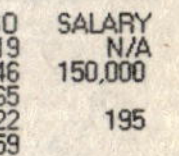

Steve Reed — No. 39/P

Full name: Steven Vincent Reed
Bats: R **Throws:** R **HT:** 6–2 **WT:** 202
Born: 3–1–66, Los Angeles, CA
High school: Chatsworth (CA)
College: Lewis and Clark State (Lewiston, ID)
His 64 appearances ranked second on the staff.

	TM	LG	POS	W	L	ERA	G	GS	CG	SH	SV	IP	H	R	ER	HR	BB	SO	SALARY
1992	SF	NL	P	1	0	2.30	18	0	0	0	0	15.2	13	5	4	2	3	11	109,000
1993	COL	NL	P	9	5	4.48	64	0	0	0	3	84.1	80	47	42	13	30	51	115,000
2	YR	TOTALS		10	5	4.14	82	0	0	0	3	100.0	93	52	46	15	33	62	
1993	Rank	MLB Ps		87		189	34	202	125	69	44	177	94	191		269	138	161	222
1994	PROJECTIONS			13	7	4.65	87	0	0	0	4	118	113	68	61	18	43	71	

Bruce Ruffin — No. 18/P

Full name: Bruce Wayne Ruffin
Bats: S **Throws:** L **HT:** 6–2 **WT:** 209
Born: 10–4–63, Lubbock, TX
High school: J.M. Hanks (El Paso, TX)
College: Texas
After August 18, Ruffin was 1–0 with a 1.25 ERA.

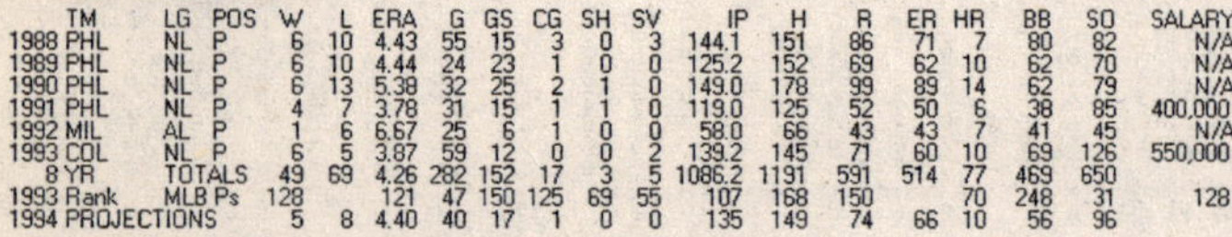

TM	LG	POS	W	L	ERA	G	GS	CG	SH	SV	IP	H	R	ER	HR	BB	SO	SALARY
1988 PHL	NL	P	6	10	4.43	55	15	3	0	3	144.1	151	86	71	7	80	82	N/A
1989 PHL	NL	P	6	10	4.44	24	23	1	0	0	125.2	152	69	62	10	62	70	N/A
1990 PHL	NL	P	6	13	5.38	32	25	2	1	0	149.0	178	99	89	14	62	79	N/A
1991 PHL	NL	P	4	7	3.78	31	15	1	1	0	119.0	125	52	50	6	38	85	400,000
1992 MIL	AL	P	1	6	6.67	25	6	1	0	0	58.0	66	43	43	7	41	45	N/A
1993 COL	NL	P	6	5	3.87	59	12	0	0	2	139.2	145	71	60	10	69	126	550,000
8 YR	TOTALS		49	69	4.26	282	152	17	3	5	1086.2	1191	591	514	77	469	650	
1993 Rank	MLB Ps		128		121	47	150	125	69	55	107	168	150		70	248	31	128
1994 PROJECTIONS			5	8	4.40	40	17	1	0	0	135	149	74	66	10	56	96	

Danny Sheaffer — No. 16/C

Full name: Daniel Sheaffer
Bats: R **Throws:** R **HT:** 6–0 **WT:** 190
Born: 8–21–61, Jacksonville, FL
Veteran minor leaguer Sheaffer struck out just 15 times in 216 AB for Colorado.

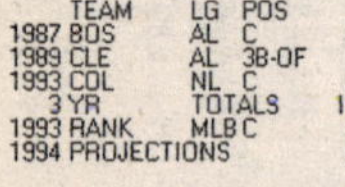

TEAM	LG	POS	G	AB	R	H	2B	3B	HR	RBI	BB	SO	SB	E	BA	SLG	SALARY
1987 BOS	AL	C	25	66	5	8	1	0	1	5	0	14	0	3	.121	.182	N/A
1989 CLE	AL	3B-OF	7	16	1	1	0	0	0	0	2	2	0	0	.063	.063	N/A
1993 COL	NL	C	82	216	26	60	9	1	4	32	8	15	2	2	.278	.384	120,000
3 YR	TOTALS		114	298	32	69	10	1	5	37	10	31	2	5	.232	.322	
1993 RANK	MLB	C	31	32	25	28	34	11	30	26	39	40	13	36	10	21	35
1994 PROJECTIONS			93	246	30	70	10	1	4	37	9	15	2	1	.285	.382	

Gary Wayne — No. 53/P

Full name: Gary Anthony Wayne
Bats: L **Throws:** L **HT:** 6–3 **WT:** 193
Born: 11–30–62, Newton, MA
High school: Crestwood (Dearborn Heights, MI)
College: Michigan
Wayne led the squad with 65 relief appearances.

TM	LG	POS	W	L	ERA	G	GS	CG	SH	SV	IP	H	R	ER	HR	BB	SO	SALARY
1989 MIN	AL	P	3	4	3.30	60	0	0	0	1	71.0	55	28	26	4	36	41	N/A
1990 MIN	AL	P	1	1	4.19	38	0	0	0	1	38.2	38	19	18	5	13	28	N/A
1991 MIN	AL	P	1	0	5.11	8	0	0	0	1	12.1	11	7	7	1	4	7	N/A
1992 MIN	AL	P	3	3	2.63	41	0	0	0	0	48.0	46	18	14	2	19	29	155,000
1993 COL	NL	P	5	3	5.05	65	0	0	0	1	62.1	68	40	35	8	26	49	325,000
5 YR	TOTALS		13	11	3.87	212	0	0	0	4	232.1	218	112	100	20	98	154	
1993 Rank	MLB Ps		149		238	28	202	125	69	70	239	205	254		229	197	67	144
1994 PROJECTIONS			3	2	4.04	48	0	0	0	0	49	50	25	22	5	19	35	

Florida *MARLINS*

1994 Scouting Report

Hitting: (1993/.248 BA, last in NL; 94 HR, last in NL)

Florida had the weakest offense in the league, but the ingredients for a potent offense are there. Gary Sheffield is a legitimate All-Star third baseman. He went from 34 HR and 100 RBI in '92 to 20 HR and 73 RBI in '93. Chuck Carr led the National League with 58 steals and scored 75 runs. But Benito Santiago hasn't had an outstanding season since '87; he posted a .230 BA with 13 HR and 50 RBI in '93.

Florida hopes Greg Colbrunn (claimed from Montreal) will add much-needed power. The Mariners will determine whether Jeff Conine or Orestes Destrade will start at first. Prospects include OFs Chuck Johnson, Nigel Wilson, Carl Everett, and Tim Clark, (MVP in the A California League).

Pitching: (1993/4.13 ERA, ninth in NL)

Charlie Hough (9–16) and Chris Hammond (11–12) will anchor the pitching rotation, along with Ryan Bowen (8–12), David Weathers, and Pat Rapp (4–6, 8–3 with AAA Edmonton). Jack Armstrong and Luis Aquino are the other candidates to start.

Brian Harvey came back from arm troubles to save 41 games for Florida. He was involved in 71.8% of his team's wins, a major league record.

Defense: (1993/.980 pct., sixth in NL)

Speedy Chuck Carr has great range in centerfield. Walt Weiss' .972 fielding percentage at SS ranked second in the NL, and his glove will be difficult to replace.

1994 Prospects:

The Marlins started off fast in '93, but were just 27–48 after the All-Star break. Although the Marlins have plenty of pitching prospects, the current starting pitching is very thin. The organization is in place, but this team is at least two years away from reaching parity with the rest of the National League. If they don't finish last in the NL East, it will be because the Mets are even worse.

Team Directory

Chairman: H. Wayne Huizenga	General Mgr.: David Dombroski
Dir. of Player Dev.: John Boles	Dir. of Scouting: Gary Hughes
Director of P.R.: Chuck Pool	Traveling Secretary: Joel Pieper

Minor League Affiliates:

Level	Team/League	1993 Record
AAA	Edmonton – Pacific Coast	72–69
AA	Portland – Eastern	1994 expansion team
A	High Desert – California	85–52
	Kane County – Midwest	75–62
	Elmira – New York/Penn.	31–44
Rookie	Gulf Coast Marlins – Gulf Coast	32–28

Purchased Sarasota in Class A Florida State League from Chicago White Sox, beginning in 1994

1993 Review

	Home		Away			Home		Away			Home		Away	
vs NL East	W	L	W	L	vs NL Cent.	W	L	W	L	vs NL West	W	L	W	L
Atlanta	2	4	3	3	Chicago	5	2	2	4	Colorado	3	3	2	4
Montreal	3	4	2	4	Cincinnati	3	3	2	4	Los Angeles	2	4	3	3
New York	1	5	3	4	Houston	2	4	1	5	San Diego	3	3	4	2
Philadelphia	3	3	1	6	Pittsburgh	4	3	2	4	S. Francisco	2	4	2	4
					St. Louis	2	4	2	5					
Total	9	16	9	17		16	16	9	22		10	14	11	13

1993 finish: 64–98 (35–46 home, 29–52 away), sixth in NL East, 33 games behind

1994 Schedule

April

S	M	T	W	Th	F	Sa
3	4	5 LA	6 LA	7 LA	8 SD	9 SD
10 SD	11	**12 HOU**	**13 HOU**	**14 HOU**	**15 SF**	**16 SF**
17 SF	18 COL	19 COL	20 COL	21	22 CIN	23 CIN
24 CIN	**25 ATL**	**26 ATL**	**27 COL**	**28 COL**	**29 CIN**	**30 CIN**

Home Away

May

S	M	T	W	Th	F	Sa
1 CIN	2	3 ATL	4 ATL	**5 PHL**	**6 PHL**	**7 PHL**
8 PHL	**9 PIT**	**10 PIT**	**11 PIT**	12	13 CHI	14 CHI
15 CHI	16 NY	17 NY	18 NY	19	**20 STL**	**21 STL**
22 STL	**23 MTL**	**24 MTL**	**25 MTL**	26	27 SF	28 SF
29 SF	30 HOU	31 HOU				

June

S	M	T	W	Th	F	Sa
			1 HOU	2	**3 SD**	**4 SD**
5 SD	**6 LA**	**7 LA**	**8 LA**	9 PIT	10 PIT	11 PIT
12 PIT	13 STL	14 STL	15 STL	**16 NY**	**17 NY**	**18 NY**
19 NY	20	**21 CHI**	**22 CHI**	**23 CHI**	24 MTL	25 MTL
26 MTL	27 PHL	28 PHL	29 PHL	**30 ATL**		

July

S	M	T	W	Th	F	Sa
					1 ATL	**2 ATL**
3 ATL	**4 CIN**	**5 CIN**	**6 CIN**	**7 COL**	**8 COL**	**9 COL**
10 COL	11 ALL-STAR BREAK	12	13	14 ATL	15 ATL	16 ATL
17 ATL	18 CIN	19 CIN	20 CIN	21	22 COL	23 COL
24 COL	**25 PHL**	**26 PHL**	**27 PHL**	28	**29 MTL**	**30 MTL**
31 MTL						

August

S	M	T	W	Th	F	Sa
	1 CHI	2 CHI	3 CHI	4 CHI	5 NY	6 NY
7 NY	**8 STL**	**9 STL**	**10 STL**	**11 STL**	**12 PIT**	**13 PIT**
14 PIT	15	16 SF	17 SF	18 SF	19 LA	20 LA
21 LA	22	**23 SD**	**24 SD**	**25 SD**	**26 LA**	**27 LA**
28 LA	29 SD	30 SD	31 SD			

Sept./Oct.

S	M	T	W	Th	F	Sa
				1	2 HOU	3 HOU
4 HOU	**5 SF**	**6 SF**	**7 SF**	8	**9 HOU**	**10 HOU**
11 HOU	12	13 PIT	14 PIT	15 PIT	16 STL	17 STL
18 STL	**19 NY**	**20 NY**	**21 NY**	22	**23 CHI**	**24 CHI**
25 CHI	26 MTL	27 MTL	28 MTL	29 PHL	30 PHL	Oc.1 PHL
Oc.2 PHL						

FLORIDA MARLINS 1994 ROSTER

Manager: Rene Lachemann (15)
Coaches: Marcel Lachemann, pitching (53); Vada Pinson, 1B (28); Doug Rader, hitting (12); Frank Reberger, bullpen (33); Cookie Rojas, 3B (1)

No.	PITCHERS	B	T	HT	WT	DOB	BIRTHPLACE	RESIDENCE
27	Aquino, Luis	R	R	6–1	190	5–19–65	Santurce, PR	Miami, FL
77	Armstrong, Jack	R	R	6–5	220	3–7–65	Englewood, NJ	Palm Beach Gard., FL
46	Bowen, Ryan	R	R	6–0	185	2–10–68	Hanford, CA	Houston, TX
56	De La Hoya, Javier	R	R	6–0	162	2–21–70	Durango, MX	North Hollywood, CA
50	Drahman, Brian	R	R	6–3	231	11–7–66	Kenton, KY	Fort Lauderdale, FL
11	Hammond, Chris	L	L	6–1	195	1–21–66	Atlanta, GA	Birmingham, AL
34	Harvey, Brian	R	R	6–2	212	6–2–63	Chattanooga, TN	Catawba, NC
	Hough, Charlie	R	R	6–2	190	1–5–48	Honolulu, HI	Broca, CA
58	Klink, Joe	R	L	5–11	175	2–3–62	Hollywood, FL	Pembroke Pines, FL
24	Lewis, Richie	R	R	5–10	175	1–25–66	Muncie, IN	Losantville, IN
44	Miller, Kurt	R	R	6–5	205	8–24–72	Tucson, AZ	Bakersfield, CA
	Mutis, Jeff	L	L	6–2	185	12–8–68	Williamsport, PA	Allentown, PA
32	Myers, Mike	L	L	6–3	197	6–26–69	Cook County, IL	Wheeling, IL
31	Nen, Robb	R	R	6–4	200	11–28–69	San Pedro, CA	Seal Beach, CA
48	Rapp, Pat	R	R	6–3	205	7–13–67	Jennings, LA	Sulphur, LA
42	Rodriguez, Rich	R	L	6–0	200	3–1–63	Downey, CA	Knoxville, TN
54	Turner, Matt	R	R	6–5	215	2–18–67	Lexington, KY	Lexington, KY
35	Weathers, Dave	R	R	6–3	205	9–25–69	Lawrenceburg, TN	Leoma, TN
38	Whisenant, Matt	S	L	6–3	200	6–8–71	Los Angeles, CA	La Canada, CA
45	Vaughn, Kip	R	R	6–0	180	7–20–69	Walnut Creek, CA	Concord, CA
No.	**CATCHERS**	**B**	**T**	**HT**	**WT**	**DOB**	**BIRTHPLACE**	**RESIDENCE**
13	Natal, Bob	R	R	5–11	190	11–13–65	Long Beach, CA	Chula Vista, CA
16	O'Halloran, Greg	L	R	6–2	205	5–21–68	Toronto, ON	Mississauga, ON
9	Santiago, Benito	R	R	6–1	185	3–9–65	Ponce, PR	Davie, FL
No.	**INFIELDERS**	**B**	**T**	**HT**	**WT**	**DOB**	**BIRTHPLACE**	**RESIDENCE**
26	Arias, Alex	R	R	6–3	185	11–20–67	New York, NY	New York, NY
8	Barberie, Bret	S	R	5–11	180	8–16–67	Long Beach, CA	Cerritos, CA
4	Colbrunn, Greg	R	R	6–0	200	7–26–69	Fontana, CA	Fontana, CA
39	Destrade, Orestes	S	R	6–4	230	5–8–62	Santiago, CU	St. Petersburg, FL
18	Magadan, Dave	L	R	6–3	205	9–30–62	Tampa, FL	Tampa, FL
37	Martinez, Ramon	S	R	6–0	165	9–8–69	Villa Gonzalez, DR	Villa Gonzalez, DR
6	Renteria, Rick	R	R	5–9	175	12–25–61	Harbor City, CA	Las Vegas, NV
10	Sheffield, Gary	R	R	5–11	190	11–18–68	Tampa, FL	St. Petersburg, FL
No.	**OUTFIELDERS**	**B**	**T**	**HT**	**WT**	**DOB**	**BIRTHPLACE**	**RESIDENCE**
21	Carr, Chuck	S	R	5–10	165	8–10–68	San Bernadino, CA	Tucson, AZ
25	Carrillo, Matias	L	L	5–11	190	2–24–63	Los Mochis, MX	Guaymas, MX
14	Clark, Tim	L	R	6–3	210	2–10–69	Philadelphia, PA	Philadelphia, PA
19	Conine, Jeff	R	R	6–1	220	6–27–66	Tacoma, WA	Rialto, CA
3	Everett, Carl	S	R	6–0	181	6–3–70	Tampa, FL	Tampa, FL
7	Moore, Kerwin	S	R	6–1	190	10–29–70	Detroit, MI	Detroit, MI
20	Tavarez, Jesus	R	R	6–0	170	3–26–71	Santo Domingo, DR	Santo Domingo, DR
17	Whitmore, Darrell	L	R	6–1	210	11–18–68	Front Royal, VA	Front Royal, VA
30	Wilson, Nigel	L	L	6–1	185	1–12–70	Oshawa, ON	Ajax, ON

Joe Robbie Stadium (43,909, grass)
Tickets: 305–930–7800
Ticket prices:

- $18 (club level section 201–210 & 233–242)
- $12 (terrace box)
- $7.50 (mezzanine reserved)
- $6.50 (outfield reserved, adult)
- $3.00 (outfield reserved, 12 & under)
- $3.50 (general admission, adult)
- $1.00 (general admission, 12 & under)

Field Dimensions (from home plate)

- To left field at foul line, 335 feet
- To center field, 410 feet
- To right field at foul line, 345 feet

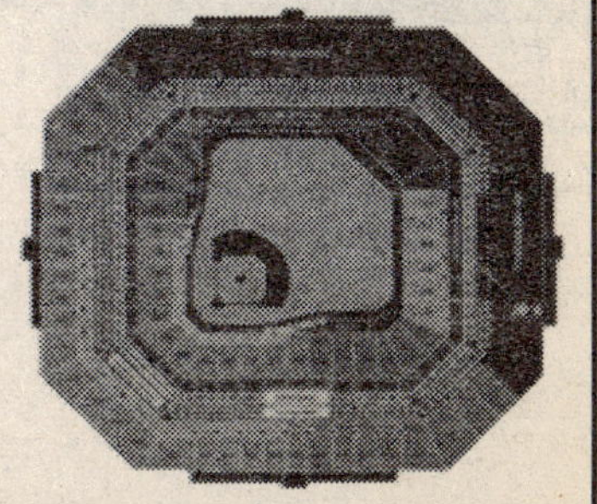

Bret Barberie No. 8/2B

Full name: Bret Edward Barberie
Bats: S **Throws:** R **HT:** 5–11 **WT:** 180
Born: 8–16–67, Long Beach, CA
High school: Gahr (CA)
College: Cerritos Junior (CA) and USC

Barberie hit .390 on artificial turf. He hit safely in 15 straight games from August 7 to August 22.

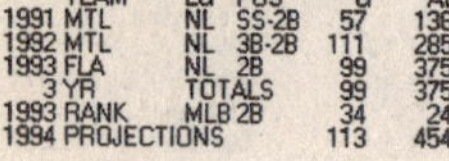
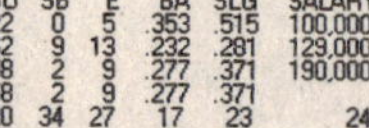

	TEAM	LG	POS	G	AB	R	H	2B	3B	HR	RBI	BB	SO	SB	E	BA	SLG	SALARY
1991	MTL	NL	SS-2B	57	136	16	48	12	2	2	18	20	22	0	5	.353	.515	100,000
1992	MTL	NL	3B-2B	111	285	26	66	11	0	1	24	47	62	9	13	.232	.281	129,000
1993	FLA	NL	2B	99	375	45	104	16	2	5	33	33	58	2	9	.277	.371	190,000
3	YR	TOTALS		99	375	45	104	16	2	5	33	33	58	2	9	.277	.371	
1993	RANK	MLB	2B	34	24	27	25	26	19	17	25	23	20	34	27	17	23	24
1994	PROJECTIONS			113	454	54	122	17	2	6	38	37	70	2	10	.269	.355	

Chuck Carr No. 21/OF

Full name: Charles Lee Glenn Carr Jr.
Bats: S **Throws:** R **HT:** 5–10 **WT:** 165
Born: 8–10–68, San Bernadino, CA
High school: Fontana (CA)

Carr was the NL stolen base champ—the first player not from St. Louis or Montreal to win the title since Pittsburgh's Omar Moreno won in 1979. Carr bunted safely 17 times in '93.

	TEAM	LG	POS	G	AB	R	H	2B	3B	HR	RBI	BB	SO	SB	E	BA	SLG	SALARY
1990	NY	NL	OF	4	2	0	0	0	0	0	0	0	2	1	0	0		N/A
1991	NY	NL	OF	12	11	1	2	0	0	0	1	0	2	1	0	.182	.182	100,000
1992	STL	NL	OF	22	64	8	14	3	0	0	3	9	6	10	0	.219	.266	N/A
1993	FLA	NL	OF	142	551	75	147	19	2	4	41	49	74	58	6	.267	.33	123,000
4	YR	TOTALS		180	628	84	163	22	2	4	45	58	84	70	6	.26	.32	
1993	RANK	MLB	OF	34	25	36	31	55	76	102	79	38	50	2	38	78	120	118
1994	PROJECTIONS			162	633	85	168	21	1	4	46	56	84	66	6	.265	.321	

Jeff Conine No. 19/OF

Full name: Jeffrey Guy Conine
Bats: R **Throws:** R **HT:** 6–1 **WT:** 220
Born: 6–27–66, Tacoma, WA
High school: Eisenhower (Rialto, CA)
College: UCLA

Only Jeff Conine and Cal Ripken played in all 162 games in '93. Florida is counting on Conine to be a star of the future.

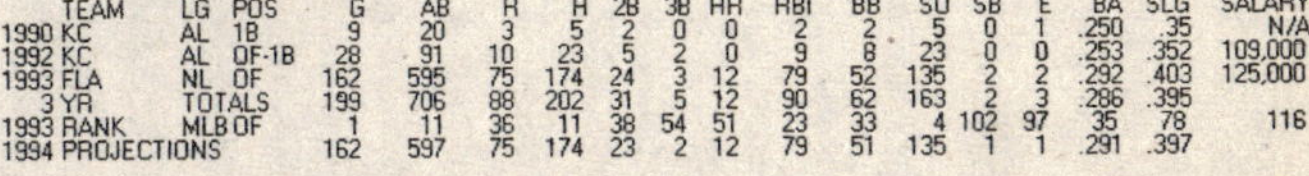

	TEAM	LG	POS	G	AB	R	H	2B	3B	HR	RBI	BB	SO	SB	E	BA	SLG	SALARY
1990	KC	AL	1B	9	20	3	5	2	0	0	2	2	5	0	1	.250	.35	N/A
1992	KC	AL	OF-1B	28	91	10	23	5	2	0	9	8	23	0	0	.253	.352	109,000
1993	FLA	NL	OF	162	595	75	174	24	3	12	79	52	135	2	2	.292	.403	125,000
3	YR	TOTALS		199	706	88	202	31	5	12	90	62	163	2	3	.286	.395	
1993	RANK	MLB	OF	1	11	36	11	38	54	51	23	33	4	102	97	35	78	116
1994	PROJECTIONS			162	597	75	174	23	2	12	79	51	135	1	1	.291	.397	

Orestes Destrade No. 39/1B

Full name: Orestes Destrade
Bats: S **Throws:** R **HT:** 6–4 **WT:** 230
Born: 5–8–62, Santiago, CU
High school: C. Columbus (Miami FL)
College: Florida College

1993 was Destrade's first full season in the majors; he spent four year's with Japan's Seibu Lions. He hit .313 on artificial turf.

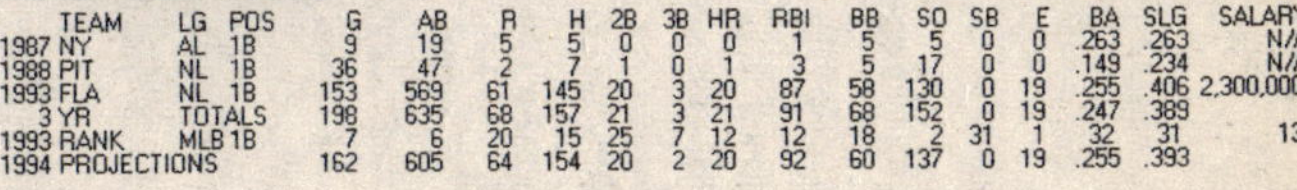

	TEAM	LG	POS	G	AB	R	H	2B	3B	HR	RBI	BB	SO	SB	E	BA	SLG	SALARY
1987	NY	AL	1B	9	19	5	5	0	0	0	1	5	5	0	0	.263	.263	N/A
1988	PIT	NL	1B	36	47	2	7	1	0	1	3	5	17	0	0	.149	.234	N/A
1993	FLA	NL	1B	153	569	61	145	20	3	20	87	58	130	0	19	.255	.406	2,300,000
3	YR	TOTALS		198	635	68	157	21	3	21	91	68	152	0	19	.247	.389	
1993	RANK	MLB	1B	7	6	20	15	25	7	12	12	18	2	31	1	32	31	13
1994	PROJECTIONS			162	605	64	154	20	2	20	92	60	137	0	19	.255	.393	

Rick Renteria No. 6/2B

Full name: Richard Avina Renteria
Bats: R **Throws:** R **HT:** 5–9 **WT:** 175
Born: 12–25–61, Harbor City, CA
Renteria was the best clutch hitter on the team, batting .347 with runners in scoring position.

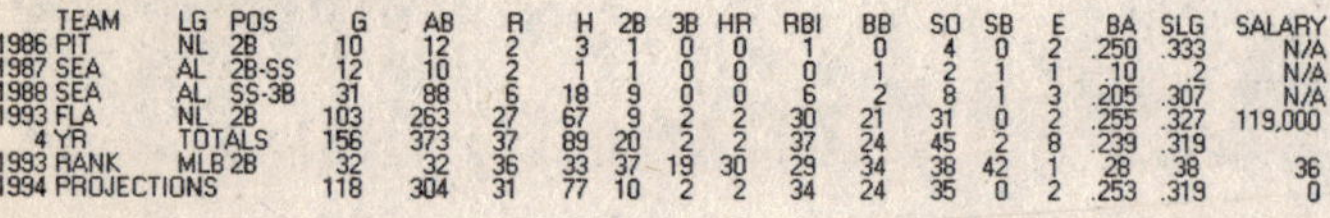

	TEAM	LG	POS	G	AB	R	H	2B	3B	HR	RBI	BB	SO	SB	E	BA	SLG	SALARY
1986	PIT	NL	2B	10	12	2	3	1	0	0	1	0	4	0	2	.250	.333	N/A
1987	SEA	AL	2B-SS	12	10	2	1	1	0	0	0	1	2	1	1	.10	.2	N/A
1988	SEA	AL	SS-3B	31	88	6	18	9	0	0	6	2	8	1	3	.205	.307	N/A
1993	FLA	NL	2B	103	263	27	67	9	2	2	30	21	31	0	2	.255	.327	119,000
4	YR	TOTALS		156	373	37	89	20	2	2	37	24	45	2	8	.239	.319	
1993	RANK	MLB	2B	32	32	36	33	37	19	30	29	34	38	42	1	28	38	36
1994	PROJECTIONS			118	304	31	77	10	2	2	34	24	35	0	2	.253	.319	0

Benito Santiago No. 9/C

Full name: Benito Rivera Santiago
Bats: R **Throws:** R **HT:** 6–1 **WT:** 185
Born: 3–9–65, Ponce, PR
High school: John F. Kennedy (Ponce, PR)
Santiago reached double figures in HRs for the seventh straight season. He led the team in triples with six, and led NL catchers in steals with ten.

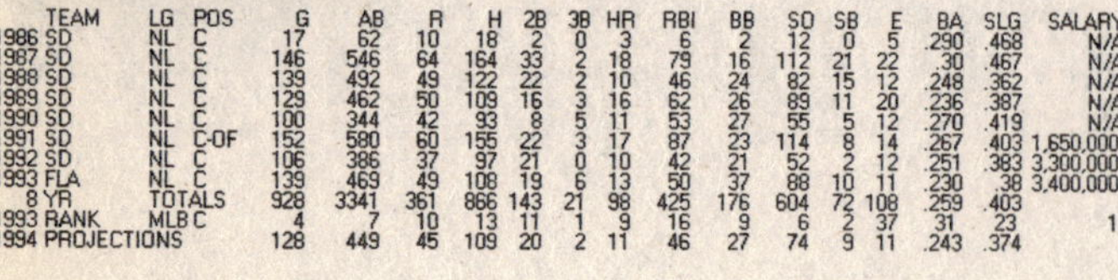

	TEAM	LG	POS	G	AB	R	H	2B	3B	HR	RBI	BB	SO	SB	E	BA	SLG	SALARY
1986	SD	NL	C	17	62	10	18	2	0	3	6	2	12	0	5	.290	.468	N/A
1987	SD	NL	C	146	546	64	164	33	2	18	79	16	112	21	22	.30	.467	N/A
1988	SD	NL	C	139	492	49	122	22	2	10	46	24	82	15	12	.248	.362	N/A
1989	SD	NL	C	129	462	50	109	16	3	16	62	26	89	11	20	.236	.387	N/A
1990	SD	NL	C	100	344	42	93	8	5	11	53	27	55	5	12	.270	.419	N/A
1991	SD	NL	C-OF	152	580	60	155	22	3	17	87	23	114	8	14	.267	.403	1,650,000
1992	SD	NL	C	106	386	37	97	21	0	10	42	21	52	2	12	.251	.383	3,300,000
1993	FLA	NL	C	139	469	49	108	19	6	13	50	37	88	10	11	.230	.38	3,400,000
8	YR	TOTALS		928	3341	361	866	143	21	98	425	176	604	72	108	.259	.403	
1993	RANK	MLB	C	4	7	10	13	11	1	9	16	9	6	2	37	31	23	1
1994	PROJECTIONS			128	449	45	109	20	2	11	46	27	74	9	11	.243	.374	

Gary Sheffield No. 10/3B

Full name: Gary Antonian Sheffield
Bats: R **Throws:** R **HT:** 5–11 **WT:** 190
Born: 11–18–68, Tampa, FL
High school: Hillsborough (Tampa, FL)
Sheffield was the youngest defending batting champ to be traded in the last 60 years when he came to Florida from San Diego.

TEAM	LG	POS	G	AB	R	H	2B	3B	HR	RBI	BB	SO	SB	E	BA	SLG	SALARY
1988 MIL	AL	SS	24	80	12	19	1	0	4	12	7	7	3	3	.238	.4	N/A
1989 MIL	AL	SS-3B	95	368	34	91	18	0	5	32	27	33	10	16	.247	.337	N/A
1990 MIL	AL	3B	125	487	67	143	30	1	10	67	44	41	25	25	.294	.421	N/A
1991 MIL	AL	3B	50	175	25	34	12	2	2	22	19	15	5	8	.194	.32	400,000
1992 SD	NL	3B	146	557	87	184	34	3	33	100	48	40	5	16	.330	.58	450,000
1993 SD-FLA	NL	3B	140	494	67	145	20	5	20	73	47	64	17	34	.294	.476	3,110,000
6 YR	TOTALS		580	2161	292	616	115	11	74	306	192	200	65	102	.285	.451	
1993 RANK	MLB	3B	16	15	12	10	19	1	6	12	11	20	2	41	8	4	3
1994 PROJECTIONS			120	449	56	126	22	2	11	57	39	46	17	25	.281	.419	

Darrell Whitmore No. 17/OF

Full name: Darrell Lamont Whitmore
Bats: L **Throws:** R **HT:** 6–1 **WT:** 210
Born: 11–18–68, Front Royal, VA
High school: Warren County (VA)
College: West Virginia
Whitmore hit .355 for AAA Edmonton, and led the Pacific Coast League with 24 doubles and 62 RBI when he was recalled.

TEAM	LG	POS	G	AB	R	H	2B	3B	HR	RBI	BB	SO	SB	E	BA	SLG	SALARY
1993 FLA	NL	OF	76	250	24	51	8	2	4	19	10	72	4	3	.204	.300	109,000
1 YR	TOTAL		76	250	24	51	8	2	4	19	10	72	4	3	.204	.300	
1993 RANK	MLB	OF	123	101	121	116	125	76	102	129	130	51	85	42	132	132	124

Ryan Bowen No. 46/P

Full name: Ryan Eugene Bowen
Bats: R **Throws:** R **HT:** 6–0 **WT:** 185
Born: 2–10–68, Hanford, CA
High school: Hanford (CA)

Bowen threw Florida's only complete game shutout May 15 vs. St. Louis. His season ended September 1 when he injured his knee covering home against San Diego.

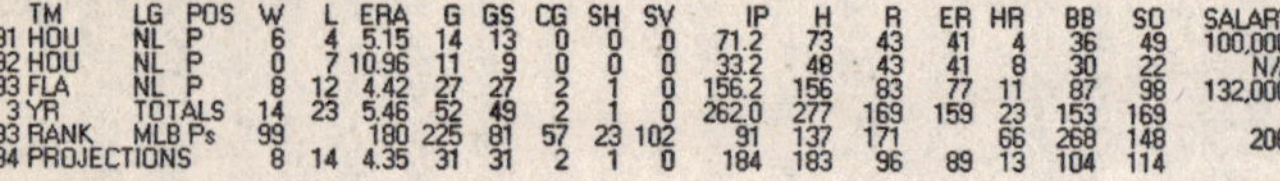

	TM	LG	POS	W	L	ERA	G	GS	CG	SH	SV	IP	H	R	ER	HR	BB	SO	SALARY
1991	HOU	NL	P	6	4	5.15	14	13	0	0	0	71.2	73	43	41	4	36	49	100,000
1992	HOU	NL	P	0	7	10.96	11	9	0	0	0	33.2	48	43	41	8	30	22	N/A
1993	FLA	NL	P	8	12	4.42	27	27	2	1	0	156.2	156	83	77	11	87	98	132,000
3	YR	TOTALS		14	23	5.46	52	49	2	1	0	262.0	277	169	159	23	153	169	
1993	RANK	MLB Ps		99		180	225	81	57	23	102	91	137	171		66	268	148	206
1994	PROJECTIONS			8	14	4.35	31	31	2	1	0	184	183	96	89	13	104	114	

Chris Hammond No. 11/P

Full name: Christopher Andrew Hammond
Bats: L **Throws:** L **HT:** 6–1 **WT:** 195
Born: 1–21–66, Atlanta, GA
High school: Vestavia Hills (B'mingham, AL)
College: Gulf Coast CC (FL) and UAB

Hammond is the only lefty in the Florida starting rotation. His 11 wins led the team, and was the third best total in expansion history.

	TM	LG	POS	W	L	ERA	G	GS	CG	SH	SV	IP	H	R	ER	HR	BB	SO	SALARY
1990	CIN	NL	P	0	2	6.35	3	3	0	0	0	11.1	13	9	8	2	12	4	N/A
1991	CIN	NL	P	7	7	4.06	20	18	0	0	0	99.2	92	51	45	4	48	50	100,000
1992	CIN	NL	P	7	10	4.21	28	26	0	0	0	147.1	149	75	69	13	55	79	130,000
1993	FLA	NL	P	11	12	4.66	32	32	1	0	0	191.0	207	106	99	18	66	108	260,000
4	YR	TOTALS		25	31	4.43	83	79	1	0	0	449.1	461	241	221	37	181	241	
1993	Rank	MLB Ps		59		206	175	39	79	69	102	55	200	189		145	125	196	157
1994	PROJECTIONS			12	12	4.63	36	36	0	0	0	216	235	120	111	20	72	123	

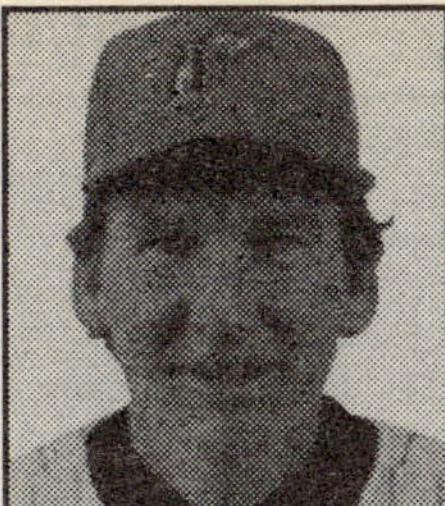

Charlie Hough P

Full name: Charles Oliver Hough
Bats: R **Throws:** R **HT:** 6–2 **WT:** 190
Born: 1–5–48, Honolulu, HI
High school: Hialeah (FL)

After going 9–16 for the Marlins (including winning their debut against the Dodgers), Hough was signed as a free agent to a minor league contract in the off–season.

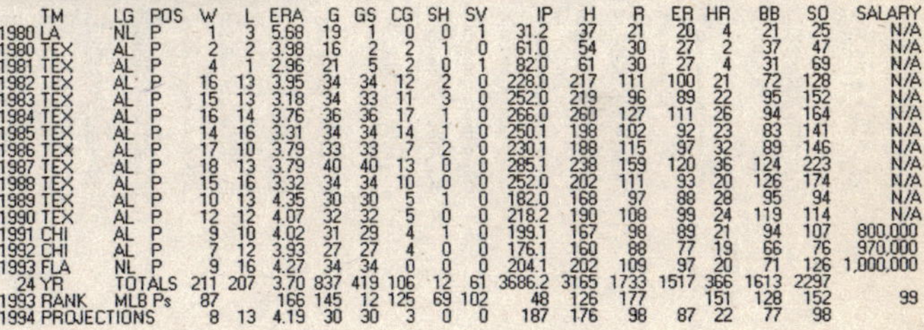

	TM	LG	POS	W	L	ERA	G	GS	CG	SH	SV	IP	H	R	ER	HR	BB	SO	SALARY
1980	LA	NL	P	1	3	5.68	19	1	0	0	1	31.2	37	21	20	4	21	25	N/A
1980	TEX	AL	P	2	2	3.98	16	2	2	1	0	61.0	54	30	27	2	37	47	N/A
1981	TEX	AL	P	4	1	2.96	21	5	2	0	1	82.0	61	30	27	4	31	69	N/A
1982	TEX	AL	P	16	13	3.95	34	34	12	2	0	228.0	217	111	100	21	72	128	N/A
1983	TEX	AL	P	15	13	3.18	34	33	11	3	0	252.0	219	96	89	22	95	152	N/A
1984	TEX	AL	P	16	14	3.76	36	36	17	1	0	266.0	260	127	111	26	94	164	N/A
1985	TEX	AL	P	14	16	3.31	34	34	14	1	0	250.1	198	102	92	23	83	141	N/A
1986	TEX	AL	P	17	10	3.79	33	33	7	2	0	230.1	188	115	97	32	89	146	N/A
1987	TEX	AL	P	18	13	3.79	40	40	13	0	0	285.1	238	159	120	36	124	223	N/A
1988	TEX	AL	P	15	16	3.32	34	34	10	0	0	252.0	202	111	93	20	126	174	N/A
1989	TEX	AL	P	10	13	4.35	30	30	5	1	0	182.0	168	97	88	28	95	94	N/A
1990	TEX	AL	P	12	12	4.07	32	32	5	0	0	218.2	190	108	99	24	119	114	N/A
1991	CHI	AL	P	9	10	4.02	31	29	4	1	0	199.1	167	98	89	21	94	107	800,000
1992	CHI	AL	P	7	12	3.93	27	27	4	0	0	176.1	160	88	77	19	66	76	970,000
1993	FLA	NL	P	9	16	4.27	34	34	0	0	0	204.1	202	109	97	20	71	126	1,000,000
24	YR	TOTALS		211	207	3.70	837	419	106	12	61	3686.2	3165	1733	1517	366	1613	2297	
1993	RANK	MLB Ps		87		166	145	12	125	69	102	48	126	177		151	128	152	99
1994	PROJECTIONS			8	13	4.19	30	30	3	0	0	187	176	98	87	22	77	98	

Pat Rapp No. 48/P

Full name: Patrick LeLand Rapp
Bats: R **Throws:** R **HT:** 6–3 **WT:** 205
Born: 7–13–67, Jennings, LA
High school: Sulphur (LA)
College: Hinds JC (MS) and So. Mississippi

Rapp was 8–3 at AAA Edmonton. Florida scored just six runs in Rapp's six losses, and was shutout three times.

	TM	LG	POS	W	L	ERA	G	GS	CG	SH	SV	IP	H	R	ER	HR	BB	SO	SALARY
1992	SF	NL	P	0	2	7.20	3	2	0	0	0	10.0	8	8	8	0	6	3	N/A
1993	FLA	NL	P	4	6	4.02	16	16	1	0	0	94.0	101	49	42	7	39	57	118,000
2	YR	TOTALS		4	8	4.33	19	18	1	0	0	104.0	109	57	50	7	45	60	
1993	RANK	MLB Ps		173		138	272	123	79	69	102	158	196	165		81	195	159	219
1994	PROJECTIONS			6	8	3.90	22	23	1	0	0	136	147	69	59	10	55	84	

Bryan Harvey No. 34/P

Full name: Bryan Stanley Harvey
Bats: R **Throws:** R **HT:** 6–2 **WT:** 212
Born: 6–2–63, Chattanooga, TN
High school: Brandys (Catawba, NC)
College: North Carolina–Charlotte
Harvey made the All-Star team. He became only the second pitcher to notch 40 saves in both leagues (with Jeff Reardon).

	TM	LG	POS	W	L	ERA	G	GS	CG	SH	SV	IP	H	R	ER	HR	BB	SO	SALARY
1987	CAL	AL	P	0	0	0.00	3	0	0	0	0	5.0	6	0	0	0	2	3	N/A
1988	CAL	AL	P	7	5	2.13	50	0	0	0	17	76.0	59	22	18	4	20	67	N/A
1989	CAL	AL	P	3	3	3.44	51	0	0	0	25	55.0	36	21	21	6	41	78	N/A
1990	CAL	AL	P	4	4	3.22	54	0	0	0	25	64.1	45	24	23	4	35	82	N/A
1991	CAL	AL	P	2	4	1.60	67	0	0	0	46	78.2	51	20	14	6	17	101	1,055,000
1992	CAL	AL	P	0	4	2.83	25	0	0	0	13	28.2	22	12	9	4	11	34	3,125,000
1993	FLA	NL	P	1	5	1.70	59	0	0	0	45	69.0	45	14	13	4	13	73	4,225,000
7	YR	TOTALS		17	25	2.34	309	0	0	0	171	376.2	264	113	98	28	139	438	
1993	Rank	MLB Ps		273		2	47	202	125	69	4	219	2	2		42	14	12	15
1994	PROJECTIONS			2	4	2.76	54	0	0	0	31	62	42	19	19	4	29	77	

Rene Lachemann No. 15/Mgr.

Full name: Rene George Lachemann
Bats: R **Throws:** R **HT:** 6–0 **WT:** 200
Born: 5–4–45, Los Angeles, CA
High school: Dorsey (Los Angeles, CA)
College: Southern California
Lachemann coached in four World Series with Oakland and Boston. He also managed at Seattle and Milwaukee.

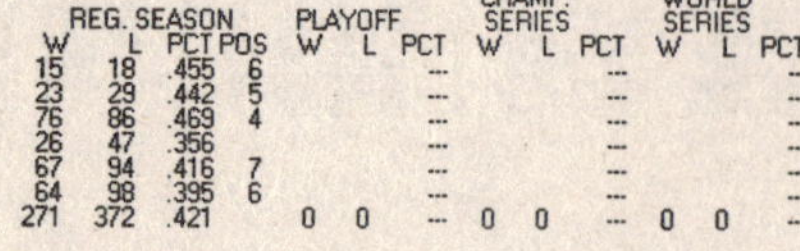

				REG. SEASON				PLAYOFF			CHAMP. SERIES			WORLD SERIES		
	YEAR	TEAM	LG	W	L	PCT	POS	W	L	PCT	W	L	PCT	W	L	PCT
1ST HALF	1981	SEA	AL	15	18	.455	6			---			---			---
2ND HALF	1981	SEA	AL	23	29	.442	5			---			---			---
	1982	SEA	AL	76	86	.469	4			---			---			---
	1983	SEA	AL	26	47	.356				---			---			---
	1984	MIL	AL	67	94	.416	7			---			---			---
	1993	FLA	NL	64	98	.395	6			---			---			---
	13	YR TOTALS		271	372	.421		0	0	---	0	0	---	0	0	---

Luis Aquino **No. 27/P**

Full name: Luis Antonio (Colon) Aquino
Bats: R **Throws:** R **HT:** 6–1 **WT:** 190
Born: 5–19–65, Santurce, PR

Aquino was 2–2 with a 3.56 ERA in 25 relief outings and 4–6 with a 3.36 ERA in 13 starts. He led the league in ERA from May 30 to June 15.

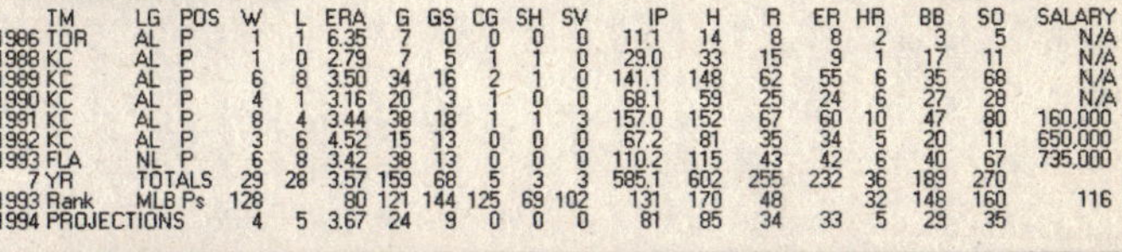

	TM	LG	POS	W	L	ERA	G	GS	CG	SH	SV	IP	H	R	ER	HR	BB	SO	SALARY
1986	TOR	AL	P	1	1	6.35	7	0	0	0	0	11.1	14	8	8	2	3	5	N/A
1988	KC	AL	P	1	0	2.79	7	5	1	1	0	29.0	33	15	9	1	17	11	N/A
1989	KC	AL	P	6	8	3.50	34	16	2	1	0	141.1	148	62	55	6	35	68	N/A
1990	KC	AL	P	4	1	3.16	20	3	1	0	0	68.1	59	25	24	6	27	28	N/A
1991	KC	AL	P	8	4	3.44	38	18	1	1	3	157.0	152	67	60	10	47	80	160,000
1992	KC	AL	P	3	6	4.52	15	13	0	0	0	67.2	81	35	34	5	20	11	650,000
1993	FLA	NL	P	6	8	3.42	38	13	0	0	0	110.2	115	43	42	6	40	67	735,000
7	YR	TOTALS		29	28	3.57	159	68	5	3	3	585.1	602	255	232	36	189	270	
1993	Rank	MLB	Ps	128		80	121	144	125	69	102	131	170	48		32	148	160	116
1994	PROJECTIONS			4	5	3.67	24	9	0	0	0	81	85	34	33	5	29	35	

Alex Arias **No. 26/IF**

Full name: Alejandro Arias
Bats: R **Throws:** R **HT:** 6–3 **WT:** 185
Born: 11–20–67, New York, NY
High school: George Washington (New York, NY)

Arias started 38 games at second and third, batting .286. He hit .302 vs. the NL East.

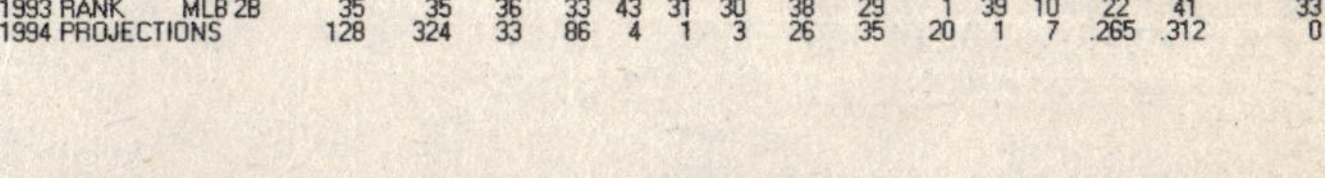

	TEAM	LG	POS	G	AB	R	H	2B	3B	HR	RBI	BB	SO	SB	E	BA	SLG	SALARY
1992	CHI	NL	SS	32	99	14	29	6	0	0	7	11	13	0	4	.293	.354	109,000
1993	FLA	NL	2B	96	249	27	67	5	1	2	20	27	18	1	6	.269	.321	123,000
2	YR	TOTALS		128	348	41	96	11	1	2	27	38	31	1	10	.276	.330	
1993	RANK	MLB	2B	35	35	36	33	43	31	30	38	29	1	39	10	22	41	33
1994	PROJECTIONS			128	324	33	86	4	1	3	26	35	20	1	7	.265	.312	0

Jack Armstrong **No. 77/P**

Full name: Jack William Armstrong
Bats: R **Throws:** R **HT:** 6–5 **WT:** 220
Born: 3–7–65, Englewood, NJ
High school: Neptune (NJ)
College: Rider (NJ) and Oklahoma

Only Doug Drabek lost more '93 games in the NL.

	TM	LG	POS	W	L	ERA	G	GS	CG	SH	SV	IP	H	R	ER	HR	BB	SO	SALARY
1988	CIN	NL	P	4	7	5.79	14	13	0	0	0	65.1	63	44	42	8	38	45	N/A
1989	CIN	NL	P	2	3	4.64	9	8	0	0	0	42.2	40	24	22	5	21	23	N/A
1990	CIN	NL	P	12	9	3.42	29	27	2	1	0	166.0	151	72	63	9	59	110	N/A
1991	CIN	NL	P	7	13	5.48	27	24	1	0	0	139.2	158	90	85	25	54	93	N/A
1992	CLE	AL	P	6	15	4.64	35	23	1	0	0	166.2	176	100	86	23	67	114	237,000
1993	FLA	NL	P	9	17	4.49	36	33	0	0	0	196.1	210	105	98	29	78	118	1,154,545
6	YR	TOTALS		40	64	4.59	150	128	4	1	0	776.2	798	435	396	99	317	503	
1993	Rank	MLB	Ps	87		190	124	30	125	69	102	53	193	179		263	182	162	91
1994	PROJECTIONS			9	18	4.44	39	36	0	0	0	217	234	115	107	32	84	130	

Matias Carrillo — No. 25/OF

Full name: Matias Garcia Carrillo
Bats: L **Throws:** L **HT:** 5–11 **WT:** 190
Born: 2–24–63, Los Mochis, MX

Florida bought Carrillo's contract from the Mexico City Tigers September 1. Carrillo led the Mexican League in HR (38) and RBI (125).

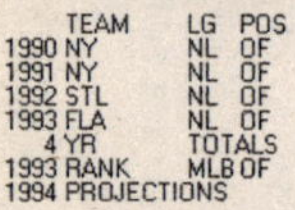
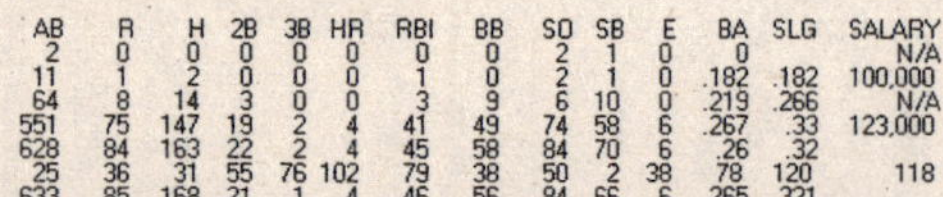

	TEAM	LG	POS	G	AB	R	H	2B	3B	HR	RBI	BB	SO	SB	E	BA	SLG	SALARY
1990	NY	NL	OF	4	2	0	0	0	0	0	0	0	2	1	0	0		N/A
1991	NY	NL	OF	12	11	1	2	0	0	0	1	0	2	1	0	.182	.182	100,000
1992	STL	NL	OF	22	64	8	14	3	0	0	3	9	6	10	0	.219	.266	N/A
1993	FLA	NL	OF	142	551	75	147	19	2	4	41	49	74	58	6	.267	.33	123,000
4	YR	TOTALS		180	628	84	163	22	2	4	45	58	84	70	6	.26	.32	
1993	RANK	MLB	OF	34	25	36	31	55	76	102	79	38	50	2	38	78	120	118
1994	PROJECTIONS			162	633	85	168	21	1	4	46	56	84	66	6	.265	.321	

Tim Clark — No. 14/OF

Bats: L **Throws:** R **HT:** 6–3 **WT:** 210
Born: 2–10–69, Philadelphia, PA
College: Louisiana State

Tim Clark was the A California League MVP and batting champ, hitting .363 with 126 RBI. He was named Marlins Organizational Player of the Year.

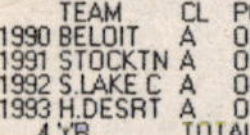
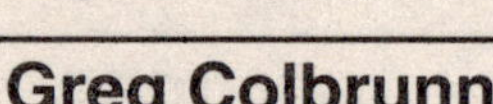

	TEAM	CL	POS	G	AB	R	H	2B	3B	HR	RBI	BB	SO	SB	BA	SLG
1990	BELOIT	A	OF	67	219	27	57	13	1	4	44	31	45	3	.260	.384
1991	STOCKTN	A	OF	125	424	51	116	19	4	9	56	57	60	9	.274	.401
1992	S.LAKE C	A	OF	69	272	57	97	24	2	11	53	28	36	1	.357	.581
1993	H.DESRT	A	OF	128	510	109	185	42	10	17	126	56	65	2	.363	.584
4	YR	TOTALS		389	1425	244	455	98	17	41	279	172	206	15	.319	.498

Greg Colbrunn — No. 4/1B

Full name: Gregory Joseph Colbrunn
Bats: R **Throws:** R **HT:** 6–0 **WT:** 200
Born: 7–26–69, Fontana, CA
High school: Fontana (CA)

Colbrunn missed all of '91 and half of '93 due to elbow problems. He was waived by Montreal.

	TEAM	LG	POS	G	AB	R	H	2B	3B	HR	RBI	BB	SO	SB	E	BA	SLG	SALARY
1992	MTL	NL	1B	52	168	12	45	8	0	2	18	6	34	3	3	.268	.351	109,000
1993	MTL	NL	1B	70	153	15	39	9	0	4	23	6	33	4	2	.255	.392	126,000
2	YR	TOTALS		122	321	27	84	17	0	6	41	12	67	7	5	.262	.371	
1993	RANK	MLB	1B	41	41	41	41	35	30	38	39	41	35	11	36	31	33	34
1994	PROJECTIONS			79	145	16	36	9	0	5	25	6	32	4	1	.248	.414	

Joe Klink — No. 58/P

Full name: Joseph Charles Klink
Bats: R **Throws:** L **HT:** 5–11 **WT:** 175
Born: 2–3–62, Hollywood, FL
High school: Chaminade (Hollywood, FL)
College: Biscayne (Opa Locka, FL)
Klink held lefthanders to a .216 average.

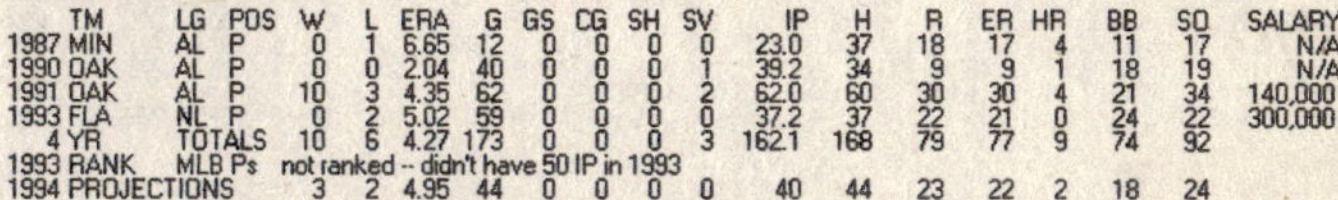

	TM	LG	POS	W	L	ERA	G	GS	CG	SH	SV	IP	H	R	ER	HR	BB	SO	SALARY
1987	MIN	AL	P	0	1	6.65	12	0	0	0	0	23.0	37	18	17	4	11	17	N/A
1990	OAK	AL	P	0	0	2.04	40	0	0	0	1	39.2	34	9	9	1	18	19	N/A
1991	OAK	AL	P	10	3	4.35	62	0	0	0	2	62.0	60	30	30	4	21	34	140,000
1993	FLA	NL	P	0	2	5.02	59	0	0	0	0	37.2	37	22	21	0	24	22	300,000
4	YR	TOTALS		10	6	4.27	173	0	0	0	3	162.1	168	79	77	9	74	92	
1993	RANK	MLB Ps	not ranked -- didn't have 50 IP in 1993																
1994	PROJECTIONS			3	2	4.95	44	0	0	0	0	40	44	23	22	2	18	24	

Richie Lewis — No. 24/P

Full name: Richie Todd Lewis
Bats: R **Throws:** R **HT:** 5–10 **WT:** 175
Born: 1–25–66, Muncie, IN
High school: South Side (Muncie, IN)
College: Florida State
Lewis' 77.1 innings led the Marlin staff.

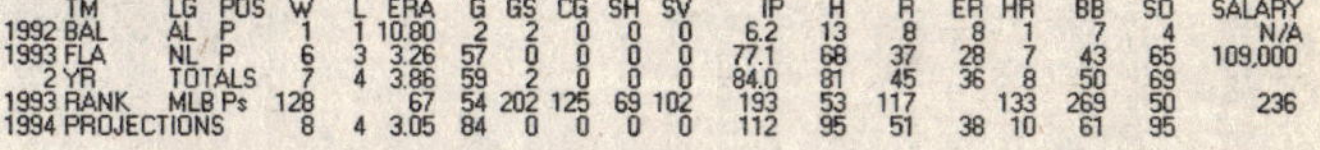

	TM	LG	POS	W	L	ERA	G	GS	CG	SH	SV	IP	H	R	ER	HR	BB	SO	SALARY
1992	BAL	AL	P	1	1	10.80	2	2	0	0	0	6.2	13	8	8	1	7	4	N/A
1993	FLA	NL	P	6	3	3.26	57	0	0	0	0	77.1	68	37	28	7	43	65	109,000
2	YR	TOTALS		7	4	3.86	59	2	0	0	0	84.0	81	45	36	8	50	69	
1993	RANK	MLB Ps		128		67	54	202	125	69	102	193	53	117		133	269	50	236
1994	PROJECTIONS			8	4	3.05	84	0	0	0	0	112	95	51	38	10	61	95	

Dave Magadan — No. 18/3B

Full name: David Joseph Magadan
Bats: L **Throws:** R **HT:** 6–3 **WT:** 205
Born: 9–30–62, Tampa, FL
High school: Jesuit (Tampa, FL)
College: Alabama
Magadan was traded from Seattle for Jeff Darwin.

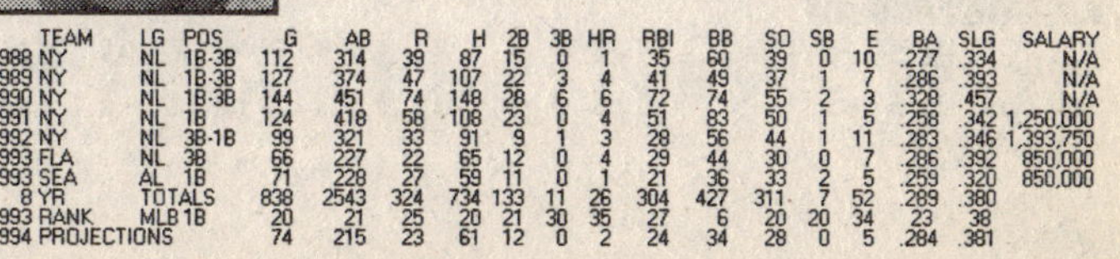

	TEAM	LG	POS	G	AB	R	H	2B	3B	HR	RBI	BB	SO	SB	E	BA	SLG	SALARY
1988	NY	NL	1B-3B	112	314	39	87	15	0	1	35	60	39	0	10	.277	.334	N/A
1989	NY	NL	1B-3B	127	374	47	107	22	3	4	41	49	37	1	7	.286	.393	N/A
1990	NY	NL	1B-3B	144	451	74	148	28	6	6	72	74	55	2	3	.328	.457	N/A
1991	NY	NL	1B	124	418	58	108	23	0	4	51	83	50	1	5	.258	.342	1,250,000
1992	NY	NL	3B-1B	99	321	33	91	9	1	3	28	56	44	1	11	.283	.346	1,393,750
1993	FLA	NL	3B	66	227	22	65	12	0	4	29	44	30	0	7	.286	.392	850,000
1993	SEA	AL	1B	71	228	27	59	11	0	1	21	36	33	2	5	.259	.320	850,000
8	YR	TOTALS		838	2543	324	734	133	11	26	304	427	311	7	52	.289	.380	
1993	RANK	MLB 1B		20	21	25	20	21	30	35	27	6	20	20	34	23	38	
1994	PROJECTIONS			74	215	23	61	12	0	2	24	34	28	0	5	.284	.381	

Bob Natal — No. 13/C

Full name: Robert Marcel Natal
Bats: R **Throws:** R **HT:** 5–11 **WT:** 190
Born: 11–13–65, Long Beach, CA
High school: Hilltop (Chula Vista, CA)
College: California–San Diego
Natal had a .996 fielding percentage at catcher.

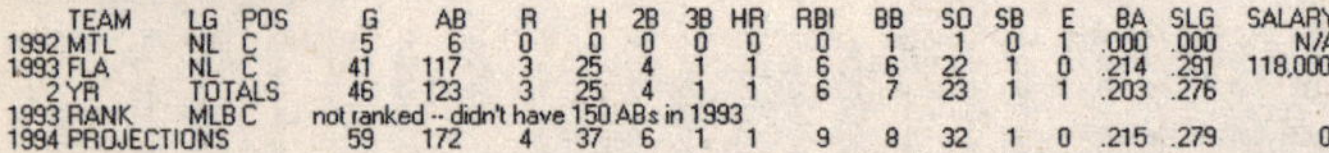

	TEAM	LG	POS	G	AB	R	H	2B	3B	HR	RBI	BB	SO	SB	E	BA	SLG	SALARY
1992	MTL	NL	C	5	6	0	0	0	0	0	0	1	1	0	1	.000	.000	N/A
1993	FLA	NL	C	41	117	3	25	4	1	1	6	6	22	1	0	.214	.291	118,000
2	YR	TOTALS		46	123	3	25	4	1	1	6	7	23	1	1	.203	.276	
1993	RANK	MLB	C	not ranked -- didn't have 150 ABs in 1993														
1994	PROJECTIONS			59	172	4	37	6	1	1	9	8	32	1	0	.215	.279	0

Rich Rodriguez — No. 42/P

Full name: Richard Anthony Rodriguez
Bats: R **Throws:** L **HT:** 6–0 **WT:** 200
Born: 3–1–63, Downey, CA
High school: Pasteje Academy (Mexico C., MX)
Rodriguez arrived in the Gary Sheffield deal. He's logged 60+ games in his last three seasons.

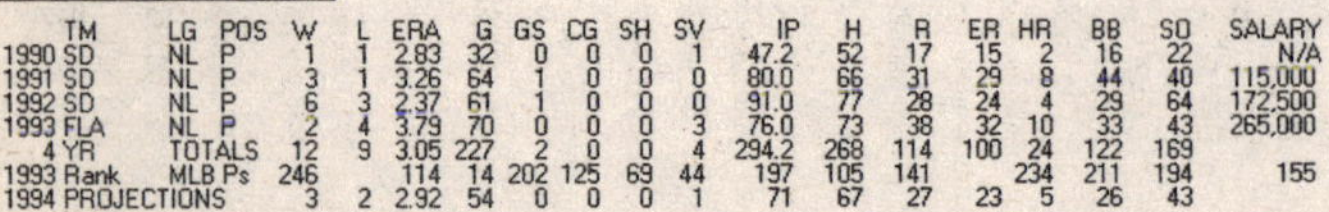

	TM	LG	POS	W	L	ERA	G	GS	CG	SH	SV	IP	H	R	ER	HR	BB	SO	SALARY
1990	SD	NL	P	1	1	2.83	32	0	0	0	1	47.2	52	17	15	2	16	22	N/A
1991	SD	NL	P	3	1	3.26	64	1	0	0	0	80.0	66	31	29	8	44	40	115,000
1992	SD	NL	P	6	3	2.37	61	1	0	0	0	91.0	77	28	24	4	29	64	172,500
1993	FLA	NL	P	2	4	3.79	70	0	0	0	3	76.0	73	38	32	10	33	43	265,000
4	YR	TOTALS		12	9	3.05	227	2	0	0	4	294.2	268	114	100	24	122	169	
1993	Rank	MLB	Ps	246		114	14	202	125	69	44	197	105	141		234	211	194	155
1994	PROJECTIONS			3	2	2.92	54	0	0	0	1	71	67	27	23	5	26	43	

Matt Turner — No. 54/P

Full name: William Matthew Turner
Bats: R **Throws:** R **HT:** 6–5 **WT:** 215
Born: 2–18–67, Lexington, KY
High school: Lafayette (Lexington, KY)
College: Middle Georgia
Turner finished 26 games without recording a save.

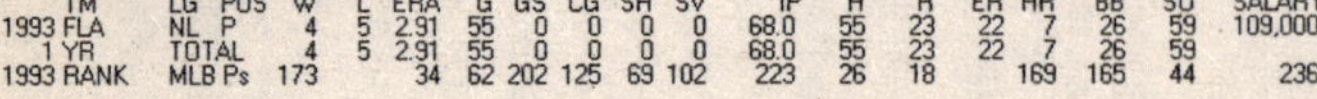

	TM	LG	POS	W	L	ERA	G	GS	CG	SH	SV	IP	H	R	ER	HR	BB	SO	SALARY
1993	FLA	NL	P	4	5	2.91	55	0	0	0	0	68.0	55	23	22	7	26	59	109,000
1	YR	TOTAL		4	5	2.91	55	0	0	0	0	68.0	55	23	22	7	26	59	
1993	RANK	MLB	Ps	173		34	62	202	125	69	102	223	26	18		169	165	44	236

Houston ASTROS

1994 Scouting Report

Hitting: (1993/.267 BA, seventh in NL; 138 HR, eighth in NL)

The Astros' leading hitters are Craig Biggio and Jeff Bagwell. They combined for 41 home runs—not a lot of home runs for the two team leaders in a year when everyone hit home runs. Astrodome or no, this team needs a bona fide power hitter to advance very far. The front office has expected Ken Caminiti to emerge as a slugger, but he hasn't filled that role, and has been mentioned in trade rumors. Houston also lacks a solid bench, but adding infielder Andy Stankiewicz will help.

For a team that plays on artificial turf, the Astros don't have very much speed. Overall, the team was just ninth in the NL in stolen bases.

Pitching: (1993/3.49 ERA, second in NL)

Houston spent heavily for pitching last year, signing Doug Drabek and Greg Swindell. Although they both had mediocre seasons in 1993, Drabek and Swindell are quality pitchers, and at least one of them should have a strong 1994 season. Darryl Kile made the All-Star team, threw a no-hitter vs. the Mets, and should continue to improve. Losing Mark Portugal in free agency will hurt, but prior to 1993, Portugal had not been an exceptional pitcher.

The bullpen is a question. Mitch Williams, acquired from the Phillies, is talented but inconsistent. Domingo Jean, obtained from the Yankees for Xavier Hernandez, may figure in the bullpen or as a fifth starter.

Defense: (1993/.979 pct., seventh in NL)

Catcher Scott Servais, first baseman Jeff Bagwell, and pitcher Doug Drabek are above-average fielders. Andujar Cedeno is a decent fielder at shortstop.

1994 Prospects:

New manager Terry Collins' job is to put some scrap in these laid-back Astros. Houston will benefit from the new divisional format—they had winning records vs. all of their new division rivals, except St. Louis, against whom they were 6–6. And if the Astros get to the playoffs, with pitchers like Kile, Harnisch, Drabek and Swindell, they'd have a chance to beat anybody in the NL in a short series. But they must solve their bullpen problems.

Team Directory

Owner & Chairman: Drayton McLane, Jr. General Mgr.: Bob Watson
Dir. of Minor Lg.Operations: Fred Nelson Dir. of Scouting: Dan O'Brien
Director of P.R.: Rob Matwick

Minor League Affiliates:

Level	Team/League	1993 Record
AAA	Tucson–Pacific Coast	83–60
AA	Jackson–Texas	73–62
A	Osceola–Florida State	56–74
	Asheville–South Atlantic	51–88
	Quad City–Midwest	56–74
	Auburn–New York/Penn.	30–46
Rookie	Gulf Coast Astros–Gulf Coast	35–24

1993 Review

	Home		Away			Home		Away			Home		Away	
vs NL East	W	L	W	L	vs NL Cent.	W	L	W	L	vs NL West	W	L	W	L
Atlanta	2	5	3	3	Chicago	4	2	4	2	Colorado	2	4	0	7
Florida	5	1	4	2	Cincinnati	4	3	3	3	Los Angeles	4	2	5	2
Montreal	3	3	2	4	Pittsburgh	3	3	4	2	San Diego	4	2	4	3
New York	6	0	5	1	St. Louis	4	2	2	4	San Fran.	1	6	2	4
Philadelphia	2	4	3	3										
Total	18	13	17	13		15	10	13	11		11	14	11	16

1993 finish: 85–77 (44–37 home, 41–40 away), third in NL West, 14 games behind

1994 Schedule

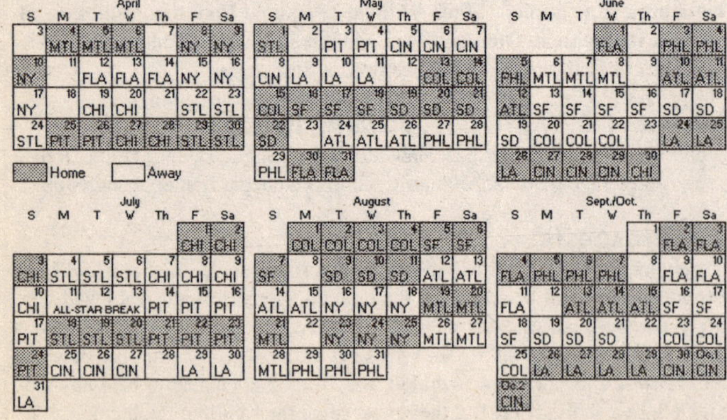

April

S	M	T	W	Th	F	Sa
3	4 MTL	5 MTL	6 MTL	7	8 NY	9 NY
10 NY	11	12 FLA	13 FLA	14 FLA	15 NY	16 NY
17 NY	18	19 CHI	20 CHI	21	22 STL	23 STL
24 STL	25 PIT	26 PIT	27 CHI	28 CHI	29 STL	30 STL

May

S	M	T	W	Th	F	Sa
1 STL	2	3 PIT	4 PIT	5 CIN	6 CIN	7 CIN
8 CIN	9 LA	10 LA	11 LA	12	13 COL	14 COL
15 COL	16 SF	17 SF	18 SF	19 SD	20 SD	21 SD
22 SD	23	24 ATL	25 ATL	26 ATL	27 PHL	28 PHL
29 PHL	30 FLA	31 FLA				

June

S	M	T	W	Th	F	Sa
			1 FLA	2	3 PHL	4 PHL
5 PHL	6 MTL	7 MTL	8 MTL	9	10 ATL	11 ATL
12 ATL	13 SF	14 SF	15 SF	16 SF	17 SD	18 SD
19 SD	20 COL	21 COL	22 COL	23	24 LA	25 LA
26 LA	27 CIN	28 CIN	29 CIN	30 CHI		

Home Away

July

S	M	T	W	Th	F	Sa
					1 CHI	2 CHI
3 CHI	4 STL	5 STL	6 STL	7 CHI	8 CHI	9 CHI
10 CHI	11 ALL-STAR BREAK	12	13	14 PIT	15 PIT	16 PIT
17 PIT	18 STL	19 STL	20 STL	21 PIT	22 PIT	23 PIT
24 PIT	25 CIN	26 CIN	27 CIN	28	29 LA	30 LA
31 LA						

August

S	M	T	W	Th	F	Sa
	1 COL	2 COL	3 COL	4 COL	5 SF	6 SF
7 SF	8	9 SD	10 SD	11 SD	12 ATL	13 ATL
14 ATL	15 ATL	16 NY	17 NY	18 NY	19 MTL	20 MTL
21 MTL	22	23 NY	24 NY	25 NY	26 MTL	27 MTL
28 MTL	29 PHL	30 PHL	31 PHL			

Sept./Oct.

S	M	T	W	Th	F	Sa
				1	2 FLA	3 FLA
4 FLA	5 PHL	6 PHL	7 PHL	8	9 FLA	10 FLA
11 FLA	12	13 ATL	14 ATL	15 ATL	16 SF	17 SF
18 SF	19 SD	20 SD	21 SD	22	23 COL	24 COL
25 COL	26 LA	27 LA	28 LA	29 LA	30 CIN	Oc.1 CIN
Oc.2 CIN						

HOUSTON ASTROS 1994 ROSTER

Manager: Terry Collins
Coaches: Matt Galante, third base coach; Ben Hines, hitting; Mel Stottlemyre, pitching; Ken Henderson, 1B & OF instructor; Julio Linares, bullpen.

No.	PITCHERS	B	T	HT	WT	DOB	BIRTHPLACE	RESIDENCE
	Dougherty, Jim	R	R	6–0	210	3–8–68	Brentwood, NY	Brentwood, NY
15	Drabek, Doug	R	R	6–1	185	7–25–62	Victoria, TX	The Woodlands, TX
46	Edens, Tom	L	R	6–2	188	6–9–61	Ontario, OR	Asotin, WA
	Gallaher, Kevin	R	R	6–3	190	8–1–68	Fairfax, VA	Fairfax, VA
27	Harnisch, Pete	R	R	6–0	207	9–23–66	Commack, NY	Freehold, NJ
	Hudek, John	S	R	6–1	200	8–8–66	Tampa, FL	Orlando, FL
	Jean, Domingo	R	R	6–2	175	1–9–69	San Pedro, DR	San Pedro, DR
59	Jones, Todd	L	R	6–3	200	4–24–68	Marietta, GA	Pell City, AL
57	Kile, Darryl	R	R	6–5	185	12–2–68	Garden Grove, CA	Corona, CA
	Morman, Alvin	L	L	6–3	210	1–6–69	Rockingham, NC	Rockingham, NC
29	Osuna, Al	R	L	6–3	200	8–10–65	Inglewood, CA	Houston, TX
37	Reynolds, Shane	R	R	6–3	210	3–26–68	Bastrop, LA	Monroe, LA
21	Swindell, Greg	R	L	6–3	225	1–2–65	Fort Worth, TX	Houston, TX
53	Williams, Brian	R	R	6–2	195	2–15–69	Lancaster, SC	Columbia, SC
	Williams, Mitch	L	L	6–4	205	11–17–64	Santa Anna, CA	Arlington, TX
No.	**CATCHERS**	**B**	**T**	**HT**	**WT**	**DOB**	**BIRTHPLACE**	**RESIDENCE**
	Eusebio, Tony	R	R	6–2	180	4–27–67	S.Jose de Los Llamos, DR	S. P. de Macoris, DR
9	Servais, Scott	R	R	6–2	195	6–4–67	LaCrosse, WI	Houston, TX
6	Taubensee, Eddie	L	R	6–4	205	10–31–68	Beeville, TX	Longwood, FL
36	Tucker, Scooter	R	R	6–2	205	11–18–66	Greenville, MS	Greenville, MS
No.	**INFIELDERS**	**B**	**T**	**HT**	**WT**	**DOB**	**BIRTHPLACE**	**RESIDENCE**
5	Bagwell, Jeff	R	R	6–0	195	5–27–68	Boston, MA	Houston, TX
7	Biggio, Craig	R	R	5–11	180	12–14–65	Smithtown, NY	Houston, TX
11	Caminiti, Ken	S	R	6–0	200	4–21–63	Hanford, CA	Richmond, TX
10	Cedeno, Andujar	R	R	6–1	168	8–21–69	La Romana, DR	La Romana, DR
3	Donnels, Chris	L	R	6–0	185	4–21–66	Los Angeles, CA	Torrance, CA
2	Miller, Orlando	R	R	6–1	180	1–13–69	Changuinola, Panama	Estafeta, Panama
	Mouton, James	R	R	5–9	175	12–29–68	Denver, CO	Sacramento, CA
	Petagine, Roberto	L	L	6–1	172	6–7–71	Nueva Esporita, VZ	Nueva Esporita, VZ
	Stankiewicz, Andy	R	R	5–9	165	8–10–64	Inglewood, CA	La Habra, CA
No.	**OUTFIELDERS**	**B**	**T**	**HT**	**WT**	**DOB**	**BIRTHPLACE**	**RESIDENCE**
64	Ansley, Willie	R	R	6–2	200	12–15–69	Dallas, TX	Houston, TX
	Castillo, Braulio	R	R	6–0	160	5–13–68	Elias Pina, DR	Santo Domingo, DR
	Felder, Mike	S	R	5–9	175	11–18–62	Vallejo, CA	Richmond, CA
12	Finley, Steve	L	L	6–2	180	3–12–65	Union City, TN	Houston, TX
26	Gonzalez, Luis	L	R	6–2	180	9–3–67	Tampa, FL	Houston, TX
60	Hatcher, Chris	R	R	6–3	220	1–7–69	Anaheim, CA	Carter Lake, IA
62	Hunter, Brian	R	R	6–4	180	3–5–71	Portland, OR	Vancouver, WA
63	Mota, Gary	R	R	6–0	195	10–6–70	Santo Domingo, DR	St. Cloud, FL
	White, Jimmy	L	R	6–1	170	12–1–72	Tampa, FL	Brandon, FL

The Astrodome (53,821, artificial)
Tickets: 713–799–9555
Ticket prices:
- $12 (field box)
- $10 (mezzanine)
- $8 (loge)
- $7 (upper box terrace)
- $6 (upper box)
- $5 (upper reserved)

Field Dimensions (from home plate)
- To left field at foul line, 330 feet
- To center field, 400 feet
- To right field at foul line, 330 feet
- (OF wall–10 feet high)

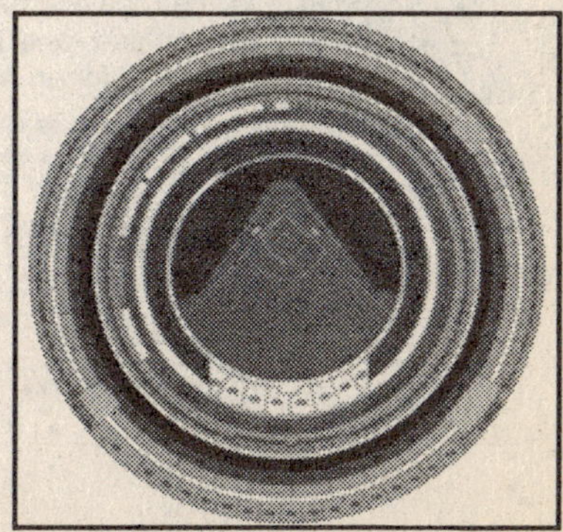

Jeff Bagwell No. 5/1B

Full name: Jeffrey Robert Bagwell
Bats: R **Throws:** R **HT:** 6–0 **WT:** 195
Born: 5–27–68, Boston, MA
High School: Xavier (Middletown, CT)
College: Hartford

Bagwell missed the last 20 games of 1993 with a broken bone in his left hand. He still finished sixth in the NL in batting.

	TEAM	LG	POS	G	AB	R	H	2B	3B	HR	RBI	BB	SO	SB	E	BA	SLG	SALARY
1991	HOU	NL	1B	156	554	79	163	26	4	15	82	75	116	7	12	.294	.437	100,000
1992	HOU	NL	1B	162	586	87	160	34	6	18	96	84	97	10	7	.273	.444	350,000
1993	HOU	NL	1B	142	535	76	171	37	4	20	88	62	73	13	9	.320	.516	655,000
3	YR	TOTALS		460	1675	242	494	97	14	53	266	221	286	30	28	.295	.464	
1993	RANK	MLB	1B	16	12	16	8	4	2	12	11	14	15	3	13	5	8	21
1994	PROJECTIONS			137	528	75	173	40	4	21	90	57	58	15	8	.328	.538	

Craig Biggio No.7/2B

Full Name: Craig Alan Biggio
Bats: R **Throws:** R **HT:** 5–11 **WT:** 180
Born: 12–14–65, Smithtown, NY
High School: Kings Park (NY)
College: Seton Hall

Led the Astros in games, at-bats, runs, hits, doubles, and home runs. His 21 HR was a record for an Astro second baseman.

	TEAM	LG	POS	G	AB	R	H	2B	3B	HR	RBI	BB	SO	SB	E	BA	SLG	SALARY
1988	HOU	NL	C	50	123	14	26	6	1	3	5	7	29	6	3	.211	.350	N/A
1989	HOU	NL	C	134	443	64	114	21	2	13	60	49	64	21	9	.257	.402	N/A
1990	HOU	NL	C	150	555	53	153	24	2	4	42	53	79	25	13	.276	.348	N/A
1991	HOU	NL	C	149	546	79	161	23	4	4	46	53	71	19	11	.295	.374	452,500
1992	HOU	NL	2B	162	613	96	170	32	3	6	39	94	95	38	12	.277	.369	1,375,000
1993	HOU	NL	2B	155	610	98	175	41	5	21	64	77	93	15	14	.287	.474	3,050,000
6	YR	TOTALS		800	2890	404	799	147	17	51	256	333	431	124	62	.276	.392	
1993	RANK	MLB	2B	1	2	3	3	1	7	1	9	3	2	10	6	11	6	5
1994	PROJECTIONS			162	650	105	187	43	4	22	68	82	97	15	14	.288	.468	

Ken Caminiti No. 11/3B

Full Name: Kenneth Gene Caminiti
Bats: S **Throws:** R **HT:** 6–0 **WT:** 200
Born: 4–21–63, Hanford, CA
High School: Leigh (San Jose, CA)
College: San Jose State

Matched his season highs for doubles and home runs, and set a career high for runs with 75. Hit safely in 22 of his last 25 games.

TEAM	LG	POS	G	AB	R	H	2B	3B	HR	RBI	BB	SO	SB	E	BA	SLG	SALARY
1987 HOU	NL	3B	63	203	10	50	7	1	3	23	12	44	0	8	.246	.335	N/A
1988 HOU	NL	3B	30	83	5	15	2	0	1	7	5	18	0	3	.181	.241	N/A
1989 HOU	NL	3B	161	585	71	149	31	3	10	72	51	93	4	22	.255	.369	N/A
1990 HOU	NL	3B	153	541	52	131	20	2	4	51	48	97	9	21	.242	.309	N/A
1991 HOU	NL	3B	152	574	65	145	30	3	13	80	46	85	4	23	.253	.383	665,000
1992 HOU	NL	3B	135	506	68	149	31	2	13	62	44	68	10	11	.294	.441	1,500,000
1993 HOU	NL	3B	143	543	75	142	31	0	13	75	49	88	8	24	.262	.390	3,150,000
7 YR	TOTALS		837	3035	346	781	152	11	57	370	255	493	35	112	.257	.371	
1993 RANK	MLB	3B	12	11	11	13	8	33	14	11	8	7	7	5	23	24	2
1994 PROJECTIONS			119	429	45	107	19	1	6	49	36	76	5	17	.249	.347	

Andujar Cedeno No. 10/SS

Full Name: Andujar Cedeno
Bats: R **Throws:** R **HT:** 6–1 **WT:** 168
Born: 8–21–69, La Romana, DR

1993 was his first full major league season. He hit .346 in June, and hit safely in 20 of 27 games in May. He also showed good power for a player in the Astrodome, with 10 HR at home in 1993.

TEAM	LG	POS	G	AB	R	H	2B	3B	HR	RBI	BB	SO	SB	E	BA	SLG	SALARY
1990 HOU	NL	SS	7	8	0	0	0	0	0	0	0	5	0	1	.000	.000	N/A
1991 HOU	NL	SS	67	251	27	61	13	2	9	36	9	74	4	18	.243	.418	100,000
1992 HOU	NL	SS	71	220	15	38	13	2	2	13	14	71	2	11	.173	.277	132,000
1993 HOU	NL	SS	149	505	69	143	24	4	11	56	48	97	9	25	.283	.412	178,000
4 YR	TOTALS		294	984	111	242	50	8	22	105	71	247	15	55	.246	.38	
1993 RANK	MLB	SS	12	13	10	11	9	9	5	11	14	4	16	4	11	11	23
1994 PROJECTIONS			162	553	75	156	26	4	11	61	52	105	9	27	.282	.403	

Mike Felder   No. 25/OF

Full name: Michael Otis Felder
Bats: S **Throws:** R **HT:** 5–9 **WT:** 175
Born: 11–18–62, Vallejo, CA
High school: J. F. Kennedy (Richmond, CA)
College: Contra Costa (San Pablo, CA)

Felder led the Mariners in triples with 5 during his first season with the team His .211 BA was his worst since 1988.

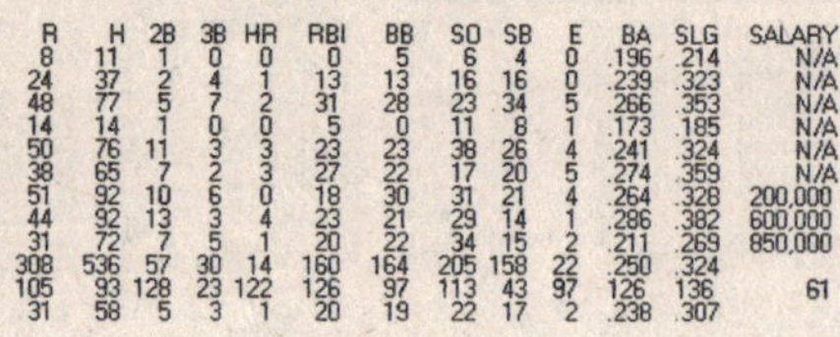

	TEAM	LG	POS	G	AB	R	H	2B	3B	HR	RBI	BB	SO	SB	E	BA	SLG	SALARY
1985	MIL	AL	OF	15	56	8	11	1	0	0	0	5	6	4	0	.196	.214	N/A
1986	MIL	AL	OF	44	155	24	37	2	4	1	13	13	16	16	0	.239	.323	N/A
1987	MIL	AL	OF	108	289	48	77	5	7	2	31	28	23	34	5	.266	.353	N/A
1988	MIL	AL	OF	50	81	14	14	1	0	0	5	0	11	8	1	.173	.185	N/A
1989	MIL	AL	OF	117	315	50	76	11	3	3	23	23	38	26	4	.241	.324	N/A
1990	MIL	AL	OF	121	237	38	65	7	2	3	27	22	17	20	5	.274	.359	N/A
1991	SF	NL	OF	132	348	51	92	10	6	0	18	30	31	21	4	.264	.328	200,000
1992	SF	NL	OF	145	322	44	92	13	3	4	23	21	29	14	1	.286	.382	600,000
1993	SEA	AL	OF	109	342	31	72	7	5	1	20	22	34	15	2	.211	.269	850,000
9	YR	TOTALS		841	2145	308	536	57	30	14	160	164	205	158	22	.250	.324	
1993	RANK	MLB	OF	84	79	105	93	128	23	122	126	97	113	43	97	126	136	61
1994	PROJECTIONS			91	244	31	58	5	3	1	20	19	22	17	2	.238	.307	

Steve Finley   No. 12/OF

Full Name: Steven Allen Finley
Bats: L **Throws:** L **HT:** 6–2 **WT:** 180
Born: 3–12–65, Union City, TN
High School: Paducah Tilghman (KY)
College: Southern Illinois

Finley suffered from Bell's palsy in spring training, which left him unable to close his left eye. He also had a hairline wrist fracture.

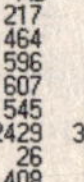
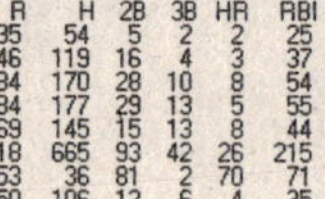
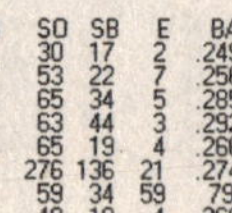
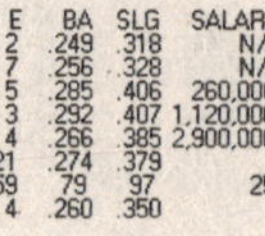

	TEAM	LG	POS	G	AB	R	H	2B	3B	HR	RBI	BB	SO	SB	E	BA	SLG	SALARY
1989	BAL	AL	OF	81	217	35	54	5	2	2	25	15	30	17	2	.249	.318	N/A
1990	BAL	AL	OF	142	464	46	119	16	4	3	37	32	53	22	7	.256	.328	N/A
1991	HOU	NL	OF	159	596	84	170	28	10	8	54	42	65	34	5	.285	.406	260,000
1992	HOU	NL	OF	162	607	84	177	29	13	5	55	58	63	44	3	.292	.407	1,120,000
1993	HOU	NL	OF	142	545	69	145	15	13	8	44	28	65	19	4	.266	.385	2,900,000
5	YR	TOTALS		686	2429	318	665	93	42	26	215	175	276	136	21	.274	.379	
1993	RANK	MLB	OF	34	26	53	36	81	2	70	71	71	59	34	59	79	97	25
1994	PROJECTIONS			121	408	50	106	12	6	4	35	25	49	19	4	.260	.350	

Luis Gonzalez No. 26/OF

Full Name: Luis Emilio Gonzalez
Bats: L **Throws:** R **HT:** 6–2 **WT:** 180
Born: 9–3–67, Tampa, FL
High School: Jefferson (Tampa, FL)
College: South Alabama

Gonzalez hit .327 after the All Star break, and had a 14–game hitting streak from July 8–23. He led the NL in sacrifice flies with 10.

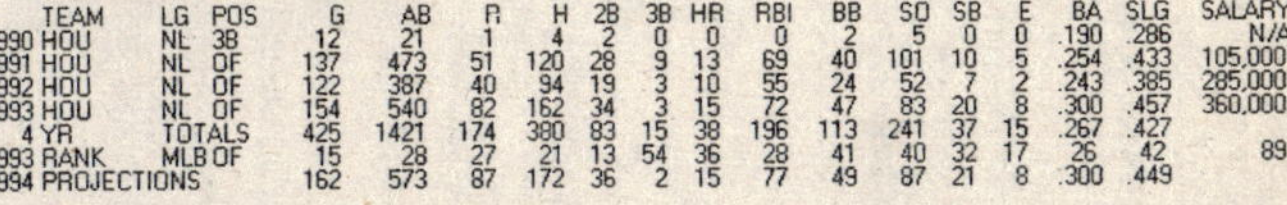

	TEAM	LG	POS	G	AB	R	H	2B	3B	HR	RBI	BB	SO	SB	E	BA	SLG	SALARY
1990	HOU	NL	3B	12	21	1	4	2	0	0	0	2	5	0	0	.190	.286	N/A
1991	HOU	NL	OF	137	473	51	120	28	9	13	69	40	101	10	5	.254	.433	105,000
1992	HOU	NL	OF	122	387	40	94	19	3	10	55	24	52	7	2	.243	.385	285,000
1993	HOU	NL	OF	154	540	82	162	34	3	15	72	47	83	20	8	.300	.457	360,000
4	YR	TOTALS		425	1421	174	380	83	15	38	196	113	241	37	15	.267	.427	
1993	RANK	MLB	OF	15	28	27	21	13	54	36	28	41	40	32	17	26	42	89
1994	PROJECTIONS			162	573	87	172	36	2	15	77	49	87	21	8	.300	.449	

Eddie Taubensee No. 6/C

Full Name: Edward Kenneth Taubensee
Bats: L **Throws:** R **HT:** 6–4 **WT:** 205
Born: 10–31–68, Beeville, TX
High School: Lake Howell (Maitland, FL)

Platooned with Scott Servais at catcher, he started 80 games. He caught 22 of 73 runners attempting to steal. He hit .207 up to May 26, and .270 after.

	TEAM	LG	POS	G	AB	R	H	2B	3B	HR	RBI	BB	SO	SB	E	BA	SLG	SALARY
1991	CLE	AL	C	26	66	5	16	2	1	0	8	5	16	0	2	.242	.303	N/A
1992	HOU	NL	C	104	297	23	66	15	0	5	28	31	78	2	5	.222	.323	122,000
1993	HOU	NL	C	94	288	26	72	11	1	9	42	21	44	1	5	.250	.389	170,000
3	YR	TOTALS		224	651	54	154	28	2	14	78	57	138	3	12	.237	.350	
1993	RANK	MLB	C	25	26	25	25	27	11	19	21	26	23	21	23	27	20	29
1994	PROJECTIONS			116	362	33	90	14	1	12	53	26	53	1	6	.249	.392	

Doug Drabek No. 15/P

Full Name: Douglas Dean Drabek
Bats: R **Throws:** R **HT:** 6–1 **WT:** 185
Born: 7–25–62, Victoria, TX
High School: St. Joseph (Victoria, TX)
College: Houston

1993 was only Drabek's third losing campaign. The Astros scored just 18 runs in the 18 decisions that he lost.

	TM	LG	POS	W	L	ERA	G	GS	CG	SH	SV	IP	H	R	ER	HR	BB	SO	SALARY
1986	NY	AL	P	7	8	4.10	27	21	0	0	0	131.2	126	64	60	13	50	76	N/A
1987	PIT	NL	P	11	12	3.88	29	28	1	1	0	176.1	165	86	76	22	46	120	N/A
1988	PIT	NL	P	15	7	3.08	33	32	3	1	0	219.1	194	83	75	21	50	127	N/A
1989	PIT	NL	P	14	12	2.80	35	34	8	5	0	244.1	215	83	76	21	69	123	N/A
1990	PIT	NL	P	22	6	2.76	33	33	9	3	0	231.1	190	78	71	15	56	131	N/A
1991	PIT	NL	P	15	14	3.07	35	35	5	2	0	234.2	245	92	80	16	62	142	3,350,000
1992	PIT	NL	P	15	11	2.77	34	34	10	4	0	256.2	218	84	79	17	54	177	4,500,000
1993	HOU	NL	P	9	18	3.79	34	34	7	2	0	237.2	242	108	100	18	60	157	4,250,000
8	YR	TOTALS		108	88	3.21	260	251	43	18	0	1732.0	1595	678	617	143	447	1053	
1993	RANK	MLB Ps		87		113	145	12	7	8	102	13	158	93		85	40	123	13
1994	PROJECTIONS			13	13	3.33	34	33	5	1	0	230	227	94	85	18	57	142	

Pete Harnisch No. 27/P

Full Name: Peter Thomas Harnisch
Bats: R **Throws:** R **HT:** 6–0 **WT:** 207
Born: 9–23–66, Commack, NY
High School: Commack (NY)
College: Fordham

Harnisch's four shutouts led the NL. And his 16 wins tied for sixth best in the NL. He threw a one-hitter vs. Chicago on July 10.

	TM	LG	POS	W	L	ERA	G	GS	CG	SH	SV	IP	H	R	ER	HR	BB	SO	SALARY
1988	BAL	AL	P	0	2	5.54	2	2	0	0	0	13.0	13	8	8	1	9	10	N/A
1989	BAL	AL	P	5	9	4.62	18	17	2	0	0	103.1	97	55	53	10	64	70	N/A
1990	BAL	AL	P	11	11	4.34	31	31	3	0	0	188.2	189	96	91	17	86	122	N/A
1991	HOU	NL	P	12	9	2.70	33	33	4	2	0	216.2	169	71	65	14	83	172	250,000
1992	HOU	NL	P	9	10	3.70	34	34	0	0	0	206.2	182	92	85	18	64	164	455,000
1993	HOU	NL	P	16	9	2.98	33	33	5	4	0	217.2	171	84	72	20	79	185	1,825,000
6	YR	TOTALS		53	50	3.56	151	150	14	6	0	946.0	821	406	374	80	385	723	
1993	RANK	MLB Ps		14		42.00	167	30	16	1	102	29	20	46		138	149	49	72
1994	PROJECTIONS			17	9	2.92	36	36	4	3	0	237	186	90	77	21	85	202	

Darryl Kile No. 57/P

Full Name: Darryl Andrew Kile
Bats: R **Throws:** R **HT:** 6–5 **WT:** 185
Born: 12–2–68, Garden Grove, CA
College: Chaffee JC (CA)

Kile was Houston's lone 1993 All-Star. He had a nine-game winning streak from May 31–July 31, and threw a no-hitter against the Mets on September 8.

TM	LG	POS	W	L	ERA	G	GS	CG	SH	SV	IP	H	R	ER	HR	BB	SO	SALARY
1991 HOU	NL	P	7	11	3.69	37	22	0	0	0	153.2	144	81	63	16	84	100	100,000
1992 HOU	NL	P	5	10	3.95	22	22	2	0	0	125.1	124	61	55	8	63	90	190,000
1993 HOU	NL	P	15	8	3.51	32	26	4	2	0	171.2	152	73	67	12	69	141	267,500
3 YR	TOTALS		27	29	3.69	91	70	6	2	0	450.2	420	215	185	36	216	331	
1993 RANK	MLB Ps		21		91.00	175	85	25	8	102	73	55	75		64	184	55	154
1994 PROJECTIONS			17	7	3.46	30	27	5	2	0	177.0	154	70	68	10	64	154	

Greg Swindell No. 21/P

Full Name: Forrest Gregory Swindell
Bats: R **Throws:** L **HT:** 6–3 **WT:** 225
Born: 1–2–65, Fort Worth, TX
High School: Sharpstown (TX)
College: Texas

Swindell was a better pitcher away from the Astrodome; he was 9–4 with a 3.06 ERA on the road, just 3–9 with a 4.90 ERA at home.

TM	LG	POS	W	L	ERA	G	GS	CG	SH	SV	IP	H	R	ER	HR	BB	SO	SALARY
1986 CLE	AL	P	5	2	4.23	9	9	1	0	0	61.2	57	35	29	9	15	46	N/A
1987 CLE	AL	P	3	8	5.10	16	15	4	1	0	102.1	112	62	58	18	37	97	N/A
1988 CLE	AL	P	18	14	3.20	33	33	12	4	0	242.0	234	97	86	18	45	180	N/A
1989 CLE	AL	P	13	6	3.37	28	28	5	2	0	184.1	170	71	69	16	51	129	N/A
1990 CLE	AL	P	12	9	4.4	34	34	3	0	0	214.2	245	110	105	27	47	135	N/A
1991 CLE	AL	P	9	16	3.48	33	33	7	0	0	238	241	112	92	21	31	169	2,025,000
1992 CIN	NL	P	12	8	2.70	31	30	5	3	0	213.2	210	72	64	14	41	138	2,500,000
1993 HOU	NL	P	12	13	4.16	31	30	1	1	0	190.1	215	98	88	24	40	124	3,750,000
8 YR	TOTALS		84	76	3.68	215	212	38	11	0	1447.0	1484	657	591	147	307	1018	
1993 RANK	MLB Ps		43		156	194	58	79	23	102	59	234	158		226	24	130	21
1994 PROJECTIONS			6	7	4.46	18	18	2	0	0	117.0	128	65	58	17	30	89	

Mitch Williams — No. 53/P

Full name: Mitchell Steven Williams
Bats: R **Throws:** R **HT:** 6–2 **WT:** 196
Born: 11–17–64, Santa Ana, CA
High school: Giles (Pearlsburg, VA)
College: Virginia Tech

Williams set a Phillie record with 43 saves, fourth in the NL. He only blew seven save opportunities in the regular season.

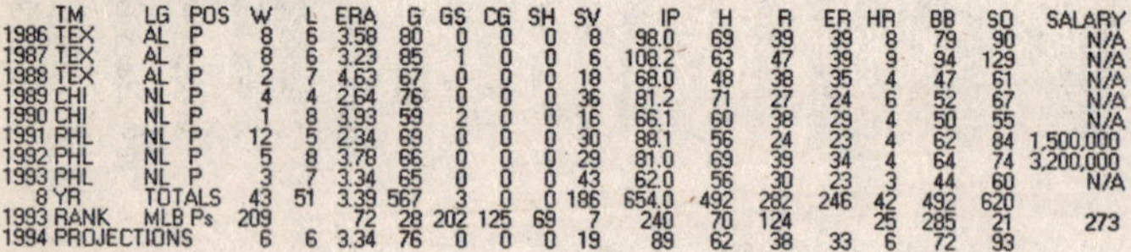

	TM	LG	POS	W	L	ERA	G	GS	CG	SH	SV	IP	H	R	ER	HR	BB	SO	SALARY
1986	TEX	AL	P	8	6	3.58	80	0	0	0	8	98.0	69	39	39	8	79	90	N/A
1987	TEX	AL	P	8	6	3.23	85	1	0	0	6	108.2	63	47	39	9	94	129	N/A
1988	TEX	AL	P	2	7	4.63	67	0	0	0	18	68.0	48	38	35	4	47	61	N/A
1989	CHI	NL	P	4	4	2.64	76	0	0	0	36	81.2	71	27	24	6	52	67	N/A
1990	CHI	NL	P	1	8	3.93	59	2	0	0	16	66.1	60	38	29	4	50	55	N/A
1991	PHL	NL	P	12	5	2.34	69	0	0	0	30	88.1	56	24	23	4	62	84	1,500,000
1992	PHL	NL	P	5	8	3.78	66	0	0	0	29	81.0	69	39	34	4	64	74	3,200,000
1993	PHL	NL	P	3	7	3.34	65	0	0	0	43	62.0	56	30	23	3	44	60	N/A
8	YR	TOTALS		43	51	3.39	567	3	0	0	186	654.0	492	282	246	42	492	620	
1993	RANK	MLB Ps		209		72	28	202	125	69	7	240	70	124		25	285	21	273
1994	PROJECTIONS			6	6	3.34	76	0	0	0	19	89	62	38	33	6	72	93	

Terry Collins — Mgr.

Full Name: Terry Lee Collins
Bats: R **Throws:** R **HT:** 5–8 **WT:** 160
Born: 5–27–49, Midland, MI

Collins was bullpen coach in Pittsburgh for two seasons. He was also a successful manager in the Pittsburgh and LA Dodger systems, winning Pacific Coast League Manager of the Year at Albuquerque in 1988

				REG. SEASON				PLAYOFF			CHAMP. SERIES			WORLD SERIES		
	YEAR	TEAM	LG	W	L	PCT	POS	W	L	PCT	W	L	PCT	W	L	PCT
1ST HALF	1982	VERO BEACH	FLA ST	38	31	.551	2			---			---			---
2ND HALF	1982	VERO BEACH	FLA ST	42	22	.656	1	1	2	.333			---			---
	1983	SAN ANTONIO	TEX	37	38	.493	3	3	2	.600	0	3	.000			---
	1983	ALBUQUERQUE	PCL	42	26	.618	1			---			---			---
1ST HALF	1984	ALBUQUERQUE	PCL	36	36	.500	5			---			---			---
2ND HALF	1984	ALBUQUERQUE	PCL	26	45	.366	5			---			---			---
1ST HALF	1985	ALBUQUERQUE	PCL	36	35	.507	4			---			---			---
2ND HALF	1985	ALBUQUERQUE	PCL	31	41	.431	4			---			---			---
1ST HALF	1986	ALBUQUERQUE	PCL	28	43	.394	5			---			---			---
2ND HALF	1986	ALBUQUERQUE	PCL	26	45	.366	5			---			---			---
1ST HALF	1987	ALBUQUERQUE	PCL	43	27	.614	1			---			---			---
2ND HALF	1987	ALBUQUERQUE	PCL	34	38	.472	4	3	0	1.000	3	1	.750			---
1ST HALF	1988	ALBUQUERQUE	PCL	48	33	.593	2			---			---			---
2ND HALF	1988	ALBUQUERQUE	PCL	48	23	.676	1	0	3	.000			---			---
	1989	BUFFALO	AA	80	62	.563	2			---			---			---
	1990	BUFFALO	AA	85	62	.578	2			---			---			---
	1991	BUFFALO	AA	81	62	.566	1			---	2	3	.400			---
	11	YR	TOTALS	834	736	.531		9	7	0.563	8	9	.471	0	0	---

Kevin Bass — No. 17/OF

Full name: Kevin Charles Bass
Bats: S **Throws:** R **HT:** 6–0 **WT:** 190
Born: 5–12–59, Redwood City, CA
High School: Menlo Park (CA)
Bass is 10th on the all–time Astros list for hits (927) and runs (428).

	TEAM	LG	POS	G	AB	R	H	2B	3B	HR	RBI	BB	SO	SB	E	BA	SLG	SALARY
1988	HOU	NL	OF	157	541	57	138	27	2	14	72	42	65	31	6	.255	.390	N/A
1989	HOU	NL	OF	87	313	42	94	19	4	5	44	29	44	11	3	.300	.435	N/A
1990	SF	NL	OF	61	214	25	54	9	1	7	32	14	26	2	3	.252	.402	N/A
1991	SF	NL	OF	124	361	43	84	10	4	10	40	36	56	7	4	.233	.366	2,000,000
1992	SF/NY	NL	OF	135	402	40	108	23	5	9	39	23	70	14	3	.269	.418	2,000,000
1993	HOU	NL	OF	111	229	31	65	18	0	3	37	26	31	7	1	.284	.402	650,000
12	YR	TOTALS		1378	4341	540	1173	221	39	107	544	305	597	141	39	.270	.413	
1993	RANK	MLB	OF	80	109	105	101	61	124	108	83	78	119	71	113	46	79	71
1994	PROJECTIONS			86	212	27	55	11	1	4	29	15	28	3	2	.259	.382	

Chris Donnels — No. 3/1B–3B

Full Name: Chris Barton Donnels
Bats: L **Throws:** R **HT:** 6–0 **WT:** 185
Born: 4–21–66, Los Angeles, CA
High School: South Torrance (CA)
College: Loyola Marymount
Donnels hit safely in 13 of his last 21 games.

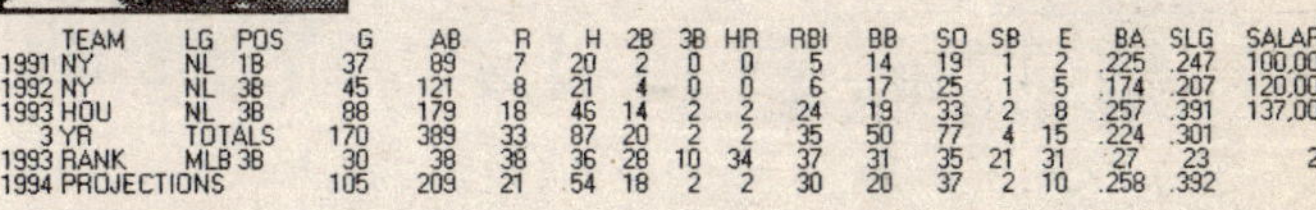

	TEAM	LG	POS	G	AB	R	H	2B	3B	HR	RBI	BB	SO	SB	E	BA	SLG	SALARY
1991	NY	NL	1B	37	89	7	20	2	0	0	5	14	19	1	2	.225	.247	100,000
1992	NY	NL	3B	45	121	8	21	4	0	0	6	17	25	1	5	.174	.207	120,000
1993	HOU	NL	3B	88	179	18	46	14	2	2	24	19	33	2	8	.257	.391	137,000
3	YR	TOTALS		170	389	33	87	20	2	2	35	50	77	4	15	.224	.301	
1993	RANK	MLB	3B	30	38	38	36	28	10	34	37	31	35	21	31	27	23	27
1994	PROJECTIONS			105	209	21	54	18	2	2	30	20	37	2	10	.258	.392	

Tom Edens — No. 46/P

Full Name: Thomas Patrick Edens
Bats: L **Throws:** R **HT:** 6–2 **WT:** 188
Born: 6–9–61, Ontario, OR
High School: Fruitland (ID)
College: Lewis–Clark State College (ID)
Edens retired 27 of 38 first batters.

	TM	LG	POS	W	L	ERA	G	GS	CG	SH	SV	IP	H	R	ER	HR	BB	SO	SALARY
1987	NY	NL	P	0	0	6.75	2	2	0	0	0	8.0	15	6	6	2	4	4	N/A
1990	MIL	AL	P	4	5	4.45	35	6	0	0	2	89.0	89	52	44	8	33	40	N/A
1991	MIN	AL	P	2	2	4.09	8	6	0	0	0	33.0	34	15	15	2	10	19	N/A
1992	MIN	AL	P	6	3	2.83	52	0	0	0	3	76.1	65	26	24	1	36	57	137,500
1993	HOU	NL	P	1	1	3.12	38	0	0	0	0	49	47	17	17	4	19	21	325,000
7	YR	TOTALS		13	11	3.74	135	14	0	0	5	255.1	250	116	106	17	102	141	
1993	RANK	MLB	Ps	not ranked -- didn't have 50 IP in 1993															
1994	PROJECTIONS			1	1	3.6	16	2	0	0	0	30	32	12	12	2	11	14	

Domingo Jean — No. 42/P

Full name: Domingo Jean
Bats: R **Throws:** R **HT:** 6–2 **WT:** 175
Born: 1–9–69, San Pedro, DR
High School: Divina Providencia (San Pedro, DR)
The Yankees were 5–1 when Jean started. His ERA was 3.00 in innings 1–3, 21.61 in innings 7–9.

	TM	LG	POS	W	L	ERA	G	GS	CG	SH	SV	IP	H	R	ER	HR	BB	SO	SALARY
1993	NY	AL	P	1	1	4.46	10	6	0	0	0	40.1	37	20	20	7	19	20	N/A
1 YR		TOTAL		1	1	4.46	10	6	0	0	0	40.1	37	20	20	7	19	20	
1993 RANK		MLB Ps		not ranked -- didn't have 50 IP in 1993															

Todd Jones — No. 59/P

Full name: Todd Barton Jones
Bats: L **Throws:** R **HT:** 6–3 **WT:** 200
Born: 4–24–68, Marietta, GA
High School: Osborne (GA)
College: Jacksonville State (AL)
Jones' ERA was 1.42 at home, 4.91 on the road.

	TM	LG	POS	W	L	ERA	G	GS	CG	SH	SV	IP	H	R	ER	HR	BB	SO	SALARY
1993	HOU	NL	P	1	2	3.13	27	0	0	0	2	37.1	28	14	13	4	15	25	109,000
1 YR		TOTAL		1	2	3.13	27	0	0	0	2	37.1	28	14	13	4	15	25	
1993 RANK		MLB Ps		not ranked -- didn't have 50 IP in 1993															

Al Osuna — No. 29/P

Full Name: Alfonso Osuna, Jr.
Bats: R **Throws:** L **HT:** 6–3 **WT:** 200
Born: 8–10–65, Inglewood, CA
High School: Gahr (Cerritos, CA)
College: Cerritos College (CA) and Stanford
Osuna was scored upon in just two of his last 27 outings.

	TM	LG	POS	W	L	ERA	G	GS	CG	SH	SV	IP	H	R	ER	HR	BB	SO	SALARY
1990	HOU	NL	P	2	0	4.76	12	0	0	0	0	11.1	10	6	6	1	6	6	N/A
1991	HOU	NL	P	7	6	3.42	71	0	0	0	12	81.2	59	39	31	5	46	68	106,000
1992	HOU	NL	P	6	3	4.23	66	0	0	0	0	61.2	52	29	29	8	38	37	235,000
1983	HOU	NL	P	13	9	3.20	44	0	0	0	2	25.1	17	10	9	3	13	21	312,500
4 YR		TOTALS		16	10	3.75	193	0	0	0	14	180	138	84	75	17	103	132	
1993 RANK		MLB Ps		not ranked -- didn't have 50 IP in 1993															
1994 PROJECTIONS				3	2	3.46	42	0	0	0	4	39	28	18	15	3	21	31	

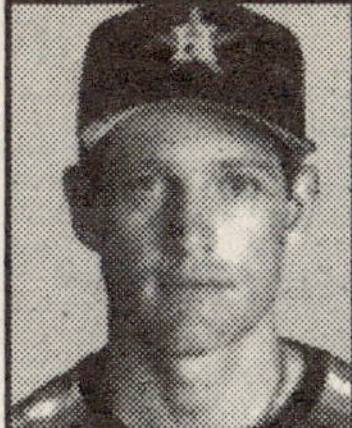

Rick Parker — No. 30/OF

Full name: Richard Alan Parker
Bats: R **Throws:** R **HT:** 6–0 **WT:** 185
Born: 3–20–63, Kansas City, MO
High School: Oak Park (MO)
College: Southwest Missouri State and Texas
Parker split time between AAA Tucson and Houston.

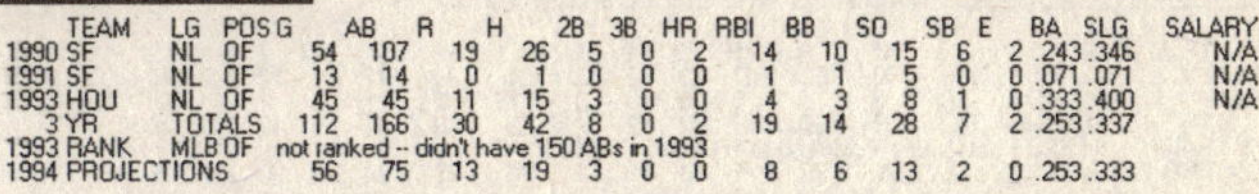

	TEAM	LG	POS	G	AB	R	H	2B	3B	HR	RBI	BB	SO	SB	E	BA	SLG	SALARY
1990	SF	NL	OF	54	107	19	26	5	0	2	14	10	15	6	2	.243	.346	N/A
1991	SF	NL	OF	13	14	0	1	0	0	0	1	1	5	0	0	.071	.071	N/A
1993	HOU	NL	OF	45	45	11	15	3	0	0	4	3	8	1	0	.333	.400	N/A
3 YR		TOTALS		112	166	30	42	8	0	2	19	14	28	7	2	.253	.337	
1993 RANK		MLB OF		not ranked -- didn't have 150 ABs in 1993														
1994 PROJECTIONS				56	75	13	19	3	0	0	8	6	13	2	0	.253	.333	

Shane Reynolds — No. 37/P

Full name: Richard Shane Reynolds
Bats: R **Throws:** R **HT:** 6–3 **WT:** 210
Born: 3–26–68, Bastrop, LA
High School: Ouachita Christian (Monroe, LA)
College: Faulkner State JC (AL) and Texas
Reynolds allowed just 1.4 walks per 9 innings in AAA.

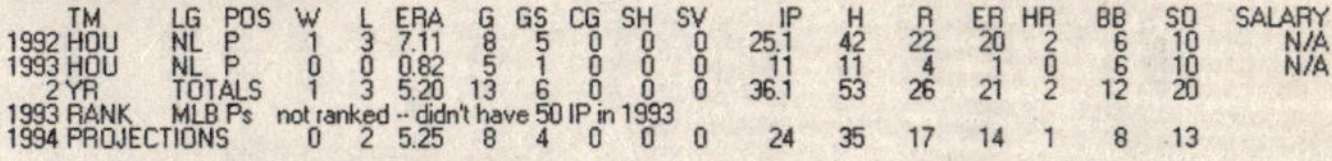

	TM	LG	POS	W	L	ERA	G	GS	CG	SH	SV	IP	H	R	ER	HR	BB	SO	SALARY
1992	HOU	NL	P	1	3	7.11	8	5	0	0	0	25.1	42	22	20	2	6	10	N/A
1993	HOU	NL	P	0	0	0.82	5	1	0	0	0	11	11	4	1	0	6	10	N/A
2 YR		TOTALS		1	3	5.20	13	6	0	0	0	36.1	53	26	21	2	12	20	
1993 RANK		MLB Ps		not ranked -- didn't have 50 IP in 1993															
1994 PROJECTIONS				0	2	5.25	8	4	0	0	0	24	35	17	14	1	8	13	

Scott Servais — No. 9/C

Full Name: Scott Daniel Servais
Bats: R **Throws:** R **HT:** 6–2 **WT:** 195
Born: 6–4–67, LaCrosse, WI
High School: Westby (WI)
College: Creighton
Servais hit 11 HRs in 85 games, including four in June.

	TEAM	LG	POS	G	AB	R	H	2B	3B	HR	RBI	BB	SO	SB	E	BA	SLG	SALARY
1991	HOU	NL	C	16	37	0	6	3	0	0	6	4	8	0	1	.162	.243	100,000
1992	HOU	NL	C	77	205	12	49	9	0	0	15	11	25	0	2	.239	.283	120,000
1993	HOU	NL	C	85	258	24	63	11	0	11	32	22	45	0	2	.244	.415	170,000
3 YR		TOTALS		178	500	36	118	23	0	11	53	37	78	0	5	.236	.348	
1993 RANK		MLB C		28	27	28	25	26	24	12	25	24	1	34	1	29	12	28
1994 PROJECTIONS				108	331	32	82	13	0	14	40	28	57	0	2	.248	.414	

Andy Stankiewicz IF

Full name: Andrew Neal Stankiewicz
Bats: R **Throws:** R **HT:** 5–9 **WT:** 165
Born: 8–10–64, Inglewood, CA
High School: St. Paul (Santa Fe Springs, CA)
College: Pepperdine
A solid infielder who should play more in Houston than he did as a Yankee.

	TEAM	LG	POS	G	AB	R	H	2B	3B	HR	RBI	BB	SO	SB	E	BA	SLG	SALARY
1992	NY	AL	SS	116	400	52	107	22	2	2	25	38	42	9	12	.268	.348	109,000
1993	NY	AL	2B	16	9	5	0	0	0	0	0	1	1	0	0	.000	.000	138,000
2	YR	TOTALS		132	409	57	107	22	2	2	25	39	43	9	12	.262	.340	
1993	RANK	MLB 2B		not ranked -- didn't have 150 ABs in 1993														
1994	PROJECTIONS			88	272	38	71	14	1	1	16	26	28	6	8	.261	.338	

Scooter Tucker No. 36/C

Full name: Eddie Jack Tucker
Bats: R **Throws:** R **HT:** 6–2 **WT:** 205
Born: 11–18–66, Greenville, MS
High school: Washington (Greenville, MS)
College: Delta State (MS)
Tucker started seven of Houston's last 18 games.

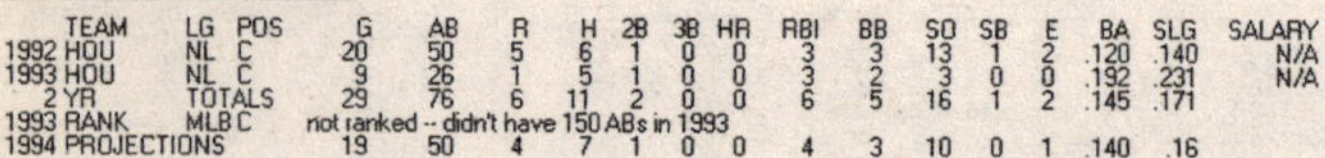

	TEAM	LG	POS	G	AB	R	H	2B	3B	HR	RBI	BB	SO	SB	E	BA	SLG	SALARY
1992	HOU	NL	C	20	50	5	6	1	0	0	3	3	13	1	2	.120	.140	N/A
1993	HOU	NL	C	9	26	1	5	1	0	0	3	2	3	0	0	.192	.231	N/A
2	YR	TOTALS		29	76	6	11	2	0	0	6	5	16	1	2	.145	.171	
1993	RANK	MLB C		not ranked -- didn't have 150 ABs in 1993														
1994	PROJECTIONS			19	50	4	7	1	0	0	4	3	10	0	1	.140	.16	

Brian Williams No. 53/P

Full Name: Brian O'Neal Williams
Bats: R **Throws:** R **HT:** 6–2 **WT:** 195
Born: 2–15–69, Lancaster, SC
High School: Lewisville (Fort Lawn, SC)
College: South Carolina
Williams filled in when Swindell was disabled.

	TM	LG	POS	W	L	ERA	G	GS	CG	SH	SV	IP	H	R	ER	HR	BB	SO	SALARY
1991	HOU	NL	P	0	1	3.75	2	2	0	0	0	12.0	11	5	5	2	4	4	N/A
1992	HOU	NL	P	7	6	3.92	16	16	0	0	0	96.1	92	44	42	10	42	54	109,000
1993	HOU	NL	P	4	4	4.83	42	5	0	0	3	82.0	76	48	44	7	38	56	140,000
3	YR	TOTALS		11	11	4.30	60	23	0	0	3	190.1	179	97	91	19	84	114	
1993	Rank	MLB Ps		173		216	106	188	125	69	44	182	85*	213*		119*	235*	112*	200
(*rank based on amount allowed per inning pitched)																			
1994	PROJECTIONS			3	3	4.29	20	7	0	0	1	63	59	32	30	6	28	38	

Los Angeles DODGERS

1994 Scouting Report

Hitting: (1993/.261, tenth in NL; 130 HR, tenth in NL)

Thanks to Dodger Stadium, that pitchers' paradise, the Dodgers' offense is always better than the stats would indicate. The Dodgers featured two legitimate power threats in 1993 Rookie of the Year Mike Piazza and 1992 Rookie of the Year Eric Karros. Piazza hit 35 HR on the way to a .318 BA with 112 RBI. Karros hit just .247, but slugged 23 HR. Unfortunately, Dodger power began and ended with Piazza and Karros. Darryl Strawberry and Eric Davis were disappointments again in '93. Strawberry's bad back limited him to a 100 AB, .140 campaign. And Davis was finally sent to Detroit.

Pitching: (1993/3.50 ERA, third in NL)

The Dodger starting rotation includes Orel Hershiser, Tom Candiotti, Kevin Gross, Ramon Martinez, and Pedro Astacio. Astacio led the team with 14 wins, while Hershiser, coming back from arm woes, had a team-high five complete games on his way to a 12–14 campaign (3.59 ERA).

Jim Gott (2.32 ERA) is the closer for the Dodgers. He saved 25 games in 62 appearances. Roger McDowell was effective out of the bullpen (54 appearances, 2.25 ERA), though. Omar Daal (47 appearances) had a 5.09 ERA and Todd Worrell had a 6.05 ERA in 35 appearances.

Defense: (1993/.979 pct., eighth in NL)

Brett Butler handled 375 chances without an error. His 1.000 fielding percentage ranked first among NL outfielders.

1994 Prospects:

The Dodgers will be stronger in '94 than in '93. Adding Delino DeShields will bolster the Dodger infield. Any contribution from Darryl Strawberry—if he stays on the team—will be an improvement over last year's dismal performance. Unfortunately, Los Angeles doesn't look like one of baseball's top teams. They don't have the overall talent of the Giants, Braves, and Phillies, or even the Houston Astros. Their pitching and defense are fine, but they need Strawberry or someone else to step up and drive in runs along with Karros and Piazza. Los Angeles finished 22 games behind the Giants in '93, and don't figure to make up those games in '94.

Team Directory

Chairman & President: Peter O'Malley
General Mgr.: Fred Claire
Dir., Minor League Operations: Charlie Blaney
Director, Scouting: Terry Reynolds
Director of P.R.: Jay Lucas
Traveling Secretary: Bill DeLary

Minor League Affiliates:

Level	Team/League	1993 Record
AAA	Albuquerque–Pacific Coast	71–72
AA	San Antonio–Texas	58–76
A	Bakersfield–California	42–94
	Vero Beach/Florida State	56–77
	Yakima–Northwest	30–46
Rookie	Great Falls–Pioneer	37–35
	Santo Domingo–Dominican Summer	39–31

1993 Review

	Home		Away			Home		Away			Home		Away	
vs NL East	W	L	W	L	vs NL Cent.	W	L	W	L	vs NL West	W	L	W	L
Atlanta	3	3	2	5	Chicago	3	3	2	4	Colorado	3	4	3	3
Florida	3	3	4	2	Cincinnati	4	2	4	3	San Diego	5	1	4	3
Montreal	4	2	2	4	Houston	2	5	2	4	S. Francisco	3	4	4	2
New York	4	2	4	2	Pittsburgh	5	1	3	3					
Philadelphia	1	5	1	5	St. Louis	1	5	5	1					
Total	15	15	13	18		15	16	16	15		11	9	11	8

1993 finish: 81–81 (41–40 home, 40–41 away), fourth in NL West, 23 games behind

1994 Schedule

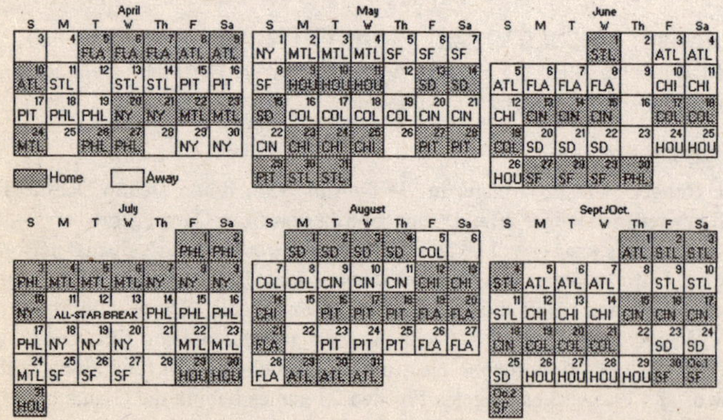

April

S	M	T	W	Th	F	Sa
3	4	5 FLA	6 FLA	7 FLA	8 ATL	9 ATL
10 ATL	11 STL	12	13 STL	14 STL	15 PIT	16 PIT
17 PIT	18 PHL	19 PHL	20 NY	21 NY	22 MTL	23 MTL
24 MTL	25	26 PHL	27 PHL	28	29 NY	30 NY

Home Away

May

S	M	T	W	Th	F	Sa
1 NY	2 MTL	3 MTL	4 MTL	5 SF	6 SF	7 SF
8 SF	9 HOU	10 HOU	11 HOU	12	13 SD	14 SD
15 SD	16 COL	17 COL	18 COL	19 COL	20 CIN	21 CIN
22 CIN	23 CHI	24 CHI	25 CHI	26	27 PIT	28 PIT
29 PIT	30 STL	31 STL				

June

S	M	T	W	Th	F	Sa
			1 STL	2	3 ATL	4 ATL
5 ATL	6 FLA	7 FLA	8 FLA	9	10 CHI	11 CHI
12 CHI	13 CIN	14 CIN	15 CIN	16	17 COL	18 COL
19 COL	20 SD	21 SD	22 SD	23	24 HOU	25 HOU
26 HOU	27 SF	28 SF	29 SF	30 PHL		

July

S	M	T	W	Th	F	Sa
					1 PHL	2 PHL
3 PHL	4 MTL	5 MTL	6 MTL	7 NY	8 NY	9 NY
10 NY	11 ALL-STAR BREAK	12	13	14 PHL	15 PHL	16 PHL
17 PHL	18 NY	19 NY	20 NY	21	22 MTL	23 MTL
24 MTL	25 SF	26 SF	27 SF	28	29 HOU	30 HOU
31 HOU						

August

S	M	T	W	Th	F	Sa
	1 SD	2 SD	3 SD	4 SD	5 COL	6
7 COL	8 COL	9 CIN	10 CIN	11 CIN	12 CHI	13 CHI
14 CHI	15	16 PIT	17 PIT	18 PIT	19 FLA	20 FLA
21 FLA	22	23 PIT	24 PIT	25 PIT	26 FLA	27 FLA
28 FLA	29 ATL	30 ATL	31 ATL			

Sept./Oct.

S	M	T	W	Th	F	Sa
				1 ATL	2 STL	3 STL
4 STL	5 ATL	6 ATL	7 ATL	8	9 STL	10 STL
11 STL	12 CHI	13 CHI	14 CHI	15 CIN	16 CIN	17 CIN
18 CIN	19 COL	20 COL	21 COL	22	23 SD	24 SD
25 SD	26 HOU	27 HOU	28 HOU	29 HOU	30 SF	Oct.1 SF
Oct.2 SF						

LOS ANGELES DODGERS 1994 ROSTER

MANAGER: Tom Lasorda (2)
COACHES: Joe Amalfitano (8), Mark Cresse (58), Joe Ferguson (13), Ben Hines (37), Ron Perranoski (16)

No.	PITCHERS	B	T	HT	WT	DOB	BIRTHPLACE	RESIDENCE
56	Astacio, Pedro	R	R	6–2	195	11–28–69	Hato Mayor, DR	Miami, FL
49	Candiotti, Tom	R	R	6–2	228	8–31–57	Walnut Creek, CA	Danville, CA
54	Daal, Omar	L	L	6–3	175	3–1–72	Maracaibo, VZ	Valencia, VZ
60	DeSilva, John	R	R	6–0	193	9–30–67	Fort Bragg, CA	Fort Bragg, CA
35	Gott, Jim	R	R	6–4	229	8–3–59	Hollywood, CA	Altadena, CA
46	Gross, Kevin	R	R	6–5	227	6–8–61	Downey, CA	Claremont, CA
57	Gross, Kip	R	R	6–2	194	8–24–64	Scottsbluff, NE	Gering, NE
63	Hansell, Greg	R	R	6–5	213	3–12–71	Bellflower, CA	La Palma, CA
55	Hershiser, Orel	R	R	6–3	198	9–16–58	Buffalo, NY	Pasadena, CA
48	Martinez, Ramon	L	R	6–4	176	4–22–68	Santo Domingo, DR	Santo Domingo, DR
17	McDowell, Roger	R	R	6–1	197	12–21–60	Cincinnati, OH	Stuart, FL
	Parra, Jose	R	R	5–11	160	11–28–72	Jacagua, DR	Santiago, DR
	Rodriguez, Felix	R	R	6–1	170	12–5–72	Montecristy, DR	Montecristy, DR
36	Trlicek, Rick	R	R	6–3	200	4–26–69	Houston, TX	Katy, TX
	VanRyn, Ben	L	L	6–5	185	8–9–71	Fort Wayne, IN	Jenison, MI
	Williams, Todd	R	R	6–3	185	2–13–71	Syracuse, NY	Syracuse, NY
	Wilson, Larry							
50	Wilson, Steve	L	L	6–4	224	12–13–64	Victoria, BC	N. Delta, BC
38	Worrell, Todd	R	R	6–5	222	9–28–59	Arcadia, CA	St. Louis, MO
No.	**CATCHERS**	**B**	**T**	**HT**	**WT**	**DOB**	**BIRTHPLACE**	**RESIDENCE**
	Brooks, Jerry	R	R	6–0	195	3–23–67	Syracuse, NY	Syracuse, NY
41	Hernandez, Carlos	R	R	5–11	218	5–24–67	Bolivar, VZ	S.M. Caracas, VZ
31	Piazza, Mike	R	R	6–3	197	9–4–68	Norristown, PA	Valley Forge, PA
No.	**INFIELDERS**	**B**	**T**	**HT**	**WT**	**DOB**	**BIRTHPLACE**	**RESIDENCE**
21	Bournigal, Rafael	R	R	5–11	165	5–12–66	Azusa, DR	Lakeland, FL
51	Busch, Mike	R	R	6–5	241	7–7–68	Davenport, IA	Houston, TX
	DeShields, Delino	L	R	6–1	175	1–15–69	Seaford, DE	West Palm Beach, FL
5	Hansen, Dave	L	R	6–0	195	11–24–68	Long Beach, CA	Long Beach, CA
23	Karros, Eric	R	R	6–4	213	11–4–67	Hackensack, NJ	Manhattan Bch, CA
30	Offerman, Jose	S	R	6–0	165	11–8–68	S.P. de Macoris, DR	S.P. de Macoris, DR
	Pye, Eddie	R	R	5–10	175	2–13–67	Columbia, TN	Columbia, TN
	Treadway, Jeff	L	R	6–0	185	1–22–63	Columbus, GA	Columbus, GA
25	Wallach, Tim	R	R	6–3	202	9–14–57	Huntington Park, CA	Yorba Linda, CA
No.	**OUTFIELDERS**	**B**	**T**	**HT**	**WT**	**DOB**	**BIRTHPLACE**	**RESIDENCE**
7	Ashley, Billy	R	R	6–7	227	7–11–70	Taylor, MI	Belleville, MI
22	Butler, Brett	L	L	5–10	161	6–15–57	Los Angeles, CA	Atlanta, GA
47	Goodwin, Tom	L	R	6–1	170	7–27–68	Fresno, CA	Fresno, CA
	Ingram, Garey	R	R	5–11	178	7–25–70	Columbus, GA	Columbus, GA
43	Mondesi, Raul	R	R	5–11	202	3–12–71	San Cristobal, DR	New York, NY
26	Rodriguez, Henry	L	L	6–1	200	11–8–67	Santo Domingo, DR	New York, NY
28	Snyder, Cory	R	R	6–3	206	11–11–62	Inglewood, CA	Laguna Hills, CA
44	Strawberry, Darryl	L	L	6–6	215	3–12–62	Los Angeles, CA	Los Angeles, CA
20	Webster, Mitch	S	L	6–1	191	5–16–59	Larned, KS	Great Bend, KS

Dodger Stadium (56,000, grass)
1000 Elysian Park Ave.
Los Angeles, CA 90012
Tickets: 213–224–1400
Ticket prices:
$15 (dugout and club level)
$13 (box seats)
$9 (reserved seats)
$6 (top deck and pavilion)
$3 (general adm., youth 12 & under)
Field Dimensions (from home plate)
To left field at foul line, 330 feet
To center field, 395 feet
To right field at foul line, 330 feet
(OF wall is 8 feet high)

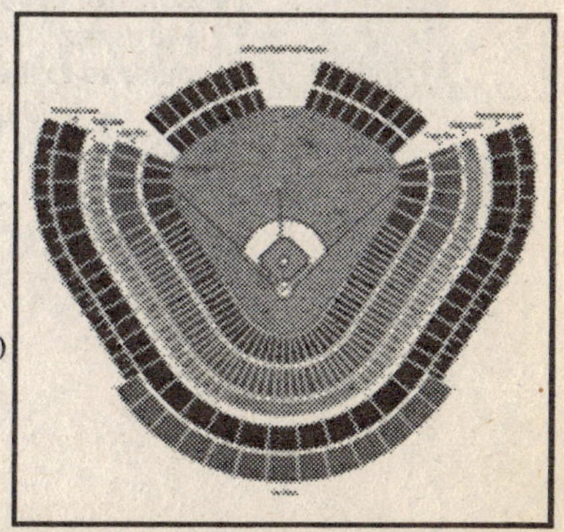

Brett Butler No.22/OF

Full name: Brett Morgan Butler
Bats: L **Throws:** L **HT:** 5–10 **WT:** 161
Born: 6–15–57, Los Angeles, CA
High school: Libertyville (IL)
College: SE Oklahoma St. and Arizona State

Butler reached base 272 times in 1993, the fifth highest total in the NL.

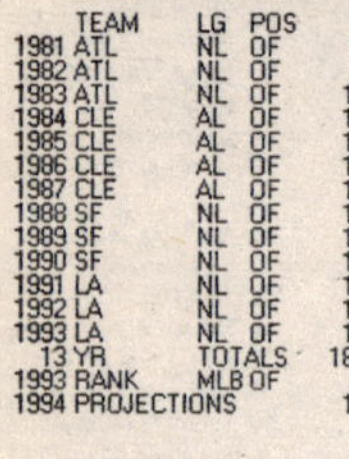
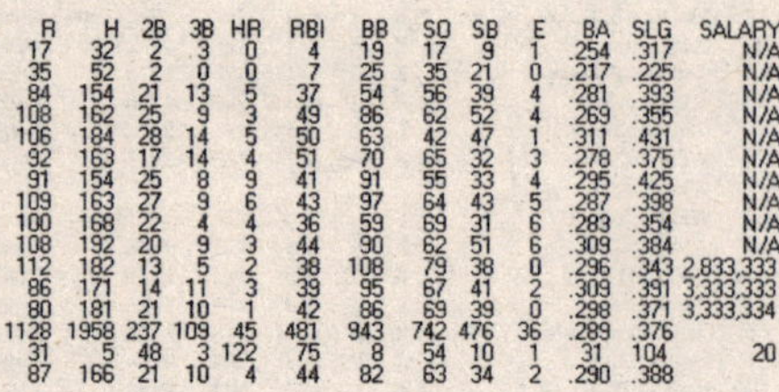

	TEAM	LG	POS	G	AB	R	H	2B	3B	HR	RBI	BB	SO	SB	E	BA	SLG	SALARY
1981	ATL	NL	OF	40	126	17	32	2	3	0	4	19	17	9	1	.254	.317	N/A
1982	ATL	NL	OF	89	240	35	52	2	0	0	7	25	35	21	0	.217	.225	N/A
1983	ATL	NL	OF	151	549	84	154	21	13	5	37	54	56	39	4	.281	.393	N/A
1984	CLE	AL	OF	159	602	108	162	25	9	3	49	86	62	52	4	.269	.355	N/A
1985	CLE	AL	OF	152	591	106	184	28	14	5	50	63	42	47	1	.311	.431	N/A
1986	CLE	AL	OF	161	587	92	163	17	14	4	51	70	65	32	3	.278	.375	N/A
1987	CLE	AL	OF	137	522	91	154	25	8	9	41	91	55	33	4	.295	.425	N/A
1988	SF	NL	OF	157	568	109	163	27	9	6	43	97	64	43	5	.287	.398	N/A
1989	SF	NL	OF	154	594	100	168	22	4	4	36	59	69	31	6	.283	.354	N/A
1990	SF	NL	OF	160	622	108	192	20	9	3	44	90	62	51	6	.309	.384	N/A
1991	LA	NL	OF	161	615	112	182	13	5	2	38	108	79	38	0	.296	.343	2,833,333
1992	LA	NL	OF	157	553	86	171	14	11	3	39	95	67	41	2	.309	.391	3,333,333
1993	LA	NL	OF	156	607	80	181	21	10	1	42	86	69	39	0	.298	.371	3,333,334
13	YR	TOTALS		1834	6776	1128	1958	237	109	45	481	943	742	476	36	.289	.376	
1993	RANK	MLB	OF	11	6	31	5	48	3	122	75	8	54	10	1	31	104	20
1994	PROJECTIONS			151	572	87	166	21	10	4	44	82	63	34	2	.290	.388	

Delino DeShields 2B

Full name: Delino Lamont DeShields
Bats: L **Throws:** R **HT:** 6–1 **WT:** 175
Born: 1–15–69, Seaford, DE
High school: Seaford (DE)

DeShields was acquired during the off-season from Montreal in exchange for Pedro Martinez. DeShields will add speed and defense to the Dodger infield.

	TEAM	LG	POS	G	AB	R	H	2B	3B	HR	RBI	BB	SO	SB	E	BA	SLG	SALARY
1990	MTL	NL	2B	129	499	69	144	28	6	4	45	66	96	42	12	.289	.393	N/A
1991	MTL	NL	2B	151	563	83	134	15	4	10	51	95	151	56	27	.238	.332	215,000
1992	MTL	NL	2B	135	530	82	155	19	8	7	56	54	108	46	15	.292	.398	302,500
1993	MTL	NL	2B	123	481	75	142	17	7	2	29	72	64	43	11	.295	.372	1,537,500
4	YR	TOTALS		538	2073	309	575	79	25	23	181	287	419	187	65	.277	.373	
1993	RANK	MLB	2B	19	15	10	10	25	3	30	32	4	16	2	24	7	22	11
1994	PROJECTIONS			129	503	75	147	21	7	4	43	64	89	43	12	.292	.388	

Eric Karros No.23/1B

Full name: Eric Peter Karros
Bats: R **Throws:** R **HT:** 6–4 **WT:** 213
Born: 11–4–67, Hackensack, NJ
High school: Patrick Henry (San Diego, CA)
College: UCLA

Karros is the first Dodger in history to hit 20 or more HR in his first two seasons.

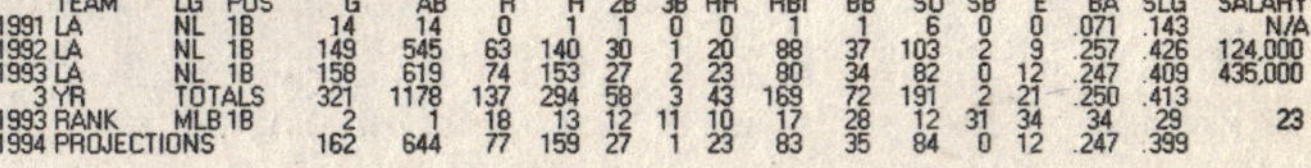

	TEAM	LG	POS	G	AB	R	H	2B	3B	HR	RBI	BB	SO	SB	E	BA	SLG	SALARY
1991	LA	NL	1B	14	14	0	1	1	0	0	1	1	6	0	0	.071	.143	N/A
1992	LA	NL	1B	149	545	63	140	30	1	20	88	37	103	2	9	.257	.426	124,000
1993	LA	NL	1B	158	619	74	153	27	2	23	80	34	82	0	12	.247	.409	435,000
3	YR	TOTALS		321	1178	137	294	58	3	43	169	72	191	2	21	.250	.413	
1993	RANK	MLB	1B	2	1	18	13	12	11	10	17	28	12	31	34	34	29	23
1994	PROJECTIONS			162	644	77	159	27	1	23	83	35	84	0	12	.247	.399	

Jose Offerman No. 30/SS

Full name: Jose Antonio Offerman
Bats: S **Throws:** R **HT:** 6–0 **WT:** 165
Born: 11–8–68, S.P. de Macoris, DR
College: Biblico Cristiano (DR)

Offerman batted .326 at Dodger Stadium and hit .308 with runners in scoring position. He set the Dodger record with 33 sacrifices in 1993.

	TEAM	LG	POS	G	AB	R	H	2B	3B	HR	RBI	BB	SO	SB	E	BA	SLG	SALARY
1990	LA	NL	SS	29	58	7	9	0	0	1	7	4	14	1	4	.155	.207	N/A
1991	LA	NL	SS	52	113	10	22	2	0	0	3	25	32	3	10	.195	.212	115,000
1992	LA	NL	SS	149	534	67	139	20	8	1	30	57	98	23	42	.260	.333	135,000
1993	LA	NL	SS	158	590	77	159	21	6	1	62	71	75	30	37	.269	.331	300,000
4	YR	TOTALS		388	1295	161	329	43	14	3	102	157	219	57	93	.254	.316	
1993	RANK	MLB	SS	5	5	5	5	13	4	31	7	5	9	1	1	20	25	18
1994	PROJECTIONS			162	616	80	167	22	5	0	63	74	76	31	38	.271	.323	

Mike Piazza — No. 31/C

Full name: Michael Joseph Piazza
Bats: R **Throws:** R **HT:** 6–3 **WT:** 197
Born: 9–4–68, Norristown, PA
High school: Phoenixville Area (PA)
College: Miami Dade–North Community

NL Rookie of the Year Piazza rewrote the Dodger record books for rookies with 35 HR and 112 RBI.

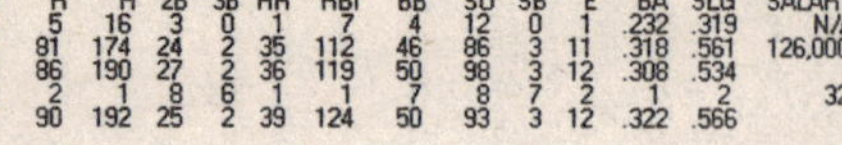

	TEAM	LG	POS	G	AB	R	H	2B	3B	HR	RBI	BB	SO	SB	E	BA	SLG	SALARY
1992	LA	NL	C	21	69	5	16	3	0	1	7	4	12	0	1	.232	.319	N/A
1993	LA	NL	C	149	547	81	174	24	2	35	112	46	86	3	11	.318	.561	126,000
2	YR	TOTALS		170	616	86	190	27	2	36	119	50	98	3	12	.308	.534	
1993	RANK	MLB	C	1	1	2	1	8	6	1	1	7	8	7	2	1	2	32
1994	PROJECTIONS			162	597	90	192	25	2	39	124	50	93	3	12	.322	.566	

Cory Snyder — No. 28/OF

Full name: James Cory Snyder
Bats: R **Throws:** R **HT:** 6–3 **WT:** 206
Born: 11–11–62, Inglewood, CA
High school: Canyon (Canyon Country, CA)
College: Brigham Young

Snyder's 137 hits were his best total since 1987 with Cleveland. He had 14 outfield assists, third best in the NL.

	TEAM	LG	POS	G	AB	R	H	2B	3B	HR	RBI	BB	SO	SB	E	BA	SLG	SALARY
1986	CLE	AL	OF-SS	103	416	58	113	21	1	24	69	16	123	2	10	.272	.500	N/A
1987	CLE	AL	OF-SS	157	577	74	136	24	2	33	82	31	166	5	15	.236	.456	N/A
1988	CLE	AL	OF	142	511	71	139	24	3	26	75	42	101	5	5	.272	.483	N/A
1989	CLE	AL	OF-SS	132	489	49	105	17	0	18	59	23	134	6	1	.215	.36	N/A
1990	CLE	AL	OF-SS	123	438	46	102	27	3	14	55	21	118	1	7	.233	.404	N/A
1991	CHI-TOR	AL	OF	71	166	14	29	4	1	3	17	9	60	0	3	.175	.265	N/A
1992	SF	NL	OF-1B	124	390	48	105	22	2	14	57	23	96	4	6	.269	.444	135,000
1993	LA	NL	OF	143	516	61	137	33	1	11	56	47	147	4	9	.266	.397	1,500,000
8	YR	TOTALS		995	3503	421	866	172	13	143	470	212	945	27	56	.247	.426	
1993	RANK	MLB	OF	32	37	67	44	15	97	55	52	41	2	85	10	80	85	48
1994	PROJECTIONS			132	481	52	114	25	1	14	56	30	133	3	5	.237	.387	

Darryl Strawberry No. 44/OF

Full name: Darryl Eugene Strawberry
Bats: L **Throws:** L **HT:** 6–6 **WT:** 215
Born: 3–12–62, Los Angeles, CA
High school: Crenshaw (Los Angeles, CA)
Veteran Strawberry played in a career low 32 games due to injuries as he struggled to return to his previous All-Star form.

	TEAM	LG	POS	G	AB	R	H	2B	3B	HR	RBI	BB	SO	SB	E	BA	SLG	SALARY
1983	NY	NL	OF	122	420	63	108	15	7	26	74	47	128	19	4	.257	.512	N/A
1984	NY	NL	OF	147	522	75	131	27	4	26	97	75	131	27	6	.251	.467	N/A
1985	NY	NL	OF	111	393	78	109	15	4	29	79	73	96	26	2	.277	.557	N/A
1986	NY	NL	OF	136	475	76	123	27	5	27	93	72	141	28	6	.259	.507	N/A
1987	NY	NL	OF	154	532	108	151	32	5	39	104	97	122	36	8	.284	.583	N/A
1988	NY	NL	OF	153	543	101	146	27	3	39	101	85	127	29	9	.269	.545	N/A
1989	NY	NL	OF	134	476	69	107	26	1	29	77	61	105	11	8	.225	.466	N/A
1990	NY	NL	OF	152	542	92	150	18	1	37	108	70	110	15	3	.277	.518	N/A
1991	LA	NL	OF	139	505	86	134	22	4	28	99	75	125	10	5	.265	.491	3,800,000
1992	LA	NL	OF	43	156	20	37	8	0	5	25	19	34	3	1	.237	.385	4,050,000
1993	LA	NL	OF	32	100	12	14	2	0	5	12	16	19	1	4	.140	.310	3,800,000
11	YR	TOTALS		1323	4664	780	1210	219	34	290	869	690	1138	205	56	.259	.508	
1993	RANK	MLB	OF	not ranked -- didn't have 150 ABs in 1993														
1994	PROJECTIONS			69	244	33	52	12	0	13	38	32	52	5	4	.213	.426	

Tim Wallach No. 25/3B

Full name: Timothy Charles Wallach
Bats: R **Throws:** R **HT:** 6–3 **WT:** 202
Born: 9–14–57, Huntington Park, CA
High school: University (Irvine, CA)
College: Saddleback JC and Cal St.–Fullerton
In his first season in LA, Wallach posted a career-low .222 BA. His 106 hits marked his tenth straight season over 100.

	TEAM	LG	POS	G	AB	R	H	2B	3B	HR	RBI	BB	SO	SB	E	BA	SLG	SALARY
1980	MTL	NL	OF-1B	5	11	1	2	0	0	1	2	1	5	0	0	.182	.455	N/A
1981	MTL	NL	OF-1B	71	212	19	50	9	1	4	13	15	37	0	1	.236	.344	N/A
1982	MTL	NL	3B-OF	158	596	89	160	31	3	28	97	36	81	6	23	.268	.471	N/A
1983	MTL	NL	3B	156	581	54	156	33	3	19	70	55	97	0	19	.269	.434	N/A
1984	MTL	NL	3B-SS	160	582	55	143	25	4	18	72	50	101	3	21	.246	.395	N/A
1985	MTL	NL	3B	155	569	70	148	36	3	22	81	38	79	9	18	.260	.450	N/A
1986	MTL	NL	3B	134	480	50	112	22	1	18	71	44	72	8	16	.233	.396	N/A
1987	MTL	NL	3B-P	153	593	89	177	42	4	26	123	37	98	9	21	.298	.514	N/A
1988	MTL	NL	3B-2B	159	592	52	152	32	5	12	69	38	88	2	18	.257	.389	N/A
1989	MTL	NL	3B-P	154	573	76	159	42	0	13	77	58	81	3	18	.277	.419	N/A
1990	MTL	NL	3B	161	626	69	185	37	5	21	98	42	80	6	21	.296	.471	N/A
1991	MTL	NL	3B	151	577	60	130	22	1	13	73	50	100	2	14	.225	.334	1,906,500
1992	MTL	NL	3B-1B	150	537	53	120	29	1	9	59	50	90	2	15	.223	.331	1,906,500
1993	LA	NL	3B	133	477	42	106	19	1	12	62	32	70	0	15	.222	.342	3,362,500
14	YR	TOTALS		1900	7006	779	1800	379	32	216	967	546	1079	50	220	.257	.413	
1993	RANK	MLB	3B	17	17	22	20	22	21	15	16	21	17	38	14	38	37	1
1994	PROJECTIONS			69	233	20	52	9	0	5	25	16	37	0	5	.223	.343	

Pedro Astacio — No. 56/P

Full name: Pedro Julio Astacio
Bats: R **Throws:** R **HT:** 6–2 **WT:** 195
Born: 11–28–69, Hato Mayor, DR
High school: Pilar Rondon (DR)

Astacio led the Dodgers staff with 14 wins in his first full season, and he held opponents to 2 ER or less in 17 of his 31 starts. The Dodgers scored just 22 runs in his 9 losses.

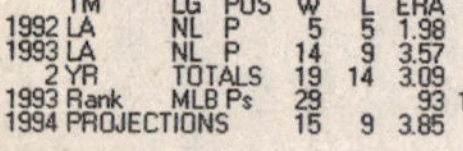

	TM	LG	POS	W	L	ERA	G	GS	CG	SH	SV	IP	H	R	ER	HR	BB	SO	SALARY
1992	LA	NL	P	5	5	1.98	11	11	4	4	0	82.0	80	23	18	1	20	43	N/A
1993	LA	NL	P	14	9	3.57	31	31	3	2	0	186.1	165	80	74	14	68	122	136,000
2	YR	TOTALS		19	14	3.09	42	42	7	6	0	268.1	245	103	92	15	88	165	
1993	Rank	MLB Ps		29		93	194	51	37	8	102	64	56	79		83	152	127	204
1994	PROJECTIONS			15	9	3.85	36	36	1	0	0	208	181	94	89	17	80	141	

Kevin Gross — No. 46/P

Full name: Kevin Frank Gross
Bats: R **Throws:** R **HT:** 6–5 **WT:** 227
Born: 6–8–61, Downey, CA
High school: Filmore (CA)
College: Cal Lutheran and Oxnard JC (CA)

Gross' 13 wins were his highest total since 1985. His 13 losses marked his ninth straight season with 10 or more.

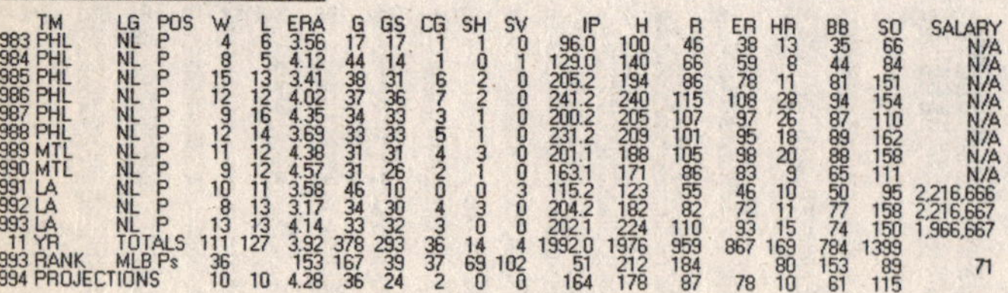

	TM	LG	POS	W	L	ERA	G	GS	CG	SH	SV	IP	H	R	ER	HR	BB	SO	SALARY
1983	PHL	NL	P	4	6	3.56	17	17	1	1	0	96.0	100	46	38	13	35	66	N/A
1984	PHL	NL	P	8	5	4.12	44	14	1	0	1	129.0	140	66	59	8	44	84	N/A
1985	PHL	NL	P	15	13	3.41	38	31	6	2	0	205.2	194	86	78	11	81	151	N/A
1986	PHL	NL	P	12	12	4.02	37	36	7	2	0	241.2	240	115	108	28	94	154	N/A
1987	PHL	NL	P	9	16	4.35	34	33	3	1	0	200.2	205	107	97	26	87	110	N/A
1988	PHL	NL	P	12	14	3.69	33	33	5	1	0	231.2	209	101	95	18	89	162	N/A
1989	MTL	NL	P	11	12	4.38	31	31	4	3	0	201.1	188	105	98	20	88	158	N/A
1990	MTL	NL	P	9	12	4.57	31	26	2	1	0	163.1	171	86	83	9	65	111	N/A
1991	LA	NL	P	10	11	3.58	46	10	0	0	3	115.2	123	55	46	10	50	95	2,216,666
1992	LA	NL	P	8	13	3.17	34	30	4	3	0	204.2	182	82	72	11	77	158	2,216,667
1993	LA	NL	P	13	13	4.14	33	32	3	0	0	202.1	224	110	93	15	74	150	1,966,667
11	YR	TOTALS		111	127	3.92	378	293	36	14	4	1992.0	1976	959	867	169	784	1399	
1993	RANK	MLB Ps		36		153	167	39	37	69	102	51	212	184		80	153	89	71
1994	PROJECTIONS			10	10	4.28	36	24	2	0	0	164	178	87	78	10	61	115	

Orel Hershiser No. 55/P

Full name: Orel Leonard Hershiser
Bats: R **Throws:** R **HT:** 6–3 **WT:** 198
Born: 9–16–58, Buffalo, NY
High school: Cherry Hills East (NJ)
College: Bowling Green (OH)

Hershiser's five complete games led the team; he held opponents to two ER or less in 19 of 33 starts. His 26 hits led all NL pitchers.

	TM	LG	POS	W	L	ERA	G	GS	CG	SH	SV	IP	H	R	ER	HR	BB	SO	SALARY
1983	LA	NL	P	0	0	3.38	8	0	0	0	1	8.0	7	6	3	1	6	5	N/A
1984	LA	NL	P	11	8	2.66	45	20	8	4	2	189.2	160	65	56	9	50	150	N/A
1985	LA	NL	P	19	3	2.03	36	34	9	5	0	239.2	179	72	54	8	68	157	N/A
1986	LA	NL	P	14	14	3.85	35	35	8	1	0	231.1	213	112	99	13	86	153	N/A
1987	LA	NL	P	16	16	3.30	37	35	10	1	1	264.2	247	105	97	17	74	190	N/A
1988	LA	NL	P	23	8	2.26	35	34	15	8	1	267.0	208	73	67	18	73	178	N/A
1989	LA	NL	P	15	15	2.31	35	33	8	4	0	256.2	226	75	66	9	77	178	N/A
1990	LA	NL	P	1	1	4.26	4	4	0	0	0	25.1	26	12	12	1	4	16	N/A
1991	LA	NL	P	7	2	3.46	21	21	0	0	0	112.0	112	43	43	3	32	73	3,166,667
1992	LA	NL	P	10	15	3.67	33	33	1	0	0	210.2	209	101	86	15	69	130	3,333,333
1993	LA	NL	P	12	14	3.59	33	33	5	1	0	215.2	201	106	86	17	72	141	4,333,333
11	YR	TOTALS		128	96	2.98	322	282	64	24	5	2020.2	1788	770	669	111	611	1371	
1993	Rank	MLB Ps		43		95	167	30	16	23	102	31	86	135		103	107	128	10
1994	PROJECTIONS			11	12	3.35	37	28	4	1	0	204	190	90	76	13	63	140	

Ramon Martinez No. 48/P

Full name: Ramon Jaime Martinez
Bats: L **Throws:** R **HT:** 6–4 **WT:** 176
Born: 4–22–68, Santo Domingo, DR
High school: L. Secundaria Las Amer. (DR)

Martinez improved from a subpar 1992, but led the NL in walks issued with 104. He reached the seventh inning in 17 of his 32 starts.

	TM	LG	POS	W	L	ERA	G	GS	CG	SH	SV	IP	H	R	ER	HR	BB	SO	SALARY
1988	LA	NL	P	1	3	3.79	9	6	0	0	0	35.2	27	17	15	0	22	23	N/A
1989	LA	NL	P	6	4	3.19	15	15	2	2	0	98.2	79	39	35	11	41	89	N/A
1990	LA	NL	P	20	6	2.92	33	33	12	3	0	234.1	191	89	76	22	67	223	N/A
1991	LA	NL	P	17	13	3.27	33	33	6	4	0	220.1	190	89	80	18	69	150	485,000
1992	LA	NL	P	8	11	4.00	25	25	1	1	0	150.2	141	82	67	11	69	101	725,000
1993	LA	NL	P	10	12	3.44	32	32	4	3	0	211.2	202	88	81	15	104	127	1,775,000
6	YR	TOTALS		62	49	3.35	147	144	25	13	0	951.1	830	404	354	77	372	713	
1993	RANK	MLB Ps		75		84	175	39	25	3	102	38	101	67		69	245	163	75
1994	PROJECTIONS			8	9	3.59	24	24	2	2	0	153	140	69	61	12	71	105	

Jim Gott No. 35/P

Full name: James William Gott
Bats: R **Throws:** R **HT:** 6–4 **WT:** 229
Born: 8–3–59, Hollywood, CA
High school: San Marino (CA)
College: Brigham Young

Gott's 25 saves led the team, and were his highest total since 1988. He did not allow a run in his first 13 appearances (19.1 IP).

	TM	LG	POS	W	L	ERA	G	GS	CG	SH	SV	IP	H	R	ER	HR	BB	SO	SALARY
1982	TOR	AL	P	5	10	4.43	30	23	1	1	0	136.0	134	76	67	15	66	82	N/A
1983	TOR	AL	P	9	14	4.74	34	30	6	1	0	176.2	195	103	93	15	68	121	N/A
1984	TOR	AL	P	7	6	4.02	35	12	1	1	2	109.2	93	54	49	7	49	73	N/A
1985	SF	NL	P	7	10	3.88	26	26	2	0	0	148.1	144	73	64	10	51	78	N/A
1986	SF	NL	P	0	0	7.62	9	2	0	0	1	13.0	16	12	11	0	13	9	N/A
1987	SF/PIT	NL	P	1	2	3.41	55	3	0	0	13	87.0	81	43	33	4	40	90	N/A
1988	PIT	NL	P	6	6	3.49	67	0	0	0	34	77.1	68	30	30	9	22	76	N/A
1989	PIT	NL	P	0	0	0.00	1	0	0	0	0	0.2	1	0	0	0	1	1	N/A
1990	LA	NL	P	3	5	2.90	50	0	0	0	3	62.0	59	27	20	5	34	44	N/A
1991	LA	NL	P	4	3	2.96	55	0	0	0	2	76.0	63	28	25	5	32	73	1,725,000
1992	LA	NL	P	3	3	2.45	68	0	0	0	6	88.0	72	27	24	4	41	75	2,125,000
1993	LA	NL	P	4	8	2.32	62	0	0	0	25	77.2	71	23	20	6	17	67	1,800,000
12	YR	TOTALS		49	67	3.73	492	96	10	3	86	1052.1	997	496	436	80	434	789	
1993	Rank	MLB Ps		173		13	42	202	125	69	15	192	78	10		94	26	45	73
1994	PROJECTIONS			2	4	3.06	40	0	0	0	9	50	48	20	17	3	21	40	

Tom Lasorda No. 2/Mgr.

Full name: Thomas Charles Lasorda
Bats: L **Throws:** L **HT:** 6–4 **WT:** 229
Born: 9–22–27, Norristown, PA
High school: Norristown (PA)

Lasorda's 17 years as Dodger manager rank only behind Don Shula's 23 years in the NFL among active pro league coaches. He's won two World Series and four NL pennants.

				REG. SEASON				PLAYOFF			CHAMP. SERIES			WORLD SERIES		
	YEAR	TEAM	LG	W	L	PCT	POS	W	L	PCT	W	L	PCT	W	L	PCT
	1980	LA	NL	92	71	.564	2			---			---			---
1ST HALF	1981	LA	NL	36	21	.632	1			---			---			---
2ND HALF	1981	LA	NL	27	26	.509	4	3	2	.600	3	2	.600	4	2	.667
	1982	LA	NL	88	74	.543	2			---			---			---
	1983	LA	NL	91	71	.562	1			---	1	3	.250			---
	1984	LA	NL	79	83	.488	4			---			---			---
	1985	LA	NL	95	67	.586	1			---	2	4	.333			---
	1986	LA	NL	73	89	.451	5			---			---			---
	1987	LA	NL	73	89	.451	4			---			---			---
	1988	LA	NL	94	67	.584	1			---	4	3	.571	4	1	.800
	1989	LA	NL	77	83	.481	4			---			---			---
	1990	LA	NL	86	76	.531	2			---			---			---
	1991	LA	NL	93	69	.574	2			---			---			---
	1992	LA	NL	63	99	.389	6			---			---			---
	1993	LA	NL	81	81	.500	4			---			---			---
	18	YR TOTALS		1422	1282	.526		3	2	.600	16	14	.533	12	11	.522

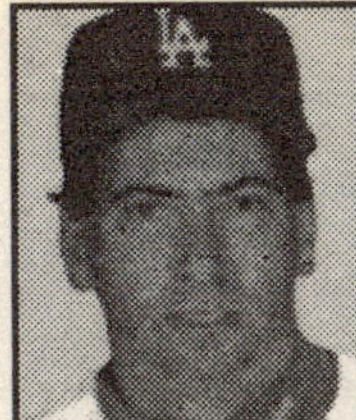

Tom Candiotti — No. 49/P

Full name: Thomas Caesar Candiotti
Bats: R **Throws:** R **HT:** 6–2 **WT:** 228
Born: 8–31–57, Walnut Creek, CA
High school: St. Mary's (Moraga, CA)
College: St. Mary's (Moraga, CA)
Candiotti's 3.12 ERA was seventh in the NL.

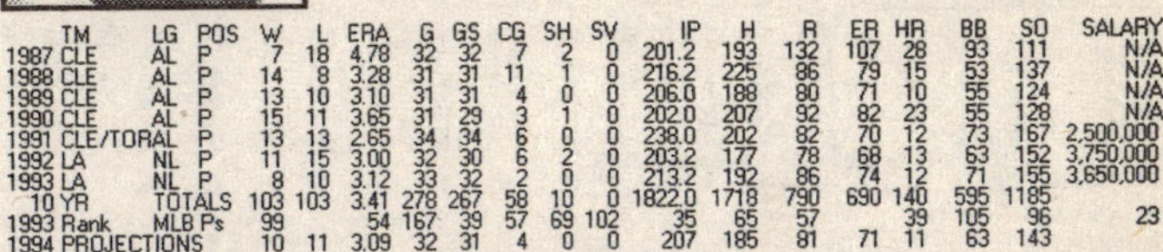

TM	LG	POS	W	L	ERA	G	GS	CG	SH	SV	IP	H	R	ER	HR	BB	SO	SALARY
1987 CLE	AL	P	7	18	4.78	32	32	7	2	0	201.2	193	132	107	28	93	111	N/A
1988 CLE	AL	P	14	8	3.28	31	31	11	1	0	216.2	225	86	79	15	53	137	N/A
1989 CLE	AL	P	13	10	3.10	31	31	4	0	0	206.0	188	80	71	10	55	124	N/A
1990 CLE	AL	P	15	11	3.65	31	29	3	1	0	202.0	207	92	82	23	55	128	N/A
1991 CLE/TOR	AL	P	13	13	2.65	34	34	6	0	0	238.0	202	82	70	12	73	167	2,500,000
1992 LA	NL	P	11	15	3.00	32	30	6	2	0	203.2	177	78	68	13	63	152	3,750,000
1993 LA	NL	P	8	10	3.12	33	32	2	0	0	213.2	192	86	74	12	71	155	3,650,000
10 YR	TOTALS		103	103	3.41	278	267	58	10	0	1822.0	1718	790	690	140	595	1185	
1993 Rank	MLB Ps		99		54	167	39	57	69	102	35	65	57		39	105	96	23
1994 PROJECTIONS			10	11	3.09	32	31	4	0	0	207	185	81	71	11	63	143	

Omar Daal — No. 54/P

Full name: Omar Daal
Bats: L **Throws:** L **HT:** 6–3 **WT:** 175
Born: 3–1–72, Maracaibo, VZ
High school: Valencia Superior (VZ)
Daal held left-handed batters to a .230 BA and stranded 36 of 48 inherited runners.

TM	LG	POS	W	L	ERA	G	GS	CG	SH	SV	IP	H	R	ER	HR	BB	SO	SALARY
1993 LA	NL	P	2	3	5.09	47	0	0	0	0	35.1	36	20	20	5	21	19	109,000
1 YR	TOTAL		2	3	5.09	47	0	0	0	0	35.1	36	20	20	5	21	19	
1993 RANK	MLB Ps	not ranked -- didn't have 50 IP in 1993																

Tom Goodwin — No. 47/OF

Full name: Thomas Jones Goodwin
Bats: L **Throws:** R **HT:** 6–1 **WT:** 170
Born: 7–27–68, Fresno, CA
College: Fresno State (CA)
Goodwin had 5 triples and 21 SB at AAA Albuquerque.

TEAM	LG	POS	G	AB	R	H	2B	3B	HR	RBI	BB	SO	SB	E	BA	SLG	SALARY
1991 LA	NL	OF	16	7	3	1	0	0	0	0	0	0	1	0	.143	.143	N/A
1992 LA	NL	OF	57	73	15	17	1	1	0	3	6	10	7	0	.233	.274	124,000
1993 LA	NL	OF	30	17	6	5	1	0	0	1	1	4	1	0	.294	.353	N/A
3 YR	TOTALS		103	97	24	23	2	1	0	4	7	14	9	0	.237	.278	
1993 RANK	MLB OF		not ranked -- didn't have 150 ABs in 1993														
1994 PROJECTIONS			34	32	8	7	0	0	0	1	2	4	3	0	.219	.281	

Kip Gross — No. 57/P

Full name: Kip Lee Gross
Bats: R **Throws:** R **HT:** 6–2 **WT:** 194
Born: 8–24–64, Scottsbluff, NE
High school: Gering (NE)
College: Murray State Junior (OK) and Nebraska
Gross had a 0.60 ERA in 10 appearances for LA.

	TM	LG	POS	W	L	ERA	G	GS	CG	SH	SV	IP	H	R	ER	HR	BB	SO	SALARY
1990	CIN	NL	P	0	0	4.26	5	0	0	0	0	6.1	6	3	3	0	2	3	N/A
1991	CIN	NL	P	6	4	3.47	29	9	1	0	0	85.2	93	43	33	8	40	40	100,000
1992	LA	NL	P	1	1	4.18	16	1	0	0	0	23.2	32	14	11	1	10	14	N/A
1993	LA	NL	P	0	0	0.60	10	0	0	0	0	15.0	13	1	1	0	4	12	N/A
4	YR	TOTALS		7	5	3.31	60	10	1	0	0	130.2	144	61	48	9	56	69	
1993	Rank	MLB Ps		not ranked -- didn't have 50 IP in 1993															
1994	PROJECTIONS			2	1	3.09	14	3	0	0	0	35	37	15	12	2	15	18	

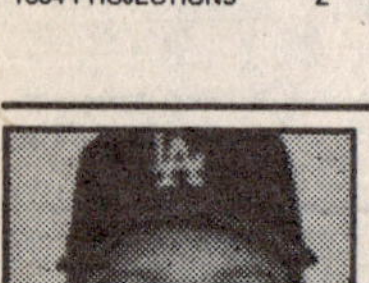

Dave Hansen — No. 5/3B

Full name: David Andrew Hansen
Bats: L **Throws:** R **HT:** 6–0 **WT:** 195
Born: 11–24–68, Long Beach, CA
High school: Rowland (CA)
Hansen's 18 pinch-hit RBI were the best in the NL for 1993, and he batted .394 in the second half.

	TEAM	LG	POS	G	AB	R	H	2B	3B	HR	RBI	BB	SO	SB	E	BA	SLG	SALARY
1990	LA	NL	3B-SS	5	7	0	1	0	0	0	1	0	3	0	1	.143	.143	N/A
1991	LA	NL	3B-SS	53	56	3	15	4	0	1	5	2	12	1	0	.268	.393	105,000
1992	LA	NL	3B	132	341	30	73	11	0	6	22	34	49	0	8	.214	.299	135,000
1993	LA	NL	3B	84	105	13	38	3	0	4	30	21	13	0	3	.362	.505	173,000
4	YR	TOTALS		274	509	46	127	18	0	11	58	57	77	1	12	.250	.350	
1993	RANK	MLB 3B		not ranked -- didn't have 150 ABs in 1993														
1994	PROJECTIONS			47	56	5	18	2	0	1	12	7	9	0	1	.321	.446	

Carlos Hernandez — No. 41/C

Full name: Carlos Alberto Hernandez
Bats: R **Throws:** R **HT:** 5–11 **WT:** 218
Born: 5–24–67, Bolivar, VZ
High school: Escuela Tecnica Ind. (VZ)
Backup catcher Hernandez batted .321 on artificial turf and .205 at Dodger Stadium.

1990	LA	NL	C	10	20	2	4	1	0	0	1	0	2	0	0	.200	.250	N/A
1991	LA	NL	C-3B	15	14	1	3	1	0	0	1	0	5	1	1	.214	.286	N/A
1992	LA	NL	C	69	173	11	45	4	0	3	17	11	21	0	7	.260	.335	135,000
1993	LA	NL	C	50	99	6	25	5	0	2	7	2	11	0	7	.253	.364	175,000
4	YR	TOTALS		144	306	20	77	11	0	5	26	13	39	1	15	.252	.337	
1993	RANK	MLB C		not ranked -- didn't have 150 ABs in 1993														
1994	PROJECTIONS			25	44	3	10	2	0	0	3	0	6	0	2	.227	.341	

Roger McDowell — No. 17/P

Full name: Roger Alan McDowell
Bats: R **Throws:** R **HT:** 6–1 **WT:** 197
Born: 12–21–60, Cincinnati, OH
High school: Colerain (Cincinnati, OH)
College: Bowling Green (OH)
McDowell's 2.25 ERA was his best since 1989.

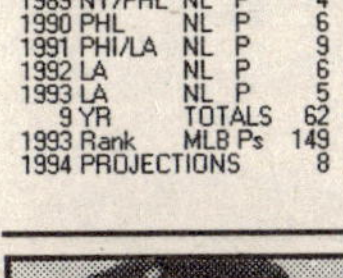

	TM	LG	POS	W	L	ERA	G	GS	CG	SH	SV	IP	H	R	ER	HR	BB	SO	SALARY
1988	NY	NL	P	5	5	2.63	62	0	0	0	16	89.0	80	31	26	1	31	46	N/A
1989	NY/PHL	NL	P	4	8	1.96	69	0	0	0	23	92.0	79	36	20	3	38	47	N/A
1990	PHL	NL	P	6	8	3.86	72	0	0	0	22	86.1	92	41	37	2	35	39	N/A
1991	PHI/LA	NL	P	9	9	2.93	71	0	0	0	10	101.1	100	40	33	4	48	50	2,000,000
1992	LA	NL	P	6	10	4.09	65	0	0	0	14	83.2	103	46	38	3	42	50	2,200,000
1993	LA	NL	P	5	3	2.25	54	0	0	0	2	68.0	76	32	17	2	30	27	1,350,000
9	YR	TOTALS		62	62	3.07	586	2	0	0	151	864.1	840	358	295	35	331	426	
1993	Rank	MLB Ps		149		7	66	202	125	69	55	223	222	109		6	215	276	86
1994	PROJECTIONS			8	5	2.78	63	0	0	0	13	107	97	41	33	5	36	54	

Raul Mondesi — No. 43/OF

Full name: Raul Mondesi
Bats: R **Throws:** R **HT:** 5–11 **WT:** 202
Born: 3–12–71, San Cristobal, DR
High school: Manual Maria Valencia (DR)
Mondesi showed promise, hitting .284 in 20 starts for the Dodgers.

	TEAM	LG	POS	G	AB	R	H	2B	3B	HR	RBI	BB	SO	SB	E	BA	SLG	SALARY
1993	LA	NL	OF	42	86	13	25	3	1	4	10	4	16	4	3	.291	.488	N/A
1	YR	TOTAL		42	86	13	25	3	1	4	10	4	16	4	3	.291	.488	
1993	RANK	MLB OF		not ranked -- didn't have 150 ABs in 1993														

Henry Rodriguez — No. 26/OF

Full name: Henry Anderson (Lorenzo) Rodriguez
Bats: L **Throws:** L **HT:** 6–1 **WT:** 200
Born: 11–8–67, Santo Domingo, DR
High school: Liceo Republica de Paraguay (DR)
Rodriguez showed power potential; 18 of his 39 hits went for extra bases.

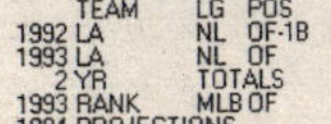
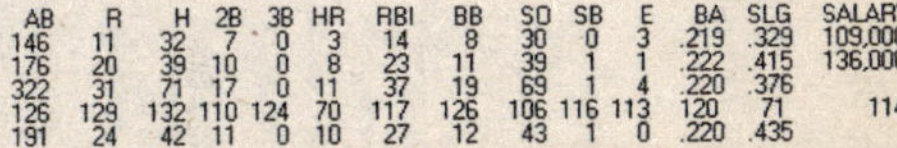

	TEAM	LG	POS	G	AB	R	H	2B	3B	HR	RBI	BB	SO	SB	E	BA	SLG	SALARY
1992	LA	NL	OF-1B	53	146	11	32	7	0	3	14	8	30	0	3	.219	.329	109,000
1993	LA	NL	OF	76	176	20	39	10	0	8	23	11	39	1	1	.222	.415	136,000
2	YR	TOTALS		129	322	31	71	17	0	11	37	19	69	1	4	.220	.376	
1993	RANK	MLB OF		123	126	129	132	110	124	70	117	126	106	116	113	120	71	114
1994	PROJECTIONS			87	191	24	42	11	0	10	27	12	43	1	0	.220	.435	

Rick Trlicek No. 36/P

Full name: Richard Alan Trlicek
Bats: R **Throws:** R **HT:** 6–3 **WT:** 200
Born: 4–26–69, Houston, TX
High school: LaGrange (TX)
In his final 18 appearances of 1993, Trlicek posted a 2.08 ERA. He held right-handers to a .184 BA.

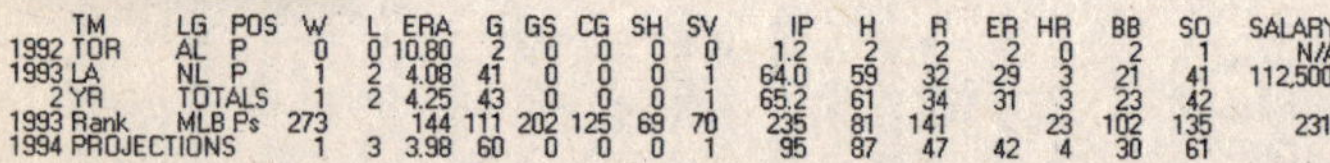

	TM	LG	POS	W	L	ERA	G	GS	CG	SH	SV	IP	H	R	ER	HR	BB	SO	SALARY
1992	TOR	AL	P	0	0	10.80	2	0	0	0	0	1.2	2	2	2	0	2	1	N/A
1993	LA	NL	P	1	2	4.08	41	0	0	0	1	64.0	59	32	29	3	21	41	112,500
2	YR	TOTALS		1	2	4.25	43	0	0	0	1	65.2	61	34	31	3	23	42	
1993	Rank	MLB Ps		273		144	111	202	125	69	70	235	81	141		23	102	135	231
1994	PROJECTIONS			1	3	3.98	60	0	0	0	1	95	87	47	42	4	30	61	

Mitch Webster No. 20/OF

Full name: Mitchell Dean Webster
Bats: S **Throws:** L **HT:** 6–1 **WT:** 191
Born: 5–16–59, Larned, KS
High school: Larned (KS)
Webster's 88 games was his lowest total since 1985. He batted .275 against left-handers.

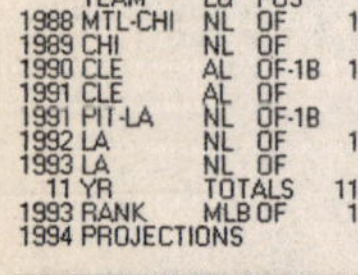

	TEAM	LG	POS	G	AB	R	H	2B	3B	HR	RBI	BB	SO	SB	E	BA	SLG	SALARY
1988	MTL-CHI	NL	OF	151	523	69	136	16	8	6	39	55	87	22	6	.260	.356	N/A
1989	CHI	NL	OF	98	272	40	70	12	4	3	19	30	55	14	6	.257	.364	N/A
1990	CLE	AL	OF-1B	128	437	58	110	20	6	12	55	20	61	22	5	.252	.407	N/A
1991	CLE	AL	OF	13	32	2	4	0	0	0	0	3	9	2	0	.125	.125	N/A
1991	PIT-LA	NL	OF-1B	94	171	21	38	8	5	2	19	18	52	0	2	.222	.363	750,000
1992	LA	NL	OF	135	262	33	70	12	5	6	35	27	49	11	3	.267	.420	115,000
1993	LA	NL	OF	88	172	26	42	6	2	2	14	11	24	4	4	.244	.337	600,000
11	YR	TOTALS		1129	3279	482	867	145	54	65	327	313	551	159	42	.264	.401	
1993	RANK	MLB	OF	105	129	115	128	133	76	114	135	126	131	85	59	109	119	75
1994	PROJECTIONS			42	75	12	17	2	1	0	6	5	13	2	2	.227	.307	

Todd Worrell No. 38/P

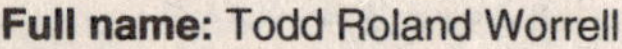

Full name: Todd Roland Worrell
Bats: R **Throws:** R **HT:** 6–5 **WT:** 222
Born: 9–28–59, Arcadia, CA
High school: Maranatha (Arcadia, CA)
College: Biola (La Miranda, CA)
Worrell's '93 ERA was 6.05 vs. 2.85 for his career.

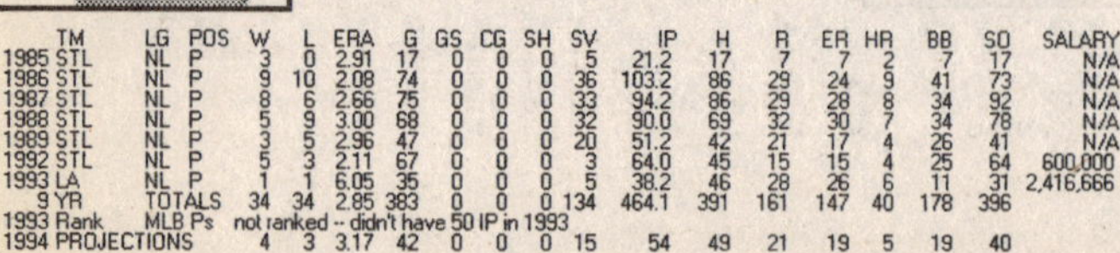

	TM	LG	POS	W	L	ERA	G	GS	CG	SH	SV	IP	H	R	ER	HR	BB	SO	SALARY
1985	STL	NL	P	3	0	2.91	17	0	0	0	5	21.2	17	7	7	2	7	17	N/A
1986	STL	NL	P	9	10	2.08	74	0	0	0	36	103.2	86	29	24	9	41	73	N/A
1987	STL	NL	P	8	6	2.66	75	0	0	0	33	94.2	86	29	28	8	34	92	N/A
1988	STL	NL	P	5	9	3.00	68	0	0	0	32	90.0	69	32	30	7	34	78	N/A
1989	STL	NL	P	3	5	2.96	47	0	0	0	20	51.2	42	21	17	4	26	41	N/A
1992	STL	NL	P	5	3	2.11	67	0	0	0	3	64.0	45	15	15	4	25	64	600,000
1993	LA	NL	P	1	1	6.05	35	0	0	0	5	38.2	46	28	26	6	11	31	2,416,666
9	YR	TOTALS		34	34	2.85	383	0	0	0	134	464.1	391	161	147	40	178	396	
1993	Rank	MLB Ps		not ranked -- didn't have 50 IP in 1993															
1994	PROJECTIONS			4	3	3.17	42	0	0	0	15	54	49	21	19	5	19	40	

Montreal *EXPOS*

1994 Scouting Report

Hitting: (1993/.257, eleventh in NL; 122 HR, eleventh in NL)

Great young outfield, with Larry Walker (.265, 22 HR, 86 RBI), Moises Alou (.286, 18 HR, 85 RBI), and Marquis Grissom (.298, 19 HR, 95 RBI). Montreal has excellent team speed, with Grissom (53 SB), Walker (29 SB), Mike Lansing (23 SB), and Alou (17 SB). In fact, the Expos led the league in stolen bases. But the rest of the team doesn't generate much offense. Montreal went through ten starters at first base last year. And the lineup cries out for another power hitter.

Prospects include 1B Cliff Floyd (projected to start at first for Montreal by '95) and OFs Rondell White and Curtis Pride. Floyd hit .329 with 26 HR, 101 RBI, and 31 steals at AA Harrisburg.

Pitching: (1993/3.55 ERA, fourth in NL)

Although Montreal will miss Dennis Martinez, who left via free agency for Cleveland, the Expos feature a promising rotation of Ken Hill (9–7), Jeff Fassero (12–5, 2.29 ERA), Kirk Reuter (8–0 as a rookie), and Chris Nabholz (9–8). Pedro Martinez (10–5, 2.61 ERA with the Dodgers) shows promise.

John Wetteland is the main closer for Montreal. The right-hander had 43 saves in 49 opportunities, and went 9–3 with a 1.37 ERA. Mel Rojas was 5–8 with 10 saves and a 2.95 ERA.

Defense: (.975 pct., twelfth in NL)

Larry Walker is often called the best right fielder in baseball. OF Marquis Grissom won his first Gold Glove in 1993.

1994 Prospects:

The Expos' 94–68 record was the best Montreal season since 1979, and the second best ever. The Expos are a young team on the rise; last year's edition featured 18 rookies, who collected 32.9% of the team's total at-bats. But Montreal is in the tough NL East, and will fight for a playoff berth against Atlanta and Philadelphia. Their pitching could be on a par with their rivals, but they can't score runs like the Braves or Phillies. Still, if either team slips, Montreal could sneak past for a wild-card berth.

Team Directory

President: Claude Brochu
General Mgr.: Dan Duquette
Director of P.R.: Richard Griffin
Chairman: L. Jacques Menard
VP, Baseball Operations: Bill Stoneman
Traveling Secretary: Erik Ostling

Minor League Affiliates:

Level	Team/League	1993 Record
AAA	Ottawa – International	73–69
AA	Harrisburg – Eastern	94–44
A	West Palm Beach – Florida State	69–67
	Burlington – Midwest	64–71
	Jamestown – New York/Penn.	31–46
Rookie	Gulf Coast Expos – Gulf Coast	27–31

1993 Review

vs NL East	Home W	Home L	Away W	Away L
Atlanta	2	4	3	3
Florida	4	2	4	3
New York	5	2	4	2
Philadelphia	4	2	2	5
Total	15	10	13	13

vs NL Cent.	Home W	Home L	Away W	Away L
Chicago	5	2	3	3
Cincinnati	4	2	4	2
Houston	4	2	3	3
Pittsburgh	5	2	3	3
St. Louis	4	2	3	4
Total	22	10	16	15

vs NL West	Home W	Home L	Away W	Away L
Colorado	5	1	4	2
Los Angeles	4	2	2	4
San Diego	6	0	4	2
S. Francisco	3	3	0	6
Total	18	6	10	14

1993 finish: 94–68 (55–26 home, 39–42 away), second in NL East, three games behind

1994 Schedule

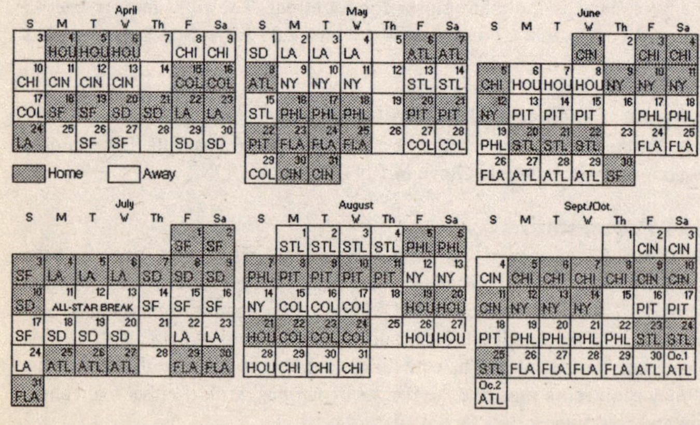

MONTREAL EXPOS 1994 ROSTER

Manager: Felipe Alou (17)
Coaches: Pierre Arsenault, bullpen (67); Tommy Harper, batting (21); Tim Johnson, bench (1); Joe Kerrigan, pitching (45); Jerry Manuel, 3B (6); Luis Pujols, 1B (31)

No.	PITCHERS	B	T	HT	WT	DOB	BIRTHPLACE	RESIDENCE
	Arteaga, Ivan	L	R	6–2	220	7–20–72	Puerto Cabello, VZ	Puerto Cabello, VZ
41	Barnes, Brian	L	L	5–9	170	3–25–67	Roanoke Rapids, NC	Roanoke Rapids, NC
	Batista, Miguel	R	R	6–1	170	2–19–71	SP de Macoris, DR	SP de Macoris, DR
	Cornelius, Reid	R	R	6–0	185	6–2–70	Thomasville, AL	West Palm Beach, FL
	Eischen, Joey	L	L	6–1	190	5–25–70	West Covina, CA	West Covina, CA
13	Fassero, Jeff	L	L	6–1	195	1–5–63	Springfield, IL	Brownsburg, IN
27	Henry, Butch	L	L	6–1	200	10–7–68	El Paso, TX	El Paso, TX
34	Heredia, Gill	R	R	6–1	205	10–26–65	Nogales, AZ	Tucson, AZ
44	Hill, Ken	R	R	6–2	200	12–14–65	Lynn, MA	Beverly, MA
53	Looney, Brian	L	L	5–10	185	9–26–69	New Haven, CT	Cheshire, CT
45	Martinez, Pedro	R	R	5–11	164	7–25–71	Manoguyabo, DR	Santo Domingo, DR
	Mathile, Mike	R	R	6–4	220	11–24–68	Toledo, OH	Tipp City, OH
43	Nabholz, Chris	L	L	6–5	210	1–5–67	Harrisburg, PA	Pottsville, PA
50	Risley, Bill	R	R	6–2	215	5–29–67	Chicago, IL	Farmington, NM
51	Rojas, Mel	R	R	5–11	195	12–10–66	Hanford, CA	Hanford, CA
42	Rueter, Kirk	L	L	6–3	195	12–1–70	Centralia, IL	Hoyleton, IL
54	Scott, Tim	R	R	6–2	205	11–16–66	Hanford, CA	Hanford, CA
31	Shaw, Jeff	R	R	6–2	200	7–7–66	Wash. C,house, OH	Wash. C,house, OH
57	Wetteland, John	R	R	6–2	215	8–21–66	San Mateo, CA	Cedar Crest, NM
No.	**CATCHERS**	**B**	**T**	**HT**	**WT**	**DOB**	**BIRTHPLACE**	**RESIDENCE**
24	Fletcher, Darrin	L	R	6–1	198	10–3–66	Elmhurst, IL	Fithian, IL
19	Laker, Tim	R	R	6–2	190	11–27–69	Encino, CA	Simi Valley, CA
2	Spehr, Tim	R	R	6–2	200	7–2–66	Excelsior Springs, MO	Waco, TX
No.	**INFIELDERS**	**B**	**T**	**HT**	**WT**	**DOB**	**BIRTHPLACE**	**RESIDENCE**
5	Berry, Sean	R	R	5–11	200	3–22–66	Santa Monica, CA	Torrance, CA
12	Cordero, Wilfredo	R	R	6–2	190	10–3–71	Mayaguez, PR	Mayaguez, PR
30	Floyd, Cliff	L	R	6–4	220	5–12–72	Chicago, IL	Markham, IL
3	Lansing, Mike	R	R	5–11	180	4–3–68	Rawlins, WY	Mulvane, KS
46	Marrero, Oreste	L	L	6–0	198	10–31–69	Bayamon, PR	Bayamon, PR
	Milligan, Randy	R	R	6–1	225	11–21–61	San Diego, CA	Baltimore, MD
39	Ready, Randy	R	R	5–11	180	1–8–60	San Mateo, CA	Cardiff, CA
23	Vander Wal, John	L	L	6–2	190	4–29–66	Grand Rapids, MI	Hudsonville, MI
14	White, Derrick	R	R	6–1	220	10–12–69	San Rafael, CA	San Rafael, CA
No.	**OUTFIELDERS**	**B**	**T**	**HT**	**WT**	**DOB**	**BIRTHPLACE**	**RESIDENCE**
18	Alou, Moises	R	R	6–3	190	7–3–66	Atlanta, GA	Santo Domingo, DR
7	Frazier, Lou	S	R	6–2	175	1–26–65	St. Louis, MO	Scottsdale, AZ
9	Grissom, Marquis	R	R	5–11	190	4–17–67	Atlanta, GA	Riverdale, GA
16	Pride, Curtis	L	R	5–11	200	12–17–68	Washington, DC	Silver Spring, MD
33	Walker, Larry	L	R	6–3	215	12–1–66	Maple Ridge, BC	West Palm Beach, FL
37	White, Rondell	R	R	6–1	205	2–23–72	Milledgeville, GA	Gray, GA

Olympic Stadium (46,500, artificial)
Tickets: 514–253–3434
Ticket prices:
- $22.00 (VIP box seats)
- $17.00 (box seats)
- $9.00 (terrace)
- $5.00 (general admission)
- $5.00 (bleachers)

Field Dimensions (from home plate)
- To left field at foul line, 325 feet
- To center field, 404 feet
- To right field at foul line, 325 feet
- (OF wall is 12 feet high)

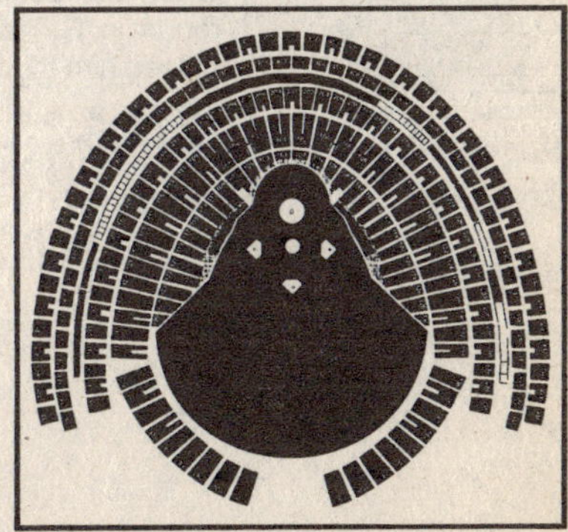

Moises Alou No.18/LF

Full name: Moises Rojas Alou
Bats: R **Throws:** R **HT:** 6–3 **WT:** 190
Born: 7–3–66, Atlanta, GA
College: Canada Coll. (Redwood City, CA)
Alou's broken leg ended his season September 16 and ended the Expos' pennant chances. He had hit .325 with 11 HR in his last 56 games.

	TEAM	LG	POS	G	AB	R	H	2B	3B	HR	RBI	BB	SO	SB	E	BA	SLG	SALARY
1990	PIT-MTL	NL	OF	16	20	4	4	0	1	0	0	0	3	0	0	.200	.300	N/A
1992	MTL	NL	OF	115	341	53	96	28	2	9	56	25	46	16	4	.282	.455	110,500
1993	MTL	NL	OF	136	482	70	138	29	6	18	85	38	53	17	4	.286	.483	210,000
4	YR	TOTALS		267	843	127	238	57	9	27	141	63	102	33	8	.282	.467	
1993	RANK	MLB	OF	50	50	50	43	21	13	30	21	54	1	36	67	42	25	106
1994	PROJECTIONS			162	582	83	166	35	6	21	103	45	63	20	4	.285	.474	0

Wil Cordero No. 12/SS

Full name: Wilfredo Nieva Cordero
Bats: R **Throws:** R **HT:** 6–2 **WT:** 190
Born: 10–3–71, Mayaguez, PR
High school: C. de Servicios (Mayaguez, PR)
Touted as a rookie of the year candidate when the season began, Cordero finished fourth in RBI among NL rookies. His 10 HR placed him third among NL shortstops.

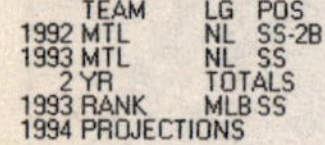

	TEAM	LG	POS	G	AB	R	H	2B	3B	HR	RBI	BB	SO	SB	E	BA	SLG	SALARY
1992	MTL	NL	SS-2B	45	126	17	38	4	1	2	8	9	31	0	8	.302	.397	109,000
1993	MTL	NL	SS	138	475	56	118	32	2	10	58	34	60	12	36	.248	.387	126,500
2	YR	TOTALS		183	601	73	156	36	3	12	66	43	91	12	44	.260	.389	
1993	RANK	MLB	SS	17	16	17	20	3	21	7	9	21	16	8	2	31	16	30
1994	PROJECTIONS			162	571	66	139	40	1	12	73	40	65	15	44	.243	.38	

Darrin Fletcher No. 24/C

Full name: Darrin Glen Fletcher
Bats: L **Throws:** R **HT:** 6–1 **WT:** 198
Born: 10–3–66, Elmhurst, IL
High school: Oakwood (IL)
College: Illinois

Fletcher established career highs in every offensive category except triples and steals. He had 21 RBI in his final 34 games.

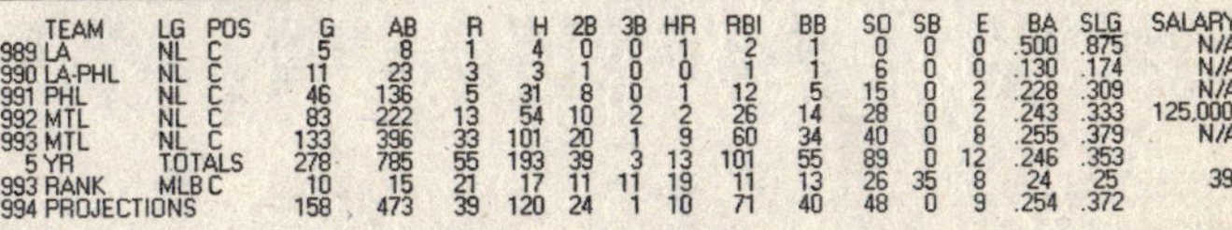

	TEAM	LG	POS	G	AB	R	H	2B	3B	HR	RBI	BB	SO	SB	E	BA	SLG	SALARY
1989	LA	NL	C	5	8	1	4	0	0	1	2	1	0	0	0	.500	.875	N/A
1990	LA-PHL	NL	C	11	23	3	3	1	0	0	1	1	6	0	0	.130	.174	N/A
1991	PHL	NL	C	46	136	5	31	8	0	1	12	5	15	0	2	.228	.309	N/A
1992	MTL	NL	C	83	222	13	54	10	2	2	26	14	28	0	2	.243	.333	125,000
1993	MTL	NL	C	133	396	33	101	20	1	9	60	34	40	0	8	.255	.379	N/A
5	YR	TOTALS		278	785	55	193	39	3	13	101	55	89	0	12	.246	.353	
1993	RANK	MLB	C	10	15	21	17	11	11	19	11	13	26	35	8	24	25	39
1994	PROJECTIONS			158	473	39	120	24	1	10	71	40	48	0	9	.254	.372	

Marquis Grissom No. 9/CF

Full name: Marquis Dion Grissom
Bats: R **Throws:** R **HT:** 5–11 **WT:** 190
Born: 4–17–67, Atlanta, GA
High school: Lakeshore (College Park, GA)
College: Florida A&M

Grissom was Montreal's only All-Star representative. His 95 RBI were tops among NL center fielders.

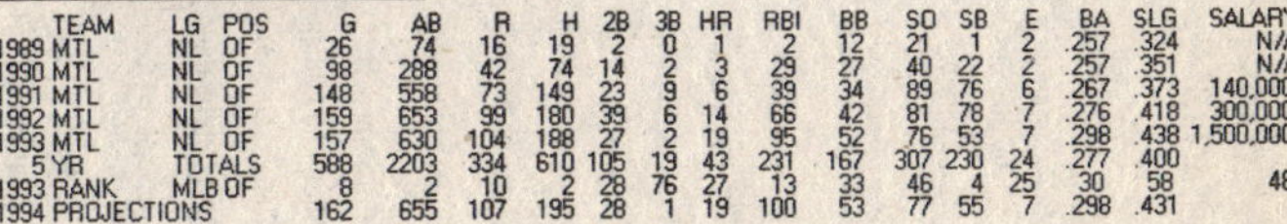

	TEAM	LG	POS	G	AB	R	H	2B	3B	HR	RBI	BB	SO	SB	E	BA	SLG	SALARY
1989	MTL	NL	OF	26	74	16	19	2	0	1	2	12	21	1	2	.257	.324	N/A
1990	MTL	NL	OF	98	288	42	74	14	2	3	29	27	40	22	2	.257	.351	N/A
1991	MTL	NL	OF	148	558	73	149	23	9	6	39	34	89	76	6	.267	.373	140,000
1992	MTL	NL	OF	159	653	99	180	39	6	14	66	42	81	78	7	.276	.418	300,000
1993	MTL	NL	OF	157	630	104	188	27	2	19	95	52	76	53	7	.298	.438	1,500,000
5	YR	TOTALS		588	2203	334	610	105	19	43	231	167	307	230	24	.277	.400	
1993	RANK	MLB	OF	8	2	10	2	28	76	27	13	33	46	4	25	30	58	48
1994	PROJECTIONS			162	655	107	195	28	1	19	100	53	77	55	7	.298	.431	

Mike Lansing No. 3/3B–SS

Full name: Michael Thomas Lansing
Bats: R **Throws:** R **HT:** 5–11 **WT:** 180
Born: 4–3–68, Rawlins, WY
High school: Natrona County
College: Wichita State (KS)
Lansing's 23 SB placed him second among NL rookies, behind Florida's Chuck Carr.

TEAM	LG	POS	G	AB	R	H	2B	3B	HR	RBI	BB	SO	SB	E	BA	SLG	SALARY
1993 MTL	NL	3B	141	491	64	141	29	1	3	45	46	56	23	24	.287	.369	109,000
1 YR	TOTAL		141	491	64	141	29	1	3	45	46	56	23	24	.287	.369	
1993 RANK	MLB	3B	15	16	15	15	12	21	33	24	12	22	1	35	10	32	34

Randy Ready No. 39/IF

Full name: Randy Max Ready
Bats: R **Throws:** R **HT:** 5–11 **WT:** 180
Born: 1–8–60, San Mateo, CA
High school: J.F. Kennedy (South Fremont, CA)
College: Cal State Heyward and Mesa (CO)
The Expos were 29–9 with this veteran starting. He started 25 games at 2B, 10 at first.

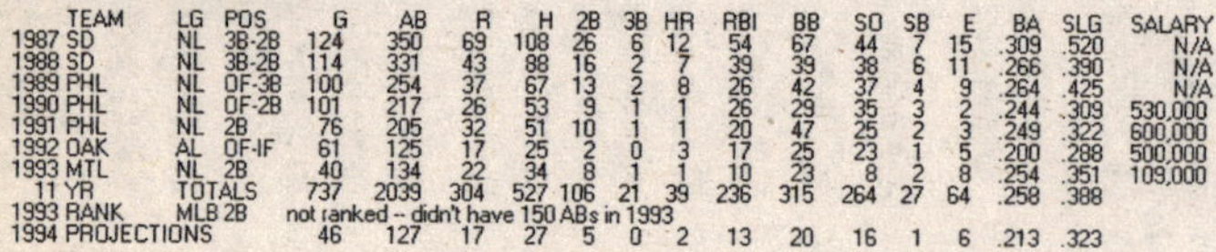

TEAM	LG	POS	G	AB	R	H	2B	3B	HR	RBI	BB	SO	SB	E	BA	SLG	SALARY
1987 SD	NL	3B-2B	124	350	69	108	26	6	12	54	67	44	7	15	.309	.520	N/A
1988 SD	NL	3B-2B	114	331	43	88	16	2	7	39	39	38	6	11	.266	.390	N/A
1989 PHL	NL	OF-3B	100	254	37	67	13	2	8	26	42	37	4	9	.264	.425	N/A
1990 PHL	NL	OF-2B	101	217	26	53	9	1	1	26	29	35	3	2	.244	.309	530,000
1991 PHL	NL	2B	76	205	32	51	10	1	1	20	47	25	2	3	.249	.322	600,000
1992 OAK	AL	OF-IF	61	125	17	25	2	0	3	17	25	23	1	5	.200	.288	500,000
1993 MTL	NL	2B	40	134	22	34	8	1	1	10	23	8	2	8	.254	.351	109,000
11 YR	TOTALS		737	2039	304	527	106	21	39	236	315	264	27	64	.258	.388	
1993 RANK	MLB	2B	not ranked -- didn't have 150 ABs in 1993														
1994 PROJECTIONS			46	127	17	27	5	0	2	13	20	16	1	6	.213	.323	

John Vander Wal No. 23/1B

Full name: John Henry Vander Wal
Bats: L **Throws:** L **HT:** 6–2 **WT:** 190
Born: 4–29–66, Grand Rapids, MI
High school: Hudsonville (MI)
College: Western Michigan
Vander Wal made just 4 errors in 106 games at first base.

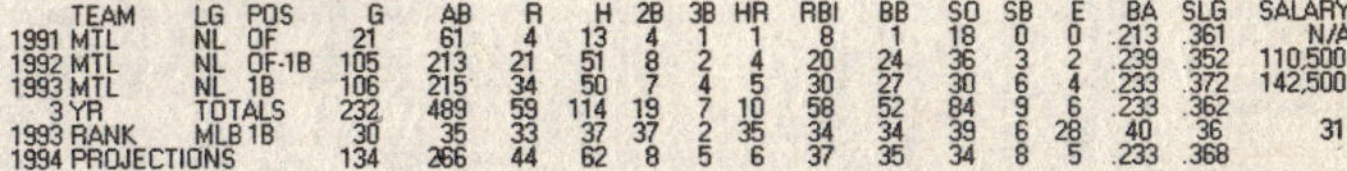

TEAM	LG	POS	G	AB	R	H	2B	3B	HR	RBI	BB	SO	SB	E	BA	SLG	SALARY
1991 MTL	NL	OF	21	61	4	13	4	1	1	8	1	18	0	0	.213	.361	N/A
1992 MTL	NL	OF-1B	105	213	21	51	8	2	4	20	24	36	3	2	.239	.352	110,500
1993 MTL	NL	1B	106	215	34	50	7	4	5	30	27	30	6	4	.233	.372	142,500
3 YR	TOTALS		232	489	59	114	19	7	10	58	52	84	9	6	.233	.362	
1993 RANK	MLB	1B	30	35	33	37	37	2	35	34	34	39	6	28	40	36	31
1994 PROJECTIONS			134	266	44	62	8	5	6	37	35	34	8	5	.233	.368	

Larry Walker No. 33/RF

Full name: Larry Kenneth Robert Walker
Bats: L **Throws:** R **HT:** 6–3 **WT:** 215
Born: 12–1–66, Maple Ridge, BC
High school: Maple Ridge (BC)
Walker is the only Expo other than Andre Dawson to have a 20 HR, 20 steal season. He had 13 outfield assists in '93, sixth in the NL, on his way to a Gold Glove season.

TEAM	LG	POS	G	AB	R	H	2B	3B	HR	RBI	BB	SO	SB	E	BA	SLG	SALARY
1989 MTL	NL	OF	20	47	4	8	0	0	0	4	5	13	1	0	.170	.170	N/A
1990 MTL	NL	OF	133	419	59	101	18	3	19	51	49	112	21	4	.241	.434	103,500
1991 MTL	NL	OF-1B	137	487	59	141	30	2	16	64	42	102	14	6	.290	.458	185,000
1992 MTL	NL	OF	143	528	85	159	31	4	23	93	41	97	18	2	.301	.506	975,000
1993 MTL	NL	OF	138	490	85	130	24	5	22	86	80	76	29	6	.265	.469	3,000,000
5 YR	TOTALS		571	1971	292	539	103	14	80	298	217	400	83	18	.273	.462	
1993 RANK	MLB	OF	45	46	24	54	38	23	16	20	13	46	19	92	81	37	24
1994 PROJECTIONS			136	465	67	124	24	3	19	67	57	96	21	5	.267	.454	

Jeff Fassero — No. 13/P

Full name: Jeffrey Joseph Fassero
Bats: L **Throws:** L **HT:** 6–1 **WT:** 195
Born: 1–5–63, Springfield, IL
High school: Griffin (Springfield, IL)
College: Lincoln Land Community (Springfield, IL) and Mississippi

Fassero was 7–4 with a 2.29 ERA in 94.1 innings as a starter.

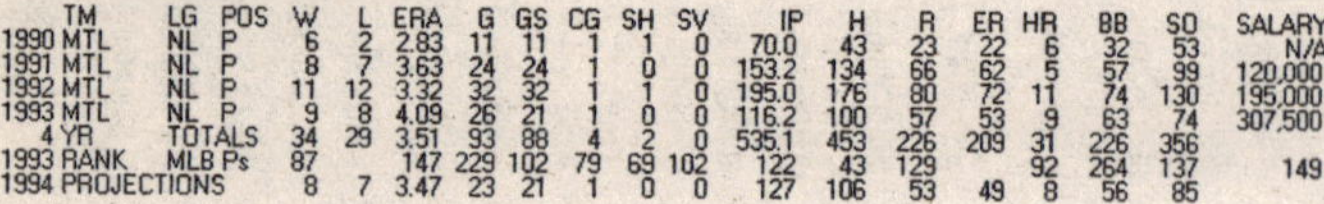

TM	LG	POS	W	L	ERA	G	GS	CG	SH	SV	IP	H	R	ER	HR	BB	SO	SALARY
1990 MTL	NL	P	6	2	2.83	11	11	1	1	0	70.0	43	23	22	6	32	53	N/A
1991 MTL	NL	P	8	7	3.63	24	24	1	0	0	153.2	134	66	62	5	57	99	120,000
1992 MTL	NL	P	11	12	3.32	32	32	1	1	0	195.0	176	80	72	11	74	130	195,000
1993 MTL	NL	P	9	8	4.09	26	21	1	0	0	116.2	100	57	53	9	63	74	307,500
4 YR	TOTALS		34	29	3.51	93	88	4	2	0	535.1	453	226	209	31	226	356	
1993 RANK	MLB Ps		87		147	229	102	79	69	102	122	43	129		92	264	137	149
1994 PROJECTIONS			8	7	3.47	23	21	1	0	0	127	106	53	49	8	56	85	

Kirk Rueter — No. 42/P

Full name: Kirk Rueter
Bats: L **Throws:** L **HT:** 6–3 **WT:** 195
Born: 12–1–70, Centralia, IL
High school: Hoyleton, IL

Reuter was 5–0 in AA, 4–2 in AAA, and 8–0 in the NL for Montreal in 1993, for a combined record of 17–6. He's the first Expo starter to win his first eight decisions.

TM	LG	POS	W	L	ERA	G	GS	CG	SH	SV	IP	H	R	ER	HR	BB	SO	SALARY
1993 MTL	NL	P	8	0	2.73	14	14	1	0	0	85.2	85	33	26	5	18	31	109,000
1 YR	TOTAL		8	0	2.73	14	14	1	0	0	85.2	85	33	26	5	18	31	
1993 RANK	MLB Ps		99		24	279	137	79	69	102	172	130	45		43	23	284	236

Ken Hill No. 44/P

Full name: Kenneth Wade Hill
Bats: R **Throws:** R **HT:** 6–2 **WT:** 200
Born: 12–14–65, Lynn, MA
High school: Lynn Classical (MA)
College: North Adams State (MA)

Hill started the season 6–0, but a strained groin hampered his effectiveness the rest of the season.

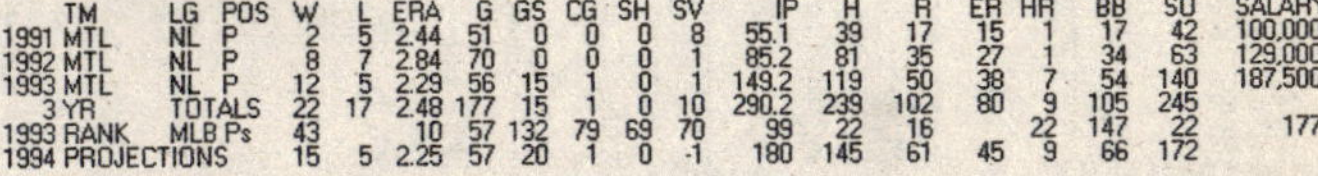

TM	LG	POS	W	L	ERA	G	GS	CG	SH	SV	IP	H	R	ER	HR	BB	SO	SALARY
1991 MTL	NL	P	2	5	2.44	51	0	0	0	8	55.1	39	17	15	1	17	42	100,000
1992 MTL	NL	P	8	7	2.84	70	0	0	0	1	85.2	81	35	27	1	34	63	129,000
1993 MTL	NL	P	12	5	2.29	56	15	1	0	1	149.2	119	50	38	7	54	140	187,500
3 YR	TOTALS		22	17	2.48	177	15	1	0	10	290.2	239	102	80	9	105	245	
1993 RANK	MLB Ps		43		10	57	132	79	69	70	99	22	16		22	147	22	177
1994 PROJECTIONS			15	5	2.25	57	20	1	0	-1	180	145	61	45	9	66	172	

Chris Nabholz No. 43/P

Full name: Christopher William Nabholz
Bats: L **Throws:** L **HT:** 6–5 **WT:** 210
Born: 1–5–67, Harrisburg, PA
High school: Pottsville Area (PA)
College: Towson State (MD)

Nabholz was third on Montreal in games started by a pitcher, behind Dennis Martinez and Ken Hill.

TM	LG	POS	W	L	ERA	G	GS	CG	SH	SV	IP	H	R	ER	HR	BB	SO	SALARY
1988 STL	NL	P	0	1	5.14	4	1	0	0	0	14.0	16	9	8	0	6	6	N/A
1989 STL	NL	P	7	15	3.80	33	33	2	1	0	196.2	186	92	83	9	99	112	N/A
1990 STL	NL	P	5	6	5.49	17	14	1	0	0	78.2	79	49	48	7	33	58	N/A
1991 STL	NL	P	11	10	3.57	30	30	0	0	0	181.1	147	76	72	15	67	121	155,000
1992 MTL	NL	P	16	9	2.68	33	33	3	3	0	218.0	187	76	65	13	75	150	620,000
1993 MTL	NL	P	9	7	3.23	28	28	2	0	0	183.2	163	84	66	7	74	90	2,000,000
6 YR	TOTALS		48	48	3.53	145	139	8	4	0	872.1	778	386	342	51	354	537	
1993 RANK	MLB Ps		87		63	220	71	57	69	102	68	59	98		15	185	242	68
1994 PROJECTIONS			4	4	3.96	16	14	1	0	0	91	86	47	40	4	37	51	

John Wetteland No. 57/P

Full name: John Karl Wetteland
Bats: R **Throws:** R **HT:** 6–2 **WT:** 215
Born: 8–21–66, San Mateo, CA
High school: Card. Newman (Santa Rosa, CA)
College: College of San Mateo

Wetteland notched 113 strikeouts in 85.1 innings, tying for most strikeouts by a major league reliever with Pedro Martinez.

	TM	LG	POS	W	L	ERA	G	GS	CG	SH	SV	IP	H	R	ER	HR	BB	SO	SALARY
1990	LA	NL	P	2	4	4.81	22	5	0	0	0	43.0	44	28	23	6	17	36	N/A
1991	LA	NL	P	1	0	0.00	6	0	0	0	0	9.0	5	2	0	0	3	9	N/A
1989	LA	NL	P	5	8	3.77	31	12	0	0	1	102.2	81	46	43	8	34	96	N/A
1992	MTL	NL	P	4	4	2.92	67	0	0	0	37	83.1	64	27	27	6	36	99	156,000
1993	MTL	NL	P	9	3	1.37	70	0	0	0	43	85.1	58	17	13	3	28	113	315,000
4	YR	TOTALS		21	19	2.95	196	17	0	0	81	323.1	252	120	106	23	118	353	
1993	RANK	MLB	Ps	87		1	14	202	125	69	7	175	3	1		12	103	2	147
1994	PROJECTIONS			5	3	2.70	53	1	0	0	26	70	55	24	21	5	27	82	

Felipe Alou No. 17/Mgr.

Full name: Felipe Rojas Alou
Bats: L **Throws:** L **HT:** 5–9 **WT:** 170
Born: 5–12–35, Haina, DR
College: University of Santo Domingo (DR)

Alou's record as Expos' manager is 164–123. 1993 was his first full season at the Montreal helm. He won 100 games faster than any manager in Expos history.

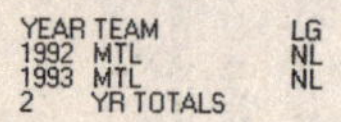
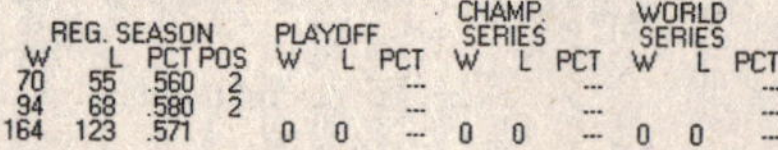

			REG. SEASON				PLAYOFF			CHAMP. SERIES			WORLD SERIES		
YEAR	TEAM	LG	W	L	PCT	POS	W	L	PCT	W	L	PCT	W	L	PCT
1992	MTL	NL	70	55	.560	2			---			---			---
1993	MTL	NL	94	68	.580	2			---			---			---
2	YR TOTALS		164	123	.571		0	0	--	0	0	--	0	0	--

Brian Barnes — No. 41/P

Full name: Brian Keith Barnes
Bats: L **Throws:** L **HT:** 5–9 **WT:** 170
Born: 3–25–67, Roanoke Rapids, NC
High school: Roanoke Rapids, NC
College: Clemson
Barnes posted a career-high 4.41 ERA in 52 games.

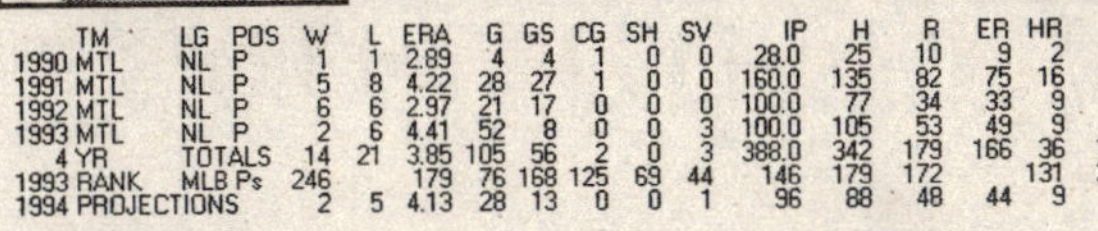

TM	LG	POS	W	L	ERA	G	GS	CG	SH	SV	IP	H	R	ER	HR	BB	SO	SALARY
1990 MTL	NL	P	1	1	2.89	4	4	1	0	0	28.0	25	10	9	2	7	23	N/A
1991 MTL	NL	P	5	8	4.22	28	27	1	0	0	160.0	135	82	75	16	84	117	103,500
1992 MTL	NL	P	6	6	2.97	21	17	0	0	0	100.0	77	34	33	9	46	65	165,000
1993 MTL	NL	P	2	6	4.41	52	8	0	0	3	100.0	105	53	49	9	48	60	182,500
4 YR	TOTALS		14	21	3.85	105	56	2	0	3	388.0	342	179	166	36	185	265	
1993 RANK	MLB Ps		246		179	76	168	125	69	44	146	179	172		131	238	163	182
1994 PROJECTIONS			2	5	4.13	28	13	0	0	1	96	88	48	44	9	46	66	

Sean Berry — No. 5/3B

Full name: Sean Robert Berry
Bats: R **Throws:** R **HT:** 5–11 **WT:** 200
Born: 3–22–66, Santa Monica, CA
High school: West Torrance (CA)
College: UCLA
Berry had 14 HR in only 299 AB.

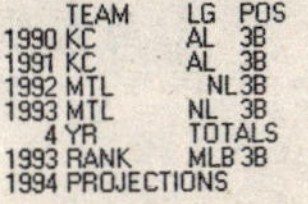

TEAM	LG	POS	G	AB	R	H	2B	3B	HR	RBI	BB	SO	SB	E	BA	SLG	SALARY
1990 KC	AL	3B	8	23	2	5	1	1	0	4	2	5	0	1	.217	.348	N/A
1991 KC	AL	3B	31	60	5	8	3	0	0	1	5	23	0	2	.133	.183	N/A
1992 MTL	NL	3B	24	57	5	19	1	0	1	4	1	11	2	4	.333	.404	115,000
1993 MTL	NL	3B	122	299	50	78	15	2	14	49	41	70	12	15	.261	.465	121,000
4 YR	TOTALS		185	439	62	110	20	3	15	58	49	109	14	22	.251	.412	
1993 RANK	MLB	3B	21	26	19	26	25	10	12	21	18	1	3	26	24	7	32
1994 PROJECTIONS			150	368	62	96	18	2	17	60	50	86	15	18	.261	.459	0

Butch Henry — No. 27/P

Full name: Floyd Buford Henry III
Bats: L **Throws:** L **HT:** 6–1 **WT:** 200
Born: 10–7–68, El Paso, TX
High school: Eastwood (El Paso, TX)
In only 103.0 IP, Henry allowed 15 HR.

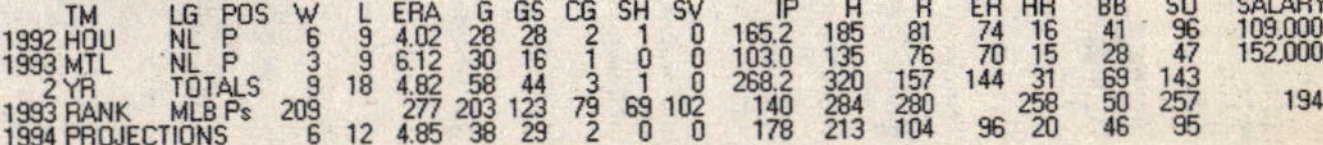

TM	LG	POS	W	L	ERA	G	GS	CG	SH	SV	IP	H	R	ER	HR	BB	SO	SALARY
1992 HOU	NL	P	6	9	4.02	28	28	2	1	0	165.2	185	81	74	16	41	96	109,000
1993 MTL	NL	P	3	9	6.12	30	16	1	0	0	103.0	135	76	70	15	28	47	152,000
2 YR	TOTALS		9	18	4.82	58	44	3	1	0	268.2	320	157	144	31	69	143	
1993 RANK	MLB Ps		209		277	203	123	79	69	102	140	284	280		258	50	257	194
1994 PROJECTIONS			6	12	4.85	38	29	2	0	0	178	213	104	96	20	46	95	

Cliff Floyd — No. 30/1B

Full name: Cornelius Clifford Floyd
Bats: L **Throws:** R **HT:** 6–4 **WT:** 220
Born: 5–12–72, Chicago, IL
High school: Thornwood (South Holland, IL)
The AA Eastern League's MVP, Floyd is the second youngest Expo to hit a home run.

TEAM	LG POS	G	AB	R	H	2B	3B	HR	RBI	BB	SO	SB	E	BA	SLG	SALARY
1993 MTL	NL 1B	10	31	3	7	0	0	1	2	0	9	0	0	.226	.323	N/A
1 YR	TOTAL	10	31	3	7	0	0	1	2	0	9	0	0	.226	.323	
1993 RANK	MLB 1B	not ranked -- didn't have 150 ABs in 1993														

Lou Frazier — No. 7/OF

Bats: S **Throws:** R **HT:** 6–2 **WT:** 175
Born: 1–26–65, St. Louis, MO
Frazier was the Expos' fourth outfielder, top pinch-runner and team pinch hit leader with 12.

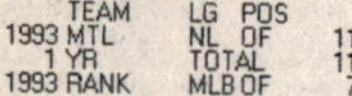
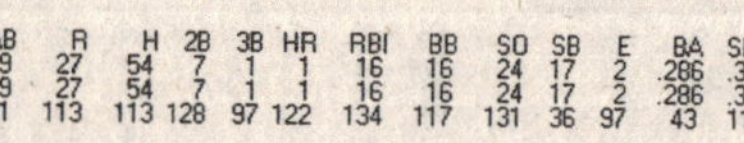

TEAM	LG POS	G	AB	R	H	2B	3B	HR	RBI	BB	SO	SB	E	BA	SLG	SALARY
1993 MTL	NL OF	112	189	27	54	7	1	1	16	16	24	17	2	.286	.349	109,000
1 YR	TOTAL	112	189	27	54	7	1	1	16	16	24	17	2	.286	.349	
1993 RANK	MLB OF	78	121	113	113	128	97	122	134	117	131	36	97	43	112	124

Pedro J. Martinez — P

Full name: Pedro Jaime Martinez
Bats: L **Throws:** R **HT:** 6–4 **WT:** 176
Born: 3–22–68, Santo Domingo, DR
High school: Liceo Sec. Las Americas (DR)
Martinez won eight consecutive decisions in '93, longest Dodger streak since Hershiser's 11 in '85.

TM	LG POS	W	L	ERA	G	GS	CG	SH	SV	IP	H	R	ER	HR	BB	SO	SALARY
1992 LA	NL P	0	1	2.25	2	1	0	0	0	8.0	6	2	2	0	1	8	N/A
1993 LA	NL P	10	5	2.61	65	2	0	0	2	107.0	76	34	31	5	57	119	119,000
2 YR	TOTALS	10	6	2.58	67	3	0	0	2	115.0	82	36	33	5	58	127	
1993 RANK	MLB Ps	75		20	28	197	125	69	55	134	8	13		21	259	7	218
1994 PROJECTIONS		15	7	2.60	96	2	0	0	3	156	111	50	45	7	85	174	

Randy Milligan 1B

Full name: Randall Andre Milligan
Bats: R **Throws:** R **HT:** 6–1 **WT:** 225
Born: 11–21–61, San Diego, CA
High school: San Diego (CA)
College: San Diego Mesa (CA)
Milligan came to Montreal from Cleveland.

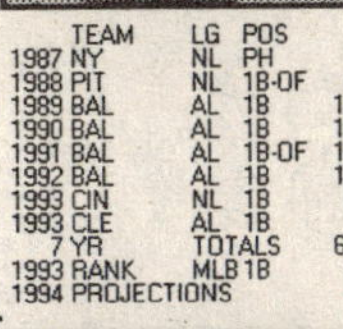
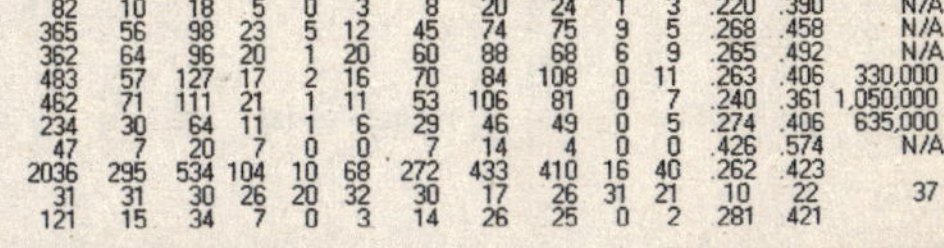

TEAM	LG	POS	G	AB	R	H	2B	3B	HR	RBI	BB	SO	SB	E	BA	SLG	SALARY
1987 NY	NL	PH	3	1	0	0	0	0	0	0	1	1	0	--	.000	.000	N/A
1988 PIT	NL	1B-OF	40	82	10	18	5	0	3	8	20	24	1	3	.220	.390	N/A
1989 BAL	AL	1B	124	365	56	98	23	5	12	45	74	75	9	5	.268	.458	N/A
1990 BAL	AL	1B	109	362	64	96	20	1	20	60	88	68	6	9	.265	.492	N/A
1991 BAL	AL	1B-OF	141	483	57	127	17	2	16	70	84	108	0	11	.263	.406	330,000
1992 BAL	AL	1B	137	462	71	111	21	1	11	53	106	81	0	7	.240	.361	1,050,000
1993 CIN	NL	1B	83	234	30	64	11	1	6	29	46	49	0	5	.274	.406	635,000
1993 CLE	AL	1B	19	47	7	20	7	0	0	7	14	4	0	0	.426	.574	N/A
7 YR	TOTALS		656	2036	295	534	104	10	68	272	433	410	16	40	.262	.423	
1993 RANK	MLB 1B		31	31	31	30	26	20	32	30	17	26	31	21	10	22	37
1994 PROJECTIONS			47	121	15	34	7	0	3	14	26	25	0	2	281	421	

Mel Rojas No. 51/P

Full name: Melquiades Rojas
Bats: R **Throws:** R **HT:** 5–11 **WT:** 195
Born: 12–10–66, Haiua, DR
High school: Liceo Mantresa (DR)
Rojas has pitched 189 innings of relief over the past two seasons. His 10 saves was a career high.

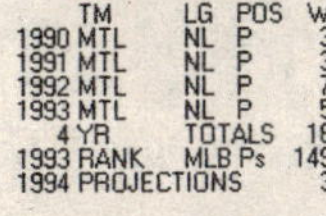

TM	LG	POS	W	L	ERA	G	GS	CG	SH	SV	IP	H	R	ER	HR	BB	SO	SALARY
1990 MTL	NL	P	3	1	3.60	23	0	0	0	1	40.0	34	17	16	5	24	26	N/A
1991 MTL	NL	P	3	3	3.75	37	0	0	0	6	48.0	42	21	20	4	13	37	115,000
1992 MTL	NL	P	7	1	1.43	68	0	0	0	10	100.2	71	17	16	2	34	70	140,000
1993 MTL	NL	P	5	8	2.95	66	0	0	0	10	88.1	80	39	29	6	30	48	300,000
4 YR	TOTALS		18	13	2.63	194	0	0	0	27	277.0	227	94	81	17	101	181	
1993 RANK	MLB Ps		149		41	26	202	125	69	25	166	73	87		61	115	211	150
1994 PROJECTIONS			3	4	3.26	42	0	0	0	5	58	52	25	21	5	22	37	

Tim Scott No. 54/P

Full name: Timothy Dale Scott
Bats: R **Throws:** R **HT:** 6–2 **WT:** 205
Born: 11–16–66, Hanford, CA
High school: Hanford (CA)
Working as a set-up man, Scott made 32 appearances after being acquired from San Diego.

TM	LG	POS	W	L	ERA	G	GS	CG	SH	SV	IP	H	R	ER	HR	BB	SO	SALARY
1991 SD	NL	P	0	0	9.00	2	0	0	0	0	1.0	2	2	1	0	0	1	N/A
1992 SD	NL	P	4	1	5.26	34	0	0	0	0	37.2	39	24	22	4	21	30	109,000
1993 MTL	NL	P	7	2	3.01	56	0	0	0	1	71.2	69	28	24	4	34	65	125,000
3 YR	TOTALS		11	3	3.83	92	0	0	0	1	110.1	110	54	47	8	55	96	
1993 RANK	MLB Ps		108		45	57	202	125	69	70	212	107	51		35	237	27	212
1994 PROJECTIONS			9	2	2.97	74	0	0	0	1	94	91	36	31	5	45	86	

Jeff Shaw — No. 31/P

Full name: Jeffrey Lee Shaw
Bats: R **Throws:** R **HT:** 6–2 **WT:** 200
Born: 7–7–66, Washington Courthouse, OH
High school: Washington Senior, (OH)
College: Cuyahoga CC (OH)
Shaw worked 47 games in middle relief.

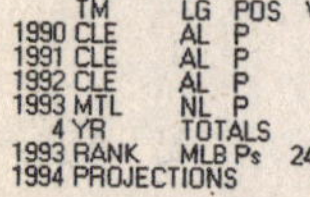
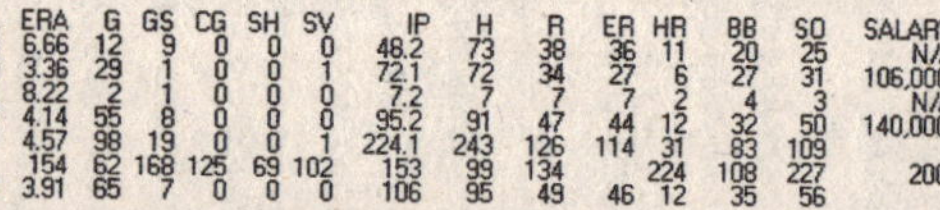

	TM	LG	POS	W	L	ERA	G	GS	CG	SH	SV	IP	H	R	ER	HR	BB	SO	SALARY
1990	CLE	AL	P	3	4	6.66	12	9	0	0	0	48.2	73	38	36	11	20	25	N/A
1991	CLE	AL	P	0	5	3.36	29	1	0	0	1	72.1	72	34	27	6	27	31	106,000
1992	CLE	AL	P	0	1	8.22	2	1	0	0	0	7.2	7	7	7	2	4	3	N/A
1993	MTL	NL	P	2	7	4.14	55	8	0	0	0	95.2	91	47	44	12	32	50	140,000
4	YR	TOTALS		5	17	4.57	98	19	0	0	1	224.1	243	126	114	31	83	109	
1993	RANK	MLB Ps		246		154	62	168	125	69	102	153	99	134		224	108	227	200
1994	PROJECTIONS			1	7	3.91	65	7	0	0	0	106	95	49	46	12	35	56	

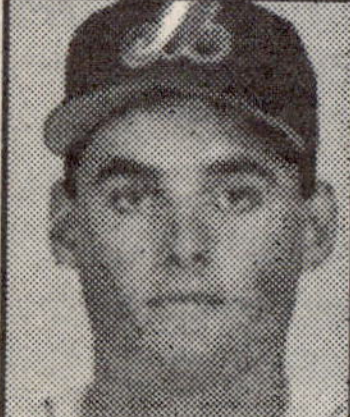

Tim Spehr — No. 2/C

Full name: Timothy Joseph Spehr
Bats: R **Throws:** R **HT:** 6–2 **WT:** 200
Born: 7–2–66, Excelsior Springs, MO
High school: Richfield (Waco, TX)
College: Arizona State
Spehr ended the season 14 for 35, with 3 doubles.

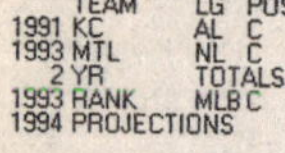
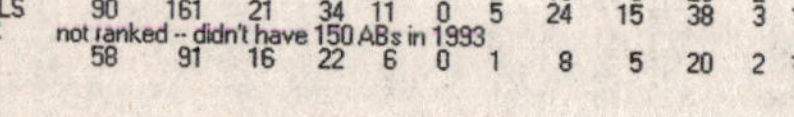

	TEAM	LG	POS	G	AB	R	H	2B	3B	HR	RBI	BB	SO	SB	E	BA	SLG	SALARY
1991	KC	AL	C	37	74	7	14	5	0	3	14	9	18	1	3	.189	.378	100,000
1993	MTL	NL	C	53	87	14	20	6	0	2	10	6	20	2	9	.230	.368	115,000
2	YR	TOTALS		90	161	21	34	11	0	5	24	15	38	3	12	.211	.373	
1993	RANK	MLB	C	not ranked -- didn't have 150 ABs in 1993														
1994	PROJECTIONS			58	91	16	22	6	0	1	8	5	20	2	11	.242	.341	0

Rondell White — No. 37/OF

Full name: Rondell Bernard White
Bats: R **Throws:** R **HT:** 6–1 **WT:** 205
Born: 2–23–72, Milledgeville, GA
High school: Jones (Gray, GA)
White started '93 in AA. As a major leaguer, he got 19 hits and 15 RBI.

	TEAM	LG	POS	G	AB	R	H	2B	3B	HR	RBI	BB	SO	SB	E	BA	SLG	SALARY
1993	MTL	NL	OF	23	73	9	19	3	1	2	15	7	16	1	0	.260	.411	N/A
1	YR	TOTAL		23	73	9	19	3	1	2	15	7	16	1	0	.260	.411	
1993	RANK	MLB	OF	not ranked -- didn't have 150 ABs in 1993														

New York METS

1994 Scouting Report

Hitting: (1993/.248 BA, thirteenth in NL; 158 HR, fourth in NL)

Bobby Bonilla is the team's biggest bat (.265, 34 HR, 87 RBI). But Eddie Murray's departure means a loss of 26 HR and 92 RBI that the Mets have to make up. Jeff Kent hit .269 with 20 HR and 79 RBI, but few expect him to surpass that level of performance. Jeromy Burnitz, a mid-season callup, was a pleasant surprise with 13 HR and 37 RBI. If GM Joe McIlvaine doesn't acquire a slugger and a leadoff hitter, you can look for only marginal improvement on 1993's anemic offense. Unfortunately, the Mets have no phenoms on the farm to fill these roles, and the club is committed to building with youth.

The Mets are very slow; they were last in the NL in steals in 1993.

Pitching: (1993/4.05 ERA, seventh in NL)

Dwight Gooden and Bret Saberhagen are All-Stars when healthy—but they've been injured often over the past two seasons. Gooden will probably bounce back strong this season, but Saberhagen may not — he's had minor, nagging injuries since he joined the team. Pete Smith (obtained in a trade with Atlanta) will help. And Frank Seminara, obtained from the Padres, may fit in the rotation.

John Franco has been plagued with injuries throughout his Mets' tenure. Most disturbingly, he suffered through several ineffective outings when he returned from the DL at the end of last season. His salad days as a reliever appear over, which creates another hole for the Mets to fill.

Defense: (.975 pct., tenth in NL)

Tim Bogar is a competent glove at SS, and Ryan Thompson is a solid defensive outfielder.

1994 Prospects:

This is a bad baseball team that can't hit or play defense. Many of their stars have disturbing injury records. There aren't five Mets that fans can count on to both remain healthy and have an improved 1994 season. A successful '94 Mets season will mean finishing ahead of Florida.

Team Directory

Chairman: Nelson Doubleday
General Mgr.: Joe McIlvaine
Director of P.R.: Jay Horwitz
President & CEO: Fred Wilpon
Senior VP/Consultant: Frank Cashen
Traveling Secretary: Bob O'Hara

Minor League Affiliates:

Level	Team/League	1993 Record
AAA	Norfolk – International	70–71
AA	Binghamton – Eastern	88–72
A	St. Lucie – Florida State	78–52
	Capital City – South Atlantic	64–77
	Pittsfield – New York/Penn.	40–35
	Kingsport – Appalachian	30–38
Rookie	Sarasota Mets – Gulf Coast	39–20

1993 Review

	Home		Away			Home		Away			Home		Away	
vs NL East	W	L	W	L	vs NL Cent.	W	L	W	L	vs NL West	W	L	W	L
Atlanta	1	5	2	4	Chicago	2	4	3	4	Colorado	4	2	2	4
Florida	4	3	5	1	Cincinnati	2	4	4	2	Los Angeles	2	4	2	4
Montreal	2	4	2	5	Houston	1	5	0	6	San Diego	2	4	3	3
Philadelphia	1	6	2	4	Pittsburgh	2	4	2	5	S. Francisco	2	4	2	4
					St. Louis	3	4	2	4					
Total	8	18	11	14		10	21	11	21		10	14	9	15

1993 finish: 59–103 (28–53 home, 31–50 away), seventh in NL East, 38 games behind

1994 Schedule

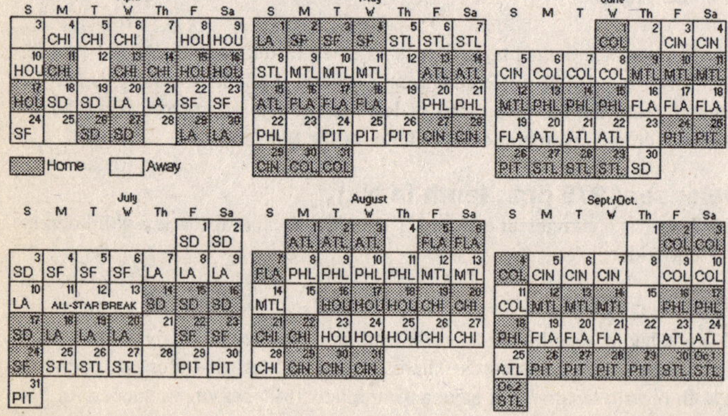

April

S	M	T	W	Th	F	Sa
3	4 CHI	5 CHI	6 CHI	7	8 HOU	9 HOU
10 HOU	11 CHI	12	13 CHI	14 CHI	15 HOU	16 HOU
17 HOU	18 SD	19 SD	20 LA	21 LA	22 SF	23 SF
24 SF	25	26 SD	27 SD	28	29 LA	30 LA

May

S	M	T	W	Th	F	Sa
1 LA	2 SF	3 SF	4 SF	5 STL	6 STL	7 STL
8 STL	9 MTL	10 MTL	11 MTL	12	13 ATL	14 ATL
15 ATL	16 FLA	17 FLA	18 FLA	19	20 PHL	21 PHL
22 PHL	23	24 PIT	25 PIT	26 PIT	27 CIN	28 CIN
29 CIN	30 COL	31 COL				

June

S	M	T	W	Th	F	Sa
			1 COL	2	3 CIN	4 CIN
5 CIN	6 COL	7 COL	8 COL	9 MTL	10 MTL	11 MTL
12 MTL	13 PHL	14 PHL	15 PHL	16 FLA	17 FLA	18 FLA
19 FLA	20 ATL	21 ATL	22 ATL	23	24 PIT	25 PIT
26 PIT	27 STL	28 STL	29 STL	30 SD		

Home Away

July

S	M	T	W	Th	F	Sa
					1 SD	2 SD
3 SD	4 SF	5 SF	6 SF	7 LA	8 LA	9 LA
10 LA	11 ALL-STAR BREAK	12	13	14 SD	15 SD	16 SD
17 SD	18 LA	19 LA	20 LA	21	22 SF	23 SF
24 SF	25 STL	26 STL	27 STL	28	29 PIT	30 PIT
31 PIT						

August

S	M	T	W	Th	F	Sa
	1 ATL	2 ATL	3 ATL	4	5 FLA	6 FLA
7 FLA	8 PHL	9 PHL	10 PHL	11 PHL	12 MTL	13 MTL
14 MTL	15	16 HOU	17 HOU	18 HOU	19 CHI	20 CHI
21 CHI	22 CHI	23 HOU	24 HOU	25 HOU	26 CHI	27 CHI
28 CHI	29 CIN	30 CIN	31 CIN			

Sept./Oct.

S	M	T	W	Th	F	Sa
				1	2 COL	3 COL
4 COL	5 CIN	6 CIN	7 CIN	8	9 COL	10 COL
11 COL	12 MTL	13 MTL	14 MTL	15	16 PHL	17 PHL
18 PHL	19 FLA	20 FLA	21 FLA	22	23 ATL	24 ATL
25 ATL	26 PIT	27 PIT	28 PIT	29 PIT	30 STL	Oct 1 STL
Oc 2 STL						

NEW YORK METS 1994 ROSTER

Manager: Dallas Green (46)
Coaches: Mike Cubbage (4); Frank Howard (55); Tom McCraw (27); Greg Pavlick (52); Steve Swisher; Bobby Wine (7)

No.	PITCHERS	B	T	HT	WT	DOB	BIRTHPLACE	RESIDENCE
63	Castillo, Juan	R	R	6–5	205	6–23–70	Caracas, VZ	Caracas, VZ
31	Franco, John	L	L	5–10	188	9–17–60	Brooklyn, NY	Staten Island, NY
16	Gooden, Dwight	R	R	6–3	210	11–16–64	Tampa, FL	St. Petersburg, FL
46	Gozzo, Mauro	R	R	6–3	212	3–7–66	New Britain, CT	Rossville, TN
35	Greer, Kenny	R	R	6–2	215	5–12–67	Boston, MA	Hull, MA
53	Hillman, Eric	L	L	6–10	225	4–27–66	Gary, IN	Arlington, VA
*	Hurst, Jonathan							
40	Innis, Jeff	R	R	6–1	168	7–5–62	Decatur, IL	Jupiter, FL
	Jacome, Jason							
28	Jones, Bob	R	R	6–4	210	2–10–70	Fresno, CA	Kerman, CA
	Linton, Doug	R	R	6–1	190	9–2–65	Santa Ana, CA	
51	Maddux, Mike	L	L	6–2	188	8–27–61	Dayton, OH	Las Vegas, NV
39	Manzanillo, Josias	R	R	6–0	190	10–16–67	S. Pedro, DR	Boston, MA
18	Saberhagen, Bret	R	R	6–1	190	4–11–64	Chic. Heights, IL	Babylon, NY
48	Schourek, Pete	L	L	6–5	205	5–10–69	Austin, TX	Fairfax, VA
	Seminara, Frank	R	R	6–2	205	5–16–67	Brooklyn, NY	Brooklyn, NY
	Smith, Pete	R	R	6–2	200	2–27–66	Weymouth, MA	Smyrna, GA
38	Telgheder, Dave	R	R	6–3	212	11–11–66	Middleton, NY	Slate Hill, NY
49	Vitko, Joe	R	R	6–8	210	2–1–70	Somerville, NJ	Ebersburg, PA
	Walker, Pete							
	Wegmann, Tom							
19	Young, Anthony	R	R	6–2	210	1–19–66	Houston, TX	Houston, TX
No.	**CATCHERS**	**B**	**T**	**HT**	**WT**	**DOB**	**BIRTHPLACE**	**RESIDENCE**
64	Fordyce, Brook	R	R	6–1	185	5–7–70	New London, CT	Old Lyme, CT
9	Hundley, Todd	S	R	5–11	185	5–27–69	Martinsville, VA	Palatine, IL
	Kmak, Joe	R	R	6–0	185	5–3–63	Napa, CA	Foster City, CA
*	Manto, Jeff	R	R	6–3	210	1–23–64	Bristol, PA	Bristol, PA
No.	**INFIELDERS**	**B**	**T**	**HT**	**WT**	**DOB**	**BIRTHPLACE**	**RESIDENCE**
23	Bogar, Tim	R	R	6–2	198	10–28–66	Indianapolis, IN	Kankakee, IL
10	Huskey, Butch	R	R	6–3	244	11–10–71	Anadarko, OK	Lawton, OK
12	Kent, Jeff	R	R	6–1	185	3–7–68	Bellflower, CA	Hunt. Beach, CA
61	Ledesma, Aaron	R	R	6–2	200	6–3–71	Union City, CA	Union City, CA
17	McKnight, Jeff	S	R	6–0	180	2–18–63	Conway, AR	Bee Branch, AR
36	Navarro, Tito	S	R	5–10	165	9–12–70	Rio Piedras, PR	Hato Rey, PR
	Veras, Quilvio							
	Zinter, Alan							
No.	**OUTFIELDERS**	**B**	**T**	**HT**	**WT**	**DOB**	**BIRTHPLACE**	**RESIDENCE**
25	Bonilla, Bobby	S	R	6–3	240	2–23–63	New York, NY	Bradenton, FL
5	Burnitz, Jeromy	L	R	6–0	190	4–15–69	Westminster, CA	Key Largo, FL
*	Cangelosi, John	S	L	5–8	160	3–10–63	Brooklyn, NY	
*	Dascenzo, Doug	S	L	5–8	160	6–30–64	Cleveland, OH	LaBelle, PA
3	Jackson, Darrin	R	R	6–0	185	8–22–63	Los Angeles, CA	Mesa, AZ
*	Linderman, Jim							
6	Orsulak, Joe	L	L	6–1	205	5–31–62	Glen Ridge, NJ	Cockeysville, MD
*	Parker, Rick							
44	Thompson, Ryan	R	R	6–3	200	11–4–67	Chesterton, MD	Rock Hall, MD

*signed to minor league contracts and invited to spring training as non-roster invitees. Also signed outfielder Pat Howell and pitcher Mike Remlinger to minor league contracts and invited them to spring training as non-roster invitees.

Shea Stadium (55,601, grass)
Tickets: 718–507–8499
Ticket prices:
- $15 (box)
- $12 (upper level box)
- $12 (loge and mezzanine reserved)
- $6.50 (bk. rows, loge & mezz. res.)
- $6.50 (upper level reserved)
- $1 (senior citizens)

Field Dimensions (from home plate)
- To left field at foul line, 338 feet
- To center field, 410 feet
- To right field at foul line, 338 feet

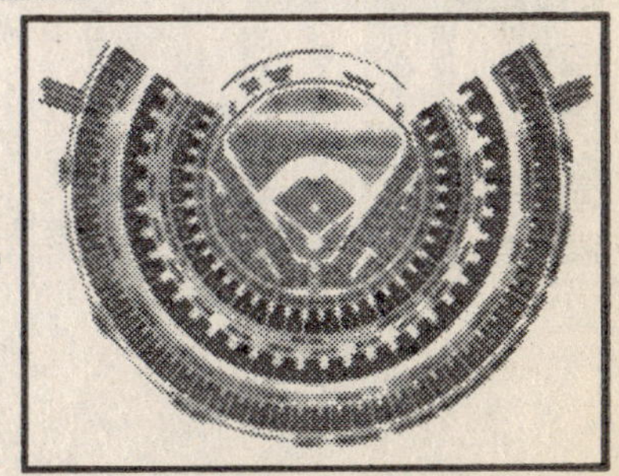

Tim Bogar No. 23/SS

Full name: Timothy Paul Bogar
Bats: R **Throws:** R **HT:** 6–2 **WT:** 198
Born: 10–28–66, Indianapolis, IN
High school: Buffalo (IL)
College: Eastern Illinois

Rookie Bogar started 60 games at shortstop for the Mets. He batted .315 with men in scoring position.

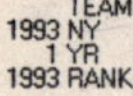

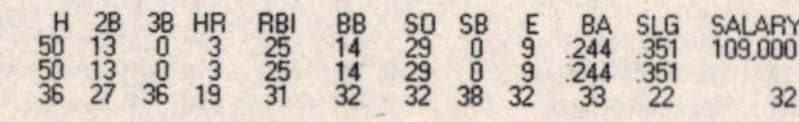

TEAM	LG	POS	G	AB	R	H	2B	3B	HR	RBI	BB	SO	SB	E	BA	SLG	SALARY
1993 NY	NL	SS	78	205	19	50	13	0	3	25	14	29	0	9	.244	.351	109,000
1 YR	TOTAL		78	205	19	50	13	0	3	25	14	29	0	9	.244	.351	
1993 RANK	MLB	SS	33	35	38	36	27	36	19	31	32	32	38	32	33	22	32

Bobby Bonilla No. 25/OF–3B

Full name: Robert Martin Antonio Bonilla Jr.
Bats: S **Throws:** R **HT:** 6–3 **WT:** 240
Born: 2–23–63, New York, NY
High school: Lehman (Bronx, NY)
College: New York Tech (Westbury, NY)

Bonilla's 34 HR was sixth best in the NL. He played in the Mets' first 139 games until a shoulder injury ended his season.

TEAM	LG	POS	G	AB	R	H	2B	3B	HR	RBI	BB	SO	SB	E	BA	SLG	SALARY
1986 CHI	AL	OF-1B	75	234	27	63	10	2	2	26	33	49	4	2	.269	.355	N/A
1986 PIT	NL	OF-1B	63	192	28	46	6	2	1	17	29	39	4	3	.240	.307	N/A
1987 PIT	NL	3B-OF	141	466	58	140	33	3	15	77	39	64	3	16	.300	.481	N/A
1988 PIT	NL	3B	159	584	87	160	32	7	24	100	85	82	3	32	.274	.476	N/A
1989 PIT	NL	3B-1B	163	616	96	173	37	10	24	86	76	93	8	35	.281	.490	N/A
1990 PIT	NL	OF-3B	160	625	112	175	39	7	32	120	45	103	4	15	.280	.518	1,250,000
1991 PIT	NL	OF-3B	157	577	102	174	44	6	18	100	90	67	2	15	.302	.492	2,400,000
1992 NY	NL	OF-1B	128	438	62	109	23	0	19	70	66	73	4	4	.249	.432	6,100,000
1993 NY	NL	OF	139	502	81	133	21	3	34	87	72	96	3	17	.265	.522	6,450,000
8 YR	TOTALS		1185	4234	653	1173	245	40	169	683	535	666	35	139	.277	.474	
1993 RANK	MLB	OF	43	41	29	50	48	54	7	19	17	30	93	2	82	12	1
1994 PROJECTIONS			136	468	67	127	25	2	22	78	59	77	3	12	.271	.481	

Jeromy Burnitz No. 5/OF

Full name: Jeromy Neal Burnitz
Bats: L **Throws:** R **HT:** 6–0 **WT:** 190
Born: 4–15–69, Westminster, CA
High school: Conroe (TX)
College: Oklahoma State

Burnitz' 13 HR ranked him third among NL rookies. He batted .445 when he swung at the first pitch, with 5 HR.

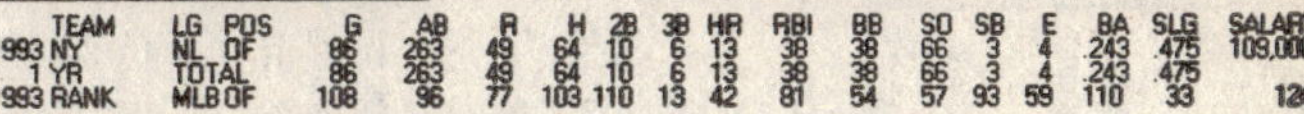

	TEAM	LG	POS	G	AB	R	H	2B	3B	HR	RBI	BB	SO	SB	E	BA	SLG	SALARY
1993	NY	NL	OF	86	263	49	64	10	6	13	38	38	66	3	4	.243	.475	109,000
1	YR	TOTAL		86	263	49	64	10	6	13	38	38	66	3	4	.243	.475	
1993	RANK	MLB	OF	108	96	77	103	110	13	42	81	54	57	93	59	110	33	124

Todd Hundley No. 9/C

Full name: Todd Randolph Hundley
Bats: S **Throws:** R **HT:** 5–11 **WT:** 185
Born: 5–27–69, Martinsville, VA
High school: William Freund (Palatine, IL)

Hundley batted .259 from the right side and .223 from the left, but hit all of his career-best 11 HR left-handed.

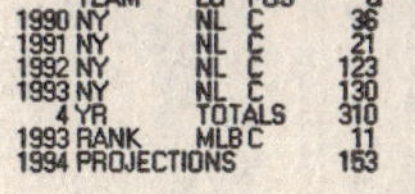
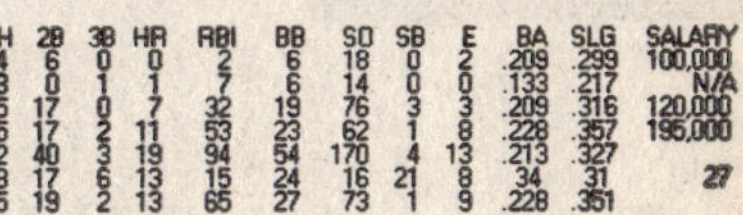

	TEAM	LG	POS	G	AB	R	H	2B	3B	HR	RBI	BB	SO	SB	E	BA	SLG	SALARY
1990	NY	NL	C	36	67	8	14	6	0	0	2	6	18	0	2	.209	.299	100,000
1991	NY	NL	C	21	60	5	8	0	1	1	7	6	14	0	0	.133	.217	N/A
1992	NY	NL	C	123	358	32	75	17	0	7	32	19	76	3	3	.209	.316	120,000
1993	NY	NL	C	130	417	40	95	17	2	11	53	23	62	1	8	.228	.357	195,000
4	YR	TOTALS		310	902	85	192	40	3	19	94	54	170	4	13	.213	.327	
1993	RANK	MLB	C	11	13	15	18	17	6	13	15	24	16	21	8	34	31	27
1994	PROJECTIONS			153	504	48	115	19	2	13	65	27	73	1	9	.228	.351	

Jeff Kent — No. 12/2B

Full name: Jeffrey Franklin Kent
Bats: R **Throws:** R **HT:** 6–1 **WT:** 185
Born: 3–7–68, Bellflower, CA
High school: Edison (Huntington Beach, CA)
College: Cal–Berkeley

Kent's 21 HR and 80 RBI were the most ever by a Mets second baseman. All 21 HR came against righthanded pitching.

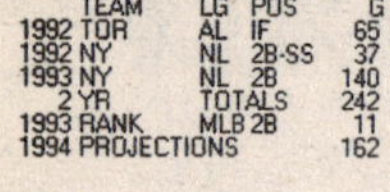

	TEAM	LG	POS	G	AB	R	H	2B	3B	HR	RBI	BB	SO	SB	E	BA	SLG	SALARY
1992	TOR	AL	IF	65	192	36	46	13	1	8	35	20	47	2	11	.240	.443	109,000
1992	NY	NL	2B-SS	37	113	16	27	8	1	3	15	7	29	0	3	.239	.407	N/A
1993	NY	NL	2B	140	496	65	134	24	0	21	80	30	88	4	22	.270	.446	195,000
2	YR	TOTALS		242	801	117	207	45	2	32	130	57	164	6	36	.258	.439	
1993	RANK	MLB	2B	11	9	14	14	13	40	1	3	26	4	29	1	20	8	23
1994	PROJECTIONS			162	582	75	158	27	0	25	94	34	99	5	26	.271	.447	

Jeff McKnight — No. 17/IF

Full name: Jefferson Alan McKnight
Bats: S **Throws:** R **HT:** 6–0 **WT:** 180
Born: 2–18–63, Conway, AR
High school: South Side (Bee Branch, AR)
College: Westark Community (Ft. Smith, AR)

In 1993, McKnight had 19 pinch hits, second best in the NL. He hit .298 after the All-Star break, and made 25 starts at 4 positions.

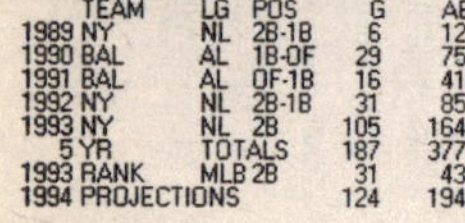

	TEAM	LG	POS	G	AB	R	H	2B	3B	HR	RBI	BB	SO	SB	E	BA	SLG	SALARY
1989	NY	NL	2B-1B	6	12	2	3	0	0	0	0	2	1	0	1	.250	.250	N/A
1990	BAL	AL	1B-OF	29	75	11	15	2	0	1	4	5	17	0	0	.200	.267	N/A
1991	BAL	AL	OF-1B	16	41	2	7	1	0	0	2	2	7	1	0	.171	.195	103,000
1992	NY	NL	2B-1B	31	85	10	23	3	1	2	13	2	8	0	3	.271	.400	N/A
1993	NY	NL	2B	105	164	19	42	3	1	2	13	13	31	0	10	.256	.323	145,000
5	YR	TOTALS		187	377	44	90	9	2	5	32	24	64	1	14	.239	.313	
1993	RANK	MLB	2B	31	43	41	42	44	31	30	43	40	38	42	22	26	400	29
1994	PROJECTIONS			124	194	22	49	3	1	2	15	15	37	0	11	.253	.309	

Joe Orsulak No. 6/OF

Full name: Joseph Michael Orsulak
Bats: L **Throws:** L **HT:** 6–1 **WT:** 205
Born: 5–31–62, Glen Ridge, NJ
High school: Parsipanny Hills (NJ)
Veteran Orsulak's 163 total bases ranked fourth on the Mets, and he led the team with a .310 BA at the All-Star break

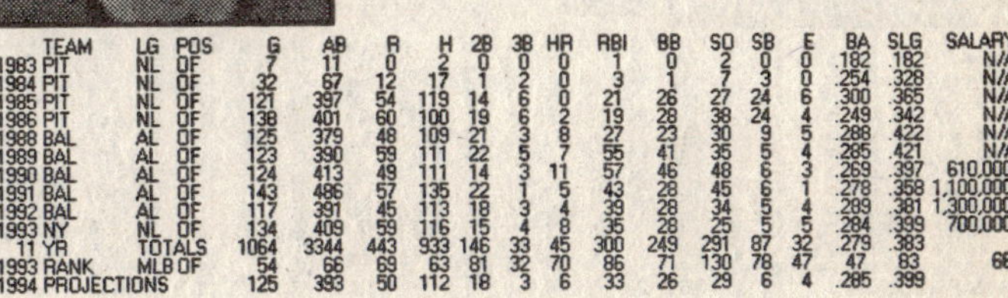

TEAM	LG	POS	G	AB	R	H	2B	3B	HR	RBI	BB	SO	SB	E	BA	SLG	SALARY
1983 PIT	NL	OF	7	11	0	2	0	0	0	1	0	2	0	0	.182	.182	N/A
1984 PIT	NL	OF	32	67	12	17	1	2	0	3	1	7	3	0	.254	.328	N/A
1985 PIT	NL	OF	121	397	54	119	14	6	0	21	26	27	24	6	.300	.365	N/A
1986 PIT	NL	OF	138	401	60	100	19	6	2	19	28	38	24	4	.249	.342	N/A
1988 BAL	AL	OF	125	379	48	109	21	3	8	27	23	30	9	5	.288	.422	N/A
1989 BAL	AL	OF	123	390	59	111	22	5	7	55	41	35	5	4	.285	.421	N/A
1990 BAL	AL	OF	124	413	49	111	14	3	11	57	46	48	6	3	.269	.397	610,000
1991 BAL	AL	OF	143	486	57	135	22	1	5	43	28	45	6	1	.278	.358	1,100,000
1992 BAL	AL	OF	117	391	45	113	18	3	4	39	28	34	5	4	.289	.381	1,300,000
1993 NY	NL	OF	134	409	59	116	15	4	8	35	28	25	5	5	.284	.399	700,000
11 YR	TOTALS		1064	3344	443	933	146	33	45	300	249	291	87	32	.279	.383	
1993 RANK	MLB	OF	54	66	69	63	81	32	70	86	71	130	78	47	47	83	66
1994 PROJECTIONS			125	393	50	112	18	3	6	33	26	29	6	4	.285	.399	

Ryan Thompson No. 44/OF

Full name: Ryan Orlando Thompson
Bats: R **Throws:** R **HT:** 6–3 **WT:** 200
Born: 11–4–67, Chesterton, MD
High school: Kent County (Rock Hall, MD)
Thompson batted a strong .270 after the All-Star break, and started in centerfield in 62 of the Mets last 63 games.

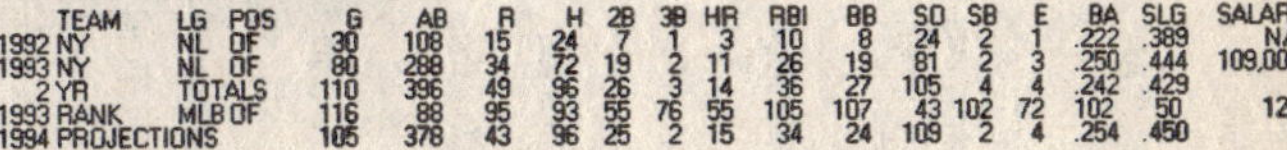

TEAM	LG	POS	G	AB	R	H	2B	3B	HR	RBI	BB	SO	SB	E	BA	SLG	SALARY
1992 NY	NL	OF	30	108	15	24	7	1	3	10	8	24	2	1	.222	.389	N/A
1993 NY	NL	OF	80	288	34	72	19	2	11	26	19	81	2	3	.250	.444	109,000
2 YR	TOTALS		110	396	49	96	26	3	14	36	27	105	4	4	.242	.429	
1993 RANK	MLB	OF	116	88	95	93	55	76	55	105	107	43	102	72	102	50	124
1994 PROJECTIONS			105	378	43	96	25	2	15	34	24	109	2	4	.254	.450	

Dwight Gooden No. 16/P

Full name: Dwight Eugene Gooden
Bats: R **Throws:** R **HT:** 6–3 **WT:** 210
Born: 11–16–64, Tampa, FL
High school: Hillsborough (Tampa, FL)
In an injury-shortened year, Gooden had 7 complete games, tied for second best in the NL, but his 15 losses were the most of his career.

TM	LG	POS	W	L	ERA	G	GS	CG	SH	SV	IP	H	R	ER	HR	BB	SO	SALARY
1984 NY	NL	P	17	9	2.60	31	31	7	3	0	218.0	161	72	63	7	73	276	N/A
1985 NY	NL	P	24	4	1.53	35	35	16	8	0	276.2	198	51	47	13	69	268	N/A
1986 NY	NL	P	17	6	2.84	33	33	12	2	0	250.0	197	92	79	17	80	200	N/A
1987 NY	NL	P	15	7	3.21	25	25	7	3	0	179.2	162	68	64	11	53	148	N/A
1988 NY	NL	P	18	9	3.19	34	34	10	3	0	248.1	242	98	88	8	57	175	N/A
1989 NY	NL	P	9	4	2.89	19	17	0	0	1	118.1	93	42	38	9	47	101	N/A
1990 NY	NL	P	19	7	3.83	34	34	2	1	0	232.2	229	106	99	10	70	223	1,866,667
1991 NY	NL	P	13	7	3.60	27	27	3	1	0	190.0	185	80	76	12	56	150	2,466,667
1992 NY	NL	P	10	13	3.67	31	31	3	0	0	206.0	197	93	84	11	70	145	4,916,667
1993 NY	NL	P	12	15	3.45	29	29	7	2	0	208.2	188	89	80	16	61	149	5,916,667
10 YR	TOTALS		154	81	3.04	298	296	67	23	1	2128.1	1852	791	718	114	636	1835	
1993 Rank	MLB Ps		43		86	213	65	7	8	102	41	67	76		89	69	98	1
1994 PROJECTIONS			11	11	3.58	29	29	4	1	0	201	190	87	80	13	62	148	

Bret Saberhagen No. 18/P

Full name: Bret William Saberhagen
Bats: R **Throws:** R **HT:** 6–1 **WT:** 190
Born: 4–11–64, Chic. Heights, IL
High school: Cleveland (Reseda, CA)
Saberhagen started poorly, but was 4–0 with a 2.97 ERA in his final 5 starts before a season-ending injury in early August.

TM	LG	POS	W	L	ERA	G	GS	CG	SH	SV	IP	H	R	ER	HR	BB	SO	SALARY
1984 KC	AL	P	10	11	3.48	38	18	2	1	1	157.2	138	71	61	13	36	73	N/A
1985 KC	AL	P	20	6	2.87	32	32	10	1	0	235.1	211	79	75	19	38	158	N/A
1986 KC	AL	P	7	12	4.15	30	25	4	2	0	156.0	165	77	72	15	29	112	N/A
1987 KC	AL	P	18	10	3.36	33	33	15	4	0	257.0	246	99	96	27	53	163	N/A
1988 KC	AL	P	14	16	3.80	35	35	9	0	0	260.2	271	122	110	18	59	171	N/A
1989 KC	AL	P	23	6	2.16	36	35	12	4	0	262.1	209	74	63	13	43	193	N/A
1990 KC	AL	P	5	9	3.27	20	20	5	0	0	135.0	146	52	49	9	28	87	1,400,000
1991 KC	AL	P	13	8	3.07	28	28	7	2	0	196.1	165	76	67	12	45	136	2,950,000
1992 NY	NL	P	3	5	3.50	17	15	1	1	0	97.2	84	39	38	6	27	81	2,950,000
1993 NY	NL	P	7	7	3.29	19	19	4	1	0	139.1	131	55	51	11	17	93	4,250,000
10 YR	TOTALS		120	90	3.24	288	260	69	16	1	1897.1	1766	744	682	143	375	1267	
1993 Rank	MLB Ps		108		68	258	108	25	23	102	108	90	54		104	2	120	13
1994 PROJECTIONS			5	7	3.37	18	18	3	0	0	123	120	48	46	8	24	87	

Frank Seminara No. 44/P

Full name: Frank Peter Seminara
Bats: R **Throws:** R **HT:** 6–2 **WT:** 205
Born: 5–16–67, Brooklyn, NY
High school: Xaverian (Brooklyn, NY)
College: Columbia (New York, NY)

Seminara struggled as a starter after a promising '92, and spent most of '93 in AAA.

	TM	LG	POS	W	L	ERA	G	GS	CG	SH	SV	IP	H	R	ER	HR	BB	SO	SALARY
1992	SD	NL	P	9	4	3.68	19	18	0	0	0	100.1	98	46	41	5	46	61	N/A
1993	SD	NL	P	3	3	4.47	18	7	0	0	0	46.1	53	30	23	5	21	22	N/A
2	YR	TOTALS		12	7	3.93	37	25	0	0	0	146.2	151	76	64	10	67	83	
1993	Rank	MLB Ps		not ranked -- didn't have 50 IP in 1993															
1994	PROJECTIONS			8	4	3.90	24	16	0	0	0	97	100	50	42	6	44	55	

Pete Smith P

Full name: Peter John Smith
Bats: R **Throws:** R **HT:** 6–2 **WT:** 200
Born: 2–27–66, Weymouth, MA
High school: Burlington (MA)

Smith had 90.2 IP for the Braves in 1993, his highest total since 1989. Acquired for Dave Gallagher, he should fit well in the Mets rotation.

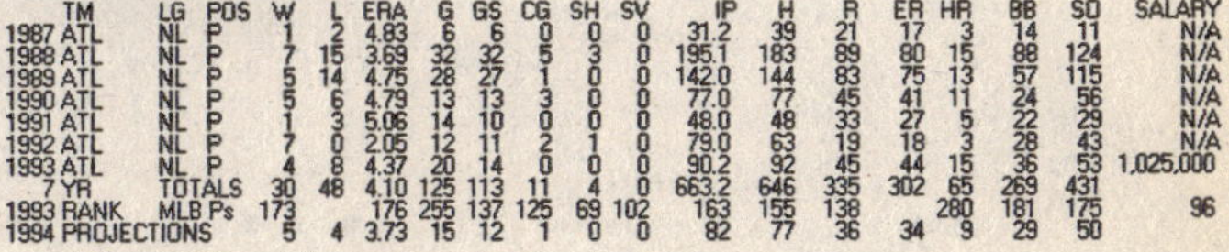

	TM	LG	POS	W	L	ERA	G	GS	CG	SH	SV	IP	H	R	ER	HR	BB	SO	SALARY
1987	ATL	NL	P	1	2	4.83	6	6	0	0	0	31.2	39	21	17	3	14	11	N/A
1988	ATL	NL	P	7	15	3.69	32	32	5	3	0	195.1	183	89	80	15	88	124	N/A
1989	ATL	NL	P	5	14	4.75	28	27	1	0	0	142.0	144	83	75	13	57	115	N/A
1990	ATL	NL	P	5	6	4.79	13	13	3	0	0	77.0	77	45	41	11	24	56	N/A
1991	ATL	NL	P	1	3	5.06	14	10	0	0	0	48.0	48	33	27	5	22	29	N/A
1992	ATL	NL	P	7	0	2.05	12	11	2	1	0	79.0	63	19	18	3	28	43	N/A
1993	ATL	NL	P	4	8	4.37	20	14	0	0	0	90.2	92	45	44	15	36	53	1,025,000
7	YR	TOTALS		30	48	4.10	125	113	11	4	0	663.2	646	335	302	65	269	431	
1993	RANK	MLB Ps		173		176	255	137	125	69	102	163	155	138		280	181	175	96
1994	PROJECTIONS			5	4	3.73	15	12	1	0	0	82	77	36	34	9	29	50	

John Franco No. 31/P

Full name: John Anthony Franco
Bats: L **Throws:** L **HT:** 5–10 **WT:** 188
Born: 9–17–60, Brooklyn, NY
High school: Lafayette (Brooklyn, NY)
College: St. John's (Jamaica, NY)

Franco battled injuries and had only 10 saves, his lowest total since 1984. His 5.20 ERA was almost double his career mark.

	TM	LG	POS	W	L	ERA	G	GS	CG	SH	SV	IP	H	R	ER	HR	BB	SO	SALARY
1984	CIN	NL	P	6	2	2.61	54	0	0	0	4	79.1	74	28	23	3	36	55	N/A
1985	CIN	NL	P	12	3	2.18	67	0	0	0	12	99.0	83	27	24	5	40	61	N/A
1986	CIN	NL	P	6	6	2.94	74	0	0	0	29	101.0	90	40	33	7	44	84	N/A
1987	CIN	NL	P	8	5	2.52	68	0	0	0	32	82.0	76	26	23	6	27	61	N/A
1988	CIN	NL	P	6	6	1.57	70	0	0	0	39	86.0	60	18	15	3	27	46	N/A
1989	CIN	NL	P	4	8	3.12	60	0	0	0	32	80.2	77	35	28	3	36	60	N/A
1990	NY	NL	P	5	3	2.53	55	0	0	0	33	67.2	66	22	19	4	21	56	1,708,333
1991	NY	NL	P	5	9	2.93	52	0	0	0	30	55.1	61	27	18	2	18	45	2,633,333
1992	NY	NL	P	6	2	1.64	31	0	0	0	15	33.0	24	6	6	1	11	20	3,333,334
1993	NY	NL	P	4	3	5.20	35	0	0	0	10	36.1	46	24	21	6	19	29	4,000,000
10	YR	TOTALS		62	47	2.62	566	0	0	0	236	720.1	657	253	210	40	279	517	
1993	Rank	MLB Ps		not ranked -- didn't have 50 IP in 1993															
1994	PROJECTIONS			5	2	3.00	40	0	0	0	19	45	45	17	15	3	17	35	

Dallas Green No. 46/Mgr.

Full name: George Dallas Green
Bats: L **Throws:** R **HT:** 6–5 **WT:** 210
Born: 8–4–34, Seaford, DE

Green's managerial career has gone from the 1980 World Series champion Phillies to being fired as manager of the Yankees in 1989. Only time will tell whether Green's hard-nosed approach will work with the Mets.

				REG. SEASON				PLAYOFF			CHAMP. SERIES			WORLD SERIES		
	YEAR	TEAM	LG	W	L	PCT	POS	W	L	PCT	W	L	PCT	W	L	PCT
	1979	PHL	AL	19	11	.633	5			---			---			---
	1980	PHL	AL	91	71	.562	1			---	3	2	.6	4	2	.667
1ST HALF	1981	PHL	AL	34	21	.618	1	2	3	0.4			---			---
2ND HALF	1981	PHL	AL	25	27	.481	3			---			---			---
	1989	NY	AL	56	65	.463	6			---			---			---
	1993	NY	NL	46	78	.371				---			---			---
	5	YR TOTALS		271	273	.498		2	3	0.40	3	2	.6	4	2	.667

John Cangelosi OF

Full name: John Anthony Cangelosi
Bats: S **Throws:** L **HT:** 5–8 **WT:** 160
Born: 3–10–63, Brooklyn, NY
High school: Miami Springs Senior (FL)
College: Miami Dade CC (FL)
Cangelosi didn't play in the major leagues in 1993.

TEAM	LG	POS	G	AB	R	H	2B	3B	HR	RBI	BB	SO	SB	E	BA	SLG	SALARY
1985 CHI	AL	OF	5	2	2	0	0	0	0	0	0	1	0	0	.000	.000	N/A
1986 CHI	AL	OF	137	438	65	103	16	3	2	32	71	61	50	9	.235	.299	N/A
1987 PIT	NL	OF	104	182	44	50	8	3	4	18	46	33	21	3	.275	.418	N/A
1988 PIT	NL	OF	75	118	18	30	4	1	0	8	17	16	9	2	.254	.305	N/A
1989 PIT	NL	OF	112	160	18	35	4	2	0	9	35	20	11	2	.219	.269	N/A
1990 PIT	NL	OF	58	76	13	15	2	0	0	1	11	12	7	0	.197	.224	N/A
1992 TEX	AL	OF	73	85	12	16	2	0	1	6	18	16	6	3	.188	.247	N/A
7 YR	TOTALS		564	1061	172	249	36	9	7	74	198	159	104	19	.235	.305	
1994 PROJECTIONS			117	260	42	62	9	2	2	19	50	38	27	4	.238	.319	

Doug Dascenzo OF

Full name: Douglas Craig Dascenzo
Bats: S **Throws:** L **HT:** 5–8 **WT:** 160
Born: 6–30–64, Cleveland, OH
High school: Brownsville (PA)
College: Fla. Coll. and Oklahoma State
Dascenzo had only 29 hits in 76 games for Texas.

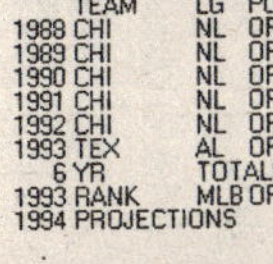

TEAM	LG	POS	G	AB	R	H	2B	3B	HR	RBI	BB	SO	SB	E	BA	SLG	SALARY
1988 CHI	NL	OF	26	75	9	16	3	0	0	4	9	4	6	0	.213	.253	N/A
1989 CHI	NL	OF	47	139	20	23	1	0	1	12	13	13	6	0	.165	.194	N/A
1990 CHI	NL	OF-P	113	241	27	61	9	5	1	26	21	18	15	0	.253	.344	100,000
1991 CHI	NL	OF-P	118	239	40	61	11	0	1	18	24	26	14	2	.255	.314	165,000
1992 CHI	NL	OF	139	376	37	96	13	4	0	20	27	32	6	5	.255	.311	240,000
1993 TEX	AL	OF	76	146	20	29	5	1	2	10	8	22	2	1	.199	.288	N/A
6 YR	TOTALS		519	1216	153	286	42	10	5	90	102	115	49	8	.235	.299	
1993 RANK	MLB OF		not ranked -- didn't have 150 ABs in 1993														
1994 PROJECTIONS			49	120	16	22	3	0	1	8	10	13	4	0	.183	.242	

Butch Huskey No. 10/3B

Full name: Robert Leon Huskey
Bats: R **Throws:** R **HT:** 6–3 **WT:** 244
Born: 11–10–71, Anadarko, OK
High school: Eisenhower (Lawton, OK)
A career .264 hitter in the minors, Huskey posted a .146 BA in 13 late-season games for New York.

TEAM	LG	POS	G	AB	R	H	2B	3B	HR	RBI	BB	SO	SB	E	BA	SLG	SALARY
1993 NY	NL	3B	13	41	2	6	1	0	0	3	1	13	0	3	.146	.171	N/A
1 YR	TOTAL		13	41	2	6	1	0	0	3	1	13	0	3	.146	.171	
1993 RANK	MLB 3B		not ranked -- didn't have 150 ABs in 1993														

Eric Hillman No. 53/P

Full name: John Eric Hillman
Bats: L **Throws:** L **HT:** 6–10 **WT:** 225
Born: 4–27–66, Gary, IN
High school: Homewood–Flossmoor (IL)
College: Eastern Illinois
Hillman lasted at least 6 innings in 15 of 22 starts.

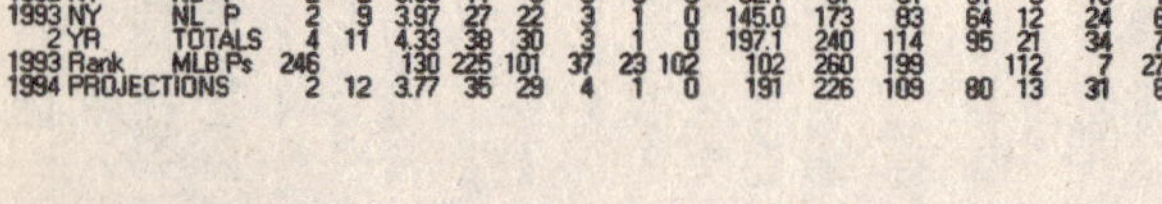

	TM	LG	POS	W	L	ERA	G	GS	CG	SH	SV	IP	H	R	ER	HR	BB	SO	SALARY
1992	NY	NL	P	2	2	5.33	11	8	0	0	0	52.1	67	31	31	9	10	16	109,000
1993	NY	NL	P	2	9	3.97	27	22	3	1	0	145.0	173	83	64	12	24	60	115,000
2	YR	TOTALS		4	11	4.33	38	30	3	1	0	197.1	240	114	95	21	34	76	
1993	Rank	MLB	Ps	246		130	225	101	37	23	102	102	260	199		112	7	273	222
1994	PROJECTIONS			2	12	3.77	35	29	4	1	0	191	226	109	80	13	31	82	

Jeff Innis No. 40/P

Full name: Jeffrey David Innis
Bats: R **Throws:** R **HT:** 6–1 **WT:** 168
Born: 7–5–62, Decatur, IL
High school: Eisenhower (Decatur, IL)
College: Illinois
Innis' 67 appearances is fourth highest in Met history.

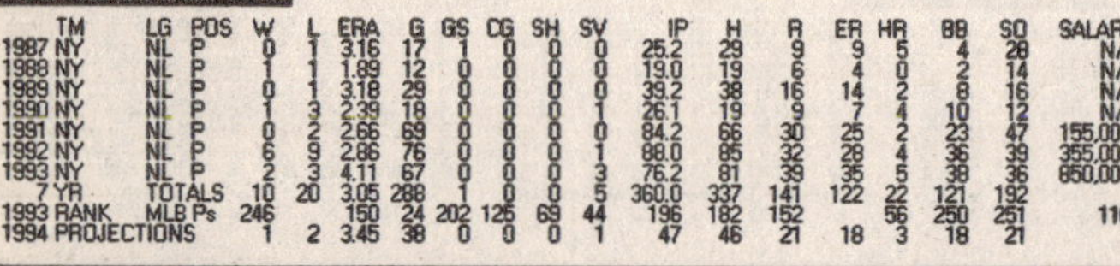

	TM	LG	POS	W	L	ERA	G	GS	CG	SH	SV	IP	H	R	ER	HR	BB	SO	SALARY
1987	NY	NL	P	0	1	3.16	17	1	0	0	0	25.2	29	9	9	5	4	28	N/A
1988	NY	NL	P	1	1	1.89	12	0	0	0	0	19.0	19	6	4	0	2	14	N/A
1989	NY	NL	P	0	1	3.18	29	0	0	0	0	39.2	38	16	14	2	8	16	N/A
1990	NY	NL	P	1	3	2.39	18	0	0	0	1	26.1	19	9	7	4	10	12	N/A
1991	NY	NL	P	0	2	2.66	69	0	0	0	0	84.2	66	30	25	2	23	47	155,000
1992	NY	NL	P	6	9	2.86	76	0	0	0	1	88.0	85	32	28	4	36	39	355,000
1993	NY	NL	P	2	3	4.11	67	0	0	0	3	76.2	81	39	35	5	38	36	850,000
7	YR	TOTALS		10	20	3.05	288	1	0	0	5	360.0	337	141	122	22	121	192	
1993	RANK	MLB	Ps	246		150	24	202	125	69	44	196	182	152		56	250	251	110
1994	PROJECTIONS			1	2	3.45	38	0	0	0	1	47	46	21	18	3	18	21	

Darrin Jackson No. 3/OF

Full name: Darrin Jay Jackson
Bats: R **Throws:** R **HT:** 6–0 **WT:** 185
Born: 8–22–63, Los Angeles, CA
High school: Culver City (CA)
Jackson's .209 BA was the lowest full-season total of his career.

	TEAM	LG	POS	G	AB	R	H	2B	3B	HR	RBI	BB	SO	SB	E	BA	SLG	SALARY
1988	CHI	NL	OF	100	188	29	50	11	3	6	20	5	28	4	2	.266	.452	N/A
1989	SD	NL	OF	70	170	17	37	7	0	4	20	13	34	1	5	.218	.329	N/A
1990	SD	NL	OF	58	113	10	29	3	0	3	9	5	24	3	1	.257	.363	145,000
1991	SD	NL	OF-P	122	359	51	94	12	1	21	49	27	66	5	2	.262	.476	260,000
1992	SD	NL	OF	155	587	72	146	23	5	17	70	26	106	14	2	.249	.392	805,000
1993	TOR	AL	OF	46	176	15	38	8	0	5	19	8	53	0	1	.216	.347	N/A
1993	NY	NL	OF	31	87	4	17	1	0	1	7	2	22	0	0	.195	.241	N/A
8	YR	TOTALS		594	1696	200	416	66	9	57	194	86	336	27	13	.245	.396	
1993	RANK	MLB	OF	121	96	132	111	118	124	87	105	130	49	127	113	129	128	36
1994	PROJECTIONS			49	144	12	30	5	0	3	15	7	36	0	2	.208	.319	

Joe Kmak — C

Full name: Joseph Robert Kmak
Bats: R **Throws:** R **HT:** 6–0 **WT:** 185
Born: 5–3–63, Napa, CA
High school: Serra (San Mateo, CA)
College: Cal–Santa Barbara
Kmak hit .303 in 24 games at AA New Orleans.

	TEAM	LG	POS	G	AB	R	H	2B	3B	HR	RBI	BB	SO	SB	E	BA	SLG	SALARY
1993	MIL	AL	C	51	110	9	24	5	0	0	7	14	13	6	0	.218	.264	N/A
1	YR	TOTAL		51	110	9	24	5	0	0	7	14	13	6	0	.218	.264	
1993	RANK	MLB C		not ranked -- didn't have 150 ABs in 1993														

Doug Linton — P

Full name: Doug Warren Linton
Bats: R **Throws:** R **HT:** 6–1 **WT:** 190
Born: 9–2–65, Santa Ana, CA
High school: Canyon (Orange, CA)
College: UC-Irvine
Linton is a non-roster spring-training invitee.

	TM	LG	POS	W	L	ERA	G	GS	CG	SH	SV	IP	H	R	ER	HR	BB	SO	SALARY
1992	TOR	AL	P	1	3	8.63	8	3	0	0	0	24.0	31	23	23	5	17	16	N/A
1993	CAL	AL	P	2	1	7.36	23	1	0	0	0	36.2	46	30	30	8	23	23	112,500
2	YR	TOTALS		3	4	7.86	31	4	0	0	0	60.2	77	53	53	13	40	39	
1993	RANK	MLB Ps		not ranked -- didn't have 50 IP in 1993															
1994	PROJECTIONS			2	0	7.07	30	0	0	0	0	42	53	33	33	9	26	26	

Mike Maddux — No. 51/P

Full name: Michael Ausley Maddux
Bats: L **Throws:** L **HT:** 6–2 **WT:** 188
Born: 8–27–61, Dayton, OH
High school: Rancho (Las Vegas, NV)
College: Texas–El Paso
Maddux led the Mets with 31 games finished.

	TM	LG	POS	W	L	ERA	G	GS	CG	SH	SV	IP	H	R	ER	HR	BB	SO	SALARY
1988	PHL	NL	P	4	3	3.76	25	11	0	0	0	88.2	91	41	37	6	34	59	N/A
1989	PHL	NL	P	1	3	5.15	16	4	2	1	1	43.2	52	29	25	3	14	26	N/A
1990	LA	NL	P	0	1	6.53	11	2	0	0	0	20.2	24	15	15	3	4	11	N/A
1991	SD	NL	P	7	2	2.46	64	1	0	0	5	98.2	78	30	27	4	27	57	110,000
1992	SD	NL	P	2	2	2.37	50	1	0	0	5	79.2	71	25	21	2	24	60	510,000
1993	NY	NL	P	3	8	3.60	58	0	0	0	5	75.0	67	34	30	3	27	57	1,012,500
8	YR	TOTALS		22	26	3.72	247	37	2	1	16	501.1	488	235	207	27	169	329	
1993	Rank	MLB Ps		209		97	50	202	125	69	33	203	61	92		17	145	77	98
1994	PROJECTIONS			2	6	4.71	30	6	0	0	2	65	69	39	34	4	25	42	

Pete Schourek No. 48/P

Full name: Peter Alan Schourek
Bats: L **Throws:** L **HT:** 6–5 **WT:** 205
Born: 5–10–69, Austin, TX
High school: Geo. C. Marshall (Falls Church, VA)
Schourek's 5.96 ERA was the worst ever by a Mets pitcher with more than 100 IP.

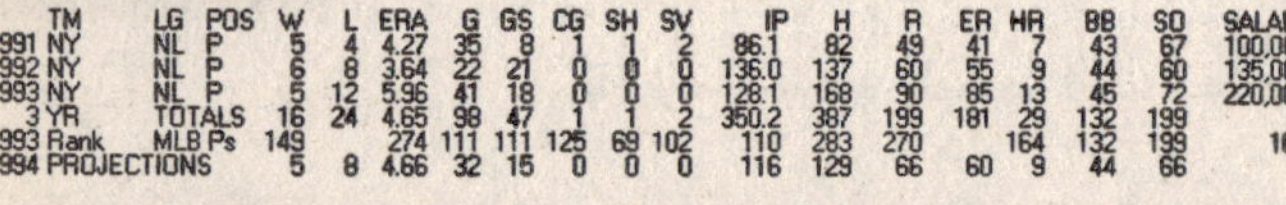

	TM	LG	POS	W	L	ERA	G	GS	CG	SH	SV	IP	H	R	ER	HR	BB	SO	SALARY
1991	NY	NL	P	5	4	4.27	35	8	1	1	2	86.1	82	49	41	7	43	67	100,000
1992	NY	NL	P	6	8	3.64	22	21	0	0	0	136.0	137	60	55	9	44	60	135,000
1993	NY	NL	P	5	12	5.96	41	18	0	0	0	128.1	168	90	85	13	45	72	220,000
3	YR	TOTALS		16	24	4.65	98	47	1	1	2	350.2	387	199	181	29	132	199	
1993	Rank	MLB	Ps	149		274	111	111	125	69	102	110	283	270		164	132	199	168
1994	PROJECTIONS			5	8	4.66	32	15	0	0	0	116	129	66	60	9	44	66	

Dave Telgheder No. 38/P

Full name: David William Telgheder
Bats: R **Throws:** R **HT:** 6–3 **WT:** 212
Born: 11–11–66, Middleton, NY
High school: Minisink Valley (Slate Hill, NY)
College: Massachusetts–Amherst
Telgheder compiled a 5–2 record in seven starts.

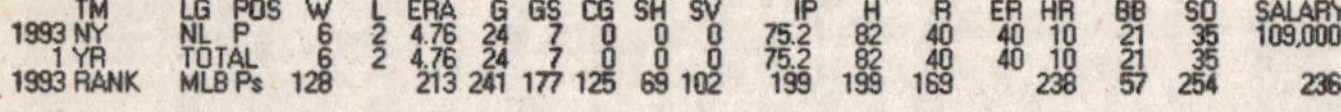

	TM	LG	POS	W	L	ERA	G	GS	CG	SH	SV	IP	H	R	ER	HR	BB	SO	SALARY
1993	NY	NL	P	6	2	4.76	24	7	0	0	0	75.2	82	40	40	10	21	35	109,000
1	YR	TOTAL		6	2	4.76	24	7	0	0	0	75.2	82	40	40	10	21	35	
1993	RANK	MLB	Ps	128		213	241	177	125	69	102	199	199	169		238	57	254	236

Anthony Young No. 19/P

Full name: Anthony Wayne Young
Bats: R **Throws:** R **HT:** 6–2 **WT:** 210
Born: 1–19–66, Houston, TX
High school: Furr (Houston, TX)
College: Houston
Young's 27 straight losses set an MLB record.

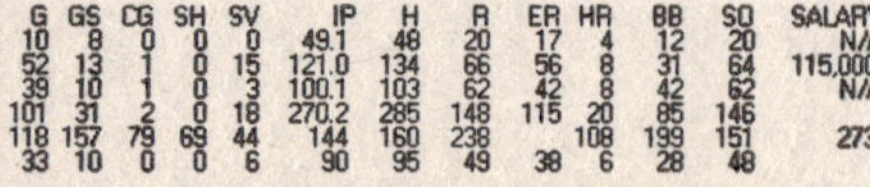

	TM	LG	POS	W	L	ERA	G	GS	CG	SH	SV	IP	H	R	ER	HR	BB	SO	SALARY
1991	NY	NL	P	2	5	3.10	10	8	0	0	0	49.1	48	20	17	4	12	20	N/A
1992	NY	NL	P	2	14	4.17	52	13	1	0	15	121.0	134	66	56	8	31	64	115,000
1993	NY	NL	P	1	16	3.77	39	10	1	0	3	100.1	103	62	42	8	42	62	N/A
3	YR	TOTALS		5	35	3.82	101	31	2	0	18	270.2	285	148	115	20	85	146	
1993	Rank	MLB	Ps	273		110	118	157	79	69	44	144	160	238		108	199	151	273
1994	PROJECTIONS			1	11	3.80	33	10	0	0	6	90	95	49	38	6	28	48	

Philadelphia PHILLIES

1994 Scouting Report

Hitting: (1993/.274, second in NL; 156 HR, fifth in NL)

The Phillies led the NL in runs scored last season. They were only 5th in HRs, but they were second in BA, first in doublès, and second in triples.

Lenny Dykstra, who led the NL by scoring 143 runs, is the key to the offense. He hit 19 HRs but, more importantly, walked a league-leading 129 times. He also stole 37 bases while finishing second in the MVP voting. John Kruk hit .316 and had 14 HRs and 85 RBIs at first base, and catcher Darren Daulton slugged 24 HRs and drove in 105 RBIs. This trio can be relied on to star for the Phillies again in 1994. Pete Incaviglia was another major contributor, hitting .274 with 24 HRs and 89 RBIs in 1993, his first year in the NL.

Pitching: (1993/3.95 ERA, sixth in NL)

The starters jumped out of the gate fast in 1993—by May 31, Tommy Greene was 7–0, Curt Schilling was 6–1, Terry Mulholland was 6–4, and Danny Jackson was 4–2. They finished with a record of 56–31. These four should be in their prime, and should do well once again.

The bullpen is a big question mark. Philadelphia's unforgiving fans blamed Mitch Williams for the team's World Series loss. So he was traded to Houston for Doug Jones and Jeff Juden in the first step of GM Lee Thomas' revamping of the bullpen. As unreliable as Williams was as a closer, the middle relief was even worse, so trading Wild Thing is only the start.

Defense: (1993/.977 pct., ninth in NL)

The Phils are not a superb defensive team. Jim Eisenreich had the third-highest fielding percentage for NL outfielders, .996, John Kruk ranked third among NL first basemen with a .993 fielding percentage, and Mickey Morandini was second among NL second basemen with a .990 mark.

1994 Prospects:

A lot of observers like Atlanta in the new NL East, but the Phillies figure to be right in the race. The Phillies have starting pitching and an ability to score runs comparable to Atlanta's. Question marks are the bullpen and team defense. Still, the Phillies figure no worse than a wild-card in 1994.

Team Directory

President & CEO: Bill Giles	Exec. VP & COO: D. Montgomery
General Mgr.: Lee Thomas	Asst. GM: Ed Wade
Director of P.R.: Larry Shenk	Traveling Secretary: Eddie Ferenz

Minor League Affiliates:

Level	Team/League	1993 Record
AAA	Scranton/Wilkes–Barre – International	60–82
AA	Reading – Eastern	62–78
A	Clearwater – Florida State	75–60
	Spartanburg – South Atlantic	62–80
	Batavia – New York/Penn.	38–39
Rookie	Martinsville – Appalachian	22–46

1993 Review

	Home		Away			Home		Away			Home		Away	
vs NL East	W	L	W	L	vs NL Cent.	W	L	W	L	vs NL West	W	L	W	L
Atlanta	3	3	3	3	Chicago	3	4	3	3	Colorado	4	2	5	1
Florida	6	1	3	3	Cincinnati	4	2	4	2	Los Angeles	5	1	5	1
Montreal	5	2	2	4	Houston	3	3	4	2	San Diego	3	3	3	3
New York	4	2	6	1	Pittsburgh	4	2	3	4	S. Francisco	2	4	2	4
					St. Louis	6	0	2	5					
Total	18	8	14	11		20	11	16	16		14	10	15	9

1993 finish: 97–65 (52–29 home, 45–36 away), first in NL East, won NLCS 4–2 over Atlanta, lost World Series 2–4 to Toronto

1994 Schedule

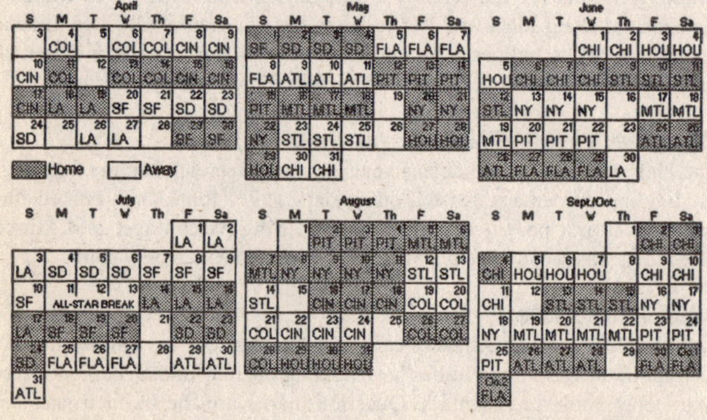

PHILADELPHIA PHILLIES 1994 ROSTER

Manager: Jim Fregosi (11)
Coaches: Larry Bowa, 3B (2); Denis Menke, hitting (14); Johnny Podres, pitching (46); Mel Roberts, 1B (26); Mike Ryan, bullpen (9); John Vukovich, dugout (18)

No.	PITCHERS	B	T	HT	WT	DOB	BIRTHPLACE	RESIDENCE
42	Borland, Toby	R	R	6–6	182	5–29–69	Quitman, LA	Quitman, LA
31	Brink, Brad	R	R	6–2	203	1–20–65	Roseville, CA	Turlock, CA
	Bottalico, Ricky	L	R	6–1	200	8–26–69	New Britain, CT	Newington, CT
57	Foster, Kevin	R	R	6–1	160	1–13–69	Evanston, IL	Evanston, IL
28	Green, Tyler	R	R	6–5	185	2–18–70	Inglewood, CO	Inglewood, CO
49	Greene, Tommy	R	R	6–5	219	4–6–67	Lumberton, NC	Richmond, VA
27	Jackson, Danny	R	L	6–3	205	1–5–62	San Antonio, TX	Overland Pk., KS
23	Jones, Doug	R	R	6–2	195	6–24–57	Covina, CA	Tucson, AZ
44	Juden, Jeff	R	R	6–7	245	1–19–71	Salem, MA	Salem, MA
48	Mason, Roger	R	R	6–6	220	9–18–58	Bellaire, MI	Bellaire, MI
45	Mulholland, Terry	R	L	6–2	215	3–9–63	Uniontown, PA	Glendale, AZ
39	Pall, Donn	R	R	6–1	180	1–11–62	Chicago, IL	Bloomingdale, IL
	Patterson, Jeff							
34	Rivera, Ben	R	R	6–6	230	1–11–68	S.P. de Macoris, DR	S.P. de Macoris, DR
38	Schilling, Curt	R	R	6–4	215	11–14–66	Anchorage, AK	Marlton, NJ
00	Slocumb, Heathcliff	R	R	6–3	220	6–7–66	Jamaica, NY	Richmond Hills, NY
	Wells, Bob							
40	West, David	L	L	6–6	230	9–1–64	Memphis, TN	Stuart, FL
41	Williams, Mike	R	R	6–2	196	7–29–69	Redford, VA	Newport, VA
No.	**CATCHERS**	**B**	**T**	**HT**	**WT**	**DOB**	**BIRTHPLACE**	**RESIDENCE**
10	Daulton, Darren	L	R	6–2	201	1–3–62	Arkansas City, KS	Safety Harbor, FL
	Lieberthal, Mike	R	R	6–0	180	1–18–72	Glendale, CA	Westlake Village, CA
23	Pratt, Todd	R	R	6–3	227	2–9–67	Bellevue, NE	Sunrise, FL
No.	**INFIELDERS**	**B**	**T**	**HT**	**WT**	**DOB**	**BIRTHPLACE**	**RESIDENCE**
5	Batiste, Kim	R	R	6–0	193	3–15–68	New Orleans, LA	Prairieville, LA
7	Duncan, Mariano	R	R	6–0	191	3–13–63	S.P. de Macoris, DR	Cherry Hill, NJ
15	Hollins, Dave	S	R	6–1	207	5–25–66	Buffalo, NY	Orchard Park, NY
17	Jordan, Ricky	R	R	6–3	205	5–26–65	Richmond, CA	Gold River, CA
29	Kruk, John	L	L	5–10	214	2–9–61	Charleston, WV	Burlington, WV
12	Morandini, Mickey	L	R	5–11	171	4–22–66	Kittanning, PA	Valparaiso, IN
16*	Quinlan, Tom	R	R	6–3	215	3–27–68	St. Paul, MN	Maplewood,MN
19	Stocker, Kevin	S	R	6–1	178	2–13–70	Spokane, WA	Spokane, WA
No.	**OUTFIELDERS**	**B**	**T**	**HT**	**WT**	**DOB**	**BIRTHPLACE**	**RESIDENCE**
44	Chamberlain, Wes	R	R	6–2	219	4–13–66	Chicago, IL	Chicago, IL
4	Dykstra, Lenny	L	L	5–10	193	2–10–63	Santa Ana, CA	Philadelphia, PA
8	Eisenreich, Jim	L	L	5–11	200	4–18–59	St. Cloud, MN	Blue Springs, MO
	Geisler, Phil	L	L	6–3	195	10–23–69	Klamath, OR	Springfield, OR
22	Incaviglia, Pete	R	R	6–1	225	4–2–64	Pebble Beach, CA	Colleyville, TX
59	Jackson, Jeff	R	R	6–2	185	1–2–72	Chicago, IL	Chicago, IL
16	Longmire, Tony	L	R	6–1	197	8–12–68	Vallejo, CA	Vallejo, CA
00	Marsh, Tom	R	R	6–2	180	12–27–65	Toledo, OH	Toledo, OH
25	Thompson, Milt	L	R	5–11	200	1–5–59	Washington, DC	Baldwin, MO

* Signed to a minor league contract and invited to spring training as a non-roster invitee

Veterans Stadium (62,586, artificial)
Tickets: 215–463–1000
Ticket prices:
- $14 (200 level box seats)
- $12 (300 and 500 level box seats)
- $9 (reserved, 600 level)
- $5 (reserved, 700 level)

Field Dimensions (from home plate)
- To left field at foul line, 330 feet
- To center field, 408 feet
- To right field at foul line, 330 feet
- (OF wall is 12' high)

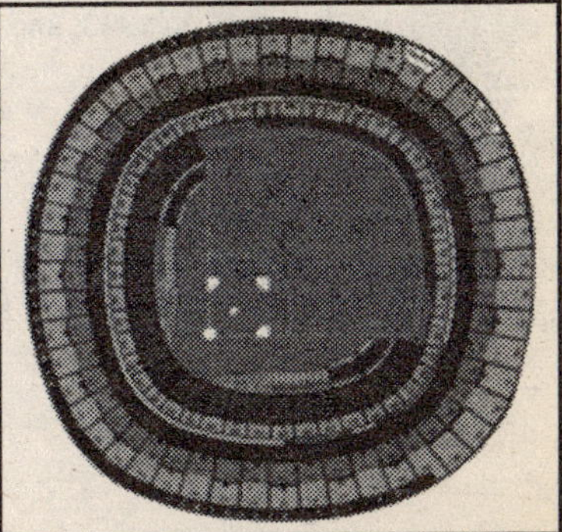

Darren Daulton No. 10/C

Full name: Darren Arthur Daulton
Bats: L **Throws:** R **HT:** 6–2 **WT:** 201
Born: 1–3–62, Arkansas City, KS
High school: Arkansas City (KS)
College: Crowley Cty. CC (KS)

Darren Daulton is looking for 1994 to be his third straight 100 RBI season.

	TEAM	LG	POS	G	AB	R	H	2B	3B	HR	RBI	BB	SO	SB	E	BA	SLG	SALARY
1983	PHL	NL		2	3	1	1	0	0	0	0	1	1	0	0	.333	.333	N/A
1985	PHL	NL		36	103	14	21	3	1	4	11	16	37	3	1	.204	.369	N/A
1986	PHL	NL		49	138	18	31	4	0	8	21	38	41	2	4	.225	.428	N/A
1987	PHL	NL		53	129	10	25	6	0	3	13	16	37	0	2	.194	.310	N/A
1988	PHL	NL		58	144	13	30	6	0	1	12	17	26	2	6	.208	.271	N/A
1989	PHL	NL		131	368	29	74	12	2	8	44	52	58	2	11	.201	.310	N/A
1990	PHL	NL	C	143	459	62	123	30	1	12	57	72	72	7	8	.268	.416	470,000
1991	PHL	NL		89	285	36	56	12	0	12	42	41	66	5	8	.196	.365	1,916,666
1992	PHL	NL		145	485	80	131	32	5	27	109	88	103	11	11	.270	.524	2,416,667
1993	PHL	NL	C	147	510	90	131	35	4	24	105	117	111	5	9	.257	.482	2,466,667
11	YR	TOTALS		853	2624	353	623	140	13	99	414	458	552	37	60	.237	.414	
1993	RANK	MLB	C	2	3	1	3	1	3	4	2	1	2	6	34	17	6	6
1994	PROJECTIONS			140	445	60	109	25	2	14	68	80	80	4	9	.245	.411	

Lenny Dykstra No. 4/CF

Full name: Leonard Kyle Dykstra
Bats: L **Throws:** L **HT:** 5–10 **WT:** 193
Born: 2–10–63, Santa Ana, CA
High school: Garden Grove (CA)

When Dykstra missed almost half of 1992, the Phils finished last. He played 161 games in 1993, and the Phils won the pennant.

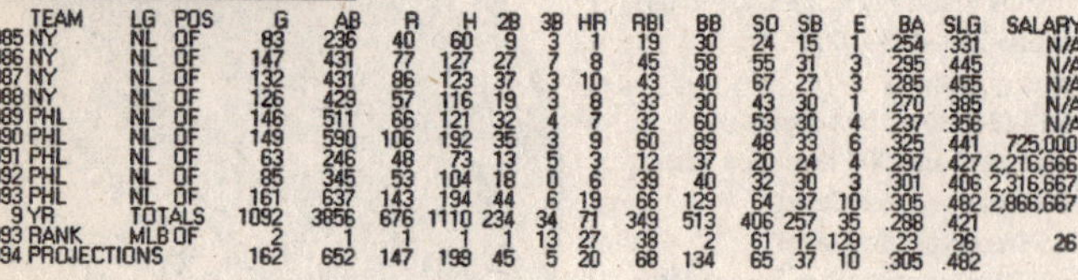

	TEAM	LG	POS	G	AB	R	H	2B	3B	HR	RBI	BB	SO	SB	E	BA	SLG	SALARY
1985	NY	NL	OF	83	236	40	60	9	3	1	19	30	24	15	1	.254	.331	N/A
1986	NY	NL	OF	147	431	77	127	27	7	8	45	58	55	31	3	.295	.445	N/A
1987	NY	NL	OF	132	431	86	123	37	3	10	43	40	67	27	3	.285	.455	N/A
1988	NY	NL	OF	126	429	57	116	19	3	8	33	30	43	30	1	.270	.385	N/A
1989	PHL	NL	OF	146	511	66	121	32	4	7	32	60	53	30	4	.237	.356	N/A
1990	PHL	NL	OF	149	590	106	192	35	3	9	60	89	48	33	6	.325	.441	725,000
1991	PHL	NL	OF	63	246	48	73	13	5	3	12	37	20	24	4	.297	.427	2,216,666
1992	PHL	NL	OF	85	345	53	104	18	0	6	39	40	32	30	3	.301	.406	2,316,667
1993	PHL	NL	OF	161	637	143	194	44	6	19	66	129	64	37	10	.305	.482	2,866,667
9	YR	TOTALS		1092	3856	676	1110	234	34	71	349	513	406	257	35	.288	.421	
1993	RANK	MLB	OF	2	1	1	1	1	13	27	38	2	61	12	129	23	26	26
1994	PROJECTIONS			162	652	147	199	45	5	20	68	134	65	37	10	.305	.482	

Jim Eisenreich No. 8/OF

Full name: James Michael Eisenreich
Bats: L **Throws:** L **HT:** 5–11 **WT:** 200
Born: 4–18–59, St. Cloud, MN
High school: St. Cloud Tech. (MN)
College: St. Cloud St. (MN)
Eisenreich's career once appeared doomed by disease, but he's come all the way back.

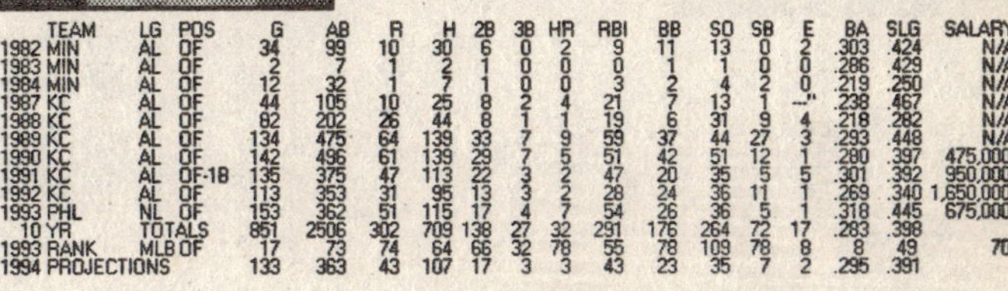

	TEAM	LG	POS	G	AB	R	H	2B	3B	HR	RBI	BB	SO	SB	E	BA	SLG	SALARY
1982	MIN	AL	OF	34	99	10	30	6	0	2	9	11	13	0	2	.303	.424	N/A
1983	MIN	AL	OF	2	7	1	2	1	0	0	0	1	1	0	0	.286	.429	N/A
1984	MIN	AL	OF	12	32	1	7	1	0	0	3	2	4	2	0	.219	.250	N/A
1987	KC	AL	OF	44	105	10	25	8	2	4	21	7	13	1	--"	.238	.467	N/A
1988	KC	AL	OF	82	202	26	44	8	1	1	19	6	31	9	4	.218	.282	N/A
1989	KC	AL	OF	134	475	64	139	33	7	9	59	37	44	27	3	.293	.448	N/A
1990	KC	AL	OF	142	496	61	139	29	7	5	51	42	51	12	1	.280	.397	475,000
1991	KC	AL	OF-1B	135	375	47	113	22	3	2	47	20	35	5	5	.301	.392	950,000
1992	KC	AL	OF	113	353	31	95	13	3	2	28	24	36	11	1	.269	.340	1,650,000
1993	PHL	NL	OF	153	362	51	115	17	4	7	54	26	36	5	1	.318	.445	675,000
10	YR	TOTALS		851	2506	302	709	138	27	32	291	176	264	72	17	.283	.398	
1993	RANK	MLB	OF	17	73	74	64	66	32	78	55	78	109	78	8	8	49	70
1994	PROJECTIONS			133	363	43	107	17	3	3	43	23	35	7	2	.295	.391	

Dave Hollins No. 15/3B

Full name: David Michael Hollins
Bats: S **Throws:** R **HT:** 6–1 **WT:** 207
Born: 5–25–66, Buffalo, NY
High school: Orchard Park (NY)
College: S. Carolina
Hollins has a strong bat (.273, 18 HR, 93 RBI in 1993).

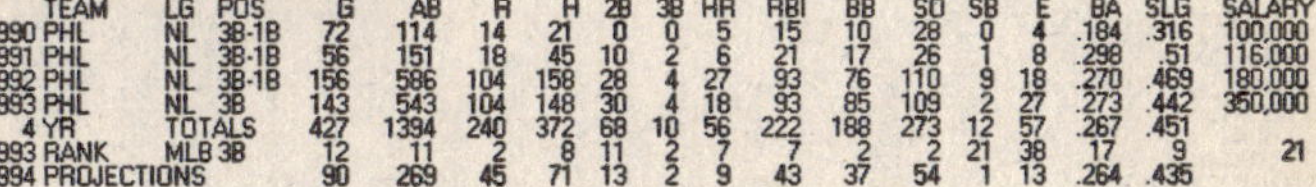

	TEAM	LG	POS	G	AB	R	H	2B	3B	HR	RBI	BB	SO	SB	E	BA	SLG	SALARY
1990	PHL	NL	3B-1B	72	114	14	21	0	0	5	15	10	28	0	4	.184	.316	100,000
1991	PHL	NL	3B-1B	56	151	18	45	10	2	6	21	17	26	1	8	.298	.51	116,000
1992	PHL	NL	3B-1B	156	586	104	158	28	4	27	93	76	110	9	18	.270	.469	180,000
1993	PHL	NL	3B	143	543	104	148	30	4	18	93	85	109	2	27	.273	.442	350,000
4	YR	TOTALS		427	1394	240	372	68	10	56	222	188	273	12	57	.267	.451	
1993	RANK	MLB	3B	12	11	2	8	11	2	7	7	2	2	21	38	17	9	21
1994	PROJECTIONS			90	269	45	71	13	2	9	43	37	54	1	13	.264	.435	

John Kruk No. 29/1B

Full name: John Martin Kruk
Bats: L **Throws:** L **HT:** 5–10 **WT:** 214
Born: 2–9–61, Charleston, WV
High school: Keyser (WV)
College: Allegany CC (MD)
John Kruk is one of the most colorful Phillies. But his bat is one of the best in the league.

	TEAM	LG	POS	G	AB	R	H	2B	3B	HR	RBI	BB	SO	SB	E	BA	SLG	SALARY
1986	SD	NL	OF-1B	122	278	33	86	16	2	4	38	45	58	2	3	.309	.424	N/A
1987	SD	NL	1B-OF	138	447	72	140	14	2	20	91	73	93	18	5	.313	.488	N/A
1988	SD	NL	1B-OF	120	378	54	91	17	1	9	44	80	68	5	3	.241	.362	N/A
1989	SD-PHL	NL	OF-1B	112	357	53	107	13	6	8	44	44	53	3	4	.300	.437	N/A
1990	PHL	NL	OF-1B	142	443	52	129	25	8	7	67	69	70	10	4	.291	.431	655,000
1991	PHL	NL	1B-OF	152	538	84	158	27	6	21	92	67	100	7	3	.294	.483	1,225,000
1992	PHL	NL	1B-OF	144	507	86	164	30	4	10	70	92	88	3	8	.323	.458	2,300,000
1993	PHL	NL	1B	150	535	100	169	33	5	14	85	111	87	6	8	.316	.475	2,500,000
8	YR	TOTALS		1080	3483	534	1044	175	34	93	531	581	617	54	38	.300	.450	
1993	RANK	MLB	1B	13	12	5	9	9	1	22	14	3	10	6	26	8	11	12
1994	PROJECTIONS			144	496	86	157	25	3	14	82	92	89	9	7	.317	.472	

Mickey Morandini No. 12/2B

Full name: Michael Robert Morandini
Bats: L **Throws:** R **HT:** 5–11 **WT:** 171
Born: 4–22–66, Kittaning, PA
High school: Leechburg Area (PA)
College: Indiana
Morandini is a solid defensive player. He had a subpar 1993 at the plate.

	TEAM	LG	POS	G	AB	R	H	2B	3B	HR	RBI	BB	SO	SB	E	BA	SLG	SALARY
1990	PHL	NL	2B	25	79	9	19	4	0	1	3	6	19	3	1	.241	.329	N/A
1991	PHL	NL	2B	98	325	38	81	11	4	1	20	29	45	13	6	.249	.317	105,000
1992	PHL	NL	2B-SS	127	422	47	112	8	8	3	30	25	64	8	6	.265	.344	180,000
1993	PHL	NL	2B	120	425	57	105	19	9	3	33	34	73	13	5	.247	.355	300,000
4	YR	TOTALS		370	1251	151	317	42	21	8	86	94	201	37	18	.253	.340	
1993	RANK	MLB	2B	21	20	18	24	21	2	26	25	21	8	13	7	36	29	22
1994	PROJECTIONS			143	511	69	126	22	11	3	40	41	86	15	6	.247	.350	

Kevin Stocker No. 19/SS

Full name: Kevin Douglas Stocker
Bats: S **Throws:** R **HT:** 6–1 **WT:** 178
Born: 2–13–70, Spokane, WA
High school: Central Valley (Spokane, WA)
College: Washington
Stocker's .324 BA at shortstop was a key reason the Phillies won the '93 pennant.

TEAM	LG POS	G	AB	R	H	2B	3B	HR	RBI	BB	SO	SB	E	BA	SLG	SALARY
1993 PHL	NL SS	70	259	46	84	12	3	2	31	30	43	5	14	.324	417	109,000
1 YR	TOTAL	70	259	46	84	12	3	2	31	30	43	5	14	.324	.417	
1993 RANK	MLB SS	38	31	24	30	29	13	26	25	24	23	21	19	2	10	34

Milt Thompson No. 25/OF

Full name: Milton Bernard Thompson
Bats: L **Throws:** R **HT:** 5–11 **WT:** 200
Born: 1–5–59, Washington, DC
High school: Magruder (DC)
College: Howard (DC)
Thompson is a good defensive outfielder. He had six outfield assists last season.

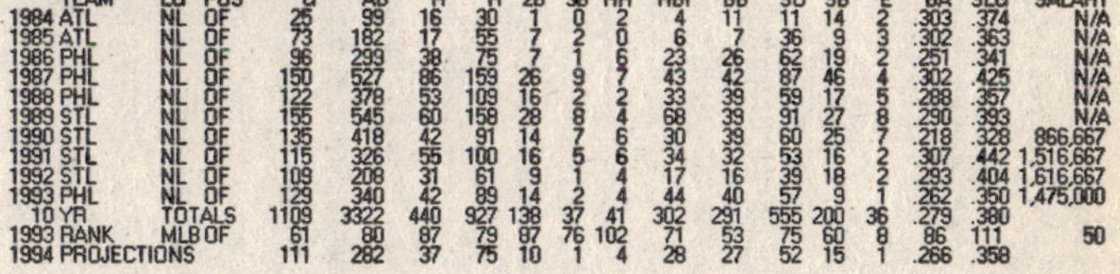

TEAM	LG	POS	G	AB	R	H	2B	3B	HR	RBI	BB	SO	SB	E	BA	SLG	SALARY
1984 ATL	NL	OF	25	99	16	30	1	0	2	4	11	11	14	2	.303	.374	N/A
1985 ATL	NL	OF	73	182	17	55	7	2	0	6	7	36	9	3	.302	.363	N/A
1986 PHL	NL	OF	96	299	38	75	7	1	6	23	26	62	19	2	.251	.341	N/A
1987 PHL	NL	OF	150	527	86	159	26	9	7	43	42	87	46	4	.302	.425	N/A
1988 PHL	NL	OF	122	378	53	109	16	2	2	33	39	59	17	5	.288	.357	N/A
1989 STL	NL	OF	155	545	60	158	28	8	4	68	39	91	27	8	.290	.393	N/A
1990 STL	NL	OF	135	418	42	91	14	7	6	30	39	60	25	7	.218	.328	866,667
1991 STL	NL	OF	115	326	55	100	16	5	6	34	32	53	16	2	.307	.442	1,516,667
1992 STL	NL	OF	109	208	31	61	9	1	4	17	16	39	18	2	.293	.404	1,616,667
1993 PHL	NL	OF	129	340	42	89	14	2	4	44	40	57	9	1	.262	.350	1,475,000
10 YR	TOTALS		1109	3322	440	927	138	37	41	302	291	555	200	36	.279	.380	
1993 RANK	MLB	OF	61	80	87	79	87	76	102	71	53	75	60	8	86	111	50
1994 PROJECTIONS			111	282	37	75	10	1	4	28	27	52	15	1	.266	.358	

Tommy Greene No. 49/P

Full name: Ira Thomas Greene
Bats: R **Throws:** R **HT:** 6–5 **WT:** 219
Born: 4–6–67, Lumberton, NC
High school: Whiteville (NC)
Tommy Greene's 16–4 '93 season was phenomenal. The Phillies are counting on him to be one of the game's biggest pitching stars.

	TM	LG	POS	W	L	ERA	G	GS	CG	SH	SV	IP	H	R	ER	HR	BB	SO	SALARY
1989	ATL	NL	P	1	2	4.10	4	4	1	1	0	26.1	22	12	12	5	6	17	N/A
1990	ATL-PHL	NL	P	3	3	5.08	15	9	0	0	0	51.1	50	31	29	8	26	21	102,500
1991	PHL	NL	P	13	7	3.38	36	27	3	2	0	207.2	177	85	78	19	66	154	115,000
1992	PHL	NL	P	3	3	5.32	13	12	0	0	0	64.1	75	39	38	5	34	39	255,000
1993	PHL	NL	P	16	4	3.42	31	30	7	2	0	200.0	175	84	76	12	62	167	390,000
5	YR	TOTALS		36	19	3.82	99	82	11	5	0	549.2	499	251	233	49	194	398	
1993	RANK	MLB	Ps	14		81	194	58	7	8	102	52	51	72		44	88	51	143
1994	PROJECTIONS			7	3	4.03	19	17	2	0	0	105	100	51	47	8	40	75	

Danny Jackson No. 27/P

Full name: Danny Lynn Jackson
Bats: R **Throws:** L **HT:** 6–3 **WT:** 205
Born: 1–5–62, San Antonio, TX
High school: Central (Aurora, CO)
College: Oklahoma
1993 was Jackson's best year in the NL since 1988, when he went 23–8 for Cincinnati.

	TM	LG	POS	W	L	ERA	G	GS	CG	SH	SV	IP	H	R	ER	HR	BB	SO	SALARY
1983	KC	AL	P	1	1	5.21	4	3	0	0	0	19.0	26	12	11	1	6	9	N/A
1984	KC	AL	P	2	6	4.26	15	11	1	0	0	76.0	84	41	36	4	35	40	N/A
1985	KC	AL	P	14	12	3.42	32	32	4	3	0	208.0	209	94	79	7	76	114	N/A
1986	KC	AL	P	11	12	3.20	32	27	4	1	1	185.2	177	83	66	13	79	115	N/A
1987	KC	AL	P	9	18	4.02	36	34	11	2	0	224.0	219	115	100	11	109	152	N/A
1988	CIN	NL	P	23	8	2.73	35	35	15	6	0	260.2	206	86	79	13	71	161	N/A
1989	CIN	NL	P	6	11	5.60	20	20	1	0	0	115.2	122	78	72	10	57	70	N/A
1990	CIN	NL	P	6	6	3.61	22	21	0	0	0	117.1	119	54	47	11	40	76	1,150,000
1991	CHI	NL	P	1	5	6.75	17	14	0	0	0	70.2	89	59	53	8	48	31	2,625,000
1992	PIT	NL	P	8	13	3.84	34	34	0	0	0	201.1	211	99	86	6	77	97	2,625,000
1993	PHL	NL	P	12	11	3.77	32	32	2	1	0	210.1	214	105	88	12	80	120	2,625,000
11	YR	TOTALS		93	103	3.82	279	263	38	13	1	1688.2	1676	826	717	96	678	985	
1993	RANK	MLB	Ps	43		108	175	39	57	23	102	40	157	140		41	163	188	46
1994	PROJECTIONS			11	12	3.67	32	32	2	1	0	206	211	99	84	8	77	110	

Terry Mulholland No. 45/P

Full name: Terrance John Mulholland
Bats: R **Throws:** L **HT:** 6–3 **WT:** 200
Born: 3/9/63, Uniontown, Pa.
High school: Laurel Highlands (PA)
College: Marietta (OH)
Mulholland was named the NL starter in the 1993 All-Star Game.

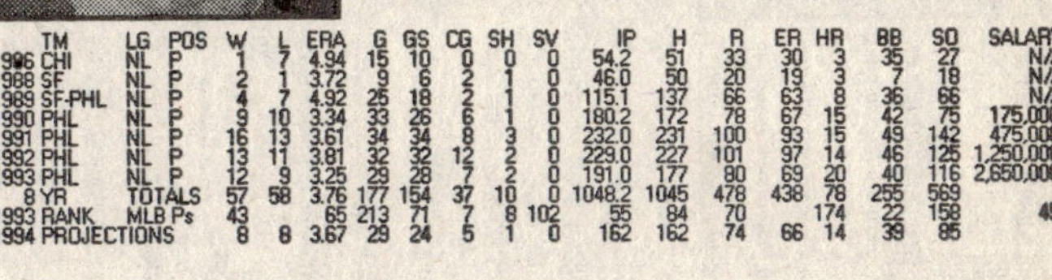

	TM	LG	POS	W	L	ERA	G	GS	CG	SH	SV	IP	H	R	ER	HR	BB	SO	SALARY
1986	CHI	NL	P	1	7	4.94	15	10	0	0	0	54.2	51	33	30	3	35	27	N/A
1988	SF	NL	P	2	1	3.72	9	6	2	1	0	46.0	50	20	19	3	7	18	N/A
1989	SF-PHL	NL	P	4	7	4.92	25	18	2	1	0	115.1	137	66	63	8	36	66	N/A
1990	PHL	NL	P	9	10	3.34	33	26	6	1	0	180.2	172	78	67	15	42	75	175,000
1991	PHL	NL	P	16	13	3.61	34	34	8	3	0	232.0	231	100	93	15	49	142	475,000
1992	PHL	NL	P	13	11	3.81	32	32	12	2	0	229.0	227	101	97	14	46	125	1,250,000
1993	PHL	NL	P	12	9	3.25	29	28	7	2	0	191.0	177	80	69	20	40	116	2,650,000
8	YR	TOTALS		57	58	3.76	177	154	37	10	0	1048.2	1045	478	438	78	255	569	
1993	RANK	MLB	Ps	43		65	213	71	7	8	102	55	84	70		174	22	158	45
1994	PROJECTIONS			8	8	3.67	29	24	5	1	0	162	162	74	66	14	39	85	

Curt Schilling No. 38/P

Full name: Curt Schilling
Bats: R **Throws:** R **HT:** 6–4 **WT:** 215
Born: 11–14–66, Anchorage, AK
High school: Shadow Mountain (OH)
College: Yavapai Junior (AZ)
Schilling was tied for second in the NL in complete games, tied for third in shutouts and was fourth in strikeouts.

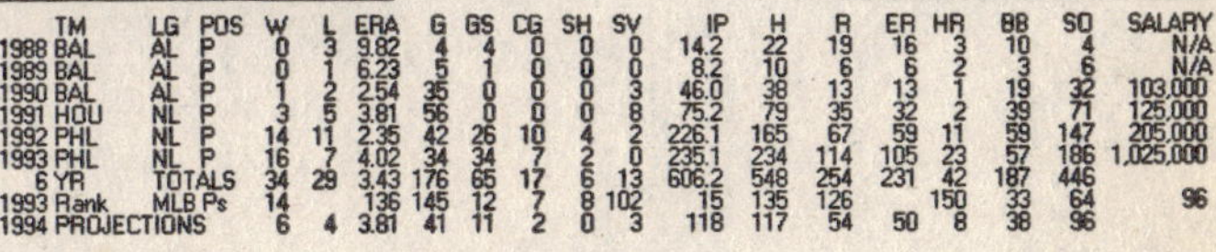

	TM	LG	POS	W	L	ERA	G	GS	CG	SH	SV	IP	H	R	ER	HR	BB	SO	SALARY
1988	BAL	AL	P	0	3	9.82	4	4	0	0	0	14.2	22	19	16	3	10	4	N/A
1989	BAL	AL	P	0	1	6.23	5	1	0	0	0	8.2	10	6	6	2	3	6	N/A
1990	BAL	AL	P	1	2	2.54	35	0	0	0	3	46.0	38	13	13	1	19	32	103,000
1991	HOU	NL	P	3	5	3.81	56	0	0	0	8	75.2	79	35	32	2	39	71	125,000
1992	PHL	NL	P	14	11	2.35	42	26	10	4	2	226.1	165	67	59	11	59	147	205,000
1993	PHL	NL	P	16	7	4.02	34	34	7	2	0	235.1	234	114	105	23	57	186	1,025,000
6	YR	TOTALS		34	29	3.43	176	65	17	6	13	606.2	548	254	231	42	187	446	
1993	Rank	MLB	Ps	14		136	145	12	7	8	102	15	135	126		150	33	64	96
1994	PROJECTIONS			6	4	3.81	41	11	2	0	3	118	117	54	50	8	38	96	

Doug Jones — No. 23/P

Full Name: Douglas Reid Jones
Bats: R **Throws:** R **HT:** 6–2 **WT:** 195
Born: 6–24–57, Covina, CA
High school: Lebanon (IN)
College: Central Arizona College and Butler

Jones arrived in Philadelphia with Jeff Juden in the Mitch Williams deal. A changeup pitcher, he had problems getting batters out in '93.

	TM	LG	POS	W	L	ERA	G	GS	CG	SH	SV	IP	H	R	ER	HR	BB	SO	SALARY
1982	MIL	AL	P	0	0	10.13	4	0	0	0	0	2.2	5	3	3	1	1	1	N/A
1986	CLE	AL	P	1	0	2.50	11	0	0	0	1	18	18	5	5	0	6	12	N/A
1987	CLE	AL	P	6	5	3.15	49	0	0	0	8	91.1	101	45	32	4	24	87	N/A
1988	CLE	AL	P	3	4	2.27	51		0	0	37	83.1	69	26	21	1	16	72	N/A
1989	CLE	AL	P	7	10	2.34	59	0	0	0	32	80.2	76	25	21	4	13	65	N/A
1990	CLE	AL	P	5	5	2.56	66	0	0	0	43	84.1	66	26	24	5	22	55	N/A
1991	CLE	AL	P	4	8	5.54	36	4	0	0	7	63.1	87	42	39	7	17	48	950,000
1992	HOU	NL	P	11	8	1.85	80	0	0	0	36	111.2	96	29	23	5	17	93	750,000
1993	HOU	NL	P	4	10	4.54	71	0	0	0	26	85.1	102	46	43	7	21	66	2,500,000
9	YR	TOTALS		41	50	3.06	427	4	0	0	190	620.2	620	247	211	34	137	499	
1993	Rank	MLB Ps		173		192	11	202	125	69	14	175	261	182		111	37	71	50
1994	PROJECTIONS			3	6	4.75	39	1	0	0	11	55	69	31	29	4	14	42	

Jim Fregosi — No. 11/Mgr.

Full name: James Louis Fregosi
Bats: R **Throws:** R **HT:** 6–2 **WT:** 197
Born: 4–4–42, San Francisco, CA
High school: Serra (San Mateo, CA)
College: Menlo (CA)

Fregosi led the Phillies from last place to first place in one season, only the third team ever to do so.

			REG. SEASON				PLAYOFF			CHAMP. SERIES			WORLD SERIES		
YEAR	TEAM	LG	W	L	PCT	POS	W	L	PCT	W	L	PCT	W	L	PCT
1978	CAL	AL	62	54	.534	2			---			---			---
1979	CAL	AL	88	74	.543	1			---	1	3	.250			---
1980	CAL	AL	65	95	.406	6			---			---			---
1981	CAL	AL	22	25	.468				---			---			---
1986	CHI	AL	45	51	.469	5			---			---			---
1987	CHI	AL	77	85	.475	5			---			---			---
1988	CHI	AL	71	90	.441	5			---			---			---
1991	PHL	NL	74	75	.497	3			---			---			---
1992	PHL	NL	70	92	.432	6			---			---			---
1993	PHL	NL	97	65	.599	1			---	4	2	.667	2	4	.333
15	YR TOTALS		671	706	.487		0	0	---	5	5	.500	2	4	.333

Kim Batiste No. 5/3B

Full name: Kimothy Emil Batiste
Bats: R **Throws:** R **HT:** 6–0 **WT:** 193
Born: 3–15–68, New Orleans, LA
High school: St. Amant (LA)
Batiste started the season as a shortstop, and ended up as the back-up third baseman.

	TEAM	LG	POS	G	AB	R	H	2B	3B	HR	RBI	BB	SO	SB	E	BA	SLG	SALARY
1991	PHL	NL	SS	10	27	2	6	0	0	0	1	1	8	0	1	.222	.222	N/A
1992	PHL	NL	SS	44	136	9	28	4	0	1	10	4	18	0	13	.206	.257	N/A
1993	PHL	NL	3B	79	156	14	44	7	1	5	29	3	29	0	10	.282	.436	122,500
3	YR	TOTALS		133	319	25	78	11	1	6	40	8	55	0	24	.245	.342	
1993	RANK	MLB	3B	34	39	41	38	37	21	29	31	41	37	38	13	11	13	31
1994	PROJECTIONS			102	199	18	56	9	1	6	38	3	36	0	13	.281	.427	

Wes Chamberlain No. 44/OF

Full name: Wesley Polk Chamberlain
Bats: R **Throws:** R **HT:** 6–2 **WT:** 219
Born: 4–13–66, Chicago, IL
High school: Simeon
College: Jackson State (MS)
Chamberlain is platooned with Eisenreich in left.

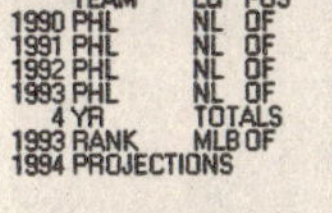

	TEAM	LG	POS	G	AB	R	H	2B	3B	HR	RBI	BB	SO	SB	E	BA	SLG	SALARY
1990	PHL	NL	OF	18	46	9	13	3	0	2	4	1	9	4	1	.283	.478	100,000
1991	PHL	NL	OF	101	383	51	92	16	3	13	50	31	73	9	3	.240	.399	105,000
1992	PHL	NL	OF	76	275	26	71	18	0	9	41	10	55	4	4	.258	.422	200,000
1993	PHL	NL	OF	96	284	34	80	20	2	12	45	17	51	2	1	.282	.493	250,000
4	YR	TOTALS		291	988	120	256	57	5	36	140	59	188	19	9	.259	.436	
1993	RANK	MLB	OF	97	91	95	85	53	76	51	68	113	84	102	8	51	22	98
1994	PROJECTIONS			63	201	23	54	13	0	7	30	9	38	3	2	.269	.458	

Mariano Duncan No. 7/2B–SS

Full name: Mariano Duncan
Bats: R **Throws:** R **HT:** 6–0 **WT:** 191
Born: 3–13–63, S.P. de Macoris, DR
High school: San Pedro de Macoris (DR)
The Phillies were 70–40 with Duncan in the starting lineup at second base or shortstop.

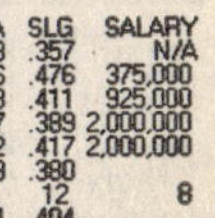

	TEAM	LG	POS	G	AB	R	H	2B	3B	HR	RBI	BB	SO	SB	E	BA	SLG	SALARY
1989	CIN	NL	SS-2B	94	258	32	64	15	2	3	21	8	51	9	14	.248	.357	N/A
1990	CIN	NL	2B-SS	125	435	67	133	22	11	10	55	24	67	13	18	.306	.476	375,000
1991	CIN	NL	2B-SS	100	333	46	86	7	4	12	40	12	57	5	9	.258	.411	925,000
1992	PHL	NL	OF-2B	142	574	71	153	40	3	8	50	17	108	23	16	.267	.389	2,000,000
1993	PHL	NL	2B	124	496	68	140	26	4	11	73	12	88	6	21	.282	.417	2,000,000
9	YR	TOTALS		912	3326	436	862	149	31	64	326	158	624	153	154	.259	.380	
1993	RANK	MLB	2B	18	9	12	12	11	12	8	4	43	4	24	42	14	12	8
1994	PROJECTIONS			130	497	69	136	24	7	9	55	24	89	19	23	.274	.404	

Tyler Green — No. 52/P

Full name: Tyler Green
Bats: R **Throws:** R **HT:** 6–5 **WT:** 180
Born: 2–18–70, Inglewood, CO
High school: Thomas Jefferson (Denver, CO)
College: Wichita State
Green was the 10th pick in the June '91 draft.

TM	LG	POS	W	L	ERA	G	GS	CG	SH	SV	IP	H	R	ER	HR	BB	SO	SALARY
1993 PHL	NL	P	0	0	7.36	3	2	0	0	0	7.1	16	9	6	1	5	7	N/A
1 YR	TOTAL		0	0	7.36	3	2	0	0	0	7.1	16	9	6	1	5	7	
1993 RANK	MLB Ps	not ranked -- didn't have 50 IP in 1993																

Pete Incaviglia — No. 22/OF

Full name: Peter Joseph Incaviglia
Bats: R **Throws:** R **HT:** 6–1 **WT:** 225
Born: 4–2–64, Pebble Beach, CA
High school: Monterey (CA)
College: Oklahoma State
Incaviglia led the team in slugging percentage.

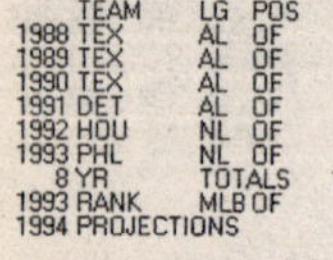

TEAM	LG	POS	G	AB	R	H	2B	3B	HR	RBI	BB	SO	SB	E	BA	SLG	SALARY
1988 TEX	AL	OF	116	418	59	104	19	3	22	54	39	153	6	2	.249	.467	N/A
1989 TEX	AL	OF	133	453	48	107	27	4	21	81	32	136	5	6	.236	.453	N/A
1990 TEX	AL	OF	153	529	59	123	27	0	24	85	45	146	3	8	.233	.420	825,000
1991 DET	AL	OF	97	337	38	72	12	1	11	38	36	92	1	3	.214	.353	500,000
1992 HOU	NL	OF	113	349	31	93	22	1	11	44	25	99	2	6	.266	.430	700,000
1993 PHL	NL	OF	116	368	60	101	16	3	24	89	21	82	1	5	.274	.530	1,100,000
8 YR	TOTALS		1020	3503	462	873	170	18	170	559	301	1061	30	57	.249	.454	
1993 RANK	MLB	OF	73	72	68	73	76	54	15	16	99	42	116	80	59	9	53
1994 PROJECTIONS			115	378	50	99	19	2	19	62	28	111	3	4	.262	.476	

Ricky Jordan — No. 17/1B

Full name: Paul Scott Jordan
Bats: R **Throws:** R **HT:** 6–3 **WT:** 205
Born: 5–26–65, Richmond, CA
High school: Grant (Sacramento, CA)
Jordan led the Phillies with 16 pinch-hits; he has a career .307 BA as a pinch hitter.

TEAM	LG	POS	G	AB	R	H	2B	3B	HR	RBI	BB	SO	SB	E	BA	SLG	SALARY
1988 PHL	NL	1B	69	273	41	84	15	1	11	43	7	39	1	5	.308	.491	N/A
1989 PHL	NL	1B	144	523	63	149	22	3	12	75	23	62	4	9	.285	.407	N/A
1990 PHL	NL	1B	92	324	32	78	21	0	5	44	13	39	2	4	.241	.352	N/A
1991 PHL	NL	1B	101	301	38	82	21	3	9	49	14	49	0	9	.272	.452	250,000
1992 PHL	NL	1B-OF	94	276	33	84	19	0	4	34	5	44	3	2	.304	.417	660,000
1993 PHL	NL	1B	90	159	21	46	4	1	5	18	8	32	0	2	.289	.421	1,000,000
6 YR	TOTALS		590	1856	228	523	102	8	46	263	70	265	10	31	.282	.420	
1993 RANK	MLB	1B	37	40	40	38	41	20	35	41	40	36	31	3	17	25	17
1994 PROJECTIONS			111	327	40	92	15	2	8	47	15	47	1	6	.281	.422	

Jeff Juden No. 44/P

Full name: Jeffrey Daniel Juden
Bats: R **Throws:** R **HT:** 6–7 **WT:** 245
Born: 1–19–71, Salem, MA
High school: Salem (MA)
GM Lee Thomas called Jeff Juden "the key" to the Mitch Williams trade, thanks to his potential.

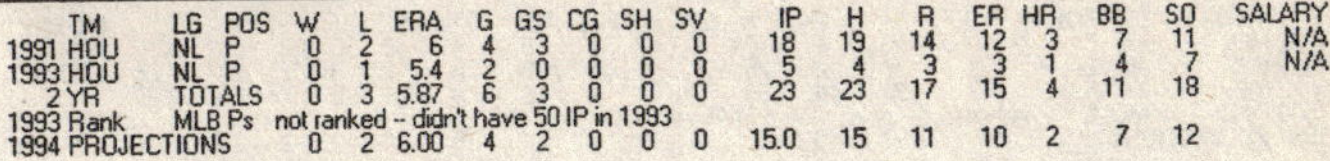

TM	LG	POS	W	L	ERA	G	GS	CG	SH	SV	IP	H	R	ER	HR	BB	SO	SALARY
1991 HOU	NL	P	0	2	6	4	3	0	0	0	18	19	14	12	3	7	11	N/A
1993 HOU	NL	P	0	1	5.4	2	0	0	0	0	5	4	3	3	1	4	7	N/A
2 YR	TOTALS		0	3	5.87	6	3	0	0	0	23	23	17	15	4	11	18	
1993 Rank	MLB Ps	not ranked -- didn't have 50 IP in 1993																
1994 PROJECTIONS			0	2	6.00	4	2	0	0	0	15.0	15	11	10	2	7	12	

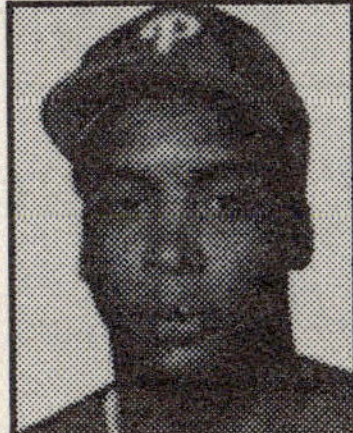

Tony Longmire No. 16/OF

Full name: Anthony Eugene Longmire
Bats: L **Throws:** R **HT:** 6–1 **WT:** 197
Born: 8–12–68, Vallejo, CA
High school: Hogan (Vallejo, CA)
Longmire hit .304 in 120 games for AAA Scranton, and set a Scranton record with 36 doubles.

TEAM	LG	POS	G	AB	R	H	2B	3B	HR	RBI	BB	SO	SB	E	BA	SLG	SALARY
1993 PHL	NL	OF	11	13	1	3	0	0	0	1	0	1	0	0	.231	.231	109,000
1 YR	TOTAL		11	13	1	3	0	0	0	1	0	1	0	0	.231	.231	
1993 RANK	MLB OF	not ranked -- didn't have 150 ABs in 1993															

Roger Mason No. 48/P

Full name: Roger Leroy Mason
Bats: R **Throws:** R **HT:** 6–6 **WT:** 220
Born: 9–18–58, Bellaire, MI
High school: Bellaire (MI)
College: Saginaw Valley State (MI)
Mason was 0–7 as a Padre, 5–5 as a Phillie.

TM	LG	POS	W	L	ERA	G	GS	CG	SH	SV	IP	H	R	ER	HR	BB	SO	SALARY
1985 SF	NL	P	1	3	2.12	5	5	1	1	0	29.2	28	13	7	1	11	26	
1986 SF	NL	P	3	4	4.80	11	11	1	0	0	60	56	35	32	5	30	43	
1987 SF	NL	P	1	1	4.50	5	5	0	0	0	26	30	15	13	4	10	18	
1989 HOU	NL	P	0	0	20.25	2	0	0	0	0	1.1	2	3	3	0	2	3	N/A
1991 PIT	NL	P	3	2	3.03	24	0	0	0	3	29.2	21	11	10	2	6	21	175,000
1992 PIT	NL	P	5	7	4.09	65	0	0	0	8	88.0	80	41	40	11	33	56	225,000
1993 PHL	NL	P	5	12	4.06	68	0	0	0	0	99.2	90	48	45	10	34	71	300,000
8 YR	TOTALS		19	30	4.07	185	23	2	1	12	356.1	330	177	161	34	136	253	
1993 RANK	MLB Ps		149		143	22	202	125	69	102	147	69	122		161	120	99	150
1994 PROJECTIONS			5	13	4.01	77	0	0	0	0	110	99	53	49	11	37	79	

Todd Pratt — No. 23/C

Full name: Todd Alan Pratt
Bats: R **Throws:** R **HT:** 6–3 **WT:** 227
Born: 2–9–67, Bellevue, NE
High school: Hilltop (Chula Vista, CA)
Primarily Darren Daulton's backup, Pratt had 5 HR and 11 RBI in his 19 starts.

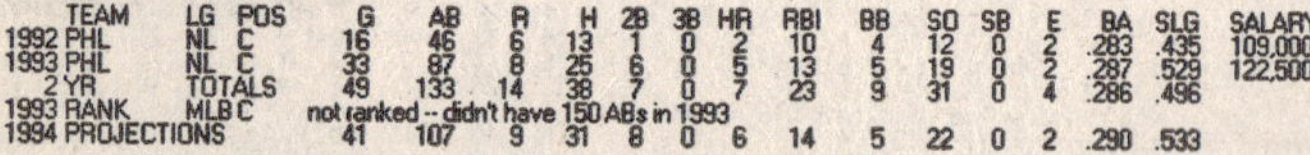

	TEAM	LG	POS	G	AB	R	H	2B	3B	HR	RBI	BB	SO	SB	E	BA	SLG	SALARY
1992	PHL	NL	C	16	46	6	13	1	0	2	10	4	12	0	2	.283	.435	109,000
1993	PHL	NL	C	33	87	8	25	6	0	5	13	5	19	0	2	.287	.529	122,500
2	YR	TOTALS		49	133	14	38	7	0	7	23	9	31	0	4	.286	.496	
1993	RANK	MLB	C	not ranked -- didn't have 150 ABs in 1993														
1994	PROJECTIONS			41	107	9	31	8	0	6	14	5	22	0	2	.290	.533	

Ben Rivera — No. 34/P

Full name: Bienvenido Rivera
Bats: R **Throws:** R **HT:** 6–6 **WT:** 230
Born: 1–11–68, S.P. de Macoris, DR
High school: San Jose (San P. de Macoris, DR)
His 12 wins in '93 were the most he's had in any pro season.

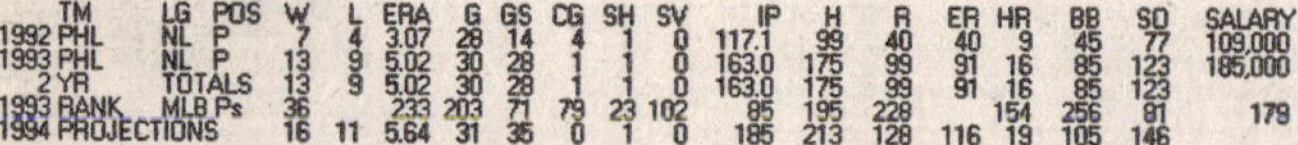

	TM	LG	POS	W	L	ERA	G	GS	CG	SH	SV	IP	H	R	ER	HR	BB	SO	SALARY
1992	PHL	NL	P	7	4	3.07	28	14	4	1	0	117.1	99	40	40	9	45	77	109,000
1993	PHL	NL	P	13	9	5.02	30	28	1	1	0	163.0	175	99	91	16	85	123	185,000
2	YR	TOTALS		13	9	5.02	30	28	1	1	0	163.0	175	99	91	16	85	123	
1993	RANK	MLB	Ps	36		233	203	71	79	23	102	85	195	228		154	256	81	179
1994	PROJECTIONS			16	11	5.64	31	35	0	1	0	185	213	128	116	19	105	146	

David West — No. 40/P

Full name: David Lee West
Bats: L **Throws:** L **HT:** 6–6 **WT:** 230
Born: 9–1–64, Memphis, TN
High school: Craigmont (TN)
His 76 appearances was a Phillie left-hander record, and tied for second in the NL.

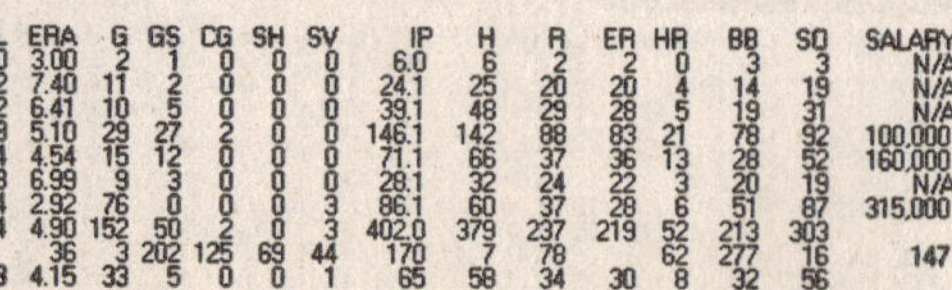

	TM	LG	POS	W	L	ERA	G	GS	CG	SH	SV	IP	H	R	ER	HR	BB	SO	SALARY
1988	NY	NL	P	1	0	3.00	2	1	0	0	0	6.0	6	2	2	0	3	3	N/A
1989	NY	NL	P	0	2	7.40	11	2	0	0	0	24.1	25	20	20	4	14	19	N/A
1989	MIN	AL	P	3	2	6.41	10	5	0	0	0	39.1	48	29	28	5	19	31	N/A
1990	MIN	AL	P	7	9	5.10	29	27	2	0	0	146.1	142	88	83	21	78	92	100,000
1991	MIN	AL	P	4	4	4.54	15	12	0	0	0	71.1	66	37	36	13	28	52	160,000
1992	MIN	AL	P	1	3	6.99	9	3	0	0	0	28.1	32	24	22	3	20	19	N/A
1993	PHL	NL	P	6	4	2.92	76	0	0	0	3	86.1	60	37	28	6	51	87	315,000
6	YR	TOTALS		22	24	4.90	152	50	2	0	3	402.0	379	237	219	52	213	303	
1993	Rank	MLB	Ps	128		36	3	202	125	69	44	170	7	78		62	277	16	147
1994	PROJECTIONS			4	3	4.15	33	5	0	0	1	65	58	34	30	8	32	56	

Pittsburgh *PIRATES*

1994 Scouting Report

Hitting: (1993/.267 BA, sixth in NL; 110 HR, thirteenth in NL)

Losing Barry Bonds left a real hole in the Pirate offense; Pittsburgh lacks both speed (eleventh in NL in stolen bases) and power. Bonds supplied both. Andy Van Slyke did his best to carry the team, batting .310 with eight home runs and 50 RBI, but injuries limited him to a half-season. Jay Bell also hit .310, and Carlos Garcia hit .269 with 12 HR while primarily batting leadoff. Still, Pittsburgh needs a real cleanup hitter to fill the void left by Bonds' departure.

Pitching: (1993/4.77 ERA, thirteenth in NL)

The Pirates haven't replaced Doug Drabek and John Smiley in their rotation. Steve Cooke led the team in wins with ten. Randy Tomlin was a disappointing 4–8, and Tim Wakefield was 6–11.

In the bullpen, the Pirates sent Stan Belinda and his 17 saves to Kansas City. Mark Dewey had seven saves in 21 appearances with a 2.36 ERA. Setup men Blas Minor and Joel Johnston had ERAs, respectively, of 4.10 and 3.38.

Defense: (1993/.983 pct., second in NL)

Pittsburgh maintained a tradition of strong defense in '93. Andy Van Slyke remains one of the best center fielders in baseball. Kevin Young was tops in the NL in fielding percentage among first basemen (.998), and shortstop Jay Bell was first in fielding percentage among NL shortstops with a .986 mark. Catcher Don Slaught's .993 fielding percentage ranked fourth in the NL among catchers.

1994 Prospects:

You can't lose the quality players that Pittsburgh has over the past few years—Bonds, Bobby Bonilla, Drabek, and Smiley—without suffering on the field. Pittsburgh's holes are directly attributable to the players they've lost. Eventually, the Pirates will develop other players, but right now, they have little to work with. Despite one of the best managers in baseball, who'll make sure Pittsburgh gives a solid effort every game, the Pirates will probably finish last in the NL Central in '94.

Team Directory

Chairman: Vincent A. Sarni	President: Mark Sauer
General Mgr.: Ted Simmons	Sen. VP, Bus. Op.: Douglas L. Bureman
VP of P.R.: Rick Cerone	Traveling Secretary: Greg Johnson

Minor League Affiliates:

Level	Team/League	1993 Record
AAA	Buffalo–American Association	71–73
AA	Carolina–Southern	74–67
A	Salem–Carolina	61–79
	Augusta–South Atlantic	59–82
	Welland, Ont.–New York/Penn.	35–42
Rookie	Bradenton Pirates–Gulf Coast	21–38

1993 Review

	Home W	Home L	Away W	Away L		Home W	Home L	Away W	Away L		Home W	Home L	Away W	Away L
vs NL East	W	L	W	L	vs NL Cent.	W	L	W	L	vs NL West	W	L	W	L
Atlanta	2	4	3	3	Chicago	4	2	4	3	Colorado	2	4	2	4
Florida	4	2	3	4	Cincinnati	3	3	1	5	Los Angeles	3	3	1	5
Montreal	3	3	2	5	Houston	2	4	3	3	San Diego	3	3	6	0
New York	5	2	4	2	St. Louis	3	4	1	5	S. Francisco	2	4	3	3
Philadelphia	4	3	2	4										
Total	18	14	14	18		12	13	9	16		10	14	12	12

1993 finish: 75–87 (40–41 home, 35–46 away), fifth in NL East, 22 games behind

1994 Schedule

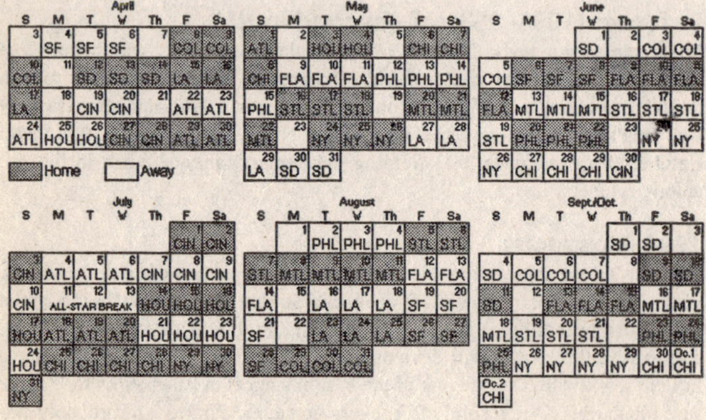

PITTSBURGH PIRATES 1994 ROSTER

MANAGER: Jim Leyland (10)

COACHES: Rich Donnelly (45), Milt May (39), Ray Miller (31), Tommy Sandt (37), Bill Verdon (19)

No.	PITCHERS	B	T	HT	WT	DOB	BIRTHPLACE	RESIDENCE
26	Cooke, Steve	R	L	6–6	220	1–14–70	Kanai, HI	Tigard, OR
52	De Los Santos, Mariano	R	R	5–10	200	7–13–70	Santo Domingo, DR	Santo Domingo, DR
50	Dewey, Mark	R	R	6–0	216	1–1–65	Grand Rapids, MI	Jenison, MI
56	Hope, John	R	R	6–3	195	12–21–70	Ft. Lauderdale, FL	Ft. Lauderdale, FL
	McCurry, Jeff	R	R	6–7	215	1–21–70	Toyko, Japan	Houston, TX
32	Miceli, Dan	R	R	6–0	207	9–9–70	Newark, NJ	Orlando, FL
55	Minor, Blas	R	R	6–3	195	3–20–66	Merced, CA	Gilbert, AZ
15	Neagle, Denny	L	L	6–2	215	9–13–68	Gambrills, MD	Gambrills, MD
34	Pena, Alejandro	R	R	6–1	203	6–25–59	Cambiaso, DR	Roswell, GA
	Ramirez, Roberto	R	L	5–11	170	8–17–72	Veracruz, MX	Veracruz,MX
41	Smith, Zane	L	L	6–1	205	12–28–60	Madison, WI	Stone Mtn., GA
29	Tomlin, Randy	L	L	5–10	170	6–14–66	Bainbridge, MA	Mars, PA
43	Wagner, Paul	R	R	6–1	185	11–14–67	Milwaukee, WI	Germantown, WI
49	Wakefield, Tim	R	R	6–2	195	8–2–66	Melbourne, FL	Melbourne, FL
	White, Rick	R	R	6–4	215	12–23–68	Springfield, OH	Springfield, OH
	Zimmerman, Mike	R	R	6–0	180	2–6–69	Brooklyn, NY	Brooklyn, NY
No.	**CATCHERS**	**B**	**T**	**HT**	**WT**	**DOB**	**BIRTHPLACE**	**RESIDENCE**
	Ensarcion, Angel	R	R	5–8	180	4–18–73	Santo Domingo, DR	Santo Domingo, DR
57	Goff, Jerry	L	R	6–3	207	4–12–64	San Rafael, CA	San Rafael, CA
	Osik, Keith	R	R	6–0	195	10–22–68	Port Jefferson, NY	Rocky Point, NY
11	Slaught, Don	R	R	6–1	190	9–11–58	Long Beach, CA	Arlington, TX
No.	**INFIELDERS**	**B**	**T**	**HT**	**WT**	**DOB**	**BIRTHPLACE**	**RESIDENCE**
48	Aude, Rich	R	R	6–5	209	7–13–71	Van Nuys, CA	Chatsworth, CA
3	Bell, Jay	R	R	6–0	185	12–11–65	Eglin AFB, FL	Gibsonia, PA
	Brown, Michael	L	L	6–7	245	11–4–71	Martinez, CA	Vacaville, CA
16	Foley, Tom	L	R	6–1	175	9–9–59	Columbus, GA	Miami, FL
13	Garcia, Carlos	R	R	6–1	185	10–15–67	Tachira, VZ	Lancaster, NY
	Hunter, Brian	R	L	6–0	195	3–4–68	El Toro, CA	Long Beach, CA
7	King, Jeff	R	R	6–1	180	12–26–64	Marion, IN	Wexford, PA
	Sandoval, Jose	R	R	5–11	170	8–25–69	Los Mochis, MX	Ahoeme, MX
44	Shelton, Ben	R	L	6–3	210	9–21–69	Chicago, IL	Oak Park, IL
51	Womack, Tony	L	R	5–9	153	9–25–69	Danville, VA	Chatham, VA
	Woodson, Tracy	R	R	6–3	216	10–5–62	Richmond, VA	
36	Young, Kevin	R	R	6–2	213	6–16–69	Alpena, MI	Kansas City, KS
No.	**OUTFIELDERS**	**B**	**T**	**HT**	**WT**	**DOB**	**BIRTHPLACE**	**RESIDENCE**
47	Bullett, Scott	L	L	6–2	190	12–25–68	Martinsburg, WV	Martinsburg, WV
	Cameron, Stanton	R	R	6–5	195	7–5–69	Knoxville, TN	Powell, TN
35	Clark, Dave	L	R	6–2	210	9–3–62	Tupelo, MS	Tupelo, MS
30	Cummings, Midre	L	R	6–0	196	10–14–71	St. Croix, VI	St. Croix, VI
28	Martin, Albert	L	L	6–2	220	11–24–67	West Covina, CA	Chandler, AZ
23	McClendon, Lloyd	R	R	6–0	212	1–11–59	Gary, IN	Merrillville, IN
6	Merced, Orlando	S	R	5–11	170	11–2–66	San Juan, PR	Ocala, FL
25	Pennyfeather, William	R	R	6–2	215	5–25–68	Perth Amboy, NJ	Perth Amboy, NJ
18	Van Slyke, Andy	L	R	6–2	195	12–21–60	Utica, NY	Chesterfield, MO

Three Rivers Stad. (47,972, artificial)
Tickets: 412–321–2827
Ticket prices:
$14.00 (club boxes)
$10.00 (terrace boxes)
$8.00 (res. seats & family sections)
$5.00 (general admission)
$2.50 (gen. adm., children 12 & under)
Field Dimensions (from home plate)
To left field at foul line, 335 feet
To center field, 400 feet
To right field at foul line, 335 feet
(OF inner fence is 10 feet high)

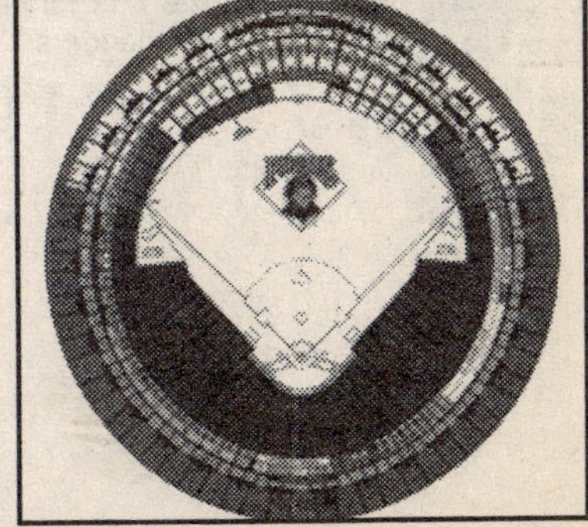

Jay Bell — No. 3/SS

Full name: Jay Stuart Bell
Bats: R **Throws:** R **HT:** 6–0 **WT:** 185
Born: 12–11–65, Eglin AFB, FL
High school: Tate (Gonzalez, FL)

Bell made the All-Star team, won his first Gold Glove, and led all NL shortstops with a .986 fielding percentage.

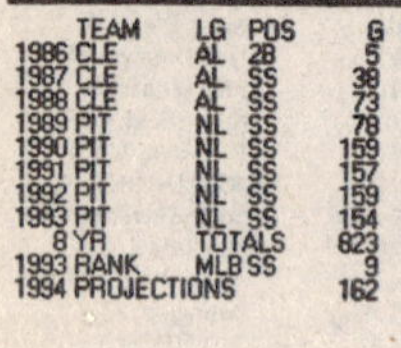

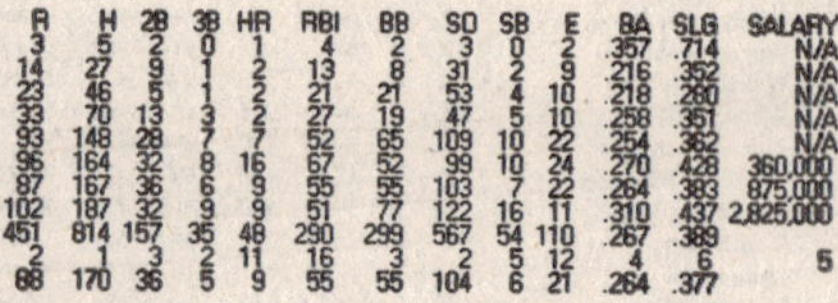

	TEAM	LG	POS	G	AB	R	H	2B	3B	HR	RBI	BB	SO	SB	E	BA	SLG	SALARY
1986	CLE	AL	2B	5	14	3	5	2	0	1	4	2	3	0	2	.357	.714	N/A
1987	CLE	AL	SS	38	125	14	27	9	1	2	13	8	31	2	9	.216	.352	N/A
1988	CLE	AL	SS	73	211	23	46	5	1	2	21	21	53	4	10	.218	.280	N/A
1989	PIT	NL	SS	78	271	33	70	13	3	2	27	19	47	5	10	.258	.351	N/A
1990	PIT	NL	SS	159	583	93	148	28	7	7	52	65	109	10	22	.254	.362	N/A
1991	PIT	NL	SS	157	608	96	164	32	8	16	67	52	99	10	24	.270	.428	360,000
1992	PIT	NL	SS	159	632	87	167	36	6	9	55	55	103	7	22	.264	.383	875,000
1993	PIT	NL	SS	154	604	102	187	32	9	9	51	77	122	16	11	.310	.437	2,825,000
8	YR	TOTALS		823	3048	451	814	157	35	48	290	299	567	54	110	.267	.389	
1993	RANK	MLB	SS	9	3	2	1	3	2	11	16	3	2	5	12	4	6	5
1994	PROJECTIONS			162	645	88	170	36	5	9	55	55	104	6	21	.264	.377	

Carlos Garcia — No. 13/2B

Full name: Carlos Jesus Garcia
Bats: R **Throws:** R **HT:** 6–1 **WT:** 185
Born: 10–15–67, Tachira, VZ
High school: Bolivar (VZ)

Garcia's 147 hits placed him third among NL rookies. He went 29 for 80 (.363) leading off the first inning and he batted .304 against left-handers.

	TEAM	LG	POS	G	AB	R	H	2B	3B	HR	RBI	BB	SO	SB	E	BA	SLG	SALARY
1990	PIT	NL	SS	4	4	1	2	0	0	0	0	0	2	0	0	.500	.500	N/A
1991	PIT	NL	SS-3B	12	24	2	6	0	2	0	1	1	8	0	1	.250	.417	N/A
1992	PIT	NL	2B-SS	22	39	4	8	1	0	0	4	0	9	0	2	.205	.231	113,000
1993	PIT	NL	2B	141	546	77	147	25	5	12	47	31	67	18	11	.269	.399	120,000
4	YR	TOTALS		179	613	84	163	26	7	12	52	32	86	18	14	.266	.390	
1993	RANK	MLB	2B	10	7	9	9	12	7	6	14	25	14	8	24	21	18	34
1994	PROJECTIONS			26	47	4	9	1	0	0	5	0	10	0	2	.191	.213	

Jeff King No. 7/3B

Full name: Jeffrey Wayne King
Bats: R **Throws:** R **HT:** 6–1 **WT:** 180
Born: 12–26–64, Marion, IN
High school: Rampart (Colo. Springs, CO)
College: Arkansas

King posted career highs in hits (180), average (.295), games (158), and doubles (35). He batted .303 with men in scoring position.

TEAM	LG	POS	G	AB	R	H	2B	3B	HR	RBI	BB	SO	SB	E	BA	SLG	SALARY
1989 PIT	NL	1B-3B	75	215	31	42	13	3	5	19	20	34	4	4	.195	.353	N/A
1990 PIT	NL	3B-1B	127	371	46	91	17	1	14	53	21	50	3	18	.245	.410	N/A
1991 PIT	NL	3B	33	109	16	26	1	1	4	18	14	15	3	2	.239	.376	215,000
1992 PIT	NL	3B-2B	130	480	56	111	21	2	14	65	27	56	4	12	.231	.371	225,000
1993 PIT	NL	3B	158	611	82	180	35	3	9	98	59	54	8	18	.295	.406	675,000
5 YR	TOTALS		523	1786	231	450	87	10	46	253	141	209	22	54	.252	.389	
1993 RANK	MLB 3B		2	2	8	1	4	6	21	3	5	24	7	31	6	18	14
1994 PROJECTIONS			141	533	61	124	22	1	15	74	28	60	4	13	.233	.362	

Albert Martin No. 28/OF

Full name: Albert Lee Martin
Bats: L **Throws:** L **HT:** 6–2 **WT:** 220
Born: 11–24–67, West Covina, CA
High school: Rowland (West Covina, CA)
College: USC

In his rookie year, King appeared in 143 games and led the Bucs with 18 HR. He batted .308 with 12 HR after the All-Star break.

TEAM	LG	POS	G	AB	R	H	2B	3B	HR	RBI	BB	SO	SB	E	BA	SLG	SALARY
1992 PIT	NL	OF	12	12	1	2	0	1	0	2	0	5	0	0	.167	.333	N/A
1993 PIT	NL	OF	143	480	85	135	26	8	18	64	42	122	16	7	.281	.481	109,000
2 YR	TOTALS		155	492	86	137	26	9	18	66	42	127	16	7	.278	.478	
1993 RANK	MLB OF		32	52	24	48	31	6	30	41	51	9	40	25	52	28	124
1994 PROJECTIONS			162	556	98	156	30	8	21	73	49	140	18	7	.281	.477	

Orlando Merced No. 6/OF

Full name: Orlando Luis Merced
Bats: S **Throws:** R **HT:** 5–11 **WT:** 170
Born: 11–2–66, San Juan, PR
High school: University Garden (PR)

Merced batted just .213 in his last 40 games, but his team-high .313 BA was the ninth best in the NL. He started 115 games and was 9 for 15 (.600) as a pinch-hitter.

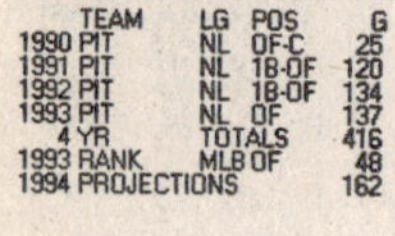
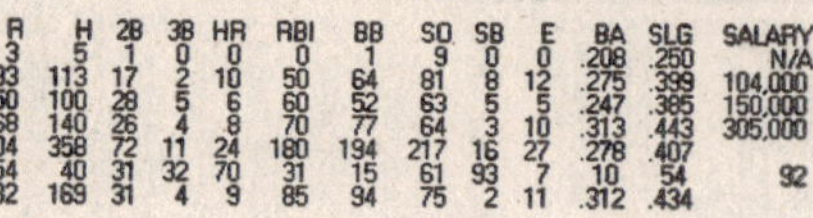

	TEAM	LG	POS	G	AB	R	H	2B	3B	HR	RBI	BB	SO	SB	E	BA	SLG	SALARY
1990	PIT	NL	OF-C	25	24	3	5	1	0	0	0	1	9	0	0	.208	.250	N/A
1991	PIT	NL	1B-OF	120	411	83	113	17	2	10	50	64	81	8	12	.275	.399	104,000
1992	PIT	NL	1B-OF	134	405	50	100	28	5	6	60	52	63	5	5	.247	.385	150,000
1993	PIT	NL	OF	137	447	68	140	26	4	8	70	77	64	3	10	.313	.443	305,000
4	YR	TOTALS		416	1287	204	358	72	11	24	180	194	217	16	27	.278	.407	
1993	RANK	MLB	OF	48	63	54	40	31	32	70	31	15	61	93	7	10	54	92
1994	PROJECTIONS			162	541	82	169	31	4	9	85	94	75	2	11	.312	.434	

Don Slaught No. 11/C

Full name: Donald Martin Slaught
Bats: R **Throws:** R **HT:** 6–1 **WT:** 190
Born: 9–11–58, Long Beach, CA
High school: Rolling Hills (P. Verdes, CA)
College: UCLA

In 1993, Slaught set career highs in hits (113) and RBI (55). His .347 BA with men in scoring position led the team.

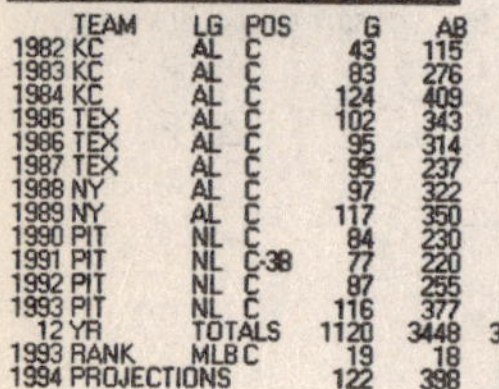
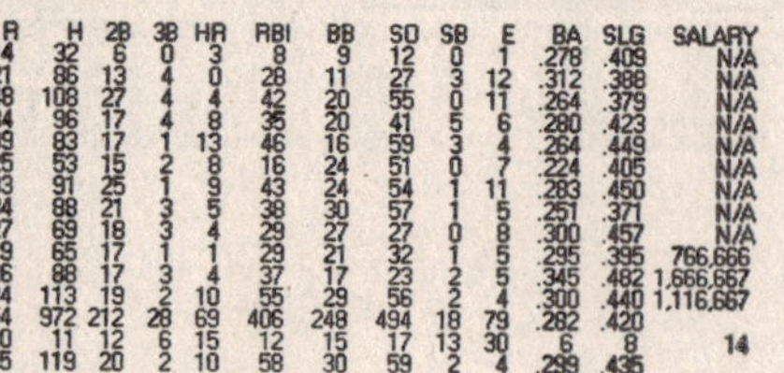

	TEAM	LG	POS	G	AB	R	H	2B	3B	HR	RBI	BB	SO	SB	E	BA	SLG	SALARY
1982	KC	AL	C	43	115	14	32	6	0	3	8	9	12	0	1	.278	.409	N/A
1983	KC	AL	C	83	276	21	86	13	4	0	28	11	27	3	12	.312	.388	N/A
1984	KC	AL	C	124	409	48	108	27	4	4	42	20	55	0	11	.264	.379	N/A
1985	TEX	AL	C	102	343	34	96	17	4	8	35	20	41	5	6	.280	.423	N/A
1986	TEX	AL	C	95	314	39	83	17	1	13	46	16	59	3	4	.264	.449	N/A
1987	TEX	AL	C	95	237	25	53	15	2	8	16	24	51	0	7	.224	.405	N/A
1988	NY	AL	C	97	322	33	91	25	1	9	43	24	54	1	11	.283	.450	N/A
1989	NY	AL	C	117	350	34	88	21	3	5	38	30	57	1	5	.251	.371	N/A
1990	PIT	NL	C	84	230	27	69	18	3	4	29	27	27	0	8	.300	.457	N/A
1991	PIT	NL	C-3B	77	220	19	65	17	1	1	29	21	32	1	5	.295	.395	766,666
1992	PIT	NL	C	87	255	26	88	17	3	4	37	17	23	2	5	.345	.482	1,666,667
1993	PIT	NL	C	116	377	34	113	19	2	10	55	29	56	2	4	.300	.440	1,116,667
12	YR	TOTALS		1120	3448	354	972	212	28	69	406	248	494	18	79	.282	.420	
1993	RANK	MLB	C	19	18	20	11	12	6	15	12	15	17	13	30	6	8	14
1994	PROJECTIONS			122	398	35	119	20	2	10	58	30	59	2	4	.299	.435	

Andy Van Slyke No. 18/OF

Full name: Andrew James Van Slyke
Bats: L **Throws:** R **HT:** 6–2 **WT:** 195
Born: 12–21–60, Utica, NY
High school: New Hartford (NY)

Van Slyke was off to a fast start, but he missed 2½ months with a broken collarbone. For the season, he collected 100 hits in only 83 games.

	TEAM	LG	POS	G	AB	R	H	2B	3B	HR	RBI	BB	SO	SB	E	BA	SLG	SALARY
1983	STL	NL	OF	101	309	51	81	15	5	8	38	46	64	21	6	.262	.421	N/A
1984	STL	NL	OF	137	361	45	88	16	4	7	50	63	71	28	8	.244	.368	N/A
1985	STL	NL	OF	146	424	61	110	25	6	13	55	47	54	34	1	.259	.439	N/A
1986	STL	NL	OF	137	418	48	113	23	7	13	61	47	85	21	8	.270	.452	N/A
1987	PIT	NL	OF	157	564	93	165	36	11	21	82	56	122	34	4	.293	.507	N/A
1988	PIT	NL	OF	154	587	101	169	23	15	25	100	57	126	30	4	.288	.506	N/A
1989	PIT	NL	OF	130	476	64	113	18	9	9	53	47	100	16	4	.237	.370	N/A
1990	PIT	NL	OF	136	493	67	140	26	6	17	77	66	89	14	8	.284	.465	N/A
1991	PIT	NL	OF	138	491	87	130	24	7	17	83	71	85	10	1	.265	.446	2,150,000
1992	PIT	NL	OF	154	614	103	199	45	12	14	89	58	99	12	5	.324	.505	4,250,000
1993	PIT	NL	OF	83	323	42	100	13	4	8	50	24	40	11	1	.310	.449	4,900,000
11	YR	TOTALS		1473	5060	762	1408	264	86	152	738	582	935	231	50	.278	.455	
1993	RANK	MLB	OF	112	82	87	74	92	32	70	60	88	101	55	113	18	46	4
1994	PROJECTIONS			107	331	46	89	14	4	7	46	44	58	20	5	.269	.411	

Kevin Young No. 36/1B

Full name: Kevin Stacey Young
Bats: R **Throws:** R **HT:** 6–2 **WT:** 213
Born: 6–16–69, Alpena, MI
High school: Washington (KS)
College: Kansas City Community and Southern Mississippi

Young sparkled in the field (only six errors), but struggled at the plate (.236 BA).

	TEAM	LG	POS	G	AB	R	H	2B	3B	HR	RBI	BB	SO	SB	E	BA	SLG	SALARY
1992	PIT	NL	3B-1B	10	7	2	4	0	0	0	4	2	0	1	1	.571	.571	N/A
1993	PIT	NL	1B	141	449	38	106	24	3	6	47	36	82	2	3	.236	.343	N/A
2	YR	TOTALS		151	456	40	110	24	3	6	51	38	82	3	4	.241	.346	
1993	RANK	MLB	1B	18	23	30	26	19	7	32	29	27	12	20	30	39	39	37
1994	PROJECTIONS			162	526	44	123	28	3	7	53	41	96	1	3	.234	.338	

Steve Cooke No. 26/P

Full name: Stephen Montague Cooke
Bats: R **Throws:** L **HT:** 6–6 **WT:** 220
Born: 1–14–70, Kanai, HI
High school: Tigard (OR)
College: Southern Idaho

Cooke's team-high 132 Ks led all rookies in the majors. He worked into the sixth inning in all but 4 of his 32 starts.

	TM	LG	POS	W	L	ERA	G	GS	CG	SH	SV	IP	H	R	ER	HR	BB	SO	SALARY
1992	PIT	NL	P	2	0	3.52	11	0	0	0	1	23.0	22	9	9	2	4	10	N/A
1993	PIT	NL	P	10	10	3.89	32	32	3	1	0	210.2	207	101	91	22	59	132	115,000
2	YR	TOTALS		12	10	3.85	43	32	3	1	1	233.2	229	110	100	24	63	142	
1993	Rank	MLB	Ps	75		125	175	39	37	23	102	39	120	119		171	61	145	222
1994	PROJECTIONS			10	11	3.93	31	36	3	0	0	227	224	110	99	24	64	144	

Paul Wagner No. 43/P

Full name: Paul Alan Wagner
Bats: R **Throws:** R **HT:** 6–1 **WT:** 185
Born: 11–14–67, Milwaukee, WI
High school: Washington (Germantown, WI)
College: Illinois State

Wagner was 6–5 with a 3.96 ERA in 17 starts. He closed 1993 strong, posting a 2.23 ERA in his final nine appearances.

	TM	LG	POS	W	L	ERA	G	GS	CG	SH	SV	IP	H	R	ER	HR	BB	SO	SALARY
1992	PIT	NL	P	2	0	0.69	6	1	0	0	0	13.0	9	1	1	0	5	5	N/A
1993	PIT	NL	P	8	8	4.27	44	17	1	1	2	141.1	143	72	67	15	42	114	112,000
2	YR	TOTALS		10	8	3.97	50	18	1	1	2	154.1	152	73	68	15	47	119	
1993	Rank	MLB	Ps	99		165	99	119	79	23	55	104	152	154		177	75	58	233
1994	PROJECTIONS			11	12	4.39	63	25	1	1	3	205	210	107	100	22	60	168	

Randy Tomlin No. 29/P

Full name: Randy Leon Tomlin
Bats: L **Throws:** L **HT:** 5–10 **WT:** 170
Born: 6–14–66, Bainbridge, MA
High school: Amherst County (VA)
College: Liberty (Lynchburg, VA)

Saddled with injuries in 1993, Tomlin pitched in only 18 games, all starts. His 4.85 ERA was the worst of his 4-year career.

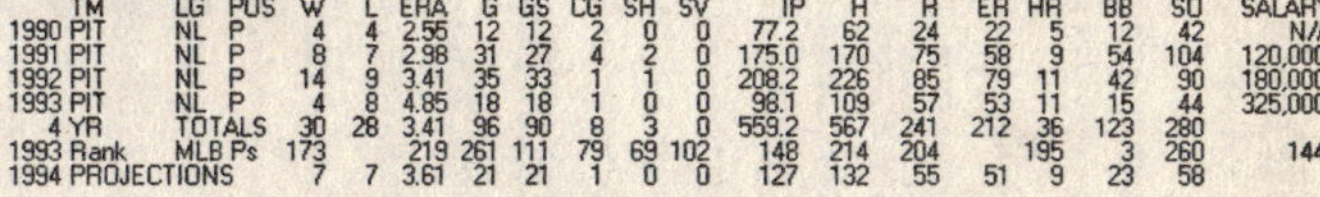

TM	LG	POS	W	L	ERA	G	GS	CG	SH	SV	IP	H	R	ER	HR	BB	SO	SALARY
1990 PIT	NL	P	4	4	2.55	12	12	2	0	0	77.2	62	24	22	5	12	42	N/A
1991 PIT	NL	P	8	7	2.98	31	27	4	2	0	175.0	170	75	58	9	54	104	120,000
1992 PIT	NL	P	14	9	3.41	35	33	1	1	0	208.2	226	85	79	11	42	90	180,000
1993 PIT	NL	P	4	8	4.85	18	18	1	0	0	98.1	109	57	53	11	15	44	325,000
4 YR	TOTALS		30	28	3.41	96	90	8	3	0	559.2	567	241	212	36	123	280	
1993 Rank	MLB Ps		173		219	261	111	79	69	102	148	214	204		195	3	260	144
1994 PROJECTIONS			7	7	3.61	21	21	1	0	0	127	132	55	51	9	23	58	

Tim Wakefield No. 49/P

Full name: Timothy Stephen Wakefield
Bats: R **Throws:** R **HT:** 6–2 **WT:** 195
Born: 8–2–66, Melbourne, FL
High school: Eau Gallie (Melbourne, FL)
College: Florida Tech (Melbourne, FL)

Wakefield struggled to regain his 1992 form (8–1, 2.15 ERA), as his ERA zoomed to 5.61. He ended '93 with back-to-back shutouts.

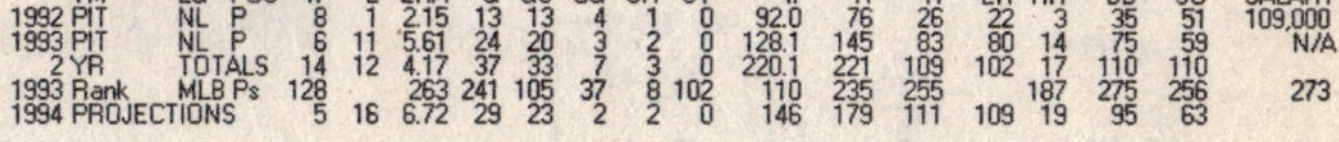

TM	LG	POS	W	L	ERA	G	GS	CG	SH	SV	IP	H	R	ER	HR	BB	SO	SALARY
1992 PIT	NL	P	8	1	2.15	13	13	4	1	0	92.0	76	26	22	3	35	51	109,000
1993 PIT	NL	P	6	11	5.61	24	20	3	2	0	128.1	145	83	80	14	75	59	N/A
2 YR	TOTALS		14	12	4.17	37	33	7	3	0	220.1	221	109	102	17	110	110	
1993 Rank	MLB Ps		128		263	241	105	37	8	102	110	235	255		187	275	256	273
1994 PROJECTIONS			5	16	6.72	29	23	2	2	0	146	179	111	109	19	95	63	

Alejandro Pena No. 34/P

Full name: Alejandro Pena
Bats: R **Throws:** R **HT:** 6–1 **WT:** 203
Born: 6–25–59, Cambiaso, DR

Pena missed '93 due to injury. His return will provide sorely needed help for the Pirate bullpen. From 1988–93, he averaged 53 appearances per year.

	TM	LG	POS	W	L	ERA	G	GS	CG	SH	SV	IP	H	R	ER	HR	BB	SO	SALARY
1981	LA	NL	P	1	1	2.88	14	0	0	0	2	25.0	18	8	8	2	11	14	N/A
1982	LA	NL	P	0	2	4.79	29	0	0	0	0	35.2	37	24	19	2	21	20	N/A
1983	LA	NL	P	12	9	2.75	34	26	4	3	1	177.0	152	67	54	7	51	120	N/A
1984	LA	NL	P	12	6	2.48	28	28	8	4	0	199.1	186	67	55	7	46	135	N/A
1985	LA	NL	P	0	1	8.31	2	1	0	0	0	4.1	7	5	4	1	3	2	N/A
1986	LA	NL	P	1	2	4.89	24	10	0	0	1	70.0	74	40	38	6	30	46	N/A
1987	LA	NL	P	2	7	3.50	37	7	0	0	11	87.1	82	41	34	9	37	76	N/A
1988	LA	NL	P	6	7	1.91	60	0	0	0	12	94.1	75	29	20	4	27	83	N/A
1989	LA	NL	P	4	3	2.13	53	0	0	0	5	76.0	62	20	18	6	18	75	N/A
1990	NY	NL	P	3	3	3.20	52	0	0	0	5	76.0	71	31	27	4	22	76	N/A
1991	NY-ATL	NL	P	8	1	2.40	59	0	0	0	15	82.1	74	23	22	6	22	62	1,000,000
1992	ATL	NL	P	1	6	4.07	41	0	0	0	15	42.0	40	19	19	7	13	34	2,650,000
12	YR	TOTALS		50	48	2.95	433	72	12	7	67	969.1	878	374	318	61	301	743	
1993	Rank	MLB Ps	not ranked -- didn't have 50 IP in 1993																
1994	PROJECTIONS			4	3	3.03	22	12	2	1	1	98	92	38	33	5	29	65	

Jim Leyland No. 10/Mgr.

Full name: James Richard Leyland
Bats: R **Throws:** R **HT:** 5–11 **WT:** 170
Born: 12–15–44, Toledo, OH
High school: Perrysburg (OH))

Leyland is a two time winner of the NL Manager of the Year award (1990 and 1992). He managed the Pirates to three straight division championships between '90 and '92.

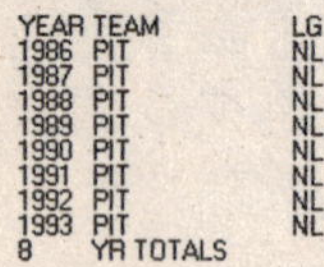

			REG. SEASON				PLAYOFF			CHAMP. SERIES			WORLD SERIES		
YEAR	TEAM	LG	W	L	PCT	POS	W	L	PCT	W	L	PCT	W	L	PCT
1986	PIT	NL	64	98	.395	6			---			---			---
1987	PIT	NL	80	82	.494	4			---			---			---
1988	PIT	NL	85	75	.531	2			---			---			---
1989	PIT	NL	74	88	.457	5			---			---			---
1990	PIT	NL	95	67	.586	1			---	2	4	.333			---
1991	PIT	NL	98	64	.605	1			---	3	4	.429			---
1992	PIT	NL	96	66	.593	1			---	3	4	.429			---
1993	PIT	NL	75	87	.463	5			---			---			---
8	YR TOTALS		667	627	.515		0	0	---	8	12	.400	0	0	---

Scott Bullett No. 47/OF

Full name: Scott Douglas Bullett
Bats: L **Throws:** L **HT:** 6–2 **WT:** 190
Born: 12–25–68, Martinsburg, WV
High school: Martinsburg (WV)
Bullett showed potential at AAA Buffalo, batting .287 with 117 hits and 28 SB in 110 games

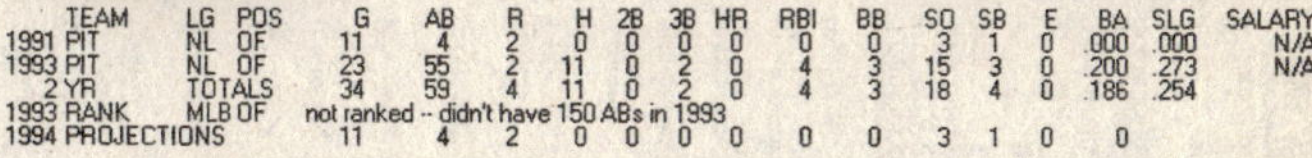

	TEAM	LG	POS	G	AB	R	H	2B	3B	HR	RBI	BB	SO	SB	E	BA	SLG	SALARY
1991	PIT	NL	OF	11	4	2	0	0	0	0	0	0	3	1	0	.000	.000	N/A
1993	PIT	NL	OF	23	55	2	11	0	2	0	4	3	15	3	0	.200	.273	N/A
2	YR	TOTALS		34	59	4	11	0	2	0	4	3	18	4	0	.186	.254	
1993	RANK	MLB	OF	not ranked -- didn't have 150 ABs in 1993														
1994	PROJECTIONS			11	4	2	0	0	0	0	0	0	3	1	0	0		

Dave Clark No. 35/OF

Full name: David Earl Clark
Bats: L **Throws:** R **HT:** 6–2 **WT:** 210
Born: 9–3–62, Tupelo, MS
High school: Shannon (MS)
College: Jackson State (MS)
Clark batted .289 in his 75 starts.

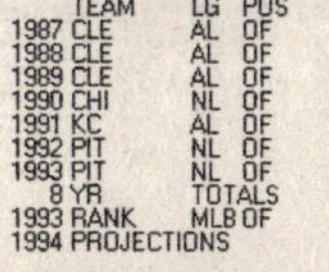
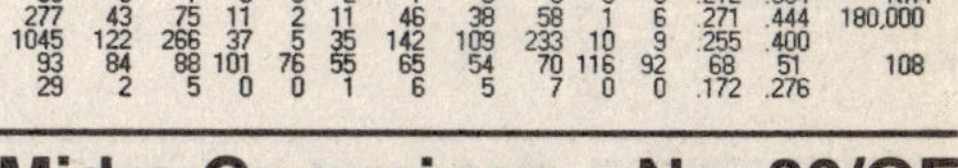

	TEAM	LG	POS	G	AB	R	H	2B	3B	HR	RBI	BB	SO	SB	E	BA	SLG	SALARY
1987	CLE	AL	OF	29	87	11	18	5	0	3	12	2	24	1	0	.207	.368	N/A
1988	CLE	AL	OF	63	156	11	41	4	1	3	18	17	28	0	2	.263	.359	N/A
1989	CLE	AL	OF	102	253	21	60	12	0	8	29	30	63	0	1	.237	.379	N/A
1990	CHI	NL	OF	84	171	22	47	4	2	5	20	8	40	7	0	.275	.409	N/A
1991	KC	AL	OF	11	10	1	2	0	0	0	1	1	1	0	0	.200	.200	N/A
1992	PIT	NL	OF	23	33	3	7	0	0	2	7	6	8	0	0	.212	.394	N/A
1993	PIT	NL	OF	110	277	43	75	11	2	11	46	38	58	1	6	.271	.444	180,000
8	YR	TOTALS		440	1045	122	266	37	5	35	142	109	233	10	9	.255	.400	
1993	RANK	MLB	OF	82	93	84	88	101	76	55	65	54	70	116	92	68	51	108
1994	PROJECTIONS			23	29	2	5	0	0	1	6	5	7	0	0	.172	.276	

Midre Cummings No. 30/OF

Full name: Midre Almeric Cummings
Bats: L **Throws:** R **HT:** 6–0 **WT:** 196
Born: 10–14–71, St. Croix, VI
High school: Miami Edison (FL)
Cummings started the season at AA Carolina, and batted .286 in 123 minor league games.

	TEAM	LG	POS	G	AB	R	H	2B	3B	HR	RBI	BB	SO	SB	E	BA	SLG	SALARY
1993	PIT	NL	OF	13	36	5	4	1	0	0	3	4	9	0	0	.111	.139	N/A
1	YR	TOTAL		13	36	5	4	1	0	0	3	4	9	0	0	.111	.139	
1993	RANK	MLB	OF	not ranked -- didn't have 150 ABs in 1993														

Mark Dewey — No. 50/P

Full name: Mark Alan Dewey
Bats: R **Throws:** R **HT:** 6–0 **WT:** 216
Born: 1–1–65, Grand Rapids, MI
High school: Jenison (MI)
Dewey registered 7 saves in 12 opportunities, and allowed only 4 of 12 inherited runners to score.

	TM	LG	POS	W	L	ERA	G	GS	CG	SH	SV	IP	H	R	ER	HR	BB	SO	SALARY
1990	SF	NL	P	1	1	2.78	14	0	0	0	0	22.2	22	7	7	1	5	11	N/A
1992	NY	NL	P	1	0	4.32	20	0	0	0	0	33.1	37	16	16	2	10	24	N/A
1993	PIT	NL	P	1	2	2.36	21	0	0	0	7	26.2	14	8	7	0	10	14	120,000
4	YR	TOTALS		3	3	3.27	55	0	0	0	7	82.2	73	31	30	3	25	49	
1993	RANK	MLB Ps		not ranked -- didn't have 50 IP in 1993															
1994	PROJECTIONS			1	2	2.33	22	0	0	0	8	27	12	8	7	0	11	14	

Jerry Goff — No. 57/C

Full name: Jerry Leroy Goff
Bats: L **Throws:** R **HT:** 6–3 **WT:** 207
Born: 4–12–64, San Rafael, CA
High school: San Rafael (CA)
College: Cal–Berkeley
Goff went 8 for 19 (.421) in his final 7 games.

	TEAM	LG	POS	G	AB	R	H	2B	3B	HR	RBI	BB	SO	SB	E	BA	SLG	SALARY
1990	MTL	NL	C-1B	52	119	14	27	1	0	3	7	21	36	0	9	.227	.311	N/A
1992	MTL	NL	PH	3	3	0	0	0	0	0	0	0	3	0	0	.000	.000	N/A
1993	PIT	NL	C	14	37	5	11	2	0	2	6	8	9	0	1	.297	.514	N/A
4	YR	TOTALS		69	159	19	38	3	0	5	13	29	48	0	10	.239	.352	
1993	RANK	MLB C		not ranked -- didn't have 150 ABs in 1993														
1994	PROJECTIONS			23	53	6	12	1	0	1	4	9	16	0	3	.226	.340	

Brian Hunter — 1B

Full name: Brian Ronald Hunter
Bats: R **Throws:** L **HT:** 6–0 **WT:** 195
Born: 3–4–68, El Toro, CA
High school: Paramount (CA)
College: Cerritos (CA)
Hunter had 26 RBI in 30 games for AAA Richmond.

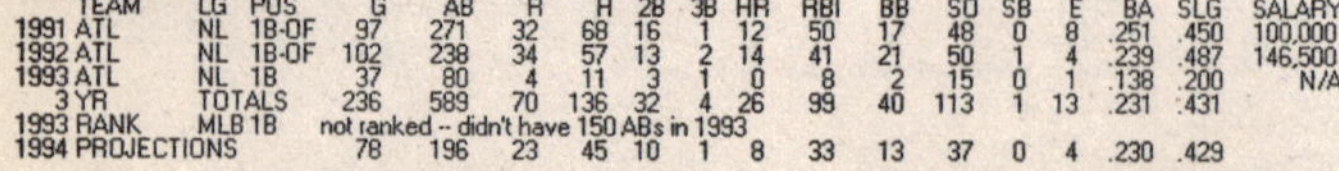

	TEAM	LG	POS	G	AB	R	H	2B	3B	HR	RBI	BB	SO	SB	E	BA	SLG	SALARY
1991	ATL	NL	1B-OF	97	271	32	68	16	1	12	50	17	48	0	8	.251	.450	100,000
1992	ATL	NL	1B-OF	102	238	34	57	13	2	14	41	21	50	1	4	.239	.487	146,500
1993	ATL	NL	1B	37	80	4	11	3	1	0	8	2	15	0	1	.138	.200	N/A
3	YR	TOTALS		236	589	70	136	32	4	26	99	40	113	1	13	.231	.431	
1993	RANK	MLB 1B		not ranked -- didn't have 150 ABs in 1993														
1994	PROJECTIONS			78	196	23	45	10	1	8	33	13	37	0	4	.230	.429	

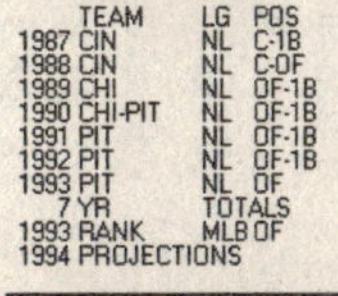

Lloyd McClendon No. 23/OF

Full name: Lloyd Glenn McClendon
Bats: R **Throws:** R **HT:** 6–0 **WT:** 212
Born: 1–11–59, Gary, IN
High school: Roosevelt (IN)
College: Valparaiso (IN)
McClendon's .221 BA was his lowest since 1990.

	TEAM	LG	POS	G	AB	R	H	2B	3B	HR	RBI	BB	SO	SB	E	BA	SLG	SALARY
1987	CIN	NL	C-1B	45	72	8	15	5	0	2	13	4	15	1	2	.208	.361	N/A
1988	CIN	NL	C-OF	72	137	9	30	4	0	3	14	15	22	4	4	.219	.314	N/A
1989	CHI	NL	OF-1B	92	259	47	74	12	1	12	40	37	31	6	6	.286	.479	N/A
1990	CHI-PIT	NL	OF-1B	53	110	6	18	3	0	2	12	14	22	1	1	.164	.245	N/A
1991	PIT	NL	OF-1B	85	163	24	47	7	0	7	24	18	23	2	3	.288	.460	260,000
1992	PIT	NL	OF-1B	84	190	26	48	8	1	3	20	28	24	1	3	.253	.353	465,000
1993	PIT	NL	OF	88	181	21	40	11	1	2	19	23	17	0	3	.221	.326	650,000
7	YR	TOTALS		519	1112	141	272	50	3	31	142	139	154	15	22	.245	.379	
1993	RANK	MLB	OF	105	123	128	131	101	97	114	129	92	135	127	72	121	122	71
1994	PROJECTIONS			71	142	12	29	6	0	2	15	17	20	1	2	.204	.303	

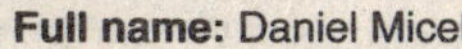

Dan Miceli No. 32/P

Full name: Daniel Miceli
Bats: R **Throws:** R **HT:** 6–0 **WT:** 207
Born: 9–9–70, Newark, NJ
High school: Dr. Phillips (Orlando, FL)
Rookie Miceli allowed no runs in his first 8 Pittsburgh appearances.

	TM	LG	POS	W	L	ERA	G	GS	CG	SH	SV	IP	H	R	ER	HR	BB	SO	SALARY
1993	PIT	NL	P	0	0	5.06	9	0	0	0	0	5.1	6	3	3	0	3	4	N/A
1	YR	TOTAL		0	0	5.06	9	0	0	0	0	5.1	6	3	3	0	3	4	
1993	RANK	MLB Ps	not ranked -- didn't have 50 IP in 1993																

Blas Minor No. 55/P

Full name: Blas Minor Jr.
Bats: R **Throws:** R **HT:** 6–3 **WT:** 195
Born: 3–20–66, Merced, CA
High school: Atwater (CA)
College: Merced JC (CA) and Arizona State
Minor led the Bucs with 65 relief appearances.

	TM	LG	POS	W	L	ERA	G	GS	CG	SH	SV	IP	H	R	ER	HR	BB	SO	SALARY
1992	PIT	NL	P	0	0	4.50	1	0	0	0	0	2.0	3	2	1	0	0	0	N/A
1993	PIT	NL	P	8	6	4.10	65	0	0	0	2	94.1	94	43	43	8	26	84	112,000
2	YR	TOTALS		8	6	4.11	66	0	0	0	2	96.1	97	45	44	8	26	84	
1993	Rank	MLB Ps		99		148	28	202	125	69	55	157	138	95		117	54	36	233
1994	PROJECTIONS			12	9	4.11	97	0	0	0	3	140	139	63	64	12	39	126	

Denny Neagle — No. 15/P

Full name: Dennis Edward Neagle Jr.
Bats: L **Throws:** L **HT:** 6–2 **WT:** 215
Born: 9–13–68, Gambrills, MD
High school: Arundel (Gambrills, MD)
College: Minnesota
Neagle had a 3.38 ERA after the All-Star break.

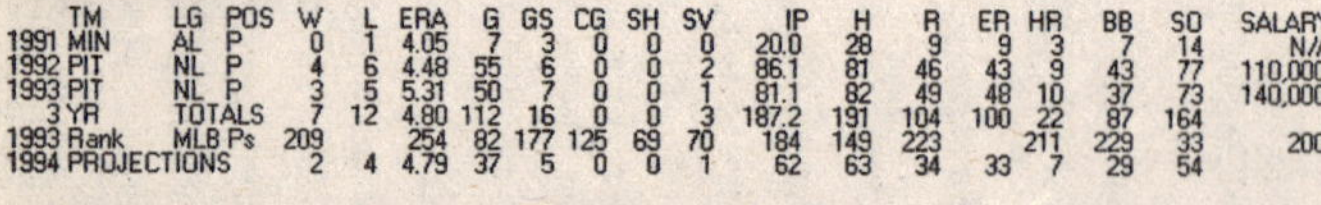

TM	LG	POS	W	L	ERA	G	GS	CG	SH	SV	IP	H	R	ER	HR	BB	SO	SALARY
1991 MIN	AL	P	0	1	4.05	7	3	0	0	0	20.0	28	9	9	3	7	14	N/A
1992 PIT	NL	P	4	6	4.48	55	6	0	0	2	86.1	81	46	43	9	43	77	110,000
1993 PIT	NL	P	3	5	5.31	50	7	0	0	1	81.1	82	49	48	10	37	73	140,000
3 YR	TOTALS		7	12	4.80	112	16	0	0	3	187.2	191	104	100	22	87	164	
1993 Rank	MLB Ps		209		254	82	177	125	69	70	184	149	223		211	229	33	200
1994 PROJECTIONS			2	4	4.79	37	5	0	0	1	62	63	34	33	7	29	54	

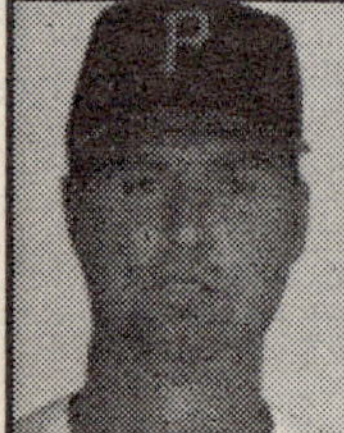

Zane Smith — No. 41/P

Full name: Zane William Smith
Bats: L **Throws:** L **HT:** 6–1 **WT:** 205
Born: 12–28–60, Madison, WI
High school: North Platte (NE)
College: Indiana State
Smith's 4.55 ERA during '93 was his career high.

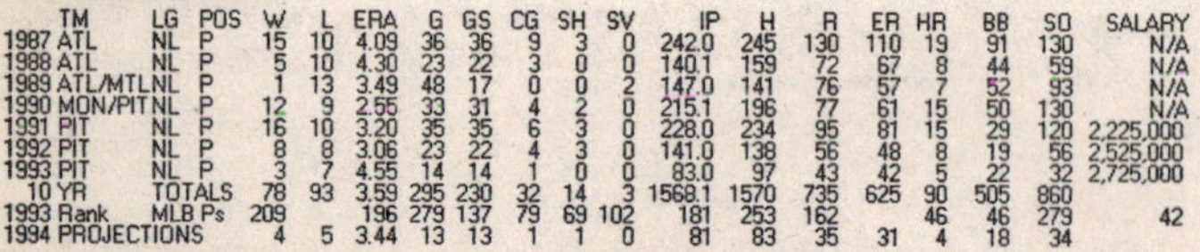

TM	LG	POS	W	L	ERA	G	GS	CG	SH	SV	IP	H	R	ER	HR	BB	SO	SALARY
1987 ATL	NL	P	15	10	4.09	36	36	9	3	0	242.0	245	130	110	19	91	130	N/A
1988 ATL	NL	P	5	10	4.30	23	22	3	0	0	140.1	159	72	67	8	44	59	N/A
1989 ATL/MTL	NL	P	1	13	3.49	48	17	0	0	2	147.0	141	76	57	7	52	93	N/A
1990 MON/PIT	NL	P	12	9	2.55	33	31	4	2	0	215.1	196	77	61	15	50	130	N/A
1991 PIT	NL	P	16	10	3.20	35	35	6	3	0	228.0	234	95	81	15	29	120	2,225,000
1992 PIT	NL	P	8	8	3.06	23	22	4	3	0	141.0	138	56	48	8	19	56	2,525,000
1993 PIT	NL	P	3	7	4.55	14	14	1	0	0	83.0	97	43	42	5	22	32	2,725,000
10 YR	TOTALS		78	93	3.59	295	230	32	14	3	1568.1	1570	735	625	90	505	860	
1993 Rank	MLB Ps		209		196	279	137	79	69	102	181	253	162		46	46	279	42
1994 PROJECTIONS			4	5	3.44	13	13	1	1	0	81	83	35	31	4	18	34	

Tracy Woodson — 3B

Full name: Tracy Michael Woodson
Bats: R **Throws:** R **HT:** 6–3 **WT:** 216
Born: 10–5–62, Richmond, VA
High school: Benedectine (Richmond, VA)
College: North Carolina State
St. Louis was 28–13 when he was a starter in '93.

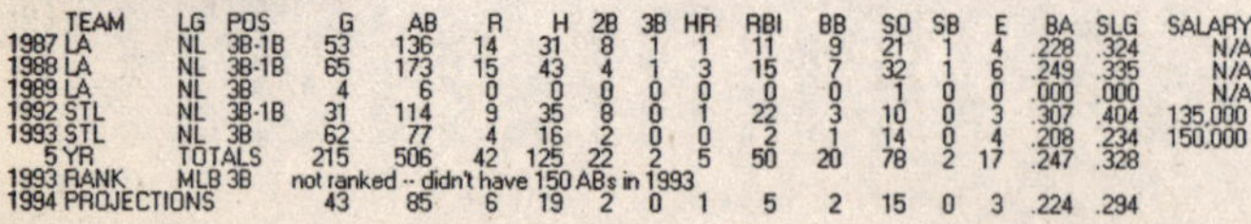

TEAM	LG	POS	G	AB	R	H	2B	3B	HR	RBI	BB	SO	SB	E	BA	SLG	SALARY
1987 LA	NL	3B-1B	53	136	14	31	8	1	1	11	9	21	1	4	.228	.324	N/A
1988 LA	NL	3B-1B	65	173	15	43	4	1	3	15	7	32	1	6	.249	.335	N/A
1989 LA	NL	3B	4	6	0	0	0	0	0	0	0	1	0	0	.000	.000	N/A
1992 STL	NL	3B-1B	31	114	9	35	8	0	1	22	3	10	0	3	.307	.404	135,000
1993 STL	NL	3B	62	77	4	16	2	0	0	2	1	14	0	4	.208	.234	150,000
5 YR	TOTALS		215	506	42	125	22	2	5	50	20	78	2	17	.247	.328	
1993 RANK	MLB 3B		not ranked -- didn't have 150 ABs in 1993														
1994 PROJECTIONS			43	85	6	19	2	0	1	5	2	15	0	3	.224	.294	

St. Louis
CARDINALS

1994 Scouting Report

Hitting: (1993/.272 BA, fourth in the NL; 118 HR, twelfth in the NL)

Offensively the '93 Cardinals were a typical Cardinal team—good team speed, hits for average, little power. In 1993, St. Louis ranked second in stolen bases in the NL. The team's leading hitter was Gregg Jefferies. Jefferies finally found a home in St. Louis, and he thrived: a .342 average with 16 HR and 83 RBI. Bernard Gilkey added a .305 BA with 16 HR and 70 RBI and Brian Jordan hit .309 with 10 HR and 44 RBI. Ozzie Smith posted a .288 BA. Unfortunately for St. Louis, Mark Whiten was the team's only legitimate power hitter (25 HR, 99 RBI). Ray Lankford was a disappointment last season, hitting just .238 with 7 HR.

Pitching: (1993/4.23 ERA, eighth in NL)

Cardinal pitching is uncharacteristically weak. Staff ace Bob Tewksbury was 17–10, but Donovan Osborne and Allen Watson are St. Louis' hopes for the future. Osborne was 10–7 with a 3.76 ERA in 26 starts last season. And Watson, 6–7 with a 4.60 ERA in 16 appearances for St. Louis, was third in the American Association in ERA when the Cardinals called him up last June. Both will get an opportunity to shine in '94.

The Cardinals need to find a closer. After Lee Smith left, no one on the roster had more than seven saves last year. Those seven belonged to Mike Perez, who was 7–2 with a 2.48 ERA in 65 appearances.

Defense: (1993/.975 pct., tenth in NL)

St. Louis usually plays good defense, but the '93 team didn't. Ozzie Smith failed to win the Gold Glove, as age started to catch up to the Wizard of Oz. The Cards have quality defensive outfielders, but Gregg Jefferies is still relying on his bat, and not his glove, to keep him in the major leagues.

1994 Prospects:

The Cardinal teams that won over the past 25 years featured defense, speed, pitching and at least one slugger who could drive the rabbits in. This year's edition doesn't promise to feature enough defense, pitching, or power to be a winner. The Cardinals will be respectable, but they don't look like a pennant contender this season.

Team Directory

Chairman: August A. Busch III	President & CEO: Stuart F. Meyer
General Mgr.: Dal Maxvill	VP, Business Operations: Mark Gorris
Director of P.R.: Jeff Wehling	Traveling Secretary: C. J. Chere

Minor League Affiliates:

Level	Team/League	1993 Record
AAA	Louisville – American Association	68–76
AA	Arkansas – Texas	67–69
A	St. Petersburg – Florida State	75–58
	Springfield – Midwest	78–58
	Savannah – South Atlantic	94–48
	Glens Falls – New York/Penn.*	37–40
Rookie	Johnson City – Appalachian	37–31

*moving to Augusta, New Jersey, and will be known as the New Jersey Cardinals in '94.

1993 Review

	Home		Away			Home		Away			Home		Away	
vs NL East	W	L	W	L	vs NL Cent.	W	L	W	L	vs NL West	W	L	W	L
Atlanta	4	2	2	4	Chicago	2	4	3	4	Colorado	3	3	4	2
Florida	5	2	4	2	Cincinnati	4	2	3	3	Los Angeles	1	5	5	1
Montreal	4	3	2	4	Houston	4	2	2	4	San Diego	5	1	0	6
New York	4	2	4	3	Pittsburgh	5	1	4	3	S. Francisco	3	3	5	1
Philadelphia	5	2	0	6										
Total	22	11	12	19		15	9	12	14		12	12	14	10

1993 finish: 87–75 (49–32 home, 38–43 away), third in NL East, ten games behind

1994 Schedule

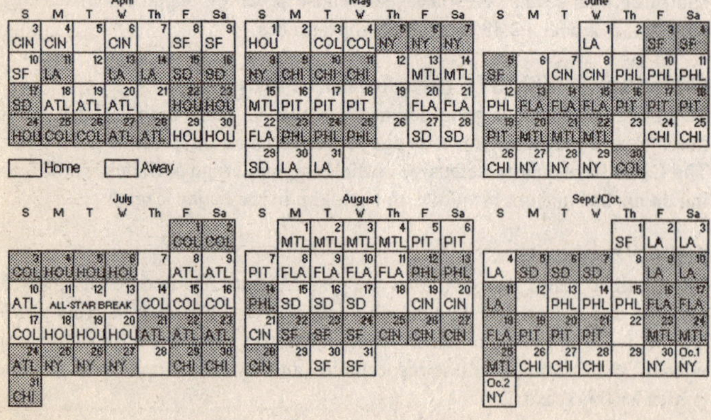

ST. LOUIS CARDINALS 1994 ROSTER

MANAGER: Joe Torre (9)

COACHES: Red Schoendienst (2), Gaylen Pitts (4), Jose Cardenal (TBD), Chris Chambliss, hitting (10), Bucky Dent, 3B (30), Joe Coleman, pitching (40)

No.	PITCHERS	B	T	HT	WT	DOB	BIRTHPLACE	RESIDENCE
43	Arocha, Rene	R	R	6–0	180	2–24–66	Havana, CU	Miami, FL
48	Batchelor, Richard	R	R	6–1	195	4–8–67	Florence, SC	Hartsville, SC
	Cimorelli, Frank	R	R	6–0	175	8–2–68	Poughkeepsie, NY	Hyde Park, NY
52	Cormier, Rheal	L	L	5–10	185	4–23–67	Moncton, Can.	New Brunswick, Can.
	Creek, Doug	L	L	5–10	205	3–1–69	Winchester, VA	Martinsburg, WV
35	Dixon, Steve	L	L	6–0	190	8–3–69	Cincinnati, OH	Louisville, KY
	Eversgerd, Bryan	R	L	6–1	190	2–11–69	Centralia, IL	Centralia, IL
	Frascatore, John	R	R	6–1	190	2–4–70	Queens, NY	Oceanside, NY
36	Kilgus, Paul	L	L	6–1	185	2–2–62	Bowling Green, KY	Bowling Green, KY
50	Murphy, Rob	L	L	6–2	215	5–26–60	Miami, FL	Miami, FL
	Olivares, Omar	R	R	6–1	193	7–6–67	Mayaguez, PR	St. Louis, MO
31	Osborne, Donovan	L	L	6–2	195	6–21–69	Roseville, CA	Carson City, NV
42	Perez, Mike	R	R	6–0	187	10–19–64	Yauco, PR	Springfield, IL
39	Tewksbury, Bob	R	R	6–4	208	11–30–60	Concord, NH	Concord, NH
41	Urbani, Tom	L	L	6–1	190	1–21–68	Santa Cruz, CA	Santa Cruz, CA
38	Watson, Allen	L	L	6–3	190	11–18–70	Jamaica, NY	Middle Village, NY
No.	CATCHERS	B	T	HT	WT	DOB	BIRTHPLACE	RESIDENCE
19	Pagnozzi, Tom	R	R	6–1	190	7–30–62	Tucson, AZ	Gilbert, AZ
22	Pappas, Eric	R	R	6–0	190	4–25–66	Chicago, IL	Chicago, IL
No.	INFIELDERS	B	T	HT	WT	DOB	BIRTHPLACE	RESIDENCE
18	Alicea, Luis	S	R	5–9	177	7–29–65	Santurce, PR	Loxahatchie, FL
33	Brewer, Rod	L	L	6–3	218	2–24–66	Eustis, FL	Zellwood, FL
	Chowlowsky, Dan	R	R	6–0	195	10–30–70	Yonkers, NY	San Jose, CA
44	Cromer, Tripp	R	R	6–2	165	11–21–67	Lake City, SC	Lexington, SC
	Deak, Darrel	S	R	6–0	180	7–5–69	Cumberland, PA	Scottsdale, AZ
	Holbert, Aaron	R	R	6–0	160	1–9–73	Torrance, CA	Long Beach, CA
9	Jefferies, Gregg	S	R	5–10	185	8–1–67	Burlingame, CA	Millbrae, CA
8	Jones, Tim	L	R	5–10	175	12–1–62	Sumter, SC	St. Louis, MO
11	Oquendo, Jose	S	R	5–10	171	7–4–63	Rio Piedras, PR	St. Louis, MO
21	Pena, Geronimo	S	R	6–1	195	3–29–67	Distrito Nacional, DR	Los Alcarrizos, DR
5	Royer, Stan	R	R	6–3	221	8–31–67	Olney, IL	Springfield, IL
1	Smith, Ozzie	S	R	5–10	168	12–26–54	Mobile, AL	St. Louis, MO
27	Zeile, Todd	R	R	6–1	190	9–9–65	Van Nuys, CA	Valencia, CA
No.	OUTFIELDERS	B	T	HT	WT	DOB	BIRTHPLACE	RESIDENCE
	Bradshaw, Terry	L	R	6–0	180	2–3–69	Franklin, VA	Zuni, VA
	Coleman, Paul	R	R	5–11	200	12–9–70	Jacksonville, TX	Frankston, TX
23	Gilkey, Bernard	R	R	6–0	190	9–24–66	St. Louis, MO	St. Louis, MO
3	Jordan, Brian	R	R	6–1	205	3–29–67	Baltimore, MD	Stone Mountain, GA
16	Lankford, Ray	L	L	5–11	198	6–5–67	Modesto, CA	Chesterfield, MO
	Mabry, John	L	R	6–4	195	10–17–70	Wilmington, DE	Warwick, MD
	Shabazz, Basil	R	R	6–0	190	1–31–72	Little Rock, AR	Pine Bluff, AR
22	Whiten, Mark	S	R	6–3	215	11–25–66	Pensacola, FL	St. Petersburg, FL

Busch Stadium (57,001, artificial)

Tickets: 314–421–3060

Ticket prices:

- $14.00 (field box, loge box rows 1–4)
- $12.00 (loge box rows 5–7, terr. box)
- $10.50 (loge reserved)
- $9.50 (terrace reserved)
- $5.50 (general admission reserved)
- $5.00 (bleachers)

Field Dimensions (from home plate)

- To left field at foul line, 330 feet
- To center field, 402 feet
- To right field at foul line, 330 feet
- (OF wall is 8' high)

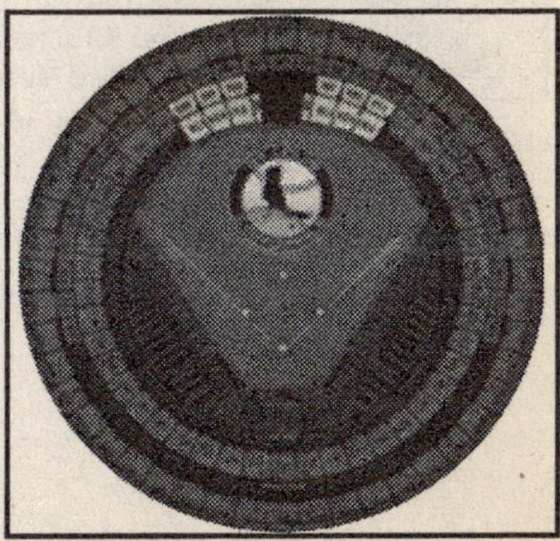

Luis Alicea No. 18/2B

Full name: Luis Rene Alicea
Bats: S **Throws:** R **HT:** 5–9 **WT:** 177
Born: 7–29–65, Santurce, PR
High school: Liceo Int. Castro (PR)
College: Florida State

In 1993 Alicea stole 11 SB in 12 attempts and batted .338 with runners in scoring position.

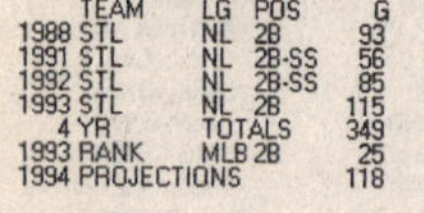
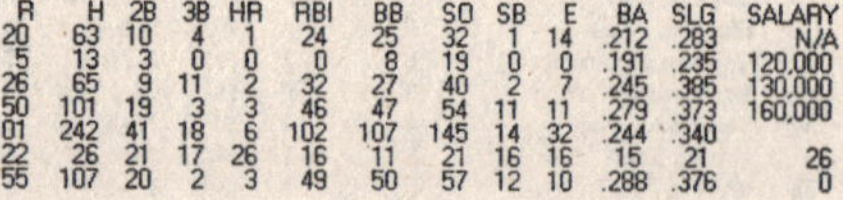

	TEAM	LG	POS	G	AB	R	H	2B	3B	HR	RBI	BB	SO	SB	E	BA	SLG	SALARY
1988	STL	NL	2B	93	297	20	63	10	4	1	24	25	32	1	14	.212	.283	N/A
1991	STL	NL	2B-SS	56	68	5	13	3	0	0	0	8	19	0	0	.191	.235	120,000
1992	STL	NL	2B-SS	85	265	26	65	9	11	2	32	27	40	2	7	.245	.385	130,000
1993	STL	NL	2B	115	362	50	101	19	3	3	46	47	54	11	11	.279	.373	160,000
4	YR	TOTALS		349	992	101	242	41	18	6	102	107	145	14	32	.244	.340	
1993	RANK	MLB	2B	25	27	22	26	21	17	26	16	11	21	16	16	15	21	26
1994	PROJECTIONS			118	372	55	107	20	2	3	49	50	57	12	10	.288	.376	0

Bernard Gilkey No. 23/OF

Full name: Otis Bernard Gilkey
Bats: R **Throws:** R **HT:** 6–0 **WT:** 190
Born: 9–24–66, St. Louis, MO
High school: University City (St. Louis, MO)

In the best year of his career, Gilkey led the Cards with 61 extra-base hits, 40 doubles, and 99 runs. He tied for the NL lead with 19 sacrifice flies.

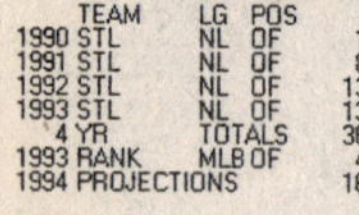
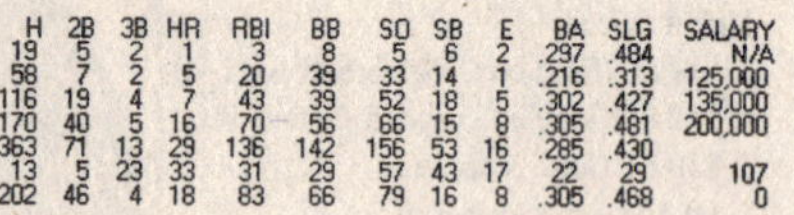

	TEAM	LG	POS	G	AB	R	H	2B	3B	HR	RBI	BB	SO	SB	E	BA	SLG	SALARY
1990	STL	NL	OF	18	64	11	19	5	2	1	3	8	5	6	2	.297	.484	N/A
1991	STL	NL	OF	81	268	28	58	7	2	5	20	39	33	14	1	.216	.313	125,000
1992	STL	NL	OF	131	384	56	116	19	4	7	43	39	52	18	5	.302	.427	135,000
1993	STL	NL	OF	137	557	99	170	40	5	16	70	56	66	15	8	.305	.481	200,000
4	YR	TOTALS		367	1273	194	363	71	13	29	136	142	156	53	16	.285	.430	
1993	RANK	MLB	OF	48	24	11	13	5	23	33	31	29	57	43	17	22	29	107
1994	PROJECTIONS			162	663	118	202	46	4	18	83	66	79	16	8	.305	.468	0

Gregg Jefferies No. 9/1B

Full name: Gregory Scott Jefferies
Bats: S **Throws:** R **HT:** 5–10 **WT:** 185
Born: 8–1–67, Burlingame, CA
High school: Sierra (San Mateo, CA)

Jefferies finished third in the league with a .342 BA. He hit .380 after June 1, and had just 32 strikeouts in 612 plate appearances.

	TEAM	LG	POS	G	AB	R	H	2B	3B	HR	RBI	BB	SO	SB	E	BA	SLG	SALARY
1987	NY	NL	PH	6	6	0	3	1	0	0	2	0	0	0	---	.500	.667	N/A
1988	NY	NL	3B-2B	29	109	19	35	8	2	6	17	8	10	5	2	.321	.596	N/A
1989	NY	NL	2B-3B	141	508	72	131	28	2	12	56	39	46	21	14	.258	.392	N/A
1990	NY	NL	2B-3B	153	604	96	171	40	3	15	68	46	40	11	16	.283	.434	200,000
1991	NY	NL	2B-3B	136	486	59	132	19	2	9	62	47	38	26	17	.272	.374	425,000
1992	KC	AL	3B-2B	152	604	66	172	36	3	10	75	43	29	19	26	.285	.404	1,150,000
1993	STL	NL	1B	142	544	89	186	24	3	16	83	62	32	46	9	.342	.485	2,650,000
7	YR	TOTALS		759	2861	401	830	156	15	68	363	245	195	128	84	.290	.426	
1993	RANK	MLB	1B	16	10	6	3	19	7	19	15	14	36	1	13	3	10	11
1994	PROJECTIONS			161	620	101	212	27	3	18	94	70	36	52	10	.342	.482	

Ray Lankford No. 16/OF

Full name: Raymond Lewis Lankford
Bats: L **Throws:** L **HT:** 5–11 **WT:** 198
Born: 6–5–67, Modesto, CA
High school: Grace Davis (Modesto, CA)
College: Modesto Junior (CA)

Lankford had a team high 81 walks (8th in the NL) and 111 strikeouts. All seven of his HR were off of right-handers.

	TEAM	LG	POS	G	AB	R	H	2B	3B	HR	RBI	BB	SO	SB	E	BA	SLG	SALARY
1990	STL	NL	OF	39	126	12	36	10	1	3	12	13	27	8	1	.286	.452	100,000
1991	STL	NL	OF	151	566	83	142	23	15	9	69	41	114	44	6	.251	.392	125,000
1992	STL	NL	OF	153	598	87	175	40	6	20	86	72	147	42	2	.293	.480	160,000
1993	STL	NL	OF	127	407	64	97	17	3	7	45	81	111	14	7	.238	.346	290,000
4	YR	TOTALS		470	1697	246	450	90	25	39	212	207	399	108	16	.265	.417	
1993	RANK	MLB	OF	65	67	60	76	66	54	78	68	11	16	48	25	114	116	94
1994	PROJECTIONS			106	377	54	102	22	3	10	47	55	95	21	3	.271	.427	

Tom Pagnozzi No. 19/C

Full name: Thomas Alan Pagnozzi
Bats: R **Throws:** R **HT:** 6–1 **WT:** 190
Born: 7–30–62, Tucson, AZ
High school: Rincon (Tucson, AZ)
College: Central Arizona and Arkansas

Pagnozzi spent most of May and June on the DL, and batted .284 after his return. He had hits in 20 of his last 26 games.

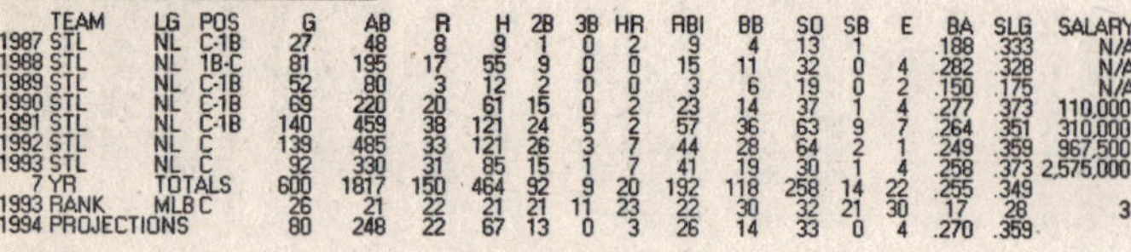

	TEAM	LG	POS	G	AB	R	H	2B	3B	HR	RBI	BB	SO	SB	E	BA	SLG	SALARY
1987	STL	NL	C-1B	27	48	8	9	1	0	2	9	4	13	1		.188	.333	N/A
1988	STL	NL	1B-C	81	195	17	55	9	0	0	15	11	32	0	4	.282	.328	N/A
1989	STL	NL	C-1B	52	80	3	12	2	0	0	3	6	19	0	2	.150	.175	N/A
1990	STL	NL	C-1B	69	220	20	61	15	0	2	23	14	37	1	4	.277	.373	110,000
1991	STL	NL	C-1B	140	459	38	121	24	5	2	57	36	63	9	7	.264	.351	310,000
1992	STL	NL	C	139	485	33	121	26	3	7	44	28	64	2	1	.249	.359	967,500
1993	STL	NL	C	92	330	31	85	15	1	7	41	19	30	1	4	.258	.373	2,575,000
7	YR	TOTALS		600	1817	150	464	92	9	20	192	118	258	14	22	.255	.349	
1993	RANK	MLB	C	26	21	22	21	21	11	23	22	30	32	21	30	17	28	3
1994	PROJECTIONS			80	248	22	67	13	0	3	26	14	33	0	4	.270	.359	

Ozzie Smith No. 1/SS

Full name: Osborne Earl Smith
Bats: S **Throws:** R **HT:** 5–10 **WT:** 168
Born: 12–26–54, Mobile, AL
High school: Locke (Los Angeles, CA)
College: Cal Poly (San Luis Obispo, CA)

Smith failed to win a Gold Glove for the first time in 14 seasons. He struck out just once per 33.5 plate appearances, best in the NL.

	TEAM	LG	POS	G	AB	R	H	2B	3B	HR	RBI	BB	SO	SB	E	BA	SLG	SALARY
1978	SD	NL	SS	159	590	69	152	17	6	1	46	47	43	40	25	.258	.312	N/A
1979	SD	NL	SS	156	587	77	124	18	6	0	27	37	37	28	20	.211	.262	N/A
1980	SD	NL	SS	158	609	67	140	18	5	0	35	71	49	57	24	.230	.276	N/A
1981	SD	NL	SS	110	450	53	100	11	2	0	21	41	37	22	16	.222	.256	N/A
1982	STL	NL	SS	140	488	58	121	24	1	2	43	68	32	25	13	.248	.314	N/A
1983	STL	NL	SS	159	552	69	134	30	6	3	50	64	36	34	21	.243	.335	N/A
1984	STL	NL	SS	124	412	53	106	20	5	1	44	56	17	35	12	.257	.337	N/A
1985	STL	NL	SS	158	537	70	148	22	3	6	54	65	27	31	14	.276	.361	N/A
1986	STL	NL	SS	153	514	67	144	19	4	0	54	79	27	31	15	.280	.333	N/A
1987	STL	NL	SS	158	600	104	182	40	4	0	75	89	36	43	10	.303	.383	N/A
1988	STL	NL	SS	153	575	80	155	27	1	3	51	74	43	57	22	.270	.336	N/A
1989	STL	NL	SS	155	593	82	162	30	8	2	50	55	37	29	17	.273	.361	N/A
1990	STL	NL	SS	143	512	61	130	21	1	1	50	61	33	32	12	.254	.305	1,975,000
1991	STL	NL	SS	150	550	96	157	30	3	3	50	83	36	35	8	.285	.367	2,225,000
1992	STL	NL	SS	132	518	73	153	20	2	0	31	59	34	43	10	.295	.342	2,000,000
1993	STL	NL	SS	141	545	75	157	22	6	1	53	43	18	21	19	.288	.356	3,000,000
16	YR	TOTALS		2349	8632	1154	2265	369	63	23	734	992	542	563	258	.262	.328	
1993	RANK	MLB	SS	15	10	7	7	12	4	31	14	16	36	2	8	8	21	4
1994	PROJECTIONS			150	552	75	153	23	3	3	52	60	29	36	18	.277	.350	

Mark Whiten No. 22/OF

Full name: Mark Anthony Whiten
Bats: S **Throws:** R **HT:** 6–3 **WT:** 215
Born: 11–25–66, Pensacola, FL
High school: Pensacola (FL)
College: Pensacola Junior (FL)
Whiten led the team with 25 HR, the most by a Cardinal since 1987. He had more RBI (99) than in the first three years of his career.

	TEAM	LG	POS	G	AB	R	H	2B	3B	HR	RBI	BB	SO	SB	E	BA	SLG	SALARY
1990	TOR	AL	OF	33	88	12	24	1	1	2	7	7	14	2	0	.273	.375	100,000
1991	TOR-CLE	AL	OF	116	407	46	99	18	7	9	45	30	85	4	7	.243	.388	115,000
1992	CLE	AL	OF	148	508	73	129	19	4	9	43	72	102	16	7	.254	.360	333,333
1993	STL	NL	OF	152	562	81	142	13	4	25	99	58	110	15	10	.253	.423	508,333
4	YR	TOTALS		449	1565	212	394	51	16	45	194	167	311	37	24	.252	.391	
1993	RANK	MLB	OF	19	22	29	38	92	32	14	10	26	17	43	7	98	66	79
1994	PROJECTIONS			162	608	87	153	14	3	26	109	62	119	16	10	.252	.413	

Todd Zeile No. 27/3B

Full name: Todd Edward Zeile
Bats: R **Throws:** R **HT:** 6–1 **WT:** 190
Born: 9–9–65, Van Nuys, CA
High school: Hart (Newhall, CA)
College: UCLA
Zeile's team-high 103 RBI ranked seventh in the NL. He hit 16 of his 17 HR after June 28, and batted .368 with the bases loaded.

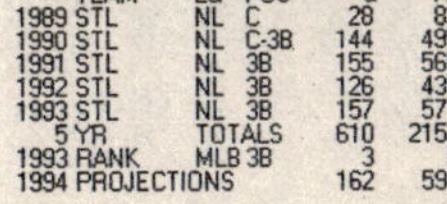

	TEAM	LG	POS	G	AB	R	H	2B	3B	HR	RBI	BB	SO	SB	E	BA	SLG	SALARY
1989	STL	NL	C	28	82	7	21	3	1	1	8	9	14	0	4	.256	.354	N/A
1990	STL	NL	C-3B	144	495	62	121	25	3	15	57	67	77	2	15	.244	.398	100,000
1991	STL	NL	3B	155	565	76	158	36	3	11	81	62	94	17	25	.280	.412	160,000
1992	STL	NL	3B	126	439	51	113	18	4	7	48	68	70	7	13	.257	.364	300,000
1993	STL	NL	3B	157	571	82	158	36	1	17	103	70	76	5	33	.277	.433	1,025,000
5	YR	TOTALS		610	2152	278	571	118	12	51	297	276	331	31	90	.265	.402	
1993	RANK	MLB	3B	3	5	8	6	3	21	8	2	4	16	15	2	15	15	13
1994	PROJECTIONS			162	594	86	164	37	0	17	108	72	78	5	33	.276	.424	

Rene Arocha No. 43/P

Full name: Rene Arocha
Bats: R **Throws:** R **HT:** 6–0 **WT:** 180
Born: 2–24–66, Havana, CU
High school: Regla (Havana, CU)
Rookie Arocha started the season 5–0 and gave up just 1.48 BB per 9 IP, second-best in the NL. He allowed a staff-high 20 HR.

	TM	LG	POS	W	L	ERA	G	GS	CG	SH	SV	IP	H	R	ER	HR	BB	SO	SALARY
1993	STL	NL	P	11	8	3.78	32	29	1	0	0	188.0	197	89	79	20	31	96	109,000
1	YR	TOTAL		11	8	3.78	32	29	1	0	0	188.0	197	89	79	20	31	96	
1993	RANK	MLB Ps		59		111	175	65	79	69	102	61	177	112		178	6	236	236

Rheal Cormier No. 52/P

Full name: Rheal Paul Cormier
Bats: L **Throws:** L **HT:** 5–10 **WT:** 185
Born: 4–23–67, Moncton, Can.
High school: Polyv. L. J. Robichaud (NB)
College: Community College of Rhode Island
Cormier shuttled between the bullpen and the starting rotation for much of 1993. He held left-handed batters to a .207 BA.

	TM	LG	POS	W	L	ERA	G	GS	CG	SH	SV	IP	H	R	ER	HR	BB	SO	SALARY
1991	STL	NL	P	4	5	4.12	11	10	2	0	0	67.2	74	35	31	5	8	38	100,000
1992	STL	NL	P	10	10	3.68	31	30	3	0	0	186.0	194	83	76	15	33	117	120,000
1993	STL	NL	P	7	6	4.33	38	21	1	0	0	145.1	163	80	70	18	27	75	155,000
3	YR	TOTALS		21	21	3.99	80	61	6	0	0	399.0	431	198	177	38	68	230	
1993	Rank	MLB Ps		108		171	121	102	79	69	102	101	226	187		215	13	233	190
1994	PROJECTIONS			7	7	4.02	26	20	2	0	0	132	143	66	59	12	22	76	

Donovan Osborne No. 31/P

Full name: Donovan Alan Osborne
Bats: L **Throws:** L **HT:** 6–2 **WT:** 195
Born: 6–21–69, Roseville, CA
High school: Carson City (NV)
College: Nevada–Las Vegas

Osborne's 3.76 ERA was the best among Cardinals starters, and he allowed only two HR to left-handed batters.

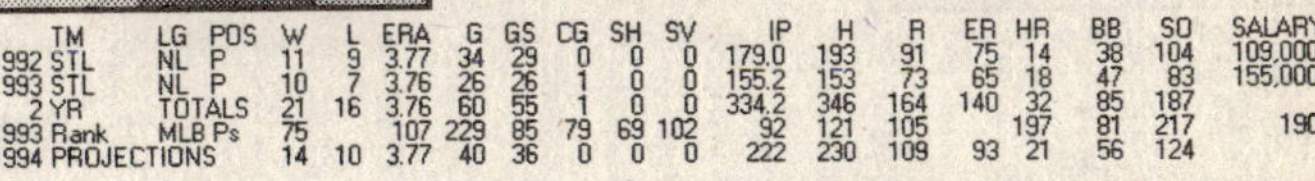

	TM	LG	POS	W	L	ERA	G	GS	CG	SH	SV	IP	H	R	ER	HR	BB	SO	SALARY
1992	STL	NL	P	11	9	3.77	34	29	0	0	0	179.0	193	91	75	14	38	104	109,000
1993	STL	NL	P	10	7	3.76	26	26	1	0	0	155.2	153	73	65	18	47	83	155,000
2	YR	TOTALS		21	16	3.76	60	55	1	0	0	334.2	346	164	140	32	85	187	
1993	Rank	MLB Ps		75		107	229	85	79	69	102	92	121	105		197	81	217	190
1994	PROJECTIONS			14	10	3.77	40	36	0	0	0	222	230	109	93	21	56	124	

Bob Tewksbury No. 39/P

Full name: Robert Alan Tewksbury
Bats: R **Throws:** R **HT:** 6–4 **WT:** 208
Born: 11–30–60, Concord, NH
High school: Merrimack (Penacook, NH)
College: Rutgers and St. Leo (FL)

Tewksbury finished seventh in the NL with a career-high 17 wins. He worked into the eighth inning in 13 of his 32 starts.

	TM	LG	POS	W	L	ERA	G	GS	CG	SH	SV	IP	H	R	ER	HR	BB	SO	SALARY
1986	NY	AL	P	9	5	3.31	23	20	2	0	0	130.1	144	58	48	8	31	49	N/A
1987	NY	AL	P	1	4	6.75	8	6	0	0	0	33.1	47	26	25	5	7	12	N/A
1987	CHI	NL	P	0	4	6.50	7	3	0	0	0	18.0	32	15	13	1	13	10	N/A
1988	CHI	NL	P	0	0	8.10	1	1	0	0	0	3.1	6	5	3	1	2	1	N/A
1989	STL	NL	P	1	0	3.30	7	4	1	1	0	30.0	25	12	11	2	10	17	N/A
1990	STL	NL	P	10	9	3.47	28	20	3	2	1	145.1	151	67	56	7	15	50	N/A
1991	STL	NL	P	11	12	3.25	30	30	3	0	0	191.0	206	86	69	13	38	75	160,000
1992	STL	NL	P	16	5	2.16	33	32	5	0	0	233.0	217	63	56	15	20	91	800,000
1993	STL	NL	P	17	10	3.83	32	32	2	0	0	213.2	258	99	91	15	20	97	2,625,000
8	YR	TOTALS		65	49	3.35	169	148	16	3	1	998.0	1086	431	372	67	156	402	
1993	Rank	MLB Ps		13		119	175	39	57	69	102	35	263	101		65	1	258	46
1994	PROJECTIONS			12	10	3.54	30	27	2	0	0	183	205	84	72	11	24	74	

Mike Perez — No. 42/P

Full name: Michael Irvin Perez
Bats: R **Throws:** R **HT:** 6–0 **WT:** 187
Born: 10–19–64, Yauco, PR
High school: Yauco (PR)
College: San Jose City (CA)
Perez replaced Lee Smith as the Cards' closer, and was 7–0 with a 2.65 ERA at home.

	TM	LG	POS	W	L	ERA	G	GS	CG	SH	SV	IP	H	R	ER	HR	BB	SO	SALARY
1990	STL	NL	P	1	0	3.95	13	0	0	0	1	13.2	12	6	6	0	3	5	N/A
1991	STL	NL	P	0	2	5.82	14	0	0	0	0	17.0	19	11	11	1	7	7	N/A
1992	STL	NL	P	9	3	1.84	77	0	0	0	0	93.0	70	23	19	4	32	46	120,000
1993	STL	NL	P	7	2	2.48	65	0	0	0	7	72.2	65	24	20	4	20	58	175,000
4	YR	TOTALS		17	7	2.57	169	0	0	0	8	196.1	166	64	56	9	62	116	
1993	Rank	MLB Ps		108		16	28	202	125	69	32	208	63	15		34	53	63	185
1994	PROJECTIONS			2	1	3.18	30	0	0	0	2	34	32	13	12	1	10	23	

Joe Torre — No. 9/Mgr.

Full name: Joseph Paul Torre
Bats: R **Throws:** R **HT:** 6–1 **WT:** 210
Born: 7–18–40, Brooklyn, NY
High school: St. Francis Prep (Br'klyn, NY)
In 11 years as a manager, Torre has only managed one team—the 1982 Braves—to a first-place finish. Those Braves lost to St. Louis in the NLCS in three straight games.

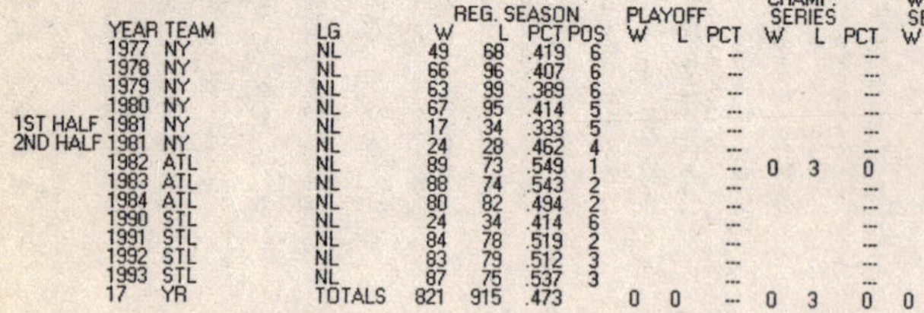

				REG. SEASON				PLAYOFF			CHAMP. SERIES			WORLD SERIES		
	YEAR	TEAM	LG	W	L	PCT	POS	W	L	PCT	W	L	PCT	W	L	PCT
	1977	NY	NL	49	68	.419	6			---			---			---
	1978	NY	NL	66	96	.407	6			---			---			---
	1979	NY	NL	63	99	.389	6			---			---			---
	1980	NY	NL	67	95	.414	5			---			---			---
1ST HALF	1981	NY	NL	17	34	.333	5			---			---			---
2ND HALF	1981	NY	NL	24	28	.462	4			---			---			---
	1982	ATL	NL	89	73	.549	1			---	0	3	0			---
	1983	ATL	NL	88	74	.543	2			---			---			---
	1984	ATL	NL	80	82	.494	2			---			---			---
	1990	STL	NL	24	34	.414	6			---			---			---
	1991	STL	NL	84	78	.519	2			---			---			---
	1992	STL	NL	83	79	.512	3			---			---			---
	1993	STL	NL	87	75	.537	3			---			---			---
	17	YR	TOTALS	821	915	.473		0	0	---	0	3	0	0	0	---

Rod Brewer No. 33/OF–1B

Full name: Rodney Lee Brewer
Bats: L **Throws:** L **HT:** 6–3 **WT:** 218
Born: 2–24–66, Eustis, FL
High school: Apopka (FL)
College: Florida
Brewer had a .324 BA at home.

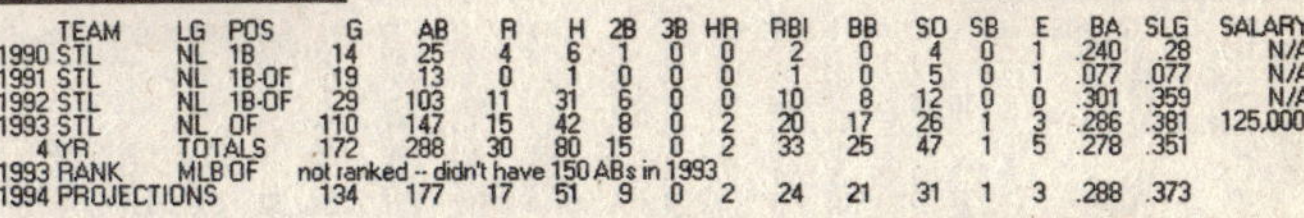

	TEAM	LG	POS	G	AB	R	H	2B	3B	HR	RBI	BB	SO	SB	E	BA	SLG	SALARY
1990	STL	NL	1B	14	25	4	6	1	0	0	2	0	4	0	1	.240	.28	N/A
1991	STL	NL	1B-OF	19	13	0	1	0	0	0	1	0	5	0	1	.077	.077	N/A
1992	STL	NL	1B-OF	29	103	11	31	6	0	0	10	8	12	0	0	.301	.359	N/A
1993	STL	NL	OF	110	147	15	42	8	0	2	20	17	26	1	3	.286	.381	125,000
4	YR	TOTALS		.172	288	30	80	15	0	2	33	25	47	1	5	.278	.351	
1993	RANK	MLB	OF	not ranked -- didn't have 150 ABs in 1993														
1994	PROJECTIONS			134	177	17	51	9	0	2	24	21	31	1	3	.288	.373	

Tim Jones No. 8/SS

Full name: William Timothy Jones
Bats: L **Throws:** R **HT:** 5–10 **WT:** 175
Born: 12–1–62, Sumter, SC
High school: Sumter (SC)
College: Citadel (Charleston, SC)
Jones batted .289 in 101 games for Louisville.

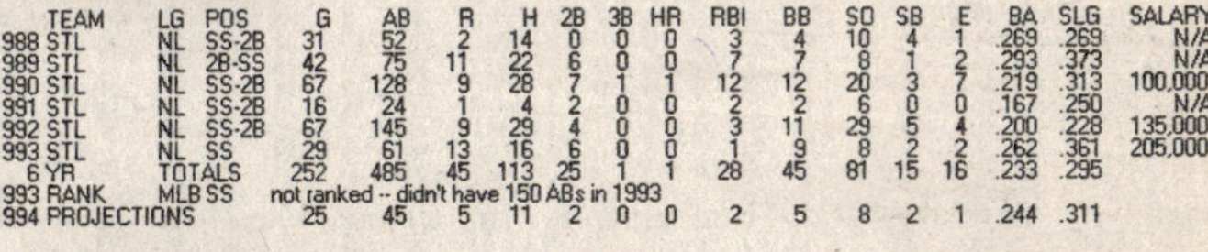

	TEAM	LG	POS	G	AB	R	H	2B	3B	HR	RBI	BB	SO	SB	E	BA	SLG	SALARY
1988	STL	NL	SS-2B	31	52	2	14	0	0	0	3	4	10	4	1	.269	.269	N/A
1989	STL	NL	2B-SS	42	75	11	22	6	0	0	7	7	8	1	2	.293	.373	N/A
1990	STL	NL	SS-2B	67	128	9	28	7	1	1	12	12	20	3	7	.219	.313	100,000
1991	STL	NL	SS-2B	16	24	1	4	2	0	0	2	2	6	0	0	.167	.250	N/A
1992	STL	NL	SS-2B	67	145	9	29	4	0	0	3	11	29	5	4	.200	.228	135,000
1993	STL	NL	SS	29	61	13	16	6	0	0	1	9	8	2	2	.262	.361	205,000
6	YR	TOTALS		252	485	45	113	25	1	1	28	45	81	15	16	.233	.295	
1993	RANK	MLB	SS	not ranked -- didn't have 150 ABs in 1993														
1994	PROJECTIONS			25	45	5	11	2	0	0	2	5	8	2	1	.244	.311	

Brian Jordan No. 3/OF

Full name: Brian O'Neal Jordan
Bats: R **Throws:** R **HT:** 6–1 **WT:** 205
Born: 3–29–67, Baltimore, MD
High school: Milford (Baltimore, MD)
College: Richmond (VA)
Jordan hit .337 after returning to St. Louis in July.

	TEAM	LG	POS	G	AB	R	H	2B	3B	HR	RBI	BB	SO	SB	E	BA	SLG	SALARY
1992	STL	NL	OF	55	193	17	40	9	4	5	22	10	48	7	1	.207	.373	N/A
1993	STL	NL	OF	67	223	33	69	10	6	10	44	12	35	6	4	.309	.543	716,667
2	YR	TOTALS		122	416	50	109	19	10	15	66	22	83	13	5	.262	.464	
1993	RANK	MLB	OF	130	112	99	95	110	13	60	71	123	110	73	59	19	6	65
1994	PROJECTIONS			73	238	41	83	10	7	12	55	13	28	5	5	.349	.601	

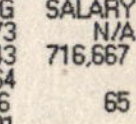

Paul Kilgus No. 36/P

Full name: Paul Nelson Kilgus
Bats: L **Throws:** L **HT:** 6–1 **WT:** 185
Born: 2–2–62, Bowling Green, KY
High school: Bowling Green (KY)
College: Kentucky
Only one of the 21 runners Kilgus inherited scored.

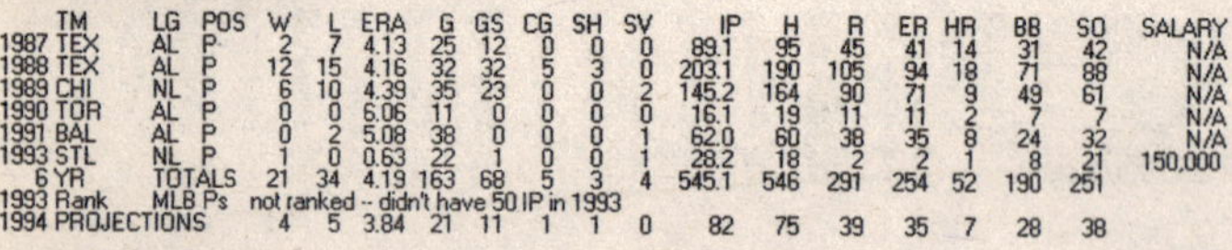

	TM	LG	POS	W	L	ERA	G	GS	CG	SH	SV	IP	H	R	ER	HR	BB	SO	SALARY
1987	TEX	AL	P	2	7	4.13	25	12	0	0	0	89.1	95	45	41	14	31	42	N/A
1988	TEX	AL	P	12	15	4.16	32	32	5	3	0	203.1	190	105	94	18	71	88	N/A
1989	CHI	NL	P	6	10	4.39	35	23	0	0	2	145.2	164	90	71	9	49	61	N/A
1990	TOR	AL	P	0	0	6.06	11	0	0	0	0	16.1	19	11	11	2	7	7	N/A
1991	BAL	AL	P	0	2	5.08	38	0	0	0	1	62.0	60	38	35	8	24	32	N/A
1993	STL	NL	P	1	0	0.63	22	1	0	0	1	28.2	18	2	2	1	8	21	150,000
6	YR	TOTALS		21	34	4.19	163	68	5	3	4	545.1	546	291	254	52	190	251	
1993	Rank	MLB Ps		not ranked -- didn't have 50 IP in 1993															
1994	PROJECTIONS			4	5	3.84	21	11	1	1	0	82	75	39	35	7	28	38	

Rob Murphy No. 50/P

Full name: Robert Alan Murphy Jr.
Bats: L **Throws:** L **HT:** 6–2 **WT:** 215
Born: 5–26–60, Miami, FL
High school: Christopher Columbus (Miami, FL)
College: Florida
Murphy appeared in a staff-high 73 games.

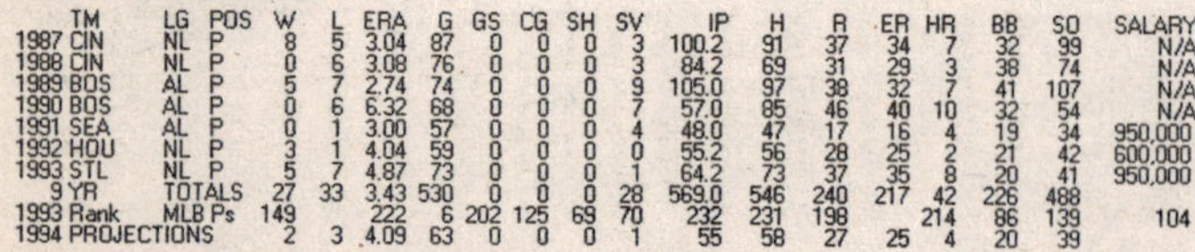

	TM	LG	POS	W	L	ERA	G	GS	CG	SH	SV	IP	H	R	ER	HR	BB	SO	SALARY
1987	CIN	NL	P	8	5	3.04	87	0	0	0	3	100.2	91	37	34	7	32	99	N/A
1988	CIN	NL	P	0	6	3.08	76	0	0	0	3	84.2	69	31	29	3	38	74	N/A
1989	BOS	AL	P	5	7	2.74	74	0	0	0	9	105.0	97	38	32	7	41	107	N/A
1990	BOS	AL	P	0	6	6.32	68	0	0	0	7	57.0	85	46	40	10	32	54	N/A
1991	SEA	AL	P	0	1	3.00	57	0	0	0	4	48.0	47	17	16	4	19	34	950,000
1992	HOU	NL	P	3	1	4.04	59	0	0	0	0	55.2	56	28	25	2	21	42	600,000
1993	STL	NL	P	5	7	4.87	73	0	0	0	1	64.2	73	37	35	8	20	41	950,000
9	YR	TOTALS		27	33	3.43	530	0	0	0	28	569.0	546	240	217	42	226	488	
1993	Rank	MLB Ps		149		222	6	202	125	69	70	232	231	198		214	86	139	104
1994	PROJECTIONS			2	3	4.09	63	0	0	0	1	55	58	27	25	4	20	39	

Omar Olivares No. 00/P

Full name: Omar Olivares
Bats: R **Throws:** R **HT:** 6–1 **WT:** 193
Born: 7–6–67, Mayaguez, PR
High school: Hostos (Mayaguez, PR)
College: Miami Dade Junior (FL)
Olivares posted a career-high 4.17 ERA.

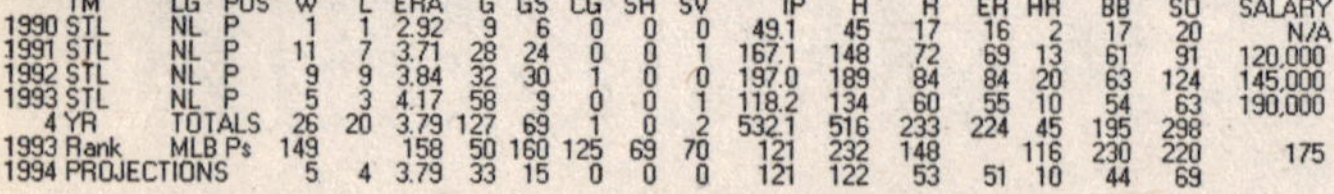

	TM	LG	POS	W	L	ERA	G	GS	CG	SH	SV	IP	H	R	ER	HR	BB	SO	SALARY
1990	STL	NL	P	1	1	2.92	9	6	0	0	0	49.1	45	17	16	2	17	20	N/A
1991	STL	NL	P	11	7	3.71	28	24	0	0	1	167.1	148	72	69	13	61	91	120,000
1992	STL	NL	P	9	9	3.84	32	30	1	0	0	197.0	189	84	84	20	63	124	145,000
1993	STL	NL	P	5	3	4.17	58	9	0	0	1	118.2	134	60	55	10	54	63	190,000
4	YR	TOTALS		26	20	3.79	127	69	1	0	2	532.1	516	233	224	45	195	298	
1993	Rank	MLB Ps		149		158	50	160	125	69	70	121	232	148		116	230	220	175
1994	PROJECTIONS			5	4	3.79	33	15	0	0	0	121	122	53	51	10	44	69	

Jose Oquendo No. 11/SS–2B

Full name: Jose Manuel Oquendo
Bats: S **Throws:** R **HT:** 5–10 **WT:** 171
Born: 7–4–63, Rio Piedras, PR
High school: Villamallo (Rio Pedras, PR)
Before a season-ending injury in August, Oquendo had just 1 error in 135 chances at SS and 2B.

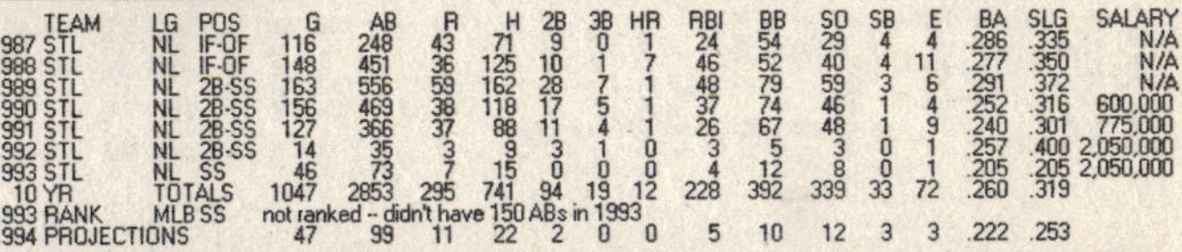

	TEAM	LG	POS	G	AB	R	H	2B	3B	HR	RBI	BB	SO	SB	E	BA	SLG	SALARY
1987	STL	NL	IF-OF	116	248	43	71	9	0	1	24	54	29	4	4	.286	.335	N/A
1988	STL	NL	IF-OF	148	451	36	125	10	1	7	46	52	40	4	11	.277	.350	N/A
1989	STL	NL	2B-SS	163	556	59	162	28	7	1	48	79	59	3	6	.291	.372	N/A
1990	STL	NL	2B-SS	156	469	38	118	17	5	1	37	74	46	1	4	.252	.316	600,000
1991	STL	NL	2B-SS	127	366	37	88	11	4	1	26	67	48	1	9	.240	.301	775,000
1992	STL	NL	2B-SS	14	35	3	9	3	1	0	3	5	3	0	1	.257	.400	2,050,000
1993	STL	NL	SS	46	73	7	15	0	0	0	4	12	8	0	1	.205	.205	2,050,000
10	YR	TOTALS		1047	2853	295	741	94	19	12	228	392	339	33	72	.260	.319	
1993	RANK	MLB	SS	not ranked -- didn't have 150 ABs in 1993														
1994	PROJECTIONS			47	99	11	22	2	0	0	5	10	12	3	3	.222	.253	

Eric Pappas No. 22/C–OF

Full name: Eric Daniel Pappas
Bats: R **Throws:** R **HT:** 6–0 **WT:** 190
Born: 4–25–66, Chicago, IL
High school: Mt. Carmel (Chicago, IL)
Filling in for the injured Pagnozzi, Pappas hit .382 with runners on third.

	TEAM	LG	POS	G	AB	R	H	2B	3B	HR	RBI	BB	SO	SB	E	BA	SLG	SALARY
1991	CHI	NL	C	7	17	1	3	0	0	0	2	1	5	0	0	.176	.176	N/A
1993	STL	NL	C	82	228	25	63	12	0	1	28	35	35	1	6	.276	.342	125,000
2	YR	TOTALS		89	245	26	66	12	0	1	30	36	40	1	6	.269	.331	
1993	RANK	MLB	C	31	30	27	26	26	25	39	30	12	29	21	15	11	33	33
1994	PROJECTIONS			107	298	33	83	16	0	1	36	46	45	1	8	.279	.342	

Geronimo Pena No. 21/2B

Full name: Geronimo Pena
Bats: S **Throws:** R **HT:** 6–1 **WT:** 195
Born: 3–29–67, Distrito Nacional, DR
High school: Distrito Nacional (DR)
Pena was the starting second baseman until a July injury. 26 of his 65 hits were for extra-bases.

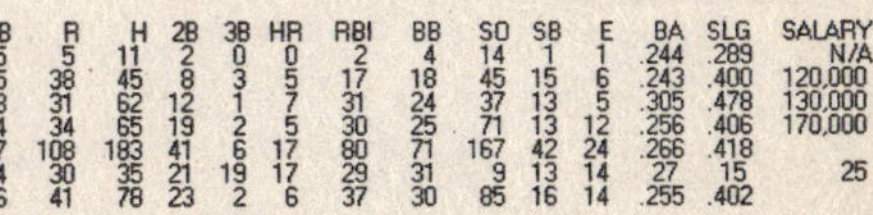

	TEAM	LG	POS	G	AB	R	H	2B	3B	HR	RBI	BB	SO	SB	E	BA	SLG	SALARY
1990	STL	NL	2B	18	45	5	11	2	0	0	2	4	14	1	1	.244	.289	N/A
1991	STL	NL	2B-OF	104	185	38	45	8	3	5	17	18	45	15	6	.243	.400	120,000
1992	STL	NL	2B	62	203	31	62	12	1	7	31	24	37	13	5	.305	.478	130,000
1993	STL	NL	2B	74	254	34	65	19	2	5	30	25	71	13	12	.256	.406	170,000
4	YR	TOTALS		258	687	108	183	41	6	17	80	71	167	42	24	.266	.418	
1993	RANK	MLB	2B	41	34	30	35	21	19	17	29	31	9	13	14	27	15	25
1994	PROJECTIONS			88	306	41	78	23	2	6	37	30	85	16	14	.255	.402	

Stan Royer — No. 5/3B–1B

Full name: Stanley Dean Royer
Bats: R **Throws:** R **HT:** 6–3 **WT:** 221
Born: 8–31–67, Olney, IL
High school: Charleston (IL)
College: Eastern Illinois
Royer hit .280 with 16 HR in 98 games in AAA.

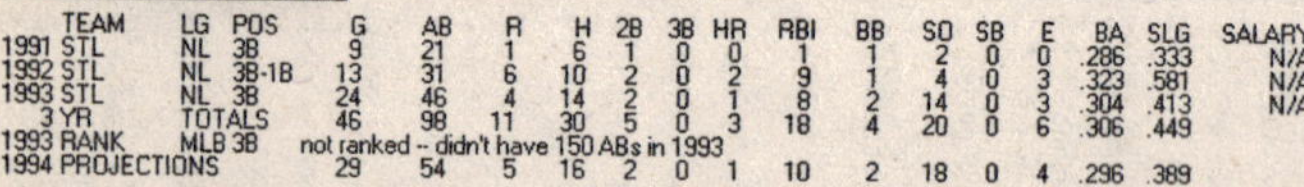

TEAM	LG	POS	G	AB	R	H	2B	3B	HR	RBI	BB	SO	SB	E	BA	SLG	SALARY
1991 STL	NL	3B	9	21	1	6	1	0	0	1	1	2	0	0	.286	.333	N/A
1992 STL	NL	3B-1B	13	31	6	10	2	0	2	9	1	4	0	3	.323	.581	N/A
1993 STL	NL	3B	24	46	4	14	2	0	1	8	2	14	0	3	.304	.413	N/A
3 YR	TOTALS		46	98	11	30	5	0	3	18	4	20	0	6	.306	.449	
1993 RANK	MLB 3B		not ranked -- didn't have 150 ABs in 1993														
1994 PROJECTIONS			29	54	5	16	2	0	1	10	2	18	0	4	.296	.389	

Allen Watson — No. 38/P

Full name: Allen Kenneth Watson
Bats: L **Throws:** L **HT:** 6–3 **WT:** 190
Born: 11–18–70, Jamaica, NY
High school: Christ the King (Middle Village, NY)
College: New York Inst. of Technology
Watson lost his last seven decisions.

TM	LG	POS	W	L	ERA	G	GS	CG	SH	SV	IP	H	R	ER	HR	BB	SO	SALARY
1993 STL	NL	P	6	7	4.60	16	15	0	0	0	86.0	90	53	44	11	28	49	109,000
1 YR	TOTAL		6	7	4.60	16	15	0	0	0	86.0	90	53	44	11	28	49	
1993 RANK	MLB Ps		128		200	272	132	125	69	102	171	175	236		228	99	189	236

San Diego *PADRES*

1994 Scouting Report

Hitting: (1993/.252 BA, twelfth in NL; 153 HR, sixth in NL)

Tony Gwynn is the team's biggest star—especially with the departures of Fred McGriff and Gary Sheffield. Gwynn's .358 average was second in the NL to Colorado's Andres Galarraga. Phil Plantier and Derek Bell are San Diego's power hitters. Plantier hit 34 homers for San Diego and Bell hit 21 HR, stole 21 bases, and hit .262.

The Padres lack speed. The Padres' 92 SB ranked eleventh in the NL. Only Derek Bell, Tony Gwynn, and Craig Shipley stole more than 10 bases last season. And San Diego hasn't replaced McGriff's power at first base.

Pitching: (1993/4.23 ERA, eleventh in NL)

Andy Benes is the Padres' ace, going 15–15. (By comparison, the rest of the staff was 46–86.) The rest of the rotation was in disarray all season, due to injuries and trades. Doug Brocail was 4–13 in 24 starts, Wally Whitehurst was 4–7 in 19 starts, and Tim Worrell was 2–7 in 16 starts. Greg W. Harris was 10–9 in 22 starts, but he was traded to Colorado. Scott Sanders is a starting prospect with potential, and should get a chance to start in '94.

The bullpen was anchored by setup man Trevor Hoffman, who came to San Diego in the Gary Sheffield deal, and closer Gene Harris. Hoffman allowed just one of 27 inherited runners to score as a Padre. Harris was 6–6 with 27 saves and converted 23 of 31 save opportunities.

Defense: (1993/.974 pct., thirteenth in NL)

SD is poor defensively. Their players aren't fast (except for Gwynn, Shipley, and Bell), so they lack range.

1994 Prospects:

The Padres are too young and too thin to improve very much on last season's 61–101 campaign. But Padre fans can take heart. The only teams to finish 43 games out in the last ten years (other than the '93 Padres) were the 1985 and 1986 Pittsburgh Pirates (43.5 and 44 games out, respectively)—a troubled team in a small market town. By 1988, Pittsburgh was an 85–75 ballclub, and by 1990, they won the first of three straight division titles.

Team Directory

Chairman: Tom Werner	President: Dick Freeman
General Mgr.: Randy Smith	Senior VP, Business Op.: Bill Adams
Director of P.R.: Jim Ferguson	Traveling Secretary: Doc Mattei

Minor League Affiliates:

Level	Team/League	1993 Record
AAA	Las Vegas – Pacific Coast	58–85
AA	Wichita – Texas	68–68
A	Rancho Cucamonga – California	64–72
	Waterloo – Midwest	54–79
	Spokane – Northwest	35–41
Rookie	Peoria Padres – Arizona	24–41

1993 review

	Home		Away			Home		Away			Home		Away	
vs NL East	W	L	W	L	vs NL Cent.	W	L	W	L	vs NL West	W	L	W	L
Atlanta	2	4	2	5	Chicago	1	5	3	3	Colorado	5	2	2	4
Florida	2	4	3	3	Cincinnati	2	4	2	5	Los Angeles	3	4	1	5
Montreal	2	4	0	6	Houston	3	4	2	4	S. Francisco	2	4	1	6
New York	3	3	4	2	Pittsburgh	0	6	3	3					
Philadelphia	3	3	3	3	St. Louis	6	0	1	5					
Total	12	18	12	19		12	19	11	20		10	10	4	15

1993 finish: 61–101 (34–47 home, 27–54 away), seventh in NL West, 43 games behind

1994 Schedule

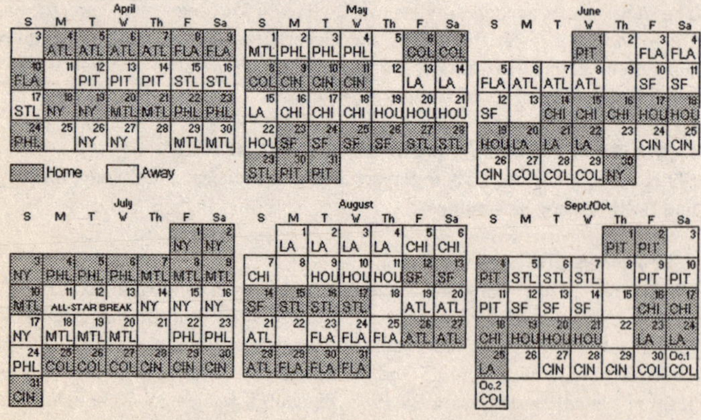

April

S	M	T	W	Th	F	Sa
3	4 ATL	5 ATL	6 ATL	7 ATL	8 FLA	9 FLA
10 FLA	11	12 PIT	13 PIT	14 PIT	15 STL	16 STL
17 STL	18 NY	19 NY	20 MTL	21 MTL	22 PHL	23 PHL
24 PHL	25	26 NY	27 NY	28	29 MTL	30 MTL

Home / Away

May

S	M	T	W	Th	F	Sa
1 MTL	2 PHL	3 PHL	4 PHL	5	6 COL	7 COL
8 COL	9 CIN	10 CIN	11 CIN	12	13 LA	14 LA
15 LA	16 CHI	17 CHI	18 CHI	19 HOU	20 HOU	21 HOU
22 HOU	23 SF	24 SF	25 SF	26 SF	27 STL	28 STL
29 STL	30 PIT	31 PIT				

June

S	M	T	W	Th	F	Sa
			1 PIT	2	3 FLA	4 FLA
5 FLA	6 ATL	7 ATL	8 ATL	9	10 SF	11 SF
12 SF	13	14 CHI	15 CHI	16 CHI	17 HOU	18 HOU
19 HOU	20 LA	21 LA	22 LA	23	24 CIN	25 CIN
26 CIN	27 COL	28 COL	29 COL	30 NY		

July

S	M	T	W	Th	F	Sa
					1 NY	2 NY
3 NY	4 PHL	5 PHL	6 PHL	7 MTL	8 MTL	9 MTL
10 MTL	11 ALL-STAR BREAK	12	13	14 NY	15 NY	16 NY
17 NY	18 MTL	19 MTL	20 MTL	21	22 PHL	23 PHL
24 PHL	25 COL	26 COL	27 COL	28 CIN	29 CIN	30 CIN
31 CIN						

August

S	M	T	W	Th	F	Sa
	1 LA	2 LA	3 LA	4 LA	5 CHI	6 CHI
7 CHI	8	9 HOU	10 HOU	11 HOU	12 SF	13 SF
14 SF	15 STL	16 STL	17 STL	18	19 ATL	20 ATL
21 ATL	22	23 FLA	24 FLA	25 FLA	26 ATL	27 ATL
28 ATL	29 FLA	30 FLA	31 FLA			

Sept./Oct.

S	M	T	W	Th	F	Sa
				1 PIT	2 PIT	3
4 PIT	5 STL	6 STL	7 STL	8	9 PIT	10 PIT
11 PIT	12 SF	13 SF	14 SF	15	16 CHI	17 CHI
18 CHI	19 HOU	20 HOU	21 HOU	22	23 LA	24 LA
25 LA	26	27 CIN	28 CIN	29 CIN	30 COL	Oc.1 COL
Oc.2 COL						

SAN DIEGO PADRES 1994 ROSTER

MANAGER: Jim Riggleman (8)
COACHES: Bruce Bochy, 3B (13); Rob Picciolo, bench (5); Dan Radison 1B (22); Merv Rettenmund, batting (16); Mike Roarke, pitching (36)

No.	PITCHERS	B	T	HT	WT	DOB	BIRTHPLACE	RESIDENCE
43	Ashby, Andy	R	R	6–5	180	7–11–67	Kansas City, MO	Kansas City, MO
38	Beckett, Robbie	R	L	6–5	235	7–16–72	Austin, TX	Austin, TX
40	Benes, Andy	R	R	6–6	240	8–20–67	Evansville, IN	Poway, CA
55	Berumen, Andres	R	R	6–1	205	4–5–71	Tijuana, MX	Banning, CA
45	Bochtler, Doug	R	R	6–3	185	7–5–70	W. Palm Beach, FL	W. Palm Beach, FL
49	Brocail, Doug	L	R	6–5	220	5–16–67	Clearfield, PA	Lamar, CO
48	Davis, Mark	L	L	6–4	210	10–19–60	Livermore, CA	Marietta, GA
38	Elliott, Donnie	R	R	6–4	190	9–20–68	Pasadena, TX	Deer Park, TX
39	Florie, Bryce	R	R	6–0	170	5–21–70	Charleston, SC	Hanahan, SC
33	Harris, Gene	R	R	5–11	190	12–5–64	Sebring, FL	San Diego, CA
51	Hoffman, Trevor	R	R	6–1	200	10–13–67	Bellflower, CA	Williamsville, NY
47	Martinez, Jose	R	R	6–2	155	4–1–71	Manoguayabo, DR	Villa Gonzalez, DR
42	Martinez, Pedro	L	L	6–2	155	11–29–68	Villa Mella, DR	Villa Mella, DR
52	Mauser, Tim	R	R	6–0	185	10–4–66	Fort Worth, TX	
27	Sanders, Scott	R	R	6–4	210	3–25–69	Thibodaux, LA	Thibodaux, LA
37	Taylor, Kerry	R	R	6–3	200	1–25–71	Bemidji, MN	Roseau, MN
41	Whitehurst, Wally	R	R	6–3	185	4–11–64	Shreveport, LA	Houma, LA
58	Worrell, Tim	R	R	6–4	210	7–5–67	Arcadia, CA	Arcadia, CA
No.	**CATCHERS**	**B**	**T**	**HT**	**WT**	**DOB**	**BIRTHPLACE**	**RESIDENCE**
11	Ausmus, Brad	R	R	5–11	185	4–14–69	New Haven, CT	Cheshire, CT
55	Johnson, Brian	R	R	6–2	195	1–8–68	Oakland, CA	Oakland, CA
No.	**INFIELDERS**	**B**	**T**	**HT**	**WT**	**DOB**	**BIRTHPLACE**	**RESIDENCE**
25	Bruno, Julio	R	R	5–10	160	10–15–72	Puerta Plata, DR	Puerta Plata, DR
26	Cianfrocco, Archi	R	R	6–5	200	10–6–66	Rome, NY	Rome, NY
12	Gardner, Jeff	L	R	5–11	175	2–4–64	Newport Beach, CA	Newport Beach, CA
7	Gutierrez, Ricky	R	R	6–1	175	5–23–70	Miami, FL	Miami, FL
53	Holbert, Ray	R	R	6–0	170	9–25–70	Torrance, CA	Moreno Valley, CA
14	Lopez, Luis	S	R	5–11	175	9–4–70	Cidra, PR	Cidra, PR
18	Shipley, Craig	R	R	6–1	190	1–7–63	Sydney, Aust.	Jupiter, FL
31	Staton, Dave	R	R	6–5	215	4–12–68	Seattle, WA	Auburn, CA
23	Velasquez, Guillermo	L	L	6–3	225	4–23–68	Mexicali, MX	Calexico, Mex.
No.	**OUTFIELDERS**	**B**	**T**	**HT**	**WT**	**DOB**	**BIRTHPLACE**	**RESIDENCE**
21	Bean, Billy	L	L	6–1	185	5–11–64	Santa Ana, CA	
14	Bell, Derek	R	R	6–2	205	12–11–68	Tampa, FL	Tampa, FL
40	Clark, Phil	R	R	6–0	180	5–6–68	Crockett, TX	Toledo, OH
19	Gwynn, Tony	L	L	5–11	215	5–9–60	Los Angeles, CA	Poway, CA
20	McDavid, Ray	L	R	6–3	190	7–20–71	San Diego, CA	San Diego, CA
56	Moore, Vince	S	L	6–1	177	9–22–71	Houston, TX	Houston, TX
10	Nieves, Melvin	S	R	6–2	186	12–28–71	San Juan, PR	Baymon, PR
9	Pegues, Steve	R	R	6–2	190	5–21–69	Pontotac, MS	Pontotac, MS
24	Plantier, Phil	L	R	5–10	195	1–27–69	Manchester, NH	San Diego, CA
58	Sanders, Tracy	R	L	6–2	200	7–26–69	Gastonia, NC	Dallas, NC

San Diego/Jack Murphy (59,722, grass)
Tickets: 619–283–4494
Ticket prices:
- $11 (field, plaza and press levels)
- $9.50 (loge, view levels)
- $7 (reserved grandstand)
- $5 (general admission)

Field Dimensions (from home plate)
- To left field at foul line, 327 feet
- To center field, 405 feet
- To right field at foul line, 327 feet
- (OF wall is 8 ft. 2 in. high)

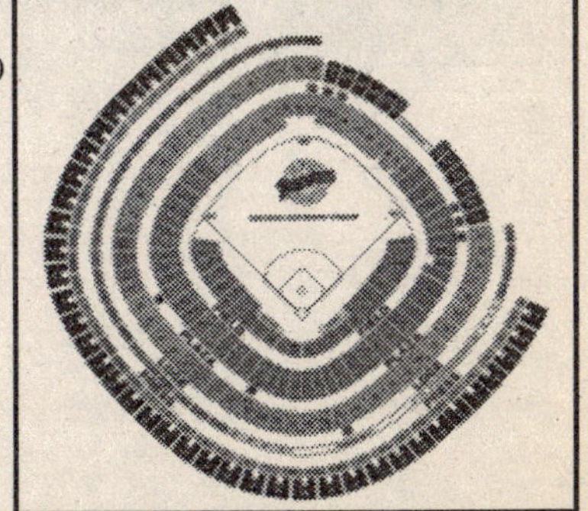

Brad Ausmus No. 11/C

Full name: Bradley David Ausmus
Bats: R **Throws:** R **HT:** 5–11 **WT:** 185
Born: 4–14–69, New Haven, CT
High school: Cheshire (CT)
College: Dartmouth

Ausmus came over from Colorado in late July, and started at C for the rest of the season. He hit safely in 14 of his last 20 games.

	TEAM	LG	POS	G	AB	R	H	2B	3B	HR	RBI	BB	SO	SB	E	BA	SLG	SALARY
1993	SD	NL	C	49	160	18	41	8	1	5	12	6	28	2	8	.256	.413	109,000
1	YR	TOTAL		49	160	18	41	8	1	5	12	6	28	2	8	.256	.413	
1993	RANK	MLB	C	40	40	36	36	35	11	27	40	40	33	13	30	19	14	36

Derek Bell No. 14/OF

Full name: Derek Nathaniel Bell
Bats: R **Throws:** R **HT:** 6–2 **WT:** 205
Born: 12–11–68, Tampa, FL
High school: King (Tampa, FL)

Last year, Bell joined Dave Winfield and Joe Carter as the only Padres to hit over 20 home runs and steal more than 20 bases (21 HR, 26 SB).

	TEAM	LG	POS	G	AB	R	H	2B	3B	HR	RBI	BB	SO	SB	E	BA	SLG	SALARY
1991	TOR	AL	OF	18	28	5	4	0	0	0	1	6	5	3	2	.143	.143	N/A
1992	TOR	AL	OF	61	161	23	39	6	3	2	15	15	34	7	0	.242	.354	112,500
1993	SD	NL	OF	150	542	73	142	19	1	21	72	23	122	26	17	.262	.417	165,000
3	YR	TOTALS		229	731	101	185	25	4	23	88	44	161	36	19	.253	.393	
1993	RANK	MLB	OF	23	27	43	38	55	97	19	28	92	9	23	135	85	69	110
1994	PROJECTIONS			162	595	79	156	20	0	23	79	23	134	27	18	.262	.412	

Archi Cianfrocco No. 26/3B

Full name: Angelo Dominic Cianfrocco
Bats: R **Throws:** R **HT:** 6–5 **WT:** 200
Born: 10–6–66, Rome, NY
High school: Rome Free Academy (NY)
Cianfrocco went just 2 for 30 after being acquired from Montreal in June, but bounced back and started 89 games for the Padres.

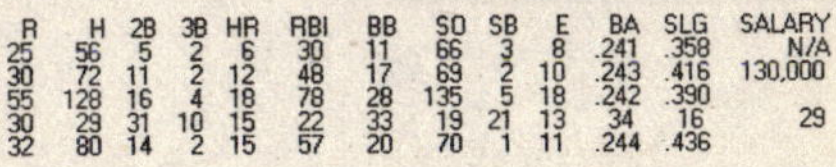

	TEAM	LG	POS	G	AB	R	H	2B	3B	HR	RBI	BB	SO	SB	E	BA	SLG	SALARY
1992	MTL	NL	1B-3B	86	232	25	56	5	2	6	30	11	66	3	8	.241	.358	N/A
1993	SD	NL	3B	96	296	30	72	11	2	12	48	17	69	2	10	.243	.416	130,000
2	YR	TOTALS		182	528	55	128	16	4	18	78	28	135	5	18	.242	.390	
1993	RANK	MLB	3B	29	27	30	29	31	10	15	22	33	19	21	13	34	16	29
1994	PROJECTIONS			101	328	32	80	14	2	15	57	20	70	1	11	.244	.436	

Jeff Gardner No. 12/2B

Full name: Jeffrey Scott Gardner
Bats: L **Throws:** R **HT:** 5–11 **WT:** 175
Born: 2–4–64, Newport Beach, CA
High school: Estancia (Costa Mesa, CA)
College: Orange Coast Junior (CA)
Gardner had a team-best 15 game hitting streak this season. He had 21 doubles, third behind McGriff and Gwynn on the team.

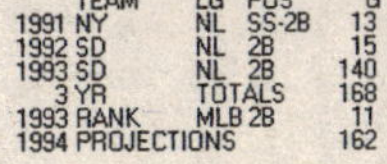

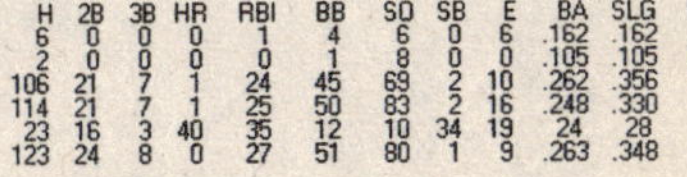

	TEAM	LG	POS	G	AB	R	H	2B	3B	HR	RBI	BB	SO	SB	E	BA	SLG	SALARY
1991	NY	NL	SS-2B	13	37	3	6	0	0	0	1	4	6	0	6	.162	.162	N/A
1992	SD	NL	2B	15	19	0	2	0	0	0	0	1	8	0	0	.105	.105	109,000
1993	SD	NL	2B	140	404	53	106	21	7	1	24	45	69	2	10	.262	.356	111,500
3	YR	TOTALS		168	460	56	114	21	7	1	25	50	83	2	16	.248	.330	
1993	RANK	MLB	2B	11	22	19	23	16	3	40	35	12	10	34	19	24	28	38
1994	PROJECTIONS			162	468	61	123	24	8	0	27	51	80	1	9	.263	.348	

Ricky Gutierrez No. 7/SS

Full name: Ricardo Gutierrez
Bats: R **Throws:** R **HT:** 6–1 **WT:** 175
Born: 5–23–70, Miami, FL
High school: American (Miami, FL)
After starting the season in the minors, Gutierrez led the Padres with 76 runs scored. He was also fourth among NL shortstops with a .971 fielding percentage.

TEAM	LG	POS	G	AB	R	H	2B	3B	HR	RBI	BB	SO	SB	E	BA	SLG	SALARY
1993 SD	NL	SS	133	438	76	110	10	5	5	26	50	97	4	14	.251	.331	109,000
1 YR	TOTAL		133	438	76	110	10	5	5	26	50	97	4	14	.251	.331	
1993 RANK	MLB	SS	20	20	7	23	31	6	15	30	11	5	25	19	30	24	34

Tony Gwynn No. 19/OF

Full name: Anthony Keith Gwynn
Bats: L **Throws:** L **HT:** 5–11 **WT:** 215
Born: 5–9–60, Los Angeles, CA
High school: Long Beach (CA)
College: San Diego State
Gwynn has hit .300 for 11 straight seasons, the best in the NL since Stan Musial's 16 straight seasons between '42 and '58.

TEAM	LG	POS	G	AB	R	H	2B	3B	HR	RBI	BB	SO	SB	E	BA	SLG	SALARY
1982 SD	NL	OF	54	190	33	55	12	2	1	17	14	16	8	1	.289	.389	N/A
1983 SD	NL	OF	86	304	34	94	12	2	1	37	23	21	7	1	.309	.372	N/A
1984 SD	NL	OF	158	606	88	213	21	10	5	71	59	23	33	4	.351	.444	N/A
1985 SD	NL	OF	154	622	90	197	29	5	6	46	45	33	14	4	.317	.408	N/A
1986 SD	NL	OF	160	642	107	211	33	7	14	59	52	35	37	4	.329	.467	N/A
1987 SD	NL	OF	157	589	119	218	36	13	7	54	82	35	56	6	.370	.511	N/A
1988 SD	NL	OF	133	521	64	163	22	5	7	70	51	40	26	5	.313	.415	N/A
1989 SD	NL	OF	158	604	82	203	27	7	4	62	56	30	40	6	.336	.424	N/A
1990 SD	NL	OF	141	573	79	177	29	10	4	72	44	23	17	5	.309	.415	1,066,667
1991 SD	NL	OF	134	530	69	168	27	11	4	62	34	19	8	3	.317	.432	2,350,000
1992 SD	NL	OF	128	520	77	165	27	3	6	41	46	16	3	5	.317	.415	2,000,000
1993 SD	NL	OF	122	489	70	175	41	3	7	59	36	19	14	5	.358	.497	4,108,333
12 YR	TOTALS		1585	6190	912	2039	316	78	66	650	542	310	263	49	.329	.438	
1993 RANK	MLB	OF	70	48	50	10	4	54	78	47	63	133	48	80	1	19	9
1994 PROJECTIONS			132	530	72	173	32	8	5	64	38	20	13	4	.326	.445	

Phil Plantier No. 24/OF

Full name: Phillip Alan Plantier
Bats: L **Throws:** R **HT:** 5–10 **WT:** 195
Born: 1–27–69, Manchester, NH
High school: Poway (CA)

Plantier's 34 HR were the most by a Padre outfielder since Dave Winfield's 34 in 1979. And his 100 RBI was only the seventh time a Padre accomplished that feat.

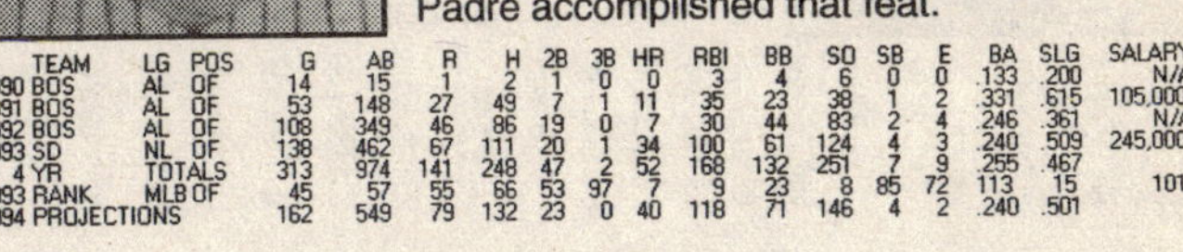

	TEAM	LG	POS	G	AB	R	H	2B	3B	HR	RBI	BB	SO	SB	E	BA	SLG	SALARY
1990	BOS	AL	OF	14	15	1	2	1	0	0	3	4	6	0	0	.133	.200	N/A
1991	BOS	AL	OF	53	148	27	49	7	1	11	35	23	38	1	2	.331	.615	105,000
1992	BOS	AL	OF	108	349	46	86	19	0	7	30	44	83	2	4	.246	.361	N/A
1993	SD	NL	OF	138	462	67	111	20	1	34	100	61	124	4	3	.240	.509	245,000
4	YR	TOTALS		313	974	141	248	47	2	52	168	132	251	7	9	.255	.467	
1993	RANK	MLB	OF	45	57	55	66	53	97	7	9	23	8	85	72	113	15	101
1994	PROJECTIONS			162	549	79	132	23	0	40	118	71	146	4	2	.240	.501	

G. Velasquez No. 23/1B

Full name: Guillermo Velasquez
Bats: L **Throws:** L **HT:** 6–3 **WT:** 225
Born: 4–23–68, Mexicali, MX

Primarily a pinch-hitter for the first half of the season, Velasquez saw more playing time after the McGriff trade. 1994 should be his first full season as a starter.

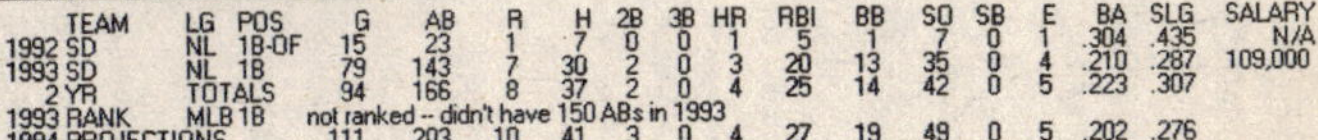

	TEAM	LG	POS	G	AB	R	H	2B	3B	HR	RBI	BB	SO	SB	E	BA	SLG	SALARY
1992	SD	NL	1B-OF	15	23	1	7	0	0	1	5	1	7	0	1	.304	.435	N/A
1993	SD	NL	1B	79	143	7	30	2	0	3	20	13	35	0	4	.210	.287	109,000
2	YR	TOTALS		94	166	8	37	2	0	4	25	14	42	0	5	.223	.307	
1993	RANK	MLB	1B	not ranked -- didn't have 150 ABs in 1993														
1994	PROJECTIONS			111	203	10	41	3	0	4	27	19	49	0	5	.202	.276	

Andy Ashby No. 43/P

Full name: Andrew Jason Ashby
Bats: R **Throws:** R **HT:** 6–5 **WT:** 180
Born: 7–11–67, Kansas City, MO
High school: Park Hill (Kansas City, MO)
College: Crowder (Neosho, MO)
After coming over in July from Colorado, Ashby compiled a 3–6 record in 12 starts as a Padre. He'll be a full-time starter in '94.

TM	LG	POS	W	L	ERA	G	GS	CG	SH	SV	IP	H	R	ER	HR	BB	SO	SALARY
1991 PHL	NL	P	1	5	6.00	8	8	0	0	0	42.0	41	28	28	5	19	26	N/A
1992 PHL	NL	P	1	3	7.54	10	8	0	0	0	37.0	42	31	31	6	21	24	109,000
1993 COL/SD	NL	P	3	10	6.80	32	21	0	0	1	123.0	168	100	93	19	56	77	150,000
3 YR	TOTALS		5	18	6.77	50	37	0	0	1	202.0	251	159	152	30	96	127	
1993 Rank	MLB Ps		209		287	175	102	125	69	70	114	286	287		270	232	146	195
1994 PROJECTIONS			3	11	6.84	40	25	0	0	1	150	210	124	114	23	68	94	

Andy Benes No. 40/P

Full name: Andrew Charles Benes
Bats: R **Throws:** R **HT:** 6–6 **WT:** 240
Born: 8–20–67, Evansville, IN
High school: Central (Evansville, IN)
College: Evansville
Benes allowed two or less earned runs in half of his starts and was named an All-Star for the first time in his career.

TM	LG	POS	W	L	ERA	G	GS	CG	SH	SV	IP	H	R	ER	HR	BB	SO	SALARY
1989 SD	NL	P	6	3	3.51	10	10	0	0	0	66.2	51	28	26	7	31	66	N/A
1990 SD	NL	P	10	11	3.60	32	31	2	0	0	192.1	177	87	77	18	69	140	130,000
1991 SD	NL	P	15	11	3.03	33	33	4	1	0	223.0	194	76	75	23	59	167	235,000
1992 SD	NL	P	13	14	3.35	34	34	2	2	0	231.1	230	90	86	14	61	169	475,000
1993 SD	NL	P	15	15	3.78	34	34	4	2	0	230.2	200	111	97	23	86	179	2,050,000
5 YR	TOTALS		59	54	3.44	143	142	12	5	0	944.0	852	392	361	85	306	721	
1993 Rank	MLB Ps		21		112	145	12	25	8	102	19	48	120		158	158	70	65
1994 PROJECTIONS			15	16	3.80	36	36	3	1	0	249	216	120	105	24	91	190	

Doug Brocail No. 49/P

Full name: Douglas Keith Brocail
Bats: L **Throws:** R **HT:** 6–5 **WT:** 220
Born: 5–16–67, Clearfield, PA
High school: Lamar (CO)
College: Lamar Community (CO)
Doug had losing streaks of 6 and 7 games in '93 after being called up from AAA, but compiled a respectable 4.56 ERA.

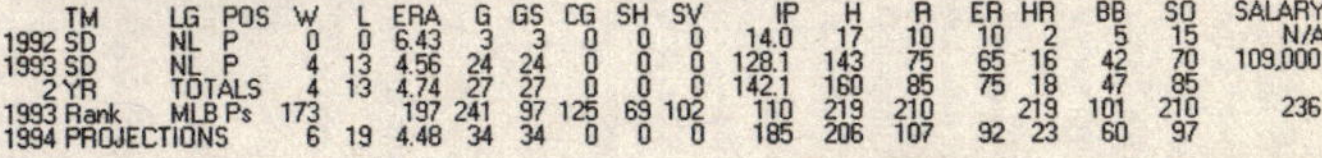

TM	LG	POS	W	L	ERA	G	GS	CG	SH	SV	IP	H	R	ER	HR	BB	SO	SALARY
1992 SD	NL	P	0	0	6.43	3	3	0	0	0	14.0	17	10	10	2	5	15	N/A
1993 SD	NL	P	4	13	4.56	24	24	0	0	0	128.1	143	75	65	16	42	70	109,000
2 YR	TOTALS		4	13	4.74	27	27	0	0	0	142.1	160	85	75	18	47	85	
1993 Rank	MLB	Ps	173		197	241	97	125	69	102	110	219	210		219	101	210	236
1994 PROJECTIONS			6	19	4.48	34	34	0	0	0	185	206	107	92	23	60	97	

Wally Whitehurst No. 41/P

Full name: Walter Richard Whitehurst
Bats: R **Throws:** R **HT:** 6–3 **WT:** 185
Born: 4–11–64, Shreveport, LA
High school: Terrobonne (Houma, LA)
College: New Orleans
Whitehurst was plagued by injuries all season, and was on the DL three separate times, but still managed to make 19 starts.

TM	LG	POS	W	L	ERA	G	GS	CG	SH	SV	IP	H	R	ER	HR	BB	SO	SALARY
1989 NY	NL	P	0	1	4.50	9	1	0	0	0	14.0	17	7	7	2	5	9	N/A
1990 NY	NL	P	1	0	3.29	38	0	0	0	2	65.2	63	27	24	5	9	46	101,000
1991 NY	NL	P	7	12	4.18	36	20	0	0	1	133.1	142	67	62	12	25	87	155,000
1992 NY	NL	P	3	9	3.62	44	11	0	0	0	97.0	99	45	39	4	33	70	235,000
1993 SD	NL	P	4	7	3.83	21	19	0	0	0	105.2	109	47	45	11	30	57	487,500
5 YR	TOTALS		15	29	3.83	148	51	0	0	3	415.2	430	193	177	34	102	269	
1993 Rank	MLB	Ps	173		118	250	108	125	69	102	136	162	89		170	64	212	136
1994 PROJECTIONS			2	5	3.64	34	10	0	0	0	89	90	39	36	6	24	57	

Gene Harris — No. 33/P

Full name: Tyrone Eugene Harris
Bats: R **Throws:** R **HT:** 5–11 **WT:** 190
Born: 12–5–64, Sebring, FL
High school: Okeechobee (FL)
College: Tulane

Harris had 12 saves and 4 wins in the Padres first 27 games, then slumped off. He finished with 23 saves in 31 chances.

	TM	LG	POS	W	L	ERA	G	GS	CG	SH	SV	IP	H	R	ER	HR	BB	SO	SALARY
1988	SD	NL	P	2	0	1.50	3	1	1	0	0	18.0	13	3	3	0	3	15	N/A
1989	SD	NL	P	8	9	2.60	56	8	0	0	6	135.0	106	43	39	8	52	106	N/A
1990	SD	NL	P	8	8	2.30	73	0	0	0	9	117.1	92	35	30	6	49	97	N/A
1991	SD	NL	P	9	5	2.23	20	20	3	2	0	133.0	116	42	33	16	27	95	342,000
1992	SD	NL	P	4	8	4.12	20	20	1	0	0	118.0	113	62	54	13	35	66	1,025,000
1993	SD/COL	NL	P	11	17	4.59	35	35	4	0	0	225.1	239	127	115	33	69	123	2,025,000
6	YR	TOTALS		42	47	3.30	207	84	9	2	15	746.2	679	312	274	76	235	502	
1993	Rank	MLB Ps		59		199	134	6	25	69	102	22	185	194		260	84	209	67
1994	PROJECTIONS			10	17	4.60	36	36	3	0	0	233	248	132	119	34	72	126	

Jim Riggleman — No. 8/Mgr.

Full name: James David Riggleman
Bats: R **Throws:** R **HT:** 5–11 **WT:** 175
Born: 12–9–52, Ft. Dix, NJ
High school: R. Montgomery (Rockville, MD)

San Diego's seventh-place finish in 1993 was the lowest finish any Riggleman team ever achieved in ten years as a minor and major league manager.

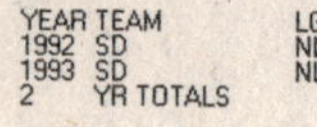
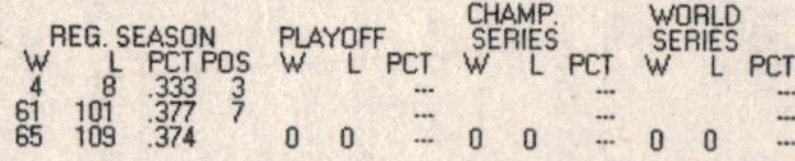

			REG. SEASON				PLAYOFF			CHAMP. SERIES			WORLD SERIES		
YEAR	TEAM	LG	W	L	PCT	POS	W	L	PCT	W	L	PCT	W	L	PCT
1992	SD	NL	4	8	.333	3			---			---			---
1993	SD	NL	61	101	.377	7			---			---			---
2	YR TOTALS		65	109	.374		0	0	---	0	0	---	0	0	---

Billy Bean — No. 21/OF

Full name: William Daro Bean
Bats: L **Throws:** L **HT:** 6–1 **WT:** 185
Born: 5–11–64, Santa Ana, CA
Bean had 9 RBIs as a pinch-hitter, the second-highest on the team.

TEAM	LG	POS	G	AB	R	H	2B	3B	HR	RBI	BB	SO	SB	E	BA	SLG	SALARY
1987 DET	AL	OF	26	66	6	17	2	0	0	4	5	11	1		.258	.288	N/A
1988 DET	AL	OF	10	11	2	2	0	1	0	0	0	2	0	0	.182	.364	N/A
1989 DET	AL	OF	9	11	0	0	0	0	0	0	2	3	0	2	.000	.000	N/A
1989 LA	NL	OF	51	71	7	14	4	0	0	3	4	10	0	0	.197	.254	N/A
1993 SD	NL	OF	88	177	19	46	9	0	5	32	6	29	2	1	.260	.395	109,000
5 YR	TOTALS		184	336	34	79	15	1	5	39	17	55	3	3	.235	.330	
1993 RANK	MLB	OF	105	125	132	123	118	124	98	92	135	124	102	8	90	89	124
1994 PROJECTIONS			100	199	21	51	10	0	6	37	6	32	2	1	.256	.397	

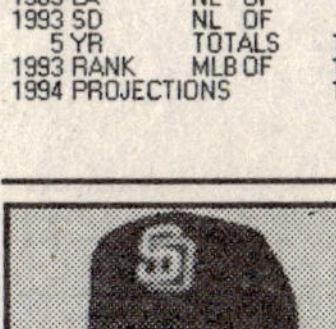

Phil Clark — No. 40/OF

Full name: Phillip Benjamin Clark
Bats: R **Throws:** R **HT:** 6–0 **WT:** 180
Born: 5–6–68, Crockett, TX
High school: Crockett (TX)
Clark started at five different positions in 1993, and hit .351 as a pinch-hitter.

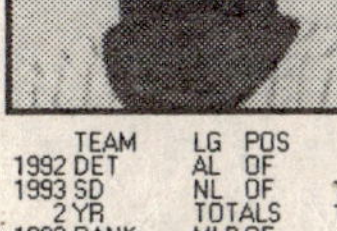

TEAM	LG	POS	G	AB	R	H	2B	3B	HR	RBI	BB	SO	SB	E	BA	SLG	SALARY
1992 DET	AL	OF	23	54	3	22	4	0	1	5	6	9	1	2	.407	.537	N/A
1993 SD	NL	OF	102	240	33	75	17	0	9	33	8	31	2	8	.313	.496	122,500
2 YR	TOTALS		125	294	36	97	21	0	10	38	14	40	3	10	.330	.503	
1993 RANK	MLB	OF	92	104	99	88	66	124	64	90	134	119	102	17	12	20	120
1994 PROJECTIONS			141	333	48	101	23	0	13	47	9	42	2	11	.303	.489	

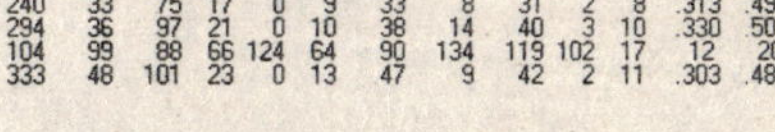

Mark Davis — No. 48/P

Full name: Mark Anthony Davis
Bats: L **Throws:** L **HT:** 6–4 **WT:** 210
Born: 10–16–60, Livermore, CA
High school: Hoover (CA)
College: Stanford
Davis had 4 saves in 6 chances for the Padres.

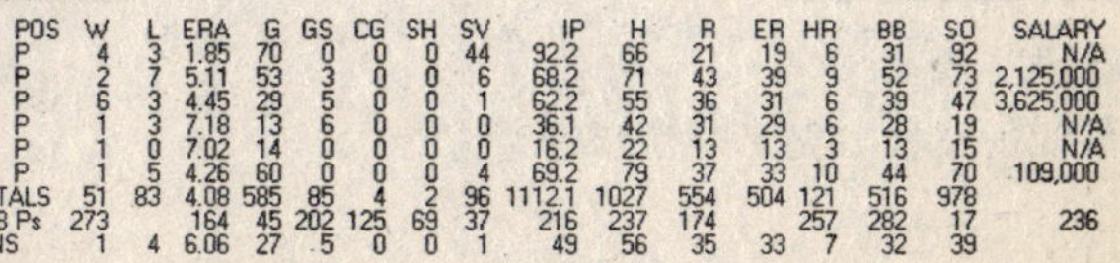

TM	LG	POS	W	L	ERA	G	GS	CG	SH	SV	IP	H	R	ER	HR	BB	SO	SALARY
1989 SD	NL	P	4	3	1.85	70	0	0	0	44	92.2	66	21	19	6	31	92	N/A
1990 KC	AL	P	2	7	5.11	53	3	0	0	6	68.2	71	43	39	9	52	73	2,125,000
1991 KC	AL	P	6	3	4.45	29	5	0	0	1	62.2	55	36	31	6	39	47	3,625,000
1992 KC	AL	P	1	3	7.18	13	6	0	0	0	36.1	42	31	29	6	28	19	N/A
1992 ATL	NL	P	1	0	7.02	14	0	0	0	0	16.2	22	13	13	3	13	15	N/A
1993 SD	NL	P	1	5	4.26	60	0	0	0	4	69.2	79	37	33	10	44	70	109,000
13 YR	TOTALS		51	83	4.08	585	85	4	2	96	1112.1	1027	554	504	121	516	978	
1993 Rank	MLB	Ps	273		164	45	202	125	69	37	216	237	174		257	282	17	236
1994 PROJECTIONS			1	4	6.06	27	5	0	0	1	49	56	35	33	7	32	39	

Pedro Martinez — No. 42/P

Full name: Pedro A. Martinez
Bats: L **Throws:** L **HT:** 6–2 **WT:** 155
Born: 11–29–68, Villa Mella, DR
High school: Ramon Matia Melle (DR)
A bright spot on the staff, he held opponents to a .172 average in 32 appearances.

	TM	LG	POS	W	L	ERA	G	GS	CG	SH	SV	IP	H	R	ER	HR	BB	SO	SALARY
1993	SD	NL	P	3	1	2.43	32	0	0	0	0	37.0	23	11	10	4	13	32	109,000
1	YR	TOTAL		3	1	2.43	32	0	0	0	0	37.0	23	11	10	4	13	32	
1993	RANK	MLB Ps		not ranked -- didn't have 50 IP in 1993															

Tim Mauser — No. 52/P

Full name: Timothy Edward Mauser
Bats: R **Throws:** R **HT:** 6–0 **WT:** 185
Born: 10–4–66, Fort Worth, TX
High school: Arlington Heights (TX)
College: Texas Christian
Mauser's ERA was 2.31 in his last 21 games.

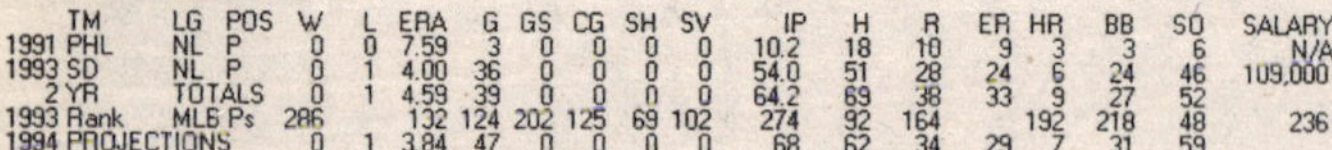

	TM	LG	POS	W	L	ERA	G	GS	CG	SH	SV	IP	H	R	ER	HR	BB	SO	SALARY
1991	PHL	NL	P	0	0	7.59	3	0	0	0	0	10.2	18	10	9	3	3	6	N/A
1993	SD	NL	P	0	1	4.00	36	0	0	0	0	54.0	51	28	24	6	24	46	109,000
2	YR	TOTALS		0	1	4.59	39	0	0	0	0	64.2	69	38	33	9	27	52	
1993	Rank	MLB Ps		286		132	124	202	125	69	102	274	92	164		192	218	48	236
1994	PROJECTIONS			0	1	3.84	47	0	0	0	0	68	62	34	29	7	31	59	

Melvin Nieves — No. 10/OF

Full name: Melvin Ramos Nieves
Bats: S **Throws:** R **HT:** 6–2 **WT:** 186
Born: 12–28–71, San Juan, PR
High school: Ives Pales Matos (Santa Rosa, PR)
Nieves struggled during his late-season callup, batting only .191 in 19 games.

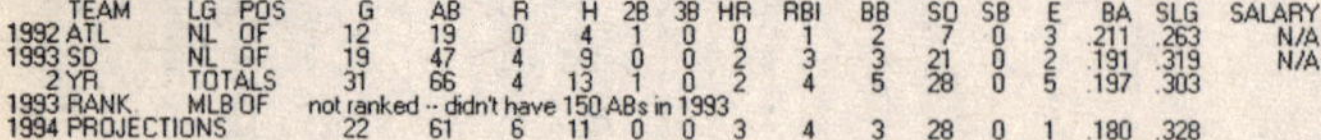

	TEAM	LG	POS	G	AB	R	H	2B	3B	HR	RBI	BB	SO	SB	E	BA	SLG	SALARY
1992	ATL	NL	OF	12	19	0	4	1	0	0	1	2	7	0	3	.211	.263	N/A
1993	SD	NL	OF	19	47	4	9	0	0	2	3	3	21	0	2	.191	.319	N/A
2	YR	TOTALS		31	66	4	13	1	0	2	4	5	28	0	5	.197	.303	
1993	RANK	MLB	OF	not ranked -- didn't have 150 ABs in 1993														
1994	PROJECTIONS			22	61	6	11	0	0	3	4	3	28	0	1	.180	.328	

Scott Sanders No. 27/P

Full name: Scott Gerald Sanders
Bats: R **Throws:** R **HT:** 6–4 **WT:** 210
Born: 3–25–69, Thibodaux, LA
High school: Thibodaux (LA)
College: Nicholls State (Thibodaux, LA)
Sanders shuttled between San Diego and AAA .

TM	LG POS	W	L	ERA	G	GS	CG	SH	SV	IP	H	R	ER	HR	BB	SO	SALARY
1993 SD	NL P	3	3	4.13	9	9	0	0	0	52.1	54	32	24	4	23	37	109,000
1 YR	TOTAL	3	3	4.13	9	9	0	0	0	52.1	54	32	24	4	23	37	
1993 RANK	MLB Ps	209		152	289	160	125	69	102	283	163	231		88	214	100	236

Craig Shipley No. 18/3B–SS

Full name: Craig Barry Shipley
Bats: R **Throws:** R **HT:** 6–1 **WT:** 190
Born: 1–7–63, Sydney, Aust.
High school: Epping (Sydney, Aust.)
College: Alabama
Shipley appeared in a career-high 103 games.

TEAM	LG POS	G	AB	R	H	2B	3B	HR	RBI	BB	SO	SB	E	BA	SLG	SALARY
1986 LA	NL SS-2B	12	27	3	3	1	0	0	4	2	5	0	3	.111	.148	N/A
1987 LA	NL SS-3B	26	35	3	9	1	0	0	2	0	6	0	3	.257	.286	N/A
1989 NY	NL SS-3B	4	7	3	1	0	0	0	0	0	1	0	0	.143	.143	N/A
1991 SD	NL SS-2B	37	91	6	25	3	0	1	6	2	14	0	7	.275	.341	100,000
1992 SD	NL SS-2B	52	105	7	26	6	0	0	7	2	21	1	1	.248	.305	117,500
1993 SD	NL SS	105	230	25	54	9	0	4	22	10	31	12	7	.235	.326	149,000
6 YR	TOTALS	236	495	47	118	20	0	5	41	16	78	13	21	.238	.309	
1993 RANK	MLB SS	26	33	34	35	34	36	16	33	34	30	8	34	36	26	28
1994 PROJECTIONS		116	255	27	60	10	0	4	24	11	34	13	7	.235	.322	

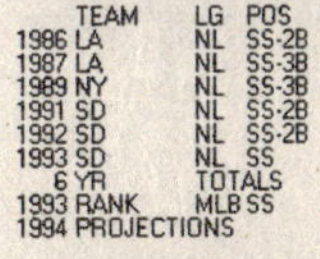

Dave Staton No. 31/1B

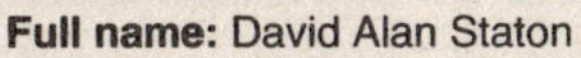

Full name: David Alan Staton
Bats: R **Throws:** R **HT:** 6–5 **WT:** 215
Born: 4–12–68, Seattle, WA
High school: Tustin (CA)
College: Orange Coast CC and Cal St.–Fullerton
Staton hit 5 home runs in only 42 AB.

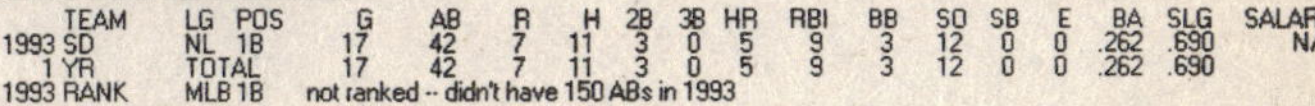

TEAM	LG POS	G	AB	R	H	2B	3B	HR	RBI	BB	SO	SB	E	BA	SLG	SALARY
1993 SD	NL 1B	17	42	7	11	3	0	5	9	3	12	0	0	.262	.690	N/A
1 YR	TOTAL	17	42	7	11	3	0	5	9	3	12	0	0	.262	.690	
1993 RANK	MLB 1B	not ranked -- didn't have 150 ABs in 1993														

Kerry Taylor — No. 37/P

Full name: Kerry Thomas Taylor
Bats: R **Throws:** R **HT:** 6–3 **WT:** 200
Born: 1–25–71, Bemidji, MN
High school: Roseau (MN)

All five of Taylor's losses came as a starter. He did not allow a home run in his final 29 games.

TM	LG	POS	W	L	ERA	G	GS	CG	SH	SV	IP	H	R	ER	HR	BB	SO	SALARY
1993 SD	NL	P	0	5	6.45	36	7	0	0	0	68.1	72	53	49	5	49	45	109,000
1 YR	TOTAL		0	5	6.45	36	7	0	0	0	68.1	72	53	49	5	49	45	
1993 RANK	MLB Ps		286		283	124	177	125	69	102	221	180	283		78	286	124	236

Tim Worrell — No. 58/P

Full name: Timothy Howard Worrell
Bats: R **Throws:** R **HT:** 6–4 **WT:** 210
Born: 7–5–67, Arcadia, CA
High school: Maronotha (Sierra Madre, CA)
College: Biola (La Mirada, CA)

In '93, his rookie year, Worrell started 16 games.

TM	LG	POS	W	L	ERA	G	GS	CG	SH	SV	IP	H	R	ER	HR	BB	SO	SALARY
1993 SD	NL	P	2	7	4.92	21	16	0	0	0	100.2	104	63	55	11	43	52	109,000
1 YR	TOTAL		2	7	4.92	21	16	0	0	0	100.2	104	63	55	11	43	52	
1993 RANK	MLB Ps		246		227	250	123	125	69	102	143	165	241		189	203	232	236

San Francisco
GIANTS

1994 Scouting Report

Hitting: (1993/.276 BA, first in NL; 168 HR, second in NL)

San Francisco's offense revolves around Barry Bonds and Matt Williams. Bonds won the National League MVP award with a .336 BA, 46 HR, and 123 RBI. But the most important Bonds investment made by the Giants may have been to hire Barry's father Bobby as the hitting instructor. The senior Bonds helped revive Matt Williams' bat, and Williams responded with a .294 average, 38 HR, and 110 RBI. Speed is below average. Robby Thompson and Willie McGee also hit over .300, and Royce Clayton and Kirt Manwaring are competent hitters. The offense won't miss Will Clark much, because he had slumped the past two seasons. Look for J.R. Phillips to be the next power-hitting Giant first baseman.

Pitching: (1993/3.61 ERA, fifth in NL)

The starting rotation features Billy Swift and John Burkett. Swift was 21–8 with a 2.82 ERA last season and Burkett was 22–7. The Giants signed Mark Portugal (18–4, 2.77 ERA) as a free agent over the off-season.

Rod Beck was the Rolaids' Relief Man award runner-up. He was 3–1 with 48 saves and a 2.16 ERA over 79.1 innings. He's been one of the best closers in baseball for several seasons. Dave Burba also saw a lot of work out of the pen (10–3, 4.25 ERA). The Giants said goodbye to Dave Righetti, and signed ex-Yankee Rich Monteleone.

Defense: (1993/.984 pct., first in NL)

The Giants' defense will be hurt by the loss of Will Clark, but second baseman Robby Thompson and third baseman Matt Williams ranked third and second, respectively, in fielding percentage at their positions. Barry Bonds is an outstanding fielder.

1994 Prospects:

The Giants are clearly the class of a weak NL West division. They finished 22 games ahead of their closest division rival, Los Angeles, last season. Perhaps more importantly, adding Portugal will strengthen their rotation for the playoffs. San Francisco has to be considered one of the leading favorites for the NL Pennant.

Team Directory

President: Peter A. Magowan
General Mgr.: Bob Quinn
Director of P.R.: Bob Rose
Executive VP: Laurance M. Baer
VP, Scouting & Player Proc.: Brian Sabean
Traveling Secretary: Dick Smith

Minor League Affiliates:

Level	Team/League	1993 Record
AAA	Phoenix – Pacific Coast	64–79
AA	Shreveport – Texas	66–70
A	San Jose – California	79–57
	Clinton – Midwest	80–54
	Everett – Northwest	42–34
Rookie	Scottsdale – Arizona	31–24

1993 Review

	Home		Away			Home		Away			Home		Away	
vs NL East	W	L	W	L	vs NL Cent.	W	L	W	L	vs NL West	W	L	W	L
Atlanta	3	4	3	3	Chicago	3	3	3	3	Colorado	4	2	6	1
Florida	4	2	4	2	Cincinnati	6	1	5	1	Los Angeles	2	4	4	3
Montreal	6	0	3	3	Houston	4	2	6	1	San Diego	6	1	4	2
New York	4	2	4	2	Pittsburgh	3	3	4	2					
Philadelphia	4	2	4	2	St. Louis	1	5	3	3					
Total	21	10	18	12		17	14	21	10		12	6	14	6

1993 finish: 103–59 (50–31 home, 53–28 away), second in NL West, one game behind

1994 Schedule

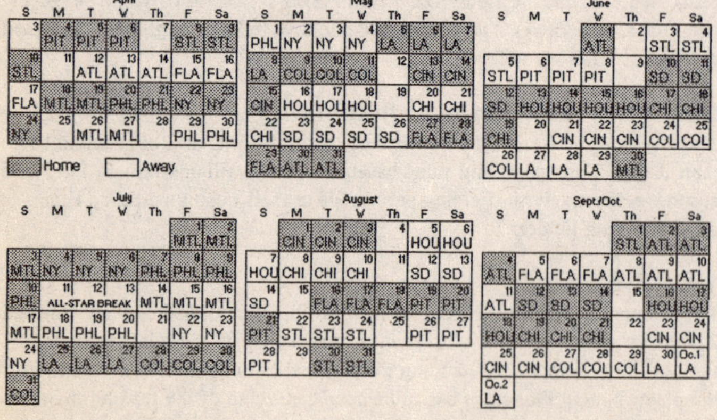

SAN FRANCISCO GIANTS 1994 ROSTER

MANAGER: Dusty Baker (12)
COACHES: Carlos Alfonso (16), Bobby Bonds (16), Bob Brenly (15), Wendell Kim (20), Bob Lillis (5), Dick Pole (48)

No.	PITCHERS	B	T	HT	WT	DOB	BIRTHPLACE	RESIDENCE
47	Beck, Rod	R	R	6–1	236	8–3–68	Burbank, CA	Scottsdale, AZ
37	Bross, Terry	R	R	6–4	230	3–30–66	El Paso, TX	Smithtown, NY
34	Burba, Dave	R	R	6–4	240	7–7–66	Dayton, OH	Springfield, OH
33	Burkett, John	R	R	6–2	211	11–28–64	New Brighton, PA	Scottsdale, AZ
	Carlson, Dan	R	R	6–1	185	1–26–70	Portland, OR	Portland, OR
52	Carter, Larry	R	R	6–5	196	5–22–65	Charleston, WV	Haughton, LA
30	Deshaies, Jim	l	l	6–5	220	6–23–60	Massena, NY	Massena, NY
60	Hancock, Chris	L	L	6–3	175	9–12–69	Lynwood, CA	Riverside, CA
41	Hickerson, Bryan	L	L	6–2	203	10–13–63	Bemidji, MN	Scottsdale, AZ
42	Jackson, Mike	R	R	6–2	223	12–22–64	Houston, TX	Spring, TX
	Monteleone, Rich	R	R	6–2	236	3–22–63	Tampa, FL	Tampa, FL
36	Munutelli, Gino	L	L	6–0	190	5–23–64	Wilmington, DE	Nashville, TN
57	McGehee, Kevin	R	R	6–0	190	1–18–69	Alexandria, LA	Pineville, LA
	Portugal, Mark	L	L	6–0	204	10–30–62	Los Angeles, CA	Missouri City, TX
21	Rogers, Kevin	S	L	6–1	198	8–20–68	Cleveland, MS	Parchman, MS
	Rosselli, Joe	R	L	6–1	170	5–28–72	Burbank, CA	Woodland Hills, CA
26	Swift, Bill	R	R	6–0	191	10–27–61	S. Portland, ME	Redmond, WA
35	Torres, Salomon	R	R	5–11	165	3–11–72	S.P. de Macoris, DR	S.P. de Macoris, DR
	VanLandingham, Bill	R	R	6–2	210	7–16–70	Columbia, TN	Franklin, TN
32	Wilson, Trevor	L	L	6–0	204	6–7–66	Torrance, CA	Scottsdale, AZ
No.	**CATCHERS**	**B**	**T**	**HT**	**WT**	**DOB**	**BIRTHPLACE**	**RESIDENCE**
54	Christopherson, Eric	R	R	6–0	195	4–25–69	Long Beach, CA	Westminster, CA
	Jensen, Marcus	S	R	6–4	195	12–14–72	Oakland, CA	Oakland, CA
8	Manwaring, Kirt	R	R	5–11	203	7–15–65	Elmira, NY	Scottsdale, AZ
No.	**INFIELDERS**	**B**	**T**	**HT**	**WT**	**DOB**	**BIRTHPLACE**	**RESIDENCE**
18	Benjamin, Mike	R	R	6–0	169	11–22–65	Euclid, OH	Chandler, AZ
14	Benzinger, Todd	S	R	6–1	190	2–11–63	Dayton, KY	Cincinnati, OH
10	Clayton, Royce	R	R	6–0	183	1–2–70	Burbank, CA	N. Inglewood, CA
21	Faries, Paul	R	R	5–10	170	2–20–65	Berkeley, CA	Moraga, CA
	Patterson, John	S	R	5–9	168	5–11–67	Key West, FL	
31	Phillips, J.R.	L	L	6–1	185	4–29–70	West Covina, CA	Scottsdale, AZ
6	Thompson, Robby	R	R	5–11	173	5–10–62	W. Palm Beach, FL	Tequesta, FL
23	Scarsone, Steve	R	R	6–2	191	4–11–66	Anaheim, CA	Anaheim, CA
9	Williams, Matt	R	R	6–2	216	11–28–65	Bishop, CA	Scottsdale, AZ
No.	**OUTFIELDERS**	**B**	**T**	**HT**	**WT**	**DOB**	**BIRTHPLACE**	**RESIDENCE**
25	Bonds, Barry	L	L	6–1	185	7–24–64	Riverside, CA	Murietta, CA
45	Carreon, Mark	R	R	6–0	195	7–9–63	Chicago, IL	Tucson, AZ
38	Faneyte, Rikkert	R	R	6–1	170	5–31–69	Amsterdam, Neth.	Amsterdam, Neth.
29	Hosey, Steve	R	R	6–3	225	4–2–69	Oakland, CA	Fresno, CA
2	Lewis, Darren	R	R	6–0	189	8–28–67	Berkeley, CA	Burlingame, CA
17	Martinez, Dave	L	L	5–10	175	9–26–64	New York, NY	Safety Harbor, FL
51	McGee, Willie	S	R	6–1	185	11–2–58	San Francisco, CA	Hercules, CA
11	Mercedes, Luis	R	R	6–3	193	2–20–68	S.P. de Macoris, DR	S.P. de Macoris, DR

Candlestick Park (62,000, grass)
Tickets: 415–467–8000
Ticket prices:
- $12.25 (lower box)
- $11.25 (upper box)
- $10.25 (lower reserved)
- $6.25 (upper reserved)
- $5.25 (pavilion)
- $2.25 (general admission)
- $1.25 (gen. adm., under 15 with adult)

Field Dimensions (from home plate)
- To left field at foul line, 335 feet
- To center field
- To right field at foul line, 328 feet
- (OF wall is 8 feet high)

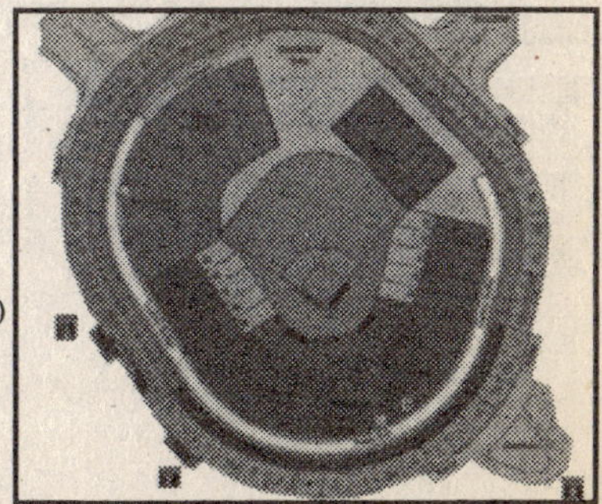

Todd Benzinger No. 14/1B

Full name: Todd Eric Benzinger
Bats: S **Throws:** R **HT:** 6–1 **WT:** 190
Born: 2–11–63, Dayton, KY
High school: New Richmond (OH)
College: Cincinnati (OH)

Veteran Benzinger will try to replace Will Clark at first base. He hit .311 as a starter in 1993.

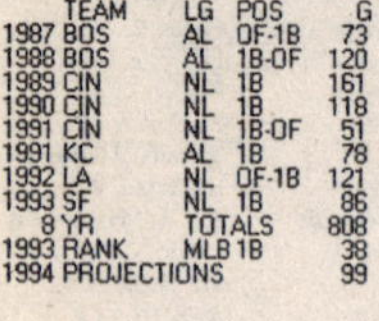
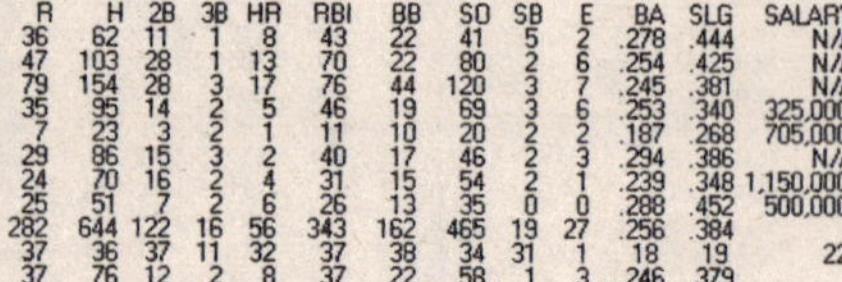

	TEAM	LG	POS	G	AB	R	H	2B	3B	HR	RBI	BB	SO	SB	E	BA	SLG	SALARY
1987	BOS	AL	OF-1B	73	223	36	62	11	1	8	43	22	41	5	2	.278	.444	N/A
1988	BOS	AL	1B-OF	120	405	47	103	28	1	13	70	22	80	2	6	.254	.425	N/A
1989	CIN	NL	1B	161	628	79	154	28	3	17	76	44	120	3	7	.245	.381	N/A
1990	CIN	NL	1B	118	376	35	95	14	2	5	46	19	69	3	6	.253	.340	325,000
1991	CIN	NL	1B-OF	51	123	7	23	3	2	1	11	10	20	2	2	.187	.268	705,000
1991	KC	AL	1B	78	293	29	86	15	3	2	40	17	46	2	3	.294	.386	N/A
1992	LA	NL	OF-1B	121	293	24	70	16	2	4	31	15	54	2	1	.239	.348	1,150,000
1993	SF	NL	1B	86	177	25	51	7	2	6	26	13	35	0	0	.288	.452	500,000
8	YR	TOTALS		808	2518	282	644	122	16	56	343	162	465	19	27	.256	.384	
1993	RANK	MLB	1B	38	38	37	36	37	11	32	37	38	34	31	1	18	19	22
1994	PROJECTIONS			99	309	37	76	12	2	8	37	22	58	1	3	.246	.379	

Barry Bonds No. 25/OF

Full name: Barry Lamar Bonds
Bats: L **Throws:** L **HT:** 6–1 **WT:** 185
Born: 7–24–64, Riverside, CA
High school: Serra (San Mateo, CA)
College: Arizona State

MVP Bonds failed to reach base in only 15 of his 156 starts. He had career bests in BA, HR, and RBI.

	TEAM	LG	POS	G	AB	R	H	2B	3B	HR	RBI	BB	SO	SB	E	BA	SLG	SALARY
1986	PIT	NL	OF	113	413	72	92	26	3	16	48	65	102	36	5	.223	.416	N/A
1987	PIT	NL	OF	150	551	99	144	34	9	25	59	54	88	32	5	.261	.492	N/A
1988	PIT	NL	OF	144	538	97	152	30	5	24	58	72	82	17	6	.283	.491	N/A
1989	PIT	NL	OF	159	580	96	144	34	6	19	58	93	93	32	6	.248	.426	N/A
1990	PIT	NL	OF	151	519	104	156	32	3	33	114	93	83	52	6	.301	.565	850,000
1991	PIT	NL	OF	153	510	95	149	28	5	25	116	107	73	43	3	.292	.514	2,300,000
1992	PIT	NL	OF	140	473	109	147	36	5	34	103	127	69	39	3	.311	.624	4,700,000
1993	SF	NL	OF	159	539	129	181	38	4	46	123	126	79	29	5	.336	.677	4,219,175
8	YR	TOTALS		1169	4123	801	1165	258	40	222	679	737	669	280	39	.283	.526	
1993	RANK	MLB	OF	3	31	2	5	7	32	1	2	3	45	19	80	3	1	7
1994	PROJECTIONS			162	547	134	189	38	3	48	130	131	75	27	4	.346	.689	

Royce Clayton No. 10/SS

Full name: Royce Spencer Clayton
Bats: R **Throws:** R **HT:** 6–0 **WT:** 183
Born: 1–2–70, Burbank, CA
High school: St. Bern. (Playa del Rey, CA)

Clayton's 70 RBI tied the Giants shortstop record. He committed 14 errors in his first 37 games, then had only 12 in his final 115 games.

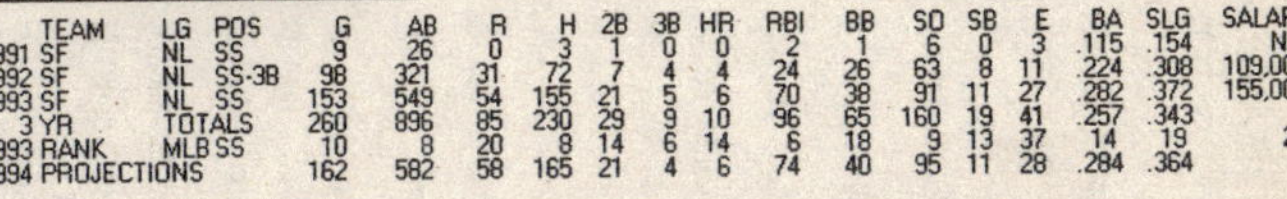

	TEAM	LG	POS	G	AB	R	H	2B	3B	HR	RBI	BB	SO	SB	E	BA	SLG	SALARY
1991	SF	NL	SS	9	26	0	3	1	0	0	2	1	6	0	3	.115	.154	N/A
1992	SF	NL	SS-3B	98	321	31	72	7	4	4	24	26	63	8	11	.224	.308	109,000
1993	SF	NL	SS	153	549	54	155	21	5	6	70	38	91	11	27	.282	.372	155,000
3	YR	TOTALS		260	896	85	230	29	9	10	96	65	160	19	41	.257	.343	
1993	RANK	MLB	SS	10	8	20	8	14	6	14	6	18	9	13	37	14	19	29
1994	PROJECTIONS			162	582	58	165	21	4	6	74	40	95	11	28	.284	.364	

Darren Lewis No. 2/OF

Full name: Darren Joel Lewis
Bats: R **Throws:** R **HT:** 6–0 **WT:** 189
Born: 8–28–67, Berkeley, CA
High school: Moreau (Hayward, CA)
College: Chabot JC (Hayward, CA) and Cal

Lewis has not made an error in the major leagues (316 games) and holds the record for most consecutive errorless games.

	TEAM	LG	POS	G	AB	R	H	2B	3B	HR	RBI	BB	SO	SB	E	BA	SLG	SALARY
1990	OAK	AL	OF	25	35	4	8	0	0	0	1	7	4	2	0	.229	.229	N/A
1991	SF	NL	OF	72	222	41	55	5	3	1	15	36	30	13	0	.248	.311	100,000
1992	SF	NL	OF	100	320	38	74	8	1	1	18	29	46	28	0	.231	.272	145,000
1993	SF	NL	OF	136	522	84	132	17	7	2	48	30	40	46	0	.253	.324	172,500
4	YR	TOTALS		333	1099	167	269	30	11	4	82	102	120	89	0	.245	.303	
1993	RANK	MLB	OF	50	35	26	51	66	11	114	61	69	101	8	131	97	123	109
1994	PROJECTIONS			162	639	103	162	20	7	1	58	34	48	56	0	.254	.311	

Kirt Manwaring No. 8/C

Full name: Kirt Dean Manwaring
Bats: R **Throws:** R **HT:** 5–11 **WT:** 203
Born: 7–15–65, Elmira, NY
High school: Horseheads (NY)
College: Coast. Carolina (Myrtle Beach, SC)

Manwaring caught 42.3% of all base stealers in 1993, the second-best percentage in the NL.

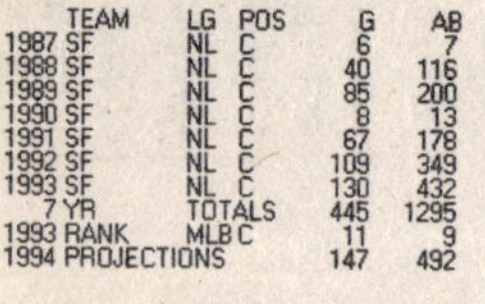
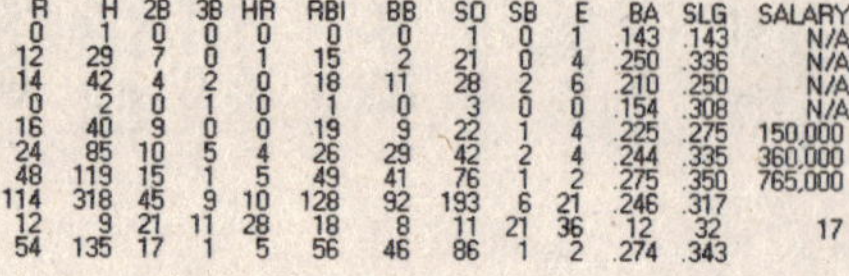

	TEAM	LG	POS	G	AB	R	H	2B	3B	HR	RBI	BB	SO	SB	E	BA	SLG	SALARY
1987	SF	NL	C	6	7	0	1	0	0	0	0	0	1	0	1	.143	.143	N/A
1988	SF	NL	C	40	116	12	29	7	0	1	15	2	21	0	4	.250	.336	N/A
1989	SF	NL	C	85	200	14	42	4	2	0	18	11	28	2	6	.210	.250	N/A
1990	SF	NL	C	8	13	0	2	0	1	0	1	0	3	0	0	.154	.308	N/A
1991	SF	NL	C	67	178	16	40	9	0	0	19	9	22	1	4	.225	.275	150,000
1992	SF	NL	C	109	349	24	85	10	5	4	26	29	42	2	4	.244	.335	360,000
1993	SF	NL	C	130	432	48	119	15	1	5	49	41	76	1	2	.275	.350	765,000
7	YR	TOTALS		445	1295	114	318	45	9	10	128	92	193	6	21	.246	.317	
1993	RANK	MLB	C	11	9	12	9	21	11	28	18	8	11	21	36	12	32	17
1994	PROJECTIONS			147	492	54	135	17	1	5	56	46	86	1	2	.274	.343	

Willie McGee No. 51/OF

Full name: Willie Dean McGee
Bats: S **Throws:** R **HT:** 6–1 **WT:** 185
Born: 11–2–58, San Francisco, CA
High school: Harry Ellis (Richmond, CA)
College: Diablo Valley (CA)

McGee batted over .300 for the fourth time in his career, even though he hit only .244 after coming off the DL in late July.

	TEAM	LG	POS	G	AB	R	H	2B	3B	HR	RBI	BB	SO	SB	E	BA	SLG	SALARY
1982	STL	NL	OF	123	422	43	125	12	8	4	56	12	58	24	11	.296	.391	N/A
1983	STL	NL	OF	147	601	75	172	22	8	5	75	26	98	39	5	.286	.374	N/A
1984	STL	NL	OF	145	571	82	166	19	11	6	50	29	80	43	6	.291	.394	N/A
1985	STL	NL	OF	152	612	114	216	26	18	10	82	34	86	56	9	.353	.503	N/A
1986	STL	NL	OF	124	497	65	127	22	7	7	48	37	82	19	3	.256	.370	N/A
1987	STL	NL	OF-SS	153	620	76	177	37	11	11	105	24	90	16	7	.285	.434	N/A
1988	STL	NL	OF	137	562	73	164	24	6	3	50	32	84	41	9	.292	.372	N/A
1989	STL	NL	OF	58	199	23	47	10	2	3	17	10	34	8	3	.236	.352	N/A
1990	STL	NL	OF	125	501	76	168	32	5	3	62	38	86	28	16	.335	.437	1,500,000
1990	OAK	AL	OF	29	113	23	31	3	2	0	15	10	18	3	1	.274	.336	1,500,000
1991	SF	NL	OF	131	497	67	155	30	3	4	43	34	74	17	6	.312	.408	3,562,500
1992	SF	NL	OF	138	474	56	141	20	2	1	36	29	88	13	6	.297	.354	3,562,500
1993	SF	NL	OF	130	475	53	143	28	1	4	46	38	67	10	5	.301	.389	2,312,500
12	YR	TOTALS		1592	6144	826	1832	285	84	61	685	353	945	317	87	.298	.402	
1993	RANK	MLB	OF	60	54	71	37	23	97	102	65	54	56	56	47	24	93	34
1994	PROJECTIONS			130	482	58	137	23	3	4	43	34	79	14	4	.284	.371	

Robby Thompson No. 6/2B

Full name: Robert Randall Thompson
Bats: R **Throws:** R **HT:** 5–11 **WT:** 173
Born: 5–10–62, W. Palm Beach, FL
High school: Forest Hill (W. Palm B., FL)
College: Palm Beach JC (Lake Worth, FL)
Thompson had a 21-game hitting streak, tied for best in the NL, and homered in 5 straight games.

TEAM	LG	POS	G	AB	R	H	2B	3B	HR	RBI	BB	SO	SB	E	BA	SLG	SALARY
1986 SF	NL	2B-SS	149	549	73	149	27	3	7	47	42	112	12	17	.271	.370	N/A
1987 SF	NL	2B	132	420	62	110	26	5	10	44	40	91	16	17	.262	.419	N/A
1988 SF	NL	2B	138	477	66	126	24	6	7	48	40	111	14	14	.264	.384	N/A
1989 SF	NL	2B	148	547	91	132	26	11	13	50	51	133	12	8	.241	.400	N/A
1990 SF	NL	2B	144	498	67	122	22	3	15	56	34	96	14	8	.245	.392	900,000
1991 SF	NL	2B	144	492	74	129	24	5	19	48	63	95	14	11	.262	.447	1,500,000
1992 SF	NL	2B	128	443	54	115	25	1	14	49	43	75	5	15	.260	.415	1,600,000
1993 SF	NL	2B	128	494	85	154	30	2	19	65	45	97	10	8	.312	.496	1,925,000
8 YR	TOTALS		1111	3920	572	1037	204	36	104	407	358	810	97	98	.265	.415	
1993 RANK	MLB 2B		16	11	5	8	5	19	4	8	12	1	17	29	5	3	9
1994 PROJECTIONS			125	487	86	154	30	1	20	67	45	95	9	6	.316	.505	

Matt Williams No. 9/3B

Full name: Matthew Derrick Williams
Bats: R **Throws:** R **HT:** 6–2 **WT:** 216
Born: 11–28–65, Bishop, CA
High school: Carson (NV)
College: Nevada–Las Vegas
Williams came back from a sub-par '92 to hit .294 with 110 RBI and a career-high 38 HR. He also reduced his strikeouts to 80.

TEAM	LG	POS	G	AB	R	H	2B	3B	HR	RBI	BB	SO	SB	E	BA	SLG	SALARY
1987 SF	NL	SS-3B	84	245	28	46	9	2	8	21	16	68	4	9	.188	.339	N/A
1988 SF	NL	3B-SS	52	156	17	32	6	1	8	19	8	41	0	7	.205	.410	N/A
1989 SF	NL	3B-SS	84	292	31	59	18	1	18	50	14	72	1	10	.202	.455	N/A
1990 SF	NL	3B	159	617	87	171	27	2	33	122	33	138	7	19	.277	.488	215,000
1991 SF	NL	3B-SS	157	589	72	158	24	5	34	98	33	128	5	16	.268	.499	600,000
1992 SF	NL	3B	146	529	58	120	13	5	20	66	39	109	7	23	.227	.384	2,000,000
1993 SF	NL	3B	145	579	105	170	33	4	38	110	27	80	1	12	.294	.561	2,250,000
7 YR	TOTALS		827	3007	398	756	130	20	159	486	170	636	25	96	.251	.467	
1993 RANK	MLB 3B		11	3	1	4	5	2	1	1	25	15	26	19	7	1	8
1994 PROJECTIONS			153	626	116	187	36	4	42	122	28	81	0	12	.299	.57	

John Burkett No. 33/P

Full name: John David Burkett
Bats: R **Throws:** R **HT:** 6–2 **WT:** 211
Born: 11–28–64, New Brighton, PA
High school: Beaver (PA)

Burkett's 22 wins were the most by a Giant in 20 years. He also yielded three or less earned runs in 25 of his 34 starts, and walked only 40 batters.

TM	LG	POS	W	L	ERA	G	GS	CG	SH	SV	IP	H	R	ER	HR	BB	SO	SALARY
1987 SF	NL	P	0	0	4.50	3	0	0	0	0	6.0	7	4	3	2	3	5	N/A
1990 SF	NL	P	14	7	3.79	33	32	2	0	1	204.0	201	92	86	18	61	118	100,000
1991 SF	NL	P	12	11	4.18	36	34	3	1	0	206.2	223	103	96	19	60	131	225,000
1992 SF	NL	P	13	9	3.84	32	32	3	1	0	189.2	194	96	81	13	45	107	375,000
1993 SF	NL	P	22	7	3.65	34	34	2	1	0	231.2	224	100	94	18	40	145	1,700,000
5 YR	TOTALS		61	34	3.87	138	132	10	3	1	838.0	849	395	360	70	209	506	
1993 RANK	MLB Ps		1		105	145	12	57	23	102	18	112	82		96	8	147	77
1994 PROJECTIONS			23	7	3.65	36	36	1	0	0	249	241	107	101	18	42	156	

Mark Portugal P

Full name: Mark Steven Portugal
Bats: L **Throws:** L **HT:** 6–0 **WT:** 204
Born: 10–30–62, Los Angeles, CA
High school: Norwalk (CA)

As a Houston Astro, Portugal had a career year. He won his final 12 decisions, the longest winning streak in the majors in '93. He was 2–0 vs. SF with a 0.57 ERA.

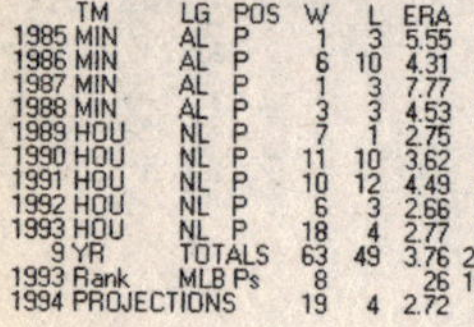

TM	LG	POS	W	L	ERA	G	GS	CG	SH	SV	IP	H	R	ER	HR	BB	SO	SALARY
1985 MIN	AL	P	1	3	5.55	6	4	0	0	0	24.1	24	16	15	3	14	12	N/A
1986 MIN	AL	P	6	10	4.31	27	15	3	0	1	112.2	112	56	54	10	50	67	N/A
1987 MIN	AL	P	1	3	7.77	13	7	0	0	0	44.0	58	40	38	13	24	28	N/A
1988 MIN	AL	P	3	3	4.53	26	0	0	0	3	57.2	60	30	29	11	17	31	N/A
1989 HOU	NL	P	7	1	2.75	20	15	2	1	0	108.0	91	34	33	7	37	86	N/A
1990 HOU	NL	P	11	10	3.62	32	32	1	0	0	196.2	187	90	79	21	67	136	217,000
1991 HOU	NL	P	10	12	4.49	32	27	1	0	1	168.1	163	91	84	19	59	120	705,000
1992 HOU	NL	P	6	3	2.66	18	16	1	1	0	101.1	76	32	30	7	41	62	1,250,000
1993 HOU	NL	P	18	4	2.77	33	33	1	1	0	208.0	194	75	64	10	77	131	2,045,000
9 YR	TOTALS		63	49	3.76	207	149	9	3	5	1021.0	965	464	426	101	386	673	
1993 Rank	MLB Ps		8		26	167	30	79	23	102	45	87	29		24	155	141	66
1994 PROJECTIONS			19	4	2.72	36	36	1	1	0	228	212	81	69	10	84	144	

Bill Swift — No. 26/P

Full name: William Charles Swift
Bats: R **Throws:** R **HT:** 6–0 **WT:** 191
Born: 10–27–61, S. Portland, ME
High school: South Portland (ME)
College: Maine

Swift's 21 wins and 157 strikeouts were career-highs. He held right-handed hitters to a .177 BA.

	TM	LG	POS	W	L	ERA	G	GS	CG	SH	SV	IP	H	R	ER	HR	BB	SO	SALARY
1985	SEA	AL	P	6	10	4.77	23	21	0	0	0	120.2	131	71	64	8	48	55	N/A
1986	SEA	AL	P	2	9	5.46	29	17	1	0	0	115.1	148	85	70	5	55	55	N/A
1988	SEA	AL	P	8	12	4.59	38	24	6	1	0	174.2	199	99	89	10	65	47	N/A
1989	SEA	AL	P	7	3	4.43	37	16	0	0	1	130.0	140	72	64	7	38	45	N/A
1990	SEA	AL	P	6	4	2.39	55	8	0	0	6	128.0	135	46	34	4	21	42	405,000
1991	SEA	AL	P	1	2	1.99	71	0	0	0	17	90.1	74	22	20	3	26	48	850,000
1992	SF	NL	P	10	4	2.08	30	22	3	2	1	164.2	144	41	38	6	43	77	2,316,667
1993	SF	NL	P	21	8	2.82	34	34	1	1	0	232.2	195	82	73	18	55	157	3,316,667
8	YR	TOTALS		61	52	3.52	317	142	11	4	25	1156.1	1166	518	452	61	351	526	
1993	Rank	MLB Ps		4		29	145	12	79	23	102	17	33	24		95	29	116	33
1994	PROJECTIONS			22	7	2.73	35	35	1	1	0	244	202	83	74	19	55	168	

Trevor Wilson — No. 32/P

Full name: Trevor Kirk Wilson
Bats: L **Throws:** L **HT:** 6–0 **WT:** 204
Born: 6–7–66, Torrance, CA
High school: Oregon City (OR)
College: Oregon State

Wilson spent nearly half the season on the DL, and started only 18 games. He posted a 2.76 ERA at home, 4.69 on the road.

	TM	LG	POS	W	L	ERA	G	GS	CG	SH	SV	IP	H	R	ER	HR	BB	SO	SALARY
1988	SF	NL	P	0	2	4.09	4	4	0	0	0	22.0	25	14	10	1	8	15	N/A
1989	SF	NL	P	2	3	4.35	14	4	0	0	0	39.1	28	20	19	2	24	22	N/A
1990	SF	NL	P	8	7	4.00	27	17	3	2	0	110.1	87	52	49	11	49	66	122,000
1991	SF	NL	P	13	11	3.56	44	29	2	1	0	202.0	173	87	80	13	77	139	205,000
1992	SF	NL	P	8	14	4.21	26	26	1	1	0	154.0	152	82	72	18	64	88	400,000
1993	SF	NL	P	7	5	3.60	22	18	1	0	0	110.0	110	45	44	8	40	57	900,000
6	YR	TOTALS		38	42	3.87	137	98	7	4	0	637.2	575	300	274	53	262	387	
1993	RANK	MLB Ps		108		97	247	111	79	69	102	132	140	63		75	151	230	106
1994	PROJECTIONS			3	3	3.79	13	8	0	0	0	57	54	26	24	3	24	31	

Rod Beck No. 47/P

Full name: Rodney Roy Beck
Bats: R **Throws:** R **HT:** 6–1 **WT:** 236
Born: 8–3–68, Burbank, CA
High school: Grant (Van Nuys, CA)

Beck's Giant-record 48 saves was the second best in the majors. He converted 48 of 52 save opportunities on the year, and set the NL record with 24 consecutive saves.

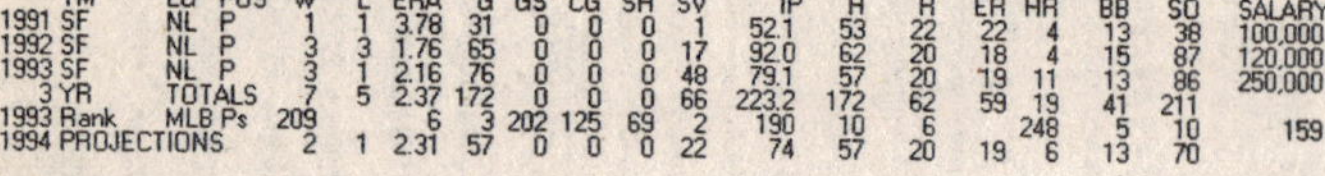

	TM	LG	POS	W	L	ERA	G	GS	CG	SH	SV	IP	H	R	ER	HR	BB	SO	SALARY
1991	SF	NL	P	1	1	3.78	31	0	0	0	1	52.1	53	22	22	4	13	38	100,000
1992	SF	NL	P	3	3	1.76	65	0	0	0	17	92.0	62	20	18	4	15	87	120,000
1993	SF	NL	P	3	1	2.16	76	0	0	0	48	79.1	57	20	19	11	13	86	250,000
3	YR	TOTALS		7	5	2.37	172	0	0	0	66	223.2	172	62	59	19	41	211	
1993	Rank	MLB Ps		209		6	3	202	125	69	2	190	10	6		248	5	10	159
1994	PROJECTIONS			2	1	2.31	57	0	0	0	22	74	57	20	19	6	13	70	

Dusty Baker No. 12/Mgr.

Full name: Johnnie B. Baker, Jr.
Bats: R **Throws:** R **HT:** 6–2 **WT:** 200
Born: 6–15–49, Riverside, CA
High school: Del Campo (Carmichael, CA)

Only the fourth manager to win over 100 games in his rookie season, Baker won more games than any rookie manager in NL history. He was named NL Manager of the Year.

			REG. SEASON				PLAYOFF			CHAMP. SERIES			WORLD SERIES		
YEAR	TEAM	LG	W	L	PCT	POS	W	L	PCT	W	L	PCT	W	L	PCT
1993	SF	AL	103	59	.636	2			---			---			---
1	YR TOTAL	TOTAL	103	59	.636		0	0	---	0	0	---	0	0	---

Mike Benjamin — No. 18/IF

Full name: Michael Paul Benjamin
Bats: R **Throws:** R **HT:** 6–0 **WT:** 169
Born: 11–22–65, Euclid, OH
High school: Bellflower (CA)
College: Arizona State
A defensive specialist, Benjamin hit just .199.

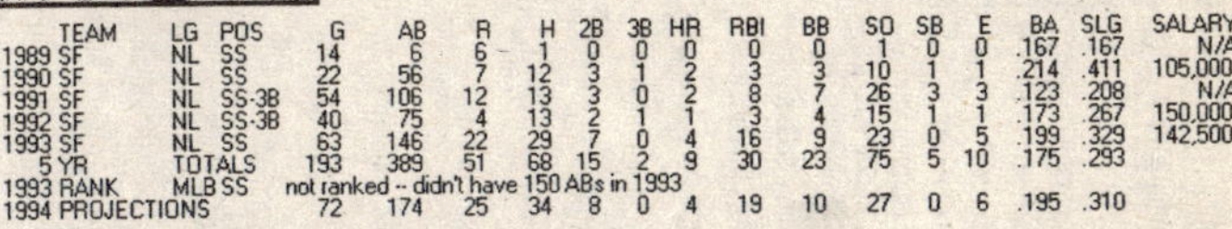

TEAM	LG	POS	G	AB	R	H	2B	3B	HR	RBI	BB	SO	SB	E	BA	SLG	SALARY
1989 SF	NL	SS	14	6	6	1	0	0	0	0	0	1	0	0	.167	.167	N/A
1990 SF	NL	SS	22	56	7	12	3	1	2	3	3	10	1	1	.214	.411	105,000
1991 SF	NL	SS-3B	54	106	12	13	3	0	2	8	7	26	3	3	.123	.208	N/A
1992 SF	NL	SS-3B	40	75	4	13	2	1	1	3	4	15	1	1	.173	.267	150,000
1993 SF	NL	SS	63	146	22	29	7	0	4	16	9	23	0	5	.199	.329	142,500
5 YR	TOTALS		193	389	51	68	15	2	9	30	23	75	5	10	.175	.293	
1993 RANK	MLB SS		not ranked -- didn't have 150 ABs in 1993														
1994 PROJECTIONS			72	174	25	34	8	0	4	19	10	27	0	6	.195	.310	

Dave Burba — No. 34/P

Full name: David Allen Burba
Bats: R **Throws:** R **HT:** 6–4 **WT:** 240
Born: 7–7–66, Dayton, OH
High school: Kenton Ridge (Springfield, OH)
Burba led the Giants with 7 wins out of the bullpen. His 10 total wins was a career high.

TM	LG	POS	W	L	ERA	G	GS	CG	SH	SV	IP	H	R	ER	HR	BB	SO	SALARY
1990 SEA	AL	P	0	0	4.50	6	0	0	0	0	8.0	8	6	4	0	2	4	N/A
1991 SEA	AL	P	2	2	3.68	22	2	0	0	1	36.2	34	16	15	6	14	16	N/A
1992 SF	NL	P	2	7	4.97	23	11	0	0	0	70.2	80	43	39	4	31	47	130,000
1993 SF	NL	P	10	3	4.25	54	5	0	0	0	95.1	95	49	45	14	37	88	140,000
4 YR	TOTALS		14	12	4.40	105	18	0	0	1	210.2	217	114	103	24	84	155	
1993 Rank	MLB Ps		75		162	66	188	125	69	102	155	139	157		262	170	23	200
1994 PROJECTIONS			12	3	4.27	66	6	0	0	0	116	116	59	55	17	45	109	

Mark Carreon — No. 45/OF

Full name: Mark Steven Carreon
Bats: R **Throws:** R **HT:** 6–0 **WT:** 195
Born: 7–9–63, Chicago, IL
High school: Salpointe (Tucson, AZ)
In 1993, Carreon batted .373 as a pinch-hitter, and hit safely in 20 of his 29 starts.

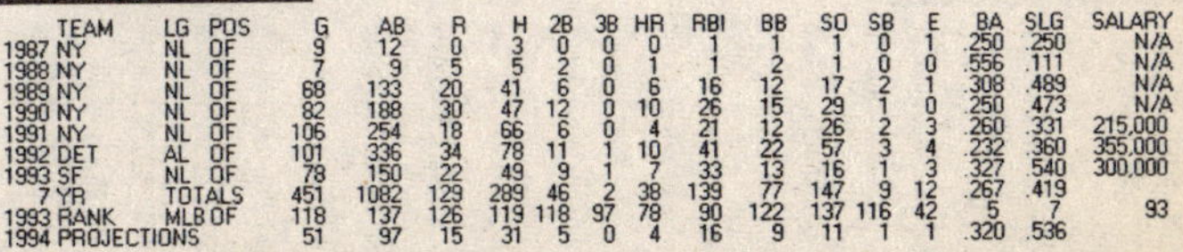

TEAM	LG	POS	G	AB	R	H	2B	3B	HR	RBI	BB	SO	SB	E	BA	SLG	SALARY
1987 NY	NL	OF	9	12	0	3	0	0	0	1	1	1	0	1	.250	.250	N/A
1988 NY	NL	OF	7	9	5	5	2	0	1	1	2	1	0	0	.556	.111	N/A
1989 NY	NL	OF	68	133	20	41	6	0	6	16	12	17	2	1	.308	.489	N/A
1990 NY	NL	OF	82	188	30	47	12	0	10	26	15	29	1	0	.250	.473	N/A
1991 NY	NL	OF	106	254	18	66	6	0	4	21	12	26	2	3	.260	.331	215,000
1992 DET	AL	OF	101	336	34	78	11	1	10	41	22	57	3	4	.232	.360	355,000
1993 SF	NL	OF	78	150	22	49	9	1	7	33	13	16	1	3	.327	.540	300,000
7 YR	TOTALS		451	1082	129	289	46	2	38	139	77	147	9	12	.267	.419	
1993 RANK	MLB OF		118	137	126	119	118	97	78	90	122	137	116	42	5	7	93
1994 PROJECTIONS			51	97	15	31	5	0	4	16	9	11	1	1	.320	.536	

Jim Deshaies No. 30/P

Full name: James Joseph Deshaies
Bats: L **Throws:** L **HT:** 6–5 **WT:** 220
Born: 6–23–60, Massena, NY
High school: Massena Central (NY)
College: Le Moyne (Syracuse, NY)
Deshaies' 13 wins were his best since 1989.

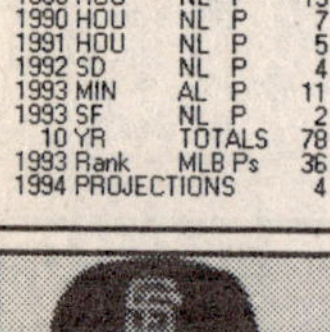
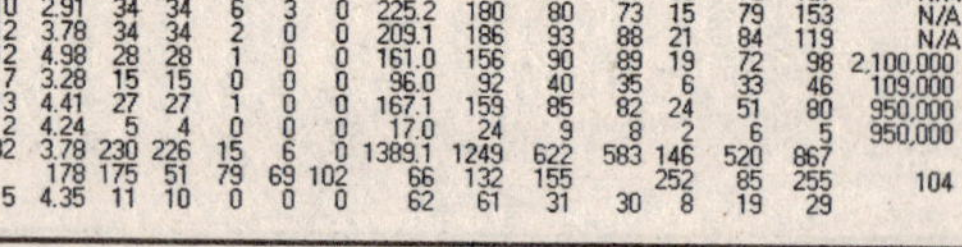

	TM	LG	POS	W	L	ERA	G	GS	CG	SH	SV	IP	H	R	ER	HR	BB	SO	SALARY
1988	HOU	AL	P	11	14	3.00	31	31	3	2	0	207.0	164	77	69	20	72	127	N/A
1989	HOU	NL	P	15	10	2.91	34	34	6	3	0	225.2	180	80	73	15	79	153	N/A
1990	HOU	NL	P	7	12	3.78	34	34	2	0	0	209.1	186	93	88	21	84	119	N/A
1991	HOU	NL	P	5	12	4.98	28	28	1	0	0	161.0	156	90	89	19	72	98	2,100,000
1992	SD	NL	P	4	7	3.28	15	15	0	0	0	96.0	92	40	35	6	33	46	109,000
1993	MIN	AL	P	11	13	4.41	27	27	1	0	0	167.1	159	85	82	24	51	80	950,000
1993	SF	NL	P	2	2	4.24	5	4	0	0	0	17.0	24	9	8	2	6	5	950,000
10	YR	TOTALS		78	82	3.78	230	226	15	6	0	1389.1	1249	622	583	146	520	867	
1993	Rank	MLB Ps		36		178	175	51	79	69	102	66	132	155		252	85	255	104
1994	PROJECTIONS			4	5	4.35	11	10	0	0	0	62	61	31	30	8	19	29	

Bryan Hickerson No. 41/P

Full name: Bryan David Hickerson
Bats: L **Throws:** L **HT:** 6–2 **WT:** 203
Born: 10–13–63, Bemidji, MN
High school: Bemidji (MN)
College: Minnesota
Hickerson was 7–3 as a spot starter.

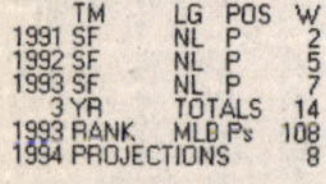
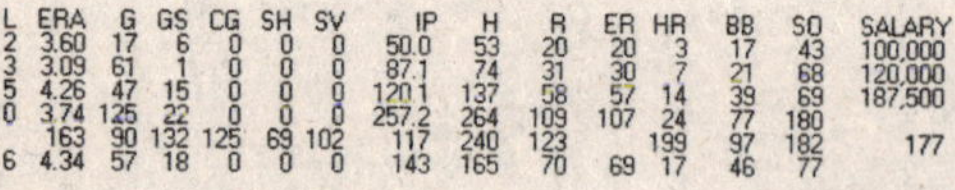

	TM	LG	POS	W	L	ERA	G	GS	CG	SH	SV	IP	H	R	ER	HR	BB	SO	SALARY
1991	SF	NL	P	2	2	3.60	17	6	0	0	0	50.0	53	20	20	3	17	43	100,000
1992	SF	NL	P	5	3	3.09	61	1	0	0	0	87.1	74	31	30	7	21	68	120,000
1993	SF	NL	P	7	5	4.26	47	15	0	0	0	120.1	137	58	57	14	39	69	187,500
3	YR	TOTALS		14	10	3.74	125	22	0	0	0	257.2	264	109	107	24	77	180	
1993	RANK	MLB Ps		108		163	90	132	125	69	102	117	240	123		199	97	182	177
1994	PROJECTIONS			8	6	4.34	57	18	0	0	0	143	165	70	69	17	46	77	

Mike Jackson No. 42/P

Full name: Michael Ray Jackson
Bats: R **Throws:** R **HT:** 6–2 **WT:** 223
Born: 12–22–64, Houston, TX
High school: Forest Brook (Houston, TX)
College: Hill Junior (Hillsboro, TX)
Jackson appeared in an NL-best 81 games in '93.

	TM	LG	POS	W	L	ERA	G	GS	CG	SH	SV	IP	H	R	ER	HR	BB	SO	SALARY
1987	PHL	NL	P	3	10	4.20	55	7	0	0	1	109.1	88	55	51	16	56	93	N/A
1988	SEA	AL	P	6	5	2.63	62	0	0	0	4	99.1	74	37	29	10	43	76	N/A
1989	SEA	AL	P	4	6	3.17	65	0	0	0	7	99.1	81	43	35	8	54	94	N/A
1990	SEA	AL	P	5	7	4.54	63	0	0	0	3	77.1	64	42	39	8	44	69	N/A
1991	SEA	AL	P	7	7	3.25	72	0	0	0	14	88.2	64	35	32	5	34	74	700,000
1992	SF	NL	P	6	6	3.73	67	0	0	0	2	82.0	76	35	34	7	33	80	1,666,667
1993	SF	NL	P	6	6	3.03	81	0	0	0	1	77.1	58	28	26	7	24	70	2,266,667
8	YR	TOTALS		37	47	3.49	474	7	0	0	32	646.2	517	280	251	63	292	559	
1993	Rank	MLB Ps		128		47	1	202	125	69	70	193	15	30		133	89	28	59
1994	PROJECTIONS			5	6	3.81	70	0	0	0	2	78	66	35	33	7	33	73	

Dave Martinez — No. 17/OF

Full name: David Martinez
Bats: L **Throws:** L **HT:** 5–10 **WT:** 175
Born: 9–26–64, New York, NY
High school: Lake Howell (Maitland, FL)
College: Valencia Community (FL)
Martinez' .241 BA was his lowest since 1986.

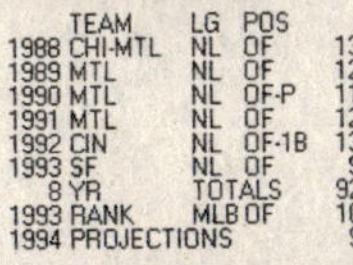

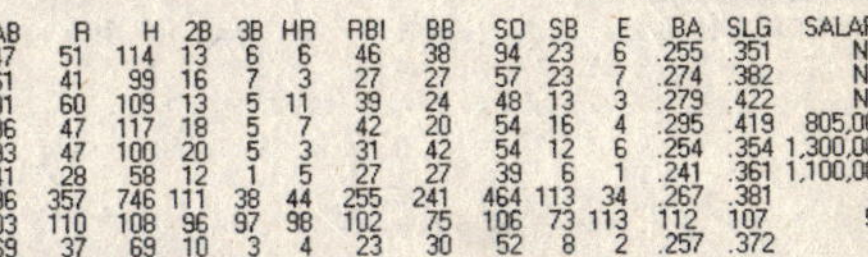

	TEAM	LG	POS	G	AB	R	H	2B	3B	HR	RBI	BB	SO	SB	E	BA	SLG	SALARY
1988	CHI-MTL	NL	OF	138	447	51	114	13	6	6	46	38	94	23	6	.255	.351	N/A
1989	MTL	NL	OF	126	361	41	99	16	7	3	27	27	57	23	7	.274	.382	N/A
1990	MTL	NL	OF-P	118	391	60	109	13	5	11	39	24	48	13	3	.279	.422	N/A
1991	MTL	NL	OF	124	396	47	117	18	5	7	42	20	54	16	4	.295	.419	805,000
1992	CIN	NL	OF-1B	135	393	47	100	20	5	3	31	42	54	12	6	.254	.354	1,300,000
1993	SF	NL	OF	91	241	28	58	12	1	5	27	27	39	6	1	.241	.361	1,100,000
8	YR	TOTALS		927	2796	357	746	111	38	44	255	241	464	113	34	.267	.381	
1993	RANK	MLB	OF	103	103	110	108	96	97	98	102	75	106	73	113	112	107	53
1994	PROJECTIONS			95	269	37	69	10	3	4	23	30	52	8	2	.257	.372	

Rich Monteleone — P

Full name: Richard Monteleone
Bats: R **Throws:** R **HT:** 6–2 **WT:** 236
Born: 3–22–63, Tampa, FL
High school: Tampa Catholic (FL)
Monteleone led the Yankee bullpen in wins for two straight seasons.

	TM	LG	POS	W	L	ERA	G	GS	CG	SH	SV	IP	H	R	ER	HR	BB	SO	SALARY
1987	SEA	AL	P	0	0	6.43	3	0	0	0	0	7.0	10	5	5	2	4	2	N/A
1988	CAL	AL	P	0	0	0.00	3	0	0	0	0	4.1	4	0	0	0	1	3	N/A
1989	CAL	AL	P	2	2	3.18	24	0	0	0	0	39.2	39	15	14	3	13	27	N/A
1990	NY	AL	P	0	1	6.14	5	0	0	0	0	7.1	8	5	5	0	2	8	N/A
1991	NY	AL	P	3	1	3.64	26	0	0	0	0	47.0	42	27	19	5	19	34	117,500
1992	NY	AL	P	7	3	3.30	47	0	0	0	0	92.2	82	35	34	7	27	62	125,000
1993	NY	AL	P	7	4	4.94	42	0	0	0	0	85.2	85	52	47	14	35	50	250,000
7	YR	TOTALS		19	11	3.93	150	0	0	0	0	283.2	270	139	124	31	101	186	
1993	Rank	MLB	Ps	108		229	106	202	125	69	102	172	130	227		276	189	177	159
1994	PROJECTIONS			4	2	4.11	30	0	0	0	0	57	55	31	26	7	22	37	

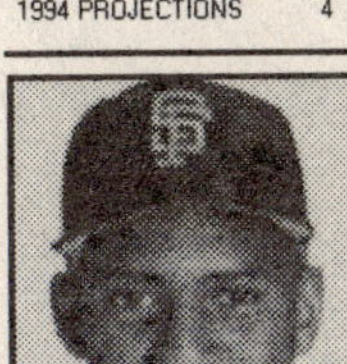

John Patterson — 2B

Full name: John Allen Patterson
Bats: S **Throws:** R **HT:** 5–9 **WT:** 168
Born: 5–11–67, Key West, FL
High school: Trevor G. Browne (Phoenix, AZ)
College: Central Arizona and Grand Canyon (AZ)
Missed most of '93 due to a shoulder problem.

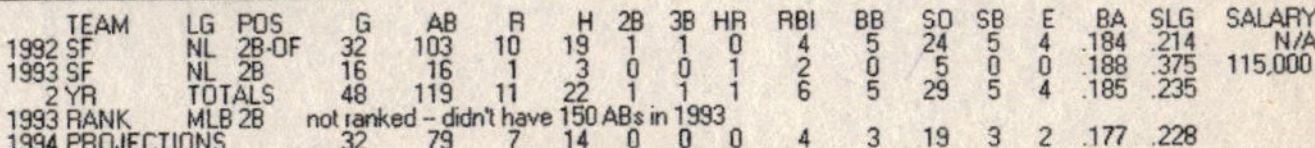

	TEAM	LG	POS	G	AB	R	H	2B	3B	HR	RBI	BB	SO	SB	E	BA	SLG	SALARY
1992	SF	NL	2B-OF	32	103	10	19	1	1	0	4	5	24	5	4	.184	.214	N/A
1993	SF	NL	2B	16	16	1	3	0	0	1	2	0	5	0	0	.188	.375	115,000
2	YR	TOTALS		48	119	11	22	1	1	1	6	5	29	5	4	.185	.235	
1993	RANK	MLB	2B	not ranked -- didn't have 150 ABs in 1993														
1994	PROJECTIONS			32	79	7	14	0	0	0	4	3	19	3	2	.177	.228	

J.R. Phillips — No. 31/1B

Full name: Charles Gene Phillips
Bats: L **Throws:** L **HT:** 6–1 **WT:** 185
Born: 4–29–70, West Covina, CA
High school: Bishop Amat (La Puente, CA)
Phillips led the Pacific Coast League with 27 HR, then batted .313 in 11 games for the Giants.

	TEAM	LG	POS	G	AB	R	H	2B	3B	HR	RBI	BB	SO	SB	E	BA	SLG	SALARY
1993	SF	NL	1B	11	16	1	5	1	1	1	4	0	5	0	1	.313	.688	N/A
1	YR	TOTAL		11	16	1	5	1	1	1	4	0	5	0	1	.313	.688	
1993	RANK	MLB	1B	not ranked -- didn't have 150 ABs in 1993														

Kevin Rogers — No. 21/P

Full name: Charles Kevin Rogers
Bats: S **Throws:** L **HT:** 6–1 **WT:** 198
Born: 8–20–68, Cleveland, MS
High school: Cleveland (MS)
College: Mississippi Delta CC (Moorhead, MS)
Rogers posted a 2.17 ERA in his final 54 games.

	TM	LG	POS	W	L	ERA	G	GS	CG	SH	SV	IP	H	R	ER	HR	BB	SO	SALARY
1992	SF	NL	P	0	2	4.24	6	6	0	0	0	34.0	37	17	16	4	13	26	N/A
1993	SF	NL	P	2	2	2.68	64	0	0	0	0	80.2	71	28	24	3	28	62	114,000
2	YR	TOTALS		2	4	3.14	70	6	0	0	0	114.2	108	45	40	7	41	88	
1993	Rank	MLB	Ps	246		22	34	202	125	69	102	187	54	22		14	127	72	228
1994	PROJECTIONS			3	2	2.45	93	-3	0	0	0	103	88	33	28	2	35	80	

AMERICAN LEAGUE

1993 Recap

AL East

Toronto outlasted the Yankees and Baltimore to win their third straight division title. Toronto struggled in July, winning just 12 of 26 games, but went 46–27 after the All-Star break. They won nine straight in September to take a 7.5 game lead over New York and put the division race out of reach.

An 11–15 September killed New York's pennant hopes. Just three games out on September 19, the Yankees dropped five of their next six against Boston, Minnesota, and Toronto to fall out of the race.

Baltimore was a streak team in '93, with a ten-game win streak, two eight-game win streaks, and an eight-game losing streak. In fact, the Orioles won eight straight in August, then immediately lost eight straight, a major league first. Their last streak killed them—1.5 games out on September 12, Baltimore lost 10 of their next 13.

Despite a dearth of starting pitching, Detroit surprised many by remaining in contention through July. Detroit started off strong, going 30–18 in May and June. But the Tigers lost ten straight from June 22 to July 1, and, after breaking that streak, won only 11 of their next 31 games to fall to fifth place. A 16–6 stretch in August moved the Tigers into third, five games out, but while Toronto went 18–10 in September and October, the Tigers were just 14–14.

Boston had a strong April (13–9), a mediocre May (14–14), and a weak June (11–16). A 20–7 July put Boston back in the race (1.5 games back), but the Red Sox were just 22–36 the rest of the way.

Cleveland opened the season reeling from the deaths of Tim Crews and Steve Olin in a boating accident during spring training. They were just 19–32 in April and in May, but went 57–54 from June 1 on, despite starting pitching woes.

After losing Paul Molitor to Toronto through free agency, Milwaukee started off slow—22–25 at the end of May—and went down from there (10–19 in June, 9–17 in July). Milwaukee finished with a 69–93 mark, their worst since 1984.

AL West

Chicago won its first division title in ten years, seizing first place for good in June. The White Sox were only 15–13 in June, but their rivals were worse: California, the division leader June 1, was 10–17, Kansas City was 13–15, and Texas was 10–16. Chicago held just a 2.5 game lead over Texas on September 13, but finished 14–5 to win the division by eight games.

Texas took three out of four from the White Sox in an August series marked by Robin Ventura charging the mound after being hit by a Nolan Ryan pitch. It started a bench-clearing brawl that Ventura got the worst of. Texas, 53–53 going into that game, went 33–23 the rest of the way. But Chicago was just as hot; when the Chisox took two out of three from Texas in September, the Rangers fell seven games out with just seven to play.

Kansas City improved from a 72–90 mark in '92 to a 84–78 record in 1993. The Royals started the season 0–5, lost four of their next six to reach 2–9, and finished April at 9–14. But they reversed themselves with a 16–9 record in May. They were only three games behind as late as August 20, but Chicago's 35–22 finish left Kansas City ten games out by season's end.

Seattle won 18 more games in '93 than in '92, the biggest improvement in the American League. The Mariners were remarkably consistent: they were within one game of .500 in every month from April to August. But Seattle was 38–40 against the AL West, and only 4–9 vs. Chicago, dooming their title chances.

Minnesota started slowly, as usual: their 8–14 mark in April was their sixth straight losing record in that month. The Twins had ten different players on the disabled list and used the DL 13 times, both team records. Minnesota sagged in the summer, going 24–33 in July and August to drop to 56–75. The '93 Twins became the first Twins team to record five consecutive losing months (April-August).

California was in first place on June 2, but posted a 10–17 record in June and a 11–17 mark in July. The Angels ended the year with a winning record against just two teams: Milwaukee (7–5) and division winner Chicago (7–6).

Oakland had its first losing record since 1986, and lost more games in a season than any Oakland team since 1982. The Athletics were so beset by pitching woes that Manager Tony La Russa even tried using pitchers in shifts.

1994 PROJECTIONS

AL EAST	AL CENTRAL	AL WEST
1. Baltimore	1. Chicago	1. Seattle
2. Toronto	2. Cleveland	2. Texas
3. New York	3. Kansas City	3. California
4. Boston	4. Minnesota	4. Oakland
5. Detroit	5. Milwaukee	

Playoffs: Baltimore over Seattle, Chicago over Toronto
Pennant Winner: Baltimore
World Series Winner: San Francisco

Realignment has made the East tougher, the West easier, and the Central somewhere in between. Look for a three-way dogfight in the AL East between Toronto, Baltimore, and New York. The Orioles really showed a desire to win it all, adding high-priced players Rafael Palmeiro and Sid Fernandez. They should have the depth to prevail. Toronto doesn't figure to three-peat. They lost Tony Fernandez and too many Jays had career-best years in 1993. The Yankees were strangely silent in the off-season, but if they find another starter, they could sneak past Toronto and Cleveland for the AL wild card. The addition of Otis Nixon and even an average year from Roger Clemens should keep Boston out of the cellar, since Detroit's pitching staff shows no sign of improving.

In the AL Central, Chicago and Cleveland will gun it out for the top spot. The Chisox starting rotation, the best in the league, should make the difference, but Cleveland added experienced veterans Dennis Martinez and Eddie Murray to help lead all of their bright young stars. Kansas City, led by Kevin Appier (18–8), may surprise people, but the Royals don't have enough power or speed to be considered serious contenders. For Minnesota and Milwaukee, a new division will mean just more of the same. Neither team figures to be in the race when the summer ends.

The Mariners and the Rangers will slug it out for the AL West title. Manager Lou Piniella has the Mariners heading in the right direction — Ken Griffey, Randy Johnson, and a healthy Edgar Martinez should carry them to a division title. Texas has strong pitching and some young sluggers, but they will miss Rafael Palmeiro's 37 HR and 105 RBI. Hampered by payroll concerns, California made no major off-season moves, and the Angels won't be in the race. Oakland, last in the league in batting average and ERA in 1993, will have to wait a few years for their young talent to develop. Even the return of Rickey Henderson won't be able to lift them out of the cellar.

AMERICAN LEAGUE EAST—1993

TEAM	W	L	PCT	GB	HOME	ROAD	EAST	WEST	LHP	RHP	X-INN
TORONTO	95	67	.586	—	48–33	47–34	50–28	45–39	23–27	72–40	6–5
NEW YORK	88	74	.543	7.0	50–31	38–43	44–34	44–40	33–24	55–50	8–9
BALTIMORE	85	77	.525	10.0	48–33	37–44	38–40	47–37	24–22	61–55	4–8
DETROIT	85	77	.525	10.0	44–37	41–40	40–38	45–39	26–18	59–59	10–2
BOSTON	80	82	.494	15.0	43–38	37–44	32–46	48–36	22–21	58–61	7–5
CLEVELAND	76	86	.469	19.0	46–35	30–51	37–41	39–45	21–24	55–62	8–6
MILWAUKEE	69	93	.426	26.0	38–43	31–50	32–46	37–47	24–32	45–61	7–11

AMERICAN LEAGUE WEST—1993

TEAM	W	L	PCT	GB	HOME	ROAD	EAST	WEST	LHP	RHP	X-INN
CHICAGO	94	68	.580	—	45–36	49–32	48–36	46–32	26–24	68–44	7–5
TEXAS	86	76	.531	7.0	50–31	36–45	49–35	37–41	16–20	70–56	6–5
KANSAS CITY	84	78	.519	9.0	43–38	41–40	43–41	41–37	22–22	62–56	8–6
SEATTLE	82	80	.506	11.0	46–35	36–45	44–40	38–40	31–22	51–58	8–9
CALIFORNIA	71	91	.438	22.0	44–37	27–54	36–48	35–43	17–23	54–68	4–8
MINNESOTA	71	91	.438	22.0	36–45	35–46	34–50	37–41	18–22	53–69	10–2
OAKLAND	68	94	.420	25.0	38–43	30–51	29–55	39–39	20–28	48–66	7–11

AMERICAN LEAGUE CLUB BATTING—1993

	AB	R	H	2B	3B	HR	RBI	BB	SO	SB	BAT	SLG	OBA
NYY	5615	821	1568	294	24	178	793	629	910	39	.279	.435	.353
TOR	5579	847	1556	317	42	159	796	588	861	170	.279	.436	.350
CLE	5619	790	1547	264	31	141	747	488	843	159	.275	.409	.335
DET	5620	899	1546	282	38	178	853	765	1122	104	.275	.434	.362
TEX	5510	835	1472	284	39	181	780	483	984	113	.267	.431	.329
BAL	5508	786	1470	287	24	157	744	655	930	73	.267	.413	.346
CHW	5483	776	1454	228	44	162	731	604	834	106	.265	.411	.338
MIN	5601	693	1480	261	27	121	642	493	850	83	.264	.385	.327
BOS	5496	686	1451	319	29	114	644	508	871	73	.264	.395	.330
KC	5522	675	1455	294	35	125	641	428	936	100	.263	.397	.320
SEA	5494	734	1429	272	24	161	681	624	901	91	.260	.406	.339
CAL	5391	684	1399	259	24	114	644	564	930	169	.260	.380	.331
MIL	5525	733	1426	240	25	125	688	555	932	138	.258	.378	.328
OAK	5543	715	1408	260	21	158	679	622	1048	131	.254	.394	.330

AMERICAN LEAGUE CLUB PITCHING—1993

	W	L	ERA	CG	SHO	SV	IP	H	R	ER	HR	BB	SO
CHI	94	68	3.70	16	11	48	1454.0	1398	664	598	125	566	974
BOS	80	82	3.77	9	11	44	1452.1	1379	698	609	127	552	997
KC	84	78	4.04	16	6	48	1445.1	1379	694	649	105	571	985
SEA	82	80	4.20	22	10	41	1453.2	1421	731	678	135	605	1083
TOR	95	67	4.21	11	11	50	1441.1	1441	742	674	134	620	1023
TEX	86	76	4.28	20	6	45	1438.1	1476	751	684	144	562	957
BAL	85	77	4.31	21	10	42	1442.2	1427	745	691	153	579	900
CAL	71	91	4.34	26	6	41	1430.1	1482	770	690	153	550	843
NYY	88	74	4.35	11	13	38	1438.1	1467	761	695	170	552	899
MIL	69	93	4.45	26	6	29	1447.0	1511	792	716	153	522	810
CLE	76	86	4.58	7	8	45	1445.2	1591	813	735	182	591	888
DET	85	77	4.65	11	7	36	1436.2	1547	837	742	188	542	828
MIN	71	91	4.71	5	3	44	1444.1	1591	830	756	148	514	901
OAK	68	94	4.90	8	2	42	1452.1	1551	846	791	157	680	864

Baltimore ORIOLES

1994 Scouting Report

Hitting: (1993/.267 BA, sixth in AL; 157 HR, eighth in AL)

Baltimore has a solid order from top to bottom. Free agent acquisition Rafael Palmeiro (.295 BA, 37 HR, 105 RBI), Chris Hoiles (.310 BA, 29 HR, 82 RBI), and Harold Baines (.313 BA, 20 HR, 78 RBI) will lead the Oriole attack in 1994. After a sub-par 1992, Cal Ripken led the squad with 90 RBI in 1993 and Mark McLemore (.284 BA, 165 hits, 21 SB) has established himself as an everyday threat. They have a hole at third base, since Mike Pagliarulo left for Japan over the winter.

Besides McLemore (21 SB) and leadoff man Brady Anderson (24 SB), the Orioles are woefully short on speed. Baltimore had 73 SB as a team, tying them with Boston for twelfth in the AL.

Pitching: (1993/4.31 ERA, seventh in AL)

The Orioles' rotation features Mike Mussina (14–6), Ben McDonald (13–14), and Jamie Moyer (12–9). McDonald got poor run support last year, and his record will improve in '94. Free agent signee Sid Fernandez has been injury-prone, but should thrive away from New York. Rookie lefty Jim O'Donoghue (7–4, 3.88 ERA in AAA) and Arthur Rhodes (5–6) should battle for the fifth starting spot.

When closer Gregg Olson (29 saves, 1.60 ERA) went out with an injury in August, the rest of the bullpen fell apart. To contend, the Orioles must find some strong middle relief to get them to setup man Jim Poole (2.15 ERA).

Defense: (1993/.984 pct., second in AL)

1993 was Baltimore's fifth straight season with 100 errors or less. Shortstop Cal Ripken, catcher Chris Hoiles, first baseman David Segui, and outfielder Brady Anderson were all in the top 5 in fielding percentage at their positions.

1994 Prospects:

Johnny Oates, 1993's AL Manager of the Year, should field a highly competitive team in 1994. Chris Hoiles and Mark McLemore must prove that 1993 was not a fluke, and Sid Fernandez has to stay healthy, but the Orioles should prevail in the tough AL East and could take the AL pennant.

Team Directory

Managing Partner: Peter G. Angelos
General Mgr.: Roland Hemond
Director of P.R.: Rick Vaughn
Vice Chrmn. for Bus. Op.: Joseph Foss
Chrmn. of Gen. Aff.: Tom Clancy
Traveling Secretary: Phil Itzoe

Minor League Affiliates:

Level	Team/League	1993 Record
AAA	Rochester – International	74–67
AA	Bowie – Eastern	72–68
A	Frederick – Carolina	78–62
	Albany – South Atlantic	71–71
Rookie	Sarasota – Gulf Coast	30–28
	Bluefield – Appalachian	44–24

1993 Review

	Home		Away			Home		Away			Home		Away	
vs AL East	W	L	W	L	vs AL Cent.	W	L	W	L	vs AL West	W	L	W	L
Boston	2	4	4	3	Chicago	2	4	2	4	California	4	2	3	3
Detroit	3	3	2	5	Cleveland	5	2	3	3	Oakland	5	1	5	1
New York	3	3	3	4	Kansas City	4	2	3	3	Seattle	5	1	2	4
Toronto	3	4	2	4	Milwaukee	5	2	3	3	Texas	2	4	2	4
					Minnesota	5	1	3	3					
Total	11	14	11	16		21	11	14	16		16	8	12	12

1993 finish: 85–77 (48–33 home, 37–44 away), third in AL East, ten games behind

1994 Schedule

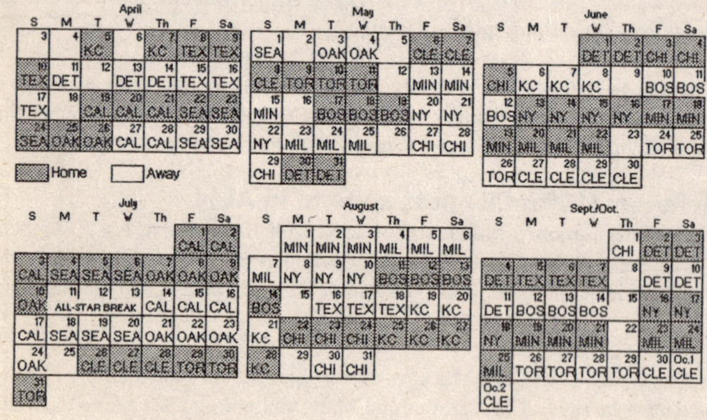

BALTIMORE ORIOLES 1994 ROSTER

MANAGER: Johnny Oates (26)
COACHES: Greg Biagini (25), Dick Bosman (17), Mike Ferraro, Elrod Hendricks (44), Davey Lopes (15), Jerry Narron, Don Buford

No.	PITCHERS	B	T	HT	WT	DOB	BIRTHPLACE	RESIDENCE
	Benitez, Armando	R	R	6–4	180	11–3–72	Ramon Santana, DR	Santo Domingo, DR
55	Cook, Mike	L	R	6–3	225	8–14–63	Charleston, SC	Charleston, SC
50	Fernandez, Sid	L	L	6–1	225	10–12–62	Honolulu, HI	Hawaii Kai, HI
	Forney, Rick	R	R	6–4	210	10–24–71	Annapolis, MD	Arnold, MD
49	Frohwirth, Todd	R	R	6–4	211	9–28–62	Milwaukee, WI	Milwaukee, WI
	Krivda, Rick	R	L	6–1	180	1–19–70	McKeesport, PA	McKeesport, PA
	Manuel, Barry	R	R	5–11	185	8–12–65	Marmour, LA	Marmour, LA
19	McDonald, Ben	R	R	6–7	213	11–24–67	Baton Rouge, LA	Denham Springs, LA
48	McGehee, Kevin	R	R	6–0	190	1–19–69	Alexandria, AL	Pineville, AL
75	Mills, Alan	S	R	6–1	192	10–18–66	Lakeland, FL	Lakeland, FL
51	Moyer, Jamie	L	L	6–6	170	11–16–62	Sellersville, PA	Grange, PA
35	Mussina, Mike	R	R	6–2	185	12–8–68	Williamsport, PA	Montoursville, PA
	O'Donoghue, John	L	L	6–6	198	5–26–69	Wilmington, DE	Elkton, MD
30	Olson, Gregg	R	R	6–4	212	10–11–66	Scribner, ME	Reisterstown, MD
56	Oquist, Mike	R	R	6–2	170	5–30–68	La Junta, CO	La Junta, CO
47	Pennington, Brad	L	L	6–5	205	4–14–69	Salem, IN	Salem, IN
45	Poole, Jim	L	L	6–2	203	4–28–66	Rochester, NY	Ellicott City, MD
53	Rhodes, Arthur	L	L	6–2	206	10–24–69	Waco, TX	Waco, TX
	Williams, Jeff	R	R	6–4	230	4–16–69	Salina, KS	Wichita, KS
No.	**CATCHERS**	**B**	**T**	**HT**	**WT**	**DOB**	**BIRTHPLACE**	**RESIDENCE**
23	Hoiles, Chris	R	R	6–0	213	3–20–65	Bowling Green, OH	Wayne, OH
41	Tackett, Jeff	R	R	6–2	205	12–1–65	Fresno, CA	Camarillo, CA
30	Zaun, Greg	S	R	5–10	170	4–14–71	Glendale, CA	Glendale, CA
No.	**INFIELDERS**	**B**	**T**	**HT**	**WT**	**DOB**	**BIRTHPLACE**	**RESIDENCE**
48	Alexander, Manny	R	R	5–10	165	3–20–71	S.P. de Macoris, DR	S.P. de Macoris, DR
	Carey, Paul	R	L	6–4	230	1–8–68	Weymouth, MA	Weymouth, MA
10	Gomez, Leo	R	R	6–0	208	3–2–67	Canovanas, PR	Canovanas, PR
36	Hulett, Tim	R	R	6–0	200	1–12–60	Springfield, IL	Springfield, IL
	Palmeiro, Rafael	L	R	6–0	188	9–24–64	Havana, CU	Arlington, TX
8	Ripken, Cal	R	R	6–4	220	8–24–60	Havre de Grace, MD	Reisterstown, MD
21	Segui, David	S	R	6–1	202	7–19–66	Kansas City, KS	Kansas City, KS
No.	**OUTFIELDERS**	**B**	**T**	**HT**	**WT**	**DOB**	**BIRTHPLACE**	**RESIDENCE**
9	Anderson, Brady	L	L	6–1	190	1–18–64	Silver Spring, MD	Poway, CA
3	Baines, Harold	L	L	6–2	195	3–15–59	Easton, MD	Easton, MD
	Buford, Damon	R	R	5–10	170	6–12–70	Baltimore, MD	Sherman Oaks, CA
12	Devereaux, Mike	R	R	6–0	195	4–10–63	Casper, WY	Owings Mills, MD
	Hammonds, Jeffrey	R	R	6–0	195	3–5–71	Plainfield, NJ	Scotch Plains, NJ
	McLemore, Mark	S	R	5–11	207	10–4–64	San Diego, CA	Gilbert, AZ
	Obando, Sherman	R	R	6–4	215	1–23–70	Changuinola, Pan.	LaDorado, Pan.
	Ochoa, Alex	R	R	6–0	175	3–29–72	Miami Lakes, FL	Miami Lakes, FL
	Smith, Mark	R	R	6–4	195	4–9–66	Houston, TX	Houston, TX
28	Voigt, Jack	R	R	6–1	175	5–17–66	Sarasota, FL	Venice, FL
	Wawruchk, James	L	L	5–11	185	4–23–70	Hartford, CT	Hartford, CT

Oriole Park at Camden Yards
(48,003, grass)
Tickets: 410–685–9800
Ticket prices:
  $15 (lower boxes); $14 (terrace boxes)
  $12 (upper boxes, LF lower boxes)
  $11 (left field upper boxes)
  $8 (reserved seats)
  $6 (left field upper reserved)
  $4 (bleachers)
Field dimensions (from home plate)
  To left field at foul line, 333 feet
  To center field, 400 feet
  To right field at foul line, 318 feet

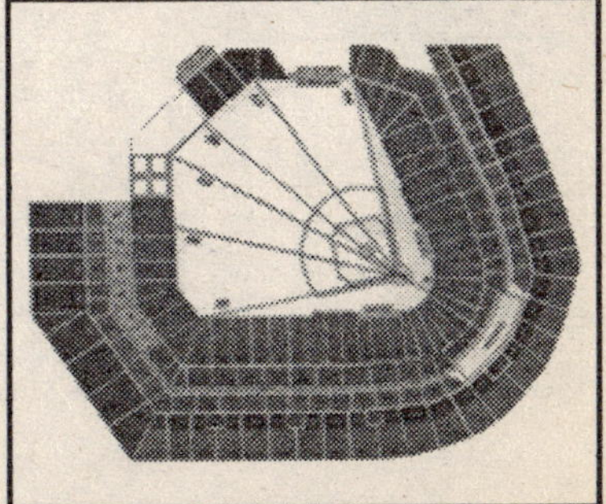

Brady Anderson No. 9/OF

Full name: Brady Kevin Anderson
Bats: L **Throws:** L **HT:** 6–1 **WT:** 190
Born: 1–18–64, Silver Spring, MD
High school: Carlsbad (CA)
College: Cal–Irvine

Anderson led the Orioles in runs (87), doubles (36), triples (8), and SB (24). He hit into only 4 double plays, second-best in the AL.

	TEAM	LG	POS	G	AB	R	H	2B	3B	HR	RBI	BB	SO	SB	E	BA	SLG	SALARY
1988	BOS-BAL	AL	OF	94	325	31	69	13	4	1	21	23	75	10	4	.212	.286	N/A
1989	BAL	AL	OF	94	266	44	55	12	2	4	16	43	45	16	3	.207	.312	N/A
1990	BAL	AL	OF	89	234	24	54	5	2	3	24	31	46	15	2	.231	.308	120,000
1991	BAL	AL	OF	113	256	40	59	12	3	2	27	38	44	12	3	.230	.324	N/A
1992	BAL	AL	OF	159	623	100	169	28	10	21	80	98	98	53	8	.271	.449	345,000
1993	BAL	AL	OF	142	560	87	147	36	8	13	66	82	99	24	2	.263	.425	1,855,000
6	YR	TOTALS		691	2264	326	553	106	29	44	234	315	407	130	22	.244	.375	
1993	RANK	MLB	OF	34	23	23	31	10	6	42	38	9	23	26	97	84	64	40
1994	PROJECTIONS			110	383	54	90	20	4	6	34	49	73	16	3	.235	.360	

Harold Baines No. 3/DH

Full name: Harold Douglas Baines
Bats: L **Throws:** L **HT:** 6–2 **WT:** 195
Born: 3–15–59, Easton, MD
High school: St. Michael's (Easton, MD)

Baines batted .340 with men on base, fifth-best in the AL. His .313 BA was the best of his career, and he hit .345 at home.

	TEAM	LG	POS	G	AB	R	H	2B	3B	HR	RBI	BB	SO	SB	E	BA	SLG	SALARY
1980	CHI	AL	OF	141	491	55	125	23	6	13	49	19	65	2	9	.255	.405	N/A
1981	CHI	AL	OF	82	280	42	80	11	7	10	41	12	41	6	2	.286	.482	N/A
1982	CHI	AL	OF	161	608	89	165	29	8	25	105	49	95	10	7	.271	.469	N/A
1983	CHI	AL	OF	156	596	76	167	33	2	20	99	49	85	7	9	.280	.443	N/A
1984	CHI	AL	OF	147	569	72	173	28	10	29	94	54	75	1	6	.304	.541	N/A
1985	CHI	AL	OF	160	640	86	198	29	3	22	113	42	89	1	2	.309	.467	N/A
1986	CHI	AL	OF	145	570	72	169	29	2	21	88	38	89	2	5	.296	.465	N/A
1987	CHI	AL	OF	132	505	59	148	26	4	20	93	46	82	0	0	.293	.479	N/A
1988	CHI-TEX	AL	OF	158	599	55	166	39	1	13	81	67	109	0	2	.277	.411	N/A
1989	TEX-OAK	AL	OF	146	505	73	156	29	1	16	72	73	79	0	2	.309	.465	N/A
1990	OAK	AL	OF	135	415	52	118	15	1	16	65	67	80	0	1	.284	.441	1,143,539
1991	OAK	AL	OF	141	488	76	144	25	1	20	90	72	67	0	1	.295	.473	1,358,333
1992	OAK	AL	OF	140	478	58	121	18	0	16	76	59	61	1	1	.253	.391	1,583,334
1993	BAL	AL	DH	118	416	64	130	22	0	20	78	57	52	0	0	.313	.510	1,200,000
14	YR	TOTALS		1962	7160	929	2060	356	46	261	1144	704	1069	30	47	.288	.460	
1993	RANK	MLB	DH	7	7	7	6	7	7	5	5	5	7	8	4	2	1	8
1994	PROJECTIONS			133	461	59	125	21	2	16	67	45	59	1	3	.271	.432	

Mike Devereaux No. 12/OF

Full name: Michael Devereaux
Bats: R **Throws:** R **HT:** 6–0 **WT:** 195
Born: 4–10–63, Casper, WY
High school: Kelly Walsh (Casper, WY)
College: Arizona State

Bothered by injuries, Devereaux slumped after a strong '92. He hit only .186 after August 13.

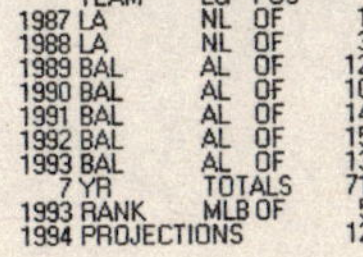

	TEAM	LG	POS	G	AB	R	H	2B	3B	HR	RBI	BB	SO	SB	E	BA	SLG	SALARY
1987	LA	NL	OF	19	54	7	12	3	0	0	4	3	10	3	0	.222	.278	N/A
1988	LA	NL	OF	30	43	4	5	1	0	0	2	2	10	0	0	.116	.140	N/A
1989	BAL	AL	OF	122	391	55	104	14	3	8	46	36	60	22	5	.266	.379	N/A
1990	BAL	AL	OF	108	367	48	88	18	1	12	49	28	48	13	5	.240	.392	145,000
1991	BAL	AL	OF	149	608	82	158	27	10	19	59	47	115	16	3	.260	.431	210,000
1992	BAL	AL	OF	156	653	76	180	29	11	24	107	44	94	10	5	.276	.464	1,000,000
1993	BAL	AL	OF	131	527	72	132	31	3	14	75	43	99	3	4	.250	.400	3,025,000
7	YR	TOTALS		715	2643	344	679	123	28	77	342	203	436	67	22	.257	.412	
1993	RANK	MLB	OF	57	34	44	51	18	54	40	25	49	23	93	59	101	80	23
1994	PROJECTIONS			120	428	58	108	21	2	11	56	35	69	12	4	.252	.390	

Leo Gomez No. 10/3B

Full name: Leonardo Gomez
Bats: R **Throws:** R **HT:** 6–0 **WT:** 208
Born: 3–2–67, Canovanas, PR
High school: Luis Hernaes Nevones (PR)

Gomez missed more than 2 months with injuries, and batted just .094 in his last 30 games

	TEAM	LG	POS	G	AB	R	H	2B	3B	HR	RBI	BB	SO	SB	E	BA	SLG	SALARY
1990	BAL	AL	3B	12	39	3	9	0	0	0	1	8	7	0	4	.231	.231	N/A
1991	BAL	AL	3B-1B	118	391	40	91	17	2	16	45	40	82	1	7	.233	.409	102,500
1992	BAL	AL	3B	137	468	62	124	24	0	17	64	63	78	2	18	.265	.425	150,000
1993	BAL	AL	3B	71	244	30	48	7	0	10	25	32	60	0	10	.197	.348	312,500
4	YR	TOTALS		338	1142	135	272	48	2	43	135	143	227	3	39	.238	.397	
1993	RANK	MLB	3B	37	31	30	35	37	33	20	35	21	21	38	26	41	36	22
1994	PROJECTIONS			73	250	31	60	10	0	9	30	34	48	0	10	.240	.388	

Chris Hoiles — No. 23/C

Full name: Christopher Allen Hoiles
Bats: R **Throws:** R **HT:** 6–0 **WT:** 213
Born: 3–20–65, Bowling Green, OH
High school: Elmwood (Wayne, OH)
College: Eastern Michigan

Hoiles had a great 1993, with career-bests in BA (.310, eleventh in the AL), HR (29), runs (80), and RBI (82).

	TEAM	LG	POS	G	AB	R	H	2B	3B	HR	RBI	BB	SO	SB	E	BA	SLG	SALARY
1989	BAL	AL	C	6	9	0	1	1	0	0	1	1	3	0	0	.111	.222	N/A
1990	BAL	AL	C-1B	23	63	7	12	3	0	1	6	5	12	0	0	.190	.286	N/A
1991	BAL	AL	C-1B	107	341	36	83	15	0	11	31	29	61	0	1	.243	.384	107,500
1992	BAL	AL	C	96	310	49	85	10	1	20	40	55	60	0	3	.274	.506	175,000
1993	BAL	AL	C	126	419	80	130	28	0	29	82	69	94	1	5	.310	.585	N/A
5	YR	TOTALS		358	1142	172	311	57	1	61	160	159	230	1	9	.272	.484	
1993	RANK	MLB	C	15	12	3	5	3	25	3	4	2	4	21	23	2	1	39
1994	PROJECTIONS			150	501	96	155	33	0	34	98	82	112	1	6	.309	.579	

Tim Hulett — No. 36/IF

Full name: Timothy Craig Hulett
Bats: R **Throws:** R **HT:** 6–0 **WT:** 200
Born: 1–12–60, Springfield, IL
High school: Lanphier (Springfield, IL)
College: Miami Dade CC (FL) and S. Florida

Veteran Hulett batted .300 for the first time, and hit .333 at Camden Yards.

	TEAM	LG	POS	G	AB	R	H	2B	3B	HR	RBI	BB	SO	SB	E	BA	SLG	SALARY
1983	CHI	AL	2B	6	5	0	1	0	0	0	0	0	0	1	2	.200	.200	N/A
1984	CHI	AL	3B-2B	8	7	1	0	0	0	0	0	1	4	1	0	.000	.000	N/A
1985	CHI	AL	3B-2B	141	395	52	106	19	4	5	37	30	81	6	24	.268	.375	N/A
1986	CHI	AL	3B-2B	150	520	53	120	16	5	17	44	21	91	4	15	.231	.379	N/A
1987	CHI	AL	3B-2B	68	240	20	52	10	0	7	28	10	41	0	9	.217	.346	N/A
1989	BAL	AL	2B-3B	33	97	12	27	5	0	3	18	10	17	0	4	.278	.423	N/A
1990	BAL	AL	3B-2B	53	153	16	39	7	1	3	16	15	41	1	4	.255	.373	207,500
1991	BAL	AL	3B-2B	79	206	29	42	9	0	7	18	13	49	0	4	.204	.350	327,500
1992	BAL	AL	3B-2B	57	142	11	41	7	2	2	21	10	31	0	7	.289	.408	380,000
1993	BAL	AL	3B	85	260	40	78	15	0	2	23	23	56	1	8	.300	.381	440,000
10	YR	TOTALS		680	2025	234	506	88	12	46	205	133	411	14	77	.250	.463	
1993	RANK	MLB	3B	31	30	23	26	25	33	34	38	28	22	26	31	5	28	19
1994	PROJECTIONS			77	235	29	57	11	0	5	23	15	48	0	7	.243	.357	

Mark McLemore No. 2/OF

Full name: Mark Tremell McLemore
Bats: S **Throws:** R **HT:** 5–11 **WT:** 207
Born: 10–4–64, San Diego, CA
High school: Morse (San Diego, CA)

McLemore led the Orioles with 49 multi-hit games and 23 infield hits. He had 13 outfield assists, tied for third-best in the AL.

	TEAM	LG	POS	G	AB	R	H	2B	3B	HR	RBI	BB	SO	SB	E	BA	SLG	SALARY
1986	CAL	AL	2B	5	4	0	0	0	0	0	0	1	2	0	0	.000	.000	N/A
1987	CAL	AL	2B	138	433	61	102	13	3	3	41	48	72	25	17	.236	.300	N/A
1988	CAL	AL	2B	77	233	38	56	11	2	2	16	25	28	13	6	.240	.330	N/A
1989	CAL	AL	2B	32	103	12	25	3	1	0	14	7	19	6	5	.243	.291	N/A
1990	CAL-CLE	AL	2B	28	60	6	9	2	0	0	2	4	15	1	4	.150	.183	N/A
1991	HOU	NL	2B	21	61	6	9	1	0	0	2	6	13	0	2	.148	.164	N/A
1992	BAL	AL	2B	101	228	40	56	7	2	0	27	21	26	11	7	.246	.294	250,000
1993	BAL	AL	2B	148	581	81	165	27	5	4	72	64	92	21	6	.284	.368	450,000
8	YR	TOTALS		550	1703	244	422	64	13	9	174	176	267	77	47	.248	.317	
1993	RANK	MLB	2B	7	5	7	5	9	7	23	5	9	3	5	32	13	24	21
1994	PROJECTIONS			162	641	89	181	29	4	3	79	69	101	22	5	.282	.354	

Rafael Palmeiro 1B

Full name: Rafael Corrales Palmeiro
Bats: L **Throws:** L **HT:** 6–0 **WT:** 188
Born: 9–24–64, Havana, CU
High school: Jackson (Miami, FL)
College: Mississippi State

Palmeiro led the AL in runs scored, and was among the top ten in games, doubles, total bases, extra base hits, homers, and slugging.

	TEAM	LG	POS	G	AB	R	H	2B	3B	HR	RBI	BB	SO	SB	E	BA	SLG	SALARY
1986	CHI	NL	1B	22	73	9	18	4	0	3	12	4	6	1	4	.247	.425	N/A
1987	CHI	NL	1B	84	221	32	61	15	1	14	30	20	26	2	1	.276	.543	N/A
1988	CHI	NL	OF	152	580	75	178	41	5	8	53	38	34	12	5	.307	.436	N/A
1989	TEX	AL	OF-1B	156	559	76	154	23	4	8	64	63	48	4	12	.275	.374	N/A
1990	TEX	AL	OF-1B	154	598	72	191	35	6	14	89	40	59	3	7	.319	.468	N/A
1991	TEX	AL	1B	159	631	115	203	49	3	26	88	68	72	4	12	.322	.532	1,475,000
1992	TEX	AL	1B	159	608	84	163	27	4	22	85	72	83	2	7	.268	.434	3,850,000
1993	TEX	AL	1B	160	597	124	176	40	2	37	105	73	85	22	5	.295	.554	4,550,000
8	YR	TOTALS		1046	3867	587	1144	234	25	132	526	378	413	50	53	.296	.472	
1993	RANK	MLB	1B	1	3	1	4	2	11	2	5	9	11	2	21	12	4	2
1994	PROJECTIONS			157	601	93	176	34	4	24	93	61	75	9	6	.293	.484	

Cal Ripken No. 8/SS

Full name: Calvin Edwin Ripken Jr.
Bats: R **Throws:** R **HT:** 6–4 **WT:** 220
Born: 8–24–60, Havre de Grace, MD
High school: Aberdeen (MD)

Ripken has now started 1,897 consecutive games. During the streak, 311 other players have started at shortstop in the majors. He hit .292 after the All-Star break.

	TEAM	LG	POS	G	AB	R	H	2B	3B	HR	RBI	BB	SO	SB	E	BA	SLG	SALARY
1981	BAL	AL	SS-3B	23	39	1	5	0	0	0	0	1	8	0	3	.128	.128	N/A
1982	BAL	AL	SS-3B	160	598	90	158	32	5	28	93	46	95	3	19	.264	.475	N/A
1983	BAL	AL	SS	162	663	121	211	47	2	27	102	58	97	0	25	.318	.517	N/A
1984	BAL	AL	SS	162	641	103	195	37	7	27	86	71	89	2	26	.304	.510	N/A
1985	BAL	AL	SS	161	642	116	181	32	5	26	110	67	68	2	26	.282	.469	N/A
1986	BAL	AL	SS	162	627	98	177	35	1	25	81	70	60	4	13	.282	.461	N/A
1987	BAL	AL	SS	162	624	97	157	28	3	27	98	81	77	3	20	.252	.436	N/A
1988	BAL	AL	SS	161	575	87	152	25	1	23	81	102	69	2	21	.264	.431	N/A
1989	BAL	AL	SS	162	646	80	166	30	0	21	93	57	72	3	8	.257	.401	N/A
1990	BAL	AL	SS	161	600	78	150	28	4	21	84	82	66	3	3	.250	.415	1,366,667
1991	BAL	AL	SS	162	650	99	210	46	5	34	114	53	46	6	11	.323	.566	2,466,667
1992	BAL	AL	SS	162	637	73	160	29	1	14	72	64	50	4	12	.251	.366	2,100,000
1993	BAL	AL	SS	162	641	87	165	26	3	24	90	65	58	1	17	.257	.420	5,150,000
13	YR	TOTALS		1962	7583	1130	2087	395	37	297	1104	817	855	33	204	.275	.455	
1993	RANK	MLB	SS	1	1	4	4	7	12	1	2	6	17	35	11	25	8	2
1994	PROJECTIONS			161	629	81	160	28	2	22	89	68	65	2	9	.254	.412	

Sid Fernandez No. 50/P

Full name: Charles Sidney Fernandez
Bats: L **Throws:** L **HT:** 6–1 **WT:** 225
Born: 10–12–62, Honolulu, HI
High school: Kaiser (Honolulu, HI)

Injured for half of 1993, Fernandez still posted an ERA under 3.00 for the Mets for the third straight year. He gave up 17 HR in only 18 starts.

	TM	LG	POS	W	L	ERA	G	GS	CG	SH	SV	IP	H	R	ER	HR	BB	SO	SALARY
1983	LA	NL	P	0	1	6.00	2	1	0	0	0	6.0	7	4	4	0	7	9	N/A
1984	NY	NL	P	6	6	3.50	15	15	0	0	0	90.0	74	40	35	8	34	62	N/A
1985	NY	NL	P	9	9	2.80	26	26	3	0	0	170.1	108	56	53	14	80	180	N/A
1986	NY	NL	P	16	6	3.52	32	31	2	1	1	204.1	161	82	80	13	91	200	N/A
1987	NY	NL	P	12	8	3.81	28	27	3	1	0	156.0	130	75	66	16	67	134	N/A
1988	NY	NL	P	12	10	3.03	31	31	1	1	0	187.0	127	69	63	15	70	189	N/A
1989	NY	NL	P	14	5	2.83	35	32	6	2	0	219.1	157	73	69	21	75	198	N/A
1990	NY	NL	P	9	14	3.46	30	30	2	1	0	179.1	130	79	69	18	67	181	N/A
1991	NY	NL	P	1	3	2.86	8	8	0	0	0	44.0	36	18	14	4	9	31	2,166,667
1992	NY	NL	P	14	11	2.73	32	32	5	2	0	214.2	162	67	65	12	67	193	160,000
1993	NY	NL	P	5	6	2.93	18	18	1	1	0	119.2	82	42	39	17	36	81	2,100,000
11	YR	TOTALS		98	79	3.15	257	251	23	9	1	1590.2	1174	605	557	138	603	1458	
1993	Rank	MLB	Ps	149		37	261	111	79	23	102	119	5	23		256	80	114	63
1994	PROJECTIONS			4	5	3.11	13	13	0	0	0	84	64	33	29	9	26	58	

Ben McDonald No.19/P

Full name: Larry Benard McDonald
Bats: R **Throws:** R **HT:** 6–7 **WT:** 213
Born: 11–24–67, Baton Rouge, LA
High school: Denham Springs (LA)
College: Louisiana State

McDonald's 3.39 ERA placed twelfth in the league. He allowed 3 ER or less in 28 of 34 starts. He hasn't missed a start since '91.

	TM	LG	POS	W	L	ERA	G	GS	CG	SH	SV	IP	H	R	ER	HR	BB	SO	SALARY
1989	BAL	AL	P	1	0	8.59	6	0	0	0	0	7.1	8	7	7	2	4	3	N/A
1990	BAL	AL	P	8	5	2.43	21	15	3	2	0	118.2	88	36	32	9	35	65	N/A
1991	BAL	AL	P	6	8	4.84	21	21	1	0	0	126.1	126	71	68	16	43	85	N/A
1992	BAL	AL	P	13	13	4.24	35	35	4	2	0	227.0	213	113	107	32	74	158	355,000
1993	BAL	AL	P	13	14	3.39	34	34	7	1	0	220.1	185	92	83	17	86	171	1,250,000
5	YR	TOTALS		41	40	3.82	117	105	15	5	0	699.2	620	319	297	76	242	482	
1993	Rank	MLB Ps		36		77	145	12	7	23	102	26	35	68		93	172	69	87
1994	PROJECTIONS			13	14	3.37	35	35	7	0	0	235	198	98	88	18	91	183	

Mike Mussina No. 35/P

Full name: Michael Cole Mussina
Bats: R **Throws:** R **HT:** 6–2 **WT:** 185
Born: 12–8–68, Williamsport, PA
High school: Montoursville (PA)
College: Stanford

Mussina placed seventh in the AL with a .700 winning percentage. He was 9–2 with a 3.05 ERA in his first 13 starts.

	TM	LG	POS	W	L	ERA	G	GS	CG	SH	SV	IP	H	R	ER	HR	BB	SO	SALARY
1991	BAL	AL	P	4	5	2.87	12	12	2	0	0	87.2	77	31	28	7	21	52	100,000
1992	BAL	AL	P	18	5	2.54	32	32	8	4	0	241.0	212	70	68	16	48	130	137,500
1993	BAL	AL	P	14	6	4.46	25	25	3	2	0	167.2	163	84	83	20	44	117	425,000
3	YR	TOTALS		36	16	3.25	69	69	13	6	0	496.1	452	185	179	43	113	299	
1993	Rank	MLB Ps		29		185	236	91	37	8	102	76	114	144		206	44	102	140
1994	PROJECTIONS			12	5	3.22	23	23	4	2	0	165	150	61	59	14	37	99	

Gregg Olson No. 30/P

Full name: Gregg William Olson
Bats: R **Throws:** R **HT:** 6–4 **WT:** 212
Born: 10–11–66, Omaha, NE
High school: Omaha Northwest (NE)
College: Auburn

Olson became the first pitcher ever to record 20+ saves in his first 5 seasons. His 29 saves were his least since 1989.

	TM	LG	POS	W	L	ERA	G	GS	CG	SH	SV	IP	H	R	ER	HR	BB	SO	SALARY
1988	BAL	AL	P	1	1	3.27	10	0	0	0	0	11.0	10	4	4	1	10	9	N/A
1989	BAL	AL	P	5	2	1.69	64	0	0	0	27	85.0	57	17	16	1	46	90	N/A
1990	BAL	AL	P	6	5	2.42	64	0	0	0	37	74.1	57	20	20	3	31	74	N/A
1991	BAL	AL	P	4	6	3.18	72	0	0	0	31	73.2	74	28	26	1	29	72	505,000
1992	BAL	AL	P	1	5	2.05	60	0	0	0	36	61.1	46	14	14	3	24	58	1,450,000
1993	BAL	AL	P	0	2	1.60	50	0	0	0	29	45.0	37	9	8	1	18	44	2,300,000
6	YR	TOTALS		17	21	2.26	320	0	0	0	160	350.1	281	92	88	10	158	347	
1993	Rank	MLB Ps	not ranked -- didn't have 50 IP in 1993																
1994	PROJECTIONS			2	1	1.72	41	0	0	0	26	47	34	10	9	1	24	47	

Johnny Oates No. 26/Mgr.

Full name: Johnny Lane Oates
Bats: L **Throws:** R **HT:** 5–11 **WT:** 185
Born: 1–21–46, Sylva, VA
High school: Prince George (VA)
College: Virginia Tech

Oates was named AL Manager of the Year, even though the Orioles slipped four games from '92.

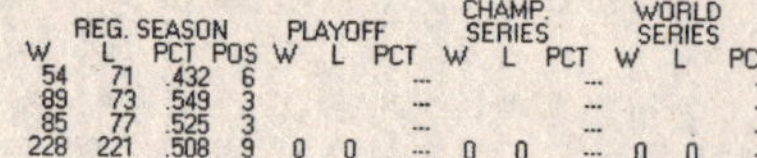

			REG. SEASON				PLAYOFF			CHAMP. SERIES			WORLD SERIES		
YEAR	TEAM	LG	W	L	PCT	POS	W	L	PCT	W	L	PCT	W	L	PCT
1991	BAL	AL	54	71	.432	6			---			---			---
1992	BAL	AL	89	73	.549	3			---			---			---
1993	BAL	AL	85	77	.525	3			---			---			---
3	YR TOTALS		228	221	.508	9	0	0	---	0	0	---	0	0	---

Damon Buford — No. 18/OF

Full name: Damon Jackson Buford
Bats: R **Throws:** R **HT:** 5–10 **WT:** 170
Born: 6–12–70, Baltimore, MD
High school: Birmingham (CA)
College: USC
Buford hit .313 in AAA Rochester.

TEAM	LG	POS	G	AB	R	H	2B	3B	HR	RBI	BB	SO	SB	E	BA	SLG	SALARY
1993 BAL	AL	OF	53	79	18	18	5	0	2	9	9	19	2	1	.228	.367	109,000
1 YR	TOTAL		53	79	18	18	5	0	2	9	9	19	2	1	.228	.367	
1993 RANK	MLB OF		not ranked -- didn't have 150 ABs in 1993														

Todd Frohwirth — No. 49/P

Full name: Todd Gerald Frohwirth
Bats: R **Throws:** R **HT:** 6–4 **WT:** 211
Born: 9–28–62, Milwaukee, WI
High school: Messmer (Milwaukee, WI)
College: Northwest Missouri State
Frohwirth's 70 appearances ranked sixth in the AL.

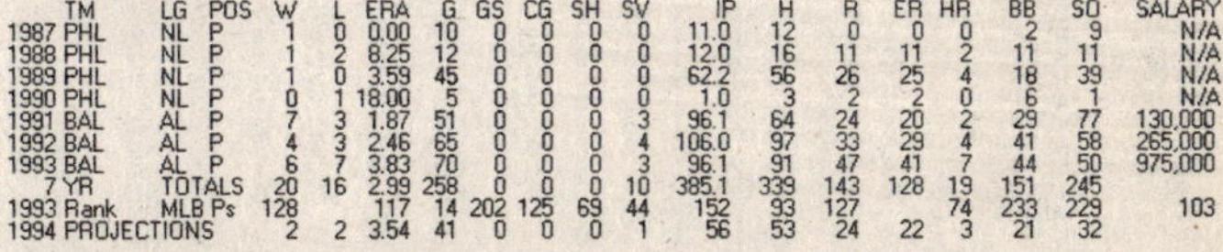

TM	LG	POS	W	L	ERA	G	GS	CG	SH	SV	IP	H	R	ER	HR	BB	SO	SALARY
1987 PHL	NL	P	1	0	0.00	10	0	0	0	0	11.0	12	0	0	0	2	9	N/A
1988 PHL	NL	P	1	2	8.25	12	0	0	0	0	12.0	16	11	11	2	11	11	N/A
1989 PHL	NL	P	1	0	3.59	45	0	0	0	0	62.2	56	26	25	4	18	39	N/A
1990 PHL	NL	P	0	1	18.00	5	0	0	0	0	1.0	3	2	2	0	6	1	N/A
1991 BAL	AL	P	7	3	1.87	51	0	0	0	3	96.1	64	24	20	2	29	77	130,000
1992 BAL	AL	P	4	3	2.46	65	0	0	0	4	106.0	97	33	29	4	41	58	265,000
1993 BAL	AL	P	6	7	3.83	70	0	0	0	3	96.1	91	47	41	7	44	50	975,000
7 YR	TOTALS		20	16	2.99	258	0	0	0	10	385.1	339	143	128	19	151	245	
1993 Rank	MLB Ps		128		117	14	202	125	69	44	152	93	127		74	233	229	103
1994 PROJECTIONS			2	2	3.54	41	0	0	0	1	56	53	24	22	3	21	32	

Jeffrey Hammonds — No. 11/OF

Full name: Jeffrey Bryan Hammonds
Bats: R **Throws:** R **HT:** 6–0 **WT:** 195
Born: 3–5–71, Plainfield, NJ
High school: Scotch Plains–Fanwood (NJ)
College: Stanford
Hammons had 19 RBI in only 33 games.

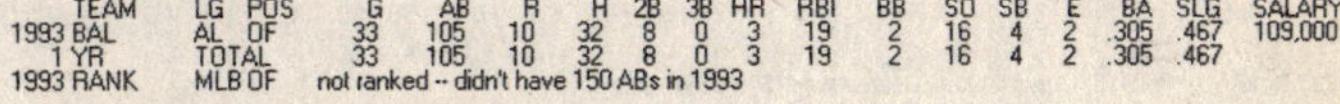

TEAM	LG	POS	G	AB	R	H	2B	3B	HR	RBI	BB	SO	SB	E	BA	SLG	SALARY
1993 BAL	AL	OF	33	105	10	32	8	0	3	19	2	16	4	2	.305	.467	109,000
1 YR	TOTAL		33	105	10	32	8	0	3	19	2	16	4	2	.305	.467	
1993 RANK	MLB OF		not ranked -- didn't have 150 ABs in 1993														

Alan Mills No. 75/P

Full name: Alan Bernard Mills
Bats: S **Throws:** R **HT:** 6–1 **WT:** 192
Born: 10–18–66, Lakeland, FL
High school: Kathleen (Lakeland, FL)
College: Tuskegee Inst. (AL) and Polk CC (FL)
Mills finished third in the AL with 100.1 IP in relief.

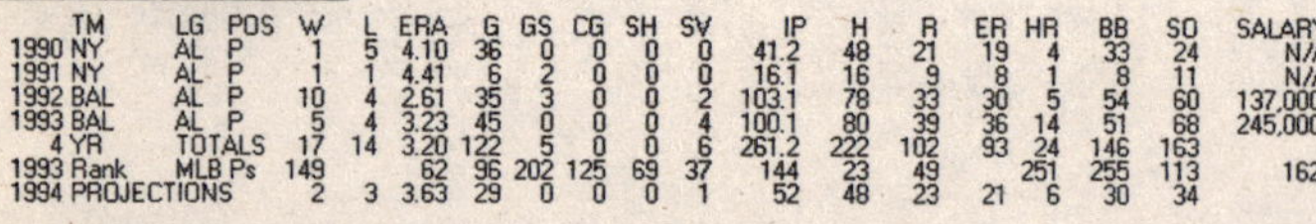

TM	LG	POS	W	L	ERA	G	GS	CG	SH	SV	IP	H	R	ER	HR	BB	SO	SALARY
1990 NY	AL	P	1	5	4.10	36	0	0	0	0	41.2	48	21	19	4	33	24	N/A
1991 NY	AL	P	1	1	4.41	6	2	0	0	0	16.1	16	9	8	1	8	11	N/A
1992 BAL	AL	P	10	4	2.61	35	3	0	0	2	103.1	78	33	30	5	54	60	137,000
1993 BAL	AL	P	5	4	3.23	45	0	0	0	4	100.1	80	39	36	14	51	68	245,000
4 YR	TOTALS		17	14	3.20	122	5	0	0	6	261.2	222	102	93	24	146	163	
1993 Rank	MLB Ps		149		62	96	202	125	69	37	144	23	49		251	255	113	162
1994 PROJECTIONS			2	3	3.63	29	0	0	0	1	52	48	23	21	6	30	34	

Jamie Moyer No. 51/P

Full name: Jamie Moyer
Bats: L **Throws:** L **HT:** 6–6 **WT:** 170
Born: 11–16–62, Sellersville, PA
High school: Souderton Area (PA)
College: St. Joseph's (Philadelphia, PA)
Moyer's 2.44 road ERA was the lowest in the AL.

TM	LG	POS	W	L	ERA	G	GS	CG	SH	SV	IP	H	R	ER	HR	BB	SO	SALARY
1986 CHI	NL	P	7	4	5.05	16	16	1	1	0	87.1	107	52	49	10	42	45	N/A
1987 CHI	NL	P	12	15	5.10	35	33	1	0	0	201.0	210	127	114	28	97	147	N/A
1988 CHI	NL	P	9	15	3.48	34	30	3	1	0	202.0	212	84	78	20	55	121	N/A
1989 TEX	AL	P	4	9	4.86	15	15	1	0	0	76.0	84	51	41	10	33	44	N/A
1990 TEX	AL	P	2	6	4.66	33	10	1	0	0	102.1	115	59	53	6	39	58	N/A
1991 STL	NL	P	0	5	5.74	8	7	0	0	0	31.1	38	21	20	5	16	20	N/A
1993 BAL	AL	P	12	9	3.43	25	25	3	1	0	152.0	154	63	58	11	38	90	200,000
7 YR	TOTALS		46	63	4.36	166	136	10	3	0	852.0	920	457	413	90	320	525	
1993 Rank	MLB Ps		43		83	236	91	37	23	102	97	154	66		73	39	170	171
1994 PROJECTIONS			7	6	4.22	24	17	1	0	0	113	125	58	53	9	39	64	

Sherman Obando No. 42/OF

Full name: Sherman Omar Obando
Bats: R **Throws:** R **HT:** 6–4 **WT:** 215
Born: 1–23–70, Changuinola, Pan.
In his first major league season, Obando batted .385 with runners in scoring position.

TEAM	LG	POS	G	AB	R	H	2B	3B	HR	RBI	BB	SO	SB	E	BA	SLG	SALARY
1993 BAL	AL	OF	31	92	8	25	2	0	3	15	4	26	0	1	.272	.391	109,000
1 YR	TOTAL		31	92	8	25	2	0	3	15	4	26	0	1	.272	.391	
1993 RANK	MLB OF		not ranked -- didn't have 150 ABs in 1993														

Brad Pennington — No. 47/P

Full name: Brad Lee Pennington
Bats: L **Throws:** L **HT:** 6–5 **WT:** 205
Born: 4–14–69, Salem, IN
High school: Eastern (IN)
College: Bellarmine (KY) and Vincennes JC (IN)
Pennington struggled to a 6.55 ERA in 34 games.

	TM	LG	POS	W	L	ERA	G	GS	CG	SH	SV	IP	H	R	ER	HR	BB	SO	SALARY
1993	BAL	AL	P	3	2	6.55	34	0	0	0	4	33.0	34	25	24	7	25	39	N/A
1	YR	TOTAL		3	2	6.55	34	0	0	0	4	33.0	34	25	24	7	25	39	
1993	RANK	MLB Ps	not ranked -- didn't have 50 IP in 1993																

Jim Poole — No. 45/P

Full name: James Richard Poole
Bats: L **Throws:** L **HT:** 6–2 **WT:** 203
Born: 4–28–66, Rochester, NY
High school: South College (Philadelphia, PA)
College: Georgia Tech
Poole held opponents to a .175 BA.

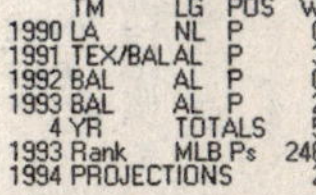

	TM	LG	POS	W	L	ERA	G	GS	CG	SH	SV	IP	H	R	ER	HR	BB	SO	SALARY
1990	LA	NL	P	0	0	4.22	16	0	0	0	0	10.2	7	5	5	1	8	6	N/A
1991	TEX/BAL	AL	P	3	2	2.36	29	0	0	0	1	42.0	29	14	11	3	12	38	105,000
1992	BAL	AL	P	0	0	0.00	6	0	0	0	0	3.1	3	3	0	0	1	3	N/A
1993	BAL	AL	P	2	1	2.15	55	0	0	0	2	50.1	30	18	12	2	21	29	150,000
4	YR	TOTALS		5	3	2.37	106	0	0	0	3	106.1	69	40	28	6	42	76	
1993	Rank	MLB Ps		246		5	62	202	125	69	55	289	1	27		16	198	180	195
1994	PROJECTIONS			2	1	1.95	64	0	0	0	2	60	35	21	13	2	24	34	

Arthur Rhodes — No. 53/P

Full name: Arthur Lee Rhodes Jr.
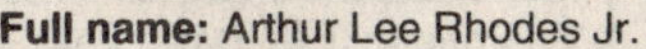
Bats: L **Throws:** L **HT:** 6–2 **WT:** 206
Born: 10–24–69, Waco, TX
High school: LaVega (Waco, TX)
Rhodes made 17 starts, the most of his career, but allowed 16 HR in just 85.2 IP.

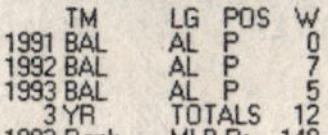

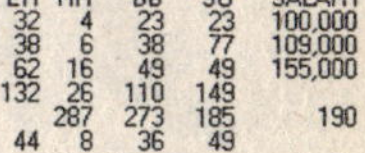

	TM	LG	POS	W	L	ERA	G	GS	CG	SH	SV	IP	H	R	ER	HR	BB	SO	SALARY
1991	BAL	AL	P	0	3	8.00	8	8	0	0	0	36.0	47	35	32	4	23	23	100,000
1992	BAL	AL	P	7	5	3.63	15	15	2	1	0	94.1	87	39	38	6	38	77	109,000
1993	BAL	AL	P	5	6	6.51	17	17	0	0	0	85.2	91	62	62	16	49	49	155,000
3	YR	TOTALS		12	14	5.50	40	40	2	1	0	216.0	225	136	132	26	110	149	
1993	Rank	MLB Ps		149		284	268	119	125	69	102	172	188	278		287	273	185	190
1994	PROJECTIONS			4	4	5.58	13	13	0	0	0	71	75	45	44	8	36	49	

David Segui — No. 21/1B

Full name: David Vincent Segui
Bats: S **Throws:** R **HT:** 6–1 **WT:** 202
Born: 7–19–66, Kansas City, KS
High school: Bishop Ward (Kansas City, KS)
College: Kansas City CC (KS) and La. Tech
Segui hit .346 with the count full.

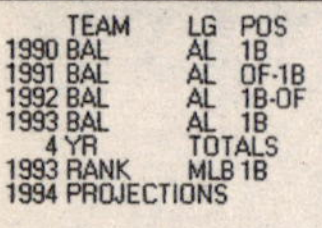
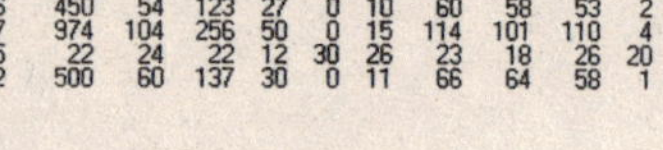

TEAM	LG	POS	G	AB	R	H	2B	3B	HR	RBI	BB	SO	SB	E	BA	SLG	SALARY
1990 BAL	AL	1B	40	123	14	30	7	0	2	15	11	15	0	3	.244	.350	100,000
1991 BAL	AL	OF-1B	86	212	15	59	7	0	2	22	12	19	1	3	.278	.340	106,000
1992 BAL	AL	1B-OF	115	189	21	44	9	0	1	17	20	23	1	1	.233	.296	150,000
1993 BAL	AL	1B	146	450	54	123	27	0	10	60	58	53	2	5	.273	.400	237,500
4 YR	TOTALS		387	974	104	256	50	0	15	114	101	110	4	12	.263	.360	
1993 RANK	MLB	1B	15	22	24	22	12	30	26	23	18	26	20	21	22	32	28
1994 PROJECTIONS			162	500	60	137	30	0	11	66	64	58	1	4	.274	.400	0

Jeff Tackett — No. 41/C

Full name: Jeffery Wilson Tackett
Bats: R **Throws:** R **HT:** 6–2 **WT:** 205
Born: 12–1–65, Fresno, CA
High school: Camarillo (CA)
Tackett started 30 games at catcher, but struggled at the plate, batting just .172.

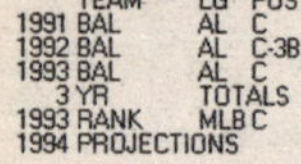
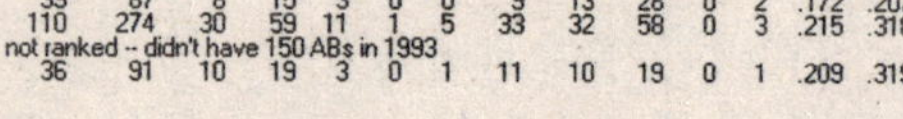

TEAM	LG	POS	G	AB	R	H	2B	3B	HR	RBI	BB	SO	SB	E	BA	SLG	SALARY
1991 BAL	AL	C	6	8	1	1	0	0	0	0	2	2	0	0	.125	.125	N/A
1992 BAL	AL	C-3B	65	179	21	43	8	1	5	24	17	28	0	1	.240	.380	109,000
1993 BAL	AL	C	39	87	8	15	3	0	0	9	13	28	0	2	.172	.207	N/A
3 YR	TOTALS		110	274	30	59	11	1	5	33	32	58	0	3	.215	.318	
1993 RANK	MLB	C	not ranked -- didn't have 150 ABs in 1993														
1994 PROJECTIONS			36	91	10	19	3	0	1	11	10	19	0	1	.209	.319	

Jack Voigt — No. 28/OF

Full name: John David Voigt
Bats: R **Throws:** R **HT:** 6–1 **WT:** 175
Born: 5–17–66, Sarasota, FL
High school: Venice (FL)
College: LSU
Rookie Voigt hit .310 in August and September.

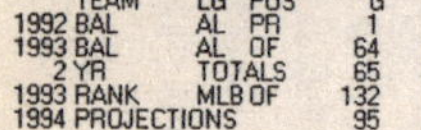
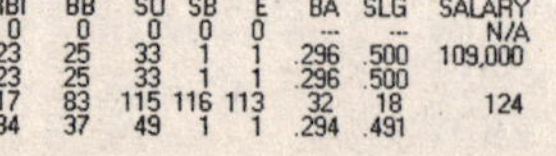

TEAM	LG	POS	G	AB	R	H	2B	3B	HR	RBI	BB	SO	SB	E	BA	SLG	SALARY
1992 BAL	AL	PR	1	0	0	0	0	0	0	0	0	0	0	0	---	---	N/A
1993 BAL	AL	OF	64	152	32	45	11	1	6	23	25	33	1	1	.296	.500	109,000
2 YR	TOTALS		65	152	32	45	11	1	6	23	25	33	1	1	.296	.500	
1993 RANK	MLB	OF	132	136	103	125	101	97	87	117	83	115	116	113	32	18	124
1994 PROJECTIONS			95	228	48	67	16	1	9	34	37	49	1	1	.294	.491	

Boston
RED SOX

1994 Scouting Report

Hitting: (1993/.264 BA, ninth in AL; 114 HR, thirteenth in AL)

Boston's offense is looking to rebound from a subpar '93. Mo Vaughn was the most dangerous hitter, batting .297 with 29 HR and 101 RBI. Mike Greenwell had a decent year, hitting .315. Andre Dawson had a broken wrist, and that limited his production.

Boston lacked a real leadoff hitter, so they signed Otis Nixon as a free-agent. The Sox also expect big years from Tim Naehring, Scott Cooper, and John Valentin. Tony Pena had an off-year, and could be done. Boston still has problems with team speed (they were twelfth in team steals). The Red Sox also lack bench strength, so injuries to starters really hurt.

Pitching: (1993/3.77 ERA, second in AL)

Boston pitching was some of the best in team history. Despite Roger Clemens' worst season and Frank Viola's elbow injury, Boston's team ERA was second in the AL. Boston got a great season from Danny Darwin (15–11, 3.26 ERA). Aaron Sele and Nate Minchey are young pitchers who the Red Sox are looking to in '94. Sele was a pleasant surprise, going 7–2 with a 2.74 ERA in 18 starts.

The bullpen features Jeff Russell (1.99 ERA with 33 saves), and setup men Paul Quantrill (3.91 ERA), Greg Harris (3.77 ERA, 5 saves), and Ken Ryan (3.60 ERA).

Defense: (1993/.980 pct., ninth in AL)

Boston's lack of speed translates into limited range, especially in the outfield. Otis Nixon's addition will give the Sox solid defense in center field.

1994 Prospects:

Boston could go either way. If the hitting rebounds and the pitching stays strong (likely if Clemens returns from his nagging injuries), Boston could contend for the division title. But if the pitching sags and the hitting doesn't come around, Boston will finish in the second division. It's risky to pin hopes on so many aging players, such as Andre Dawson, Otis Nixon, and Danny Darwin. At least one of them is likely to show his age this year.

Team Directory

General Partner: John Harrington
VP of Transportation: Jack Rogers
Executive Vice President of Baseball Operations: Lou Gorman
VP of P.R.: Dick Bresciani

Minor League Affiliates:

Level	Team/League	1993 Record
AAA	Pawtucket – International	60–82
AA	New Britain – Eastern	52–88
A	Lynchburg – Carolina	65–74
	Ft. Lauderdale – Florida St.	46–85
	Utica – New York/Penn.	38–38
Rookie	Ft. Myers Red Sox – Gulf Coast	32–28
	Ft. Myers Red Sox – Instructional League	15–16

1993 Review

	Home		Away			Home		Away			Home		Away	
vs AL East	W	L	W	L	vs AL Cent.	W	L	W	L	vs AL West	W	L	W	L
Baltimore	3	4	4	2	Chicago	4	2	3	3	California	6	0	1	5
Detroit	4	3	2	4	Cleveland	3	4	2	4	Oakland	5	1	4	2
New York	3	3	3	4	Kansas City	0	6	5	1	Seattle	3	3	4	2
Toronto	2	4	1	6	Milwaukee	2	4	3	4	Texas	4	2	2	4
					Minnesota	4	2	3	3					
Total	12	14	10	16		13	18	16	15		18	6	11	13

1993 finish: 80–82 (43–38 home, 37–44 away), fifth in AL East, 15 games behind

1994 Schedule

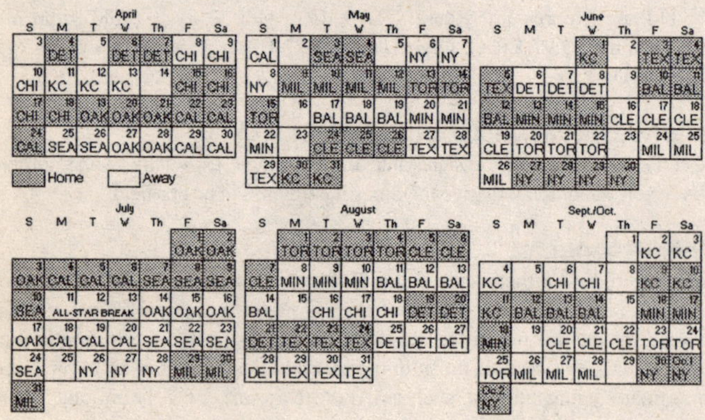

April

S	M	T	W	Th	F	Sa
3	4 DET	5	6 DET	7 DET	8 CHI	9 CHI
10 CHI	11 KC	12 KC	13 KC	14	15 CHI	16 CHI
17 CHI	18 CHI	19 OAK	20 OAK	21 OAK	22 CAL	23 CAL
24 CAL	25 SEA	26 SEA	27 OAK	28 OAK	29 CAL	30 CAL

May

S	M	T	W	Th	F	Sa
1 CAL	2	3 SEA	4 SEA	5	6 NY	7 NY
8 NY	9 MIL	10 MIL	11 MIL	12 MIL	13 TOR	14 TOR
15 TOR	16	17 BAL	18 BAL	19 BAL	20 MIN	21 MIN
22 MIN	23	24 CLE	25 CLE	26 CLE	27 TEX	28 TEX
29 TEX	30 KC	31 KC				

June

S	M	T	W	Th	F	Sa
			1 KC	2	3 TEX	4 TEX
5 TEX	6 DET	7 DET	8 DET	9	10 BAL	11 BAL
12 BAL	13 MIN	14 MIN	15 MIN	16 CLE	17 CLE	18 CLE
19 CLE	20 TOR	21 TOR	22 TOR	23	24 MIL	25 MIL
26 MIL	27 NY	28 NY	29 NY	30 NY		

July

S	M	T	W	Th	F	Sa
					1 OAK	2 OAK
3 OAK	4 CAL	5 CAL	6 CAL	7 SEA	8 SEA	9 SEA
10 SEA	11 ALL-STAR BREAK	12	13	14 OAK	15 OAK	16 OAK
17 OAK	18 CAL	19 CAL	20 CAL	21 SEA	22 SEA	23 SEA
24 SEA	25	26 NY	27 NY	28 NY	29 MIL	30 MIL
31 MIL						

August

S	M	T	W	Th	F	Sa
	1 TOR	2 TOR	3 TOR	4 TOR	5 CLE	6 CLE
7 CLE	8 MIN	9 MIN	10 MIN	11 BAL	12 BAL	13 BAL
14 BAL	15	16 CHI	17 CHI	18 CHI	19 DET	20 DET
21 DET	22 TEX	23 TEX	24 TEX	25 DET	26 DET	27 DET
28 DET	29 TEX	30 TEX	31 TEX			

Sept./Oct.

S	M	T	W	Th	F	Sa
				1	2 KC	3 KC
4 KC	5	6 CHI	7 CHI	8	9 KC	10 KC
11 KC	12 BAL	13 BAL	14 BAL	15	16 MIN	17 MIN
18 MIN	19	20 CLE	21 CLE	22 CLE	23 TOR	24 TOR
25 TOR	26 MIL	27 MIL	28 MIL	29	30 NY	Oc.1 NY
Oc.2 NY						

BOSTON RED SOX 1994 ROSTER

MANAGER: Butch Hobson (17)

COACHES: Gary Allenson, 3B (32); Mike Easler, hitting (34); Mike Roarke, pitching; John Wathan, bullpen; Frank White, 1B.

No.	PITCHERS	B	T	HT	WT	DOB	BIRTHPLACE	RESIDENCE
	Bailey, Cory	R	R	6–1	208	1–24–71	Herrin, IL	Marion, IL
29	Bankhead, Scott	R	R	5–10	185	7–31–63	Raleigh, NC	Asheboro, NC
	Caruso, Joe	R	R	6–3	185	9–16–70	Brooklyn, NY	Petaluma, CA
	Ciccarella, Joe	L	L	6–3	200	12–29–69	Cincinnati, OH	Huntington, CA
21	Clemens, Roger	R	R	6–4	220	8–4–62	Dayton, OH	Katy, TX
54	Conroy, Brian	S	R	6–2	180	8–29–68	Needham, MA	Needham, MA
44	Darwin, Danny	R	R	6–3	205	10–25–55	Bonham, TX	Valley View, TX
	Finnvold, Gar	R	R	6–5	195	3–11–68	Boynton Beach, FL	Boca Raton, FL
49	Fossas, Tony	L	L	6–0	197	9–23–67	Havana, CU	Ft. Lauderdale, FL
27	Harris, Greg	S	R	6–0	175	11–2–55	Lynwood, CA	Las Vegas, NV
	Henkel, Rob	R	R	6–3	180	11–23–70	Dallas, TX	Norris, TN
55	Hesketh, Joe	L	L	6–2	173	2–15–59	Lackawanna, NY	Palm Harbor, FL
19	Melendez, Jose	R	R	6–2	175	9–2–66	Nagubo, PR	Nagubo, PR
49	Quantrill, Paul	L	R	6–1	185	11–3–68	London, Ont.	Port Hope, Ont.
24	Russell, Jeff	R	R	6–3	205	9–2–61	Cincinnati, OH	Colleyville, TX
50	Ryan, Ken	R	R	6–3	215	10–24–68	Pawtucket, RI	Seekonk, MA
34	Sele, Aaron	R	R	6–5	205	6–25–70	Golden Valley, MN	Suquamish, WA
56	Taylor, Scott	L	L	6–1	190	8–2–67	Defiance, OH	Defiance, OH
	Vanegmond, Tim	R	R	6–2	180	5–31–69	Shreveport, LA	Senoia, GA
16	Viola, Frank	L	L	6–4	210	4–19–60	East Meadow, NY	Longwood, FL
No.	**CATCHERS**	**B**	**T**	**HT**	**WT**	**DOB**	**BIRTHPLACE**	**RESIDENCE**
15	Flaherty, John	R	R	6–1	195	10–21–67	New York, NY	West Nyack, NY
	Hatteberg, Scott	L	R	6–1	185	12–14–69	Salem, OR	Yakima, WA
3	Melvin, Bob	R	R	6–4	207	10–28–61	Palo Alto, CA	Germantown, PA
No.	**INFIELDERS**	**B**	**T**	**HT**	**WT**	**DOB**	**BIRTHPLACE**	**RESIDENCE**
45	Cooper, Scott	L	R	6–3	205	10–13–67	St. Louis, MO	St. Charles, MO
5	Fletcher, Scott	R	R	5–11	175	7–30–58	Fort Walton Beach, FL	Arlington, TX
11	Naehring, Tim	R	R	6–2	205	2–1–67	Cincinnati, OH	Cincinnati, OH
51	Ortiz, Luis	R	R	6–0	185	5–25–70	Santo Domingo, DR	Santo Domingo, DR
13	Valentin, John	R	R	6–0	180	2–18–67	Jersey City, NJ	Jersey City, NJ
42	Vaughn, Mo	L	R	6–1	225	12–15–67	Norwalk, CT	Braintree, MA
No.	**OUTFIELDERS**	**B**	**T**	**HT**	**WT**	**DOB**	**BIRTHPLACE**	**RESIDENCE**
38	Blosser, Greg	L	L	6–3	200	6–26–71	Bradenton, FL	Sarasota, FL
10	Dawson, Andre	R	R	6–3	197	7–10–54	Miami, FL	Miami, FL
39	Greenwell, Mike	L	R	6–0	205	7–18–63	Louisville, KY	Cape Coral, FL
22	Hatcher, Billy	R	R	5–10	190	10–4–60	Williams, AZ	Cincinnati, OH
	Malave, Jose	R	R	6–2	184	5–31–71	Cumana, VZ	Cumana, VZ
58	McNeely, Jeff	R	R	6–2	190	10–18–69	Monroe, NC	Monroe, NC
	Nixon, Otis	S	R	6–2	180	1–9–59	Evergreen, NC	Alpharetta, GA
18	Quintana, Carlos	R	R	6–2	220	8–26–65	Estado Miranda, Ven.	Estado Miranda, Ven.
28	Zupcic, Bob	R	R	6–4	225	8–18–66	Pittsburgh, PA	Levittown, PA

Fenway Park (34,142, grass)

Tickets: 617–267–8661

Ticket prices:

- $20 (field box)
- $18 (roof box)
- $16 (RF roof box)
- $16 (upper box)
- $12 (grandstand)
- $8 (bleachers, standing room)

Field dimensions (from home plate)

- To left field at foul line, 315 feet
- To center field, 420 feet
- To right field at foul line, 302 feet

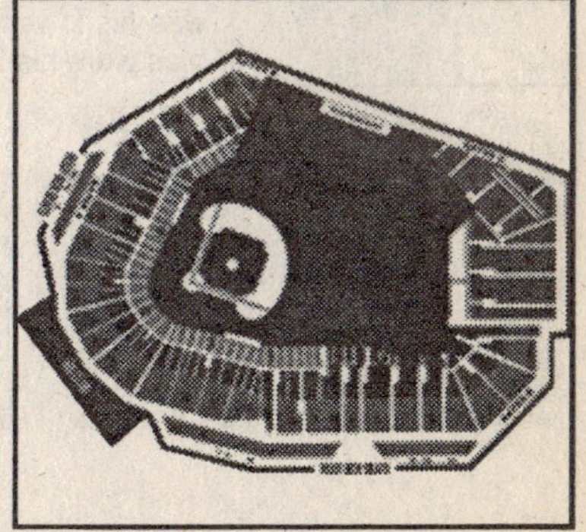

Scott Cooper No. 45/3B

Full name: Scott Kendrick Cooper
Bats: L **Throws:** R **HT:** 6–3 **WT:** 205
Born: 10–13–67, St. Louis, MO
High school: Pattonsville (St. Louis, MO)

Cooper replaced Wade Boggs at 3B, and posted a solid .279 BA. He tailed off, hitting .250 over his last 61 games. He made a team-high 26 errors.

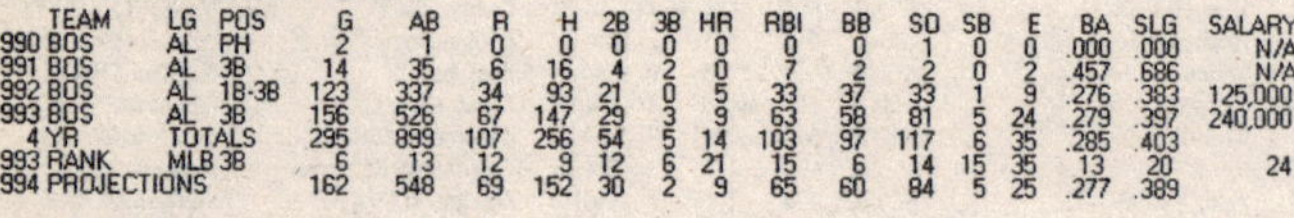

	TEAM	LG	POS	G	AB	R	H	2B	3B	HR	RBI	BB	SO	SB	E	BA	SLG	SALARY
1990	BOS	AL	PH	2	1	0	0	0	0	0	0	0	1	0	0	.000	.000	N/A
1991	BOS	AL	3B	14	35	6	16	4	2	0	7	2	2	0	2	.457	.686	N/A
1992	BOS	AL	1B-3B	123	337	34	93	21	0	5	33	37	33	1	9	.276	.383	125,000
1993	BOS	AL	3B	156	526	67	147	29	3	9	63	58	81	5	24	.279	.397	240,000
4	YR	TOTALS		295	899	107	256	54	5	14	103	97	117	6	35	.285	.403	
1993	RANK	MLB	3B	6	13	12	9	12	6	21	15	6	14	15	35	13	20	24
1994	PROJECTIONS			162	548	69	152	30	2	9	65	60	84	5	25	.277	.389	

Andre Dawson No. 10/DH

Full name: Andre Nolan Dawson
Bats: R **Throws:** R **HT:** 6–3 **WT:** 197
Born: 7–10–54, Miami, FL
High school: Southwest Miami Senior (FL)
College: Florida A&M

Dawson had bursts of power, but his 13 HR was his lowest full-season total. His 29 doubles were his best since 1988.

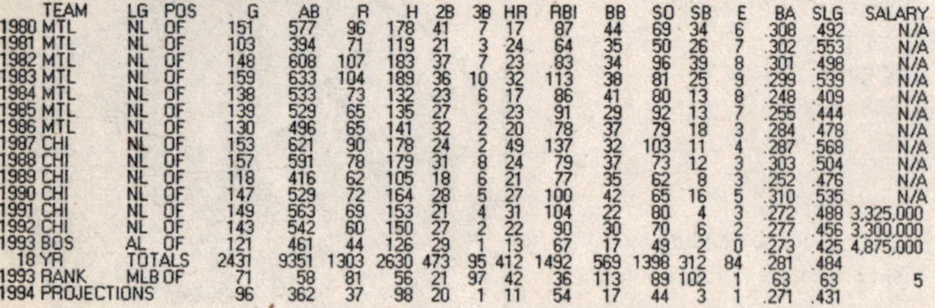

	TEAM	LG	POS	G	AB	R	H	2B	3B	HR	RBI	BB	SO	SB	E	BA	SLG	SALARY
1980	MTL	NL	OF	151	577	96	178	41	7	17	87	44	69	34	6	.308	.492	N/A
1981	MTL	NL	OF	103	394	71	119	21	3	24	64	35	50	26	7	.302	.553	N/A
1982	MTL	NL	OF	148	608	107	183	37	7	23	83	34	96	39	8	.301	.498	N/A
1983	MTL	NL	OF	159	633	104	189	36	10	32	113	38	81	25	9	.299	.539	N/A
1984	MTL	NL	OF	138	533	73	132	23	6	17	86	41	80	13	8	.248	.409	N/A
1985	MTL	NL	OF	139	529	65	135	27	2	23	91	29	92	13	7	.255	.444	N/A
1986	MTL	NL	OF	130	496	65	141	32	2	20	78	37	79	18	3	.284	.478	N/A
1987	CHI	NL	OF	153	621	90	178	24	2	49	137	32	103	11	4	.287	.568	N/A
1988	CHI	NL	OF	157	591	78	179	31	8	24	79	37	73	12	3	.303	.504	N/A
1989	CHI	NL	OF	118	416	62	105	18	6	21	77	35	62	8	3	.252	.476	N/A
1990	CHI	NL	OF	147	529	72	164	28	5	27	100	42	65	16	5	.310	.535	N/A
1991	CHI	NL	OF	149	563	69	153	21	4	31	104	22	80	4	3	.272	.488	3,325,000
1992	CHI	NL	OF	143	542	60	150	27	2	22	90	30	70	6	2	.277	.456	3,300,000
1993	BOS	AL	OF	121	461	44	126	29	1	13	67	17	49	2	0	.273	.425	4,875,000
18	YR	TOTALS		2431	9351	1303	2630	473	95	412	1492	569	1398	312	84	.281	.484	
1993	RANK	MLB	OF	71	58	81	56	21	97	42	36	113	89	102	1	63	63	5
1994	PROJECTIONS			96	362	37	98	20	1	11	54	17	44	3	1	.271	.431	

Scott Fletcher No. 5/2B

Full name: Scott Brian Fletcher
Bats: R **Throws:** R **HT:** 5–11 **WT:** 175
Born: 7–30–58, Fort Walton Beach, FL
High school: Wadsworth (OH)
College: Toledo (OH), Valencia JC (FL), and Georgia Southern

Fletcher struck out once per every 15.1 plate appearances, fifth best in the AL.

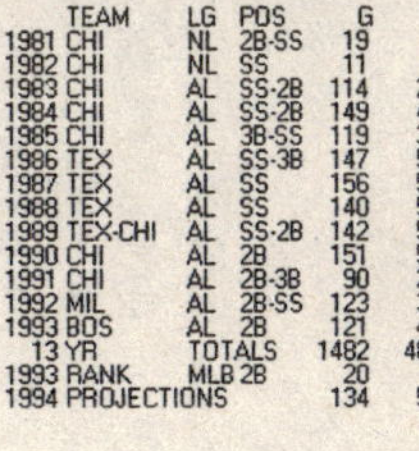

	TEAM	LG	POS	G	AB	R	H	2B	3B	HR	RBI	BB	SO	SB	E	BA	SLG	SALARY
1981	CHI	NL	2B-SS	19	46	6	10	4	0	0	1	2	4	0	3	.217	.304	N/A
1982	CHI	NL	SS	11	24	4	4	0	0	0	1	4	5	1	0	.167	.167	N/A
1983	CHI	AL	SS-2B	114	262	42	62	16	5	3	31	29	22	5	16	.237	.370	N/A
1984	CHI	AL	SS-2B	149	456	46	114	13	3	3	35	46	46	10	19	.250	.311	N/A
1985	CHI	AL	3B-SS	119	301	38	77	8	1	2	31	35	47	5	8	.256	.309	N/A
1986	TEX	AL	SS-3B	147	530	82	159	34	5	3	50	47	59	12	16	.300	.400	N/A
1987	TEX	AL	SS	156	588	82	169	28	4	5	63	61	66	13	23	.287	.374	N/A
1988	TEX	AL	SS	140	515	59	142	19	4	0	47	62	34	8	11	.276	.328	N/A
1989	TEX-CHI	AL	SS-2B	142	546	77	138	25	2	1	43	64	60	2	15	.253	.311	N/A
1990	CHI	AL	2B	151	509	54	123	18	3	4	56	45	63	1	9	.242	.312	N/A
1991	CHI	AL	2B-3B	90	248	14	51	10	1	1	28	17	26	0	3	.206	.266	1,300,000
1992	MIL	AL	2B-SS	123	386	53	106	18	3	3	51	30	33	17	9	.275	.360	200,000
1993	BOS	AL	2B	121	480	81	137	31	5	5	45	37	35	16	11	.285	.402	N/A
13	YR	TOTALS		1482	4891	638	1292	224	36	30	482	479	500	90	143	.264	.343	
1993	RANK	MLB	2B	20	16	7	13	4	7	17	17	18	35	9	24	12	16	43
1994	PROJECTIONS			134	513	72	139	25	3	2	45	54	43	8	12	.271	.345	

Mike Greenwell No. 39/OF

Full name: Michael Lewis Greenwell
Bats: L **Throws:** R **HT:** 6–0 **WT:** 205
Born: 7–18–63, Louisville, KY
High school: North Fort Myers (FL)

Bouncing back from injuries, Greenwell batted .315 (seventh in the AL), his best mark since 1988. He had only 19 RBI in his final 63 games.

	TEAM	LG	POS	G	AB	R	H	2B	3B	HR	RBI	BB	SO	SB	E	BA	SLG	SALARY
1985	BOS	AL	OF	17	31	7	10	1	0	4	8	3	4	1	0	.323	.742	N/A
1986	BOS	AL	OF	31	35	4	11	2	0	0	4	5	7	0	0	.314	.371	N/A
1987	BOS	AL	OF-C	125	412	71	135	31	6	19	89	35	40	5	6	.328	.570	N/A
1988	BOS	AL	OF	158	590	86	192	39	8	22	119	87	38	16	6	.325	.531	N/A
1989	BOS	AL	OF	145	578	87	178	36	0	14	95	56	44	13	8	.308	.443	N/A
1990	BOS	AL	OF	159	610	71	181	30	6	14	73	65	43	8	7	.297	.434	N/A
1991	BOS	AL	OF	147	544	76	163	26	6	9	83	43	35	15	3	.300	.419	2,550,000
1992	BOS	AL	OF	49	180	16	42	2	0	2	18	18	19	2	0	.233	.278	3,050,000
1993	BOS	AL	OF	146	540	77	170	38	6	13	72	54	46	5	2	.315	.480	3,425,000
9	YR	TOTALS		977	3520	495	1082	205	32	97	561	366	276	65	32	.307	.466	
1993	RANK	MLB	OF	27	28	33	13	7	13	42	28	31	94	78	26	9	30	19
1994	PROJECTIONS			138	510	78	161	35	4	15	85	48	43	7	5	.316	.490	

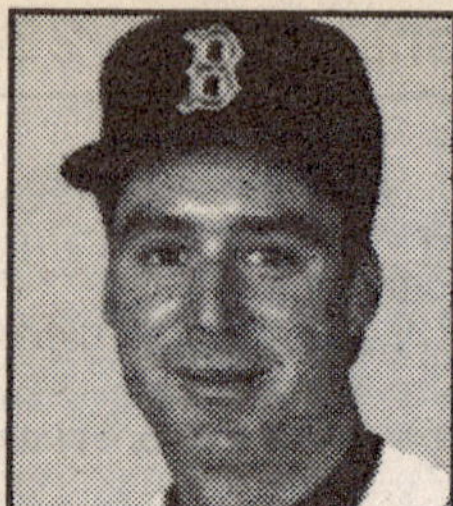

Bob Melvin — No. 3/C

Full name: Robert Paul Melvin
Bats: R **Throws:** R **HT:** 6–4 **WT:** 207
Born: 10–28–61, Palo Alto, CA
High school: Menlo–Atherton (CA)
College: Canada College (Redwood, CA)
Melvin's .222 BA was his worst since 1987. He made 50 starts at catcher for the Sox.

	TEAM	LG	POS	G	AB	R	H	2B	3B	HR	RBI	BB	SO	SB	E	BA	SLG	SALARY
1985	DET	AL	C	41	82	10	18	4	1	0	4	3	21	0	2	.220	.293	N/A
1986	SF	NL	C-3B	89	268	24	60	14	2	5	25	15	69	3	6	.224	.347	N/A
1987	SF	NL	C-1B	84	246	31	49	8	0	11	31	17	44	0	1	.199	.366	N/A
1988	SF	NL	C-1B	92	273	23	64	13	1	8	27	13	46	0	7	.234	.377	N/A
1989	BAL	AL	C	85	278	22	67	10	1	1	32	15	53	1	3	.241	.295	N/A
1990	BAL	AL	C-1B	93	301	30	73	14	1	5	37	11	53	0	1	.243	.346	N/A
1991	BAL	AL	C	79	228	11	57	10	0	1	23	11	46	0	1	.250	.307	650,000
1992	KC	AL	C-1B	32	70	5	22	5	0	0	6	5	13	0	1	.314	.386	900,000
1993	BOS	AL	C	77	176	13	39	7	0	3	23	7	44	0	2	.222	.313	725,000
9	YR	TOTALS		672	1922	169	449	85	6	34	208	97	389	4	24	.234	.337	
1993	RANK	MLB	C	33	39	41	39	39	25	35	35	40	23	35	36	36	36	18
1994	PROJECTIONS			50	109	9	26	5	0	1	11	5	26	0	1	.239	.321	

Otis Nixon — OF

Full name: Otis Junior Nixon
Bats: B **Throws:** R **HT:** 6–2 **WT:** 180
Born: 1–9–59, Evergreen, NC
High school: Columbus (NC)
College: Louisburg (NC))
Nixon was signed in the off-season as a free-agent. Boston expects Nixon to add much-needed speed at the top of the lineup.

	TEAM	LG	POS	G	AB	R	H	2B	3B	HR	RBI	BB	SO	SB	E	BA	SLG	SALARY
1983	NY	AL	OF	13	14	2	2	0	0	0	0	1	5	2	1	.143	.143	N/A
1984	CLE	AL	OF	49	91	16	14	0	0	0	1	8	11	12	0	.154	.154	N/A
1985	CLE	AL	OF	104	162	34	38	4	0	3	9	8	27	20	4	.235	.315	N/A
1986	CLE	AL	OF	105	95	33	25	4	1	0	8	13	12	23	3	.263	.326	N/A
1987	CLE	AL	OF	19	17	2	1	0	0	0	1	3	4	2	0	.059	.059	N/A
1988	MTL	NL	OF	90	271	47	66	8	2	0	15	28	42	46	1	.244	.288	N/A
1989	MTL	NL	OF	126	258	41	56	7	2	0	21	33	36	37	2	.217	.260	N/A
1990	MTL	NL	OF-SS	119	231	46	58	6	2	1	20	28	33	50	1	.251	.307	N/A
1991	ATL	NL	OF	124	401	81	119	10	1	0	26	47	40	72	3	.297	.327	585,000
1992	ATL	NL	OF	120	456	79	134	14	2	2	22	39	54	41	3	.294	.346	735,000
1993	ATL	NL	OF	134	461	77	124	12	3	1	24	61	63	47	3	.269	.315	2,815,000
11	YR	TOTALS		1003	2457	458	637	65	13	7	147	269	327	352	21	.259	.305	
1993	RANK	MLB	OF	54	58	33	58	96	54	122	113	23	64	7	72	71	126	27
1994	PROJECTIONS			116	377	68	103	10	2	0	21	45	48	55	2	.273	.313	

Carlos Quintana No. 18/OF

Full name: Carlos Narcis Quintana
Bats: R **Throws:** R **HT:** 6–2 **WT:** 220
Born: 8–26–65, Estado Miranda, VZ
High school: Mamparal Miranda (VZ)

Back after missing all of 1992, Quintana slumped to a lowly .244 BA. He batted only .226 away from Fenway.

	TEAM	LG	POS	G	AB	R	H	2B	3B	HR	RBI	BB	SO	SB	E	BA	SLG	SALARY
1988	BOS	AL	OF	5	6	1	2	0	0	0	2	2	3	0	0	.333	.333	N/A
1989	BOS	AL	OF-1B	34	77	6	16	5	0	0	6	7	12	0	2	.208	.273	N/A
1990	BOS	AL	1B-OF	149	512	56	147	28	0	7	67	52	74	1	17	.287	.383	N/A
1991	BOS	AL	1B-OF	149	478	69	141	21	1	11	71	61	66	1	9	.295	.412	285,000
1993	BOS	AL	1B	101	303	31	74	5	0	1	19	31	52	1	3	.244	.271	340,000
5	YR	TOTALS		438	1376	163	380	59	1	19	165	153	207	3	31	.276	.362	
1993	RANK	MLB	1B	32	30	35	32	40	30	41	40	31	28	27	30	36	41	25
1994	PROJECTIONS			46	128	12	30	3	0	0	9	13	22	0	1	.234	.273	

John Valentin No. 13/SS

Full name: John William Valentin
Bats: R **Throws:** R **HT:** 6–0 **WT:** 180
Born: 2–18–67, Jersey City, NJ
High school: St. Anthony's (Jersey City, NJ)
College: Seton Hall (South Orange, NJ)

Valentin's team-high 40 doubles tied him for third in the AL. His 20 errors were the second most by an AL shortstop.

	TEAM	LG	POS	G	AB	R	H	2B	3B	HR	RBI	BB	SO	SB	E	BA	SLG	SALARY
1992	BOS	AL	SS	58	185	21	51	13	0	5	25	20	17	1	10	.276	.427	109,000
1993	BOS	AL	SS	144	468	50	130	40	3	11	66	49	77	3	20	.278	.447	N/A
2	YR	TOTALS		202	653	71	181	53	3	16	91	69	94	4	30	.277	.441	
1993	RANK	MLB	SS	13	17	19	16	1	12	5	5	13	8	29	7	18	3	36
1994	PROJECTIONS			162	527	55	146	45	3	12	74	54	92	3	21	.277	.442	

Mo Vaughn No. 42/1B

Full name: Maurice Samuel Vaughn
Bats: L **Throws:** R **HT:** 6–1 **WT:** 225
Born: 12–15–67, Norwalk, CT
High school: Trinity Pawling (Pawling, NY)
College: Seton Hall (South Orange, NJ)

Vaughn led the team in HR (29), RBI (101), and walks (79). He batted .351 with runners in scoring position and hit .332 at Fenway.

	TEAM	LG	POS	G	AB	R	H	2B	3B	HR	RBI	BB	SO	SB	E	BA	SLG	SALARY
1991	BOS	AL	1B	74	219	21	57	12	0	4	32	26	43	2	6	.260	.370	100,000
1992	BOS	AL	1B	113	355	42	83	16	2	13	57	47	67	3	15	.234	.400	155,000
1993	BOS	AL	1B	152	539	86	160	34	1	29	101	79	130	4	16	.297	.525	290,000
3	YR	TOTALS		339	1113	149	300	62	3	46	190	152	240	9	37	.270	.455	
1993	RANK	MLB	1B	10	11	7	11	8	20	6	6	7	2	11	4	11	7	26
1994	PROJECTIONS			162	587	97	176	37	0	33	112	87	144	3	17	.300	.532	

Roger Clemens No. 21/P

Full name: William Roger Clemens
Bats: R **Throws:** R **HT:** 6–4 **WT:** 220
Born: 8–4–62, Dayton, OH
High school: Spring Woods (Houston, TX)
College: Texas

Clemens suffered through his first sub-.500 season. He's still had 7.5 K–9 IP, fourth best in the AL, racking up a total of 160.

	TM	LG	POS	W	L	ERA	G	GS	CG	SH	SV	IP	H	R	ER	HR	BB	SO	SALARY
1984	BOS	AL	P	9	4	4.32	21	20	5	1	0	133.1	146	67	64	13	29	126	N/A
1985	BOS	AL	P	7	5	3.29	15	15	3	1	0	98.1	83	38	36	5	37	74	N/A
1986	BOS	AL	P	24	4	2.48	33	33	10	1	0	254.0	179	77	70	21	67	238	N/A
1987	BOS	AL	P	20	9	2.97	36	36	18	7	0	281.2	248	100	93	19	83	256	N/A
1988	BOS	AL	P	18	12	2.93	35	35	14	8	0	264.0	217	93	86	17	62	291	N/A
1989	BOS	AL	P	17	11	3.13	35	35	8	3	0	253.1	215	101	88	20	93	230	N/A
1990	BOS	AL	P	21	6	1.93	31	31	7	4	0	228.1	193	59	49	7	54	209	N/A
1991	BOS	AL	P	18	10	2.62	35	35	13	4	0	271.1	219	93	79	15	65	241	2,600,000
1992	BOS	AL	P	18	11	2.41	32	32	11	5	0	246.2	203	80	66	11	62	208	4,555,250
1993	BOS	AL	P	11	14	4.46	29	29	2	1	0	191.2	175	99	95	17	67	160	4,655,250
10	YR	TOTALS		163	86	2.94	302	301	91	35	0	2222.2	1878	807	726	145	619	2033	
1993	Rank	MLB	Ps	59		186	213	65	57	23	102	54	75	160		128	131	52	9
1994	PROJECTIONS			9	7	4.18	21	21	3	1	0	140	134	68	65	11	44	120	

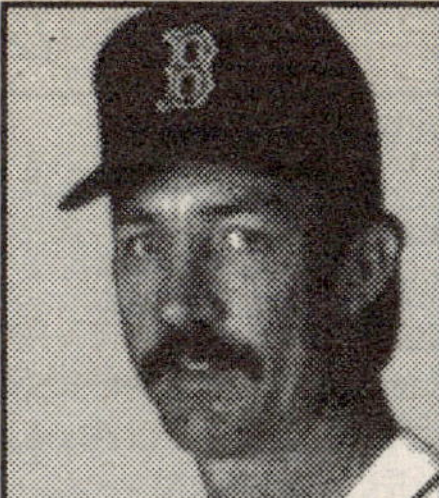

Danny Darwin No. 44/P

Full name: Danny Wayne Darwin
Bats: R **Throws:** R **HT:** 6–3 **WT:** 205
Born: 10–25–55, Bonham, TX
High school: Bonham (TX)
College: Grayson County (Denison, TX)

Darwin set career-highs in wins and IP and was ninth in the AL in ERA (3.26). He also gave up 31 HR, third most in the AL.

	TM	LG	POS	W	L	ERA	G	GS	CG	SH	SV	IP	H	R	ER	HR	BB	SO	SALARY
1982	TEX	AL	P	10	8	3.44	56	1	0	0	7	89.0	95	38	34	6	37	61	N/A
1983	TEX	AL	P	8	13	3.49	28	26	9	2	0	183.0	175	86	71	9	62	92	N/A
1984	TEX	AL	P	8	12	3.94	35	32	5	1	0	223.2	249	110	98	19	54	123	N/A
1985	MIL	AL	P	8	18	3.80	39	29	11	1	2	217.2	212	112	92	34	65	125	N/A
1986	MIL	AL	P	6	8	3.52	27	14	5	1	0	130.1	120	62	51	13	35	80	N/A
1986	HOU	NL	P	5	2	2.32	12	8	1	1	0	54.1	50	19	14	3	9	40	N/A
1987	HOU	NL	P	9	10	3.59	33	30	3	0	0	195.2	184	87	78	17	69	134	N/A
1988	HOU	NL	P	8	13	3.84	44	20	3	0	3	192.0	189	86	82	20	48	129	N/A
1989	HOU	NL	P	11	4	2.36	68	0	0	0	7	122.0	92	34	32	8	33	104	N/A
1990	HOU	NL	P	11	4	2.21	48	17	3	0	2	162.2	136	42	40	11	31	109	N/A
1991	BOS	AL	P	3	6	5.16	12	12	0	0	0	68.0	71	39	39	15	15	42	N/A
1992	BOS	AL	P	9	9	3.96	51	15	2	0	3	161.1	159	76	71	11	53	124	3,250,000
1993	BOS	AL	P	15	11	3.26	34	34	2	1	0	229.1	196	93	83	31	49	130	2,750,000
16	YR	TOTALS		138	135	3.47	585	269	51	9	32	2371.2	2202	1028	915	218	698	1561	
1993	Rank	MLB Ps		21		66	145	12	57	23	102	20	42	60		241	25	193	40
1994	PROJECTIONS			15	11	3.24	35	36	2	1	0	242	207	98	87	32	52	137	

Frank Viola No. 16/P

Full name: Frank John Viola, Jr.
Bats: L **Throws:** L **HT:** 6–4 **WT:** 210
Born: 4–19–60, East Meadow, NY
High school: East Meadow (NY)
College: St. John's (Jamaica, NY)

Viola was 6–0 with a 2.24 ERA in his final 11 starts. He gave up only 2 HR at Fenway.

	TM	LG	POS	W	L	ERA	G	GS	CG	SH	SV	IP	H	R	ER	HR	BB	SO	SALARY
1982	MIN	AL	P	4	10	5.21	22	22	3	1	0	126.0	152	77	73	22	38	84	N/A
1983	MIN	AL	P	7	15	5.49	35	34	4	0	0	210.0	242	141	128	34	92	127	N/A
1984	MIN	AL	P	18	12	3.21	35	35	10	4	0	257.2	225	101	92	28	73	149	N/A
1985	MIN	AL	P	18	14	4.09	36	36	9	0	0	250.2	262	136	114	26	68	135	N/A
1986	MIN	AL	P	16	13	4.51	37	37	7	1	0	245.2	257	136	123	37	83	191	N/A
1987	MIN	AL	P	17	10	2.90	36	36	7	1	0	251.2	230	91	81	29	66	197	N/A
1988	MIN	AL	P	24	7	2.64	35	35	7	2	0	255.1	236	80	75	20	54	193	N/A
1989	MIN	AL	P	8	12	3.79	24	24	7	1	0	175.2	171	80	74	17	47	138	N/A
1989	NY	NL	P	5	5	3.38	12	12	2	1	0	85.1	75	35	32	5	27	73	N/A
1990	NY	NL	P	20	12	2.67	35	35	7	3	0	249.2	227	83	74	15	60	182	N/A
1991	NY	NL	P	13	15	3.97	35	35	3	0	0	231.1	259	112	102	25	54	132	3,166,667
1992	BOS	AL	P	13	12	3.44	35	35	6	1	0	238.0	214	99	91	13	89	121	4,733,333
1993	BOS	AL	P	11	8	3.14	29	29	2	1	0	183.2	180	76	64	12	72	91	4,833,333
12	YR	TOTALS		174	145	3.66	406	405	74	16	0	2760.2	2730	1247	1123	283	823	1813	
1993	Rank	MLB Ps		59		57	213	65	57	23	102	68	117	65		57	174	240	8
1994	PROJECTIONS			7	10	3.91	25	25	4	1	0	161	167	77	70	17	52	104	

Jeff Russell No. 24/P

Full name: Jeffrey Lee Russell
Bats: R **Throws:** R **HT:** 6–3 **WT:** 205
Born: 9–2–61, Cincinnati, OH
High school: Wyoming (Cincinnati, OH)
College: Gulf Coast Community (FL)

Russell registered 33 saves (his best since 1987, seventh-best in the AL) in 37 chances, and he allowed only 1 HR in 46.2 IP.

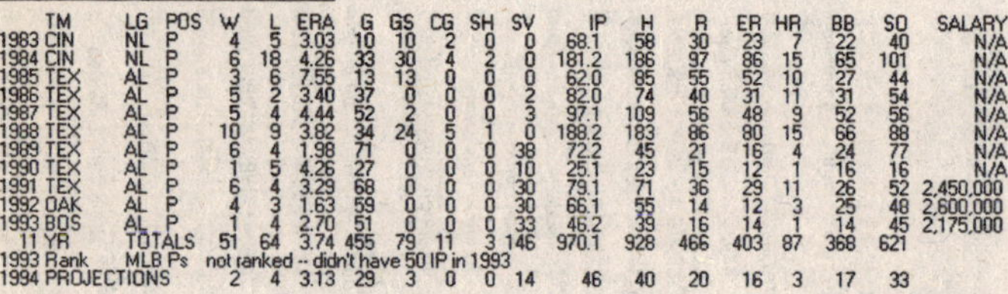

TM	LG	POS	W	L	ERA	G	GS	CG	SH	SV	IP	H	R	ER	HR	BB	SO	SALARY
1983 CIN	NL	P	4	5	3.03	10	10	2	0	0	68.1	58	30	23	7	22	40	N/A
1984 CIN	NL	P	6	18	4.26	33	30	4	2	0	181.2	186	97	86	15	65	101	N/A
1985 TEX	AL	P	3	6	7.55	13	13	0	0	0	62.0	85	55	52	10	27	44	N/A
1986 TEX	AL	P	5	2	3.40	37	0	0	0	2	82.0	74	40	31	11	31	54	N/A
1987 TEX	AL	P	5	4	4.44	52	2	0	0	3	97.1	109	56	48	9	52	56	N/A
1988 TEX	AL	P	10	9	3.82	34	24	5	1	0	188.2	183	86	80	15	66	88	N/A
1989 TEX	AL	P	6	4	1.98	71	0	0	0	38	72.2	45	21	16	4	24	77	N/A
1990 TEX	AL	P	1	5	4.26	27	0	0	0	10	25.1	23	15	12	1	16	16	N/A
1991 TEX	AL	P	6	4	3.29	68	0	0	0	30	79.1	71	36	29	11	26	52	2,450,000
1992 OAK	AL	P	4	3	1.63	59	0	0	0	30	66.1	55	14	12	3	25	48	2,600,000
1993 BOS	AL	P	1	4	2.70	51	0	0	0	33	46.2	39	16	14	1	14	45	2,175,000
11 YR	TOTALS		51	64	3.74	455	79	11	3	146	970.1	928	466	403	87	368	621	
1993 Rank	MLB Ps	not ranked -- didn't have 50 IP in 1993																
1994 PROJECTIONS			2	4	3.13	29	3	0	0	14	46	40	20	16	3	17	33	

Butch Hobson No. 17/Mgr.

Full name: Clell Lavern Hobson, Jr.
Bats: R **Throws:** R **HT:** 6–1 **WT:** 190
Born: 8–17–51, Tuscaloosa, AL
High school: Bessemer (AL)
College: Alabama

Hobson got Boston out to a surprisingly fast start last season, but the Red Sox sagged in mid season, going 3–15 between June 1–20.

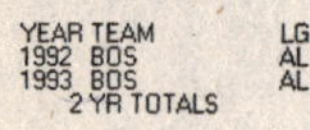
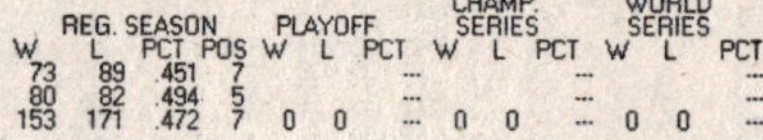

		REG. SEASON				PLAYOFF			CHAMP. SERIES			WORLD SERIES		
YEAR TEAM	LG	W	L	PCT	POS	W	L	PCT	W	L	PCT	W	L	PCT
1992 BOS	AL	73	89	.451	7			---			---			---
1993 BOS	AL	80	82	.494	5			---			---			---
2 YR TOTALS		153	171	.472	7	0	0	---	0	0	---	0	0	---

Scott Bankhead No. 29/P

Full name: Michael Scott Bankhead
Bats: R **Throws:** R **HT:** 5–10 **WT:** 185
Born: 7–31–63, Raleigh, NC
High school: Reidsville (NC)
College: North Carolina
Bankhead held 15 of 19 leads or ties.

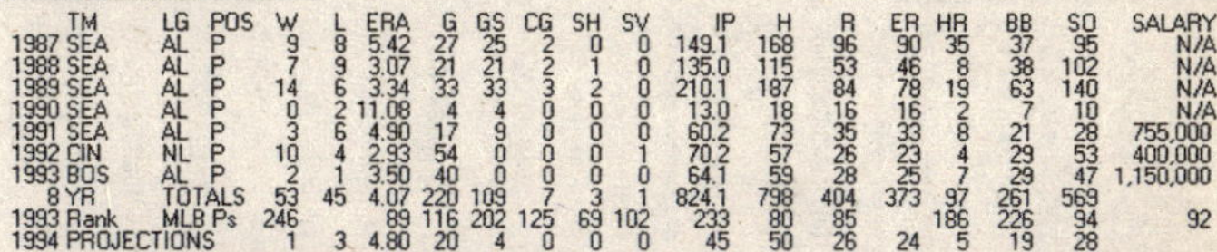

TM	LG	POS	W	L	ERA	G	GS	CG	SH	SV	IP	H	R	ER	HR	BB	SO	SALARY
1987 SEA	AL	P	9	8	5.42	27	25	2	0	0	149.1	168	96	90	35	37	95	N/A
1988 SEA	AL	P	7	9	3.07	21	21	2	1	0	135.0	115	53	46	8	38	102	N/A
1989 SEA	AL	P	14	6	3.34	33	33	3	2	0	210.1	187	84	78	19	63	140	N/A
1990 SEA	AL	P	0	2	11.08	4	4	0	0	0	13.0	18	16	16	2	7	10	N/A
1991 SEA	AL	P	3	6	4.90	17	9	0	0	0	60.2	73	35	33	8	21	28	755,000
1992 CIN	NL	P	10	4	2.93	54	0	0	0	1	70.2	57	26	23	4	29	53	400,000
1993 BOS	AL	P	2	1	3.50	40	0	0	0	0	64.1	59	28	25	7	29	47	1,150,000
8 YR	TOTALS		53	45	4.07	220	109	7	3	1	824.1	798	404	373	97	261	569	
1993 Rank	MLB Ps		246		89	116	202	125	69	102	233	80	85		186	226	94	92
1994 PROJECTIONS			1	3	4.80	20	4	0	0	0	45	50	26	24	5	19	28	

Greg Blosser No. 38/OF

Full name: Gregory Brent Blosser
Bats: L **Throws:** L **HT:** 6–3 **WT:** 200
Born: 6–26–71, Bradenton, FL
High school: Sarasota (FL)
Blosser led AAA Pawtucket with 23 HR, but had only 2 hits in 17 games with Boston.

TEAM	LG	POS	G	AB	R	H	2B	3B	HR	RBI	BB	SO	SB	E	BA	SLG	SALARY
1993 BOS	AL	OF	17	28	1	2	1	0	0	1	2	7	1	0	.071	.107	155,000
1 YR	TOTAL		17	28	1	2	1	0	0	1	2	7	1	0	.071	.107	
1993 RANK	MLB OF		not ranked -- didn't have 150 ABs in 1993														

John Flaherty No. 15/C

Full name: John Timothy Flaherty
Bats: R **Throws:** R **HT:** 6–1 **WT:** 195
Born: 10–21–67, New York, NY
High school: St. Joseph's Reg. (Montvale, NJ)
College: George Washington (Washington, DC)
Flaherty hit .271 with 22 doubles at Pawtucket.

TEAM	LG	POS	G	AB	R	H	2B	3B	HR	RBI	BB	SO	SB	E	BA	SLG	SALARY
1992 BOS	AL	C	35	66	3	13	2	0	0	2	3	7	0	2	.197	.227	N/A
1993 BOS	AL	C	13	25	3	3	2	0	0	2	2	6	0	0	.120	.200	N/A
2 YR	TOTALS		48	91	6	16	4	0	0	4	5	13	0	2	.176	.220	
1993 RANK	MLB C		not ranked -- didn't have 150 ABs in 1993														
1994 PROJECTIONS			32	60	4	10	2	0	0	2	3	8	0	1	.167	.217	

Tony Fossas — No. 49/P

Full name: Emilio Antonio Fossas
Bats: L **Throws:** L **HT:** 6–0 **WT:** 197
Born: 9–23–67, Havana, CU
High school: St. Mary's (Brookline, MA)
College: South Florida (Tampa, FL)
Fossas held first batters to a .200 BA.

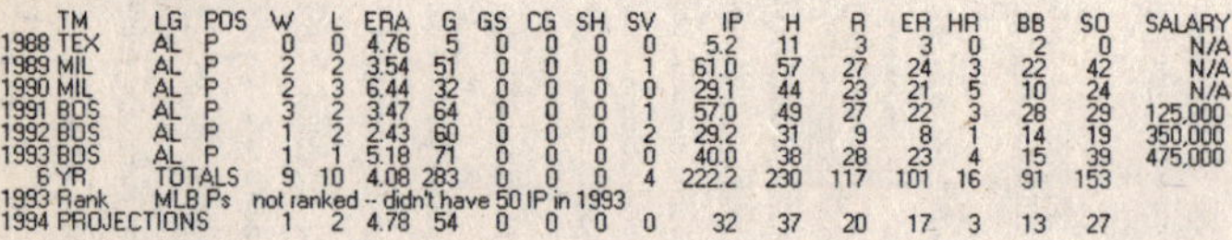

TM	LG	POS	W	L	ERA	G	GS	CG	SH	SV	IP	H	R	ER	HR	BB	SO	SALARY
1988 TEX	AL	P	0	0	4.76	5	0	0	0	0	5.2	11	3	3	0	2	0	N/A
1989 MIL	AL	P	2	2	3.54	51	0	0	0	1	61.0	57	27	24	3	22	42	N/A
1990 MIL	AL	P	2	3	6.44	32	0	0	0	0	29.1	44	23	21	5	10	24	N/A
1991 BOS	AL	P	3	2	3.47	64	0	0	0	1	57.0	49	27	22	3	28	29	125,000
1992 BOS	AL	P	1	2	2.43	60	0	0	0	2	29.2	31	9	8	1	14	19	350,000
1993 BOS	AL	P	1	1	5.18	71	0	0	0	0	40.0	38	28	23	4	15	39	475,000
6 YR	TOTALS		9	10	4.08	283	0	0	0	4	222.2	230	117	101	16	91	153	
1993 Rank	MLB Ps		not ranked -- didn't have 50 IP in 1993															
1994 PROJECTIONS			1	2	4.78	54	0	0	0	0	32	37	20	17	3	13	27	

Greg Harris — No. 27/P

Full name: Gregory Allen Harris
Bats: S **Throws:** R **HT:** 6–0 **WT:** 175
Born: 11–2–55, Lynwood, CA
High school: Los Alamitos (CA)
College: Long Beach City (CA)
Harris' 80 appearances set a new Red Sox record.

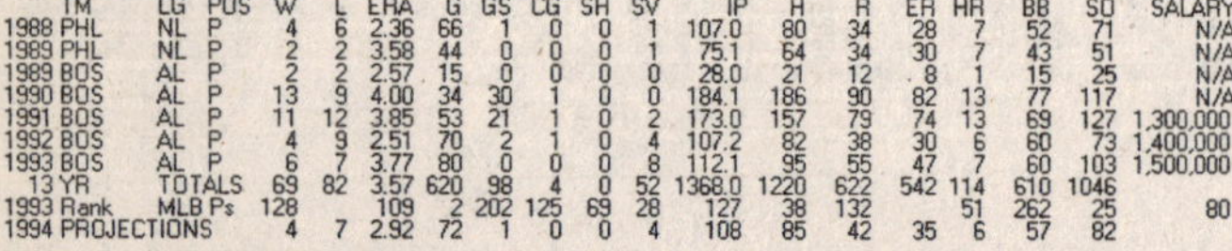

TM	LG	POS	W	L	ERA	G	GS	CG	SH	SV	IP	H	R	ER	HR	BB	SO	SALARY
1988 PHL	NL	P	4	6	2.36	66	1	0	0	1	107.0	80	34	28	7	52	71	N/A
1989 PHL	NL	P	2	2	3.58	44	0	0	0	1	75.1	64	34	30	7	43	51	N/A
1989 BOS	AL	P	2	2	2.57	15	0	0	0	0	28.0	21	12	8	1	15	25	N/A
1990 BOS	AL	P	13	9	4.00	34	30	1	0	0	184.1	186	90	82	13	77	117	N/A
1991 BOS	AL	P	11	12	3.85	53	21	1	0	2	173.0	157	79	74	13	69	127	1,300,000
1992 BOS	AL	P	4	9	2.51	70	2	1	0	4	107.2	82	38	30	6	60	73	1,400,000
1993 BOS	AL	P	6	7	3.77	80	0	0	0	8	112.1	95	55	47	7	60	103	1,500,000
13 YR	TOTALS		69	82	3.57	620	98	4	0	52	1368.0	1220	622	542	114	610	1046	
1993 Rank	MLB Ps		128		109	2	202	125	69	28	127	38	132		51	262	25	80
1994 PROJECTIONS			4	7	2.92	72	1	0	0	4	108	85	42	35	6	57	82	

Billy Hatcher — No. 22/OF

Full name: William Augustus Hatcher
Bats: R **Throws:** R **HT:** 5–10 **WT:** 190
Born: 10–4–60, Williams, AZ
High school: Williams (AZ)
College: Yavapai Community (Prescott, AZ)
Hatcher only hit .248 after the All-Star break.

TEAM	LG	POS	G	AB	R	H	2B	3B	HR	RBI	BB	SO	SB	E	BA	SLG	SALARY
1988 HOU	NL		145	530	79	142	25	4	7	52	37	56	32	5	.268	.370	N/A
1989 HOU-PIT	NL		135	481	59	111	19	3	4	51	30	62	24	2	.231	.308	N/A
1990 CIN	NL	OF	139	504	68	139	28	5	5	25	33	42	30	1	.276	.381	N/A
1991 CIN	NL	OF	138	442	45	116	25	3	4	41	26	55	11	5	.262	.360	1,200,000
1992 CIN	NL	OF	43	94	10	27	3	0	2	10	5	11	0	1	.287	.383	1,600,000
1992 BOS	AL	OF	75	315	37	75	16	2	1	23	17	41	4	5	.238	.311	N/A
1993 BOS	AL	OF	136	508	71	146	24	3	9	57	28	46	14	2	.287	.400	1,000,000
10 YR	TOTALS		1140	4029	534	1072	195	28	51	368	249	447	210	30	.266	.366	
1993 RANK	MLB OF		50	39	45	34	38	54	64	50	71	94	48	97	41	82	58
1994 PROJECTIONS			140	514	72	142	25	4	7	44	32	48	25	2	.276	.383	

Joe Hesketh — No. 55/P

Full name: Joseph Thomas Hesketh
Bats: L **Throws:** L **HT:** 6–2 **WT:** 173
Born: 2–15–59, Lackawanna, NY
High school: Central (Hamburg, NY)
College: Buffalo (NY)
Hesketh was 2–1 with a 2.81 ERA in relief.

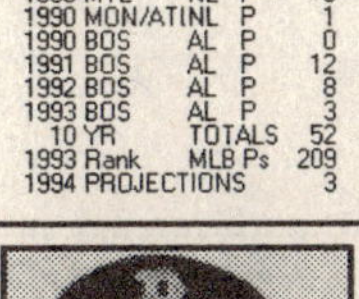
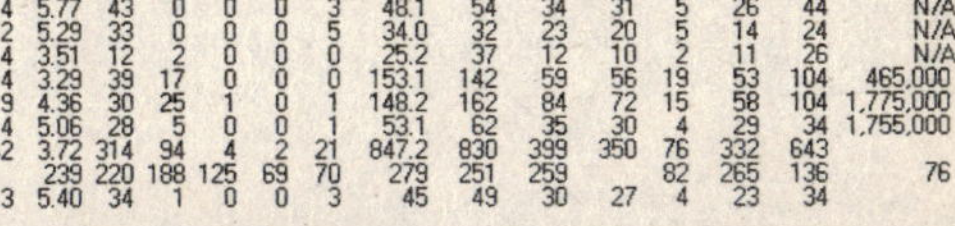

	TM	LG	POS	W	L	ERA	G	GS	CG	SH	SV	IP	H	R	ER	HR	BB	SO	SALARY
1988	MTL	NL	P	4	3	2.85	60	0	0	0	9	72.2	63	30	23	1	35	64	N/A
1989	MTL	NL	P	6	4	5.77	43	0	0	0	3	48.1	54	34	31	5	26	44	N/A
1990	MON/ATI	NL	P	1	2	5.29	33	0	0	0	5	34.0	32	23	20	5	14	24	N/A
1990	BOS	AL	P	0	4	3.51	12	2	0	0	0	25.2	37	12	10	2	11	26	N/A
1991	BOS	AL	P	12	4	3.29	39	17	0	0	0	153.1	142	59	56	19	53	104	465,000
1992	BOS	AL	P	8	9	4.36	30	25	1	0	1	148.2	162	84	72	15	58	104	1,775,000
1993	BOS	AL	P	3	4	5.06	28	5	0	0	1	53.1	62	35	30	4	29	34	1,755,000
10	YR	TOTALS		52	42	3.72	314	94	4	2	21	847.2	830	399	350	76	332	643	
1993	Rank	MLB Ps		209		239	220	188	125	69	70	279	251	259		82	265	136	76
1994	PROJECTIONS			3	3	5.40	34	1	0	0	3	45	49	30	27	4	23	34	

Jeff McNeely — No. 58/OF

Full name: Jeffrey Lavern McNeely
Bats: R **Throws:** R **HT:** 6–2 **WT:** 190
Born: 10–18–69, Monroe, NC
High school: Monroe (NC)
College: Spartanburg Methodist (SC)
McNeely had six SB in 21 games for Boston.

	TEAM	LG	POS	G	AB	R	H	2B	3B	HR	RBI	BB	SO	SB	E	BA	SLG	SALARY
1993	BOS	AL	OF	21	37	10	11	1	1	0	1	7	9	6	2	.297	.378	N/A
1	YR	TOTAL		21	37	10	11	1	1	0	1	7	9	6	2	.297	.378	
1993	RANK	MLB	OF	not ranked -- didn't have 150 ABs in 1993														

Tim Naehring — No. 11/IF

Full name: Timothy James Naehring
Bats: R **Throws:** R **HT:** 6–2 **WT:** 205
Born: 2–1–67, Cincinnati, OH
High school: LaSalle (Cincinnati, OH)
College: Miami (Oxford, OH)
In 30 starts at four positions, Naehring hit .337.

	TEAM	LG	POS	G	AB	R	H	2B	3B	HR	RBI	BB	SO	SB	E	BA	SLG	SALARY
1990	BOS	AL	SS-3B	24	85	10	23	6	0	2	12	8	15	0	9	.271	.412	N/A
1991	BOS	AL	SS-3B	20	55	1	6	1	0	0	3	6	15	0	3	.109	.127	125,000
1992	BOS	AL	SS-2B	72	186	12	43	8	0	3	14	18	31	0	3	.231	.323	130,000
1993	BOS	AL	2B	39	127	14	42	10	0	1	17	10	26	1	2	.331	.433	200,000
4	YR	TOTALS		155	453	37	114	25	0	6	46	42	87	1	17	.252	.347	
1993	RANK	MLB	2B	not ranked -- didn't have 150 ABs in 1993														
1994	PROJECTIONS			27	89	8	23	5	0	1	10	8	18	0	4	.258	.360	

Paul Quantrill — No. 49/P

Full name: Paul John Quantrill
Bats: L **Throws:** R **HT:** 6–1 **WT:** 185
Born: 11–3–68, London, Ont.
High school: Okemos (MI)
College: Wisconsin
Only five of the 36 runners he inherited scored.

TM	LG	POS	W	L	ERA	G	GS	CG	SH	SV	IP	H	R	ER	HR	BB	SO	SALARY
1993 BOS	AL	P	6	12	3.91	49	14	1	1	1	138.0	151	73	60	13	44	66	150,000
1992 BOS	AL	P	2	3	2.19	27	0	0	0	1	49.1	55	18	12	1	15	24	109,000
2 YR	TOTALS		8	15	3.46	76	14	1	1	2	187.1	206	91	72	14	59	90	
1993 Rank	MLB	Ps	128		127	84	137	79	23	70	109	208	170		144	94	248	195
1994 PROJECTIONS			8	16	4.15	60	21	1	1	1	182	199	100	84	19	58	87	

Aaron Sele — No. 34/P

Full name: Aaron Helmer Sele
Bats: R **Throws:** R **HT:** 6–5 **WT:** 205
Born: 6–25–70, Golden Valley, MN
High school: North Kitsap (WA)
College: Washington State
Sele won his first six major league decisions.

TM	LG	POS	W	L	ERA	G	GS	CG	SH	SV	IP	H	R	ER	HR	BB	SO	SALARY
1993 BOS	AL	P	7	2	2.74	18	18	0	0	0	111.2	100	42	34	5	48	93	109,000
1 YR	TOTAL		7	2	2.74	18	18	0	0	0	111.2	100	42	34	5	48	93	
1993 Rank	MLB	Ps	108		25	261	111	125	69	102	128	64	39		20	206	53	236

Bob Zupcic — No. 28/OF

Full name: Robert Zupcic
Bats: R **Throws:** R **HT:** 6–4 **WT:** 225
Born: 8–18–66, Pittsburgh, PA
High school: Bishop Egan (Fairless Hills, PA)
College: Oral Roberts (Tulsa, OK)
Utilityman Zupcic hit .279 at Fenway.

TEAM	LG	POS	G	AB	R	H	2B	3B	HR	RBI	BB	SO	SB	E	BA	SLG	SALARY
1991 BOS	AL	OF	18	25	3	4	0	0	1	3	1	6	0	2	.160	.280	N/A
1992 BOS	AL	OF	124	392	46	108	19	1	3	43	25	60	2	6	.276	.352	109,000
1993 BOS	AL	OF	141	286	40	69	24	2	2	26	27	54	5	4	.241	.360	222,000
3 YR	TOTALS		283	703	89	181	43	3	6	72	53	120	7	12	.257	.353	
1993 RANK	MLB	OF	38	90	90	95	38	76	114	105	75	79	78	59	111	108	103
1994 PROJECTIONS			94	234	29	60	14	1	2	24	17	40	2	4	.256	.350	

California ANGELS

1994 Scouting Report

Hitting: (1993/.264 BA, twelfth in AL; 114 HR, thirteenth in AL)

The Angles have lots of young hitters who should only get better in '94. Tim Salmon was AL rookie of the year, hitting .283 with 31 HR, 95 RBI, and 93 runs scored. Damion Easley, another budding star, hit .313 for California. Chad Curtis hit .285. Chili Davis' 27 HR and 112 RBI was a pleasant surprise. California needs another big RBI producer in the middle of the lineup, but J.T. Snow could fill that role in '94; he hit 16 HR in 129 games in '93. Chris Turner, Eduardo Perez, and Rod Correia are young players that the Angels are counting on for the team's future.

Pitching: (1993/4.34 ERA, eighth in AL)

California has two of the best starting pitchers in baseball in Chuck Finley (16–14, 3.15 ERA, 187 SO) and Mark Langston (16–11, 3.20 ERA, 196 SO). The starters dropped off in quality after Langston. California picked up Joe Magrane last season and hope he can return to his St. Louis-form. Phil Leftwich is a young pitcher with a bright future; he had a 3.79 ERA in 12 starts last season.

The Angels have a bullpen by committee, with Mike Butcher (2.86 ERA, 8 saves, 10 opportunities), Joe Grahe (2.86 ERA, 11 saves, 13 opportunities), and Steve Frey (2.98 ERA, 13 saves, 16 opportunities).

Defense: (1993/.980 pct., ninth in AL)

Gary DiSarcina ranked fifth in the AL among shortstops with a .975 fielding percentage. And J.T. Snow's .996 fielding percentage ranked sixth among AL first basemen.

1994 Prospects:

The AL West is up for grabs among teams not often associated with success. California, Texas, and Seattle have one postseason appearance in their collective histories: California in the ALCS in '86. If Magrane and Leftwich live up to their potential, California could have the best pitching in the division. And if J.T. Snow emerges as an RBI threat, the Angels could score enough runs to win the division, but it's more likely they'll watch Seattle and Texas slug it out in September.

Team Directory

Chairman: Gene Autry

Executive VP: Jackie Autry

VP, Media Relations: Tim Mead

President & CEO: Richard Brown

General Manager: Whitey Herzog

Traveling Secretary: Frank Sims

Minor League Affiliates:

Level	Team/League	1993 Record
AAA	Vancouver — Pacific Coast	72–68
AA	Midland — Texas	67–68
A	Palm Springs — California	61–75
	Cedar Rapids — Midwest	54–80
	Boise — Northwest	43–35
Rookie	Mesa Angels — Arizona	29–26

1993 Review

	Home		Away			Home		Away			Home		Away	
vs AL East	W	L	W	L	vs AL Cent.	W	L	W	L	vs AL West	W	L	W	L
Baltimore	3	3	2	4	Chicago	3	4	4	2	Oakland	4	3	2	4
Boston	5	1	0	6	Cleveland	4	2	1	5	Seattle	3	3	3	4
Detroit	2	4	2	4	Kansas City	3	3	3	4	Texas	4	3	2	4
New York	4	2	2	4	Milwaukee	3	3	4	2					
Toronto	3	3	1	5	Minnesota	3	3	1	6					
Total	17	13	7	23		16	15	13	19		11	9	7	12

1993 finish: 71–91 (44–37 home, 27–54 away), tied for fifth in AL West, 23 games behind

1994 Schedule

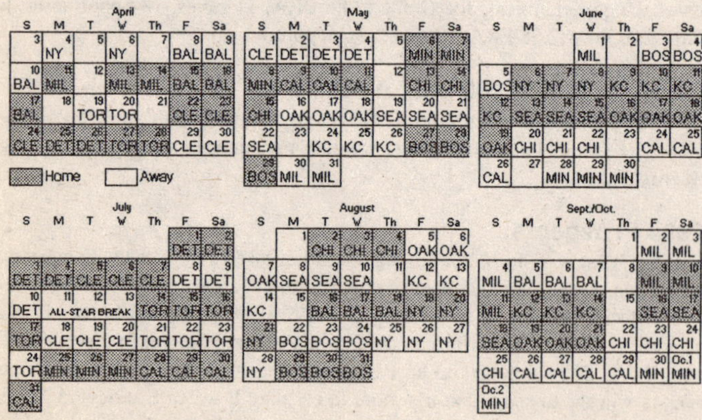

April

S	M	T	W	Th	F	Sa
3	4 NY	5	6 NY	7	8 BAL	9 BAL
10 BAL	11 MIL	12	13 MIL	14 MIL	15 BAL	16 BAL
17 BAL	18	19 TOR	20 TOR	21	22 CLE	23 CLE
24 CLE	25 DET	26 DET	27 TOR	28 TOR	29 CLE	30 CLE

Home Away

May

S	M	T	W	Th	F	Sa
1 CLE	2 DET	3 DET	4 DET	5	6 MIN	7 MIN
8 MIN	9 CAL	10 CAL	11 CAL	12	13 CHI	14 CHI
15 CHI	16 OAK	17 OAK	18 OAK	19 SEA	20 SEA	21 SEA
22 SEA	23	24 KC	25 KC	26 KC	27 BOS	28 BOS
29 BOS	30 MIL	31 MIL				

June

S	M	T	W	Th	F	Sa
			1 MIL	2	3 BOS	4 BOS
5 BOS	6 NY	7 NY	8 NY	9 KC	10 KC	11 KC
12 KC	13 SEA	14 SEA	15 SEA	16 OAK	17 OAK	18 OAK
19 OAK	20 CHI	21 CHI	22 CHI	23	24 CAL	25 CAL
26 CAL	27	28 MIN	29 MIN	30 MIN		

July

S	M	T	W	Th	F	Sa
					1 DET	2 DET
3 DET	4 DET	5 CLE	6 CLE	7 CLE	8 DET	9 DET
10 DET	11 ALL-STAR BREAK	12	13	14 TOR	15 TOR	16 TOR
17 TOR	18 CLE	19 CLE	20 CLE	21 TOR	22 TOR	23 TOR
24 TOR	25 MIN	26 MIN	27 MIN	28 CAL	29 CAL	30 CAL
31 CAL						

August

S	M	T	W	Th	F	Sa
	1	2 CHI	3 CHI	4 CHI	5 OAK	6 OAK
7 OAK	8 SEA	9 SEA	10 SEA	11	12 KC	13 KC
14 KC	15	16 BAL	17 BAL	18 BAL	19 NY	20 NY
21 NY	22 BOS	23 BOS	24 BOS	25 NY	26 NY	27 NY
28 NY	29 BOS	30 BOS	31 BOS			

Sept./Oct.

S	M	T	W	Th	F	Sa
				1	2 MIL	3 MIL
4 MIL	5 BAL	6 BAL	7 BAL	8	9 MIL	10 MIL
11 MIL	12 KC	13 KC	14 KC	15	16 SEA	17 SEA
18 SEA	19 OAK	20 OAK	21 OAK	22 CHI	23 CHI	24 CHI
25 CHI	26 CAL	27 CAL	28 CAL	29 CAL	30 MIN	Oc.1 MIN
Oc.2 MIN						

CALIFORNIA ANGELS 1994 ROSTER

MANAGER: Buck Rodgers
COACHES: Rod Carew, hitting; Chuck Hernandez, pitching; Bobby Knopp, 1B; Ken Macha, 3B; Max Oliveras, bullpen; Jimmy Reese, conditioning.

No.	PITCHERS	B	T	HT	WT	DOB	BIRTHPLACE	RESIDENCE
56	Anderson, Brian	S	L	6–1	190	4–26–72	Geneva, OH	Geneva, OH
23	Butcher, Mike	R	R	6–1	200	5–10–65	Davenport, IA	Rock Island, IL
38	Farrell, John	R	R	6–4	210	8–4–62	Neptune, NJ	Westlake, OH
31	Finley, Chuck	L	L	6–6	214	11–26–62	Monroe, LA	Newport Beach, CA
41	Frey, Steve	R	L	5–9	170	7–29–63	Southampton, PA	Newtown, PA
	Gamez, Bob	L	L	6–5	185	11–18–68	Los Angeles, CA	Newark, CA
19	Grahe, Joe	R	R	6–0	200	8–14–67	W. Palm Beach, CA	Palm Beach Gardens, FL
48	Hathaway, Hilly	L	L	6–4	195	9–12–69	Jacksonville, FL	Jacksonville, FL
42	Holzener, Mark	L	L	6–0	165	8–20–69	Littleton, CO	Littleton, CO
60	Janicki, Pete	R	R	6–4	190	1–28–71	Parma, OH	Rancho Cucamonga, CA
12	Langston, Mark	R	L	6–2	184	8–20–60	San Diego, CA	Anaheim Hills, CA
45	Leftwich, Phil	R	R	6–5	205	5–19–69	Lynchburg, VA	Mesa, AZ
18	Lewis, Scott	R	R	6–3	178	12–5–65	Grants Pass, OR	Tustin, CA
32	Magrane, Joe	R	L	6–6	230	7–2–64	Des Moines, IA	Chesterfield, MO
27	Perciva, Troy	R	R	6–3	200	8–9–69	Fontana, CA	Moreno Valley, CA
	Sebach, Kyle	R	R	6–4	198	9–6–71	San Diego, CA	Santee, CA
40	Springer, Russ	R	R	6–4	195	11–7–68	Alexandria, LA	Pollock, LA
20	Swing, Paul	R	R	6–0	185	12–21–66	Inglewood, CA	Mesa, AZ
34	Valera, Julio	R	R	6–2	215	10–13–68	San Sebastian, PR	San Sebastian, PR
57	Vasquez, Julian	R	R	6–3	185	5–24–68	Puerto Plata, DR	Puerto Plata, DR
21	Watson, Ron	L	R	6–5	240	9–12–68	Newton, MA	Gilford, NH
No.	**CATCHERS**	**B**	**T**	**HT**	**WT**	**DOB**	**BIRTHPLACE**	**RESIDENCE**
	Delasandro, Mark	R	R	6–0	195	5–14–68	Chicago, IL	Chicago, IL
11	Myers, Greg	L	R	6–2	215	4–14–66	Riverside, CA	Riverside, CA
53	Turner, Chris	R	R	6–1	190	3–23–69	Bowling Green, KY	Bowling Green, KY
No.	**INFIELDERS**	**B**	**T**	**HT**	**WT**	**DOB**	**BIRTHPLACE**	**RESIDENCE**
	Brumley, Mike	S	R	5–10	175	4–9–63	Oklahoma City, OK	Tulsa, OK
5	Correia, Rod	R	R	5–11	180	9–13–67	Providence, RI	Rehoboth, VA
24	DiSarcina, Gary	R	R	6–1	178	11–19–67	Malden, MA	East Grandwich, MA
1	Easley, Damion	R	R	5–11	185	1–11–69	New York, NY	Glendale, AZ
	Gonzales, Rene	R	R	6–3	215	9–3–62	Austin, TX	Balboa Island, CA
10	Lovullo, Torey	S	R	6–0	185	7–25–65	Santa Monica, CA	Northridge, CA
	Owen, Spike	S	R	5–10	170	4–19–61	Cleburne, TX	Austin, TX
24	Perez, Eduardo	R	R	6–4	215	9–11–59	Cincinnati, OH	Santurce, PR
6	Snow, J.T.	S	L	6–2	202	2–28–68	Long Beach, CA	Corona del Mar, CA
No.	**OUTFIELDERS**	**B**	**T**	**HT**	**WT**	**DOB**	**BIRTHPLACE**	**RESIDENCE**
	Anderson, Garrett	R	R	6–3	190	6–30–72	Los Angeles, CA	Granada Hills, CA
9	Curtis, Chad	R	R	5–10	175	11–6–68	Marion, IN	Benson, AZ
44	Davis, Chili	S	R	6–3	217	1–17–60	Kingston, JM	Scottsdale, AZ
46	Edmonds, Jim	L	L	6–1	190	6–2–70	Fullerton, CA	Diamond Bar, CA
8	Flora, Kevin	R	R	6–0	185	6–10–69	Fontana, CA	Chandler, AZ
15	Salmon, Tim	R	R	6–3	220	8–24–68	Long Beach, CA	Phoenix, AZ
	Sweeney, Mark	L	L	6–1	195	10–26–69	Framingham, MA	Holliston, MA

Anaheim Stadium (64,593, grass)
Tickets: 714-634-2000
Ticket prices:
- $13 (field and club MVP)
- $11 (field and club box)
- $10 (terrace MVP)
- $9 (terrace box)
- $8 (view level, lower box)
- $7 (view level, upper box)
- $5 (Outfield pavilion)

Field Dimensions (from home plate)
- To left field at foul line, 333 feet
- To center field, 404 feet
- To right field at foul line, 333 feet
- (OF wall is 8 feet high)

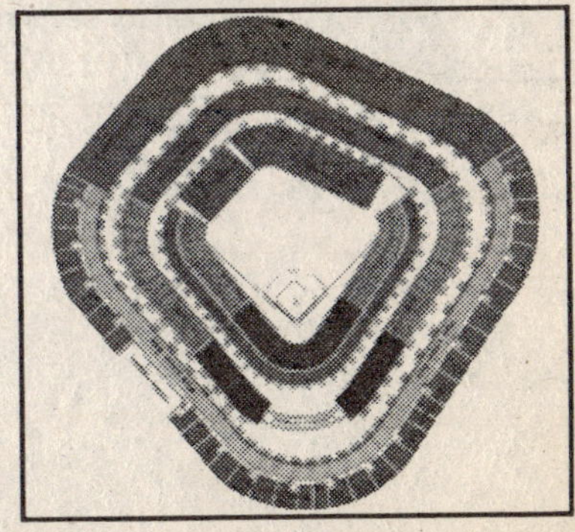

Mike Brumley IF-OF

Full name: Anthony Michael Brumley
Bats: S **Throws:** R **HT:** 5–10 **WT:** 175
Born: 4–9–63, Oklahoma City, OK
High school: Union (Broken Arrow, OK)
Brumley spent most of '93 in AAA Tucson, where his .353 BA was second in the league.

	TEAM	LG	POS	G	AB	R	H	2B	3B	HR	RBI	BB	SO	SB	E	BA	SLG	SALARY
1987	CHI	NL	SS	39	104	8	21	2	2	1	9	10	30	7	5	.202	.288	N/A
1989	DET	AL	SS	92	212	33	42	5	2	1	11	14	45	8	12	.198	.255	N/A
1990	SEA	AL	SS	62	147	19	33	5	4	0	7	10	22	2	5	.224	.313	N/A
1991	BOS	AL	SS	63	118	16	25	5	0	0	5	10	22	2	7	.212	.254	175,000
1992	BOS	AL	PH	2	1	0	0	0	0	0	0	0	0	0	0	.000	.000	N/A
1993	HOU	NL	3B	8	10	1	3	0	0	0	2	1	3	0	0	.300	.300	N/A
6	YR	TOTALS		266	592	77	124	17	8	2	34	45	122	19	29	.209	.275	
1993	RANK	MLB	3B	not ranked -- didn't have 150 ABs in 1993														
1994	PROJECTIONS			34	74	11	15	1	0	0	4	5	16	2	4	.203	.257	

Chad Curtis No. 9/OF

Full name: Chad David Curtis
Bats: R **Throws:** R **HT:** 5–10 **WT:** 175
Born: 11–6–68, Marion, IN
High school: Benson (AZ)
College: Yavapai, Cochise and G.Canyon (AZ)
Curtis batted .324 vs. lefties. His 13 assists tied for second among AL outfielders.

	TEAM	LG	POS	G	AB	R	H	2B	3B	HR	RBI	BB	SO	SB	E	BA	SLG	SALARY
1992	CAL	AL	OF	139	441	59	114	16	2	10	46	51	71	43	6	.259	.372	109,000
1993	CAL	AL	OF	152	583	94	166	25	3	6	59	70	89	48	9	.285	.369	220,000
2	YR	TOTALS		291	1024	153	280	41	5	16	105	121	160	91	15	.273	.370	
1993	RANK	MLB	OF	19	14	13	17	34	54	87	47	18	37	6	10	45	105	104
1994	PROJECTIONS			158	654	111	192	29	3	4	65	79	98	50	10	.294	.365	

Chili Davis No. 44/DH

Full name: Charles Theodore Davis
Bats: S **Throws:** R **HT:** 6–3 **WT:** 217
Born: 1–17–60, Kingston, JM
High school: Dorsey (Los Angeles, CA)
Davis' 27 HR and 112 RBI were career highs. He drove in 90+ RBI for the third time in four seasons with the Angels.

	TEAM	LG	POS	G	AB	R	H	2B	3B	HR	RBI	BB	SO	SB	E	BA	SLG	SALARY
1981	SF	NL	OF	8	15	1	2	0	0	0	0	1	2	2	0	.133	.133	N/A
1982	SF	NL	OF	154	641	86	167	27	6	19	76	45	115	24	12	.261	.410	N/A
1983	SF	NL	OF	137	486	54	113	21	2	11	59	55	108	10	9	.233	.352	N/A
1984	SF	NL	OF	137	499	87	157	21	6	21	81	42	74	12	9	.315	.507	N/A
1985	SF	NL	OF	136	481	53	130	25	2	13	56	62	74	15	6	.270	.412	N/A
1986	SF	NL	OF	153	526	71	146	28	3	13	70	84	96	16	9	.278	.416	N/A
1987	SF	NL	OF	149	500	80	125	22	1	24	76	72	109	16	7	.250	.442	N/A
1988	CAL	AL	OF	158	600	81	161	29	3	21	93	56	118	9	19	.268	.432	N/A
1989	CAL	AL	OF	154	560	81	152	24	1	22	90	61	109	3	6	.271	.436	N/A
1990	CAL	AL	OF	113	412	58	109	17	1	12	58	61	89	1	3	.265	.398	N/A
1991	MIN	AL	OF	153	534	84	148	34	1	29	93	95	117	5	0	.277	.507	1,700,000
1992	MIN	AL	OF	138	444	63	128	27	2	12	66	73	76	4	0	.288	.439	2,800,000
1993	CAL	AL	DH	153	573	74	139	32	0	27	112	71	135	4	0	.243	.440	2,400,000
13 YR	TOTALS			1743	6271	873	1677	307	28	224	930	778	1222	121	80	.267	.432	
1993	RANK	MLB	DH	2	2	4	5	3	7	2	1	3	2	4	4	7	5	7
1994	PROJECTIONS			152	544	78	138	26	0	24	92	68	117	7	4	.254	.439	

Gary DiSarcina No. 24/SS

Full name: Gary Thomas DiSarcina
Bats: R **Throws:** R **HT:** 6–1 **WT:** 178
Born: 11–19–67, Malden, MA
High school: Billerica (MA)
College: Massachusetts
DiSarcina has walked only 35 times in 934 at bats. His season ended August 26 when he broke his thumb.

	TEAM	LG	POS	G	AB	R	H	2B	3B	HR	RBI	BB	SO	SB	E	BA	SLG	SALARY
1989	CAL	AL	SS	2	0	0	0	0	0	0	0	0	0	0	0	---	---	N/A
1990	CAL	AL	SS	18	57	8	8	1	1	0	0	3	10	1	4	.140	.193	N/A
1991	CAL	AL	SS	18	57	5	12	2	0	0	3	3	4	0	4	.211	.246	N/A
1992	CAL	AL	SS	157	518	48	128	19	0	3	42	20	50	9	25	.247	.301	117,500
1993	CAL	AL	SS	126	416	44	99	20	1	3	45	15	38	5	14	.238	.313	265,000
5 YR	TOTALS			321	1048	105	247	42	2	6	90	41	102	15	47	.236	.297	
1993	RANK	MLB	SS	20	20	24	23	16	29	19	19	30	26	21	18	35	30	19
1994	PROJECTIONS			54	176	19	39	7	0	1	16	7	17	2	7	.222	.29	

Rene Gonzales No. 88/3B

Full name: Rene Adrian Gonzales
Bats: R **Throws:** R **HT:** 6–3 **WT:** 215
Born: 9–3–62, Austin, TX
High school: Rosemead (CA)
College: Glendale City (CA) and Cal State–LA
Gonzales played at all four infield positions in '93.

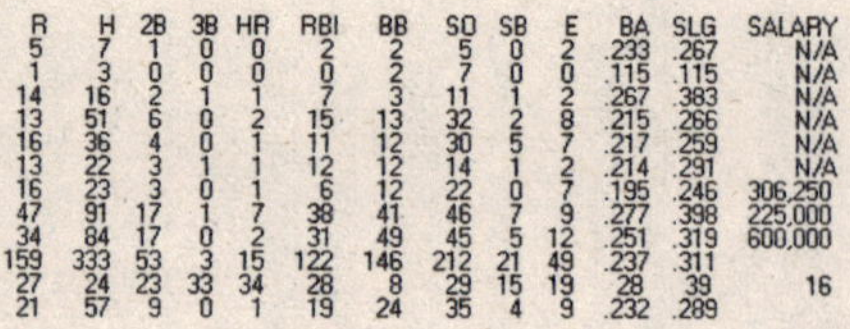

	TEAM	LG	POS	G	AB	R	H	2B	3B	HR	RBI	BB	SO	SB	E	BA	SLG	SALARY
1984	MTL	NL	SS	29	30	5	7	1	0	0	2	2	5	0	2	.233	.267	N/A
1986	MTL	NL	SS-3B	11	26	1	3	0	0	0	0	2	7	0	0	.115	.115	N/A
1987	BAL	AL	3B-2B	37	60	14	16	2	1	1	7	3	11	1	2	.267	.383	N/A
1988	BAL	AL	IF-OF	92	237	13	51	6	0	2	15	13	32	2	8	.215	.266	N/A
1989	BAL	AL	2B-3B	71	166	16	36	4	0	1	11	12	30	5	7	.217	.259	N/A
1990	BAL	AL	2B-3B	67	103	13	22	3	1	1	12	12	14	1	2	.214	.291	N/A
1991	TOR	AL	IF	71	118	16	23	3	0	1	6	12	22	0	7	.195	.246	306,250
1992	CAL	AL	IF	104	329	47	91	17	1	7	38	41	46	7	9	.277	.398	225,000
1993	CAL	AL	3B	118	335	34	84	17	0	2	31	49	45	5	12	.251	.319	600,000
9	YR	TOTALS		600	1404	159	333	53	3	15	122	146	212	21	49	.237	.311	
1993	RANK	MLB	3B	23	23	27	24	23	33	34	28	8	29	15	19	28	39	16
1994	PROJECTIONS			93	246	21	57	9	0	1	19	24	35	4	9	.232	.289	

Torey Lovullo No. 10/2B

Full name: Salvatore Anthony Lovullo
Bats: S **Throws:** R **HT:** 6–0 **WT:** 185
Born: 7–25–65, Santa Monica, CA
High school: Montclair Pr. (S. Fernando, CA)
College: UCLA
Lovullo hit .238, 1 HR, 11 RBI in innings 1–6, .271, 5HR, 19 RBI after the sixth inning.

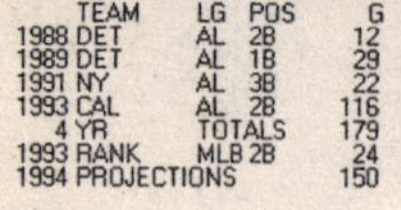

	TEAM	LG	POS	G	AB	R	H	2B	3B	HR	RBI	BB	SO	SB	E	BA	SLG	SALARY
1988	DET	AL	2B	12	21	2	8	1	1	1	2	1	2	0	0	.381	.667	N/A
1989	DET	AL	1B	29	87	8	10	2	0	1	4	14	20	0	1	.115	.172	N/A
1991	NY	AL	3B	22	51	0	9	2	0	0	2	5	7	0	3	.176	.216	N/A
1993	CAL	AL	2B	116	367	42	92	20	0	6	30	36	49	7	11	.251	.354	109,000
4	YR	TOTALS		179	526	52	119	25	1	8	38	56	78	7	15	.226	.323	
1993	RANK	MLB	2B	24	26	29	27	18	40	16	29	20	27	21	16	33	30	39
1994	PROJECTIONS			150	482	55	120	26	0	7	39	47	64	9	14	.249	.346	

Greg Myers No. 11/C

Full name: Gregory Richard Myers
Bats: L **Throws:** R **HT:** 6–2 **WT:** 215
Born: 4–14–66, Riverside, CA
High school: Riverside Polytechnical (CA)

Myers has walked only 22 times in his last 320 times at bat. He threw out 23 of 90 potential base stealers, and committed just six errors in 419 total chances.

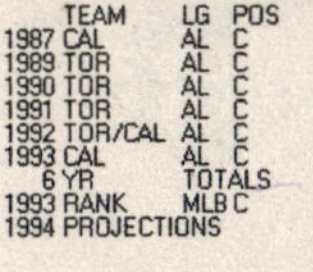
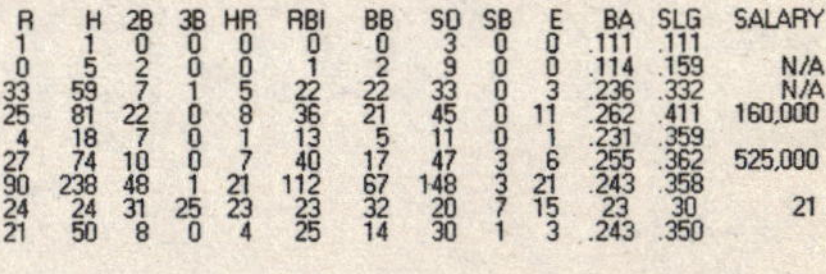

	TEAM	LG	POS	G	AB	R	H	2B	3B	HR	RBI	BB	SO	SB	E	BA	SLG	SALARY
1987	CAL	AL	C	7	9	1	1	0	0	0	0	0	3	0	0	.111	.111	
1989	TOR	AL	C	17	44	0	5	2	0	0	1	2	9	0	0	.114	.159	N/A
1990	TOR	AL	C	87	250	33	59	7	1	5	22	22	33	0	3	.236	.332	N/A
1991	TOR	AL	C	107	309	25	81	22	0	8	36	21	45	0	11	.262	.411	160,000
1992	TOR/CAL	AL	C	30	78	4	18	7	0	1	13	5	11	0	1	.231	.359	
1993	CAL	AL	C	108	290	27	74	10	0	7	40	17	47	3	6	.255	.362	525,000
6	YR	TOTALS		356	980	90	238	48	1	21	112	67	148	3	21	.243	.358	
1993	RANK	MLB	C	21	25	24	24	31	25	23	23	32	20	7	15	23	30	21
1994	PROJECTIONS			75	206	21	50	8	0	4	25	14	30	1	3	.243	.350	

Tim Salmon No. 15/OF

Full name: Timothy James Salmon
Bats: R **Throws:** R **HT:** 6–3 **WT:** 220
Born: 8–24–68, Long Beach, CA
High school: Greenway (Phoenix, AZ)
College: Grand Canyon (Phoenix, AZ)

The only others to hit 30 HR in their first Angels season are Reggie Jackson, Frank Robinson, and Doug DeCinces.

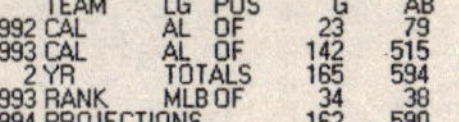
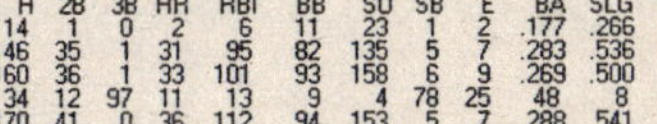

	TEAM	LG	POS	G	AB	R	H	2B	3B	HR	RBI	BB	SO	SB	E	BA	SLG	SALARY
1992	CAL	AL	OF	23	79	8	14	1	0	2	6	11	23	1	2	.177	.266	109,000
1993	CAL	AL	OF	142	515	93	146	35	1	31	95	82	135	5	7	.283	.536	127,500
2	YR	TOTALS		165	594	101	160	36	1	33	101	93	158	6	9	.269	.500	
1993	RANK	MLB	OF	34	38	14	34	12	97	11	13	9	4	78	25	48	8	115
1994	PROJECTIONS			162	590	108	170	41	0	36	112	94	153	5	7	.288	.541	

J.T. Snow — No. 6/1B

Full name: Jack Thomas Snow Jr.
Bats: S **Throws:** L **HT:** 6–2 **WT:** 202
Born: 2–28–68, Long Beach, CA
High school: Los Alamitos (CA)
College: Arizona
Snow's father is former Rams wide receiver Jack Snow. He hit .343 with 6 HR and 17 RBI in April, only .188 from May to July.

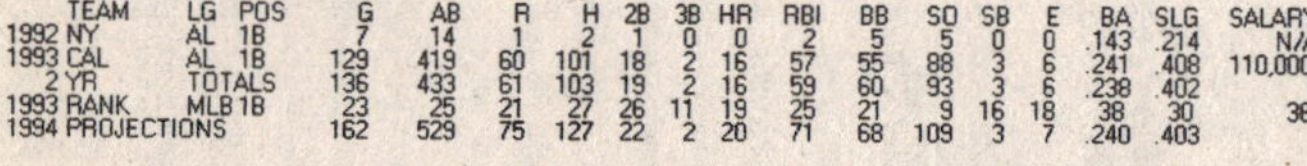

TEAM	LG	POS	G	AB	R	H	2B	3B	HR	RBI	BB	SO	SB	E	BA	SLG	SALARY
1992 NY	AL	1B	7	14	1	2	1	0	0	2	5	5	0	0	.143	.214	N/A
1993 CAL	AL	1B	129	419	60	101	18	2	16	57	55	88	3	6	.241	.408	110,000
2 YR	TOTALS		136	433	61	103	19	2	16	59	60	93	3	6	.238	.402	
1993 RANK	MLB 1B		23	25	21	27	26	11	19	25	21	9	16	18	38	30	36
1994 PROJECTIONS			162	529	75	127	22	2	20	71	68	109	3	7	.240	.403	

Chuck Finley — No. 31/P

Full name: Charles Edward Finley
Bats: L **Throws:** L **HT:** 6–6 **WT:** 214
Born: 11–26–62, Monroe, LA
High school: West Monroe (LA)
College: Northeast Louisiana State
Finley led the AL in complete games. In six full seasons as a starter, he has allowed fewer hits than innings pitched five times.

TM	LG	POS	W	L	ERA	G	GS	CG	SH	SV	IP	H	R	ER	HR	BB	SO	SALARY
1986 CAL	AL	P	3	1	3.30	25	0	0	0	0	46.1	40	17	17	2	23	37	N/A
1987 CAL	AL	P	2	7	4.67	35	3	0	0	0	90.2	102	54	47	7	43	63	N/A
1988 CAL	AL	P	9	15	4.17	31	31	2	0	0	194.1	191	95	90	15	82	111	N/A
1989 CAL	AL	P	16	9	2.57	29	29	9	1	0	199.2	171	64	57	13	82	156	N/A
1990 CAL	AL	P	18	9	2.40	32	32	7	2	0	236.0	210	77	63	17	81	177	N/A
1991 CAL	AL	P	18	9	3.80	34	34	4	2	0	227.1	205	102	96	23	101	171	2,500,000
1992 CAL	AL	P	7	12	3.96	31	31	4	1	0	204.1	212	99	90	24	98	124	4,375,000
1993 CAL	AL	P	16	14	3.15	35	35	13	2	0	251.1	243	108	88	22	82	187	5,375,000
8 YR	TOTALS		89	76	3.40	252	195	39	8	0	1450.0	1374	616	548	123	592	1026	
1993 RANK	MLB Ps		14		58	134	6	1	8	102	8	111	80		125	100	86	4
1994 PROJECTIONS			15	13	3.12	33	36	12	1	0	254	247	109	88	22	82	189	

Mark Langston No. 12/P

Full name: Mark Edward Langston
Bats: R **Throws:** L **HT:** 6–2 **WT:** 184
Born: 8–20–60, San Diego, CA
High school: Buchser (Santa Clara, CA)
College: San Jose State

In his first 15 starts, he was 9–1 with three blown saves by the bullpen. He allowed 22 earned runs in his last 33.1 innings.

	TM	LG	POS	W	L	ERA	G	GS	CG	SH	SV	IP	H	R	ER	HR	BB	SO	SALARY
1984	SEA	AL	P	17	10	3.40	35	33	5	2	0	225.0	188	99	85	16	118	204	N/A
1985	SEA	AL	P	7	14	5.47	24	24	2	0	0	126.2	122	85	77	22	91	72	N/A
1986	SEA	AL	P	12	14	4.85	37	36	9	0	0	239.1	234	142	129	30	123	245	N/A
1987	SEA	AL	P	19	13	3.84	35	35	14	3	0	272.0	242	132	116	30	114	262	N/A
1988	SEA	AL	P	15	11	3.34	35	35	9	3	0	261.1	222	108	97	32	110	235	N/A
1989	SEA	AL	P	4	5	3.56	10	10	2	1	0	73.1	60	30	29	3	19	60	N/A
1989	MTL	NL	P	12	9	2.39	24	24	6	4	0	176.2	138	57	47	13	93	175	N/A
1990	CAL	AL	P	10	17	4.40	33	33	5	1	0	223.0	215	120	109	13	104	195	N/A
1991	CAL	AL	P	19	8	3.00	34	34	7	0	0	246.1	190	89	82	30	96	183	3,550,000
1992	CAL	AL	P	13	14	3.66	32	32	9	2	0	229.0	206	103	93	14	74	174	3,550,000
1993	CAL	AL	P	16	11	3.20	35	35	7	0	0	256.1	220	100	91	22	85	196	3,550,000
10	YR	TOTALS		144	126	3.69	334	331	75	16	0	2329.0	2037	1065	955	225	1027	2001	
1993	RANK	MLB Ps		14		60.00	134	6	7	69	102	5	44	50		120	104	75	25
1994	PROJECTIONS			15	11	3.79	35	34	7	0	0	240.0	214	113	101	22	108	215	

Joe Magrane No. 32/P

Full name: Joseph David Magrane
Bats: R **Throws:** L **HT:** 6–6 **WT:** 230
Born: 7–2–64, Des Moines, IA
High school: Rowan (Morehead, KY)
College: Arizona

Magrane was 5–1 with a 2.47 ERA in June for St. Louis. He was 3–1 with a 3.76 ERA in September for California.

	TM	LG	POS	W	L	ERA	G	GS	CG	SH	SV	IP	H	R	ER	HR	BB	SO	SALARY
1987	STL	NL	P	9	7	3.54	27	26	4	2	0	170.1	157	75	67	9	60	101	N/A
1988	STL	NL	P	5	9	2.18	24	24	4	3	0	165.1	133	57	40	6	51	100	N/A
1989	STL	NL	P	18	9	2.91	34	33	9	3	0	234.2	219	81	76	5	72	127	N/A
1990	STL	NL	P	10	17	3.59	31	31	3	2	0	203.1	204	86	81	10	59	100	N/A
1992	STL	NL	P	1	2	4.02	5	5	0	0	0	31.1	34	15	14	2	15	20	820,000
1993	STL	NL	P	8	10	4.97	22	20	0	0	0	116.0	127	68	64	15	37	38	N/A
1993	CAL	AL	P	3	2	3.94	8	8	0	0	0	48.0	48	27	21	4	21	24	109,000
6	YR	TOTALS		54	56	3.37	151	147	20	10	0	969.0	922	409	363	51	315	510	
1993	RANK	MLB Ps		59		205	203	71	125	69	102	84	191	203		198	135	281	236
1994	PROJECTIONS			4	4	4.57	11	11	0	0	0	65	69	36	33	7	24	27	

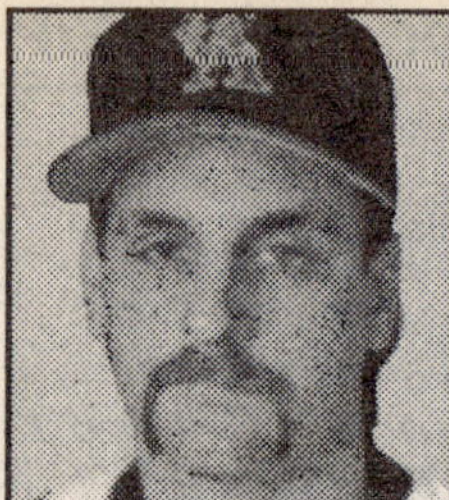

Steve Frey No. 41/P

Full name: Steven Francis Frey
Bats: R **Throws:** L **HT:** 5–9 **WT:** 170
Born: 7–29–63, Southampton, PA
High school: Wm. Tennant (PA)
College: Bucks County CC (Newtown, PA)

Opponents hit only .230 against Frey (righties .230, lefties .231). They hit .298 with no runners on base, only .198 with runners on.

	TM	LG	POS	W	L	ERA	G	GS	CG	SH	SV	IP	H	R	ER	HR	BB	SO	SALARY
1989	MTL	NL	P	3	2	5.48	20	0	0	0	0	21.1	29	15	13	4	11	15	N/A
1990	MTL	NL	P	8	2	2.10	51	0	0	0	9	55.2	44	15	13	4	29	29	N/A
1991	MTL	NL	P	0	1	4.99	31	0	0	0	1	39.2	43	31	22	3	23	21	N/A
1992	CAL	AL	P	4	2	3.57	51	0	0	0	4	45.1	39	18	18	6	22	24	155,000
1993	CAL	AL	P	2	3	2.98	55	0	0	0	13	48.1	41	20	16	1	26	22	525,000
5	YR	TOTALS		17	10	3.51	208	0	0	0	27	210.1	196	99	82	18	111	111	
1993	RANK	MLB Ps	not ranked -- didn't have 50 IP in 1993																
1994	PROJECTIONS			2	2	3.68	45	0	0	0	6	44	41	23	18	3	23	22	

Buck Rodgers No. 7/Mgr.

Full name: Robert Leroy Rodgers
Bats: B **Throws:** R **HT:** 6–1 **WT:** 190
Born: 8–16–38, Delaware, OH
High school: Prospect (OH)
College: Ohio Wesleyan and Ohio Northern

Rodgers was the NL Manager of the Year with Montreal in 1987. He was third in the 1990 NL Manager of the Year voting.

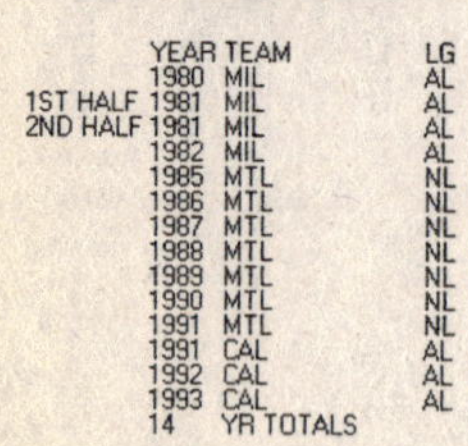

				REG. SEASON				PLAYOFF			CHAMP. SERIES			WORLD SERIES		
	YEAR	TEAM	LG	W	L	PCT	POS	W	L	PCT	W	L	PCT	W	L	PCT
	1980	MIL	AL	13	10	.565	3			---			---			---
1ST HALF	1981	MIL	AL	31	25	.554	3			---			---			---
2ND HALF	1981	MIL	AL	31	22	.585	1			---			---			---
	1982	MIL	AL	23	24	.489				---			---			---
	1985	MTL	NL	84	77	.522	3			---			---			---
	1986	MTL	NL	78	83	.484	4			---			---			---
	1987	MTL	NL	91	71	.562	3			---			---			---
	1988	MTL	NL	81	81	.500	3			---			---			---
	1989	MTL	NL	81	81	.500	4			---			---			---
	1990	MTL	NL	85	77	.525	3			---			---			---
	1991	MTL	NL	20	29	.408				---			---			---
	1991	CAL	AL	20	18	.526	7			---			---			---
	1992	CAL	AL	72	90	.444	5			---			---			---
	1993	CAL	AL	71	91	.438	5			---			---			---
	14	YR TOTALS		781	779	.501		0	0	---	0	0	---	0	0	---

Mike Butcher No. 23/P

Full name: Michael Dana Butcher
Bats: R **Throws:** R **HT:** 6–1 **WT:** 200
Born: 5–10–65, Davenport, IA
High school: United Township (IL)
College: North Eastern Oklahoma Junior
Five of his eight saves came in one-run games.

	TM	LG	POS	W	L	ERA	G	GS	CG	SH	SV	IP	H	R	ER	HR	BB	SO	SALARY
1992	CAL	AL	P	2	2	3.25	19	0	0	0	0	27.2	29	11	10	3	13	24	109,000
1993	CAL	AL	P	1	0	2.86	23	0	0	0	8	28.1	21	12	9	2	15	24	115,000
2	YR	TOTALS		3	2	3.05	42	0	0	0	8	56.0	50	23	19	5	28	48	
1993	RANK	MLB Ps		not ranked -- didn't have 50 IP in 1993															
1994	PROJECTIONS			0	0	2.57	25	0	0	0	12	28	17	12	8	1	16	24	

Rod Correia No. 5/SS

Full name: Ronald Douglas Correia
Bats: R **Throws:** R **HT:** 5–11 **WT:** 180
Born: 9–13–67, Providence, RI
High school: Dighton-Rebobath (RI)
College: SE Mass and UMass at Dartmouth
Correia hit .326 vs. lefties, .235 vs. righties.

	TEAM	LG	POS	G	AB	R	H	2B	3B	HR	RBI	BB	SO	SB	E	BA	SLG	SALARY
1993	CAL	AL	SS	64	128	12	34	5	0	0	9	6	20	2	3	.266	.305	109,000
1	YR	TOTAL		64	128	12	34	5	0	0	9	6	20	2	3	.266	.305	
1993	RANK	MLB	SS	not ranked -- didn't have 150 ABs in 1993														

Damion Easley No. 1/2B

Full name: Jacinto Damion Easley
Bats: R **Throws:** R **HT:** 5–11 **WT:** 185
Born: 1–11–69, New York, NY
High school: Lakewood (CA)
College: Long Beach City
California's fifth opening day 2B in last six years.

	TEAM	LG	POS	G	AB	R	H	2B	3B	HR	RBI	BB	SO	SB	E	BA	SLG	SALARY
1992	CAL	AL	3B	47	151	14	39	5	0	1	12	8	26	9	5	.258	.311	109,000
1993	CAL	AL	2B	73	230	33	72	13	2	2	22	28	35	6	6	.313	.413	112,500
2	YR	TOTALS		120	381	47	111	18	2	3	34	36	61	15	11	.291	.373	
1993	RANK	MLB	2B	42	36	31	30	29	19	30	36	28	35	24	32	4	13	37
1994	PROJECTIONS			86	269	42	88	17	3	2	27	38	39	4	6	.327	.435	

Jim Edmonds No. 46/OF

Full name: James Patrick Edmonds
Bats: L **Throws:** L **HT:** 6–1 **WT:** 190
Born: 6–2–70, Fullerton, CA
High school: Diamond Bar (CA)
His 11 game hitting streak was the team's best in '93.

	TEAM	LG	POS	G	AB	R	H	2B	3B	HR	RBI	BB	SO	SB	E	BA	SLG	SALARY
1993	CAL	AL	OF	18	61	5	15	4	1	0	4	2	16	0	1	.246	.344	N/A
1	YR	TOTAL		18	61	5	15	4	1	0	4	2	16	0	1	.246	.344	
1993	RANK	MLB	OF	not ranked -- didn't have 150 ABs in 1993														

John Farrell No. 38/P

Full name: John Edward Farrell
Bats: R **Throws:** R **HT:** 6–4 **WT:** 210
Born: 8–4–62, Neptune, NJ
High school: Shore Reg. (W. Long Branch, NJ)
College: Oklahoma State
In his 11 losses, California scored just 17 runs.

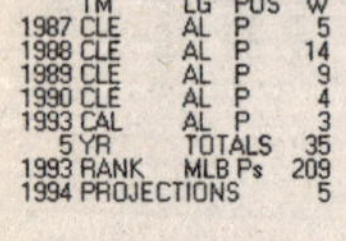

	TM	LG	POS	W	L	ERA	G	GS	CG	SH	SV	IP	H	R	ER	HR	BB	SO	SALARY
1987	CLE	AL	P	5	1	3.39	10	9	1	0	0	69.0	68	29	26	7	22	28	N/A
1988	CLE	AL	P	14	10	4.24	31	30	4	0	0	210.1	216	106	99	15	67	92	N/A
1989	CLE	AL	P	9	14	3.63	31	31	7	2	0	208.0	196	97	84	14	71	132	N/A
1990	CLE	AL	P	4	5	4.28	17	17	1	0	0	96.2	108	49	46	10	33	44	N/A
1993	CAL	AL	P	3	12	7.35	21	17	0	0	0	90.2	110	74	74	22	44	45	N/A
5	YR	TOTALS		35	42	4.39	110	104	13	2	0	674.2	698	355	329	68	237	341	
1993	RANK	MLB	Ps	209		290	250	119	125	69	102	163	264	288		290	242	239	273
1994	PROJECTIONS			5	9	4.50	20	19	2	0	0	122	124	66	61	14	45	68	

Joe Grahe No. 19/P

Full name: Joseph Milton Grahe
Bats: R **Throws:** R **HT:** 6–0 **WT:** 200
Born: 8–14–67, W. Palm Beach, CA
High school: Palm Beach Gardens (FL)
College: Miami (FL)
Righties hit .211 against him, lefties .317.

	TM	LG	POS	W	L	ERA	G	GS	CG	SH	SV	IP	H	R	ER	HR	BB	SO	SALARY
1990	CAL	AL	P	3	4	4.98	8	8	0	0	0	43.1	51	30	24	3	23	25	N/A
1991	CAL	AL	P	3	7	4.81	18	10	1	0	0	73.0	84	43	39	2	33	40	107,000
1992	CAL	AL	P	5	6	3.52	46	7	0	0	21	94.2	85	37	37	5	39	39	125,000
1993	CAL	AL	P	4	1	2.86	45	0	0	0	11	56.2	54	22	18	5	25	31	230,000
4	YR	TOTALS		15	18	3.97	117	25	1	0	32	267.2	274	132	118	15	120	135	
1993	RANK	MLB	Ps	173		31	96	202	125	69	23	263	100	47		127	215	207	166
1994	PROJECTIONS			4	3	3.66	33	5	0	0	10	64.0	63	29	26	4	29	31	

Hilly Hathaway No. 48/P

Full name: Hillary Houston Hathaway
Bats: L **Throws:** L **HT:** 6–4 **WT:** 195
Born: 9–12–69, Jacksonville, FL
High school: Sandalwood (FL)
College: Bradenton Community (FL)
At AAA Vancouver, he was 7–0 with a 4.00 ERA

	TM	LG	POS	W	L	ERA	G	GS	CG	SH	SV	IP	H	R	ER	HR	BB	SO	SALARY
1992	CAL	AL	P	0	0	7.94	2	1	0	0	0	5.2	8	5	5	1	3	1	N/A
1993	CAL	AL	P	4	3	5.02	11	11	0	0	0	57.1	71	35	32	6	26	11	109,000
2	YR	TOTALS		4	3	5.29	13	12	0	0	0	63.0	79	40	37	7	29	12	
1993	RANK	MLB Ps		173		232	287	155	125	69	102	259.0	273	230		173	227	290	236
1994	PROJECTIONS			6	4	4.88	15	16	0	0	0	83.0	102	50	45	8	37	16	

Phil Leftwich No. 45/P

Full name: Phillip Dale Leftwich
Bats: R **Throws:** R **HT:** 6–5 **WT:** 205
Born: 5–19–69, Lynchburg, VA
High school: Brookville (VA)
College: Radford (VA)
Leftwich won five of his last six decisions.

	TM	LG	POS	W	L	ERA	G	GS	CG	SH	SV	IP	H	R	ER	HR	BB	SO	SALARY
1993	CAL	AL	P	4	6	3.79	12	12	1	0	0	80.2	81	35	34	5	27	31	109,000
1	YR	TOTAL		4	6	3.79	12	12	1	0	0	80.2	81	35	34	5	27	31	
1993	RANK	MLB Ps		173		115	286	150	79	69	102	187	146	84		48	109	280	236

Spike Owen No. 17/SS

Full name: Spike Lee Owen
Bats: S **Throws:** R **HT:** 5–10 **WT:** 170
Born: 4–19–61, Cleburne, TX
High School: Cleburne (TX)
College: Texas
Owen batted just .234 with 14 errors.

	TEAM	LG	POS	G	AB	R	H	2B	3B	HR	RBI	BB	SO	SB	E	BA	SLG	SALARY
1988	BOS	AL	SS	89	257	40	64	14	1	5	18	27	27	0	10	.249	.370	N/A
1989	MTL	NL	SS	142	437	52	102	17	4	6	41	76	44	3	13	.233	.332	N/A
1990	MTL	NL	SS	149	453	55	106	24	5	5	35	70	60	8	6	.234	.342	N/A
1991	MTL	NL	SS	139	424	39	108	22	8	3	26	42	61	2	8	.255	.366	1,033,333
1992	MTL	NL	SS	122	386	52	104	16	3	7	40	50	30	9	9	.269	.381	1,133,334
1993	NY	AL	SS	103	334	41	78	16	2	2	20	29	30	3	14	.234	.311	2,250,000
11	YR	TOTALS		1380	4444	540	1078	189	54	42	374	502	480	77	136	.243	.338	
1993	RANK	MLB	SS	30	30	27	31	21	21	26	36	25	1	30	19	38	32	6
1994	PROJECTIONS			90	299	39	67	13	2	3	19	26	33	4	11	.224	.314	

Eduardo Perez — No. 24/3B

Full name: Eduardo Antancio Perez
Bats: R **Throws:** R **HT:** 6–4 **WT:** 215
Born: 9–11–59, Cincinnati, OH
High school: Robinson (PR)
College: Florida State
Tony Perez' son, he hit .306 at AAA Vancouver.

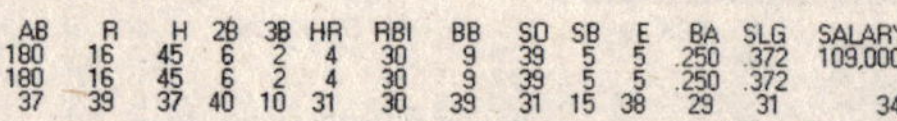

	TEAM	LG	POS	G	AB	R	H	2B	3B	HR	RBI	BB	SO	SB	E	BA	SLG	SALARY
1993	CAL	AL	3B	52	180	16	45	6	2	4	30	9	39	5	5	.250	.372	109,000
1	YR	TOTAL		52	180	16	45	6	2	4	30	9	39	5	5	.250	.372	
1993	RANK	MLB	3B	40	37	39	37	40	10	31	30	39	31	15	38	29	31	34

Chris Turner — No. 53/C

Full name: Christopher Wan Turner
Bats: R **Throws:** R **HT:** 6–1 **WT:** 190
Born: 3–23–69, Bowling Green, KY
High school: Warren Central (KY)
College: Western Kentucky
Turner hit .324 on road, just .222 at home.

	TEAM	LG	POS	G	AB	R	H	2B	3B	HR	RBI	BB	SO	SB	E	BA	SLG	SALARY
1993	CAL	AL	C	25	75	9	21	5	0	1	13	9	16	1	1	.280	.387	109,000
1	YR	TOTAL		25	75	9	21	5	0	1	13	9	16	1	1	.280	.387	
1993	RANK	MLB	C	not ranked -- didn't have 150 ABs in 1993														

Julio Valera — No. 45/P

Full name: Julio Enrique Valera
Bats: R **Throws:** R **HT:** 6–2 **WT:** 215
Born: 10–13–68, San Sebastian, PR
High school: M. M. Luciago (San Sebastian, PR)
Lefthanders hit .396 against Valera in '93. Valera blew 3 of 7 save opportunities.

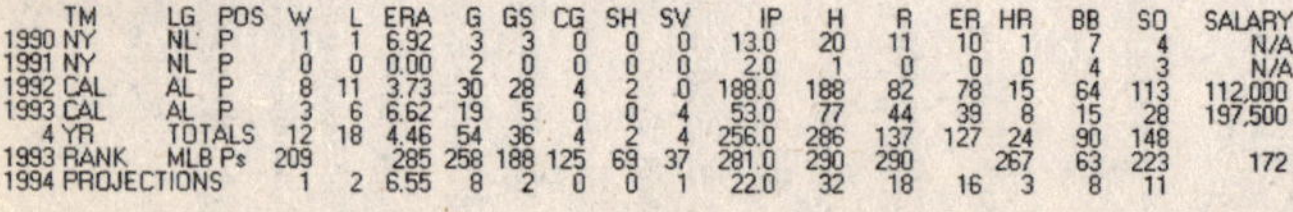

	TM	LG	POS	W	L	ERA	G	GS	CG	SH	SV	IP	H	R	ER	HR	BB	SO	SALARY
1990	NY	NL	P	1	1	6.92	3	3	0	0	0	13.0	20	11	10	1	7	4	N/A
1991	NY	NL	P	0	0	0.00	2	0	0	0	0	2.0	1	0	0	0	4	3	N/A
1992	CAL	AL	P	8	11	3.73	30	28	4	2	0	188.0	188	82	78	15	64	113	112,000
1993	CAL	AL	P	3	6	6.62	19	5	0	0	4	53.0	77	44	39	8	15	28	197,500
4	YR	TOTALS		12	18	4.46	54	36	4	2	4	256.0	286	137	127	24	90	148	
1993	RANK	MLB	Ps	209		285	258	188	125	69	37	281.0	290	290		267	63	223	172
1994	PROJECTIONS			1	2	6.55	8	2	0	0	1	22.0	32	18	16	3	8	11	

Chicago WHITE SOX

1994 Scouting Report

Hitting: (1993/.265 BA, seventh in AL; 162 HR, fourth in AL)

Chicago's offense starts with AL MVP Frank Thomas. Thomas' 41 HR was a White Sox team record. He also set team records in extra base hits (77) and slugging percentage (.607). Unfortunately, opponents found they could work around Thomas and pitch to the rest of the lineup. Robin Ventura batted cleanup for Chicago, and hit .262 with 22 HR and 94 RBI. Lance Johnson had a strong '93 campaign, hitting .311 and stealing 35 bases. Ozzie Guillen returned from a knee injury to hit .280 with 23 doubles. But Chicago will have to replace Ellis Burks (lost via free agency). Free agent signee Julio Franco (.289 BA, 84 RBI) provides some punch in the DH slot.

Pitching: (1993/3.70 ERA, first in AL)

Chicago has deep, young starting pitching, with Cy Young winner Jack McDowell (22–10, 3.37 ERA), Wilson Alvarez (15–8, 2.95), Alex Fernandez (18–9, 3.13 ERA), and Jason Bere (12–5, 3.47 ERA).

The White Sox bullpen is led by closer Roberto Hernandez, with 38 saves in '93. Other key relievers include Scott Radinsky (73 appearances, 4.28 ERA), and Jeff Schwarz (41 appearances, 3.71 ERA).

Defense: (1993/.982 pct., sixth in AL)

Lance Johnson had a .980 fielding percentage in center field. But Ellis Burks was Chicago's strongest outfield arm. Robin Ventura is a Gold Glove fielder at third. Ron Karkovice throws out 50 percent of steal attempts, nearly twice the major league average.

1994 Prospects:

The White Sox have tried to improve themselves by subtraction—getting rid of clubhouse malcontent George Bell. Franco should pick up the slack at DH, but they haven't replaced Burks. Jack McDowell showed signs of a tired arm at the end of '93, and that's a worry. Chicago still should have too much talent for division rivals Cleveland and Kansas City—but they don't figure to win the pennant, and they could lose the division if someone else has a breakout year.

Team Directory

Chairman: Jerry Reinsdorf
Vice Chairman: Eddie Einhorn
Sr. VP, Major Lg. Oper.: Ron Schueler
Senior VP, Baseball: Jack Gould
Director of P.R.: Doug Abel
Traveling Secretary: Glen Rosenbaum

Minor League Affiliates:

Level	Team/League	1993 Record
AAA	Nashville–American Association	81–62
AA	Birmingham–Southern	78–64
A	Sarasota–Florida State*	77–57
	South Bend–Midwest	77–59
	Hickory–South Atlantic	52–88
Rookie	Sarasota–Gulf Coast	32–27

* Sold to Florida; will be replaced by Prince William of the Carolina League (A) in '94.

1993 Review

	Home		Away			Home		Away			Home		Away	
vs AL East	W	L	W	L	vs AL Cent.	W	L	W	L	vs AL West	W	L	W	L
Baltimore	4	2	4	2	Cleveland	6	0	3	3	California	2	4	4	3
Boston	3	3	2	4	Kansas City	2	5	4	2	Oakland	3	3	4	3
Detroit	2	4	5	1	Milwaukee	4	2	5	1	Seattle	4	3	5	1
New York	2	4	2	4	Minnesota	5	2	5	1	Texas	5	1	3	4
Toronto	3	3	3	3										
Total	14	16	16	14		17	9	17	7		14	11	16	11

1993 finish: 94–68 (45–36 home, 49–32 away), first in AL West; lost to Toronto 2–4 in ALCS

1994 Schedule

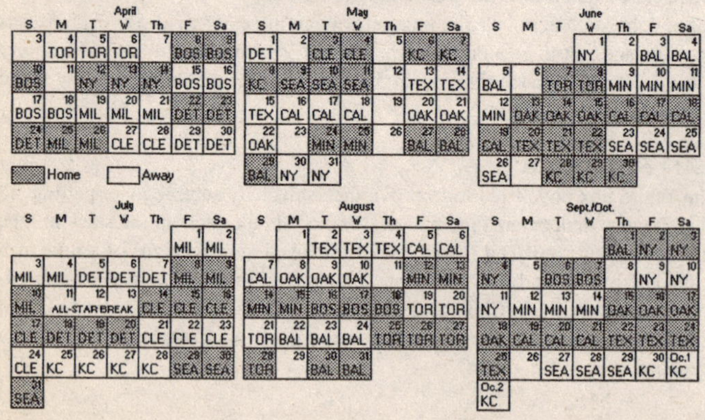

CHICAGO WHITE SOX 1994 ROSTER

MANAGER: Gene Lamont (33)
COACHES: Terry Bevington (18), Jackie Brown (41), Walt Hriniak (6), Doug Mansolino (17), Joe Nossek (15), Dewey Robinson (55)

No.	PITCHERS	B	T	HT	WT	DOB	BIRTHPLACE	RESIDENCE
	Andujar, Luis							
40	Alvarez, Wilson	L	L	6–1	235	3–24–70	Maracaibo, VZ	Maracaibo, VZ
	Baldwin, James							
51	Bere, Jason	R	R	6–3	185	5–26–71	Cambridge, MA	Wilmington, MA
	Boehringer, Brian							
42	Bolton, Rodney	R	R	6–2	190	9–23–68	Chattanooga, TN	Chattanooga, TN
48	DeLeon, Jose	R	R	6–3	226	12–20–60	Rancho Viejo, DR	Boca Raton, FL
	Ellis, Robert	R	R	6–5	215	12–25–70	Baton Rouge, LA	Baton Rouge, LA
32	Fernandez, Alex	R	R	6–1	215	8–13–69	Miami Beach, FL	Miami Lakes, FL
39	Hernandez, Roberto	R	R	6 4	235	11–11–64	Santurce, PR	Cobo Rojo, PR
58	Howard, Chris	R	L	6–0	185	11–18–65	Lynn MA	Nahant, MA
25	McCaskill, Kirk	R	R	6–1	205	4–9–61	Kapuskasing, Ont.	Corona del Mar, CA
29	McDowell, Jack	R	R	6–5	188	1–16–66	Van Nuys, CA	Chicago, IL
31	Radinsky, Scott	L	L	6–3	204	3–3–68	Glendale, CA	Simi Valley, CA
45	Ruffcorn, Scott	R	R	6–4	210	12–21–69	New Braunfels, TX	Austin, TX
	Schrenk, Steve	R	R	6–3	185	11–20–68	Great Lakes, IL	Aurora, ON
49	Schwarz, Jeff	R	R	6–5	190	5–20–64	Ft. Pierce, FL	Ft. Pierce, FL
	Thomas, Larry							
No.	**CATCHERS**	**B**	**T**	**HT**	**WT**	**DOB**	**BIRTHPLACE**	**RESIDENCE**
20	Karkovice, Ron	R	R	6–1	219	8–8–63	Union, NJ	Orlando, FL
10	LaValliere, Mike	L	R	5–9	210	8–18–60	Charlotte, NC	Bradenton, FL
68	Lindsey, Doug	R	R	6–2	232	9–22–67	Austin, TX	Austin, TX
5	Merullo, Matt	L	R	6–2	200	8–4–65	Ridgefield, CT	Ridgefield, CT
No.	**INFIELDERS**	**B**	**T**	**HT**	**WT**	**DOB**	**BIRTHPLACE**	**RESIDENCE**
38	Beltre, Esteban	R	R	5–10	172	12–26–67	Ingenio Quisfuella, DR	S.P. de Macoris, DR
	Coomer, Ron	R	R	5–11	195	11–18–66	Crest Hill, IL	Crest Hill, IL
28	Cora, Joey	S	R	5–8	155	5–14–65	Caguas, PR	Caguas, PR
52	Denson, Drew	R	R	6–5	220	11–16–65	Cincinnati, OH	Cincinnati, OH
	DiSarcina, Glenn							
	Durham, Ray							
14	Grebeck, Craig	R	R	5–7	148	12–29–64	Johnstown, PA	Cerritos, CA
13	Guillen, Ozzie	L	R	5–11	164	1–20–64	Oculare del Tuy, VZ	Caracas, VZ
53	Martin, Norberto	R	R	5–10	164	12–10–66	Santo Domingo, PR	Hato Ray, PR
35	Thomas, Frank	R	R	6–5	257	5–27–68	Columbus, GA	Burr Ridge, IL
23	Ventura, Robin	L	R	6–1	198	7–14–67	Santa Maria, CA	Santa Maria, CA
57	Wilson, Brandon	R	R	6–1	170	2–26–69	Owensboro, KY	Owensboro, KY
No.	**OUTFIELDERS**	**B**	**T**	**HT**	**WT**	**DOB**	**BIRTHPLACE**	**RESIDENCE**
	Franco, Julio	R	R	6–1	190	8–23–61	S.P. de Macoris, DR	Arlington, TX
12	Huff, Michael	R	R	6–1	190	8–11–63	Honolulu, HI	Chicago, IL
1	Johnson, Lance	L	L	5–11	160	7–6–63	Cincinnati, OH	Mobile, AL
24	Newson, Warren	L	L	5–7	202	7–3–64	Newnan, GA	Newnan, GA
44	Pasqua, Dan	L	L	6–0	218	10–17–61	Yonkers, NY	Palos Park, IL
30	Raines, Tim	S	R	5–8	186	9–16–59	Sanford, FL	Sanford, FL
7	Sax, Steve	R	R	5–11	189	1–29–60	Sacramento, CA	Loomis, CA

Comiskey Park (44,321, grass)
Tickets: 312–924–1000
Ticket prices:
- $18 (club level)
- $15 (lower deck box)
- $12 (upper deck box)
- $11 (lower deck reserved)
- $8 (upper deck reserved)
- $8 (bleacher reserved)

Field Dimensions (from home plate)
- To left field at foul line, 347 feet
- To center field, 400 feet
- To right field at foul line, 347 feet
- (OF wall is 8 feet high)

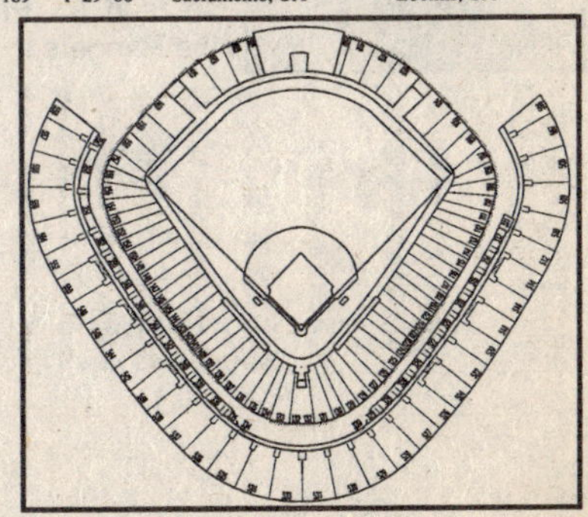

Joey Cora — No. 28/2B

Full name: Jose Manuel Cora
Bats: S **Throws:** R **HT:** 5–8 **WT:** 155
Born: 5–14–65, Caguas, PR
College: Vanderbilt (Nashville, TN)

Cora finished second in the AL with 13 triples. He batted .279 in the leadoff spot.

TEAM	LG	POS	G	AB	R	H	2B	3B	HR	RBI	BB	SO	SB	E	BA	SLG	SALARY
1987 SD	NL	2B-SS	77	241	23	57	7	2	0	13	28	26	15	10	.237	.282	N/A
1989 SD	NL	SS-3B	12	19	5	6	1	0	0	1	1	0	1	2	.316	.368	N/A
1990 SD	NL	2B-SS	51	100	12	27	3	0	0	2	6	9	8	11	.270	.300	N/A
1991 CHI	AL	2B-SS	100	228	37	55	2	3	0	18	20	21	11	10	.241	.276	120,000
1992 CHI	AL	2B-SS	68	122	27	30	7	1	0	9	22	13	10	3	.246	.320	235,000
1993 CHI	AL	2B	153	579	95	155	15	13	2	51	67	63	20	19	.268	.349	465,000
6 YR	TOTALS		461	1289	199	330	35	19	2	94	144	132	65	55	.256	.317	
1993 RANK	MLB	2B	3	6	4	6	27	1	30	11	5	17	6	4	23	31	20
1994 PROJECTIONS			162	623	104	167	15	13	1	55	71	67	19	19	.268	.339	

Julio Franco — 2B/DH

Full name: Julio Cesar Franco
Bats: R **Throws:** R **HT:** 6–1 **WT:** 190
Born: 8–23–61, San Pedro de Macoris, DR
High school: Divine Providence (DR)

Franco, a free agent acquisition from Texas, helps Chicago at 2B and at DH, two trouble spots in '93. Franco was exclusively a DH for the Rangers in '93.

TEAM	LG	POS	G	AB	R	H	2B	3B	HR	RBI	BB	SO	SB	E	BA	SLG	SALARY
1982 PHL	NL	SS-2B	16	29	3	8	1	0	0	3	2	4	0	0	.276	.310	N/A
1983 CLE	AL	SS	149	560	68	153	24	8	8	80	27	50	32	28	.273	.388	N/A
1984 CLE	AL	SS	160	658	82	188	22	5	3	79	43	68	19	36	.286	.348	N/A
1985 CLE	AL	SS-2B	160	636	97	183	33	4	6	90	54	74	13	36	.288	.381	N/A
1986 CLE	AL	SS-2B	149	599	80	183	30	5	10	74	32	66	10	19	.306	.422	N/A
1987 CLE	AL	SS-2B	128	495	86	158	24	3	8	52	57	56	32	18	.319	.428	N/A
1988 CLE	AL	2B	152	613	88	186	23	6	10	54	56	72	25	14	.303	.409	N/A
1989 TEX	AL	2B	150	548	80	173	31	5	13	92	66	69	21	13	.316	.462	N/A
1990 TEX	AL	2B	157	582	96	172	27	1	11	69	82	83	31	19	.296	.402	N/A
1991 TEX	AL	2B	146	589	108	201	27	3	15	78	65	78	36	14	.341	.474	2,375,000
1992 TEX	AL	2B	35	107	19	25	7	0	2	8	15	17	1	3	.234	.355	2,387,500
1993 TEX	AL	DH	144	532	85	154	31	3	14	84	62	95	9	0	.289	.438	3,000,000
12 YR	TOTALS		1546	5948	892	1784	280	43	100	763	561	732	229	200	.300	.412	
1993 RANK	MLB	DH	4	5	3	2	4	2	7	4	4	4	2	4	3	6	4
1994 PROJECTIONS			151	583	78	165	25	5	8	81	44	71	20	21	.283	.388	

Ozzie Guillen No. 13/SS

Full name: Oswaldo Guillen
Bats: L **Throws:** R **HT:** 5–11 **WT:** 164
Born: 1–20–64, Oculare del Tuy, VZ
After missing most of 1992 with a knee injury, Guillen returned in 1993 to post a career-high in doubles (23), but had only 5 SB, the lowest full-season total of his career.

	TEAM	LG	POS	G	AB	R	H	2B	3B	HR	RBI	BB	SO	SB	E	BA	SLG	SALARY
1985	CHI	AL	SS	150	491	71	134	21	9	1	33	12	36	7	12	.273	.358	N/A
1986	CHI	AL	SS	159	547	58	137	19	4	2	47	12	52	8	22	.250	.311	N/A
1987	CHI	AL	SS	149	560	64	156	22	7	2	51	22	52	25	19	.279	.354	N/A
1988	CHI	AL	SS	156	566	58	148	16	7	0	39	25	40	25	20	.261	.314	N/A
1989	CHI	AL	SS	155	597	63	151	20	8	1	54	15	48	36	22	.253	.318	N/A
1990	CHI	AL	SS	160	516	61	144	21	4	1	58	26	37	13	17	.279	.341	782,529
1991	CHI	AL	SS	154	524	52	143	20	3	3	49	11	38	21	21	.273	.340	1,600,000
1992	CHI	AL	SS	12	40	5	8	4	0	0	7	1	5	1	0	.200	.300	1,900,000
1993	CHI	AL	SS	134	457	44	128	23	4	4	50	10	41	5	16	.280	.374	2,000,000
9	YR	TOTALS		1229	4298	476	1149	166	46	14	388	134	349	141	149	.267	.337	
1993	RANK	MLB	SS	18	18	24	17	10	9	16	17	34	23	21	13	15	17	7
1994	PROJECTIONS			101	348	35	91	15	2	2	34	7	32	4	12	.261	.336	

Michael Huff No. 12/OF

Full name: Michael Kale Huff
Bats: R **Throws:** R **HT:** 6–1 **WT:** 190
Born: 8–11–63, Honolulu, HI
High school: New Trier East (Winnetka, IL)
College: Northwestern (Chicago, IL)
Strong prospect Huff should replace Ellis Burks in the outfield. In 1993 he batted .294 with 18 SB in 92 games with AAA Nashville.

	TEAM	LG	POS	G	AB	R	H	2B	3B	HR	RBI	BB	SO	SB	E	BA	SLG	SALARY
1989	LA	NL	OF	12	25	4	5	1	0	1	2	3	6	0	0	.200	.360	N/A
1991	CLE-CHI	AL	OF-2B	102	243	42	61	10	2	3	25	37	48	14	2	.251	.346	100,000
1992	CHI	AL	OF	60	115	13	24	5	0	0	8	10	24	1	0	.209	.252	145,000
1993	CHI	AL	OF	43	44	4	8	2	0	1	6	9	15	1	0	.182	.295	N/A
4	YR	TOTALS		217	427	63	98	18	2	5	41	59	93	16	2	.230	.316	
1993	RANK	MLB	OF	not ranked -- didn't have 150 ABs in 1993														
1994	PROJECTIONS			52	104	16	24	4	0	1	11	16	23	5	0	.231	.337	

Lance Johnson No. 1/OF

Full name: Kenneth Lance Johnson
Bats: L **Throws:** L **HT:** 5–11 **WT:** 160
Born: 7–6–63, Cincinnati, OH
High school: Princeton (Cincinnati, OH)
College: Triton JC (IL) and South Alabama

Johnson led the AL in triples for the third straight season. His .311 BA was tenth-best in the AL and his 35 SB ranked sixth.

	TEAM	LG	POS	G	AB	R	H	2B	3B	HR	RBI	BB	SO	SB	E	BA	SLG	SALARY
1987	STL	NL	OF	33	59	4	13	2	1	0	7	4	6	6	2	.220	.288	N/A
1988	CHI	AL	OF	33	124	11	23	4	1	0	6	6	11	6	2	.185	.234	N/A
1989	CHI	AL	OF	50	180	28	54	8	2	0	16	17	24	16	2	.300	.367	N/A
1990	CHI	AL	OF	151	541	76	154	18	9	1	51	33	45	36	10	.285	.357	N/A
1991	CHI	AL	OF	159	588	72	161	14	13	0	49	26	58	26	2	.274	.342	275,000
1992	CHI	AL	OF	157	567	67	158	15	12	3	47	34	33	41	6	.279	.363	325,000
1993	CHI	AL	OF	147	540	75	168	18	14	0	47	36	33	35	9	.311	.396	2,666,666
7	YR	TOTALS		730	2599	333	731	79	52	4	223	156	210	166	33	.281	.356	
1993	RANK	MLB	OF	26	28	36	15	61	1	135	63	63	115	14	10	14	88	30
1994	PROJECTIONS			162	604	84	188	19	14	0	51	39	35	38	9	.311	.389	0

Ron Karkovice No. 20/C

Full name: Ronald Joseph Karkovice
Bats: R **Throws:** R **HT:** 6–1 **WT:** 219
Born: 8–8–63, Union, NJ
High school: Boone (Orlando, FL)

Karkovice led AL catchers by throwing out 48 of 96 base stealers (50%), but his BA dipped to .228, his worst mark since 1988.

	TEAM	LG	POS	G	AB	R	H	2B	3B	HR	RBI	BB	SO	SB	E	BA	SLG	SALARY
1986	CHI	AL	C	37	97	13	24	7	0	4	13	9	37	1	1	.247	.443	N/A
1987	CHI	AL	C	39	85	7	6	0	0	2	7	7	40	3	3	.071	.141	N/A
1988	CHI	AL	C	46	115	10	20	4	0	3	9	7	30	4	1	.174	.287	N/A
1989	CHI	AL	C	71	182	21	48	9	2	3	24	10	56	0	5	.264	.385	N/A
1990	CHI	AL	C	68	183	30	45	10	0	6	20	16	52	2	2	.246	.399	108,000
1991	CHI	AL	C-OF	75	167	25	41	13	0	5	22	15	42	0	4	.246	.413	310,000
1992	CHI	AL	C-OF	123	342	39	81	12	1	13	50	30	89	10	6	.237	.392	500,000
1993	CHI	AL	C	128	403	60	92	17	1	20	54	29	126	2	5	.228	.424	1,566,666
8	YR	TOTALS		587	1574	205	357	72	4	56	199	123	472	22	27	.227	.384	
1993	RANK	MLB	C	14	14	6	19	17	11	6	14	15	1	13	23	33	10	10
1994	PROJECTIONS			139	441	65	100	18	1	22	59	31	137	2	5	.227	.422	

Tim Raines No. 30/OF

Full name: Timothy Raines
Bats: B **Throws:** R **HT:** 5–8 **WT:** 186
Born: 9–16–59, Sanford, FL
High school: Seminole (Sanford, FL)

Raines is now fourth on the all-time stolen base list. He had 40 hits in his last 115 at-bats (.348) and stole 11 bases in his last 30 games.

TEAM	LG	POS	G	AB	R	H	2B	3B	HR	RBI	BB	SO	SB	E	BA	SLG	SALARY
1979 MTL	NL	PR	6	0	3	0	0	0	0	0	0	0	2	---	---	---	N/A
1980 MTL	NL	2B-OF	15	20	5	1	0	0	0	0	6	3	5	0	.050	.050	N/A
1981 MTL	NL	OF-2B	88	313	61	95	13	7	5	37	45	31	71	4	.304	.438	N/A
1982 MTL	NL	OF-2B	156	647	90	179	32	8	4	43	75	83	78	8	.277	.369	N/A
1983 MTL	NL	OF-2B	156	615	133	183	32	8	11	71	97	70	90	4	.298	.429	N/A
1984 MTL	NL	OF-2B	160	622	106	192	38	9	8	60	87	69	75	6	.309	.437	N/A
1985 MTL	NL	OF	150	575	115	184	30	13	11	41	81	60	70	2	.320	.475	N/A
1986 MTL	NL	OF	151	580	91	194	35	10	9	62	78	60	70	6	.334	.476	N/A
1987 MTL	NL	OF	139	530	123	175	34	8	18	68	90	52	50	4	.330	.526	N/A
1988 MTL	NL	OF	109	429	66	116	19	7	12	48	53	44	33	3	.270	.431	N/A
1989 MTL	NL	OF	145	517	76	148	29	6	9	60	93	48	41	1	.286	.418	N/A
1990 MTL	NL	OF	130	457	65	131	11	5	9	62	70	43	49	6	.287	.392	N/A
1991 CHI	AL	OF	155	609	102	163	20	6	5	50	83	68	51	3	.268	.345	3,500,000
1992 CHI	AL	OF	144	551	102	162	22	9	7	54	81	48	45	2	.294	.405	3,500,000
1993 CHI	AL	OF	115	415	75	127	16	4	16	54	64	35	21	0	.306	.480	3,500,000
15 YR	TOTALS		1819	6880	1213	2050	331	100	124	710	1003	714	751	49	.298	.429	
1993 RANK	MLB OF		75	65	36	55	76	32	33	55	21	110	29	131	21	31	18
1994 PROJECTIONS			118	433	68	124	15	5	12	54	62	40	34	3	.286	.432	

Frank Thomas No. 35/1B

Full name: Frank Edward Thomas
Bats: R **Throws:** R **HT:** 6–5 **WT:** 257
Born: 5–27–68, Columbus, GA
High school: Columbus (GA)
College: Auburn

AL MVP Thomas made the AL top 10 in BA (.317), HR (41), RBI (128), and walks (122). He's had 100+ walks in '91, '92 and '93.

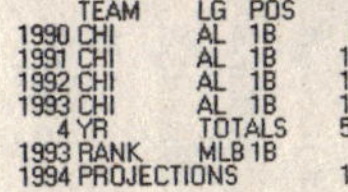

TEAM	LG	POS	G	AB	R	H	2B	3B	HR	RBI	BB	SO	SB	E	BA	SLG	SALARY
1990 CHI	AL	1B	60	191	39	63	11	3	7	31	44	54	0	5	.330	.529	100,000
1991 CHI	AL	1B	158	559	104	178	31	2	32	109	138	112	1	2	.318	.553	120,000
1992 CHI	AL	1B	160	573	108	185	46	2	24	115	122	88	6	13	.323	.536	600,000
1993 CHI	AL	1B	153	549	106	174	36	0	41	128	112	54	4	15	.317	.607	975,000
4 YR	TOTALS		531	1872	357	600	124	7	104	383	416	308	11	35	.321	.561	
1993 RANK	MLB 1B		7	9	4	5	5	30	1	1	2	25	11	5	6	1	18
1994 PROJECTIONS			162	587	112	185	38	0	45	139	118	49	4	15	.315	.610	

Robin Ventura No. 23/3B

Full name: Robin Mark Ventura
Bats: L **Throws:** R **HT:** 6–1 **WT:** 198
Born: 7–14–67, Santa Maria, CA
High school: Righetti (Santa Maria, CA)
College: Oklahoma State

Ventura has had over 90 RBI in the last three seasons. In 1993 he had 105 walks, sixth-best in the AL.

	TEAM	LG	POS	G	AB	R	H	2B	3B	HR	RBI	BB	SO	SB	E	BA	SLG	SALARY
1989	CHI	AL	3B	16	45	5	8	3	0	0	7	8	6	0	2	.178	.244	N/A
1990	CHI	AL	3B-1B	150	493	48	123	17	1	5	54	55	53	1	25	.249	.318	100,000
1991	CHI	AL	3B-1B	157	606	92	172	25	1	23	100	80	67	2	18	.284	.442	150,000
1992	CHI	AL	3B-1B	157	592	85	167	38	1	16	93	93	71	2	23	.282	.431	600,000
1993	CHI	AL	3B	157	554	85	145	27	1	22	94	105	82	1	14	.262	.433	1,820,000
5	YR	TOTALS		637	2290	315	615	110	4	66	348	341	279	6	82	.269	.407	
1993	RANK	MLB	3B	3	7	6	10	14	21	4	6	1	11	26	17	22	14	11
1994	PROJECTIONS			107	364	46	92	15	0	9	51	56	47	0	13	.253	.374	

Wilson Alvarez No. 40/P

Full name: Wilson Eduardo Alvarez
Bats: L **Throws:** L **HT:** 6–1 **WT:** 235
Born: 3–24–70, Maracaibo, VZ

In his first full season as a starter, Alvarez had a career-high 15 wins and led the AL with 122 walks. He was 7–0 with a 1.55 ERA in his last 8 starts

	TM	LG	POS	W	L	ERA	G	GS	CG	SH	SV	IP	H	R	ER	HR	BB	SO	SALARY
1989	TEX	AL	P	0	1	---	1	0	0	0	0	0.0	3	3	3	2	2	0	N/A
1991	CHI	AL	P	3	2	3.51	10	9	2	1	0	56.1	47	26	22	9	29	32	100,000
1992	CHI	AL	P	5	3	5.20	34	9	0	0	1	100.1	103	64	58	12	65	66	130,000
1993	CHI	AL	P	15	8	2.95	31	31	1	1	0	207.2	168	78	68	14	122	155	180,000
4	YR	TOTALS		23	14	3.73	76	49	3	2	1	364.1	321	171	151	37	218	253	
1993	RANK	MLB	Ps	21		40	194	51	79	23	102	46	27	38		59	276	84	184
1994	PROJECTIONS			17	8	2.91	36	36	0	0	0	241	195	90	78	15	142	180	

Alex Fernandez No. 32/P

Full name: Alexander Fernandez
Bats: R **Throws:** R **HT:** 6–1 **WT:** 215
Born: 8–13–69, Miami Beach, FL
High school: Pace (Miami, FL)
College: Miami (FL)
Fernandez posted a career-best 18–9 record. He led the team with 169 strikeouts and was 10–3 after a White Sox loss.

	TM	LG	POS	W	L	ERA	G	GS	CG	SH	SV	IP	H	R	ER	HR	BB	SO	SALARY
1990	CHI	AL	P	5	5	3.80	13	13	3	0	0	87.2	89	40	37	6	34	61	100,000
1991	CHI	AL	P	9	13	4.51	34	32	2	0	0	191.2	186	100	96	16	88	145	120,000
1992	CHI	AL	P	8	11	4.27	29	29	4	2	0	187.2	199	100	89	21	50	95	2,216,667
1993	CHI	AL	P	18	9	3.13	34	34	3	1	0	247.1	221	95	86	27	67	169	868,333
4	YR	TOTALS		40	38	3.68	110	108	12	3	0	714.1	695	335	308	70	239	470	
1993	Rank	MLB Ps		8		56	145	12	37	23	102	9	62	44		188	48	111	109
1994	PROJECTIONS			19	9	3.07	36	36	2	0	0	264	234	99	90	29	69	180	

Jack McDowell No. 29/P

Full name: Jack Burns McDowell
Bats: R **Throws:** R **HT:** 6–5 **WT:** 188
Born: 1–16–66, Van Nuys, CA
High school: Notre Dame (Van Nuys, CA)
College: Stanford
Cy Young winner McDowell tied for the ML lead with 22 wins. Since 1990, he has more wins (73) than any other pitcher.

	TM	LG	POS	W	L	ERA	G	GS	CG	SH	SV	IP	H	R	ER	HR	BB	SO	SALARY
1987	CHI	AL	P	3	0	1.93	4	4	0	0	0	28.0	16	6	6	1	6	15	N/A
1988	CHI	AL	P	5	10	3.97	26	26	1	0	0	158.2	147	85	70	12	68	84	N/A
1990	CHI	AL	P	14	9	3.82	33	33	4	0	0	205.0	189	93	87	20	77	165	125,000
1991	CHI	AL	P	17	10	3.41	35	35	15	3	0	253.2	212	97	96	19	82	191	175,000
1992	CHI	AL	P	20	10	3.18	34	34	13	1	0	260.2	247	95	92	21	75	178	1,600,000
1993	CHI	AL	P	22	10	3.37	34	34	10	4	0	256.2	261	104	96	20	69	158	4,000,000
6	YR	TOTALS		81	49	3.46	166	166	43	8	0	1162.2	1072	480	447	93	377	791	
1993	Rank	MLB Ps		1		73	145	12	3	1	102	4	156	59		98	47	154	17
1994	PROJECTIONS			13	9	3.67	31	31	5	1	0	206	199	94	84	17	71	135	

Roberto Hernandez No. 39/P

Full name: Roberto Manuel Hernandez
Bats: R **Throws:** R **HT:** 6–4 **WT:** 235
Born: 11–11–64, Santurce, PR
High school: New Hampton (NH)
College: South Carolina–Aiken

In his first full season as a closer, Hernandez placed fourth in the AL with 38 saves. He had a 1.74 ERA in his last 42 outings.

	TM	LG	POS	W	L	ERA	G	GS	CG	SH	SV	IP	H	R	ER	HR	BB	SO	SALARY
1991	CHI	AL	P	1	0	7.80	9	3	0	0	0	15.0	18	15	13	1	7	6	100,000
1992	CHI	AL	P	7	3	1.65	43	0	0	0	12	71.0	45	15	13	4	20	68	112,000
1993	CHI	AL	P	3	4	2.29	70	0	0	0	38	78.2	66	21	20	6	20	71	195,000
3	YR	TOTALS		11	7	2.51	122	3	0	0	50	164.2	129	51	46	11	47	145	
1993	Rank	MLB Ps		209		11	14	202	125	69	10	191	34	7		87	42	30	173
1994	PROJECTIONS			3	2	2.50	40	1	0	0	16	54	43	17	15	3	15	48	

Gene Lamont No. 33/Mgr.

Full name: Gene William Lamont
Bats: B **Throws:** R **HT:** 6–1 **WT:** 190
Born: 12–25–46, Rockford, IL
High school: Hiawatha (Kirkland, IL)
College: Northern Illinois and Western Illinois

In just his second season at the White Sox helm, Lamont managed Chicago to their first division title in ten years.

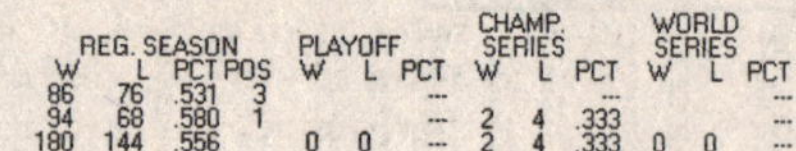

			REG. SEASON				PLAYOFF			CHAMP. SERIES			WORLD SERIES		
YEAR	TEAM	LG	W	L	PCT	POS	W	L	PCT	W	L	PCT	W	L	PCT
1992	CHI	AL	86	76	.531	3			---			---			---
1993	CHI	AL	94	68	.580	1			---	2	4	.333			---
2	YR TOTALS		180	144	.556		0	0	---	2	4	.333	0	0	---

Esteban Beltre No. 38/IF

Full name: Esteban Velera Beltre
Bats: R **Throws:** R **HT:** 5–10 **WT:** 172
Born: 12–26–67, Ingenio Quisfuella, DR
Beltre made the American Association All-Star team at shortstop for AAA Nashville. He hit .292 with eight home runs and 52 RBI.

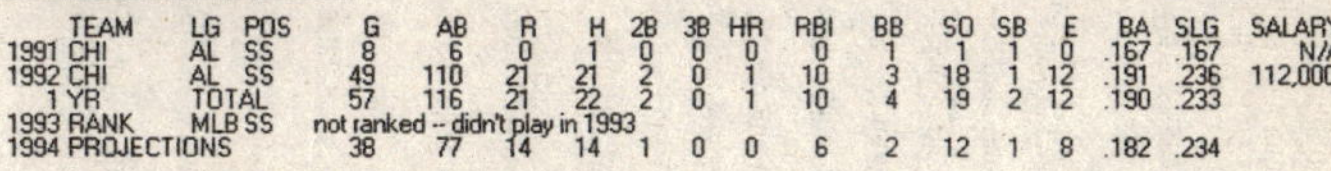

	TEAM	LG	POS	G	AB	R	H	2B	3B	HR	RBI	BB	SO	SB	E	BA	SLG	SALARY
1991	CHI	AL	SS	8	6	0	1	0	0	0	0	1	1	1	0	.167	.167	N/A
1992	CHI	AL	SS	49	110	21	21	2	0	1	10	3	18	1	12	.191	.236	112,000
1	YR	TOTAL		57	116	21	22	2	0	1	10	4	19	2	12	.190	.233	
1993	RANK	MLB	SS	not ranked -- didn't play in 1993														
1994	PROJECTIONS			38	77	14	14	1	0	0	6	2	12	1	8	.182	.234	

Jason Bere No. 51/P

Full name: Jason Phillip Bere
Bats: R **Throws:** R **HT:** 6–3 **WT:** 185
Born: 5–26–71, Cambridge, MA
High school: Wilmington (MA)
College: Middlesex Community (Burlington, MA)
Bere led all AL rookie pitchers in wins (12).

	TM	LG	POS	W	L	ERA	G	GS	CG	SH	SV	IP	H	R	ER	HR	BB	SO	SALARY
1993	CHI	AL	P	12	5	3.47	24	24	1	0	0	142.2	109	60	55	12	81	129	109,000
1	YR	TOTAL		12	5	3.47	24	24	1	0	0	142.2	109	60	55	12	81	129	
1993	RANK	MLB	Ps	43		87	241	97	79	69	102	103	16	73		115	272	29	236

Craig Grebeck No. 14/IF

Full name: Craig Allen Grebeck
Bats: R **Throws:** R **HT:** 5–7 **WT:** 148
Born: 12–29–64, Johnstown, PA
High school: Lakewood (CA)
College: Cal State–Dominguez Hills
Grebeck batted just .226, his lowest since '90.

	TEAM	LG	POS	G	AB	R	H	2B	3B	HR	RBI	BB	SO	SB	E	BA	SLG	SALARY
1990	CHI	AL	3B-SS	59	119	7	20	3	1	1	9	8	24	0	3	.168	.235	100,000
1991	CHI	AL	3B-2B	107	224	37	63	16	3	6	31	38	40	1	10	.281	.460	125,000
1992	CHI	AL	SS-3B	88	287	24	77	21	2	3	35	30	34	0	8	.268	.387	200,000
1993	CHI	AL	3B	72	190	25	43	5	0	1	12	26	26	1	5	.226	.268	632,500
4	YR	TOTALS		326	820	93	203	45	6	11	87	102	124	2	26	.248	.357	
1993	RANK	MLB	3B	35	36	36	39	41	33	40	40	26	39	26	38	36	41	15
1994	PROJECTIONS			73	198	18	46	9	1	1	18	21	28	0	5	.232	.318	

Jose DeLeon — No. 48/P

Full name: Jose Chestaro De Leon
Bats: R **Throws:** R **HT:** 6–3 **WT:** 226
Born: 12–20–60, Rancho Viejo, LaVega, DR
High school: Perth Amboy (NJ)
Acquired in '93 for Bobby Thigpen, nine of his 11 appearances for the White Sox were scoreless.

	TM	LG	POS	W	L	ERA	G	GS	CG	SH	SV	IP	H	R	ER	HR	BB	SO	SALARY
1989	STL	NL	P	16	12	3.05	36	36	5	3	0	244.2	173	96	83	16	80	201	N/A
1990	STL	NL	P	7	19	4.43	32	32	0	0	0	182.2	168	96	90	15	86	164	N/A
1991	STL	NL	P	5	9	2.71	28	28	1	0	0	162.2	144	57	49	15	61	118	2,366,667
1992	PHL	NL	P	2	8	4.37	32	18	0	0	0	117.1	111	63	57	7	48	79	N/A
1993	PHL	NL	P	3	0	3.26	24	3	0	0	0	47.0	39	25	17	5	27	34	N/A
1993	CHI	AL	P	0	0	1.74	11	0	0	0	0	10.1	5	2	2	2	3	6	550,000
11	YR	TOTALS		78	113	3.70	328	264	21	7	4	1754.1	1441	801	722	136	775	1462	
1993	RANK	MLB Ps		209		43	134	196	125	69	102	259	18	110		209	257	103	128
1994	PROJECTIONS			1	1	4.13	14	1	0	0	0	24	20	14	11	3	15	17	

Mike LaValliere — No. 10/C

Full name: Michael Eugene LaValliere
Bats: L **Throws:** R **HT:** 5–9 **WT:** 210
Born: 8–18–60, Charlotte, NC
High school: Trinity (Manchester, NH)
College: Lowell (MA)
Mike caught on when Karkovice went on the DL.

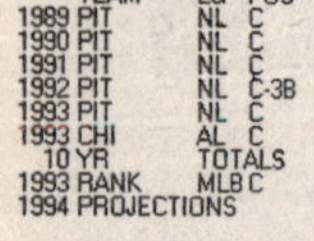

	TEAM	LG	POS	G	AB	R	H	2B	3B	HR	RBI	BB	SO	SB	E	BA	SLG	SALARY
1989	PIT	NL	C	68	190	15	60	10	0	2	23	29	24	0	3	.316	.400	N/A
1990	PIT	NL	C	96	279	27	72	15	0	3	31	44	20	0	5	.258	.344	655,000
1991	PIT	NL	C	108	336	25	97	11	2	3	41	33	27	2	1	.289	.360	925,000
1992	PIT	NL	C-3B	95	293	22	75	13	1	2	29	44	21	0	3	.256	.328	1,850,000
1993	PIT	NL	C	1	5	0	1	0	0	0	0	0	0	0	0	.200	.200	N/A
1993	CHI	AL	C	37	97	6	25	2	0	0	8	4	14	0	0	.258	.278	109,000
10	YR	TOTALS		774	2236	172	600	99	5	16	251	292	214	5	31	.268	.339	
1993	RANK	MLB C		not ranked -- didn't have 150 ABs in 1993														
1994	PROJECTIONS			14	36	2	8	0	0	0	2	2	5	0	0	.222	.25	

Kirk McCaskill — No. 25/P

Full name: Kirk Edward McCaskill
Bats: R **Throws:** R **HT:** 6–1 **WT:** 205
Born: 4–9–61, Kapuskasing, Ont.
High school: Trinity Pawling (Trinity, NY)
College: Vermont
McCaskill came out of the bullpen 16 times in '93.

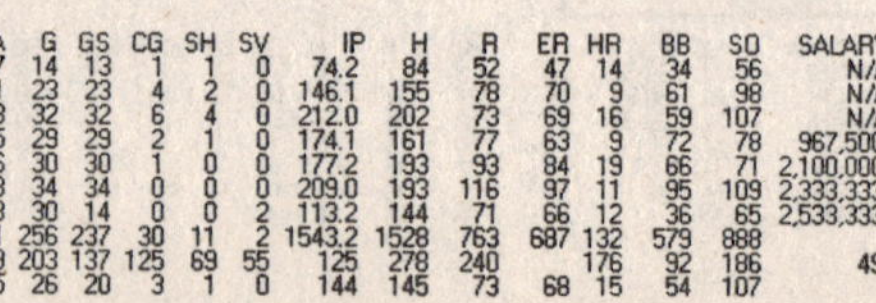

	TM	LG	POS	W	L	ERA	G	GS	CG	SH	SV	IP	H	R	ER	HR	BB	SO	SALARY
1987	CAL	AL	P	4	6	5.67	14	13	1	1	0	74.2	84	52	47	14	34	56	N/A
1988	CAL	AL	P	8	6	4.31	23	23	4	2	0	146.1	155	78	70	9	61	98	N/A
1989	CAL	AL	P	15	10	2.93	32	32	6	4	0	212.0	202	73	69	16	59	107	N/A
1990	CAL	AL	P	12	11	3.25	29	29	2	1	0	174.1	161	77	63	9	72	78	967,500
1991	CAL	AL	P	10	19	4.26	30	30	1	0	0	177.2	193	93	84	19	66	71	2,100,000
1992	CHI	AL	P	12	13	4.18	34	34	0	0	0	209.0	193	116	97	11	95	109	2,333,333
1993	CHI	AL	P	4	8	5.23	30	14	0	0	2	113.2	144	71	66	12	36	65	2,533,333
9	YR	TOTALS		94	95	4.01	256	237	30	11	2	1543.2	1528	763	687	132	579	888	
1993	Rank	MLB Ps		173		249	203	137	125	69	55	125	278	240		176	92	186	49
1994	PROJECTIONS			8	8	4.25	26	20	3	1	0	144	145	73	68	15	54	107	

Matt Merullo No. 5/C

Full name: Matthew Bates Merullo
Bats: L **Throws:** R **HT:** 6–2 **WT:** 200
Born: 8–4–65, Ridgefield, CT
High school: Fairfield Prep (CT)
College: North Carolina–Chapel Hill
Merullo hit .332 in 103 games at AAA Nashville.

TEAM	LG	POS	G	AB	R	H	2B	3B	HR	RBI	BB	SO	SB	E	BA	SLG	SALARY
1989 CHI	AL	C	31	81	5	18	1	0	1	8	6	14	0	3	.222	.272	N/A
1991 CHI	AL	C-1B	80	140	8	32	1	0	5	21	9	18	0	2	.229	.343	108,500
1992 CHI	AL	C	24	50	3	9	1	1	0	3	1	8	0	2	.180	.240	N/A
1993 CHI	AL	DH	8	20	1	1	0	0	0	0	0	1	0	0	.050	.050	N/A
4 YR	TOTALS		143	291	17	60	3	1	6	32	16	41	0	7	.206	.285	
1993 RANK	MLB	DH	not ranked -- didn't have 150 ABs in 1993														
1994 PROJECTIONS			39	80	4	17	0	0	2	9	5	11	0	1	.213	.288	

Warren Newson No. 24/DH

Full name: Warren D. Newson
Bats: L **Throws:** L **HT:** 5–7 **WT:** 202
Born: 7–3–64, Newnan, GA
High school: Newnan (GA)
College: Middle Georgia Junior
Newson batted .300 in 26 games for Chicago.

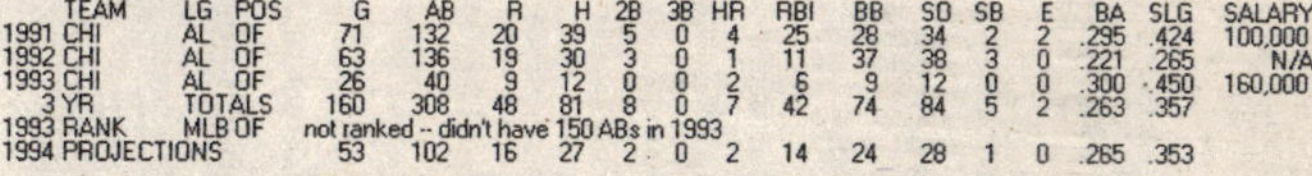

TEAM	LG	POS	G	AB	R	H	2B	3B	HR	RBI	BB	SO	SB	E	BA	SLG	SALARY
1991 CHI	AL	OF	71	132	20	39	5	0	4	25	28	34	2	2	.295	.424	100,000
1992 CHI	AL	OF	63	136	19	30	3	0	1	11	37	38	3	0	.221	.265	N/A
1993 CHI	AL	OF	26	40	9	12	0	0	2	6	9	12	0	0	.300	.450	160,000
3 YR	TOTALS		160	308	48	81	8	0	7	42	74	84	5	2	.263	.357	
1993 RANK	MLB	OF	not ranked -- didn't have 150 ABs in 1993														
1994 PROJECTIONS			53	102	16	27	2	0	2	14	24	28	1	0	.265	.353	

Dan Pasqua No. 44/OF

Full name: Daniel Anthony Pasqua
Bats: L **Throws:** L **HT:** 6–0 **WT:** 218
Born: 10–17–61, Yonkers, NY
High school: Old Tappan (NJ)
College: William Paterson (Wayne, NJ)
Pasqua hit just .106 with men in scoring position.

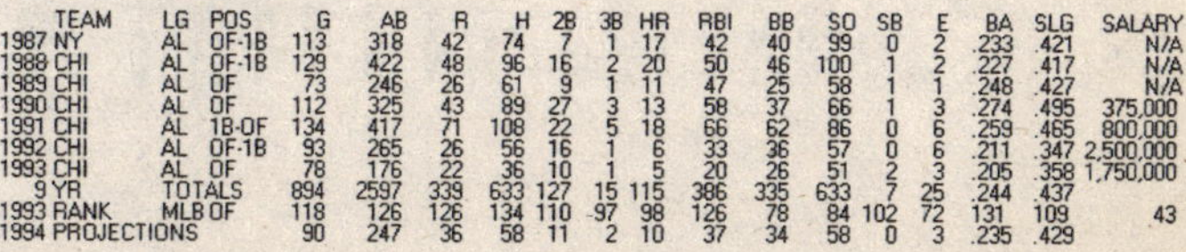

TEAM	LG	POS	G	AB	R	H	2B	3B	HR	RBI	BB	SO	SB	E	BA	SLG	SALARY
1987 NY	AL	OF-1B	113	318	42	74	7	1	17	42	40	99	0	2	.233	.421	N/A
1988 CHI	AL	OF-1B	129	422	48	96	16	2	20	50	46	100	1	2	.227	.417	N/A
1989 CHI	AL	OF	73	246	26	61	9	1	11	47	25	58	1	1	.248	.427	N/A
1990 CHI	AL	OF	112	325	43	89	27	3	13	58	37	66	1	3	.274	.495	375,000
1991 CHI	AL	1B-OF	134	417	71	108	22	5	18	66	62	86	0	6	.259	.465	800,000
1992 CHI	AL	OF-1B	93	265	26	56	16	1	6	33	36	57	0	6	.211	.347	2,500,000
1993 CHI	AL	OF	78	176	22	36	10	1	5	20	26	51	2	3	.205	.358	1,750,000
9 YR	TOTALS		894	2597	339	633	127	15	115	386	335	633	7	25	.244	.437	
1993 RANK	MLB	OF	118	126	126	134	110	97	98	126	78	84	102	72	131	109	43
1994 PROJECTIONS			90	247	36	58	11	2	10	37	34	58	0	3	.235	.429	

Scott Radinsky — No. 31/P

Full name: Scott David Radinsky
Bats: L **Throws:** L **HT:** 6–3 **WT:** 204
Born: 3–3–68, Glendale, CA
High school: Simi Valley (CA)
Radinsky has averaged over 67 appearances per year in his four-year career.

	TM	LG	POS	W	L	ERA	G	GS	CG	SH	SV	IP	H	R	ER	HR	BB	SO	SALARY
1990	CHI	AL	P	6	1	4.82	62	0	0	0	4	52.1	47	29	28	1	36	46	100,000
1991	CHI	AL	P	5	5	2.02	67	0	0	0	8	71.1	53	18	16	4	23	49	130,000
1992	CHI	AL	P	3	7	2.73	68	0	0	0	15	59.1	54	21	18	3	34	48	190,000
1993	CHI	AL	P	8	2	4.28	73	0	0	0	4	54.2	61	33	26	3	19	44	1,050,000
4	YR	TOTALS		22	15	3.33	270	0	0	0	31	237.2	215	101	88	11	112	187	
1993	Rank	MLB Ps		99		168	6	202	125	69	37	273	221	224		33	129	60	95
1994	PROJECTIONS			5	4	2.95	69	0	0	0	9	61	56	24	20	3	25	47	

Steve Sax — No. 7/OF

Full name: Stephen Louis Sax
Bats: R **Throws:** R **HT:** 5–11 **WT:** 189
Born: 1–29–60, Sacramento, CA
High school: J. Marshall (W. Sacramento, CA)
Former All-Star Sax had his second straight poor season, appearing in only 57 games.

	TEAM	LG	POS	G	AB	R	H	2B	3B	HR	RBI	BB	SO	SB	E	BA	SLG	SALARY
1988	LA	NL	2B	160	632	70	175	19	4	5	57	45	51	42	14	.277	.343	N/A
1989	NY	AL	2B	158	651	88	205	26	3	5	63	52	44	43	10	.315	.387	N/A
1990	NY	AL	2B	155	615	70	160	24	2	4	42	49	46	43	10	.260	.325	950,000
1991	NY	AL	2B-3B	158	652	85	198	38	2	10	56	41	38	31	10	.304	.414	1,633,334
1992	CHI	AL	2B	143	567	74	134	26	4	4	47	43	42	30	20	.236	.317	3,575,000
1993	CHI	AL	OF	57	119	20	28	5	0	1	8	8	6	7	0	.235	.303	1,975,000
13	YR	TOTALS		1762	6916	911	1943	278	46	54	549	556	582	444	190	.281	.358	
1993	RANK	MLB OF		not ranked -- didn't have 150 ABs in 1993														
1994	PROJECTIONS			81	284	35	73	10	0	2	19	21	22	18	4	.257	.324	

Jeff Schwarz — No. 49/P

Full name: Jeff Schwarz
Bats: R **Throws:** R **HT:** 6–5 **WT:** 190
Born: 5–20–64, Ft. Pierce, FL
High school: Ft. Pierce, FL
Schwarz allowed just 17 earned runs in his last 42 innings pitched for a 3.64 ERA

	TM	LG	POS	W	L	ERA	G	GS	CG	SH	SV	IP	H	R	ER	HR	BB	SO	SALARY
1993	CHI	AL	P	2	2	3.71	41	0	0	0	0	51.0	35	21	21	1	38	41	109,000
1	YR	TOTAL		2	2	3.71	41	0	0	0	0	51.0	35	21	21	1	38	41	
1993	RANK	MLB Ps		246		106	111	202	125	69	102	285	6	64		4	288	61	236

Cleveland *INDIANS*

1994 Scouting Report

Hitting: (.275 BA, third in AL; 141 HR, ninth in AL)

The Indians' key offensive players are Carlos Baerga, Albert Belle, Kenny Lofton, and Sandy Alomar. Just 24 in '93, Baerga got 200 hits on his way to a .321 BA, with 21 HR and 114 RBI. Albert Belle led the majors in RBI, driving in 129, with 38 HR. Lofton hit .325 and led the AL in SB with 70.

The Indians' offense should improve in 1994. Catcher Sandy Alomar missed 60 percent of the season due to injury, but hit .270 when he played. Plugging in free agent signee Eddie Murray's 90–plus RBI at DH should help. Wayne Kirby is good defensively, but Manny Ramirez (Baseball America's Minor League Player of the Year) will eventually take over RF.

Pitching: (1993/4.58 ERA, eleventh in AL)

Jose Mesa was the team's best pitcher in 1993. He was only 10–12, but he worked 208.2 innings. Injuries sidelined Charles Nagy (right shoulder), Alan Embree, and Dave Mlicki (right shoulder). Tom Kramer, a rookie in 1993, was 7–3 for Cleveland. The Indians hope aging free agent Dennis Martinez will help. Julian Tavarez (AA Carolina League Player of the Year), Albie Lopez, and Chad Ogea (who tied for first in the AAA International League in wins with 13) are promising prospects.

After Steve Olin's death, Eric Plunk emerged as the bullpen ace; his 70 appearances and 15 saves led Cleveland. But rookie Jerry DiPoto contributed 11 saves, and Derek Lilliquist had 10 saves (a career-high).

Defense: (1993/.976 pct., last in AL)

Kirby and Belle have outstanding arms in the outfield.

1994 Prospects:

If the Indians are ever going to become a true contender, this is the year for it. Last year's boating tragedy involving pitchers Tim Crews and Steve Olin not only ruined the team's psyche, it crippled its bullpen. The result — a 19–32 record through May 31. The Tribe was 57–54 from June 1 on. This is a young team with a solid core that could do well, if it can overcome questionable pitching.

Team Directory

Chairman: Richard E. Jacobs
General Mgr.: John Hart
Manager of Media Relations: John Maroon
Exec. VP, Business: Dennis Lehman
Dir., Player Procurement: Mickey White
Traveling Secretary: Mike Seghi

Minor League Affiliates:

Level	Team/League	1993 Record
AAA	Charlotte – International	86–55
AA	Canton/Akron – Eastern	75–63
A	Kinston – Carolina	71–67
	Columbus, Ga. – South Atlantic	86–56
	Watertown – New York/Penn.	46–32
Rookie	Burlington – Appalachian	44–24

1993 Review

	Home		Away			Home		Away			Home		Away	
vs AL East	W	L	W	L	vs AL Cent.	W	L	W	L	vs AL West	W	L	W	L
Baltimore	3	3	2	5	Chicago	3	3	0	6	California	5	1	2	4
Boston	4	2	4	3	Kansas City	4	2	3	3	Oakland	4	2	4	2
Detroit	3	3	3	4	Milwaukee	5	2	3	3	Seattle	3	3	0	6
New York	4	3	2	4	Minnesota	2	4	2	4	Texas	4	2	3	3
Toronto	2	5	2	4										
Total	16	16	13	20		14	11	8	16		16	8	9	15

1993 finish: 76–86 (46–35 home, 30–51 away), sixth in AL East, 19 games behind

1994 Schedule

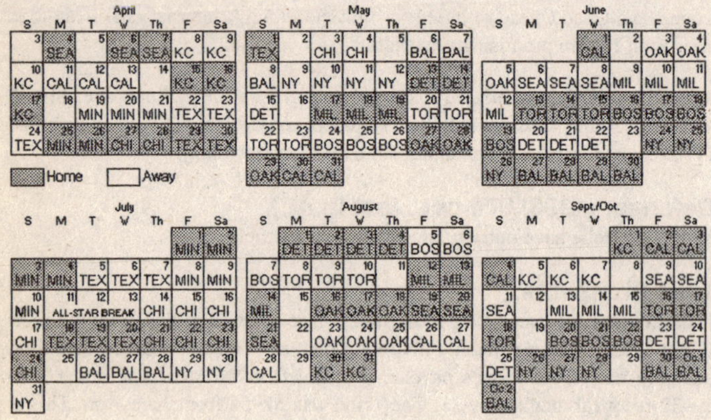

CLEVELAND INDIANS 1994 ROSTER

Manager: Mike Hargrove (21)
Coaches: Buddy Bell, infield coach ; Luis Isaac, bullpen coach; Charlie Manuel, hitting instructor; Phil Regan, pitching coach; Dave Nelson, 1B (14); Jeff Newman, 3B/assistant coach (55).

No.	PITCHERS	B	T	HT	WT	DOB	BIRTHPLACE	RESIDENCE
	Bryant, Shawn	R	L	6–3	205	6–10–69	Oklahoma City, OK	Oklahoma City, OK
	Carter, John	R	R	6–1	195	2–16–72	Chicago, IL	Chicago, IL
54	Clark, Mark	R	R	6–5	225	5–12–68	Bath, IL	Bath, IL
	Crawford, Carlos	R	R	6–1	185	10–4–71	Charlotte, NC	Charlotte, NC
45	DiPoto, Jerry	R	R	6–2	200	5–24–68	Jersey City, NJ	Leawood, KS
	Embree, Alan	L	L	6–2	185	1–23–70	Vancouver, WA	Brush Prairie, WA
48	Grimsley, Jason	R	R	6–3	182	8–7–67	Cleveland, TX	Cleveland, TX
53	Hernandez, Jeremy	R	R	6–6	205	7–6–66	Burbank, CA	Yuma, AZ
29	Kramer, Tom	S	R	6–0	205	1–9–68	Cincinnati, OH	St. Bernard, OH
28	Lilliquist, Derek	L	L	5–10	195	2–20–66	Winter Park, FL	Vero Beach, FL
	Lopez, Albie	R	R	6–1	205	8–18–71	Mesa, AZ	Mesa, AZ
32	Martinez, Dennis	R	R	6–1	180	5–14–55	Granada, Nic.	Miami, FL
	McCarthy, Greg	L	L	6–2	193	11–30–68	Norwalk, CT	Shelton, CT
49	Mesa, Jose	R	R	6–3	225	5–22–66	Winter Park, FL	Vero Beach, FL
23	Mlicki, Dave	R	R	6–4	190	6–8–68	Cleveland, OH	Galloway, OH
41	Nagy, Charles	L	R	6–3	200	5–5–67	Fairfield, CT	Westlake, OH
38	Plunk, Eric	R	R	6–6	220	9–3–63	Wilmington, CA	Riverside, CA
50	Tavarez, Julian	R	R	6–2	165	5–22–73	Santiago, DR	Santiago, DR
46	Wertz, Bill	R	R	6–6	220	1–15–67	Cleveland, OH	Cleveland, OH
No.	**CATCHERS**	**B**	**T**	**HT**	**WT**	**DOB**	**BIRTHPLACE**	**RESIDENCE**
15	Alomar, Jr., Sandy	R	R	6–5	215	6–18–66	Salinas, PR	Westlake, OH
	Levis, Jesse	L	R	5–9	180	4–14–68	Philadelphia, PA	Philadelphia, PA
No.	**INFIELDERS**	**B**	**T**	**HT**	**WT**	**DOB**	**BIRTHPLACE**	**RESIDENCE**
9	Baerga, Carlos	S	R	5–11	200	11–4–68	San Juan, PR	Westlake, OH
	Bell, David	R	R	6–4	200	9–14–72	Cincinnati, OH	Cincinnati, OH
10	Espinoza, Alvaro	R	R	6–0	190	2–19–62	Valencia, VZ	Bergenfield, NJ
16	Fermin, Felix	R	R	5–11	170	10–9–63	Mao Valverde, DR	Santiago, DR
44	Jefferson, Reggie	S	L	6–4	215	9–25–68	Tallahassee, FL	Tallahassee, FL
20	Lewis, Mark	R	R	6–1	190	11–30–69	Hamilton, OH	Hamilton, OH
33	Murray, Eddie	S	R	6–2	222	2–24–56	Los Angeles, CA	Canyon County, CA
	Perry, Herbert	R	R	6–2	210	9–15–69	Mayo, FL	Mayo, FL
11	Sorrento, Paul	L	R	6–2	220	11–17–65	Somerville, MA	Peabody, MA
25	Thome, Jim	L	R	6–4	220	8–27–70	Peoria, IL	Peoria, IL
No.	**OUTFIELDERS**	**B**	**T**	**HT**	**WT**	**DOB**	**BIRTHPLACE**	**RESIDENCE**
	Amaro, Ruben	S	R	5–10	175	2–12–65	Philadelphia, PA	Philadelphia, PA
8	Belle, Albert	R	R	6–2	210	8–25–66	Shreveport. LA	Euclid, OH
35	Kirby, Wayne	L	R	5–10	185	1–22–64	Williamsburg, VA	Yorktown, VA
7	Lofton, Kenny	L	L	6–0	180	5–31–67	East Chicago, IN	Tucson, AZ
22	Maldonado, Candy	R	R	6–0	205	9–5–60	Humacao, PR	Arecibo, PR
24	Ramirez, Manny	R	R	6–0	190	5–30–72	Santo Domingo, DR	New York, NY
	Ramirez, Omar	R	R	5–9	170	9–2–70	Santiago, DR	Santiago, DR
	Ramos, Ken	L	L	6–1	185	6–8–67	Sidney, NE	Pueblo, CO

Cleveland Indians Baseball Park
(41,911, grass)
Ticket prices:
- $28.00 (club seating)
- $16.00 (field box)
- $14.00 (lower box, view box)
- $12.00 (lower res.,mezz., upper box)
- $10.00 (upper reserved)
- $6 (res. general admission)
- $6 (bleachers)

Field Dimensions (from home plate)
- To left field at foul line, 325 feet
- To center field, 400 feet
- To right field at foul line, 325 feet
- (OF wall is 19' high in LF, 8' high in CF and RF)

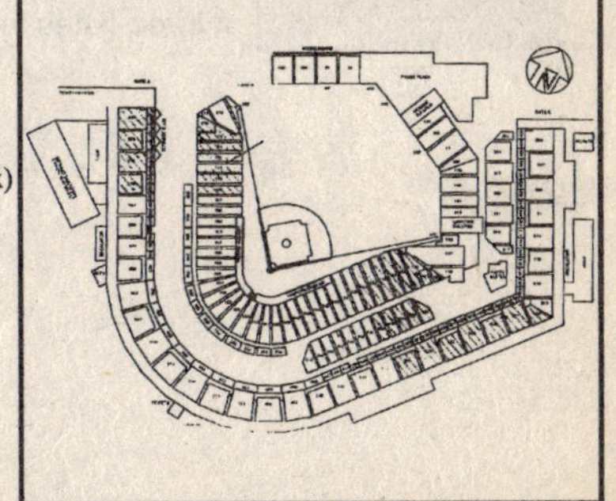

Sandy Alomar, Jr. 15/C

Full name: Santos Valazquez Alomar, Jr.
Bats: R **Throws:** R **HT:** 6–5 **WT:** 215
Born: 6–18–66, Salinas, PR
High school: L. Munoz Rivera (Salinas, PR)

Alomar, one of the best defensive catchers in baseball, has thrown out 87 of 254 potential base stealers (34%). He missed most of 1993 due to injuries to his back and knee.

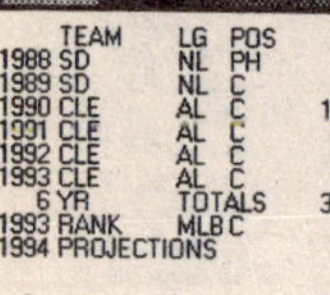
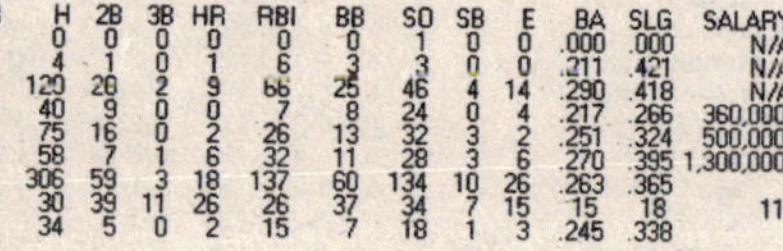

	TEAM	LG	POS	G	AB	R	H	2B	3B	HR	RBI	BB	SO	SB	E	BA	SLG	SALARY
1988	SD	NL	PH	1	1	0	0	0	0	0	0	0	1	0	0	.000	.000	N/A
1989	SD	NL	C	7	19	1	4	1	0	1	6	3	3	0	0	.211	.421	N/A
1990	CLE	AL	C	132	445	60	129	26	2	9	66	25	46	4	14	.290	.418	N/A
1991	CLE	AL	C	51	184	10	40	9	0	0	7	8	24	0	4	.217	.266	360,000
1992	CLE	AL	C	89	299	22	75	16	0	2	26	13	32	3	2	.251	.324	500,000
1993	CLE	AL	C	64	215	24	58	7	1	6	32	11	28	3	6	.270	.395	1,300,000
6	YR	TOTALS		344	1163	117	306	59	3	18	137	60	134	10	26	.263	.365	
1993	RANK	MLB	C	40	33	29	30	39	11	26	26	37	34	7	15	15	18	11
1994	PROJECTIONS			40	139	11	34	5	0	2	15	7	18	1	3	.245	.338	

Carlos Baerga No. 9/2B

Full name: Carlos Obed Baerga
Bats: S **Throws:** R **HT:** 5–11 **WT:** 200
Born: 11–4–68, San Juan, PR
High school: Barbara Ann Rooshart (PR)

Baerga is only the second Indian second baseman to put together back to back 20 HR seasons. The other was Joe Gordon, who did it three times in a row from 1947–1949.

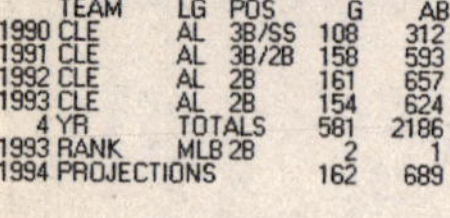

	TEAM	LG	POS	G	AB	R	H	2B	3B	HR	RBI	BB	SO	SB	E	BA	SLG	SALARY
1990	CLE	AL	3B/SS	108	312	46	81	17	2	7	47	16	57	0	17	.260	.394	N/A
1991	CLE	AL	3B/2B	158	593	80	171	28	2	11	69	48	74	3	27	.288	.398	165,000
1992	CLE	AL	2B	161	657	92	205	32	1	20	105	35	76	10	19	.312	.455	500,000
1993	CLE	AL	2B	154	624	105	200	28	6	21	114	34	68	15	17	.321	.486	1,225,000
4	YR	TOTALS		581	2186	323	657	105	11	59	335	133	275	28	80	.301	.440	
1993	RANK	MLB	2B	2	1	2	1	8	5	1	1	21	12	10	5	3	5	12
1994	PROJECTIONS			162	689	116	224	29	6	23	127	37	68	17	16	.325	.485	

Albert Belle No. 8/OF

Full name: Albert Jojuan Belle
Bats: R **Throws:** R **HT:** 6–2 **WT:** 210
Born: 8–25–66, Shreveport, LA
High school: Huntington (Shreveport, LA)
College: Louisiana State

Belle's 38 HR were the most by an Indian since Rocky Colavito's 42 in 1959. He was second in the AL with 16 outfield assists.

	TEAM	LG	POS	G	AB	R	H	2B	3B	HR	RBI	BB	SO	SB	E	BA	SLG	SALARY
1989	CLE	AL	OF	62	218	22	49	8	4	7	37	12	55	2	2	.225	.394	N/A
1990	CLE	AL	OF	9	23	1	4	0	0	1	3	1	6	0	0	.174	.304	N/A
1991	CLE	AL	OF	123	461	60	130	31	2	28	95	25	99	3	9	.282	.540	100,000
1992	CLE	AL	OF	153	585	81	152	23	1	34	112	52	128	8	3	.260	.477	175,000
1993	CLE	AL	OF	159	594	93	172	36	3	38	129	76	96	23	5	.290	.552	1,625,000
5	YR	TOTALS		506	1881	257	507	98	10	108	376	166	384	36	19	.270	.505	
1993	RANK	MLB	OF	3	12	14	12	10	54	5	1	16	30	27	47	38	5	45
1994	PROJECTIONS			162	608	97	178	37	1	40	133	80	94	24	4	.293	.554	

Alvaro Espinoza No. 10/3B

Full name: Alvaro Alberto Espinoza
Bats: R **Throws:** R **HT:** 6–0 **WT:** 190
Born: 2–19–62, Valencia, VZ
High school: Pedro Gual (Venezuela)

Espinoza hit .345 vs. lefties, just .227 vs. righties. Espinoza also batted better on the road than at home (.331 away vs. .218 at home).

	TEAM	LG	POS	G	AB	R	H	2B	3B	HR	RBI	BB	SO	SB	E	BA	SLG	SALARY
1985	MIN	AL	SS	1	0	0	0	0	0	0	0	0	0	0	-	---	---	N/A
1986	MIN	AL	2B-SS	32	57	5	15	2	0	0	9	1	9	0	5	.263	.298	N/A
1987	MIN	AL	SS-3B	37	42	4	9	1	0	0	1	1	10	0	4	.214	.238	N/A
1988	NY	AL	2B-SS	3	3	0	0	0	0	0	0	0	0	0	0	.000	.000	N/A
1989	NY	AL	SS	146	503	51	142	23	1	0	41	14	60	3	22	.282	.332	N/A
1990	NY	AL	SS	150	438	31	98	12	2	2	20	16	54	1	17	.224	.274	N/A
1991	NY	AL	SS-3B	148	480	51	123	23	2	5	33	16	57	4	21	.256	.344	610,000
1993	CLE	AL	3B	129	263	34	73	15	0	4	27	8	36	2	12	.278	.380	500,000
8	YR	TOTALS		646	1786	176	460	76	5	11	131	56	226	10	81	.258	.324	
1993	RANK	MLB	3B	19	28	27	28	25	33	31	32	40	33	21	19	14	29	17
1994	PROJECTIONS			66	120	14	32	6	0	1	12	3	18	0	7	.267	.350	

Felix Fermin No. 16/SS

Full name: Felix Jose Fermin
Bats: R **Throws:** R **HT:** 5–11 **WT:** 170
Born: 10–9–63, Mao Valverde, DR
College: U.C.E. (S.P. de Macoris, DR)

Fermin's strikeout ratio—just one strikeout per 36.7 plate appearances—was the best in the major leagues. The next best was Brian Harper's one strikeout per 19.8 PAs.

	TEAM	LG	POS	G	AB	R	H	2B	3B	HR	RBI	BB	SO	SB	E	BA	SLG	SALARY
1987	PIT	NL	SS	23	68	6	17	0	0	0	4	4	9	0	2	.250	.250	N/A
1988	PIT	NL	SS	43	87	9	24	0	2	0	2	8	10	3	6	.276	.322	N/A
1989	CLE	AL	SS-2B	156	484	50	115	9	1	0	21	41	27	6	26	.238	.260	N/A
1990	CLE	AL	SS	148	414	47	106	13	2	1	40	26	22	3	16	.256	.304	N/A
1991	CLE	AL	SS	129	424	30	111	13	2	0	31	26	27	5	12	.262	.302	575,000
1992	CLE	AL	SS-3B	79	215	27	58	7	2	0	13	18	10	0	8	.270	.321	950,000
1993	CLE	AL	SS	140	480	48	126	16	2	2	45	24	14	4	23	.263	.317	975,000
7	YR	TOTALS		718	2172	217	557	58	11	3	156	147	119	21	93	.256	.297	
1993	RANK	MLB	SS	16	15	22	18	20	21	25	19	25	37	25	5	23	29	13
1994	PROJECTIONS			156	538	54	141	18	2	2	50	26	14	4	26	.262	.314	

Wayne Kirby No. 35/OF

Full name: Wayne Leonard Kirby
Bats: L **Throws:** R **HT:** 5–10 **WT:** 185
Born: 1–22–64, Williamsburg, VA
High school: Tabb (VA)
College: Newport News (VA)

A 29–year old rookie in '93, Kirby's 19 outfield assists led the AL. He compiled a .983 fielding percentage.

	TEAM	LG	POS	G	AB	R	H	2B	3B	HR	RBI	BB	SO	SB	E	BA	SLG	SALARY
1991	CLE	AL	OF	21	43	4	9	2	0	0	5	2	6	1	0	.209	.256	N/A
1992	CLE	AL	OF	21	18	9	3	1	0	1	1	3	2	0	0	.167	.389	N/A
1993	CLE	AL	OF	131	458	71	123	19	5	6	60	37	58	17	5	.269	.371	123,000
3	YR	TOTALS		173	519	84	135	22	5	7	66	42	66	18	5	.260	.362	
1993	RANK	MLB	OF	57	60	45	59	55	23	87	45	59	70	36	47	73	102	118
1994	PROJECTIONS			162	578	90	156	23	5	7	75	46	72	21	5	.270	.363	

Kenny Lofton — No. 7/OF

Full name: Kenneth Lofton
Bats: L **Throws:** L **HT:** 6–0 **WT:** 180
Born: 5–31–67, East Chicago, IN
High school: Washington (East Chicago, IN)
College: Arizona

Lofton had 19 bunt singles last year. His only HR in '93 was his first career grand slam, off Chicago's Tom Bolton at home June 29.

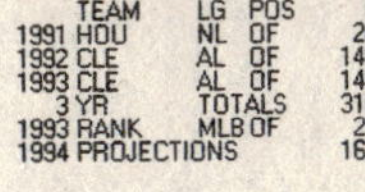
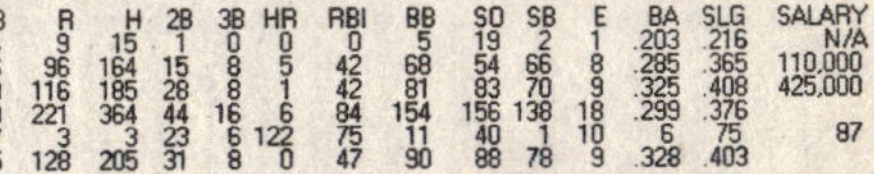

	TEAM	LG	POS	G	AB	R	H	2B	3B	HR	RBI	BB	SO	SB	E	BA	SLG	SALARY
1991	HOU	NL	OF	20	74	9	15	1	0	0	0	5	19	2	1	.203	.216	N/A
1992	CLE	AL	OF	148	576	96	164	15	8	5	42	68	54	66	8	.285	.365	110,000
1993	CLE	AL	OF	148	569	116	185	28	8	1	42	81	83	70	9	.325	.408	425,000
3	YR	TOTALS		316	1219	221	364	44	16	6	84	154	156	138	18	.299	.376	
1993	RANK	MLB	OF	25	17	3	3	23	6	122	75	11	40	1	10	6	75	87
1994	PROJECTIONS			162	625	128	205	31	8	0	47	90	88	78	9	.328	.403	

Eddie Murray — DH

Full name: Eddie Clarence Murray
Bats: S **Throws:** R **HT:** 6–2 **WT:** 222
Born: 2–24–56, Los Angeles, CA
High school: Locke (Los Angeles, CA)
College: Cal State Los Angeles

Murray is second among active players in HR to Dave Winfield's 453. His 17 grand slams tie him for third on the all-time list.

	TEAM	LG	POS	G	AB	R	H	2B	3B	HR	RBI	BB	SO	SB	E	BA	SLG	SALARY
1978	BAL	AL	1B-3B	161	610	85	174	32	3	27	95	70	97	6	6	.285	.480	N/A
1979	BAL	AL	1B	159	606	90	179	30	2	25	99	72	78	10	10	.295	.475	N/A
1980	BAL	AL	1B	158	621	100	186	36	2	32	116	54	71	7	9	.300	.519	N/A
1981	BAL	AL	1B	99	378	57	111	21	2	22	78	40	43	2	1	.294	.534	N/A
1982	BAL	AL	1B	151	550	87	174	30	1	32	110	70	82	7	4	.316	.549	N/A
1983	BAL	AL	1B	156	582	115	178	30	3	33	111	86	90	5	10	.306	.538	N/A
1984	BAL	AL	1B	162	588	97	180	26	3	29	110	107	87	10	13	.306	.509	N/A
1985	BAL	AL	1B	156	583	111	173	37	1	31	124	84	68	5	19	.297	.523	N/A
1986	BAL	AL	1B	137	495	61	151	25	1	17	84	78	49	3	13	.305	.463	N/A
1987	BAL	AL	1B	160	618	89	171	28	3	30	91	73	80	1	10	.277	.477	N/A
1988	BAL	AL	1B	161	603	75	171	27	2	28	84	75	78	5	11	.284	.474	N/A
1989	LA	NL	1B-3B	160	594	66	147	29	1	20	88	87	85	7	6	.247	.401	N/A
1990	LA	NL	1B	155	558	96	184	22	3	26	95	82	64	8	10	.330	.520	N/A
1991	LA	NL	1B-3B	153	576	69	150	23	1	19	96	55	74	10	7	.260	.403	2,635,000
1992	NY	NL	1B	156	551	64	144	37	2	16	93	66	74	4	12	.261	.423	4,125,000
1993	NY	NL	1B	154	610	77	174	28	1	27	100	40	61	2	18	.285	.467	3,375,000
17	YR	TOTALS		2598	9734	1420	2820	490	33	441	1662	1187	1285	92	163	.290	.483	
1993	RANK	MLB	1B	5	2	15	5	11	20	7	8	25	21	20	40	19	14	7
1994	PROJECTIONS			156	585	69	155	31	1	21	93	64	73	4	12	.265	.431	

Paul Sorrento No. 11/1B

Full name: Paul Anthony Sorrento
Bats: L **Throws:** R **HT:** 6–2 **WT:** 220
Born: 11–17–65, Somerville, MA
High school: St. John's Prep.(Danvers, MA)
College: Florida State
Sorrento was third on the Indians in HR and RBI, and fourth in runs scored and doubles.

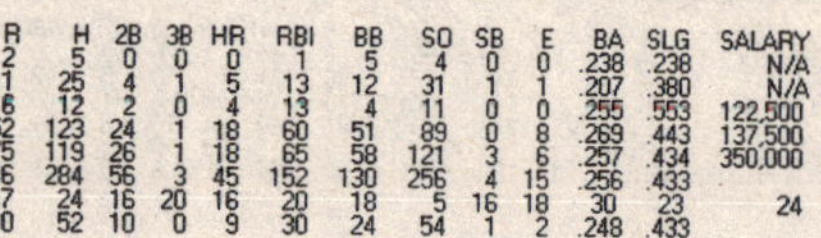

TEAM	LG	POS	G	AB	R	H	2B	3B	HR	RBI	BB	SO	SB	E	BA	SLG	SALARY
1989 MIN	AL	1B	14	21	2	5	0	0	0	1	5	4	0	0	.238	.238	N/A
1990 MIN	AL	1B	41	121	11	25	4	1	5	13	12	31	1	1	.207	.380	N/A
1991 MIN	AL	1B	26	47	6	12	2	0	4	13	4	11	0	0	.255	.553	122,500
1992 CLE	AL	1B	140	458	52	123	24	1	18	60	51	89	0	8	.269	.443	137,500
1993 CLE	AL	1B	148	463	75	119	26	1	18	65	58	121	3	6	.257	.434	350,000
5 YR	TOTALS		369	1110	146	284	56	3	45	152	130	256	4	15	.256	.433	
1993 RANK	MLB	1B	14	20	17	24	16	20	16	20	18	5	16	18	30	23	24
1994 PROJECTIONS			71	210	30	52	10	0	9	30	24	54	1	2	.248	.433	

Dennis Martinez No. 32/P

Full name: Jose Dennis Martinez
Bats: R **Throws:** R **HT:** 6–1 **WT:** 180
Born: 5–14–55, Granada, Nic.
"El Presidente" started the season 2–5 for Montreal, then went 13–4 the rest of the way. As a 10–5 player, he vetoed a trade to Atlanta on August 26, and was 4–1 from then on. Martinez allowed 27 HR in '93.

TM	LG	POS	W	L	ERA	G	GS	CG	SH	SV	IP	H	R	ER	HR	BB	SO	SALARY
1979 BAL	AL	P	15	16	3.66	40	39	18	3	0	292.1	279	129	119	28	78	132	N/A
1980 BAL	AL	P	6	4	3.96	25	12	2	0	1	100.0	103	44	44	12	44	42	N/A
1981 BAL	AL	P	14	5	3.32	25	24	9	2	0	179.0	173	84	66	10	62	88	N/A
1982 BAL	AL	P	16	12	4.21	40	39	10	2	0	252.0	262	123	118	30	87	111	N/A
1983 BAL	AL	P	7	16	5.53	32	25	4	0	0	153.0	209	108	94	21	45	71	N/A
1984 BAL	AL	P	6	9	5.02	34	20	2	0	0	141.2	145	81	79	26	37	77	N/A
1985 BAL	AL	P	13	11	5.15	33	31	3	1	0	180.0	203	110	103	29	63	68	N/A
1986 BAL	AL	P	0	0	6.75	4	0	0	0	0	6.2	11	5	5	0	2	2	N/A
1986 MTL	NL	P	3	6	4.59	19	15	1	1	0	98.0	103	52	50	11	28	63	N/A
1987 MTL	NL	P	11	4	3.30	22	22	2	1	0	144.2	133	59	53	9	40	84	N/A
1988 MTL	NL	P	15	13	2.72	34	34	9	2	0	235.1	215	94	71	21	55	120	N/A
1989 MTL	NL	P	16	7	3.18	34	33	5	2	0	232.0	227	88	82	21	49	142	N/A
1990 MTL	NL	P	10	11	2.95	32	32	7	2	0	226.0	191	80	74	16	49	156	N/A
1991 MTL	NL	P	14	11	2.39	31	31	9	5	0	222.0	187	70	59	9	62	123	3,348,333
1992 MTL	NL	P	16	11	2.47	32	32	6	0	0	226.1	172	75	62	12	60	147	3,333,333
1993 MTL	NL	P	15	9	3.85	35	34	2	0	1	224.2	211	110	96	27	64	138	2,833,334
18 YR	TOTALS		208	165	3.64	558	476	110	23	6	3384.1	3261	1527	1367	313	990	1831	
1993 RANK	MLB	Ps	21		120	134	12	57	69	70.	23	89	132		207	66	155	38
1994 PROJECTIONS			14	7	3.76	34	23	5	0	1	189	180	93	79	15	63	111	

Jose Mesa No. 49/P

Full name: Jose Ramon Mesa
Bats: R **Throws:** R **HT:** 6–3 **WT:** 225
Born: 5–22–66, Winter Park, FL
High school: Santa School (Azua, DR)

In only his second major league season, Mesa led the Indians in wins, starts, complete games, innings pitched, and strikeouts. He was 7–5 at home, 3–7 away.

	TM	LG	POS	W	L	ERA	G	GS	CG	SH	SV	IP	H	R	ER	HR	BB	SO	SALARY
1987	BAL	AL	P	1	3	6.03	6	5	0	0	0	31.1	38	23	21	7	15	17	
1990	BAL	AL	P	3	2	3.86	7	7	0	0	0	46.2	37	20	20	2	27	24	N/A
1991	BAL	AL	P	6	11	5.97	23	23	2	1	0	123.2	151	86	82	11	62	64	107,000
1992	BAL-CLE	AL	P	7	12	4.59	28	27	1	1	0	160.2	169	86	82	14	70	62	135,000
1993	CLE	AL	P	10	12	4.92	34	33	3	0	0	208.2	232	122	114	21	62	118	325,000
5	YR	TOTALS		27	40	5.03	98	95	6	2	0	571.0	627	337	319	55	236	285	
1993	Rank	MLB Ps		75		226	145	30	37	69	102	41.0	217	211		162	74	195	144
1994	PROJECTIONS			10	12	4.90	36	36	2	0	0	226.0	252	132	123	22	66	128	

Charles Nagy No. 41/P

Full name: Charles Harrison Nagy
Bats: L **Throws:** R **HT:** 6–3 **WT:** 200
Born: 5–5–67, Fairfield, CT
High school: Roger Ludlowe (Fairfield, CT)
College: Connecticut

The ace of the staff, an injured right shoulder put Nagy on the DL from May 17 until the season's final game.

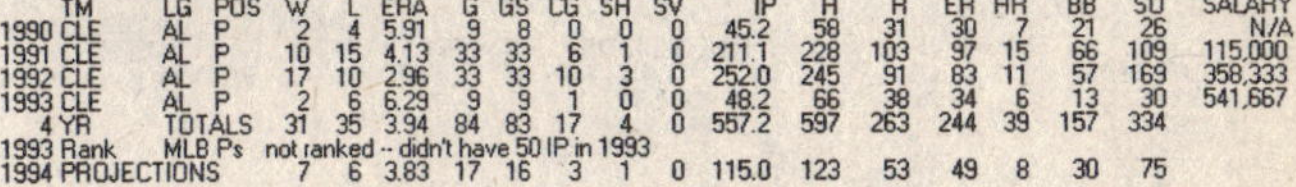

	TM	LG	POS	W	L	ERA	G	GS	CG	SH	SV	IP	H	R	ER	HR	BB	SO	SALARY
1990	CLE	AL	P	2	4	5.91	9	8	0	0	0	45.2	58	31	30	7	21	26	N/A
1991	CLE	AL	P	10	15	4.13	33	33	6	1	0	211.1	228	103	97	15	66	109	115,000
1992	CLE	AL	P	17	10	2.96	33	33	10	3	0	252.0	245	91	83	11	57	169	358,333
1993	CLE	AL	P	2	6	6.29	9	9	1	0	0	48.2	66	38	34	6	13	30	541,667
4	YR	TOTALS		31	35	3.94	84	83	17	4	0	557.2	597	263	244	39	157	334	
1993	Rank	MLB Ps	not ranked -- didn't have 50 IP in 1993																
1994	PROJECTIONS			7	6	3.83	17	16	3	1	0	115.0	123	53	49	8	30	75	

Jerry DiPoto No. 45/P

Full name: Gerard Peter DiPoto III
Bats: R **Throws:** R **HT:** 6–2 **WT:** 200
Born: 5–24–68, Jersey City, NJ
High school: Toms River (NJ)
College: Virginia Commonwealth

DiPoto's 11 saves were the most saves by an Indians rookie since Tom Buskey posted a team-record 18 in 1974.

TM	LG	POS	W	L	ERA	G	GS	CG	SH	SV	IP	H	R	ER	HR	BB	SO	SALARY
1993 CLE	AL	P	4	4	2.40	46	0	0	0	11	56.1	57	21	15	0	30	41	109,000
1 YR	TOTAL		4	4	2.40	46	0	0	0	11	56.1	57	21	15	0	30	41	
1993 Rank	MLB Ps		173		15.00	93	202	125	69	23	266.0	153	34		1	258	95	236

Mike Hargrove No. 21/Mgr.

Full name: Dudley Michael Hargrove
Bats: L **Throws:** L **HT:** 6–0 **WT:** 195
Born: 10–26–49, Perryton, TX
High school: Perryton (TX)
College: Northwestern State (OK)

Hargrove received one first place vote and ten third place votes in the '93 AL Manager of the Year voting.

		REG. SEASON				PLAYOFF			CHAMP. SERIES			WORLD SERIES		
YEAR TEAM	LG	W	L	PCT	POS	W	L	PCT	W	L	PCT	W	L	PCT
1991 CLE	AL	32	53	0.376	7			---			---			---
1992 CLE	AL	76	86	0.469	4			---			---			---
1993 CLE	AL	76	86	0.469	6			---			---			---
3 YR	TOTALS	184	225	0.45		0	0	---	0	0	---	0	0	---

Ruben Amaro OF

Full name: Ruben Amaro, Jr.
Bats: S **Throws:** R **HT:** 5–10 **WT:** 175
Born: 2–12–65, Philadelphia, PA
High school: Wm. Penn Charter (Phila., PA)
College: Stanford
Amaro came to Cleveland from the Phillies.

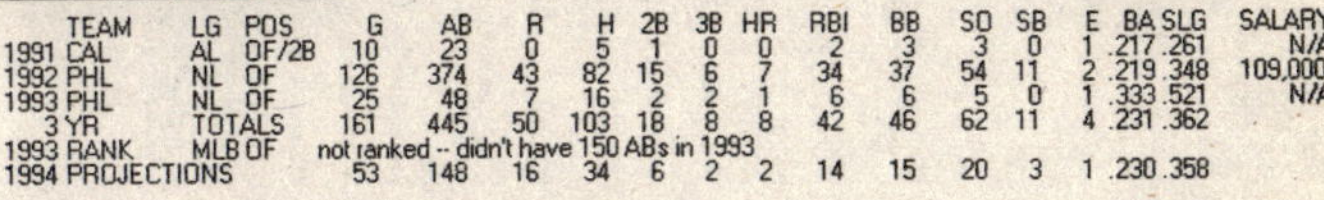

	TEAM	LG	POS	G	AB	R	H	2B	3B	HR	RBI	BB	SO	SB	E	BA	SLG	SALARY
1991	CAL	AL	OF/2B	10	23	0	5	1	0	0	2	3	3	0	1	.217	.261	N/A
1992	PHL	NL	OF	126	374	43	82	15	6	7	34	37	54	11	2	.219	.348	109,000
1993	PHL	NL	OF	25	48	7	16	2	2	1	6	6	5	0	1	.333	.521	N/A
3	YR	TOTALS		161	445	50	103	18	8	8	42	46	62	11	4	.231	.362	
1993	RANK	MLB	OF	not ranked -- didn't have 150 ABs in 1993														
1994	PROJECTIONS			53	148	16	34	6	2	2	14	15	20	3	1	.230	.358	

Mark Clark No. 54/P

Full name: Mark William Clark
Bats: R **Throws:** R **HT:** 6–5 **WT:** 225
Born: 5–12–68, Bath, IL
High school: Balyki (Bath, IL)
College: Lincoln Land CC (IL)
Clark had a 1.91 ERA after September 9.

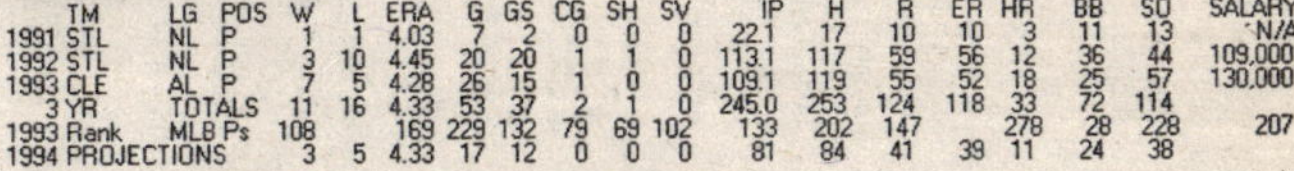

	TM	LG	POS	W	L	ERA	G	GS	CG	SH	SV	IP	H	R	ER	HR	BB	SO	SALARY
1991	STL	NL	P	1	1	4.03	7	2	0	0	0	22.1	17	10	10	3	11	13	N/A
1992	STL	NL	P	3	10	4.45	20	20	1	1	0	113.1	117	59	56	12	36	44	109,000
1993	CLE	AL	P	7	5	4.28	26	15	1	0	0	109.1	119	55	52	18	25	57	130,000
3	YR	TOTALS		11	16	4.33	53	37	2	1	0	245.0	253	124	118	33	72	114	
1993	Rank	MLB	Ps	108		169	229	132	79	69	102	133	202	147		278	28	228	207
1994	PROJECTIONS			3	5	4.33	17	12	0	0	0	81	84	41	39	11	24	38	

Jeremy Hernandez No. 53/P

Full name: Jeremy Stuart Hernandez
Bats: R **Throws:** R **HT:** 6–6 **WT:** 205
Born: 6–7–66, Burbank, CA
High school: Francis Poly (Sun Valley, CA)
College: Cal State Northridge
Hernandez was 8 for 13 in save opportunities.

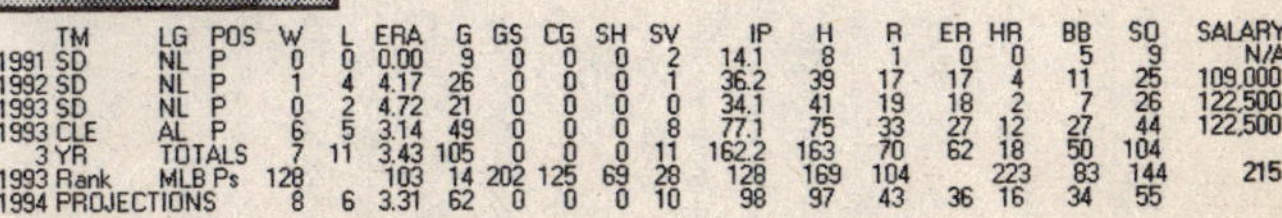

	TM	LG	POS	W	L	ERA	G	GS	CG	SH	SV	IP	H	R	ER	HR	BB	SO	SALARY
1991	SD	NL	P	0	0	0.00	9	0	0	0	2	14.1	8	1	0	0	5	9	N/A
1992	SD	NL	P	1	4	4.17	26	0	0	0	1	36.2	39	17	17	4	11	25	109,000
1993	SD	NL	P	0	2	4.72	21	0	0	0	0	34.1	41	19	18	2	7	26	122,500
1993	CLE	AL	P	6	5	3.14	49	0	0	0	8	77.1	75	33	27	12	27	44	122,500
3	YR	TOTALS		7	11	3.43	105	0	0	0	11	162.2	163	70	62	18	50	104	
1993	Rank	MLB	Ps	128		103	14	202	125	69	28	128	169	104		223	83	144	215
1994	PROJECTIONS			8	6	3.31	62	0	0	0	10	98	97	43	36	16	34	55	

Reggie Jefferson No. 44/DH

Full name: Reginald Jirod Jefferson
Bats: S **Throws:** L **HT:** 6–4 **WT:** 215
Born: 9–25–68, Tallahassee, FL
High school: Lincoln (Tallahassee, FL)
Jefferson batted .270, with 9 HR and 25 RBI vs. righties, just .196 with 1 HR and 9 RBI vs. lefties.

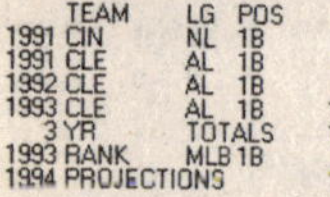

	TEAM	LG	POS	G	AB	R	H	2B	3B	HR	RBI	BB	SO	SB	E	BA	SLG	SALARY
1991	CIN	NL	1B	5	7	1	1	0	0	1	1	1	2	0	0	.143	.571	N/A
1991	CLE	AL	1B	26	101	10	20	3	0	2	12	3	22	0	2	.198	.287	N/A
1992	CLE	AL	1B	24	89	8	30	6	2	1	6	1	17	0	1	.337	.483	N/A
1993	CLE	AL	1B	113	366	35	91	11	2	10	34	28	78	1	3	.249	.372	142,500
3	YR	TOTALS		168	563	54	142	20	4	14	53	33	118	1	6	.252	.377	
1993	RANK	MLB	1B	28	29	32	20	33	11	26	32	33	14	27	30	33	37	31
1994	PROJECTIONS			149	485	46	121	14	2	13	45	37	103	1	4	.249	.367	

Tom Kramer No. 29/P

Full name: Thomas Joseph Kramer
Bats: S **Throws:** R **HT:** 6–0 **WT:** 205
Born: 1–9–68, Cincinnati, OH
High school: Roger Bacon (Cincinnati, OH)
College: Logan Junior (IL)
Lefties batted .234 against Kramer, righties .303.

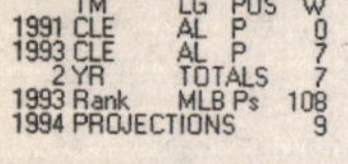
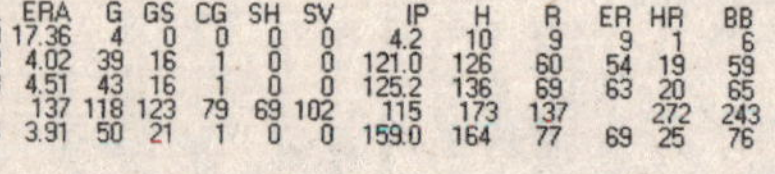
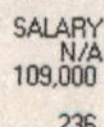

	TM	LG	POS	W	L	ERA	G	GS	CG	SH	SV	IP	H	R	ER	HR	BB	SO	SALARY
1991	CLE	AL	P	0	0	17.36	4	0	0	0	0	4.2	10	9	9	1	6	4	N/A
1993	CLE	AL	P	7	3	4.02	39	16	1	0	0	121.0	126	60	54	19	59	71	109,000
2	YR	TOTALS		7	3	4.51	43	16	1	0	0	125.2	136	69	63	20	65	75	
1993	Rank	MLB	Ps	108		137	118	123	79	69	102	115	173	137		272	243	174	236
1994	PROJECTIONS			9	4	3.91	50	21	1	0	0	159.0	164	77	69	25	76	93	

Derek Lilliquist No. 28/P

Full name: Derek Jansen Lilliquist
Bats: L **Throws:** L **HT:** 5–10 **WT:** 195
Born: 2–20–66, Winter Park, FL
High school: Sarasota (FL)
College: Georgia
Lilliquist's 10 saves in '93 were a career high.

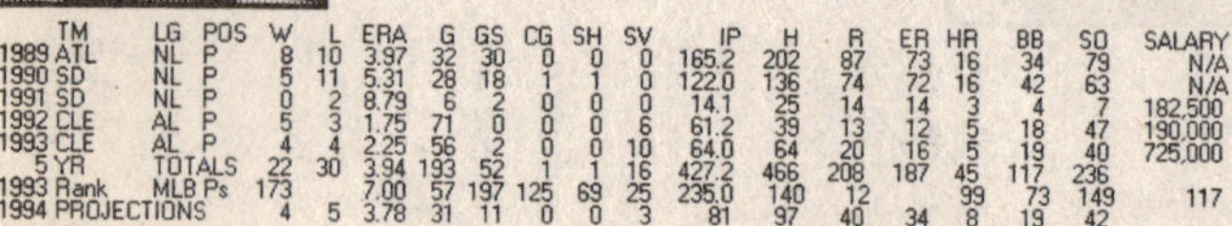

	TM	LG	POS	W	L	ERA	G	GS	CG	SH	SV	IP	H	R	ER	HR	BB	SO	SALARY
1989	ATL	NL	P	8	10	3.97	32	30	0	0	0	165.2	202	87	73	16	34	79	N/A
1990	SD	NL	P	5	11	5.31	28	18	1	1	0	122.0	136	74	72	16	42	63	N/A
1991	SD	NL	P	0	2	8.79	6	2	0	0	0	14.1	25	14	14	3	4	7	182,500
1992	CLE	AL	P	5	3	1.75	71	0	0	0	6	61.2	39	13	12	5	18	47	190,000
1993	CLE	AL	P	4	4	2.25	56	2	0	0	10	64.0	64	20	16	5	19	40	725,000
5	YR	TOTALS		22	30	3.94	193	52	1	1	16	427.2	466	208	187	45	117	236	
1993	Rank	MLB	Ps	173		7.00	57	197	125	69	25	235.0	140	12		99	73	149	117
1994	PROJECTIONS			4	5	3.78	31	11	0	0	3	81	97	40	34	8	19	42	

Candy Maldonado No. 22/DH

Full name: Candido Maldonado
Bats: R **Throws:** R **HT:** 6–0 **WT:** 205
Born: 9–5–60, Humacao, PR
High school: Trina Padilla de Sanz (Arecibo, PR)
Maldonado hit safely in 17 of his 28 games with Cleveland.

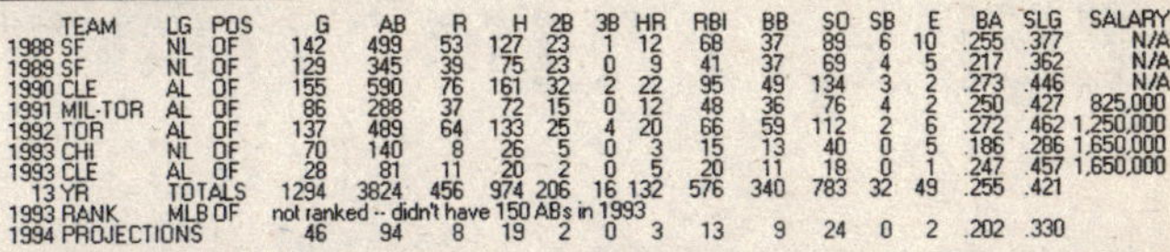

	TEAM	LG	POS	G	AB	R	H	2B	3B	HR	RBI	BB	SO	SB	E	BA	SLG	SALARY
1988	SF	NL	OF	142	499	53	127	23	1	12	68	37	89	6	10	.255	.377	N/A
1989	SF	NL	OF	129	345	39	75	23	0	9	41	37	69	4	5	.217	.362	N/A
1990	CLE	AL	OF	155	590	76	161	32	2	22	95	49	134	3	2	.273	.446	N/A
1991	MIL-TOR	AL	OF	86	288	37	72	15	0	12	48	36	76	4	2	.250	.427	825,000
1992	TOR	AL	OF	137	489	64	133	25	4	20	66	59	112	2	6	.272	.462	1,250,000
1993	CHI	NL	OF	70	140	8	26	5	0	3	15	13	40	0	5	.186	.286	1,650,000
1993	CLE	AL	OF	28	81	11	20	2	0	5	20	11	18	0	1	.247	.457	1,650,000
13	YR	TOTALS		1294	3824	456	974	206	16	132	576	340	783	32	49	.255	.421	
1993	RANK	MLB	OF	not ranked -- didn't have 150 ABs in 1993														
1994	PROJECTIONS			46	94	8	19	2	0	3	13	9	24	0	2	.202	.330	

Dave Mlicki No. 23/P

Full name: David John Mlicki
Bats: R **Throws:** R **HT:** 6–4 **WT:** 190
Born: 6–8–68, Cleveland, OH
High school: Cheyenne Mtn. (Colo. Springs, CO)
College: Oklahoma State
Injuries limited Mlicki to just three starts in '93.

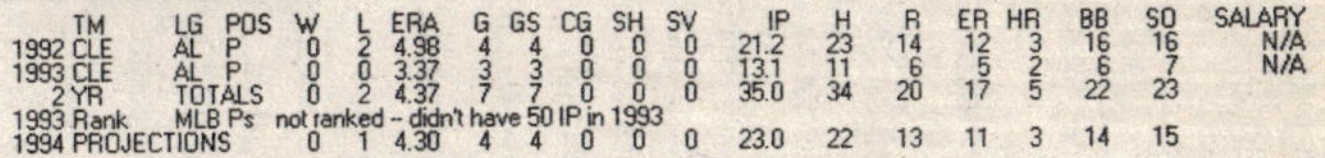

	TM	LG	POS	W	L	ERA	G	GS	CG	SH	SV	IP	H	R	ER	HR	BB	SO	SALARY
1992	CLE	AL	P	0	2	4.98	4	4	0	0	0	21.2	23	14	12	3	16	16	N/A
1993	CLE	AL	P	0	0	3.37	3	3	0	0	0	13.1	11	6	5	2	6	7	N/A
2	YR	TOTALS		0	2	4.37	7	7	0	0	0	35.0	34	20	17	5	22	23	
1993	Rank	MLB	Ps	not ranked -- didn't have 50 IP in 1993															
1994	PROJECTIONS			0	1	4.30	4	4	0	0	0	23.0	22	13	11	3	14	15	

Eric Plunk No. 38/P

Full name: Eric Vaughan Plunk
Bats: R **Throws:** R **HT:** 6–6 **WT:** 220
Born: 9–3–63, Wilmington, CA
High school: Bellflower (CA)
His 70 appearances and 15 saves led Cleveland.

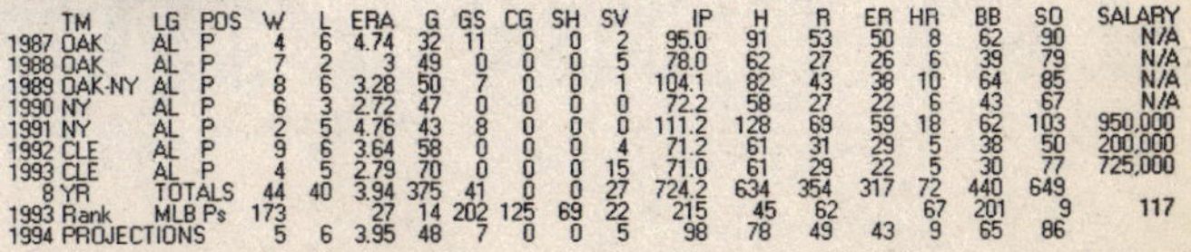

	TM	LG	POS	W	L	ERA	G	GS	CG	SH	SV	IP	H	R	ER	HR	BB	SO	SALARY
1987	OAK	AL	P	4	6	4.74	32	11	0	0	2	95.0	91	53	50	8	62	90	N/A
1988	OAK	AL	P	7	2	3	49	0	0	0	5	78.0	62	27	26	6	39	79	N/A
1989	OAK-NY	AL	P	8	6	3.28	50	7	0	0	1	104.1	82	43	38	10	64	85	N/A
1990	NY	AL	P	6	3	2.72	47	0	0	0	0	72.2	58	27	22	6	43	67	N/A
1991	NY	AL	P	2	5	4.76	43	8	0	0	0	111.2	128	69	59	18	62	103	950,000
1992	CLE	AL	P	9	6	3.64	58	0	0	0	4	71.2	61	31	29	5	38	50	200,000
1993	CLE	AL	P	4	5	2.79	70	0	0	0	15	71.0	61	29	22	5	30	77	725,000
8	YR	TOTALS		44	40	3.94	375	41	0	0	27	724.2	634	354	317	72	440	649	
1993	Rank	MLB	Ps	173		27	14	202	125	69	22	215	45	62		67	201	9	117
1994	PROJECTIONS			5	6	3.95	48	7	0	0	5	98	78	49	43	9	65	86	

Manny Ramirez — No. 24/OF

Full name: Manuel Aristides Ramirez
Bats: R **Throws:** R **HT:** 5–11 **WT:** 165
Born: 3–21–75, Miranda, VZ
Ramirez was Baseball America's Minor League Player of the Year. He hit .333 with 31 HR and 115 RBI in AA and AAA in '93.

TEAM	LG	POS	G	AB	R	H	2B	3B	HR	RBI	BB	SO	SB	E	BA	SLG	SALARY
1993 CLE	AL	OF	22	53	5	9	1	0	2	5	2	8	0	0	.170	.302	N/A
1 YR	TOTAL		22	53	5	9	1	0	2	5	2	8	0	0	.170	.302	
1993 RANK	MLB OF		not ranked -- didn't have 150 ABs in 1993														

Jim Thome — No. 25/3B

Full name: James Howard Thome
Bats: L **Throws:** R **HT:** 6–4 **WT:** 220
Born: 8–27–70, Peoria, IL
High school: Limestone (IL)
College: Illinois Central
He led the AAA Int'l League in batting and RBI.

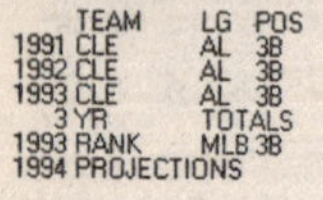

TEAM	LG	POS	G	AB	R	H	2B	3B	HR	RBI	BB	SO	SB	E	BA	SLG	SALARY
1991 CLE	AL	3B	27	98	7	25	4	2	1	9	5	16	1	8	.255	.367	N/A
1992 CLE	AL	3B	40	117	8	24	3	1	2	12	10	34	2	11	.205	.299	N/A
1993 CLE	AL	3B	47	154	28	41	11	0	7	22	29	36	2	6	.266	.474	135,000
3 YR	TOTALS		114	369	43	90	18	3	10	43	44	86	5	25	.244	.390	
1993 RANK	MLB	3B	41	40	33	40	31	33	24	39	24	1	21	5	21	6	28
1994 PROJECTIONS			53	172	35	46	13	0	9	26	37	42	2	5	.267	.500	0

Bill Wertz — No. 46/P

Full name: William Charles Wertz
Bats: R **Throws:** R **HT:** 6–6 **WT:** 220
Born: 1–15–67, Cleveland, OH
High school: Cleveland Central Catholic (OH)
College: Ohio State
Wertz was 7–2 with a 1.95 ERA for AAA Charlotte

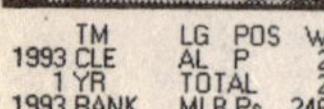
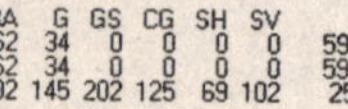
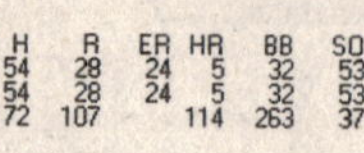
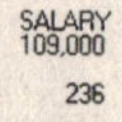

TM	LG	POS	W	L	ERA	G	GS	CG	SH	SV	IP	H	R	ER	HR	BB	SO	SALARY
1993 CLE	AL	P	2	3	3.62	34	0	0	0	0	59.2	54	28	24	5	32	53	109,000
1 YR	TOTAL		2	3	3.62	34	0	0	0	0	59.2	54	28	24	5	32	53	
1993 RANK	MLB	Ps	246		102	145	202	125	69	102	251	72	107		114	263	37	236

Detroit *TIGERS*

1994 Scouting Report

Hitting: (1993/.275, fourth in AL; 178 HR, second in AL)

Detroit has a variety of offensive threats. Travis Fryman made the All-Star team. He finished the season at .300, 22 HR, and 97 RBI. Cecil Fielder hit 30 HR and drove in 117 runs. Mickey Tettleton added 32 HR and 110 RBI. Alan Trammell visited the fountain of youth, going .329 with 12 HR in his seventeenth season. His infield partner, Lou Whitaker, hit .290 with 9 HR and 67 RBI. Chris Gomez hit .250 as a rookie. Eric Davis came to Detroit from Los Angeles and started to look like the Eric Davis of old, hitting .253 with six HR in 23 games for Detroit.

Milt Cuyler had a horrible campaign, playing in just 82 games and hitting .213 with no homers. He figures to bounce back in '94.

Pitching: (1993/4.65 ERA, twelfth in AL)

John Doherty, David Wells, and Bill Gullickson are the leading starters for Detroit. Doherty led the team in wins with 14. Wells started the season 9–1 with a 2.68 ERA through June 19, but faded to an 11–9 mark with a 4.19 ERA for the season. Gullickson won 13 games with a 5.39 ERA

Mike Henneman holds down the closer role; he led the team with 24 saves. Detroit also has Joe Boever (2.74 ERA, three saves) coming out of the bullpen.

Defense: (1993/.979 pct., eleventh in AL)

Eric Davis is a good defensive outfielder.

1994 Prospects:

The Tigers surprised observers in '93 with a fast start. Detroit was in first in the AL East with a 43–27 record on June 28. But the offense was regularly scoring runs in double digits, a pace no team could hope to continue. Unfortunately, the pitching collapsed in the second half, and Detroit was 42–50 the rest of the way. The Tigers will score too many runs this year to finish too far back (Detroit 20, Seattle 3 was a baseball score last year, not the Lions over the Seahawks), but they lack the pitching to seriously threaten Toronto.

Team Directory

Chairman: Michael Ilitch
General Mgr.: Jerry Walker
Director of P.R.: Greg Shea
Chief Financial Officer: Gerald Pasternak
Sr. Director, Asst. GM: Gary Vitto
Traveling Secretary: Bill Brown

Minor League Affiliates:

Level	Team/League	1993 Record
AAA	Toledo–International	65–77
AA	London, Ont.–Eastern	63–75
A	Fayetteville–South Atlantic	75–66
	Lakeland–Florida State	65–63
	Niagara Falls–New York/Penn.	47–31
Rookie	Bristol–Appalachian	28–39

1993 Review

	Home		Away			Home		Away			Home		Away	
vs AL East	W	L	W	L	vs AL Cent.	W	L	W	L	vs AL West	W	L	W	L
Baltimore	5	2	3	3	Chicago	1	5	4	2	California	4	2	4	2
Boston	4	2	3	4	Cleveland	4	3	3	3	Oakland	5	1	3	3
New York	3	4	1	5	Kansas City	2	4	3	3	Seattle	5	1	2	4
Toronto	3	3	3	4	Milwaukee	4	2	4	3	Texas	3	3	3	3
					Minnesota	1	5	5	1					
Total	15	11	10	16		12	19	19	12		17	7	12	12

1993 finish: 85–77 (44–37 home, 41–40 away), third in AL East, ten games behind

1994 Schedule

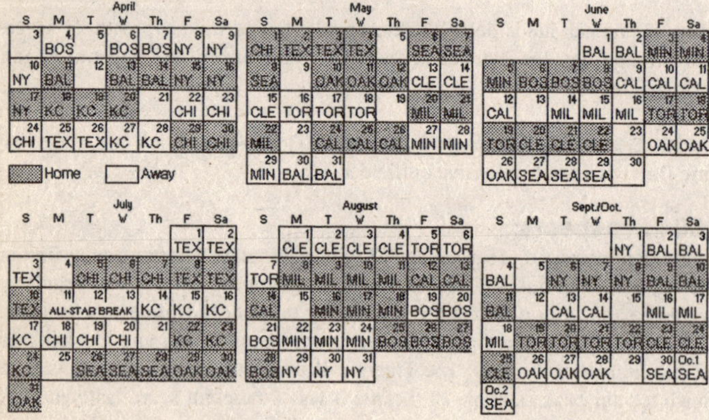

April

S	M	T	W	Th	F	Sa
3	4 BOS	5	6 BOS	7 BOS	8 NY	9 NY
10 NY	11 BAL	12	13 BAL	14 BAL	15 NY	16 NY
17 NY	18 KC	19 KC	20 KC	21	22 CHI	23 CHI
24 CHI	25 TEX	26 TEX	27 KC	28 KC	29 CHI	30 CHI

Home Away

May

S	M	T	W	Th	F	Sa
1 CHI	2 TEX	3 TEX	4 TEX	5	6 SEA	7 SEA
8 SEA	9	10 OAK	11 OAK	12 OAK	13 CLE	14 CLE
15 CLE	16 TOR	17 TOR	18 TOR	19	20 MIL	21 MIL
22 MIL	23	24 CAL	25 CAL	26 CAL	27 MIN	28 MIN
29 MIN	30 BAL	31 BAL				

June

S	M	T	W	Th	F	Sa
			1 BAL	2 BAL	3 MIN	4 MIN
5 MIN	6 BOS	7 BOS	8 BOS	9 CAL	10 CAL	11 CAL
12 CAL	13	14 MIL	15 MIL	16 MIL	17 TOR	18 TOR
19 TOR	20 CLE	21 CLE	22 CLE	23	24 OAK	25 OAK
26 OAK	27 SEA	28 SEA	29 SEA	30		

July

S	M	T	W	Th	F	Sa
					1 TEX	2 TEX
3 TEX	4	5 CHI	6 CHI	7 CHI	8 TEX	9 TEX
10 TEX	11 ALL-STAR BREAK	12	13	14 KC	15 KC	16 KC
17 KC	18 CHI	19 CHI	20 CHI	21	22 KC	23 KC
24 KC	25	26 SEA	27 SEA	28 SEA	29 OAK	30 OAK
31 OAK						

August

S	M	T	W	Th	F	Sa
	1 CLE	2 CLE	3 CLE	4 CLE	5 TOR	6 TOR
7 TOR	8 MIL	9 MIL	10 MIL	11 MIL	12 CAL	13 CAL
14 CAL	15	16 MIN	17 MIN	18 MIN	19 BOS	20 BOS
21 BOS	22 MIN	23 MIN	24 MIN	25 BOS	26 BOS	27 BOS
28 BOS	29 NY	30 NY	31 NY			

Sept./Oct.

S	M	T	W	Th	F	Sa
				1 NY	2 BAL	3 BAL
4 BAL	5	6 NY	7 NY	8 NY	9 BAL	10 BAL
11 BAL	12	13 CAL	14 CAL	15	16 MIL	17 MIL
18 MIL	19 TOR	20 TOR	21 TOR	22 TOR	23 CLE	24 CLE
25 CLE	26 OAK	27 OAK	28 OAK	29	30 SEA	Oc.1 SEA
Oc.2 SEA						

DETROIT TIGERS 1994 ROSTER

MANAGER: Sparky Anderson (11)
COACHES: Billy Consolo (50), Gene Roof (52), Larry Herndon (54), Dick Tracewski (53), Billy Muffett (56), Dan Whitmer (59)

No.	PITCHERS	B	T	HT	WT	DOB	BIRTHPLACE	RESIDENCE
	Bergman, Sean	R	R	6-4	205	4-11-70	Joliet, IL	Joliet, IL
	Blomdahl, Benjamin	R	R	6-2	185	12-30-70	Long Beach, CA	Riverside, CA
	Boever, Joe	R	R	6-1	200	10-4-60	St. Louis, MO	Largo, FL
49	Bolton, Tom	L	L	6-3	185	5-6-62	Nashville, TN	Smyrna, TN
15	Davis, Storm	R	R	6-4	225	12-26-61	Dallas, TX	Atlantic Beach, FL
44	Doherty, John	R	R	6-4	210	6-11-67	Bronx, NY	Tuckahoe, NY
	Gardiner, Michael	S	R	6-0	200	10-19-65	Sarnia, ONT	Conton, MA
34	Gohr, Greg	R	R	6-3	205	10-29-67	Santa Clara, CA	Campbell, CA
42	Groom, Buddy	L	L	6-2	200	7-10-65	Dallas, TX	Red Oak, TX
36	Gullickson, Bill	R	R	6-3	225	2-20-59	Marshall, MN	Brentwood, TN
39	Henneman, Mike	R	R	6-4	205	12-11-61	St. Charles, MO	Colleyville, TX
27	Knudsen, Kurt	R	R	6-3	200	2-20-67	Arlington Hts, IL	Carmichael, CA
30	Krueger, Bill	L	L	6-5	205	4-24-58	Waukegan, IL	Seattle, WA
23	Leiter, Mark	R	R	6-3	210	4-13-63	Joliet, IL	West Caldwell, NJ
	Lima, Jose	R	R	6-2	170	9-30-72	Santiago, DR	Santiago, DR
	Lira, Felipe	R	R	6-0	170	4-26-72	Miranda, VZ	Miranda, VZ
	MacDonald, Robert	L	L	6-3	208	4-27-65	East Orange, NJ	Safety Harbor, FL
21	Moore, Mike	R	R	6-4	205	11-26-59	Early, OK	Tempe, AZ
16	Wells, David	L	L	6-4	225	5-20-63	Torrence, CA	
	Withem, Shannon	R	R	6-3	185	9-27-72	Ann Arbor, MI	Ipsilanti, MI
No.	**CATCHERS**	**B**	**T**	**HT**	**WT**	**DOB**	**BIRTHPLACE**	**RESIDENCE**
19	Kreuter, Chad	R	R	6-2	195	8-26-64	Greenbrae, CA	Arlington, TX
12	Rowland, Rich	R	R	6-1	215	2-25-67	Cloverdale, CA	Cloverdale, CA
20	Tettleton, Mickey	S	R	6-2	212	9-16-60	Oklahoma City, OK	Scottsdale, AZ
No.	**INFIELDERS**	**B**	**T**	**HT**	**WT**	**DOB**	**BIRTHPLACE**	**RESIDENCE**
9	Barnes, Skeeter	R	R	5-10	180	3-7-57	Cincinnati, OH	Indianapolis, IN
13	Brogna, Rico	L	L	6-2	200	4-18-70	Turner Falls, MA	Watertown, CT
	Clark, Anthony	S	R	6-8	205	6-15-72	El Cajon, CA	El Cajon, CA
	Dubose, Brian	L	R	6-3	208	5-17-71	Detroit, MI	Detroit, MI
45	Fielder, Cecil	R	R	6-3	250	9-21-63	Los Angeles, CA	Irving, TX
24	Fryman, Travis	R	R	6-1	194	3-25-69	Lexington, KY	Pensacola, FL
35	Gomez, Christopher	R	R	6-1	183	6-16-71	Los Angeles, CA	Lakewood, CA
7	Livingstone, Scott	L	R	6-0	198	7-15-65	Dallas, TX	Dallas, TX
3	Trammell, Alan	R	R	6-0	185	2-21-58	Garden Grove, CA	Bloomfield Hills, MI
	Phillips, Tony	S	R	5-10	175	4-25-59	Atlanta, GA	Scottsdale, AZ
1	Whitaker, Lou	L	R	5-11	180	5-12-57	New York, NY	Lakeland, FL
No.	**OUTFIELDERS**	**B**	**T**	**HT**	**WT**	**DOB**	**BIRTHPLACE**	**RESIDENCE**
29	Bautista, Danny	R	R	5-11	170	5-24-72	Santo Domingo, DR	Santo Domingo, DR
22	Cuyler, Milt	S	R	5-10	185	10-7-68	Macon, GA	Farmington Hills, MI
33	Davis, Eric	R	R	6-3	185	5-29-62	Los Angeles, CA	Woodland Hills, CA
25	Hare, Shawn	L	L	6-1	200	3-26-67	St. Louis, MO	Rochester Hills, MI
	Pemberton, Rudy	R	R	6-1	185	12-7-69	S.P. de Macoris, DR	S.P. de Macoris, DR
	Thurman, Gary	R	R	5-10	175	11-12-64	Indianapolis, IN	Overland Park, KS

Tiger Stadium (52,416)
Tickets: 313-962-4000
Ticket prices: (1993 prices; 1994 prices not available at press time)

- $14 (box seats)
- $11 (reserved seats)
- $7 (grandstand reserved seats)
- $4 (bleacher seats)

Field Dimensions (from home plate)

- To left field at foul line, 340 feet
- To center field, 440 feet
- To right field at foul line, 325 feet
- (OF wall is 9 feet high)

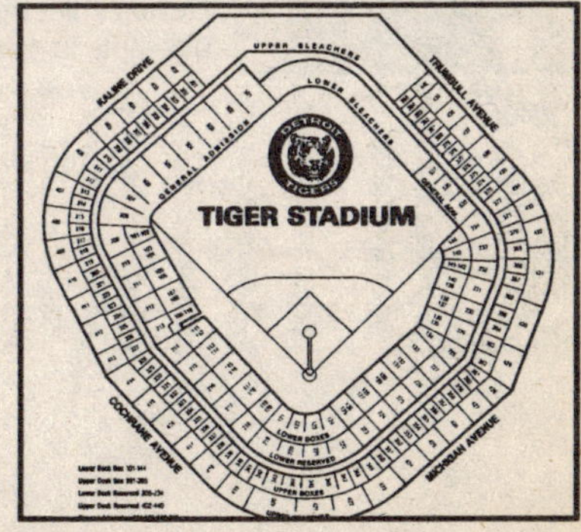

Milt Cuyler No. 22/OF

Full name: Milton Cuyler Jr.
Bats: S **Throws:** R **HT:** 5–10 **WT:** 185
Born: 10–7–68, Macon, GA
High school: Southwest Macon (GA)
College: Macon Junior (GA)
Cuyler's season was cut short by a knee injury in August, and his .213 BA was a career-low.

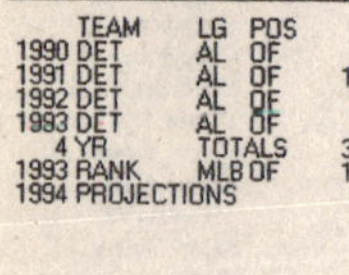
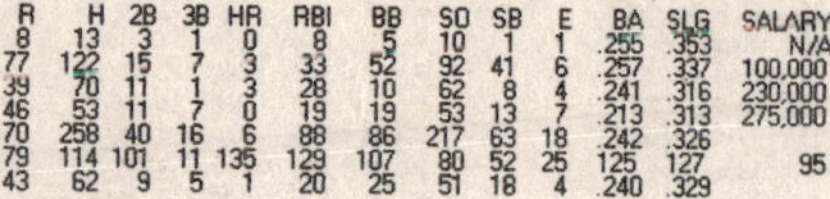

	TEAM	LG	POS	G	AB	R	H	2B	3B	HR	RBI	BB	SO	SB	E	BA	SLG	SALARY
1990	DET	AL	OF	19	51	8	13	3	1	0	8	5	10	1	1	.255	.353	N/A
1991	DET	AL	OF	154	475	77	122	15	7	3	33	52	92	41	6	.257	.337	100,000
1992	DET	AL	OF	89	291	39	70	11	1	3	28	10	62	8	4	.241	.316	230,000
1993	DET	AL	OF	82	249	46	53	11	7	0	19	19	53	13	7	.213	.313	275,000
4	YR	TOTALS		344	1066	170	258	40	16	6	88	86	217	63	18	.242	.326	
1993	RANK	MLB	OF	114	102	79	114	101	11	135	129	107	80	52	25	125	127	95
1994	PROJECTIONS			85	258	43	62	9	5	1	20	25	51	18	4	.240	.329	

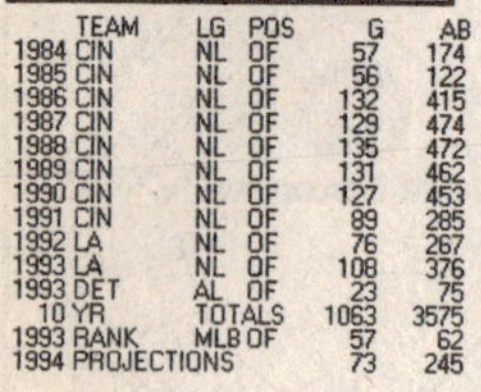

Eric Davis No. 33/OF

Full name: Eric Keith Davis
Bats: R **Throws:** R **HT:** 6–3 **WT:** 185
Born: 5–29–62, Los Angeles, CA
High school: Fremont (Los Angeles, CA)
Acquired from the Dodgers in August, Davis, if healthy, will add even more power to Detroit's lineup. He also stole 35 bases in 39 attempts in 1993.

	TEAM	LG	POS	G	AB	R	H	2B	3B	HR	RBI	BB	SO	SB	E	BA	SLG	SALARY
1984	CIN	NL	OF	57	174	33	39	10	1	10	30	24	48	10	1	.224	.466	N/A
1985	CIN	NL	OF	56	122	26	30	3	3	8	18	7	39	16	1	.246	.516	N/A
1986	CIN	NL	OF	132	415	97	115	15	3	27	71	68	100	80	7	.277	.523	N/A
1987	CIN	NL	OF	129	474	120	139	23	4	37	100	84	134	50	4	.293	.593	N/A
1988	CIN	NL	OF	135	472	81	129	18	3	26	93	65	124	35	6	.273	.489	N/A
1989	CIN	NL	OF	131	462	74	130	14	2	34	101	68	116	21	5	.281	.541	N/A
1990	CIN	NL	OF	127	453	84	118	26	2	24	86	60	100	21	2	.260	.486	2,100,000
1991	CIN	NL	OF	89	285	39	67	10	0	11	33	48	92	14	3	.235	.386	3,600,000
1992	LA	NL	OF	76	267	21	61	8	1	5	32	36	71	19	5	.228	.322	3,600,000
1993	LA	NL	OF	108	376	57	88	17	0	14	53	41	88	33	2	.234	.391	N/A
1993	DET	AL	OF	23	75	14	19	1	1	6	15	14	18	2	1	.253	.533	N/A
10	YR	TOTALS		1063	3575	646	935	145	20	202	632	515	930	301	37	.262	.483	
1993	RANK	MLB	OF	57	62	45	69	61	97	23	34	30	18	14	72	116	72	39
1994	PROJECTIONS			73	245	36	58	9	0	10	33	34	66	16	2	.237	.404	

Cecil Fielder No. 45/1B

Full name: Cecil Grant Fielder
Bats: R **Throws:** R **HT:** 6–3 **WT:** 250
Born: 9–21–63, Los Angeles, CA
High school: Nogales (Los Angeles, CA)
One of the game's top sluggers, Fielder has averaged 40 HR and 126 RBI in his four Tiger seasons. He had 2 HR in a game five times in 1993.

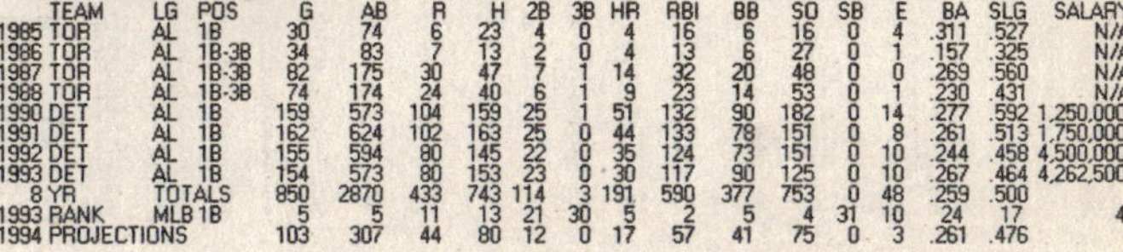

	TEAM	LG	POS	G	AB	R	H	2B	3B	HR	RBI	BB	SO	SB	E	BA	SLG	SALARY
1985	TOR	AL	1B	30	74	6	23	4	0	4	16	6	16	0	4	.311	.527	N/A
1986	TOR	AL	1B-3B	34	83	7	13	2	0	4	13	6	27	0	1	.157	.325	N/A
1987	TOR	AL	1B-3B	82	175	30	47	7	1	14	32	20	48	0	0	.269	.560	N/A
1988	TOR	AL	1B-3B	74	174	24	40	6	1	9	23	14	53	0	1	.230	.431	N/A
1990	DET	AL	1B	159	573	104	159	25	1	51	132	90	182	0	14	.277	.592	1,250,000
1991	DET	AL	1B	162	624	102	163	25	0	44	133	78	151	0	8	.261	.513	1,750,000
1992	DET	AL	1B	155	594	80	145	22	0	35	124	73	151	0	10	.244	.458	4,500,000
1993	DET	AL	1B	154	573	80	153	23	0	30	117	90	125	0	10	.267	.464	4,262,500
8	YR	TOTALS		850	2870	433	743	114	3	191	590	377	753	0	48	.259	.500	
1993	RANK	MLB	1B	5	5	11	13	21	30	5	2	5	4	31	10	24	17	4
1994	PROJECTIONS			103	307	44	80	12	0	17	57	41	75	0	3	.261	.476	

Travis Fryman No. 24/3B-SS

Full name: Travis David Fryman
Bats: R **Throws:** R **HT:** 6–1 **WT:** 194
Born: 3–25–69, Lexington, KY
High school: Tate (KY)
Fryman had an All-Star season, with career highs in BA (.300), HR (22), RBI (97), and doubles (37). He made 13 of his 23 errors before May 25.

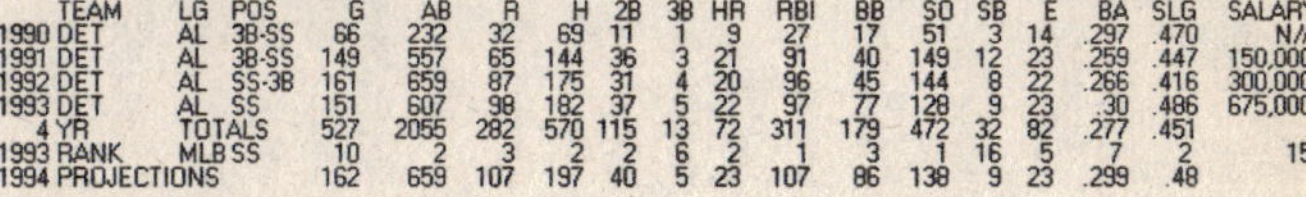

	TEAM	LG	POS	G	AB	R	H	2B	3B	HR	RBI	BB	SO	SB	E	BA	SLG	SALARY
1990	DET	AL	3B-SS	66	232	32	69	11	1	9	27	17	51	3	14	.297	.470	N/A
1991	DET	AL	3B-SS	149	557	65	144	36	3	21	91	40	149	12	23	.259	.447	150,000
1992	DET	AL	SS-3B	161	659	87	175	31	4	20	96	45	144	8	22	.266	.416	300,000
1993	DET	AL	SS	151	607	98	182	37	5	22	97	77	128	9	23	.30	.486	675,000
4	YR	TOTALS		527	2055	282	570	115	13	72	311	179	472	32	82	.277	.451	
1993	RANK	MLB	SS	10	2	3	2	2	6	2	1	3	1	16	5	7	2	15
1994	PROJECTIONS			162	659	107	197	40	5	23	107	86	138	9	23	.299	.48	

Chad Kreuter No. 19/C

Full name: Chadden Michael Kreuter
Bats: R **Throws:** R **HT:** 6–2 **WT:** 195
Born: 8–26–64, Greenbrae, CA
High school: Redwood (CA)
College: Pepperdine

Kreuter threw out 33 of 87 attempted base stealers. His 107 hits, 15 HR, and 51 RBI were career highs.

	TEAM	LG	POS	G	AB	R	H	2B	3B	HR	RBI	BB	SO	SB	E	BA	SLG	SALARY
1988	TEX	AL	C	16	51	3	14	2	1	1	5	7	13	0	1	.275	.412	N/A
1989	TEX	AL	C	87	158	16	24	3	0	5	9	27	40	U	4	.152	.266	N/A
1990	TEX	AL	C	22	22	2	1	1	0	0	2	8	9	0	1	.045	.091	N/A
1991	TEX	AL	C	3	4	0	0	0	0	0	0	0	1	0	0	.000	.000	N/A
1992	DET	AL	C	67	190	22	48	9	0	2	16	20	38	0	5	.253	.332	155,000
1993	DET	AL	C	119	374	59	107	23	3	15	51	49	92	2	7	.286	.484	240,000
6	YR	TOTALS		314	799	102	194	38	4	23	83	111	193	2	18	.243	.387	
1993	RANK	MLB	C	17	19	7	15	9	5	8	16	5	5	13	12	8	6	25
1994	PROJECTIONS			136	427	68	122	26	3	17	58	56	105	2	8	.286	.48	

Scott Livingstone No. 7/DH

Full name: Scott Louis Livingstone
Bats: L **Throws:** R **HT:** 6–0 **WT:** 198
Born: 7–15–65, Dallas, TX
College: Texas A&M

Although his .293 BA was a career-high, Livingstone's overall production slipped slightly in 1993, as his HRs fell from 21 to 10.

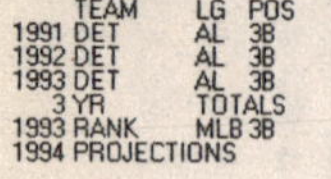

	TEAM	LG	POS	G	AB	R	H	2B	3B	HR	RBI	BB	SO	SB	E	BA	SLG	SALARY
1991	DET	AL	3B	44	127	19	37	5	0	2	11	10	25	2	2	.291	.378	100,000
1992	DET	AL	3B	117	354	43	100	21	0	4	46	21	36	1	10	.282	.376	120,000
1993	DET	AL	3B	98	304	39	89	10	2	2	39	19	32	1	6	.293	.359	230,000
3	YR	TOTALS		259	785	101	226	36	2	8	96	50	93	4	18	.288	.369	
1993	RANK	MLB	3B	27	25	25	22	33	10	34	26	31	36	26	36	9	35	25
1994	PROJECTIONS			86	261	33	75	12	0	2	32	16	31	1	6	.287	.368	

Mickey Tettleton No. 20/1B-C

Full name: Mickey Lee Tettleton
Bats: S **Throws:** R **HT:** 6–2 **WT:** 212
Born: 9–16–60, Oklahoma City, OK
High school: Southeast (Oklahoma City, OK)
College: Oklahoma State

Tettleton's career-best 33 HR placed him eighth in the AL. His 110 RBI and 109 walks were also in the top ten.

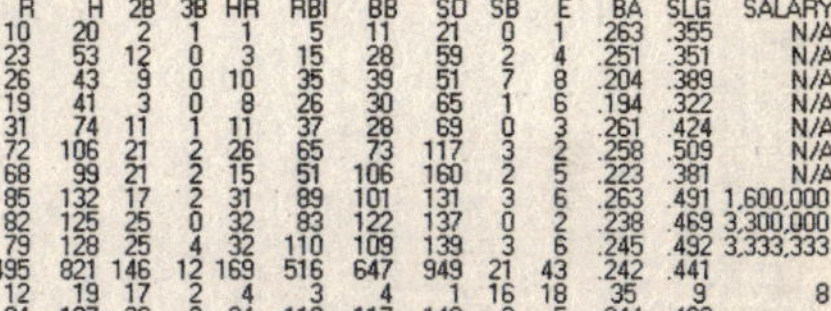

	TEAM	LG	POS	G	AB	R	H	2B	3B	HR	RBI	BB	SO	SB	E	BA	SLG	SALARY
1984	OAK	AL	C	33	76	10	20	2	1	1	5	11	21	0	1	.263	.355	N/A
1985	OAK	AL	C	78	211	23	53	12	0	3	15	28	59	2	4	.251	.351	N/A
1986	OAK	AL	C	90	211	26	43	9	0	10	35	39	51	7	8	.204	.389	N/A
1987	OAK	AL	C-1B	82	211	19	41	3	0	8	26	30	65	1	6	.194	.322	N/A
1988	BAL	AL	C	86	283	31	74	11	1	11	37	28	69	0	3	.261	.424	N/A
1989	BAL	AL	C	117	411	72	106	21	2	26	65	73	117	3	2	.258	.509	N/A
1990	BAL	AL	C-1B	135	444	68	99	21	2	15	51	106	160	2	5	.223	.381	N/A
1991	DET	AL	C-OF	154	501	85	132	17	2	31	89	101	131	3	6	.263	.491	1,600,000
1992	DET	AL	C-1B	157	525	82	125	25	0	32	83	122	137	0	2	.238	.469	3,300,000
1993	DET	AL	1B	152	522	79	128	25	4	32	110	109	139	3	6	.245	.492	3,333,333
10	YR	TOTALS		1084	3395	495	821	146	12	169	516	647	949	21	43	.242	.441	
1993	RANK	MLB	1B	10	15	12	19	17	2	4	3	4	1	16	18	35	9	8
1994	PROJECTIONS			162	562	84	137	26	3	34	119	117	149	2	5	.244	.482	

Alan Trammell No. 3/SS

Full name: Alan Stuart Trammell
Bats: R **Throws:** R **HT:** 6–0 **WT:** 185
Born: 2–21–58, Garden Grove, CA
High school: Kearney (San Diego, CA)

Veteran Trammell came back from a 1992 ankle injury to lead the team with a .329 BA, his best since 1987. He put together a team-high sixteen-game hitting streak.

	TEAM	LG	POS	G	AB	R	H	2B	3B	HR	RBI	BB	SO	SB	E	BA	SLG	SALARY
1978	DET	AL	SS	139	448	49	120	14	6	2	34	45	56	3	14	.268	.339	N/A
1979	DET	AL	SS	142	460	68	127	11	4	6	50	43	55	17	26	.276	.357	N/A
1980	DET	AL	SS	146	560	107	168	21	5	9	65	69	63	12	13	.300	.404	N/A
1981	DET	AL	SS	105	392	52	101	15	3	2	31	49	31	10	9	.258	.327	N/A
1982	DET	AL	SS	157	489	66	126	34	3	9	57	52	47	19	16	.258	.395	N/A
1983	DET	AL	SS	142	505	83	161	31	2	14	66	57	64	30	13	.319	.471	N/A
1984	DET	AL	SS	139	555	85	174	34	5	14	69	60	63	19	10	.314	.468	N/A
1985	DET	AL	SS	149	605	79	156	21	7	13	57	50	71	14	15	.258	.380	N/A
1986	DET	AL	SS	151	574	107	159	33	7	21	75	59	57	25	22	.277	.469	N/A
1987	DET	AL	SS	151	597	109	205	34	3	28	105	60	47	21	19	.343	.551	N/A
1988	DET	AL	SS	128	466	73	145	24	1	15	69	46	46	7	11	.311	.464	N/A
1989	DET	AL	SS	121	449	54	109	20	3	5	43	45	45	10	9	.243	.334	N/A
1990	DET	AL	SS	146	559	71	170	37	1	14	89	68	55	12	14	.304	.449	N/A
1991	DET	AL	SS-3B	101	375	57	93	20	0	9	55	37	39	11	9	.248	.373	2,200,000
1992	DET	AL	SS	29	102	11	28	7	1	1	11	15	4	2	3	.275	.392	2,400,000
1993	DET	AL	SS	112	401	72	132	25	3	12	60	38	38	12	9	.329	.496	1,827,500
17	YR	TOTALS		2077	7580	1149	2182	381	54	174	936	797	793	224	214	.288	.421	
1993	RANK	MLB	SS	23	22	9	15	8	12	4	8	17	26	8	32	1	1	10
1994	PROJECTIONS			137	450	68	128	23	3	9	55	44	46	16	17	.284	.411	

Lou Whitaker No. 1/2B

Full name: Louis Rodman Whitaker
Bats: L **Throws:** R **HT:** 5–11 **WT:** 180
Born: 5–12–57, New York, NY
High school: Martinsville (WV)
The 36-year-old Whitaker's power output has dropped off (9 HR), but he posted his highest average (.290) since 1983.

	TEAM	LG	POS	G	AB	R	H	2B	3B	HR	RBI	BB	SO	SB	E	BA	SLG	SALARY
1978	DET	AL	2B	139	484	71	138	12	7	3	58	61	65	7	17	.285	.357	N/A
1979	DET	AL	2B	127	423	75	121	14	8	3	42	78	66	20	9	.286	.378	N/A
1980	DET	AL	2B	145	477	88	111	19	1	1	45	73	79	8	12	.233	.283	N/A
1981	DET	AL	2B	109	335	48	88	14	4	5	36	40	42	5	9	.263	.373	N/A
1982	DET	AL	2B	152	560	76	160	22	8	15	65	48	58	11	10	.286	.434	N/A
1983	DET	AL	2B	161	643	94	206	40	6	12	72	67	70	17	13	.320	.457	N/A
1984	DET	AL	2B	143	558	90	161	25	1	13	56	62	63	6	15	.289	.407	N/A
1985	DET	AL	2B	152	609	102	170	29	8	21	73	80	56	6	11	.279	.456	N/A
1986	DET	AL	2B	144	584	95	157	26	6	20	73	63	70	13	11	.269	.437	N/A
1987	DET	AL	2B	149	604	110	160	38	6	16	59	71	108	13	17	.265	.427	N/A
1988	DET	AL	2B	115	403	54	111	18	2	12	55	66	61	2	8	.275	.419	N/A
1989	DET	AL	2B	148	509	77	128	21	1	28	85	89	59	6	11	.251	.462	N/A
1990	DET	AL	2B	132	472	75	112	22	2	18	60	74	71	8	6	.237	.407	N/A
1991	DET	AL	2B	138	470	94	131	26	2	23	78	90	45	4	4	.279	.489	2,000,000
1992	DET	AL	2B	130	453	77	126	26	0	19	71	81	46	6	9	.278	.461	2,200,000
1993	DET	AL	2B	119	383	72	111	32	1	9	67	78	46	3	11	.290	.449	3,433,333
17	YR	TOTALS		2214	7999	1283	2199	385	63	218	997	1125	1011	137	173	.275	.421	
1993	RANK	MLB	2B	22	23	11	19	3	31	9	7	2	29	31	16	8	7	4
1994	PROJECTIONS			120	403	67	114	21	3	8	54	74	57	8	9	.283	.414	

John Doherty No. 44/P

Full name: John Harold Doherty
Bats: R **Throws:** R **HT:** 6–4 **WT:** 210
Born: 6–11–67, Bronx, NY
High school: Eastchester (NY)
College: Concordia (Bronxville, NY)
Doherty's 14 wins led the Tigers. He pitched at least 7 full innings in 14 of his 30 starts, and allowed only 48 walks for the year.

	TM	LG	POS	W	L	ERA	G	GS	CG	SH	SV	IP	H	R	ER	HR	BB	SO	SALARY
1992	DET	AL	P	7	4	3.88	47	11	0	0	3	116.0	131	61	50	4	25	37	109,000
1993	DET	AL	P	14	11	4.44	32	31	3	2	0	184.2	205	104	91	19	48	63	170,000
2	YR	TOTALS		21	15	4.22	79	42	3	2	3	300.2	336	165	141	23	73	100	
1993	Rank	MLB	Ps	29		182	175	51	37	8	102	65	216	193		168	43	286	188
1994	PROJECTIONS			14	12	4.57	21	36	3	2	0	191	212	109	97	22	51	66	

Bill Gullickson No. 36/P

Full name: William Lee Gullickson
Bats: R **Throws:** R **HT:** 6–3 **WT:** 225
Born: 2–20–59, Marshall, MN
High school: Joliet (IL)

Gullickson registered 13 wins in spite of a 5.37 ERA, and was 6–0 in August. This was his tenth straight season with more than ten wins.

	TM	LG	POS	W	L	ERA	G	GS	CG	SH	SV	IP	H	R	ER	HR	BB	SO	SALARY
1979	MTL	NL	P	0	0	0.00	1	0	0	0	0	1.0	2	0	0	0	0	0	N/A
1980	MTL	NL	P	10	5	3.00	24	19	5	2	0	141.0	127	53	47	6	50	120	N/A
1981	MTL	NL	P	7	9	2.81	22	22	3	2	0	157.0	142	54	49	3	34	115	N/A
1982	MTL	NL	P	12	14	3.57	34	34	6	0	0	236.2	231	101	94	25	61	155	N/A
1983	MTL	NL	P	17	12	3.75	34	34	10	1	0	242.1	230	108	101	19	59	120	N/A
1984	MTL	NL	P	12	9	3.61	32	32	3	0	0	226.2	230	100	91	27	37	100	N/A
1985	MTL	NL	P	14	12	3.52	29	29	4	1	0	181.1	187	78	71	8	47	68	N/A
1986	CIN	NL	P	15	12	3.38	37	37	6	2	0	244.2	245	103	92	24	60	121	N/A
1987	CIN	NL	P	10	11	4.85	27	27	3	1	0	165.0	172	99	89	33	39	89	N/A
1987	NY	AL	P	4	2	4.88	8	8	1	0	0	48.0	46	29	26	7	11	28	N/A
1990	HOU	NL	P	10	14	3.82	32	32	2	1	0	193.1	221	100	82	21	61	73	1,826,000
1991	DET	AL	P	20	9	3.90	35	35	4	0	0	226.1	256	109	98	22	44	91	1,825,000
1992	DET	AL	P	14	13	4.34	34	34	4	1	0	221.2	228	109	107	35	50	64	1,925,000
1993	DET	AL	P	13	9	5.37	28	28	2	0	0	159.1	186	106	95	28	44	70	2,300,000
13	YR	TOTALS		158	131	3.84	377	371	53	11	0	2444.1	2503	1149	1042	258	597	1214	
1993	Rank	MLB Ps		36		257	220	71	57	69	102	89	252	260		284	56	264	58
1994	PROJECTIONS			5	3	5.22	12	12	1	0	0	69	78	45	40	11	18	32	

David Wells No. 16/P

Full name: David Lee Wells
Bats: L **Throws:** L **HT:** 6–4 **WT:** 225
Born: 5–20–63, Torrance, CA
High school: Point Loma (San Diego, CA)

Wells dominated opponents early, starting off 9–1 with a 2.68 ERA through June 19. His 30 starts was a career high. An inflamed left elbow put him on the DL in August.

	TM	LG	POS	W	L	ERA	G	GS	CG	SH	SV	IP	H	R	ER	HR	BB	SO	SALARY
1987	TOR	AL	P	4	3	3.99	18	2	0	0	1	29.1	37	14	13	0	12	32	N/A
1988	TOR	AL	P	3	5	4.62	41	0	0	0	4	64.1	65	36	33	12	31	56	N/A
1989	TOR	AL	P	7	4	2.40	54	0	0	0	2	86.1	66	25	23	5	28	78	N/A
1990	TOR	AL	P	11	6	3.14	43	25	0	0	3	189.0	165	72	66	14	45	115	N/A
1991	TOR	AL	P	15	10	3.72	40	28	2	0	1	198.1	188	88	82	24	49	106	800,000
1992	TOR	AL	P	7	9	5.40	41	14	0	0	2	120.0	138	84	72	16	36	62	2,063,000
1993	DET	AL	P	11	9	4.19	32	30	0	0	0	187.0	183	93	87	26	42	139	1,450,000
7	YR	TOTALS		58	46	3.87	269	99	2	0	13	874.1	842	412	376	97	243	588	
1993	RANK	MLB Ps		59		159	175	58	125	69	102	62	116	139		250	27	88	83
1994	PROJECTIONS			8	7	4.12	42	14	0	0	1	131	129	67	60	15	35	93	

Mike Henneman No. 39/P

Full name: Michael Alan Henneman
Bats: R **Throws:** R **HT:** 6–4 **WT:** 205
Born: 12–11–61, St. Charles, MO
High school: St. Pius X (Festus, MO)
College: Oklahoma State

Henneman saved 24 games in 29 opportunities during 1993, and his 2.64 ERA was his best since 1988.

	TM	LG	POS	W	L	ERA	G	GS	CG	SH	SV	IP	H	R	ER	HR	BB	SO	SALARY
1987	DET	AL	P	11	3	2.98	55	0	0	0	7	96.2	86	36	32	8	30	75	N/A
1988	DET	AL	P	9	6	1.87	65	0	0	0	22	91.1	72	23	19	7	24	58	N/A
1989	DET	AL	P	11	4	3.70	60	0	0	0	8	90.0	84	46	37	4	51	69	N/A
1990	DET	AL	P	8	6	3.05	69	0	0	0	22	94.1	90	36	32	4	33	50	335,000
1991	DET	AL	P	10	2	2.88	60	0	0	0	21	84.1	81	29	27	2	34	61	1,100,000
1992	DET	AL	P	2	6	3.96	60	0	0	0	24	77.1	75	36	34	6	20	58	2,437,500
1993	DET	AL	P	5	3	2.64	63	0	0	0	24	71.2	69	28	21	4	32	58	4,333,333
7	YR	TOTALS		56	30	3.00	432	0	0	0	128	605.2	557	234	202	35	224	429	
1993	Rank	MLB Ps		149		21	38	202	125	69	17	212	107	51		35	223	57	10
1994	PROJECTIONS			8	4	2.51	61	0	0	0	17	86	75	29	24	6	28	63	

Sparky Anderson No. 11/Mgr.

Full name: George Lee Anderson
Bats: R **Throws:** R **HT:** 5–9 **WT:** 168
Born: 6–15–49, Riverside, CA
High school: Del Campo (Fair Oaks, CA)
College: American River (CA)

Anderson never won NL Manager of the Year with the Big Red Machine, but won AL Manager of the Year twice with Detroit.

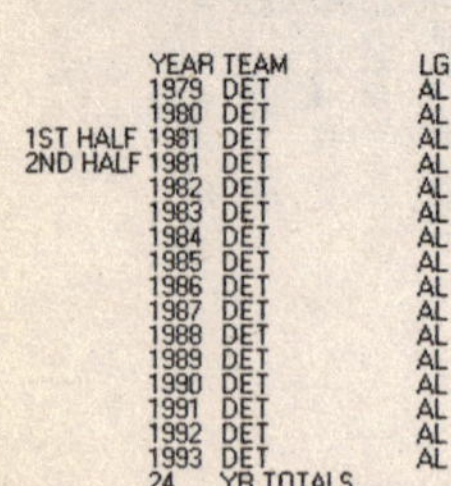

				REG. SEASON				PLAYOFF			CHAMP. SERIES			WORLD SERIES		
	YEAR	TEAM	LG	W	L	PCT	POS	W	L	PCT	W	L	PCT	W	L	PCT
	1979	DET	AL	56	50	.528	5			---			---			---
	1980	DET	AL	84	78	.519	5			---			---			---
1ST HALF	1981	DET	AL	31	26	.544	4			---			---			---
2ND HALF	1981	DET	AL	29	23	.558	3			---			---			---
	1982	DET	AL	83	79	.512	4			---			---			---
	1983	DET	AL	92	70	.568	2			---			---			---
	1984	DET	AL	104	58	.642	1			---	3	0	1.000	4	1	.800
	1985	DET	AL	84	77	.522	3			---			---			---
	1986	DET	AL	87	75	.537	3			---			---			---
	1987	DET	AL	98	64	.605	1			---	1	4	.200			---
	1988	DET	AL	88	74	.543	2			---			---			---
	1989	DET	AL	59	103	.364	7			---			---			---
	1990	DET	AL	79	83	.488	3			---			---			---
	1991	DET	AL	84	78	.519	2			---			---			---
	1992	DET	AL	75	87	.463	6			---			---			---
	1993	DET	AL	85	162	.344	3			---			---			---
	24	YR TOTALS		2081	1773	.540	66	0	0	---	18	9	.667	16	12	.571

Joe Boever No. 37/P

Full name: Michael Alan Henneman
Bats: R **Throws:** R **HT:** 6–4 **WT:** 205
Born: 12–11–61, St. Charles, MO
High school: St. Pius X (Festus, MO)
College: Oklahoma State
Didn't allow a run in 13 of 19 Tiger appearances.

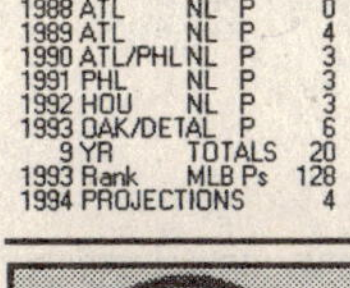
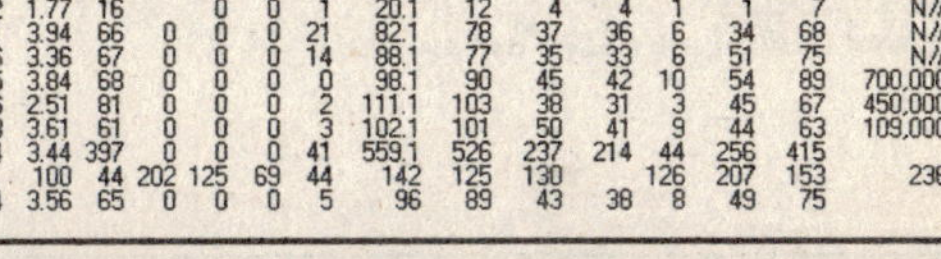

TM	LG	POS	W	L	ERA	G	GS	CG	SH	SV	IP	H	R	ER	HR	BB	SO	SALARY
1987 ATL	NL	P	1	0	7.36	14	0	0	0	0	18.1	29	15	15	4	12	18	N/A
1988 ATL	NL	P	0	2	1.77	16		0	0	1	20.1	12	4	4	1	1	7	N/A
1989 ATL	NL	P	4	11	3.94	66	0	0	0	21	82.1	78	37	36	6	34	68	N/A
1990 ATL/PHL	NL	P	3	6	3.36	67	0	0	0	14	88.1	77	35	33	6	51	75	N/A
1991 PHL	NL	P	3	5	3.84	68	0	0	0	0	98.1	90	45	42	10	54	89	700,000
1992 HOU	NL	P	3	6	2.51	81	0	0	0	2	111.1	103	38	31	3	45	67	450,000
1993 OAK/DET	AL	P	6	3	3.61	61	0	0	0	3	102.1	101	50	41	9	44	63	109,000
9 YR	TOTALS		20	34	3.44	397	0	0	0	41	559.1	526	237	214	44	256	415	
1993 Rank	MLB Ps		128		100	44	202	125	69	44	142	125	130		126	207	153	236
1994 PROJECTIONS			4	4	3.56	65	0	0	0	5	96	89	43	38	8	49	75	

Skeeter Barnes No. 9/1B–OF

Full name: William Henry Barnes III
Bats: R **Throws:** R **HT:** 5–10 **WT:** 180
Born: 3–7–57, Cincinnati, OH
High school: Woodward (Cincinnati, OH)
College: Cincinnati
Barnes appeared at seven different positions.

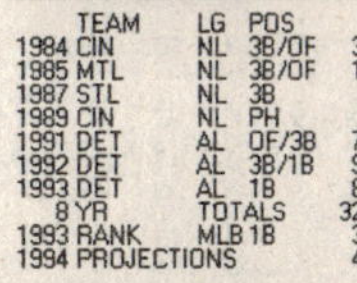
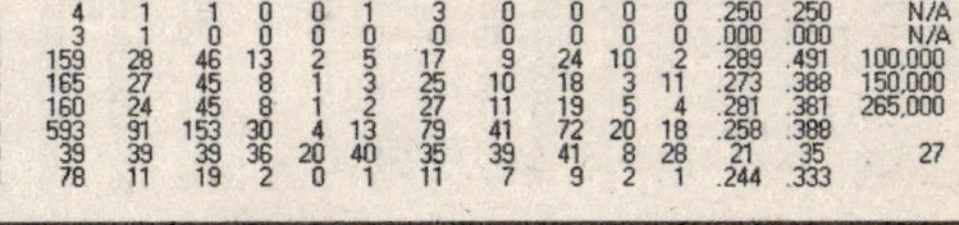

TEAM	LG	POS	G	AB	R	H	2B	3B	HR	RBI	BB	SO	SB	E	BA	SLG	SALARY
1984 CIN	NL	3B/OF	32	42	5	5	0	0	1	3	4	6	0	0	.119	.190	N/A
1985 MTL	NL	3B/OF	19	26	0	4	1	0	0	0	0	2	0	0	.154	.192	N/A
1987 STL	NL	3B	4	4	1	1	0	0	1	3	0	0	0	0	.250	.250	N/A
1989 CIN	NL	PH	5	3	1	0	0	0	0	0	0	0	0	0	.000	.000	N/A
1991 DET	AL	OF/3B	75	159	28	46	13	2	5	17	9	24	10	2	.289	.491	100,000
1992 DET	AL	3B/1B	95	165	27	45	8	1	3	25	10	18	3	11	.273	.388	150,000
1993 DET	AL	1B	84	160	24	45	8	1	2	27	11	19	5	4	.281	.381	265,000
8 YR	TOTALS		329	593	91	153	30	4	13	79	41	72	20	18	.258	.388	
1993 RANK	MLB	1B	39	39	39	39	36	20	40	35	39	41	8	28	21	35	27
1994 PROJECTIONS			43	78	11	19	2	0	1	11	7	9	2	1	.244	.333	

Tom Bolton No. 49/P

Full name: Thomas Edward Bolton
Bats: L **Throws:** L **HT:** 6–3 **WT:** 185
Born: 5–6–62, Nashville, TN
High school: Antioch (TN)
Bolton was 5–2 as a starter and 1–4 out of the bullpen in 1993. He appeared in 43 games.

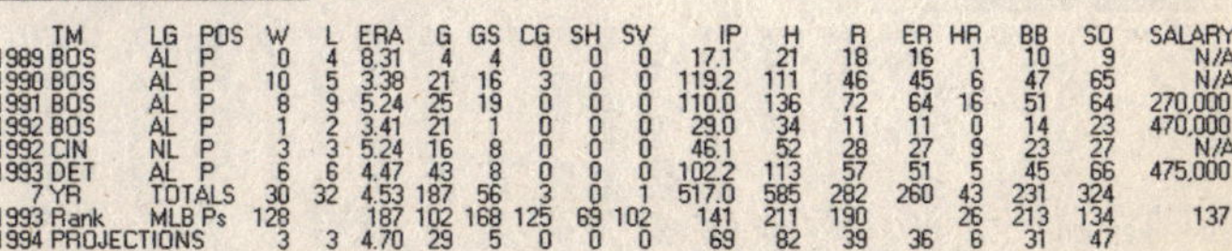

TM	LG	POS	W	L	ERA	G	GS	CG	SH	SV	IP	H	R	ER	HR	BB	SO	SALARY
1989 BOS	AL	P	0	4	8.31	4	4	0	0	0	17.1	21	18	16	1	10	9	N/A
1990 BOS	AL	P	10	5	3.38	21	16	3	0	0	119.2	111	46	45	6	47	65	N/A
1991 BOS	AL	P	8	9	5.24	25	19	0	0	0	110.0	136	72	64	16	51	64	270,000
1992 BOS	AL	P	1	2	3.41	21	1	0	0	0	29.0	34	11	11	0	14	23	470,000
1992 CIN	NL	P	3	3	5.24	16	8	0	0	0	46.1	52	28	27	9	23	27	N/A
1993 DET	AL	P	6	6	4.47	43	8	0	0	0	102.2	113	57	51	5	45	66	475,000
7 YR	TOTALS		30	32	4.53	187	56	3	0	1	517.0	585	282	260	43	231	324	
1993 Rank	MLB Ps		128		187	102	168	125	69	102	141	211	190		26	213	134	137
1994 PROJECTIONS			3	3	4.70	29	5	0	0	0	69	82	39	36	6	31	47	

Rico Brogna — No. 13/1B

Full name: Rico Joseph Brogna
Bats: L **Throws:** L **HT:** 6–2 **WT:** 200
Born: 4–18–70, Turner Falls, MA
High school: Watertown (CT)
Prospect Brogna batted .273 at AAA Toledo, and led the team with 132 hits.

TEAM	LG	POS	G	AB	R	H	2B	3B	HR	RBI	BB	SO	SB	E	BA	SLG	SALARY
1992 DET	AL	1B	9	26	3	5	1	0	1	3	3	5	0	1	.192	.346	N/A
1 YR	TOTAL		9	26	3	5	1	0	1	3	3	5	0	1	.192	.346	
1993 RANK	MLB 1B		not ranked -- didn't play in 1993														

Storm Davis — No. 48/P

Full name: George Earl Davis
Bats: R **Throws:** R **HT:** 6–4 **WT:** 225
Born: 12–26–61, Dallas, TX
High school: University Christian (J'ville, FL)
Veteran Davis was used exclusively in relief by the Tigers, and notched 4 saves in 4 opportunities.

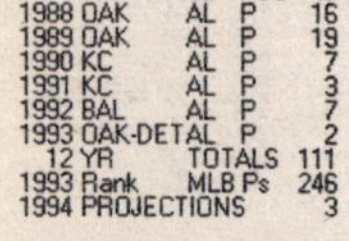

TM	LG	POS	W	L	ERA	G	GS	CG	SH	SV	IP	H	R	ER	HR	BB	SO	SALARY
1988 OAK	AL	P	16	7	3.70	33	33	1	0	0	201.2	211	86	83	16	91	127	N/A
1989 OAK	AL	P	19	7	4.36	31	31	1	0	0	169.1	187	91	82	19	68	91	N/A
1990 KC	AL	P	7	10	4.74	21	20	0	0	0	112.0	129	66	59	9	35	62	N/A
1991 KC	AL	P	3	9	4.96	51	9	1	1	2	114.1	140	69	63	11	46	53	2,275,000
1992 BAL	AL	P	7	3	3.43	48	2	0	0	4	89.1	79	35	34	5	36	53	2,466,667
1993 OAK-DET	AL	P	2	8	5.05	43	8	0	0	4	98.0	93	57	55	9	48	73	109,000
12 YR	TOTALS		111	92	4.04	407	239	30	5	11	1732.2	1756	843	777	133	653	1010	
1993 Rank	MLB Ps		246		237	102	168	125	69	37	149	96	207		137	244	85	236
1994 PROJECTIONS			3	6	4.77	37	6	0	0	2	83	80	46	44	6	40	54	

Bill Krueger — No. 30/P

Full name: William Culp Krueger
Bats: L **Throws:** L **HT:** 6–5 **WT:** 215
Born: 4–24–58, Waukegan, IL
High school: McMinnville (OR)
College: Portland (OR)
Krueger's 3.40 ERA was his best ever.

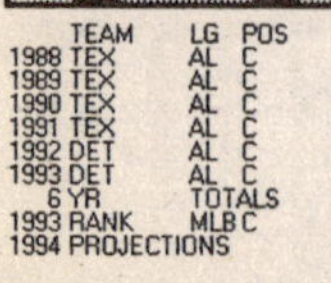

TEAM	LG	POS	G	AB	R	H	2B	3B	HR	RBI	BB	SO	SB	E	BA	SLG	SALARY
1988 TEX	AL	C	16	51	3	14	2	1	1	5	7	13	0	1	.275	.412	N/A
1989 TEX	AL	C	87	158	16	24	3	0	5	9	27	40	0	4	.152	.266	N/A
1990 TEX	AL	C	22	22	2	1	1	0	0	2	8	9	0	1	.045	.091	N/A
1991 TEX	AL	C	3	4	0	0	0	0	0	0	0	1	0	0	.000	.000	N/A
1992 DET	AL	C	67	190	22	48	9	0	2	16	20	38	0	5	.253	.332	155,000
1993 DET	AL	C	119	374	59	107	23	3	15	51	49	92	2	7	.286	.484	240,000
6 YR	TOTALS		314	799	102	194	38	4	23	83	111	193	2	18	.243	.387	
1993 RANK	MLB	C	17	19	7	15	9	5	8	16	5	5	13	12	8	6	25
1994 PROJECTIONS			136	427	68	122	26	3	17	58	56	105	2	8	.286	.48	

Mike Gardiner P

Full name: Michael James Gardiner
Bats: S **Throws:** R **HT:** 6–0 **WT:** 200
Born: 10–19–65, Sarnia, ONT
High school: Sarnia Collegiate (ONT.)
College: Indiana State
Gardiner was unscored upon in 7 of his 10 games.

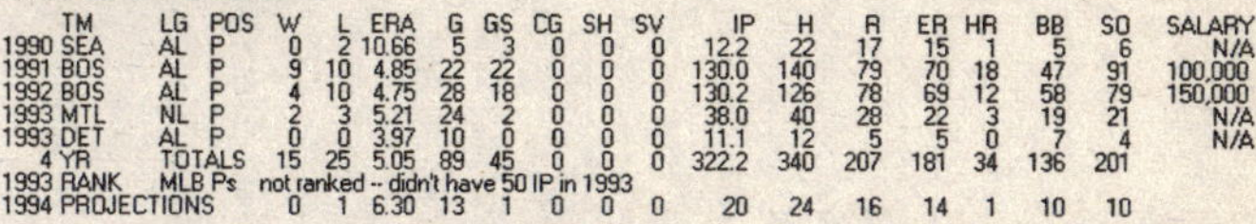

	TM	LG	POS	W	L	ERA	G	GS	CG	SH	SV	IP	H	R	ER	HR	BB	SO	SALARY
1990	SEA	AL	P	0	2	10.66	5	3	0	0	0	12.2	22	17	15	1	5	6	N/A
1991	BOS	AL	P	9	10	4.85	22	22	0	0	0	130.0	140	79	70	18	47	91	100,000
1992	BOS	AL	P	4	10	4.75	28	18	0	0	0	130.2	126	78	69	12	58	79	150,000
1993	MTL	NL	P	2	3	5.21	24	2	0	0	0	38.0	40	28	22	3	19	21	N/A
1993	DET	AL	P	0	0	3.97	10	0	0	0	0	11.1	12	5	5	0	7	4	N/A
4	YR	TOTALS		15	25	5.05	89	45	0	0	0	322.2	340	207	181	34	136	201	
1993	RANK	MLB Ps		not ranked -- didn't have 50 IP in 1993															
1994	PROJECTIONS			0	1	6.30	13	1	0	0	0	20	24	16	14	1	10	10	

Mark Leiter No. 23/P

Full name: Mark Edward Leiter
Bats: R **Throws:** R **HT:** 6–3 **WT:** 210
Born: 4–13–63, Joliet, IL
High school: Central Regional (Bayville, NJ)
College: Connors State (Warner, OK)
Leiter was slowed by shoulder problems in 1993.

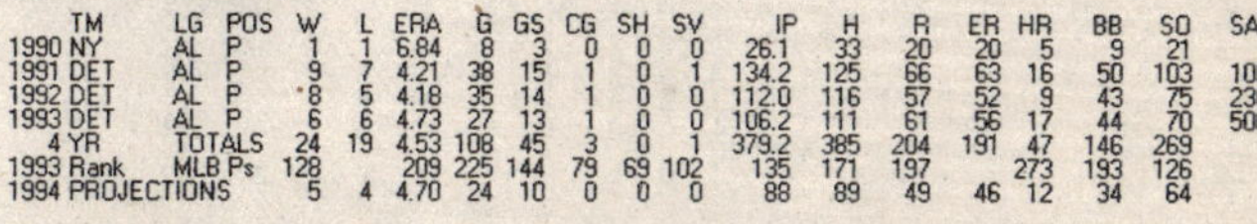

	TM	LG	POS	W	L	ERA	G	GS	CG	SH	SV	IP	H	R	ER	HR	BB	SO	SALARY
1990	NY	AL	P	1	1	6.84	8	3	0	0	0	26.1	33	20	20	5	9	21	N/A
1991	DET	AL	P	9	7	4.21	38	15	1	0	1	134.2	125	66	63	16	50	103	100,000
1992	DET	AL	P	8	5	4.18	35	14	1	0	0	112.0	116	57	52	9	43	75	230,000
1993	DET	AL	P	6	6	4.73	27	13	1	0	0	106.2	111	61	56	17	44	70	500,000
4	YR	TOTALS		24	19	4.53	108	45	3	0	1	379.2	385	204	191	47	146	269	
1993	Rank	MLB Ps		128		209	225	144	79	69	102	135	171	197		273	193	126	132
1994	PROJECTIONS			5	4	4.70	24	10	0	0	0	88	89	49	46	12	34	64	

Robert MacDonald No. 38/P

Full name: Robert Joseph MacDonald
Bats: L **Throws:** L **HT:** 6–3 **WT:** 208
Born: 4–27–65, East Orange, NJ
High school: Point Pleasant Beach (NJ)
College: Rutgers (NJ)
His 68 appearances was tenth-best in the AL.

	TM	LG	POS	W	L	ERA	G	GS	CG	SH	SV	IP	H	R	ER	HR	BB	SO	SALARY
1990	TOR	AL	P	0	0	0.00	4	0	0	0	0	2.1	0	0	0	0	2	0	N/A
1991	TOR	AL	P	3	3	2.85	45	0	0	0	0	53.2	51	19	17	5	25	24	110,000
1992	TOR	AL	P	1	0	4.37	27	0	0	0	0	47.1	50	24	23	4	16	26	N/A
1993	DET	AL	P	3	3	5.35	68	0	0	0	3	65.2	67	42	39	8	33	39	225,000
4	YR	TOTALS		7	6	4.21	144	0	0	0	3	169.0	168	85	79	17	76	89	
1993	Rank	MLB Ps		209		256	22	202	125	69	44	230	159	253		208	254	167	167
1994	PROJECTIONS			3	3	5.40	84	0	0	0	3	80	83	52	48	10	40	48	

Mike Moore — No. 21/P

Full name: Michael Wayne Moore
Bats: R **Throws:** R **HT:** 6–4 **WT:** 205
Born: 11–26–59, Early, OK
High school: Early (OK)
College: Oral Roberts (Tulsa, OK)
Moore led the league with 35 HR allowed.

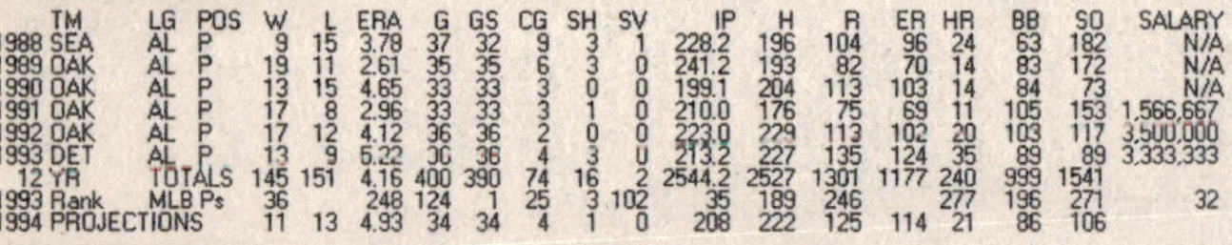

	TM	LG	POS	W	L	ERA	G	GS	CG	SH	SV	IP	H	R	ER	HR	BB	SO	SALARY
1988	SEA	AL	P	9	15	3.78	37	32	9	3	1	228.2	196	104	96	24	63	182	N/A
1989	OAK	AL	P	19	11	2.61	35	35	6	3	0	241.2	193	82	70	14	83	172	N/A
1990	OAK	AL	P	13	15	4.65	33	33	3	0	0	199.1	204	113	103	14	84	73	N/A
1991	OAK	AL	P	17	8	2.96	33	33	3	1	0	210.0	176	75	69	11	105	153	1,566,667
1992	OAK	AL	P	17	12	4.12	36	36	2	0	0	223.0	229	113	102	20	103	117	3,500,000
1993	DET	AL	P	13	9	5.22	36	36	4	3	0	213.2	227	135	124	35	89	89	3,333,333
12	YR	TOTALS		145	151	4.16	400	390	74	16	2	2544.2	2527	1301	1177	240	999	1541	
1993	Rank	MLB Ps		36		248	124	1	25	3	102	35	189	246		277	196	271	32
1994	PROJECTIONS			11	13	4.93	34	34	4	1	0	208	222	125	114	21	86	106	

Rich Rowland — No. 12/C

Full name: Rich Garnet Rowland
Bats: R **Throws:** R **HT:** 6–1 **WT:** 215
Born: 2–25–67, Cloverdale, CA
College: Mendocino (CA)
Rowland started 12 games at catcher.

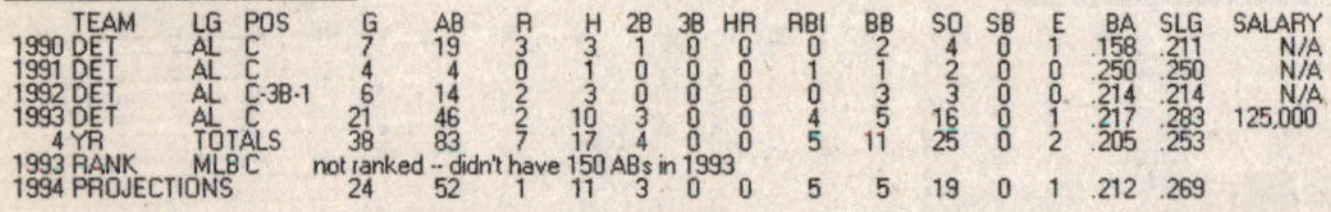

	TEAM	LG	POS	G	AB	R	H	2B	3B	HR	RBI	BB	SO	SB	E	BA	SLG	SALARY
1990	DET	AL	C	7	19	3	3	1	0	0	0	2	4	0	1	.158	.211	N/A
1991	DET	AL	C	4	4	0	1	0	0	0	1	1	2	0	0	.250	.250	N/A
1992	DET	AL	C-3B-1	6	14	2	3	0	0	0	0	3	3	0	0	.214	.214	N/A
1993	DET	AL	C	21	46	2	10	3	0	0	4	5	16	0	1	.217	.283	125,000
4	YR	TOTALS		38	83	7	17	4	0	0	5	11	25	0	2	.205	.253	
1993	RANK	MLB	C	not ranked -- didn't have 150 ABs in 1993														
1994	PROJECTIONS			24	52	1	11	3	0	0	5	5	19	0	1	.212	.269	

Gary Thurman — No. 15/OF

Full name: Gary Montez Thurman Jr.
Bats: R **Throws:** R **HT:** 5–10 **WT:** 175
Born: 11–12–64, Indianapolis, IN
High school: Indianapolis North Central (IN)
College: Texas A&M
Thurman was 7 for 7 in stolen base attempts.

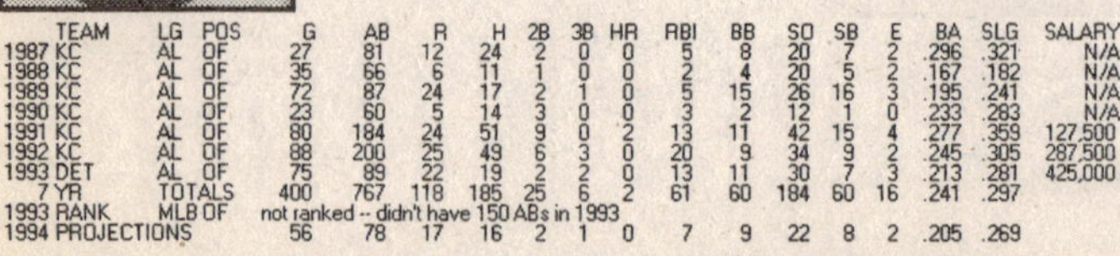

	TEAM	LG	POS	G	AB	R	H	2B	3B	HR	RBI	BB	SO	SB	E	BA	SLG	SALARY
1987	KC	AL	OF	27	81	12	24	2	0	0	5	8	20	7	2	.296	.321	N/A
1988	KC	AL	OF	35	66	6	11	1	0	0	2	4	20	5	2	.167	.182	N/A
1989	KC	AL	OF	72	87	24	17	2	1	0	5	15	26	16	3	.195	.241	N/A
1990	KC	AL	OF	23	60	5	14	3	0	0	3	2	12	1	0	.233	.283	N/A
1991	KC	AL	OF	80	184	24	51	9	0	2	13	11	42	15	4	.277	.359	127,500
1992	KC	AL	OF	88	200	25	49	6	3	0	20	9	34	9	2	.245	.305	287,500
1993	DET	AL	OF	75	89	22	19	2	2	0	13	11	30	7	3	.213	.281	425,000
7	YR	TOTALS		400	767	118	185	25	6	2	61	60	184	60	16	.241	.297	
1993	RANK	MLB	OF	not ranked -- didn't have 150 ABs in 1993														
1994	PROJECTIONS			56	78	17	16	2	1	0	7	9	22	8	2	.205	.269	

Kansas City
ROYALS

1994 Scouting Report

Hitting: (1993/.263 BA, tenth in AL; 125 HR, tenth in AL)

Kansas City's offense underachieved in '93. The team counted on Kevin McReynolds to drive in runs, but he only hit .245 with 11 HR and 42 RBI. Mike Macfarlane had a team-high 20 HR and 67 RBI. Gary Gaetti hit just .245 with 14 HR. The Royals lost Keith Miller for most of the season due to shoulder and elbow problems, and Felix Jose (.253) was plagued with shoulder problems throughout the season. Kansas City lacks speed to compensate for their lack of power; they were ninth in the AL in stolen bases with 100.

The Royals sorely need a power-hitter to drive in runs, especially after George Brett's retirement leaves them without a true DH. But Kansas City seems to be resting their hopes on Kevin McReynolds rebounding, and Keith Miller and Felix Jose coming back from their injury problems.

Pitching: (1993/4.04 ERA, third in AL)

Kansas City's starters are as good as any in the AL. Kevin Appier was 18–8 for Kansas City, with a 2.56 ERA and five complete games. David Cone had tough luck in '93, going 11–14 with a 3.33 ERA. He led the staff with 254 innings. Tom "Flash" Gordon was 12–6 with a 3.58 ERA.

Closer Jeff Montgomery saved 45 games in 63 appearances, with a 2.27 ERA. John Habyan (4.15 ERA) made 48 appearances and Billy Brewer (3.46 ERA) made 46 appearances out of the bullpen as setup men for Montgomery.

Defense: (1993/.984 pct., second in AL)

The Royals have the league's best defense up the middle. Shortstop Greg Gagne and second baseman Jose Lind were tops in the AL in fielding percentage at their positions.

1994 Prospects:

Although their pitching will keep them close, the Royals lack the offense to compete with Chicago and Cleveland in the AL Central.

Team Directory

Chairman: David D. Glass	President: Mike Herman
General Mgr.: Herk Robinson	VP–Treasurer: Charles Hughes
VP, P.R.: Dean Vogelaar	Traveling Secretary: Dave Witty

Minor League Affiliates:

Level	Team/League	1993 Record
AAA	Omaha–American Association	70–74
AA	Memphis–Southern	63–77
A	Wilmington–Carolina	74–65
	Rockford–Midwest	78–54
	Eugene–Northwest	40–36
Rookie	Gulf Coast Royals–Gulf Coast	29–30

1993 Review

	Home W	Home L	Away W	Away L		Home W	Home L	Away W	Away L		Home W	Home L	Away W	Away L
vs AL East	W	L	W	L	vs AL Cent.	W	L	W	L	vs AL West	W	L	W	L
Baltimore	3	3	2	4	Chicago	2	4	5	2	California	4	3	3	3
Boston	1	5	6	0	Cleveland	3	3	2	4	Oakland	4	2	2	5
Detroit	3	3	4	2	Milwaukee	3	3	2	4	Seattle	4	2	3	4
New York	4	2	2	4	Minnesota	3	4	4	2	Texas	4	3	3	3
Toronto	5	1	3	3										
Total	16	14	17	13		11	14	13	12		16	10	11	15

1993 finish: 84–78 (43–38 home, 41–40 away), third in AL West, ten games behind

1994 Schedule

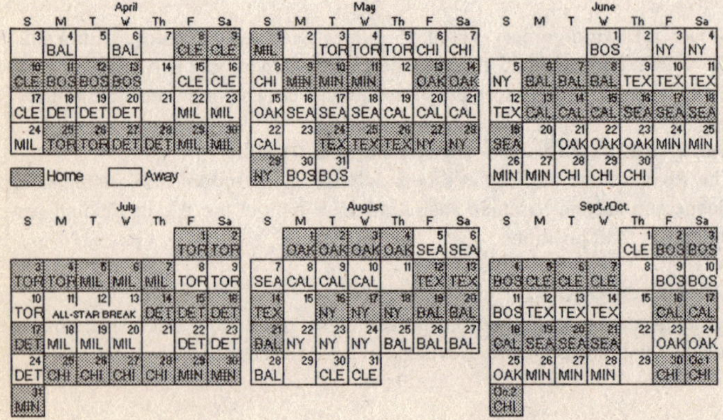

KANSAS CITY ROYALS 1994 ROSTER

MANAGER: Hal McRae (11)
COACHES: Steve Boros, Glenn Ezell (44), Guy Hansen (46), Bruce Kison (42), Lee May (45)

No.	PITCHERS	B	T	HT	WT	DOB	BIRTHPLACE	RESIDENCE
55	Appier, Kevin	R	R	6–2	200	12–6–67	Lancaster, CA	Overland Park, KS
50	Belinda, Stan	R	R	6–3	187	8–6–66	Huntingdon, PA	Alexandria, PA
29	Brewer, Billy	L	L	6–1	175	4–15–68	Ft. Worth, TX	Longview, TX
51	Burgos, Enrique	L	L	6–4	230	10–7–65	Chomera, PN	Panama City, PN
17	Cone, David	L	R	6–1	190	1–2–63	Kansas City, MO	Kansas City, MO
36	Gordon,Tom	R	R	5–9	180	11–18–67	Sebring, FL	Avon Park, FL
27	Granger, Jeff	R	L	6–4	200	12–16–71	San Pedro, CA	Orange, TX
	Gubicza, Mark	R	R	5–9	180	8–14–62	Philadelphia, PA	Philadelphia, PA
41	Habyan, John	R	R	6–2	195	1–29–64	Bayshore, NY	Bel Air, MD
33	Haney, Chris	L	L	6–3	185	11–16–68	Baltimore, MD	Barboursville, VA
58	Harris, Doug	R	R	6–4	190	9–27–69	Carlisle, PA	Carlisle, PA
57	Magnante, Mike	L	L	6–1	180	6–17–65	Glendale, CA	Burbank, CA
28	Meacham, Rusty	R	R	6–2	165	1–27–68	Stuart, FL	Stuart, FL
21	Montgomery, Jeff	R	R	5–11	180	1–7–62	Wellston, OH	Cincinnati, OH
58	Pichardo, Hipolito	R	R	6–1	160	8–22–69	Esperanza, DR	Esperanza, DR
No.	**CATCHERS**	**B**	**T**	**HT**	**WT**	**DOB**	**BIRTHPLACE**	**RESIDENCE**
	Jennings, Lance	R	R	6–0	190	10–3–71	Redlands, CA	Modesto, CA
15	Macfarlane, Mike	R	R	6–1	205	4–12–64	Stockton, CA	Overland Park, KS
24	Mayne, Brent	L	R	6–1	190	4–19–68	Loma Linda, CA	Costa Mesa, CA
	Strickland, Chad	R	R	6–1	185	8–22–69	Esperanza, DR	Esperanza, DR
No.	**INFIELDERS**	**B**	**T**	**HT**	**WT**	**DOB**	**BIRTHPLACE**	**RESIDENCE**
	Caraballo, Gary	R	R	5–11	205	7–11–71	Brooklyn, NY	Yauco, PR
	Gaetti, Gary	R	R	6–0	200	8–19–58	Centralia, IL	Eden Prairie, MN
7	Gagne, Greg	R	R	5–11	175	11–12–61	Fall River, MA	Rehoboth, MA
	Halter, Shane	R	R	5–10	160	11–8–69	LaPlata, MD	Papillon, NE
48	Hamelin, Bob	L	L	6–0	230	11–29–67	Elizabeth, NJ	Charlotte, NC
25	Hiatt, Phil	R	R	6–3	190	5–1–69	Pensacola, FL	Pensacola, FL
6	Howard, David	S	R	6–0	165	2–26–67	Sarasota, FL	Sarasota, FL
12	Joyner, Wally	L	L	6–2	205	6–16–62	Atlanta, GA	Lee's Summit, MO
13	Lind, Jose	R	R	5–11	175	5–1–64	Toabaja, PR	Dorado, PR
16	Miller, Keith	R	R	5–11	185	6–12–63	Midland, MI	Frankenmuth, MI
	Randa, Joe	R	R	5–11	190	12–18–69	Milwaukee, WI	Delafield, WI
3	Shumpert, Terry	R	R	5–11	190	8–16–66	Paducah, KY	Paducah, KY
	Vitello, Joe	R	R	6–2	215	4–11–70	Cambridge, MA	Stoneham, MA
8	Wilson, Craig	R	R	5–11	210	11–28–64	Anne Arundel CO., MD	Annapolis, MD
No.	**OUTFIELDERS**	**B**	**T**	**HT**	**WT**	**DOB**	**BIRTHPLACE**	**RESIDENCE**
	Burton, Darren	S	R	6–1	185	9–16–72	Somerset, KY	Somerset, KY
14	Gwynn, Chris	L	L	6–0	210	10–13–64	Los Angeles, CA	Alta Loma, CA
34	Jose, Felix	S	R	6–1	220	5–8–65	Santo Domingo, DR	Boca Raton, FL
40	Koslofski, Kevin	L	R	5–8	165	9–24–66	Decatur, IL	Maroa, IL
56	McRae, Brian	S	R	6–0	185	8–27–67	Bradenton, FL	Leawood, KS
22	McReynolds, Kevin	R	R	6–1	215	10–16–59	Little Rock, AR	Little Rock, AR
	Norman, Les	R	R	6–1	185	2–25–69	Warren, MI	Greenfield, IL

Royals Stadium (40,625, artificial)
Tickets: 816–921–8000
Ticket prices:
- $14 (club box)
- $13 (field box)
- $11 (plaza reserved)
- $10 (view upper box)
- $9 (view upper reserved)
- $6 (general admission)

Field Dimensions (from home plate)
- To left field at foul line, 330 feet
- To center field, 410 feet
- To right field at foul line, 330 feet
- (OF wall is 12 feet high)

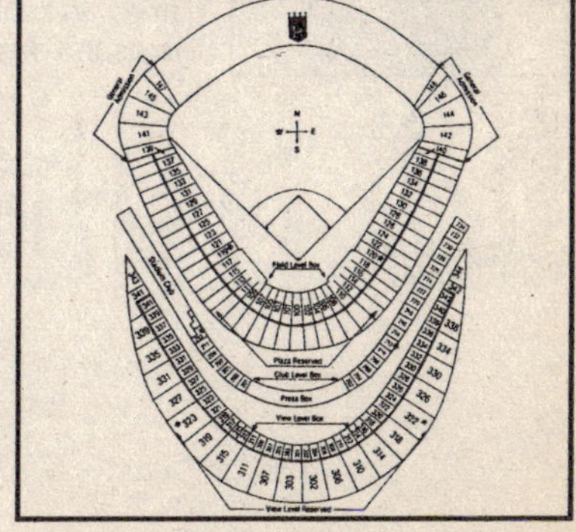

Greg Gagne No. 7/SS

Full name: Gregory Carpenter Gagne
Bats: R **Throws:** R **HT:** 5–11 **WT:** 175
Born: 11–12–61, Fall River, MA
High school: Somerset (MA)

Gagne batted .280 in his first season with the Royals, and played in a team-high 159 games. He also led AL shortstops with a .986 fielding percentage.

TEAM	LG	POS	G	AB	R	H	2B	3B	HR	RBI	BB	SO	SB	E	BA	SLG	SALARY
1983 MIN	AL	SS	10	27	2	3	1	0	0	3	0	6	0	2	.111	.148	N/A
1984 MIN	AL	PH	2	1	0	0	0	0	0	0	0	0	0	--"	.000	.000	N/A
1985 MIN	AL	SS	114	293	37	66	15	3	2	23	20	57	10	14	.225	.317	N/A
1986 MIN	AL	SS-2B	156	472	63	118	22	6	12	54	30	108	12	26	.250	.398	N/A
1987 MIN	AL	SS-OF	137	437	68	116	28	7	10	40	25	84	6	18	.265	.430	N/A
1988 MIN	AL	SS-OF	149	461	70	109	20	6	14	48	27	110	15	18	.236	.397	N/A
1989 MIN	AL	SS-OF	149	460	69	125	29	7	9	48	17	80	11	18	.272	.424	N/A
1990 MIN	AL	SS-OF	138	388	38	91	22	3	7	38	24	76	8	14	.235	.361	N/A
1991 MIN	AL	SS-3B	139	408	52	108	23	3	8	42	26	72	11	9	.265	.395	1,733,333
1992 MIN	AL	SS	146	439	53	108	23	0	7	39	19	83	6	18	.246	.346	1,933,334
1993 KC	AL	SS	159	540	66	151	32	3	10	57	33	93	10	10	.280	.406	3,366,666
11 YR	TOTALS		1299	3926	518	995	215	38	79	392	221	769	89	147	.253	.388	
1993 RANK	MLB	SS	3	11	12	9	3	12	7	10	22	6	14	29	16	12	3
1994 PROJECTIONS			162	551	66	154	32	2	9	57	33	94	9	9	.279	.394	

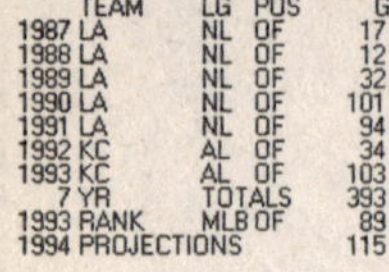

Chris Gwynn No. 14/OF

Full name: Christopher Karlton Gwynn
Bats: L **Throws:** L **HT:** 6–0 **WT:** 210
Born: 10–13–64, Los Angeles, CA
High school: Long Beach Polytechnic (CA)
College: San Diego State

As a platoon player, Gwynn hit .300 in 106 games, including 74 starts in the outfield and five as the designated hitter.

TEAM	LG	POS	G	AB	R	H	2B	3B	HR	RBI	BB	SO	SB	E	BA	SLG	SALARY
1987 LA	NL	OF	17	32	2	7	1	0	0	2	1	7	0	0	.219	.250	N/A
1988 LA	NL	OF	12	11	1	2	0	0	0	0	1	2	0	0	.182	.182	N/A
1989 LA	NL	OF	32	68	8	16	4	1	0	7	2	9	1	0	.235	.324	N/A
1990 LA	NL	OF	101	141	19	40	2	1	5	22	7	28	0	0	.284	.418	125,000
1991 LA	NL	OF	94	139	18	35	5	1	5	22	10	23	1	0	.252	.410	260,000
1992 KC	AL	OF	34	84	10	24	3	2	1	7	3	10	0	0	.286	.405	425,000
1993 KC	AL	OF	103	287	36	86	14	4	1	25	24	34	0	1	.300	.387	505,000
7 YR	TOTALS		393	762	94	210	29	9	12	85	48	113	2	1	.276	.385	
1993 RANK	MLB	OF	89	89	93	81	87	32	122	110	88	113	127	113	28	94	80
1994 PROJECTIONS			115	323	40	97	15	4	1	28	27	37	0	1	.300	.381	0

Phil Hiatt — No. 25/3B

Full name: Philip Farrell Hiatt
Bats: R **Throws:** R **HT:** 6–3 **WT:** 190
Born: 5–1–69, Pensacola, FL
High school: Riverview (FL)
College: Manatee CC (Bradenton, FL)

Hiatt started 66 games at 3B, but batted a weak .218 for the season. He should battle Keith Miller for the 3B spot in spring training.

TEAM	LG	POS	G	AB	R	H	2B	3B	HR	RBI	BB	SO	SB	E	BA	SLG	SALARY
1993 KC	AL	3B	81	238	30	52	12	1	7	36	16	82	6	16	.218	.366	N/A
1 YR	TOTAL		81	238	30	52	12	1	7	36	16	82	6	16	.218	.366	
1993 RANK	MLB	3B	32	32	30	34	30	21	24	27	34	11	10	13	40	33	40

Felix Jose — No. 34/OF

Full name: Domingo Felix Jose
Bats: S **Throws:** R **HT:** 6–1 **WT:** 220
Born: 5–8–65, Santo Domingo, DR
High school: E. F. Reyez de Munoz (DR)

Due to a nagging shoulder injury, Jose batted a lowly .069 from the right side. He posted a .253 average overall with a team-high 31 SB.

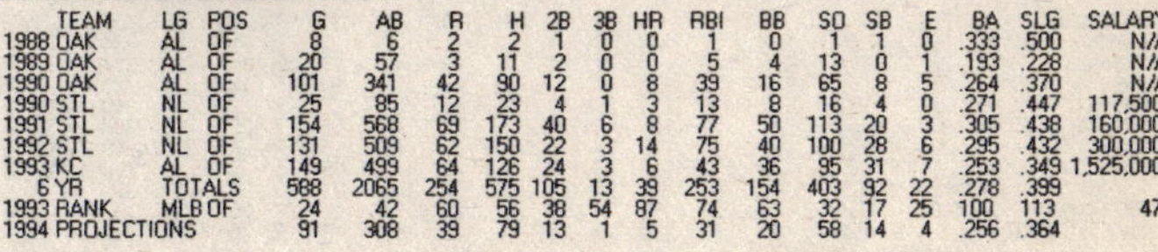

TEAM	LG	POS	G	AB	R	H	2B	3B	HR	RBI	BB	SO	SB	E	BA	SLG	SALARY
1988 OAK	AL	OF	8	6	2	2	1	0	0	1	0	1	1	0	.333	.500	N/A
1989 OAK	AL	OF	20	57	3	11	2	0	0	5	4	13	0	1	.193	.228	N/A
1990 OAK	AL	OF	101	341	42	90	12	0	8	39	16	65	8	5	.264	.370	N/A
1990 STL	NL	OF	25	85	12	23	4	1	3	13	8	16	4	0	.271	.447	117,500
1991 STL	NL	OF	154	568	69	173	40	6	8	77	50	113	20	3	.305	.438	160,000
1992 STL	NL	OF	131	509	62	150	22	3	14	75	40	100	28	6	.295	.432	300,000
1993 KC	AL	OF	149	499	64	126	24	3	6	43	36	95	31	7	.253	.349	1,525,000
6 YR	TOTALS		588	2065	254	575	105	13	39	253	154	403	92	22	.278	.399	
1993 RANK	MLB	OF	24	42	60	56	38	54	87	74	63	32	17	25	100	113	47
1994 PROJECTIONS			91	308	39	79	13	1	5	31	20	58	14	4	.256	.364	

Wally Joyner No. 12/1B

Full name: Wallace Keith Joyner
Bats: L **Throws:** L **HT:** 6–2 **WT:** 205
Born: 6–16–62, Atlanta, GA
High school: Rednan (Stone Mountain, GA)
College: Brigham Young
After a poor 1992 season, Joyner recovered to bat .292 in 141 games. He had a team-high 36 doubles.

	TEAM	LG	POS	G	AB	R	H	2B	3B	HR	RBI	BB	SO	SB	E	BA	SLG	SALARY
1986	CAL	AL	1B	154	593	82	172	27	3	22	100	57	58	5	15	.290	.457	N/A
1987	CAL	AL	1B	149	564	100	161	33	1	34	117	72	64	8	10	.285	.528	N/A
1988	CAL	AL	1B	158	597	81	176	31	2	13	85	55	51	8	8	.295	.419	N/A
1989	CAL	AL	1B	159	593	78	167	30	2	16	79	46	58	3	4	.282	.420	N/A
1990	CAL	AL	1B	83	310	35	83	15	0	8	41	41	34	2	4	.268	.394	1,750,000
1991	CAL	AL	1B	143	551	79	166	34	3	21	96	52	66	2	8	.301	.488	2,100,000
1992	KC	AL	1B	149	572	66	154	36	2	9	66	55	50	11	10	.269	.386	4,200,000
1993	KC	AL	1B	141	497	83	145	36	3	15	65	66	67	5	7	.292	.467	4,400,000
8	YR	TOTALS		1136	4277	604	1224	242	16	138	649	444	448	44	66	.286	.447	
1993	RANK	MLB	1B	18	17	9	15	5	7	21	20	12	18	8	17	13	16	3
1994	PROJECTIONS			124	459	61	127	29	1	10	57	54	50	6	7	.277	.416	

Jose Lind No. 13/2B

Full name: Jose Salgado Lind
Bats: R **Throws:** R **HT:** 5–11 **WT:** 175
Born: 5–1–64, Toabaja, PR
High school: Jose Alegria (Dorado, PR)
Lind batted .267 with runners in scoring position, and led the Royals with 13 sacrifice bunts. Lind won his second Gold Glove in 1993.

	TEAM	LG	POS	G	AB	R	H	2B	3B	HR	RBI	BB	SO	SB	E	BA	SLG	SALARY
1987	PIT	NL	2B	35	143	21	46	8	4	0	11	8	12	2	1	.322	.434	
1988	PIT	NL	2B	154	611	82	160	24	4	2	49	42	75	15	11	.262	.324	N/A
1989	PIT	NL	2B	153	578	52	134	21	3	2	48	39	64	15	18	.232	.289	N/A
1990	PIT	NL	2B	152	514	46	134	28	5	1	48	35	52	8	7	.261	.340	270,000
1991	PIT	NL	2B	150	502	53	133	16	6	3	54	30	56	7	9	.265	.339	575,000
1992	PIT	NL	2B	135	468	38	110	14	1	0	39	26	29	3	6	.235	.269	2,000,000
1993	KC	AL	2B	136	431	33	107	13	2	0	37	13	36	3	4	.248	.288	2,400,000
7	YR	TOTALS		915	3247	325	824	124	25	8	286	193	324	53	56	.254	.315	
1993	RANK	MLB	2B	34	33	28	31	29	30	22	26	26	22	31	36	9	6	30
1994	PROJECTIONS			108	395	45	104	15	3	0	32	21	41	6	5	.263	.324	

Mike Macfarlane No. 15/C

Full name: Michael Andrew Macfarlane
Bats: R **Throws:** R **HT:** 6–1 **WT:** 205
Born: 4–12–64, Stockton, CA
High school: Lincoln (Stockton, CA)
College: Santa Clara

An impressive surprise, Macfarlane won the starting catching job in May and had a career-high 20 HR and 67 RBI.

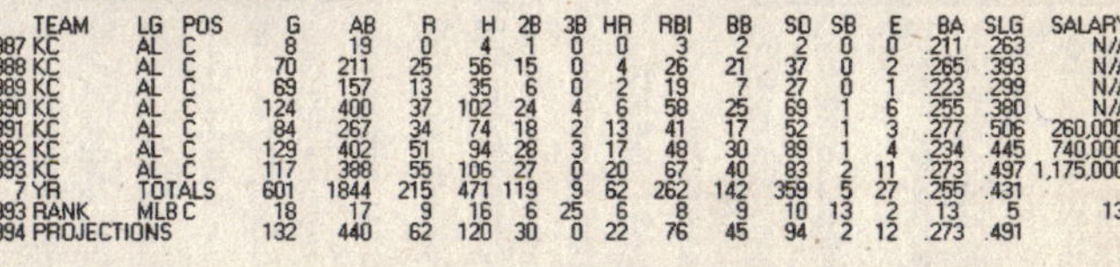

	TEAM	LG	POS	G	AB	R	H	2B	3B	HR	RBI	BB	SO	SB	E	BA	SLG	SALARY
1987	KC	AL	C	8	19	0	4	1	0	0	3	2	2	0	0	.211	.263	N/A
1988	KC	AL	C	70	211	25	56	15	0	4	26	21	37	0	2	.265	.393	N/A
1989	KC	AL	C	69	157	13	35	6	0	2	19	7	27	0	1	.223	.299	N/A
1990	KC	AL	C	124	400	37	102	24	4	6	58	25	69	1	6	.255	.380	N/A
1991	KC	AL	C	84	267	34	74	18	2	13	41	17	52	1	3	.277	.506	260,000
1992	KC	AL	C	129	402	51	94	28	3	17	48	30	89	1	4	.234	.445	740,000
1993	KC	AL	C	117	388	55	106	27	0	20	67	40	83	2	11	.273	.497	1,175,000
7	YR	TOTALS		601	1844	215	471	119	9	62	262	142	359	5	27	.255	.431	
1993	RANK	MLB	C	18	17	9	16	6	25	6	8	9	10	13	2	13	5	13
1994	PROJECTIONS			132	440	62	120	30	0	22	76	45	94	2	12	.273	.491	

Brian McRae No. 56/OF

Full name: Brian Wesley McRae
Bats: S **Throws:** R **HT:** 6–0 **WT:** 185
Born: 8–27–67, Bradenton, FL
High school: Blue Springs (MO)

Despite a late-season slump, McRae led the team in hits with 177. He also had a team-high 9 triples and 48 multiple-hit games.

	TEAM	LG	POS	G	AB	R	H	2B	3B	HR	RBI	BB	SO	SB	E	BA	SLG	SALARY
1990	KC	AL	OF	46	168	21	48	8	3	2	23	9	29	4	0	.286	.405	N/A
1991	KC	AL	OF	152	629	86	164	28	9	8	64	24	99	20	3	.261	.372	124,000
1992	KC	AL	OF	149	533	63	119	23	5	4	52	42	88	18	3	.223	.308	275,000
1993	KC	AL	OF	153	627	78	177	28	9	12	69	37	105	23	7	.282	.413	378,500
4	YR	TOTALS		500	1957	248	508	87	26	26	208	112	321	65	13	.260	.370	
1993	RANK	MLB	OF	17	4	32	8	23	5	51	33	59	21	27	25	50	73	88
1994	PROJECTIONS			162	670	83	189	29	9	12	72	39	112	24	7	.282	.406	

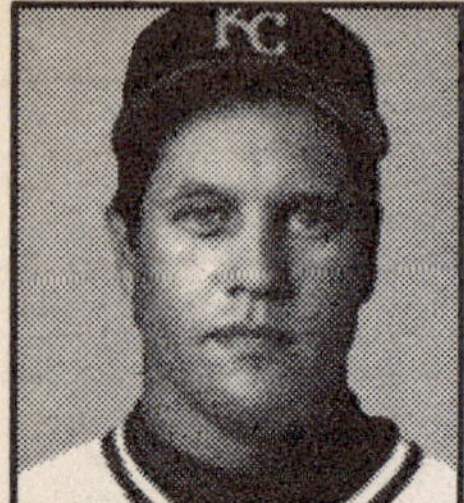

Kevin McReynolds No. 22/OF

Full name: Walter Kevin McReynolds
Bats: R **Throws:** R **HT:** 6–1 **WT:** 215
Born: 10–16–59, Little Rock, AR
High school: Sylvan Hills (AR)
College: Arkansas

McReynolds .245 BA average was his lowest since '85. His 42 RBI and 11 HR were also career-lows.

	TEAM	LG	POS	G	AB	R	H	2B	3B	HR	RBI	BB	SO	SB	E	BA	SLG	SALARY
1983	SD	NL	OF	39	140	15	31	3	1	4	14	12	29	2	1	.221	.343	N/A
1984	SD	NL	OF	147	525	68	146	26	6	20	75	34	69	3	4	.278	.465	N/A
1985	SD	NL	OF	152	564	61	132	24	4	15	75	43	81	4	3	.234	.371	N/A
1986	SD	NL	OF	158	560	89	161	31	6	26	96	66	83	8	8	.288	.504	N/A
1987	NY	NL	OF	151	590	86	163	32	5	29	95	39	70	14	4	.276	.495	N/A
1988	NY	NL	OF	147	552	82	159	30	2	27	99	38	56	21	4	.288	.496	N/A
1989	NY	NL	OF	148	545	74	148	25	3	22	85	46	74	15	10	.272	.450	N/A
1990	NY	NL	OF	147	521	75	140	23	1	24	82	71	61	9	3	.269	.455	1,266,667
1991	NY	NL	OF	143	522	65	135	32	1	16	74	49	46	6	2	.259	.416	2,266,667
1992	KC	AL	OF	109	373	45	92	25	0	13	49	67	48	7	3	.247	.418	3,416,667
1993	KC	AL	OF	110	351	44	86	22	4	11	42	37	56	2	2	.245	.425	3,666,667
11	YR	TOTALS		1451	5243	704	1393	273	33	207	786	502	673	91	44	.266	.449	
1993	RANK	MLB	OF	82	75	81	81	45	32	55	75	59	78	102	97	108	65	15
1994	PROJECTIONS			97	337	41	84	19	2	10	43	32	43	3	1	.249	.409	

Kevin Appier No. 55/P

Full name: Robert Kevin Appier
Bats: R **Throws:** R **HT:** 6–2 **WT:** 200
Born: 12–6–67, Lancaster, CA
High school: Antelope Valley (CA)
College: Antelope Valley JC and Fresno State

Appier posted an AL-best 2.56 ERA with 186 Ks. He won 16 of his last 21 decisions.

	TM	LG	POS	W	L	ERA	G	GS	CG	SH	SV	IP	H	R	ER	HR	BB	SO	SALARY
1989	KC	AL	P	1	4	9.14	6	5	0	0	0	21.2	34	22	22	3	12	10	N/A
1990	KC	AL	P	12	8	2.76	32	24	3	3	0	185.2	179	67	57	13	54	127	100,000
1991	KC	AL	P	13	10	3.42	34	31	6	3	0	207.2	205	97	79	13	61	158	215,000
1992	KC	AL	P	15	8	2.46	30	30	3	0	0	208.1	167	59	57	10	68	150	390,000
1993	KC	AL	P	18	8	2.56	34	34	5	1	0	238.2	183	74	68	8	81	186	2,000,000
5	YR	TOTALS		59	38	2.95	136	124	17	7	0	862.0	768	319	283	47	276	631	
1993	Rank	MLB	Ps	8		18	145	12	16	23	102	12	17	11		9	114	68	68
1994	PROJECTIONS			19	7	2.47	36	36	5	0	0	259	195	77	71	8	86	204	

David Cone No. 17/P

Full name: David Brian Cone
Bats: L **Throws:** R **HT:** 6–1 **WT:** 190
Born: 1–2–63, Kansas City, MO
High school: Rockhurst (Kansas City, MO)
Cone ranked in the league's top ten in ERA and complete games. He suffered from poor run support, especially in April and May, as he lost 7 of his first 10 starts.

	TM	LG	POS	W	L	ERA	G	GS	CG	SH	SV	IP	H	R	ER	HR	BB	SO	SALARY
1986	KC	AL	P	0	0	5.56	11	0	0	0	0	22.2	29	14	14	2	13	21	N/A
1987	NY	NL	P	5	6	3.71	21	13	1	0	1	99.1	87	46	41	11	44	68	N/A
1988	NY	NL	P	20	3	2.22	35	28	8	4	0	231.1	178	67	57	10	80	213	N/A
1989	NY	NL	P	14	8	3.52	34	33	7	2	0	219.2	183	92	86	20	74	190	N/A
1990	NY	NL	P	14	10	3.23	31	30	6	2	0	211.2	177	84	76	21	65	233	1,300,000
1991	NY	NL	P	14	14	3.29	34	34	5	2	0	232.2	204	95	85	13	73	241	2,350,000
1992	NY	NL	P	13	7	2.88	27	27	7	5	0	196.2	162	75	63	12	82	214	4,250,000
1992	TOR	AL	P	4	3	2.55	8	7	0	0	0	53.0	39	16	15	3	29	47	N/A
1993	KC	AL	P	11	14	3.33	34	34	6	1	0	254.0	205	102	94	20	114	191	5,000,000
8	YR	TOTALS		95	65	3.14	235	206	40	16	1	1521.0	1264	591	531	112	574	1418	
1993	Rank	MLB Ps		59		70	145	12	15	23	102	7	25	56		102	224	82	5
1994	PROJECTIONS			11	14	3.30	34	36	5	0	0	267	215	107	98	20	119	200	

Hipolito Pichardo No. 58/P

Full name: Hipolito Antonio Pichardo
Bats: R **Throws:** R **HT:** 6–1 **WT:** 160
Born: 8–22–69, Esperanza, DR
High school: Liceo Enriguillo (DR)
Pichardo started 25 games for the Royals in 1993. His ERA was a respectable 4.04, but opponents batted .282 against him.

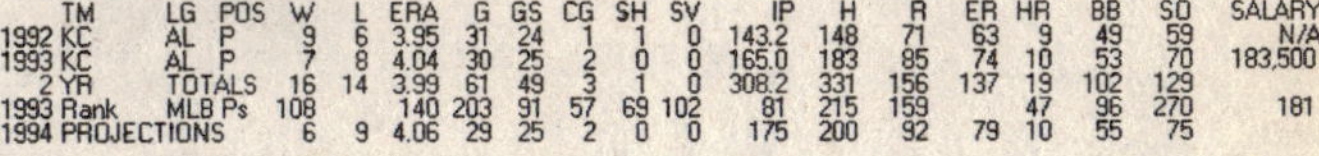

	TM	LG	POS	W	L	ERA	G	GS	CG	SH	SV	IP	H	R	ER	HR	BB	SO	SALARY
1992	KC	AL	P	9	6	3.95	31	24	1	1	0	143.2	148	71	63	9	49	59	N/A
1993	KC	AL	P	7	8	4.04	30	25	2	0	0	165.0	183	85	74	10	53	70	183,500
2	YR	TOTALS		16	14	3.99	61	49	3	1	0	308.2	331	156	137	19	102	129	
1993	Rank	MLB Ps		108		140	203	91	57	69	102	81	215	159		47	96	270	181
1994	PROJECTIONS			6	9	4.06	29	25	2	0	0	175	200	92	79	10	55	75	

Jeff Montgomery No. 21/P

Full name: Jeffrey Thomas Montgomery
Bats: R **Throws:** R **HT:** 5–11 **WT:** 180
Born: 1–7–62, Wellston, OH
High school: Wellston (OH)
College: Marshall (Huntington, WV)

Montgomery, the Royals only All-Star, was the top reliever in the AL for 1993 with 45 saves and a 2.27 ERA.

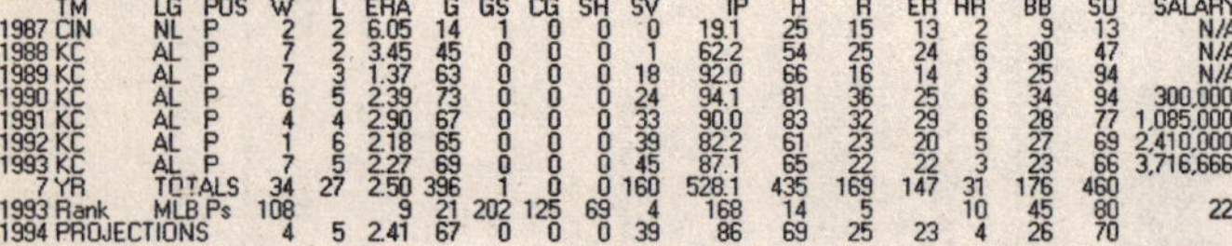

	TM	LG	POS	W	L	ERA	G	GS	CG	SH	SV	IP	H	R	ER	HR	BB	SO	SALARY
1987	CIN	NL	P	2	2	6.05	14	1	0	0	0	19.1	25	15	13	2	9	13	N/A
1988	KC	AL	P	7	2	3.45	45	0	0	0	1	62.2	54	25	24	6	30	47	N/A
1989	KC	AL	P	7	3	1.37	63	0	0	0	18	92.0	66	16	14	3	25	94	N/A
1990	KC	AL	P	6	5	2.39	73	0	0	0	24	94.1	81	36	25	6	34	94	300,000
1991	KC	AL	P	4	4	2.90	67	0	0	0	33	90.0	83	32	29	6	28	77	1,085,000
1992	KC	AL	P	1	6	2.18	65	0	0	0	39	82.2	61	23	20	5	27	69	2,410,000
1993	KC	AL	P	7	5	2.27	69	0	0	0	45	87.1	65	22	22	3	23	66	3,716,666
7	YR	TOTALS		34	27	2.50	396	1	0	0	160	528.1	435	169	147	31	176	460	
1993	Rank	MLB Ps		108		9	21	202	125	69	4	168	14	5		10	45	80	22
1994	PROJECTIONS			4	5	2.41	67	0	0	0	39	86	69	25	23	4	26	70	

Hal McRae No. 11/Mgr.

Full name: Harold Abraham McRae
Bats: R **Throws:** R **HT:** 5–11 **WT:** 185
Born: 7–10–45, Avon Park, FL
High school: Douglas (Sebring, FL)
College: Florida A&M

Hal McRae is the tenth full-time manager in Royals' history. McRae never managed in the minors.

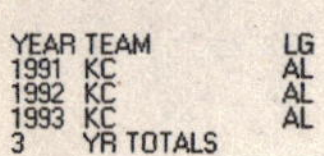

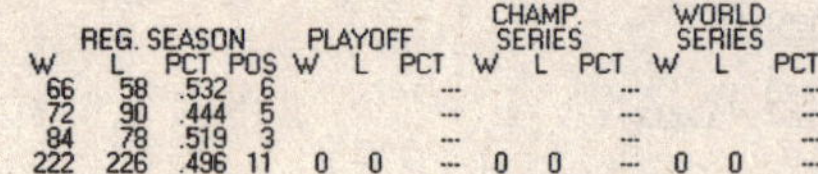

			REG. SEASON				PLAYOFF			CHAMP. SERIES			WORLD SERIES		
YEAR	TEAM	LG	W	L	PCT	POS	W	L	PCT	W	L	PCT	W	L	PCT
1991	KC	AL	66	58	.532	6			---			---			---
1992	KC	AL	72	90	.444	5			---			---			---
1993	KC	AL	84	78	.519	3			---			---			---
3	YR TOTALS		222	226	.496	11	0	0	---	0	0	---	0	0	---

Stan Belinda — No. 50/P

Full name: Stanley Peter Belinda
Bats: R **Throws:** R **HT:** 6–3 **WT:** 187
Born: 8–6–66, Huntingdon, PA
High school: State College Area (PA)
College: Allegheny Community (Cumberland, MD)
Belinda appeared in 23 games as a setup man.

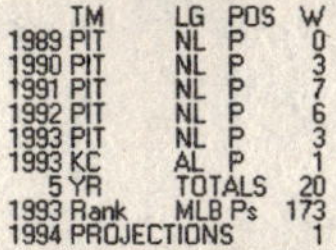
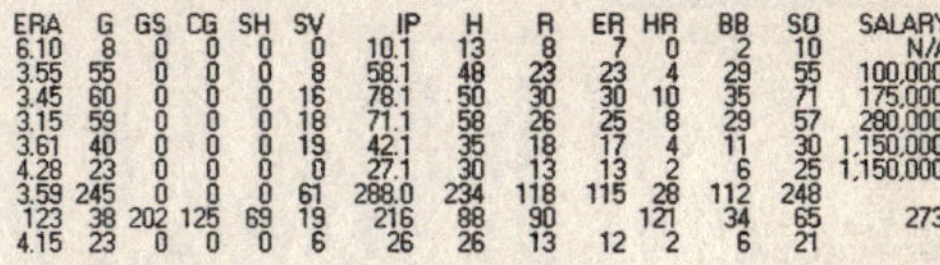

	TM	LG	POS	W	L	ERA	G	GS	CG	SH	SV	IP	H	R	ER	HR	BB	SO	SALARY
1989	PIT	NL	P	0	1	6.10	8	0	0	0	0	10.1	13	8	7	0	2	10	N/A
1990	PIT	NL	P	3	4	3.55	55	0	0	0	8	58.1	48	23	23	4	29	55	100,000
1991	PIT	NL	P	7	5	3.45	60	0	0	0	16	78.1	50	30	30	10	35	71	175,000
1992	PIT	NL	P	6	4	3.15	59	0	0	0	18	71.1	58	26	25	8	29	57	280,000
1993	PIT	NL	P	3	1	3.61	40	0	0	0	19	42.1	35	18	17	4	11	30	1,150,000
1993	KC	AL	P	1	1	4.28	23	0	0	0	0	27.1	30	13	13	2	6	25	1,150,000
5	YR	TOTALS		20	16	3.59	245	0	0	0	61	288.0	234	118	115	28	112	248	
1993	Rank	MLB	Ps	173		123	38	202	125	69	19	216	88	90		121	34	65	273
1994	PROJECTIONS			1	1	4.15	23	0	0	0	6	26	26	13	12	2	6	21	

Billy Brewer — No. 29/P

Full name: William Robert Brewer
Bats: L **Throws:** L **HT:** 6–1 **WT:** 175
Born: 4–15–68, Ft. Worth, TX
High school: Spring Hill (Longview, TX)
College: Dallas Baptist (TX)
Brewer finished 14 games for the Royals.

	TM	LG	POS	W	L	ERA	G	GS	CG	SH	SV	IP	H	R	ER	HR	BB	SO	SALARY
1993	KC	AL	P	2	2	3.46	46	0	0	0	0	39.0	31	16	15	6	20	28	109,000
1	YR	TOTAL		2	2	3.46	46	0	0	0	0	39.0	31	16	15	6	20	28	
1993	RANK	MLB	Ps	not ranked -- didn't have 50 IP in 1993															

Gary Gaetti — 1B-3B

Full name: Gary Joseph Gaetti
Bats: R **Throws:** R **HT:** 6–2 **WT:** 203
Born: 8–19–58, Centralia, IL
High school: Centralia (IL)
College: Land Lake (IL) and N'west Missouri St.
Gaetti hit 14 HR in 82 games in '93.

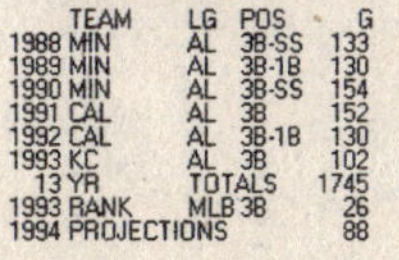

	TEAM	LG	POS	G	AB	R	H	2B	3B	HR	RBI	BB	SO	SB	E	BA	SLG	SALARY
1988	MIN	AL	3B-SS	133	468	66	141	29	2	28	88	36	85	7	7	.301	.551	N/A
1989	MIN	AL	3B-1B	130	498	63	125	11	4	19	75	25	87	6	10	.251	.404	N/A
1990	MIN	AL	3B-SS	154	577	61	132	27	5	16	85	36	101	6	18	.229	.376	N/A
1991	CAL	AL	3B	152	586	58	144	22	1	18	66	33	104	5	17	.246	.379	2,700,000
1992	CAL	AL	3B-1B	130	456	41	103	13	2	12	48	21	79	3	22	.226	.342	2,700,000
1993	KC	AL	3B	102	331	40	81	20	1	14	50	21	87	1	7	.245	.438	109,000
13	YR	TOTALS		1745	6362	785	1604	307	29	245	922	433	1147	83	186	.252	.425	
1993	RANK	MLB	3B	26	24	23	25	19	21	12	20	29	8	26	35	31	11	34
1994	PROJECTIONS			88	311	35	72	15	2	10	46	19	64	2	8	.232	.399	

Tom Gordon — No. 36/P

Full name: Thomas Gordon
Bats: R **Throws:** R **HT:** 5–9 **WT:** 180
Born: 11–18–67, Sebring, FL
High school: Avon Park (FL)
Gordon won 12 games for the Royals, and won back his starting role by the end of 1993.

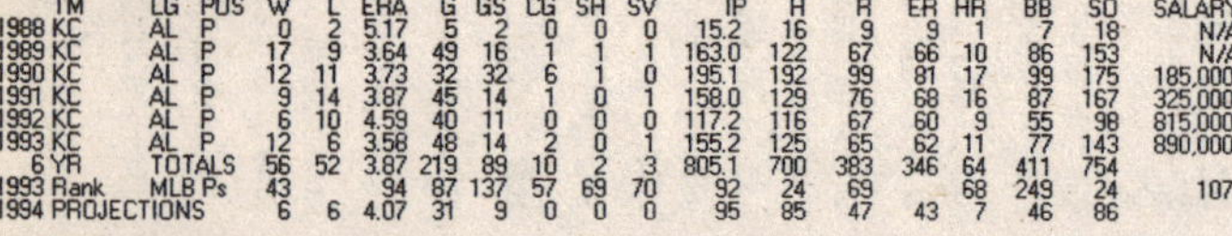

	TM	LG	POS	W	L	ERA	G	GS	CG	SH	SV	IP	H	R	ER	HR	BB	SO	SALARY
1988	KC	AL	P	0	2	5.17	5	2	0	0	0	15.2	16	9	9	1	7	18	N/A
1989	KC	AL	P	17	9	3.64	49	16	1	1	1	163.0	122	67	66	10	86	153	N/A
1990	KC	AL	P	12	11	3.73	32	32	6	1	0	195.1	192	99	81	17	99	175	185,000
1991	KC	AL	P	9	14	3.87	45	14	1	0	1	158.0	129	76	68	16	87	167	325,000
1992	KC	AL	P	6	10	4.59	40	11	0	0	0	117.2	116	67	60	9	55	98	815,000
1993	KC	AL	P	12	6	3.58	48	14	2	0	1	155.2	125	65	62	11	77	143	890,000
6	YR	TOTALS		56	52	3.87	219	89	10	2	3	805.1	700	383	346	64	411	754	
1993	Rank	MLB Ps		43		94	87	137	57	69	70	92	24	69		68	249	24	107
1994	PROJECTIONS			6	6	4.07	31	9	0	0	0	95	85	47	43	7	46	86	

Mark Gubicza — No. 23/P

Full name: Mark Steven Gubicza
Bats: R **Throws:** R **HT:** 5–9 **WT:** 180
Born: 8–14–62, Philadelphia, PA
High school: Wm. Penn Charter (Phila., PA)
Gubicza had a 0–4 record as a starter before going to the the bullpen.

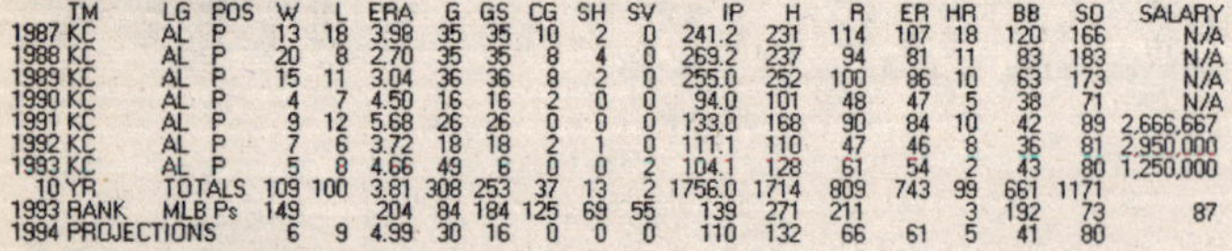

	TM	LG	POS	W	L	ERA	G	GS	CG	SH	SV	IP	H	R	ER	HR	BB	SO	SALARY
1987	KC	AL	P	13	18	3.98	35	35	10	2	0	241.2	231	114	107	18	120	166	N/A
1988	KC	AL	P	20	8	2.70	35	35	8	4	0	269.2	237	94	81	11	83	183	N/A
1989	KC	AL	P	15	11	3.04	36	36	8	2	0	255.0	252	100	86	10	63	173	N/A
1990	KC	AL	P	4	7	4.50	16	16	2	0	0	94.0	101	48	47	5	38	71	N/A
1991	KC	AL	P	9	12	5.68	26	26	0	0	0	133.0	168	90	84	10	42	89	2,666,667
1992	KC	AL	P	7	6	3.72	18	18	2	1	0	111.1	110	47	46	8	36	81	2,950,000
1993	KC	AL	P	5	8	4.66	49	6	0	0	2	104.1	128	61	54	2	43	80	1,250,000
10	YR	TOTALS		109	100	3.81	308	253	37	13	2	1756.0	1714	809	743	99	661	1171	
1993	RANK	MLB Ps		149		204	84	184	125	69	55	139	271	211		3	192	73	87
1994	PROJECTIONS			6	9	4.99	30	16	0	0	0	110	132	66	61	5	41	80	

John Habyan — No. 41/P

Full name: John Gabriel Habyan
Bats: R **Throws:** R **HT:** 6–2 **WT:** 195
Born: 1–29–64, Bayshore, NY
High school: St. John the Baptist (W. Islip, NY)
Between the Yankees and the Royals, Habyan had 48 appearances, with 1 save and 2 wins.

	TM	LG	POS	W	L	ERA	G	GS	CG	SH	SV	IP	H	R	ER	HR	BB	SO	SALARY
1987	BAL	AL	P	6	7	4.80	27	13	0	0	1	116.1	110	67	62	20	40	64	N/A
1988	BAL	AL	P	1	0	4.30	7		0	0	0	14.2	22	10	7	2	4	4	N/A
1990	NY	AL	P	0	0	2.08	6	0	0	0	0	8.2	10	2	2	0	2	4	N/A
1991	NY	AL	P	4	2	2.30	66	0	0	0	2	90.0	73	28	23	2	20	70	105,000
1992	NY	AL	P	5	6	3.84	56	0	0	0	7	72.2	84	32	31	6	21	44	500,000
1993	NY-KC	AL	P	2	1	4.15	48	0	0	0	1	56.1	59	27	26	6	20	39	600,000
8	YR	TOTALS		20	19	3.81	218	18	0	0	11	387.2	385	184	164	39	125	241	
1993	Rank	MLB Ps		246		155	87	202	125	69	70	266	176	118		179	137	109	126
1994	PROJECTIONS			1	1	4.22	20	2	0	0	0	32	35	18	15	3	14	19	

Bob Hamelin — No. 48/1B

Full name: Robert James Hamelin III
Bats: L **Throws:** L **HT:** 6–0 **WT:** 230
Born: 11–29–67, Elizabeth, NJ
High school: Irvine (CA)
College: Rancho Santiage Junior (CA) and UCLA
Hamelin had 29 HR and 84 RBI at AAA Omaha.

TEAM	LG POS	G	AB	R	H	2B	3B	HR	RBI	BB	SO	SB	E	BA	SLG	SALARY
1993 KC	AL 1B	16	49	2	11	3	0	2	5	6	15	0	2	.224	.408	N/A
1 YR	TOTAL	16	49	2	11	3	0	2	5	6	15	0	2	.224	.408	
1993 RANK	MLB 1B	not ranked -- didn't have 150 ABs in 1993														

Chris Haney — No. 33/P

Full name: Christopher Deane Haney
Bats: L **Throws:** L **HT:** 6–3 **WT:** 185
Born: 11–16–68, Baltimore, MD
High school: Grange County (VA)
College: North Carolina–Charlotte
Haney had 9 wins in 23 starts.

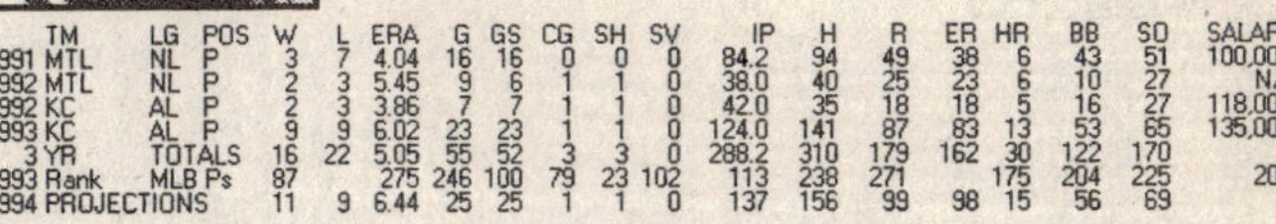

TM	LG POS	W	L	ERA	G	GS	CG	SH	SV	IP	H	R	ER	HR	BB	SO	SALARY
1991 MTL	NL P	3	7	4.04	16	16	0	0	0	84.2	94	49	38	6	43	51	100,000
1992 MTL	NL P	2	3	5.45	9	6	1	1	0	38.0	40	25	23	6	10	27	N/A
1992 KC	AL P	2	3	3.86	7	7	1	1	0	42.0	35	18	18	5	16	27	118,000
1993 KC	AL P	9	9	6.02	23	23	1	1	0	124.0	141	87	83	13	53	65	135,000
3 YR	TOTALS	16	22	5.05	55	52	3	3	0	288.2	310	179	162	30	122	170	
1993 Rank	MLB Ps	87		275	246	100	79	23	102	113	238	271		175	204	225	205
1994 PROJECTIONS		11	9	6.44	25	25	1	1	0	137	156	99	98	15	56	69	

Brent Mayne — No. 24/C

Full name: Brent Danem Mayne
Bats: L **Throws:** R **HT:** 6–1 **WT:** 190
Born: 4–19–68, Loma Linda, CA
High school: Costa Mesa (CA)
College: Orange Coast JC and Cal State–Fullerton
Mayne finished with a career-high .254 BA.

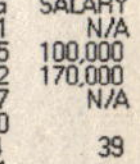

TEAM	LG POS	G	AB	R	H	2B	3B	HR	RBI	BB	SO	SB	E	BA	SLG	SALARY
1990 KC	AL C	5	13	2	3	0	0	0	1	3	3	0	1	.231	.231	N/A
1991 KC	AL C	85	231	22	58	8	0	3	31	23	42	2	6	.251	.325	100,000
1992 KC	AL C-3B	82	213	16	48	10	0	0	18	11	26	0	3	.225	.272	170,000
1993 KC	AL C	71	205	22	52	9	1	2	22	18	31	3	2	.254	.337	N/A
4 YR	TOTALS	243	662	62	161	27	1	5	72	55	102	5	12	.243	.310	
1993 RANK	MLB C	36	35	33	35	34	11	37	37	31	30	7	36	26	34	39
1994 PROJECTIONS		52	143	13	34	6	0	0	13	10	20	1	2	.238	.301	

Rusty Meacham — No. 28/P

Full name: Russell Loren Meacham
Bats: R **Throws:** R **HT:** 6–2 **WT:** 165
Born: 1–27–68, Stuart, FL
High school: Stuart (FL)
Due to injuries, Meacham pitched in only 15 games for the Royals in '93, down from 64 in '92.

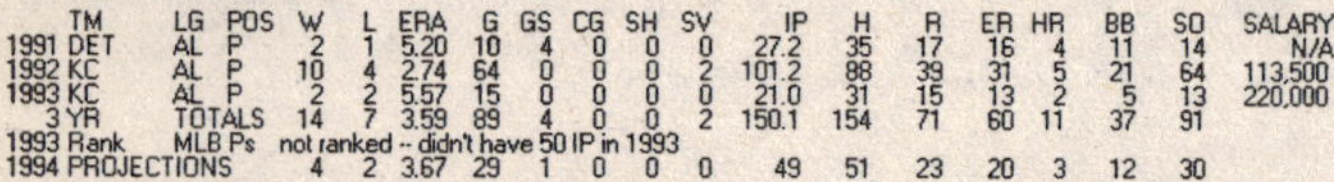

TM	LG	POS	W	L	ERA	G	GS	CG	SH	SV	IP	H	R	ER	HR	BB	SO	SALARY
1991 DET	AL	P	2	1	5.20	10	4	0	0	0	27.2	35	17	16	4	11	14	N/A
1992 KC	AL	P	10	4	2.74	64	0	0	0	2	101.2	88	39	31	5	21	64	113,500
1993 KC	AL	P	2	2	5.57	15	0	0	0	0	21.0	31	15	13	2	5	13	220,000
3 YR	TOTALS		14	7	3.59	89	4	0	0	2	150.1	154	71	60	11	37	91	
1993 Rank	MLB Ps		not ranked -- didn't have 50 IP in 1993															
1994 PROJECTIONS			4	2	3.67	29	1	0	0	0	49	51	23	20	3	12	30	

Keith Miller — No. 16/3B

Full name: Keith Alan Miller
Bats: R **Throws:** R **HT:** 5–11 **WT:** 185
Born: 6–12–63, Midland, MI
High school: All Saints (Bay City, MI)
College: Oral Roberts (Tulsa, OK)
Miller's .167 BA in 37 games was a career-low.

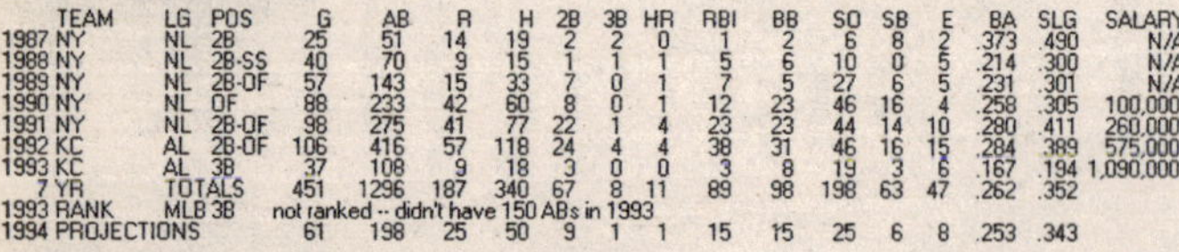

TEAM	LG	POS	G	AB	R	H	2B	3B	HR	RBI	BB	SO	SB	E	BA	SLG	SALARY
1987 NY	NL	2B	25	51	14	19	2	2	0	1	2	6	8	2	.373	.490	N/A
1988 NY	NL	2B-SS	40	70	9	15	1	1	1	5	6	10	0	5	.214	.300	N/A
1989 NY	NL	2B-OF	57	143	15	33	7	0	1	7	5	27	6	5	.231	.301	N/A
1990 NY	NL	OF	88	233	42	60	8	0	1	12	23	46	16	4	.258	.305	100,000
1991 NY	NL	2B-OF	98	275	41	77	22	1	4	23	23	44	14	10	.280	.411	260,000
1992 KC	AL	2B-OF	106	416	57	118	24	4	4	38	31	46	16	15	.284	.389	575,000
1993 KC	AL	3B	37	108	9	18	3	0	0	3	8	19	3	6	.167	.194	1,090,000
7 YR	TOTALS		451	1296	187	340	67	8	11	89	98	198	63	47	.262	.352	
1993 RANK	MLB 3B		not ranked -- didn't have 150 ABs in 1993														
1994 PROJECTIONS			61	198	25	50	9	1	1	15	15	25	6	8	.253	.343	

Craig Wilson — No. 8/3B

Full name: Craig Wilson
Bats: R **Throws:** R **HT:** 5–11 **WT:** 210
Born: 11–28–64, Anne Arundel CO., MD
High school: Annapolis (MD)
College: Anne Arundel Community (MD)
Wilson made 11 starts at 3B, and batted .265.

TEAM	LG	POS	G	AB	R	H	2B	3B	HR	RBI	BB	SO	SB	E	BA	SLG	SALARY
1989 STL	NL	3B	6	4	1	1	0	0	0	1	1	2	0	1	.250	.250	N/A
1990 STL	NL	3B-OF	55	121	13	30	2	0	0	7	8	14	0	1	.248	.264	100,000
1991 STL	NL	3B-OF	60	82	5	14	2	0	0	13	6	10	0	2	.171	.195	130,000
1992 STL	NL	3B-2B	61	106	6	33	6	0	0	13	10	18	1	3	.311	.368	N/A
1993 KC	AL	3B	21	49	6	13	1	0	1	3	7	6	1	1	.265	.347	N/A
5 YR	TOTALS		203	362	31	91	11	0	1	37	32	50	2	8	.251	.290	
1993 RANK	MLB 3B		not ranked -- didn't have 150 ABs in 1993														
1994 PROJECTIONS			29	45	4	9	1	0	0	5	4	6	0	1	.200	.244	

Milwaukee BREWERS

1994 Scouting Report

Hitting: (1993/.258 BA, thirteenth in AL; 125 HR, tenth in AL)

The Brewers are looking to players like Dave Nilsson, John Jaha, and Juan Bell to be the stars of the future. Injuries prevented Nilsson from having a successful season, but Jaha hit 19 HR and batted .303 after July 20, and Bell set career highs in every category. As Milwaukee turns to youth, their veterans were disappointing. Greg Vaughn was Milwaukee's biggest offensive threat, hitting .267 with 30 HR and 97 RBI, but B.J. Surhoff hit .274 with seven homers, and Tom Brunansky (.183, 6 HR, 29 RBI) had his worst major league season in '93.

Milwaukee parted ways with Kevin Seitzer and Robin Yount. Darryl Hamilton (.310, 9 HR, 48 RBI in 520 AB) will take over in CF.

Pitching: (1993/4.45 ERA, tenth in AL)

Milwaukee doesn't have much starting pitching. The Brewers need Jaime Navarro (11–12, 5.33 ERA in '93) to have a good season. Once again, Milwaukee missed Ted Higuera; he's been plagued with injuries over the last few years. If he can return to the form he once had, Milwaukee's pitching will improve considerably.

Doug Henry, the bullpen ace, saved only 17 games and compiled a 5.56 ERA in 54 appearances. Graeme Lloyd was effective out of the bullpen (55 appearances, 2.83 ERA), as was veteran Jesse Orosco (57 appearances, 3.18 ERA, eight saves).

Defense: (1993/.979 pct., thirteenth in AL)

Milwaukee lost one of the best defensive outfielders in the league in Robin Yount. Hamilton is a solid glove in the outfield, and B.J. Surhoff's .949 fielding percentage ranked fifth among AL third basemen.

1994 Prospects:

Milwaukee, like many small market teams facing a cash crunch, is just trying to stay competitive. They have a number of young players who can only get better. But this year, Milwaukee will be fortunate if they can beat out Kansas City or Minnesota for fourth place in the five-team AL Central Division.

Team Directory

President & CEO: Allan H. "Bud" Selig
General Mgr.: Sal Bando
Director of P.R.: Tom Skibosh
Senior VP: Harry Dalton
Asst. VP, Baseball Op.: Bruce Manno
Traveling Secretary: Steve Ethire

Minor League Affiliates:

Level	Team/League	1993 Record
AAA	New Orleans–American Association	80–64
AA	El Paso–Texas	76–59
A	Stockton–California	79–57
	Beloit–Midwest	60–74
Rookie	Helena–Pioneer	43–30
	Chandler Brewers–Arizona	29–27

1993 Review

	Home		Away			Home		Away			Home		Away	
vs AL East	W	L	W	L	vs AL Cent.	W	L	W	L	vs AL West	W	L	W	L
Baltimore	3	3	2	5	Chicago	1	5	2	4	California	2	4	3	3
Boston	4	3	4	2	Cleveland	3	3	2	5	Oakland	6	0	1	5
Detroit	3	4	2	4	Kansas City	4	2	3	3	Seattle	2	4	2	4
New York	2	5	2	4	Minnesota	5	1	2	4	Texas	2	4	2	4
Toronto	1	5	4	3										
Total	13	20	14	18		13	11	9	16		12	12	8	16

1993 finish: 69–93 (38–43 home, 31–50 away), seventh in AL East, 26 games behind

1994 Schedule

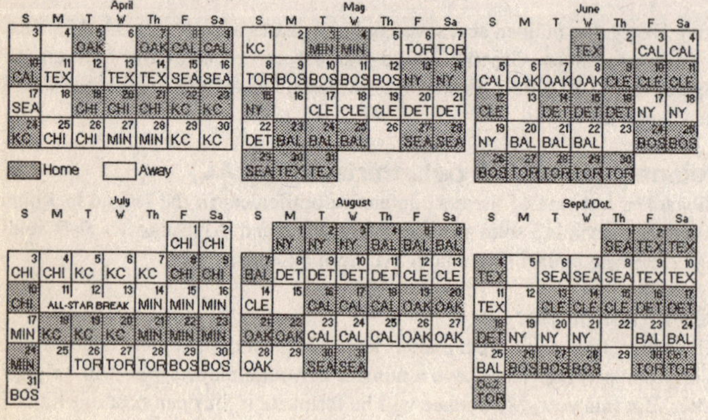

MILWAUKEE BREWERS 1994 ROSTER

Manager: Phil Garner

Coaches: Bill Castro, bullpen (35); Gene Clines, batting (12); Duffy Dyer, 3B (10); Tim Foli, IF & 1B (14); Don Rowe, pitching (45)

No.	PITCHERS	B	T	HT	WT	DOB	BIRTHPLACE	RESIDENCE
25	Bones, Ricky	R	R	6-0	190	4-7-69	Salinas, PR	Guayama, PR
57	Boze, Marshall	R	R	6-1	212	5-23-71	San Manuel, AZ	Springfield, IL
59	Browne, Byron	R	R	6-7	190	8-8-70	Camden, NJ	Phoeniz, AZ
21	Eldred, Cal	R	R	6-4	235	11-24-67	Cedar Rapids, IA	Center Point, IA
36	Fetters, Mike	R	R	6-4	215	12-19-64	Van Nuys, CA	Kailua, HI
58	Gamez, Francisco	R	R	6-2	185	4-2-70	Hermsillo, MX	Tucson, AZ
28	Henry, Doug	R	R	6-4	205	12-10-63	Sacramento, CA	Hartland, WI
49	Higuera, Ted	S	L	5-10	180	11-9-58	Los Mochis, MX	Los Mochis, MX
55	Hill, Tyrone	L	L	6-6	195	3-7-72	Yucaipa, CA	Yucaipa, CA
40	Ignasiak, Michael	S	R	5-11	190	3-12-66	Anchorville, MI	Casco, MI
43	Kiefer, Mark	R	R	6-4	184	11-13-68	Orange, CA	Kingsland, TX
37	Lloyd, Graeme	L	L	6-7	230	4-9-67	Victoria, Aust.	Guarwarre, Aust.
50	McAndrew, Jamie	R	R	6-2	190	9-2-67	Williamsport, PA	Ft. Myers, FL
38	Miranda, Angel	L	L	6-1	195	11-9-69	Arecibo, PR	Arecibo, PR
31	Navarro, Jaime	R	R	6-4	225	3-27-67	Bayamon, PR	Orlando, FL
39	Novoa, Rafael	L	L	6-1	190	10-26-67	New York, NY	Phoenix, AZ
47	Orosco, Jesse	R	L	6-2	205	4-21-57	Santa Barbara, CA	Poway, CA
60	Rogers, Charlie	L	L	6-0	180	8-21-68	Arlington Hts, IL	Bremen, AL
54	Taylor, Scott	R	R	6-3	200	10-3-66	Topeka, KS	Wichita, KS
46	Wegman, Bill	R	R	6-5	235	12-19-62	Cincinnati, OH	Cincinnati, OH
No.	**CATCHERS**	**B**	**T**	**HT**	**WT**	**DOB**	**BIRTHPLACE**	**RESIDENCE**
22	Lampkin, Tom	L	R	5-11	190	3-4-64	Cincinnati, OH	Camas, WA
65	Metheny, Mike	R	R	6-3	205	9-22-70	Columbus, OH	Reynoldsburg, OH
11	Nilsson, Dave	L	R	6-3	215	12-14-69	Brisbane, Aust.	Everton Hills, Aust.
64	Stefanski, Mike	R	R	6-2	190	9-12-69	Flint, MI	Redford, MI
No.	**INFIELDERS**	**B**	**T**	**HT**	**WT**	**DOB**	**BIRTHPLACE**	**RESIDENCE**
26	Bell, Juan	S	R	5-11	175	3-29-68	S.P. de Macoris, DR	S.P. de Macoris, DR
27	Cirillo, Jeff	R	R	6-2	190	9-23-69	Pasadena, CA	Van Nuys, CA
32	Jaha, John	R	R	6-1	205	5-27-66	Portland, OR	Portland, OR
16	Listach, Pat	S	R	5-9	170	9-12-67	Natchitoches, LA	Woodway, TX
9	Spiers, Bill	L	R	6-2	190	6-5-66	Orangeburg, SC	Elleree, SC
5	Surhoff, B.J.	L	R	6-1	200	8-4-64	Bronx, NY	Franklin, WI
2	Valentin, Jose	S	R	5-10	175	10-12-69	Manati, PR	Manati, PR
No.	**OUTFIELDERS**	**B**	**T**	**HT**	**WT**	**DOB**	**BIRTHPLACE**	**RESIDENCE**
1	Diaz, Alex	S	R	5-11	180	10-5-68	Brooklyn, NY	S. Sebastian, PR
24	Hamilton, Darryl	L	R	6-1	180	12-3-64	Baton Rouge, LA	Sugarland, TX
30	Mieske, Matt	R	R	6-0	185	2-13-68	Midland, MI	Livernois, MI
33	O'Leary, Troy	L	L	6-0	190	8-4-69	Compton, CA	Realto, CA
29	Reimer, Kevin	L	R	6-2	230	6-28-64	Macon, GA	Enderby, BC
51	Singleton, Duane	L	R	6-1	170	8-6-72	Staten Island, NY	Staten Island, NY
23	Vaughn, Greg	R	R	6-0	205	7-3-65	Sacramento, CA	Elk Grove, CA
52	Wachter, Derek	R	R	6-2	195	8-28-70	Bethpage, NY	Miller Place, NY
24	Ward, Turner	S	R	6-2	200	4-11-65	Orlando, FL	Satsuma, AL

County Stadium (53,192, grass)

Tickets: 414-933-1818

Ticket prices

- $18 (del. mez. & mez. diamond)
- $17 (diamond box); $15 (mezz.)
- $14 (lower box); $12 (upper box)
- $11 (lower grandstand)
- $8 (upper grandstand)
- $7 (general admission)
- $4 (bleachers)

Field Dimensions (from home plate)

- To left field at foul line, 315 feet
- To center field, 402 feet
- To right field at foul line, 315 feet

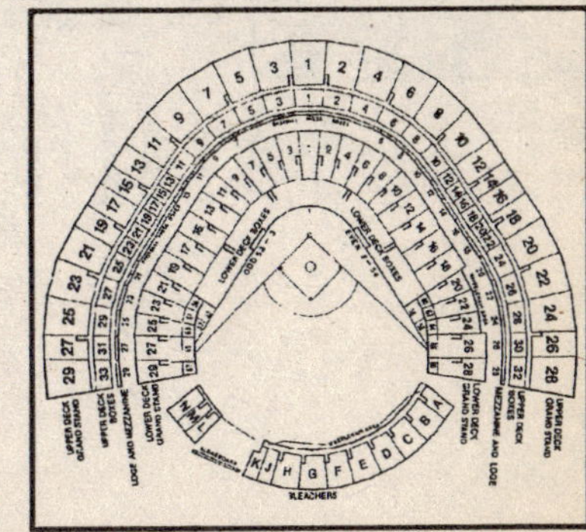

Darryl Hamilton No. 24/OF

Full name: Darryl Quinn Hamilton
Bats: L **Throws:** R **HT:** 6–1 **WT:** 180
Born: 12–3–64, Baton Rouge, LA
High school: University (Baton Rouge, LA)
College: Nicholls State (LA)

Hamilton led the Brewers in BA (.310) and SB (21) and his 51 multi-hit games tied for ninth in the AL.

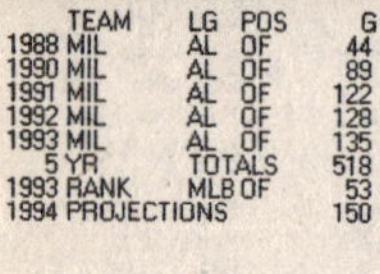
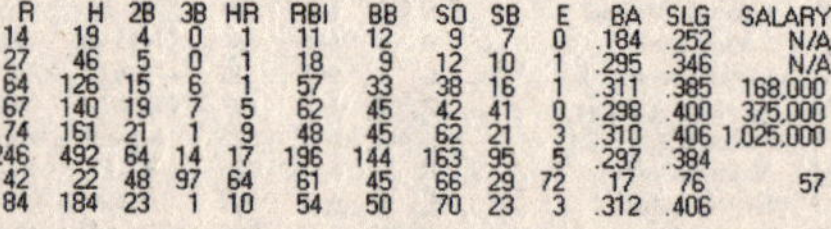

TEAM	LG	POS	G	AB	R	H	2B	3B	HR	RBI	BB	SO	SB	E	BA	SLG	SALARY
1988 MIL	AL	OF	44	103	14	19	4	0	1	11	12	9	7	0	.184	.252	N/A
1990 MIL	AL	OF	89	156	27	46	5	0	1	18	9	12	10	1	.295	.346	N/A
1991 MIL	AL	OF	122	405	64	126	15	6	1	57	33	38	16	1	.311	.385	168,000
1992 MIL	AL	OF	128	470	67	140	19	7	5	62	45	42	41	0	.298	.400	375,000
1993 MIL	AL	OF	135	520	74	161	21	1	9	48	45	62	21	3	.310	.406	1,025,000
5 YR	TOTALS		518	1654	246	492	64	14	17	196	144	163	95	5	.297	.384	
1993 RANK	MLB	OF	53	36	42	22	48	97	64	61	45	66	29	72	17	76	57
1994 PROJECTIONS			150	589	84	184	23	1	10	54	50	70	23	3	.312	.406	

John Jaha No. 2/1B

Full name: John Emil Jaha
Bats: R **Throws:** R **HT:** 6–1 **WT:** 205
Born: 5–27–66, Portland, OR
High school: David Douglas (Portland, OR)

In 1993, Jaha started slowly, then hit .303 over his last 60 games. Of his 19 HR, 15 were solo shots.

TEAM	LG	POS	G	AB	R	H	2B	3B	HR	RBI	BB	SO	SB	E	BA	SLG	SALARY
1992 MIL	AL	1B-OF	47	133	17	30	3	1	2	10	12	30	10	0	.226	.308	109,000
1993 MIL	AL	1B	153	515	78	136	21	0	19	70	51	109	13	10	.264	.416	118,000
2 YR	TOTALS		200	648	95	166	24	1	21	80	63	139	23	10	.256	.394	
1993 RANK	MLB	1B	7	16	13	18	23	30	14	19	22	6	3	10	27	27	35
1994 PROJECTIONS			162	555	84	148	23	0	21	78	55	116	11	11	.267	.422	

Pat Listach No. 16/SS

Full name: Patrick Alan Listach
Bats: S **Throws:** R **HT:** 5–9 **WT:** 170
Born: 9–12–67, Natchitoches, LA
High school: Natchitoches Central (LA)
College: Arizona State

Listach, the 1992 AL Rookie of the Year had only 18 SB, down from 54 in '92, and his BA dipped almost 50 points.

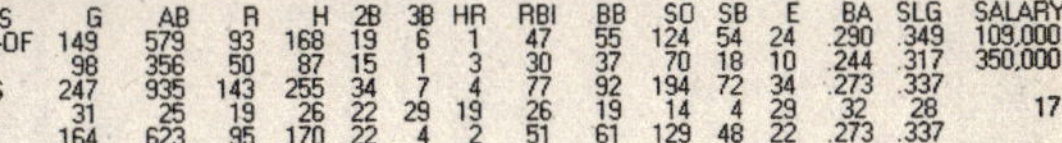

TEAM	LG	POS	G	AB	R	H	2B	3B	HR	RBI	BB	SO	SB	E	BA	SLG	SALARY
1992 MIL	AL	SS-OF	149	579	93	168	19	6	1	47	55	124	54	24	.290	.349	109,000
1993 MIL	AL	SS	98	356	50	87	15	1	3	30	37	70	18	10	.244	.317	350,000
2 YR	TOTALS		247	935	143	255	34	7	4	77	92	194	72	34	.273	.337	
1993 RANK	MLB	SS	31	25	19	26	22	29	19	26	19	14	4	29	32	28	17
1994 PROJECTIONS			164	623	95	170	22	4	2	51	61	129	48	22	.273	.337	

Dave Nilsson No. 11/C

Full name: David Wayne Nilsson
Bats: L **Throws:** R **HT:** 6–3 **WT:** 215
Born: 12–14–69, Brisbane, Aust.
High school: Kendron (Brisbane, Aust.)

Due to two stints on the DL, Nilsson started only 85 games behind the plate. He batted .301 over his last 33 games.

TEAM	LG	POS	G	AB	R	H	2B	3B	HR	RBI	BB	SO	SB	E	BA	SLG	SALARY
1992 MIL	AL	C-1B	51	164	15	38	8	0	4	25	17	18	2	2	.232	.354	109,000
1993 MIL	AL	C	100	296	35	76	10	2	7	40	37	36	3	9	.257	.375	122,500
2 YR	TOTALS		151	460	50	114	18	2	11	65	54	54	5	11	.248	.367	
1993 RANK	MLB	C	23	24	18	23	31	6	23	23	10	28	7	6	19	27	34
1994 PROJECTIONS			124	362	45	95	11	3	8	47	47	45	3	12	.262	.376	

Kevin Reimer — No. 29/DH

Full name: Kevin Michael Reimer
Bats: L **Throws:** R **HT:** 6–2 **WT:** 230
Born: 6–28–64, Macon, GA
High school: A.L. Fortune (Enderby, BC)
College: Orange Coast (CA) and Cal–Fullerton

Reimer had 0 HR and just 8 RBI after the All-Star break.

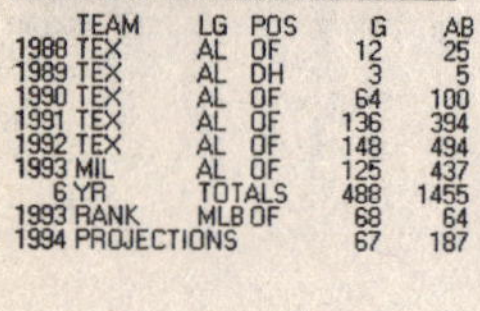
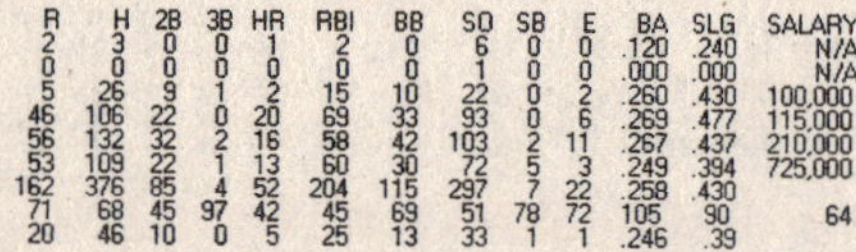

	TEAM	LG	POS	G	AB	R	H	2B	3B	HR	RBI	BB	SO	SB	E	BA	SLG	SALARY
1988	TEX	AL	OF	12	25	2	3	0	0	1	2	0	6	0	0	.120	.240	N/A
1989	TEX	AL	DH	3	5	0	0	0	0	0	0	0	1	0	0	.000	.000	N/A
1990	TEX	AL	OF	64	100	5	26	9	1	2	15	10	22	0	2	.260	.430	100,000
1991	TEX	AL	OF	136	394	46	106	22	0	20	69	33	93	0	6	.269	.477	115,000
1992	TEX	AL	OF	148	494	56	132	32	2	16	58	42	103	2	11	.267	.437	210,000
1993	MIL	AL	OF	125	437	53	109	22	1	13	60	30	72	5	3	.249	.394	725,000
6	YR	TOTALS		488	1455	162	376	85	4	52	204	115	297	7	22	.258	.430	
1993	RANK	MLB	OF	68	64	71	68	45	97	42	45	69	51	78	72	105	90	64
1994	PROJECTIONS			67	187	20	46	10	0	5	25	13	33	1	1	.246	.39	

Bill Spiers — No. 9/2B

Full name: William James Spiers III
Bats: L **Throws:** R **HT:** 6–2 **WT:** 190
Born: 6–5–66, Orangeburg, SC
High school: W. Hampton Acad. (CA)
College: Clemson

Spiers .238 BA in 1993 was the lowest of his career, and he had only 14 extra-base hits. He started 94 games at three positions.

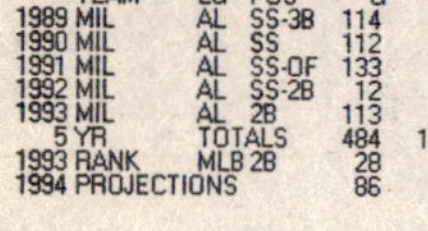

	TEAM	LG	POS	G	AB	R	H	2B	3B	HR	RBI	BB	SO	SB	E	BA	SLG	SALARY
1989	MIL	AL	SS-3B	114	345	44	88	9	3	4	33	21	63	10	21	.255	.333	N/A
1990	MIL	AL	SS	112	363	44	88	15	3	2	36	16	46	11	12	.242	.317	135,000
1991	MIL	AL	SS-OF	133	414	71	117	13	6	8	54	34	55	14	17	.283	.401	250,000
1992	MIL	AL	SS-2B	12	16	2	5	2	0	0	2	1	4	1	0	.313	.438	750,000
1993	MIL	AL	2B	113	340	43	81	8	4	2	36	29	51	9	13	.238	.303	750,000
5	YR	TOTALS		484	1478	204	379	47	16	16	161	101	219	45	63	.256	.342	
1993	RANK	MLB	2B	28	29	28	28	38	12	30	23	27	25	18	12	38	42	15
1994	PROJECTIONS			86	256	38	67	7	3	3	30	21	36	8	10	.262	.359	

B.J. Surhoff No. 5/3B

Full name: William James Surhoff
Bats: L **Throws:** R **HT:** 6–1 **WT:** 200
Born: 8–4–64, Bronx, NY
High school: Rye (NY)
College: North Carolina

Surhoff led the team with a career-best 38 doubles. He was the ninth hardest batter in the AL to strike out (1/12.7 AB).

TEAM	LG	POS	G	AB	R	H	2B	3B	HR	RBI	BB	SO	SB	E	BA	SLG	SALARY
1987 MIL	AL	C-3B	115	395	50	118	22	3	7	68	36	30	11	11	.299	.423	N/A
1988 MIL	AL	C-3B	139	493	47	121	21	0	5	38	31	49	21	8	.245	.318	N/A
1989 MIL	AL	C-3B	126	436	42	108	17	4	5	55	25	29	14	10	.248	.339	N/A
1990 MIL	AL	C-3B	135	474	55	131	21	4	6	59	41	37	18	12	.276	.376	N/A
1991 MIL	AL	C-3B	143	505	57	146	19	4	5	68	26	33	5	4	.289	.372	1,085,000
1992 MIL	AL	C-1B	139	480	63	121	19	1	4	62	46	41	14	6	.252	.321	2,500,000
1993 MIL	AL	3B	148	552	66	151	38	3	7	79	36	47	12	18	.274	.391	2,478,289
7 YR	TOTALS		945	3335	380	896	157	19	39	429	241	266	95	69	.269	.362	
1993 RANK	MLB	3B	8	8	14	7	2	6	24	10	19	28	3	10	16	22	7
1994 PROJECTIONS			152	574	68	155	40	3	7	80	36	49	12	19	.270	.387	

Greg Vaughn No. 23/OF

Full name: Gregory Lamont Vaughn
Bats: R **Throws:** R **HT:** 6–0 **WT:** 205
Born: 7–3–65, Sacramento, CA
High school: J.F. Kennedy (Sac'mento, CA)
College: Miami (FL)

Vaughn was the only Brewer All-Star in 1993, leading the team in HR for the third straight year.

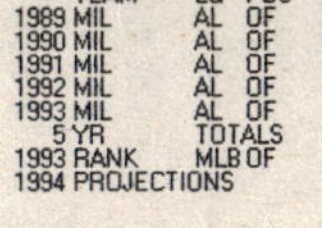

TEAM	LG	POS	G	AB	R	H	2B	3B	HR	RBI	BB	SO	SB	E	BA	SLG	SALARY
1989 MIL	AL	OF	38	113	18	30	3	0	5	23	13	23	4	2	.265	.425	N/A
1990 MIL	AL	OF	120	382	51	84	26	2	17	61	33	91	7	7	.220	.432	100,000
1991 MIL	AL	OF	145	542	81	132	24	5	27	98	62	125	2	2	.244	.456	190,000
1992 MIL	AL	OF	141	501	77	114	18	2	23	78	60	123	15	3	.228	.409	500,000
1993 MIL	AL	OF	154	569	97	152	28	2	30	97	89	118	10	3	.267	.482	1,777,500
5 YR	TOTALS		598	2107	324	512	99	11	102	357	257	480	38	17	.243	.446	
1993 RANK	MLB	OF	15	17	12	29	23	76	12	12	7	11	56	72	76	27	42
1994 PROJECTIONS			162	604	102	161	30	1	32	101	95	125	10	2	.267	.478	

Turner Ward No. 24/OF

Full name: Turner Max Ward
Bats: S **Throws:** R **HT:** 6–2 **WT:** 200
Born: 4–11–65, Orlando, FL
High school: Satsuma (AL)
College: South Alabama

Off-season pick-up Ward posted a career-low .192 BA for Toronto in 1993, but batted .242 on the road.

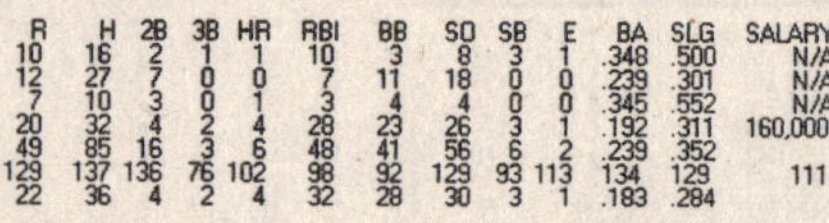

	TEAM	LG	POS	G	AB	R	H	2B	3B	HR	RBI	BB	SO	SB	E	BA	SLG	SALARY
1990	CLE	AL	OF	14	46	10	16	2	1	1	10	3	8	3	1	.348	.500	N/A
1991	CLE-TOR	AL	OF	48	113	12	27	7	0	0	7	11	18	0	0	.239	.301	N/A
1992	TOR	AL	OF	18	29	7	10	3	0	1	3	4	4	0	0	.345	.552	N/A
1993	TOR	AL	OF	72	167	20	32	4	2	4	28	23	26	3	1	.192	.311	160,000
4	YR	TOTALS		152	355	49	85	16	3	6	48	41	56	6	2	.239	.352	
1993	RANK	MLB	OF	128	132	129	137	136	76	102	98	92	129	93	113	134	129	111
1994	PROJECTIONS			86	197	22	36	4	2	4	32	28	30	3	1	.183	.284	

Cal Eldred No. 21/P

Full name: Calvin John Eldred
Bats: R **Throws:** R **HT:** 6–4 **WT:** 235
Born: 11–24–67, Cedar Rapids, IA
High school: Urbana Community (IA)
College: Iowa

In 1993, Eldred became the first Brewer to lead the AL in IP with 258. His 180 K was the fourth highest total in team history.

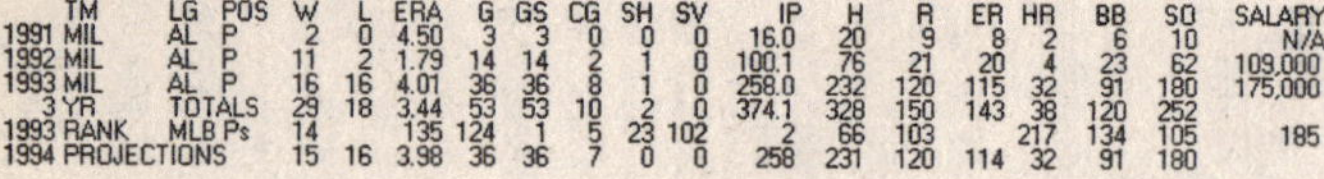

	TM	LG	POS	W	L	ERA	G	GS	CG	SH	SV	IP	H	R	ER	HR	BB	SO	SALARY
1991	MIL	AL	P	2	0	4.50	3	3	0	0	0	16.0	20	9	8	2	6	10	N/A
1992	MIL	AL	P	11	2	1.79	14	14	2	1	0	100.1	76	21	20	4	23	62	109,000
1993	MIL	AL	P	16	16	4.01	36	36	8	1	0	258.0	232	120	115	32	91	180	175,000
3	YR	TOTALS		29	18	3.44	53	53	10	2	0	374.1	328	150	143	38	120	252	
1993	RANK	MLB	Ps	14		135	124	1	5	23	102	2	66	103		217	134	105	185
1994	PROJECTIONS			15	16	3.98	36	36	7	0	0	258	231	120	114	32	91	180	

Ricky Bones No. 25/P

Full name: Ricardo Bones
Bats: R **Throws:** R **HT:** 6–0 **WT:** 190
Born: 4–7–69, Salinas, PR
High school: Guayama (PR)

Bones' 4.86 ERA was the worst of his career, but he pitched six or more innings in 20 of his 31 starts. He had an equal number of walks and strikeouts (63).

TM	LG	POS	W	L	ERA	G	GS	CG	SH	SV	IP	H	R	ER	HR	BB	SO	SALARY
1991 SD	NL	P	4	6	4.83	11	11	0	0	0	54.0	57	33	29	3	18	31	100,000
1992 MIL	AL	P	9	10	4.57	31	28	0	0	0	163.1	169	90	83	27	48	65	109,000
1993 MIL	AL	P	11	11	4.86	32	31	3	0	0	203.2	222	122	110	28	63	63	190,000
3 YR	TOTALS		24	27	4.75	74	70	3	0	0	421.0	448	245	222	58	129	159	
1993 RANK	MLB Ps		59		220	175	51	37	69	102	49	204	221		244	87	287	175
1994 PROJECTIONS			12	11	4.89	37	36	3	0	0	245	269	146	133	35	75	71	

Jaime Navarro No. 31/P

Full name: Jaime Navarro
Bats: R **Throws:** R **HT:** 6–4 **WT:** 225
Born: 3–27–67, Bayamon, PR
High school: Luis Pales Matos (PR)
College: Miami Dade Center

Navarro allowed a Brewers-record 127 earned runs, the most in the AL. He pitched over 200 innings for the third straight year.

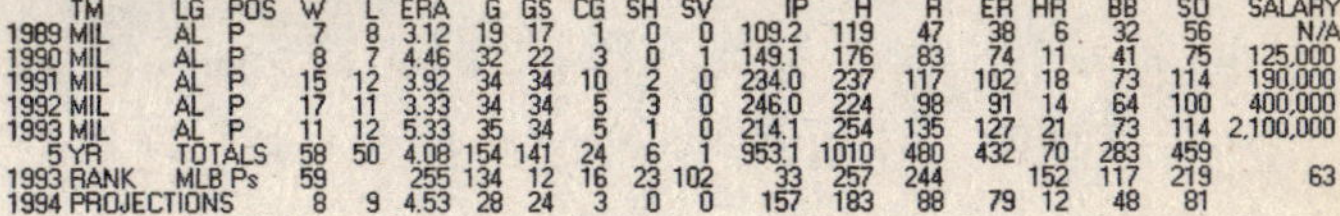

TM	LG	POS	W	L	ERA	G	GS	CG	SH	SV	IP	H	R	ER	HR	BB	SO	SALARY
1989 MIL	AL	P	7	8	3.12	19	17	1	0	0	109.2	119	47	38	6	32	56	N/A
1990 MIL	AL	P	8	7	4.46	32	22	3	0	1	149.1	176	83	74	11	41	75	125,000
1991 MIL	AL	P	15	12	3.92	34	34	10	2	0	234.0	237	117	102	18	73	114	190,000
1992 MIL	AL	P	17	11	3.33	34	34	5	3	0	246.0	224	98	91	14	64	100	400,000
1993 MIL	AL	P	11	12	5.33	35	34	5	1	0	214.1	254	135	127	21	73	114	2,100,000
5 YR	TOTALS		58	50	4.08	154	141	24	6	1	953.1	1010	480	432	70	283	459	
1993 RANK	MLB Ps		59		255	134	12	16	23	102	33	257	244		152	117	219	63
1994 PROJECTIONS			8	9	4.53	28	24	3	0	0	157	183	88	79	12	48	81	

Doug Henry No. 28/P

Full name: Richard Douglas Henry
Bats: R **Throws:** R **HT:** 6–4 **WT:** 205
Born: 12–10–63, Sacramento, CA
High school: Tennyson (CA)
College: Arizona State

Henry was the Brewers save leader for the third straight season. After the All-Star break, he posted a 7.32 ERA with only 1 save.

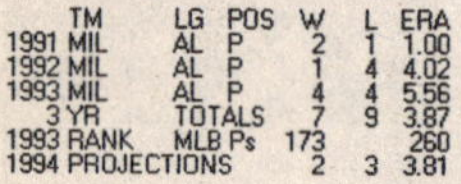
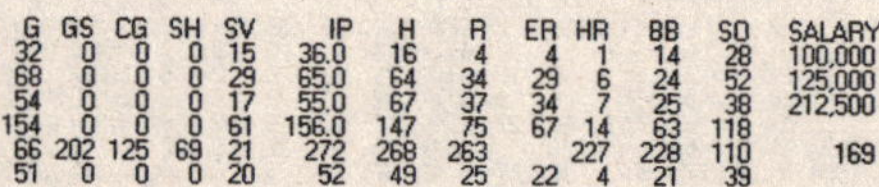

	TM	LG	POS	W	L	ERA	G	GS	CG	SH	SV	IP	H	R	ER	HR	BB	SO	SALARY
1991	MIL	AL	P	2	1	1.00	32	0	0	0	15	36.0	16	4	4	1	14	28	100,000
1992	MIL	AL	P	1	4	4.02	68	0	0	0	29	65.0	64	34	29	6	24	52	125,000
1993	MIL	AL	P	4	4	5.56	54	0	0	0	17	55.0	67	37	34	7	25	38	212,500
3	YR	TOTALS		7	9	3.87	154	0	0	0	61	156.0	147	75	67	14	63	118	
1993	RANK	MLB Ps		173		260	66	202	125	69	21	272	268	263		227	228	110	169
1994	PROJECTIONS			2	3	3.81	51	0	0	0	20	52	49	25	22	4	21	39	

Phil Garner No. 26/Mgr.

Full name: Philip Mason Garner
Bats: R **Throws:** R **HT:** 5–10 **WT:** 177
Born: 4–30–49, Jefferson City, TN
High school: Beardon (Knoxville, TN)
College: Tennessee

Garner's first Brewer team improved nine games, but his '93 team lost 13 more games than the '92 squad.

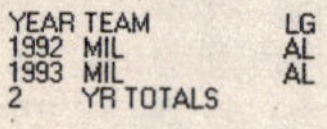
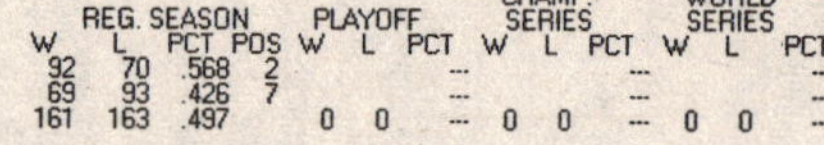

			REG. SEASON				PLAYOFF			CHAMP. SERIES			WORLD SERIES		
YEAR	TEAM	LG	W	L	PCT	POS	W	L	PCT	W	L	PCT	W	L	PCT
1992	MIL	AL	92	70	.568	2			---			---			---
1993	MIL	AL	69	93	.426	7			---			---			---
2	YR TOTALS		161	163	.497		0	0	---	0	0	---	0	0	---

Juan Bell No. 26/2B

Full name: Juan Bell
Bats: S **Throws:** R **HT:** 5–11 **WT:** 175
Born: 3–29–68, S.P. de Macoris, DR
High school: G. F. Deligne (SPD Macoris, DR)
Bell batted .404 in his first 15 games as a Brewer, but hit just .201 after June 20.

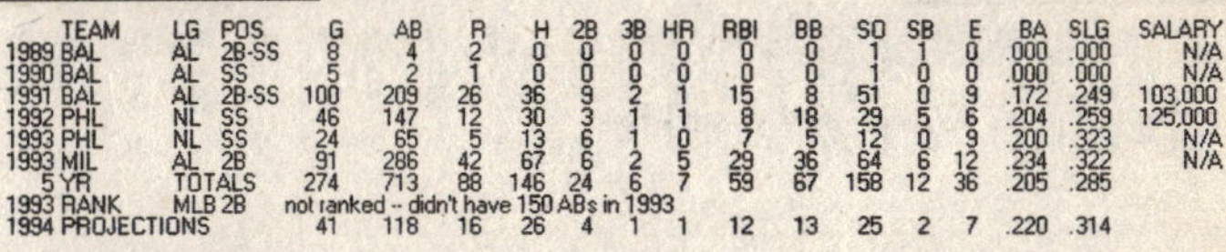

	TEAM	LG	POS	G	AB	R	H	2B	3B	HR	RBI	BB	SO	SB	E	BA	SLG	SALARY
1989	BAL	AL	2B-SS	8	4	2	0	0	0	0	0	0	1	1	0	.000	.000	N/A
1990	BAL	AL	SS	5	2	1	0	0	0	0	0	0	1	0	0	.000	.000	N/A
1991	BAL	AL	2B-SS	100	209	26	36	9	2	1	15	8	51	0	9	.172	.249	103,000
1992	PHL	NL	SS	46	147	12	30	3	1	1	8	18	29	5	6	.204	.259	125,000
1993	PHL	NL	SS	24	65	5	13	6	1	0	7	5	12	0	9	.200	.323	N/A
1993	MIL	AL	2B	91	286	42	67	6	2	5	29	36	64	6	12	.234	.322	N/A
5	YR	TOTALS		274	713	88	146	24	6	7	59	67	158	12	36	.205	.285	
1993	RANK	MLB 2B		not ranked -- didn't have 150 ABs in 1993														
1994	PROJECTIONS			41	118	16	26	4	1	1	12	13	25	2	7	.220	.314	

Alex Diaz No. 1/OF

Full name: Alexis Diaz
Bats: S **Throws:** R **HT:** 5–11 **WT:** 180
Born: 10–5–68, Brooklyn, NY
High school: M. Mendez Liciaga (PR)
Diaz struggled in April (.143 BA) before being hurt, but hit .364 in 21 games late in the season.

	TEAM	LG	POS	G	AB	R	H	2B	3B	HR	RBI	BB	SO	SB	E	BA	SLG	SALARY
1992	MIL	AL	OF	22	9	5	1	0	0	0	1	0	0	3	0	.111	.111	109,000
1993	MIL	AL	OF	32	69	9	22	2	0	0	1	0	12	5	1	.319	.348	110,000
2	YR	TOTALS		54	78	14	23	2	0	0	2	0	12	8	1	.295	.321	
1993	RANK	MLB OF		not ranked -- didn't have 150 ABs in 1993														
1994	PROJECTIONS			37	99	11	32	3	0	0	1	0	18	6	1	.323	.354	

Ted Higuera No. 49/P

Full name: Teodoro Valenzuela Higuera
Bats: S **Throws:** L **HT:** 5–10 **WT:** 180
Born: 11–9–58, Los Mochis, MX
High school: Los Mochis (Sinaloa, MX)
Higuera made 8 starts, marking his return to the majors after two years of injuries and rehabilitation.

	TM	LG	POS	W	L	ERA	G	GS	CG	SH	SV	IP	H	R	ER	HR	BB	SO	SALARY
1986	MIL	AL	P	20	11	2.79	34	34	15	4	0	248.1	226	84	77	26	74	207	N/A
1987	MIL	AL	P	18	10	3.85	35	35	14	3	0	261.2	236	120	112	24	87	240	N/A
1988	MIL	AL	P	16	9	2.45	31	31	8	1	0	227.1	168	66	62	15	59	192	N/A
1989	MIL	AL	P	9	6	3.46	22	22	2	1	0	135.1	125	56	52	9	48	91	N/A
1990	MIL	AL	P	11	10	3.76	27	27	4	1	0	170.0	167	80	71	16	50	129	2,125,000
1991	MIL	AL	P	3	2	4.46	7	6	0	0	0	36.1	37	18	18	2	10	33	2,750,000
1993	MIL	AL	P	1	3	7.20	8	8	0	0	0	30.0	43	24	24	4	16	27	3,250,000
8	YR	TOTALS		93	59	3.46	196	193	50	12	0	1321.1	1188	553	508	118	407	1046	
1993	RANK	MLB Ps		not ranked -- didn't have 50 IP in 1993															
1994	PROJECTIONS			13	8	3.57	25	25	9	2	0	179	168	76	71	18	59	158	

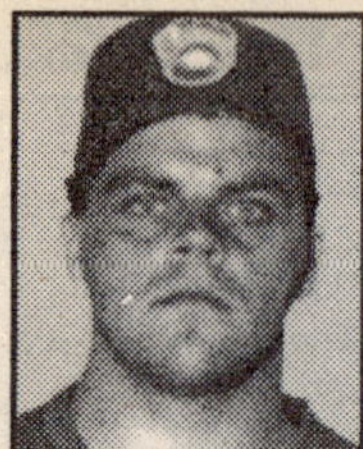

Michael Ignasiak No. 40/P

Full name: Michael James Ignasiak
Bats: S **Throws:** R **HT:** 5–11 **WT:** 190
Born: 3–12–66, Anchorville, MI
High school: St. Mary's (Orchard Lakes, MI)
College: Michigan
Ignasiak held opposing batters to a .241 BA.

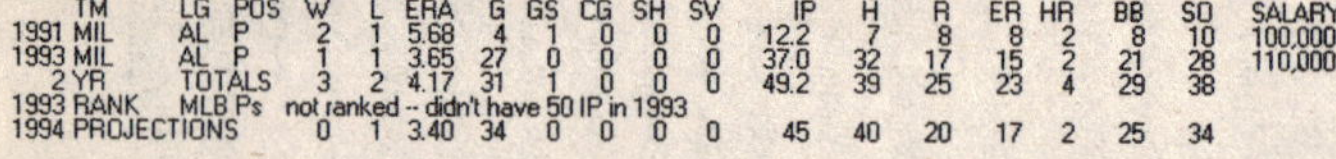

TM	LG	POS	W	L	ERA	G	GS	CG	SH	SV	IP	H	R	ER	HR	BB	SO	SALARY
1991 MIL	AL	P	2	1	5.68	4	1	0	0	0	12.2	7	8	8	2	8	10	100,000
1993 MIL	AL	P	1	1	3.65	27	0	0	0	0	37.0	32	17	15	2	21	28	110,000
2 YR	TOTALS		3	2	4.17	31	1	0	0	0	49.2	39	25	23	4	29	38	
1993 RANK	MLB Ps	not ranked -- didn't have 50 IP in 1993																
1994 PROJECTIONS			0	1	3.40	34	0	0	0	0	45	40	20	17	2	25	34	

Tom Lampkin No. 22/C

Full name: Thomas Michael Lampkin
Bats: L **Throws:** R **HT:** 5–11 **WT:** 190
Born: 3–4–64, Cincinnati, OH
High school: Blanchet (Seattle, WA)
College: Portland (OR)
Lampkin threw out 14 of 40 base stealers.

TEAM	LG	POS	G	AB	R	H	2B	3B	HR	RBI	BB	SO	SB	E	BA	SLG	SALARY
1988 CLE	AL	C	4	4	0	0	0	0	0	0	1	0	0	0	.000	.000	N/A
1990 SD	NL	C	26	63	4	14	0	1	1	4	4	9	0	3	.222	.302	N/A
1991 SD	NL	C-1B	38	58	4	11	3	1	0	3	3	9	0	0	.190	.276	N/A
1992 SD	NL	C-OF	9	17	3	4	0	0	0	0	6	1	2	0	.235	.235	N/A
1993 MIL	AL	C	73	162	22	32	8	0	4	25	20	26	7	6	.198	.321	120,000
5 YR	TOTALS		150	304	33	61	11	2	5	32	34	45	9	9	.201	.299	
1993 RANK	MLB C		35	40	33	41	36	25	30	32	28	37	4	15	39	35	35
1994 PROJECTIONS			84	188	25	37	9	0	4	29	23	30	8	7	.197	.309	

Graeme Lloyd No. 37/P

Full name: Graeme John Lloyd
Bats: L **Throws:** L **HT:** 6–7 **WT:** 230
Born: 4–9–67, Victoria, Aust.
High school: Geelong Technical (Victoria, Aust.)
Lloyd's 55 appearances set a team rookie record. He allowed just 2 HR in his last 61.2 IP.

TM	LG	POS	W	L	ERA	G	GS	CG	SH	SV	IP	H	R	ER	HR	BB	SO	SALARY
1993 MIL	AL	P	3	4	2.83	55	0	0	0	0	63.2	64	24	20	5	13	31	109,000
1 YR	TOTAL		3	4	2.83	55	0	0	0	0	63.2	64	24	20	5	13	31	
1993 RANK	MLB Ps		209		30	62	202	125	69	102	237	147	40		100	20	243	236

Mike Metheny No. 65/C

Full name: Michael Scott Metheny
Bats: R **Throws:** R **HT:** 6–3 **WT:** 205
Born: 9–22–70, Columbus, OH
High school: Reynoldsburg (OH)
College: Michigan
Metheny hit .254 with 21 doubles at New Orleans.

	TEAM	LG	POS	G	AB	R	H	2B	3B	HR	RBI	BB	SO	SB	E	BA	SLG
1993	EL PASO	TEX		107	339	39	86	21	2	2	28	17	73	1	9	.254	.345

Matt Mieske No. 30/OF

Full name: Matthew Todd Mieske
Bats: R **Throws:** R **HT:** 6–0 **WT:** 185
Born: 2–13–68, Midland, MI
High school: Bay City Western (Auburn, MI)
College: Western Michigan
Mieske had 3 HR in 58 late-season AB.

	TEAM	LG	POS	G	AB	R	H	2B	3B	HR	RBI	BB	SO	SB	E	BA	SLG	SALARY
1993	MIL	AL	OF	23	58	9	14	0	0	3	7	4	14	0	3	.241	.397	N/A
1 YR		TOTAL		23	58	9	14	0	0	3	7	4	14	0	3	.241	.397	
1993	RANK	MLB	OF	not ranked -- didn't have 150 ABs in 1993														

Angel Miranda No. 38/P

Full name: Angel Luis Miranda
Bats: L **Throws:** L **HT:** 6–1 **WT:** 195
Born: 11–9–69, Arecibo, PR
High school: Maria Cedillo (Arecibo, PR)
Miranda posted a 3.30 ERA and averaged 6.6 K per 9 IP in his first major league season.

	TM	LG	POS	W	L	ERA	G	GS	CG	SH	SV	IP	H	R	ER	HR	BB	SO	SALARY
1993	MIL	AL	P	4	5	3.30	22	17	2	0	0	120.0	100	53	44	12	52	88	109,000
1 YR		TOTAL		4	5	3.30	22	17	2	0	0	120.0	100	53	44	12	52	88	
1993	RANK	MLB	Ps	173		69	247	119	57	69	102	118	32	88		160	209	91	236

Rafael Novoa No. 39/P

Full name: Rafael Angel Novoa
Bats: L **Throws:** L **HT:** 6–1 **WT:** 190
Born: 10–26–67, New York, NY
High school: Fordham Prep (NY)
College: Villanova (PA)
He was 0–2 with a 3.62 ERA in his first five starts.

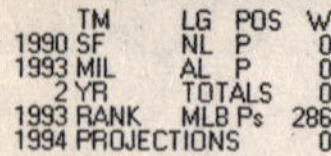

TM	LG	POS	W	L	ERA	G	GS	CG	SH	SV	IP	H	R	ER	HR	BB	SO	SALARY
1990 SF	NL	P	0	1	6.75	7	2	0	0	1	18.2	21	14	14	3	13	14	N/A
1993 MIL	AL	P	0	3	4.50	15	7	2	0	0	56.0	58	32	28	7	22	17	109,000
2 YR	TOTALS		0	4	5.06	22	9	2	0	1	74.2	79	46	42	10	35	31	
1993 RANK	MLB Ps		286		191	278	177	57	69	102	268	167	196		221	177	288	236
1994 PROJECTIONS			0	3	4.29	17	8	2	0	0	65	67	36	31	8	24	17	

Jesse Orosco No. 47/P

Full name: Jesse Orosco
Bats: R **Throws:** L **HT:** 6–2 **WT:** 205
Born: 4–21–57, Santa Barbara, CA
High school: Santa Barbara (CA)
College: Santa Barbara City (CA)
Orosco led the Brewers in appearances with 57.

TM	LG	POS	W	L	ERA	G	GS	CG	SH	SV	IP	H	R	ER	HR	BB	SO	SALARY
1986 NY	NL	P	8	6	2.33	58	0	0	0	21	81.0	64	23	21	6	35	62	N/A
1987 NY	NL	P	3	9	4.44	58	0	0	0	16	77.0	78	41	38	5	31	78	N/A
1988 LA	NL	P	3	2	2.72	55	0	0	0	9	53.0	41	18	16	4	30	43	N/A
1989 CLE	AL	P	3	4	2.08	69	0	0	0	3	78.0	54	20	18	7	26	79	N/A
1990 CLE	AL	P	5	4	3.90	55	0	0	0	2	64.2	58	35	28	9	38	55	940,000
1991 CLE	AL	P	2	0	3.74	47	0	0	0	0	45.2	52	20	19	4	15	36	900,000
1992 MIL	AL	P	3	1	3.23	59	0	0	0	1	39.0	33	15	14	5	13	40	1,075,000
1993 MIL	AL	P	3	5	3.18	57	0	0	0	8	56.2	47	25	20	2	17	67	1,000,000
14 YR	TOTALS		66	63	2.86	714	4	0	0	130	932.1	765	340	296	71	379	826	
1993 RANK	MLB Ps		209		59	54	202	125	69	28	263	30	86		13	78	5	99

Bill Wegman No. 46/P

Full name: William Edward Wegman
Bats: R **Throws:** R **HT:** 6–5 **WT:** 235
Born: 12–19–62, Cincinnati, OH
High school: Oak Hill (Cincinnati, OH)
Wegman's career-high 14 losses tied him for fourth in the AL.

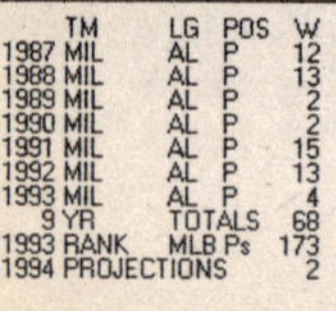
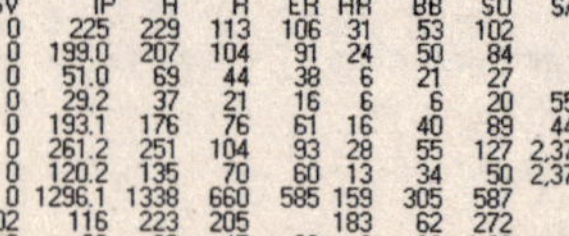

TM	LG	POS	W	L	ERA	G	GS	CG	SH	SV	IP	H	R	ER	HR	BB	SO	SALARY
1987 MIL	AL	P	12	11	4.24	34	33	7	0	0	225	229	113	106	31	53	102	N/A
1988 MIL	AL	P	13	13	4.12	32	31	4	1	0	199.0	207	104	91	24	50	84	N/A
1989 MIL	AL	P	2	6	6.71	11	8	0	0	0	51.0	69	44	38	6	21	27	N/A
1990 MIL	AL	P	2	2	4.85	8	5	1	1	0	29.2	37	21	16	6	6	20	550,000
1991 MIL	AL	P	15	7	2.84	28	28	7	2	0	193.1	176	76	61	16	40	89	440,000
1992 MIL	AL	P	13	14	3.20	35	35	7	0	0	261.2	251	104	93	28	55	127	2,375,000
1993 MIL	AL	P	4	14	4.48	20	18	5	0	0	120.2	135	70	60	13	34	50	2,375,000
9 YR	TOTALS		68	79	4.06	206	193	33	4	0	1296.1	1338	660	585	159	305	587	
1993 RANK	MLB Ps		173		188	255	111	16	69	102	116	223	205		183	62	272	55
1994 PROJECTIONS			2	7	5.18	13	10	2	0	0	66	80	45	38	8	20	32	

Minnesota *TWINS*

1994 Scouting Report

Hitting: (1993/.264 BA, eighth in AL; 121 HR, twelfth in AL)

Kirby Puckett, Chuck Knoblauch, Kent Hrbek, and Dave Winfield all hit under their career averages in '93. Hrbek, in particular, was 41 points below his lifetime average. Even Puckett's .296 BA (with 22 HR and 89 RBI) was 22 points under his career average.

Minnesota needs to find a third baseman. Mike Pagliarulo, who started 79 games at third, went to Baltimore and is now playing in Japan. Top Twins prospects include OF Dave McCarty (.385 at AAA Portland), SS Denny Hocking (.267 at AA Nashville), 3B Scott Stahoviak (.272 at Nashville), and C Derek Parks (.311 at Portland).

Pitching: (1993/4.71 ERA, eleventh in AL)

Minnesota's 4.71 team ERA was the second highest in team history. Kevin Tapani (12–15, 4.43 ERA) became the staff ace, leading the Twins in wins, starts, complete games, and strikeouts. Scott Erickson lost 19 games. Willie Banks was 11–12, but was traded to the Cubs after the season.

The bullpen features closer Rick Aguilera (4–3, 3.11 ERA, 34 saves) and setup man Larry Casian (5–3, 3.02 ERA in 54 appearances). They get lots of work; Minnesota set a major league record of 103 straight games without a complete game in '93. (Erickson's complete game 5–4 loss to Boston snapped the string August 4.)

Defense: (1993/.984 pct., fourth in AL)

Kirby Puckett is a Gold Glove outfielder. First baseman Kent Hrbek and second baseman Chuck Knoblauch ranked fourth and second, respectively, in fielding percentage at their positions.

1994 Prospects:

Minnesota has too many established hitters to finish eleventh in the AL in runs scored, as they did in 1993. But they lack the starting pitching to contend. The Twins figure to finish behind Chicago and Cleveland in the AL Central, but ahead of Milwaukee.

Team Directory

Owner: Carl R. Pohlad
General Mgr.:Andy McPhail
Director of P.R.: Rob Antony
President: Jerry Bell
VP, Player Procurement: Terry Ryan
Traveling Secretary: Remzi Kiratli

Minor League Affiliates:

Level	Team/League	1993 Record
AAA	Portland – Pacific Coast	87–56
AA	Nashville – Southern	72–70
A	Fort Myers – Florida State	55–79
	Fort Wayne – Midwest	68–67
Rookie	Elizabethton – Appalachian	37–30
	Ft. Myers Twins – Gulf Coast	23–36

1993 Review

	Home		Away			Home		Away			Home		Away	
vs AL East	W	L	W	L	vs AL Cent.	W	L	W	L	vs AL West	W	L	W	L
Baltimore	3	3	1	5	Chicago	1	5	2	5	California	6	1	3	3
Boston	3	3	2	4	Cleveland	4	2	4	2	Oakland	3	4	5	1
Detroit	1	5	5	1	Kansas City	2	4	4	3	Seattle	2	5	2	4
New York	2	4	2	4	Milwaukee	4	2	1	5	Texas	4	2	3	4
Toronto	1	5	1	5										
Total	10	20	11	19		11	13	11	15		15	12	13	12

1993 finish: 71–91 (36–45 home, 35–46 away), tied for fifth in AL West, 23 games behind

1994 Schedule

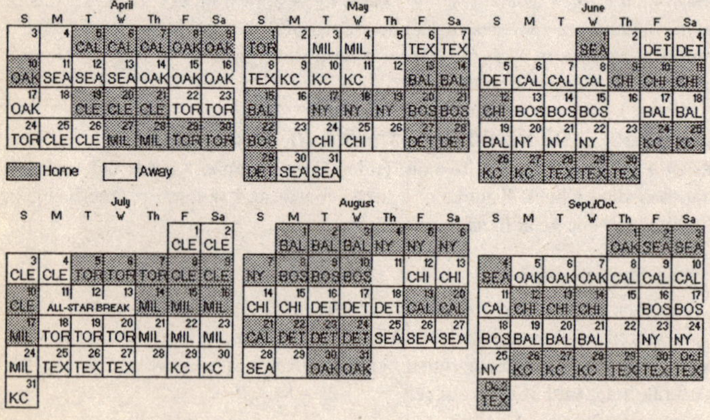

MINNESOTA TWINS 1994 ROSTER

Manager: Tom Kelly (10)
Coaches: Terry Crowley, batting (46); Ron Gardenhire, 3B (43); Rick Stelmaszek, bullpen (42); Dick Such, pitching (45); Wayne Terwilliger, 1B (45)

No.	PITCHERS	B	T	HT	WT	DOB	BIRTHPLACE	RESIDENCE
38	Aguilera, Rick	R	R	6–5	203	12–31–61	San Gabriel, CA	Chanhassen, MN
57	Brummett, Greg	R	R	6–0	186	4–20–67	Wichita, KS	Wichita, KS
	Caridad, Ron	R	R	5–10	181	3–22–72	Caracas, VZ	Miami, FL
48	Casian, Larry	R	L	6–0	173	10–28–65	Lynwood, CA	Salem, OR
	Correa, Jose	R	R	6–2	193	6–2–72	Guarenas, VZ	Guarenas, VZ
19	Erickson, Scott	R	R	6–4	222	2–2–68	Long Beach, CA	Sunnyvale, CA
18	Guardado, Eddie	R	L	6–0	193	10–2–70	Stockton, CA	Stockton, CA
53	Guthrie, Mark	R	L	6–4	206	9–22–65	Buffalo, NY	Bradenton, FL
20	Mahomes, Pat	R	R	6–4	210	8–9–70	Bryan, TX	Lindale, TX
47	Merriman, Brett	R	R	6–2	216	7–15–66	Jacksonville, IL	Chandler, AZ
55	Munoz, Oscar	R	R	6–3	210	9–25–69	Hialeah, FL	Hialeah, FL
	Pulido, Carlos	L	L	6–0	194	8–5–71	Caracas, VZ	Caracas, VZ
	Ritchie, Todd	R	R	6–3	190	11–7–71	Portsmouth, VA	Duncanville, TX
50	Stevens, Dave	R	R	6–3	210	3–4–70	Fullerton, CA	La Habra, CA
36	Tapani, Kevin	R	R	6–0	188	2–18–64	Des Moines, IA	Eden Prairie, MN
21	Trombley, Mike	R	R	6–2	208	4–14–67	Springfield, MA	Naples, FL
51	Willis, Carl	L	R	6–4	213	12–28–60	Danville, VA	Durham, NC
No.	**CATCHERS**	**B**	**T**	**HT**	**WT**	**DOB**	**BIRTHPLACE**	**RESIDENCE**
	Durant, Mike	R	R	6–2	200	9–14–69	Columbus, OH	Columbus, OH
16	Parks, Derek	R	R	6–0	217	9–29–68	Covina, CA	Ran. Cucamonga, CA
9	Walbeck, Matt	S	R	5–11	190	10–2–69	Sacramento, CA	Sacramento, CA
15	Webster, Lenny	R	R	5–9	195	2–10–65	New Orleans, LA	Charlotte, NC
No.	**INFIELDERS**	**B**	**T**	**HT**	**WT**	**DOB**	**BIRTHPLACE**	**RESIDENCE**
39	Dunn, Steve	L	L	6–4	225	4–18–70	Champaign, IL	Fairfax, VA
4	Hale, Chip	L	R	5–11	191	12–2–64	Santa Clara, CA	Tucson, AZ
7	Hocking, Denny	S	R	5–10	176	4–2–70	Torrance, CA	Torrance, CA
14	Hrbek, Kent	L	R	6–4	260	5–21–60	Minneapolis, MN	Bloomington, MN
11	Knoblauch, Chuck	R	R	5–9	181	7–7–68	Houston, TX	Houston, TX
31	Leius, Scott	R	R	6–3	208	9–24–65	Yonkers, NY	Minnetonka, MN
2	Meares, Pat	R	R	6–0	184	9–6–68	Salina, KS	Wichita, KS
17	Reboulet, Jeff	R	R	6–0	169	4–30–64	Dayton, OH	Kettering, OH
	Scott, Gary	R	R	6–0	175	8–22–68	New Rochelle, NY	Pelham, NY
37	Stahoviak, Scott	L	R	6–5	208	3–6–70	Waukegan, IL	Grayslake, IL
No.	**OUTFIELDERS**	**B**	**T**	**HT**	**WT**	**DOB**	**BIRTHPLACE**	**RESIDENCE**
25	Becker, Rich	S		5–10	180	2–1–72	Aurora, IL	Aurora, IL
26	Bruett, J.T.	L	L	5–11	180	10–8–67	Milwaukee, WI	Plymouth, MN
40	Cordova, Marty	R	R	6–0	200	7–10–69	Las Vegas, NV	Las Vegas, NV
24	Mack, Shane	R	R	6–0	190	12–7–63	Los Angeles, CA	Chanhassen, MN
	Martinez, Chito	L	L	5–10	185	12–19–65	Belize	
8	McCarty, David	R		6–5	207	11–23–69	Houston, TX	Houston, TX
5	Munoz, Pedro	R	R	5–10	203	9–19–68	Ponce, PR	Ponce, PR
34	Puckett, Kirby	R	R	5–9	215	3–14–61	Chicago, IL	Edina, MN
32	Winfield, Dave	R	R	6–6	245	10–3–51	St. Paul, MN	Ft. Myers, FL

Hubert Humphrey Metrodome (55,883, artificial)

Tickets: 612–375–7444

Ticket prices:

- $17 (VIP level)
- $15 (lower deck club level)
- $12 (lower deck reserved)
- $11 (upper deck club level)
- $10 (upper deck reserved)
- $7 (g.a., lower deck)
- $4 (g.a., upper deck)

Field Dimensions (from home plate)

- To left field at foul line, 343 feet
- To center field, 408 feet
- To right field at foul line, 327 feet

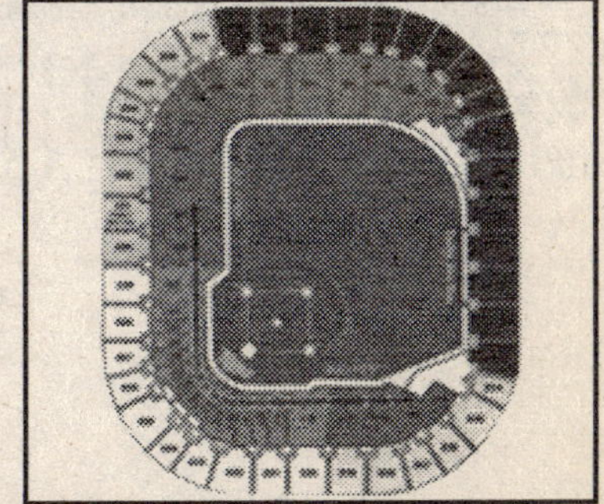

Kent Hrbek No. 14/1B

Full name: Kent Alan Hrbek
Bats: L **Throws:** R **HT:** 6–4 **WT:** 260
Born: 5–21–60, Minneapolis, MN
High school: Bloomington Kennedy (MN)

Hrbek's 152 HR in the Metrodome and 10 more in Seattle's Kingdome give him 162 indoor HR, tops in major league history. He had a .995 fielding percentage in '93.

	TEAM	LG	POS	G	AB	R	H	2B	3B	HR	RBI	BB	SO	SB	E	BA	SLG	SALARY
1981	MIN	AL	1B	24	67	5	16	5	0	1	7	5	9	0	0	.239	.358	N/A
1982	MIN	AL	1B	140	532	82	160	21	4	23	92	54	80	3	9	.301	.485	N/A
1983	MIN	AL	1B	141	515	75	153	41	5	16	84	57	71	4	13	.297	.489	N/A
1984	MIN	AL	1B	149	559	80	174	31	3	27	107	65	87	1	14	.311	.522	N/A
1985	MIN	AL	1B	158	593	78	165	31	2	21	93	67	87	1	8	.278	.444	N/A
1986	MIN	AL	1B	149	550	85	147	27	1	29	91	71	81	2	10	.267	.478	N/A
1987	MIN	AL	1B	143	477	85	136	20	1	34	90	84	60	5	5	.285	.545	N/A
1988	MIN	AL	1B	143	510	75	159	31	0	25	76	67	54	0	3	.312	.520	N/A
1989	MIN	AL	1B	109	375	59	102	17	0	25	84	53	35	3	4	.272	.517	N/A
1990	MIN	AL	1B-3B	143	492	61	141	26	0	22	79	69	45	5	3	.287	.474	N/A
1991	MIN	AL	1B	132	462	72	131	20	1	20	89	67	48	4	8	.284	.461	2,600,000
1992	MIN	AL	1B	112	394	52	96	20	0	15	58	71	56	5	3	.244	.409	3,100,000
1993	MIN	AL	1B	123	392	60	95	11	1	25	83	71	57	4	5	.242	.467	3,100,000
13	YR	TOTALS		1666	5918	869	1675	301	18	283	1033	801	770	37	85	.283	.483	
1993	RANK	MLB	1B	24	27	21	28	33	20	8	15	10	23	11	21	37	15	9
1994	PROJECTIONS			86	284	39	69	12	0	13	49	49	40	3	2	.243	.43	

Chuck Knoblauch No. 11/2B

Full name: Edward Charles Knoblauch
Bats: R **Throws:** R **HT:** 5–9 **WT:** 181
Born: 7–7–68, Houston, TX
High school: Bellaire (Houston, TX)
College: Texas A&M

Knoblauch led the Twins in steals for the third straight season. He tied for the team lead in triples, sacrifice flies and hit-by-pitches.

	TEAM	LG	POS	G	AB	R	H	2B	3B	HR	RBI	BB	SO	SB	E	BA	SLG	SALARY
1991	MIN	AL	2B	151	565	78	159	24	6	1	50	59	40	25	18	.281	.350	100,000
1992	MIN	AL	2B-SS	155	600	104	178	19	6	2	56	88	60	34	6	.297	.358	325,000
1993	MIN	AL	2B	153	602	82	167	27	4	2	41	65	44	29	9	.277	.346	500,000
3	YR	TOTALS		459	1767	264	504	70	16	5	147	212	144	88	33	.285	.351	
1993	RANK	MLB	2B	3	3	6	4	9	12	30	20	7	31	3	27	16	33	19
1994	PROJECTIONS			153	589	88	168	23	5	1	49	70	48	29	11	.285	.351	

Shane Mack No. 24/OF

Full name: Shane Lee Mack
Bats: R **Throws:** R **HT:** 6–0 **WT:** 190
Born: 12–7–63, Los Angeles, CA
High school: Gahr (Cerritos, CA)
College: UCLA

Mack was named AL Player of the Week for the first time when he went 8 for 20 with 3 HR and 10 RBI June 7–13.

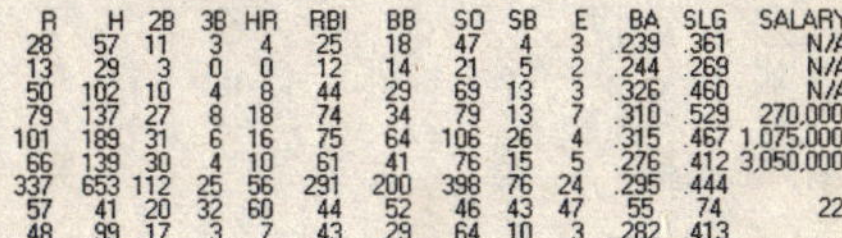

	TEAM	LG	POS	G	AB	R	H	2B	3B	HR	RBI	BB	SO	SB	E	BA	SLG	SALARY
1987	SD	NL	OF	105	238	28	57	11	3	4	25	18	47	4	3	.239	.361	N/A
1988	SD	NL	OF	56	119	13	29	3	0	0	12	14	21	5	2	.244	.269	N/A
1990	MIN	AL	OF	125	313	50	102	10	4	8	44	29	69	13	3	.326	.460	N/A
1991	MIN	AL	OF	143	442	79	137	27	8	18	74	34	79	13	7	.310	.529	270,000
1992	MIN	AL	OF	156	600	101	189	31	6	16	75	64	106	26	4	.315	.467	1,075,000
1993	MIN	AL	OF	128	503	66	139	30	4	10	61	41	76	15	5	.276	.412	3,050,000
6	YR	TOTALS		713	2215	337	653	112	25	56	291	200	398	76	24	.295	.444	
1993	RANK	MLB	OF	62	40	57	41	20	32	60	44	52	46	43	47	55	74	22
1994	PROJECTIONS			119	351	48	99	17	3	7	43	29	64	10	3	.282	.413	

Pat Meares No. 2/SS

Full name: Patrick James Meares
Bats: R **Throws:** R **HT:** 6–0 **WT:** 184
Born: 9–6–68, Salina, KS
High school: Sacred Heart (Salinas, CA)
College: Wichita State (KS)

Meares started 103 games at shortstop as a rookie. He had ten errors in his first 36 games, but just nine in his last 75.

	TEAM	LG	POS	G	AB	R	H	2B	3B	HR	RBI	BB	SO	SB	E	BA	SLG	SALARY
1993	MIN	AL	SS	111	346	33	87	14	3	0	33	7	52	4	19	.251	.309	109,000
1	YR	TOTAL		111	346	33	87	14	3	0	33	7	52	4	19	.251	.309	
1993	RANK	MLB	SS	25	27	31	27	25	13	38	23	38	1	25	30	29	35	34

Pedro Munoz No. 5/OF

Full name: Pedro Javier Munoz
Bats: R **Throws:** R **HT:** 5–10 **WT:** 203
Born: 9–19–68, Ponce, PR
High school: Dr. Pila (Ponce, PR)
11 of Munoz' 13 HR were hit on the road. His 27 game hitless streak from July 28 to August 13 was the longest of the season by a Twin.

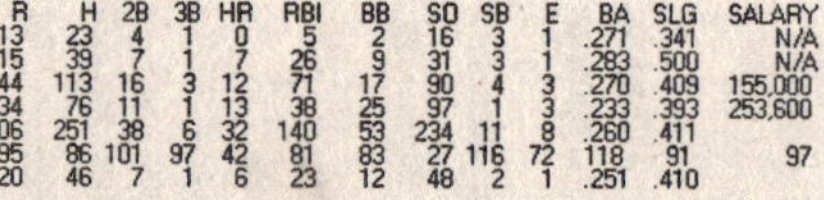

	TEAM	LG	POS	G	AB	R	H	2B	3B	HR	RBI	BB	SO	SB	E	BA	SLG	SALARY
1990	MIN	AL	OF	22	85	13	23	4	1	0	5	2	16	3	1	.271	.341	N/A
1991	MIN	AL	OF	51	138	15	39	7	1	7	26	9	31	3	1	.283	.500	N/A
1992	MIN	AL	OF	127	418	44	113	16	3	12	71	17	90	4	3	.270	.409	155,000
1993	MIN	AL	OF	104	326	34	76	11	1	13	38	25	97	1	3	.233	.393	253,600
4	YR	TOTALS		304	967	106	251	38	6	32	140	53	234	11	8	.260	.411	
1993	RANK	MLB	OF	88	81	95	86	101	97	42	81	83	27	116	72	118	91	97
1994	PROJECTIONS			59	183	20	46	7	1	6	23	12	48	2	1	.251	.410	

Kirby Puckett No. 34/OF

Full name: Kirby Puckett
Bats: R **Throws:** R **HT:** 5–9 **WT:** 215
Born: 3–14–61, Chicago, IL
High school: Calumet (Chicago, IL)
College: Bradley (Peoria, IL) and Triton Junior (River Grove, IL)
Puckett hit 20 HR for the first time since '88. He had 56 multi-hit games, fifth in the AL.

	TEAM	LG	POS	G	AB	R	H	2B	3B	HR	RBI	BB	SO	SB	E	BA	SLG	SALARY
1984	MIN	AL	OF	128	557	63	165	12	5	0	31	16	69	14	3	.296	.336	N/A
1985	MIN	AL	OF	161	691	80	199	29	13	4	74	41	87	21	8	.288	.385	N/A
1986	MIN	AL	OF	161	680	119	223	37	6	31	96	34	99	20	6	.328	.537	N/A
1987	MIN	AL	OF	157	624	96	207	32	5	28	99	32	91	12	5	.332	.534	N/A
1988	MIN	AL	OF	158	657	109	234	42	5	24	121	23	83	6	3	.356	.545	N/A
1989	MIN	AL	OF	159	635	75	215	45	4	9	85	41	59	11	4	.339	.465	N/A
1990	MIN	AL	OF-2B	146	551	82	164	40	3	12	80	57	73	5	4	.298	.446	N/A
1991	MIN	AL	OF	152	611	92	195	29	6	15	89	31	78	11	6	.319	.460	3,166,667
1992	MIN	AL	OF-3B	160	639	104	210	38	4	19	110	44	97	17	3	.329	.490	2,966,667
1993	MIN	AL	OF	156	622	89	184	39	3	22	89	47	93	8	2	.296	.474	5,300,000
10	YR	TOTALS		1538	6267	909	1996	343	54	164	874	366	829	125	44	.318	.469	
1993	RANK	MLB	OF	11	5	22	4	6	54	16	16	41	33	66	97	33	35	3
1994	PROJECTIONS			155	622	85	198	37	4	15	87	39	76	10	4	.318	.466	

Jeff Reboulet No. 17/3B

Full name: Jeffrey Allen Reboulet
Bats: R **Throws:** R **HT:** 6–0 **WT:** 169
Born: 4–30–64, Dayton, OH
High school: Alter (Kettering, OH)
College: Triton Junior (IL) and La. State

Both Reboulet and Kirby Puckett are members of the Triton Junior College Hall of Fame.

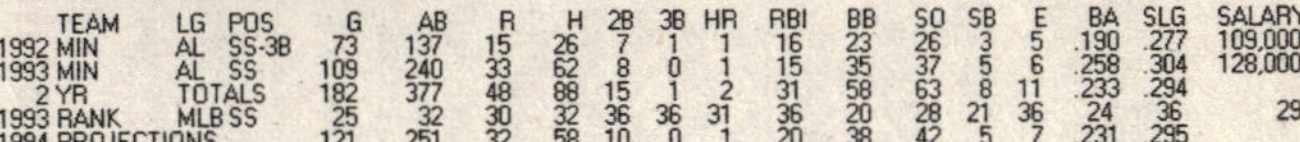

TEAM	LG	POS	G	AB	R	H	2B	3B	HR	RBI	BB	SO	SB	E	BA	SLG	SALARY
1992 MIN	AL	SS-3B	73	137	15	26	7	1	1	16	23	26	3	5	.190	.277	109,000
1993 MIN	AL	SS	109	240	33	62	8	0	1	15	35	37	5	6	.258	.304	128,000
2 YR	TOTALS		182	377	48	88	15	1	2	31	58	63	8	11	.233	.294	
1993 RANK	MLB	SS	25	32	30	32	36	36	31	36	20	28	21	36	24	36	29
1994 PROJECTIONS			121	251	32	58	10	0	1	20	38	42	5	7	.231	.295	

Lenny Webster No. 15/C

Full name: Leonard Irell Webster
Bats: R **Throws:** R **HT:** 5–9 **WT:** 195
Born: 2–10–65, New Orleans, LA
High school: Lutcher (LA)
College: Grambling State

Webster threw out 38 percent of potential base stealers (13 of 34).

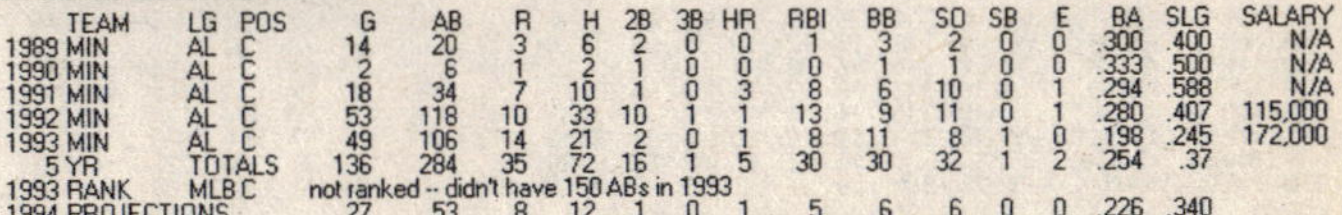

TEAM	LG	POS	G	AB	R	H	2B	3B	HR	RBI	BB	SO	SB	E	BA	SLG	SALARY
1989 MIN	AL	C	14	20	3	6	2	0	0	1	3	2	0	0	.300	.400	N/A
1990 MIN	AL	C	2	6	1	2	1	0	0	0	1	1	0	0	.333	.500	N/A
1991 MIN	AL	C	18	34	7	10	1	0	3	8	6	10	0	1	.294	.588	N/A
1992 MIN	AL	C	53	118	10	33	10	1	1	13	9	11	0	1	.280	.407	115,000
1993 MIN	AL	C	49	106	14	21	2	0	1	8	11	8	1	0	.198	.245	172,000
5 YR	TOTALS		136	284	35	72	16	1	5	30	30	32	1	2	.254	.37	
1993 RANK	MLB	C	not ranked -- didn't have 150 ABs in 1993														
1994 PROJECTIONS			27	53	8	12	1	0	1	5	6	6	0	0	.226	.340	

Dave Winfield No. 32/DH

Full name: David Mark Winfield
Bats: R **Throws:** R **HT:** 6–6 **WT:** 245
Born: 10–3–51, St. Paul, MN
High school: St. Paul Central (MN)
College: Minnesota

He is one of only three players with 450 HR, 3,000 hits, and 200 SB (the others are Hank Aaron and Willie Mays).

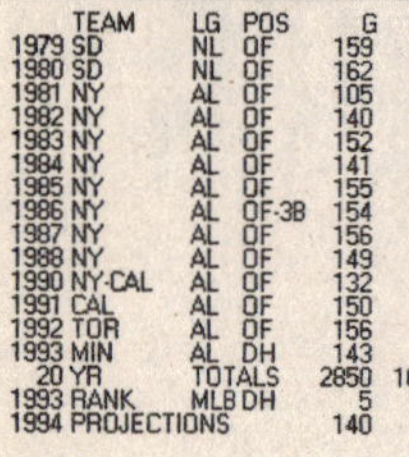
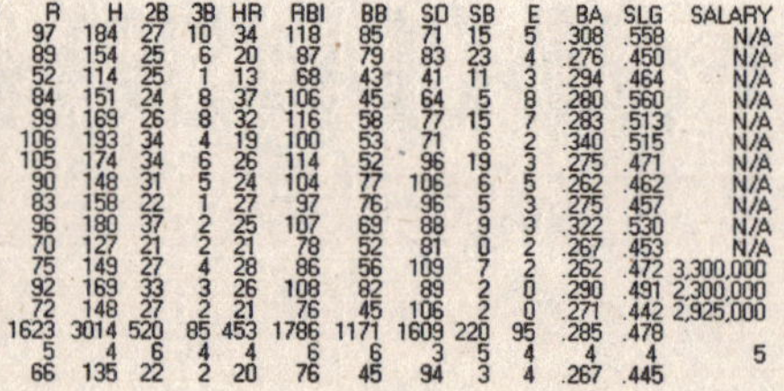

	TEAM	LG	POS	G	AB	R	H	2B	3B	HR	RBI	BB	SO	SB	E	BA	SLG	SALARY
1979	SD	NL	OF	159	597	97	184	27	10	34	118	85	71	15	5	.308	.558	N/A
1980	SD	NL	OF	162	558	89	154	25	6	20	87	79	83	23	4	.276	.450	N/A
1981	NY	AL	OF	105	388	52	114	25	1	13	68	43	41	11	3	.294	.464	N/A
1982	NY	AL	OF	140	539	84	151	24	8	37	106	45	64	5	8	.280	.560	N/A
1983	NY	AL	OF	152	598	99	169	26	8	32	116	58	77	15	7	.283	.513	N/A
1984	NY	AL	OF	141	567	106	193	34	4	19	100	53	71	6	2	.340	.515	N/A
1985	NY	AL	OF	155	633	105	174	34	6	26	114	52	96	19	3	.275	.471	N/A
1986	NY	AL	OF-3B	154	565	90	148	31	5	24	104	77	106	6	5	.262	.462	N/A
1987	NY	AL	OF	156	575	83	158	22	1	27	97	76	96	5	3	.275	.457	N/A
1988	NY	AL	OF	149	559	96	180	37	2	25	107	69	88	9	3	.322	.530	N/A
1990	NY-CAL	AL	OF	132	475	70	127	21	2	21	78	52	81	0	2	.267	.453	N/A
1991	CAL	AL	OF	150	568	75	149	27	4	28	86	56	109	7	2	.262	.472	3,300,000
1992	TOR	AL	OF	156	583	92	169	33	3	26	108	82	89	2	0	.290	.491	2,300,000
1993	MIN	AL	DH	143	547	72	148	27	2	21	76	45	106	2	0	.271	.442	2,925,000
20	YR	TOTALS		2850	10594	1623	3014	520	85	453	1786	1171	1609	220	95	.285	.478	
1993	RANK	MLB	DH	5	4	5	4	6	4	4	6	6	3	5	4	4	4	5
1994	PROJECTIONS			140	506	66	135	22	2	20	76	45	94	3	4	.267	.445	

Scott Erickson No. 19/P

Full name: Scott Gavin Erickson
Bats: R **Throws:** R **HT:** 6–4 **WT:** 222
Born: 2–2–68, Long Beach, CA
High school: Homestead (Cupertino, CA)
College: San Jose City and Arizona

Erickson's 19 losses led the majors, and was second to Pedro Ramos' 20 losses in Twins' history.

	TM	LG	POS	W	L	ERA	G	GS	CG	SH	SV	IP	H	R	ER	HR	BB	SO	SALARY
1990	MIN	AL	P	8	4	2.87	19	17	1	0	0	113.0	108	49	36	9	51	53	N/A
1991	MIN	AL	P	20	8	3.18	32	32	5	3	0	204.0	189	80	72	13	71	108	143,500
1992	MIN	AL	P	13	12	3.40	32	32	5	3	0	212.0	197	86	80	18	83	101	425,000
1993	MIN	AL	P	8	19	5.19	34	34	1	0	0	218.2	266	138	126	17	71	116	535,000
4	YR	TOTALS		49	43	3.78	117	115	12	6	0	747.2	760	353	314	57	276	378	
1993	RANK	MLB	Ps	99		245	145	12	79	69	102	28	265	245		97	98	221	130
1994	PROJECTIONS			9	11	3.98	28	27	2	1	0	181.0	190	91	80	14	68	90	

Eddie Guardado No. 18/P

Full name: Edward Adrian Guardado
Bats: R **Throws:** L **HT:** 6–0 **WT:** 193
Born: 10–2–70, Stockton, CA
College: San Joaquin Delta Junior
Guardado was 4–0 with a 1.24 ERA in ten starts at AA Nashville.

TM	LG	POS	W	L	ERA	G	GS	CG	SH	SV	IP	H	R	ER	HR	BB	SO	SALARY
1993 MIN	AL	P	3	8	6.18	19	16	0	0	0	94.2	123	68	65	13	36	46	109,000
1 YR	TOTAL		3	8	6.18	19	16	0	0	0	94.2	123	68	65	13	36	46	
1993 RANK	MLB Ps		209		278	258	123	125	69	102	156	281	277		243	162	244	236

Kevin Tapani No. 36/P

Full name: Kevin Ray Tapani
Bats: R **Throws:** R **HT:** 6–0 **WT:** 188
Born: 2–18–64, Des Moines, IA
High school: Escanaba Area (MI)
College: Central Michigan
After the All-Star break, Tapani was 9–4 with a 3.12 ERA. He hasn't missed a start due to injury in 105 straight outings.

TM	LG	POS	W	L	ERA	G	GS	CG	SH	SV	IP	H	R	ER	HR	BB	SO	SALARY
1989 NY	NL	P	0	0	3.68	3	0	0	0	0	7.1	5	3	3	1	4	2	N/A
1989 MIN	AL	P	2	2	3.86	5	5	0	0	0	32.2	34	15	14	2	8	21	N/A
1990 MIN	AL	P	12	8	4.07	28	28	1	1	0	159.1	164	75	72	12	29	101	N/A
1991 MIN	AL	P	16	9	2.99	34	34	4	1	0	244.0	225	84	81	23	40	135	197,500
1992 MIN	AL	P	16	11	3.97	34	34	4	1	0	220.0	226	103	97	17	48	138	485,000
1993 MIN	AL	P	12	15	4.43	36	35	3	1	0	225.2	243	123	111	21	57	150	2,000,000
5 YR	TOTALS		58	45	3.83	140	136	12	4	0	889.0	897	403	378	76	186	547	
1993 RANK	MLB Ps		43		181	124	6	37	23	102	21	197	186		142	41	121	68
1994 PROJECTIONS			8	8	4.24	23	22	1	0	0	138.0	147	71	65	11	31	90	

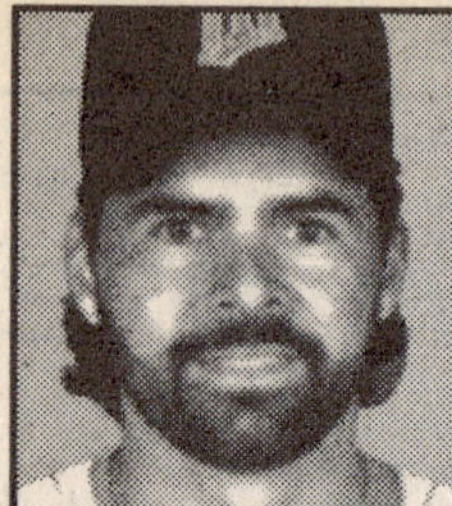

Rick Aguilera No. 38/P

Full name: Richard Warren Aguilera
Bats: R **Throws:** R **HT:** 6–5 **WT:** 203
Born: 12–31–61, San Gabriel, CA
High school: Edgewood (West Covina, CA)
College: Brigham Young

Opponents only hit .223 against Aguilera in '93, best on the team. He's had 30+ saves for four straight years.

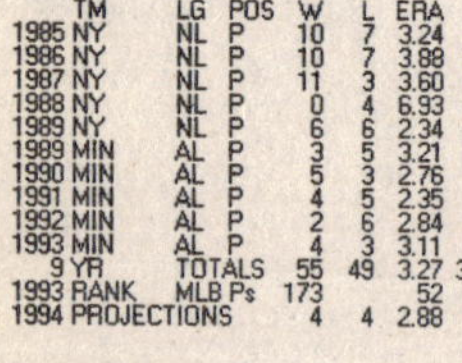
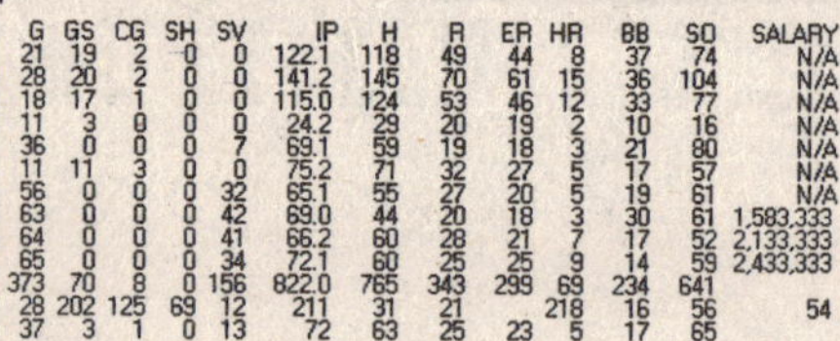

	TM	LG	POS	W	L	ERA	G	GS	CG	SH	SV	IP	H	R	ER	HR	BB	SO	SALARY
1985	NY	NL	P	10	7	3.24	21	19	2	0	0	122.1	118	49	44	8	37	74	N/A
1986	NY	NL	P	10	7	3.88	28	20	2	0	0	141.2	145	70	61	15	36	104	N/A
1987	NY	NL	P	11	3	3.60	18	17	1	0	0	115.0	124	53	46	12	33	77	N/A
1988	NY	NL	P	0	4	6.93	11	3	0	0	0	24.2	29	20	19	2	10	16	N/A
1989	NY	NL	P	6	6	2.34	36	0	0	0	7	69.1	59	19	18	3	21	80	N/A
1989	MIN	AL	P	3	5	3.21	11	11	3	0	0	75.2	71	32	27	5	17	57	N/A
1990	MIN	AL	P	5	3	2.76	56	0	0	0	32	65.1	55	27	20	5	19	61	N/A
1991	MIN	AL	P	4	5	2.35	63	0	0	0	42	69.0	44	20	18	3	30	61	1,583,333
1992	MIN	AL	P	2	6	2.84	64	0	0	0	41	66.2	60	28	21	7	17	52	2,133,333
1993	MIN	AL	P	4	3	3.11	65	0	0	0	34	72.1	60	25	25	9	14	59	2,433,333
9	YR	TOTALS		55	49	3.27	373	70	8	0	156	822.0	765	343	299	69	234	641	
1993	RANK	MLB Ps		173		52	28	202	125	69	12	211	31	21		218	16	56	54
1994	PROJECTIONS			4	4	2.88	37	3	1	0	13	72	63	25	23	5	17	65	

Tom Kelly No. 10/Mgr.

Full name: Jay Thomas Kelly
Bats: L **Throws:** L **HT:** 5–11 **WT:** 185
Born: 8–15–50, Graceville, MN
High school: St. Mary's (S. Amboy, NJ)
College: Mesa CC (AZ) and Monmouth College (NJ)

Kelly is one of just six active managers to lead a team to three 90-win seasons.

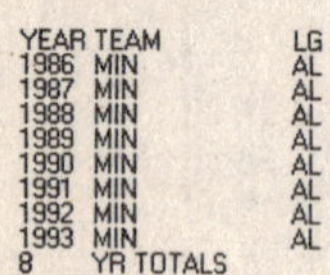

			REG. SEASON				PLAYOFF			CHAMP. SERIES			WORLD SERIES		
YEAR	TEAM	LG	W	L	PCT	POS	W	L	PCT	W	L	PCT	W	L	PCT
1986	MIN	AL	12	11	.522	6			---			---			---
1987	MIN	AL	85	77	.525	1			---	4	1	.800	4	3	.571
1988	MIN	AL	91	71	.562	2			---			---			---
1989	MIN	AL	80	82	.494	5			---			---			---
1990	MIN	AL	74	88	.457	7			---			---			---
1991	MIN	AL	95	67	.586	1			---	4	1	.800	4	3	.571
1992	MIN	AL	90	72	.556	2			---			---			---
1993	MIN	AL	71	91	.438	6			---			---			---
8	YR TOTALS		598	559	.517	24	0	0	---	8	2	.800	8	6	.571

Rich Becker No. 25/OF

Full name: Richard Goodhard Becker
Bats: S **Throws:** L **HT:** 5–10 **WT:** 180
Born: 2–1–72, Aurora, IL
High school: Aurora West (IL)
Becker was USA Today's Twins Minor League Player of the Year.

TEAM	LG	POS	G	AB	R	H	2B	3B	HR	RBI	BB	SO	SB	E	BA	SLG	SALARY
1993 MIN	AL	OF	3	7	3	2	2	0	0	0	5	4	1	1	.286	.571	N/A
1 YR	TOTAL		3	7	3	2	2	0	0	0	5	4	1	1	.286	.571	
1993 RANK	MLB OF		not ranked -- didn't have 150 ABs in 1993														

Larry Casian No. 48/P

Full name: Lawrence Paul Casian
Bats: R **Throws:** L **HT:** 6–0 **WT:** 173
Born: 10–28–65, Lynwood, CA
High school: Lakewood (CA)
College: Oral Roberts and Cal State Fullerton
Allowed just 3 earned runs in his first 39 games.

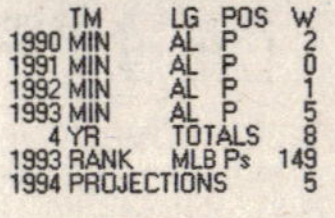

TM	LG	POS	W	L	ERA	G	GS	CG	SH	SV	IP	H	R	ER	HR	BB	SO	SALARY
1990 MIN	AL	P	2	1	3.22	5	3	0	0	0	22.1	26	9	8	2	4	11	N/A
1991 MIN	AL	P	0	0	7.36	15	0	0	0	0	18.1	28	16	15	4	7	6	N/A
1992 MIN	AL	P	1	0	2.7	6	0	0	0	0	6.2	7	2	2	0	1	2	N/A
1993 MIN	AL	P	5	3	3.02	54	0	0	0	1	56.2	59	23	19	1	14	31	115,000
4 YR	TOTALS		8	4	3.81	80	3	0	0	1	104.0	120	50	44	7	26	50	
1993 RANK	MLB Ps		149		46	66	202	125	69	70	263	172	61		2	38	207	222
1994 PROJECTIONS			5	3	2.95	66	0	0	0	1	64.0	67	26	21	0	16	36	

Mark Guthrie No. 53/P

Full name: Mark Andrew Guthrie
Bats: R **Throws:** L **HT:** 6–4 **WT:** 206
Born: 9–22–65, Buffalo, NY
High school: Venice (FL)
College: Louisiana State
Injury limited Guthrie to just 22 innings in '93.

TM	LG	POS	W	L	ERA	G	GS	CG	SH	SV	IP	H	R	ER	HR	BB	SO	SALARY
1989 MIN	AL	P	2	4	4.55	13	8	0	0	0	57.1	66	32	29	7	21	38	N/A
1990 MIN	AL	P	7	9	3.79	24	21	3	1	0	144.2	154	65	61	8	39	101	N/A
1991 MIN	AL	P	7	5	4.32	41	12	0	0	2	98.0	116	52	47	11	41	72	160,000
1992 MIN	AL	P	2	3	2.88	54	0	0	0	5	75.0	59	27	24	7	23	76	270,000
1993 MIN	AL	P	2	1	4.71	22	0	0	0	0	21.0	20	11	11	2	16	15	725,000
5 YR	TOTALS		20	22	3.91	154	41	3	1	7	396.0	415	187	172	35	140	302	
1993 RANK	MLB Ps		not ranked -- didn't have 50 IP in 1993															
1994 PROJECTIONS			5	5	4.03	29	11	1	0	0	87.0	96	42	39	7	32	62	

Chip Hale — No. 4/2B

Full name: Walter William Hale III
Bats: L **Throws:** R **HT:** 5–11 **WT:** 191
Born: 12–2–64, Santa Clara, CA
High school: Campolindo (Moraga, CA)
College: Arizona
Hale hit safely in the last ten games of '93.

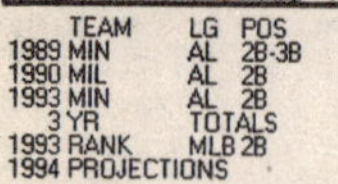
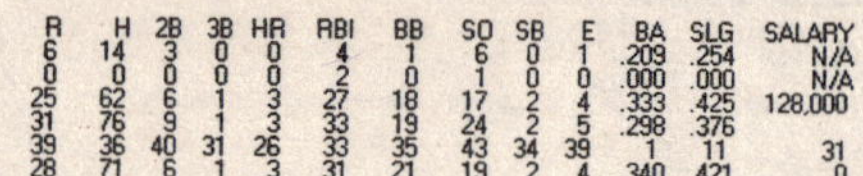

TEAM	LG	POS	G	AB	R	H	2B	3B	HR	RBI	BB	SO	SB	E	BA	SLG	SALARY
1989 MIN	AL	2B-3B	28	67	6	14	3	0	0	4	1	6	0	1	.209	.254	N/A
1990 MIL	AL	2B	1	2	0	0	0	0	0	2	0	1	0	0	.000	.000	N/A
1993 MIN	AL	2B	69	186	25	62	6	1	3	27	18	17	2	4	.333	.425	128,000
3 YR	TOTALS		98	255	31	76	9	1	3	33	19	24	2	5	.298	.376	
1993 RANK	MLB 2B		43	41	39	36	40	31	26	33	35	43	34	39	1	11	31
1994 PROJECTIONS			77	209	28	71	6	1	3	31	21	19	2	4	.340	.421	0

Denny Hocking — No. 7/SS

Full name: Dennis Lee Hocking
Bats: S **Throws:** R **HT:** 5–10 **WT:** 176
Born: 4–2–70, Torrance, CA
High school: West Torrance (CA)
College: El Camino CC (West Torrance, CA)
Hocking was a 52nd round draft choice.

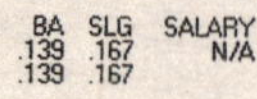

TEAM	LG	POS	G	AB	R	H	2B	3B	HR	RBI	BB	SO	SB	E	BA	SLG	SALARY
1993 MIN	AL	SS	15	36	7	5	1	0	0	0	6	8	1	1	.139	.167	N/A
1 YR	TOTAL		15	36	7	5	1	0	0	0	6	8	1	1	.139	.167	
1993 RANK	MLB SS		not ranked -- didn't have 150 ABs in 1993														

Scott Leius — No. 31/SS

Full name: Scott Thomas Leius
Bats: R **Throws:** R **HT:** 6–3 **WT:** 208
Born: 9–24–65, Yonkers, NY
High school: Mamaroneck (NY)
College: Concordia (Bronxville, NY)
Rotator cuff problems limited Leius' season.

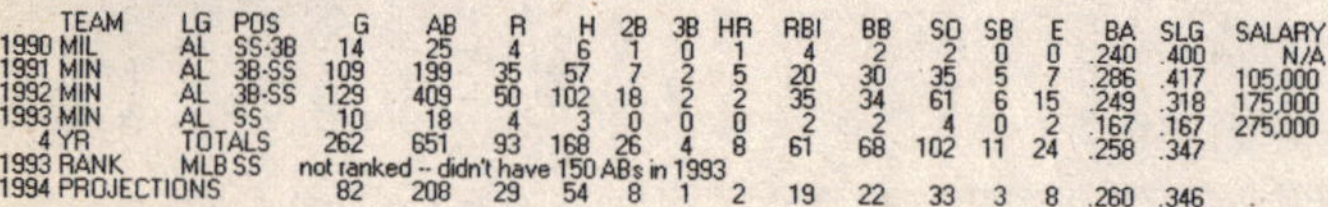

TEAM	LG	POS	G	AB	R	H	2B	3B	HR	RBI	BB	SO	SB	E	BA	SLG	SALARY
1990 MIL	AL	SS-3B	14	25	4	6	1	0	1	4	2	2	0	0	.240	.400	N/A
1991 MIN	AL	3B-SS	109	199	35	57	7	2	5	20	30	35	5	7	.286	.417	105,000
1992 MIN	AL	3B-SS	129	409	50	102	18	2	2	35	34	61	6	15	.249	.318	175,000
1993 MIN	AL	SS	10	18	4	3	0	0	0	2	2	4	0	2	.167	.167	275,000
4 YR	TOTALS		262	651	93	168	26	4	8	61	68	102	11	24	.258	.347	
1993 RANK	MLB SS		not ranked -- didn't have 150 ABs in 1993														
1994 PROJECTIONS			82	208	29	54	8	1	2	19	22	33	3	8	.260	.346	

Chito Martinez OF

Full name: Reynaldo Ignacio Martinez
Bats: L **Throws:** L **HT:** 5–10 **WT:** 185
Born: 12–19–65, Belize
High school: Brother Martinez (New Orleans, LA)
Martinez started '93 with Baltimore, but tore a ligament in his right knee in April.

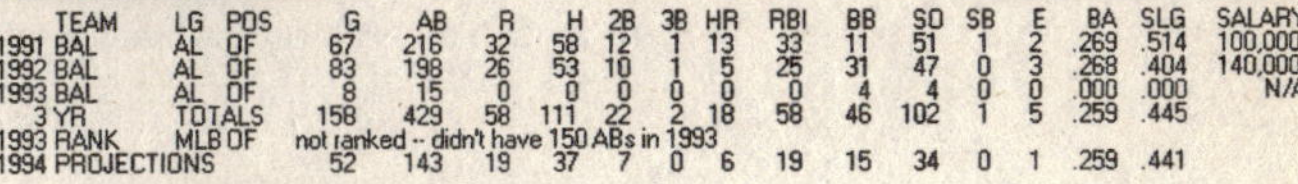

	TEAM	LG	POS	G	AB	R	H	2B	3B	HR	RBI	BB	SO	SB	E	BA	SLG	SALARY
1991	BAL	AL	OF	67	216	32	58	12	1	13	33	11	51	1	2	.269	.514	100,000
1992	BAL	AL	OF	83	198	26	53	10	1	5	25	31	47	0	3	.268	.404	140,000
1993	BAL	AL	OF	8	15	0	0	0	0	0	0	4	4	0	0	.000	.000	N/A
3	YR	TOTALS		158	429	58	111	22	2	18	58	46	102	1	5	.259	.445	
1993	RANK	MLB	OF	not ranked -- didn't have 150 ABs in 1993														
1994	PROJECTIONS			52	143	19	37	7	0	6	19	15	34	0	1	.259	.441	

David McCarty No. 8/OF

Full name: David Andrew McCarty
Bats: R **Throws:** L **HT:** 6–5 **WT:** 207
Born: 11–23–69, Houston, TX
High school: Sharpstown Senior (Houston, TX)
College: Stanford
Hit safely in 18 of his first 19 major league games.

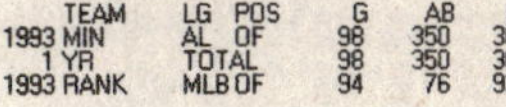
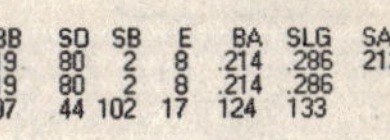

	TEAM	LG	POS	G	AB	R	H	2B	3B	HR	RBI	BB	SO	SB	E	BA	SLG	SALARY
1993	MIN	AL	OF	98	350	36	75	15	2	2	21	19	80	2	8	.214	.286	212,500
1	YR	TOTAL		98	350	36	75	15	2	2	21	19	80	2	8	.214	.286	
1993	RANK	MLB	OF	94	76	93	88	81	76	114	123	107	44	102	17	124	133	105

Derek Parks No. 16/C

Full name: Derek Gavin Parks
Bats: R **Throws:** R **HT:** 6–0 **WT:** 217
Born: 9–29–68, Covina, CA
High school: Montclair (CA)
Parks was the starting catcher in the '93 AAA All-Star game.

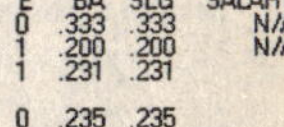

	TEAM	LG	POS	G	AB	R	H	2B	3B	HR	RBI	BB	SO	SB	E	BA	SLG	SALARY
1992	MIN	AL	C	7	6	1	2	0	0	0	0	1	1	0	0	.333	.333	N/A
1993	MIN	AL	C	7	20	3	4	0	0	0	1	1	2	0	1	.200	.200	N/A
2	YR	TOTALS		14	26	4	6	0	0	0	1	2	3	0	1	.231	.231	
1993	RANK	MLB	C	not ranked -- didn't have 150 ABs in 1993														
1994	PROJECTIONS			9	17	2	4	0	0	0	0	1	2	0	0	.235	.235	

Scott Stahoviak — No. 37/IF

Full name: Scott Edmund Stahoviak
Bats: L **Throws:** R **HT:** 6–5 **WT:** 208
Born: 3–6–70, Waukegan, IL
High school: Carmel Mundelin (IL)
College: Creighton
Stahoviak hit .456 for Creighton.

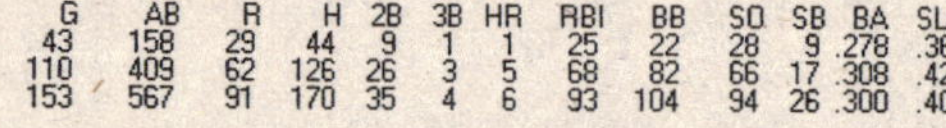

TEAM	CL	POS	G	AB	R	H	2B	3B	HR	RBI	BB	SO	SB	BA	SLG
1991 VISALIA	A	3B	43	158	29	44	9	1	1	25	22	28	9	.278	.367
1992 VISALIA	A	3B	110	409	62	126	26	3	5	68	82	66	17	.308	.423
2 YR	TOTAL		153	567	91	170	35	4	6	93	104	94	26	.300	.407

Mike Trombley — No. 21/P

Full name: Michael Scott Trombley
Bats: R **Throws:** R **HT:** 6–2 **WT:** 208
Born: 4–14–67, Springfield, MA
High school: Minnechaug Reg. (Wilbraham, MA)
College: Duke
Trombley was 3–1, with a 4.10 ERA, in relief.

TM	LG	POS	W	L	ERA	G	GS	CG	SH	SV	IP	H	R	ER	HR	BB	SO	SALARY
1992 MIN	AL	P	3	2	3.30	10	7	0	0	0	46.1	43	20	17	5	17	38	109,000
1993 MIN	AL	P	6	6	4.88	44	10	0	0	2	114.1	131	72	62	15	41	85	124,000
2 YR	TOTALS		9	8	4.43	54	17	0	0	2	160.2	174	92	79	20	58	123	
1993 Rank	MLB Ps		128		223	99	157	125	69	55	123	243	243		232	142	87	214
1994 PROJECTIONS			7	8	5.11	61	11	0	0	3	148.0	175	98	84	20	53	108	

Carl Willis — No. 51/P

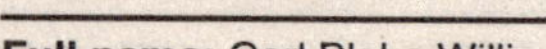

Full name: Carl Blake Willis
Bats: L **Throws:** R **HT:** 6–4 **WT:** 213
Born: 12–28–60, Danville, VA
High school: Piedmont Acad. (Providence, NC)
College: North Carolina–Wilmington
Allowed just 5 earned runs in his last 33 games.

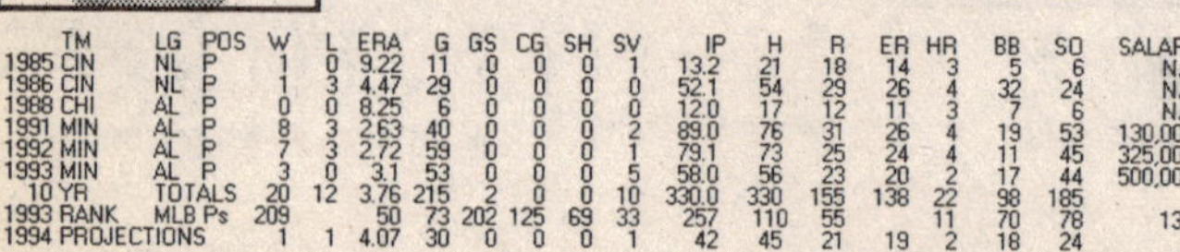

TM	LG	POS	W	L	ERA	G	GS	CG	SH	SV	IP	H	R	ER	HR	BB	SO	SALARY
1985 CIN	NL	P	1	0	9.22	11	0	0	0	1	13.2	21	18	14	3	5	6	N/A
1986 CIN	NL	P	1	3	4.47	29	0	0	0	0	52.1	54	29	26	4	32	24	N/A
1988 CHI	AL	P	0	0	8.25	6	0	0	0	0	12.0	17	12	11	3	7	6	N/A
1991 MIN	AL	P	8	3	2.63	40	0	0	0	2	89.0	76	31	26	4	19	53	130,000
1992 MIN	AL	P	7	3	2.72	59	0	0	0	1	79.1	73	25	24	4	11	45	325,000
1993 MIN	AL	P	3	0	3.1	53	0	0	0	5	58.0	56	23	20	2	17	44	500,000
10 YR	TOTALS		20	12	3.76	215	2	0	0	10	330.0	330	155	138	22	98	185	
1993 RANK	MLB Ps		209		50	73	202	125	69	33	257	110	55		11	70	78	132
1994 PROJECTIONS			1	1	4.07	30	0	0	0	1	42	45	21	19	2	18	24	

New York YANKEES

1994 Scouting Report

Hitting: (1993/.279, first in AL; 178 HR, second in AL)

Wade Boggs surprised the critics by having a strong 1993 campaign, hitting .302 for the Yankees. But Boggs is the slowest leadoff hitter in baseball, and the Yankees are looking for a hitter who could allow Boggs to hit second. Don Mattingly had a strong 1993, too, hitting .291. But he tailed off toward the end of the season, hitting just .250 in September and October.

Mike Stanley was a big surprise in 1993. The catcher slugged 26 HR, a career high. Can he repeat that feat? Danny Tartabull has been a big disappointment–he's been injury plagued, and there are whispers he won't play the outfield. He's available for the right price.

Pitching: (1993/4.35 ERA, ninth in AL)

Adding Jimmy Key has bolstered the Yankee pitching staff. But Jim Abbott's been a disappointment. If he learns a new pitch, he could improve enough to boost the Yankees into first. Melido Perez was a disappointment in 1993, but he could rebound in 1994.

New York is looking to shore up its bullpen. The Yanks bid adieu to Steve Farr, and Steve Howe showed signs that age is finally catching up with him. The Yankees got Lee Smith late in 1993, but did not offer him salary arbitration. Xavier Hernandez, obtained from Houston, may figure in a major role.

Defense: (1993/.983 pct., 5th in AL)

Don Mattingly is a perennial Gold Glover at first base. Mike Stanley ranked first in fielding percentage among AL catchers. Paul O'Neill is an above-average defensive outfielder. Wade Boggs led AL third basemen in fielding percentage.

1994 Prospects:

The Yankees look like a playoff team in 1994. The bullpen is a big question mark—but it won't be worse than it was in 1993, when the Yankees won 88 games. Abbott and Perez won't both be as bad in 1994 as they were in 1993, and the Yanks have plenty of offense.

Team Directory

Principal Owner: G. M. Steinbrenner III
General Mgr.: Gene Michael
Director of P.R.: Jeff Idelson
Exec. VP, Operations: John C. Lawn
VP, Player Dev. & Scouting: Bill Livesey
Traveling Secretary: David Szen

Minor League Affiliates:

Level	Team/League	1993 Record
AAA	Columbus, Oh. – International	78–62
AA	Albany/Colonie – Eastern	70–68
A	Prince William – Carolina	67–73
	Greensboro – South Atlantic	85–56
	Oneonta – New York/Penn.	36–40
Rookie	Tampa Yankees – Gulf Coast	30–29

1993 Review

	Home		Away			Home		Away			Home		Away	
vs AL East	W	L	W	L	vs AL Cent.	W	L	W	L	vs AL West	W	L	W	L
Baltimore	4	3	3	3	Chicago	4	2	4	2	California	4	2	2	4
Boston	4	3	3	3	Cleveland	4	2	3	4	Oakland	4	2	2	4
Detroit	5	1	4	3	Kansas City	4	2	2	4	Seattle	4	2	3	3
Toronto	3	4	2	4	Milwaukee	4	2	5	2	Texas	2	4	1	5
					Minnesota	4	2	4	2					
Total	16	11	12	13		20	10	18	14		14	10	8	

1993 finish: 88–74 (50–31 home, 38–43 away), second in AL East, 7 games behind

1994 Schedule

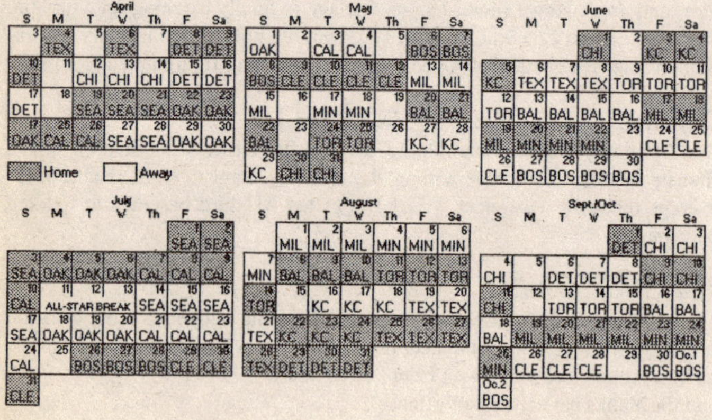

April

S	M	T	W	Th	F	Sa
3	4 TEX	5	6 TEX	7	8 DET	9 DET
10 DET	11	12 CHI	13 CHI	14 CHI	15 DET	16 DET
17 DET	18	19 SEA	20 SEA	21 SEA	22 OAK	23 OAK
24 OAK	25 CAL	26 CAL	27 SEA	28 SEA	29 OAK	30 OAK

Home Away

May

S	M	T	W	Th	F	Sa
1 OAK	2	3 CAL	4 CAL	5	6 BOS	7 BOS
8 BOS	9 CLE	10 CLE	11 CLE	12 CLE	13 MIL	14 MIL
15 MIL	16	17 MIN	18 MIN	19	20 BAL	21 BAL
22 BAL	23	24 TOR	25 TOR	26	27 KC	28 KC
29 KC	30 CHI	31 CHI				

June

S	M	T	W	Th	F	Sa
			1 CHI	2	3 KC	4 KC
5 KC	6 TEX	7 TEX	8 TEX	9 TOR	10 TOR	11 TOR
12 TOR	13 BAL	14 BAL	15 BAL	16 BAL	17 MIL	18 MIL
19 MIL	20 MIN	21 MIN	22 MIN	23	24 CLE	25 CLE
26 CLE	27 BOS	28 BOS	29 BOS	30 BOS		

July

S	M	T	W	Th	F	Sa
					1 SEA	2 SEA
3 SEA	4 OAK	5 OAK	6 OAK	7 CAL	8 CAL	9 CAL
10 CAL	11 ALL-STAR BREAK	12	13	14 SEA	15 SEA	16 SEA
17 SEA	18 OAK	19 OAK	20 OAK	21 CAL	22 CAL	23 CAL
24 CAL	25	26 BOS	27 BOS	28 BOS	29 CLE	30 CLE
31 CLE						

August

S	M	T	W	Th	F	Sa
	1 MIL	2 MIL	3 MIL	4 MIN	5 MIN	6 MIN
7 MIN	8 BAL	9 BAL	10 BAL	11 TOR	12 TOR	13 TOR
14 TOR	15	16 KC	17 KC	18 KC	19 TEX	20 TEX
21 TEX	22 KC	23 KC	24 KC	25 TEX	26 TEX	27 TEX
28 TEX	29 DET	30 DET	31 DET			

Sept./Oct.

S	M	T	W	Th	F	Sa
				1 DET	2 CHI	3 CHI
4 CHI	5	6 DET	7 DET	8 DET	9 CHI	10 CHI
11 CHI	12	13 TOR	14 TOR	15 TOR	16 BAL	17 BAL
18 BAL	19 MIL	20 MIL	21 MIL	22 MIL	23 MIN	24 MIN
25 MIN	26 CLE	27 CLE	28 CLE	29	30 BOS	Oc.1 BOS
Oc.2 BOS						

NEW YORK YANKEES 1994 ROSTER

Manager: Buck Showalter
Coaches: Clete Boyer, 3B (6); Rick Down, batting (48); Tony Cloninger (40); Willie Randolph; Billy Connors, pitching; Brian Butterfield.

No.	PITCHERS	B	T	HT	WT	DOB	BIRTHPLACE	RESIDENCE
25	Abbott, Jim	L	L	6–3	210	9–19–67	Flint, MI	New York, NY
43	Assenmacher, Paul	L	L	6–3	210	12–10–60	Allen Park, MI	Stone Mountain, GA
35	Gibson, Paul	R	L	6–1	185	1–4–60	Center Moriches, NY	Center Moriches, NY
	Hernandez, Xavier	L	R	6–2	185	8–16–65	Port Arthur, TX	Missouri City, TX
34	Hitchcock, Sterling	L	L	6–1	192	4–29–71	Fayetteville, NC	Seffner, FL
57	Howe, Steve	L	L	5–11	198	3–10–58	Pontiac, MI	Whitefish, MT
53	Hutton, Mark	R	R	6–6	240	2–6–70	S. Adelaide, S. Aust.	W. Lakes, S. Aust.
28	Kamieniecki, Scott	R	R	6–0	195	4–19–64	Mt. Clemens, MI	Flint, MI
22	Key, Jimmy	R	L	6–1	185	4–22–61	Huntsville, AL	Tarpon Springs, FL
	Militello, Sam	R	R	6–3	195	11–26–69	Tampa, FL	Tampa, FL
54	Munoz, Bobby	R	R	6–7	237	3–3–68	Rio Pedras, PR	Hialeah, FL
33	Perez, Melido	R	R	6–4	210	2–15–66	San Cristobal, DR	Costa Verde, DR
	Rivera, Mariano	R	R	6–4	168	11–29–69	Panama City, Panama	LaChorrera, Panama
27	Wickman, Bob	R	R	6–1	212	2–6–69	Green Bay, WI	Abrams, WI
No.	**CATCHERS**	**B**	**T**	**HT**	**WT**	**DOB**	**BIRTHPLACE**	**RESIDENCE**
38	Nokes, Matt	L	R	6–1	210	10–31–63	San Diego, CA	San Diego, CA
20	Stanley, Mike	R	R	6–0	192	6–25–63	Ft. Lauderdale, FL	Oviedo, FL
No.	**INFIELDERS**	**B**	**T**	**HT**	**WT**	**DOB**	**BIRTHPLACE**	**RESIDENCE**
12	Boggs, Wade	L	R	6–2	197	6–15–58	Omaha, NE	Tampa, FL
	Davis, Russell	R	R	6–0	170	9–13–69	Birmingham, AL	Hueytown, AL
	Eenhoorn, Robert	R	R	6–3	170	2–9–68	Rotterdam, Neth.	Rotterdam, Neth.
	Fox, Andy	L	R	6–4	185	1–12–71	Sacramento, CA	Sacramento, CA
2	Gallego, Mike	R	R	5–8	175	10–31–60	Whittier, CA	Yorba Linda, CA
	Jordan, Kevin	R	R	6–1	185	10–9–69	San Francisco, CA	San Francisco, CA
14	Kelly, Pat	R	R	6–0	182	10–14–67	Philadelphia, PA	Clearwater Beach, FL
13	Leyritz, Jim	R	R	6–0	195	12–27–63	Lakewood, OH	Plantation, FL
24	Maas, Kevin	L	L	6–3	204	1–20–65	Castro Valley, CA	Castro Valley, CA
23	Mattingly, Don	L	L	6–0	200	4–20–61	Evansville, IN	Evansville, IN
	Seefried, Tate	L	R	6–4	180	4–22–72	Seattle, WA	El Segundo, CA
	Silvestri, Dave	R	R	6–0	196	9–29–67	St. Louis, MO	Chesterfield, MO
18	Velarde, Randy	R	R	6–0	192	11–24–62	Midland, TX	Midland, TX
No.	**OUTFIELDERS**	**B**	**T**	**HT**	**WT**	**DOB**	**BIRTHPLACE**	**RESIDENCE**
39	Humphreys, Michael	R	R	6–0	195	4–10–67	Dallas, TX	Desoto, TX
	Leach, Jalal	L	L	6–2	200	3–14–69	San Francisco, CA	Novato, CA
	Masse, Billy	R	R	6–1	185	7–6–66	Manchester, CT	Wethersfield, CT
21	O'Neill, Paul	L	L	6–4	215	2–25–63	Columbus, OH	Cincinnati, OH
	Robertson, Jason	L	L	6–2	200	3–24–71	Chicago, IL	Country Club Hills, IL
45	Tartabull, Danny	R	R	6–1	204	10–30–62	Miami, FL	Malibu, CA
51	Williams, Bernie	S	R	6–2	200	9–13–68	San Juan, PR	Guayhabo, PR
36	Williams, Gerald	R	R	6–2	190	8–10–66	New Orleans, LA	LaPlace, LA

Yankee Stadium (57,545, grass)
Tickets: 212–293–6000
Ticket prices:
- $17 (lower and loge box seats)
- $15.50 (tier box seats)
- $14.50 (lower reserves)
- $11.50 (tier reserves)
- $6.50 (bleachers)

Field Dimensions (from home plate)
- To left field at foul line, 318 feet
- To center field, 408 feet
- To right field at foul line, 314 feet
- (OF wall–7'5" in LF, 7'3" in CF, 9' in RF)

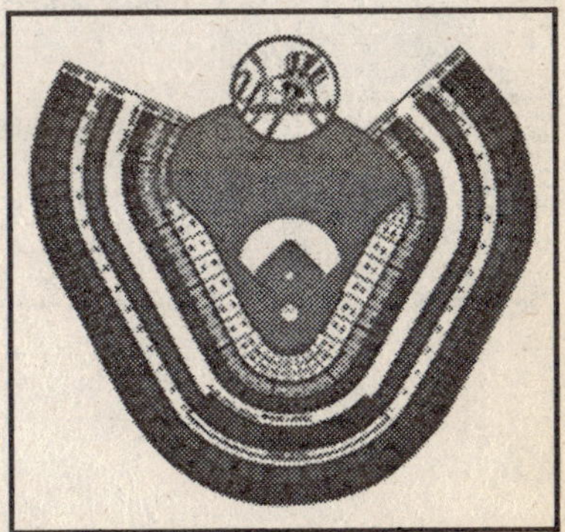

Wade Boggs No. 12/3B

Full name: Wade Anthony Boggs
Bats: L **Throws:** R **HT:** 6–2 **WT:** 197
Born: 6–15–58, Omaha, NE
High School: H.B. Plant (Tampa, FL)
College: Hillsborough CC (FL)

140 of Boggs' 169 hits were singles. He hit .291 with runners in scoring position and .400 with the bases loaded. He hit .375 as a DH.

	TEAM	LG	POS	G	AB	R	H	2B	3B	HR	RBI	BB	SO	SB	E	BA	SLG	SALARY
1982	BOS	AL	3B	104	338	51	118	14	1	5	44	35	21	1	8	.349	.441	N/A
1983	BOS	AL	3B	153	582	100	210	44	7	5	74	92	36	3	27	.361	.486	N/A
1984	BOS	AL	3B	158	625	109	203	31	4	6	55	89	44	3	20	.325	.416	N/A
1985	BOS	AL	3B	161	653	107	240	42	3	8	78	96	61	2	17	.368	.478	N/A
1986	BOS	AL	3B	149	580	107	207	47	2	8	71	105	44	0	19	.357	.486	N/A
1987	BOS	AL	3B	147	551	108	200	40	6	24	89	105	48	1	14	.363	.588	N/A
1988	BOS	AL	3B	155	584	128	214	45	6	5	58	125	34	2	11	.366	.490	N/A
1989	BOS	AL	3B	156	621	113	205	51	7	3	54	107	51	2	17	.330	.449	N/A
1990	BOS	AL	3B	155	619	89	187	44	5	6	63	87	68	0	20	.302	.418	N/A
1991	BOS	AL	3B	144	546	93	181	42	2	8	51	89	32	1	12	.332	.460	2,700,000
1992	BOS	AL	3B	143	514	62	133	22	4	7	50	74	31	1	15	.259	.358	2,700,000
1993	NY	AL	3B	143	560	83	169	26	1	2	59	74	49	0	12	.302	.363	2,950,000
12	YR	TOTALS		1768	6773	1150	2267	448	48	87	746	1078	519	16	192	.335	.454	
1993	RANK	MLB	3B	12	6	7	5	16	21	34	17	3	25	38	19	4	34	5
1994	PROJECTIONS			130	470	65	140	20	2	4	51	61	33	0	11	.298	.379	

Mike Gallego No. 2/IF

Full name: Michael Anthony Gallego
Bats: R **Throws:** R **HT:** 5–8 **WT:** 175
Born: 10–31–60, Whittier, CA
High School: St. Paul (Yorba Linda, CA)
College: UCLA

1993's .283 BA, 54 RBI were career bests.

	TEAM	LG	POS	G	AB	R	H	2B	3B	HR	RBI	BB	SO	SB	E	BA	SLG	SALARY
1987	OAK	AL	2B	72	124	18	31	6	0	2	14	12	21	0	8	.250	.347	N/A
1988	OAK	AL	2B	129	277	38	58	8	0	2	20	34	53	2	8	.209	.260	N/A
1989	OAK	AL	SS	133	357	45	90	14	2	3	30	35	43	7	19	.252	.328	N/A
1990	OAK	AL	2B	140	389	36	80	13	2	3	34	35	50	5	13	.206	.272	N/A
1991	OAK	AL	2B	159	482	67	119	15	4	12	49	67	84	6	12	.247	.369	565,000
1992	NY	AL	2B	53	173	24	44	7	1	3	14	20	22	0	6	.254	.358	1,950,000
1993	NY	AL	SS	119	403	63	114	20	1	10	54	50	65	3	13	.283	.412	1,575,000
9	YR	TOTALS		901	2319	306	562	90	11	36	228	266	358	24	71	.242	.337	
1993	RANK	MLB	SS	22	21	14	21	16	29	7	12	10	15	29	22	12	10	11
1994	PROJECTIONS			130	383	48	94	15	1	5	39	40	52	5	15	.245	.337	

Pat Kelly No. 14/2B

Full name: Patrick Franklin Kelly
Bats: R **Throws:** R **HT:** 6–0 **WT:** 182
Born: 10–14–67, Philadelphia, PA
High School: Catasaqua (PA)
College: West Chester State (PA)

1993 was the best season of Kelly's short major league career. He hit .273 with 7 HR, 51 RBI and 14 stolen bases, all career highs.

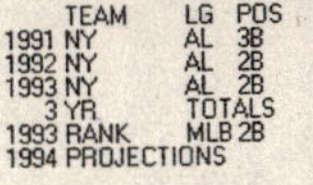
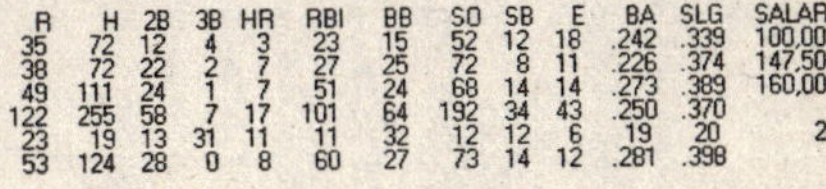

	TEAM	LG	POS	G	AB	R	H	2B	3B	HR	RBI	BB	SO	SB	E	BA	SLG	SALARY
1991	NY	AL	3B	96	298	35	72	12	4	3	23	15	52	12	18	.242	.339	100,000
1992	NY	AL	2B	106	318	38	72	22	2	7	27	25	72	8	11	.226	.374	147,500
1993	NY	AL	2B	127	406	49	111	24	1	7	51	24	68	14	14	.273	.389	160,000
3	YR	TOTALS		329	1022	122	255	58	7	17	101	64	192	34	43	.250	.370	
1993	RANK	MLB	2B	17	21	23	19	13	31	11	11	32	12	12	6	19	20	26
1994	PROJECTIONS			137	442	53	124	28	0	8	60	27	73	14	12	.281	.398	

Jim Leyritz No. 13/IF–OF

Full name: James Joseph Leyritz
Bats: R **Throws:** R **HT:** 6–0 **WT:** 195
Born: 12–27–63, Lakewood, OH
College: Middle Georgia JC and Kentucky

Leyritz' .309 BA, 14 HR, and 53 RBIs in 1993 were all career highs. He hit .484 in April.

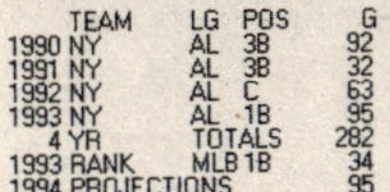
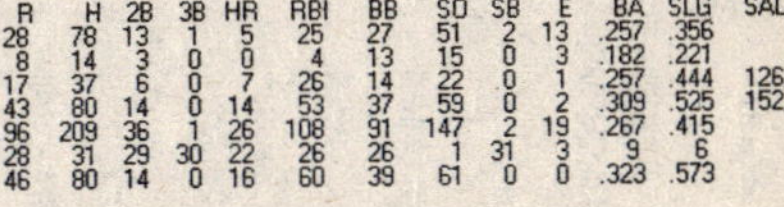

	TEAM	LG	POS	G	AB	R	H	2B	3B	HR	RBI	BB	SO	SB	E	BA	SLG	SALARY
1990	NY	AL	3B	92	303	28	78	13	1	5	25	27	51	2	13	.257	.356	N/A
1991	NY	AL	3B	32	77	8	14	3	0	0	4	13	15	0	3	.182	.221	N/A
1992	NY	AL	C	63	144	17	37	6	0	7	26	14	22	0	1	.257	.444	126,500
1993	NY	AL	1B	95	259	43	80	14	0	14	53	37	59	0	2	.309	.525	152,000
4	YR	TOTALS		282	783	96	209	36	1	26	108	91	147	2	19	.267	.415	
1993	RANK	MLB	1B	34	33	28	31	29	30	22	26	26	1	31	3	9	6	30
1994	PROJECTIONS			95	248	46	80	14	0	16	60	39	61	0	0	.323	.573	

Don Mattingly No. 23/1B

Full name: Donald Arthur Mattingly
Bats: L **Throws:** L **HT:** 6–0 **WT:** 200
Born: 4–20–61, Evansville, IN
High School: Ritz Memorial (Evansville, IN)
Mattingly's 1993 season–with a .291 BA, 17 HR and 86 RBI–was his best since '89. He also set a team record for fielding percentage by a first baseman (.998).

	TEAM	LG	POS	G	AB	R	H	2B	3B	HR	RBI	BB	SO	SB	E	BA	SLG	SALARY
1982	NY	AL	OF	7	12	0	2	0	0	0	1	0	1	0	0	.167	.167	N/A
1983	NY	AL	OF	91	279	34	79	15	4	4	32	21	31	0	3	.283	.409	N/A
1984	NY	AL	1B	153	603	91	207	44	2	23	110	41	33	1	6	.343	.537	N/A
1985	NY	AL	1B	159	652	107	211	48	3	35	145	56	41	2	7	.324	.567	N/A
1986	NY	AL	1B	162	677	117	238	53	2	31	113	53	35	0	7	.352	.573	N/A
1987	NY	AL	1B	141	569	93	186	38	2	30	115	51	38	1	5	.327	.559	N/A
1988	NY	AL	1B	144	599	94	186	37	0	18	88	41	29	1	9	.311	.462	N/A
1989	NY	AL	1B	158	631	79	191	37	2	23	113	51	30	3	7	.303	.477	N/A
1990	NY	AL	1B	102	394	40	101	16	0	5	42	28	20	1	3	.256	.335	N/A
1991	NY	AL	1B	152	587	64	169	35	0	9	68	46	42	2	5	.288	.394	3,420,000
1992	NY	AL	1B	157	640	89	184	40	0	14	86	39	43	3	4	.288	.416	3,620,000
1993	NY	AL	1B	134	530	78	154	27	2	17	86	61	42	0	3	.291	.445	3,820,000
12	YR	TOTALS		1560	6173	886	1908	390	17	209	999	488	385	14	59	.309	.479	
1993	RANK	MLB	1B	21	14	13	12	12	11	17	13	16	1	31	7	15	20	6
1994	PROJECTIONS			129	503	60	141	26	0	10	65	45	34	1	3	.28	.396	

Paul O'Neill No. 21/OF

Full name: Paul Andrew O'Neill
Bats: L **Throws:** L **HT:** 6–4 **WT:** 215
Born: 2–25–63, Columbus, OH
High School: Brookhaven (Columbus, OH)
College: Otterbein (OH)
O'Neill hit a career high .311 with 20 HR and 75 RBI. His 34 doubles led the Yankees, and his 155 hits was second behind Boggs.

	TEAM	LG	POS	G	AB	R	H	2B	3B	HR	RBI	BB	SO	SB	E	BA	SLG	SALARY
1985	CIN	NL	OF	5	12	1	4	1	0	0	1	0	2	0	0	.333	.417	N/A
1986	CIN	NL	OF	3	2	0	0	0	0	0	0	1	1	0	0	.000	.000	N/A
1987	CIN	NL	OF	84	160	24	41	14	1	7	28	18	29	2	4	.256	.488	N/A
1988	CIN	NL	OF	145	485	58	122	25	3	16	73	38	65	8	6	.252	.414	N/A
1989	CIN	NL	OF	117	428	49	118	24	2	15	74	46	64	20	4	.276	.446	N/A
1990	CIN	NL	OF	145	503	59	136	28	0	16	78	53	103	13	2	.270	.421	N/A
1991	CIN	NL	OF	152	532	71	136	36	0	28	91	73	107	12	2	.256	.481	975,000
1992	CIN	NL	OF	148	496	59	122	19	1	14	66	77	85	6	1	.246	.373	2,833,333
1993	NY	AL	OF	141	498	71	155	34	1	20	75	44	69	2	2	.311	.504	3,833,333
9	YR	TOTALS		940	3116	392	834	181	8	116	486	350	525	63	21	.268	.443	
1993	RANK	MLB	OF	38	44	45	26	13	97	23	25	46	54	102	97	13	17	12
1994	PROJECTIONS			143	495	62	137	29	1	17	75	45	79	7	3	.277	.446	

Mike Stanley No. 20/C

Full name: Michael Robert Stanley
Bats: R **Throws:** R **HT:** 6–0 **WT:** 192
Born: 6–25–63, Ft. Lauderdale, FL
High School: St. Thomas Aquinas (FL)
College: Florida

In 1993, Stanley became one of only ten major league catchers ever to hit .300 with 25 HRs. His 14 HR vs LHP led the team.

TEAM	LG	POS	G	AB	R	H	2B	3B	HR	RBI	BB	SO	SB	E	BA	SLG	SALARY
1986 TEX	AL	3B	15	30	4	10	3	0	1	1	3	7	1	1	.333	.533	N/A
1987 TEX	AL	C	78	216	34	59	8	1	6	37	31	48	3	7	.273	.403	N/A
1988 TEX	AL	C	94	249	21	57	8	0	3	27	37	62	0	4	.229	.297	N/A
1989 TEX	AL	C	67	122	9	30	3	1	1	11	12	29	1	3	.246	.311	N/A
1990 TEX	AL	C	103	189	21	47	8	1	2	19	30	25	1	4	.249	.333	N/A
1991 TEX	AL	C	95	181	25	45	13	1	3	25	34	44	0	6	.249	.381	145,000
1992 NY	AL	C	68	173	24	43	7	0	8	27	33	45	0	6	.249	.428	145,000
1993 NY	AL	C	130	423	70	129	17	1	26	84	57	85	1	3	.305	.534	675,000
8 YR	TOTALS		650	1583	208	420	67	5	50	231	237	345	7	34	.265	.409	
1993 RANK	MLB	C	11	10	5	6	17	11	4	3	3	9	21	34	3	4	19
1994 PROJECTIONS			144	472	78	143	18	1	29	94	63	94	1	3	.303	.530	

Danny Tartabull No. 45/DH

Full name: Danilo Tartabull
Bats: R **Throws:** R **HT:** 6–1 **WT:** 204
Born: 10–30–62, Miami, FL
High School: Carol City (Miami, FL)

Tartabull tied his career high with 102 RBI, despite missing a month with a bruised kidney (suffered in an outfield collision) and being plagued with a variety of other injuries.

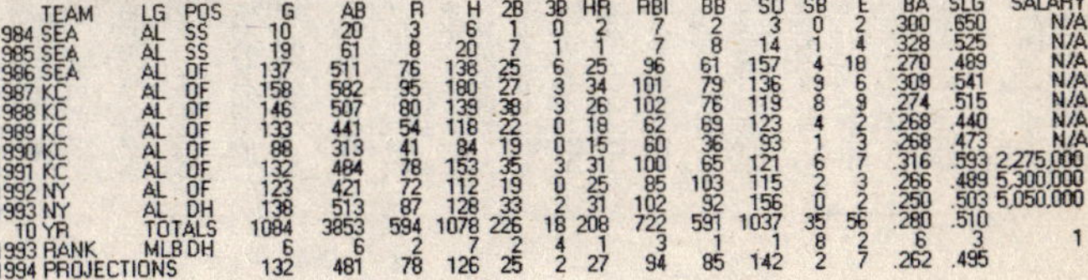

TEAM	LG	POS	G	AB	R	H	2B	3B	HR	RBI	BB	SO	SB	E	BA	SLG	SALARY
1984 SEA	AL	SS	10	20	3	6	1	0	2	7	2	3	0	2	.300	.650	N/A
1985 SEA	AL	SS	19	61	8	20	7	1	1	7	8	14	1	4	.328	.525	N/A
1986 SEA	AL	OF	137	511	76	138	25	6	25	96	61	157	4	18	.270	.489	N/A
1987 KC	AL	OF	158	582	95	180	27	3	34	101	79	136	9	6	.309	.541	N/A
1988 KC	AL	OF	146	507	80	139	38	3	26	102	76	119	8	9	.274	.515	N/A
1989 KC	AL	OF	133	441	54	118	22	0	18	62	69	123	4	2	.268	.440	N/A
1990 KC	AL	OF	88	313	41	84	19	0	15	60	36	93	1	3	.268	.473	N/A
1991 KC	AL	OF	132	484	78	153	35	3	31	100	65	121	6	7	.316	.593	2,275,000
1992 NY	AL	OF	123	421	72	112	19	0	25	85	103	115	2	3	.266	.489	5,300,000
1993 NY	AL	DH	138	513	87	128	33	2	31	102	92	156	0	2	.250	.503	5,050,000
10 YR	TOTALS		1084	3853	594	1078	226	18	208	722	591	1037	35	56	.280	.510	
1993 RANK	MLB	DH	6	6	2	7	2	4	1	3	1	1	8	2	6	3	1
1994 PROJECTIONS			132	481	78	126	25	2	27	94	85	142	2	7	.262	.495	

Bernie Williams No. 51/OF

Full name: Bernabe Williams
Bats: S **Throws:** R **HT:** 6–2 **WT:** 200
Born: 9–13–68, San Juan, PR
High School: Escuela Libre de Musica (San Juan, PR)

Williams had a 21-game hitting streak from August 1 to August 23, longest by a Yankee since Don Mattingly's 23-game streak in '86.

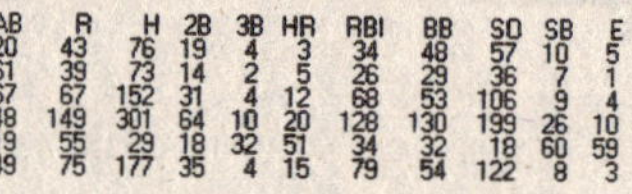

	TEAM	LG	POS	G	AB	R	H	2B	3B	HR	RBI	BB	SO	SB	E	BA	SLG	SALARY
1991	NY	AL	OF	85	320	43	76	19	4	3	34	48	57	10	5	.238	.350	100,000
1992	NY	AL	OF	62	261	39	73	14	2	5	26	29	36	7	1	.280	.406	125,000
1993	NY	AL	OF	139	567	67	152	31	4	12	68	53	106	9	4	.268	.400	150,000
3	YR	TOTALS		286	1148	149	301	64	10	20	128	130	199	26	10	.262	.388	
1993	RANK	MLB	OF	43	19	55	29	18	32	51	34	32	18	60	59	75	81	112
1994	PROJECTIONS			157	649	75	177	35	4	15	79	54	122	8	3	.273	.408	

Jim Abbott No. 25/P

Full name: James Anthony Abbott
Bats: L **Throws:** L **HT:** 6–3 **WT:** 210
Born: 9–19–67, Flint, MI
High School: Flint Central (MI)
College: Michigan

Abbott's no-hitter against Cleveland was the high point of an otherwise disappointing season. He lost five of his last seven decisions.

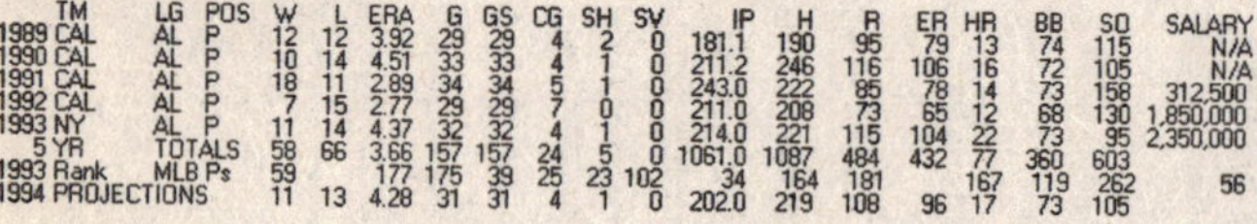

	TM	LG	POS	W	L	ERA	G	GS	CG	SH	SV	IP	H	R	ER	HR	BB	SO	SALARY
1989	CAL	AL	P	12	12	3.92	29	29	4	2	0	181.1	190	95	79	13	74	115	N/A
1990	CAL	AL	P	10	14	4.51	33	33	4	1	0	211.2	246	116	106	16	72	105	N/A
1991	CAL	AL	P	18	11	2.89	34	34	5	1	0	243.0	222	85	78	14	73	158	312,500
1992	CAL	AL	P	7	15	2.77	29	29	7	0	0	211.0	208	73	65	12	68	130	1,850,000
1993	NY	AL	P	11	14	4.37	32	32	4	1	0	214.0	221	115	104	22	73	95	2,350,000
5	YR	TOTALS		58	66	3.66	157	157	24	5	0	1061.0	1087	484	432	77	360	603	
1993	Rank	MLB	Ps	59		177	175	39	25	23	102	34	164	181		167	119	262	56
1994	PROJECTIONS			11	13	4.28	31	31	4	1	0	202.0	219	108	96	17	73	105	

Scott Kamieniecki No. 28/P

Full name: Scott Andrew Kamieniecki
Bats: R **Throws:** R **HT:** 6–0 **WT:** 195
Born: 4–19–64, Mt. Clemens, MI
High School: Redford St. Mary's (Detroit, MI)
College: Michigan

Kamieniecki's string of 12 straight wins at Yankee Stadium was broken in a 6–2 loss to Boston September 16.

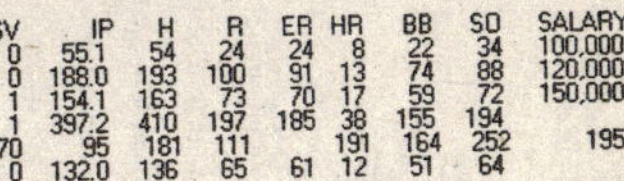

	TM	LG	POS	W	L	ERA	G	GS	CG	SH	SV	IP	H	R	ER	HR	BB	SO	SALARY
1991	NY	AL	P	4	4	3.90	9	9	0	0	0	55.1	54	24	24	8	22	34	100,000
1992	NY	AL	P	6	14	4.36	28	28	4	0	0	188.0	193	100	91	13	74	88	120,000
1993	NY	AL	P	10	7	4.08	30	20	2	0	1	154.1	163	73	70	17	59	72	150,000
3	YR	TOTALS		20	25	4.19	67	57	6	0	1	397.2	410	197	185	38	155	194	
1993	Rank	MLB Ps		75		145	203	105	57	69	70	95	181	111		191	164	252	195
1994	PROJECTIONS			6	8	4.16	22	19	2	0	0	132.0	136	65	61	12	51	64	

Jimmy Key No. 22/P

Full name: James Edward Key
Bats: R **Throws:** L **HT:** 6–1 **WT:** 185
Born: 4–22–61, Huntsville, AL
High School: Butler (Huntsville, AL)
College: Clemson

Key was 18–6 with a 3.00 ERA, and went 11–3 in starts after Yankee losses. He finished fourth in the Cy Young voting.

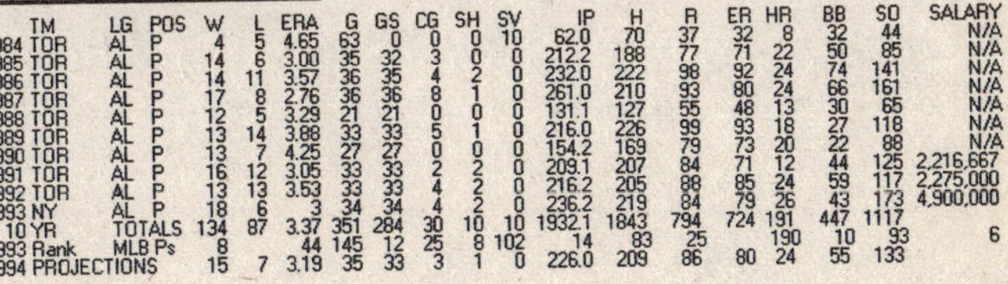

	TM	LG	POS	W	L	ERA	G	GS	CG	SH	SV	IP	H	R	ER	HR	BB	SO	SALARY
1984	TOR	AL	P	4	5	4.65	63	0	0	0	10	62.0	70	37	32	8	32	44	N/A
1985	TOR	AL	P	14	6	3.00	35	32	3	0	0	212.2	188	77	71	22	50	85	N/A
1986	TOR	AL	P	14	11	3.57	36	35	4	2	0	232.0	222	98	92	24	74	141	N/A
1987	TOR	AL	P	17	8	2.76	36	36	8	1	0	261.0	210	93	80	24	66	161	N/A
1988	TOR	AL	P	12	5	3.29	21	21	0	0	0	131.1	127	55	48	13	30	65	N/A
1989	TOR	AL	P	13	14	3.88	33	33	5	1	0	216.0	226	99	93	18	27	118	N/A
1990	TOR	AL	P	13	7	4.25	27	27	0	0	0	154.2	169	79	73	20	22	88	N/A
1991	TOR	AL	P	16	12	3.05	33	33	2	2	0	209.1	207	84	71	12	44	125	2,216,667
1992	TOR	AL	P	13	13	3.53	33	33	4	2	0	216.2	205	88	85	24	59	117	2,275,000
1993	NY	AL	P	18	6	3	34	34	4	2	0	236.2	219	84	79	26	43	173	4,900,000
10	YR	TOTALS		134	87	3.37	351	284	30	10	10	1932.1	1843	794	724	191	447	1117	
1993	Rank	MLB Ps		8		44	145	12	25	8	102	14	83	25		190	10	93	6
1994	PROJECTIONS			15	7	3.19	35	33	3	1	0	226.0	209	86	80	24	55	133	

Xavier Hernandez P

Full name: Francis Xavier Hernandez
Bats: L **Throws:** R **HT:** 6–2 **WT:** 185
Born: 8–16–65, Port Arthur, TX
High School: Tho. Jefferson (Port Arthur, TX)
College: Southwestern Louisiana
His 72 appearances was seventh in the NL.

	TM	LG	POS	W	L	ERA	G	GS	CG	SH	SV	IP	H	R	ER	HR	BB	SO	SALARY
1989	TOR	AL	P	1	0	4.76	7	0	0	0	0	22.2	25	15	12	2	8	7	N/A
1990	HOU	NL	P	2	1	4.62	34	1	0	0	0	62.1	60	34	32	8	24	24	N/A
1991	HOU	NL	P	2	7	4.71	32	6	0	0	3	63.0	66	34	33	6	32	55	122,500
1992	HOU	NL	P	9	1	2.11	77	0	0	0	7	111.0	81	31	26	5	42	96	175,000
1993	HOU	NL	P	4	5	2.61	72	0	0	0	9	96.2	75	37	28	6	28	101	990,000
5	YR	TOTALS		18	14	3.31	222	7	0	0	19	355.2	307	151	131	27	134	283	
1993	Rank	MLB Ps		173		19	9	202	125	69	27	151	19	43		49	68	13	102
1994	PROJECTIONS			2	4	3.82	46	2	0	0	4	73.0	67	35	31	6	28	60	

Buck Showalter No. 11/Mgr.

Full name: William Nathaniel Showalter III
Bats: L **Throws:** L **HT:** 5–10 **WT:** 185
Born: 5–23–56, DeFuniak, FL
Showalter finished second in the AL Manager of the Year voting. New York improved 12 games over 1992, his first at the Yankee helm. He was named Eastern League Manager of the Year in '89.

			REG. SEASON				PLAYOFF			CHAMP. SERIES			WORLD SERIES		
YEAR	TEAM	LG	W	L	PCT	POS	W	L	PCT	W	L	PCT	W	L	PCT
1992	NY	AL	76	86	.469	4			---			---			---
1993	NY	AL	88	74	.543	2			---			---			---
2	YR TOTALS		164	160	.506		0	0	---	0	0	---	0	0	---

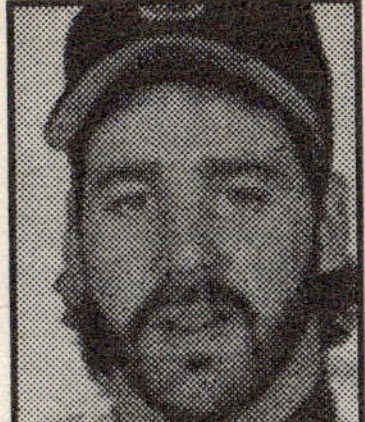

Paul Assenmacher — No. 43/P

Full name: Paul Andre Assenmacher
Bats: L **Throws:** L **HT:** 6–3 **WT:** 210
Born: 12–10–60, Allen Park, MI
High School: Aquinas (Southgate, MI)
College: Aquinas (Grand Rapids, MI)
Assenmacher was 0–1 in Yankee save situations.

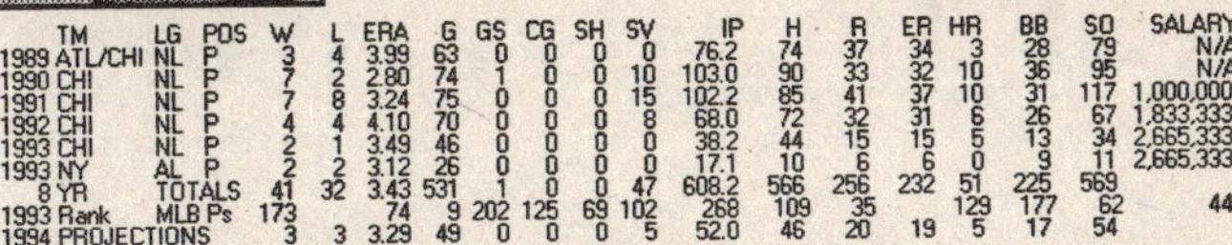

TM	LG	POS	W	L	ERA	G	GS	CG	SH	SV	IP	H	R	ER	HR	BB	SO	SALARY
1989 ATL/CHI	NL	P	3	4	3.99	63	0	0	0	0	76.2	74	37	34	3	28	79	N/A
1990 CHI	NL	P	7	2	2.80	74	1	0	0	10	103.0	90	33	32	10	36	95	N/A
1991 CHI	NL	P	7	8	3.24	75	0	0	0	15	102.2	85	41	37	10	31	117	1,000,000
1992 CHI	NL	P	4	4	4.10	70	0	0	0	8	68.0	72	32	31	6	26	67	1,833,333
1993 CHI	NL	P	2	1	3.49	46	0	0	0	0	38.2	44	15	15	5	13	34	2,665,333
1993 NY	AL	P	2	2	3.12	26	0	0	0	0	17.1	10	6	6	0	9	11	2,665,333
8 YR	TOTALS		41	32	3.43	531	1	0	0	47	608.2	566	256	232	51	225	569	
1993 Rank	MLB Ps		173		74	9	202	125	69	102	268	109	35		129	177	62	44
1994 PROJECTIONS			3	3	3.29	49	0	0	0	5	52.0	46	20	19	5	17	54	

Paul Gibson — No. 35/P

Full name: Paul Marshall Gibson
Bats: R **Throws:** L **HT:** 6–1 **WT:** 185
Born: 1–4–60, Center Moriches, NY
High School: Center Moriches (NY)
College: Suffolk CC (NY)
Yankees were 6–14 in Gibson's 20 appearances

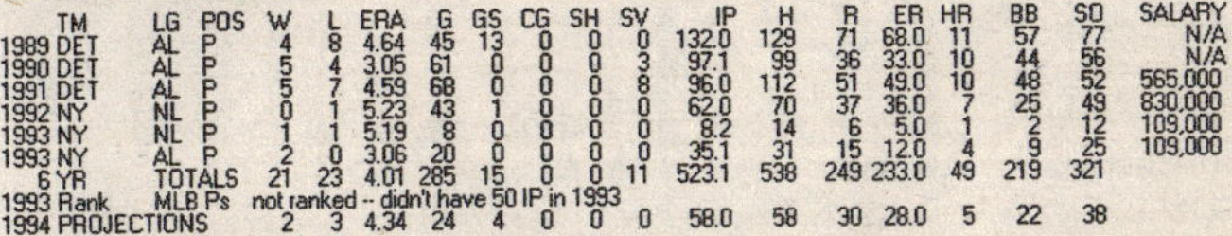

TM	LG	POS	W	L	ERA	G	GS	CG	SH	SV	IP	H	R	ER	HR	BB	SO	SALARY
1989 DET	AL	P	4	8	4.64	45	13	0	0	0	132.0	129	71	68.0	11	57	77	N/A
1990 DET	AL	P	5	4	3.05	61	0	0	0	3	97.1	99	36	33.0	10	44	56	N/A
1991 DET	AL	P	5	7	4.59	68	0	0	0	8	96.0	112	51	49.0	10	48	52	565,000
1992 NY	NL	P	0	1	5.23	43	1	0	0	0	62.0	70	37	36.0	7	25	49	830,000
1993 NY	NL	P	1	1	5.19	8	0	0	0	0	8.2	14	6	5.0	1	2	12	109,000
1993 NY	AL	P	2	0	3.06	20	0	0	0	0	35.1	31	15	12.0	4	9	25	109,000
6 YR	TOTALS		21	23	4.01	285	15	0	0	11	523.1	538	249	233.0	49	219	321	
1993 Rank	MLB Ps		not ranked -- didn't have 50 IP in 1993															
1994 PROJECTIONS			2	3	4.34	24	4	0	0	0	58.0	58	30	28.0	5	22	38	

Steve Howe — No. 57/P

Full name: Steven Roy Howe
Bats: L **Throws:** L **HT:** 5–11 **WT:** 198
Born: 3–10–58, Pontiac, MI
High School: Clarkson (Pontiac, MI)
College: Michigan
Howe led Yankee relievers in losses with five.

TM	LG	POS	W	L	ERA	G	GS	CG	SH	SV	IP	H	R	ER	HR	BB	SO	SALARY
1985 LA	NL	P	1	1	4.91	19	0	0	0	3	22.0	30	17	12	2	5	11	
1985 MIN	AL	P	2	3	6.16	13	0	0	0	0	19.0	28	16	13	1	7	10	
1987 TEX	AL	P	3	3	4.31	24	0	0	0	1	31.1	33	15	15	2	8	19	
1991 NY	AL	P	3	1	1.68	37	0	0	0	3	48.1	39	12	9	1	7	34	500,000
1992 NY	AL	P	3	0	2.45	20	0	0	0	6	22.0	9	7	6	1	3	12	N/A
1993 NY	AL	P	3	5	4.97	51	0	0	0	4	50.2	58	31	28	7	10	19	2,500,000
9 YR	TOTALS		38	37	2.82	376	0	0	0	73	500.1	473	190	157	22	109	277	
1993 Rank	MLB Ps		209		231	80	202	125	69	37	287	242	232		245	19	283	50
1994 PROJECTIONS			3	2	4.24	31	0	0	0	3	34.0	33	17	16	3	7	16	

Mark Hutton — No. 53/P

Full name: Mark Steven Hutton
Bats: R **Throws:** R **HT:** 6–6 **WT:** 240
Born: 2–6–70, S. Adelaide, S. Australia
Hutton was 10–4 with a 3.18 ERA in 21 starts at AAA Columbus.

TM	LG	POS	W	L	ERA	G	GS	CG	SH	SV	IP	H	R	ER	HR	BB	SO	SALARY
1993 NY	AL	P	1	1	5.73	7	4	0	0	0	22.0	24	17	14	2	17	12	N/A
1 YR	TOTAL		1	1	5.73	7	4	0	0	0	22.0	24	17	14	2	17	12	
1993 RANK	MLB Ps		not ranked -- didn't have 50 IP in 1993															

Kevin Maas — No. 24/1B

Full name: Kevin Christian Maas
Bats: L **Throws:** L **HT:** 6–3 **WT:** 204
Born: 1–20–65, Castro Valley, CA
High School: Bishop O'Dowd (CA)
College: California
Maas hit .300 vs. lefties, .191, 9 HR vs. righties.

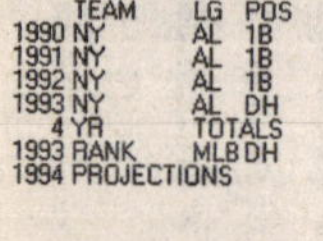

TEAM	LG	POS	G	AB	R	H	2B	3B	HR	RBI	BB	SO	SB	E	BA	SLG	SALARY
1990 NY	AL	1B	79	254	42	64	9	0	21	41	43	76	1	9	.252	.535	N/A
1991 NY	AL	1B	148	500	69	110	14	1	23	63	83	128	5	6	.220	.390	250,000
1992 NY	AL	1B	98	286	35	71	12	0	11	35	25	63	3	2	.248	.406	255,000
1993 NY	AL	DH	59	151	20	31	4	0	9	25	24	32	1	2	.205	.411	N/A
4 YR	TOTALS		384	1191	166	276	39	1	64	164	175	299	10	19	.232	.427	
1993 RANK	MLB	DH	9	9	9	9	9	7	9	9	8	9	6	2	9	8	
1994 PROJECTIONS			95	301	43	68	9	0	17	43	50	78	2	5	.226	.435	

Sam Militello — No. 34/P

Full name: Sam Salvatore Militello, Jr.
Bats: R **Throws:** R **HT:** 6–3 **WT:** 195
Born: 11–26–69, Tampa, FL
High School: Thomas Jefferson (Tampa, FL)
College: Univ. of Tampa (FL)
Militello had just ten 1993 appearances.

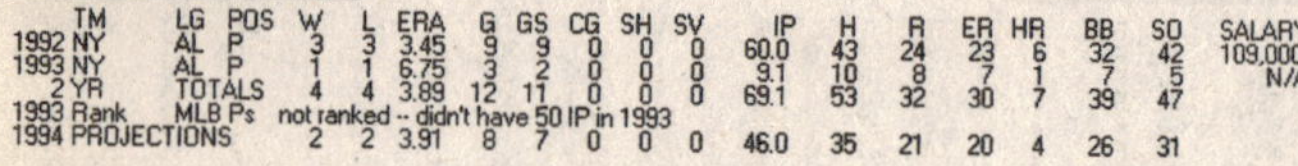

TM	LG	POS	W	L	ERA	G	GS	CG	SH	SV	IP	H	R	ER	HR	BB	SO	SALARY
1992 NY	AL	P	3	3	3.45	9	9	0	0	0	60.0	43	24	23	6	32	42	109,000
1993 NY	AL	P	1	1	6.75	3	2	0	0	0	9.1	10	8	7	1	7	5	N/A
2 YR	TOTALS		4	4	3.89	12	11	0	0	0	69.1	53	32	30	7	39	47	
1993 Rank	MLB Ps		not ranked -- didn't have 50 IP in 1993															
1994 PROJECTIONS			2	2	3.91	8	7	0	0	0	46.0	35	21	20	4	26	31	

Bobby Munoz — No. 54/P

Full name: Roberto Munoz
Bats: R **Throws:** R **HT:** 6–7 **WT:** 237
Born: 3–3–68, Rio Pedras, PR
High School: Hialeah Miami Lakes
College: West Palm Beach JC and Polk CC
Munoz didn't enter a game in a save situation all year.

	TM	LG	POS	W	L	ERA	G	GS	CG	SH	SV	IP	H	R	ER	HR	BB	SO	SALARY
1993	NY	AL	P	3	3	5.32	38	0	0	0	0	45.2	48	27	27	1	26	33	N/A
1	YR	TOTAL		3	3	5.32	38	0	0	0	0	45.2	48	27	27	1	26	33	
1993	Rank	MLB Ps	not ranked -- didn't have 50 IP in 1993																

Matt Nokes — No. 38/C

Full name: Matthew Dodge Nokes
Bats: L **Throws:** R **HT:** 6–1 **WT:** 210
Born: 10–31–63, San Diego, CA
High School: Patrick Henry (San Diego, CA)
New York was 27–20 (with a 3.93 ERA) when Nokes started at catcher.

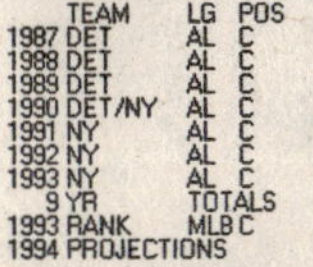

	TEAM	LG	POS	G	AB	R	H	2B	3B	HR	RBI	BB	SO	SB	E	BA	SLG	SALARY
1987	DET	AL	C	135	461	69	133	14	2	32	87	35	70	2	5	.289	.536	N/A
1988	DET	AL	C	122	382	53	96	18	0	16	53	34	58	0	7	.251	.424	N/A
1989	DET	AL	C	87	268	15	67	10	0	9	39	17	37	1	6	.250	.388	N/A
1990	DET/NY	AL	C	136	351	33	87	9	1	11	40	24	47	2	2	.248	.373	N/A
1991	NY	AL	C	135	456	52	122	20	0	24	77	25	49	3	6	.268	.469	887,500
1992	NY	AL	C	121	384	42	86	9	1	22	59	37	62	0	4	.224	.424	2,500,000
1993	NY	AL	C	76	217	25	54	8	0	10	35	16	31	0	2	.249	.424	2,500,000
9	YR	TOTALS		838	2596	294	664	91	4	127	397	190	364	8	34	.256	.441	
1993	RANK	MLB	C	34	31	27	34	36	25	15	25	33	30	35	36	28	11	4
1994	PROJECTIONS			34	98	10	24	3	0	4	14	6	13	0	1	.245	.418	

Melido Perez — No. 33/P

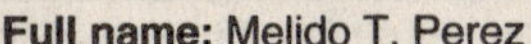

Full name: Melido T. Perez
Bats: R **Throws:** R **HT:** 6–4 **WT:** 210
Born: 2–15–66, San Cristobal, DR
High School: S. Greg. de Nigua (S. Domingo, DR)
Perez' ERA went from from 2.87 in 1992 to 5.19 in 1993. Perez had 10 CG in 1992, none in 1993.

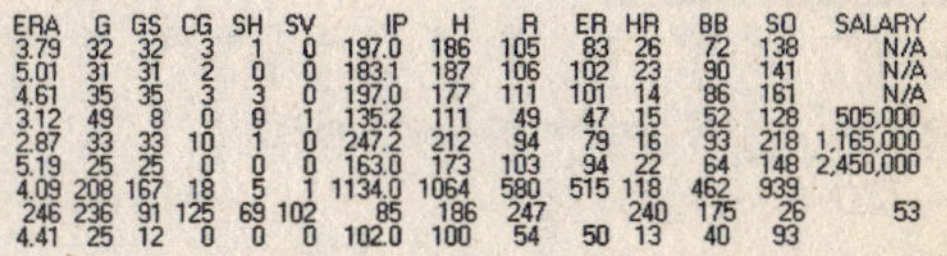

	TM	LG	POS	W	L	ERA	G	GS	CG	SH	SV	IP	H	R	ER	HR	BB	SO	SALARY
1988	CHI	AL	P	12	10	3.79	32	32	3	1	0	197.0	186	105	83	26	72	138	N/A
1989	CHI	AL	P	11	14	5.01	31	31	2	0	0	183.1	187	106	102	23	90	141	N/A
1990	CHI	AL	P	13	14	4.61	35	35	3	3	0	197.0	177	111	101	14	86	161	N/A
1991	CHI	AL	P	8	7	3.12	49	8	0	0	1	135.2	111	49	47	15	52	128	505,000
1992	NY	AL	P	13	16	2.87	33	33	10	1	0	247.2	212	94	79	16	93	218	1,165,000
1993	NY	AL	P	6	14	5.19	25	25	0	0	0	163.0	173	103	94	22	64	148	2,450,000
7	YR	TOTALS		64	76	4.09	208	167	18	5	1	1134.0	1064	580	515	118	462	939	
1993	Rank	MLB Ps		128		246	236	91	125	69	102	85	186	247		240	175	26	53
1994	PROJECTIONS			5	7	4.41	25	12	0	0	0	102.0	100	54	50	13	40	93	

Dave Silvestri — No. 47/IF

Full name: David Joseph Silvestri
Bats: R **Throws:** R **HT:** 6–0 **WT:** 196
Born: 9–29–67, St. Louis, MO
High school: Parkway Central (St. Louis, MO)
College: Missouri
Silvestri hit .269 with 20 HR at AAA Columbus.

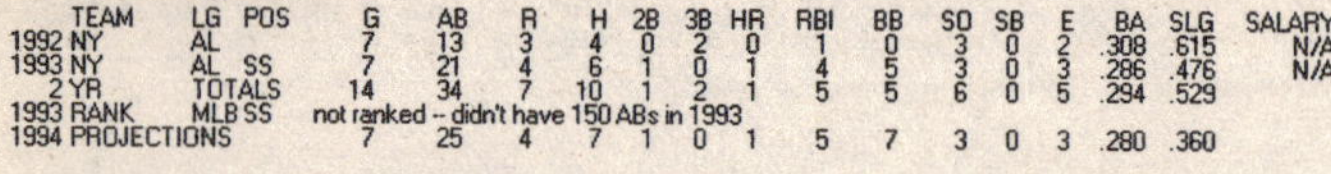

	TEAM	LG	POS	G	AB	R	H	2B	3B	HR	RBI	BB	SO	SB	E	BA	SLG	SALARY
1992	NY	AL		7	13	3	4	0	2	0	1	0	3	0	2	.308	.615	N/A
1993	NY	AL	SS	7	21	4	6	1	0	1	4	5	3	0	3	.286	.476	N/A
2	YR	TOTALS		14	34	7	10	1	2	1	5	5	6	0	5	.294	.529	
1993	RANK	MLB	SS	not ranked -- didn't have 150 ABs in 1993														
1994	PROJECTIONS			7	25	4	7	1	0	1	5	7	3	0	3	.280	.360	

Bob Wickman — No. 27/P

Full name: Robert Joe Wickman
Bats: R **Throws:** R **HT:** 6–1 **WT:** 212
Born: 2–6–69, Green Bay, WI
High School: Oconto Falls (WI)
College: University of Wisconsin–Whitewater
Wickman is 20–5 in his first two Yankee seasons.

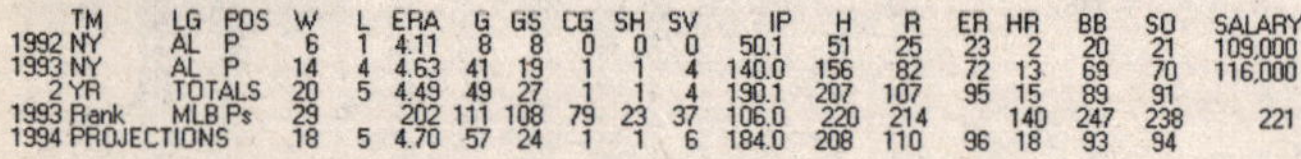

	TM	LG	POS	W	L	ERA	G	GS	CG	SH	SV	IP	H	R	ER	HR	BB	SO	SALARY
1992	NY	AL	P	6	1	4.11	8	8	0	0	0	50.1	51	25	23	2	20	21	109,000
1993	NY	AL	P	14	4	4.63	41	19	1	1	4	140.0	156	82	72	13	69	70	116,000
2	YR	TOTALS		20	5	4.49	49	27	1	1	4	190.1	207	107	95	15	89	91	
1993	Rank	MLB	Ps	29		202	111	108	79	23	37	106.0	220	214		140	247	238	221
1994	PROJECTIONS			18	5	4.70	57	24	1	1	6	184.0	208	110	96	18	93	94	

Gerald Williams — No. 36/OF

Full name: Gerald Floyd Williams
Bats: R **Throws:** R **HT:** 6–2 **WT:** 190
Born: 8–10–66, New Orleans, LA
College: Grambling State (LA)
Williams spent most of '93 in AAA Columbus, where he hit .283. He hit just .149 for New York.

	TEAM	LG	POS	G	AB	R	H	2B	3B	HR	RBI	BB	SO	SB	E	BA	SLG	SALARY
1992	NY	AL	OF	15	27	7	8	2	0	3	6	0	3	2	2	.296	.704	N/A
1993	NY	AL	OF	42	67	11	10	2	3	0	6	1	14	2	2	.149	.269	109,000
2	YR	TOTALS		57	94	18	18	4	3	3	12	1	17	4	4	.191	.394	
1993	RANK	MLB	OF	not ranked -- didn't have 150 ABs in 1993														
1994	PROJECTIONS			38	62	12	12	2	2	2	8	0	11	2	2	.194	.387	

Oakland ATHLETICS

1994 Scouting Report

Hitting: (1993/.254 BA, fourteenth in AL; 158 HR, seventh in AL)

The A's are loaded with promising young players like Brent Gates (.290 BA, 29 doubles) and Troy Neel (.290 BA, 19 HR). Mark McGwire started '93 on a tear, but played in only 27 games due to injury. Terry Steinbach was hitting a solid .285 when he broke his wrist in August. Ruben Sierra provided some power with 22 HR and 101 RBI, but batted a lowly .233. Free agent signee Stan Javier (.291 BA) should start in the OF, but he's not a power threat. Prospects Kurt Abbott (.319 BA at AAA) and Marcos Armas (.290 BA, 89 RBI at AAA) could see major playing time in 1994.

The A's will welcome the return of Rickey Henderson's speed. Sierra had 25 SB, but no one else at Oakland or AAA Tacoma had more than 20.

Pitching: (1993/4.90 ERA, fourteenth in AL)

Only the expansion Rockies had a higher ERA than Oakland last year. Starters Bob Welch and Ron Darling are past their prime, leaving Bobby Witt (14–13, 4.21 ERA) as the staff ace. Prospect-of-the-decade Todd Van Poppel (6–6, 5.04 ERA) has yet to live up to his promise. Youngsters Miguel Jimenez (10–6, 2.94 ERA at AA) and Steve Karsay (3–3, 4.04 ERA) could crack the rotation this spring.

Is age finally catching up with Dennis Eckersley? The best closer in history had a poor year (for him) with 36 saves and a 4.16 ERA. Middle relievers Vince Horsman and Kelly Downs both had ERAs over 5.00.

Defense: (1993/.982 pct., seventh in AL)

Mike Bordick was second among AL second basemen with a .982 fielding percentage, and Brent Gates ranked fifth among AL shortstops at .981.

1994 Prospects:

The A's are a fine example of the problems facing small-market teams. They were last in the AL in both pitching and hitting in 1993, but can't afford many high-priced free agents. Oakland has gotten off to a good start rebuilding from within, but there's still a long way to go. Even if McGwire returns to form, Oakland will not be able to keep pace with Seattle and Texas.

Team Directory

Owner: Walter A. Haas, Jr.
Chairman & CEO: Walter J. Haas
VP, Baseball Operations: Sandy Alderson
Executive VP: Andy Dolich
Dir. of Baseball Information: Jay Alves
Dir. of Team Travel: Mickey Morabito

Minor League Affiliates:

Level	Team/League	1993 Record
AAA	Tacoma – Pacific Coast	69–74
AA	Huntsville – Southern	71–70
A	Modesto – California	72–64
	Madison – Midwest	77–58
	Southern Oregon – Northwest	37–39
Rookie	Scottsdale Athletics – Arizona	35–20

1993 Review

	Home		Away	
vs AL East	W	L	W	L
Baltimore	1	5	1	5
Boston	2	4	1	5
Detroit	3	3	1	5
New York	4	2	2	4
Toronto	1	5	4	2
Total	11	19	9	21

	Home		Away	
vs AL Cent.	W	L	W	L
Chicago	3	4	3	3
Cleveland	2	4	2	4
Kansas City	5	2	2	4
Milwaukee	5	1	0	6
Minnesota	1	5	4	3
	16	16	11	20

	Home		Away	
vs AL West	W	L	W	L
California	4	2	3	4
Seattle	3	3	6	1
Texas	4	3	1	5
	11	8	10	10

1993 finish: 68–94 (38–43 home, 30–51 away), seventh in AL West, 26 games behind

1994 Schedule

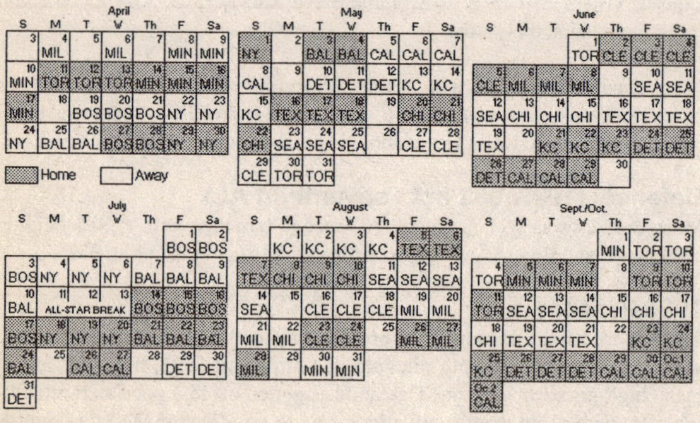

OAKLAND ATHLETICS 1994 ROSTER

MANAGER: Tony LaRussa (10)
COACHES: Dave Duncan (18), Art Kusnyer (5), Jim Lefebvre (6), Dave McKay (8), Tommie Reynolds (47)

No.	PITCHERS	B	T	HT	WT	DOB	BIRTHPLACE	RESIDENCE
62	Baker, Scott	L	L	6–2	175	5–18–70	San Jose, CA	Las Vegas, NV
53	Briscoe, John	R	R	6–3	185	9–22–67	La Grange, IL	Richardson, TX
17	Darling, Ron	R	R	6–3	195	8–19–60	Honolulu, HI	New York, NY
31	Downs, Kelly	R	R	6–4	200	10–25–60	Ogden, UT	Centerville, UT
43	Eckersley, Dennis	R	R	6–2	195	10–3–54	Oakland, CA	Sudbury, MA
57	Hillegas, Shawn	R	R	6–2	223	8–21–64	Dos Palos, CA	Phoenix, AZ
26	Horsman, Vince	R	L	6–2	180	3–9–67	Halifax, Nova Scotia	Dunedin, FL
47	Jiminez, Miguel	R	R	6–2	205	8–19–69	New York, NY	New York, NY
50	Karsay, Steve	R	R	6–3	205	3–24–72	College Point, NY	College Point, NY
61	Shaw, Curtis	L	L	6–1	190	8–16–69	Charlotte, NC	Bartlesville, OK
51	Smithberg, Roger	R	R	6–3	210	3–21–6	Elgin, IL	Elgin, IL
	Sturtze, Tanyon	R	R	6–5	190	10–12–70	Worcester, MA	Worcester, MA
59	Van Poppel, Todd	R	R	6–5	210	12–9–71	Hinsdale, IL	Arlington, TX
35	Welch, Bob	R	R	6–3	198	11–3–56	Detroit, MI	Scottsdale, AZ
32	Witt, Bobby	R	R	6–2	205	5–11–64	Arlington, VA	Colleyville, TX
No.	**CATCHERS**	**B**	**T**	**HT**	**WT**	**DOB**	**BIRTHPLACE**	**RESIDENCE**
48	Helfand, Eric	L	R	6–0	195	3–25–69	Erie, PA	Tempe, AZ
2	Hemond, Scott	R	R	6–0	215	11–18–65	Taunton, MA	Dunedin, FL
39	Mercedes, Henry	R	R	5–11	185	7–23–69	Santo Domingo, DR	Santo Domingo, DR
45	Molina, Islay	R	R	6–1	200	6–3–71	New York, NY	Miami, FL
36	Steinbach, Terry	R	R	6–1	195	3–2–62	New Ulm, MN	Plymouth, MN
	Williams, George	S	R	5–10	190	4–22–66	Lacrosse, WI	Lacrosse, WI
No.	**INFIELDERS**	**B**	**T**	**HT**	**WT**	**DOB**	**BIRTHPLACE**	**RESIDENCE**
11	Abbott, Kurt	R	R	6–0	170	6–2–69	Zaneville, OH	St. Petersburg, FL
23	Aldrete, Mike	R	R	5–11	185	1–29–61	Carmel, CA	Monterey, CA
38	Armas, Marcos	R	R	6–5	190	8–5–69	Puerto Pirtu, VZ	Puerto Pirtu, VZ
14	Bordick, Mike	R	R	5–11	175	7–21–65	Marquette, MI	Auburn, ME
	Cruz, Fausto	R	R	5–10	165	5–1–72	Monte Cristy, DR	Monte Cristy, DR
13	Gates, Brent	S	R	6–1	180	3–14–70	Grand Rapids, MI	Phoenix, AZ
25	McGwire, Mark	R	R	6–5	225	10–1–63	Pomona, CA	Alamo, CA
16	Neel, Troy	L	R	6–4	215	9–14–65	Freeport, TX	Austin, TX
3	Paquette, Craig	R	R	6–0	190	3–28–69	Long Beach, CA	Garden Grove, CA
No.	**OUTFIELDERS**	**B**	**T**	**HT**	**WT**	**DOB**	**BIRTHPLACE**	**RESIDENCE**
12	Blankenship, Lance	R	R	6–0	185	12–8–63	Portland, OR	San Ramon, CA
7	Brosius, Scott	R	R	6–1	185	6–15–66	Hillsboro, OR	Portland, OR
	Henderson, Rickey	R	L	5–10	190	12–25–58	Chicago, IL	Hillsborough, CA
	Herrera, Jose	L	L	6–0	165	8–30–72	Santo Domingo, DR	Santo Domingo, DR
	Javier, Stan	S	R	6–0	185	9–1–65	S.F. de Macoris, DR	Santo Domingo, DR
49	Lydy, Scott	R	R	6–5	190	10–26–68	Mesa, AZ	Chandler, AZ
21	Sierra, Ruben	S	R	6–1	200	10–6–65	Rio Piedras, PR	Carolina, PR
	Young, Ernie	R	R	6–1	190	7–8–68	Chicago, IL	Chicago, IL

Oakland–Alameda County Coliseum
(46,942, grass)
Tickets: 510–638–4900
Ticket prices:
$14 (field level)
$13 (plaza level)
$7 (upper reserved)
$4.50 (bleachers)
Field Dimensions (from home plate)
To left field at foul line, 330 feet
To center field, 400 feet
To right field at foul line, 330 feet
(OF wall is 8 feet high)

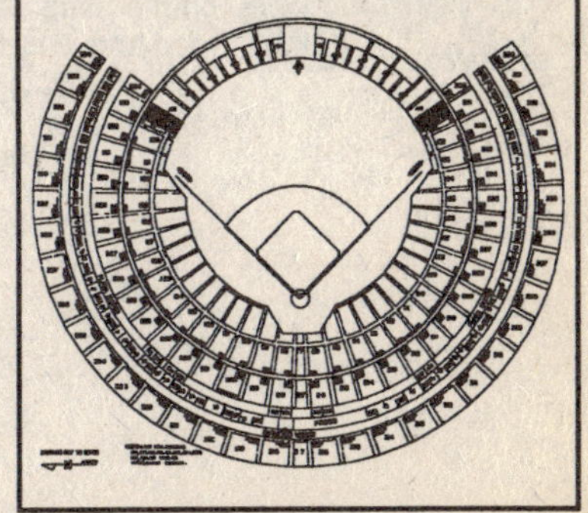

Mike Bordick — No. 14/SS

Full name: Michael Todd Bordick
Bats: R **Throws:** R **HT:** 5–11 **WT:** 175
Born: 7–21–65, Marquette, MI
High school: Hampton Academy (ME)
College: Maine–Orono

Bordick's .982 fielding percentage ranked second among AL shortstops, but his average dropped to .249 from .300 in 1992.

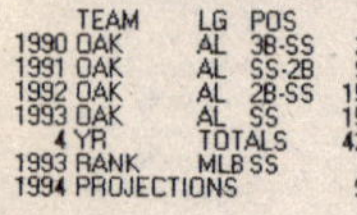
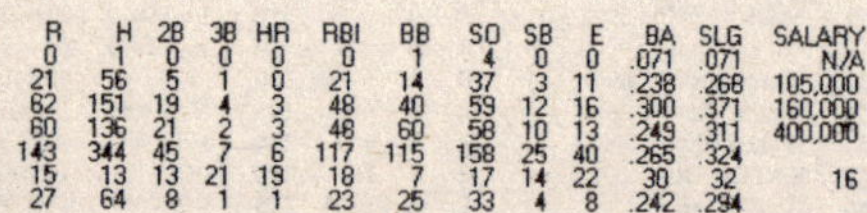

	TEAM	LG	POS	G	AB	R	H	2B	3B	HR	RBI	BB	SO	SB	E	BA	SLG	SALARY
1990	OAK	AL	3B-SS	25	14	0	1	0	0	0	0	1	4	0	0	.071	.071	N/A
1991	OAK	AL	SS-2B	90	235	21	56	5	1	0	21	14	37	3	11	.238	.268	105,000
1992	OAK	AL	2B-SS	154	504	62	151	19	4	3	48	40	59	12	16	.300	.371	160,000
1993	OAK	AL	SS	159	546	60	136	21	2	3	48	60	58	10	13	.249	.311	400,000
4	YR	TOTALS		428	1299	143	344	45	7	6	117	115	158	25	40	.265	.324	
1993	RANK	MLB	SS	3	9	15	13	13	21	19	18	7	17	14	22	30	32	16
1994	PROJECTIONS			91	265	27	64	8	1	1	23	25	33	4	8	.242	.294	

Brent Gates — No. 13/2B

Full name: Brent Robert Gates
Bats: S **Throws:** R **HT:** 6–1 **WT:** 180
Born: 3–14–70, Grand Rapids, MI
High school: Grandville (MI)
College: Minnesota

In an impressive debut, Gates ranked second on the team with 69 RBI. He hit .314 on the road and .315 from the seventh inning on.

	TEAM	LG	POS	G	AB	R	H	2B	3B	HR	RBI	BB	SO	SB	E	BA	SLG	SALARY
1993	OAK	AL	2B	139	535	64	155	29	2	7	69	56	75	7	14	.290	.391	109,000
1	YR	TOTAL		139	535	64	155	29	2	7	69	56	75	7	14	.290	.391	
1993	RANK	MLB	2B	13	8	15	6	6	19	11	6	10	7	21	6	9	19	39

Rickey Henderson No. 24/OF

Full name: Rickey Henley Henderson
Bats: L **Throws:** R **HT:** 5–10 **WT:** 190
Born: 12–25–58, Chicago, IL
High school: Technical (Oakland, CA)
Henderson led the A's in average (.327), runs (75), homers (17), and stolen bases (29) when he was traded to Toronto. A wrist injury held him to a .215 BA with the Blue Jays.

	TEAM	LG	POS	G	AB	R	H	2B	3B	HR	RBI	BB	SO	SB	E	BA	SLG	SALARY
1979	OAK	AL	OF	89	351	49	96	13	3	1	26	34	39	33	6	.274	.336	N/A
1980	OAK	AL	OF	158	591	111	179	22	4	9	53	117	54	100	7	.303	.399	N/A
1981	OAK	AL	OF	108	423	89	135	18	7	6	35	64	68	56	7	.319	.437	N/A
1982	OAK	AL	OF	149	536	119	143	24	4	10	51	116	94	130	9	.267	.382	N/A
1983	OAK	AL	OF	145	513	105	150	25	7	9	48	103	80	108	3	.292	.421	N/A
1984	OAK	AL	OF	142	502	113	147	27	4	16	58	86	81	66	11	.293	.458	N/A
1985	NY	AL	OF	143	547	146	172	28	5	24	72	99	65	80	9	.314	.516	N/A
1986	NY	AL	OF	153	608	130	160	31	5	28	74	89	81	87	6	.263	.469	N/A
1987	NY	AL	OF	95	358	78	104	17	3	17	37	80	52	41	4	.291	.497	N/A
1988	NY	AL	OF	140	554	118	169	30	2	6	50	82	54	93	12	.305	.399	N/A
1989	NY/OAK	AL	OF	150	541	113	148	26	3	12	57	126	68	77	4	.274	.399	N/A
1990	OAK	AL	OF	136	489	119	159	33	3	28	61	97	60	65	5	.325	.577	N/A
1991	OAK	AL	OF	134	470	105	126	17	1	18	57	98	73	58	8	.268	.423	3,250,000
1992	OAK	AL	OF	117	396	77	112	18	3	15	46	95	56	48	4	.283	.457	3,250,000
1993	TOR	AL	OF	134	481	114	139	22	2	21	59	120	65	53	7	.289	.474	3,550,000
15	YR	TOTALS		1993	7360	1586	2139	351	56	220	784	1406	990	1095	102	.291	.443	
1993	RANK	MLB	OF	54	51	5	41	45	76	19	47	4	59	4	25	39	36	17
1994	PROJECTIONS			139	516	112	152	25	3	12	52	101	66	84	7	.295	.428	

Stan Javier No. 25/OF

Full name: Stanley Julian Javier
Bats: B **Throws:** R **HT:** 6-0 **WT:** 185
Born: 1-9-64, San Francisco de Macoris, DR
High school: La Altagracia (SF de Macoris, DR)
Son of former Cardinal IF Julian Javier, he hit .343 with 3 HR and 27 RBI in 50 second–half games.

	TEAM	LG	POS	G	AB	R	H	2B	3B	HR	RBI	BB	SO	SB	E	BA	SLG	SALARY
1984	NY	AL	OF	7	7	1	1	0	0	0	0	0	1	0	0	.143	.143	N/A
1986	OAK	AL	OF	59	114	13	23	8	0	0	8	16	27	8	0	.202	.272	N/A
1987	OAK	AL	OF	81	151	22	28	3	1	2	9	19	33	3	3	.185	.258	N/A
1988	OAK	AL	OF	125	397	49	102	13	3	2	35	32	63	20	5	.257	.320	N/A
1989	OAK	AL	OF	112	310	42	77	12	3	1	28	31	45	12	2	.248	.316	N/A
1990	OAK	AL	OF	19	33	4	8	0	2	0	3	3	6	0	0	.242	.364	310,000
1990	LA	NL	OF	104	276	56	84	9	4	3	24	37	44	15	0	.304	.399	310,000
1991	LA	NL	OF	121	176	21	36	5	3	1	11	16	36	7	3	.205	.284	650,000
1992	LA-PHL	NL	OF	130	334	42	83	17	1	1	29	37	54	18	3	.249	.314	715,000
1993	CAL	AL	OF	92	237	33	69	10	4	3	28	27	33	12	4	.291	.405	600,000
10	YR	TOTALS		912	2201	303	562	85	21	19	197	224	363	96	22	.255	.339	
1993	RANK	MLB	OF	101	107	99	95	110	32	108	98	75	115	54	67	36	77	75
1994	PROJECTIONS			98	188	25	44	6	2	2	16	20	34	7	3	.234	.324	

Mark McGwire No. 25/1B

Full name: Mark David McGwire
Bats: R **Throws:** R **HT:** 6–5 **WT:** 225
Born: 10–1–63, Pomona, CA
High school: Damien (CA)
College: USC

McGwire had 24 RBI in 25 games before a heel injury ended his season. He has 226 HR since 1987, second only to Fred McGriff.

	TEAM	LG	POS	G	AB	R	H	2B	3B	HR	RBI	BB	SO	SB	E	BA	SLG	SALARY
1986	OAK	AL	1B	18	53	10	10	1	0	3	9	4	18	0	6	.189	.377	N/A
1987	OAK	AL	1B-3B	151	557	97	161	28	4	49	118	71	131	1	13	.289	.618	N/A
1988	OAK	AL	1B-OF	155	550	87	143	22	1	32	99	76	117	0	9	.260	.478	N/A
1989	OAK	AL	1B	143	490	74	113	17	0	33	95	83	94	1	6	.231	.467	N/A
1990	OAK	AL	1B	156	523	87	123	16	0	39	108	110	116	2	5	.235	.489	N/A
1991	OAK	AL	1B	154	483	62	97	22	0	22	75	93	116	2	4	.201	.383	2,875,000
1992	OAK	AL	1B	139	467	87	125	22	0	42	104	90	105	0	6	.268	.585	2,650,000
1993	OAK	AL	1B	27	84	16	28	6	0	9	24	21	19	0	0	.333	.726	4,000,000
8	YR	TOTALS		943	3207	520	800	134	5	229	632	548	716	6	49	.249	.509	
1993	RANK	MLB	1B	not ranked -- didn't have 150 ABs in 1993														
1994	PROJECTIONS			65	231	41	66	11	1	20	50	32	56	0	6	.286	.610	

Troy Neel No. 16/DH

Full name: Troy Lee Neel
Bats: L **Throws:** R **HT:** 6–4 **WT:** 210
Born: 9–14–65, Freeport, TX
High school: Brazoswood (TX)
College: Texas A&M and Howard (TX)

Neel led the team with a .354 BA against left-handers. He hit .326 with 15 HR and 50 RBI after June 17.

	TEAM	LG	POS	G	AB	R	H	2B	3B	HR	RBI	BB	SO	SB	E	BA	SLG	SALARY
1992	OAK	AL	OF-1B	24	53	8	14	3	0	3	9	5	15	0	3	.264	.491	N/A
1993	OAK	AL	1B	123	427	59	124	21	0	19	63	49	101	3	5	.290	.473	130,000
2	YR	TOTALS		147	480	67	138	24	0	22	72	54	116	3	8	.288	.475	
1993	RANK	MLB	1B	24	24	23	20	23	30	14	22	23	8	16	21	16	13	33
1994	PROJECTIONS			162	578	79	168	28	0	25	84	66	135	3	5	.291	.469	0

Craig Paquette No. 20/3B

Full name: Craig Howard Paquette
Bats: R **Throws:** R **HT:** 6–0 **WT:** 190
Born: 3–28–69, Long Beach, CA
High school: R. Alamitos (Garden Gr., CA)
College: Golden West, (Huntington B., CA)

Rookie Paquette started fast with 19 RBI in his first 20 games, but he batted just .193 after the All-Star break.

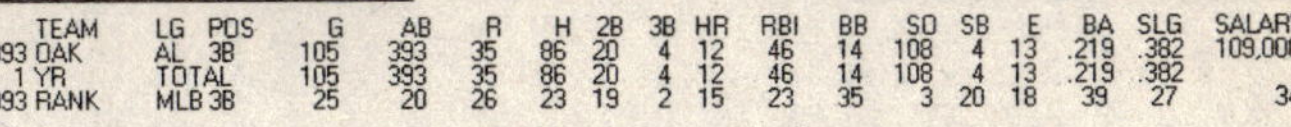

TEAM	LG POS	G	AB	R	H	2B	3B	HR	RBI	BB	SO	SB	E	BA	SLG	SALARY
1993 OAK	AL 3B	105	393	35	86	20	4	12	46	14	108	4	13	.219	.382	109,000
1 YR	TOTAL	105	393	35	86	20	4	12	46	14	108	4	13	.219	.382	
1993 RANK	MLB 3B	25	20	26	23	19	2	15	23	35	3	20	18	39	27	34

Ruben Sierra No. 29/OF

Full name: Ruben Angel Sierra
Bats: S **Throws:** R **HT:** 6–1 **WT:** 200
Born: 10–6–65, Rio Piedras, PR
High school: Dr. Secario Rosario (PR)

Sierra had the fourth 100+ RBI season of his career, but posted a .233 BA, his worst ever. He had a career-high 25 SB in just 30 attempts.

TEAM	LG POS	G	AB	R	H	2B	3B	HR	RBI	BB	SO	SB	E	BA	SLG	SALARY
1986 TEX	AL OF	113	382	50	101	13	10	16	55	22	65	7	6	.264	.476	N/A
1987 TEX	AL OF	158	643	97	169	35	4	30	109	39	114	16	11	.263	.470	N/A
1988 TEX	AL OF	156	615	77	156	32	2	23	91	44	91	18	7	.254	.424	N/A
1989 TEX	AL OF	162	634	101	194	35	14	29	119	43	82	8	9	.306	.543	N/A
1990 TEX	AL OF	159	608	70	170	37	2	16	96	49	86	9	10	.280	.426	N/A
1991 TEX	AL OF	161	661	110	203	44	5	25	116	56	91	16	7	.307	.502	2,650,000
1992 OAK	AL OF	151	601	83	167	34	7	17	87	45	68	14	7	.278	.443	5,000,000
1993 OAK	AL OF	158	630	77	147	23	5	22	101	52	97	25	7	.233	.390	4,200,000
8 YR	TOTALS	1218	4774	665	1307	253	49	178	774	350	694	113	64	.274	.459	
1993 RANK	MLB OF	6	2	33	31	44	23	16	8	33	27	25	25	117	92	8
1994 PROJECTIONS		144	548	76	147	23	9	22	91	39	81	13	7	.268	.469	

Terry Steinbach No. 36/C

Full name: Terry Lee Steinbach
Bats: R **Throws:** R **HT:** 6–1 **WT:** 195
Born: 3–2–62, New Ulm, MN
High school: New Ulm (MN)
College: Minnesota

In an injury-shortened 1993, Steinbach hit a career-high .285, but only batted .194 with men in scoring position.

	TEAM	LG	POS	G	AB	R	H	2B	3B	HR	RBI	BB	SO	SB	E	BA	SLG	SALARY
1986	OAK	AL	C	6	15	3	5	0	0	2	4	1	0	0	1	.333	.733	N/A
1987	OAK	AL	C-3B	122	391	66	111	16	3	16	56	32	66	1	10	.284	.463	N/A
1988	OAK	AL	C-3B	104	351	42	93	19	1	9	51	33	47	3	9	.265	.402	N/A
1989	OAK	AL	C-OF	130	454	37	124	13	1	7	42	30	66	1	11	.273	.352	N/A
1990	OAK	AL	C-1B	114	379	32	95	15	2	9	57	19	66	0	5	.251	.372	N/A
1991	OAK	AL	C-1B	129	456	50	125	31	1	6	67	22	70	2	15	.274	.386	1,050,000
1992	OAK	AL	C-1B	128	438	48	122	20	1	12	53	45	58	2	10	.279	.411	2,050,000
1993	OAK	AL	C	104	389	47	111	19	1	10	43	25	65	3	7	.285	.416	2,815,000
8	YR	TOTALS		837	2873	325	786	133	10	71	373	207	438	12	68	.274	.401	
1993	RANK	MLB	C	22	16	14	12	12	11	15	19	21	14	7	12	9	12	2
1994	PROJECTIONS			112	398	42	109	17	1	8	45	29	59	2	9	.274	.387	

Ron Darling No. 17/P

Full name: Ronald Maurice Darling
Bats: R **Throws:** R **HT:** 6–3 **WT:** 195
Born: 8–19–60, Honolulu, HI
High school: St. John's (Worcester, MA)
College: Yale

Veteran Darling slumped sharply after a strong 1992, slumping in wins (5), strikeouts (95), and ERA (5.16).

	TM	LG	POS	W	L	ERA	G	GS	CG	SH	SV	IP	H	R	ER	HR	BB	SO	SALARY
1983	NY	NL	P	1	3	2.80	5	5	1	0	0	35.1	31	11	11	0	17	23	N/A
1984	NY	NL	P	12	9	3.81	33	33	2	2	0	205.2	179	97	87	17	104	136	N/A
1985	NY	NL	P	16	6	2.90	36	35	4	2	0	248.0	214	93	80	21	114	167	N/A
1986	NY	NL	P	15	6	2.81	34	34	4	2	0	237.0	203	84	74	21	81	184	N/A
1987	NY	NL	P	12	8	4.29	32	32	2	0	0	207.2	183	111	99	24	96	167	N/A
1988	NY	NL	P	17	9	3.25	34	34	7	4	0	240.2	218	97	87	24	60	161	N/A
1989	NY	NL	P	14	14	3.52	33	33	4	0	0	217.1	214	100	85	19	70	153	N/A
1990	NY	NL	P	7	9	4.50	33	18	1	0	0	126.0	135	73	63	20	44	99	N/A
1991	NY/MTL	NL	P	5	8	4.37	20	20	0	0	0	119.1	121	66	58	15	33	69	1,966,667
1991	OAK	AL	P	3	7	4.08	12	12	0	0	0	75.0	64	34	34	7	38	60	3,250,000
1992	OAK	AL	P	15	10	3.66	33	33	4	3	0	206.1	198	98	84	15	72	99	2,100,000
1993	OAK	AL	P	5	9	5.16	31	29	3	0	0	178.0	198	107	102	22	72	95	2,250,000
11	YR	TOTALS		122	98	3.71	336	318	32	13	0	2096.1	1958	971	864	205	801	1413	
1993	Rank	MLB	Ps	149		243	194	65	37	69	102	71	218	222		213	186	216	60
1994	PROJECTIONS			5	8	4.72	28	22	1	0	0	141	151	82	74	19	49	87	

Bob Welch No. 35/P

Full name: Robert Lynn Welch
Bats: R **Throws:** R **HT:** 6–3 **WT:** 198
Born: 11–3–56, Detroit, MI
High school: Hazel Park (Ferndale, MI)
College: Eastern Michigan
Welch's nine wins were his worst since 1986, and his 5.29 ERA was his highest ever. The A's were just 8–20 in games he started.

	TM	LG	POS	W	L	ERA	G	GS	CG	SH	SV	IP	H	R	ER	HR	BB	SO	SALARY
1980	LA	NL	P	14	9	3.29	32	32	3	2	0	213.2	190	85	78	15	79	141	N/A
1981	LA	NL	P	9	5	3.44	23	23	2	1	0	141.1	141	56	54	11	41	88	N/A
1982	LA	NL	P	16	11	3.36	36	36	9	3	0	235.2	199	94	88	19	81	176	N/A
1983	LA	NL	P	15	12	2.65	31	31	4	3	0	204.0	164	73	60	13	72	156	N/A
1984	LA	NL	P	13	13	3.78	31	29	3	1	0	178.2	191	86	75	11	58	126	N/A
1985	LA	NL	P	14	4	2.31	23	23	8	3	0	167.1	141	49	43	16	35	96	N/A
1986	LA	NL	P	7	13	3.28	33	33	7	3	0	235.2	227	95	86	14	55	183	N/A
1987	LA	NL	P	15	9	3.22	35	35	6	4	0	251.2	204	94	90	21	86	196	N/A
1988	OAK	AL	P	17	9	3.64	36	36	4	2	0	244.2	237	107	99	22	81	158	N/A
1989	OAK	AL	P	17	8	3.00	33	33	1	0	0	209.2	191	82	70	13	78	137	N/A
1990	OAK	AL	P	27	6	2.95	35	35	2	2	0	238.0	214	90	78	26	77	127	N/A
1991	OAK	AL	P	12	13	4.58	35	35	7	1	0	220.0	220	124	112	25	91	101	3,450,000
1992	OAK	AL	P	11	7	3.27	20	20	0	0	0	123.2	114	47	45	13	43	47	3,450,000
1993	OAK	AL	P	9	11	5.29	30	28	0	0	0	166.2	208	102	98	25	56	63	3,450,000
16	YR	TOTALS		208	140	3.38	481	454	61	28	8	3023.1	2815	1254	1137	257	991	1925	
1993	Rank	MLB Ps		87		252	203	71	125	69	102	78	274	233		265	112	282	29
1994	PROJECTIONS			9	7	4.09	24	23	0	0	0	143	154	68	65	16	46	66	

Bobby Witt No. 32/P

Full name: Robert Andrew Witt
Bats: R **Throws:** R **HT:** 6–2 **WT:** 205
Born: 5–11–64, Arlington, VA
High school: Canton (MA)
College: Oklahoma
Witt led the staff with in wins (14), strikeouts (131), IP (220.0), and complete games (5). He pitched 6 or more innings in 22 of 33 starts.

	TM	LG	POS	W	L	ERA	G	GS	CG	SH	SV	IP	H	R	ER	HR	BB	SO	SALARY
1986	TEX	AL	P	11	9	5.48	31	31	0	0	0	157.2	130	104	96	18	143	174	N/A
1987	TEX	AL	P	8	10	4.91	26	25	1	0	0	143.0	114	82	78	10	140	160	N/A
1988	TEX	AL	P	8	10	3.92	22	22	13	2	0	174.1	134	83	76	13	101	148	N/A
1989	TEX	AL	P	12	13	5.14	31	31	5	1	0	194.1	182	123	111	14	114	166	N/A
1990	TEX	AL	P	17	10	3.36	33	32	7	1	0	222.0	197	98	83	12	110	221	N/A
1991	TEX	AL	P	3	7	6.09	17	16	1	1	0	88.2	84	66	60	4	74	82	1,383,333
1992	TEX/OAK	AL	P	10	14	4.29	31	31	0	0	0	193.0	183	99	92	16	114	125	2,383,333
1993	OAK	AL	P	14	13	4.21	35	33	5	1	0	220.0	226	112	103	16	91	131	3,033,334
8	YR	TOTALS		83	86	4.52	226	221	32	6	0	1393.0	1250	767	699	103	887	1207	
1993	Rank	MLB Ps		29		161	134	30	16	23	102	27	161	153		75	194	165	37
1994	PROJECTIONS			12	13	4.54	32	31	3	0	0	202	197	111	102	15	106	140	

Dennis Eckersley No. 43/P

Full name: Dennis Lee Eckersley
Bats: R **Throws:** R **HT:** 6–2 **WT:** 195
Born: 10–3–54, Oakland, CA
High school: Washington (Fremont, CA)
Despite posting a 4.16 ERA, his highest since 1986, Eckersley became the first reliever to record 30+ saves in 6 straight seasons.

	TM	LG	POS	W	L	ERA	G	GS	CG	SH	SV	IP	H	R	ER	HR	BB	SO	SALARY
1981	BOS	AL	P	9	8	4.27	23	23	8	2	0	154.0	160	82	73	9	35	79	N/A
1982	BOS	AL	P	13	13	3.73	33	33	11	3	0	224.1	228	101	93	31	43	127	N/A
1983	BOS	AL	P	9	13	5.61	28	28	2	0	0	176.1	223	119	110	27	39	77	N/A
1984	BOS	AL	P	4	4	5.01	9	9	2	0	0	64.2	71	38	36	10	13	33	N/A
1984	CHI	NL	P	10	8	3.03	24	24	2	0	0	160.1	152	59	54	11	36	81	N/A
1985	CHI	NL	P	11	7	3.08	25	25	6	2	0	169.1	145	61	58	15	19	117	N/A
1986	CHI	NL	P	6	11	4.57	33	32	1	0	0	201.0	226	109	102	21	43	137	N/A
1987	OAK	AL	P	6	8	3.03	54	2	0	0	16	115.2	99	41	39	11	17	113	N/A
1988	OAK	AL	P	4	2	2.35	60	0	0	0	45	72.2	52	20	19	5	11	70	N/A
1989	OAK	AL	P	4	0	1.56	51	0	0	0	33	57.2	32	10	10	5	3	55	N/A
1990	OAK	AL	P	4	2	0.61	63	0	0	0	48	73.1	41	9	5	2	4	73	N/A
1991	OAK	AL	P	5	4	2.96	67	0	0	0	43	76.0	60	26	25	11	9	87	3,000,000
1992	OAK	AL	P	7	1	1.91	69	0	0	0	51	80.0	62	17	17	5	11	93	3,000,000
1993	OAK	AL	P	2	4	4.16	64	0	0	0	36	67.0	67	32	31	7	13	80	3,800,000
19	YR	TOTALS		183	149	3.45	804	361	100	20	275	3038.1	2814	1256	1164	314	692	2198	
1993	Rank	MLB Ps		246		157	34	202	125	69	11	226	140	115		172	17	4	18
1994	PROJECTIONS			5	5	4.36	55	0	3	0	27	95	99	50	46	8	20	64	

Tony La Russa No. 10/Mgr.

Full name: Anthony La Russa Jr.
Bats: R **Throws:** R **HT:** 6–0 **WT:** 185
Born: 10–4–44, Tampa, FL
High school: Jefferson (Tampa, FL)
Tony La Russa has been named AL Manager of the Year three times—1983, 1988, and 1992. He's won five division titles, three AL pennants, and one World Series.

				REG. SEASON				PLAYOFF			CHAMP. SERIES			WORLD SERIES		
	YEAR	TEAM	LG	W	L	PCT	POS	W	L	PCT	W	L	PCT	W	L	PCT
1ST HALF	1981	CHI	AL	31	22	.585	3			---			---			---
2ND HALF	1981	CHI	AL	23	30	.434	6			---			---			---
	1982	CHI	AL	87	75	.537	3			---			---			---
	1983	CHI	AL	99	63	.611	1			---	1	3	.250			---
	1984	CHI	AL	74	88	.457	5			---			---			---
	1985	CHI	AL	85	77	.525	3			---			---			---
	1986	CHI	AL	26	38	.406				---			---			---
	1986	OAK	AL	45	34	.570	3			---			---			---
	1987	OAK	AL	81	81	.500	3			---			---			---
	1988	OAK	AL	104	58	.642	1			---	4	0	1.000	1	4	.200
	1989	OAK	AL	99	63	.611	1			---	4	1	.800	4	0	1.000
	1990	OAK	AL	103	59	.636	1			---	4	0	1.000	0	4	.000
	1991	OAK	AL	84	78	.519	4			---			---			---
	1992	OAK	AL	96	66	.593	1			---	2	4	.333			---
	1993	OAK	AL	68	94	.420	7			---			---			---
	15	YR TOTALS		1202	1043	.535	45	0	0	---	15	8	.652	5	8	.385

Kurt Abbott No. 11/SS

Full name: Kurt Thomas Abbott
Bats: R **Throws:** R **HT:** 6–0 **WT:** 170
Born: 6–2–69, Zaneville, OH
High school: Dixie Hollins (St. Petersburg, FL)
College: St. Petersburg (FL)
Abbott was an All-Star at AAA with a .319 BA.

TEAM	LG	POS	G	AB	R	H	2B	3B	HR	RBI	BB	SO	SB	E	BA	SLG	SALARY
1993 OAK	AL	OF	20	61	11	15	1	0	3	9	3	20	2	2	.246	.410	N/A
1 YR	TOTAL		20	61	11	15	1	0	3	9	3	20	2	2	.246	.410	
1993 RANK	MLB OF	not ranked -- didn't have 150 ABs in 1993															

Mike Aldrete No. 23/1B–OF

Full name: Michael Peter Aldrete
Bats: L **Throws:** L **HT:** 5–11 **WT:** 185
Born: 1–29–61, Carmel, CA
High school: Monterey (CA)
College: Stanford
Aldrete filled in when Mark McGwire injured his heel.

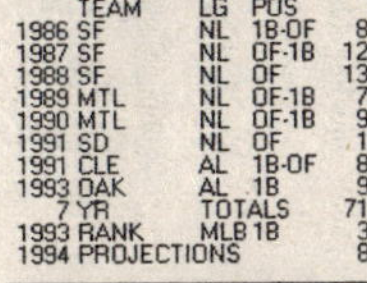
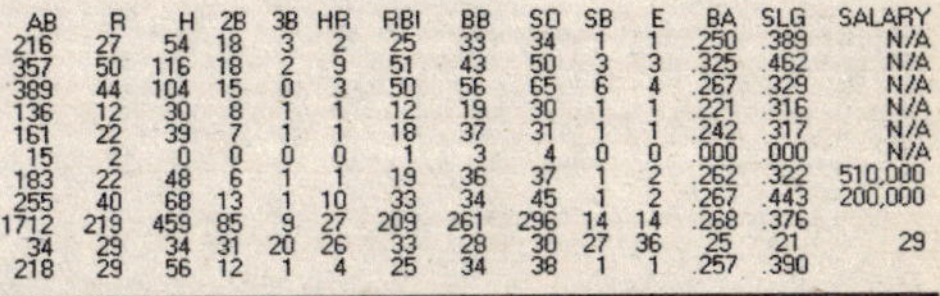

TEAM	LG	POS	G	AB	R	H	2B	3B	HR	RBI	BB	SO	SB	E	BA	SLG	SALARY
1986 SF	NL	1B-OF	84	216	27	54	18	3	2	25	33	34	1	1	.250	.389	N/A
1987 SF	NL	OF-1B	126	357	50	116	18	2	9	51	43	50	3	3	.325	.462	N/A
1988 SF	NL	OF	139	389	44	104	15	0	3	50	56	65	6	4	.267	.329	N/A
1989 MTL	NL	OF-1B	76	136	12	30	8	1	1	12	19	30	1	1	.221	.316	N/A
1990 MTL	NL	OF-1B	96	161	22	39	7	1	1	18	37	31	1	1	.242	.317	N/A
1991 SD	NL	OF	12	15	2	0	0	0	0	1	3	4	0	0	.000	.000	N/A
1991 CLE	AL	1B-OF	85	183	22	48	6	1	1	19	36	37	1	2	.262	.322	510,000
1993 OAK	AL	1B	95	255	40	68	13	1	10	33	34	45	1	2	.267	.443	200,000
7 YR	TOTALS		713	1712	219	459	85	9	27	209	261	296	14	14	.268	.376	
1993 RANK	MLB 1B		34	34	29	34	31	20	26	33	28	30	27	36	25	21	29
1994 PROJECTIONS			88	218	29	56	12	1	4	25	34	38	1	1	.257	.390	

Marcos Armas No. 38/1B

Full name: Marcos Rafael Armas
Bats: R **Throws:** R **HT:** 6–5 **WT:** 190
Born: 8–5–69, Puerto Pirtu, VZ
Armas showed potential at AAA Tacoma, posting a .290 BA and banging out 27 doubles.

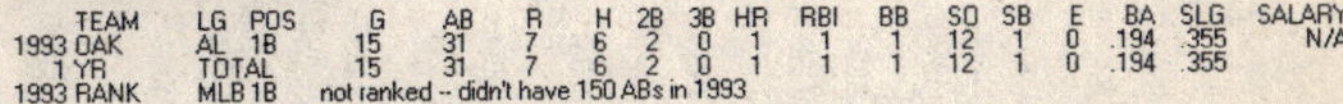

TEAM	LG	POS	G	AB	R	H	2B	3B	HR	RBI	BB	SO	SB	E	BA	SLG	SALARY
1993 OAK	AL	1B	15	31	7	6	2	0	1	1	1	12	1	0	.194	.355	N/A
1 YR	TOTAL		15	31	7	6	2	0	1	1	1	12	1	0	.194	.355	
1993 RANK	MLB 1B	not ranked -- didn't have 150 ABs in 1993															

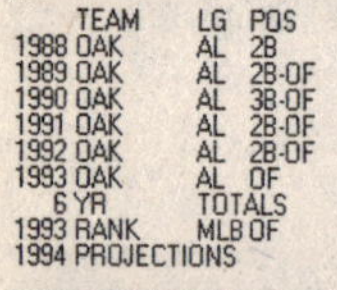

Lance Blankenship No. 12/OF

Full name: Lance Robert Blankenship
Bats: R **Throws:** R **HT:** 6–0 **WT:** 185
Born: 12–6–63, Portland, OR
High school: Ygnacio Valley (Concord, CA)
College: California
Blankenship walked 67 times in 94 games.

TEAM	LG	POS	G	AB	R	H	2B	3B	HR	RBI	BB	SO	SB	E	BA	SLG	SALARY
1988 OAK	AL	2B	10	3	1	0	0	0	0	0	0	1	0	0	.000	.000	N/A
1989 OAK	AL	2B-OF	58	125	22	29	5	1	1	4	8	31	5	1	.232	.312	N/A
1990 OAK	AL	3B-OF	86	136	18	26	3	0	0	10	20	23	3	5	.191	.213	N/A
1991 OAK	AL	2B-OF	90	185	33	46	8	0	3	21	23	42	12	3	.249	.341	125,000
1992 OAK	AL	2B-OF	123	349	59	84	24	1	3	34	82	57	21	6	.241	.341	165,000
1993 OAK	AL	OF	94	252	43	48	8	1	2	23	67	64	13	5	.190	.254	627,500
6 YR	TOTALS		461	1050	176	233	48	3	9	92	200	218	54	20	.222	.299	
1993 RANK	MLB	OF	99	100	84	121	125	97	114	117	19	61	52	47	135	137	73
1994 PROJECTIONS			80	187	32	41	7	0	2	16	32	45	10	3	.219	.294	

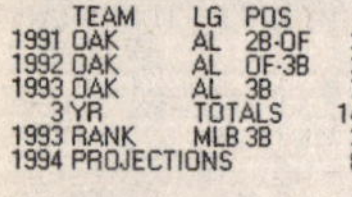

Scott Brosius No. 2/IF–OF

Full name: Scott David Brosius
Bats: R **Throws:** R **HT:** 6–1 **WT:** 185
Born: 8–15–66, Hillsboro, OR
High school: Rex Putnam (Milwaukie, OR)
College: Linfield (McMinnville, OR)
Brosius hit .342 from the seventh inning on.

TEAM	LG	POS	G	AB	R	H	2B	3B	HR	RBI	BB	SO	SB	E	BA	SLG	SALARY
1991 OAK	AL	2B-OF	36	68	9	16	5	0	2	4	3	11	3	0	.235	.397	100,000
1992 OAK	AL	OF-3B	38	87	13	19	2	0	4	13	3	13	3	1	.218	.379	113,000
1993 OAK	AL	3B	70	213	26	53	10	1	6	25	14	37	6	2	.249	.390	130,000
3 YR	TOTALS		144	368	48	88	17	1	12	42	20	61	12	3	.239	.389	
1993 RANK	MLB	3B	38	35	34	33	33	21	28	35	35	32	10	41	30	25	29
1994 PROJECTIONS			81	261	31	65	11	1	7	32	17	45	7	2	.249	.379	0

Kelly Downs No. 31/P

Full name: Kelly Robert Downs
Bats: R **Throws:** R **HT:** 6–4 **WT:** 200
Born: 10–25–60, Ogden, UT
High school: Viewmont (Bountiful, UT)
Downs was 0–6 with a 7.02 ERA as a starter.

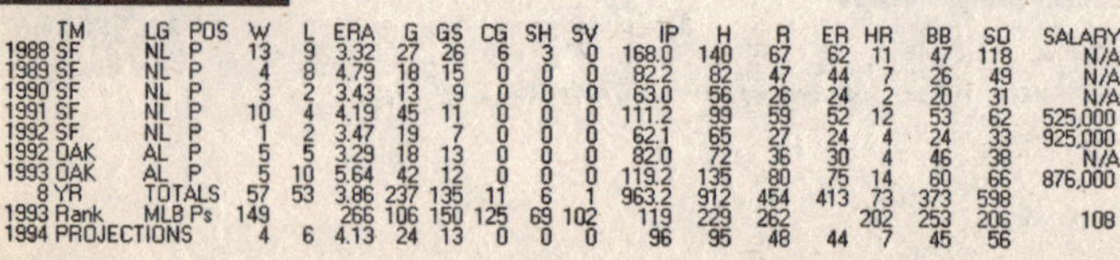

TM	LG	POS	W	L	ERA	G	GS	CG	SH	SV	IP	H	R	ER	HR	BB	SO	SALARY
1988 SF	NL	P	13	9	3.32	27	26	6	3	0	168.0	140	67	62	11	47	118	N/A
1989 SF	NL	P	4	8	4.79	18	15	0	0	0	82.2	82	47	44	7	26	49	N/A
1990 SF	NL	P	3	2	3.43	13	9	0	0	0	63.0	56	26	24	2	20	31	N/A
1991 SF	NL	P	10	4	4.19	45	11	0	0	0	111.2	99	59	52	12	53	62	525,000
1992 SF	NL	P	1	2	3.47	19	7	0	0	0	62.1	65	27	24	4	24	33	925,000
1992 OAK	AL	P	5	5	3.29	18	13	0	0	0	82.0	72	36	30	4	46	38	N/A
1993 OAK	AL	P	5	10	5.64	42	12	0	0	0	119.2	135	80	75	14	60	66	876,000
8 YR	TOTALS		57	53	3.86	237	135	11	6	1	963.2	912	454	413	73	373	598	
1993 Rank	MLB	Ps	149		266	106	150	125	69	102	119	229	262		202	253	206	108
1994 PROJECTIONS			4	6	4.13	24	13	0	0	0	96	95	48	44	7	45	56	

Scott Hemond No. 2/C

Full name: Scott Matthew Hemond
Bats: R **Throws:** R **HT:** 6–0 **WT:** 205
Born: 11–16–65, Taunton, MA
High school: Dunedin (FL)
College: South Florida
Hemond batted .282 after the All-Star break.

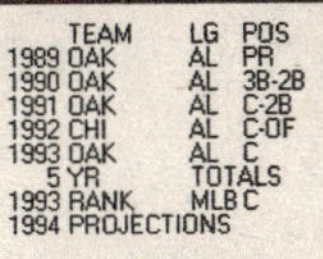
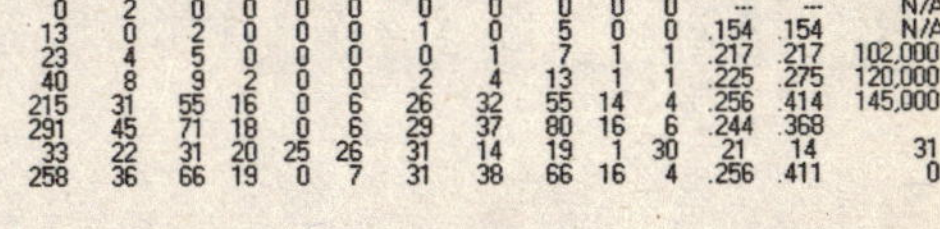

TEAM	LG	POS	G	AB	R	H	2B	3B	HR	RBI	BB	SO	SB	E	BA	SLG	SALARY
1989 OAK	AL	PR	4	0	2	0	0	0	0	0	0	0	0	0	---	---	N/A
1990 OAK	AL	3B-2B	7	13	0	2	0	0	0	1	0	5	0	0	.154	.154	N/A
1991 OAK	AL	C-2B	23	23	4	5	0	0	0	0	1	7	1	1	.217	.217	102,000
1992 CHI	AL	C-OF	25	40	8	9	2	0	0	2	4	13	1	1	.225	.275	120,000
1993 OAK	AL	C	91	215	31	55	16	0	6	26	32	55	14	4	.256	.414	145,000
5 YR	TOTALS		150	291	45	71	18	0	6	29	37	80	16	6	.244	.368	
1993 RANK	MLB C		27	33	22	31	20	25	26	31	14	19	1	30	21	14	31
1994 PROJECTIONS			108	258	36	66	19	0	7	31	38	66	16	4	.256	.411	0

Shawn Hillegas No. 57/P

Full name: Shawn Patrick Hillegas
Bats: R **Throws:** R **HT:** 6–2 **WT:** 223
Born: 8–21–64, Dos Palos, CA
High school: Forest Hills (Sidman. PA)
College: Middle Georgia
Hillegas finished the year at AAA Tacoma.

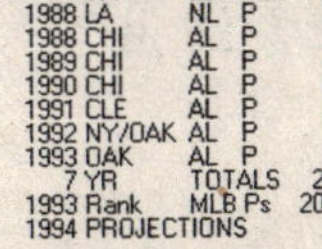

TM	LG	POS	W	L	ERA	G	GS	CG	SH	SV	IP	H	R	ER	HR	BB	SO	SALARY
1988 LA	NL	P	3	4	4.13	11	10	0	0	0	56.2	54	26	26	5	17	30	N/A
1988 CHI	AL	P	3	2	3.15	6	6	0	0	0	40.0	30	16	14	4	18	26	N/A
1989 CHI	AL	P	7	11	4.74	50	13	0	0	3	119.2	132	67	63	12	51	76	N/A
1990 CHI	AL	P	0	0	0.79	7	0	0	0	0	11.1	4	1	1	0	5	5	N/A
1991 CLE	AL	P	3	4	4.34	51	3	0	0	7	83.0	67	42	40	7	46	66	200,000
1992 NY/OAK	AL	P	1	8	5.23	26	9	1	1	0	86.0	104	57	50	13	37	49	N/A
1993 OAK	AL	P	3	6	6.97	18	11	0	0	0	60.2	78	48	47	8	33	29	N/A
7 YR	TOTALS		24	38	4.61	181	62	1	1	10	515.1	521	284	264	54	238	332	
1993 Rank	MLB Ps		209		288	261	155	125	69	102	246	280	284		237	266	249	273
1994 PROJECTIONS			2	2	4.86	10	5	0	0	0	37	37	21	20	4	18	20	

Vince Horsman No. 26/P

Full name: Vincent Stanley Joseph Horsman
Bats: R **Throws:** L **HT:** 6–2 **WT:** 180
Born: 3–9–67, Halifax, Nova Scotia
High school: Prince Andrew (Dartmouth, NS)
Horsman allowed just 7 of 35 inherited runners to score and held righty opponents to a .216 BA.

TM	LG	POS	W	L	ERA	G	GS	CG	SH	SV	IP	H	R	ER	HR	BB	SO	SALARY
1991 TOR	AL	P	0	0	0.00	4	0	0	0	0	4.0	2	0	0	0	3	2	N/A
1992 OAK	AL	P	2	1	2.49	58	0	0	0	1	43.1	39	13	12	3	21	18	109,000
1993 OAK	AL	P	2	0	5.40	40	0	0	0	0	25.0	25	15	15	2	15	17	147,500
3 YR	TOTALS		4	1	3.36	102	0	0	0	1	72.1	66	28	27	5	39	37	
1993 Rank	MLB Ps	not ranked -- didn't have 50 IP in 1993																
1994 PROJECTIONS			1	0	3.38	34	0	0	0	0	24.0	22	9	9	1	13	12	

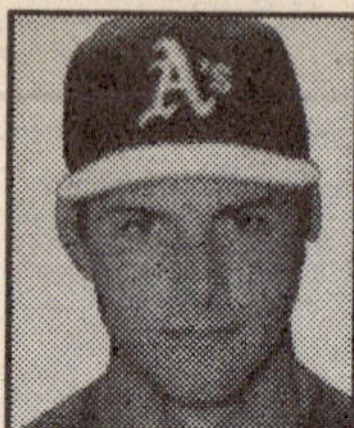

Steve Karsay — No. 50/P

Full name: Scott Karsay
Bats: R **Throws:** R **HT:** 6–3 **WT:** 180
Born: 3–24–72, College Point, NY
Acquired in the Rickey Henderson trade, Karsay was 2–0 with a 2.25 ERA in his last 4 starts for the A's.

TM	LG	POS	W	L	ERA	G	GS	CG	SH	SV	IP	H	R	ER	HR	BB	SO	SALARY
1993 OAK	AL	P	3	3	4.04	8	8	0	0	0	49.0	49	23	22	4	16	33	109,000
1 YR	TOTAL		3	3	4.04	8	8	0	0	0	49.0	49	23	22	4	16	33	
1993 RANK	MLB Ps		not ranked -- didn't have 50 IP in 1993															

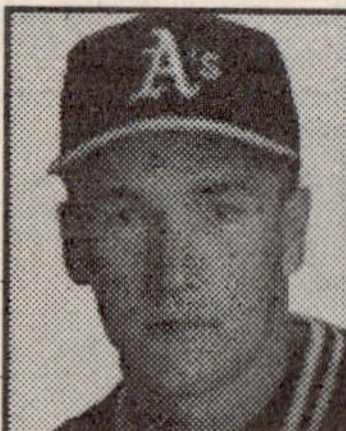

Scott Lydy — No. 49/OF

Full name: Donald Scott Lydy
Bats:R **Throws:** R **HT:** 6–5 **WT:** 195
Born: 10–26–68, Mesa, AZ
High school: Mountain View (Mesa, AZ)
College: South Mountain Junior (Mesa, AZ)
Lydy batted .293 in 95 games for AAA Tacoma.

TEAM	LG	POS	G	AB	R	H	2B	3B	HR	RBI	BB	SO	SB	E	BA	SLG	SALARY
1993 OAK	AL	OF	41	102	11	23	5	0	2	7	8	39	2	3	.225	.333	109,000
1 YR	TOTAL		41	102	11	23	5	0	2	7	8	39	2	3	.225	.333	
1993 RANK	MLB	OF	not ranked -- didn't have 150 ABs in 1993														

Todd Van Poppel — No. 59/P

Full name: Todd Matthew Van Poppel
Bats: R **Throws:** R **HT:** 6–5 **WT:** 210
Born: 12–9–71, Hinsdale, IL
High school: St. Martin (Arlington, TX)
Van Poppel issued 62 walks in 84.0 IP, but held opponents to a .234 BA.

TM	LG	POS	W	L	ERA	G	GS	CG	SH	SV	IP	H	R	ER	HR	BB	SO	SALARY
1991 OAK	AL	P	0	0	9.64	1	1	0	0	0	4.2	7	5	5	1	2	6	N/A
1993 OAK	AL	P	6	6	5.04	16	16	0	0	0	84.0	76	50	47	10	62	47	454,000
2 YR	TOTALS		6	6	5.28	17	17	0	0	0	88.2	83	55	52	11	64	53	
1993 Rank	MLB Ps		128		235	272	123	125	69	102	178	71	218		205	287	201	138
1994 PROJECTIONS			8	8	4.99	21	21	0	0	0	110	99	65	61	13	82	60	

Seattle *MARINERS*

1994 Scouting Report

Hitting: (1993/.260 BA, eleventh in AL; 161 HR, fifth in AL)

Piniella's first Mariner team won 18 more games than the year before, the largest improvement in the AL and third best in the majors. Ken Griffey was the team's best player with a .309 BA, 45 HR, and 109 RBI. Jay Buhner contributed a .272 average with 27 HR and 98 RBI. Edgar Martinez , the defending AL batting champ, missed most of '93 due to a hamstring injury. His return will certainly improve Seattle's offense. Seattle was 38–18 vs. left handed starters. But thanks to the Mariners lack of a left-handed bat, the team was just 47–62 vs. righties.

Pitching: (1993/4.20 ERA, fourth in AL)

The Mariner rotation includes AL strikeout king Randy Johnson (19–8, 3.24 ERA, 308 Ks), Dave Fleming (12–5, 4.36), Chris Bosio (9–9, 3.45), and Roger Salkeld (0–0, 2.51 in two '93 starts). Johnson and Fleming are outsanding, but Bosio and Salkeld will have to have big seasons if Seattle is to break out of the pack.

The bullpen is a trouble spot. Closer Norm Charlton was injured and became a free agent. Ted Power will probably assume that role for 1994. The team's leading setup man was Jeff Nelson (71 appearances, 4.35 ERA).

Defense: (1993/.985 pct., first in AL)

Seattle's .98543 fielding percentage was seventh best in major league history. However, Seattle declined to offer arbitration to Dave Valle, the number two catcher in the AL in fielding percentage, and his departure will probably hurt the defense. Mike Blowers' .951 mark was fourth best among AL third basemen. Ken Griffey is a Gold Glove outfielder.

1994 Prospects:

Seattle took a huge step forward in Piniella's first year. And they're fortunate—Texas is the only serious competition in the AL West. If Edgar Martinez comes back and key Rangers such as Will Clark, Jose Canseco, or Gary Redus don't—1993 could be an AL West championship year for Seattle.

Team Directory

CEO: John Ellis	President & COO: Chuck Armstrong
General Mgr.: Woody Woodward	VP, Finance and Adm.: Brian Beggs
Director of P.R.: Dave Aust	Traveling Secretary: Craig Detweiler

Minor League Affiliates:

Level	Team/League	1993 Record
AAA	Calgary – Pacific Coast	68–72
AA	Jacksonville – Southern	59–81
A	Riverside – California	76–61
	Appleton – Midwest	62–73
	Bellingham – Northwest	44–32
Rookie	Peoria Mariners – Arizona	18–36

1993 Review

	Home		Away			Home		Away			Home		Away	
vs AL East	W	L	W	L	vs AL Cent.	W	L	W	L	vs AL West	W	L	W	L
Baltimore	4	2	1	5	Chicago	1	5	3	4	California	4	3	3	3
Boston	2	4	3	3	Cleveland	6	0	3	3	Oakland	1	6	3	3
Detroit	4	2	1	5	Kansas City	4	3	2	4	Texas	5	1	3	4
New York	3	3	2	4	Milwaukee	4	2	4	2					
Toronto	4	2	3	3	Minnesota	4	2	5	2					
Total	17	13	10	20		19	12	17	15		10	10	9	10

1994 finish: 82–80 (46–35 home, 36–45 away), fourth in AL West, 12 games behind

1994 Schedule

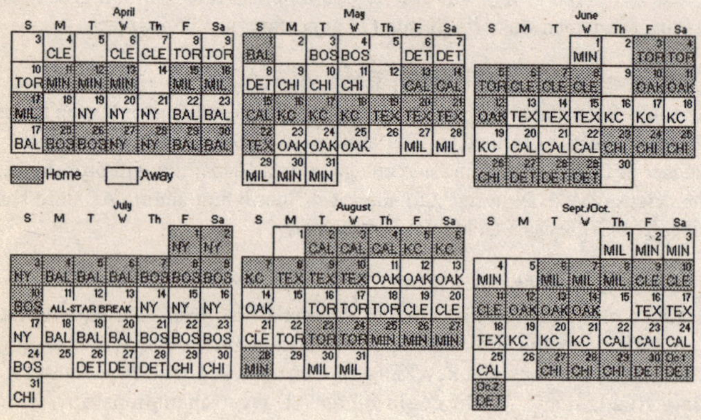

April

S	M	T	W	Th	F	Sa
3	4 CLE	5	6 CLE	7 CLE	8 TOR	9 TOR
10 TOR	11 MIN	12 MIN	13 MIN	14	15 MIL	16 MIL
17 MIL	18	19 NY	20 NY	21 NY	22 BAL	23 BAL
17 BAL	25 BOS	26 BOS	27 NY	28 NY	29 BAL	30 BAL

Home Away

May

S	M	T	W	Th	F	Sa
1 BAL	2	3 BOS	4 BOS	5	6 DET	7 DET
8 DET	9 CHI	10 CHI	11 CHI	12	13 CAL	14 CAL
15 CAL	16 KC	17 KC	18 KC	19 TEX	20 TEX	21 TEX
22 TEX	23 OAK	24 OAK	25 OAK	26	27 MIL	28 MIL
29 MIL	30 MIN	31 MIN				

June

S	M	T	W	Th	F	Sa
			1 MIN	2	3 TOR	4 TOR
5 TOR	6 CLE	7 CLE	8 CLE	9	10 OAK	11 OAK
12 OAK	13 TEX	14 TEX	15 TEX	16 KC	17 KC	18 KC
19 KC	20 CAL	21 CAL	22 CAL	23 CHI	24 CHI	25 CHI
26 CHI	27 DET	28 DET	29 DET	30		

July

S	M	T	W	Th	F	Sa
					1 NY	2 NY
3 NY	4 BAL	5 BAL	6 BAL	7 BOS	8 BOS	9 BOS
10 BOS	11 ALL-STAR BREAK	12	13	14 NY	15 NY	16 NY
17 NY	18 BAL	19 BAL	20 BAL	21 BOS	22 BOS	23 BOS
24 BOS	25	26 DET	27 DET	28 DET	29 CHI	30 CHI
31 CHI						

August

S	M	T	W	Th	F	Sa
	1	2 CAL	3 CAL	4 CAL	5 KC	6 KC
7 KC	8 TEX	9 TEX	10 TEX	11 OAK	12 OAK	13 OAK
14 OAK	15	16 TOR	17 TOR	18 TOR	19 CLE	20 CLE
21 CLE	22 TOR	23 TOR	24 TOR	25 MIN	26 MIN	27 MIN
28 MIN	29	30 MIL	31 MIL			

Sept./Oct.

S	M	T	W	Th	F	Sa
				1 MIL	2 MIN	3 MIN
4 MIN	5	6 MIL	7 MIL	8 MIL	9 CLE	10 CLE
11 CLE	12 OAK	13 OAK	14 OAK	15	16 TEX	17 TEX
18 TEX	19 KC	20 KC	21 KC	22 CAL	23 CAL	24 CAL
25 CAL	26	27 CHI	28 CHI	29 CHI	30 DET	Oct 1 DET
Oc.2 DET						

SEATTLE MARINERS 1994 ROSTER

MANAGER: Lou Piniella (14)
COACHES: Lee Elia (3), Sammy Ellis (32), Ken Griffey (30), John McLaren (7), Sam Perlozzo

No.	PITCHERS	B	T	HT	WT	DOB	BIRTHPLACE	RESIDENCE
59	Ayala, Bobby	R	R	6–3	200	7–8–69	Ventura, CA	Oxnard, CA
29	Bosio, Chris	R	R	6–3	225	4–3–63	Carmichael, CA	Shingle Springs, CA
	Buckley, Travis	R	R	6–4	210	6–15–70	Ottawa, KS	Overland Park, KS
	Clayton, Craig	R	R	6–0	185	11–29–70	Bellflower, CA	Anaheim, CA
57	Converse, Jim	L	R	5–9	180	8–17–71	San Francisco, CA	Citrus Heights, CA
47	Cummings, John	L	L	6–3	200	5–10–69	Torrance, CA	Laguna, CA
	Darwin, Jeff	R	R	6–3	180	7–6–69	Sherman, TX	Bonham, TX
55	DeLucia, Rich	R	R	6–0	185	10–7–64	Reading, PA	Columbia, SC
35	Fleming, Dave	L	L	6–3	200	11–7–69	Queens, NY	Mahopac, NY
	Harris, Reggie	R	R	6–1	190	8–12–68	Waynesboro, VA	Waynesboro, VA
	Holman, Brad	R	R	6–8	235	2–9–68	Kansas City, MO	Wichita, KS
51	Johnson, Randy	R	L	6–10	225	9–10–63	Walnut Creek, CA	Seattle, WA
50	King, Kevin	L	L	6–4	200	2–11–69	Atwater, CA	Tulsa, OK
40	Nelson, Jeff	R	R	6–8	235	11–17–66	Baltimore, MD	Baltimore, MD
12	Planteberg, Erik	S	L	6–1	180	10–30–68	Renton, WA	Bellevue, WA
48	Power, Ted	R	R	6–4	215	11–31–55	Guthrie, OK	Cincinnati, OH
41	Salkeld, Roger	R	R	6–5	215	3–6–71	Burbank, CA	Saugus, CA
26	Wainhouse, Dave	L	R	6–2	185	11–7–67	Toronto, OT	Mercer Island, WA
No.	**CATCHERS**	**B**	**T**	**HT**	**WT**	**DOB**	**BIRTHPLACE**	**RESIDENCE**
	Deak, Brian	R	R	6–0	183	10–25–67	Harrisburg, PA	Scottsdale, AZ
15	Haselman, Bill	R	R	6–3	215	5–25–66	Long Branch, NJ	Saratoga, CA
	Howard, Chris	R	R	6–2	220	2–27–66	San Diego, CA	Houston, TX
4	Sasser, Mackey	L	R	6–1	210	8–3–62	Fort Gaines, GA	Lynn Haven, FL
6	Wilson, Dan	R	R	6–3	190	3–25–69	Arlington Hts., IL	St. Louis Park, MN
No.	**INFIELDERS**	**B**	**T**	**HT**	**WT**	**DOB**	**BIRTHPLACE**	**RESIDENCE**
8	Amaral, Rich	R	R	6–0	175	4–1–62	Visalia, CA	Costa Mesa, CA
16	Blowers, Mike	R	R	6–2	210	4–24–65	Wurzburg, GM	Tacoma, WA
15	Litton, Greg	R	R	6–0	175	7–13–64	New Orleans, LA	Pensacola, FL
	Manahan, Anthony	R	R	6–0	190	12–15–68	Elizabeth, NJ	Scottsdale, AZ
11	Martinez, Edgar	R	R	5–11	190	1–2–63	New York, NY	Kirkland, WA
23	Martinez, Tino	L	R	6–2	210	12–7–67	Tampa, FL	Tampa, FL
20	Pirkl, Greg	R	R	6–5	225	8–7–70	Long Beach, CA	Los Alamitos, CA
	Rodriguez, Alex	R	R	6–3	190	7–27–75	New York, NY	Miami, FL
	Santana, Ruben	R	R	6–2	175	3–7–70	Santo Domingo, DR	Santo Domingo, DR
13	Vizquel, Omar	S	R	5–9	165	4–24–67	Caracas, VN	Caracas, VN
No.	**OUTFIELDERS**	**B**	**T**	**HT**	**WT**	**DOB**	**BIRTHPLACE**	**RESIDENCE**
	Anthony, Eric	L	L	6–2	195	11–8–67	San Diego, CA	Houston, TX
19	Buhner, Jay	R	R	6–3	210	8–13–64	Louisville, KY	League City, TX
24	Griffey Jr., Ken	L	L	6–3	205	11–21–69	Donora, PA	Renton, WA
28	Newfield, Marc	R	R	6–4	205	10–19–72	Sacramento, CA	Huntington B., CA
27	Tinsley, Lee	S	R	5–10	185	3–4–69	Shelbyville, KY	Shelbyville, KY
1	Turang, Brian	R	R	5–10	170	6–14–67	Long Beach, CA	Long Beach, CA

The Kingdome (58,879, artificial)
Tickets: 206–628–3555
Ticket prices:
- $15 (box)
- $12 (club)
- $8 (view)
- $6 (view–children 14 & under, family sections and general admission)
- $4 (family sect. and g.a., 14 & under)

Field Dimensions (from home plate)
- To left field at foul line, 331 feet
- To center field, 405 feet
- To right field at foul line, 312 feet

(OF wall is 11.5' in LF & CF, 23' in RF)

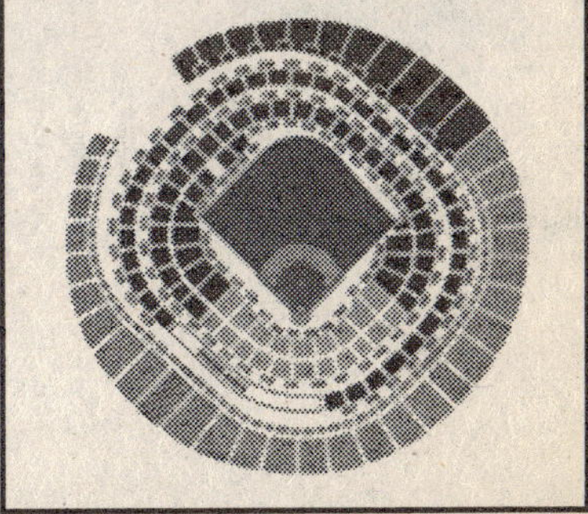

Rich Amaral No. 8/2B

Full name: Richard Louis Amaral
Bats: R **Throws:** R **HT:** 6–0 **WT:** 175
Born: 4–1–62, Visalia, CA
High school: Estancia (Costa Mesa, CA)
College: Orange Coast (CA) and UCLA

In his first full season, Amaral batted an impressive .290. He also had Seattle's best average against lefties – .372.

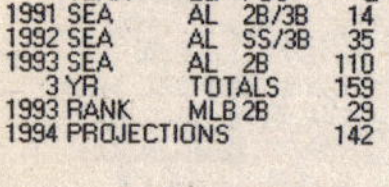
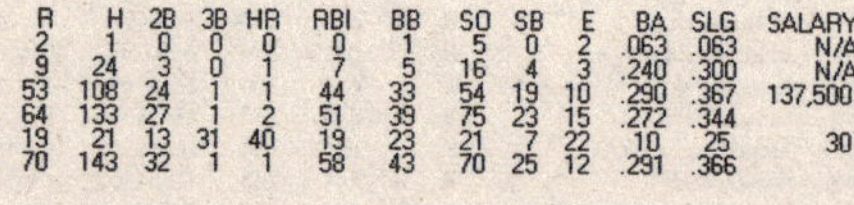

	TEAM	LG	POS	G	AB	R	H	2B	3B	HR	RBI	BB	SO	SB	E	BA	SLG	SALARY
1991	SEA	AL	2B/3B	14	16	2	1	0	0	0	0	1	5	0	2	.063	.063	N/A
1992	SEA	AL	SS/3B	35	100	9	24	3	0	1	7	5	16	4	3	.240	.300	N/A
1993	SEA	AL	2B	110	373	53	108	24	1	1	44	33	54	19	10	.290	.367	137,500
3	YR	TOTALS		159	489	64	133	27	1	2	51	39	75	23	15	.272	.344	
1993	RANK	MLB	2B	29	25	19	21	13	31	40	19	23	21	7	22	10	25	30
1994	PROJECTIONS			142	492	70	143	32	1	1	58	43	70	25	12	.291	.366	

Eric Anthony No. 24/OF

Full name: Eric Todd Anthony
Bats: L **Throws:** L **HT:** 6–2 **WT:** 195
Born: 11–8–67, San Diego, CA
High School: Sharstown (Houston, TX)

Anthony started off fast, hitting .338 in April, but due to tendinitis in his shoulder, only played 19 games in September and October.

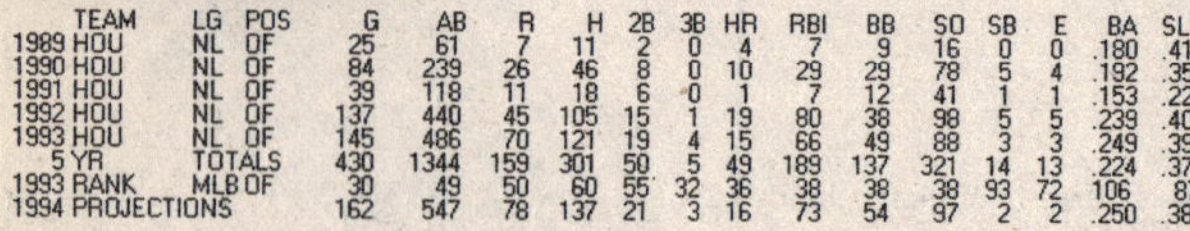

	TEAM	LG	POS	G	AB	R	H	2B	3B	HR	RBI	BB	SO	SB	E	BA	SLG	SALARY
1989	HOU	NL	OF	25	61	7	11	2	0	4	7	9	16	0	0	.180	.410	N/A
1990	HOU	NL	OF	84	239	26	46	8	0	10	29	29	78	5	4	.192	.351	N/A
1991	HOU	NL	OF	39	118	11	18	6	0	1	7	12	41	1	1	.153	.229	N/A
1992	HOU	NL	OF	137	440	45	105	15	1	19	80	38	98	5	5	.239	.407	115,000
1993	HOU	NL	OF	145	486	70	121	19	4	15	66	49	88	3	3	.249	.397	350,000
5	YR	TOTALS		430	1344	159	301	50	5	49	189	137	321	14	13	.224	.378	
1993	RANK	MLB	OF	30	49	50	60	55	32	36	38	38	38	93	72	106	87	90
1994	PROJECTIONS			162	547	78	137	21	3	16	73	54	97	2	2	.250	.388	

Mike Blowers No. 16/3B

Full name: Michael Roy Blowers
Bats: R **Throws:** R **HT:** 6–2 **WT:** 210
Born: 4–24–65, Wurzburg, GM
High school: Bethel (WA)
College: Tacoma CC (WA) and Washington

Blowers had his best season, with a .280 BA, 15 HR, and 57 RBI. He belted grand slams in back to back games May 16 and 17.

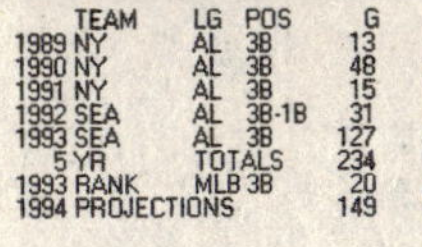

TEAM	LG	POS	G	AB	R	H	2B	3B	HR	RBI	BB	SO	SB	E	BA	SLG	SALARY
1989 NY	AL	3B	13	38	2	10	0	0	0	3	3	13	0	4	.263	.263	N/A
1990 NY	AL	3B	48	144	16	27	4	0	5	21	12	50	1	10	.188	.319	N/A
1991 NY	AL	3B	15	35	3	7	0	0	1	1	4	3	0	3	.200	.286	N/A
1992 SEA	AL	3B-1B	31	73	7	14	3	0	1	2	6	20	0	1	.192	.274	135,000
1993 SEA	AL	3B	127	379	55	106	23	3	15	57	44	98	1	15	.280	.475	109,000
5 YR	TOTALS		234	669	83	164	30	3	22	84	69	184	2	33	.245	.398	
1993 RANK	MLB	3B	20	21	16	20	18	6	10	18	13	5	26	14	12	5	34
1994 PROJECTIONS			149	447	65	125	27	3	18	67	52	115	1	17	.280	.474	

Jay Buhner No. 19/OF

Full name: Jay Campbell Buhner
Bats: R **Throws:** R **HT:** 6–3 **WT:** 210
Born: 8–13–64, Louisville, KY
High school: Clear Creek (League City, TX)
College: McClennan CC (Waco, TX)

Buhner has hit over 25 home runs in each of the last three seasons. He ended 1993 with a ten-game hitting streak.

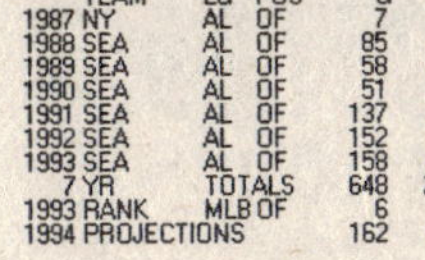

TEAM	LG	POS	G	AB	R	H	2B	3B	HR	RBI	BB	SO	SB	E	BA	SLG	SALARY
1987 NY	AL	OF	7	22	0	5	2	0	0	1	1	6	0	0	.227	.318	N/A
1988 SEA	AL	OF	85	261	36	56	13	1	13	38	28	93	1	3	.215	.421	N/A
1989 SEA	AL	OF	58	204	27	56	15	1	9	33	19	55	1	4	.275	.490	N/A
1990 SEA	AL	OF	51	163	16	45	12	0	7	33	17	50	2	2	.276	.479	N/A
1991 SEA	AL	OF	137	406	64	99	14	4	27	77	53	117	0	5	.244	.498	247,500
1992 SEA	AL	OF	152	543	69	132	16	3	25	79	71	146	0	2	.243	.422	1,445,000
1993 SEA	AL	OF	158	563	91	153	28	3	27	98	100	144	2	6	.272	.476	2,772,500
7 YR	TOTALS		648	2162	303	546	100	12	108	359	289	611	6	22	.253	.460	
1993 RANK	MLB	OF	6	21	19	27	23	54	13	11	5	3	102	38	66	32	28
1994 PROJECTIONS			162	578	93	156	28	2	27	100	102	147	1	6	.270	.465	

Ken Griffey Jr. No. 24/OF

Full name: George Kenneth Griffey Jr.
Bats: L **Throws:** L **HT:** 6–3 **WT:** 205
Born: 11–21–69, Donora, PA
High school: Moeller (Cincinnati, OH)
Griffey reached 100 HR in 1993, the sixth youngest player ever to do so. He led the AL in total bases and extra base hits, and ranked second in HR and slugging percentage.

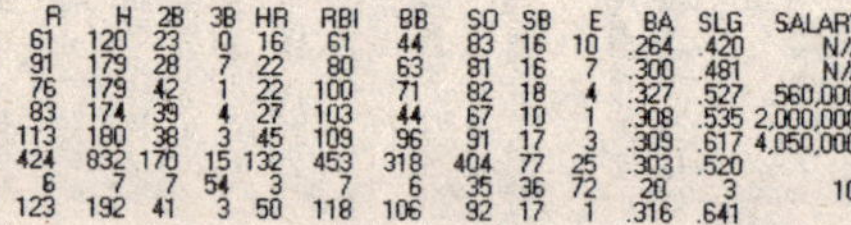

	TEAM	LG	POS	G	AB	R	H	2B	3B	HR	RBI	BB	SO	SB	E	BA	SLG	SALARY
1989	SEA	AL	OF	127	455	61	120	23	0	16	61	44	83	16	10	.264	.420	N/A
1990	SEA	AL	OF	155	597	91	179	28	7	22	80	63	81	16	7	.300	.481	N/A
1991	SEA	AL	OF	154	548	76	179	42	1	22	100	71	82	18	4	.327	.527	560,000
1992	SEA	AL	OF	142	565	83	174	39	4	27	103	44	67	10	1	.308	.535	2,000,000
1993	SEA	AL	OF	156	582	113	180	38	3	45	109	96	91	17	3	.309	.617	4,050,000
5	YR	TOTALS		734	2747	424	832	170	15	132	453	318	404	77	25	.303	.520	
1993	RANK	MLB	OF	11	15	6	7	7	54	3	7	6	35	36	72	20	3	10
1994	PROJECTIONS			161	607	123	192	41	3	50	118	106	92	17	1	.316	.641	

Bill Haselman No. 15/C

Full name: William Joseph Haselman
Bats: R **Throws:** R **HT:** 6–3 **WT:** 215
Born: 5–25–66, Long Branch, NJ
High school: Saratoga (CA)
College: UCLA
Haselman appeared in 58 games and hit .255.

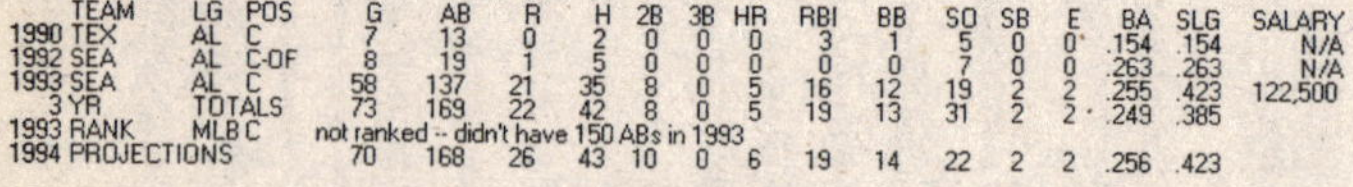

	TEAM	LG	POS	G	AB	R	H	2B	3B	HR	RBI	BB	SO	SB	E	BA	SLG	SALARY
1990	TEX	AL	C	7	13	0	2	0	0	0	3	1	5	0	0	.154	.154	N/A
1992	SEA	AL	C-OF	8	19	1	5	0	0	0	0	0	7	0	0	.263	.263	N/A
1993	SEA	AL	C	58	137	21	35	8	0	5	16	12	19	2	2	.255	.423	122,500
3	YR	TOTALS		73	169	22	42	8	0	5	19	13	31	2	2	.249	.385	
1993	RANK	MLB	C	not ranked -- didn't have 150 ABs in 1993														
1994	PROJECTIONS			70	168	26	43	10	0	6	19	14	22	2	2	.256	.423	

Edgar Martinez No. 11/3B

Full name: Edgar Martinez
Bats: R **Throws:** R **HT:** 5–11 **WT:** 190
Born: 1–2–63, New York, NY
High school: Dorado (PR)
Martinez, the 1992 AL batting champ, missed 112 games due to injuries, and batted just .237 when he was in the lineup.

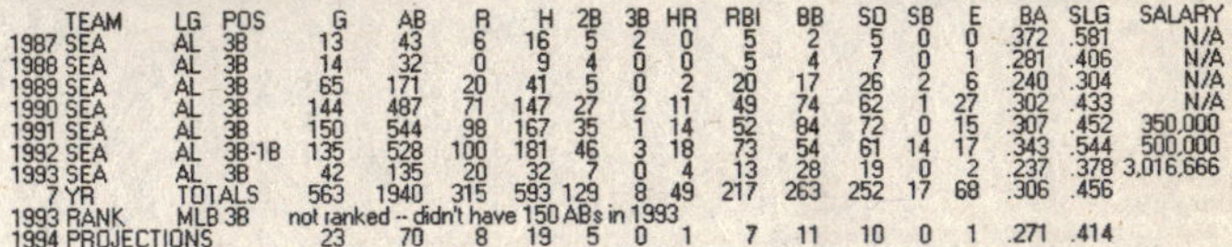

	TEAM	LG	POS	G	AB	R	H	2B	3B	HR	RBI	BB	SO	SB	E	BA	SLG	SALARY
1987	SEA	AL	3B	13	43	6	16	5	2	0	5	2	5	0	0	.372	.581	N/A
1988	SEA	AL	3B	14	32	0	9	4	0	0	5	4	7	0	1	.281	.406	N/A
1989	SEA	AL	3B	65	171	20	41	5	0	2	20	17	26	2	6	.240	.304	N/A
1990	SEA	AL	3B	144	487	71	147	27	2	11	49	74	62	1	27	.302	.433	N/A
1991	SEA	AL	3B	150	544	98	167	35	1	14	52	84	72	0	15	.307	.452	350,000
1992	SEA	AL	3B-1B	135	528	100	181	46	3	18	73	54	61	14	17	.343	.544	500,000
1993	SEA	AL	3B	42	135	20	32	7	0	4	13	28	19	0	2	.237	.378	3,016,666
7	YR	TOTALS		563	1940	315	593	129	8	49	217	263	252	17	68	.306	.456	
1993	RANK	MLB 3B		not ranked -- didn't have 150 ABs in 1993														
1994	PROJECTIONS			23	70	8	19	5	0	1	7	11	10	0	1	.271	.414	

Tino Martinez No. 23/1B

Full name: Constantino Martinez
Bats: L **Throws:** R **HT:** 6–2 **WT:** 210
Born: 12–7–67, Tampa, FL
High school: Jefferson (Tampa, FL)
College: Tampa
Martinez ranked third on the team with 17 HR, even though he missed the season's last 50 games with a knee injury.

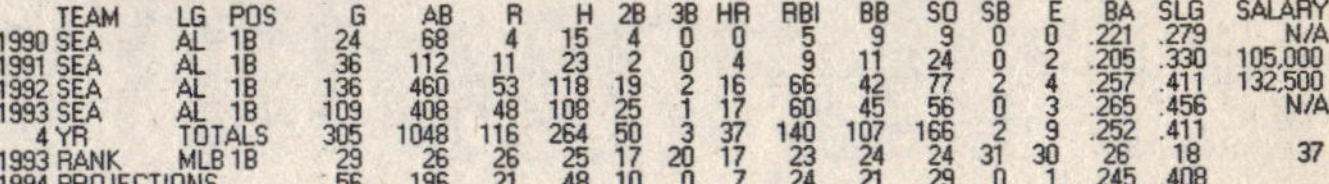

	TEAM	LG	POS	G	AB	R	H	2B	3B	HR	RBI	BB	SO	SB	E	BA	SLG	SALARY
1990	SEA	AL	1B	24	68	4	15	4	0	0	5	9	9	0	0	.221	.279	N/A
1991	SEA	AL	1B	36	112	11	23	2	0	4	9	11	24	0	2	.205	.330	105,000
1992	SEA	AL	1B	136	460	53	118	19	2	16	66	42	77	2	4	.257	.411	132,500
1993	SEA	AL	1B	109	408	48	108	25	1	17	60	45	56	0	3	.265	.456	N/A
4	YR	TOTALS		305	1048	116	264	50	3	37	140	107	166	2	9	.252	.411	
1993	RANK	MLB 1B		29	26	26	25	17	20	17	23	24	24	31	30	26	18	37
1994	PROJECTIONS			56	196	21	48	10	0	7	24	21	29	0	1	.245	.408	

Omar Vizquel — No. 13/IF

Full name: Omar Enrique Vizquel
Bats: S **Throws:** R **HT:** 5–9 **WT:** 165
Born: 4–24–67, Caracas, VN
High school: Francisco Espejo (Caracas, VN)
Vizquel's 158 games were the most ever by a Seattle shortstop. He batted a solid .255, but 125 of his 143 hits were singles.

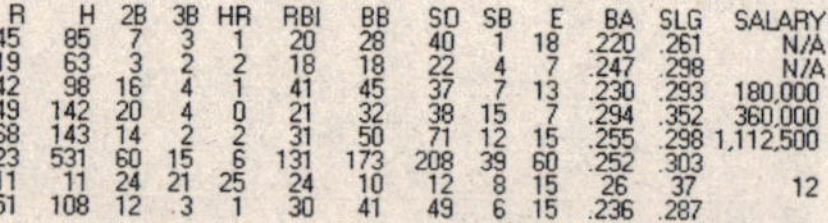

	TEAM	LG	POS	G	AB	R	H	2B	3B	HR	RBI	BB	SO	SB	E	BA	SLG	SALARY
1989	SEA	AL	SS	143	387	45	85	7	3	1	20	28	40	1	18	.220	.261	N/A
1990	SEA	AL	SS	81	255	19	63	3	2	2	18	18	22	4	7	.247	.298	N/A
1991	SEA	AL	SS-2B	142	426	42	98	16	4	1	41	45	37	7	13	.230	.293	180,000
1992	SEA	AL	SS	136	483	49	142	20	4	0	21	32	38	15	7	.294	.352	360,000
1993	SEA	AL	SS	158	560	68	143	14	2	2	31	50	71	12	15	.255	.298	1,112,500
5	YR	TOTALS		660	2111	223	531	60	15	6	131	173	208	39	60	.252	.303	
1993	RANK	MLB	SS	5	6	11	11	24	21	25	24	10	12	8	15	26	37	12
1994	PROJECTIONS			147	457	51	108	12	3	1	30	41	49	6	15	.236	.287	

Bobby Ayala — No. 59/P

Full name: Robert Joseph Ayala
Bats: R **Throws:** R **HT:** 6–3 **WT:** 200
Born: 7–8–69, Ventura, CA
High school: Rio Mesa (Oxnard, CA)
In Cincinnati, Ayala posted a 5–4 record with a 3.61 ERA in relief, and stranded 17 of 23 inherited runners. He struggled as a starter, with an ERA of 8.41 and a 2–6 record.

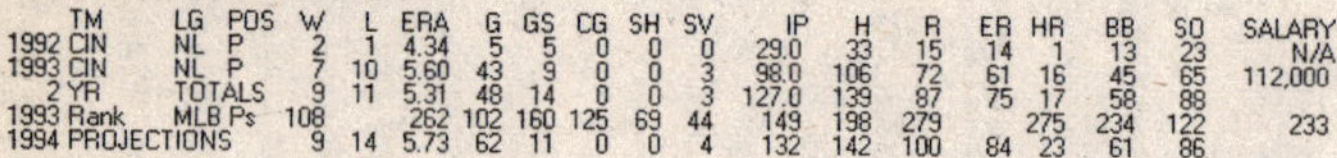

	TM	LG	POS	W	L	ERA	G	GS	CG	SH	SV	IP	H	R	ER	HR	BB	SO	SALARY
1992	CIN	NL	P	2	1	4.34	5	5	0	0	0	29.0	33	15	14	1	13	23	N/A
1993	CIN	NL	P	7	10	5.60	43	9	0	0	3	98.0	106	72	61	16	45	65	112,000
2	YR	TOTALS		9	11	5.31	48	14	0	0	3	127.0	139	87	75	17	58	88	
1993	Rank	MLB	Ps	108		262	102	160	125	69	44	149	198	279		275	234	122	233
1994	PROJECTIONS			9	14	5.73	62	11	0	0	4	132	142	100	84	23	61	86	

Chris Bosio No. 29/P

Full name: Christopher Louis Bosio
Bats: R **Throws:** R **HT:** 6–3 **WT:** 225
Born: 4–3–63, Carmichael, CA
High school: Cordova (CA)
College: Sacramento City (CA)

After no-hitting the Red Sox on April 22, Bosio spent 40 games on the DL. He was 6–5 with a 3.25 ERA after the All-Star break.

TM	LG	POS	W	L	ERA	G	GS	CG	SH	SV	IP	H	R	ER	HR	BB	SO	SALARY
1986 MIL	AL	P	0	4	7.01	10	4	0	0	0	34.2	41	27	27	9	13	29	N/A
1987 MIL	AL	P	11	8	5.24	46	19	2	1	2	170.0	187	102	99	18	50	150	N/A
1988 MIL	AL	P	7	15	3.36	38	22	9	1	6	182.0	190	80	68	13	38	84	N/A
1989 MIL	AL	P	15	10	2.95	33	33	8	2	0	234.2	225	90	77	16	48	173	N/A
1990 MIL	AL	P	4	9	4.00	20	20	4	1	0	132.2	131	67	59	15	38	76	N/A
1991 MIL	AL	P	14	10	3.25	32	32	5	1	0	204.2	187	80	74	15	58	117	875,000
1992 MIL	AL	P	16	6	3.62	33	33	4	2	0	231.1	223	100	93	21	44	120	2,287,000
1993 SEA	AL	P	9	9	3.45	29	24	3	1	1	164.1	138	75	63	14	59	119	2,750,000
8 YR	TOTALS		76	71	3.72	241	187	35	9	9	1354.1	1322	621	560	121	348	868	
1993 Rank	MLB Ps		87		85	213	97	37	23	70	82	36	96		118	143	97	40
1994 PROJECTIONS			8	8	4.24	31	21	3	1	1	155	152	81	73	15	49	115	

Randy Johnson No. 51/P

Full name: Randall David Johnson
Bats: R **Throws:** L **HT:** 6–10 **WT:** 225
Born: 9–10–63, Walnut Creek, CA
High school: Livermore (CA)
College: USC

Johnson led the majors in strikeouts for the second straight year with a team record 308. His 10.86Ks/9 IP was fourth best in history.

TM	LG	POS	W	L	ERA	G	GS	CG	SH	SV	IP	H	R	ER	HR	BB	SO	SALARY
1988 MTL	NL	P	3	0	2.42	4	4	1	0	0	26.0	23	8	7	3	7	25	N/A
1989 MTL	NL	P	0	4	6.67	7	6	0	0	0	29.2	29	25	22	2	26	26	N/A
1989 SEA	AL	P	7	9	4.40	22	22	2	0	0	131.0	118	75	64	11	70	104	N/A
1990 SEA	AL	P	14	11	3.65	33	33	5	2	0	219.2	174	103	89	26	120	194	N/A
1991 SEA	AL	P	13	10	3.98	33	33	2	1	0	201.1	151	96	89	15	152	228	350,000
1992 SEA	AL	P	12	14	3.77	31	31	6	2	0	210.1	154	104	88	13	144	241	1,392,500
1993 SEA	AL	P	19	8	3.24	35	34	10	3	1	255.1	185	97	92	22	99	308	2,625,000
6 YR	TOTALS		68	56	3.78	165	163	26	8	1	1073.1	834	508	451	92	618	1126	
1993 RANK	MLB Ps		6		64	134	12	3	3	70	6	11	41		122	169	3	46
1994 PROJECTIONS			19	8	3.23	36	36	10	2	0	270	195	102	97	23	105	327	

Ted Power No. 48/P

Full name: Ted Henry Power
Bats: R **Throws:** R **HT:** 6–4 **WT:** 215
Born: 11–31–55, Guthrie, OK
High school: Cincinnati, OH
Power came over from Cleveland and had 13 saves as the closer for the Mariners. He posted a 0.79 ERA in his first 14 games with Seattle.

	TM	LG	POS	W	L	ERA	G	GS	CG	SH	SV	IP	H	R	ER	HR	BB	SO	SALARY
1981	LA	NL	P	1	3	3.21	5	2	0	0	0	14.0	16	6	5	0	7	7	N/A
1982	LA	NL	P	1	1	6.68	12	4	0	0	0	33.2	38	27	25	4	23	15	N/A
1983	CIN	NL	P	5	6	4.54	49	6	1	0	2	111.0	120	62	56	10	49	57	N/A
1984	CIN	NL	P	9	7	2.82	78	0	0	0	11	108.2	93	37	34	4	46	81	N/A
1985	CIN	NL	P	8	6	2.70	64	0	0	0	27	80.0	65	27	24	2	45	42	N/A
1986	CIN	NL	P	10	6	3.70	56	10	0	0	1	129.0	115	59	53	13	52	95	N/A
1987	CIN	NL	P	10	13	4.50	34	34	2	1	0	204.0	213	115	102	28	71	133	N/A
1988	KC/DET	AL	P	6	7	5.91	26	14	2	2	0	99.0	121	67	65	8	38	57	N/A
1989	STL	NL	P	7	7	3.71	23	15	0	0	0	97.0	96	47	40	7	21	43	N/A
1990	PIT	NL	P	1	3	3.66	40	0	0	0	7	51.2	50	23	21	5	17	42	N/A
1991	CIN	NL	P	5	3	3.62	68	0	0	0	3	87.0	87	37	35	6	31	51	500,000
1992	CLE	AL	P	3	3	2.54	64	0	0	0	6	99.1	88	33	28	7	35	51	125,000
1993	SEA	AL	P	2	4	5.36	45	0	0	0	13	45.1	57	28	27	3	17	27	109,000
13	YR	TOTALS		68	69	4.00	564	85	5	3	70	1159.2	1159	568	516	97	452	701	
1993	Rank	MLB Ps	not ranked -- didn't have 50 IP in 1993																
1994	PROJECTIONS			1	2	5.70	20	2	0	0	4	30	37	20	19	2	15	16	

Lou Piniella No. 14/Mgr.

Full name: Louis Victor Piniella
Bats: R **Throws:** R **HT:** 6–2 **WT:** 199
Born: 10–7–64, Reading, PA
High school: Jesuit (Tampa, FL)
College: Tampa (FL)
Piniella's winning percentage is the fifth highest among active managers with five years experience.

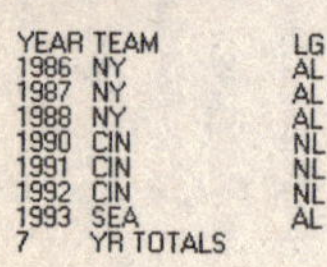

			REG. SEASON				PLAYOFF			CHAMP. SERIES			WORLD SERIES		
YEAR	TEAM	LG	W	L	PCT	POS	W	L	PCT	W	L	PCT	W	L	PCT
1986	NY	AL	90	72	.556	2			---			---			---
1987	NY	AL	89	73	.549	4			---			---			---
1988	NY	AL	45	48	.484	5			---			---			---
1990	CIN	NL	91	71	.562	1			---	4	2	.667	4	0	1.000
1991	CIN	NL	74	88	.457	5			---			---			---
1992	CIN	NL	90	72	.556	2			---			---			---
1993	SEA	AL	82	80	.506	4			---			---			---
7	YR TOTALS		561	504	.527	19	0	0	---	4	2	.667	4	0	1.000

Jeff Darwin — P

Full name: Jeffrey Scott Darwin
Bats: R **Throws:** R **HT:** 6–3 **WT:** 180
Born: 7–6–69, Sherman, TX
High school: Bonham (TX))
College: Alvin CC (TX)
Darwin had a 2.97 ERA at AA Jacksonville.

	TM	LG	POS	W	L	ERA	G	GS	CG	SH	SV	IP	H	R	ER	HR	BB	SO
1993	J'VILLE	SOU	P	3	5	2.97	27	0	0	0	7	36.1	29	17	12	1	17	39

Rich DeLucia — No. 55/P

Full name: Richard Anthony DeLucia
Bats: R **Throws:** R **HT:** 6–0 **WT:** 185
Born: 10–7–64, Reading, PA
High school: Wyomissing Area (PA)
College: Tennessee
DeLucia finished the season at AAA Calgary.

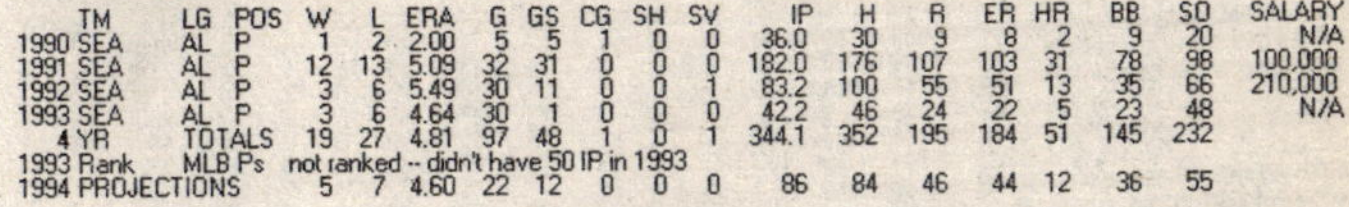

	TM	LG	POS	W	L	ERA	G	GS	CG	SH	SV	IP	H	R	ER	HR	BB	SO	SALARY
1990	SEA	AL	P	1	2	2.00	5	5	1	0	0	36.0	30	9	8	2	9	20	N/A
1991	SEA	AL	P	12	13	5.09	32	31	0	0	0	182.0	176	107	103	31	78	98	100,000
1992	SEA	AL	P	3	6	5.49	30	11	0	0	1	83.2	100	55	51	13	35	66	210,000
1993	SEA	AL	P	3	6	4.64	30	1	0	0	0	42.2	46	24	22	5	23	48	N/A
4	YR	TOTALS		19	27	4.81	97	48	1	0	1	344.1	352	195	184	51	145	232	
1993	Rank	MLB Ps		not ranked -- didn't have 50 IP in 1993															
1994	PROJECTIONS			5	7	4.60	22	12	0	0	0	86	84	46	44	12	36	55	

Dave Fleming — No. 35/P

Full name: David Anthony Fleming
Bats: L **Throws:** L **HT:** 6–3 **WT:** 200
Born: 11–7–69, Queens, NY
High school: Mahopac (NY)
College: Georgia
Seattle won 18 of Fleming's 26 starts.

	TM	LG	POS	W	L	ERA	G	GS	CG	SH	SV	IP	H	R	ER	HR	BB	SO	SALARY
1991	SEA	AL	P	1	0	6.62	9	3	0	0	0	17.2	19	13	13	3	3	11	N/A
1992	SEA	AL	P	17	10	3.39	33	33	7	4	0	228.1	225	95	86	13	60	112	109,000
1993	SEA	AL	P	12	5	4.36	26	26	1	1	0	167.1	189	84	81	15	67	75	300,000
3	YR	TOTALS		30	15	3.92	68	62	8	5	0	413.1	433	192	180	31	130	198	
1993	Rank	MLB Ps		43		175	229	85	79	23	102	77	233	145		130	183	259	150
1994	PROJECTIONS			10	5	3.94	22	20	2	1	0	137	144	64	60	10	43	66	

Brad Holman — P

Full name:
Bats: R **Throws:** R **HT:** 6–8 **WT:** 235
Born: 2–9–68, Kansas City, MO

Holman split his season between AAA Calgary (8–4, 4.74 ERA in 21 games) and Seattle (1–3, 3.72 ERA in 19 games). He held AL opponents to a .208 average.

	TM	LG	POS	W	L	ERA	G	GS	CG	SH	SV	IP	H	R	ER	HR	BB	SO	SALARY
1993	SEA	AL	P	1	3	3.72	19	0	0	0	3	36.1	27	17	15	1	16	17	N/A
1	YR	TOTAL		1	3	3.72	19	0	0	0	3	36.1	27	17	15	1	16	17	
1993	RANK	MLB Ps	not ranked -- didn't have 50 IP in 1993																

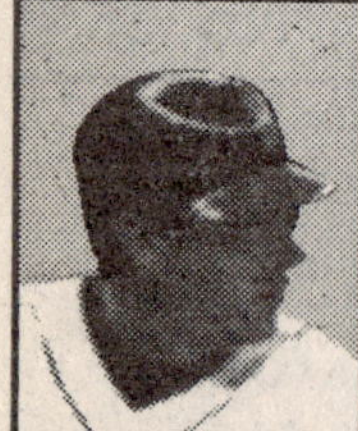

Greg Litton — No. 15/IF–OF

Full name: Jon Gregory Litton
Bats: R **Throws:** R **HT:** 6–0 **WT:** 175
Born: 7–13–64, New Orleans, LA
High school: Woodham (Pensacola, FL)
College: Pensecola Junior (FL)

Litton handled 188 chances without an error.

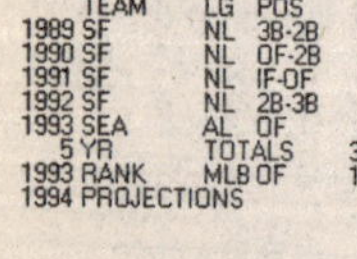

	TEAM	LG	POS	G	AB	R	H	2B	3B	HR	RBI	BB	SO	SB	E	BA	SLG	SALARY
1989	SF	NL	3B-2B	71	143	12	36	5	3	4	17	7	29	0	3	.252	.413	N/A
1990	SF	NL	OF-2B	93	204	17	50	9	1	1	24	11	45	1	1	.245	.314	N/A
1991	SF	NL	IF-OF	59	127	13	23	7	1	1	15	11	25	0	2	.181	.276	165,000
1992	SF	NL	2B-3B	68	140	9	32	5	0	4	15	11	33	0	4	.229	.350	215,000
1993	SEA	AL	OF	72	174	25	52	17	0	3	25	18	30	0	0	.299	.448	225,000
5	YR	TOTALS		363	788	76	193	43	5	13	96	58	162	1	10	.245	.362	
1993	RANK	MLB	OF	128	128	118	115	66	124	108	110	110	122	127	131	29	48	102
1994	PROJECTIONS			72	180	27	55	19	0	2	26	20	30	0	0	.306	.444	

Jeff Nelson — No. 40/P

Full name: Jeffrey Allan Nelson
Bats: R **Throws:** R **HT:** 6–8 **WT:** 235
Born: 11–17–66, Baltimore, MD
High school: Catonsville (MD)
College: Catonsville Community (MD)

Nelson's 71 appearances ranked third in the AL.

	TM	LG	POS	W	L	ERA	G	GS	CG	SH	SV	IP	H	R	ER	HR	BB	SO	SALARY
1992	SEA	AL	P	1	7	3.44	66	0	0	0	6	81.0	71	34	31	7	44	46	109,000
1993	SEA	AL	P	5	3	4.35	71	0	0	0	1	60.0	57	30	29	5	34	61	195,000
2	YR	TOTALS		6	10	3.83	137	0	0	0	7	141.0	128	64	60	12	78	107	
1993	Rank	MLB Ps		149		173	11	202	125	69	70	249	97	141		113	271	15	173
1994	PROJECTIONS			4	6	3.83	91	0	0	0	4	94	85	42	40	8	52	71	

Marc Newfield — No. 28/OF

Full name: Marc Newfield
Bats: R **Throws:** R **HT:** 6–4 **WT:** 205
Born: 10–19–72, Sacramento, CA
High school: Huntington Beach (CA)
Newfield was the fourth-youngest player in the majors at season's end.

TEAM	LG	POS	G	AB	R	H	2B	3B	HR	RBI	BB	SO	SB	E	BA	SLG	SALARY
1993 SEA	AL	OF	22	66	5	15	3	0	1	7	2	8	0	0	.227	.318	109,000
1 YR	TOTAL		22	66	5	15	3	0	1	7	2	8	0	0	.227	.318	
1993 RANK	MLB OF		not ranked -- didn't have 150 ABs in 1993														

Alex Rodriguez — SS

Full name: Alex Rodriguez
Bats: R **Throws:** R **HT:** 6–3 **WT:** 190
Born: 7–27–75, New York, NY
High school: Westminster Christian (Miami, FL)
Rodriguez was the No. 1 pick in the '93 free agent draft. In high school, he hit .505 with nine HR.

TEAM	LG	POS	G	AB	R	H	2B	3B	HR	RBI	BB	SO	SB	E	BA	SLG	SALARY
NO PROFESSIONAL BASEBALL EXPERIENCE																	

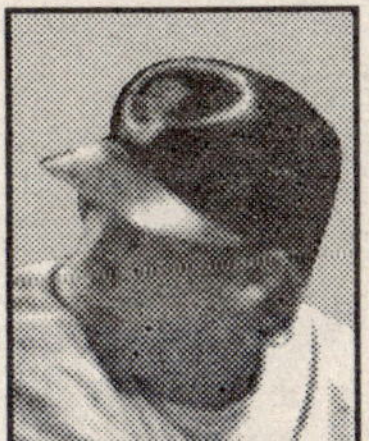

Mackey Sasser — No. 4/C

Full name: Mack Daniel Sasser Jr.
Bats: L **Throws:** R **HT:** 6–1 **WT:** 210
Born: 8–3–62, Fort Gaines, GA
High school: Godby (Tallahassee, FL)
College: Geo. Wallace CC (AL) and Troy St.(AL)
Sasser hit just .121 in the last two months of '93.

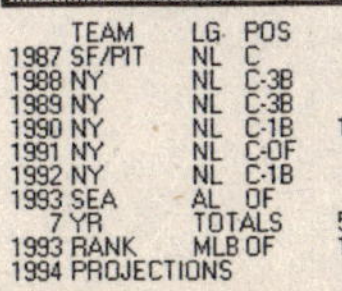

TEAM	LG	POS	G	AB	R	H	2B	3B	HR	RBI	BB	SO	SB	E	BA	SLG	SALARY
1987 SF/PIT	NL	C	14	27	2	5	0	0	0	2	0	2	0	0	.185	.185	N/A
1988 NY	NL	C-3B	60	123	9	35	10	1	1	17	6	9	0	6	.285	.407	N/A
1989 NY	NL	C-3B	72	182	17	53	14	2	1	22	7	15	0	3	.291	.407	N/A
1990 NY	NL	C-1B	100	270	31	83	14	0	6	41	15	19	0	14	.307	.426	N/A
1991 NY	NL	C-OF	96	228	18	62	14	2	5	35	9	19	0	3	.272	.417	505,000
1992 NY	NL	C-1B	92	141	7	34	6	0	2	18	3	10	0	1	.241	.326	775,000
1993 SEA	AL	OF	83	188	18	41	10	2	1	21	15	30	1	3	.218	.309	475,000
7 YR	TOTALS		517	1159	102	313	68	7	16	156	55	104	1	30	.270	.382	
1993 RANK	MLB OF		112	122	135	129	110	76	122	123	121	122	116	72	123	130	86
1994 PROJECTIONS			78	150	11	36	8	1	1	18	8	16	0	3	.240	.34	

Brian Turang — No. 1/OF

Full name: Brian Craig Turang
Bats: R **Throws:** R **HT:** 5–10 **WT:** 170
Born: 6–14–67, Long Beach, CA
High school: Millikan (Long Beach, CA)
College: L. Beach (CA) and Loyola M'mount (CA)
Turang batted .324 for AAA Calgary.

	TEAM	LG	POS	G	AB	R	H	2B	3B	HR	RBI	BB	SO	SB	E	BA	SLG	SALARY
1993	SEA	AL	OF	40	140	22	35	11	1	0	7	17	20	6	1	.250	.343	109,000
1	YR	TOTAL		40	140	22	35	11	1	0	7	17	20	6	1	.250	.343	
1993	RANK	MLB	OF	not ranked -- didn't have 150 ABs in 1993														

Dan Wilson — No. 6/C

Full name: Daniel Allen Wilson
Bats: R **Throws:** R **HT:** 6–3 **WT:** 190
Born: 3–25–69, Arlington Hts., IL
High school: Barrington (IL)
College: Minnesota
In 36 games as a Red, Wilson batted a weak .224.

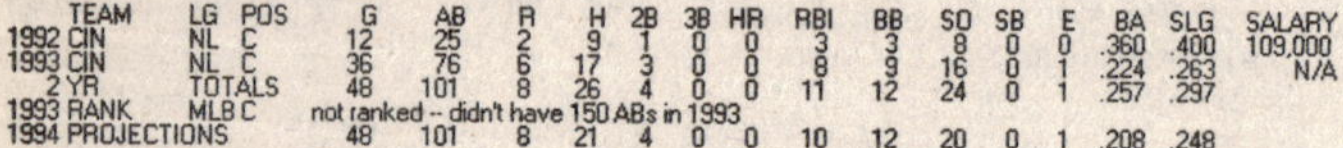

	TEAM	LG	POS	G	AB	R	H	2B	3B	HR	RBI	BB	SO	SB	E	BA	SLG	SALARY
1992	CIN	NL	C	12	25	2	9	1	0	0	3	3	8	0	0	.360	.400	109,000
1993	CIN	NL	C	36	76	6	17	3	0	0	8	9	16	0	1	.224	.263	N/A
2	YR	TOTALS		48	101	8	26	4	0	0	11	12	24	0	1	.257	.297	
1993	RANK	MLB	C	not ranked -- didn't have 150 ABs in 1993														
1994	PROJECTIONS			48	101	8	21	4	0	0	10	12	20	0	1	.208	.248	

Texas
RANGERS

1994 Scouting Report

Hitting: (1993/.267 BA, fifth in AL; 181 HR, first in AL)

The Rangers' offense features some of baseball's best power hitters in Juan Gonzalez (.310, 46 HR, 118 RBI), free agent acquisition Will Clark (.283, 14 HR, 73 RBI), Jose Canseco (.255, 10 HR, 46 RBI in 60 games), and Dean Palmer (33 HR). Texas is hoping that Clark will return to his old form—and make the fans forget free agent departure Rafael Palmeiro, who had his best season in his walk year — .295, 37 HR, 105 RBI. Jose Canseco's return is iffy; he suffered a serious injury to his right elbow in a relief appearance against Boston in a 15–1 blowout, and the injury could be career-ending. Ivan Rodriguez' continued development will help the Rangers' pennant chances. Rodriguez hit .273 with 10 HR and 66 RBI. He'll only be 22 come opening day '94, but he'll be starting his fourth major league season.

Pitching: (1993/4.28 ERA, sixth in AL)

Kevin Brown is one of baseball's best pitchers. He's won 36 games over the last two seasons, and finished second in the AL in shutouts with three. He's especially tough in the late innings, with opponents hitting just .198 against him from the seventh inning on. Roger Pavlik is a promising young pitcher; he went 12–6 for Texas, despite spending April and half of May in AAA.

In the bullpen, Tom Henke is a reliable closer—but he's getting up in years. If his fastball fades, he'll be in trouble.

Defense: (1993/.979 pct., eleventh in AL)

Dean Palmer committed 29 errors in 148 games at third base. Interestingly, Will Clark's arrival won't bolster the defense much; the man he replaces, Rafael Palmiero, turned in a .997 fielding percentage at first (second in the AL).

1994 Prospects:

If everything breaks right, Texas will have all the elements to go all the way: solid starting pitching, a reliable closer, a core of power hitters, and speed at the top of the lineup. But they're counting on Canseco, Clark, and Gary Redus to come back from injuries. Texas also lacks a stellar defense. Still, they should at least contend in the weak AL West.

Team Directory

General Partner: George W. Bush
President: J. Thomas Schieffer
VP, P.R.: John Blake

General Partner: Edward W. Rose
General Mgr.: Tom Grieve
Traveling Secretary: Dan Schimek

Minor League Affiliates:

Level	Team/League	1993 Record
AAA	Oklahoma City – American Association	54–90
AA	Tulsa – Texas	66–69
A	Charlotte – Florida State	84–49
	Charleston, SC – South Atlantic	65–77
	Erie – New York/Penn.*	36–41
Rookie	Gulf Coast Rangers – Gulf Coast	40–20

*will move from Erie, Pennsylvania to Dutchess County, New York in 1994.

1993 Review

	Home		Away	
vs AL East	W	L	W	L
Baltimore	4	2	4	2
Boston	4	2	2	4
Detroit	3	3	3	3
New York	5	1	4	2
Toronto	3	3	4	2
Total	19	11	17	13

	Home		Away	
vs AL Cent.	W	L	W	L
Chicago	4	3	1	5
Cleveland	3	3	2	4
Kansas City	3	3	3	4
Milwaukee	4	2	4	2
Minnesota	4	3	2	4
Total	18	14	12	19

	Home		Away	
vs AL West	W	L	W	L
California	4	2	3	4
Oakland	5	1	3	4
Seattle	4	3	1	5
Total	13	6	7	13

1993 finish: 86–76 (50–31 home, 36–45 away), second in AL West, eight games behind

1994 Schedule

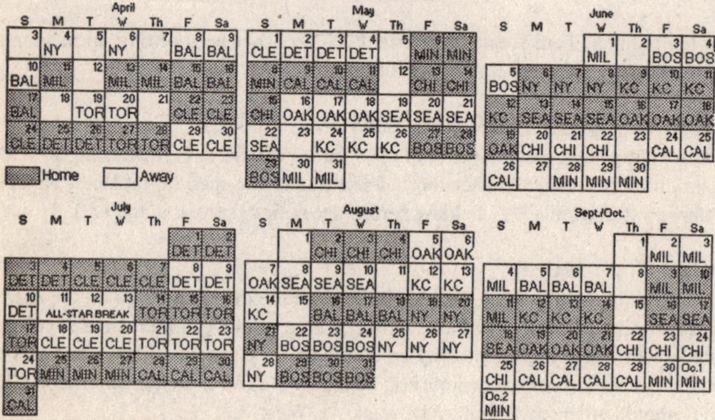

TEXAS RANGERS 1994 ROSTER

Manager: Kevin Kennedy (44)
Coaches: Mickey Hatcher (43), Perry Hill (47), Jackie Moore (42), Dave Oliver (26), Claude Osteen (48), and Willie Upshaw (46)

No.	PITCHERS	B	T	HT	WT	DOB	BIRTHPLACE	RESIDENCE
51	Bronkey, Jeff	R	R	6–3	210	9–18–65	Kabul, Afg.	Klamath Falls, OH
1	Brown, Kevin	R	R	6–4	195	3–14–65	McIntyre, GA	Macon, GA
53	Burrows, Terry	L	L	6–1	185	11–28–68	Lake Charles, LA	Lake Charles, LA
	Brumley, Duff	R	R	6–4	185	8–25–70	Cleveland, TN	Cleveland, TN
31	Carpenter, Cris	R	R	6–1	185	4–5–65	St. Augustine, FL	Lainesville, GA
24	Dreyer, Steve	R	R	6–3	180	11–19–69	Amos, IA	Cedar Falls, IA
30	Fajardo, Hector	R	R	6–4	200	11–6–70	Michoacan, MX	Michoacan, MX
50	Henke, Tom	R	R	6–5	225	12–21–57	Kansas City, MO	Jefferson City, MO
	Honeycutt, Rick	L	L	6–1	191	6–29–54	Chattanooga, TN	Signal Mountain, TN
	Hurst, James	L	L	6–0	160	6–1–67	Plantation, FL	Sebring, FL
28	Oliver, Darren	R	L	6–0	170	10–6–70	Kansas City, MO	Rio Linda, CA
59	Pavlik, Roger	R	R	6–2	220	10–4–67	Houston, TX	Houston, TX
37	Rogers, Kenny	L	L	6–1	205	11–10–64	Savannah, GA	Arlington, TX
	Santana, Julio	R	R	6–0	175	1–20–73	S. P. de Macoris, DR	S. P. de Macoris, DR
35	Smith, Dan	L	L	6–5	195	4–20–69	St. Paul, MN	Apple Valley, MN
27	Whiteside, Matt	R	R	6–0	195	8–8–67	Charleston, MO	Charleston, MO
No.	**CATCHERS**	**B**	**T**	**HT**	**WT**	**DOB**	**BIRTHPLACE**	**RESIDENCE**
7	Rodriguez, Ivan	R	R	5–9	205	11–30–71	Vega Baja, PR	Vega Baja, PR
30	*McNamara, Jim	L	R	6–4	210	6–10–65	Nashua, NH	Vienna, VA
	Scioscia, Mike	L	R	6–2	220		Upper Darby, PA	
No.	**INFIELDERS**	**B**	**T**	**HT**	**WT**	**DOB**	**BIRTHPLACE**	**RESIDENCE**
	Clark, Will	L	L	6–0	196	3–13–64	New Orleans, LA	New Orleans, LA
1	Frye, Jeff	R	R	5–9	165	8–31–66	Oakland, CA	Arlington, TX
22	Gil, Benji	R	R	6–2	182	10–6–72	Tijuana, MX	San Diego, CA
9	Huson, Jeff	L	R	6–3	180	8–15–64	Scottsdale, AZ	Bedford, TX
2	Lee, Manuel	S	R	6–2	205	6–17–65	SP de Macoris, DR	SP de Macoris, DR
16	Palmer, Dean	R	R	6–2	195	12–27–68	Tallahassee, FL	Tallahassee, FL
10	Shave, Jon	R	R	6–0	180	11–4–67	Waycross, GA	Fernandina Beach, FL
20	Strange, Doug	S	R	6–2	170	4–13–64	Greenville, SC	Scottsdale, AZ
No.	**OUTFIELDERS**	**B**	**T**	**HT**	**WT**	**DOB**	**BIRTHPLACE**	**RESIDENCE**
33	Canseco, Jose	R	R	6–4	240	7–2–64	Havana, CU	Miami, FL
40	Ducey, Rob	L	R	6–2	180	5–24–65	Toronto, ON	Palm Harbor, FL
19	Gonzalez, Juan	R	R	6–3	210	10–16–69	Vaga Baja, PR	Vaga Baja, PR
	Greer, Rusty	L	L	6–0	190	1–21–69	Ft. Rucker, AL	Albertville, AL
18	Harris, Donald	R	R	6–1	185	11–12–67	Waco, TX	Waco, TX
15	Hulse, David	L	L	5–11	170	2–25–68	San Angelo, TX	San Angelo, TX
4	James, Chris	R	R	6–1	202	10–4–62	Rusk, TX	Alto, TX
	Lowery, Terrell	R	R	6–3	175	10–25–70	Oakland, CA	Oakland, CA
17	Peltier, Dan	L	L	6–1	200	6–30–68	Clifton Park, NY	Eden Prairie, MN
5	Redus, Gary	R	R	6–1	195	11–1–56	Tanner, AL	Decatur, AL
	Wilson, Desi	L	L	6–7	230	8–9–89	Glen Cove, NJ	Glen Cove, NJ

* signed to minor league contract and invited to spring training

The Ballpark in Arlington (48,100, grass)
Tickets: 817–273–5000
Ticket prices:
- $16 (field box, club level box)
- $14 (terrace box, club level reserve)
- $10 (upper box)
- $9 (upper reserve)
- $8 (lower reserve, upper/lower porch)
- $6 (reserve grandstand)
- $4 (outfield bleachers)

Field Dimensions (from home plate)
- To left field at foul line, 334 feet
- To center field, 388 feet
- To right field at foul line, 325 feet
- (OF wall is 15' in LF, 8' in CF & RF)

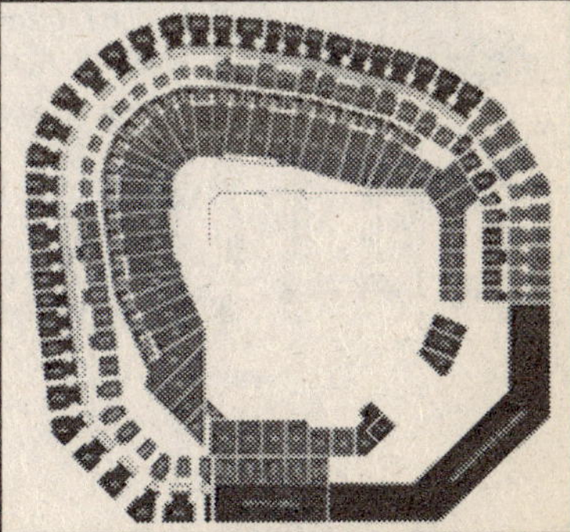

Jose Canseco No. 33/OF

Full name: Jose Canseco, Jr.
Bats: R **Throws:** R **HT:** 6–4 **WT:** 240
Born: 7–2–64, Havana, CU
High school: Coral Park (Miami, FL)

Canseco's elbow injury has endangered a promising career. Last season, Canseco became the first player since Ted Williams in 1947 to have 750 RBI in his first 1000 games.

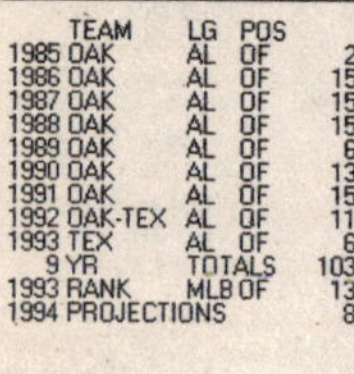
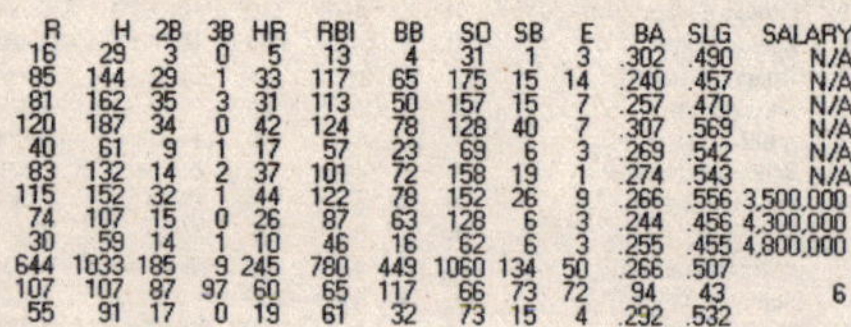

	TEAM	LG	POS	G	AB	R	H	2B	3B	HR	RBI	BB	SO	SB	E	BA	SLG	SALARY
1985	OAK	AL	OF	29	96	16	29	3	0	5	13	4	31	1	3	.302	.490	N/A
1986	OAK	AL	OF	157	600	85	144	29	1	33	117	65	175	15	14	.240	.457	N/A
1987	OAK	AL	OF	159	630	81	162	35	3	31	113	50	157	15	7	.257	.470	N/A
1988	OAK	AL	OF	158	610	120	187	34	0	42	124	78	128	40	7	.307	.569	N/A
1989	OAK	AL	OF	65	227	40	61	9	1	17	57	23	69	6	3	.269	.542	N/A
1990	OAK	AL	OF	131	481	83	132	14	2	37	101	72	158	19	1	.274	.543	N/A
1991	OAK	AL	OF	154	572	115	152	32	1	44	122	78	152	26	9	.266	.556	3,500,000
1992	OAK-TEX	AL	OF	119	439	74	107	15	0	26	87	63	128	6	3	.244	.456	4,300,000
1993	TEX	AL	OF	60	231	30	59	14	1	10	46	16	62	6	3	.255	.455	4,800,000
9 YR		TOTALS		1032	3886	644	1033	185	9	245	780	449	1060	134	50	.266	.507	
1993 RANK		MLB	OF	136	108	107	107	87	97	60	65	117	66	73	72	94	43	6
1994 PROJECTIONS				82	312	55	91	17	0	19	61	32	73	15	4	.292	.532	

Will Clark 1B

Full name: William Nuschler Clark, Jr.
Bats: L **Throws:** L **HT:** 6–0 **WT:** 196
Born: 3–13–64, New Orleans, LA
High school: Jesuit (New Orleans, LA)
College: Mississippi State

Clark hit .318 with 13 HR and 54 RBI in his last 87 games. San Francisco was 87–41 when he started, 16–18 when he didn't.

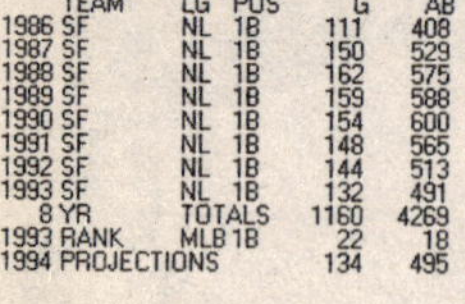

	TEAM	LG	POS	G	AB	R	H	2B	3B	HR	RBI	BB	SO	SB	E	BA	SLG	SALARY
1986	SF	NL	1B	111	408	66	117	27	2	11	41	34	76	4	11	.287	.444	N/A
1987	SF	NL	1B	150	529	89	163	29	5	35	91	49	98	5	13	.308	.580	N/A
1988	SF	NL	1B	162	575	102	162	31	6	29	109	100	129	9	12	.282	.508	N/A
1989	SF	NL	1B	159	588	104	196	38	9	23	111	74	103	8	10	.333	.546	N/A
1990	SF	NL	1B	154	600	91	177	25	5	19	95	62	97	8	12	.295	.448	N/A
1991	SF	NL	1B	148	565	84	170	32	7	29	116	51	91	4	4	.301	.536	3,775,000
1992	SF	NL	1B	144	513	69	154	40	1	16	73	73	82	12	10	.300	.476	4,250,000
1993	SF	NL	1B	132	491	82	139	27	2	14	73	63	68	2	14	.283	.432	4,750,000
8 YR		TOTALS		1160	4269	687	1278	249	37	176	709	506	744	52	86	.299	.499	
1993 RANK		MLB	1B	22	18	10	17	12	11	22	18	13	17	20	6	20	24	1
1994 PROJECTIONS				134	495	84	150	30	4	16	75	57	82	4	11	.303	.481	

Juan Gonzalez No. 19/OF

Full name: Juan Alberto Vazquez Gonzalez
Bats: R **Throws:** R **HT:** 6–3 **WT:** 210
Born: 10–16–69, Vaga Baja, PR
High school: Vega Baja (PR)

Gonzalez is the first American Leaguer to lead outright in HR in consecutive seasons since Boston's Jim Rice in 1977–78.

	TEAM	LG	POS	G	AB	R	H	2B	3B	HR	RBI	BB	SO	SB	E	BA	SLG	SALARY
1989	TEX	AL	OF	24	60	6	9	3	0	1	7	6	17	0	2	.150	.250	N/A
1990	TEX	AL	OF	25	90	11	26	7	1	4	12	2	18	0	0	.289	.522	N/A
1991	TEX	AL	OF	142	545	78	144	34	1	27	102	42	118	4	6	.264	.479	120,000
1992	TEX	AL	OF	155	584	77	152	24	2	43	109	35	143	0	10	.260	.529	280,000
1993	TEX	AL	OF	140	536	105	166	33	1	46	118	37	99	4	4	.310	.632	525,000
5	YR	TOTALS		486	1815	277	497	101	5	121	348	122	395	8	22	.274	.535	
1993	RANK	MLB	OF	41	33	9	17	15	97	1	5	59	23	85	59	16	2	78
1994	PROJECTIONS			162	627	123	195	38	0	54	139	42	114	3	3	.311	.630	

David Hulse No. 15/OF

Full name: David Lindsey Hulse
Bats: L **Throws:** L **HT:** 5–11 **WT:** 170
Born: 2–25–68, San Angelo, TX
High school: San Angelo Central (TX)
College: Schreiner (TX)

Hulse's .290 BA was the second highest ever for a Texas rookie (behind Mike Hargrove's .323 in 1974).

	TEAM	LG	POS	G	AB	R	H	2B	3B	HR	RBI	BB	SO	SB	E	BA	SLG	SALARY
1992	TEX	AL	OF	32	92	14	28	4	0	0	2	3	18	3	1	.304	.348	109,000
1993	TEX	AL	OF	114	407	71	118	9	10	1	29	26	57	29	3	.290	.369	120,000
2	YR	TOTALS		146	499	85	146	13	10	1	31	29	75	32	4	.293	.365	
1993	RANK	MLB	OF	77	67	45	61	118	3	122	96	78	75	19	72	37	106	121
1994	PROJECTIONS			97	332	56	97	8	6	0	20	19	50	21	2	.292	.364	

Manuel Lee No. 2/IF

Full name: Manuel Lora Lee
Bats: S **Throws:** R **HT:** 6–2 **WT:** 205
Born: 6–17–65, San Pedro de Macoris, DR
High school: Jose Joaquin Perez (DR)
Due to injuries, Lee played in just 73 games, his fewest since 1987. He hit .304 in his final 33 games.

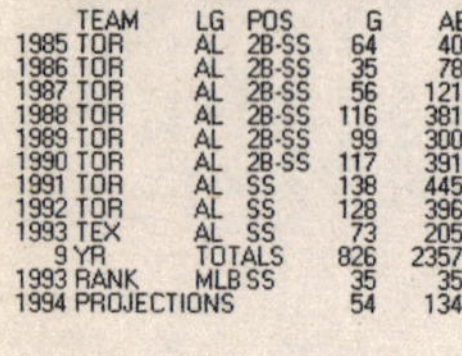

	TEAM	LG	POS	G	AB	R	H	2B	3B	HR	RBI	BB	SO	SB	E	BA	SLG	SALARY
1985	TOR	AL	2B-SS	64	40	9	8	0	0	0	0	2	9	1	3	.200	.200	N/A
1986	TOR	AL	2B-SS	35	78	8	16	0	1	1	7	4	10	0	2	.205	.269	N/A
1987	TOR	AL	2B-SS	56	121	14	31	2	3	1	11	6	13	2	5	.256	.347	N/A
1988	TOR	AL	2B-SS	116	381	38	111	16	3	2	38	26	64	3	12	.291	.365	N/A
1989	TOR	AL	2B-SS	99	300	27	78	9	2	3	34	20	60	4	11	.260	.333	N/A
1990	TOR	AL	2B-SS	117	391	45	95	12	4	6	41	26	90	3	4	.243	.340	N/A
1991	TOR	AL	SS	138	445	41	104	18	3	0	29	24	107	7	19	.234	.288	712,500
1992	TOR	AL	SS	128	396	49	104	10	1	3	39	50	73	6	7	.263	.316	1,000,000
1993	TEX	AL	SS	73	205	31	45	3	1	1	12	22	39	2	10	.220	.259	1,842,406
9	YR	TOTALS		826	2357	262	592	70	18	17	211	180	465	28	73	.251	.318	
1993	RANK	MLB	SS	35	35	32	38	38	29	31	38	26	24	33	29	38	38	9
1994	PROJECTIONS			54	134	17	30	1	1	1	10	10	20	1	5	.224	.284	

Dean Palmer No. 16/3B

Full name: Dean William Palmer
Bats: R **Throws:** R **HT:** 6–2 **WT:** 195
Born: 12–27–68, Tallahassee, FL
High school: Florida (Tallahassee, FL)
Second only to Matt Williams' 38 HR for homers by a major league third baseman, Palmer's .245 BA was fourth lowest among 73 qualifiers for the AL batting title.

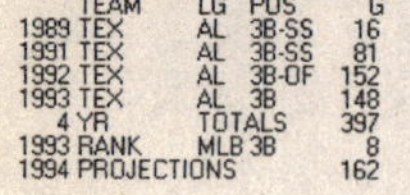
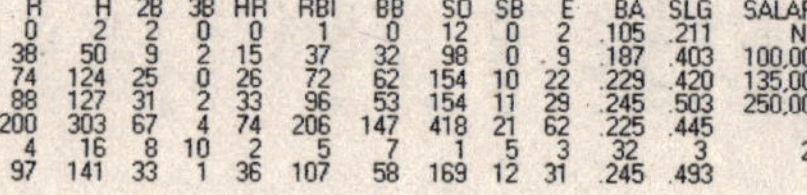

	TEAM	LG	POS	G	AB	R	H	2B	3B	HR	RBI	BB	SO	SB	E	BA	SLG	SALARY
1989	TEX	AL	3B-SS	16	19	0	2	2	0	0	1	0	12	0	2	.105	.211	N/A
1991	TEX	AL	3B-SS	81	268	38	50	9	2	15	37	32	98	0	9	.187	.403	100,000
1992	TEX	AL	3B-OF	152	541	74	124	25	0	26	72	62	154	10	22	.229	.420	135,000
1993	TEX	AL	3B	148	519	88	127	31	2	33	96	53	154	11	29	.245	.503	250,000
4	YR	TOTALS		397	1347	200	303	67	4	74	206	147	418	21	62	.225	.445	
1993	RANK	MLB	3B	8	14	4	16	8	10	2	5	7	1	5	3	32	3	23
1994	PROJECTIONS			162	576	97	141	33	1	36	107	58	169	12	31	.245	.493	

Gary Redus No. 5/OF

Full name: Gary Eugene Redus
Bats: R **Throws:** R **HT:** 6–1 **WT:** 195
Born: 11–1–56, Tanner, AL
High school: Alter (Kettering OH)
College: Louisiana State

Redus hit .317 in 40 games after the All-Star break until he pulled his left hamstring, ending his season.

	TEAM	LG	POS	G	AB	R	H	2B	3B	HR	RBI	BB	SO	SB	E	BA	SLG	SALARY
1982	CIN	NL	OF	20	83	12	18	3	2	1	7	5	21	11	1	.217	.337	N/A
1983	CIN	NL	OF	125	453	90	112	20	9	17	51	71	111	39	7	.247	.444	N/A
1984	CIN	NL	OF	123	394	69	100	21	3	7	22	52	71	48	7	.254	.376	N/A
1985	CIN	NL	OF	101	246	51	62	14	4	6	28	44	52	48	2	.252	.415	N/A
1986	PHL	NL	OF	90	340	62	84	22	4	11	33	47	78	25	4	.247	.432	N/A
1987	CHI	AL	OF	130	475	78	112	26	6	12	48	69	90	52	6	.236	.392	N/A
1988	CHI	AL	OF	77	262	42	69	10	4	6	34	33	52	26	2	.263	.401	N/A
1988	PIT	NL	OF	30	71	12	14	2	0	2	4	15	19	5	2	.197	.310	N/A
1989	PIT	NL	1B-OF	98	279	42	79	18	7	6	33	40	51	25	9	.283	.462	N/A
1990	PIT	NL	1B-OF	96	227	32	56	15	3	6	23	33	38	11	8	.247	.419	N/A
1991	PIT	NL	1B-OF	98	252	45	62	12	2	7	24	28	39	17	6	.246	.393	600,000
1992	PIT	NL	1B-OF	76	176	26	45	7	3	3	12	17	25	11	1	.256	.381	825,000
1993	TEX	AL	OF	77	222	28	64	12	4	6	31	23	35	4	3	.288	.459	500,000
12	YR	TOTALS		1141	3480	589	877	182	51	90	350	477	682	322	58	.252	.411	
1993	RANK	MLB	OF	121	114	110	103	96	32	87	94	92	110	85	72	40	41	81
1994	PROJECTIONS			92	240	41	62	12	3	6	27	31	42	23	3	.258	.421	

Ivan Rodriguez No. 7/C

Full name: Ivan Rodriguez
Bats: R **Throws:** R **HT:** 5–9 **WT:** 205
Born: 11–30–71, Vega Baja, PR
High school: Lina Padron Rivera (PR)

Rodriguez' .273 BA was fourth among qualifying AL catchers and his 66 RBI are the most ever by a Texas catcher.

	TEAM	LG	POS	G	AB	R	H	2B	3B	HR	RBI	BB	SO	SB	E	BA	SLG	SALARY
1991	TEX	AL	C	88	280	24	74	16	0	3	27	5	42	0	10	.264	.354	100,000
1992	TEX	AL	C	123	420	39	109	16	1	8	37	24	73	0	15	.260	.360	135,000
1993	TEX	AL	C	137	473	56	129	28	4	10	66	29	70	8	8	.273	.412	275,000
3	YR	TOTALS		348	1173	119	312	60	5	21	130	58	185	8	33	.266	.379	
1993	RANK	MLB	C	7	6	8	6	3	3	15	9	15	12	3	8	14	16	24
1994	PROJECTIONS			153	537	66	147	32	5	12	79	37	79	10	7	.274	.419	

Doug Strange No. 20/2B

Full name: Joseph Douglas Strange
Bats: S **Throws:** R **HT:** 6–2 **WT:** 170
Born: 4–13–64, Greenville, SC
High school: Wade Hampton (Gr'nville, SC)
College: North Carolina State
Strange started in just four of the Rangers' first 23 games, 124 of their last 139 contests.

	TEAM	LG	POS	G	AB	R	H	2B	3B	HR	RBI	BB	SO	SB	E	BA	SLG	SALARY
1989	DET	AL	3B-2B	64	196	16	42	4	1	1	14	17	36	3	19	.214	.260	N/A
1991	CHI	NL	3B	3	9	0	4	1	0	0	1	0	1	1	1	.444	.556	N/A
1992	CHI	NL	3B-2B	52	94	7	15	1	0	1	5	10	15	1	6	.160	.202	N/A
1993	TEX	AL	2B	145	484	58	124	29	0	7	60	43	69	6	13	.256	.360	125,000
4	YR	TOTALS		264	783	81	185	35	1	9	80	70	121	11	39	.236	.318	
1993	RANK	MLB	2B	8	14	17	15	6	40	11	10	14	10	24	12	25	27	32
1994	PROJECTIONS			161	541	66	140	34	0	8	69	48	75	6	11	.259	.366	

Kevin Brown No. 1/P

Full name: James Kevin Brown
Bats: R **Throws:** R **HT:** 6–4 **WT:** 195
Born: 3–14–65, McIntyre, GA
High school: Wilkinson Cty. (Irwinton, GA)
College: Georgia Tech
Brown is especially tough in the late innings, with opponents hitting just .198 against him from the seventh inning on.

	TM	LG	POS	W	L	ERA	G	GS	CG	SH	SV	IP	H	R	ER	HR	BB	SO	SALARY
1986	TEX	AL	P	1	0	3.60	1	1	0	0	0	5.0	6	2	2	0	0	4	N/A
1988	TEX	AL	P	1	1	4.24	4	4	1	0	0	23.1	33	15	11	2	8	12	N/A
1989	TEX	AL	P	12	9	3.35	28	28	7	0	0	191.0	167	81	71	10	70	104	N/A
1990	TEX	AL	P	12	10	3.60	26	26	6	2	0	180.0	175	84	72	13	60	88	N/A
1991	TEX	AL	P	9	12	4.40	33	33	0	0	0	210.2	233	116	103	17	90	96	320,000
1992	TEX	AL	P	21	11	3.32	35	35	11	1	0	265.2	262	117	98	11	76	173	1,200,000
1993	TEX	AL	P	15	12	3.59	34	34	12	3	0	233.0	228	105	93	14	74	142	2,800,000
8	YR	TOTALS		71	55	3.65	161	161	37	6	0	1108.2	1104	520	450	67	378	619	
1993	Rank	MLB	Ps	21		96	145	12	2	3	102	16	115	91		45	93	157	39
1994	PROJECTIONS			12	11	3.8	31	31	6	1	0	211.0	209	100	89	13	78	114	

Roger Pavlik No. 59/P

Full name: Roger Allen Pavlik
Bats: R **Throws:** R **HT:** 6–2 **WT:** 220
Born: 10–4–67, Houston, TX
High school: Aldine (Houston, TX)
Pavlik's 3.41 ERA was the best among Texas starting pitchers. Texas was 19–7 in games he started, and won all of his last ten starts.

	TM	LG	POS	W	L	ERA	G	GS	CG	SH	SV	IP	H	R	ER	HR	BB	SO	SALARY
1992	TEX	AL	P	4	4	4.21	13	12	1	0	0	62.0	66	32	29	3	34	45	109,000
1993	TEX	AL	P	12	6	3.41	26	26	2	0	0	166.1	151	67	63	18	80	131	130,000
2	YR	TOTALS		16	10	3.63	39	38	3	0	0	228.1	217	99	92	21	114	176	
1993	Rank	MLB Ps		43		79	229	85	57	69	102	79	74	58		185	239	66	207
1994	PROJECTIONS			16	7	3.30	32	33	2	0	0	218.0	193	84	80	25	103	174	

Kenny Rogers No. 37/P

Full name: Kenneth Scott Rogers
Bats: L **Throws:** L **HT:** 6–1 **WT:** 205
Born: 11–10–64, Savannah, GA
High school: Plant City (FL)
Rogers' 16 wins was a record for a Texas lefty. He went 6–1 in August and was 12–5 with a 3.07 ERA in his last 21 starts.

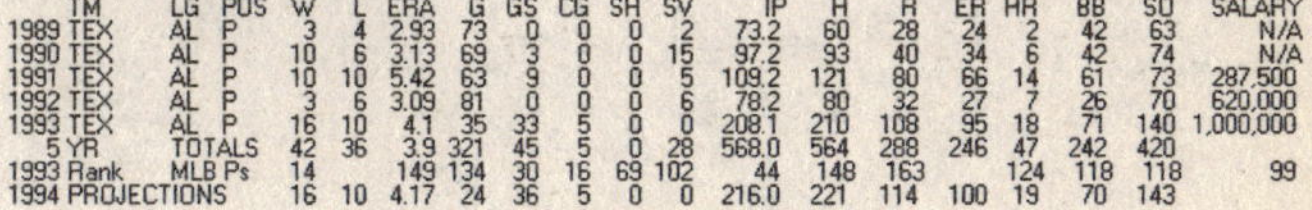

	TM	LG	POS	W	L	ERA	G	GS	CG	SH	SV	IP	H	R	ER	HR	BB	SO	SALARY
1989	TEX	AL	P	3	4	2.93	73	0	0	0	2	73.2	60	28	24	2	42	63	N/A
1990	TEX	AL	P	10	6	3.13	69	3	0	0	15	97.2	93	40	34	6	42	74	N/A
1991	TEX	AL	P	10	10	5.42	63	9	0	0	5	109.2	121	80	66	14	61	73	287,500
1992	TEX	AL	P	3	6	3.09	81	0	0	0	6	78.2	80	32	27	7	26	70	620,000
1993	TEX	AL	P	16	10	4.1	35	33	5	0	0	208.1	210	108	95	18	71	140	1,000,000
5	YR	TOTALS		42	36	3.9	321	45	5	0	28	568.0	564	288	246	47	242	420	
1993	Rank	MLB Ps		14		149	134	30	16	69	102	44	148	163		124	118	118	99
1994	PROJECTIONS			16	10	4.17	24	36	5	0	0	216.0	221	114	100	19	70	143	

Tom Henke No. 50/P

Full name: Thomas Anthony Henke
Bats: R **Throws:** R **HT:** 6–5 **WT:** 225
Born: 12–21–57, Kansas City, MO
High school: Blair Oaks (Jefferson City, MO)
College: East Central (MO)

Henke has had an ERA under 3.00 for seven straight seasons. Opponents hit just .205 against him.

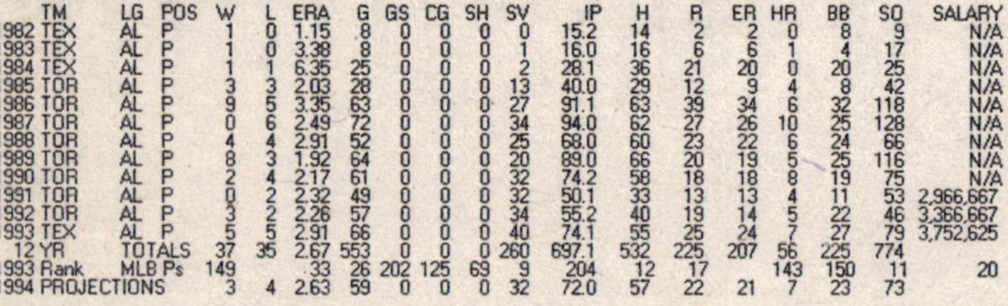

	TM	LG	POS	W	L	ERA	G	GS	CG	SH	SV	IP	H	R	ER	HR	BB	SO	SALARY
1982	TEX	AL	P	1	0	1.15	8	0	0	0	0	15.2	14	2	2	0	8	9	N/A
1983	TEX	AL	P	1	0	3.38	8	0	0	0	1	16.0	16	6	6	1	4	17	N/A
1984	TEX	AL	P	1	1	6.35	25	0	0	0	2	28.1	36	21	20	0	20	25	N/A
1985	TOR	AL	P	3	3	2.03	28	0	0	0	13	40.0	29	12	9	4	8	42	N/A
1986	TOR	AL	P	9	5	3.35	63	0	0	0	27	91.1	63	39	34	6	32	118	N/A
1987	TOR	AL	P	0	6	2.49	72	0	0	0	34	94.0	62	27	26	10	25	128	N/A
1988	TOR	AL	P	4	4	2.91	52	0	0	0	25	68.0	60	23	22	6	24	66	N/A
1989	TOR	AL	P	8	3	1.92	64	0	0	0	20	89.0	66	20	19	5	25	116	N/A
1990	TOR	AL	P	2	4	2.17	61	0	0	0	32	74.2	58	18	18	8	19	75	N/A
1991	TOR	AL	P	0	2	2.32	49	0	0	0	32	50.1	33	13	13	4	11	53	2,966,667
1992	TOR	AL	P	3	2	2.26	57	0	0	0	34	55.2	40	19	14	5	22	46	3,366,667
1993	TEX	AL	P	5	5	2.91	66	0	0	0	40	74.1	55	25	24	7	27	79	3,752,625
12	YR	TOTALS		37	35	2.67	553	0	0	0	260	697.1	532	225	207	56	225	774	
1993	Rank	MLB Ps		149		33	26	202	125	69	9	204	12	17		143	150	11	20
1994	PROJECTIONS			3	4	2.63	59	0	0	0	32	72.0	57	22	21	7	23	73	

Kevin Kennedy No. 44/Mgr.

Full name: Kevin Curtis Kennedy
Bats: R **Throws:** R **HT:** 6–3 **WT:** 220
Born: 5–26–54, Los Angeles, CA
High school: Taft (Woodland Hills, CA)
College: Cal State–Northridge

Kennedy managed Texas to its most wins since 1986 in his first season managing in the major leagues.

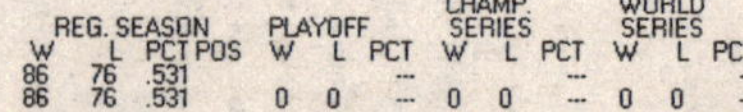

			REG. SEASON				PLAYOFF			CHAMP. SERIES			WORLD SERIES		
YEAR	TEAM	LG	W	L	PCT	POS	W	L	PCT	W	L	PCT	W	L	PCT
1993	TEX	AL	86	76	.531				---			---			---
1	YR TOTAL		86	76	.531		0	0	---	0	0	---	0	0	---

Jeff Bronkey No. 51/P

Full name: Jacob Jeffrey Bronkey
Bats: R **Throws:** R **HT:** 6–3 **WT:** 210
Born: 9–18–65, Kabul, Afg.
High school: Klamath Union (Klamath Falls, OH)
College: Oklahoma State
He was recalled from the minors five times in '93.

TM	LG	POS	W	L	ERA	G	GS	CG	SH	SV	IP	H	R	ER	HR	BB	SO	SALARY
1993 TEX	AL	P	1	1	4.00	21	0	0	0	1	36.0	39	20	16	4	11	18	N/A
1 YR	TOTAL		1	1	4.00	21	0	0	0	1	36.0	39	20	16	4	11	18	
1993 Rank	MLB Ps	not ranked -- didn't have 50 IP in 1993																

Cris Carpenter No. 31/P

Full name: Cris Howell Carpenter
Bats: R **Throws:** R **HT:** 6–1 **WT:** 185
Born: 4–5–65, St. Augustine, FL
High school: Gainesville (FL)
College: Georgia
Carpenter was 4–1 in 27 relief appearances.

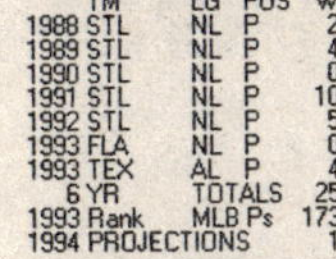

TM	LG	POS	W	L	ERA	G	GS	CG	SH	SV	IP	H	R	ER	HR	BB	SO	SALARY
1988 STL	NL	P	2	3	4.72	8	8	1	0	0	47.2	56	27	25	3	9	24	N/A
1989 STL	NL	P	4	4	3.18	36	5	0	0	0	68.0	70	30	24	4	26	35	N/A
1990 STL	NL	P	0	0	4.50	4	0	0	0	0	8.0	5	4	4	2	2	6	N/A
1991 STL	NL	P	10	4	4.23	59	0	0	0	0	66.0	53	31	31	6	20	47	120,000
1992 STL	NL	P	5	4	2.97	73	0	0	0	1	88.0	69	29	29	10	27	46	150,000
1993 FLA	NL	P	0	1	2.89	29	0	0	0	0	37.1	29	15	12	1	13	26	N/A
1993 TEX	AL	P	4	1	4.22	27	0	0	0	1	32.0	35	15	15	4	12	27	725,000
6 YR	TOTALS		25	17	3.63	236	13	1	0	2	347.0	317	151	140	30	109	211	
1993 Rank	MLB Ps		173		90	57	202	125	69	70	218	82	83		71	146		
1994 PROJECTIONS			1	0	3.60	20	0	0	0	0	25.0	23	11	10	2	9	19	

Steve Dreyer No. 24/P

Full name: Steven William Dreyer
Bats: R **Throws:** R **HT:** 6–3 **WT:** 180
Born: 11–19–69, Ames, IA
High school: Ames (IA)
College: Northern Iowa
Dreyer won his big league debut vs. Seattle.

TM	LG	POS	W	L	ERA	G	GS	CG	SH	SV	IP	H	R	ER	HR	BB	SO	SALARY
1993 TEX	AL	P	3	3	5.71	10	6	0	0	0	41.0	48	26	26	7	20	23	109,000
1 YR	TOTAL		3	3	5.71	10	6	0	0	0	41.0	48	26	26	7	20	23	
1993 RANK	MLB Ps	not ranked -- didn't have 50 IP in 1993																

Rob Ducey — No. 40/OF

Full name: Robert Thomas Ducey
Bats: L **Throws:** R **HT:** 6–2 **WT:** 180
Born: 5–24–65, Toronto, ON
High school: Glanview Park (Toronto, ON)
College: Seminole CC (FL)
Ducey hit .319 as a leadoff hitter.

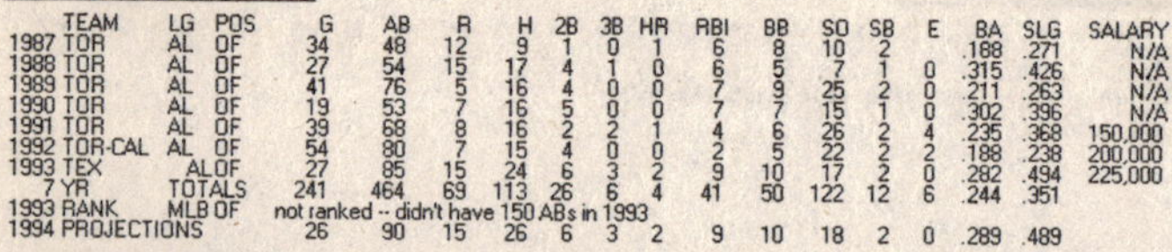

	TEAM	LG	POS	G	AB	R	H	2B	3B	HR	RBI	BB	SO	SB	E	BA	SLG	SALARY
1987	TOR	AL	OF	34	48	12	9	1	0	1	6	8	10	2		.188	.271	N/A
1988	TOR	AL	OF	27	54	15	17	4	1	0	6	5	7	1	0	.315	.426	N/A
1989	TOR	AL	OF	41	76	5	16	4	0	0	7	9	25	2	0	.211	.263	N/A
1990	TOR	AL	OF	19	53	7	16	5	0	0	7	7	15	1	0	.302	.396	N/A
1991	TOR	AL	OF	39	68	8	16	2	2	1	4	6	26	2	4	.235	.368	150,000
1992	TOR-CAL	AL	OF	54	80	7	15	4	0	0	2	5	22	2	2	.188	.238	200,000
1993	TEX	AL	OF	27	85	15	24	6	3	2	9	10	17	2	0	.282	.494	225,000
7	YR	TOTALS		241	464	69	113	26	6	4	41	50	122	12	6	.244	.351	
1993	RANK	MLB	OF	not ranked -- didn't have 150 ABs in 1993														
1994	PROJECTIONS			26	90	15	26	6	3	2	9	10	18	2	0	.289	.489	

Benji Gil — No. 22/SS

Full name: Romar Benjamin Gil
Bats: R **Throws:** R **HT:** 6–2 **WT:** 182
Born: 10–6–72, Tijuana, MX
High school: Castle Park (Chula Vista, CA)
Gil opened the season as SS, but hit only .172 and was sent to AA Tulsa, where he hit .275.

	TEAM	LG	POS	G	AB	R	H	2B	3B	HR	RBI	BB	SO	SB	E	BA	SLG	SALARY
1993	TEX	AL	SS	22	57	3	7	0	0	0	2	5	22	1	5	.123	.123	N/A
1	YR	TOTAL		22	57	3	7	0	0	0	2	5	22	1	5	.123	.123	
1993	RANK	MLB	SS	not ranked -- didn't have 150 ABs in 1993														

Donald Harris — No. 18/OF

Full name: Donald Harris
Bats: R **Throws:** R **HT:** 6–1 **WT:** 185
Born: 11–12–67, Waco, TX
High school: Jefferson–Moore (Waco, TX)
College: McLennan CC (TX)
Harris hit just .143 in his last 22 games for Texas.

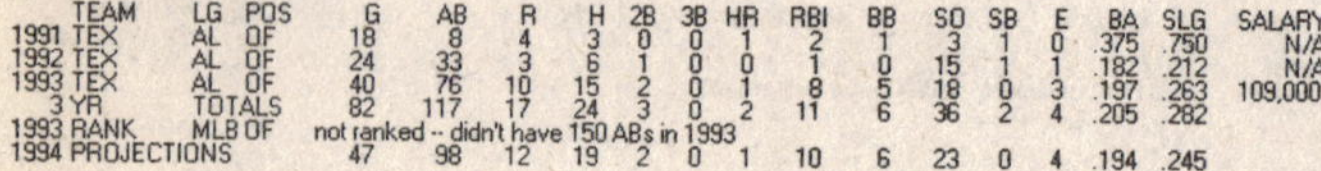

	TEAM	LG	POS	G	AB	R	H	2B	3B	HR	RBI	BB	SO	SB	E	BA	SLG	SALARY
1991	TEX	AL	OF	18	8	4	3	0	0	1	2	1	3	1	0	.375	.750	N/A
1992	TEX	AL	OF	24	33	3	6	1	0	0	1	0	15	1	1	.182	.212	N/A
1993	TEX	AL	OF	40	76	10	15	2	0	1	8	5	18	0	3	.197	.263	109,000
3	YR	TOTALS		82	117	17	24	3	0	2	11	6	36	2	4	.205	.282	
1993	RANK	MLB	OF	not ranked -- didn't have 150 ABs in 1993														
1994	PROJECTIONS			47	98	12	19	2	0	1	10	6	23	0	4	.194	.245	

Rick Honeycutt — P

Full name: Frederick Wayne Honeycutt
Bats: L **Throws:** L **HT:** 6–1 **WT:** 191
Born: 6–29–54, Chattanooga, TN
High school: Lakeview (Fort Oglethorpe, GA)
College: Tennessee
Honeycutt was signed as a free agent.

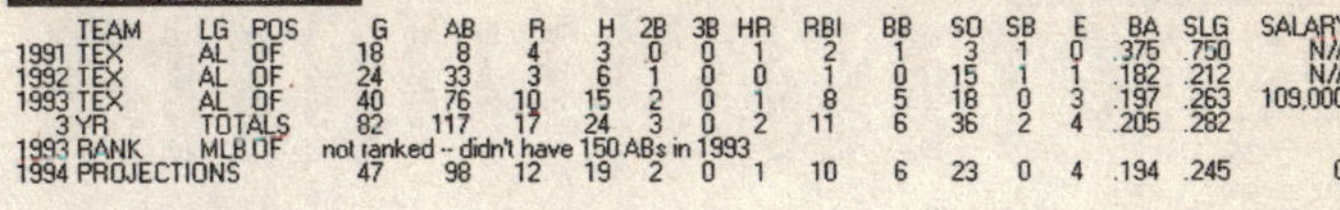

	TEAM	LG	POS	G	AB	R	H	2B	3B	HR	RBI	BB	SO	SB	E	BA	SLG	SALARY
1991	TEX	AL	OF	18	8	4	3	0	0	1	2	1	3	1	0	.375	.750	N/A
1992	TEX	AL	OF	24	33	3	6	1	0	0	1	0	15	1	1	.182	.212	N/A
1993	TEX	AL	OF	40	76	10	15	2	0	1	8	5	18	0	3	.197	.263	109,000
3	YR	TOTALS		82	117	17	24	3	0	2	11	6	36	2	4	.205	.282	
1993	RANK	MLB	OF	not ranked -- didn't have 150 ABs in 1993														
1994	PROJECTIONS			47	98	12	19	2	0	1	10	6	23	0	4	.194	.245	0

Chris James — No. 4/OF

Full name: Donald Christopher James
Bats: R **Throws:** R **HT:** 6–1 **WT:** 190
Born: 10–4–62, Rusk, TX
High school: Stratford (Houston, TX)
College: Blinn (TX)
Hit .438 against righties after coming to Texas.

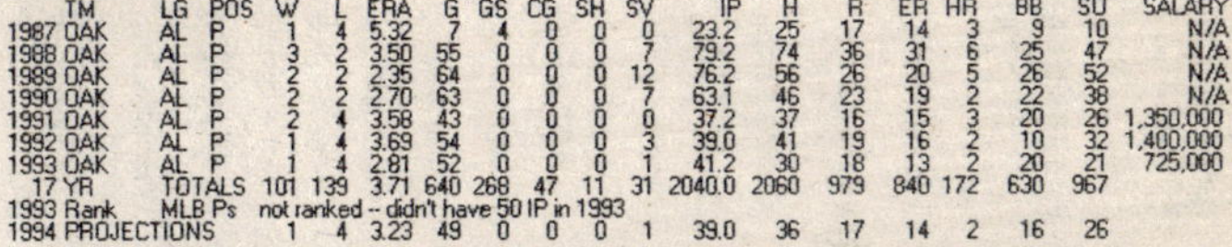

	TM	LG	POS	W	L	ERA	G	GS	CG	SH	SV	IP	H	R	ER	HR	BB	SO	SALARY
1987	OAK	AL	P	1	4	5.32	7	4	0	0	0	23.2	25	17	14	3	9	10	N/A
1988	OAK	AL	P	3	2	3.50	55	0	0	0	7	79.2	74	36	31	6	25	47	N/A
1989	OAK	AL	P	2	2	2.35	64	0	0	0	12	76.2	56	26	20	5	26	52	N/A
1990	OAK	AL	P	2	2	2.70	63	0	0	0	7	63.1	46	23	19	2	22	38	N/A
1991	OAK	AL	P	2	4	3.58	43	0	0	0	0	37.2	37	16	15	3	20	26	1,350,000
1992	OAK	AL	P	1	4	3.69	54	0	0	0	3	39.0	41	19	16	2	10	32	1,400,000
1993	OAK	AL	P	1	4	2.81	52	0	0	0	1	41.2	30	18	13	2	20	21	725,000
17	YR	TOTALS		101	139	3.71	640	268	47	11	31	2040.0	2060	979	840	172	630	967	
1993	Rank	MLB	Ps	not ranked -- didn't have 50 IP in 1993															
1994	PROJECTIONS			1	4	3.23	49	0	0	0	1	39.0	36	17	14	2	16	26	

Darren Oliver — No. 28/P

Full name: Darren Christopher Oliver
Bats: R **Throws:** L **HT:** 6–1 **WT:** 170
Born: 10–6–70, Kansas City, MO
High school: Rio Linda (CA)
Oliver was 7–5 at AA Tulsa with a 1.96 ERA as a reliever.

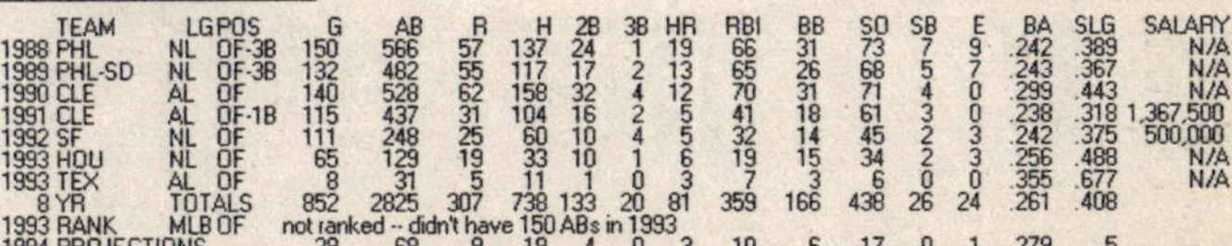

	TEAM	LG	POS	G	AB	R	H	2B	3B	HR	RBI	BB	SO	SB	E	BA	SLG	SALARY
1988	PHL	NL	OF-3B	150	566	57	137	24	1	19	66	31	73	7	9	.242	.389	N/A
1989	PHL-SD	NL	OF-3B	132	482	55	117	17	2	13	65	26	68	5	7	.243	.367	N/A
1990	CLE	AL	OF	140	528	62	158	32	4	12	70	31	71	4	0	.299	.443	N/A
1991	CLE	AL	OF-1B	115	437	31	104	16	2	5	41	18	61	3	0	.238	.318	1,367,500
1992	SF	NL	OF	111	248	25	60	10	4	5	32	14	45	2	3	.242	.375	500,000
1993	HOU	NL	OF	65	129	19	33	10	1	6	19	15	34	2	3	.256	.488	N/A
1993	TEX	AL	OF	8	31	5	11	1	0	3	7	3	6	0	0	.355	.677	N/A
8	YR	TOTALS		852	2825	307	738	133	20	81	359	166	438	26	24	.261	.408	
1993	RANK	MLB	OF	not ranked -- didn't have 150 ABs in 1993														
1994	PROJECTIONS			29	68	9	19	4	0	3	10	6	17	0	1	.279	.5	

Dan Peltier — No. 17/OF

Full name: Daniel Edward Peltier
Bats: L **Throws:** L **HT:** 6–1 **WT:** 200
Born: 6–30–68, Clifton Park, NY
High school: Shenedowa (Clifton Park, NY)
College: Notre Dame
Peltier hit .314 at home, just .216 on the road.

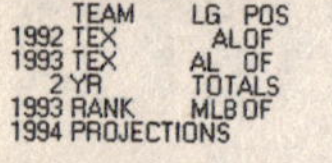
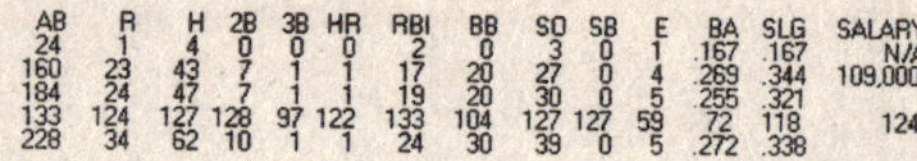

	TEAM	LG	POS	G	AB	R	H	2B	3B	HR	RBI	BB	SO	SB	E	BA	SLG	SALARY
1992	TEX	AL	OF	12	24	1	4	0	0	0	2	0	3	0	1	.167	.167	N/A
1993	TEX	AL	OF	65	160	23	43	7	1	1	17	20	27	0	4	.269	.344	109,000
2	YR	TOTALS		77	184	24	47	7	1	1	19	20	30	0	5	.255	.321	
1993	RANK	MLB	OF	131	133	124	127	128	97	122	133	104	127	127	59	72	118	124
1994	PROJECTIONS			91	228	34	62	10	1	1	24	30	39	0	5	.272	.338	

Mike Scioscia — C

Full name: Michael Lorri Scioscia
Bats: L **Throws:** R **HT:** 6–2 **WT:** 220
Born: 11–27–58, Upper Darby, PA
High school: Springfield (PA)
College: Penn State
Texas signed Scioscia to back up Ivan Rodriguez.

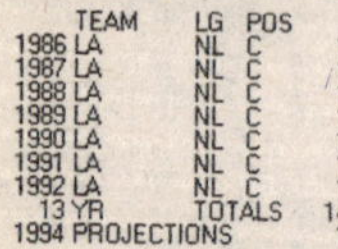
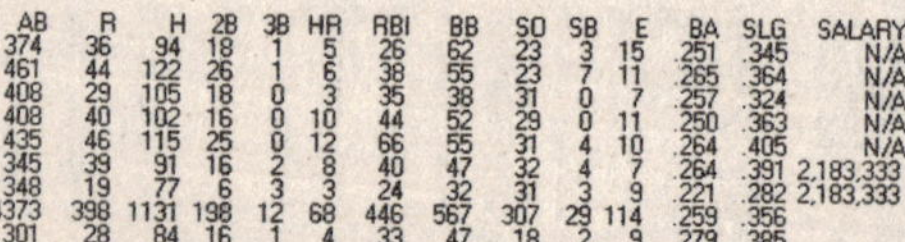

	TEAM	LG	POS	G	AB	R	H	2B	3B	HR	RBI	BB	SO	SB	E	BA	SLG	SALARY
1986	LA	NL	C	122	374	36	94	18	1	5	26	62	23	3	15	.251	.345	N/A
1987	LA	NL	C	142	461	44	122	26	1	6	38	55	23	7	11	.265	.364	N/A
1988	LA	NL	C	130	408	29	105	18	0	3	35	38	31	0	7	.257	.324	N/A
1989	LA	NL	C	133	408	40	102	16	0	10	44	52	29	0	11	.250	.363	N/A
1990	LA	NL	C	135	435	46	115	25	0	12	66	55	31	4	10	.264	.405	N/A
1991	LA	NL	C	119	345	39	91	16	2	8	40	47	32	4	7	.264	.391	2,183,333
1992	LA	NL	C	117	348	19	77	6	3	3	24	32	31	3	9	.221	.282	2,183,333
13	YR	TOTALS		1441	4373	398	1131	198	12	68	446	567	307	29	114	.259	.356	
1994	PROJECTIONS			103	301	28	84	16	1	4	33	47	18	2	9	.279	.385	

Matt Whiteside — No. 27/P

Full name: Matthew Christopher Whiteside
Bats: R **Throws:** R **HT:** 6–0 **WT:** 195
Born: 8–8–67, Charleston, MO
High school: Charleston (MO)
College: Arkansas State
His 60 appearances was second on the staff.

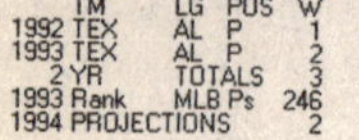
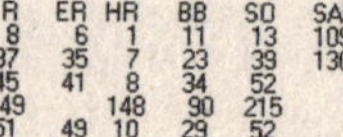

	TM	LG	POS	W	L	ERA	G	GS	CG	SH	SV	IP	H	R	ER	HR	BB	SO	SALARY
1992	TEX	AL	P	1	1	1.93	20	0	0	0	4	28.0	26	8	6	1	11	13	109,000
1993	TEX	AL	P	2	1	4.32	60	0	0	0	1	73.0	78	37	35	7	23	39	130,000
2	YR	TOTALS		3	2	3.65	80	0	0	0	5	101.0	104	45	41	8	34	52	
1993	Rank	MLB	Ps	246		170	45	202	125	69	70	207	192	149		148	90	215	207
1994	PROJECTIONS			2	1	4.64	80	0	0	0	0	95.0	104	51	49	10	29	52	

Toronto BLUE JAYS

1994 Scouting Report

Hitting: (1993/.279 BA, second in AL; 159 HR, fourth in AL)

Toronto's offense is as strong as any in baseball. John Olerud led the league in hitting last season, and he should have another strong year in '94. Paul Molitor will be 38 next season, but he's always been a consistent hitter, so there's no reason to expect a decline from him. Roberto Alomar is in his prime. And Joe Carter is still one of the game's best sluggers. Devon White (34 SB) provides speed at the top of the lineup.

As talent-laden as the Jays are, they've got several prospects ready to move up. Carlos Delgado is ready to replace Pat Borders at catcher. Alex Gonzalez will become the Blue Jays' SS before the end of 1994. And Rob Butler is penciled in for LF next year.

Pitching: (1993/4.21 ERA, fifth in AL)

The Blue Jays' pitching is the only potential problem area. Juan Guzman is the team's best pitcher, and has many strong years ahead. But Jack Morris and Dave Stewart will be 39 and 37 by the end of the '94 season, and both are showing signs of slowing down. Pat Hentgen (19–9) will have to prove 1993 was not a fluke. Todd Stottlemyre is erratic—but he's not 30 yet, so he'll have a place on the team. Signs are that GM Pat Gillick will have to acquire more starting pitching.

As for the bullpen, Duane Ward proved to be a solid closer, but the Jays didn't really find an adequate replacement for him as a setup man, and middle relief is shaky.

Defense: (1993/.982 pct., sixth in AL)

The Blue Jays play solid defense. They're "strong up the middle," with Pat Borders behind the plate, Tony Fernandez and Roberto Alomar at SS and 2B, and Devon White in center field.

1994 Prospects:

Toronto stayed pretty quiet over the off-season, while Baltimore made major player moves. But the Blue Jays have won two years in a row, and GM Pat Gillick may be the best since Branch Rickey. The Blue Jays may or may not three-peat, but the road to the pennant will go through Toronto.

Team Directory

Chairman: Peter N. T. Widdrington

President & CEO: Paul Beeston

VP, Baseball Operations: Pat Gillick

Asst. GM: Gord Ash

Director of P.R.: Howard Starkman

Traveling Secretary: John Brioux

Minor League Affiliates:

Level	Team/League	1993 Record
AAA	Syracuse – International	59–82
AA	Knoxville – Southern	71–71
A	Hagerstown – South Atlantic	74–68
	Dunedin – Florida State	68–64
	St. Catharines – New York/Penn.	49–29
Rookie	Medicine Hat – Pioneer	39–34
	Gulf Coast Blue Jays – Gulf Coast	22–38

1993 Review

	Home		Away			Home		Away			Home		Away	
vs AL East	W	L	W	L	vs AL Cent.	W	L	W	L	vs AL West	W	L	W	L
Baltimore	4	2	4	3	Chicago	3	3	3	3	California	5	1	3	3
Boston	6	1	4	2	Cleveland	4	2	5	2	Oakland	2	4	5	1
Detroit	4	3	3	3	Kansas City	3	3	1	5	Seattle	3	3	2	4
New York	4	2	4	3	Milwaukee	3	4	5	1	Texas	2	4	3	3
					Minnesota	5	1	5	1					
Total	18	8	15	11		18	13	19	12		12	12	13	11

1993 finish: 95–67 (48–33 home, 47–34 away), first in AL East; defeated Chicago 4–2 for AL Pennant; defeated Philadelphia 4–2 in World Series

1994 Schedule

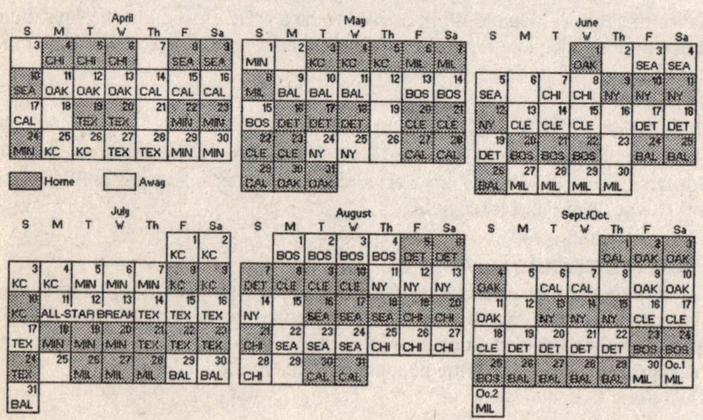

April

S	M	T	W	Th	F	Sa
3	4 CHI	5 CHI	6 CHI	7	8 SEA	9 SEA
10 SEA	11 OAK	12 OAK	13 OAK	14 CAL	15 CAL	16 CAL
17 CAL	18	19 TEX	20 TEX	21	22 MIN	23 MIN
24 MIN	25 KC	26 KC	27 TEX	28 TEX	29 MIN	30 MIN

Home Away

May

S	M	T	W	Th	F	Sa
1 MIN	2	3 KC	4 KC	5 KC	6 MIL	7 MIL
8 MIL	9 BAL	10 BAL	11 BAL	12	13 BOS	14 BOS
15 BOS	16 DET	17 DET	18 DET	19	20 CLE	21 CLE
22 CLE	23 CLE	24 NY	25 NY	26	27 CAL	28 CAL
29 CAL	30 OAK	31 OAK				

June

S	M	T	W	Th	F	Sa
			1 OAK	2	3 SEA	4 SEA
5 SEA	6	7 CHI	8 CHI	9 NY	10 NY	11 NY
12 NY	13 CLE	14 CLE	15 CLE	16	17 DET	18 DET
19 DET	20 BOS	21 BOS	22 BOS	23	24 BAL	25 BAL
26 BAL	27 MIL	28 MIL	29 MIL	30 MIL		

July

S	M	T	W	Th	F	Sa
					1 KC	2 KC
3 KC	4 KC	5 MIN	6 MIN	7 MIN	8 KC	9 KC
10 KC	11 ALL-STAR BREAK	12	13	14 TEX	15 TEX	16 TEX
17 TEX	18 MIN	19 MIN	20 MIN	21 TEX	22 TEX	23 TEX
24 TEX	25	26 MIL	27 MIL	28 MIL	29 BAL	30 BAL
31 BAL						

August

S	M	T	W	Th	F	Sa
	1 BOS	2 BOS	3 BOS	4 BOS	5 DET	6 DET
7 DET	8 CLE	9 CLE	10 CLE	11 NY	12 NY	13 NY
14 NY	15	16 SEA	17 SEA	18 SEA	19 CHI	20 CHI
21 CHI	22 SEA	23 SEA	24 SEA	25 CHI	26 CHI	27 CHI
28 CHI	29	30 CAL	31 CAL			

Sept./Oct.

S	M	T	W	Th	F	Sa
				1 CAL	2 OAK	3 OAK
4 OAK	5	6 CAL	7 CAL	8	9 OAK	10 OAK
11 OAK	12	13 NY	14 NY	15 NY	16 CLE	17 CLE
18 CLE	19 DET	20 DET	21 DET	22 DET	23 BOS	24 BOS
25 BOS	26 BAL	27 BAL	28 BAL	29 BAL	30 MIL	Oc.1 MIL
Oc.2 MIL						

TORONTO BLUE JAYS 1994 ROSTER

MANAGER: Cito Gaston (43)
COACHES: Bob Bailor (3), Rich Hacker (7), Galen Cisco (42), Gene Tenace (18), John Sullivan (8), Larry Hisle (39)

No.	PITCHERS	B	T	HT	WT	DOB	BIRTHPLACE	RESIDENCE
44	Brow, Scott	R	R	6-3	200	3-17-69	Butte, MT	Hillsboro, OR
49	Castillo, Tony	L	L	5-10	188	3-1-63	Lara, VZ	Lara, VZ
50	Cox, Danny	R	R	6-4	225	9-21-59	Northampton, Eng.	Freeburg, IL
	Daniels, Huck	S	L	5-11	185	2-25-69	Austin, CA	Fairfield, CA
32	Flener, Huck	S	L	5-11	185	2-25-69	Austin, TX	Fairfield, CA
	Gray, Dennis	L	L	5-6	210	12-24-69	Riverside, CA	Beaumont, CA
66	Guzman, Juan	R	R	5-11	195	10-28-66	Santo Domingo, DR	Manoguayabo, DR
41	Hentgen, Pat	R	R	6-2	200	11-13-68	Detroit, MI	Fraser, MI
28	Leiter, Al	L	L	6-3	215	10-23-65	Toms River, NJ	Plantation, FL
55	Menhart, Paul	R	R	6-2	190	3-25-69	St. Louis, MO	Conyers, GA
38	Small, Aaron	R	R	6-5	195	11-23-71	Oxnard, CA	Victorville, CA
	Spoljaric, Paul	R	L	6-3	205	9-24-70	Kelowna, BC	Kelowna, BC
34	Stewart, Dave	R	R	6-2	200	2-19-57	Oakland, CA	Emeryville, CA
30	Stottlemyre, Todd	L	R	6-3	200	5-20-65	Yakima, WA	Oldsmar, FL
40	Timlin, Mike	R	R	6-4	210	3-10-66	Midland, TX	Oldsmar, FL
31	Ward, Duane	R	R	6-4	215	5-28-64	Parkview, NM	Las Vegas, NV
54	Williams, Woody	R	R	6-0	190	8-19-66	Houston, TX	Alvin, TX
No.	**CATCHERS**	**B**	**T**	**HT**	**WT**	**DOB**	**BIRTHPLACE**	**RESIDENCE**
10	Borders, Pat	R	R	6-2	200	5-14-63	Columbus, OH	Lake Wales, FL
6	Delgado, Carlos	L	R	6-3	215	6-25-72	Aguadilla, PR	Aguadilla, PR
27	Knorr, Randy	R	R	6-2	218	11-12-68	San Gabriel, CA	Covina, CA
53	Martinez, Angel	R	R	6-4	200	10-3-72	Villa Mella, DR	Santo Domingo, DR
No.	**INFIELDERS**	**B**	**T**	**HT**	**WT**	**DOB**	**BIRTHPLACE**	**RESIDENCE**
12	Alomar, Roberto	S	R	6-0	185	2-5-68	Ponce, PR	Ponce, PR
	Bittle, Howard	R	R	6-0	208	3-25-72	Biloxi, MS	Biloxi, MS
	Buto, Tilson	R	R	6-0	170	5-28-72	Santo Domingo, DR	Santo Domingo, DR
70	Cedeno, Domingo	S	R	6-1	165	11-4-68	La Romana, DR	La Romana, DR
19	Martinez, Domingo	R	R	6-2	215	8-4-67	Santo Domingo, DR	Santo Domingo, DR
4	Molitor, Paul	R	R	6-0	185	8-22-56	St. Paul, MN	Mequon, WI
9	Olerud, John	L	L	6-5	220	8-5-68	Seattle, WA	Bellevue, WA
22	Schofield, Dick	R	R	5-10	179	11-21-62	Springfield, IL	Laguna Hills, CA
5	Sojo, Luis	R	R	5-11	174	1-3-66	Barquisimeto, VZ	Barquisimeto, VZ
33	Sprague, Ed	R	R	6-2	215	7-25-67	Castro Valley, CA	Stockton, CA
	Zosky, Eddie	R	R	6-0	175	2-10-68	Whittier, CA	Fresno, CA
No.	**OUTFIELDERS**	**B**	**T**	**HT**	**WT**	**DOB**	**BIRTHPLACE**	**RESIDENCE**
23	Bowers, Brent	L	R	6-3	190	5-2-71	Oak Lawn, IL	Bridgeview, IL
2	Butler, Rob	L	L	5-11	185	4-10-70	East York, ON	Toronto, ON
21	Canate, Willie	R	R	6-0	170	12-11-71	Maracaibo, VZ	Maracaibo, VZ
29	Carter, Joe	R	R	6-3	225	3-7-60	Oklahoma City, KS	Leawood, KS
11	Coles, Darnell	R	R	6-1	185	6-2-62	San Bernardino, CA	Safety Harbor, FL
56	Green, Shawn	L	L	6-4	190	11-10-72	Des Plains, IL	Irvine, CA
	Hofield, Rick	L	L	6-2	180	3-25-70	Bronx, NY	Norwalk, CT
17	Perez, Robert	R	R	6-3	205	6-4-69	Bolivar, VZ	Bolivar, VZ
25	White, Devon	S	R	6-2	195	12-29-62	Kingston, Jamaica	Gilbert, AZ

Sky Dome (52,268, artificial)
Tickets: 416-341-1000
Ticket prices (1993 ticket prices; 1994 ticket prices NA at press time):
- $19.50 (esplanade IF, club level OF)
- $15.00 (skydeck IF, esplanade OF)
- $11 (skydeck); $5 (skydeck outfield)

Field Dimensions (from home plate)
- To left field at foul line, 328 feet
- To center field, 400 feet
- To right field at foul line, 328 feet

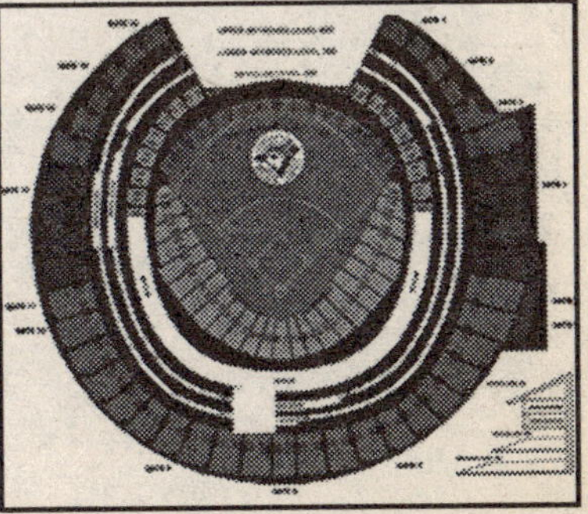

Roberto Alomar No. 12/2B

Full name: Roberto Velazquez Alomar
Bats: S **Throws:** R **HT:** 6–0 **WT:** 185
Born: 2–5–68, Ponce, PR
Alomar had career-bests in BA (.326), hits (192), and HR (17). He batted .327 on the road, fifth-best in the AL, and his team-high 55 SB ranked second in the league.

	TEAM	LG	POS	G	AB	R	H	2B	3B	HR	RBI	BB	SO	SB	E	BA	SLG	SALARY
1988	SD	NL	2B	143	545	84	145	24	6	9	41	47	83	24	16	.266	.382	N/A
1989	SD	NL	2B	158	623	82	184	27	1	7	56	53	76	42	28	.295	.376	N/A
1990	SD	NL	2B/SS	147	586	80	168	27	5	6	60	48	72	24	19	.287	.381	400,000
1991	TOR	AL	2B	161	637	88	188	41	11	9	69	57	86	53	15	.295	.436	1,250,000
1992	TOR	AL	2B	152	571	105	177	27	8	8	76	87	52	49	5	.310	.427	2,833,333
1993	TOR	AL	2B	153	589	109	192	35	6	17	93	80	67	55	14	.326	.492	4,883,333
6	YR	TOTALS		914	3551	548	1054	181	37	56	395	372	436	247	97	.297	.416	
1993	RANK	MLB	2B	3	4	1	2	2	5	5	2	1	14	1	6	2	4	2
1994	PROJECTIONS			154	596	113	199	36	6	18	101	85	64	60	13	.334	.505	

Pat Borders No. 10/C

Full name: Patrick Lance Borders
Bats: R **Throws:** R **HT:** 6–2 **WT:** 200
Born: 5–14–63, Columbus, OH
High school: Lake Wales (FL)
For the second straight year, Borders led the AL in games caught with 134. His 124 hits, 55 RBI, and 30 doubles were career-bests.

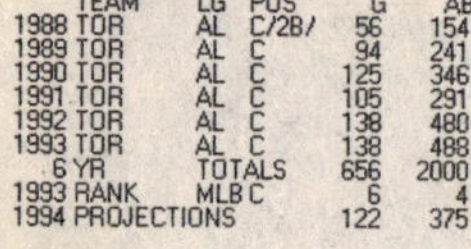

	TEAM	LG	POS	G	AB	R	H	2B	3B	HR	RBI	BB	SO	SB	E	BA	SLG	SALARY
1988	TOR	AL	C/2B/	56	154	15	42	6	3	5	21	3	24	0	7	.273	.448	N/A
1989	TOR	AL	C	94	241	22	62	11	1	3	29	11	45	2	6	.257	.349	N/A
1990	TOR	AL	C	125	346	36	99	24	2	15	49	18	57	0	4	.286	.497	180,000
1991	TOR	AL	C	105	291	22	71	17	0	5	36	11	45	0	4	.244	.354	700,000
1992	TOR	AL	C	138	480	47	116	26	2	13	53	33	75	1	8	.242	.385	950,000
1993	TOR	AL	C	138	488	38	124	30	0	9	55	20	66	2	13	.254	.371	2,500,000
6	YR	TOTALS		656	2000	180	514	114	8	50	243	96	312	5	42	.257	.397	
1993	RANK	MLB	C	6	4	17	8	2	25	19	12	28	13	13	1	25	29	4
1994	PROJECTIONS			122	375	32	98	23	0	9	46	16	56	0	7	.261	.405	

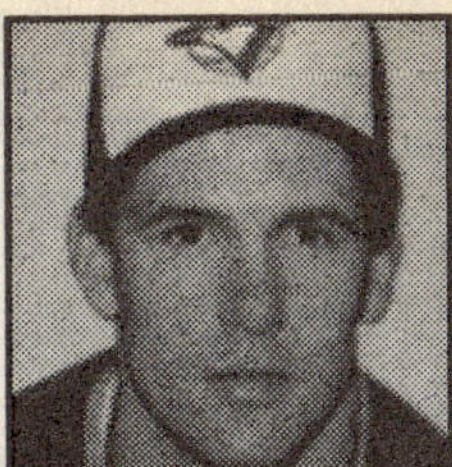

Rob Butler — No. 2/OF

Full name: Rob Butler
Bats: L **Throws:** L **HT:** 5–11 **WT:** 185
Born: 4–10–70, East York, ON

Rookie Butler will try to replace the departed Rickey Henderson. He batted .284 in 55 games at AAA Syracuse, and .271 in 17 games with the Blue Jays.

	TEAM	LG	POS	G	AB	R	H	2B	3B	HR	RBI	BB	SO	SB	E	BA	SLG	SALARY
1993	TOR	AL	OF	17	48	8	13	4	0	0	2	7	12	2	1	.271	.354	109,000
1	YR	TOTAL		17	48	8	13	4	0	0	2	7	12	2	1	.271	.354	
1993	RANK	MLB	OF	not ranked -- didn't have 150 ABs in 1993														

Joe Carter — No. 29/OF

Full name: Joseph Chris Carter
Bats: R **Throws:** R **HT:** 6–3 **WT:** 225
Born: 3–7–60, Oklahoma City, OK
High school: Millwood (Oklahoma City, OK)
College: Wichita State

Carter has had at least 24 HR in each of the last eight years, and his 121 RBI was third best in the AL.

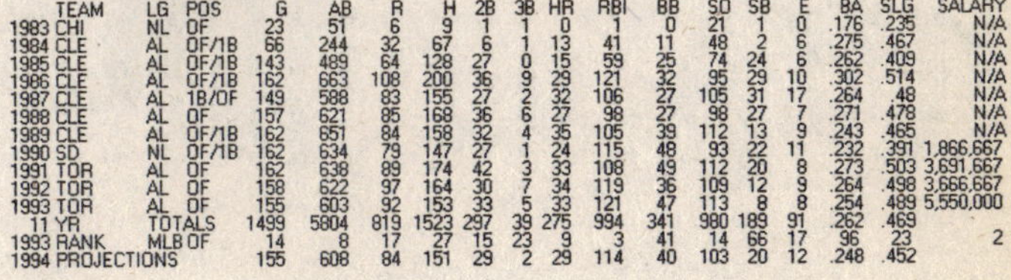

	TEAM	LG	POS	G	AB	R	H	2B	3B	HR	RBI	BB	SO	SB	E	BA	SLG	SALARY
1983	CHI	NL	OF	23	51	6	9	1	1	0	1	0	21	1	0	.176	.235	N/A
1984	CLE	AL	OF/1B	66	244	32	67	6	1	13	41	11	48	2	6	.275	.467	N/A
1985	CLE	AL	OF/1B	143	489	64	128	27	0	15	59	25	74	24	6	.262	.409	N/A
1986	CLE	AL	OF/1B	162	663	108	200	36	9	29	121	32	95	29	10	.302	.514	N/A
1987	CLE	AL	1B/OF	149	588	83	155	27	2	32	106	27	105	31	17	.264	.48	N/A
1988	CLE	AL	OF	157	621	85	168	36	6	27	98	27	98	27	7	.271	.478	N/A
1989	CLE	AL	OF/1B	162	651	84	158	32	4	35	105	39	112	13	9	.243	.465	N/A
1990	SD	NL	OF/1B	162	634	79	147	27	1	24	115	48	93	22	11	.232	.391	1,866,667
1991	TOR	AL	OF	162	638	89	174	42	3	33	108	49	112	20	8	.273	.503	3,691,667
1992	TOR	AL	OF	158	622	97	164	30	7	34	119	36	109	12	9	.264	.498	3,666,667
1993	TOR	AL	OF	155	603	92	153	33	5	33	121	47	113	8	8	.254	.489	5,550,000
11	YR	TOTALS		1499	5804	819	1523	297	39	275	994	341	980	189	91	.262	.469	
1993	RANK	MLB	OF	14	8	17	27	15	23	9	3	41	14	66	17	96	23	2
1994	PROJECTIONS			155	608	84	151	29	2	29	114	40	103	20	12	.248	.452	

Paul Molitor — No. 4/DH

Full name: Paul Leo Molitor
Bats: R **Throws:** R **HT:** 6–0 **WT:** 185
Born: 8–22–56, St. Paul, MN
High school: Cretin (St. Paul, MN)
College: Minnesota

At 37, Molitor was the oldest player in history to have more than 20 HR and 20 SB. He had his third straight year batting over .320.

	TEAM	LG	POS	G	AB	R	H	2B	3B	HR	RBI	BB	SO	SB	E	BA	SLG	SALARY
1979	MIL	AL	2B/SS	140	584	88	188	27	16	9	62	48	48	33	16	.322	.469	N/A
1980	MIL	AL	2B/SS	111	450	81	137	29	2	9	37	48	48	34	20	.304	.438	N/A
1981	MIL	AL	OF	64	251	45	67	11	0	2	19	25	29	10	3	.267	.335	N/A
1982	MIL	AL	3B/SS	160	666	136	201	26	8	19	71	69	93	41	32	.302	.450	N/A
1983	MIL	AL	3B	152	608	95	164	28	6	15	47	59	74	41	16	.270	.410	N/A
1984	MIL	AL	3B	13	46	3	10	1	0	0	6	2	8	1	2	.217	.239	N/A
1985	MIL	AL	3B	140	576	93	171	28	3	10	48	54	80	21	19	.297	.408	N/A
1986	MIL	AL	3B/OF	105	437	62	123	24	6	9	55	40	81	20	15	.281	.426	N/A
1987	MIL	AL	3B/2B	118	465	114	164	41	5	16	75	69	67	45	5	.353	.566	N/A
1988	MIL	AL	3B/2B	154	609	115	190	34	6	13	60	71	54	41	17	.312	.452	N/A
1989	MIL	AL	3B/2B	155	615	84	194	35	4	11	56	64	67	27	18	.315	.439	N/A
1990	MIL	AL	2B	103	418	64	119	27	6	12	45	37	51	18	10	.285	.464	2,600,000
1991	MIL	AL	1B	158	665	133	216	32	13	17	75	77	62	19	6	.325	.489	3,305,833
1992	MIL	AL	1B	158	609	89	195	36	7	12	89	73	66	31	2	.320	.461	3,433,334
1993	TOR	AL	DH	160	636	121	211	37	5	22	111	77	71	22	3	.332	.509	3,575,000
16	YR	TOTALS		2016	8156	1396	2492	442	91	182	901	832	953	434	206	.306	.449	
1993	RANK	MLB	DH	1	1	1	1	1	1	3	2	2	5	1	1	1	2	3
1994	PROJECTIONS			159	637	115	202	33	6	17	90	73	76	31	12	.317	.473	

John Olerud — No. 9/1B

Full name: John Garrett Olerud
Bats: L **Throws:** L **HT:** 6–5 **WT:** 220
Born: 8–5–68, Seattle, WA
High school: Interlake (Bellevue, WA)
College: Washington State

MVP runner-up Olerud flirted with .400 for much of 1993. He is one of only 5 major leaguers to have never played in the minors.

	TEAM	LG	POS	G	AB	R	H	2B	3B	HR	RBI	BB	SO	SB	E	BA	SLG	SALARY
1989	TOR	AL	1B	6	8	2	3	0	0	0	0	0	1	0	0	.375	.375	N/A
1990	TOR	AL	1B	111	358	43	95	15	1	14	48	57	75	0	2	.265	.430	100,000
1991	TOR	AL	1B	139	454	64	116	30	1	17	68	68	84	0	5	.256	.438	291,667
1992	TOR	AL	1B	138	458	68	130	28	0	16	66	70	61	1	7	.284	.450	387,500
1993	TOR	AL	1B	158	551	109	200	54	2	24	107	114	65	0	10	.363	.599	1,537,000
5	YR	TOTALS		552	1829	286	544	127	4	71	289	309	286	1	24	.297	.488	
1993	RANK	MLB	1B	2	8	3	1	1	11	9	4	1	19	31	10	2	3	15
1994	PROJECTIONS			162	567	112	205	55	1	24	110	117	66	0	10	.362	.589	

Dick Schofield No. 22/SS

Full name: Richard Craig Schofield
Bats: R **Throws:** R **HT:** 5–10 **WT:** 179
Born: 11–21–62, Springfield, IL
High school: Sacred Heart (Springfield, IL)

Due to injuries, Schofield played in his fewest games (36) since 1983. He batted a weak .127 in 16 road games.

	TEAM	LG	POS	G	AB	R	H	2B	3B	HR	RBI	BB	SO	SB	E	BA	SLG	SALARY
1983	CAL	AL	SS	21	54	4	11	2	0	3	4	6	8	0	7	.204	.407	N/A
1984	CAL	AL	SS	140	400	39	77	10	3	4	21	33	79	5	12	.193	.263	N/A
1985	CAL	AL	SS	147	438	50	96	19	3	8	41	35	70	11	25	.219	.331	N/A
1986	CAL	AL	SS	139	458	67	114	17	6	13	57	48	55	23	18	.249	.397	N/A
1987	CAL	AL	SS/2B	134	479	52	120	17	3	9	46	37	63	19	9	.251	.355	N/A
1988	CAL	AL	SS	155	527	61	126	11	6	6	34	40	57	20	13	.239	.317	N/A
1989	CAL	AL	SS	91	302	42	69	11	2	4	26	28	47	9	7	.228	.318	N/A
1990	CAL	AL	SS	99	310	41	79	8	1	1	18	52	61	3	17	.255	.297	N/A
1991	CAL	AL	SS	134	427	44	96	9	3	0	31	50	69	8	15	.225	.260	1,483,334
1992	CAL	AL	SS	1	3	0	1	0	0	0	0	1	0	0	0	.333	.333	N/A
1992	NY	NL	SS	142	420	52	86	18	2	4	36	60	82	11	7	.205	.286	1,500,000
1993	TOR	AL	SS	36	110	11	21	1	2	0	5	16	25	3	4	.191	.236	800,000
11	YR	TOTALS		1239	3928	463	896	123	31	52	319	406	616	112	134	.228	.315	
1993	RANK	MLB	SS	not ranked -- didn't have 150 ABs in 1993														
1994	PROJECTIONS			19	55	5	11	1	0	1	3	7	11	1	3	.20	.291	

Ed Sprague No. 33/3B

Full name: Edward Nelson Sprague
Bats: R **Throws:** R **HT:** 6–2 **WT:** 215
Born: 7–25–67, Castro Valley, CA
High school: St. Mary's (Stockton, CA)
College: Stanford

In his first full season at Toronto, Sprague started 150 games at third base. He hit .284 from the seventh inning on.

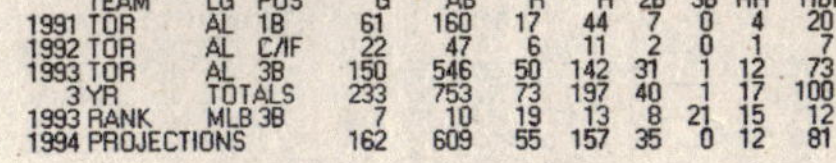

	TEAM	LG	POS	G	AB	R	H	2B	3B	HR	RBI	BB	SO	SB	E	BA	SLG	SALARY
1991	TOR	AL	1B	61	160	17	44	7	0	4	20	19	43	0	14	.275	.394	100,000
1992	TOR	AL	C/IF	22	47	6	11	2	0	1	7	3	7	0	1	.234	.340	117,500
1993	TOR	AL	3B	150	546	50	142	31	1	12	73	32	85	1	17	.260	.386	182,500
3	YR	TOTALS		233	753	73	197	40	1	17	100	54	135	1	32	.262	.385	
1993	RANK	MLB	3B	7	10	19	13	8	21	15	12	21	10	26	12	25	26	26
1994	PROJECTIONS			162	609	55	157	35	0	12	81	32	89	0	16	.258	.374	

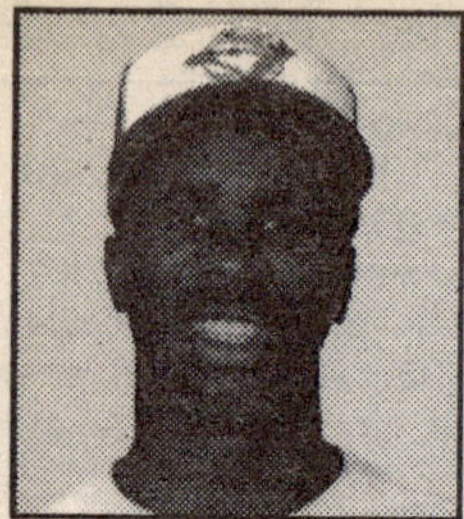

Devon White No. 25/OF

Full name: Devon Markes White
Bats: S **Throws:** R **HT:** 6–2 **WT:** 195
Born: 12–29–62, Kingston, Jamaica
High school: Park West (NY)

White's career-high 41 doubles were second best in the AL, and his 116 runs ranked third. He had over 30 SB for the third straight season.

	TEAM	LG	POS	G	AB	R	H	2B	3B	HR	RBI	BB	SO	SB	E	BA	SLG	SALARY
1985	CAL	AL	OF	21	7	7	1	0	0	0	0	1	3	3	0	.143	.143	N/A
1986	CAL	AL	OF	29	51	8	12	1	1	1	3	6	8	13	2	.235	.353	N/A
1987	CAL	AL	OF	159	639	103	168	33	5	24	87	39	135	32	9	.263	.443	N/A
1988	CAL	AL	OF	122	455	76	118	22	2	11	51	23	84	17	9	.259	.389	N/A
1989	CAL	AL	OF	156	636	86	156	18	13	12	56	31	129	44	5	.245	.371	N/A
1990	CAL	AL	OF	125	443	57	96	17	3	11	44	44	116	21	9	.217	.343	580,000
1991	TOR	AL	OF	156	642	110	181	40	10	17	60	55	135	33	1	.282	.455	750,000
1992	TOR	AL	OF	153	641	98	159	26	7	17	60	47	133	37	7	.248	.390	2,333,333
1993	TOR	AL	OF	146	598	116	163	42	6	15	52	57	127	34	3	.273	.438	3,608,333
9	YR	TOTALS		1067	4112	661	1054	199	47	108	413	303	870	234	45	.256	.406	
1993	RANK	MLB	OF	27	9	3	20	3	13	36	58	28	7	16	72	65	57	16
1994	PROJECTIONS			151	625	100	159	28	8	14	56	45	129	38	5	.254	.398	

Juan Guzman No. 66/P

Full name: Juan Andres Correa Guzman
Bats: R **Throws:** R **HT:** 5–11 **WT:** 195
Born: 10–28–66, Santo Domingo, DR
High school: Liceo las Americas (DR)

Guzman had the best winning percentage in the AL (.824) due to great run support (6.2/game). He set the AL-record with 26 wild pitches.

	TM	LG	POS	W	L	ERA	G	GS	CG	SH	SV	IP	H	R	ER	HR	BB	SO	SALARY
1991	TOR	AL	P	10	3	2.99	23	23	1	0	0	138.2	98	53	46	6	66	123	100,000
1992	TOR	AL	P	16	5	2.64	28	28	1	0	0	180.2	135	56	53	6	72	165	220,000
1993	TOR	AL	P	14	3	3.99	33	33	2	1	0	221.0	211	107	98	17	110	194	500,000
3	YR	TOTALS		40	11	3.28	84	84	4	1	0	540.1	444	216	197	29	248	482	
1993	Rank	MLB	Ps	29		131	167	30	57	23	102	25	102	125		90	252	40	132
1994	PROJECTIONS			15	3	4.17	36	36	2	1	0	248	248	125	115	20	124	217	

Pat Hentgen No. 41/P

Full name: Patrick George Hentgen
Bats: R **Throws:** R **HT:** 6–2 **WT:** 200
Born: 11–13–68, Detroit, MI
High school: Fraser (MI)

In his first full season, Hentgen led the Jays with 19 wins, second-best in the AL. He gave up a team-high 26 HR, and lasted at least 6 innings in 14 of his last 15 starts.

TM	LG	POS	W	L	ERA	G	GS	CG	SH	SV	IP	H	R	ER	HR	BB	SO	SALARY
1991 TOR	AL	P	0	0	2.45	3	1	0	0	0	7.1	5	2	2	1	3	3	N/A
1992 TOR	AL	P	5	2	5.36	28	2	0	0	0	50.1	49	30	30	7	32	39	109,000
1993 TOR	AL	P	19	9	3.87	34	32	3	0	0	216.1	215	103	93	27	74	122	182,500
3 YR	TOTALS		24	11	4.11	65	35	3	0	0	274.0	269	135	125	35	109	164	
1993 Rank	MLB Ps		6		122	145	39	37	69	102	30	134	114		220	121	198	182
1994 PROJECTIONS			21	10	3.87	37	36	3	0	0	244	244	116	105	30	83	138	

Dave Stewart No. 34/P

Full name: David Keith Stewart
Bats: R **Throws:** R **HT:** 6–2 **WT:** 200
Born: 2–19–57, Oakland, CA
High school: St. Elizabeth (Oakland, CA)
College: Merritt (CA) and Cal State-Hayward

Veteran Stewart started 26 games, his lowest total since 1986. He did not throw a complete game, but held opponents to a .242 BA.

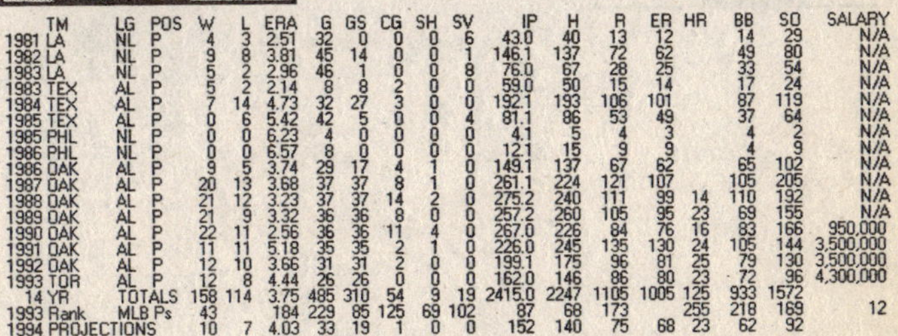

TM	LG	POS	W	L	ERA	G	GS	CG	SH	SV	IP	H	R	ER	HR	BB	SO	SALARY
1981 LA	NL	P	4	3	2.51	32	0	0	0	6	43.0	40	13	12		14	29	N/A
1982 LA	NL	P	9	8	3.81	45	14	0	0	1	146.1	137	72	62		49	80	N/A
1983 LA	NL	P	5	2	2.96	46	1	0	0	8	76.0	67	28	25		33	54	N/A
1983 TEX	AL	P	5	2	2.14	8	8	2	0	0	59.0	50	15	14		17	24	N/A
1984 TEX	AL	P	7	14	4.73	32	27	3	0	0	192.1	193	106	101		87	119	N/A
1985 TEX	AL	P	0	6	5.42	42	5	0	0	4	81.1	86	53	49		37	64	N/A
1985 PHL	NL	P	0	0	6.23	4	0	0	0	0	4.1	5	4	3		4	2	N/A
1986 PHL	NL	P	0	0	6.57	8	0	0	0	0	12.1	15	9	9		4	9	N/A
1986 OAK	AL	P	9	5	3.74	29	17	4	1	0	149.1	137	67	62		65	102	N/A
1987 OAK	AL	P	20	13	3.68	37	37	8	1	0	261.1	224	121	107		105	205	N/A
1988 OAK	AL	P	21	12	3.23	37	37	14	2	0	275.2	240	111	99	14	110	192	N/A
1989 OAK	AL	P	21	9	3.32	36	36	8	0	0	257.2	260	105	95	23	69	155	N/A
1990 OAK	AL	P	22	11	2.56	36	36	11	4	0	267.0	226	84	76	16	83	166	950,000
1991 OAK	AL	P	11	11	5.18	35	35	2	1	0	226.0	245	135	130	24	105	144	3,500,000
1992 OAK	AL	P	12	10	3.66	31	31	2	0	0	199.1	175	96	81	25	79	130	3,500,000
1993 TOR	AL	P	12	8	4.44	26	26	0	0	0	162.0	146	86	80	23	72	96	4,300,000
14 YR	TOTALS		158	114	3.75	485	310	54	9	19	2415.0	2247	1105	1005	125	933	1572	
1993 Rank	MLB Ps		43		184	229	85	125	69	102	87	68	173		255	218	169	12
1994 PROJECTIONS			10	7	4.03	33	19	1	0	0	152	140	75	68	23	62	92	

Duane Ward — No. 31/P

Full name: Roy Duane Ward
Bats: R **Throws:** R **HT:** 6–4 **WT:** 215
Born: 5–28–64, Parkview, NM
High school: Farmington (NM)

Closer Ward became the first Blue Jay to lead the AL in saves with a team-record 45. He saved at least one game against every AL team but the Royals.

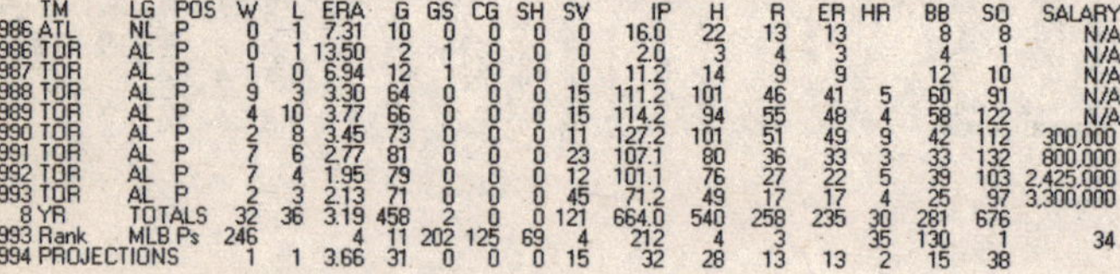

	TM	LG	POS	W	L	ERA	G	GS	CG	SH	SV	IP	H	R	ER	HR	BB	SO	SALARY
1986	ATL	NL	P	0	1	7.31	10	0	0	0	0	16.0	22	13	13		8	8	N/A
1986	TOR	AL	P	0	1	13.50	2	1	0	0	0	2.0	3	4	3		4	1	N/A
1987	TOR	AL	P	1	0	6.94	12	1	0	0	0	11.2	14	9	9		12	10	N/A
1988	TOR	AL	P	9	3	3.30	64	0	0	0	15	111.2	101	46	41	5	60	91	N/A
1989	TOR	AL	P	4	10	3.77	66	0	0	0	15	114.2	94	55	48	4	58	122	N/A
1990	TOR	AL	P	2	8	3.45	73	0	0	0	11	127.2	101	51	49	9	42	112	300,000
1991	TOR	AL	P	7	6	2.77	81	0	0	0	23	107.1	80	36	33	3	33	132	800,000
1992	TOR	AL	P	7	4	1.95	79	0	0	0	12	101.1	76	27	22	5	39	103	2,425,000
1993	TOR	AL	P	2	3	2.13	71	0	0	0	45	71.2	49	17	17	4	25	97	3,300,000
8	YR	TOTALS		32	36	3.19	458	2	0	0	121	664.0	540	258	235	30	281	676	
1993	Rank	MLB Ps		246		4	11	202	125	69	4	212	4	3		35	130	1	34
1994	PROJECTIONS			1	1	3.66	31	0	0	0	15	32	28	13	13	2	15	38	

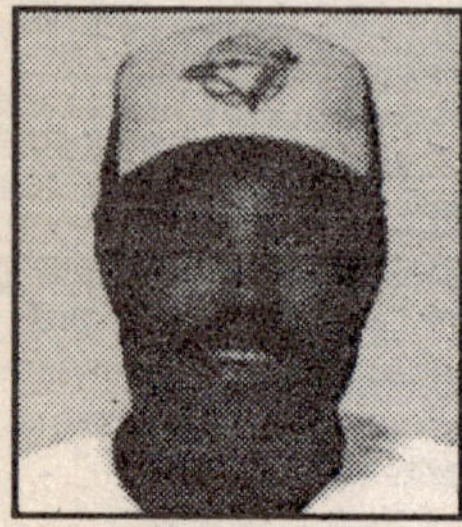

Cito Gaston — No. 43/Mgr.

Full name: Clarence Edwin Gaston
Bats: R **Throws:** R **HT:** 6–4 **WT:** 210
Born: 3–17–44, San Antonio, TX
High school: Holy Cross (Corpus Christi, TX)

Earl Weaver, Whitey Herzog, Tony LaRussa, and Cito Gaston all won three straight AL division championships—but only Gaston won back-to-back World Series.

			REG. SEASON				PLAYOFF			CHAMP. SERIES			WORLD SERIES		
YEAR	TEAM	LG	W	L	PCT	POS	W	L	PCT	W	L	PCT	W	L	PCT
1989	TOR	AL	77	49	.611	1			---	1	4	.200			---
1990	TOR	AL	86	76	.531	2			---			---			---
1991	TOR	AL	91	71	.562	1			---	1	4	.200			---
1992	TOR	AL	96	66	.593	1			---	4	2	.667	4	2	.667
1993	TOR	AL	95	67	.586	1			---	4	2	.667	4	2	.667
5	YR TOTALS		445	329	.575		0	0	---	10	12	.455	8	4	.667

Willie Canate No. 21/OF

Full name: Willie Canate
Bats: R **Throws:** R **HT:** 6–0 **WT:** 170
Born: 12–11–71, Maracaibo, VZ
Canate struck out 15 times in only 47 AB for the Jays. He batted .250 on the road.

TEAM	LG	POS	G	AB	R	H	2B	3B	HR	RBI	BB	SO	SB	E	BA	SLG	SALARY
1993 TOR	AL	OF	38	47	12	10	0	0	1	3	6	15	1	0	.213	.277	109,000
1 YR	TOTAL		38	47	12	10	0	0	1	3	6	15	1	0	.213	.277	
1993 RANK	MLB OF		not ranked -- didn't have 150 ABs in 1993														

Tony Castillo No. 49/P

Full name: Antonio Castillo
Bats: L **Throws:** L **HT:** 5–10 **WT:** 188
Born: 3–1–63, Lara, VZ
High school: Lara (VZ)
Castillo made 51 appearances, his most since 1990, and had a road ERA of 1.27.

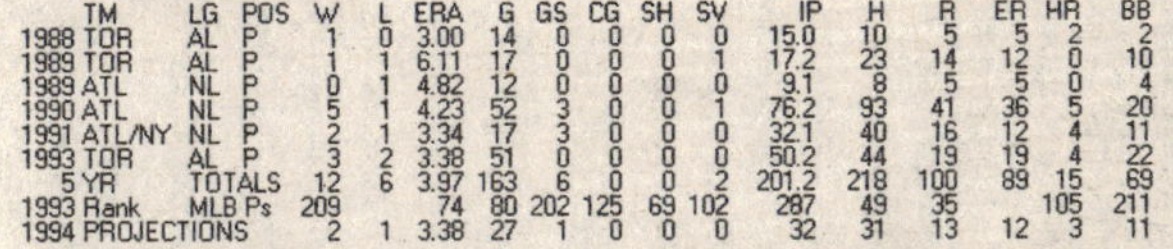

TM	LG	POS	W	L	ERA	G	GS	CG	SH	SV	IP	H	R	ER	HR	BB	SO	SALARY
1988 TOR	AL	P	1	0	3.00	14	0	0	0	0	15.0	10	5	5	2	2	14	N/A
1989 TOR	AL	P	1	1	6.11	17	0	0	0	1	17.2	23	14	12	0	10	10	N/A
1989 ATL	NL	P	0	1	4.82	12	0	0	0	0	9.1	8	5	5	0	4	5	N/A
1990 ATL	NL	P	5	1	4.23	52	3	0	0	1	76.2	93	41	36	5	20	64	100,000
1991 ATL/NY	NL	P	2	1	3.34	17	3	0	0	0	32.1	40	16	12	4	11	18	165,000
1993 TOR	AL	P	3	2	3.38	51	0	0	0	0	50.2	44	19	19	4	22	28	185,000
5 YR	TOTALS		12	6	3.97	163	6	0	0	2	201.2	218	100	89	15	69	139	
1993 Rank	MLB Ps		209		74	80	202	125	69	102	287	49	35		105	211	205	179
1994 PROJECTIONS			2	1	3.38	27	1	0	0	0	32	31	13	12	3	11	20	

Domingo Cedeno No. 70/SS

Full name: Domingo Cedeno
Bats: S **Throws:** R **HT:** 6–1 **WT:** 165
Born: 11–4–68, La Romana, DR
High school: La Romana (DR)
Cedeno batted .272 with 15 SB in 103 games for AAA Syracuse.

TEAM	LG	POS	G	AB	R	H	2B	3B	HR	RBI	BB	SO	SB	E	BA	SLG	SALARY
1993 TOR	AL	SS	15	46	5	8	0	0	0	7	1	10	1	1	.174	.174	N/A
1 YR	TOTAL		15	46	5	8	0	0	0	7	1	10	1	1	.174	.174	
1993 RANK	MLB SS		not ranked -- didn't have 150 ABs in 1993														

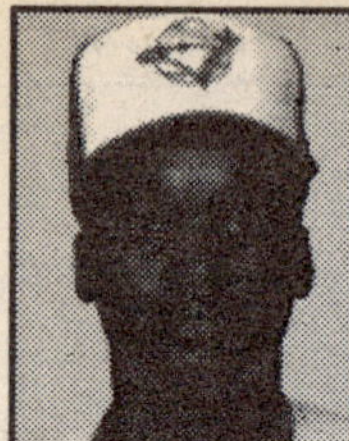

Darnell Coles — No. 11/OF

Full name: Darnell Coles
Bats: R **Throws:** R **HT:** 6–1 **WT:** 185
Born: 6–2–62, San Bernardino, CA
High school: Eisenhower (Rialto, CA)
Utilityman Coles started at 4 different positions. He batted .277 against the AL West.

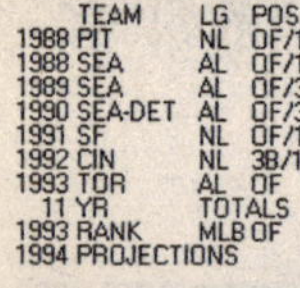

	TEAM	LG	POS	G	AB	R	H	2B	3B	HR	RBI	BB	SO	SB	E	BA	SLG	SALARY
1988	PIT	NL	OF/1B	68	211	20	49	13	1	5	36	20	41	1	83	.232	.374	N/A
1988	SEA	AL	OF/1B	55	195	32	57	10	1	10	34	17	26	3	0	.292	.508	N/A
1989	SEA	AL	OF/3B	146	535	54	135	21	3	10	59	27	61	5	0	.252	.359	N/A
1990	SEA-DET	AL	OF/3B	89	215	22	45	7	1	3	20	16	38	0	0	.209	.293	N/A
1991	SF	NL	OF/1B	11	14	1	3	0	0	0	0	0	2	0	0	.214	.214	N/A
1992	CIN	NL	3B/1B	55	141	16	44	11	2	3	18	3	15	1	0	.312	.482	1,600,000
1993	TOR	AL	OF	64	194	26	49	9	1	4	26	16	29	1	7	.253	.371	500,000
11	YR	TOTALS		825	2588	304	641	128	13	67	335	211	394	20	151	.248	.385	
1993	RANK	MLB	OF	132	120	115	119	118	97	102	105	117	124	116	25	99	103	81
1994	PROJECTIONS			69	183	21	46	9	1	3	21	11	27	0	2	.251	.366	

Danny Cox — No. 50/P

Full name: Danny Bradford Cox
Bats: R **Throws:** R **HT:** 6–4 **WT:** 225
Born: 9–21–59, Northampton, Eng.
High school: Warner Robbins (GA)
College: C'hoochee Valley (AL) and Troy State (AL)
Cox's 3.12 ERA was his lowest since 1986.

	TM	LG	POS	W	L	ERA	G	GS	CG	SH	SV	IP	H	R	ER	HR	BB	SO	SALARY
1985	STL	NL	P	18	9	2.88	35	35	10	4	0	241.0	226	91	77	19	64	131	N/A
1986	STL	NL	P	12	13	2.90	32	32	8	0	0	220.0	189	85	71	14	60	108	N/A
1987	STL	NL	P	11	9	3.88	31	31	2	0	0	199.1	224	99	86	17	71	101	N/A
1988	STL	NL	P	3	8	3.98	13	13	0	0	0	86.0	89	40	38	6	25	47	N/A
1991	PHL	NL	P	4	6	4.57	23	17	0	0	0	102.1	98	57	52	14	39	46	220,000
1992	PHL/PIT	NL	P	5	3	4.60	25	7	0	0	3	62.2	66	37	32	5	27	48	625,000
1993	TOR	AL	P	7	6	3.12	44	0	0	0	2	83.2	73	31	29	8	29	84	625,000
9	YR	TOTALS		72	71	3.54	244	174	21	5	5	1234.1	1228	559	485	98	392	671	
1993	RANK	MLB	Ps	108		55	99	202	125	69	55	179	50	33		147	126	18	124
1994	PROJECTIONS			4	6	3.43	23	8	0	0	0	84	84	36	32	6	25	55	

Carlos Delgado — No. 6/C

Full name: Carlos Juan Delgado
Bats: L **Throws:** R **HT:** 6–3 **WT:** 215
Born: 6–25–72, Aguadilla, PR
High school: Jose de Diego (PR)
Delgado caught 107 games for AA Knoxville, posting an impressive .303 BA with 25 HR.

	TEAM	LG	POS	G	AB	R	H	2B	3B	HR	RBI	BB	SO	SB	E	BA	SLG	SALARY
1993	TOR	AL	C	2	1	0	0	0	0	0	0	1	0	0	0	.000	.000	N/A
1	YR	TOTAL		2	1	0	0	0	0	0	0	1	0	0	0	.000	.000	
1993	RANK	MLB	C	not ranked -- didn't have 150 ABs in 1993														

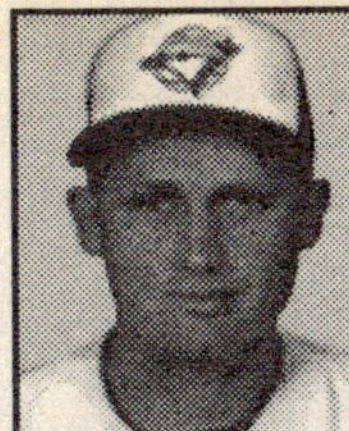

Randy Knorr — No. 27/C

Full name: Randy Duane Knorr
Bats: R **Throws:** R **HT:** 6–2 **WT:** 218
Born: 11–12–68, San Gabriel, CA
High school: Baldwin Park (CA)
In his first full season with the Jays, Knorr hit .091 before the All-Star break, .368 afterwards.

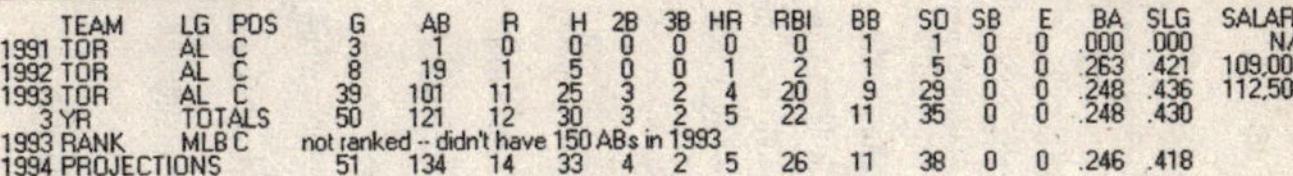

	TEAM	LG	POS	G	AB	R	H	2B	3B	HR	RBI	BB	SO	SB	E	BA	SLG	SALARY
1991	TOR	AL	C	3	1	0	0	0	0	0	0	1	1	0	0	.000	.000	N/A
1992	TOR	AL	C	8	19	1	5	0	0	1	2	1	5	0	0	.263	.421	109,000
1993	TOR	AL	C	39	101	11	25	3	2	4	20	9	29	0	0	.248	.436	112,500
3	YR	TOTALS		50	121	12	30	3	2	5	22	11	35	0	0	.248	.430	
1993	RANK	MLB	C	not ranked -- didn't have 150 ABs in 1993														
1994	PROJECTIONS			51	134	14	33	4	2	5	26	11	38	0	0	.246	.418	

Al Leiter — No. 28/P

Full name: Alois Terry Leiter
Bats: L **Throws:** L **HT:** 6–3 **WT:** 215
Born: 10–23–65, Toms River, NJ
High school: Central Regional (Bayville, NJ)
Leiter had career highs in wins (9) and IP (105.0). His ERA after the All-Star break was 2.75.

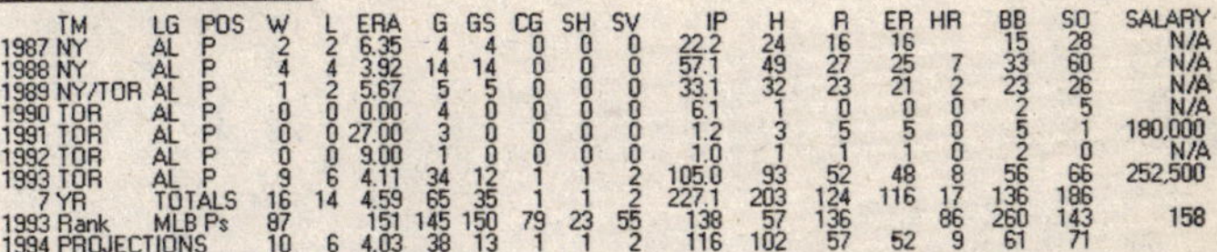

	TM	LG	POS	W	L	ERA	G	GS	CG	SH	SV	IP	H	R	ER	HR	BB	SO	SALARY
1987	NY	AL	P	2	2	6.35	4	4	0	0	0	22.2	24	16	16		15	28	N/A
1988	NY	AL	P	4	4	3.92	14	14	0	0	0	57.1	49	27	25	7	33	60	N/A
1989	NY/TOR	AL	P	1	2	5.67	5	5	0	0	0	33.1	32	23	21	2	23	26	N/A
1990	TOR	AL	P	0	0	0.00	4	0	0	0	0	6.1	1	0	0	0	2	5	N/A
1991	TOR	AL	P	0	0	27.00	3	0	0	0	0	1.2	3	5	5	0	5	1	180,000
1992	TOR	AL	P	0	0	9.00	1	0	0	0	0	1.0	1	1	1	0	2	0	N/A
1993	TOR	AL	P	9	6	4.11	34	12	1	1	2	105.0	93	52	48	8	56	66	252,500
7	YR	TOTALS		16	14	4.59	65	35	1	1	2	227.1	203	124	116	17	136	186	
1993	Rank	MLB	Ps	87		151	145	150	79	23	55	138	57	136		86	260	143	158
1994	PROJECTIONS			10	6	4.03	38	13	1	1	2	116	102	57	52	9	61	71	

Luis Sojo — No. 5/IF

Full name: Luis Sojo
Bats: R **Throws:** R **HT:** 5–11 **WT:** 174
Born: 1–3–66, Barquisimeto, VZ
High school: Barquisimeto (VZ)
Sojo struck out just 2 times in 47 AB with the Jays.

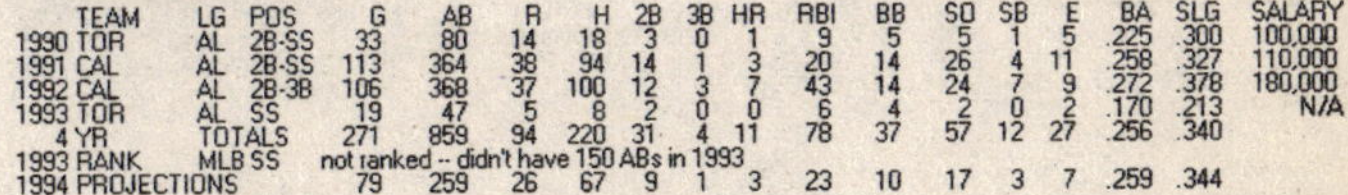

	TEAM	LG	POS	G	AB	R	H	2B	3B	HR	RBI	BB	SO	SB	E	BA	SLG	SALARY
1990	TOR	AL	2B-SS	33	80	14	18	3	0	1	9	5	5	1	5	.225	.300	100,000
1991	CAL	AL	2B-SS	113	364	38	94	14	1	3	20	14	26	4	11	.258	.327	110,000
1992	CAL	AL	2B-3B	106	368	37	100	12	3	7	43	14	24	7	9	.272	.378	180,000
1993	TOR	AL	SS	19	47	5	8	2	0	0	6	4	2	0	2	.170	.213	N/A
4	YR	TOTALS		271	859	94	220	31	4	11	78	37	57	12	27	.256	.340	
1993	RANK	MLB	SS	not ranked -- didn't have 150 ABs in 1993														
1994	PROJECTIONS			79	259	26	67	9	1	3	23	10	17	3	7	.259	.344	

Todd Stottlemyre — No. 30/P

Full name: Todd Vernon Stottlemyre
Bats: L **Throws:** R **HT:** 6–3 **WT:** 200
Born: 5–20–65, Yakima, WA
High school: David (Yakima, WA)
College: Nevada–Las Vegas
Stottlemyre had his first sub–.500 year since '88.

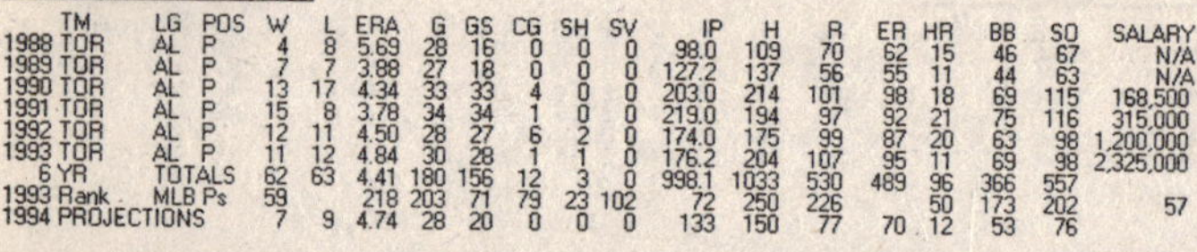

	TM	LG	POS	W	L	ERA	G	GS	CG	SH	SV	IP	H	R	ER	HR	BB	SO	SALARY
1988	TOR	AL	P	4	8	5.69	28	16	0	0	0	98.0	109	70	62	15	46	67	N/A
1989	TOR	AL	P	7	7	3.88	27	18	0	0	0	127.2	137	56	55	11	44	63	N/A
1990	TOR	AL	P	13	17	4.34	33	33	4	0	0	203.0	214	101	98	18	69	115	168,500
1991	TOR	AL	P	15	8	3.78	34	34	1	0	0	219.0	194	97	92	21	75	116	315,000
1992	TOR	AL	P	12	11	4.50	28	27	6	2	0	174.0	175	99	87	20	63	98	1,200,000
1993	TOR	AL	P	11	12	4.84	30	28	1	1	0	176.2	204	107	95	11	69	98	2,325,000
6	YR	TOTALS		62	63	4.41	180	156	12	3	0	998.1	1033	530	489	96	366	557	
1993	Rank	MLB Ps		59		218	203	71	79	23	102	72	250	226		50	173	202	57
1994	PROJECTIONS			7	9	4.74	28	20	0	0	0	133	150	77	70	12	53	76	

Mike Timlin — No. 40/P

Full name: Michael August Timlin
Bats: R **Throws:** R **HT:** 6–4 **WT:** 210
Born: 3–10–66, Midland, TX
High school: Midland (TX)
College: Southwestern (Georgetown, TX)
Timlin averaged 7.92 K/9 IP in 53 appearances.

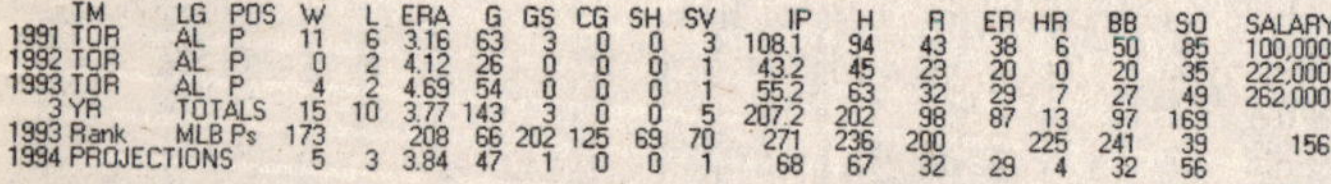

	TM	LG	POS	W	L	ERA	G	GS	CG	SH	SV	IP	H	R	ER	HR	BB	SO	SALARY
1991	TOR	AL	P	11	6	3.16	63	3	0	0	3	108.1	94	43	38	6	50	85	100,000
1992	TOR	AL	P	0	2	4.12	26	0	0	0	1	43.2	45	23	20	0	20	35	222,000
1993	TOR	AL	P	4	2	4.69	54	0	0	0	1	55.2	63	32	29	7	27	49	262,000
3	YR	TOTALS		15	10	3.77	143	3	0	0	5	207.2	202	98	87	13	97	169	
1993	Rank	MLB Ps		173		208	66	202	125	69	70	271	236	200		225	241	39	156
1994	PROJECTIONS			5	3	3.84	47	1	0	0	1	68	67	32	29	4	32	56	

Woody Williams — No. 54/P

Full name: Gregory Scott Williams
Bats: R **Throws:** R **HT:** 6–0 **WT:** 190
Born: 8–19–66, Houston, TX
High school: CY–Fair (TX)
College: Houston
Williams held lefthanded batters to a .241 BA.

	TM	LG	POS	W	L	ERA	G	GS	CG	SH	SV	IP	H	R	ER	HR	BB	SO	SALARY
1993	TOR	AL	P	3	1	4.38	30	0	0	0	0	37.0	40	18	18	2	22	24	N/A
1	YR	TOTAL		3	1	4.38	30	0	0	0	0	37.0	40	18	18	2	22	24	
1993	RANK	MLB Ps		not ranked -- didn't have 50 IP in 1993															

1993 League Championship Series and World Series Recap

AMERICAN LEAGUE

The Chicago White Sox (94–68) won their first division crown in 10 years on the strength of American League MVP Frank Thomas (.317, 106 runs, 41 HR, 128 RBI) and the arms of a young pitching staff that included Cy Young Award winner Jack McDowell (22–10, 3.57 ERA), Alex Fernandez (18–9, 3.13), Wilson Alvarez (15–8, 2.95), and Jason Bere (12–5, 3.47).

The Toronto Blue Jays (95–67) used a potent offense to capture their third straight Eastern title and fourth in five years. They had the league's top two batters in John Olerud (.363) and Paul Molitor (.332), plus Joe Carter (33 HR, 121 RBI), Roberto Alomar (109 runs, 17 HR, 93 RBI), and Devon White (116 runs, 34 stolen bases). Pat Hentgen (19–9) was their biggest winner during the season, but it was the veteran Dave Stewart (12–8) and Juan Guzman (14–3) who combined for the four victories over the White Sox which gave the Jays their second straight pennant. Stewart, signed as a free agent after seven years with the Oakland A's, won Games 2 and 6 and raised his playoff record to 8–0, the best in history, to gain his second ALCS MVP Award.

Chicago's Tim Raines and Toronto's Devon White, who each went 12 for 27 in the series, broke the ALCS record of 11 hits set by Boston's Marty Barrett in 1986.

GAME 1

Toronto	0 0 0	2 3 0	2 0 0	7	17	1
Chicago	0 0 0	3 0 0	0 0 0	3	6	1

Guzman, Cox (7), Ward (9), and Borders; McDowell, DeLeon (7), Radinsky (8), McCaskill (9), and Karkovice. W—Guzman, L—McDowell. HR—Molitor.

GAME 2

Toronto	1 0 0	2 0 0	0 0 0	3	8	0
Chicago	1 0 0	0 0 0	0 0 0	3	7	2

Stewart, Leiter (7), Ward (9), and Borders; A. Fernandez, Hernandez (9), and Karkovice, LaValliere (7). W—Stewart, L—A. Fernandez.

GAME 3

				R H E
Chicago	0 0 5	1 0 0	0 0 0	6 12 0
Toronto	0 0 1	0 0 0	0 0 0	1 7 1

Alvarez and Karkovice; Hentgen, Cox (4), Eichorn (7), Castillo (9), and Borders. W—Alvarez, L—Hentgen.

GAME 4

Chicago	0 2 0	0 0 3	1 0 1	7 11 0
Toronto	0 0 3	0 0 1	0 0 0	4 9 0

Bere, Belcher (3), McCaskill (7), Radinsky (8), Hernandez (9), and Karkovice; Stottlemyre, Leiter (7), Timlin (7), and Borders. W—Belcher, L–Stottlemyre.

GAME 5

Chicago	0 0 0	0 1 0	0 0 2	3 5 1
Toronto	1 1 1	1 0 0	1 0 x	5 14 0

McDowell, DeLeon (3), Radinsky (7), Hernandez (7), and Karkovice; Guzman, Castillo (8), Ward (9), and Borders. W—Guzman, L—McDowell. HR—Ventura, Burks.

GAME 6

Toronto	0 2 0	1 0 0	0 0 3	6 10 0
Chicago	0 0 2	0 0 0	0 0 1	3 5 3

Stewart, Ward (8), and Borders; A. Fernandez, McCaskill (8), Radinsky (9), Hernandez (9), and LaValliere, Karkovice (8). W—Stewart, L—A. Fernandez. HR—White, Newson.

TORONTO BLUE JAYS' HITTING

	AB	R	H	2B	3B	HR	RBI	AVG.
Alomar	24	3	7	1	0	0	4	.292
Borders	24	1	6	1	0	0	3	.250
Carter	27	2	7	0	0	0	2	.259
Fernandez, T.	22	1	7	0	0	0	1	.318
Henderson	24	4	3	2	0	0	0	.120
Molitor	23	7	9	2	1	1	5	.391
Olerud	23	5	8	1	0	0	3	.348
Sprague	21	0	6	0	1	0	4	.286
White	27	3	12	1	1	1	2	.444
Total	**216**	**26**	**65**	**8**	**3**	**2**	**24**	**.301**

CHICAGO WHITE SOX' HITTING

	AB	R	H	2B	3B	HR	RBI	AVG.
Burks	23	4	7	1	0	1	3	.304
Cora	22	1	3	0	0	0	1	.136
Grebeck	1	0	1	0	0	0	0	1.000
Guillen	22	4	6	1	0	0	2	.273
Jackson	10	1	0	0	0	0	0	.000
Johnson	23	2	5	1	1	1	6	.217
Karkovice	15	0	0	0	0	0	0	.000
LaValliere	3	0	1	0	0	0	0	.333
Newson	5	1	1	0	0	1	1	.200
Pasqua	6	1	0	0	0	0	0	.000
Raines	27	5	12	3	0	0	1	.444
Thomas	17	2	6	0	0	1	3	.353
Ventura	20	2	4	0	0	1	5	.200
Totals	**194**	**23**	**46**	**6**	**1**	**5**	**22**	**.237**

TORONTO BLUE JAYS' PITCHING

	G	IP	H	R	ER	BB	SO	ERA
Castillo	2	2.0	0	0	0	1	1	0.00
Cox	2	5.0	3	0	0	2	5	0.00
Eichorn	1	2.0	1	0	0	1	1	0.00
Guzman (2–0)	2	13.0	8	4	3	9	9	2.08
Hentgen (0–1)	1	3.0	9	6	6	2	3	18.00
Leiter	2	2.2	4	1	1	2	2	3.38
Stewart (2–0)	2	13.1	8	3	3	8	8	2.03
Stottlemyre (0–1)	1	6.0	6	5	5	4	4	7.50
Timlin	1	2.1	3	1	1	0	2	3.86
Ward, D.	4	4.2	4	3	3	3	8	5.79
Totals	**6**	**54.0**	**46**	**23**	**22**	**32**	**43**	**3.67**

CHICAGO WHITE SOX' PITCHING

	G	IP	H	R	ER	BB	SO	ERA
Alvarez (1–0)	1	9.0	7	1	1	2	6	1.00
Belcher (1–0)	1	3.2	3	1	1	3	1	2.45
Bere	1	2.1	5	3	3	2	3	11.57
DeLeon	2	4.2	7	1	1	1	6	1.93
Fernandez, A. (0–2)	2	15.0	15	6	3	6	10	1.80
Hernandez	4	4.0	4	0	0	0	1	0.00
McCaskill	3	3.2	3	0	0	1	3	0.00
McDowell (0–2)	2	9.0	18	10	9	5	5	10.00
Radinsky	4	1.2	3	4	2	1	1	10.80
Totals	**6**	**53.0**	**65**	**26**	**19**	**21**	**36**	**3.57**

COMPOSITE SCORE BY INNINGS

Toronto	**2 3 5**	**6 3 1**	**3 0 3**	**26**
Chicago	**1 2 7**	**4 1 3**	**1 0 4**	**23**

Errors: Toronto 2 (Henderson, Olerud), Chicago 7 (McDowell, Pasqua, Radinsky, Ventura, Cora 3). Double Plays: Toronto 7, Chicago 5. LOB: Toronto 56, Chicago 50. Stolen Bases: Toronto 7 (Henderson 2, Borders, Alomar 4), Chicago 3 (Guillen, Raines, Johnson). Caught stealing: Toronto 2 (White, Henderson), Chicago 2 (Raines, Burks). Sacrifices: Toronto 1 (T. Fernandez), Chicago 5 (Karkovice 2, Cora 2, Guillen). Sacrifice flies: Toronto 1 (Sprague), Chicago 1 (Ventura). Saves: Toronto 2 (D. Ward), Chicago 1 (Hernandez)

NATIONAL LEAGUE

The Atlanta Braves needed every one of their 104 regular-season victories to edge the San Francisco Giants for the Western Division title on the final day of the season. Bolstered by the addition of Fred McGriff (37 HR, 101 RBI) on July 20, the Braves went on to win 51 of their final 68 games. David Justice (40 HR, 120 RBI) and Ron Gant (36 HR, 117 RBI) supplied additional firepower, while the pitching staff featured Cy Young Award winner Greg Maddux (20–10), Tom Glavine (22–6), Steve Avery (18–6), and John Smoltz (15–11).

The Philadelphia Phillies, whose 97–55 record was a 27-game improvement from the previous season, rose from last place in the National League East in 1992 to first in 1993. Undaunted by the prospect of playing the team with the best record in baseball, the Phillies defeated the Braves in six games to capture the pennant, thus becoming the first team from their division to advance to the World Series since the St. Louis Cardinals in 1987.

Although the Braves had the vaunted starting rotation, it was the less-heralded Philadelphia starters who rose to the occasion. NLCS MVP Curt Schilling did not get a decision, but sparkled in the two games he pitched (1.69 ERA in 16 innings), both of which the Phillies won in extra innings, while Danny Jackson allowed only one earned run in seven innings to win Game 4, and Tommy Greene held the Braves to three earned runs in seven innings in the series finale.

GAME 1

Atlanta	**001**	**100**	**0010**	**3**	**9**	**0**
Philadelphia	**100**	**101**	**0001**	**5**	**11**	**1**

Avery, Mercker (7), McMichael (9), and Berryhill; Schilling, Williams (9), and Daulton; W—Williams, L—McMichael. HR—Incaviglia.

GAME 2

Atlanta	**206**	**010**	**041**	**14**	**16**	**0**
Philadelphia	**000**	**200**	**001**	**3**	**7**	**2**

Maddux, Stanton (8), Wohlers (9) and Berryhill; Greene, Thigpen (3), Rivera (4), Mason (6), West (8), Andersen (9) and Daulton; W—Maddux, L—Greene. HR—Dykstra, Hollins, Blauser, McGriff, Pendleton, Berryhill.

GAME 3

Philadelphia	**000**	**101**	**011**	**4**	**10**	**1**
Atlanta	**000**	**005**	**40x**	**9**	**12**	**0**

Mulholland, Mason (6), Andersen (7), West (7), Thigpen (8), and Daulton; Glavine, Mercker (8), McMichael (9), and Berryhill. W—Glavine, L—Mulholland. HR—Kruk.

GAME 4

Philadelphia	**000**	**200**	**000**	**2**	**8**	**1**
Atlanta	**010**	**000**	**000**	**1**	**10**	**1**

Jackson, Williams (8), and Daulton; Smoltz, Mercker (7), Wohlers (9), and Olson. W—Jackson, L—Smoltz.

GAME 5

Philadelphia	**100**	**100**	**0011**	**4**	**6**	**1**
Atlanta	**000**	**000**	**0030**	**3**	**7**	**1**

Schilling, Williams (9), Andersen (10), and Daulton; Avery, Mercker (8), McMichael (9), Wohlers (10), and Berryhill, Cabrera (10). W—Williams, L—Wohlers. HR—Dykstra, Daulton.

GAME 6

Atlanta	**000**	**010**	**200**	**3**	**5**	**3**
Philadelphia	**002**	**022**	**00x**	**6**	**7**	**1**

Greene, West (8), and Daulton; Maddux, Mercker (6), McMichael (7), Wohlers (7) and Berryhill. W—Greene, L—Maddux. HR—Blauser, Hollins.

PHILADELPHIA PHILLIES' HITTING

	AB	R	H	2B	3B	HR	RBI	AVG.
Batiste	1	0	1	0	0	0	1	1.000
Chamberlain	11	1	4	3	0	0	1	.364
Daulton	19	2	5	1	0	1	3	.263
Duncan	15	3	4	0	2	0	0	.267
Dykstra	25	5	7	1	0	2	2	.280
Eisenreich	15	0	2	1	0	0	1	.133
Greene	0	1	0	0	0	0	0	.000
Hollins	20	2	4	1	0	2	4	.200
Incaviglia	12	2	2	0	0	1	1	.167

PHILADELPHIA PHILLIES' HITTING (CONT.)

	AB	R	H	2B	3B	HR	RBI	AVG.
Jackson	4	0	1	0	0	0	1	.250
Jordan	1	0	0	0	0	0	0	.000
Kruk	24	4	6	2	1	1	5	.250
Longmire	1	0	0	0	0	0	0	.000
Morandini	16	1	4	0	1	0	2	.250
Mulholland	2	0	0	0	0	0	0	.000
Pratt	1	0	0	0	0	0	0	.000
Schilling	5	0	0	0	0	0	0	.000
Stocker	22	0	4	1	0	0	1	.182
Thompson	13	2	3	1	0	0	0	.231
Totals	**207**	**23**	**47**	**11**	**4**	**7**	**22**	**.227**

ATLANTA BRAVES' HITTING

	AB	R	H	2B	3B	HR	RBI	AVG.
Avery	4	1	2	1	0	0	0	.500
Belliard	1	1	0	0	0	0	0	.000
Berryhill	19	2	4	0	0	1	3	.211
Blauser	25	5	7	1	0	2	4	.250
Bream	1	1	1	0	0	0	0	1.000
Cabrera	3	0	2	0	0	0	1	.667
Gant	27	4	5	3	0	0	3	.185
Glavine	3	0	0	0	0	0	0	.000
Justice	21	2	3	1	0	0	4	.143
Lemke	24	2	5	2	0	0	4	.208
Maddux	4	1	1	0	0	0	0	.250
McGriff	23	6	10	2	0	1	4	.435
Nixon	23	3	8	2	0	0	4	.348
Olson	3	0	1	1	0	0	0	.333
Pecota	3	1	1	0	0	0	0	.333
Pendleton	26	4	9	1	0	1	5	.346
Sanders	3	0	0	0	0	0	0	.000
Smoltz	1	0	0	0	0	0	0	.000
Tarasco	1	0	0	0	0	0	0	.000
Totals	**215**	**33**	**59**	**14**	**0**	**5**	**32**	**.274**

PHILADELPHIA PHILLIES' PITCHING

	G	IP	H	R	ER	BB	SO	ERA
Andersen	3	2.1	4	4	4	1	3	15.43
Greene (1–1)	2	9.1	12	10	10	7	7	9.64
Jackson (1–0)	1	7.2	9	1	1	2	6	1.17
Mason	2	3.0	1	0	0	0	2	0.00
Mulholland (0–1)	1	5.0	9	5	4	1	2	7.20
Rivera	1	2.0	1	1	1	1	2	4.50
Schilling	2	16.0	11	4	3	5	19	1.69
Thigpen	2	1.2	1	1	1	1	3	5.40

PHILADELPHIA PHILLIES' PITCHING (CONT.)

	G	IP	H	R	ER	BB	SO	ERA
West	3	3.2	5	5	4	2	5	13.50
Williams (2–0)	4	5.1	6	2	1	2	5	1.69
Totals	**6**	**55**	**59**	**33**	**29**	**22**	**54**	**4.75**

ATLANTA BRAVES' PITCHING

	G	IP	H	R	ER	BB	SO	ERA
Avery	2	13.0	9	5	4	6	10	2.77
Glavine (1–0)	1	7.0	6	2	2	0	5	2.57
Maddux (1–1)	2	12.2	11	8	7	7	11	4.97
McMichael (0–1)	4	4.0	7	3	3	2	1	6.75
Mercker	5	5.0	3	1	1	2	4	1.80
Smoltz (0–1)	1	6.1	8	2	0	5	10	0.00
Stanton	1	1.0	1	0	0	1	0	0.00
Wohlers (0–1)	4	5.1	2	2	2	3	10	3.38
Totals	**6**	**54.1**	**47**	**23**	**19**	**26**	**51**	**3.15**

COMPOSITE SCORE BY INNINGS

Atlanta	**2 1 7**	**1 2 5**	**6 4 5**	**0**	**33**
Philadelphia	**2 0 2**	**7 2 2**	**2 1 3**	**2**	**23**

Errors: Philadelphia 7 (Duncan, Morandini, Stocker, Thompson, M. Williams, Batiste 2), Atlanta 5 (Maddux, Gant, Justice, Lemke 2). Double Plays: Philadelphia 2, Atlanta 1. LOB: Philadelphia 52, Atlanta 47. Stolen Bases: Philadelphia 2 (Morandini, Hollins). Caught stealing: Atlanta 3 (Gant, Nixon 2). Sacrifices: Philadelphia 3 (Schilling, Greene 2), Atlanta 5 (Belliard, Maddux 2, Nixon 2). Sacrifice flies: Philadelphia 2 (Stocker, Chamberlain), Atlanta 2 (Justice). Saves: Philadelphia 1 (Williams), Toronto 2 (Ward). Philadelphia 3 (Andersen, M. Williams 2).

WORLD SERIES

The Toronto Blue Jays defeated the Philadelphia Phillies, four games to two, and became the first team since the 1977–78 New York Yankees to repeat as World Series champions. Far from a purist's delight, the Series saw 81 runs scored in the six games, with the Blue Jays battering the Phillies for 45 runs while surrendering 36. Toronto's Paul Molitor, who scored 10 runs, drove in eight, and went 12 for 24, was named the Most Valuable Player.

GAME 1

Devon White scored three runs and drove in two, with a solo home run and a double, to lead Toronto to an 8–5 triumph. White's home run with two out in the bottom of the fifth inning tied the score at 4–4, and his double in the seventh, an inning after John Olerud's solo homer had given the Blue Jays a 5–4 lead, drove in the first of three insurance runs to seal the victory. Al

Leiter pitched 2 2/3 scoreless innings in middle relief for the win and Duane Ward recorded the final four outs to pick up the save.

Philadelphia	2	0	1	0	1	0	0	0	1	5	11	1
Toronto	0	2	1	0	1	1	3	0	x	8	10	3

Schilling, West (7), Andersen (7), Mason (8), and Daulton; Guzman, Leiter (6), Ward (8), and Borders. W—Leiter, L—Schilling. HR—Duncan, White, Olerud.

GAME 2

Jim Eisenreich's three-run home run capped a five-run third inning and Lenny Dykstra added a solo shot in the seventh as the Phillies beat Toronto 6–4, to even the Series a one game apiece. Eisenreich's shot came off starter Dave Stewart, whose World Series career record dropped to 2–4. Terry Mulholland, who surrendered Joe Carter's two-run homer in the fourth, pitched the first 5 2/3 innings for the victory and Mitch Williams the final 1 2/3 for the save.

Philadelphia	0	0	5	0	0	0	1	0	0	6	12	0
Toronto	0	0	0	2	0	1	0	1	0	4	8	0

Stewart, Castillo (7), Eichorn (8), Timlin (8) and Borders; Mulholland, Mason (6), Williams (8) and Daulton; W—Mulholland, L—Stewart. HR—Dykstra, Eisenreich, Carter.

GAME 3

The Series shifted to Philadelphia, which meant the DH was not in effect. And with the Phillies starting left-hander Danny Jackson, Jays manager Cito Gaston opted to bench the American League's leading batter, lefty John Olerud, and start the right-handed–hitting Paul Molitor, the runner-up to Olerud for the batting title, at first base. Molitor responded with three hits, including a two-run triple in the first and a solo homer in the third, three runs, and three RBIs to lead Toronto to a 10–3 victory. Roberto Alomar added four hits and Pat Hentgen earned the win by allowing just one run on five hits over six innings. The Blue Jays set a World Series record with three sacrifice flies in the game.

Toronto	3	0	1	0	0	1	3	0	2	10	13	1
Philadelphia	0	0	0	0	0	1	1	0	1	3	9	0

Jackson, Rivera (6), Thigpen (7), and Daulton; Hentgen, Cox (7), Ward (9), and Borders. W—Hentgen, L—Jackson. HR—Molitor, Thompson.

GAME 4

Devon White's two-run triple capped a six-run eighth inning as Toronto rallied from five runs back to defeat the Phillies, 15–14, in the highest-scoring game in postseason history. The Phillies, after pounding 14 hits through the first seven innings, were shut down in order over the final two frames by relievers Mike Timlin and Duane Ward, with Ward earning his second save of the Series. White had 4 RBI and teammate Tony Fernandez had five. Milt Thompson drove in five runs for the Phillies, and Lenny Dykstra, with two two-run homers, knocked in four.

Toronto	**3 0 4**	**0 0 2**	**0 6 0**		**15 18 0**
Philadelphia	**4 2 0**	**1 5 1**	**1 0 0**		**14 14 1**

Greene, Mason (3), West (6), Andersen (7), Williams (8), Thigpen (9), and Daulton; Stottlemyre, Leiter (3), Castillo (5), Timlin (8), Ward (8), and Borders. W—Castillo, L—Williams. HR—Dykstra 2, Daulton.

GAME 5

Philadelphia's Curt Schilling tossed a five-hit complete-game shutout to defeat Toronto, 2–0, and keep his team's Series hopes alive. Schilling, who struck out six, was supported by John Kruk's RBI groundout in the first inning and Kevin Stocker's RBI double in the second. The Jays mounted a scoring threat in the eighth, putting their first two runners on the corners. But Schilling fielded Rickey Henderson's grounder to cut down pinch runner Willie Canate who tried to score from third, then struck out Devon White and retired Roberto Alomar on a grounder to end the inning.

Toronto	**0 0 0**	**0 0 0**	**0 0 0**		**0 5 1**
Philadelphia	**1 1 0**	**0 0 0**	**0 0 0**		**2 5 1**

Guzman, Cox (8), and Borders, Knorr (8); Schilling and Daulton. W—Schilling, L—Guzman.

GAME 6

Joe Carter's three-run homer in the bottom of the ninth inning gave Toronto its second consecutive Series championship. Carter drove a 2–2 fastball from Mitch Williams over the left-field fence, rallying the Jays from a 6–5 deficit. Only one previous World Series had ended on a home run—in 1960 between Pittsburgh and New York, which was decided in the bottom of the ninth of Game 7 on a solo shot by the Pirates' Bill Mazeroski.

Philadelphia	**0 0 0**	**1 0 0**	**5 0 0**		**6 7 0**
Toronto	**3 0 0**	**1 1 0**	**0 0 3**		**8 10 2**

Mulholland, Mason (6), West (8), Andersen (8), Williams (8) and Daulton; Stewart, Cox (7), Leiter (7), Ward (9) and Borders. W—Ward, L—Williams. HR—Dykstra, Molitor, Carter.

TORONTO BLUE JAYS' HITTING

	AB	R	H	2B	3B	HR	RBI	AVG.
Alomar	25	5	12	2	1	0	6	.480
Borders	23	2	7	0	0	0	1	.304
Butler	2	1	1	0	0	0	0	.500
Carter	25	6	7	1	0	2	8	.280
Castillo	1	0	0	0	0	0	0	.000
Cox	1	0	0	0	0	0	0	.000
Fernandez	21	2	7	1	0	0	9	.333
Guzman	2	0	0	0	0	0	0	.000
Henderson	22	6	5	2	0	0	2	.227
Hentgen	3	0	0	0	0	0	0	.000
Leiter	1	0	1	1	0	0	0	1.000
Molitor	24	10	12	2	2	2	8	.500
Olerud	17	5	4	1	0	1	2	.235
Sprague	15	0	1	0	0	0	2	.067
White	24	8	7	3	2	1	7	.292
Total	**206**	**45**	**64**	**13**	**5**	**6**	**45**	**.311**

PHILADELPHIA PHILLIES' HITTING

	AB	R	H	2B	3B	HR	RBI	AVG.
Chamberlain	2	0	0	0	0	0	0	.000
Daulton	23	4	5	2	0	1	4	.217
Duncan	29	5	10	0	1	0	2	.345
Dykstra	23	9	8	1	0	4	8	.348
Eisenreich	26	3	6	0	0	1	7	.231
Greene	1	1	1	0	0	0	0	1.000
Hollins	23	5	6	1	0	0	2	.261
Incaviglia	8	0	1	0	0	0	1	.125
Jackson	1	0	0	0	0	0	0	.000
Jordan	10	0	2	0	0	0	0	.200
Kruk	23	4	8	1	0	0	4	.348
Mason	1	0	0	0	0	0	0	.000
Morandini	5	1	1	0	0	0	0	.200
Schilling	2	0	1	0	0	0	0	.500
Stocker	19	1	4	1	0	0	1	.211
Thompson	16	3	5	1	1	1	6	.313
Totals	**212**	**36**	**58**	**7**	**2**	**7**	**35**	**.274**

TORONTO BLUE JAYS' PITCHING

	G	IP	H	R	ER	BB	SO	ERA
Castillo (1–0)	2	3.1	6	3	3	3	1	8.10
Cox	3	3.1	6	3	3	5	6	8.10
Eichorn	1	0.1	1	0	0	1	0	0.00
Guzman (0–1)	2	12.0	10	6	5	8	12	3.75
Hentgen (1–0)	1	6.0	5	1	1	3	6	1.50
Leiter (1–0)	3	7.0	12	6	6	2	5	7.71
Stewart (0–1)	2	12.0	10	9	9	8	8	6.75
Stottlemyre	1	2.0	3	9	6	4	1	27.00
Timlin	2	2.1	2	0	0	0	4	0.00
Ward (1–0)	4	4.2	3	2	1	0	7	1.93
Totals	**6**	**53.0**	**58**	**36**	**34**	**34**	**50**	**5.77**

PHILADELPHIA PHILLIES' HITTING

	G	IP	H	R	ER	BB	SO	ERA
Andersen	4	3.2	5	5	5	3	3	12.77
Greene	1	2.1	7	7	7	4	1	27.00
Jackson (0–1)	1	5.0	6	4	4	1	1	7.20
Mason	4	7.2	4	1	1	1	7	1.17
Mulholland (1–0)	2	10.2	14	8	8	3	5	6.75
Rivera	1	1.1	4	4	4	2	3	27.00
Schilling (1–1)	2	15.1	13	7	6	5	9	3.52
Thigpen	2	2.2	1	0	0	1	0	0.00
West	3	1.0	5	3	3	1	0	27.00
Williams (0–2)	3	2.2	5	6	6	4	1	20.25
Totals	**6**	**52.1**	**64**	**45**	**44**	**25**	**30**	**7.57**

COMPOSITE SCORE BY INNINGS

Philadelphia	**7**	**3**	**6**	**2**	**6**	**2**	**8**	**0**	**2**	**36**
Toronto	**9**	**2**	**6**	**3**	**2**	**5**	**6**	**7**	**5**	**45**

Errors: Philadelphia 2 (Duncan, Thompson), Toronto 7 (Borders, Alomar 2, Carter 2, Sprague 2). Double Plays: Philadelphia 5, Toronto 5. LOB: Philadelphia 54, Toronto 39. Stolen Bases: Philadelphia 7 (Duncan 3, Dykstra 4), Toronto 7 (Molitor, Henderson, White, Alomar 4). Caught stealing: Philadelphia 1 (Stocker), Toronto 4 (Fernandez, Henderson, Alomar 2). Sacrifices: Philadelphia 1 (Schilling). Sacrifice flies: Philadelphia 1 (Incaviglia), Toronto 7 (Olerud, Fernandez, Sprague 2, Carter 3). HBP: by Thigpen (Henderson), by West (Molitor), by Castillo (Daulton), by Andersen (Fernandez), Balk: Stewart. PB: Daulton. Saves: Philadelphia 1 (Williams), Toronto 2 (Ward).

American League Statistics

American League Hitters

	TEAM	POS	G	AB	R	H	2B	3B	HR	RBI	BB	SO	SB	E	BA	SLG	FLD
Abbott, Kurt	OAK	OF	20	61	11	15	1	0	3	9	3	20	2	2	.246	.410	.961
Aldrete, Mike	OAK	1B	95	255	40	68	13	1	10	33	34	45	1	2	.267	.443	.995
Alexander, Manny	BAL	SS	3	0	1	0	0	0	0	0	0	0	0	0	—	—	—
Alomar, Roberto	TOR	2B	153	589	109	192	35	6	17	93	80	67	55	14	.326	.492	.980
Alomar, Sandy	CLE	C	64	215	24	58	7	1	6	32	11	28	3	6	.270	.395	.984
Amaral, Rich	SEA	2B	110	373	53	108	24	1	1	44	33	54	19	10	.290	.367	.978
Anderson, Brady	BAL	OF	142	560	87	147	36	8	13	66	82	99	24	2	.263	.425	.993
Armas, Marcos	OAK	1B	15	31	7	6	2	0	1	1	1	12	1	0	.194	.355	1.000
Backman, Wally	SEA	3B	10	29	2	4	0	0	0	0	1	8	0	3	.138	.138	.864
Baerga, Carlos	CLE	2B	154	624	105	200	28	6	21	114	34	68	15	17	.321	.486	.979
Baines, Harold	BAL	DH	118	416	64	130	22	0	20	78	57	52	0	0	.313	.510	—
Balboni, Steve	TEX	DH	2	5	0	3	0	0	0	0	0	2	0	0	.600	.600	—
Barnes, Skeeter	DET	1B	84	160	24	45	8	1	2	27	11	19	5	4	.281	.381	.980
Bautista, Danny	DET	OF	17	61	6	19	3	0	1	9	1	10	3	0	.311	.410	1.000
Becker, Rich	MIN	OF	3	7	3	2	2	0	0	0	5	4	1	1	.286	.571	.875
Belle, Albert	CLE	OF	159	594	93	172	36	3	38	129	76	96	23	5	.290	.552	.986
Bell, George	CHI	DH	102	410	36	89	17	2	13	64	13	49	1	0	.217	.363	—
Bell, Juan	MIL	2B	91	286	42	67	6	2	5	29	36	64	6	12	.234	.322	.971
Blankenship, Lance	OAK	OF	94	252	43	48	8	1	2	23	67	64	13	5	.190	.254	.982
Blosser, Greg	BOS	OF	17	28	1	2	1	0	0	1	2	7	1	0	.071	.107	1.000
Blowers, Mike	SEA	3B	127	379	55	106	23	3	15	57	44	98	1	15	.280	.475	.952
Boggs, Wade	NY	3B	143	560	83	169	26	1	2	59	74	49	0	12	.302	.363	.970
Boone, Bret	SEA	2B	76	271	31	68	12	2	12	38	17	52	2	3	.251	.443	.991
Borders, Pat	TOR	C	138	488	38	124	30	0	9	55	20	66	2	13	.254	.371	.986

Bordick, Mike	OAK	SS	159	546	60	136	21	2	3	48	60	58	10	13	.249	.311	.982
Brett, George	KC	DH	145	560	69	149	31	3	19	75	39	67	7	0	.266	.434	—
Brito, Bernardo	MIN	OF	27	54	8	13	2	0	4	9	1	20	0	0	.241	.500	1.000
Brooks, Hubie	KC	OF	75	168	14	48	12	0	1	24	11	27	0	2	.286	.375	.975
Brosius, Scott	OAK	3B	70	213	26	53	10	1	6	25	14	37	6	2	.249	.390	.990
Browne, Jerry	OAK	OF	76	260	27	65	13	0	2	19	22	17	4	6	.250	.323	.967
Bruett, J.T.	MIN	OF	17	20	2	5	2	0	0	1	1	4	0	2	.250	.350	.857
Brunansky, Tom	MIL	OF	80	224	20	41	7	3	6	29	25	59	3	2	.183	.321	.987
Buford, Damon	BAL	OF	53	79	18	18	5	0	2	9	9	19	2	1	.228	.367	.984
Buhner, Jay	SEA	OF	158	563	91	153	28	3	27	98	100	144	2	6	.272	.476	.978
Burks, Ellis	CHI	OF	146	499	75	137	24	4	17	74	60	97	6	6	.275	.441	.982
Bush, Randy	MIN	1B	35	45	1	7	2	0	0	3	7	13	0	0	.156	.200	1.000
Butler, Rob	TOR	OF	17	48	8	13	4	0	0	2	7	12	2	1	.271	.354	.970
Byrd, Jim	BOS	DH	2	0	0	0	0	0	0	0	0	0	0	0	—	—	—
Calderon, Ivan	CHI	OF	82	239	26	50	10	2	1	22	21	33	4	0	.209	.280	1.000
Canate, Willie	TOR	OF	38	47	12	10	0	0	1	3	6	15	1	0	.213	.277	1.000
Canseco, Jose	TEX	OF	60	231	30	59	14	1	10	46	16	62	6	3	.255	.455	.970
Carey, Paul	BAL	1B	18	47	1	10	1	0	0	3	5	14	0	2	.213	.234	.970
Carter, Joe	TOR	OF	155	603	92	153	33	5	33	121	47	113	8	8	.254	.489	.974
Cedeno, Domingo	TOR	SS	15	46	5	8	0	0	0	7	1	10	1	1	.174	.174	.980
Coles, Darnell	TOR	OF	64	194	26	49	9	1	4	26	16	29	1	7	.253	.371	.933
Cooper, Scott	BOS	3B	156	526	67	147	29	3	9	63	58	81	5	24	.279	.397	.937
Cora, Joey	CHI	2B	153	579	95	155	15	13	2	51	67	63	20	19	.268	.349	.974
Correia, Rod	CAL	SS	64	128	12	34	5	0	0	9	6	20	2	3	.266	.305	.986
Cotto, Henry	SEA	OF	54	105	10	20	1	0	2	7	2	22	5	1	.190	.257	.983
Curtis, Chad	CAL	OF	152	583	94	166	25	3	6	59	70	89	48	9	.285	.369	.980
Cuyler, Milt	DET	OF	82	249	46	53	11	7	0	19	19	53	13	7	.213	.313	.968
Dascenzo, Doug	TEX	OF	76	146	20	29	5	1	2	10	8	22	2	1	.199	.288	.990

	TEAM	POS	G	AB	R	H	2B	3B	HR	RBI	BB	SO	SB	E	BA	SLG	FLD
Davis, Butch	TEX	OF	62	159	24	39	10	4	3	20	5	28	3	4	.245	.415	.960
Davis, Chili	CAL	DH	153	573	74	139	32	0	27	112	71	135	4	0	.243	.440	—
Davis, Eric	DET	OF	23	75	14	19	1	1	6	15	14	18	2	1	.253	.533	.981
Davis, Glenn	BAL	1B	30	113	8	20	3	0	1	9	7	29	0	2	.177	.230	.990
Dawson, Andre	BOS	OF	121	461	44	126	29	1	13	67	17	49	2	0	.273	.425	1.000
Deer, Rob	DET–BOS	OF	128	466	66	98	17	1	21	55	58	169	5	8	.210	.386	.973
Delgado, Carlos	TOR	C	2	1	0	0	0	0	0	0	1	0	0	0	.000	.000	1.000
Denson, Drew	CHI	1B	4	5	0	1	0	0	0	0	0	2	0	1	.200	.200	.800
Devereaux, Mike	BAL	OF	131	527	72	132	31	3	14	75	43	99	3	4	.250	.400	.988
Diaz, Alex	MIL	OF	32	69	9	22	2	0	0	1	0	12	5	1	.319	.348	.979
Diaz, Mario	TEX	SS	71	205	24	56	10	1	2	24	8	13	1	3	.273	.361	.988
Disarcina, Gary	CAL	SS	126	416	44	99	20	1	3	45	15	38	5	14	.238	.313	.975
Doran, Bill	MIL	2B	28	60	7	13	4	0	0	6	6	3	1	2	.217	.283	.973
Ducey, Rob	TEX	OF	27	85	15	24	6	3	2	9	10	17	2	0	.282	.494	1.000
Easley, Damion	CAL	2B	73	230	33	72	13	2	2	22	28	35	6	6	.313	.413	.978
Edmonds, Jim	CAL	OF	18	61	5	15	4	1	0	4	2	16	0	1	.246	.344	.980
Espinoza, Alvaro	CLE	3B	129	263	34	73	15	0	4	27	8	36	2	12	.278	.380	.949
Felder, Mike	SEA	OF	109	342	31	72	7	5	1	20	22	34	15	2	.211	.269	.987
Fermin, Felix	CLE	SS	140	480	48	126	16	2	2	45	24	14	4	23	.263	.317	.960
Fernandez, Tony	TOR	SS	94	353	45	108	18	9	4	50	31	26	15	7	.306	.442	.985
Fielder, Cecil	DET	1B	154	573	80	153	23	0	30	117	90	125	0	10	.267	.464	.991
Fisk, Carlton	CHI	C	25	53	2	10	0	0	1	4	2	11	0	0	.189	.245	1.000
Flaherty, John	BOS	C	13	25	3	3	2	0	0	2	2	6	0	0	.120	.200	1.000
Fletcher, Scott	BOS	2B	121	480	81	137	31	5	5	45	37	35	16	11	.285	.402	.982
Fox, Eric	OAK	OF	29	56	5	8	1	0	1	5	2	7	0	0	.143	.214	1.000
Franco, Julio	TEX	DH	144	532	85	154	31	3	14	84	62	95	9	0	.289	.438	—

Fryman, Travis	DET	SS	151	607	98	182	37	5	22	97	77	128	9	23	.300	.486	.960
Gaetti, Gary	KC	3B	102	331	40	81	20	1	14	50	21	87	1	7	.245	.438	.980
Gagne, Greg	KC	SS	159	540	66	151	32	3	10	57	33	93	10	10	.280	.406	.986
Gallego, Mike	NY	SS	119	403	63	114	20	1	10	54	50	65	3	13	.283	.412	.976
Gates, Brent	OAK	2B	139	535	64	155	29	2	7	69	56	75	7	14	.290	.391	.981
Gibson, Kirk	DET	OF	116	403	62	105	18	6	13	62	44	87	15	1	.261	.432	.987
Gil, Benji	TEX	SS	22	57	3	7	0	0	0	2	5	22	1	5	.123	.123	.954
Gladden, Dan	DET	OF	91	356	52	95	16	2	13	56	21	50	8	3	.267	.433	.986
Gomez, Chris	DET	SS	46	128	11	32	7	1	0	11	9	17	2	5	.250	.320	.974
Gomez, Leo	BAL	3B	71	244	30	48	7	0	10	25	32	60	0	10	.197	.348	.951
Gonzales, Larry	CAL	C	2	2	0	1	0	0	0	1	1	0	0	0	.500	.500	1.000
Gonzales, Rene	CAL	3B	118	335	34	84	17	0	2	31	49	45	5	12	.251	.319	.971
Gonzalez, Juan	TEX	OF	140	536	105	166	33	1	46	118	37	99	4	4	.310	.632	.985
Grebeck, Craig	CHI	3B	72	190	25	43	5	0	1	12	26	26	1	5	.226	.268	.982
Greenwell, Mike	BOS	OF	146	540	77	170	38	6	13	72	54	46	5	2	.315	.480	.993
Green, Shawn	TOR	OF	3	6	0	0	0	0	0	0	0	1	0	0	.000	.000	1.000
Griffey, Jr., Ken	SEA	OF	156	582	113	180	38	3	45	109	96	91	17	3	.309	.617	.991
Griffin, Alfredo	TOR	SS	46	95	15	20	3	0	0	3	3	13	0	4	.211	.242	.969
Gruber, Kelly	CAL	3B	18	65	10	18	3	0	3	9	2	11	0	4	.277	.462	.939
Guillen, Ozzie	CHI	SS	134	457	44	128	23	4	4	50	10	41	5	16	.280	.374	.972
Gwynn, Chris	KC	OF	103	287	36	86	14	4	1	25	24	34	0	1	.300	.387	.994
Hale, Chip	MIN	2B	69	186	25	62	6	1	3	27	18	17	2	4	.333	.425	.962
Hamelin, Bob	KC	1B	16	49	2	11	3	0	2	5	6	15	0	2	.224	.408	.986
Hamilton, Darryl	MIL	OF	135	520	74	161	21	1	9	48	45	62	21	3	.310	.406	.992
Hammonds, Jeffrey	BAL	OF	33	105	10	32	8	0	3	19	2	16	4	2	.305	.467	.961
Harper, Brian	MIN	C	147	530	52	161	26	1	12	73	29	29	1	10	.304	.425	.988
Harris, Donald	TEX	OF	40	76	10	15	2	0	1	8	5	18	0	3	.197	.263	.943
Haselman, Bill	SEA	C	58	137	21	35	8	0	5	16	12	19	2	2	.255	.423	.992

	TEAM	POS	G	AB	R	H	2B	3B	HR	RBI	BB	SO	SB	E	BA	SLG	FLD
Hatcher, Billy	BOS	OF	136	508	71	146	24	3	9	57	28	46	14	2	.287	.400	.993
Helfand, Eric	OAK	C	8	13	1	3	0	0	0	1	0	1	0	0	.231	.231	1.000
Hemond, Scott	OAK	C	91	215	31	55	16	0	6	26	32	55	14	4	.256	.414	.991
Henderson, Dave	OAK	OF	107	382	37	84	19	0	20	53	32	113	0	2	.220	.427	.991
Henderson, Rickey	OAK–TOR	OF	134	481	114	139	22	2	21	59	120	65	53	7	.289	.474	.974
Hiatt, Phil	KC	3B	81	238	30	52	12	1	7	36	16	82	6	16	.218	.366	.909
Hill, Glenallen	CLE	OF	66	174	19	39	7	2	5	25	11	50	7	4	.224	.374	.940
Hocking, Dennis	MIN	SS	15	36	7	5	1	0	0	0	6	8	1	1	.139	.167	.977
Hoiles, Chris	BAL	C	126	419	80	130	28	0	29	82	69	94	1	5	.310	.585	.993
Horn, Sam	CLE	DH	12	33	8	15	1	0	4	8	1	5	0	0	.455	.848	—
Howard, Chris	SEA	C	4	1	0	0	0	0	0	0	0	0	0	0	.000	.000	1.000
Howard, David	KC	2B	15	24	5	8	0	1	0	2	2	5	1	3	.333	.417	.938
Howard, Thomas	CLE	OF	74	178	26	42	7	0	3	23	12	42	5	2	.236	.326	.977
Howitt, Dann	SEA	OF	32	76	6	16	3	1	2	8	4	18	0	0	.211	.355	1.000
Hrbek, Kent	MIN	1B	123	392	60	95	11	1	25	83	71	57	4	5	.242	.467	.995
Huff, Mike	CHI	OF	43	44	4	8	2	0	1	6	9	15	1	0	.182	.295	1.000
Hulett, Tim	BAL	3B	85	260	40	78	15	0	2	23	23	56	1	8	.300	.381	.967
Hulse, David	TEX	OF	114	407	71	118	9	10	1	29	26	57	29	3	.290	.369	.988
Humphreys, Mike	NY	OF	25	35	6	6	2	1	1	6	4	11	2	0	.171	.371	1.000
Huson, Jeff	TEX	SS	23	45	3	6	1	1	0	2	0	10	0	6	.133	.200	.917
Jackson, Bo	CHI	OF	85	284	32	66	9	0	16	45	23	106	0	1	.232	.433	.989
Jackson, Darrin	TOR	OF	46	176	15	38	8	0	5	19	8	53	0	1	.216	.347	.989
Jaha, John	MIL	1B	153	515	78	136	21	0	19	70	51	109	13	10	.264	.416	.992
James, Chris	TEX	OF	8	31	5	11	1	0	3	7	3	6	0	0	.355	.677	1.000
James, Dion	NY	OF	115	343	62	114	21	2	7	36	31	31	0	5	.332	.466	.967
Javier, Stan	CAL	OF	92	237	33	69	10	4	3	28	27	33	12	4	.291	.405	.977

Jefferson, Reggie	CLE	1B	113	366	35	91	11	2	10	34	28	78	1	3	.249	.372	.976
Johnson, Lance	CHI	OF	147	540	75	168	18	14	0	47	36	33	35	9	.311	.396	.980
Jorgensen, Terry	MIN	3B	59	152	15	34	7	0	1	12	10	21	1	3	.224	.289	.981
Jose, Feilx	KC	OF	149	499	64	126	24	3	6	43	36	95	31	7	.253	.349	.972
Joyner, Wally	KC	1B	141	497	83	145	36	3	15	65	66	67	5	7	.292	.467	.994
Karkovice, Ron	CHI	C	128	403	60	92	17	1	20	54	29	126	2	5	.228	.424	.994
Kelly, Pat	NY	2B	127	406	49	111	24	1	7	51	24	68	14	14	.273	.389	.978
Kirby, Wayne	CLE	OF	131	458	71	123	19	5	6	60	37	58	17	5	.269	.371	.983
Kmak, Joe	MIL	C	51	110	9	24	5	0	0	7	14	13	6	0	.218	.264	1.000
Knoblauch, Chuck	MIN	2B	153	602	82	167	27	4	2	41	65	44	29	9	.277	.346	.988
Knorr, Randy	TOR	C	39	101	11	25	3	2	4	20	9	29	0	0	.248	.436	1.000
Koslofski, Kevin	KC	OF	15	26	4	7	0	0	1	2	4	5	0	0	.269	.385	1.000
Kreuter, Chad	DET	C	119	374	59	107	23	3	15	51	49	92	2	7	.286	.484	.988
Lampkin, Tom	MIL	C	73	162	22	32	8	0	4	25	20	26	7	6	.198	.321	.978
Larkin, Gene	MIN	OF	56	144	17	38	7	1	1	19	21	16	0	2	.264	.347	.988
Lavalliere, Mike	CHI	C	37	97	6	25	2	0	0	8	4	14	0	0	.258	.278	1.000
Lee, Derek	MIN	OF	15	33	3	5	1	0	0	4	1	4	0	0	.152	.182	1.000
Lee, Manuel	TEX	SS	73	205	31	45	3	1	1	12	22	39	2	10	.220	.259	.968
Leius, Scott	MIN	SS	10	18	4	3	0	0	0	2	2	4	0	2	.167	.167	.947
Leonard, Mark	BAL	OF	10	15	1	1	1	0	0	3	3	7	0	1	.067	.133	.833
Levis, Jesse	CLE	C	31	63	7	11	2	0	0	4	2	10	0	1	.175	.206	.991
Lewis, Mark	CLE	SS	14	52	6	13	2	0	1	5	0	7	3	2	.250	.346	.964
Leyritz, Jim	NY	1B	95	259	43	80	14	0	14	53	37	59	0	2	.309	.525	.994
Lindsey, Doug	CHI	C	2	1	0	0	0	0	0	0	0	0	0	0	.000	.000	1.000
Lind, Jose	KC	2B	136	431	33	107	13	2	0	37	13	36	3	4	.248	.288	.994
Listach, Pat	MIL	SS	98	356	50	87	15	1	3	30	37	70	18	10	.244	.317	.976
Litton, Greg	SEA	OF	72	174	25	52	17	0	3	25	18	30	0	0	.299	.448	1.000
Livingstone, Scott	DET	3B	98	304	39	89	10	2	2	39	19	32	1	6	.293	.359	.955

	TEAM	POS	G	AB	R	H	2B	3B	HR	RBI	BB	SO	SB	E	BA	SLG	FLD
Lofton, Kenny	CLE	OF	148	569	116	185	28	8	1	42	81	83	70	9	.325	.408	.979
Lovullo, Torey	CAL	2B	116	367	42	92	20	0	6	30	36	49	7	11	.251	.354	.976
Lydy, Scott	OAK	OF	41	102	11	23	5	0	2	7	8	39	2	3	.225	.333	.958
Lyons, Steve	BOS	OF	28	23	4	3	1	0	0	0	2	5	1	0	.130	.174	1.000
Maas, Kevin	NY	DH	59	151	20	31	4	0	9	25	24	32	1	2	.205	.411	.984
Macfarlane, Mike	KC	C	117	388	55	106	27	0	20	67	40	83	2	11	.273	.497	.985
Mack, Shane	MIN	OF	128	503	66	139	30	4	10	61	41	76	15	5	.276	.412	.986
Magadan, Dave	SEA	1B	71	228	27	59	11	0	1	21	36	33	2	5	.259	.320	.988
Maksudian, Mike	MIN	1B	5	12	2	2	1	0	0	2	4	2	0	0	.167	.250	1.000
Maldonado, Candy	CLE	OF	28	81	11	20	2	0	5	20	11	18	0	1	.247	.457	.976
Martinez, Carlos	CLE	3B	80	262	26	64	10	0	5	31	20	29	1	9	.244	.340	.959
Martinez, Chito	BAL	OF	8	15	0	0	0	0	0	0	4	4	0	0	.000	.000	1.000
Martinez, Domingo	TOR	1B	8	14	2	4	0	0	1	3	1	7	0	0	.286	.500	1.000
Martinez, Edgar	SEA	3B	42	135	20	32	7	0	4	13	28	19	0	2	.237	.378	.889
Martinez, Tino	SEA	1B	109	408	48	108	25	1	17	60	45	56	0	3	.265	.456	.997
Martin, Norberto	CHI	2B	8	14	3	5	0	0	0	2	1	1	0	1	.357	.357	.957
Mattingly, Don	NY	1B	134	530	78	154	27	2	17	86	61	42	0	3	.291	.445	.998
Mayne, Brent	KC	C	71	205	22	52	9	1	2	22	18	31	3	2	.254	.337	.995
McCarty, Dave	MIN	OF	98	350	36	75	15	2	2	21	19	80	2	8	.214	.286	.983
McGwire, Mark	OAK	1B	27	84	16	28	6	0	9	24	21	19	0	0	.333	.726	1.000
McIntosh, Tim	MIL	C	1	0	0	0	0	0	0	0	0	0	0	0	—	—	—
McLemore, Mark	BAL	2B	148	581	81	165	27	5	4	72	64	92	21	6	.284	.368	.986
McNeely, Jeff	BOS	OF	21	37	10	11	1	1	0	1	7	9	6	2	.297	.378	.913
McRae, Brian	KC	OF	153	627	78	177	28	9	12	69	37	105	23	7	.282	.413	.983
McReynolds, Kevin	KC	OF	110	351	44	86	22	4	11	42	37	56	2	2	.245	.425	.990
Meares, Pat	MIN	SS	111	346	33	87	14	3	0	33	7	52	4	19	.251	.309	.961

Melvin, Bob	BOS	C	77	176	13	39	7	0	3	23	7	44	0	2	.222	.313	.994
Mercedes, Henry	OAK	C	20	47	5	10	2	0	0	3	2	15	1	1	.213	.255	.987
Mercedes, Luis	BAL	OF	10	24	1	7	2	0	0	0	5	4	1	0	.292	.375	1.000
Merullo, Matt	CHI	DH	8	20	1	1	0	0	0	0	0	1	0	0	.050	.050	—
Meulens, Hensley	NY	OF	30	53	8	9	1	1	2	5	8	19	0	0	.170	.340	1.000
Mieske, Matt	MIL	OF	23	58	9	14	0	0	3	7	4	14	0	3	.241	.397	.935
Miller, Keith	KC	3B	37	108	9	18	3	0	0	3	8	19	3	6	.167	.194	.898
Milligan, Randy	CLE	1B	19	47	7	20	7	0	0	7	14	4	0	0	.426	.574	1.000
Molitor, Paul	TOR	DH	160	636	121	211	37	5	22	111	77	71	22	3	.332	.509	.985
Munoz, Pedro	MIN	OF	104	326	34	76	11	1	13	38	25	97	1	3	.233	.393	.983
Myers, Greg	CAL	C	108	290	27	74	10	0	7	40	17	47	3	6	.255	.362	.986
Naehring, Tim	BOS	2B	39	127	14	42	10	0	1	17	10	26	1	2	.331	.433	.978
Neel, Troy	OAK	1B	123	427	59	124	21	0	19	63	49	101	3	5	.290	.473	.981
Newfield, Marc	SEA	OF	22	66	5	15	3	0	1	7	2	8	0	0	.227	.318	—
Newson, Warren	CHI	OF	26	40	9	12	0	0	2	6	9	12	0	0	.300	.450	1.000
Nilsson, Dave	MIL	C	100	296	35	76	10	2	7	40	37	36	3	9	.257	.375	.982
Nokes, Matt	NY	C	76	217	25	54	8	0	10	35	16	31	0	2	.249	.424	.992
Obando, Sherman	BAL	OF	31	92	8	25	2	0	3	15	4	26	0	1	.272	.391	.929
O'Brien, Pete	SEA	1B	72	210	30	54	7	0	7	27	26	21	0	1	.257	.390	.988
O'Leary, Troy	MIL	OF	19	41	3	12	3	0	0	3	5	9	0	0	.293	.366	1.000
Olerud, John	TOR	1B	158	551	109	200	54	2	24	107	114	65	0	10	.363	.599	.992
O'Neill, Paul	NY	OF	141	498	71	155	34	1	20	75	44	69	2	2	.311	.504	.992
Ortiz, Junior	CLE	C	95	249	19	55	13	0	0	20	11	26	1	5	.221	.273	.990
Ortiz, Luis	BOS	3B	9	12	0	3	0	0	0	1	0	2	0	0	.250	.250	1.000
Orton, John	CAL	C	37	95	5	18	5	0	1	4	7	24	1	4	.189	.274	.981
Owen, Spike	NY	SS	103	334	41	78	16	2	2	20	29	30	3	14	.234	.311	.968
Pagliarulo, Mike	MIN–BAL	3B	116	370	55	112	25	4	9	44	26	49	6	8	.303	.465	.972
Palmeiro, Rafael	TEX	1B	160	597	124	176	40	2	37	105	73	85	22	5	.295	.554	.997

	TEAM	POS	G	AB	R	H	2B	3B	HR	RBI	BB	SO	SB	E	BA	SLG	FLD
Palmer, Dean	TEX	3B	148	519	88	127	31	2	33	96	53	154	11	29	.245	.503	.922
Paquette, Craig	OAK	3B	105	393	35	86	20	4	12	46	14	108	4	13	.219	.382	.950
Parent, Mark	BAL	C	22	54	7	14	2	0	4	12	3	14	0	1	.259	.519	.989
Parks, Derek	MIN	C	7	20	3	4	0	0	0	1	1	2	0	1	.200	.200	.970
Parrish, Lance	CLE	C	10	20	2	4	1	0	1	2	4	5	1	3	.200	.400	.950
Pasqua, Dan	CHI	OF	78	176	22	36	10	1	5	20	26	51	2	3	.205	.358	.986
Peltier, Dan	TEX	OF	65	160	23	43	7	1	1	17	20	27	0	4	.269	.344	.955
Pena, Tony	BOS	C	126	304	20	55	11	0	4	19	25	46	1	4	.181	.257	.995
Perez, Eduardo	CAL	3B	52	180	16	45	6	2	4	30	9	39	5	5	.250	.372	.962
Petralli, Geno	TEX	C	59	133	16	32	5	0	1	13	22	17	2	2	.241	.301	.990
Phillips, Tony	DET	OF	151	566	113	177	27	0	7	57	132	102	16	13	.313	.398	.974
Pirkl, Greg	SEA	1B	7	23	1	4	0	0	1	4	0	4	0	0	.174	.304	1.000
Polonia, Luis	CAL	OF	152	576	75	156	17	6	1	32	48	53	55	5	.271	.326	.984
Puckett, Kirby	MIN	OF	156	622	89	184	39	3	22	89	47	93	8	2	.296	.474	.994
Pulliam, Harvey	KC	OF	27	62	7	16	5	0	1	6	2	14	0	1	.258	.387	.971
Quintana, Carlos	BOS	1B	101	303	31	74	5	0	1	19	31	52	1	3	.244	.271	.993
Raines, Tim	CHI	OF	115	415	75	127	16	4	16	54	64	35	21	0	.306	.480	1.000
Ramirez, Manny	CLE	OF	22	53	5	9	1	0	2	5	2	8	0	0	.170	.302	1.000
Reboulet, Jeff	MIN	SS	109	240	33	62	8	0	1	15	35	37	5	6	.258	.304	.983
Redus, Gary	TEX	OF	77	222	28	64	12	4	6	31	23	35	4	3	.288	.459	.977
Reimer, Kevin	MIL	OF	125	437	53	109	22	1	13	60	30	72	5	3	.249	.394	.962
Reynolds, Harold	BAL	2B	145	485	64	122	20	4	4	47	66	47	12	10	.252	.334	.986
Richardson, Jeff	BOS	2B	15	24	3	5	2	0	0	2	1	3	0	0	.208	.292	1.000
Riles, Ernest	BOS	2B	94	143	15	27	8	0	5	20	20	40	1	0	.189	.350	1.000
Ripken, Billy	TEX	2B	50	132	12	25	4	0	0	11	11	19	0	2	.189	.220	.990
Ripken, Cal	BAL	SS	162	641	87	165	26	3	24	90	65	58	1	17	.257	.420	.977

Rivera, Luis	BOS	SS	62	130	13	27	8	1	1	7	11	36	1	6	.208	.308	.967
Rodriguez, Ivan	TEX	C	137	473	56	129	28	4	10	66	29	70	8	8	.273	.412	.991
Rossy, Rico	KC	2B	46	86	10	19	4	0	2	12	9	11	0	1	.221	.337	.992
Rowland, Rich	DET	C	21	46	2	10	3	0	0	4	5	16	0	1	.217	.283	.988
Russell, John	TEX	C	18	22	1	5	1	0	1	3	2	10	0	0	.227	.409	1.000
Salmon, Tim	CAL	OF	142	515	93	146	35	1	31	95	82	135	5	7	.283	.536	.980
Santovenia, Nelson	KC	C	4	8	0	1	0	0	0	0	1	2	0	0	.125	.125	1.000
Sasser, Mackey	SEA	OF	83	188	18	41	10	2	1	21	15	30	1	3	.218	.309	.955
Sax, Steve	CHI	OF	57	119	20	28	5	0	1	8	8	6	7	0	.235	.303	1.000
Schofield, Dick	TOR	SS	36	110	11	21	1	2	0	5	16	25	3	4	.191	.236	.976
Segui, David	BAL	1B	146	450	54	123	27	0	10	60	58	53	2	5	.273	.400	.996
Seitzer, Kevin	MIL	3B	120	417	45	112	16	2	11	57	44	48	7	12	.269	.396	.973
Shave, Jon	TEX	SS	17	47	3	15	2	0	0	7	0	8	1	3	.319	.362	.952
Sheets, Larry	SEA	OF	11	17	0	2	1	0	0	1	2	1	0	0	.118	.176	1.000
Shumpert, Terry	KC	2B	8	10	0	1	0	0	0	0	2	2	1	0	.100	.100	1.000
Sierra, Ruben	OAK	OF	158	630	77	147	23	5	22	101	52	97	25	7	.233	.390	.977
Silvestri, Dave	NY	SS	7	21	4	6	1	0	1	4	5	3	0	3	.286	.476	.906
Smith, Lonnie	BAL	OF	9	24	8	5	1	0	2	3	8	10	0	0	.208	.500	1.000
Snow, J.T.	CAL	1B	129	419	60	101	18	2	16	57	55	88	3	6	.241	.408	.995
Sojo, Luis	TOR	SS	19	47	5	8	2	0	0	6	4	2	0	2	.170	.213	.967
Sorrento, Paul	CLE	1B	148	463	75	119	26	1	18	65	58	121	3	6	.257	.434	.995
Spiers, Bill	MIL	2B	113	340	43	81	8	4	2	36	29	51	9	13	.238	.303	.972
Sprague, Ed	TOR	3B	150	546	50	142	31	1	12	73	32	85	1	17	.260	.386	.955
Stahoviak, Scott	MIN	3B	20	57	1	11	4	0	0	1	3	22	0	4	.193	.263	.922
Stankiewicz, Andy	NY	2B	16	9	5	0	0	0	0	0	1	1	0	0	.000	.000	1.000
Stanley, Mike	NY	C	130	423	70	129	17	1	26	84	57	85	1	3	.305	.534	.996
Steinbach, Terry	OAK	C	104	389	47	111	19	1	10	43	25	65	3	7	.285	.416	.988
Stillwell, Kurt	CAL	2B	22	61	2	16	2	2	0	3	4	11	2	5	.262	.361	.951

	TEAM	POS	G	AB	R	H	2B	3B	HR	RBI	BB	SO	SB	E	BA	SLG	FLD
Strange, Doug	TEX	2B	145	484	58	124	29	0	7	60	43	69	6	13	.256	.360	.980
Suero, William	MIL	2B	15	14	0	4	0	0	0	0	1	3	0	1	.286	.286	.950
Surhoff, B.J.	MIL	3B	148	552	66	151	38	3	7	79	36	47	12	18	.274	.391	.956
Sveum, Dale	OAK	1B	30	79	12	14	2	1	2	6	16	21	0	3	.177	.304	.980
Tackett, Jeff	BAL	C	39	87	8	15	3	0	0	9	13	28	0	2	.172	.207	.989
Tartabull, Danny	NY	DH	138	513	87	128	33	2	31	102	92	156	0	2	.250	.503	.978
Tettleton, Mickey	DET	1B	152	522	79	128	25	4	32	110	109	139	3	6	.245	.492	.992
Thomas, Frank	CHI	1B	153	549	106	174	36	0	41	128	112	54	4	15	.317	.607	.989
Thome, Jim	CLE	3B	47	154	28	41	11	0	7	22	29	36	2	6	.266	.474	.950
Thon, Dickie	MIL	SS	85	245	23	66	10	1	1	33	22	39	6	7	.269	.331	.966
Thurman, Gary	DET	OF	75	89	22	19	2	2	0	13	11	30	7	3	.213	.281	.950
Tingley, Ron	CAL	C	58	90	7	18	7	0	0	12	9	22	1	1	.200	.278	.995
Tinsley, Lee	SEA	OF	11	19	2	3	1	0	1	2	2	9	0	1	.158	.368	.900
Trammell, Alan	DET	SS	112	401	72	132	25	3	12	60	38	38	12	9	.329	.496	.975
Treadway, Jeff	CLE	3B	97	221	25	67	14	1	2	27	14	21	1	10	.303	.403	.940
Turang, Brian	SEA	OF	40	140	22	35	11	1	0	7	17	20	6	1	.250	.343	.987
Turner, Chris	CAL	C	25	75	9	21	5	0	1	13	9	16	1	1	.280	.387	.992
Valentin, John	BOS	SS	144	468	50	130	40	3	11	66	49	77	3	20	.278	.447	.971
Valentin, John	MIL	SS	19	53	10	13	1	2	1	7	7	16	1	6	.245	.396	.922
Valle, Dave	SEA	C	135	423	48	109	19	0	13	63	48	56	1	5	.258	.395	.995
Van Burkleo, Ty	CAL	1B	12	33	2	5	3	0	1	1	6	9	1	0	.152	.333	1.000
Vaughn, Greg	MIL	OF	154	569	97	152	28	2	30	97	89	118	10	3	.267	.482	.986
Vaughn, Mo	BOS	1B	152	539	86	160	34	1	29	101	79	130	4	16	.297	.525	.987
Velarde, Randy	NY	OF	85	226	28	68	13	2	7	24	18	39	2	9	.301	.469	.956
Ventura, Robin	CHI	3B	157	554	85	145	27	1	22	94	105	82	1	14	.262	.433	.966
Vina, Fernando	SEA	2B	24	45	5	10	2	0	0	2	4	3	6	0	.222	.267	1.000

Vizquel, Omar	SEA	SS	158	560	68	143	14	2	2	31	50	71	12	15	.255	.298	.980
Voigt, Jose	BAL	OF	64	152	32	45	11	1	6	23	25	33	1	1	.296	.500	.991
Walewander, Jim	CAL	SS	12	8	2	1	0	0	0	3	5	1	1	0	.125	.125	1.000
Walton, Jerome	CAL	OF	5	2	2	0	0	0	0	0	1	2	1	0	.000	.000	1.000
Ward, Turner	TOR	OF	72	167	20	32	4	2	4	28	23	26	3	1	.192	.311	.990
Webster, Lenny	MIN	C	49	106	14	21	2	0	1	8	11	8	1	0	.198	.245	1.000
Whitaker, Lou	DET	2B	119	383	72	111	32	1	9	67	78	46	3	11	.290	.449	.981
White, Devon	TOR	OF	146	598	116	163	42	6	15	52	57	127	34	3	.273	.438	.993
Wilkerson, Curtis	KC	2B	12	28	1	4	0	0	0	0	1	6	2	0	.143	.143	1.000
Williams, Bernie	NY	OF	139	567	67	152	31	4	12	68	53	106	9	4	.268	.400	.989
Williams, Gerald	NY	OF	42	67	11	10	2	3	0	6	1	14	2	2	.149	.269	.956
Wilson, Craig	KC	3B	21	49	6	13	1	0	1	3	7	6	1	1	.265	.347	.968
Winfield, Dave	MIN	DH	143	547	72	148	27	2	21	76	45	106	2	0	.271	.442	1.000
Wrona, Rick	CHI	C	4	8	0	1	0	0	0	1	0	4	0	0	.125	.125	1.000
Yount, Robin	MIL	OF	127	454	62	117	25	3	8	51	44	93	9	1	.258	.379	.997
Zupcic, Bob	BOS	OF	141	286	40	69	24	2	2	26	27	54	5	4	.241	.360	.979

American Legue Pitchers

	TEAM	W	L	ERA	G	GS	CG	GF	SH	SV	IP	H	R	ER	HR	BB	SO
Abbott, Jim	NY	11	14	4.37	32	32	4	0	1	0	214.0	221	115	104	22	73	95
Abbott, Paul	CLE	0	1	6.38	5	5	0	0	0	0	18.1	19	15	13	5	11	7
Aguilera, Rick	MIN	4	3	3.11	65	0	0	61	0	34	72.1	60	25	25	9	14	59
Alvarez, Wilson	CHI	15	8	2.95	31	31	1	0	1	0	207.2	168	78	68	14	122	155
Anderson, Brian	CAL	0	0	3.97	4	1	0	3	0	0	11.1	11	5	5	1	2	4
Appier, Kevin	KC	18	8	2.56	34	34	5	0	1	0	238.2	183	74	68	8	81	186
Assenmacher, Paul	NY	2	2	3.12	26	0	0	6	0	0	17.1	10	6	6	0	9	11
Austin, James	MIL	1	2	3.82	31	0	0	8	0	0	33.0	28	15	14	3	13	15
Ayrault, Bob	SEA	1	1	3.20	14	0	0	6	0	0	19.2	18	8	7	1	6	7
Bailey, Cory	BOS	0	1	3.45	11	0	0	5	0	0	15.2	12	7	6	0	12	11

	TEAM	W	L	ERA	G	GS	CG	GF	SH	SV	IP	H	R	ER	HR	BB	SO
Bankhead, Scott	BOS	2	1	3.50	40	0	0	4	0	0	64.1	59	28	25	7	29	47
Banks, Willie	MIN	11	12	4.04	31	30	0	1	0	0	171.1	186	91	77	17	78	138
Belcher, Tim	CHI	3	5	4.40	12	11	1	0	1	0	71.2	64	36	35	8	27	34
Belinda, Stan	KC	1	1	4.28	23	0	0	7	0	0	27.1	30	13	13	2	6	25
Bere, Jason	CHI	12	5	3.47	24	24	1	0	0	0	142.2	109	60	55	12	81	129
Bergman, Sean	DET	1	4	5.67	9	6	1	1	0	0	39.2	47	29	25	6	23	19
Bielecki, Mike	CLE	4	5	5.90	13	13	0	0	0	0	68.2	90	47	45	8	23	38
Boddicker, Mike	KC–MIL	3	5	5.67	10	10	1	0	0	0	54.0	77	35	34	6	15	24
Boever, Joe	DET	6	3	3.61	61	0	0	22	0	3	102.1	101	50	41	9	44	63
Bohanon, Brian	TEX	4	4	4.76	36	8	0	4	0	0	92.2	107	54	49	8	46	45
Bolton, Rodney	CHI	2	6	7.44	9	8	0	0	0	0	42.1	55	40	35	4	16	17
Bolton, Tom	DET	6	6	4.47	43	8	0	9	0	0	102.2	113	57	51	5	45	66
Bones, Ricky	MIL	11	11	4.86	32	31	3	1	0	0	203.2	222	122	110	28	63	63
Bosio, Chris	SEA	9	9	3.45	29	24	3	2	1	1	164.1	138	75	63	14	59	119
Brewer, Billy	KC	2	2	3.46	46	0	0	14	0	0	39.0	31	16	15	6	20	28
Briscoe, John	OAK	1	0	8.03	17	0	0	6	0	0	24.2	26	25	22	2	26	24
Bronkey, Jeff	TEX	1	1	4.00	21	0	0	6	0	1	36.0	39	20	16	4	11	18
Brown, J. Kevin	TEX	15	12	3.59	34	34	12	0	3	0	233.0	228	105	93	14	74	142
Brow, Scott	TOR	1	1	6.00	6	3	0	1	0	0	18.0	19	15	12	2	10	7
Brummett, Greg	MIN	2	1	5.74	5	5	0	0	0	0	26.2	29	17	17	3	15	10
Burgos, Enrique	KC	0	1	9.00	5	0	0	3	0	0	5.0	5	5	5	0	6	6
Burns, Todd	TEX	0	4	4.57	25	5	0	8	0	0	65.0	63	36	33	6	32	35
Butcher, Mike	CAL	1	0	2.86	23	0	0	11	0	8	28.1	21	12	9	2	15	24
Cadaret, Greg	KC	1	1	2.93	13	0	0	3	0	0	15.1	14	5	5	0	7	2
Campbell, Kevin	OAK	0	0	7.31	11	0	0	4	0	0	16.0	20	13	13	1	11	9
Carpenter, Cris	TEX	4	1	4.22	27	0	0	8	0	1	32.0	35	15	15	4	12	27

Cary, Chuck	CHI	1	0	5.23	16	0	0	4	0	0	20.2	22	12	12	1	11	10
Casian, Larry	MIN	5	3	3.02	54	0	0	8	0	1	56.2	59	23	19	1	14	31
Castillo, Tony	TOR	3	2	3.38	51	0	0	10	0	0	50.2	44	19	19	4	22	28
Charlton, Norm	SEA	1	3	2.34	34	0	0	29	0	18	34.2	22	12	9	4	17	48
Christopher, Mike	CLE	0	0	3.86	9	0	0	3	0	0	11.2	14	6	5	3	2	8
Clark, Mark	CLE	7	5	4.28	26	15	1	1	0	0	109.1	119	55	52	18	25	57
Clemens, Roger	BOS	11	14	4.46	29	29	2	0	1	0	191.2	175	99	95	17	67	160
Cone, David	KC	11	14	3.33	34	34	6	0	1	0	254.0	205	102	94	20	114	191
Converse, Jim	SEA	1	3	5.31	4	4	0	0	0	0	20.1	23	12	12	0	14	10
Cook, Andy	NY	0	1	5.06	4	0	0	3	0	0	5.1	4	3	3	1	7	4
Cook, Dennis	CLE	5	5	5.67	25	6	0	2	0	0	54.0	62	36	34	9	16	34
Cook, Mike	BAL	0	0	0.00	2	0	0	0	0	0	3.0	1	0	0	0	2	3
Cox, Danny	TOR	7	6	3.12	44	0	0	13	0	2	83.2	73	31	29	8	29	84
Crim, Chuck	CAL	2	2	5.87	11	0	0	3	0	0	15.1	17	11	10	2	5	10
Cummings, John	SEA	0	6	6.02	10	8	1	0	0	0	46.1	59	34	31	6	16	19
Darling, Ron	OAK	5	9	5.16	31	29	3	1	0	0	178.0	198	107	102	22	72	95
Darwin, Danny	BOS	15	11	3.26	34	34	2	0	1	0	229.1	196	93	83	31	49	130
Davis, Storm	DET	2	8	5.05	43	8	0	12	0	4	98.0	93	57	55	9	48	73
Dayley, Ken	TOR	0	0	0.00	2	0	0	0	0	0	0.2	1	2	0	0	4	2
DeLeon, Jose	CHI	0	0	1.74	11	0	0	1	0	0	10.1	5	2	2	2	3	6
DeLucia, Rich	SEA	3	6	4.64	30	1	0	11	0	0	42.2	46	24	22	5	23	48
Deshaies, Jim	MIN	11	13	4.41	27	27	1	0	0	0	167.1	159	85	82	24	51	80
DeSilva, John	DET	0	0	9.00	1	0	0	1	0	0	1.0	2	1	1	0	0	0
DiPino, Frank	KC	1	1	6.89	11	0	0	5	0	0	15.2	21	12	12	2	6	5
DiPoto, Jerry	CLE	4	4	2.40	46	0	0	26	0	11	56.1	57	21	15	0	30	41
Doherty, John	DET	14	11	4.44	32	31	3	1	2	0	184.2	205	104	91	19	48	63
Dopson, John	BOS	7	11	4.97	34	28	1	3	1	0	155.2	170	93	86	16	59	89
Downs, Kelly	OAK	5	10	5.64	42	12	0	12	0	0	119.2	135	80	75	14	60	66

	TEAM	W	L	ERA	G	GS	CG	GF	SH	SV	IP	H	R	ER	HR	BB	SO
Drahman, Brian	CHI	0	0	0.00	5	0	0	4	0	1	5.1	7	0	0	0	2	3
Dreyer, Steve	TEX	3	3	5.71	10	6	0	1	0	0	41.0	48	26	26	7	20	23
Eckersley, Dennis	OAK	2	4	4.16	64	0	0	52	0	36	67.0	67	32	31	7	13	80
Eichhorn, Mark	TOR	3	1	2.72	54	0	0	16	0	0	72.2	76	26	22	3	22	47
Eldred, Cal	MIL	16	16	4.01	36	36	8	0	1	0	258.0	232	120	115	32	91	180
Erickson, Scott	MIN	8	19	5.19	34	34	1	0	0	0	218.2	266	138	126	17	71	116
Fajardo, Hector	TEX	0	0	0.00	1	0	0	1	0	0	0.2	0	0	0	0	0	1
Farrell, John	CAL	3	12	7.35	21	17	0	1	0	0	90.2	110	74	74	22	44	45
Farr, Steve	NY	2	2	4.21	49	0	0	37	0	25	47.0	44	22	22	8	28	39
Fernandez, Alex	CHI	18	9	3.13	34	34	3	0	1	0	247.1	221	95	86	27	67	169
Fetters, Mike	MIL	3	3	3.34	45	0	0	14	0	0	59.1	59	29	22	4	22	23
Finley, Chuck	CAL	16	14	3.15	35	35	13	0	2	0	251.1	243	108	88	22	82	187
Fleming, Dave	SEA	12	5	4.36	26	26	1	0	1	0	167.1	189	84	81	15	67	75
Flener, Huck	TOR	0	0	4.05	6	0	0	1	0	0	6.2	7	3	3	0	4	2
Fossas, Tony	BOS	1	1	5.18	71	0	0	19	0	0	40.0	38	28	23	4	15	39
Frey, Steve	CAL	2	3	2.98	55	0	0	28	0	13	48.1	41	20	16	1	26	22
Frohwirth, Todd	BAL	6	7	3.83	70	0	0	30	0	3	96.1	91	47	41	7	44	50
Garces, Richard	MIN	0	0	0.00	3	0	0	1	0	0	4.0	4	2	0	0	2	3
Gardiner, Mike	DET	0	0	3.97	10	0	0	1	0	0	11.1	12	5	5	0	7	4
Gardner, Mark	KC	4	6	6.19	17	16	0	0	0	0	91.2	92	65	63	17	36	54
Gibson, Paul	NY	2	0	3.06	20	0	0	9	0	0	35.1	31	15	12	4	9	25
Gohr, Greg	DET	0	0	5.96	16	0	0	9	0	0	22.2	26	15	15	1	14	23
Gordon, Tom	KC	12	6	3.58	48	14	2	18	0	1	155.2	125	65	62	11	77	143
Gossage, Goose	OAK	4	5	4.53	39	0	0	12	0	1	47.2	49	24	24	6	26	40
Grahe, Joe	CAL	4	1	2.86	45	0	0	32	0	11	56.2	54	22	18	5	25	31
Granger, Jeff	KC	0	0	27.00	1	0	0	0	0	0	1.0	3	3	3	0	2	1

Grater, Mark	DET	0	0	5.40	6	0	0	1	0	0	5.0	6	3	3	0	4	4
Grimsley, Jason	CLE	3	4	5.31	10	6	0	1	0	0	42.1	52	26	25	3	20	27
Groom, Buddy	DET	0	2	6.14	19	3	0	8	0	0	36.2	48	25	25	4	13	15
Guardado, Eddie	MIN	3	8	6.18	19	16	0	2	0	0	94.2	123	68	65	13	36	46
Gubicza, Mark	KC	5	8	4.66	49	6	0	12	0	2	104.1	128	61	54	2	43	80
Gullickson, Bill	DET	13	9	5.37	28	28	2	0	0	0	159.1	186	106	95	28	44	70
Guthrie, Mark	MIN	2	1	4.71	22	0	0	2	0	0	21.0	20	11	11	2	16	15
Guzman, Juan	TOR	14	3	3.99	33	33	2	0	1	0	221.0	211	107	98	17	110	194
Haas, Dave	DET	1	2	6.11	20	0	0	5	0	0	28.0	45	20	19	9	8	17
Habyan, John	NY–KC	2	1	4.15	48	0	0	23	0	1	56.1	59	27	26	6	20	39
Hampton, Mike	SEA	1	3	9.53	13	3	0	2	0	1	17.0	28	20	18	3	17	8
Haney, Chris	KC	9	9	6.02	23	23	1	0	1	0	124.0	141	87	83	13	53	65
Hanson, Erik	SEA	11	12	3.47	31	30	7	0	0	0	215.0	215	91	83	17	60	163
Harris, Greg A.	BOS	6	7	3.77	80	0	0	24	0	8	112.1	95	55	47	7	60	103
Hartley, Mike	MIN	1	2	4.00	53	0	0	21	0	1	81.0	86	38	36	4	36	57
Hathaway, Hilly	CAL	4	3	5.02	11	11	0	0	0	0	57.1	71	35	32	6	26	11
Heaton, Neal	NY	1	0	6.00	18	0	0	9	0	0	27.0	34	19	18	6	11	15
Henke, Tom	TEX	5	5	2.91	66	0	0	60	0	40	74.1	55	25	24	7	27	79
Henneman, Mike	DET	5	3	2.64	63	0	0	50	0	24	71.2	69	28	21	4	32	58
Henry, Dwayne	SEA	2	1	6.67	31	1	0	15	0	2	54.0	56	40	40	6	35	35
Henry, Doug	MIL	4	4	5.56	54	0	0	41	0	17	55.0	67	37	34	7	25	38
Hentgen, Pat	TOR	19	9	3.87	34	32	3	0	0	0	216.1	215	103	93	27	74	122
Hernandez, Je	CLE	6	5	3.14	49	0	0	22	0	8	77.1	75	33	27	12	27	44
Hernandez, Roberto	CHI	3	4	2.29	70	0	0	67	0	38	78.2	66	21	20	6	20	71
Hesketh, Joe	BOS	3	4	5.06	28	5	0	8	0	1	53.1	62	35	30	4	29	34
Higuera, Teddy	MIL	1	3	7.20	8	8	0	0	0	0	30.0	43	24	24	4	16	27
Hillegas, Shawn	OAK	3	6	6.97	18	11	0	4	0	0	60.2	78	48	47	8	33	29
Hitchcock, Sterling	NY	1	2	4.65	6	6	0	0	0	0	31.0	32	18	16	4	14	26

	TEAM	W	L	ERA	G	GS	CG	GF	SH	SV	IP	H	R	ER	HR	BB	SO
Holman, Brian	SEA	1	3	3.72	19	0	0	9	0	3	36.1	27	17	15	1	16	17
Holzemer, Mark	CAL	0	3	8.87	5	4	0	1	0	0	23.1	34	24	23	2	13	10
Honeycutt, Rick	OAK	1	4	2.81	52	0	0	7	0	1	41.2	30	18	13	2	20	21
Horsman, Vince	OAK	2	0	5.40	40	0	0	5	0	0	25.0	25	15	15	2	15	17
Howard, Chris	CHI	1	0	0.00	3	0	0	0	0	0	2.1	2	0	0	0	3	1
Howe, Steve	NY	3	5	4.97	51	0	0	19	0	4	50.2	58	31	28	7	10	19
Hutton, Mark	NY	1	1	5.73	7	4	0	2	0	0	22.0	24	17	14	2	17	12
Ignasiak, Mike	MIL	1	1	3.65	27	0	0	4	0	0	37.0	32	17	15	2	21	28
Jean, Domingo	NY	1	1	4.46	10	6	0	1	0	0	40.1	37	20	20	7	19	20
Jimenez, Miguel	OAK	1	0	4.00	5	4	0	0	0	0	27.0	27	12	12	5	16	13
Johnson, Dave	DET	1	1	12.96	6	0	0	2	0	0	8.1	13	13	12	3	5	7
Johnson, Jeff	NY	0	2	30.38	2	2	0	0	0	0	2.2	12	10	9	1	2	0
Johnson, Randy	SEA	19	8	3.24	35	34	10	1	3	1	255.1	185	97	92	22	99	308
Jones, Barry	CHI	0	1	8.59	6	0	0	1	0	0	7.1	14	8	7	2	3	7
Kamieniecki, Scott	NY	10	7	4.08	30	20	2	4	0	1	154.1	163	73	70	17	59	72
Karsay, Steve	TOR–OAK	3	3	4.04	8	8	0	0	0	0	49.0	49	23	22	4	16	33
Key, Jimmy	NY	18	6	3.00	34	34	4	0	2	0	236.2	219	84	79	26	43	173
Kiefer, Mark	MIL	0	0	0.00	6	0	0	4	0	1	9.1	3	0	0	0	5	7
Kiely, John	DET	0	2	7.71	8	0	0	5	0	0	11.2	13	11	10	2	13	5
King, Kevin	SEA	0	1	6.17	13	0	0	3	0	0	11.2	9	8	8	3	4	8
Knudsen, Kurt	DET	3	2	4.78	30	0	0	7	0	2	37.2	41	22	20	9	16	29
Kramer, Tom	CLE	7	3	4.02	39	16	1	6	0	0	121.0	126	60	54	19	59	71
Krueger, Bill	DET	6	4	3.40	32	7	0	7	0	0	82.0	90	43	31	6	30	60
Langston, Mark	CAL	16	11	3.20	35	35	7	0	0	0	256.1	220	100	91	22	85	196
Leach, Terry	CHI	0	0	2.81	14	0	0	8	0	1	16.0	15	5	5	0	2	3
Leary, Tim	SEA	11	9	5.05	33	27	0	6	0	0	169.1	202	104	95	21	58	68

Lefferts, Craig	TEX	3	9	6.05	52	8	0	9	0	0	83.1	102	57	56	17	28	58
Leftwich, Phil	CAL	4	6	3.79	12	12	1	0	0	0	80.2	81	35	34	5	27	31
Leibrandt, Charlie	TEX	9	10	4.55	26	26	1	0	0	0	150.1	169	84	76	15	45	89
Leiter, Al	TOR	9	6	4.11	34	12	1	4	1	2	105.0	93	52	48	8	56	66
Leiter, Mark	DET	6	6	4.73	27	13	1	4	0	0	106.2	111	61	56	17	44	70
Lewis, Scott	CAL	1	2	4.22	15	4	0	2	0	0	32.0	37	16	15	3	12	10
Lilliquist, Derek	CLE	4	4	2.25	56	2	0	28	0	10	64.0	64	20	16	5	19	40
Linton, Doug	TOR–CAL	2	1	7.36	23	1	0	6	0	0	36.2	46	30	30	8	23	23
Lloyd, Graeme	MIL	3	4	2.83	55	0	0	12	0	0	63.2	64	24	20	5	13	31
Lopez, Albie	CLE	3	1	5.98	9	9	0	0	0	0	49.2	49	34	33	7	32	25
MacDonald, Bob	DET	3	3	5.35	68	0	0	24	0	3	65.2	67	42	39	8	33	39
Magnante, Mike	KC	1	2	4.08	7	6	0	0	0	0	35.1	37	16	16	3	11	16
Magrane, Joe	CAL	3	2	3.94	8	8	0	0	0	0	48.0	48	27	21	4	21	24
Mahomes, Pat	MIN	1	5	7.71	12	5	0	4	0	0	37.1	47	34	32	8	16	23
Maldonado, Carlos	MIL	2	2	4.58	29	0	0	9	0	1	37.1	40	20	19	2	17	18
Manzanillo, Josias	MIL	1	1	9.53	10	1	0	4	0	1	17.0	22	20	18	1	10	10
Maysey, Matt	MIL	1	2	5.73	23	0	0	12	0	1	22.0	28	14	14	4	13	10
McCaskill, Kirk	CHI	4	8	5.23	30	14	0	6	0	2	113.2	144	71	66	12	36	65
McDonald, Ben	BAL	13	14	3.39	34	34	7	0	1	0	220.1	185	92	83	17	86	171
McDowell, Jack	CHI	22	10	3.37	34	34	10	0	4	0	256.2	261	104	96	20	69	158
McGehee, Kevin	BAL	0	0	5.94	5	0	0	1	0	0	16.2	18	11	11	5	7	7
Meacham, Rusty	KC	2	2	5.57	15	0	0	11	0	0	21.0	31	15	13	2	5	13
Melendez, Jose	BOS	2	1	2.25	9	0	0	5	0	0	16.0	10	4	4	2	5	14
Merriman, Brett	MIN	1	1	9.67	19	0	0	10	0	0	27.0	36	29	29	3	23	14
Mesa, Jose	CLE	10	12	4.92	34	33	3	0	0	0	208.2	232	122	114	21	62	118
Milacki, Bob	CLE	1	1	3.38	5	2	0	0	0	0	16.0	19	8	6	3	11	7
Militello, Sam	NY	1	1	6.75	3	2	0	0	0	0	9.1	10	8	7	1	7	5
Mills, Alan	BAL	5	4	3.23	45	0	0	18	0	4	100.1	80	39	36	14	51	68

	TEAM	W	L	ERA	G	GS	CG	GF	SH	SV	IP	H	R	ER	HR	BB	SO
Minchey, Nate	BOS	1	2	3.55	5	5	1	0	0	0	33.0	35	16	13	5	8	18
Miranda, Angel	MIL	4	5	3.30	22	17	2	0	0	0	120.0	100	53	44	12	52	88
Mlicki, Dave	CLE	0	0	3.38	3	3	0	0	0	0	13.1	11	6	5	2	6	7
Mohler, Mike	OAK	1	6	5.60	42	9	0	4	0	0	64.1	57	45	40	10	44	42
Monteleone, Rich	NY	7	4	4.94	42	0	0	11	0	0	85.2	85	52	47	14	35	50
Montgomery, Jeff	KC	7	5	2.27	69	0	0	63	0	45	87.1	65	22	22	3	23	66
Moore, Mike	DET	13	9	5.22	36	36	4	0	3	0	213.2	227	135	124	35	89	89
Morris, Jack	TOR	7	12	6.19	27	27	4	0	1	0	152.2	189	116	105	18	65	103
Moyer, Jamie	BAL	12	9	3.43	25	25	3	0	1	0	152.0	154	63	58	11	38	90
Munoz, Bobby	NY	3	3	5.32	38	0	0	12	0	0	45.2	48	27	27	1	26	33
Munoz, Mike	DET	0	1	6.00	8	0	0	3	0	0	3.0	4	2	2	1	6	1
Mussina, Mike	BAL	14	6	4.46	25	25	3	0	2	0	167.2	163	84	83	20	44	117
Mutis, Jeff	CLE	3	6	5.78	17	13	1	1	1	0	81.0	93	56	52	14	33	29
Nagy, Charles	CLE	2	6	6.29	9	9	1	0	0	0	48.2	66	38	34	6	13	30
Navarro, Jaime	MIL	11	12	5.33	35	34	5	0	1	0	214.1	254	135	127	21	73	114
Nelson, Gene	TEX	0	5	3.12	52	0	0	22	0	5	60.2	60	28	21	3	24	35
Nelson, Jeff	SEA	5	3	4.35	71	0	0	13	0	1	60.0	57	30	29	5	34	61
Nen, Robb	TEX	1	1	6.35	9	3	0	3	0	0	22.2	28	17	16	1	26	12
Nielsen, Jerry	CAL	0	0	8.03	10	0	0	3	0	0	12.1	18	13	11	1	4	8
Novoa, Rafael	MIL	0	3	4.50	15	7	2	0	0	0	56.0	58	32	28	7	22	17
Nunez, Edwin	OAK	3	6	3.81	56	0	0	16	0	1	75.2	89	36	32	2	29	58
O'Donoghue, John	BAL	0	1	4.58	11	1	0	3	0	0	19.2	22	12	10	4	10	16
Ojeda, Bob	CLE	2	1	4.40	9	7	0	0	0	0	43.0	48	22	21	5	21	27
Oliver, Darren	TEX	0	0	2.70	2	0	0	0	0	0	3.1	2	1	1	1	1	4
Olson, Gregg	BAL	0	2	1.60	50	0	0	45	0	29	45.0	37	9	8	1	18	44
Ontiveros, Steve	SEA	0	2	1.00	14	0	0	8	0	0	18.0	18	3	2	0	6	13

Oquist, Mike	BAL	0	0	3.86	5	0	0	2	0	0	11.2	12	5	5	0	4	8
Orosco, Jesse	MIL	3	5	3.18	57	0	0	27	0	8	56.2	47	25	20	2	17	67
Pall, Donn	CHI	2	3	3.22	39	0	0	9	0	1	58.2	62	25	21	5	11	29
Patterson, Bob	TEX	2	4	4.78	52	0	0	29	0	1	52.2	59	28	28	8	11	46
Patterson, Ken	CAL	1	1	4.58	46	0	0	9	0	1	59.0	54	30	30	7	35	36
Pavlik, Roger	TEX	12	6	3.41	26	26	2	0	0	0	166.1	151	67	63	18	80	131
Pennington, Brad	BAL	3	2	6.55	34	0	0	16	0	4	33.0	34	25	24	7	25	39
Perez, Melido	NY	6	14	5.19	25	25	0	0	0	0	163.0	173	103	94	22	64	148
Pichardo, Hipolito	KC	7	8	4.04	30	25	2	2	0	0	165.0	183	85	74	10	53	70
Plantenberg, Erik	SEA	0	0	6.52	20	0	0	4	0	1	9.2	11	7	7	0	12	3
Plunk, Eric	CLE	4	5	2.79	70	0	0	40	0	15	71.0	61	29	22	5	30	77
Poole, Jim	BAL	2	1	2.15	55	0	0	11	0	2	50.1	30	18	12	2	21	29
Powell, Dennis	SEA	0	0	4.15	33	2	0	7	0	0	47.2	42	22	22	7	24	32
Power, Ted	SEA	2	4	5.36	45	0	0	24	0	13	45.1	57	28	27	3	17	27
Quantrill, Paul	BOS	6	12	3.91	49	14	1	8	1	1	138.0	151	73	60	13	44	66
Radinsky, Scott	CHI	8	2	4.28	73	0	0	24	0	4	54.2	61	33	26	3	19	44
Rasmussen, Dennis	KC	1	2	7.45	9	4	0	3	0	0	29.0	40	25	24	4	14	12
Reed, Rick	TEX	1	0	5.87	3	0	0	0	0	0	7.2	12	5	5	1	2	5
Rhodes, Arthur	BAL	5	6	6.51	17	17	0	0	0	0	85.2	91	62	62	16	49	49
Rogers, Kenny	TEX	16	10	4.10	35	33	5	0	0	0	208.1	210	108	95	18	71	140
Ruffcorn, Scott	CHI	0	2	8.10	3	2	0	1	0	0	10.0	9	11	9	2	10	2
Russell, Jeff	BOS	1	4	2.70	51	0	0	48	0	33	46.2	39	16	14	1	14	45
Ryan, Ken	BOS	7	2	3.60	47	0	0	26	0	1	50.0	43	23	20	2	29	49
Ryan, Nolan	TEX	5	5	4.88	13	13	0	0	0	0	66.1	54	47	36	5	40	46
Salkeld, Roger	SEA	0	0	2.51	3	2	0	0	0	0	14.1	13	4	4	0	4	13
Sampen, Bill	KC	2	2	5.89	18	0	0	3	0	0	18.1	25	12	12	1	9	9
Sanderson, Scott	CAL	7	11	4.46	21	21	4	0	1	0	135.1	153	77	67	15	27	66
Schooler, Mike	TEX	3	0	5.55	17	0	0	0	0	0	24.1	30	17	15	3	10	16

	TEAM	W	L	ERA	G	GS	CG	GF	SH	SV	IP	H	R	ER	HR	BB	SO
Schwarz, Jeff	CHI	2	2	3.71	41	0	0	10	0	0	51.0	35	21	21	1	38	41
Scott, Darryl	CAL	1	2	5.85	16	0	0	2	0	0	20.0	19	13	13	1	11	13
Scudder, Scott	CLE	0	1	9.00	2	1	0	1	0	0	4.0	5	4	4	0	4	1
Sele, Aaron	BOS	7	2	2.74	18	18	0	0	0	0	111.2	100	42	34	5	48	93
Shinall, Zak	SEA	0	0	3.38	1	0	0	0	0	0	2.2	4	1	1	1	2	0
Slocumb, Heathcliff	CLE	3	1	4.28	20	0	0	5	0	0	27.1	28	14	13	3	16	18
Slusarski, Joe	OAK	0	0	5.19	2	1	0	0	0	0	8.2	9	5	5	1	11	1
Smithberg, Roger	OAK	1	2	2.75	13	0	0	9	0	3	19.2	13	7	6	2	7	4
Smith, Lee	NY	0	0	0.00	8	0	0	8	0	3	8.0	4	0	0	0	5	11
Springer, Russ	CAL	1	6	7.20	14	9	1	3	0	0	60.0	73	48	48	11	32	31
Stewart, Dave	TOR	12	8	4.44	26	26	0	0	0	0	162.0	146	86	80	23	72	96
Stieb, Dave	CHI	1	3	6.04	4	4	0	0	0	0	22.1	27	17	15	1	14	11
Stottlemyre, Todd	TOR	11	12	4.84	30	28	1	0	1	0	176.2	204	107	95	11	69	98
Sutcliffe, Rick	BAL	10	10	5.75	29	28	3	0	0	0	166.0	212	112	106	23	74	80
Swan, Russ	SEA	3	3	9.15	23	0	0	6	0	0	19.2	25	20	20	2	18	10
Swingle, Paul	CAL	0	1	8.38	9	0	0	2	0	0	9.2	15	9	9	2	6	6
Tanana, Frank	NY	0	2	3.20	3	3	0	0	0	0	19.2	18	10	7	2	7	12
Tapani, Kevin	MIN	12	15	4.43	36	35	3	0	1	0	225.2	243	123	111	21	57	150
Tavarez, Julian	CLE	2	2	6.57	8	7	0	0	0	0	37.0	53	29	27	7	13	19
Taylor, Scott	BOS	0	1	8.18	16	0	0	3	0	0	11.0	14	10	10	1	12	8
Telford, Anthony	BAL	0	0	9.82	3	0	0	2	0	0	7.1	11	8	8	3	1	6
Thigpen, Bobby	CHI	0	0	5.71	25	0	0	11	0	1	34.2	51	25	22	5	12	19
Timlin, Mike	TOR	4	2	4.69	54	0	0	27	0	1	55.2	63	32	29	7	27	49
Trombley, Mike	MIN	6	6	4.88	44	10	0	8	0	2	114.1	131	72	62	15	41	85
Tsamis, George	MIN	1	2	6.19	41	0	0	18	0	1	68.1	86	51	47	9	27	30
Valenzuela, Fernando	BAL	8	10	4.94	32	31	5	0	2	0	178.2	179	104	98	18	79	78

Valera, Julio	CAL	3	6	6.62	19	5	0	8	0	4	53.0	77	44	39	8	15	28
Van Poppel, Todd	OAK	6	6	5.04	16	16	0	0	0	0	84.0	76	50	47	10	62	47
Viola, Frank	BOS	11	8	3.14	29	29	2	0	1	0	183.2	180	76	64	12	72	91
Wainhouse, Dave	SEA	0	0	27.00	3	0	0	0	0	0	2.1	7	7	7	1	5	2
Ward, Duane	TOR	2	3	2.13	71	0	0	70	0	45	71.2	49	17	17	4	25	97
Wegman, Bill	MIL	4	14	4.48	20	18	5	0	0	0	120.2	135	70	60	13	34	50
Welch, Bob	OAK	9	11	5.29	30	28	0	0	0	0	166.2	208	102	98	25	56	63
Wells, David	DET	11	9	4.19	32	30	0	0	0	0	187.0	183	93	87	26	42	139
Wertz, Bill	CLE	2	3	3.62	34	0	0	7	0	0	59.2	54	28	24	5	32	53
Whiteside, Matt	TEX	2	1	4.32	60	0	0	10	0	1	73.0	78	37	35	7	23	39
Wickander, Kevin	CLE	0	0	4.15	11	0	0	1	0	0	8.2	15	7	4	3	3	3
Wickman, Bob	NY	14	4	4.63	41	19	1	9	1	4	140.0	156	82	72	13	69	70
Williamson, Mark	BAL	7	5	4.91	48	1	0	12	0	0	88.0	106	54	48	5	25	45
Williams, Woody	TOR	3	1	4.38	30	0	0	9	0	0	37.0	40	18	18	2	22	24
Willis, Carl	MIN	3	0	3.10	53	0	0	21	0	5	58.0	56	23	20	2	17	44
Witt, Bobby	OAK	14	13	4.21	35	33	5	0	1	0	220.0	226	112	103	16	91	131
Witt, Mike	NY	3	2	5.27	9	9	0	0	0	0	41.0	39	26	24	7	22	30
Young, Curt	OAK	1	1	4.30	3	3	0	0	0	0	14.2	14	7	7	5	6	4
Young, Cliff	CLE	3	3	4.62	21	7	0	3	0	1	60.1	74	35	31	9	18	31
Young, Matt	CLE	1	6	5.21	22	8	0	2	0	0	74.1	75	45	43	8	57	65

National League Statistics

National League Hitters

	TEAM	POS	G	AB	R	H	2B	3B	HR	RBI	BB	SO	SB	E	BA	SLG	FLD
Alicea, Luis	STL	2B	115	362	50	101	19	3	3	46	47	54	11	11	.279	.373	.978
Allanson, Andy	SF	C	13	24	3	4	1	0	0	2	1	2	0	0	.167	.208	1.000
Alou, Moises	MTL	OF	136	482	70	138	29	6	18	85	38	53	17	4	.286	.483	.985

	TEAM	POS	G	AB	R	H	2B	3B	HR	RBI	BB	SO	SB	E	BA	SLG	FLD
Amaro, Ruben	PHL	OF	25	48	7	16	2	2	1	6	6	5	0	1	.333	.521	.963
Anthony, Eric	HOU	OF	145	486	70	121	19	4	15	66	49	88	3	3	.249	.397	.988
Arias, Alex	FLA	2B	96	249	27	67	5	1	2	20	27	18	1	6	.269	.321	.975
Ashley, Billy	LA	OF	14	37	0	9	0	0	0	0	2	11	0	0	.243	.243	1.000
Aude, Rich	PIT	1B	13	26	1	3	1	0	0	4	1	7	0	1	.115	.154	.980
Ausmus, Brad	COL–SD	C	49	160	18	41	8	1	5	12	6	28	2	8	.256	.413	.975
Baez, Kevin	NY	SS	52	126	10	23	9	0	0	7	13	17	0	6	.183	.254	.967
Bagwell, Jeff	HOU	1B	142	535	76	171	37	4	20	88	62	73	13	9	.320	.516	.993
Barberie, Bret	FLA	2B	99	375	45	104	16	2	5	33	33	58	2	9	.277	.371	.982
Bass, Kevin	HOU	OF	111	229	31	65	18	0	3	37	26	31	7	1	.284	.402	.989
Batiste, Kim	PHL	3B	79	156	14	44	7	1	5	29	3	29	0	10	.282	.436	.947
Bean, Billy	SD	OF	88	177	19	46	9	0	5	32	6	29	2	1	.260	.395	.992
Belliard, Rafael	ATL	SS	91	79	6	18	5	0	0	6	4	13	0	1	.228	.291	.993
Bell, Derek	SD	OF	150	542	73	142	19	1	21	72	23	122	26	17	.262	.417	.956
Bell, Jay	PIT	SS	154	604	102	187	32	9	9	51	77	122	16	11	.310	.437	.986
Bell, Juan	PHL	SS	24	65	5	13	6	1	0	7	5	12	0	9	.200	.323	.909
Benavides, Freddie	COL	SS	74	213	20	61	10	3	3	26	6	27	3	13	.286	.404	.952
Benjamin, Mike	SF	SS	63	146	22	29	7	0	4	16	9	23	0	5	.199	.329	.976
Benzinger, Todd	SF	1B	86	177	25	51	7	2	6	26	13	35	0	0	.288	.452	1.000
Berroa, Geronimo	FLA	OF	14	34	3	4	1	0	0	0	2	7	0	2	.118	.147	.833
Berryhill, Damon	ATL	C	115	335	24	82	18	2	8	43	21	64	0	6	.245	.382	.990
Berry, Sean	MTL	3B	122	299	50	78	15	2	14	49	41	70	12	15	.261	.465	.936
Bichette, Dante	COL	OF	141	538	93	167	43	5	21	89	28	99	14	9	.310	.526	.973
Biggio, Craig	HOU	2B	155	610	98	175	41	5	21	64	77	93	15	14	.287	.474	.982
Blauser, Jeff	ATL	SS	161	597	110	182	29	2	15	73	85	109	16	19	.305	.436	.970
Bogar, Tim	NY	SS	78	205	19	50	13	0	3	25	14	29	0	9	.244	.351	.973

Bolick, Frank	MTL	1B	95	213	25	45	13	0	4	24	23	37	1	8	.211	.329	.980
Bonds, Barry	SF	OF	159	539	129	181	38	4	46	123	126	79	29	5	.336	.677	.984
Bonilla, Bobby	NY	OF	139	502	81	133	21	3	34	87	72	96	3	17	.265	.522	.954
Boston, Darryl	COL	OF	124	291	46	76	15	1	14	40	26	57	1	2	.261	.464	.985
Bournigal, Rafael	LA	SS	8	18	0	9	1	0	0	3	0	2	0	0	.500	.556	1.000
Branson, Jeff	CIN	SS	125	381	40	92	15	1	3	22	19	73	4	11	.241	.310	.976
Bream, Sid	ATL	1B	117	277	33	72	14	1	9	35	31	43	4	3	.260	.415	.996
Brewer, Rod	STL	OF	110	147	15	42	8	0	2	20	17	26	1	3	.286	.381	.981
Briley, Greg	FLA	OF	120	170	17	33	6	0	3	12	12	42	6	1	.194	.282	.986
Brooks, Jerry	LA	OF	9	9	2	2	1	0	1	1	0	2	0	0	.222	.667	—
Brown, Jarvis	SD	OF	47	133	21	31	9	2	0	8	15	26	3	2	.233	.331	.982
Brumfield, Jacob	CIN	OF	103	272	40	73	17	3	6	23	21	47	20	7	.268	.419	.965
Brumley, Mike	HOU	3B	8	10	1	3	0	0	0	2	1	3	0	0	.300	.300	1.000
Buechele, Steve	CHI	3B	133	460	53	125	27	2	15	65	48	87	1	8	.272	.437	.976
Bullett, Scott	PIT	OF	23	55	2	11	0	2	0	4	3	15	3	0	.200	.273	1.000
Burnitz, Jeromy	NY	OF	86	263	49	64	10	6	13	38	38	66	3	4	.243	.475	.977
Butler, Brett	LA	OF	156	607	80	181	21	10	1	42	86	69	39	0	.298	.371	1.000
Cabrera, Francisco	ATL	1B	70	83	8	20	3	0	4	11	8	21	0	0	.241	.422	1.000
Caminiti, Ken	HOU	3B	143	543	75	142	31	0	13	75	49	88	8	24	.262	.390	.942
Candaele, Casey	HOU	2B	75	121	18	29	8	0	1	7	10	14	2	3	.240	.331	.966
Canseco, Ozzie	STL	OF	6	17	0	3	0	0	0	0	1	3	0	1	.176	.176	.500
Caraballo, Ramon	ATL	2B	6	0	0	0	0	0	0	0	0	0	0	0	—	—	1.000
Carreon, Mark	SF	OF	78	150	22	49	9	1	7	33	13	16	1	3	.327	.540	.951
Carrillo, Matias	FLA	OF	24	55	4	14	6	0	0	3	1	7	0	0	.255	.364	1.000
Carr, Chuck	FLA	OF	142	551	75	147	19	2	4	41	49	74	58	6	.267	.330	.985
Castellano, Pedro	COL	3B	34	71	12	13	2	0	3	7	8	16	1	4	.183	.338	.957
Castilla, Vinny	COL	SS	105	337	36	86	9	7	9	30	13	45	2	11	.255	.404	.975
Cedeno, Andujar	HOU	SS	149	505	69	143	24	4	11	56	48	97	9	25	.283	.412	.955

	TEAM	POS	G	AB	R	H	2B	3B	HR	RBI	BB	SO	SB	E	BA	SLG	FLD
Chamberlain, Wes	PHL	OF	96	284	34	80	20	2	12	45	17	51	2	1	.282	.493	.993
Cianfrocco, Archi	MTL–SD	3B	96	296	30	72	11	2	12	48	17	69	2	10	.243	.416	.971
Clark, Dave	PIT	OF	110	277	43	75	11	2	11	46	38	58	1	6	.271	.444	.957
Clark, Jerald	COL	OF	140	478	65	135	26	6	13	67	20	60	9	12	.282	.444	.977
Clark, Phil	SD	OF	102	240	33	75	17	0	9	33	8	31	2	8	.313	.496	.972
Clark, Will	SF	1B	132	491	82	139	27	2	14	73	63	68	2	14	.283	.432	.911
Clayton, Royce	SF	SS	153	549	54	155	21	5	6	70	38	91	11	27	.282	.372	.963
Colbert, Craig	SF	C	23	37	2	6	2	0	1	5	3	13	0	1	.162	.297	.983
Colbrunn, Greg	MTL	1B	70	153	15	39	9	0	4	23	6	33	4	2	.255	.392	.995
Coleman, Vince	NY	OF	92	373	64	104	14	8	2	25	21	58	38	3	.279	.375	.982
Cole, Alex	COL	OF	126	348	50	89	9	4	0	24	43	58	30	4	.256	.305	.982
Conine, Jeff	FLA	OF	162	595	75	174	24	3	12	79	52	135	2	2	.292	.403	.995
Cordero, Wilfredo	MTL	SS	138	475	56	118	32	2	10	58	34	60	12	36	.248	.387	.937
Costo, Tim	CIN	1B	31	98	13	22	5	0	3	12	4	17	0	1	.224	.367	.982
Cotto, Henry	FLA	OF	54	135	15	40	7	0	3	14	3	18	11	2	.296	.415	.977
Cromer, Tripp	STL	SS	10	23	1	2	0	0	0	0	1	6	0	3	.087	.087	.912
Cummings, Midre	PIT	OF	13	36	5	4	1	0	0	3	4	9	0	0	.111	.139	1.000
Daugherty, Jack	HOU–CIN	OF	50	62	7	14	2	0	2	9	11	15	0	1	.226	.355	.971
Daulton, Darren	PHL	C	147	510	90	131	35	4	24	105	117	111	5	9	.257	.482	.991
Davis, Eric	LA	OF	108	376	57	88	17	0	14	53	41	88	33	2	.234	.391	.991
Decker, Steve	FLA	C	8	15	0	0	0	0	0	1	3	3	0	1	.000	.000	.968
Deshields, Delino	MTL	2B	123	481	75	142	17	7	2	29	72	64	43	11	.295	.372	.983
Destrade, Orestes	FLA	1B	153	569	61	145	20	3	20	87	58	130	0	19	.255	.406	.987
Donnels, Chris	HOU	3B	88	179	18	46	14	2	2	24	19	33	2	8	.257	.391	.965
Dorsett, Brian	CIN	C	25	63	7	16	4	0	2	12	3	14	0	0	.254	.413	1.000
Duncan, Mariano	PHL	2B	124	496	68	140	26	4	11	73	12	88	6	21	.282	.417	.958

Dunston, Shawon	CHI	SS	7	10	3	4	2	0	0	2	0	1	0	0	.400	.600	1.000
Dykstra, Lenny	PHL	OF	161	637	143	194	44	6	19	66	129	64	37	10	.305	.482	.979
Eisenreich, Jim	PHL	OF	153	362	51	115	17	4	7	54	26	36	5	1	.318	.445	.996
Espy, Cecil	CIN	OF	40	60	6	14	2	0	0	5	14	13	2	2	.233	.267	.931
Everett, Carl	FLA	OF	11	19	0	2	0	0	0	0	1	9	1	1	.105	.105	.857
Faneyte, Rikkert	SF	OF	7	15	2	2	0	0	0	0	2	4	0	0	.133	.133	1.000
Faries, Paul	SF	2B	15	36	6	8	2	1	0	4	1	4	2	1	.222	.333	.980
Fariss, Monty	FLA	OF	18	29	3	5	2	1	0	2	5	13	0	0	.172	.310	1.000
Felix, Junior	FLA	OF	57	214	25	51	11	1	7	22	10	50	2	6	.238	.397	.94
Fernandez, Tony	NY	SS	48	173	20	39	5	2	1	14	25	19	6	6	.225	.295	.975
Finley, Steve	HOU	OF	142	545	69	145	15	13	8	44	28	65	19	4	.266	.385	.988
Fletcher, Darrin	MTL	C	133	396	33	101	20	1	9	60	34	40	0	8	.255	.379	.988
Floyd, Cliff	MTL	1B	10	31	3	7	0	0	1	2	0	9	0	0	.226	.323	1.000
Foley, Tom	PIT	2B	86	194	18	49	11	1	3	22	11	26	0	5	.253	.366	.978
Frazier, Lou	MTL	OF	112	189	27	54	7	1	1	16	16	24	17	2	.286	.349	.982
Gainer, Jay	COL	1B	23	41	4	7	0	0	3	6	4	12	1	1	.171	.390	.982
Galarraga, Andres	COL	1B	120	470	71	174	35	4	22	98	24	73	2	11	.370	.602	.990
Gallagher, Dave	NY	OF	99	201	34	55	12	2	6	28	20	18	1	0	.274	.443	1.000
Gant, Ron	ATL	OF	157	606	113	166	27	4	36	117	67	117	26	11	.274	.510	.962
Garcia, Carlos	PIT	2B	141	546	77	147	25	5	12	47	31	67	18	11	.269	.399	.983
Gardner, Jeff	SD	2B	140	404	53	106	21	7	1	24	45	69	2	10	.262	.356	.981
Geren, Bob	SD	C	58	145	8	31	6	0	3	6	13	28	0	2	.214	.317	.993
Gilkey, Bernard	STL	OF	137	557	99	170	40	5	16	70	56	66	15	8	.305	.481	.971
Girardi, Joe	COL	C	86	310	35	90	14	5	3	31	24	41	6	6	.290	.397	.989
Goff, Jerry	PIT	C	14	37	5	11	2	0	2	6	8	9	0	1	.297	.514	.984
Gonzalez, Luis	HOU	OF	154	540	82	162	34	3	15	72	47	83	20	8	.300	.457	.978
Goodwin, Tom	LA	OF	30	17	6	5	1	0	0	1	1	4	1	0	.294	.353	1.000
Gordon, Keith	CIN	OF	3	6	0	1	0	0	0	0	0	2	0	0	.167	.167	1.000

	TEAM	POS	G	AB	R	H	2B	3B	HR	RBI	BB	SO	SB	E	BA	SLG	FLD
Grace, Mark	CHI	1B	155	594	86	193	39	4	14	98	71	32	8	5	.325	.475	.997
Greene, Willie	CIN	SS	15	50	7	8	1	1	2	5	2	19	0	1	.160	.340	.982
Gregg, Tommy	CIN	OF	10	12	1	2	0	0	0	1	0	0	0	0	.167	.167	1.000
Grissom, Marquis	MTL	OF	157	630	104	188	27	2	19	95	52	76	53	7	.298	.438	.984
Gutierrez, Ricky	SD	SS	133	438	76	110	10	5	5	26	50	97	4	14	.251	.331	.973
Gwynn, Tony	SD	OF	122	489	70	175	41	3	7	59	36	19	14	5	.358	.497	.981
Hansen, Dave	LA	3B	84	105	13	38	3	0	4	30	21	13	0	3	.362	.505	.927
Harris, Lenny	LA	2B	107	160	20	38	6	1	2	11	15	15	3	3	.238	.325	.982
Hayes, Charlie	COL	3B	157	573	89	175	45	2	25	98	43	82	11	20	.305	.522	.954
Hernandez, Carlos	LA	C	50	99	6	25	5	0	2	7	2	11	0	7	.253	.364	.966
Hernandez, Cesar	CIN	OF	27	24	3	2	0	0	0	1	1	8	1	1	.083	.083	.970
Higgins, Kevin	SD	C	71	181	17	40	4	1	0	13	16	17	0	6	.221	.254	.983
Hill, Glenallen	CHI	OF	31	87	14	30	7	0	10	22	6	21	1	2	.345	.770	.957
Hollins, Dave	PHL	3B	143	543	104	148	30	4	18	93	85	109	2	27	.273	.442	.914
Hosey, Steve	SF	OF	3	2	0	1	1	0	0	1	1	1	0	0	.500	1.000	—
Housie, Wayne	NY	OF	18	16	2	3	1	0	0	1	1	1	0	0	.188	.250	—
Howard, Thomas	CIN	OF	38	141	22	39	8	3	4	13	12	21	5	1	.277	.461	.987
Hughes, Keith	CIN	OF	3	4	0	0	0	0	0	0	0	0	0	0	.000	.000	—
Hundley, Todd	NY	C	130	417	40	95	17	2	11	53	23	62	1	8	.228	.357	.988
Hunter, Brian R.	ATL	1B	37	80	4	11	3	1	0	8	2	15	0	1	.138	.200	.995
Huskey, Butch	NY	3B	13	41	2	6	1	0	0	3	1	13	0	3	.146	.171	.923
Incaviglia, Pete	PHL	OF	116	368	60	101	16	3	24	89	21	82	1	5	.274	.530	.971
Jackson, Darrin	NY	OF	31	87	4	17	1	0	1	7	2	22	0	0	.195	.241	1.000
James, Chris	HOU	OF	65	129	19	33	10	1	6	19	15	34	2	3	.256	.488	.958
Jefferies, Gregg	STL	1B	142	544	89	186	24	3	16	83	62	32	46	9	.342	.485	.993
Jennings, Doug	CHI	1B	42	52	8	13	3	1	2	8	3	10	0	0	.250	.462	1.000

Johnson, Erik	SF	2B	4	5	1	2	2	0	0	0	0	1	0	0	.400	.800	1.000
Johnson, Howard	NY	3B	72	235	32	56	8	2	7	26	43	43	6	11	.238	.379	.944
Jones, Chipper	ATL	SS	8	3	2	2	1	0	0	0	1	1	0	0	.667	1.000	1.000
Jones, Chris	COL	OF	86	209	29	57	11	4	6	31	10	48	9	2	.273	.450	.983
Jones, Tim	STL	SS	29	61	13	16	6	0	0	1	9	8	2	2	.262	.361	.980
Jordan, Brian	STL	OF	67	223	33	69	10	6	10	44	12	35	6	4	.309	.543	.973
Jordan, Ricky	PHL	1B	90	159	21	46	4	1	5	18	8	32	0	2	.289	.421	.990
Justice, Dave	ATL	OF	157	585	90	158	15	4	40	120	78	90	3	5	.270	.515	.985
Karros, Eric	LA	1B	158	619	74	153	27	2	23	80	34	82	0	12	.247	.409	.992
Kelly, Roberto	CIN	OF	78	320	44	102	17	3	9	35	17	43	21	1	.319	.475	.995
Kent, Jeff	NY	2B	140	496	65	134	24	0	21	80	30	88	4	22	.270	.446	.965
Kessinger, Keith	CIN	SS	11	27	4	7	1	0	1	3	4	4	0	2	.259	.407	.935
King, Jeff	PIT	3B	158	611	82	180	35	3	9	98	59	54	8	18	.295	.406	.963
Klesko, Ryan	ATL	1B	22	17	3	6	1	0	2	5	3	4	0	0	.353	.765	1.000
Koelling, Brian	CIN	2B	7	15	2	1	0	0	0	0	0	2	0	1	.067	.067	.947
Kruk, John	PHL	1B	150	535	100	169	33	5	14	85	111	87	6	8	.316	.475	.993
Laker, Tim	MTL	C	43	86	3	17	2	1	0	7	2	16	2	2	.198	.244	.987
Lake, Steve	CHI	C	44	120	11	27	6	0	5	13	4	19	0	3	.225	.400	.985
Landrum, Ced	NY	OF	22	19	2	5	1	0	0	1	0	5	0	0	.263	.316	—
Lankford, Ray	STL	OF	127	407	64	97	17	3	7	45	81	111	14	7	.238	.346	.978
Lansing, Mike	MTL	3B	141	491	64	141	29	1	3	45	46	56	23	24	.287	.369	.952
Larkin, Barry	CIN	SS	100	384	57	121	20	3	8	51	51	33	14	16	.315	.445	.965
Lavalliere, Mike	PIT	C	1	5	0	1	0	0	0	0	0	0	0	0	.200	.200	1.000
Lemke, Mark	ATL	2B	151	493	52	124	19	2	7	49	65	50	1	14	.252	.341	.982
Lewis, Darren	SF	OF	136	522	84	132	17	7	2	48	30	40	46	0	.253	.324	1.000
Lindeman, Jim	HOU	1B	9	23	2	8	3	0	0	0	0	7	0	0	.348	.478	1.000
Lindsey, Doug	PHL	C	2	2	0	1	0	0	0	0	0	1	0	0	.500	.500	1.000
Liriano, Nelson	COL	SS	48	151	28	46	6	3	2	15	18	22	6	6	.305	.424	.966

	TEAM	POS	G	AB	R	H	2B	3B	HR	RBI	BB	SO	SB	E	BA	SLG	FLD
Longmire, Tony	PHL	OF	11	13	1	3	0	0	0	1	0	1	0	0	.231	.231	1.000
Lopez, Javier	ATL	C	8	16	1	6	1	1	1	2	0	2	0	1	.375	.750	.975
Lopez, Luis	SD	2B	17	43	1	5	1	0	0	1	0	8	0	1	.116	.140	.983
Lyden, Mitch	FLA	C	6	10	2	3	0	0	1	1	0	3	0	0	.300	.600	1.000
Maclin, Lonnie	STL	OF	12	13	2	1	0	0	0	1	0	5	1	0	.077	.077	1.000
Magadan, Dave	FLA	3B	66	227	22	65	12	0	4	29	44	30	0	7	.286	.392	.962
Maldonado, Candy	CHI	OF	70	140	8	26	5	0	3	15	13	40	0	5	.186	.286	.914
Manto, Jeff	PHL	3B	8	18	0	1	0	0	0	0	0	3	0	0	.056	.056	1.000
Manwaring, Kirt	SF	C	130	432	48	119	15	1	5	49	41	76	1	2	.275	.350	.998
Marrero, Oreste	MTL	1B	32	81	10	17	5	1	1	4	14	16	1	2	.210	.333	.991
Martinez, Dave	SF	OF	91	241	28	58	12	1	5	27	27	39	6	1	.241	.361	.993
Martin, Albert	PIT	OF	143	480	85	135	26	8	18	64	42	122	16	7	.281	.481	.975
May, Derrick	CHI	OF	128	465	62	137	25	2	10	77	31	41	10	7	.295	.422	.970
Mcclendon, Lloyd	PIT	OF	88	181	21	40	11	1	2	19	23	17	0	3	.221	.326	.972
McGee, Willie	SF	OF	130	475	53	143	28	1	4	46	38	67	10	5	.301	.389	.979
McGriff, Fred	SD/ATL	1B	151	557	111	162	29	2	37	101	76	106	5	17	.291	.549	.987
McGriff, Terry	FLA	C	3	7	0	0	0	0	0	0	1	2	0	0	.000	.000	1.000
McIntosh, Tim	MTL	OF	20	21	2	2	1	0	0	2	0	7	0	0	.095	.143	.929
McKnight, Jeff	NY	2B	105	164	19	42	3	1	2	13	13	31	0	10	.256	.323	.946
McNamara, Jim	SF	C	4	7	0	1	0	0	0	1	0	1	0	0	.143	.143	1.000
Mejia, Roberto	COL	2B	65	229	31	53	14	5	5	20	13	63	4	12	.231	.402	.963
Mercedes, Luis	SF	OF	18	25	1	4	0	1	0	3	1	3	0	0	.160	.240	1.000
Merced, Orlando	PIT	OF	137	447	68	140	26	4	8	70	77	64	3	10	.313	.443	.981
Millette, Joe	PHL	SS	10	10	3	2	0	0	0	2	1	2	0	0	.200	.200	1.000
Milligan, Randy	CIN	1B	83	234	30	64	11	1	6	29	46	49	0	5	.274	.406	.991
Mitchell, Kevin	CIN	OF	93	323	56	110	21	3	19	64	25	48	1	7	.341	.601	.957

Mondesi, Raul	LA	OF	42	86	13	25	3	1	4	10	4	16	4	3	.291	.488	.951
Montoyo, Charlie	MTL	2B	4	5	1	2	1	0	0	3	0	0	0	0	.400	.600	—
Morandini, Mickey	PHL	2B	120	425	57	105	19	9	3	33	34	73	13	5	.247	.355	.990
Morris, Hal	CIN	1B	101	379	48	120	18	0	7	49	34	51	2	5	.317	.420	.994
Murphy, Dale	COL	OF	26	42	1	6	1	0	0	7	5	15	0	0	.143	.167	1.000
Murray, Eddie	NY	1B	154	610	77	174	28	1	27	100	40	61	2	18	.285	.467	.988
Natal, Bob	FLA	C	41	117	3	25	4	1	1	6	6	22	1	0	.214	.291	1.000
Navarro, Tito	NY	SS	12	17	1	1	0	0	0	1	0	4	0	0	.059	.059	1.000
Nieves, Melvin	ATL–SD	OF	19	47	4	9	0	0	2	3	3	21	0	2	.191	.319	.931
Nixon, Otis	ATL	OF	134	461	77	124	12	3	1	24	61	63	47	3	.269	.315	.990
O'Brien, Charlie	NY	C	67	188	15	48	11	0	4	23	14	14	1	5	.255	.378	.986
Offerman, Jose	LA	SS	158	590	77	159	21	6	1	62	71	75	30	37	.269	.331	.950
Oliver, Joe	CIN	C	139	482	40	115	28	0	14	75	27	91	0	7	.239	.384	.992
Olson, Greg	ATL	C	83	262	23	59	10	0	4	24	29	27	1	6	.225	.309	.988
Oquendo, Jose	STL	SS	46	73	7	15	0	0	0	4	12	8	0	1	.205	.205	.993
Orsulak, Joe	NY	OF	134	409	59	116	15	4	8	35	28	25	5	5	.284	.399	.980
Owens, Jayhawk	COL	C	33	86	12	18	5	0	3	6	6	30	1	7	.209	.372	.957
Pagnozzi, Tom	STL	C	92	330	31	85	15	1	7	41	19	30	1	4	.258	.373	.991
Pappas, Erik	STL	C	82	228	25	63	12	0	1	28	35	35	1	6	.276	.342	.984
Parker, Rich	HOU	OF	45	45	11	15	3	0	0	4	3	8	1	0	.333	.400	1.000
Patterson, John	SF	2B	16	16	1	3	0	0	1	2	0	5	0	0	.188	.375	—
Pecota, Bill	ATL	3B	72	62	17	20	2	1	0	5	2	5	1	0	.323	.387	1.000
Pena, Geronimo	STL	2B	74	254	34	65	19	2	5	30	25	71	13	12	.256	.406	.966
Pendleton, Terry	ATL	3B	161	633	81	172	33	1	17	84	36	97	5	19	.272	.408	.959
Pennyfeather, William	PIT	OF	21	34	4	7	1	0	0	2	0	6	0	0	.206	.235	1.000
Perry, Gerald	STL	1B	96	98	21	33	5	0	4	16	18	23	1	2	.337	.510	.976
Phillips, J.R.	SF	1B	11	16	1	5	1	1	1	4	0	5	0	1	.313	.688	.971
Piazza, Mike	LA	C	149	547	81	174	24	2	35	112	46	86	3	11	.318	.561	.989

	TEAM	POS	G	AB	R	H	2B	3B	HR	RBI	BB	SO	SB	E	BA	SLG	FLD
Plantier, Phil	SD	OF	138	462	67	111	20	1	34	100	61	124	4	3	.240	.509	.990
Polidor, Gus	FLA	2B	7	6	0	1	1	0	0	0	0	2	0	0	.167	.333	1.000
Pose, Scott	FLA	OF	15	41	0	8	2	0	0	3	2	4	0	0	.195	.244	1.000
Pratt, Todd	PHL	C	33	87	8	25	6	0	5	13	5	19	0	2	.287	.529	.989
Pride, Curtis	MTL	OF	10	9	3	4	1	1	1	5	0	3	1	0	.444	1.111	1.000
Prince, Tom	PIT	C	66	179	14	35	14	0	2	24	13	38	1	5	.196	.307	.984
Ready, Randy	MTL	2B	40	134	22	34	8	1	1	10	23	8	2	8	.254	.351	.966
Reed, Jeff	SF	C	66	119	10	31	3	0	6	12	16	22	0	0	.261	.437	1.000
Reed, Jody	LA	2B	132	445	48	123	21	2	2	31	38	40	1	5	.276	.346	.993
Renteria, Rich	FLA	2B	103	263	27	67	9	2	2	30	21	31	0	2	.255	.327	.992
Rhodes, Karl	CHI	OF	20	54	12	15	2	1	3	7	11	9	2	1	.278	.519	.971
Roberson, Kevin	CHI	OF	62	180	23	34	4	1	9	27	12	48	0	3	.189	.372	.963
Roberts, Bip	CIN	2B	83	292	46	70	13	0	1	18	38	46	26	6	.240	.295	.982
Rodriguez, Henry	LA	OF	76	176	20	39	10	0	8	23	11	39	1	1	.222	.415	.993
Ronan, Marc	STL	C	6	12	0	1	0	0	0	0	0	5	0	0	.083	.083	1.000
Royer, Stan	STL	3B	24	46	4	14	2	0	1	8	2	14	0	3	.304	.413	.927
Sabo, Chris	CIN	3B	148	552	86	143	33	2	21	82	43	105	6	11	.259	.440	.967
Samuel, Juan	CIN	2B	103	261	31	60	10	4	4	26	23	53	9	10	.230	.345	.970
Sanchez, Rey	CHI	SS	105	344	35	97	11	2	0	28	15	22	1	15	.282	.326	.969
Sandberg, Ryne	CHI	2B	117	456	67	141	20	0	9	45	37	62	9	7	.309	.412	.988
Sanders, Deion	ATL	OF	95	272	42	75	18	6	6	28	16	42	19	2	.276	.452	.986
Sanders, Reggie	CIN	OF	138	496	90	136	16	4	20	83	51	118	27	8	.274	.444	.975
Santiago, Benito	FLA	C	139	469	49	108	19	6	13	50	37	88	10	11	.230	.380	.987
Saunders, Doug	NY	2B	28	67	8	14	2	0	0	0	3	4	0	4	.209	.239	.957
Scarsone, Steve	SF	2B	44	103	16	26	9	0	2	15	4	32	0	1	.252	.398	.990
Servais, Scott	HOU	C	85	258	24	63	11	0	11	32	22	45	0	2	.244	.415	.996

Sharperson, Mike	LA	2B	73	90	13	23	4	0	2	10	5	17	2	5	.256	.367	.931
Sheaffer, Danny	COL	C	82	216	26	60	9	1	4	32	8	15	2	2	.278	.384	.995
Sheffield, Gary	SD–FLA	3B	140	494	67	145	20	5	20	73	47	64	17	34	.294	.476	.899
Shelton, Ben	PIT	OF	15	24	3	6	1	0	2	7	3	3	0	1	.250	.542	.950
Sherman, Darrell	SD	OF	37	63	8	14	1	0	0	2	6	8	2	0	.222	.238	1.000
Shields, Tommy	CHI	2B	20	34	4	6	1	0	0	1	2	10	0	0	.176	.206	1.000
Shipley, Craig	SD	SS	105	230	25	54	9	0	4	22	10	31	12	7	.235	.326	.967
Siddall, Joe	MTL	C	19	20	0	2	1	0	0	1	1	5	0	0	.100	.150	1.000
Slaught, Don	PIT	C	116	377	34	113	19	2	10	55	29	56	2	4	.300	.440	.993
Smith, Dwight	CHI	OF	111	310	51	93	17	5	11	35	25	51	8	8	.300	.494	.955
Smith, Lonnie	PIT	OF	94	199	35	57	5	4	6	24	43	42	9	2	.286	.442	.981
Smith, Ozzie	STL	SS	141	545	75	157	22	6	1	53	43	18	21	19	.288	.356	.974
Snyder, Cory	LA	OF	143	516	61	137	33	1	11	56	47	147	4	9	.266	.397	.966
Sosa, Sammy	CHI	OF	159	598	92	156	25	5	33	93	38	135	36	9	.261	.485	.976
Spehr, Tim	MTL	C	53	87	14	20	6	0	2	10	6	20	2	9	.230	.368	.954
Stairs, Matt	MTL	OF	6	8	1	3	1	0	0	2	0	1	0	0	.375	.500	1.000
Staton, Dave	SD	1B	17	42	7	11	3	0	5	9	3	12	0	0	.262	.690	1.000
Stillwell, Kurt	SD	SS	57	121	9	26	4	0	1	11	11	22	4	9	.215	.273	.924
Stocker, Kevin	PHL	SS	70	259	46	84	12	3	2	31	30	43	5	14	.324	.417	.958
Strawberry, Darryl	LA	OF	32	100	12	14	2	0	5	12	16	19	1	4	.140	.310	.905
Tarasco, Tony	ATL	OF	24	35	6	8	2	0	0	2	0	5	0	0	.229	.286	1.000
Tatum, Jimmy	COL	1B	92	98	7	20	5	0	1	12	5	27	0	2	.204	.286	.962
Taubensee, Eddie	HOU	C	94	288	26	72	11	1	9	42	21	44	1	5	.250	.389	.992
Teufel, Tim	SD	2B	96	200	26	50	11	2	7	31	27	39	2	3	.250	.430	.987
Thompson, Milt	PHL	OF	129	340	42	89	14	2	4	44	40	57	9	1	.262	.350	.994
Thompson, Robby	SF	2B	128	494	85	154	30	2	19	65	45	97	10	8	.312	.496	.988
Thompson, Ryan	NY	OF	80	288	34	72	19	2	11	26	19	81	2	3	.250	.444	.987
Tomberlin, Andy	PIT	OF	27	42	4	12	0	1	1	5	2	14	0	0	.286	.405	1.000

	TEAM	POS	G	AB	R	H	2B	3B	HR	RBI	BB	SO	SB	E	BA	SLG	FLD
Tubbs, Greg	CIN	OF	35	59	10	11	0	0	1	2	14	10	3	1	.186	.237	.975
Tucker, Scooter	HOU	C	9	26	1	5	1	0	0	3	2	3	0	0	.192	.231	1.000
Uribe, Jose	HOU	SS	45	53	4	13	1	0	0	3	8	5	1	5	.245	.264	.945
Van Slyke, Andy	PIT	OF	83	323	42	100	13	4	8	50	24	40	11	1	.310	.449	.995
Vanderwal, John	MTL	1B	106	215	34	50	7	4	5	30	27	30	6	4	.233	.372	.986
Varsho, Gary	CIN	OF	77	95	8	22	6	0	2	11	9	19	1	0	.232	.358	1.000
Velasquez, Guillermo	SD	1B	79	143	7	30	2	0	3	20	13	35	0	4	.210	.287	.984
Villanueva, Hector	STL	C	17	55	7	8	1	0	3	9	4	17	0	0	.145	.327	1.000
Vizcaino, Jose	CHI	SS	151	551	74	158	19	4	4	54	46	71	12	17	.287	.358	.974
Walbeck, Matt	CHI	C	11	30	2	6	2	0	1	6	1	6	0	0	.200	.367	1.000
Walker, Chico	NY	2B	115	213	18	48	7	1	5	19	14	29	7	8	.225	.338	.949
Walker, Larry	MTL	OF	138	490	85	130	24	5	22	86	80	76	29	6	.265	.469	.982
Wallach, Tim	LA	3B	133	477	42	106	19	1	12	62	32	70	0	15	.222	.342	.959
Walters, Dan	SD	C	27	94	6	19	3	0	1	10	7	13	0	5	.202	.266	.970
Webster, Mitch	LA	OF	88	172	26	42	6	2	2	14	11	24	4	4	.244	.337	.950
Wedge, Eric	COL	C	9	11	2	2	0	0	0	1	0	4	0	0	.182	.182	1.000
Wehner, John	PIT	OF	29	35	3	5	0	0	0	0	6	10	0	0	.143	.143	1.000
Weiss, Walt	FLA	SS	158	500	50	133	14	2	1	39	79	73	7	15	.266	.308	.977
Whiten, Mark	STL	OF	152	562	81	142	13	4	25	99	58	110	15	10	.253	.423	.971
White, Derrick	MTL	1B	17	49	6	11	3	0	2	4	2	12	2	1	.224	.408	.993
White, Rondell	MTL	OF	23	73	9	19	3	1	2	15	7	16	1	0	.260	.411	1.000
Whitmore, Darrell	FLA	OF	76	250	24	51	8	2	4	19	10	72	4	3	.204	.300	.979
Wilkins, Rick	CHI	SS	136	446	78	135	23	1	30	73	50	99	2	3	.303	.561	.996
Williams, Matt	SF	3B	145	579	105	170	33	4	38	110	27	80	1	12	.294	.561	.970
Wilson, Dan	CIN	C	36	76	6	17	3	0	0	8	9	16	0	1	.224	.263	.994
Wilson, Glenn	PIT	OF	10	14	0	2	0	0	0	0	0	9	0	1	.143	.143	.875

Wilson, Nigel	FLA	OF	7	16	0	0	0	0	0	0	0	11	0	0	.000	.000	1.000
Wilson, Willie	CHI	OF	105	221	29	57	11	3	1	11	11	40	7	1	.258	.348	.991
Womack, Tony	PIT	SS	15	24	5	2	0	0	0	0	3	3	2	1	.083	.083	.971
Woodson, Tracy	STL	3B	62	77	4	16	2	0	0	2	1	14	0	4	.208	.234	.953
Wood, Ted	MTL	OF	13	26	4	5	1	0	0	3	3	3	0	0	.192	.231	1.000
Yelding, Eric	CHI	2B	69	108	14	22	5	1	1	10	11	22	3	4	.204	.296	.972
Young, Eric	COL	OF	144	490	82	132	16	8	3	42	63	41	42	18	.269	.353	.971
Young, Gerald	COL	OF	19	19	5	1	0	0	0	1	4	1	0	2	.053	.053	.882
Young, Kevin	PIT	1B	141	449	38	106	24	3	6	47	36	82	2	3	.236	.343	.998
Zambrano, Eddie	CHI	OF	8	17	1	5	0	0	0	2	1	3	0	1	.294	.294	.933
Zeile, Todd	STL	3B	157	571	82	158	36	1	17	103	70	76	5	33	.277	.433	.923

National League Pitchers

	TEAM	W	L	ERA	G	GS	CG	GF	SH	SV	IP	H	R	ER	HR	BB	SO
Agosto, Juan	HOU	0	0	6.00	6	0	0	3	0	0	6.0	8	4	4	1	0	3
Aldred, Scott	COL–MTL	1	0	9.00	8	0	0	2	0	0	12.0	19	14	12	2	10	9
Andersen, Larry	PHL	3	2	2.92	64	0	0	13	0	0	61.2	54	22	20	4	21	67
Anderson, Mike	CIN	0	0	18.56	3	0	0	0	0	0	5.1	12	11	11	3	3	4
Aquino, Luis	FLA	6	8	3.42	38	13	0	5	0	0	110.2	115	43	42	6	40	67
Armstrong, Jack	FLA	9	17	4.49	36	33	0	2	0	0	196.1	210	105	98	29	78	118
Arocha, Rene	STL	11	8	3.78	32	29	1	0	0	0	188.0	197	89	79	20	31	96
Ashby, Andy	COL–SD	3	10	6.80	32	21	0	3	0	1	123.0	168	100	93	19	56	77
Assenmacher, Paul	CHI	2	1	3.49	46	0	0	15	0	0	38.2	44	15	15	5	13	34
Astacio, Pedro	LA	14	9	3.57	31	31	3	0	2	0	186.1	165	80	74	14	68	122
Avery, Steve	ATL	18	6	2.94	35	35	3	0	1	0	223.1	216	81	73	14	43	125
Ayala, Bobby	CIN	7	10	5.60	43	9	0	8	0	3	98.0	106	72	61	16	45	65
Ayrault, Bob	PHL	2	0	9.58	10	0	0	3	0	0	10.1	18	11	11	1	10	8
Ballard, Jeff	PIT	4	1	4.86	25	5	0	4	0	0	53.2	70	31	29	3	15	16
Barnes, Brian	MTL	2	6	4.41	52	8	0	8	0	3	100.0	105	53	49	9	48	60

	TEAM	W	L	ERA	G	GS	CG	GF	SH	SV	IP	H	R	ER	HR	BB	SO
Batchelor, Richard	STL	0	0	8.10	9	0	0	2	0	0	10.0	14	12	9	1	3	4
Bautista, Jose	CHI	10	3	2.82	58	7	1	14	0	2	111.2	105	38	35	11	27	63
Beck, Rod	SF	3	1	2.16	76	0	0	71	0	48	79.1	57	20	19	11	13	86
Bedrosian, Steve	ATL	5	2	1.63	49	0	0	12	0	0	49.2	34	11	9	4	14	33
Belcher, Tim	CIN	9	6	4.47	22	22	4	0	2	0	137.0	134	72	68	11	47	101
Belinda, Stan	PIT	3	1	3.61	40	0	0	37	0	19	42.1	35	18	17	4	11	30
Bell, Eric	HOU	0	1	6.14	10	0	0	2	0	0	7.1	10	5	5	0	2	2
Benes, Andy	SD	15	15	3.78	34	34	4	0	2	0	230.2	200	111	97	23	86	179
Black, Bud	SF	8	2	3.56	16	16	0	0	0	0	93.2	89	44	37	13	33	45
Blair, Willie	COL	6	10	4.75	46	18	1	5	0	0	146.0	184	90	77	20	42	84
Borbon, Pedro	ATL	0	0	21.60	3	0	0	0	0	0	1.2	3	4	4	0	3	2
Boskie, Shawn	CHI	5	3	3.43	39	2	0	10	0	0	65.2	63	30	25	7	21	39
Bottenfield, Kent	MTL–COL	5	10	5.07	37	25	1	2	0	0	159.2	179	102	90	24	71	63
Boucher, Denis	SD–MTL	3	1	1.91	5	5	0	0	0	0	28.1	24	7	6	1	3	14
Bowen, Ryan	FLA	8	12	4.42	27	27	2	0	1	0	156.2	156	83	77	11	87	98
Brantley, Jeff	SF	5	6	4.28	53	12	0	9	0	0	113.2	112	60	54	19	46	76
Brennan, Bill	CHI	2	1	4.20	8	1	0	0	0	0	15.0	16	8	7	2	8	11
Brink, Brad	PHL	0	0	3.00	2	0	0	1	0	0	6.0	3	2	2	1	3	8
Brocail, Doug	SD	4	13	4.56	24	24	0	0	0	0	128.1	143	75	65	16	42	70
Bross, Terry	SF	0	0	9.00	2	0	0	1	0	0	2.0	3	2	2	1	1	1
Browning, Tom	CIN	7	7	4.74	21	20	0	0	0	0	114.0	159	61	60	15	20	53
Brummett, Greg	SF	2	3	4.70	8	8	0	0	0	0	46.0	53	25	24	9	13	20
Bullinger, Jim	CHI	1	0	4.32	15	0	0	6	0	1	16.2	18	9	8	1	9	10
Burba, Dave	SF	10	3	4.25	54	5	0	9	0	0	95.1	95	49	45	14	37	88
Burkett, John	SF	22	7	3.65	34	34	2	0	1	0	231.2	224	100	94	18	40	145
Burns, Todd	STL	0	4	6.16	24	0	0	5	0	0	30.2	32	21	21	8	9	10

Bushing, Chris	CIN	0	0	12.46	6	0	0	2	0	0	4.1	9	7	6	1	4	3
Cadaret, Greg	CIN	2	1	4.96	34	0	0	15	0	1	32.2	40	19	18	3	23	23
Candelaria, John	PIT	0	3	8.24	24	0	0	6	0	1	19.2	25	19	18	2	9	17
Candiotti, Tom	LA	8	10	3.12	33	32	2	0	0	0	213.2	192	86	74	12	71	155
Carpenter, Cris	FLA	0	1	2.89	29	0	0	9	0	0	37.1	29	15	12	1	13	26
Castillo, Frank	CHI	5	8	4.84	29	25	2	0	0	0	141.1	162	83	76	20	39	84
Cooke, Steve	PIT	10	10	3.89	32	32	3	0	1	0	210.2	207	101	91	22	59	132
Cormier, Rheal	STL	7	6	4.33	38	21	1	4	0	0	145.1	163	80	70	18	27	75
Corsi, Jim	FLA	0	2	6.64	15	0	0	6	0	0	20.1	28	15	15	1	10	7
Daal, Omar	LA	2	3	5.09	47	0	0	12	0	0	35.1	36	20	20	5	21	19
Davis, Mark	SD	1	5	4.26	60	0	0	13	0	4	69.2	79	37	33	10	44	70
DeLeon, Jose	PHL	3	0	3.26	24	3	0	6	0	0	47.0	39	25	17	5	27	34
Deshaies, Jim	SF	2	2	4.24	5	4	0	1	0	0	17.0	24	9	8	2	6	5
DeSilva, John	LA	0	0	6.75	3	0	0	2	0	0	5.1	6	4	4	0	1	6
Dewey, Mark	NY–PIT	1	2	2.36	21	0	0	17	0	7	26.2	14	8	7	0	10	14
Dibble, Rob	CIN	1	4	6.48	45	0	0	37	0	19	41.2	34	33	30	8	42	49
Dixon, Steve	STL	0	0	33.75	4	0	0	0	0	0	2.2	7	10	10	1	5	2
Drabek, Doug	HOU	9	18	3.79	34	34	7	0	2	0	237.2	242	108	100	18	60	157
Draper, Mike	NY	1	1	4.25	29	1	0	11	0	0	42.1	53	22	20	2	14	16
Edens, Tom	HOU	1	1	3.12	38	0	0	20	0	0	49.0	47	17	17	4	19	21
Eiland, Dave	SD	0	3	5.21	10	9	0	0	0	0	48.1	58	33	28	5	17	14
Ettles, Mark	SD	1	0	6.50	14	0	0	5	0	0	18.0	23	16	13	4	4	9
Fassero, Jeff	MTL	12	5	2.29	56	15	1	10	0	1	149.2	119	50	38	7	54	140
Fernandez, Sid	NY	5	6	2.93	18	18	1	0	1	0	119.2	82	42	39	17	36	81
Fletcher, Paul	PHL	0	0	0.00	1	0	0	0	0	0	0.1	0	0	0	0	0	0
Foster, Kevin	PHL	0	1	14.85	2	1	0	0	0	0	6.2	13	11	11	3	7	6
Foster, Steve	CIN	2	2	1.75	17	0	0	7	0	0	25.2	23	8	5	1	5	16
Franco, John	NY	4	3	5.20	35	0	0	30	0	10	36.1	46	24	21	6	19	29

	TEAM	W	L	ERA	G	GS	CG	GF	SH	SV	IP	H	R	ER	HR	BB	SO
Fredrickson, Scott	COL	0	1	6.21	25	0	0	4	0	0	29.0	33	25	20	3	17	20
Freeman, Marvin	ATL	2	0	6.08	21	0	0	5	0	0	23.2	24	16	16	1	10	25
Gardiner, Mark	MTL	2	3	5.21	24	2	0	3	0	0	38.0	40	28	22	3	19	21
Gibson, Paul	NY	1	1	5.19	8	0	0	1	0	0	8.2	14	6	5	1	2	12
Glavine, Tom	ATL	22	6	3.20	36	36	4	0	2	0	239.1	236	91	85	16	90	120
Gomez, Pat	SD	1	2	5.12	27	1	0	6	0	0	31.2	35	19	18	2	19	26
Gooden, Dwight	NY	12	15	3.45	29	29	7	0	2	0	208.2	188	89	80	16	61	149
Gott, Jim	LA	4	8	2.32	62	0	0	45	0	25	77.2	71	23	20	6	17	67
Gozzo, Mauro	NY	0	1	2.57	10	0	0	5	0	1	14.0	11	5	4	1	5	6
Grant, Mark	HOU–COL	0	1	7.46	20	0	0	9	0	1	25.1	34	24	21	4	11	14
Green, Tyler	PHL	0	0	7.36	3	2	0	1	0	0	7.1	16	9	6	1	5	7
Greene, Tommy	PHL	16	4	3.42	31	30	7	0	2	0	200.0	175	84	76	12	62	167
Greer, Ken	NY	1	0	0.00	1	0	0	1	0	0	1.0	0	0	0	0	0	2
Gross, Kevin	LA	13	13	4.14	33	32	3	1	0	0	202.1	224	110	93	15	74	150
Gross, Kip	LA	0	0	0.60	10	0	0	0	0	0	15.0	13	1	1	0	4	12
Guetterman, Lee	STL	3	3	2.93	40	0	0	14	0	1	46.0	41	18	15	1	16	19
Guzman, Jose	CHI	12	10	4.34	30	30	2	0	1	0	191.0	188	98	92	25	74	163
Hammond, Chris	FLA	11	12	4.66	32	32	1	0	0	0	191.0	207	106	99	18	66	108
Harkey, Mike	CHI	10	10	5.26	28	28	1	0	0	0	157.1	187	100	92	17	43	67
Harnisch, Pete	HOU	16	9	2.98	33	33	5	0	4	0	217.2	171	84	72	20	79	185
Harris, Gene	SD	6	6	3.03	59	0	0	48	0	23	59.1	57	27	20	3	37	39
Harris, Greg W.	SD–COL	11	17	4.59	35	35	4	0	0	0	225.1	239	127	115	33	69	123
Harvey, Brian	FLA	1	5	1.70	59	0	0	54	0	45	69.0	45	14	13	4	13	73
Henry, Butch	MTL–COL	3	9	6.12	30	16	1	4	0	0	103.0	135	76	70	15	28	47
Henry, Dwayne	CIN	0	1	3.86	3	0	0	1	0	0	4.2	6	8	2	0	4	2
Heredia, Gil	MTL	4	2	3.92	20	9	1	2	0	2	57.1	66	28	25	4	14	40

Hernandez, Jeremy	SD	0	2	4.72	21	0	0	9	0	0	34.1	41	19	18	2	7	26
Hernandez, Xavier	HOU	4	5	2.61	72	0	0	29	0	9	96.2	75	37	28	6	28	101
Hershiser, Orel	LA	12	14	3.59	33	33	5	0	1	0	215.2	201	106	86	17	72	141
Hibbard, Greg	CHI	15	11	3.96	31	31	1	0	0	0	191.0	209	96	84	19	47	82
Hickerson, Bryan	SF	7	5	4.26	47	15	0	5	0	0	120.1	137	58	57	14	39	69
Hill, Ken	MTL	9	7	3.23	28	28	2	0	0	0	183.2	163	84	66	7	74	90
Hill, Milt	CIN	3	0	5.65	19	0	0	2	0	0	28.2	34	18	18	5	9	23
Hillman, Eric	NY	2	9	3.97	27	22	3	1	1	0	145.0	173	83	64	12	24	60
Hoffman, Trevor	FLA–SD	4	6	3.90	67	0	0	26	0	5	90.0	80	43	39	10	39	79
Holmes, Darren	COL	3	3	4.05	62	0	0	51	0	25	66.2	56	31	30	6	20	60
Hope, John	PIT	0	2	4.03	7	7	0	0	0	0	38.0	47	19	17	2	8	8
Hough, Charlie	FLA	9	16	4.27	34	34	0	0	0	0	204.1	202	109	97	20	71	126
Howell, Jay	ATL	3	3	2.31	54	0	0	22	0	0	58.1	48	16	15	3	16	37
Hurst, Bruce	SD–COL	0	2	7.62	5	5	0	0	0	0	13.0	15	12	11	1	6	9
Innis, Jeff	NY	2	3	4.11	67	0	0	30	0	3	76.2	81	39	35	5	38	36
Jackson, Danny	PHL	12	11	3.77	32	32	2	0	1	0	210.1	214	105	88	12	80	120
Jackson, Mike	SF	6	6	3.03	81	0	0	17	0	1	77.1	58	28	26	7	24	70
Johnston, Joel	PIT	2	4	3.38	33	0	0	16	0	2	53.1	38	20	20	7	19	31
Johnstone, Jay	FLA	0	2	5.91	7	0	0	3	0	0	10.2	16	8	7	1	7	5
Jones, Bob	NY	2	4	3.65	9	9	0	0	0	0	61.2	61	35	25	6	22	35
Jones, Doug	HOU	4	10	4.54	71	0	0	60	0	26	85.1	102	46	43	7	21	66
Jones, Jimmy	MTL	4	1	6.35	12	6	0	3	0	0	39.2	47	34	28	6	9	21
Jones, Todd	HOU	1	2	3.13	27	0	0	8	0	2	37.1	28	14	13	4	15	25
Juden, Jeff	HOU	0	1	5.40	2	0	0	1	0	0	5.0	4	3	3	1	4	7
Kaiser, Jeff	NY–CIN	0	0	7.88	9	0	0	3	0	0	8.0	10	7	7	1	5	9
Kile, Darryl	HOU	15	8	3.51	32	26	4	0	2	0	171.2	152	73	67	12	69	141
Kilgus, Paul	STL	1	0	0.63	22	1	0	7	0	1	28.2	18	2	2	1	8	21
Klink, Joe	FLA	0	2	5.02	59	0	0	10	0	0	37.2	37	22	21	0	24	22

	TEAM	W	L	ERA	G	GS	CG	GF	SH	SV	IP	H	R	ER	HR	BB	SO
Knudson, M	COL	0	0	22.24	4	0	0	2	0	0	5.2	16	14	14	4	5	3
Lancaster, Les	STL	4	1	2.93	50	0	0	12	0	0	61.1	56	24	20	5	21	36
Landrum, Bill	CIN	0	2	3.74	18	0	0	6	0	0	21.2	18	9	9	1	6	14
Layana, Tim	SF	0	0	22.50	1	0	0	0	0	0	2.0	7	5	5	1	1	1
Leskanic, Curt	COL	1	5	5.37	18	8	0	1	0	0	57.0	59	40	34	7	27	30
Lewis, Richie	FLA	6	3	3.26	57	0	0	14	0	0	77.1	68	37	28	7	43	65
Looney, Brian	MTL	0	0	3.00	3	1	0	1	0	0	6.0	8	2	2	0	2	7
Luebbers, Larry	CIN	2	5	4.54	14	14	0	0	0	0	77.1	74	49	39	7	38	38
Maddux, Greg	ATL	20	10	2.36	36	36	8	0	1	0	267.0	228	85	70	14	52	197
Maddux, Mike	NY	3	8	3.60	58	0	0	31	0	5	75.0	67	34	30	3	27	57
Magrane, Joe	STL	8	10	4.97	22	20	0	2	0	0	116.0	127	68	64	15	37	38
Manzanillo, Josias	NY	0	0	3.00	6	0	0	2	0	0	12.0	8	7	4	1	9	11
Martinez, Dennis	MTL	15	9	3.85	35	34	2	1	0	1	224.2	211	110	96	27	64	138
Martinez, Pedro J.	LA	10	5	2.61	65	2	0	20	0	2	107.0	76	34	31	5	57	119
Martinez, Pedro A.	SD	3	1	2.43	32	0	0	9	0	0	37.0	23	11	10	4	13	32
Martinez, Ramon	LA	10	12	3.44	32	32	4	0	3	0	211.2	202	88	81	15	104	127
Mason, Roger	SD–PHL	5	12	4.06	68	0	0	29	0	0	99.2	90	48	45	10	34	71
Mauser, Tim	PHL–SD	0	1	4.00	36	0	0	16	0	0	54.0	51	28	24	6	24	46
McClure, Bob	FLA	1	1	7.11	14	0	0	1	0	0	6.1	13	5	5	2	5	6
McDowell, Roger	LA	5	3	2.25	54	0	0	19	0	2	68.0	76	32	17	2	30	27
McElroy, Chuck	CHI	2	2	4.56	49	0	0	11	0	0	47.1	51	30	24	4	25	31
McMichael, Greg	ATL	2	3	2.06	74	0	0	40	0	19	91.2	68	22	21	3	29	89
Menendez, Tony	PIT	2	0	3.00	14	0	0	3	0	0	21.0	20	8	7	4	4	13
Mercker, Kent	ATL	3	1	2.86	43	6	0	9	0	0	66.0	52	24	21	2	36	59
Miceli, Danny	PIT	0	0	5.06	9	0	0	1	0	0	5.1	6	3	3	0	3	4
Miller, Paul	PIT	0	0	5.40	3	2	0	1	0	0	10.0	15	6	6	2	2	2

Minor, Blas	PIT	8	6	4.10	65	0	0	18	0	2	94.1	94	43	43	8	26	84
Minutelli, Gino	SF	0	1	3.77	9	0	0	4	0	0	14.1	7	9	6	2	15	10
Moeller, Dennis	PIT	1	0	9.92	10	0	0	3	0	0	16.1	26	20	18	2	7	13
Moore, Marcus	COL	3	1	6.84	27	0	0	8	0	0	26.1	30	25	20	4	20	13
Morgan, Mike	CHI	10	15	4.03	32	32	1	0	1	0	207.2	206	100	93	15	74	111
Mulholland, Terry	PHL	12	9	3.25	29	28	7	0	2	0	191.0	177	80	69	20	40	116
Munoz, Mike	COL	2	1	4.50	21	0	0	7	0	0	18.0	21	12	9	1	9	16
Murphy, Rob	STL	5	7	4.87	73	0	0	23	0	1	64.2	73	37	35	8	20	41
Myers, Randy	CHI	2	4	3.11	73	0	0	69	0	53	75.1	65	26	26	7	26	86
Nabholz, Chris	MTL	9	8	4.09	26	21	1	2	0	0	116.2	100	57	53	9	63	74
Neagle, Denny	PIT	3	5	5.31	50	7	0	13	0	1	81.1	82	49	48	10	37	73
Nen, Robb	FLA	1	0	7.02	15	1	0	2	0	0	33.1	35	28	26	5	20	27
Nichols, Rod	LA	0	1	5.68	4	0	0	2	0	0	6.1	9	5	4	1	2	3
Nied, David	COL	5	9	5.17	16	16	1	0	0	0	87.0	99	53	50	8	42	46
Olivares, Omar	STL	5	3	4.17	58	9	0	11	0	1	118.2	134	60	55	10	54	63
Osborne, Donovan	STL	10	7	3.76	26	26	1	0	0	0	155.2	153	73	65	18	47	83
Osuna, Al	HOU	1	1	3.20	44	0	0	6	0	2	25.1	17	10	9	3	13	21
Otto, Dave	PIT	3	4	5.03	28	8	0	7	0	0	68.0	85	40	38	9	28	30
Painter, Lance	COL	2	2	6.00	10	6	1	2	0	0	39.0	52	26	26	5	9	16
Pall, Donn	PHL	1	0	2.55	8	0	0	2	0	0	17.2	15	7	5	1	3	11
Parrett, Jeff	COL	3	3	5.38	40	6	0	13	0	1	73.2	78	47	44	6	45	66
Perez, Mike	STL	7	2	2.48	65	0	0	25	0	7	72.2	65	24	20	4	20	58
Petkovsek, Mark	PIT	3	0	6.96	26	0	0	8	0	0	32.1	43	25	25	7	9	14
Plesac, Dan	CHI	2	1	4.74	57	0	0	12	0	0	62.2	74	37	33	10	21	47
Portugal, Mark	HOU	18	4	2.77	33	33	1	0	1	0	208.0	194	75	64	10	77	131
Powell, Ross	CIN	0	3	4.41	9	1	0	1	0	0	16.1	13	8	8	1	6	17
Pugh, Tim	CIN	10	15	5.26	31	27	3	3	1	0	164.1	200	102	96	19	59	94
Rapp, Pat	FLA	4	6	4.02	16	16	1	0	0	0	94.0	101	49	42	7	39	57

	TEAM	W	L	ERA	G	GS	CG	GF	SH	SV	IP	H	R	ER	HR	BB	SO
Reardon, Jeff	CIN	4	6	4.09	58	0	0	32	0	8	61.2	66	34	28	4	10	35
Reed, Steve	COL	9	5	4.48	64	0	0	14	0	3	84.1	80	47	42	13	30	51
Reynolds, Shane	HOU	0	0	0.82	5	1	0	0	0	0	11.0	11	4	1	0	6	10
Reynoso, Armando	COL	12	11	4.00	30	30	4	0	0	0	189.0	206	101	84	22	63	117
Righetti, Dave	SF	1	1	5.70	51	0	0	15	0	1	47.1	58	31	30	11	17	31
Rijo, Jose	CIN	14	9	2.48	36	36	2	0	1	0	257.1	218	76	71	19	62	227
Risley, Bill	MTL	0	0	6.00	2	0	0	1	0	0	3.0	2	3	2	1	2	2
Rivera, Ben	PHL	13	9	5.02	30	28	1	1	1	0	163.0	175	99	91	16	85	123
Robertson, Rich	PIT	0	1	6.00	9	0	0	2	0	0	9.0	15	6	6	0	4	5
Rodriguez, Rich	SD–FLA	2	4	3.79	70	0	0	21	0	3	76.0	73	38	32	10	33	43
Rogers, Kevin	SF	2	2	2.68	64	0	0	24	0	0	80.2	71	28	24	3	28	62
Rojas, Mel	MTL	5	8	2.95	66	0	0	25	0	10	88.1	80	39	29	6	30	48
Roper, John	CIN	2	5	5.63	16	15	0	0	0	0	80.0	92	51	50	10	36	54
Rueter, Kirk	MTL	8	0	2.73	14	14	1	0	0	0	85.2	85	33	26	5	18	31
Ruffin, Bruce	COL	6	5	3.87	59	12	0	8	0	2	139.2	145	71	60	10	69	126
Ruffin, Johnny	CIN	2	1	3.58	21	0	0	5	0	2	37.2	36	16	15	4	11	30
Ruskin, Steve	CIN	0	0	18.00	4	0	0	0	0	0	1.0	3	2	2	1	2	0
Saberhagen, Bret	NY	7	7	3.29	19	19	4	0	1	0	139.1	131	55	51	11	17	93
Sanders, Scott	SD	3	3	4.13	9	9	0	0	0	0	52.1	54	32	24	4	23	37
Sanderson, Scott	SF	4	2	3.51	11	8	0	1	0	0	48.2	48	20	19	12	7	36
Sanford, Mo	COL	1	2	5.30	11	6	0	1	0	0	35.2	37	25	21	4	27	36
Scanlan, Bob	CHI	4	5	4.54	70	0	0	13	0	0	75.1	79	41	38	6	28	44
Schilling, Curt	PHL	16	7	4.02	34	34	7	0	2	0	235.1	234	114	105	23	57	186
Schourek, Pete	NY	5	12	5.96	41	18	0	6	0	0	128.1	168	90	85	13	45	72
Scott, Tim	SD–MTL	7	2	3.01	56	0	0	18	0	1	71.2	69	28	24	4	34	65
Seanez, Rudy	SD	0	0	13.50	3	0	0	3	0	0	3.1	8	6	5	1	2	1

Seminara, Frank	SD	3	3	4.47	18	7	0	0	0	0	46.1	53	30	23	5	21	22
Service, Scott	CIN	2	2	4.30	29	0	0	7	0	2	46.0	44	24	22	6	16	43
Shaw, Jeff	MTL	2	7	4.14	55	8	0	13	0	0	95.2	91	47	44	12	32	50
Shepherd, Keith	COL	1	3	6.98	14	1	0	3	0	1	19.1	26	16	15	4	4	7
Shouse, Brian	PIT	0	0	9.00	6	0	0	1	0	0	4.0	7	4	4	1	2	3
Slocumb, Heathcliff	CHI	1	0	3.38	10	0	0	4	0	0	10.2	7	5	4	0	4	4
Smiley, John	CIN	3	9	5.62	18	18	2	0	0	0	105.2	117	69	66	15	31	60
Smith, Bryn	COL	2	4	8.49	11	5	0	2	0	0	29.2	47	29	28	2	11	9
Smith, Lee	STL	2	4	4.50	55	0	0	48	0	43	50.0	49	25	25	11	9	49
Smith, Pete	ATL	4	8	4.37	20	14	0	2	0	0	90.2	92	45	44	15	36	53
Smith, Zane	PIT	3	7	4.55	14	14	1	0	0	0	83.0	97	43	42	5	22	32
Smoltz, John	ATL	15	11	3.62	35	35	3	0	1	0	243.2	208	104	98	23	100	208
Spradlin, Jerry	CIN	2	1	3.49	37	0	0	16	0	2	49.0	44	20	19	4	9	24
Stanton, Mike	ATL	4	6	4.67	63	0	0	41	0	27	52.0	51	35	27	4	29	43
Swift, Bill	SF	21	8	2.82	34	34	1	0	1	0	232.2	195	82	73	18	55	157
Swindell, Greg	HOU	12	13	4.16	31	30	1	0	1	0	190.1	215	98	88	24	40	124
Tanana, Frank	NY	7	15	4.48	29	29	0	0	0	0	183.0	198	100	91	26	48	104
Taylor, Kerry	SD	0	5	6.45	36	7	0	9	0	0	68.1	72	53	49	5	49	45
Telgheder, Dave	NY	6	2	4.76	24	7	0	7	0	0	75.2	82	40	40	10	21	35
Tewksbury, Bob	STL	17	10	3.83	32	32	2	0	0	0	213.2	258	99	91	15	20	97
Thigpen, Bobby	PHL	3	1	6.05	17	0	0	5	0	0	19.1	23	13	13	2	9	10
Toliver, Fred	PIT	1	0	3.74	12	0	0	3	0	0	21.2	20	10	9	2	8	14
Tomlin, Randy	PIT	4	8	4.85	18	18	1	0	0	0	98.1	109	57	53	11	15	44
Torres, Salomon	SF	3	5	4.03	8	8	0	0	0	0	44.2	37	21	20	5	27	23
Trachsel, Steve	CHI	0	2	4.58	3	3	0	0	0	0	19.2	16	10	10	4	3	14
Trlicek, Rick	LA	1	2	4.08	41	0	0	18	0	1	64.0	59	32	29	3	21	41
Turner, Matt	FLA	4	5	2.91	55	0	0	26	0	0	68.0	55	23	22	7	26	59
Urbani, Tom	STL	1	3	4.65	18	9	0	2	0	0	62.0	73	44	32	4	26	33

	TEAM	W	L	ERA	G	GS	CG	GF	SH	SV	IP	H	R	ER	HR	BB	SO
Valdez, Sergio	MTL	0	0	9.00	4	0	0	1	0	0	3.0	4	4	3	1	1	2
Wagner, Paul	PIT	8	8	4.27	44	17	1	9	1	2	141.1	143	72	67	15	42	114
Wakefield, Tim	PIT	6	11	5.61	24	20	3	1	2	0	128.1	145	83	80	14	75	59
Walk, Bob	PIT	13	14	5.68	32	32	3	0	0	0	187.0	214	121	118	23	70	80
Walton, Bruce	MTL	0	0	9.53	4	0	0	3	0	0	5.2	11	6	6	1	3	0
Watson, Allen	STL	6	7	4.60	16	15	0	1	0	0	86.0	90	53	44	11	28	49
Wayne, Gary	COL	5	3	5.05	65	0	0	21	0	1	62.1	68	40	35	8	26	49
Weathers, Dave	FLA	2	3	5.12	14	6	0	2	0	0	45.2	57	26	26	3	13	34
Wendell, Turk	CHI	1	2	4.37	7	4	0	1	0	0	22.2	24	13	11	0	8	15
West, David	PHL	6	4	2.92	76	0	0	27	0	3	86.1	60	37	28	6	51	87
Weston, Mickey	NY	0	0	7.94	4	0	0	0	0	0	5.2	11	5	5	0	1	2
Wetteland, John	MTL	9	3	1.37	70	0	0	58	0	43	85.1	58	17	13	3	28	113
Whitehurst, Wally	SD	4	7	3.83	21	19	0	1	0	0	105.2	109	47	45	11	30	57
Wickander, Kevin	CIN	1	0	6.75	33	0	0	8	0	0	25.1	32	20	19	5	19	20
Williams, Brian	HOU	4	4	4.83	42	5	0	12	0	3	82.0	76	48	44	7	38	56
Williams, Mike	PHL	1	3	5.29	17	4	0	2	0	0	51.0	50	32	30	5	22	33
Williams, Mitch	PHL	3	7	3.34	65	0	0	57	0	43	62.0	56	30	23	3	44	60
Wilson, Steve	LA	1	0	4.56	25	0	0	4	0	1	25.2	30	13	13	2	14	23
Wilson, Trevor	SF	7	5	3.60	22	18	1	1	0	0	110.0	110	45	44	8	40	57
Wohlers, Mark	ATL	6	2	4.50	46	0	0	13	0	0	48.0	37	25	24	2	22	45
Worrell, Todd	LA	1	1	6.05	35	0	0	22	0	5	38.2	46	28	26	6	11	31
Worrell, Tim	SD	2	7	4.92	21	16	0	1	0	0	100.2	104	63	55	11	43	52
Young, Anthony	NY	1	16	3.77	39	10	1	19	0	3	100.1	103	62	42	8	42	62
Young, Pete	MTL	1	0	3.38	4	0	0	2	0	0	5.1	4	2	2	1	0	3

Award Winners

Most Valuable Player

1931	AL	Lefty Grove, Philadelphia	p	31–4	2.06 ERA	5 SV	
	NL	Frank Frisch, St. Louis	2b	.311 BA	4 HR	82 RBI	28 SB
1932	AL	Jimmie Foxx, Philadelphia	1b	.364 BA	58 HR	169 RBI	3 SB
	NL	Chuck Klein, Philadelphia	of	.348 BA	38 HR	137 RBI	20 SB
1933	AL	Jimmie Foxx, Philadelphia	1b	.356 BA	48 HR	163 RBI	2 SB
	NL	Carl Hubbell, New York	p	21–12	2.30 ERA	5 SV	
1934	AL	Mickey Cochrane, Detroit	c	.320 BA	2 HR	76 RBI	8 SB
	NL	Dizzy Dean, St. Louis	p	30–7	2.66 ERA	7 SV	
1935	AL	Hank Greenberg, Detroit	1b	.328 BA	36 HR	170 RBI	4 SB
	NL	Gabby Hartnett, Chicago	c	.344 BA	13 HR	91 RBI	1 SB
1936	AL	Lou Gehrig, New York	1b	.354 BA	49 HR	152 RBI	3 SB
	NL	Carl Hubbell, New York	p	26–6	2.31 ERA	3 SV	
1937	AL	Charley Gehringer, Detroit	2b	.371 BA	14 HR	96 RBI	11 SB
	NL	Joe Medwick, St. Louis	of	.374 BA	31 HR	154 RBI	4 SB
1938	AL	Jimmie Foxx, Boston	1b	.349 BA	50 HR	175 RBI	5 SB
	NL	Ernie Lombardi, Cincinnati	c	.342 BA	19 HR	95 RBI	0 SB
1939	AL	Joe DiMaggio, New York	of	.381 BA	31 HR	133 RBI	3 SB
	NL	Bucky Walters, Cincinnati	p	27–11	2.29 ERA	0 SV	
1940	AL	Hank Greenberg, Detroit	1b	.340 BA	41 HR	150 RBI	6 SB
	NL	Frank McCormack, Cincinnati	1b	.309 BA	19 HR	127 RBI	2 SB
1941	AL	Joe DiMaggio, New York	of	.357 BA	30 HR	125 RBI	4 SB
	NL	Dolph Camilli, Brooklyn	1b	.285 BA	34 HR	120 RBI	3 SB
1942	AL	Joe Gordon, New York	2b	.322 BA	18 HR	103 RBI	12 SB
	NL	Mort Cooper, St. Louis	p	22–7	1.78 ERA	0 SV	
1943	AL	Spud Chandler, New York	p	20–4	1.64 ERA	0 SV	
	NL	Stan Musial, St. Louis	of	.357 BA	13 HR	81 RBI	7 SB
1944	AL	Hal Newhouser, Detroit	p	29–9	2.22 ERA	2 SV	
	NL	Marty Marion, St. Louis	ss	.267 BA	6 HR	63 RBI	1 SB
1945	AL	Hal Newhouser, Detroit	p	25–9	1.81 ERA	2 SV	
	NL	Phil Cavaretta, Chicago	1b	.355 BA	6 HR	97 RBI	5 SB
1946	AL	Ted Williams, Boston	of	.342 BA	38 HR	123 RBI	0 SB
	NL	Stan Musial, St. Louis	1b	.365 BA	16 HR	103 RBI	9 SB
1947	AL	Joe DiMaggio, New York	of	.315 BA	20 HR	97 RBI	3 SB
	NL	Bob Elliott, Boston	3b	.317 BA	22 HR	113 RBI	3 SB
1948	AL	Lou Boudreau, Cleveland	ss	.355 BA	18 HR	106 RBI	3 SB
	NL	Stan Musial, St. Louis	of	.376 BA	39 HR	131 RBI	7 SB
1949	AL	Ted Williams, Boston	of	.343 BA	43 HR	159 RBI	1 SB
	NL	Jackie Robinson, Brooklyn	2b	.342 BA	16 HR	124 RBI	37 SB
1950	AL	Phil Rizzuto, New York	ss	.324 BA	7 HR	66 RBI	12 SB
	NL	Jim Konstanty, Philadelphia	p	16–7	2.66 ERA	22 SV	
1951	AL	Yogi Berra, New York	c	.294 BA	27 HR	88 RBI	5 SB
	NL	Roy Campanella, Brooklyn	c	.325 BA	33 HR	108 RBI	4 SB
1952	AL	Bobby Shantz, Philadelphia	p	24–7	2.48 ERA	0 SV	
	NL	Hank Sauer, Chicago	of	.270 BA	37 HR	121 RBI	1 SB

1953	AL	Al Rosen, Cleveland	3b	.336 BA	43 HR	145 RBI	8 SB
	NL	Roy Campanella, Brooklyn	c	.312 BA	41 HR	142 RBI	2 SB
1954	AL	Yogi Berra, New York	c	.307 BA	22 HR	125 RBI	1 SB
	NL	Willie Mays, New York	of	.345 BA	41 HR	110 RBI	8 SB
1955	AL	Yogi Berra, New York	c	.272 BA	27 HR	108 RBI	0 SB
	NL	Roy Campanella, Brooklyn	c	.318 BA	32 HR	107 RBI	1 SB
1956	AL	Mickey Mantle, New York	of	.353 BA	52 HR	130 RBI	10 SB
	NL	Don Newcombe, Brooklyn	p	27–7	3.06 ERA	0 SV	
1957	AL	Mickey Mantle, New York	of	.365 BA	34 HR	94 RBI	16 SB
	NL	Hank Aaron, Milwaukee	of	.322 BA	44 HR	132 RBI	1 SB
1958	AL	Jackie Jensen, Boston	of	.286 BA	35 HR	122 RBI	9 SB
	NL	Ernie Banks, Chicago	ss	.313 BA	47 HR	129 RBI	4 SB
1959	AL	Nellie Fox, Chicago	2b	.306 BA	2 HR	70 RBI	5 SB
	NL	Ernie Banks, Chicago	ss	.304 BA	45 HR	143 RBI	2 SB
1960	AL	Roger Maris, New York	of	.283 BA	39 HR	112 RBI	0 SB
	NL	Dick Groat, Philadelphia	ss	.325 BA	2 HR	50 RBI	0 SB
1961	AL	Roger Maris, New York	of	.269 BA	61 HR	142 RBI	2 SB
	NL	Frank Robinson, Cincinnati	of	.323 BA	37 HR	124 RBI	22 SB
1962	AL	Mickey Mantle, New York	of	.321 BA	30 HR	89 RBI	9 SB
	NL	Maury Wills, Los Angeles	ss	.299 BA	6 HR	48 RBI	104 SB
1963	AL	Elston Howard, New York	c	.287 BA	28 HR	85 RBI	0 SB
	NL	Sandy Koufax, Los Angeles	p	25–5	1.88 ERA	0 SV	
1964	AL	Brooks Robinson, Baltimore	3b	.317 BA	28 HR	118 RBI	1 SB
	NL	Ken Boyer, St. Louis	3b	.295 BA	24 HR	119 RBI	3 SB
1965	NL	Willie Mays, San Francisco	of	.317 BA	52 HR	112 RBI	9 SB
	AL	Zoilo Versalles, Minnesota	ss	.273 BA	19 HR	77 RBI	27 SB
1966	AL	Frank Robinson, Baltimore	of	.316 BA	49 HR	122 RBI	8 SB
	NL	Roberto Clemente, Pittsburgh	of	.317 BA	29 HR	119 RBI	7 SB
1967	AL	Carl Yastremski, Boston	of	.326 BA	44 HR	121 RBI	10 SB
	NL	Orlando Cepeda, St. Louis	1b	.325 BA	25 HR	111 RBI	11 SB
1968	AL	Denny McLain, Detroit	p	31–6	1.96 ERA	0 SV	
	NL	Bob Gibson, St. Louis	p	22–9	1.12 ERA	0 SV	
1969	AL	Harmon Killebrew, Minn.	1b–3b	.276 BA	49 HR	140 RBI	8 SB
	NL	Willie McCovey, San Francisco	1b	.320 BA	45 HR	126 RBI	0 SB
1970	AL	Boog Powell, Baltimore	1b	.297 BA	35 HR	114 RBI	1 SB
	NL	Johnny Bench, Cincinnati	c	.293 BA	2 HR	27 RBI	5 SB
1971	AL	Vida Blue, Oakland	p	24–8	1.82 ERA	0 SV	
	NL	Joe Torre, St. Louis	3b	.363 BA	24 HR	137 RBI	4 SB
1972	AL	Dick Allen, Chicago	1b	.308 BA	37 HR	113 RBI	19 SB
	NL	Johnny Bench, Cincinnati	c	.270 BA	40 HR	125 RBI	6 SB
1973	AL	Reggie Jackson, Oakland	of	.293 BA	32 HR	117 RBI	22 SB
	NL	Pete Rose, Cincinnati	of	.338 BA	5 HR	64 RBI	10 SB
1974	AL	Jeff Burroughs, Texas	of	.301 BA	25 HR	118 RBI	2 SB
	NL	Steve Garvey, Los Angeles	1b	.312 BA	21 HR	111 RBI	5 SB
1975	AL	Fred Lynn, Boston	of	.331 BA	21 HR	105 RBI	10 SB
	NL	Joe Morgan, Cincinnati	2b	.327 BA	17 HR	94 RBI	67 SB
1976	AL	Thurman Munson, New York	c	.302 BA	17 HR	105 RBI	14 SB
	NL	Joe Morgan, Cincinnati	2b	.320 BA	27 HR	111 RBI	60 SB

1977	AL	Rod Carew, Minnesota	1b	.388 BA	14 HR	100 RBI	23 SB
	NL	George Foster, Cincinnati	of	.32 BA	52 HR	149 RBI	6 SB
1978	AL	Jim Rice, Boston	of	.315 BA	46 HR	139 RBI	7 SB
	NL	Dave Parker, Pittsburgh	of	.334 BA	30 HR	117 RBI	20 SB
1979	AL	Don Baylor, California	of	.296 BA	36 HR	139 RBI	22 SB
	NL	Keith Hernandez, St. Louis	1b	.344 BA	11 HR	105 RBI	11 SB
	NL	Willie Stargell, Pittsburgh	1b	.281 BA	32 HR	82 RBI	0 SB
1980	AL	George Brett, Kansas City	3b	.390 BA	24 HR	118 RBI	15 SB
	NL	Mike Schmidt, Philadelphia	3b	.286 BA	48 HR	121 RBI	12 SB
1981	AL	Rollie Fingers, Milwaukee	p	6–3	1.04 ERA	28 SV	
	NL	Mike Schmidt, Philadelphia	3b	.316 BA	31 HR	91 RBI	12 SB
1982	AL	Robin Yount, Milwaukee	of	.331 BA	29 HR	114 RBI	19 SB
	NL	Dale Murphy, Atlanta	of	.281 BA	36 HR	109 RBI	23 SB
1983	AL	Cal Ripken, Jr., Baltimore	ss	.318 BA	27 HR	102 RBI	0 SB
	NL	Dale Murphy, Atlanta	of	.302 BA	36 HR	121 RBI	30 SB
1984	AL	Willie Hernandez, Detroit	p	9–3	1.92 ERA	32 SV	
	NL	Ryne Sandberg, Chicago	2b	.314 BA	19 HR	84 RBI	32 SB
1985	AL	Don Mattingly, New York	1b	.324 BA	35 HR	145 RBI	2 SB
	NL	Willie McGee, St. Louis	of	.353 BA	7 HR	48 RBI	56 SB
1986	AL	Roger Clemens, Boston	p	24–4	2.48 ERA	0 SV	
	NL	Mike Schmidt, Philadelphia	3b	.290 BA	37 HR	119 RBI	1 SB
1987	AL	George Bell, Toronto	of	.308 BA	47 HR	134 RBI	5 SB
	NL	Andre Dawson, Chicago	of	.287 BA	49 HR	137 RBI	11 SB
1988	AL	Jose Canseco, Oakland	of	.307 BA	42 HR	124 RBI	40 SB
	NL	Kirk Gibson, Los Angeles	of	.290 BA	25 HR	76 RBI	31 SB
1989	AL	Robin Yount, Milwaukee	of	.318 BA	21 HR	103 RBI	14 SB
	NL	Kevin Mitchell, San Francisco	of	.291 BA	47 HR	125 RBI	3 SB
1990	AL	Rickey Henderson, Oakland	of	.325 BA	28 HR	61 RBI	65 SB
	NL	Barry Bonds, Pittsburgh	of	.301 BA	33 HR	114 RBI	52 SB
1991	AL	Cal Ripken, Jr., Baltimore	ss	.323 BA	34 HR	114 RBI	6 SB
	NL	Terry Pendleton, Atlanta	3b	.319 BA	22 HR	86 RBI	10 SB
1992	AL	Dennis Eckersley, Oakland	p	7–1	1.91 ERA	51 SV	
	NL	Barry Bonds, Pittsburgh	of	.311 BA	34 HR	103 RBI	39 SB
1993	AL	Frank Thomas, Chicago	1B	.317 BA	41 HR	128 RBI	4 SB
	NL	Barry Bonds, San Francisco	of	.336 BA	46 HR	123 RBI	29 SB

Cy Young Award

1957	Warren Spahn, Milwaukee	21–11	2.69 ERA	3 SV
1958	Bob Turley, New York (AL)	21–7	2.97 ERA	1 SV
1959	Early Wynn, Chicago (AL)	22–10	3.17 ERA	0 SV
1960	Vernon Law, Pittsburgh	20–9	3.08 ERA	0 SV
1961	Whitey Ford, New York (AL)	25–4	3.21 ERA	0 SV
1962	Don Drysdale, Los Angeles	25–9	2.83 ERA	1 SV
1963	Sandy Koufax, Los Angeles	25–5	1.88 ERA	0 SV
1964	Dean Chance, Los Angeles	20–9	1.65 ERA	4 SV
1965	Sandy Koufax, Los Angeles	26–8	2.04 ERA	2 SV
1966	Sandy Koufax, Los Angeles	27–9	1.73 ERA	0 SV

1967	AL	Jim Lonborg, Boston	22–9	3.16 ERA	0 SV
	NL	Mike McCormick, San Francisco	22–10	2.85 ERA	0 SV
1968	AL	Denny McLain, Detroit	31–6	1.96 ERA	0 SV
	NL	Bob Gibson, St. Louis	22–9	1.12 ERA	0 SV
1969	AL	Denny McLain, Detroit	24–9	2.80 ERA	0 SV
	AL	Mike Cuellar, Baltimore	23–11	2.38 ERA	0 SV
	NL	Tom Seaver, New York	25–7	2.21 ERA	0 SV
1970	AL	Jim Perry, Minnesota	24–12	3.04 ERA	0 SV
	NL	Bob Gibson, St. Louis	23–7	3.12 ERA	0 SV
1971	AL	Vida Blue, Oakland	24–8	1.82 ERA	0 SV
	NL	Fergie Jenkins, Chicago	24–13	2.77 ERA	0 SV
1972	AL	Gaylord Perry, Cleveland	24–16	1.92 ERA	1 SV
	NL	Steve Carlton, Philadelphia	27–10	1.97 ERA	0 SV
1973	AL	Jim Palmer, Baltimore	22–9	2.40 ERA	1 SV
	NL	Tom Seaver, New York	19–10	2.08 ERA	0 SV
1974	AL	Jim Hunter, Oakland	25–12	2.49 ERA	0 SV
	NL	Mike Marshall, Los Angeles	15–12	2.42 ERA	21 SV
1975	AL	Jim Palmer, Baltimore	23–11	2.09 ERA	1 SV
	NL	Tom Seaver, New York	22–9	2.38 ERA	0 SV
1976	AL	Jim Palmer, Baltimore	22–13	2.51 ERA	0 SV
	NL	Randy Jones, San Diego	22–14	2.74 ERA	0 SV
1977	AL	Sparky Lyle, New York	13–5	2.17 ERA	26 SV
	NL	Steve Carlton, Philadelphia	23–10	2.64 ERA	0 SV
1978	AL	Ron Guidry, New York	25–3	1.74 ERA	0 SV
	NL	Gaylord Perry, San Diego	21–6	2.73 ERA	0 SV
1979	AL	Mike Flanagan, Baltimore	23–9	3.08 ERA	0 SV
	NL	Bruce Sutter, Chicago	6–6	2.22 ERA	37 SV
1980	AL	Steve Stone, Baltimore	25–7	3.23 ERA	0 SV
	NL	Steve Carlton, Philadelphia	24–9	2.34 ERA	0 SV
1981	AL	Rollie Fingers, Milwaukee	6–3	1.04 ERA	28 SV
	NL	Fernando Valenzuela, Los Angeles	13–7	2.48 ERA	0 SV
1982	AL	Pete Vuckovich, Milwaukee	18–6	3.34 ERA	0 SV
	NL	Steve Carlton, Philadelphia	23–11	3.10 ERA	0 SV
1983	AL	LaMarr Hoyt, Chicago	24–10	3.66 ERA	0 SV
	NL	John Denny, Philadelphia	19–6	2.37 ERA	0 SV
1984	AL	Willie Hernandez, Detroit	9–3	1.92 ERA	32 SV
	NL	Rick Sutcliffe, Chicago	20–6	3.97 ERA	0 SV
1985	AL	Bret Saberhagen, Kansas City	20–6	2.87 ERA	0 SV
	NL	Dwight Gooden, New York	24–4	1.53 ERA	0 SV
1986	AL	Roger Clemens, Boston	24–4	2.48 ERA	0 SV
	NL	Mike Scott, Houston	18–10	2.22 ERA	0 SV
1987	AL	Roger Clemens, Boston	20–9	2.97 ERA	0 SV
	NL	Steve Bedrosian, Philadelphia	5–3	2.83 ERA	40 SV
1988	AL	Frank Viola, Minnesota	24–7	2.64 ERA	0 SV
	NL	Orel Hershiser, Los Angeles	23–8	2.26 ERA	1 SV
1989	AL	Bret Saberhagen, Kansas City	23–6	2.16 ERA	0 SV
	NL	Mark Davis, San Diego	4–3	1.85 ERA	44 SV

1990	AL	Bob Welch, Oakland	27–6	2.95 ERA	0 SV
	NL	Doug Drabek, Pittsburgh	22–6	2.76 ERA	0 SV
1991	AL	Roger Clemens, Boston	18–10	2.62 ERA	0 SV
	NL	Tom Glavine, Atlanta	20–11	2.55 ERA	0 SV
1992	AL	Dennis Eckersley, Oakland	7–1	1.91 ERA	51 SV
	NL	Greg Maddux, Chicago	20–11	2.18 ERA	0 SV
1993	AL	Jack McDowell, Chicago	22–10	3.37 ERA	0 SV
	NL	Greg Maddux, Atlanta	20–10	2.36 ERA	0 SV

Jackie Robinson Rookie of the Year Award

1949	AL	Roy Sievers, St. Louis	of	.306 BA	16 HR	91 RBI	1 SB
	NL	Don Newcombe, Brooklyn	p	17–8	3.17 ERA	1 SV	
1950	AL	Walt Dropo, Boston	1b	.322 BA	34 HR	144 RBI	0 SB
	NL	Sam Jethroe, Boston	of	.273 BA	18 HR	58 RBI	35 SB
1951	AL	Gil McDougald, New York	3b	.306 BA	14 HR	63 RBI	14 SB
	NL	Willie Mays, New York	of	.274 BA	20 HR	68 RBI	7 SB
1952	AL	Harry Byrd, Philadelphia	p	15–15	3.31 ERA	2 SV	
	NL	Joe Black, Brooklyn	p	15–4	2.15	15 SV	
1953	AL	Harvey Kuenn, Detroit	ss	.308 BA	2 HR	48 RBI	6 SB
	NL	Jim Gilliam, Brooklyn	2b	.278 BA	6 HR	63 RBI	21 SB
1954	AL	Bob Grim, New York	p	20–6	3.26 ERA	0 SV	
	NL	Wally Moon, St. Louis	of	.304 BA	12 HR	76 RBI	18 SB
1955	AL	Herb Score, Cleveland	p	16–10	2.85 ERA	0 SV	
	NL	Bill Virdon, St. Louis	of	.281 BA	17 HR	68 RBI	2 SB
1956	AL	Luis Aparicio, Chicago	ss	.266 BA	3 HR	56 RBI	21 SB
	NL	Frank Robinson, Cincinnati	of	.290 BA	38 HR	83 RBI	8 SB
1957	AL	Tony Kubek, New York	ss	.297 BA	3 HR	39 RBI	6 SB
	NL	Jack Sanford, Philadelphia	p	19–8	3.08 ERA	0 SV	
1958	AL	Albie Pearson, Washington	of	.275 BA	3 HR	33 RBI	7 SB
	NL	Orlando Cepeda, San Fran.	1b	.312 BA	25 HR	96 RBI	15 SB
1959	AL	Bob Allison, Washington	of	.261 BA	30 HR	85 RBI	13 SB
	NL	Willie McCovey, San Fran.	1b	.354 BA	13 HR	38 RBI	2 SB
1960	AL	Ron Hansen, Baltimore	ss	.255 BA	22 HR	86 RBI	3 SB
	NL	Frank Howard, Los Angeles	of	.268 BA	23 HR	77 RBI	0 SB
1961	AL	Don Schwall, Boston	p	15–7	3.22 ERA	0 SV	
	NL	Billy Williams, Chicago	of	.278 BA	25 HR	86 RBI	6 SB
1962	AL	Tom Tresh, New York	of–ss	.286 BA	20 HR	93 RBI	4 SB
	NL	Ken Hubbs, Chicago	2b	.260 BA	5 HR	49 RBI	3 SB
1963	AL	Gary Peters, Chicago	p	19–8	2.33 ERA	1 SV	
	NL	Pete Rose, Cinncinati	2b	.273 BA	6 HR	41 RBI	13 SB
1964	AL	Tony Oliva, Minnesota	of	.323 BA	32 HR	94 RBI	12 SB
	NL	Dick Allen, Philadelphia	3b	.318 BA	29 HR	91 RBI	3 SB
1965	AL	Curt Blefary, Baltimore	of	.260 BA	22 HR	70 RBI	4 SB
	NL	Jim Lefebvre, Los Angeles	2b	.250 BA	12 HR	69 RBI	3 SB
1966	AL	Tommie Agee, Chicago	of	.273 BA	22 HR	86 RBI	44 SB
	NL	Tommy Helms, Cincinnati	2b	.284 BA	9 HR	49 RBI	3 SB

1967	AL	Rod Carew, Minnesota	2b	.292 BA	8 HR	51 RBI	5 SB
	NL	Tom Seaver, New York	p	16–13	2.76 ERA	0 SV	
1968	AL	Stan Bahnsen, New York	p	17–12	2.05 ERA	0 SV	
	NL	Johnny Bench, Cincinnati	c	.275 BA	15 HR	82 RBI	1 SB
1969	AL	Lou Piniella, Kansas City	of	.282 BA	11 HR	68 RBI	2 SB
	NL	Ted Sizemore, Los Angeles	2b	.271 BA	4 HR	46 RBI	5 SB
1970	AL	Thurman Munson, New York	c	.302 BA	6 HR	53 RBI	5 SB
	NL	Carl Morton, Montreal	p	18–11	3.60 ERA	0 SV	
1971	AL	Chris Chambliss, Cleveland	1b	.275 BA	9 HR	48 RBI	2 SB
	NL	Earl Williams, Atlanta	c	.260 BA	33 HR	87 RBI	0 SB
1972	AL	Carlton Fisk, Boston	c	.293 BA	22 HR	61 RBI	5 SB
	NL	Jon Matlack, New York	p	15–10	2.32 ERA	0 SV	
1973	AL	Al Bumbry, Baltimore	of	.337 BA	7 HR	34 RBI	23 SB
	NL	Gary Matthews, San Fran.	of	.300 BA	12 HR	58 RBI	17 SB
1974	AL	Mike Hargrove, Texas	1b	.323 BA	4 HR	66 RBI	0 SB
	NL	Bake McBride, St. Louis	of	.309 BA	6 HR	56 RBI	0 SB
1975	AL	Fred Lynn, Boston	of	.331 BA	21 HR	105 RBI	10 SB
	NL	John Montefusco, San Fran.	p	15–9	2.88 ERA	0 SV	
1976	AL	Mark Fidrych, Detroit	p	19–9	2.34 ERA	0 SV	
	NL	Pat Zachry, Cincinnati	p	14–7	2.74 ERA	0 SV	
	NL	Butch Metzger, San Diego	p	11–4	2.92 ERA	16 SV	
1977	AL	Eddie Murray, Baltimore	dh–1b	.283 BA	27 HR	88 RBI	0 SB
	NL	Andre Dawson, Montreal	of	.282 BA	19 HR	65 RBI	21 SB
1978	AL	Lou Whitaker, Detroit	2b	.285 BA	3 HR	58 RBI	7 SB
	NL	Bob Horner, Atlanta	3b	.266 BA	23 HR	63 RBI	0 SB
1979	AL	Alfredo Griffin, Toronto	ss	.287 BA	2 HR	31 RBI	21 SB
	AL	John Castino, Minnesota	3b	.285 BA	5 HR	52 RBI	5 SB
	NL	Rick Sutcliffe, Los Angeles	p	17–10	3.46 ERA	0 SV	
1980	AL	Joe Charboneau, Cleveland	of	.289 BA	23 HR	87 RBI	2 SB
	NL	Steve Howe, Los Angeles	p	7–9	2.66 ERA	17 SV	
1981	AL	Dave Righetti, New York	p	8–4	2.05 ERA	0 SV	
	NL	Fernando Valenzuela, LA	p	13–7	2.48 ERA	0 SV	
1982	AL	Cal Ripken, Baltimore	ss	.264 BA	28 HR	93 RBI	0 SB
	NL	Steve Sax, Los Angeles	2b	.282 BA	4 HR	47 RBI	49 SB
1983	AL	Ron Kittle, Chicago	of	.254 BA	35 HR	100 RBI	8 SB
	NL	Darryl Strawberry, New York	of	.257 BA	26 HR	74 RBI	19 SB
1984	AL	Alvin Davis, Seattle	1b	.284 BA	27 HR	116 RBI	5 SB
	NL	Dwight Gooden, New York	p	17–9	2.60 ERA	0 SV	
1985	AL	Ozzie Guillen, Chicago	ss	.273 BA	1 HR	33 RBI	7 SB
	NL	Vince Coleman, St. Louis	of	.267 BA	1 HR	40 RBI	110 SB
1986	AL	Jose Canseco, Oakland	of	.240 BA	33 HR	117 RBI	15 SB
	NL	Todd Worrell, St. Louis	p	9–10	2.08 ERA	36 SV	
1987	AL	Mark McGwire, Oakland	1b	.289 BA	49 HR	118 RBI	1 SB
	NL	Benito Santiago, San Diego	c	.300 BA	18 HR	79 RBI	21 SB
1988	AL	Walt Weiss, Oakland	ss	.250 BA	3 HR	39 RBI	4 SB
	NL	Chris Sabo, Cincinnati	3b	.271 BA	11 HR	44 RBI	46 SB
1989	AL	Gregg Olson, Baltimore	p	5–2	1.69 ERA	27 SV	
	NL	Jerome Walton, Chicago	of	.293 BA	5 HR	46 RBI	24 SB

1990	AL	Sandy Alomar, Jr., Cleveland	c	.290 BA	9 HR	66 RBI	4 SB
	NL	Dave Justice, Atlanta	of	.282 BA	28 HR	78 RBI	11 SB
1991	AL	Chuck Knoblauch, Cleveland	2b	.281 BA	1 HR	50 RBI	25 SB
	NL	Jeff Bagwell, Houston	1b	.294 BA	15 HR	82 RBI	7 SB
1992	AL	Pat Listach, Milwaukee	ss	.290 BA	1 HR	47 RBI	54 SB
	NL	Eric Karros, Los Angeles	1b	.257 BA	20 HR	88 RBI	2 SB
1993	AL	Tim Salmon, California	of	.283 BA	31 HR	95 RBI	5 SB
	NL	Mike Piazza, Los Angeles	c	.318 BA	35 HR	112 RBI	3 SB

Gold Glove Award

Pitchers

Year	National League	American League
1957	(NO SELECTION)	Bobby Shantz, New York
1958	Harvey Haddix, Cincinnati	Bobby Shantz, New York
1959	Harvey Haddix, Pittsburgh	Bobby Shantz, New York
1960	Harvey Haddix, Pittsburgh	Bobby Shantz, New York
1961	Bobby Shantz, Pittsburgh	Frank Lary, Detroit
1962	Bobby Shantz, St. Louis	Jim Kaat, Minnesota
1963	Bobby Shantz, St. Louis	Jim Kaat, Minnesota
1964	Bobby Shantz, Philadelphia	Jim Kaat, Minnesota
1965	Bob Gibson, St. Louis	Jim Kaat, Minnesota
1966	Bob Gibson, St. Louis	Jim Kaat, Minnesota
1967	Bob Gibson, St. Louis	Jim Kaat, Minnesota
1968	Bob Gibson, St. Louis	Jim Kaat, Minnesota
1969	Bob Gibson, St. Louis	Jim Kaat, Minnesota
1970	Bob Gibson, St. Louis	Jim Kaat, Minnesota
1971	Bob Gibson, St. Louis	Jim Kaat, Minnesota
1972	Bob Gibson, St. Louis	Jim Kaat, Minnesota
1973	Bob Gibson, St. Louis	Jim Kaat, Minnesota
1974	Andy Messersmith, Los Angeles	Jim Kaat, Chicago
1975	Andy Messersmith, Los Angeles	Jim Kaat, Chicago
1976	Jim Kaat, Philadelphia	Jim Palmer, Baltimore
1977	Jim Kaat, Philadelphia	Jim Palmer, Baltimore
1978	Phil Niekro, Atlanta	Jim Palmer, Baltimore
1979	Phil Niekro, Atlanta	Jim Palmer, Baltimore
1980	Phil Niekro, Atlanta	Mike Norris, Oakland
1981	Steve Carlton, Philadelphia	Mike Norris, Oakland
1982	Phil Niekro, Atlanta	Ron Guidry, New York
1983	Phil Niekro, Atlanta	Ron Guidry, New York
1984	Joaquin Andujar, St. Louis	Ron Guidry, New York
1985	Rick Reuschel, Pittsburgh	Ron Guidry, New York
1986	Fernando Valenzuela, Los Angeles	Ron Guidry, New York
1987	Rick Reuschel, San Francisco	Mark Langston, Seattle
1988	Orel Hershiser, Los Angeles	Mark Langston, Seattle
1989	Ron Darling, New York	Bret Saberhagen, Kansas City
1990	Greg Maddux, Chicago	Mike Boddicker, Boston

1991	Greg Maddux, Chicago	Mark Langston, California
1992	Greg Maddux, Chicago	Mark Langston, California
1993	Greg Maddux, Chicago	Mark Langston, California

Catchers

Year	National League	American League
1957	(NO SELECTION)	Sherm Lollar, Chicago
1958	Del Crandall, Milwaukee	Sherm Lollar, Chicago
1959	Del Crandall, Milwaukee	Sherm Lollar, Chicago
1960	Del Crandall, Milwaukee	Earl Battey, Washington
1961	John Roseboro, Los Angeles	Earl Battey, Minnesota
1962	Del Crandall, Milwaukee	Earl Battey, Minnesota
1963	Johnny Edwards, Cincinnati	Elston Howard, New York
1964	Johnny Edwards, Cincinnati	Elston Howard, New York
1965	Joe Torre, Milwaukee	Bill Freehan, Detroit
1966	John Roseboro, Los Angeles	Bill Freehan, Detroit
1967	Randy Hundley, Chicago	Bill Freehan, Detroit
1968	Johnny Bench, Cincinnati	Bill Freehan, Detroit
1969	Johnny Bench, Cincinnati	Bill Freehan, Detroit
1970	Johnny Bench, Cincinnati	Ray Fosse, Cleveland
1971	Johnny Bench, Cincinnati	Ray Fosse, Cleveland
1972	Johnny Bench, Cincinnati	Carlton Fisk, Boston
1973	Johnny Bench, Cincinnati	Thurman Munson, New York
1974	Johnny Bench, Cincinnati	Thurman Munson, New York
1975	Johnny Bench, Cincinnati	Thurman Munson, New York
1976	Johnny Bench, Cincinnati	Jim Sundberg, Texas
1977	Johnny Bench, Cincinnati	Jim Sundberg, Texas
1978	Bob Boone, Philadelphia	Jim Sundberg, Texas
1979	Bob Boone, Philadelphia	Jim Sundberg, Texas
1980	Gary Carter, Montreal	Jim Sundberg, Texas
1981	Gary Carter, Montreal	Jim Sundberg, Texas
1982	Gary Carter, Montreal	Bob Boone, California
1983	Tony Pena, Pittsburgh	Lance Parrish, Detroit
1984	Tony Pena, Pittsburgh	Lance Parrish, Detroit
1985	Tony Pena, Pittsburgh	Lance Parrish, Detroit
1986	Jody Davis, Chicago	Bob Boone, California
1987	Mike LaValliere, Pittsburgh	Bob Boone, California
1988	Benito Santiago, San Diego	Bob Boone, California
1989	Benito Santiago, San Diego	Bob Boone, California
1990	Benito Santiago, San Diego	Sandy Alomar, Cleveland
1991	Tom Pagnozzi, St. Louis	Tony Pena, Boston
1992	Tom Pagnozzi, St. Louis	Ivan Rodriguez, Texas
1993	Kirt Manwaring, San Francisco	Ivan Rodriguez, Texas

First Baseman

Year	National League	American League
1957	Gil Hodges, Brooklyn	(NO SELECTION)
1958	Gil Hodges, Los Angeles	Vic Power, Cleveland
1959	Gil Hodges, Los Angeles	Vic Power, Cleveland
1960	Bill White, St. Louis	Vic Power, Cleveland
1961	Bill White, St. Louis	Vic Power, Cleveland
1962	Bill White, St. Louis	Vic Power, Minnesota
1963	Bill White, St. Louis	Vic Power, Minnesota
1964	Bill White, St. Louis	Vic Power, Los Angeles
1965	Bill White, St. Louis	Joe Pepitone, New York
1966	Bill White, Philadelphia	Joe Pepitone, New York
1967	Wes Parker, Los Angeles	George Scott, Boston
1968	Wes Parker, Los Angeles	George Scott, Boston
1969	Wes Parker, Los Angeles	Joe Pepitone, New York
1970	Wes Parker, Los Angeles	Jim Spencer, California
1971	Wes Parker, Los Angeles	George Scott, Boston
1972	Wes Parker, Los Angeles	George Scott, Milwaukee
1973	Mike Jorgenson, Montreal	George Scott, Milwaukee
1974	Steve Garvey, Los Angeles	George Scott, Milwaukee
1975	Steve Garvey, Los Angeles	George Scott, Milwaukee
1976	Steve Garvey, Los Angeles	George Scott, Milwaukee
1977	Steve Garvey, Los Angeles	Jim Spencer, Chicago
1978	Keith Hernandez, St. Louis	Chris Chambliss, New York
1979	Keith Hernandez, St. Louis	Cecil Cooper, Milwaukee
1980	Keith Hernandez, St. Louis	Cecil Cooper, Milwaukee
1981	Keith Hernandez, St. Louis	Mike Squires, Chicago
1982	Keith Hernandez, St. Louis	Eddie Murray, Baltimore
1983	Keith Hernandez, St. Louis–New York	Eddie Murray, Baltimore
1984	Keith Hernandez, New York	Eddie Murray, Baltimore
1985	Keith Hernandez, New York	Don Mattingly, New York
1986	Keith Hernandez, New York	Don Mattingly, New York
1987	Keith Hernandez, New York	Don Mattingly, New York
1988	Keith Hernandez, New York	Don Mattingly, New York
1989	Andres Galarraga, Montreal	Don Mattingly, New York
1990	Andres Galarraga, Montreal	Mark McGwire, Oakland
1991	Will Clark, San Francisco	Don Mattingly, New York
1992	Mark Grace, Chicago	Don Mattingly, New York
1993	Mark Grace, Chicago	Don Mattingly, New York

Second Basemen

Year	National League	American League
1957	(NO SELECTION)	Nellie Fox, Chicago
1958	Bill Mazeroski, Pittsburgh	Frank Bolling, Detroit
1959	Charlie Neal, Los Angeles	Nellie Fox, Chicago
1960	Bill Mazeroski, Pittsburgh	Nellie Fox, Chicago
1961	Bill Mazeroski, Pittsburgh	Bobby Richardson, New York

1962	Ken Hubbs, Chicago	Bobby Richardson, New York
1963	Bill Mazeroski, Pittsburgh	Bobby Richardson, New York
1964	Bill Mazeroski, Pittsburgh	Bobby Richardson, New York
1965	Bill Mazeroski, Pittsburgh	Bobby Richardson, New York
1966	Bill Mazeroski, Pittsburgh	Bobby Knoop, California
1967	Bill Mazeroski, Pittsburgh	Bobby Knoop, California
1968	Glenn Beckert, Chicago	Bobby Knoop, California
1969	Felix Millan, Atlanta	Dave Johnson, Baltimore
1970	Tommy Helms, Cincinnati	Dave Johnson, Baltimore
1971	Tommy Helms, Cincinnati	Dave Johnson, Baltimore
1972	Felix Millan, Atlanta	Doug Griffin, Boston
1973	Joe Morgan, Cincinnati	Bobby Grich, Baltimore
1974	Joe Morgan, Cincinnati	Bobby Grich, Baltimore
1975	Joe Morgan, Cincinnati	Bobby Grich, Baltimore
1976	Joe Morgan, Cincinnati	Bobby Grich, Baltimore
1977	Joe Morgan, Cincinnati	Frank White, Kansas City
1978	Davey Lopes, Los Angeles	Frank White, Kansas City
1979	Manny Trillo, Philadelphia	Frank White, Kansas City
1980	Doug Flynn, New York	Frank White, Kansas City
1981	Manny Trillo, Philadelphia	Frank White, Kansas City
1982	Manny Trillo, Philadelphia	Frank White, Kansas City
1983	Ryne Sandberg, Chicago	Lou Whitaker, Detroit
1984	Ryne Sandberg, Chicago	Lou Whitaker, Detroit
1985	Ryne Sandberg, Chicago	Lou Whitaker, Detroit
1986	Ryne Sandberg, Chicago	Frank White, Kansas City
1987	Ryne Sandberg, Chicago	Frank White, Kansas City
1988	Ryne Sandberg, Chicago	Harold Reynolds, Seattle
1989	Ryne Sandberg, Chicago	Harold Reynolds, Seattle
1990	Ryne Sandberg, Chicago	Harold Reynolds, Seattle
1991	Ryne Sandberg, Chicago	Roberto Alomar, Toronto
1992	Jose Lind, Pittsburgh	Roberto Alomar, Toronto
1993	Robby Thompson, San Francisco	Roberto Alomar, Toronto

Third Basemen

Year	National League	American League
1957	(NO SELECTION)	Frank Malzone, Boston
1958	Ken Boyer, St. Louis	Frank Malzone, Boston
1959	Ken Boyer, St. Louis	Frank Malzone, Boston
1960	Ken Boyer, St. Louis	Brooks Robinson, Baltimore
1961	Ken Boyer, St. Louis	Brooks Robinson, Baltimore
1962	Jim Davenport, San Francisco	Brooks Robinson, Baltimore
1963	Ken Boyer, St. Louis	Brooks Robinson, Baltimore
1964	Ron Santo, Chicago	Brooks Robinson, Baltimore
1965	Ron Santo, Chicago	Brooks Robinson, Baltimore
1966	Ron Santo, Chicago	Brooks Robinson, Baltimore
1967	Ron Santo, Chicago	Brooks Robinson, Baltimore
1968	Ron Santo, Chicago	Brooks Robinson, Baltimore

1969	Clete Boyer, Atlanta	Brooks Robinson, Baltimore
1970	Doug Rader, Houston	Brooks Robinson, Baltimore
1971	Doug Rader, Houston	Brooks Robinson, Baltimore
1972	Doug Rader, Houston	Brooks Robinson, Baltimore
1973	Doug Rader, Houston	Brooks Robinson, Baltimore
1974	Doug Rader, Houston	Brooks Robinson, Baltimore
1975	Ken Reitz, St. Louis	Brooks Robinson, Baltimore
1976	Mike Schmidt, Philadelphia	Aurelio Rodriguez, Detroit
1977	Mike Schmidt, Philadelphia	Graig Nettles, New York
1978	Mike Schmidt, Philadelphia	Graig Nettles, New York
1979	Mike Schmidt, Philadelphia	Buddy Bell, Texas
1980	Mike Schmidt, Philadelphia	Buddy Bell, Texas
1981	Mike Schmidt, Philadelphia	Buddy Bell, Texas
1982	Mike Schmidt, Philadelphia	Buddy Bell, Texas
1983	Mike Schmidt, Philadelphia	Buddy Bell, Texas
1984	Mike Schmidt, Philadelphia	Buddy Bell, Texas
1985	Tim Wallach, Montreal	George Brett, Kansas City
1986	Mike Schmidt, Philadelphia	Gary Gaetti, Minnesota
1987	Terry Pendleton, St. Louis	Gary Gaetti, Minnesota
1988	Tim Wallach, Montreal	Gary Gaetti, Minnesota
1989	Terry Pendleton, St. Louis	Gary Gaetti, Minnesota
1990	Tim Wallach, Montreal	Kelly Gruber, Toronto
1991	Matt Williams, San Francisco	Robin Ventura, Chicago
1992	Terry Pendleton, St. Louis	Robin Ventura, Chicago
1993	Matt Williams, San Francisco	Robin Ventura, Chicago

Shortstop

Year	National League	American League
1957	Roy McMillan, Cincinnati	(NO SELECTION)
1958	Roy McMillan, Cincinnati	Luis Aparicio, Chicago
1959	Roy McMillan, Cincinnati	Luis Aparicio, Chicago
1960	Ernie Banks, Chicago	Luis Aparicio, Chicago
1961	Maury Wills, Los Angeles	Luis Aparicio, Chicago
1962	Maury Wills, Los Angeles	Luis Aparicio, Chicago
1963	Bobby Wine, Philadelphia	Zoilo Versalles, Minnesota
1964	Ruben Amaro, Philadelphia	Luis Aparicio, Baltimore
1965	Leo Cardenas, Cincinnati	Zoilo Versalles, Minnesota
1966	Gene Alley, Pittsburgh	Luis Aparicio, Baltimore
1967	Gene Alley, Pittsburgh	Jim Fregosi, California
1968	Dal Maxvill, St. Louis	Luis Aparicio, Chicago
1969	Don Kessinger, Chicago	Mark Belanger, Baltimore
1970	Don Kessinger, Chicago	Luis Aparicio, Chicago
1971	Buddy Harrelson, New York	Mark Belanger, Baltimore
1972	Larry Bowa, Philadelphia	Eddie Brinkman, Detroit
1973	Roger Metzger, Houston	Mark Belanger, Baltimore
1974	Dave Concepcion, Cincinnati	Mark Belanger, Baltimore
1975	Dave Concepcion, Cincinnati	Mark Belanger, Baltimore

1976	Dave Concepcion, Cincinnati	Mark Belanger, Baltimore
1977	Dave Concepcion, Cincinnati	Mark Belanger, Baltimore
1978	Larry Bowa, Philadelphia	Mark Belanger, Baltimore
1979	Dave Concepcion, Cincinnati	Rick Burleson, Boston
1980	Ozzie Smith, San Diego	Alan Trammell, Detroit
1981	Ozzie Smith, San Diego	Alan Trammell, Detroit
1982	Ozzie Smith, St. Louis	Robin Yount, Milwaukee
1983	Ozzie Smith, St. Louis	Alan Trammell, Detroit
1984	Ozzie Smith, St. Louis	Alan Trammell, Detroit
1985	Ozzie Smith, St. Louis	Alfredo Griffin, Oakland
1986	Ozzie Smith, St. Louis	Tony Fernandez, Toronto
1987	Ozzie Smith, St. Louis	Tony Fernandez, Toronto
1988	Ozzie Smith, St. Louis	Tony Fernandez, Toronto
1989	Ozzie Smith, St. Louis	Tony Fernandez, Toronto
1990	Ozzie Smith, St. Louis	Ozzie Guillen, Chicago
1991	Ozzie Smith, St. Louis	Cal Ripken, Baltimore
1992	Ozzie Smith, St. Louis	Cal Ripken, Baltimore
1993	Jay Bell, Pittsburgh	Omar Vizquel, Seattle

National League Outfielders

1957	Willie Mays, New York	(NO OTHER SELECTIONS)	
1958	Frank Robinson, Cinc.	Willie Mays, San Fran.	Hank Aaron, Milwaukee
1959	J. Brandt, San Francisco	Willie Mays, San Fran.	Hank Aaron, Milwaukee
1960	Wally Moon, Los Angeles	Willie Mays, San Fran.	Hank Aaron, Milwaukee
1961	Willie Mays, San Fran.	Roberto Clemente, Pitt.	Vada Pinson, Cincinnati
1962	Willie Mays, San Fran.	Roberto Clemente, Pitt.	Bill Virdon, Pittsburgh
1963	Willie Mays, San Fran.	Roberto Clemente, Pitt.	Curt Flood, St. Louis
1964	Willie Mays, San Fran.	Roberto Clemente, Pitt.	Curt Flood, St. Louis
1965	Willie Mays, San Fran.	Roberto Clemente, Pitt.	Curt Flood, St. Louis
1966	Willie Mays, San Fran.	Curt Flood, St. Louis	Roberto Clemente, Pitt.
1967	Roberto Clemente, Pitt.	Curt Flood, St. Louis	Willie Mays, San Fran.
1968	Willie Mays, San Fran.	Roberto Clemente, Pitt.	Curt Flood, St. Louis
1969	Roberto Clemente, Pitt.	Curt Flood, St. Louis	Pete Rose, Cincinnati
1970	Roberto Clemente, Pitt.	Tommie Agee, NY	Pete Rose, Cincinnati
1971	Roberto Clemente, Pitt.	Bobby Bonds, San Fran.	Willie Davis, Los Angeles
1972	Roberto Clemente, Pitt.	Cesar Cedeno, Houston	Willie Davis, Los Angeles
1973	Bobby Bonds, San Fran.	Cesar Cedeno, Houston	Willie Davis, Los Angeles
1974	Cesar Cedeno, Houston	Cesar Geronimo, Cinc.	Bobby Bonds, San Fran.
1975	Cesar Cedeno, Houston	Cesar Geronimo, Cinc.	Garry Maddox, Phila.
1976	Cesar Cedeno, Houston	Cesar Geronimo, Cinc.	Garry Maddox, Phila.
1977	Cesar Geronimo, Cinc.	Garry Maddox, Phila.	Dave Parker, Pittsburgh
1978	Garry Maddox, Phila.	Dave Parker, Pittsburgh	E. Valentine, Montreal
1979	Garry Maddox, Phila.	Dave Parker, Pittsburgh	Dave Winfield, San Diego
1980	Andre Dawson, Montreal	Garry Maddox, Phila.	Dave Winfield, San Diego
1981	Andre Dawson, Montreal	Garry Maddox, Phila.	Dusty Baker, Los Angeles
1982	Andre Dawson, Montreal	Dale Murphy, Atlanta	Garry Maddox, Phila.
1983	Andre Dawson, Montreal	Dale Murphy, Atlanta	Willie McGee, St. Louis

1984	Dale Murphy, Atlanta	Bob Dernier, Chicago	Andre Dawson, Montreal
1985	Willie McGee, St. Louis	Dale Murphy, Atlanta	Andre Dawson, Montreal
1986	Tony Gwynn, San Diego	Dale Murphy, Atlanta	Willie McGee, St. Louis
1987	Eric Davis, Cincinnati	Tony Gwynn, San Diego	Andre Dawson, Chicago
1988	Andy Van Slyke, Pitt.	Eric Davis, Cincinnati	Andre Dawson, Chicago
1989	Andy Van Slyke, Pitt.	Eric Davis, Cincinnati	Tony Gwynn, San Diego
1990	Andy Van Slyke, Pitt.	Tony Gwynn, San Diego	Barry Bonds, Pittsburgh
1991	Barry Bonds, Pittsburgh	Tony Gwynn, San Diego	Andy Van Slyke, Pitt.
1992	Barry Bonds, SF	Marquis Grissom, Mont.	Larry Walker, Montreal

American League Outfielders

1957	Minnie Minoso, Chicago	Al Kaline, Detroit (RF)	(NO OTHER SELECTION)
1958	Norm Siebern, NY	Jim Piersall, Boston	Al Kaline, Detroit
1959	Minnie Minoso, Cleveland	Al Kaline, Detroit	Jackie Jensen, Boston
1960	Minnie Minoso, Chicago	Jim Landis, Chicago	Roger Maris, New York
1961	Al Kaline, Detroit	Jim Piersall, Cleveland	Jim Landis, Chicago
1962	Jim Landis, Chicago	Mickey Mantle, NY	Al Kaline, Detroit
1963	Al Kaline, Detroit	Carl Yastrzemski, Bost.	Jim Landis, Chicago
1964	Al Kaline, Detroit	Jim Landis, Chicago	Vic Davalillo, Cleveland
1965	Al Kaline, Detroit	Tom Tresh, New York	Carl Yastrzemski, Boston
1966	Al Kaline, Detroit	Tommie Agee, Chicago	Tony Oliva, Minnesota
1967	Carl Yastrzemski, Bost.	Paul Blair, Baltimore	Al Kaline, Detroit
1968	Mickey Stanley, Detroit	Carl Yastrzemski, Bost.	Reggie Smith, Boston
1969	Paul Blair, Baltimore	Mickey Stanley, Detroit	Carl Yastrzemski, Boston
1970	Mickey Stanley, Detroit	Paul Blair, Baltimore	Ken Berry, Chicago
1971	Paul Blair, Baltimore	Amos Otis, Kansas City	Carl Yastrzemski, Boston
1972	Paul Blair, Baltimore	Bobby Murcer, NY	Ken Berry, California
1973	Paul Blair, Baltimore	Amos Otis, Kansas City	Mickey Stanley, Detroit
1974	Paul Blair, Baltimore	Amos Otis, Kansas City	Joe Rudi, Oakland
1975	Paul Blair, Baltimore	Joe Rudi, Oakland	Fred Lynn, Boston
1976	Joe Rudi, Oakland	Dwight Evans, Boston	Rick Manning, Cleveland
1977	J. Beniquez, Texas	Carl Yastrzemski, Boston	Al Cowens, Kansas City
1978	Fred Lynn, Boston	Dwight Evans, Boston	Rick Miller, California
1979	Dwight Evans, Boston	Sixto Lezcano, Milw.	Fred Lynn, Boston
1980	Fred Lynn, Boston	Dwayne Murphy, Oak.	Willie Wilson, Kansas C.
1981	Dwayne Murphy, Oak.	Dwight Evans, Boston	Rickey Henderson, Oak.
1982	Dwight Evans, Boston	Dave Winfield, NY	Dwayne Murphy, Oak.
1983	Dwight Evans, Boston	Dave Winfield, NY	Dwayne Murphy, Oak.
1984	Dwight Evans, Boston	Dave Winfield, NY	Dwayne Murphy, Oak.
1985	Gary Pettis, California	Dave Winfield, NY	Dwight Evans, Boston & Dwayne Murphy, Oak.
1986	Gary Pettis, California	Jesse Barfield, Toronto	Kirby Puckett, Minnesota
1987	Jesse Barfield, Toronto	Kirby Puckett, Minn.	Dave Winfield, New York
1988	Kirby Puckett, Minn.	Devon White, California	Gary Pettis, Detroit
1989	Devon White, California	Gary Pettis, Detroit	Kirby Puckett, Minnesota
1990	Gary Pettis, Texas	Ken Griffey Jr., Seattle	Ellis Burks, Boston
1991	Ken Griffey Jr., Seattle	Devon White, Toronto	Kirby Puckett, Minnesota

1992	Ken Griffey Jr., Seattle	Devon White, Toronto	Kirby Puckett, Minnesota
1993	Ken Griffey Jr., Seattle	Devon White, Toronto	Kenny Lofton, Cleveland

World Series Winners

Year	AL Champion	NL Champion	World Series Champion		
1903	Boston Red Sox	Pittsburgh Pirates	Boston Red Sox	5	3
1905	Philadelphia Athletics	New York Giants	New York Giants	4	1
1906	Chicago White Sox	Chicago Cubs	Chicago White Sox	4	2
1907	Detroit Tigers	Chicago Cubs	Chicago Cubs	4	0–1
1908	Detroit Tigers	Chicago Cubs	Chicago Cubs	4	1
1909	Detroit Tigers	Pittsburgh Pirates	Pittsburgh Pirates	4	3
1910	Philadelphia Athletics	Chicago Cubs	Philadelphia Athletics	4	1
1911	Philadelphia Athletics	New York Giants	Philadelphia Athletics	4	2
1912	Boston Red Sox	New York Giants	Boston Red Sox	4	3–1
1913	Philadelphia Athletics	New York Giants	Philadelphia Athletics	4	1
1914	Philadelphia Athletics	Boston Braves	Boston Braves	4	0
1915	Boston Red Sox	Philadelphia Phillies	Boston Red Sox	4	1
1916	Boston Red Sox	Brooklyn Dodgers	Boston Red Sox	4	1
1917	Chicago White Sox	New York Giants	Chicago White Sox	4	2
1918	Boston Red Sox	Chicago Cubs	Boston Red Sox	4	2
1919	Chicago White Sox	Cincinnati Reds	Cincinnati Reds	5	3
1920	Cleveland Indians	Brooklyn Dodgers	Cleveland Indians	5	2
1921	New York Yankees	New York Giants	New York Yankees	5	3
1922	New York Yankees	New York Giants	New York Yankees	4	0–1
1923	New York Yankees	New York Giants	New York Yankees	4	2
1924	Washington Senators	New York Giants	Washington Senators	4	2
1925	Washington Senators	Pittsburgh Pirates	Pittsburgh Pirates	4	3
1926	New York Yankees	St. Louis Cardinals	St. Louis Cardinals	4	3
1927	New York Yankees	Pittsburgh Pirates	New York Yankees	4	0
1928	New York Yankees	St. Louis Cardinals	New York Yankees	4	0
1929	Philadelphia Athletics	Chicago Cubs	Philadelphia Athletics	4	2
1930	Philadelphia Athletics	St. Louis Cardinals	Philadelphia Athletics	4	2
1931	Philadelphia Athletics	St. Louis Cardinals	St. Louis Cardinals	4	3
1932	New York Yankees	Chicago Cubs	New York Yankees	4	0
1933	Washington Senators	New York Giants	New York Giants	4	1
1934	Detroit Tigers	St. Louis Cardinals	St. Louis Cardinals	4	3
1935	Detroit Tigers	Chicago Cubs	Detroit Tigers	4	2
1936	New York Yankees	New York Giants	New York Yankees	4	2
1937	New York Yankees	New York Giants	New York Yankees	4	1
1938	New York Yankees	Chicago Cubs	New York Yankees	4	0
1939	New York Yankees	Cincinnati Reds	New York Yankees	4	0
1940	Detroit Tigers	Cincinnati Reds	Cincinnati Reds	4	3
1941	New York Yankees	Brooklyn Dodgers	New York Yankees	4	1
1942	New York Yankees	St. Louis Cardinals	St. Louis Cardinals	4	1
1943	New York Yankees	St. Louis Cardinals	New York Yankees	4	1
1944	St. Louis Browns	St. Louis Cardinals	St. Louis Cardinals	4	2

Year	AL Champion	NL Champion	World Series Champion		
1945	Detroit Tigers	Chicago Cubs	Detroit Tigers	4	3
1946	Boston Red Sox	St. Louis Cardinals	St. Louis Cardinals	4	3
1947	New York Yankees	Chicago Cubs	New York Yankees	4	3
1948	Cleveland Indians	Boston Braves	Cleveland Indians	4	2
1949	New York Yankees	Brooklyn Dodgers	New York Yankees	4	1
1950	New York Yankees	Philadelphia Phillies	New York Yankees	4	0
1951	New York Yankees	New York Giants	New York Yankees	4	2
1952	New York Yankees	Brooklyn Dodgers	New York Yankees	4	3
1953	New York Yankees	Brooklyn Dodgers	New York Yankees	4	2
1954	Cleveland Indians	New York Giants	New York Giants	4	0
1955	New York Yankees	Brooklyn Dodgers	Brooklyn Dodgers	4	3
1956	New York Yankees	Brooklyn Dodgers	New York Yankees	4	3
1957	New York Yankees	Milwaukee Braves	Milwaukee Braves	4	3
1958	New York Yankees	Milwaukee Braves	New York Yankees	4	3
1959	Chicago White Sox	Los Angeles Dodgers	Los Angeles Dodgers	4	2
1960	New York Yankees	Pittsburgh Pirates	Pittsburgh Pirates	4	3
1961	New York Yankees	Cincinnati Reds	New York Yankees	4	1
1962	New York Yankees	San Francisco Giants	New York Yankees	4	3
1963	New York Yankees	Los Angeles Dodgers	Los Angeles Dodgers	4	2
1964	New York Yankees	St. Louis Cardinals	St. Louis Cardinals	4	3
1965	Minnesota Twins	Los Angeles Dodgers	Los Angeles Dodgers	4	3
1966	Baltimore Orioles	Los Angeles Dodgers	Baltimore Orioles	4	0
1967	Boston Red Sox	St. Louis Cardinals	St. Louis Cardinals	4	3
1968	Detroit Tigers	St. Louis Cardinals	Detroit Tigers	4	3
1969	Baltimore Orioles	New York Mets	New York Mets	4	1
1970	Baltimore Orioles	Cincinnati Reds	Baltimore Orioles	4	1
1971	Baltimore Orioles	Pittsburgh Pirates	Pittsburgh Pirates	4	3
1972	Oakland A's	Cincinnati Reds	Oakland A's	4	3
1973	Oakland A's	New York Mets	Oakland A's	4	3
1974	Oakland A's	Los Angeles Dodgers	Oakland A's	4	1
1975	Boston Red Sox	Cincinnati Reds	Cincinnati Reds	4	3
1976	New York Yankees	Cincinnati Reds	Cincinnati Reds	4	0
1977	New York Yankees	Los Angeles Dodgers	New York Yankees	4	2
1978	New York Yankees	Los Angeles Dodgers	New York Yankees	4	2
1979	Baltimore Orioles	Pittsburgh Pirates	Pittsburgh Pirates	4	3
1980	Kansas City Royals	Philadelphia Phillies	Philadelphia Phillies	4	2
1981	New York Yankees	Los Angeles Dodgers	Los Angeles Dodgers	4	2
1982	Milwaukee Brewers	St. Louis Cardinals	St. Louis Cardinals	4	3
1983	Baltimore Orioles	Philadelphia Phillies	Baltimore Orioles	4	1
1984	Detroit Tigers	San Diego Padres	Detroit Tigers	4	1
1985	Kansas City Royals	St. Louis Cardinals	Kansas City Royals	4	3
1986	Boston Red Sox	New York Mets	New York Mets	4	3
1987	Minnesota Twins	St. Louis Cardinals	Minnesota Twins	4	3
1988	Oakland A's	Los Angeles Dodgers	Los Angeles Dodgers	4	1
1989	Oakland A's	San Francisco Giants	Oakland A's	4	0
1990	Oakland A's	Cincinnati Reds	Cincinnati Reds	4	0
1991	Minnesota Twins	Atlanta Braves	Minnesota Twins	4	3

Year	AL Champion	NL Champion	World Series Champion		
1992	Toronto Blue Jays	Atlanta Braves	Toronto Blue Jays	4	2
1993	Toronto Blue Jays	Philadelphia Phillies	Toronto Blue Jays	4	2

Major League Records

Lifetime

Games

1	Pete Rose	3562
2	Carl Yastrzemski	3308
3	Hank Aaron	3298

At Bats

1	Pete Rose	14053
2	Hank Aaron	12364
3	Carl Yastrzemski	11988

Runs

1	Ty Cobb	2245
2	Hank Aaron	2174
	Babe Ruth	2174
4	Pete Rose	2165
5	Willie Mays	2062
6	Stan Musial	1949
7	Lou Gehrig	1888
8	Tris Speaker	1882
9	Mel Ott	1859
10	Frank Robinson	1829

Hits

1	Pete Rose	4256
2	Ty Cobb	4190
3	Hank Aaron	3771
4	Stan Musial	3630
5	Tris Speaker	3514
6	Carl Yastrzemski	3419
7	Honus Wagner	3415
8	Eddie Collins	3310
9	Willie Mays	3283
10	Nap Lajoie	3242

Doubles

1	Tris Speaker	792
2	Pete Rose	746
3	Stan Musial	725

Triples

1	Sam Crawford	309
2	Ty Cobb	295
3	Honus Wagner	252

Home Runs

1	Hank Aaron	755
2	Babe Ruth	714
3	Willie Mays	660
4	Frank Robinson	586
5	Harmon Killebrew	573
6	Reggie Jackson	563
7	Mike Schmidt	548
8	Mickey Mantle	536
9	Jimmie Foxx	534
10	Willie McCovey	521
	Ted Williams	521

Total Bases

1	Hank Aaron	6856
2	Stan Musial	6134
3	Willie Mays	6066
4	Ty Cobb	5855
5	Babe Ruth	5793
6	Pete Rose	5752
7	Carl Yastrzemski	5539
8	Frank Robinson	5373
9	Tris Speaker	5101
10	Lou Gehrig	5060

Runs Batted In

1	Hank Aaron	2297
2	Babe Ruth	2213
3	Lou Gehrig	1995
4	Stan Musial	1951
5	Ty Cobb	1937
6	Jimmie Foxx	1922
7	Willie Mays	1903
8	Cap Anson	1879
9	Mel Ott	1860
10	Carl Yastrzemski	1844

Walks

1	Babe Ruth	2056
2	Ted Williams	2019
3	Joe Morgan	1865
4	Carl Yastrzemski	1845
5	Mickey Mantle	1733
6	Mel Ott	1708
7	Eddie Yost	1614
8	Darrell Evans	1605
9	Stan Musial	1599
10	Pete Rose	1566

Strikeouts

1	Reggie Jackson	2597
2	Willie Stargell	1936
3	Mike Schmidt	1883
4	Tony Perez	1867
5	Dave Kingman	1816
6	Bobby Bonds	1757
7	Dale Murphy	1748
8	Lou Brock	1730
9	Mickey Mantle	1710
10	Harmon Killebrew	1699

Batting Average

1	Ty Cobb	.366
2	Rogers Hornsby	.358
3	Joe Jackson	.356
4	Ed Delahanty	.346
5	Tris Speaker	.345
6	Ted Williams	.344
7	Billy Hamilton	.344
8	Willie Keeler	.343
9	Dan Brouthers	.342
10	Babe Ruth	.342

Batting Average (BY POSITION)

First Base

1	Dan Brouthers	.342
2	Bill Terry	.341
3	George Sisler	.340
4	Lou Gehrig	.340
5	Cap Anson	.329

Second Base

1	Rogers Hornsby	.358
2	Nap Lajoie	.338
3	Eddie Collins	.333
4	Charlie Gehringer	.320
5	Frankie Frisch	.316

Shortstop

1	Honus Wagner	.327
2	Arky Vaughan	.318
3	Joe Sewell	.312
4	Luke Appling	.310
5	Ed McKean	.302

Third Base

1	Wade Boggs	.335
2	Pie Traynor	.320
3	Denny Lyons	.310
4	George Brett	.308
5	Frank Baker	.307

Outfield

1	Ty Cobb	.366
2	Joe Jackson	.356
3	Ed Delahanty	.346
4	Tris Speaker	.345
5	Ted Williams	.344

Catcher

1	Mickey Cochrane	.320
2	Bill Dickey	.313
3	Spud Davis	.308
4	Ernie Lombardi	.306
5	Gabby Hartnett	.297

Slugging Average

1	Babe Ruth	.690
2	Ted Williams	.634
3	Lou Gehrig	.632
4	Jimmie Foxx	.609
5	Hank Greenberg	.605
6	Joe DiMaggio	.579
7	Rogers Hornsby	.577
8	Johnny Mize	.562
9	Stan Musial	.559
10	Willie Mays	.557

Stolen Bases

1	Rickey Henderson	1095
2	Lou Brock	938
3	Billy Hamilton	912
4	Ty Cobb	891
5	Tim Raines	751
6	Eddie Collins	744
7	Arlie Latham	739
8	Max Carey	738
9	Honus Wagner	722
10	Joe Morgan	689

Wins

1	Cy Young	511
2	Walter Johnson	417
3	Pete Alexander	373
	Christy Mathewson	373
5	Warren Spahn	363
6	Kid Nichols	361
7	Jim Galvin	360
8	Tim Keefe	342
9	Steve Carlton	329
10	John Clarkson	328

Losses

1	Cy Young	316
2	Jim Galvin	308
3	Nolan Ryan	292
4	Walter Johnson	279
5	Phil Niekro	274
6	Gaylord Perry	265
7	Don Sutton	256
8	Jack Powell	254
9	Eppa Rixey	251
10	Bert Blyleven	250

Games

1	Hoyt Wilhelm	1070
2	Kent Tekulve	1050
3	Lindy McDaniel	987
4	Rich Gossage	966
5	Rollie Fingers	944
6	Gene Garber	931
7	Cy Young	906
8	Sparky Lyle	899
9	Jim Kaat	898
10	Don McMahon	874

Games Started

1	Cy Young	815
2	Nolan Ryan	773
3	Don Sutton	756
4	Phil Niekro	716
5	Steve Carlton	709
6	Tommy John	700
7	Gaylord Perry	690
8	Bert Blyleven	685
9	Jim Galvin	682
10	Walter Johnson	665
	Warren Spahn	665

Shutouts

1	Walter Johnson	110
2	Pete Alexander	90
3	Christy Mathewson	79
4	Cy Young	76
5	Eddie Plank	69
6	Warren Spahn	63
7	Nolan Ryan	61
	Tom Seaver	61
9	Bert Blyleven	60
10	Don Sutton	58

Saves

1	Lee Smith	401
2	Jeff Reardon	365
3	Rollie Fingers	341
4	Rich Gossage	309
5	Bruce Sutter	300
6	Dennis Eckersley	275
7	Tom Henke	260
8	Dave Righetti	252
9	Dan Quisenberry	244
10	Sparky Lyle	238

Innings Pitched

1	Cy Young	7354.2
2	Jim Galvin	5941.1
3	Walter Johnson	5923.2
4	Phil Niekro	5404.1
5	Nolan Ryan	5387.0
6	Gaylord Perry	5350.1
7	Don Sutton	5282.1
8	Warren Spahn	5243.2
9	Steve Carlton	5217.1
10	Pete Alexander	5189.1

Strikeouts

1	Nolan Ryan	5714
2	Steve Carlton	4136
3	Bert Blyleven	3701
4	Tom Seaver	3640
5	Don Sutton	3574
6	Gaylord Perry	3534
7	Walter Johnson	3509
8	Phil Niekro	3342
9	Fergie Jenkins	3192
10	Bob Gibson	3117

Earned Run Average

1	Ed Walsh	1.82
2	Addie Joss	1.89
3	Mordecai Brown	2.06
4	Monte Ward	2.10
5	Christy Mathewson	2.13
6	Rube Waddell	2.16
7	Walter Johnson	2.17
8	Orval Overall	2.23
9	Tommy Bond	2.25
10	Ed Reulbach	2.28
	Will White	2.28

Single season

At Bats

1	Willie Wilson	1980	705
2	Juan Samuel	1984	701
3	Dave Cash	1975	699

Runs

1	Billy Hamilton	1894	192
2	Tom Brown	1891	177
	Babe Ruth	1921	177

Hits

1	George Sisler	1920	257
2	Lefty O'Doul	1929	254
	Bill Terry	1930	254

Doubles

1	Earl Webb	1931	67
2	George Burns	1926	64
	Joe Medwick	1936	64

Triples

1	Chief Wilson	1912	36
2	Dave Orr	1886	31
	Heinie Reitz	1894	31

Home Runs

1	Roger Maris	1961	61
2	Babe Ruth	1927	60
3	Babe Ruth	1921	59
4	Jimmie Foxx	1932	58
	Hank Greenberg	1938	58
6	Hack Wilson	1930	56
7	Babe Ruth	1920	54
	Babe Ruth	1928	54
	Ralph Kiner	1949	54
	Mickey Mantle	1961	54

Total Bases

1	Babe Ruth	1921	457
2	Rogers Hornsby	1922	450
3	Lou Gehrig	1927	447

Runs Batted In

1	Hack Wilson	1930	190
2	Lou Gehrig	1931	184
3	Hank Greenberg	1937	183

Walks

1	Babe Ruth	1923	170
2	Ted Williams	1947	162
	Ted Williams	1949	162

Strikeouts

1	Bobby Bonds	1970	189
2	Bobby Bonds	1969	187
3	Rob Deer	1987	186

Batting Average

1	Hugh Duffy	1894	.440
2	Tip O'Neill	1887	.435
3	Ross Barnes	1876	.429
4	Nap Lajoie	1901	.426
5	Willie Keeler	1897	.424
6	Rogers Hornsby	1924	.424
7	George Sisler	1922	.420
8	Ty Cobb	1911	.420
9	Fred Dunlap	1884	.412
10	Ty Cobb	1912	.410

Slugging Average

1	Babe Ruth	1920	.847
2	Babe Ruth	1921	.846
3	Babe Ruth	1927	.772
4	Lou Gehrig	1927	.765
5	Babe Ruth	1923	.764
6	Rogers Hornsby	1925	.756
7	Jimmie Foxx	1932	.749
8	Babe Ruth	1924	.739
9	Babe Ruth	1926	.737
10	Ted Williams	1941	.735

Pinch Hits

1	Jose Morales	1976	25
2	Dave Philley	1961	24
	Vic Davalillo	1970	24
	Rusty Staub	1983	24

Stolen Bases

1	Hugh Nicol	1887	138
2	Rickey Henderson	1982	130
3	Arlie Latham	1887	129
4	Lou Brock	1974	118
5	Charlie Comiskey	1887	117
6	Monte Ward	1887	111
	Billy Hamilton	1889	111
	Billy Hamilton	1891	111
9	Vince Coleman	1985	110

Year–by–Year Statistical Leaders

Year	NL Batting Avg. leaders Player, Team	BA	AL Batting Avg. leaders Player, Team	BA
1876	Ross Barnes, Chicago	.429	none	
1877	James "Deacon" White, Boston	.387	none	
1878	Paul Hines, Providence	.358	none	
1879	Paul Hines, Providence	.357	none	
1880	George Gore, Chicago	.360	none	
1881	Adrian "Cap" Anson, Chicago	.399	none	
1882	"Big Dan" Brouthers, Buffalo	.368	none	
1883	"Big Dan" Brouthers, Buffalo	.374	none	
1884	Mike "King" Kelly, Chicago	.354	none	
1885	Roger Connor, N.Y. Giants	.371	none	
1886	Mike "King" Kelly, Chicago	.388	none	
1887	Sam Thompson, Detroit	.372	none	
1888	Adrian "Cap" Anson, Chicago	.344	none	
1889	"Big Dan" Brouthers, Boston	.373	none	
1890	Jack Glasscock, NY Giants	.336	none	
1891	Billy Hamilton, Philadelphia	.340	none	
1892	"Big Dan" Brouthers, Brooklyn	.335	none	
1893	Billy Hamilton, Philadelphia	.380	none	
1894	Hugh Duffy, Boston	.440	none	
1895	Jesse Burkett, Cleveland	.409	none	
1896	Jesse Burkett, Cleveland	.410	none	
1897	"Wee Willie" Keeler, Baltimore	.424	none	
1898	"Wee Willie" Keeler, Baltimore	.385	none	
1899	Big Ed" Delahanty, Phila.	.410	none	
1900	"Honus" Wagner, Pittsburgh	.381	none	
1901	Jesse Burkett, St. Louis	.376	Napoleon Lajoie, Philadelphia	.422
1902	Ginger Beaumont, Pittsburgh	.357	Ed Delahanty, Washington	.376
1903	"Honus" Wagner, Pittsburgh	.355	Napoleon Lajoie, Cleveland	.355
1904	"Honus" Wagner, Pittsburgh	.349	Napoleon Lajoie, Cleveland	.381
1905	Cy Seymour, Cincinnati	.377	Elmer Flick, Cleveland	.306
1906	"Honus" Wagner, Pittsburgh	.339	George Stone, St. Louis	.358
1907	"Honus" Wagner, Pittsburgh	.350	Ty Cobb, Detroit	.350
1908	"Honus" Wagner, Pittsburgh	.354	Ty Cobb, Detroit	.324
1909	"Honus" Wagner, Pittsburgh	.339	Ty Cobb, Detroit	.377
1910	Sherry Magee, Philadelphia	.331	Ty Cobb, Detroit	.385
1911	"Honus" Wagner, Pittsburgh	.334	Ty Cobb, Detroit	.420
1912	Heinie Zimmerman, Chicago	.372	Ty Cobb, Detroit	.410
1913	Jake Daubert, Brooklyn	.350	Ty Cobb, Detroit	.390
1914	Jake Daubert, Brooklyn	.329	Ty Cobb, Detroit	.368
1915	Larry Doyle, N. Y. Giants	.320	Ty Cobb, Detroit	.369
1916	Hal Chase, Cincinnati	.339	Tris Speaker, Cleveland	.386
1917	Edd Roush, Cincinnati	.341	Ty Cobb, Detroit	.383
1918	Zack Wheat, Brooklyn	.335	Ty Cobb, Detroit	.382

Year	NL Batting Avg. leaders Player, Team	BA	AL Batting Avg. leaders Player, Team	BA
1919	Edd Roush, Cincinnati	.321	Ty Cobb, Detroit	.384
1920	Rogers Hornsby, St. Louis	.370	George Sisler, St. Louis	.407
1921	Rogers Hornsby, St. Louis	.397	Harry Heilmann, Detroit	.394
1922	Rogers Hornsby, St. Louis	.401	George Sisler, St. Louis	.420
1923	Rogers Hornsby, St. Louis	.384	Harry Heilmann, Detroit	.403
1924	Rogers Hornsby, St. Louis	.424	Babe Ruth, New York	.378
1925	Rogers Hornsby, St. Louis	.403	Harry Heilmann, Detroit	.393
1926	Paul "Big Poison" Waner, Pitts.	.336	Heinie Manush, Detroit	.378
1927	Paul "Big Poison" Waner, Pitts.	.380	Harry Heilmann, Detroit	.398
1928	Rogers Hornsby, St. Louis	.387	Goose Goslin, Washington	.379
1929	"Lefty" O'Doul, Philadelphia	.398	Lew Fonseca, Cleveland	.369
1930	Bill Terry, N. Y. Giants	.401	Al Simmons, Philadelphia	.381
1931	Chick Hafey, St. Louis	.349	Al Simmons, Philadelphia	.390
1932	"Lefty" O'Doul, Brooklyn	.368	Dale Alexander, Boston–Detroit	.367
1933	Chuck Klein, Philadelphia	.368	Jimmy Foxx, Philadelphia	.356
1934	Paul "Big Poison" Waner, Pitts.	.362	Lou Gehrig, New York	.363
1935	Floyd "Arky" Vaughan, Pitts.	.385	Buddy Myer, Washington	.349
1936	Paul "Big Poison" Waner, Pitts.	.373	Luke Appling, Chicago	.388
1937	Joe "Ducky" Medwick, St. Louis	.374	Charlie Gehringer, Detroit	.371
1938	Ernie Lombardi, Cincinnati	.342	Jimmie Foxx, Boston	.349
1939	Johnny Mize, St. Louis	.349	Joe DiMaggio, New York	.381
1940	Stan Hack, Chicago	.317	Joe DiMaggio, New York	.352
1941	Pete Reiser, Brooklyn	.343	Ted Williams, Boston	.406
1942	Enos "Country" Slaughter, St. L.	.318	Ted Williams, Boston	.356
1943	Stan Musial, St. Louis	.357	Luke Appling, Chicago	.328
1944	Fred "Dixie" Walker, Brooklyn	.357	Lou Boudreau, Cleveland	.327
1945	Phil Cavarretta, Chicago	.355	Snuffy Stirnweiss, New York	.309
1946	Stan Musial, St. Louis	.365	Mickey Vernon, Washington	.353
1947	Harry Walker, St. L.–Phila.	.363	Ted Williams, Boston	.343
1948	Stan Musial, St. Louis	.376	Ted Williams, Boston	.369
1949	Jackie Robinson, Brooklyn	.342	Ted Williams, Boston	.343
			George Kell, Detroit	.343
1950	Stan Musial, St. Louis	.346	Billy Goodman, Boston	.354
1951	Stan Musial, St. Louis	.355	Ferris Fain, Philadelphia	.344
1952	Stan Musial, St. Louis	.336	Ferris Fain, Philadelphia	.327
1953	Carl Furillo, Brooklyn	.344	Mickey Vernon, Washington	.337
1954	Willie Mays, N. Y. Giants	.345	Bobby Avila, Cleveland	.341
1955	Richie Ashburn, Philadelphia	.338	Al Kaline, Detroit	.340
1956	Hank Aaron, Milwaukee	.328	Mickey Mantle, New York	.353
1957	Stan Musial, St. Louis	.351	Ted Williams, Boston	.388
1958	Richie Ashburn, Philadelphia	.350	Ted Williams, Boston	.328
1959	Hank Aaron, Milwaukee	.355	Harvey Kuenn, Detroit	.353
1960	Dick Groat, Pittsburgh	.325	Pete Runnels, Boston	.320
1961	Roberto Clemente, Pittsburgh	.351	Norm Cash, Detroit	.361
1962	Tommy Davis, Los Angeles	.346	Pete Runnels, Boston	.326

NL Batting Avg. leaders / AL Batting Avg. leaders

Year	Player, Team	BA	Player, Team	BA
1963	Tommy Davis, Los Angeles	.326	Carl Yastrzemski, Boston	.321
1964	Roberto Clemente, Pittsburgh	.339	Tony Oliva, Minnesota	.323
1965	Roberto Clemente, Pittsburgh	.329	Tony Oliva, Minnesota	.321
1966	Matty Alou, Pittsburgh	.342	Frank Robinson, Baltimore	.316
1967	Roberto Clemente, Pittsburgh	.357	Carl Yastrzemski, Boston	.326
1968	Pete Rose, Cincinnati	.335	Carl Yastrzemski, Boston	.301
1969	Pete Rose, Cincinnati	.348	Rod Carew, Minnesota	.332
1970	Rico Carty, Atlanta	.366	Alex Johnson, California	.329
1971	Joe Torre, St. Louis	.363	Tony Oliva, Minnesota	.337
1972	Billy Williams, Chicago	.333	Rod Carew, Minnesota	.318
1973	Pete Rose, Cincinnati	.338	Rod Carew, Minnesota	.350
1974	Ralph Garr, Atlanta	.353	Rod Carew, Minnesota	.364
1975	Bill Madlock, Chicago	.354	Rod Carew, Minnesota	.359
1976	Bill Madlock, Chicago	.339	George Brett, Kansas City	.333
1977	Dave Parker, Pittsburgh	.338	Rod Carew, Minnesota	.388
1978	Dave Parker, Pittsburgh	.334	Rod Carew, Minnesota	.333
1979	Keith Hernandez, St. Louis	.344	Fred Lynn, Boston	.333
1980	Bill Buckner, Chicago	.324	George Brett, Kansas City	.390
1981	Pete Rose, Philadelphia	.325	Carney Lansford, Boston	.326
			Tom Paciorek, Seattle	.326
1982	Al Oliver, Montreal	.331	Willie Wilson, Kansas City	.332
1983	Bill Madlock, Philadelphia	.323	Wade Boggs, Boston	.361
1984	Tony Gwynn, San Diego	.351	Don Mattingly, New York	.343
1985	Willie McGee, St. Louis	.353	Wade Boggs, Boston	.368
1986	Tim Raines, Montreal	.334	Wade Boggs, Boston	.357
1987	Tony Gwynn, San Diego	.370	Wade Boggs, Boston	.363
1988	Tony Gwynn, San Diego	.313	Wade Boggs, Boston	.366
1989	Tony Gwynn, San Diego	.336	Kirby Puckett, Minnesota	.339
1990	Willie McGee, St. Louis	.335	George Brett, Kansas City	.329
1991	Terry Pendleton, Atlanta	.319	Julio Franco, Texas	.341
1992	Gary Sheffield, San Diego	.330	Edgar Martinez, Seattle	.343
1993	Andres Galarraga, Colorado	.370	John Olerud, Toronto	.363

NL Home Run leaders / AL Home Run leaders

Year	Player, Team	HRs	Player, Team	HRs
1876	George Hall, Philadelphia	5	none	
1877	Lip Pike, Cincinnati	4	none	
1878	Paul Hines, Providence	4	none	
1879	Charley Jones, Boston	9	none	
1880	Jim O'Rourke, Boston	6	none	
	Harry Stovey, Worcester	6		
1881	"Big Dan" Brouthers, Buffalo	8	none	
1882	George Wood, Detroit	7	none	
1883	"Buck" Ewing, N. Y. Giants	10	none	
1884	Ned Williamson, Chicago	27	none	

Year	NL Home Run leaders Player, Team	HRs	AL Home Run leaders Player, Team	HRs
1885	Abner Dalrymple, Chicago	11	none	
1886	"Big Dan" Brouthers, Detroit	11	none	
	Hardy Richardson, Detroit	11		
1887	Billy O'Brien, Washington	19	none	
1888	Jimmy Ryan, Chicago	16	none	
1889	Sam Thompson, Philadelphia	20	none	
1890	"Oyster" Burns, Brooklyn	13	none	
	Walt Wilmot, Chicago	13		
1890	Mike Tiernan, N. Y. Giants	13	none	
1891	Mike Tiernan, N. Y. Giants	17	none	
1892	"Bug" Holliday, Cincinnati	13	none	
1893	"Big Ed" Delahanty, Philadelphia	19	none	
1894	Hugh Duffy, Boston	18	none	
1895	Sam Thompson, Philadelphia	18	none	
1896	"Big Ed" Delahanty, Philadelphia	13	none	
	Bill Joyce, Wash.–N. Y. Giants	13		
1897	Hugh Duffy, Boston	11	none	
1898	Jimmy Collins, Boston	15	none	
1899	"Buck" Freeman, Washington	25	none	
1900	Herman Long, Boston	12	none	
1901	Sam Crawford, Cincinnati	16	Napoleon Lajoie, Philadelphia	13
1902	Tommy Leach, Pittsburgh	6	Socks Seybold, Philadelphia	16
1903	Jimmy Sheckard, Brooklyn	9	Buck Freeman, Boston	13
1904	Harry Lumley, Brooklyn	9	Harry Davis, Philadelphia	10
1905	Fred Odwell, Cincinnati	9	Harry Davis, Philadelphia	8
1906	Tim Jordan, Brooklyn	12	Harry Davis, Philadelphia	12
1907	Dave Brain, Boston	10	Harry Davis, Philadelphia	8
1908	Tim Jordan, Brooklyn	12	Sam Crawford, Detroit	7
1909	John "Red" Murray, N. Y. Giants	7	Ty Cobb, Detroit	9
1910	Fred Beck, Boston	10	Jake Stahl, Boston	10
	Frank Schulte, Chicago	10		
1911	Frank Schulte, Chicago	21	Frank Baker, Philadelphia	11
1912	Heinie Zimmerman, Chicago	14	Frank Baker, Philadelphia	10
			Tris Speaker, Boston	10
1913	"Gavvy" Cravath, Philadelphia	19	Frank Baker, Philadelphia	12
1914	"Gavvy" Cravath, Philadelphia	19	Frank Baker, Philadelphia	9
1915	"Gavvy" Cravath, Philadelphia	24	Braggo Roth, Chicago–Cleveland	7
1916	"Cy" Williams, Chicago	12	Wally Pipp, New York	12
	Dave Robertson, N. Y. Giants	12		
1917	Dave Robertson, N. Y. Giants	12	Wally Pipp, New York	9
1918	"Gavvy" Cravath, Philadelphia	8	Babe Ruth, Boston	11
			Tilly Walker, Philadelphia	11
1919	"Gavvy" Cravath, Philadelphia	12	Babe Ruth, Boston	29
1920	"Cy" Williams, Philadelphia	15	Babe Ruth, New York	54
1921	George Kelly, N. Y. Giants	23	Babe Ruth, New York	59

Year	NL Home Run leaders Player, Team	HR	AL Home Run leaders Player, Team	HR
1922	Rogers Hornsby, St. Louis	42	Ken Williams, St. Louis	39
1923	"Cy" Williams, Philadelphia	41	Babe Ruth, New York	41
1924	Jack Fournier, Brooklyn	27	Babe Ruth, New York	46
1925	Rogers Hornsby, St. Louis	39	Bob Meusel, New York	33
1926	Lewis "Hack" Wilson, Chicago	21	Babe Ruth, New York	47
1927	Lewis "Hack" Wilson, Chicago	30	Babe Ruth, New York	60
	"Cy" Williams, Philadelphia	30		
1928	Lewis "Hack" Wilson, Chicago	31	Babe Ruth, New York	54
	"Sunny Jim" Bottomley, St. Louis	31		
1929	Chuck Klein, Philadelphia	43	Babe Ruth, New York	46
1930	Lewis "Hack" Wilson, Chicago	56	Babe Ruth, New York	49
1931	Chuck Klein, Philadelphia	31	Babe Ruth, New York	46
			Lou Gehrig, New York	46
1932	Mel Ott, N. Y. Giants	38	Jimmy Foxx, Philadelphia	58
	Chuck Klein, Philadelphia	38		
1933	Chuck Klein, Philadelphia	28	Jimmy Foxx, Philadelphia	48
1934	Mel Ott, N. Y. Giants	35	Lou Gehrig, New York	49
	"Ripper" Collins, St. Louis	35		
1935	Wally Barger, Boston	34	Jimmy Foxx, Philadelphia	36
			Hank Greenberg, Detroit	36
1936	Mel Ott, N. Y. Giants	33	Lou Gehrig, New York	49
1937	Mel Ott, N. Y. Giants	31	Joe DiMaggio, New York	46
	Joe "Ducky" Medwick, St. Louis	31		
1938	Mel Ott, N. Y. Giants	36	Hank Greenberg, Detroit	58
1939	Johnny Mize, St. Louis	28	Jimmie Foxx, Boston	35
1940	Johnny Mize, St. Louis	43	Hank Greenberg, Detroit	41
1941	Dolph Camilli, Brooklyn	34	Ted Williams, Boston	37
1942	Mel Ott, N. Y. Giants	30	Ted Williams, Boston	36
1943	Bill Nicholson, Chicago	29	Rudy York, Detroit	34
1944	Bill Nicholson, Chicago	33	Nick Etten, New York	22
1945	Tommy Holmes, Boston	28	Vern Stephens, St. Louis	24
1946	Ralph Kiner, Pittsburgh	23	Hank Greenberg, Detroit	44
1947	Johnny Mize, N. Y. Giants	51	Ted Williams, Boston	32
	Ralph Kiner, Pittsburgh	51		
1948	Johnny Mize, N. Y. Giants	40	Joe DiMaggio, New York	39
	Ralph Kiner, Pittsburgh	40		
1949	Ralph Kiner, Pittsburgh	54	Ted Williams, Boston	43
1950	Ralph Kiner, Pittsburgh	47	Al Rosen, Cleveland	37
1951	Ralph Kiner, Pittsburgh	42	Gus Zernial, Chicago–Phila.	33
1952	Hank Sauer, Chicago	37	Larry Doby, Cleveland	32
	Ralph Kiner, Pittsburgh	37		
1953	Eddie Matthews, Milwaukee	47	Al Rosen, Cleveland	43
1954	Ted Kluszewski, Cincinnati	49	Larry Doby, Cleveland	32
1955	Willie Mays, N. Y. Giants	51	Mickey Mantle, New York	37
1956	Duke Snider, Brooklyn	43	Mickey Mantle, New York	52

Year	NL Home Run leaders Player, Team	HRs	AL Home Run leaders Player, Team	HRs
1957	Hank Aaron, Milwaukee	44	Roy Sievers, Washington	42
1958	Ernie Banks, Chicago	47	Mickey Mantle, New York	42
1959	Eddie Matthews, Milwaukee	46	Harmon Killebrew, Washington	42
			Rocky Colavito, Cleveland	42
1960	Ernie Banks, Chicago	41	Mickey Mantle, New York	40
1961	Orlando Cepeda, San Francisco	46	Roger Maris, New York	61
1962	Willie Mays, San Francisco	49	Harmon Killebrew, Minnesota	48
1963	Hank Aaron, Milwaukee	44	Harmon Killebrew, Minnesota	45
	Willie McCovey, San Francisco	44		
1964	Willie Mays, San Francisco	47	Harmon Killebrew, Minnesota	49
1965	Willie Mays, San Francisco	52	Tony Conigliaro, Boston	32
1966	Hank Aaron, Atlanta	44	Frank Robinson, Baltimore	49
1967	Hank Aaron, Atlanta	39	Carl Yastrzemski, Boston	44
			Harmon Killebrew, Minnesota	44
1968	Willie McCovey, San Francisco	36	Frank Howard, Washington	44
1969	Willie McCovey, San Francisco	46	Harmon Killebrew, Minnesota	49
1970	Johnny Bench, Cincinnati	45	Frank Howard, Washington	44
1971	Willie Stargell, Pittsburgh	48	Bill Melton, Chicago	33
1972	Johnny Bench, Cincinnati	40	Dick Allen, Chicago	37
1973	Willie Stargell, Pittsburgh	44	Reggie Jackson, Oakland	32
1974	Mike Schmidt, Philadelphia	36	Dick Allen, Chicago	32
1975	Mike Schmidt, Philadelphia	38	Reggie Jackson, Oakland	36
			George Scott, Milwaukee	36
1976	Mike Schmidt, Philadelphia	38	Graig Nettles, New York	32
1977	George Foster, Cincinnati	52	Jim Rice, Boston	39
1978	George Foster, Cincinnati	40	Jim Rice, Boston	46
1979	Dave Kingman, Chicago	48	Gorman Thomas, Milwaukee	45
1980	Mike Schmidt, Philadelphia	48	Reggie Jackson, New York	41
			Ben Oglivie, Milwaukee	41
1981	Mike Schmidt, Philadelphia	31	Bobby Grich, California	22
			Tony Armas, Oakland	22
			Dwight Evans, Boston	22
			Eddie Murray, Baltimore	22
1982	Dave Kingman, New York Mets	37	Reggie Jackson, California	39
			Gorman Thomas, Milwaukee	39
1983	Mike Schmidt, Philadelphia	40	Jim Rice, Boston	39
1984	Dale Murphy, Atlanta	36	Tony Armas, Boston	43
	Mike Schmidt, Philadelphia	36		
1985	Dale Murphy, Atlanta	37	Darrell Evans, Detroit	40
1986	Mike Schmidt, Philadelphia	37	Jesse Barfield, Toronto	40
1987	Andre Dawson, Chicago	49	Mark McGwire, Oakland	49
1988	Darryl Strawberry, N.Y. Mets	39	Jose Canseco, Oakland	42
1989	Kevin Mitchell, San Francisco	47	Fred McGriff, Toronto	36
1990	Ryne Sandberg, Chicago	40	Cecil Fielder, Detroit	51

NL Home Run leaders / AL Home Run leaders

Year	NL Player, Team	HRs	AL Player, Team	HRs
1991	Howard Johnson, N. Y. Mets	38	Cecil Fielder, Detroit	44
			Jose Canseco, Oakland	44
1992	Fred McGriff, San Diego	35	Juan Gonzalez, Texas	43
1993	Barry Bonds, San Francisco	46	Juan Gonzalez, Texas	46

NL Runs Batted In leaders / AL Runs Batted In leaders

Year	NL Player, Team	RBIs	AL Player, Team	RBIs
1876	James "Deacon" White, Chicago	60	none	
1877	James "Deacon" White, Boston	49	none	
1878	Paul Hines, Providence	50	none	
1879	John O'Rourke, Boston	62	none	
1880	Adrian "Cap" Anson, Chicago	74	none	
1881	Adrian "Cap" Anson, Chicago	82	none	
1882	Adrian "Cap" Anson, Chicago	83	none	
1883	"Big Dan" Brouthers, Buffalo	97	none	
1884	Adrian "Cap" Anson, Chicago	102	none	
1885	Adrian "Cap" Anson, Chicago	108	none	
1886	Adrian "Cap" Anson, Chicago	147	none	
1887	Sam Thompson, Detroit	166	none	
1888	Adrian "Cap" Anson, Chicago	84	none	
1889	Roger Connor, N. Y. Giants	130	none	
1890	"Oyster" Burns, Brooklyn	128	none	
1891	Adrian "Cap" Anson, Chicago	120	none	
1892	"Big Dan" Brouthers, Brooklyn	124	none	
1893	"Big Ed" Delahanty, Phila.	146	none	
1894	Hugh Duffy, Boston	145	none	
1895	Sam Thompson, Philadelphia	165	none	
1896	"Big Ed" Delahanty, Phila.	126	none	
1897	George Davis, N. Y. Giants	136	none	
1898	Nap Lajoie, Philadelphia	127	none	
1899	"Big Ed" Delahanty, Phila.	137	none	
1900	Elmer Flick, Philadelphia	110	none	
1901	"Honus" Wagner, Pittsburgh	126	Napoleon Lajoie, Philadelphia	125
1902	"Honus" Wagner, Pittsburgh	91	Buck Freeman, Boston	121
1903	Sam Mertes, N. Y. Giants	104	Buck Freeman, Boston	104
1904	Bill Dahlen, N. Y. Giants	80	Napoleon Lajoie, Cleveland	102
1905	Cy Seymour, Cincinnati	121	Harry Davis, Philadelphia	83
1906	Harry Steinfeldt, Chicago	83	Harry Davis, Philadelphia	96
	Jim Nealon, Pittsburgh	83		
1907	Sherry Magee, Philadelphia	85	Ty Cobb, Detroit	116
1908	"Honus" Wagner, Pittsburgh	109	Ty Cobb, Detroit	108
1909	"Honus" Wagner, Pittsburgh	100	Ty Cobb, Detroit	107
1910	Sherry Magee, Philadelphia	123	Sam Crawford, Detroit	120
1911	Frank Schulte, Chicago	107	Ty Cobb, Detroit	144
	"Chief" Wilson, Pittsburgh	107		

Year	NL Runs Batted In leaders Player, Team	RBIs	AL Runs Batted In leaders Player, Team	RBIs
1912	"Honus" Wagner, Pittsburgh	102	Frank Baker, Philadelphia	133
1913	"Gavvy" Cravath, Philadelphia	128	Frank Baker, Philadelphia	126
1914	Sherry Magee, Philadelphia	103	Sam Crawford, Detroit	104
1915	"Gavvy" Cravath, Philadelphia	115	B. Veach, Detroit	112
			Sam Crawford, Detroit	112
1916	Heinie Zimmerman, Chic.–N.Y.	83	Del Pratt, St. Louis	103
1917	Heinie Zimmerman, New York	102	Bobby Veach, Detroit	103
1918	Sherry Magee, Cincinnati	76	Bobby Veach, Detroit	78
1919	Hy Myers, Brooklyn	73	Babe Ruth, Boston	114
1920	George Kelly, N. Y. Giants	94	Babe Ruth, New York	137
	Rogers Hornsby, St. Louis	94		
1921	Rogers Hornsby, St. Louis	126	Babe Ruth, New York	171
1922	Rogers Hornsby, St. Louis	152	Ken Williams, St. Louis	155
1923	Emil Meusel, N. Y. Giants	125	Babe Ruth, New York	130
			Tris Speaker, Cleveland	130
1924	George Kelly, N. Y. Giants	136	Goose Goslin, Washington	129
1925	Rogers Hornsby, St. Louis	143	Bob Meusel, New York	138
1926	Sunny Jim" Bottomley, St. L.	120	Babe Ruth, New York	145
1927	Paul "Big Poison" Waner, Pitt.	131	Lou Gehrig, New York	175
1928	Sunny Jim" Bottomley, St. L.	136	Babe Ruth, New York	142
			Lou Gehrig, New York	142
1929	Lewis "Hack" Wilson, Chicago	159	Al Simmons, Philadelphia	157
1930	Lewis "Hack" Wilson, Chicago	190	Lou Gehrig, New York	174
1931	Chuck Klein, Philadelphia	121	Lou Gehrig, New York	184
1932	Don Hurst, Philadelphia	143	Jimmy Foxx, Philadelphia	169
1933	Chuck Klein, Philadelphia	120	Jimmy Foxx, Philadelphia	163
1934	Mel Ott, N. Y. Giants	135	Lou Gehrig, New York	165
1935	Wally Berger, Boston	130	Hank Greenberg, Detroit	170
1936	Joe "Ducky" Medwick, St. L.	138	Hal Trosky, Cleveland	162
1937	Joe "Ducky" Medwick, St. L.	154	Hank Greenberg, Detroit	183
1938	Joe "Ducky" Medwick, St. L.	122	Jimmie Foxx, Boston	175
1939	Frank McCormick, Cincinnati	128	Ted Williams, Boston	145
1940	Johnny Mize, St. Louis	137	Hank Greenberg, Detroit	150
1941	Dolph Camilli, Brooklyn	120	Joe DiMaggio, New York	125
1942	Johnny Mize, N. Y. Giants	110	Ted Williams, Boston	137
1943	Bill Nicholson, Chicago	128	Rudy York, Detroit	118
1944	Bill Nicholson, Chicago	122	Vern Stephens, St. Louis	109
1945	Fred "Dixie" Walker, Brooklyn	124	Nick Etten, New York	111
1946	Enos Slaughter, St. Louis	130	Hank Greenberg, Detroit	127
1947	Johnny Mize, N. Y. Giants	138	Ted Williams, Boston	114
1948	Stan Musial, St. Louis	131	Joe DiMaggio, New York	155
1949	Ralph Kiner, Pittsburgh	127	Ted Williams, Boston	159
			Vern Stephens, Boston	159
1950	Del Ennis, Philadelphia	126	Walt Dropo, Boston	144
			Vern Stephens, Boston	144

Year	NL Runs Batted In leaders Player, Team	RBIs	AL Runs Batted In leaders Player, Team	RBIs
1951	Monte Irvin, N. Y. Giants	121	Gus Zernial, Chicago–Phila.	129
1952	Hank Sauer, Chicago	121	Al Rosen, Cleveland	105
1953	Roy Campanella, Brooklyn	142	Al Rosen, Cleveland	145
1954	Ted Kluszewski, Cincinnati	141	Larry Doby, Cleveland	126
1955	Duke Snider, Brooklyn	136	Ray Boone, Detroit	116
			Jackie Jensen, Boston	116
1956	Stan Musial, St. Louis	109	Mickey Mantle, New York	130
1957	Hank Aaron, Milwaukee	132	Roy Sievers, Washington	114
1958	Ernie Banks, Chicago	129	Jackie Jensen, Boston	122
1959	Ernie Banks, Chicago	143	Jackie Jensen, Boston	112
1960	Hank Aaron, Milwaukee	126	Roger Maris, New York	112
1961	Orlando Cepeda, San Francisco	142	Roger Maris, New York	142
1962	Tommy Davis, Los Angeles	153	Harmon Killebrew, Minnesota	126
1963	Hank Aaron, Milwaukee	130	Dick Stuart, Boston	118
1964	Ken Boyer, St. Louis	119	Brooks Robinson, Baltimore	118
1965	Deron Johnson, Cincinnati	130	Rocky Colavito, Cleveland	108
1966	Hank Aaron, Atlanta	127	Frank Robinson, Baltimore	122
1967	Orlando Cepeda, St. Louis	111	Carl Yastrzemski, Boston	121
1968	Willie McCovey, San Francisco	105	Ken Harrelson, Boston	109
1969	Willie McCovey, San Francisco	126	Harmon Killebrew, Minnesota	140
1970	Johnny Bench, Cincinnati	148	Frank Howard, Washington	126
1971	Joe Torre, St. Louis	137	Harmon Killebrew, Minnesota	119
1972	Johnny Bench, Cincinnati	125	Dick Allen, Chicago	113
1973	Willie Stargell, Pittsburgh	119	Reggie Jackson, Oakland	117
1974	Johnny Bench, Cincinnati	129	Jeff Burroughs, Texas	118
1975	Greg Luzinski, Philadelphia	120	George Scott, Milwaukee	109
1976	George Foster, Cincinnati	121	Lee May, Baltimore	109
1977	George Foster, Cincinnati	149	Larry Hisle, Minnesota	119
1978	George Foster, Cincinnati	120	Jim Rice, Boston	139
1979	Dave Winfield, San Diego	118	Don Baylor, California	139
1980	Mike Schmidt, Philadelphia	121	Cecil Cooper, Milwaukee	122
1981	Mike Schmidt, Philadelphia	91	Eddie Murray, Baltimore	78
1982	Dale Murphy, Atlanta	109	Hal McRae, Kansas City	133
	Al Oliver, Montreal	109		
1983	Dale Murphy, Atlanta	121	Jim Rice, Boston	126
			Cecil Cooper, Milwaukee	126
1984	Gary Carter, Montreal	106	Tony Armas, Boston	123
	Mike Schmidt, Philadelphia	106		
1985	Dave Parker, Cincinnati	125	Don Mattingly, New York	145
1986	Mike Schmidt, Philadelphia	119	Joe Carter, Cleveland	121
1987	Andre Dawson, Chicago	137	George Bell, Toronto	134
1988	Will Clark, San Francisco	109	Jose Canseco, Oakland	124
1989	Kevin Mitchell, San Francisco	125	Ruben Sierra, Texas	119
1990	Matt Williams, San Francisco	122	Cecil Fielder, Detroit	132
1991	Howard Johnson, N. Y. Giants	117	Cecil Fielder, Detroit	133

NL Runs Batted In leaders / AL Runs Batted In leaders

Year	Player, Team	RBIs	Player, Team	RBIs
1992	Darren Daulton, Philadelphia	109	Cecil Fielder, Detroit	124
1993	Barry Bonds, San Francisco	123	Albert Belle, Cleveland	129

NL Stolen Base leaders / AL Stolen Base leaders

Year	Player, Team	SBs	Player, Team	SBs
1886	Ed Andrews, Philadelphia	56	none	
1887	John "Monte" Ward, New York	111	none	
1888	"Dummy" Hoy, Washington	82	none	
1889	Jim Fogarty, Philadelphia	99	none	
1890	Billy Hamilton, Philadelphia	102	none	
1891	Billy Hamilton, Philadelphia	111	none	
1892	John "Monte" Ward, Brooklyn	88	none	
1893	Tom Brown, Louisville	66	none	
1894	Billy Hamilton, Philadelphia	98	none	
1895	Billy Hamilton, Philadelphia	97	none	
1896	Joe Kelley, Baltimore	87	none	
1897	Bill Lange, Chicago	73	none	
1898	"Big Ed" Delahanty, Phila.	58	none	
1899	Jimmy Sheckard, Baltimore	77	none	
1900	George Van Haltren, New York	45	none	
	"Patsy" Donovan, St. Louis	45		
1901	"Honus" Wagner, Pittsburgh	49	Frank Isbell, Chicago	52
1902	"Honus" Wagner, Pittsburgh	42	Topsy Hartsel, Philadelphia	47
1903	Jimmy Sheckard, Brooklyn	67	Harry Bay, Cleveland	45
	Frank "Husk" Chance, Chicago	67		
1904	"Honus" Wagner, Pittsburgh	53	Elmer Flick, Cleveland	42
1905	Billy Maloney, Chicago	59	Danny Hoffman, Philadelphia	46
	Art Devlin, N. Y. Giants	59		
1906	Frank "Husk" Chance, Chicago	57	John Anderson, Washington	39
			Elmer Flick, Washington	39
1907	"Honus" Wagner, Pittsburgh	61	Ty Cobb, Detroit	49
1908	"Honus" Wagner, Pittsburgh	53	Patsy Dougherty, Chicago	47
1909	Bob Bescher, Cincinnati	54	Ty Cobb, Detroit	76
1910	Bob Bescher, Cincinnati	70	Eddie Collins, Philadelphia	81
1911	Bob Bescher, Cincinnati	80	Ty Cobb, Detroit	83
1912	Bob Bescher, Cincinnati	67	Clyde Milan, Washington	88
1913	Max "Scoops" Carey, Pitt.	61	Clyde Milan, Washington	75
1914	George J. Burns, N. Y. Giants	62	Fritz Maisel, New York	74
1915	Max "Scoops" Carey, Pitt.	36	Ty Cobb, Detroit	96
1916	Max "Scoops" Carey, Pitt.	63	Ty Cobb, Detroit	68
1917	Max "Scoops" Carey, Pitt.	46	Ty Cobb, Detroit	55
1918	Max "Scoops" Carey, Pitt.	58	George Sisler, St. Louis	45
1919	George J. Burns, N. Y. Giants	40	Eddie Collins, Chicago	33
1920	Max "Scoops" Carey, Pittsburgh	52	Sam Rice, Washington	63
1921	Frankie Frisch, N. Y. Giants	49	George Sisler, St. Louis	35

Year	NL Stolen Base leaders Player, Team	SBs	AL Stolen Base leaders Player, Team	SBs
1922	Max "Scoops" Carey, Pittsburgh	51	George Sisler, St. Louis	51
1923	Max "Scoops" Carey, Pittsburgh	51	Eddie Collins, Chicago	47
1924	Max "Scoops" Carey, Pittsburgh	49	Eddie Collins, Chicago	42
1925	Max "Scoops" Carey, Pittsburgh	46	Johnny Mostil, Chicago	43
1926	Hazen "Kiki" Cuyler, Pittsburgh	35	Johnny Mostil, Chicago	35
1927	Frankie Frisch, St. Louis	48	George Sisler, St. Louis	27
1928	Hazen "Kiki" Cuyler, Chicago	37	Buddy Myer, Boston	30
1929	Hazen "Kiki" Cuyler, Chicago	43	Charlie Gehringer, Detroit	28
1930	Hazen "Kiki" Cuyler, Chicago	37	Marty McManus, Detroit	23
1931	Frankie Frisch, St. Louis	28	Ben Chapman, New York	61
1932	Chuck Klein, Philadelphia	20	Ben Chapman, New York	38
1933	John "Pepper" Martin, St. Louis	26	Ben Chapman, New York	27
1934	John "Pepper" Martin, St. Louis	23	Billy Werber, Boston	40
1935	Augie Galan, Chicago	22	Billy Werber, Boston	29
1936	John "Pepper" Martin, St. Louis	23	Lyn Lary, St. Louis	37
1937	Augie Galan, Chicago	23	Billy Werber, Philadelphia	35
			Ben Chapman, Boston–Wash.	35
1938	Stan Hack, Chicago	16	Frank Crosetti, New York	27
1939	Stan Hack, Chicago	17	George Case, Washington	51
	Lee Handley, Pittsburgh	17		
1940	Lonny Frey, Cincinnati	22	George Case, Washington	35
1941	Danny Murtaugh, Philadelphia	18	George Case, Washington	33
1942	Pete Reiser, Brooklyn	20	George Case, Washington	44
1943	Floyd "Arky" Vaughan, Br'klyn	20	George Case, Washington	61
1944	Johnny Barrett, Pittsburgh	28	Snuffy Stirnweiss, New York	55
1945	"Red" Schoendienst, St. Louis	26	Snuffy Stirnweiss, New York	33
1946	Pete Reiser, Brooklyn	34	George Case, Cleveland	28
1947	Jackie Robinson, Brooklyn	29	Bob Dillinger, St. Louis	34
1948	Richie Ashburn, Philadelphia	32	Bob Dillinger, St. Louis	28
1949	Jackie Robinson, Brooklyn	37	Bob Dillinger, St. Louis	20
1950	Sam Jethroe, Boston	35	Dom DiMaggio, Boston	15
1951	Sam Jethroe, Boston	35	Minnie Minoso, Chicago–Cleve.	31
1952	"Pee Wee" Reese, Brooklyn	30	Minnie Minoso, Chicago	22
1953	Bill Bruton, Milwaukee	26	Minnie Minoso, Chicago	25
1954	Bill Bruton, Milwaukee	34	Jackie Jensen, Boston	22
1955	Bill Bruton, Milwaukee	25	Jim Rivera, Chicago	25
1956	Willie Mays, N. Y. Giants	40	Luis Aparicio, Chicago	21
1957	Willie Mays, N. Y. Giants	38	Luis Aparicio, Chicago	28
1958	Willie Mays, San Francisco	31	Luis Aparicio, Chicago	29
1959	Willie Mays, San Francisco	27	Luis Aparicio, Chicago	56
1960	Maury Wills, Los Angeles	50	Luis Aparicio, Chicago	51
1961	Maury Wills, Los Angeles	35	Luis Aparicio, Chicago	53
1962	Maury Wills, Los Angeles	104	Luis Aparicio, Chicago	31
1963	Maury Wills, Los Angeles	40	Luis Aparicio, Baltimore	40
1964	Maury Wills, Los Angeles	53	Luis Aparicio, Baltimore	57

NL Stolen Base leaders / AL Stolen Base leaders

Year	NL Player, Team	SBs	AL Player, Team	SBs
1965	Maury Wills, Los Angeles	94	Bert Campaneris, Kansas City	51
1966	Lou Brock, St. Louis	74	Bert Campaneris, Kansas City	52
1967	Lou Brock, St. Louis	52	Bert Campaneris, Kansas City	55
1968	Lou Brock, St. Louis	62	Bert Campaneris, Oakland	62
1969	Lou Brock, St. Louis	53	Tommy Harper, Seattle	73
1970	Bobby Tolan, Cincinnati	57	Bert Campaneris, Oakland	42
1971	Lou Brock, St. Louis	64	Amos Otis, Kansas City	52
1972	Lou Brock, St. Louis	63	Bert Campaneris, Oakland	52
1973	Lou Brock, St. Louis	70	Tommy Harper, Boston	54
1974	Lou Brock, St. Louis	118	Billy North, Oakland	54
1975	Davey Lopes, Los Angeles	77	Mickey Rivers, California	70
1976	Davey Lopes, Los Angeles	63	Billy North, Oakland	75
1977	Frank Taveras, Pittsburgh	70	Fred Patek, Kansas City	53
1978	Omar Moreno, Pittsburgh	71	Ron LeFlore, Detroit	68
1979	Omar Moreno, Pittsburgh	77	Willie Wilson, Kansas City	83
1980	Ron LeFlore, Montreal	97	Rickey Henderson, Oakland	100
1981	Tim Raines, Montreal	71	Rickey Henderson, Oakland	56
1982	Tim Raines, Montreal	78	Rickey Henderson, Oakland	130
1983	Tim Raines, Montreal	90	Rickey Henderson, Oakland	108
1984	Tim Raines, Montreal	75	Rickey Henderson, Oakland	66
1985	Vince Coleman, St. Louis	110	Rickey Henderson, New York	80
1986	Vince Coleman, St. Louis	107	Rickey Henderson, New York	87
1987	Vince Coleman, St. Louis	109	Harold Reynolds, Seattle	60
1988	Vince Coleman, St. Louis	81	Rickey Henderson, New York	93
1989	Vince Coleman, St. Louis	65	Rickey Henderson, New York–Oak.	77
1990	Vince Coleman, St. Louis	77	Rickey Henderson, Oakland	65
1991	Marquis Grissom, Montreal	76	Rickey Henderson, Oakland	58
1992	Marquis Grissom, Montreal	78	Kenny Lofton, Cleveland	66
1993	Chuck Carr, Florida	58	Kenny Lofton, Cleveland	70

NL Wins leaders / AL Wins leaders

Year	NL Player, Team	Wins	AL Player, Team	Wins
1876	Al Spalding, Chicago	47	none	
1877	Tommy Bond, Boston	40	none	
1878	Tommy Bond, Boston	40	none	
1879	John "Monte" Ward, Providence	47	none	
1880	Jim McCormick, Cleveland	45	none	
1881	Jim Whitney, Boston	31	none	
	Larry Corcoran, Chicago	31		
1882	Jim McCormick, Cleveland	36	none	
1883	"Ol' Hoss" Radbourn, Prov	.48	none	
1884	"Ol' Hoss" Radbourn, Prov.	59	none	
1885	John Clarkson, Chicago	53	none	
1886	Charles "Lady" Baldwin, Detroit	42	none	
	Tim Keefe, N. Y. Giants	42		

Year	NL Wins leaders Player, Team	Wins	AL Wins leaders Player, Team	Wins
1887	John Clarkson, Chicago	38	none	
1888	Tim Keefe, N. Y. Giants	35	none	
1889	John Clarkson, Boston	49	none	
1890	Bill Hutchinson, Chicago	42	none	
1891	Bill Hutchinson, Chicago	44	none	
1892	Bill Hutchinson, Chicago	37	none	
1893	Frank Killen, Pittsburgh	36	none	
1894	Amos Rusie, N. Y. Giants	36	none	
1895	Cy Young, Cleveland	35	none	
1896	Nichols, Boston	30	none	
1896	Frank Killen, Pittsburgh	30	none	
1897	Nichols, Boston	31	none	
1898	Nichols, Boston	31	none	
1899	McGinnity, Baltimore	28	none	
1899	Jim Hughes, Brooklyn	28	none	
1900	Joe McGinnity, Brooklyn	28	none	
1901	Bill Donovan, Brooklyn	25	Cy Young, Boston	33
1902	Jack Chesbro, Pittsburgh	28	Cy Young, Boston	32
1903	Joe McGinnity, N. Y. Giants	31	Cy Young, Boston	28
1904	Joe McGinnity, N. Y. Giants	35	Jack Chesbro, New York	41
1905	Christy Mathewson, N. Y. Giants	31	Rube Waddell, Philadelphia	26
1906	Joe McGinnity, N. Y. Giants	27	Al Orth, New York	27
1907	Christy Mathewson, N. Y. Giants	24	Addie Joss, Cleveland	27
			Doc White, Chicago	27
1908	Christy Mathewson, N. Y. Giants	37	Ed Walsh, Chicago	40
1909	"Three Finger" Brown, Chicago	27	George Mullin, Detroit	29
1910	Christy Mathewson, N. Y. Giants	27	Jack Coombs, Philadelphia	31
1911	Grover C. Alexander, Phila.	28	Jack Coombs, Philadelphia	28
1912	Larry Cheney, Chicago	26	"Smokey" Joe Wood, Boston	34
	Rube Marquard, N. Y. Giants	26		
1913	Tom Seaton, Philadelphia	27	Walter Johnson, Washington	36
1914	Richard Rudolph, Boston	27	Walter Johnson, Washington	28
	Grover C. Alexander, Phila.	27		
1915	Grover C. Alexander, Phila.	31	Walter Johnson, Washington	28
1916	Grover C. Alexander, Phila.	33	Walter Johnson, Washington	25
1917	Grover C. Alexander, Phila.	30	Eddie Cicotte, Chicago	28
1918	James "Hippo" Vaughn, Chi.	22	Walter Johnson, Washington	23
1919	Jesse Barnes, N. Y. Giants	25	Eddie Cicotte, Chicago	29
1920	Grover C. Alexander, Chicago	27	Jim Bagby, Cleveland	31
1921	Burleigh Grimes, Brooklyn	22	Carl Mays, New York	27
	Wilbur Cooper, Pittsburgh	22	Urban Shocker, St. Louis	27
1922	Eppa Rixey, Cincinnati	25	Eddie Rommel, Philadelphia	27
1923	Dolf Luque, Cincinnati	27	George Uhle, Cleveland	26
1924	Arthur "Dazzy" Vance, Br'klyn	28	Walter Johnson, Washington	23
1925	Arthur "Dazzy" Vance, Br'klyn	22	Eddie Rommel, Philadelphia	21

Year	NL Wins leaders Player, Team	Wins	AL Wins leaders Player, Team	Wins
1926	Pete Donahue, Cincinnati	20	George Uhle, Cleveland	27
	Remy "Ray" Kremer, Pittsburgh	20		
	Lee Meadows, Pittsburgh	20		
	Flint Rhem, St. Louis	20		
1927	Charlie Root, Chicago	26	Waite Hoyt, New York	22
			Ted Lyons, Chicago	22
1928	Rube Benton, N. Y. Giants	25	Lefty Grove, Philadelphia	24
	Burleigh Grimes, Pittsburgh	25	George Pipgras, New York	24
1929	Perce "Pat" Malone, Chicago	22	George Earnshaw, Philadelphia	24
1930	Perce "Pat" Malone, Chicago	20	Lefty Grove, Philadelphia	28
	Remy "Ray" Kremer, Pittsburgh	20		
1931	J. Elliott, Philadelphia	19	Lefty Grove, Philadelphia	31
	Henry "Heinie" Meine, Pitt.	19		
	Billy Hallahan, St. Louis	19		
1932	Lonnie Warneke, Chicago	22	General Crowder, Washington	26
1933	Carl Hubbell, N. Y. Giants	23	General Crowder, Washington	24
			Lefty Grove, Philadelphia	24
1934	Jay "Dizzy" Dean, St. Louis	30	Lefty Gomez, New York	26
1935	Jay "Dizzy" Dean, St. Louis	28	Wes Ferrell, Boston	25
1936	Carl Hubbell, N. Y. Giants	26	Tommy Bridges, Detroit	23
1937	Carl Hubbell, N. Y. Giants	22	Lefty Gomez, New York	21
1938	Bill Lee, Chicago	22	Red Ruffing, New York	21
1939	Bucky Walters, Cincinnati	27	Bob Feller, Cleveland	24
1940	Bucky Walters, Cincinnati	22	Bob Feller, Cleveland	27
1941	Whit Wyatt, Brooklyn	22	Bob Feller, Cleveland	25
	Kirby Higbe, Brooklyn	22		
1942	Mort Cooper, St. Louis	22	Tex Hughson, Boston	22
1943	Elmer Riddle, Cincinnati	21	Spud Chandler, New York	20
	Truett "Rip" Sewell, Pittsburgh	21	Dizzy Trout, Detroit	20
	Mort Cooper, St. Louis	21		
1944	Bucky Walters, Cincinnati	23	Hal Newhouser, Detroit	29
1945	Red Barrett, Boston–St. Louis	23	Hal Newhouser, Detroit	25
1946	Howie Pollet, St. Louis	21	Hal Newhouser, Detroit	26
			Bob Feller, Cleveland	26
1947	Ewell Blackwell, Cincinnati	22	Bob Feller, Cleveland	20
1948	Johnny Sain, Boston	24	Hal Newhouser, Detroit	21
1949	Warren Spahn, Boston	21	Mel Parnell, Boston	25
1950	Warren Spahn, Boston	21	Bob Lemon, Cleveland	23
1951	Sal Maglie, N. Y. Giants	23	Bob Feller, Cleveland	22
	Larry Jansen, N. Y. Giants	23		
1952	Robin Roberts, Philadelphia	28	Bobby Shantz, Philadelphia	24
1953	Warren Spahn, Milwaukee	23	Bob Porterfield, Washington	22
	Robin Roberts, Philadelphia	23		
1954	Robin Roberts, Philadelphia	23	Bob Lemon, Cleveland	23
			Early Wynn, Cleveland	23

	NL Wins leaders		AL Wins leaders	
Year	Player, Team	Wins	Player, Team	Wins
1955	Robin Roberts, Philadelphia	23	Bob Lemon, Cleveland	18
			Frank Sullivan, Boston	18
			Whitey Ford, New York	18
1956	Don Newcombe, Brooklyn	27	Frank Lary, Detroit	21
1957	Warren Spahn, Milwaukee	21	Jim Bunning, Detroit	20
			Billy Pierce, Chicago	20
1958	Warren Spahn, Milwaukee	22	Bob Turley, New York	21
	Bob Friend, Pittsburgh	22		
1959	Warren Spahn, Milwaukee	21	Early Wynn, Chicago	22
	Lew Burdette, Milwaukee	21		
	Sam Jones, San Francisco	21		
1960	Warren Spahn, Milwaukee	21	Jim Perry, Cleveland	18
	Ernie Broglio, St. Louis	21	Chuck Estrada, Baltimore	18
1961	Warren Spahn, Milwaukee	21	Whitey Ford, New York	25
1962	Don Drysdale, Los Angeles	25	Ralph Terry, New York	23
1963	Sandy Koufax, Los Angeles	25	Whitey Ford, New York	24
	Juan Marichal, San Francisco	25		
1964	Larry Jackson, Chicago	24	Gary Peters, Chicago	20
			Dean Chance, Los Angeles	20
1965	Sandy Koufax, Los Angeles	26	Mudcat Grant, Minnesota	21
1966	Sandy Koufax, Los Angeles	27	Jim Kaat, Minnesota	25
1967	Mike McCormick, San Francisco	22	Jim Lonborg, Boston	22
			Earl Wilson, Detroit	22
1968	Juan Marichal, San Francisco	26	Denny McLain, Detroit	31
1969	Tom Seaver, New York Mets	25	Denny McLain, Detroit	24
1970	Gaylord Perry, San Francisco	23	Mike Cuellar, Baltimore	24
	Bob Gibson, St. Louis	23	Jim Perry, Minnesota	24
			Dave McNally, Baltimore	24
1971	Ferguson Jenkins, Chicago	24	Mickey Lolich, Detroit	25
1972	Steve Carlton, Philadelphia	27	Gaylord Perry, Cleveland	24
			Wilbur Wood, Chicago	24
1973	Ron Bryant, San Francisco	24	Wilbur Wood, Chicago	24
1974	Phil Niekro, Atlanta	20	Catfish Hunter, Oakland	25
	Andy Messersmith, Los Angeles	20	Ferguson Jenkins, Texas	25
1975	Tom Seaver, New York Mets	22	Catfish Hunter, New York	23
			Jim Palmer, Baltimore	23
1976	Randy Jones, San Diego	22	Jim Palmer, Baltimore	22
1977	Steve Carlton, Philadelphia	23	Jim Palmer, Baltimore	20
			Dennis Leonard, Kansas City	20
			Dave Goltz, Minnesota	20
1978	Gaylord Perry, San Diego	21	Ron Guidry, New York	25
1979	Phil Niekro, Atlanta	21	Mike Flanagan, Baltimore	23
	Joe Niekro, Houston	21		
1980	Steve Carlton, Philadelphia	24	Steve Stone, Baltimore	25

Year	NL Wins leaders Player, Team	Wins	AL Wins leaders Player, Team	Wins
1981	Tom Seaver, Cincinnati	14	Pete Vuckovich, Milwaukee	14
			Dennis Martinez, Baltimore	14
			Steve McCatty, Oakland	14
			Jack Morris, Detroit	14
1982	Steve Carlton, Philadelphia	23	LaMarr Hoyt, Chicago	19
1983	John Denny, Philadelphia	19	LaMarr Hoyt, Chicago	24
1984	Joaquin Andujar, St. Louis	20	Mike Boddicker, Baltimore	20
1985	Dwight Gooden, New York Mets	24	Ron Guidry, New York	22
1986	Fernando Valenzuela, Los Ang.	21	Roger Clemens, Boston	24
1987	Rick Sutcliffe, Chicago	18	Roger Clemens, Boston	20
			Dave Stewart, Oakland	20
1988	Danny Jackson, Cincinnati	23	Frank Viola, Minnesota	24
	Orel Hershiser, Los Angeles	23		
1989	Mike Scott, Houston	20	Bret Saberhagen, Kansas City	23
1990	Doug Drabek, Pittsburgh	22	Bob Welch, Oakland	27
1991	Tom Glavine, Atlanta	20	Scott Erickson, Minnesota	20
	John Smiley, Pittsburgh	20	Bill Gullickson, Detroit	20
1992	Tom Glavine, Atlanta	20	Kevin Brown, Texas	21
	Greg Maddux, Chicago	20	Jack Morris, Toronto	21
1993	John Burkett, San Francisco	22	Jack McDowell, Chicago	22
	Tom Glavine, Atlanta	22		

Year	NL ERA leaders Player, Team	ERA	AL ERA leaders Player, Team	ERA
1876	"Foghorn" Bradley, St. Louis	1.23	none	
1877	Tommy Bond, Boston	2.11	none	
1878	"Monte" Ward, Providence	1.51	none	
1879	Tommy Bond, Boston	1.96	none	
1880	Tim Keefe, Troy	0.86	none	
1881	"Stump" Weidman, Detroit	1.80	none	
1882	Larry Corcoran, Chicago	1.95	none	
1883	Jim McCormick, Cleveland	1.84	none	
1884	"Ol' Hoss" Radbourn, Prov.	1.38	none	
1885	Tim Keefe, N. Y. Giants	1.58	none	
1886	Charlie Ferguson, Phila.	1.98	none	
1887	Dan Casey, Philadelphia	2.86	none	
1888	Tim Keefe, N. Y. Giants	1.74	none	
1889	John Clarkson, Boston	2.73	none	
1890	Billy Rhines, Cincinnati	1.95	none	
1891	John Ewing, N. Y. Giants	2.27	none	
1892	Cy Young, Cleveland	1.93	none	
1893	Ted Breitenstein, St. Louis	3.18	none	
1894	Amos Rusie, N. Y. Giants	2.78	none	
1895	Al Maul, Washington	2.45	none	
1896	Billy Rhines, Cincinnati	2.45	none	

Year	NL ERA leaders Player, Team	ERA	AL ERA leaders Player, Team	ERA
1897	Amos Rusie, N. Y. Giants	2.54	none	
1898	Clark Griffith, Chicago	1.88	none	
1899	Vic Willis, Boston	2.50	none	
1900	"Rube" Waddell, Pittsburgh	2.37	none	
1901	Jesse Tannehill, Pittsburgh	2.18	Cy Young, Boston	1.62
1902	Jack Taylor, Chicago	1.33	Ed Siever, Detroit	1.91
1903	Sam Leever, Pittsburgh	2.06	Earl Moore, Cleveland	1.77
1904	Joe McGinnity, N. Y. Giants	1.61	Addie Joss, Cleveland	1.59
1905	Christy Mathewson, New York	1.27	Rube Waddell, Philadelphia	1.48
1906	"Three Fingers" Brown, Chi.	1.04	Doc White, Chicago	1.52
1907	Jack Pfiester, Chicago	1.15	Ed Walsh, Chicago	1.60
1908	Christy Mathewson, New York	1.43	Addie Joss, Cleveland	1.16
1909	Christy Mathewson, New York	1.14	Harry Krause, Philadelphia	1.39
1910	King Cole, Chicago	1.80	Ed Walsh, Chicago	1.27
1911	Christy Mathewson, New York	1.99	Vean Gregg, Cleveland	1.81
1912	"Jeff" Tesreau, N. Y. Giants	1.96	Walter Johnson, Washington	1.39
1913	Christy Mathewson, New York	2.06	Walter Johnson, Washington	1.09
1914	Bill Doak, St. Louis	1.72	Dutch Leonard, Boston	1.01
1915	Grover C. Alexander, Phila.	1.22	"Smokey" Joe Wood, Boston	1.49
1916	Grover C. Alexander, Phila.	1.55	Babe Ruth, Boston	1.75
1917	Fred Anderson, N. Y. Giants	1.44	Eddie Cicotte, Chicago	1.53
1918	James "Hippo" Vaughn, Chi.	1.74	Walter Johnson, Washington	1.27
1919	Grover C. Alexander, Chicago	1.72	Walter Johnson, Washington	1.49
1920	Grover C. Alexander, Chicago	1.91	Bob Shawkey, New York	2.45
1921	Bill Doak, St. Louis	2.59	Red Faber, Chicago	2.48
1922	Phil Douglas, N. Y. Giants	2.63	Red Faber, Chicago	2.80
1923	Dolf Luque, Cincinnati	1.93	Stan Coveleski, Cleveland	2.76
1924	"Dazzy" Vance, Brooklyn	2.16	Walter Johnson, Washington	2.72
1925	Dolf Luque, Cincinnati	2.63	Stan Coveleski, Washington	2.84
1926	Remy "Ray" Kremer, Pitts.	2.61	Lefty Grove, Philadelphia	2.51
1927	Remy "Ray" Kremer, Pitts.	2.47	Waite Hoyt, New York	2.63
1928	"Dazzy" Vance, Brooklyn	2.09	Garland Braxton, Wash.	2.51
1929	Bill Walker, N. Y. Giants	3.09	Lefty Grove, Philadelphia	2.81
1930	"Dazzy" Vance, Brooklyn	2.61	Lefty Grove, Philadelphia	2.54
1931	Bill Walker, N. Y. Giants	2.26	Lefty Grove, Philadelphia	2.06
1932	Lonnie Warneke, Chicago	2.37	Lefty Grove, Philadelphia	2.84
1933	Carl Hubbell, N. Y. Giants	1.66	Monte Pearson, Cleveland	2.33
1934	Carl Hubbell, N. Y. Giants	2.30	Lefty Gomez, New York	2.33
1935	Cy Blanton, Pittsburgh	2.58	Lefty Grove, Boston	2.70
1936	Carl Hubbell, N. Y. Giants	2.31	Lefty Grove, Boston	2.81
1937	James Turner, Boston	2.38	Lefty Gomez, New York	2.33
1938	Bill Lee, Chicago	2.66	Lefty Grove, Boston	3.08
1939	Bucky Walters, Cincinnati	2.29	Lefty Grove, Boston	2.54
1940	Bucky Walters, Cincinnati	2.48	Ernie Bonham, New York	1.90
1941	Elmer Riddle, Cincinnati	2.24	Thornton Lee, Chicago	2.37

NL ERA leaders / AL ERA leaders

Year	NL Player, Team	ERA	AL Player, Team	ERA
1942	Mort Cooper, St. Louis	1.78	Ted Lyons, Chicago	2.10
1943	Max Lanier, St. Louis	1.90	Spud Chandler, New York	1.64
1944	Ed Heusser, Cincinnati	2.38	Dizzy Trout, Detroit	2.12
1945	Ray Prim, Chicago	2.40	Hal Newhouser, Detroit	1.81
1946	Howie Pollet, St. Louis	2.10	Hal Newhouser, Detroit	1.94
1947	Warren Spahn, Boston	2.33	Spud Chandler, New York	2.46
1948	Harry Brecheen, St. Louis	2.24	Gene Bearden, Cleveland	2.43
1949	Dave Koslo, N. Y. Giants	2.50	Mel Parnell, Boston	2.77
1950	Sal Maglie, N. Y. Giants	2.71	Early Wynn, Cleveland	3.20
1951	Chet Nichols, Boston	2.88	Saul Rogovin, Chicago–Detroit	2.78
1952	Hoyt Wilhelm, N. Y. Giants	2.43	Allie Reynolds, New York	2.06
1953	Warren Spahn, Milwaukee	2.10	Ed Lopat, New York	2.42
1954	Johnny Antonelli, N. Y. Giants	2.30	Mike Garcia, Cleveland	2.64
1955	Bob Friend, Pittsburgh	2.83	Billy Pierce, Chicago	1.97
1956	Lew Burdette, Milwaukee	2.70	Whitey Ford, New York	2.47
1957	Johnny Podres, Brooklyn	2.66	Bobby Shantz, New York	2.45
1958	Stu Miller, San Francisco	2.47	Whitey Ford, New York	2.01
1959	Sam Jones, San Francisco	2.83	Hoyt Wilhelm, Baltimore	2.19
1960	Mike McCormick, San Fran.	2.70	Frank Baumann, Chicago	2.67
1961	Warren Spahn, Milwaukee	3.02	Dick Donovan, Washington	2.40
1962	Sandy Koufax, Los Angeles	2.54	Hank Aguirre, Detroit	2.21
1963	Sandy Koufax, Los Angeles	1.88	Gary Peters, Chicago	2.33
1964	Sandy Koufax, Los Angeles	1.74	Dean Chance, Los Angeles	1.65
1965	Sandy Koufax, Los Angeles	2.04	Sam McDowell, Cleveland	2.18
1966	Sandy Koufax, Los Angeles	1.73	Gary Peters, Chicago	1.98
1967	Phil Niekro, Atlanta	1.87	Joel Horlen, Chicago	2.06
1968	Bob Gibson, St. Louis	1.12	Luis Tiant, Cleveland	1.60
1969	Juan Marichal, San Francisco	2.10	Dick Bosman, Washington	2.19
1970	Tom Seaver, New York Mets	2.82	Diego Segui, Oakland	2.56
1971	Tom Seaver, New York Mets	1.76	Vida Blue, Oakland	1.82
1972	Steve Carlton, Philadelphia	1.97	Luis Tiant, Cleveland	1.91
1973	Tom Seaver, New York Mets	2.08	Jim Palmer, Baltimore	2.40
1974	Buzz Capra, Atlanta	2.28	Catfish Hunter, Oakland	2.49
1975	Randy Jones, San Diego	2.24	Jim Palmer, Baltimore	2.09
1976	John Denny, St. Louis	2.52	Mark Fidrych, Detroit	2.34
1977	John Candelaria, Pittsburgh	2.34	Frank Tanana, California	2.54
1978	Craig Swan, New York Mets	2.43	Ron Guidry, New York	1.74
1979	J.R. Richard, Houston	2.71	Ron Guidry, New York	2.78
1980	Don Sutton, Los Angeles	2.20	Rudy May, New York	2.47
1981	Nolan Ryan, Houston	1.69	Steve McCatty, Oakland	2.32
1982	Steve Rogers, Montreal	2.40	Rick Sutcliffe, Cleveland	2.96
1983	Atlee Hammaker, San Fran.	2.25	Rick Honeycutt, Texas	2.42
1984	Alejandro Pena, Los Angeles	2.48	Mike Boddicker, Baltimore	2.79
1985	Dwight Gooden, N. Y. Mets	1.53	Dave Stieb, Toronto	2.48
1986	Mike Scott, Houston	2.22	Roger Clemens, Boston	2.48

NL ERA leaders / AL ERA leaders

Year	NL Player, Team	ERA	AL Player, Team	ERA
1987	Nolan Ryan, Houston	2.76	Jimmy Key, Toronto	2.76
1988	Joe Magrane, St. Louis	2.18	Allan Anderson, Minnesota	2.45
			Teddy Higuera, Milwaukee	2.45
1989	Scott Garrelts, San Francisco	2.28	Bret Saberhagen, Kansas City	2.16
1990	Danny Darwin, Houston	2.21	Roger Clemens, Boston	1.93
1991	Dennis Martinez, Montreal	2.39	Roger Clemens, Boston	2.62
1992	Bill Swift, San Francisco	2.08	Roger Clemens, Boston	2.41
1993	Greg Maddux, Atlanta	2.36	Kevin Appier, Kansas City	2.56

NL strikeout leaders / AL strikeout leaders

Year	NL Player, Team	SO	AL Player, Team	SO
1876	Jim Devlin, Louisville	122	none	
1877	Tommy Bond, Boston	170	none	
1878	Tommy Bond, Boston	182	none	
1879	"Monte" Ward, Providence	239	none	
1880	Larry Corcoran, Chicago	268	none	
1881	George Derby, Detroit	212	none	
1882	"Ol' Hoss" Radbourn, Prov.	201	none	
1883	Jim Whitney, Boston	345	none	
1884	"Ol' Hoss" Radbourn, Prov.	441	none	
1885	John Clarkson, Chicago	308	none	
1886	"Lady" Baldwin, Detroit	323	none	
1887	John Clarkson, Chicago	237	none	
1888	Tim Keefe, N. Y. Giants	333	none	
1889	John Clarkson, Boston	284	none	
1890	Amos Rusie, N. Y. Giants	341	none	
1891	Amos Rusie, N. Y. Giants	337	none	
1892	Bill Hutchinson, Chicago	316	none	
1893	Amos Rusie, N. Y. Giants	208	none	
1894	Amos Rusie, N. Y. Giants	195	none	
1895	Amos Rusie, N. Y. Giants	201	none	
1896	Cy Young, Cleveland	140	none	
1897	James "Doc" McJames, Wash.	156	none	
1898	Cy Seymour, N. Y. Giants	239	none	
1899	Frank "Noodles" Hahn, Cinc.	145	none	
1900	"Rube" Waddell, Pittsburgh	130	none	
1901	Frank "Noodles" Hahn, Cinc.	239	Cy Young, Boston	158
1902	Vic Willis, Boston	225	Rube Waddell, Philadelphia	210
1903	Christy Mathewson, New York	267	Rube Waddell, Philadelphia	302
1904	Christy Mathewson, New York	212	Rube Waddell, Philadelphia	349
1905	Christy Mathewson, New York	206	Rube Waddell, Philadelphia	287
1906	Fred Beebe, Chicago–St. Louis	171	Rube Waddell, Philadelphia	196
1907	Christy Mathewson, New York	178	Rube Waddell, Philadelphia	232
1908	Christy Mathewson, New York	259	Ed Walsh, Chicago	269
1909	Orval Overall, Chicago	205	F. Smith, Chicago	177

Year	NL strikeout leaders Player, Team	SO	AL strikeout leaders Player, Team	SO
1910	Earl Moore, Philadelphia	185	Walter Johnson, Washington	313
1911	Rube Marquard, N. Y. Giants	237	Ed Walsh, Chicago	255
1912	Grover C. Alexander, Phila.	195	Walter Johnson, Washington	303
1913	Tom Seaton, Philadelphia	168	Walter Johnson, Washington	243
1914	Grover C. Alexander, Phila.	214	Walter Johnson, Washington	225
1915	Grover C. Alexander, Phila.	241	Walter Johnson, Washington	203
1916	Grover C. Alexander, Phila.	167	Walter Johnson, Washington	228
1917	Grover C. Alexander, Phila.	200	Walter Johnson, Washington	188
1918	James "Hippo" Vaughn, Chi.	148	Walter Johnson, Washington	162
1919	James "Hippo" Vaughn, Chi.	141	Walter Johnson, Washington	147
1920	Grover C. Alexander, Chi.	173	Stan Coveleski, Cleveland	133
1921	Burleigh Grimes, Brooklyn	136	Walter Johnson, Washington	143
1922	Arthur "Dazzy" Vance, Br'klyn	134	Urban Shocker, St. Louis	149
1923	Arthur "Dazzy" Vance, Br'klyn	197	Walter Johnson, Washington	130
1924	Arthur "Dazzy" Vance, Br'klyn	262	Walter Johnson, Washington	158
1925	Arthur "Dazzy" Vance, Br'klyn	221	Lefty Grove, Philadelphia	116
1926	Arthur "Dazzy" Vance, Br'klyn	140	Lefty Grove, Philadelphia	194
1927	Arthur "Dazzy" Vance, Br'klyn	184	Lefty Grove, Philadelphia	174
1928	Arthur "Dazzy" Vance, Br'klyn	200	Lefty Grove, Philadelphia	183
1929	Perce "Pat" Malone, Chicago	166	Lefty Grove, Philadelphia	170
1930	Bill Hallahan, St. Louis	177	Lefty Grove, Philadelphia	209
1931	Billy Hallahan, St. Louis	159	Lefty Grove, Philadelphia	175
1932	Jay "Dizzy" Dean, St. Louis	191	Red Ruffing, New York	190
1933	Jay "Dizzy" Dean, St. Louis	199	Lefty Gomez, New York	163
1934	Jay "Dizzy" Dean, St. Louis	195	Lefty Gomez, New York	158
1935	Jay "Dizzy" Dean, St. Louis	182	Tommy Bridges, Detroit	163
1936	Van Lingle Mungo, Brooklyn	238	Tommy Bridges, Detroit	175
1937	Carl Hubbell, N. Y. Giants	159	Lefty Gomez, New York	194
1938	Clay Bryant, Chicago	135	Bob Feller, Cleveland	240
1939	Claude Passeau, Phila.–Cinc.	137	Bob Feller, Cleveland	246
1940	Kirby Higbe, Philadelphia	137	Bob Feller, Cleveland	261
1941	Johnny Vander Meer, Cinc.	202	Bob Feller, Cleveland	260
1942	Johnny Vander Meer, Cinc.	186	Bobo Newsom, Washington	113
			Tex Hughson, Boston	113
1943	Johnny Vander Meer, Cinc.	174	Allie Reynolds, Cleveland	151
1944	Bill Voiselle, N. Y. Giants	161	Hal Newhouser, Detroit	187
1945	Elwin "Preacher" Roe, Pitt.	148	Hal Newhouser, Detroit	212
1946	Johnny Schmitz, Chicago	135	Bob Feller, Cleveland	348
1947	Ewell Blackwell, Cincinnati	193	Bob Feller, Cleveland	196
1948	Harry Brecheen, St. Louis	149	Bob Feller, Cleveland	164
1949	Warren Spahn, Boston	151	Virgil Trucks, Detroit	153
1950	Warren Spahn, Boston	191	Bob Lemon, Cleveland	170
1951	Warren Spahn, Boston	164	Vic Raschi, New York	164
	Don Newcombe, Brooklyn	164		
1952	Warren Spahn, Boston	183	Allie Reynolds, New York	160

NL strikeout leaders / AL strikeout leaders

Year	NL Player, Team	SO	AL Player, Team	SO
1953	Robin Roberts, Philadelphia	198	Billy Pierce, Chicago	186
1954	Robin Roberts, Philadelphia	185	Bob Turley, Baltimore	185
1955	Sam Jones, Chicago	198	Herb Score, Cleveland	245
1956	Sam Jones, Chicago	176	Herb Score, Cleveland	263
1957	Jack Sanford, Philadelphia	188	Early Wynn, Cleveland	184
1958	Sam Jones, St. Louis	225	Early Wynn, Chicago	179
1959	Don Drysdale, Los Angeles	242	Jim Bunning, Detroit	201
1960	Don Drysdale, Los Angeles	246	Jim Bunning, Detroit	201
1961	Sandy Koufax, Los Angeles	269	Camilo Pascual, Minnesota	221
1962	Don Drysdale, Los Angeles	232	Camilo Pascual, Minnesota	206
1963	Sandy Koufax, Los Angeles	306	Camilo Pascual, Minnesota	202
1964	Bob Veale, Pittsburgh	250	Al Downing, New York	217
1965	Sandy Koufax, Los Angeles	382	Sam McDowell, Cleveland	325
1966	Sandy Koufax, Los Angeles	317	Sam McDowell, Cleveland	225
1967	Jim Bunning, Philadelphia	253	Jim Lonborg, Boston	246
1968	Bob Gibson, St. Louis	268	Sam McDowell, Cleveland	283
1969	Ferguson Jenkins, Chicago	273	Sam McDowell, Cleveland	279
1970	Tom Seaver, New York Mets	283	Sam McDowell, Cleveland	304
1971	Tom Seaver, New York Mets	289	Mickey Lolich, Detroit	308
1972	Steve Carlton, Philadelphia	310	Nolan Ryan, California	329
1973	Tom Seaver, New York Mets	251	Nolan Ryan, California	383
1974	Steve Carlton, Philadelphia	240	Nolan Ryan, California	367
1975	Tom Seaver, New York Mets	243	Frank Tanana, California	269
1976	Tom Seaver, New York Mets	235	Nolan Ryan, California	327
1977	Phil Niekro, Atlanta	262	Nolan Ryan, California	341
1978	J.R. Richard, Houston	303	Nolan Ryan, California	260
1979	J.R. Richard, Houston	313	Nolan Ryan, California	223
1980	Steve Carlton, Philadelphia	286	Len Barker, Cleveland	187
1981	Fernando Valenzuela, Los Ang.	180	Len Barker, Cleveland	127
1982	Steve Carlton, Philadelphia	286	Floyd Bannister, Seattle	209
1983	Steve Carlton, Philadelphia	275	Jack Morris, Detroit	232
1984	Dwight Gooden, N. Y. Mets	276	Mark Langston, Seattle	204
1985	Dwight Gooden, N. Y Mets	268	Bert Blyleven, Cleveland–Minn.	206
1986	Mike Scott, Houston	306	Mark Langston, Seattle	245
1987	Nolan Ryan, Houston	270	Mark Langston, Seattle	262
1988	Nolan Ryan, Houston	228	Roger Clemens, Boston	291
1989	Jose DeLeon, St. Louis	201	Nolan Ryan, Texas	301
1990	David Cone, New York Mets	233	Nolan Ryan, Texas	232
1991	David Cone, New York Mets	241	Roger Clemens, Boston	241
1992	John Smoltz, Atlanta	215	Randy Johnson, Seattle	241
1993	Jose Rijo, Cincinnati	227	Randy Johnson, Seattle	308